0003
98-0021-S

DEPOSITORY RECEIPT

MAR 2 6 1998

Indian River Community College
LIBRARY

AGS 9800

D1218701

4/29/98
gift
$10⁰⁰ xx

Loblolly Pine

The Ecology and Culture of Loblolly Pine

(Pinus taeda L.)

Robert P. Schultz, retired

U.S. Department of Agriculture

Forest Service

Southern Forest Experiment Station

New Orleans, Louisiana

Agricultural Handbook 713

December 1997

S
21
A37
1997

U.S. Department of Agriculture, Forest Service
Washington, D.C.

The United States Department of Agriculture (USDA) prohibits discrimination in its programs on the basis of race, color, national origin, sex, religion, age, disability, political beliefs, and marital or familial status. (Not all prohibited bases apply to all programs.) Persons with disabilities who require alternative means for communication of program information (braille, large print, audiotape, etc.) should contact USDA's TARGET CENTER at (202) 720-2600 (voice and TDD).

To file a complaint, write the Secretary of Agriculture, U.S. Department of Agriculture, Washington, DC 20250, or call 1-800-245-6340 (voice) or (202) 720-1127 (TAD). USDA is an equal employment opportunity employer.

This publication reports research involving pesticides; it does not contain recommendations for their use, nor does it imply that the uses discussed here have been registered by appropriate State and/or Federal agencies before they can be recommended. Pesticide registrations and formulations may change, and readers should contact the manufacturer, a local distributor, or local county extension agent for correct information on usage of a particular pesticide. **Caution: Pesticides can be injurious to humans, domestic animals, desirable plants, fish, and other wildlife—if they are not handled properly**. Use all pesticides selectively and carefully. Follow recommended practices for the disposal of surplus pesticides and pesticide containers.

The mention of commercial products in this publication is solely for the information of the reader and endorsement is not intended by the U.S. Department of Agriculture or the USDA Forest Service.

For sale by the U.S. Government Printing Office
Superintendent of Documents, Mail Stop: SSOP, Washington, DC 20402-9328
ISBN 0-16-049279-3

Contents

· ·

Foreword

In 1985, when I was Deputy Chief of Research for the U.S. Department of Agriculture, Forest Service, I discussed with Tom Ellis, Director of the Southern Forest Experiment Station (1984 to 1992), and Bob Schultz, Assistant Director (1976 to 1992), the possibility of publishing a new monograph on the ecology and culture of loblolly pine. There had been an enormous increase in knowledge about the species since the publication of W.G. Wahlenberg's "Loblolly Pine" in 1960. I was eager that Forest Service scientists summarize and disseminate the available information about loblolly pine. The Forest Service had long been a leader in research on the species, and Forest Service researchers W.W. Ashe and W.G. Wahlenberg had authored important monographs on loblolly pine. This is not to suggest that the Forest Service operated alone—substantial contributions to knowledge about loblolly pine came from the newly emerging and strengthened forestry schools and forest industries of the South following World War II.

There were other reasons for producing a new summary. Loblolly pine is the most important forest tree species in the United States and one of the most important in the world. It provided much of the raw material for enormous expansion of forest industries in the South and is important for rehabilitation of degraded lands, as a component of consumptive and nonconsumptive wildlife habitats, and for watershed protection in the Coastal Plain and Piedmont of the southeastern United States. It now grows abundantly on very large areas once occupied by unproductive cut-over and burned-over forests, worn-out cotton and tobacco fields, and submarginal pastures—areas in which there was a great deal of rural poverty. Bob Schultz agreed to undertake preparation of the new monograph. The results, as you will see, are impressive. Some 5,800 articles published since 1960 have been reviewed. The book reflects both the growth of knowledge and changing perceptions about loblolly pine ecology, protection, and management during the last 30 years.

A greatly expanded discussion of loblolly pine genetics and breeding is presented in this manuscript. Schultz devotes an entire chapter to site preparation for artificial regeneration, a subject little understood in 1960. Up-to-date information about growth and yield, resource inventory, and plantation and natural stand management is presented. Nontimber values of loblolly pine for wildlife, grazing, watershed protection, and rehabilitation of degraded lands receive considerable emphasis. The volume also includes an entire chapter on the international importance of loblolly pine, an area of interest likely to grow still more. Physical properties of loblolly pine wood are discussed only briefly, and uses of loblolly pine are not discussed. These subjects were extensively covered by Peter Koch in his two-volume treatise on utilization of southern pines, published in 1972.

A concluding observation: the premier story of forest conservation the world over, in my estimation, is the resurgence of forest resources in the southeastern United States. Nowhere else has such a large area been restored to high forest productivity, and nowhere else has forest conservation contributed so much to economic vitality and environmental well-being. This restoration has been based very largely on an accumulation of scientific and technological know-how about the management, protection, and utilization of loblolly pine. This monograph will enjoy the same prominent place on book shelves and be accorded the same classical standing as its predecessors.

Robert E. Buckman
Professor, College of Forestry
Oregon State University
Corvallis, Oregon

Preface

Colonization, farming, and intensive logging in the 1800's, followed by fire control and extensive planting of loblolly pine in the 1900's, converted the southern pinery from predominantly longleaf pine to predominantly loblolly pine in less than 100 years. Because of its rapid growth on a wide variety of sites, its ecological role in rejuvenating damaged soils and minimizing erosion, and its outstanding value for a variety of commodity and noncommodity uses, loblolly pine has grown exponentially in popularity since the turn of the 20th century. Loblolly pine had become so important to the economy of North Carolina by the first decade of the 20th century that an entire book, "Loblolly or North Carolina Pine," was devoted to discussing the growth and management of the species (Ashe 1915). Beginning in the 1930's, the increasing importance of loblolly pine to the economy of the entire South led to the development of private, federal, and university research programs. This research produced an extensive body of knowledge and led to the publication of a classic book entitled "Loblolly Pine: Its Use, Ecology, Regeneration, Protection, Growth and Management" (Wahlenberg 1960).

Since 1960, almost 6,000 documents have been published throughout the world, highlighting new research results and identifying valuable and practical implications for intensive or extensive management of loblolly pine, which has become the single most important forest tree species in the Nation. Successful tree improvement programs, plantings, and natural regeneration in many countries around the world indicate excellent opportunities for future growth and usefulness of the species on an international scale.

This book adds to the technical foundations laid by Ashe and Wahlenberg. It summarizes the results of an exhaustive search and review of literature published between 1960 and 1990. Noteworthy references and technical innovations since then have been added. The objectives are to provide a better understanding of the ecology of this remarkable conifer and to highlight individual tree, stand, and land management alternatives useful to resource managers, students, researchers, and others.

Unless other species are specifically referred to, the reader should assume that discussion throughout the book is about loblolly pine. Unless otherwise noted, all measurements are in metric units for consistency and ease of use on an international basis. A table of conversion factors is included on page XII.

Because the literature is extensive, I have had to be selective in choosing specific examples, and some worthy articles have not been cited. I apologize to authors of these excellent research contributions.

Robert P. Schultz
Metairie, Louisiana

LOBLOLLY PINE (*PINUS TAEDA* L.)

Acknowledgments

· ·

The author gratefully acknowledges Dr. Thomas E. Ellis, Director, U.S. Department of Agriculture, Forest Service, Southern Forest Experiment Station, New Orleans, Louisiana, and Dr. Robert E. Buckman, Deputy Chief of Research (1976 to 1986), U.S. Department of Agriculture, Forest Service, Washington, DC, without whose dedicated support and leadership this book would never have been initiated. They freed me from most administrative responsibilities during the critical 2-year period when I was reviewing the literature and writing a first draft.

Rebecca Nisley was managing editor for the book's editing and production through the Washington Office and Carol Lowe supervised the editing at the Southern Station. I owe special thanks to Dale McDaniel, who edited the final draft; to Sharon Delaneuville, who checked and organized thousands of citations and prepared many figures and tables; and to Kathleen Newsom, who volunteered many long hours to work on the final literature citation section. Susan Branham and Alan Salmon also provided substantial editorial assistance. Numerous other individuals provided dedicated and highly professional technical and administrative support. Virginia (Ginger) Brown with the INFOSOUTH staff at the University of Georgia organized a systematic and detailed electronic search of world literature and diligently worked to provide hard copies of worldwide literature associated with loblolly pine—a monumental task. Marian Nichols, Ellen Moore, Joyce Even, Gwen Marcus, and Minnie Haten ordered and electronically cataloged publications and maintained the internal integrity of a massive literature database. The Forest Inventory and Analysis research units of the Southern and Southeastern Forest Experiment Stations provided current data and excellent figures of loblolly pine resources throughout the South.

The following is an alphabetical listing of many of those who contributed to the success of this book by providing suggestions for organization, technically reviewing all or parts of various chapters, and supplying materials. I owe a sincere debt of gratitude to each of them.

Acknowledgments

NAME	ORGANIZATION	LOCATION
James Baker	USDA Forest Service	Monticello, AR
Virgil Baldwin	USDA Forest Service	Alexandria, LA
Richard Barnes	Oxford University	Oxford, England
James Barnett	USDA Forest Service	Alexandria, LA
Roger Belanger	USDA Forest Service	Athens, GA
Wayne Berisford	University of Georgia	Athens, GA
Frank Bonner	USDA Forest Service	Starkville, MS
William Boyer	USDA Forest Service	Auburn, AL
David Bramlett	USDA Forest Service	Macon, GA
Harold Burkhart	Virginia Polytechnic University	Blacksburg, VA
Paul Burns	Louisiana State University	Baton Rouge, LA

Acknowledgments

NAME	ORGANIZATION	LOCATION
Michael Cain	USDA Forest Service	Monticello, AR
Richard Conner	USDA Forest Service	Nacogdoches, TX
Douglas Crutchfield	Westvaco	Summerville, SC
Edward de Steiguer	USDA Forest Service	Research Triangle Park, NC
Tommy Dell	USDA Forest Service, retired	New Orleans, LA
Roger Dennington	USDA Forest Service	Atlanta, GA
James Dickson	USDA Forest Service	Nacogdoches, TX
Vinson Duvall	USDA Forest Service, retired	New Orleans, LA
Susan Eggen	USDA Forest Service	Starkville, MS
Robert Farrar	USDA Forest Service, retired	Starkville, MS
Richard Fitzgerald	USDA Forest Service	Washington, DC
Carlyle Franklin	North Carolina State University	Raleigh, NC
Ronald Froelich	USDA Forest Service, deceased	Gulfport, MS
Michael Golden	Auburn University	Auburn, AL
Michael Greenwood	University of Maine	Orono, ME
William Harms	USDA Forest Service	Charleston, SC
Constance Harrington	USDA Forest Service	Monticello, AR
Roy Hedden	Clemson University	Clemson, SC
Charles Hodges	USDA Forest Service, retired	Research Triangle Park, NC
John Hodges	Mississippi State University	Starkville, MS
William Hyde	Duke University	Durham, NC
Earle Jones	USDA Forest Service	Macon, GA
Jaques Jorgensen	USDA Forest Service	Research Triangle Park, NC
Robert Kellison	North Carolina State University	Raleigh, NC
Susan Kossuth	USDA Forest Service	Gainesville, FL
John Kraus	USDA Forest Service, retired	Macon, GA
Stanley Krugman	USDA Forest Service, retired	Washington, DC
George Kuhlman	USDA Forest Service	Athens, GA

Acknowledgments

NAME	ORGANIZATION	LOCATION
Clark Lantz	USDA Forest Service	Atlanta, GA
Michael Lennartz	USDA Forest Service	Washington, DC
Clifford Lewis	USDA Forest Service, retired	Gainesville, FL
F. Thomas Lloyd	USDA Forest Service	Clemson, SC
Peter Lorio	USDA Forest Service	Alexandria, LA
Sebastiano Machado	Federal University of Parana	Curitiba, Brazil
Donald Marx	USDA Forest Service	Athens, GA
Gene McGee	USDA Forest Service, retired	Sewanee, TN
William McKee	USDA Forest Service	Athens, GA
Robert McLemore	USDA Forest Service, retired	Alexandria, LA
Ralph Meldahl	Auburn University	Auburn, AL
James Miller	USDA Forest Service	Auburn, AL
Thomas Miller	USDA Forest Service, retired	Gainesville, FL
Paul Murphy	USDA Forest Service	Monticello, AR
John Nord	USDA Forest Service	Athens, GA
Henry Pearson	USDA Forest Service, retired	Alexandria, LA
Joseph Saucier	USDA Forest Service	Athens, GA
Ronald Schmidtling	USDA Forest Service	Gulfport, MS
Rudi Seitz	Federal University of Parana	Curitiba, Brazil
Michael Shelton	USDA Forest Service	Monticello, AR
Glenn Snow	USDA Forest Service, retired	Gulfport, MS
Jan Troensegaard	Food and Agriculture Organization of the United Nations (FAO)	Rome, Italy
Hans van Buijtenen	Texas A & M University	College Station, TX
David Van Lear	Clemson University	Clemson, SC
John Vann	USDA Forest Service	Atlanta, GA
John Vozzo	USDA Forest Service	Starkville, MS
Charles Walkinshaw	USDA Forest Service	Alexandria, LA
Harry Yates	USDA Forest Service	Athens, GA

Abbreviations
Used Throughout This Book

FAO	=	Food and Agriculture Organization of the United Nations
IUFRO	=	International Union of Forestry Research Organizations
TAPPI	=	Technical Association of the Pulp and Paper Industry
USDA	=	United States Department of Agriculture
dbh	=	diameter at breast height

Conversion Factors
for "English" and Metric Units

	English units	Metric units	Conversion factors	
			English to metric	Metric to English
Area	acre (ac)	hectare (ha)	0.405	2.471
	square feet (ft^2)	square meter (m^2)	0.093	10.764
	sq ft/ac	m^2/ha	0.2296	4.356
	square inch (in^2)	square centimeter (cm^2)	6.452	0.155
Length	feet (ft)	meter (m)	0.305	3.281
	inch (in)	centimeter (cm)	2.54	0.394
	mile (mi)	kilometer (km)	1.609	0.621
Light	footcandle	lumen/m2	10.76	0.093
Mass	ounce (oz)	gram (g)	28.35	0.035
	pound (lb)	kilogram (kg)	0.454	2.205
	English ton (ton)	metric tonne (t)	0.9072	1.102
Pressure	atmosphere (atm)	kg/cm^2	1.033	0.9678
Volume	bushel	m^3	0.035	28.400
	ft^3	m^3	0.028	35.314
	cord (90 ft^3)	m^3	2.55	0.392
Yield	board ft/ac	m^3/ha	0.014	71.457
Yield	cord/ac	m^3/ha	6.298	0.159
	ft^3/ac	m^3/ha	0.07	14.291
	lb/ac	kg/ha	1.12	0.891
	ton/ac	t/ha	2.240	0.446

Part 1

Ecology
Of Loblolly Pine

Chapter 1

Introduction

Contents

Introduction

Background

Loblolly pine (*Pinus taeda* L.) is an ideal tree for site restoration and forest management (figure 1-1). It is the most hardy and versatile of all southern pines, in terms of its ability to reproduce and grow rapidly on diverse sites. It seeds profusely, regenerates easily, provides large yields per hectare, provides many different marketable products at a relatively early age, and makes good wildlife habitat when stands of many ages are growing in close proximity. It grows naturally in various combinations with longleaf pine, *P. palustris* Mill.; shortleaf pine, *P. echinata* Mill.; and slash pine, *P. elliottii* Engelm.; and with most southern hardwoods. It reaches maturity by age 80 and rarely lives beyond age 300 even under the best conditions. In the absence of disturbance, succession results in nearly complete elimination of loblolly pine and the formation of mixed hardwood forests. Loblolly pine is presently the leading timber species in the United States, predominating on more than 13.4

Figure 1-1—Natural uneven-aged loblolly pine stand on a highly productive site in southeast Arkansas.

Table 1-1—Species in the genus *Pinus* subsection *Australes* and species range

Scientific name	Common name	General range
Pinus caribaea Morelet	Caribbean pine	Caribbean Seaboard of Central America, Cuba, the Bahamas
P. cubensis Griseb.	Cuban pine	Oriente Province of Cuba
P. echinata Mill.	Shortleaf pine	Southeastern U.S.
P. elliottii Engelm.	Slash pine	Coastal Plain of southeastern U.S.
P. glabra Walt.	Spruce pine	Coastal Plain of southeastern U.S.
P. occidentalis Sw.	West Indian pine	Hispaniola, eastern Cuba
P. palustris Mill.	Longleaf pine	Coastal Plain of southeastern U.S.
P. pungens Lamb.	Table Mountain pine	Appalachian Mountains
P. rigida Mill.	Pitch pine	Eastern U.S.
P. serotina Michx.	Pond pine	Coastal Plain of southeastern U.S.
P. taeda L.	Loblolly pine	Coastal Plain & Piedmont of southeastern U.S.

Source: adapted from Critchfield and Little (1966).

million ha (hectares) of southern forest lands. Its growing stock volume in 1989 was 1.4 billion m³ (cubic meters), half of the growing stock of all southern yellow pine. Total biomass in loblolly pine presently exceeds 1 billion dry metric tons (Cost and others 1990). Loblolly pine is in the *Australes* subsection of the genus *Pinus*. This subsection contains eight species native to the southeastern and eastern United States, two native to the West Indies, and one native to both the West Indies and adjacent Central America (table 1-1).

The natural range of loblolly pine extends from Texas eastward to Florida and northward to Delaware. This range is generally continuous with the exceptions of the Mississippi River flood plain and a disjunct population in Texas called the "lost pines" (figure 1-2). Loblolly pine's extensive range overlaps the natural ranges of longleaf pine; shortleaf pine; slash pine; pitch pine, *P. rigida* Mill.; pond pine, *P. serotina* Michx.; and Virginia pine, *P. virginiana* Mill. Completely mixed stands occur in many areas, and natural hybridization is relatively common.

The natural range of loblolly pine is fairly well delineated by isolines (figure 1-3) connecting similar rates of annual actual evapotranspiration (AE), which is a measurement of the simultaneous availability of water and solar energy in an environment during any given period. The main distribution of the species is defined by AE values of 1,050 mm of moisture on the south and 813 mm on the north. Actual evapotranspiration isolines of 762 mm and 813 mm identify a transition zone in which loblolly pine survives with varying success. The iso-

line of 737 mm is a good indicator of the northern and western limits of loblolly pine. This isoline reflects the dry conditions of the lost pines area of Texas and low-energy conditions in Maryland and Delaware. Loblolly pine is absent from the Mississippi Delta primarily because of edaphic conditions. In central Florida, loblolly pine occurs in the transition zone bounded by AE values of 1,050 and 1,150 mm. South of this, loblolly pine is unable to compete due to a combination of climatic, physiographic, and pyric conditions (Manogaran 1975, Rosenzweig 1968).

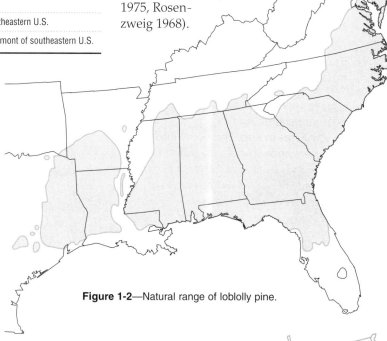

Figure 1-2—Natural range of loblolly pine.

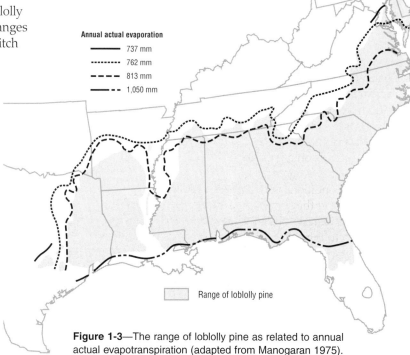

Annual actual evaporation
— 737 mm
····· 762 mm
– – – 813 mm
–·–·– 1,050 mm

▨ Range of loblolly pine

Figure 1-3—The range of loblolly pine as related to annual actual evapotranspiration (adapted from Manogaran 1975).

History of Loblolly Pine

The Original Forests

In the original forests of the South, loblolly pine was a minor species both on the uplands, which were dominated by longleaf pine or mixed upland hardwoods, and in the wet river bottoms and swamps, which were dominated by mixed bottomland hardwoods. It was, however, an important species on moist sites that were not subject to regular burning. Its association with other species varied greatly, depending on region and site. In total, there were probably no more than 2 million ha of predominantly loblolly pine forests in the South before the arrival of the Europeans in North America.

In the Coastal Plain, loblolly pine grew best mixed with hardwoods along stream margins and around swamps on sites that were not subject to long periods of flooding or to serious fires. Under natural conditions, it rarely formed pure stands, and these seldom exceeded more than a few acres in size. The occurrence of most pure loblolly pine stands was attributable to effects of natural disasters such as fires and hurricanes or to land clearing by Native Americans. When natural disasters created openings, seeds from nearby trees quickly became established. However, because loblolly pine has limited tolerance to fire, it generally could not compete with longleaf pine on well-drained Coastal Plain lands subject to regular fires.

Loblolly pine was also a minor component of the original Piedmont forests, which were largely composed of mixed hardwoods. During the 1800's, many Piedmont forests were cleared, burned, and planted to cotton, *Gossypium* spp. Successive cycles of cropping, erosion, and abandonment, and finally destruction of the cotton industry by the boll weevil, *Anthonomus grandis grandis* Boheman, in the 1880's, made as much as half of the Piedmont a wasteland of abandoned fields. These conditions permitted the light-seeded loblolly pines, which were scattered among hardwood stands along the myriad of drains, to seed in and form pure stands in old fields. Fire control efforts in the early 1900's protected these stands and further promoted the expansion of loblolly pine stands on a wide array of sites throughout the species' natural range.

The diverse conditions under which loblolly pine grows greatly affect the species' size, shape, form, character, and even its common names. The name "loblolly" was probably given to the species because it often grew in low spots or swales along the coast of Virginia and the Carolinas. These wet areas were commonly referred to as "loblollies" by early colonials. Until the early 1900's, loblolly pine, which grew throughout the Coastal Plain and Piedmont of North Carolina, was often called "North Carolina pine." Its other common name, "oldfield pine," reflected the species' ability to regenerate rapidly on abandoned

cultivated land or homesites. Loblolly pine regularly grew intermingled with longleaf, shortleaf, and slash pines. Confusion with these species gave rise to many other names. In swampy areas, loblolly pine was often called "swamp pine," "rosemary pine," or "slash pine." Other local names included "short straw pine," "sap pine," "foxtail pine," "cornstalk pine," and "black-bark pine." The last name was used most frequently in the Carolina pocosins. Until the mid-1800's, loblolly pine was commonly called "longleaf" in the Piedmont counties of Virginia.

Even the scientific name of loblolly pine was somewhat controversial. The word "*taeda*," meaning torch, which was bestowed on loblolly by Linnaeus in 1753, is more appropriate for longleaf pine. Torches were made primarily from resin-soaked longleaf pine heartwood, called "lightwood." They provided an important source of light at night in colonial homes throughout the southern Coastal Plain. Longleaf pine, which commonly grows in pure stands on the drier sites and mixed with loblolly pine on intermediate sites, was given the species name *palustris* (from the Latin word "*palus*" or "*paluster*") meaning swamp. In retrospect, these two great southern pines should more appropriately have had the other's species name.

Antebellum Logging

Captain John Smith and other early 17th-century settlers in Virginia quickly recognized the value of loblolly pine for farm building and ship construction. The wood found many uses because it was relatively easy to cut and form and because the heartwood was very durable. Its large size permitted the formation of heavy timbers with a relatively small amount of hand hewing. An entire building—including the roof if baldcypress, *Taxodium distichum* (L.) Rich., was unavailable—and its furnishings might be constructed of pine. Tall straight trees were coveted. In some places, English law required that ship masts be made from loblolly pines. Only straight, unblemished pines 66 to 76 cm in diameter at the large end, 46 to 53 cm at the small end, and 20 to 30 m in length could meet the exacting standards. Skilled axmen hewed these trees into octagonal timbers with broadaxes.

Continuous harvesting and land clearing for farming all along the Atlantic and Gulf Coasts and major rivers consumed many of the virgin loblolly pines, which often grew near the shores of navigable waters. However, because access was poor, trees growing in and around wet interior sites were relatively safe from early land clearing and survived to regenerate the species.

In early logging operations, prime trees were felled with a poleax, which had a single cutting edge and weighed about 2 kg. Logs were dragged short distances to work areas by oxen, mules, or horses and then roughly squared with a broadax. Early French, English, and Span-

Figure 1-4—Big-wheels and oxen pulling a pine log from an Alabama swamp in 1926.

ish settlers constructed crude sawpits or scaffolds to cut squared timbers into boards. Only a few boards could be cut in a day, and much skill and stamina were needed to maintain uniform board widths. These primitive sawmills shipped lumber to London and to the growing towns of New York, Boston, and Philadelphia as early as 1749.

Sash mills appeared in the late colonial period and continued in use until the 1840's. Sash saw blades were fixed in a rectangular frame that provided stability and made it possible to cut from 17 to 28 m³ (3,000 to 5,000 board feet) of pine lumber per day.

Installation of the first steam sawmills along the tidewater in the 1830's changed the entire complexion of logging. Because these new mills required large supplies of timber in order to operate continuously, they were invariably erected at river estuaries or along the banks of bayous that extended a few miles into the interior. Again, loblolly pine stands were the most accessible and among the first to be cut.

The only easy way to move large numbers of logs was by water. Axmen (commonly known as "choppers") cut loblolly pines near rivers and streams, and oxen skidded the logs to riverbanks for water transport to mills. When axes were used, pine trees were cut at waist height. Expert choppers were very skillful and possessed great endurance. Many could smooth the ends of logs very

effectively. Average axmen could cut about 10 trees per day, but some could cut twice as many. About 15 to 18 logs, averaging 12 m in length and 50 cm in diameter, were taken from an average hectare of piney woods. Logs had to be free of knots, be at least 45.0 cm in diameter at the small end and no shorter than 4.9 m, and contain no more than 2.5 cm of sapwood to meet mill requirements. Caralogs (also called "go-devils," "big-wheels," or "log carts"), with two wheels up to 2.4 m in diameter and over 15 cm wide, were common log carriers through the middle and late 1800's (figure 1-4). Oxen were the preferred draft animals because they were less susceptible than horses or mules to bogging down in swamps, required less feed than horses or mules, and could forage on the open range at no cost to the owners when not working. After the Civil War, more modern methods of felling (crosscut saws) and transportation (eight-wheeled wagons and railroads, used initially with logtracks, figure 1-5) and contract labor replaced the early primitive techniques.

Records suggest that logs were floated from cutting areas to sawmills even before 1840. Logs were skidded a maximum of 8 km on each side of rivers. They were branded at streambanks by their owners for identification and to restrict theft during floating or rafting to mills. The logs were rafted together with chains or boards so that very dense ones would not sink and be lost. Usually, both logging and rafting were done by the same people. In the Coastal Plain, good rainfall permitted log movement down the larger streams year round. Logs were stored along smaller streams and released after heavy rainstorms.

By 1927, only 5.1 million ha of the original virgin pine lands of over 49 million ha remained uncut. This set the stage for the loblolly pine forests we know today.

Figure 1-5—Primitive log train (**left**) on train road with round pine logs for rails in south Alabama, 1902 (photograph by E.A. Smith and R.S. Hodges, Geological Survey of Alabama). Train on iron tracks (**right**) being loaded with southern pine logs brought to the landing with oxen, beams, and a big-wheel. A white-colored lead animal was often chosen so that the driver could keep track of the lead team even in the dark (photograph from the Andrew D. Lytle Collection, Louisiana and Lower Mississippi Valley Collections, LSU Libraries, Louisiana State University, Baton Rouge, LA 70803).

Species Range

Loblolly pine occurs naturally in 15 southern and mid-Atlantic states and has a wider geographic range than any other southern pine except shortleaf. Its range extends from latitude 39° 21' N in Delaware and nearby coastal regions of New Jersey and eastern Maryland south to latitude 28° N in central Florida and west to eastern Texas, the southeastern tip of Oklahoma, and southern Arkansas (figure 1-6). Small outlying populations occur in southwestern North Carolina, east-central Arkansas, and northeastern and southeastern Texas. The latter population, the "lost pines," is at the western boundary of the species' range. This disjunct population is 160 km west of the contiguous range of the species. The overall east–west range extends from about longitude 75° W to about longitude 97° 30' W (Little 1971). The range includes the Atlantic and Gulf Coastal Plain, the Piedmont Plateau, and the southern extremities of the Ridge and Valley, the Highland Rim, and the Cumberland Plateau provinces of the Appalachian Highlands. Loblolly pine grows at elevations ranging from sea level on the Coastal Plain to nearly 900 m in northern Alabama and Georgia. It does not grow naturally in the Mississippi River Valley. This gap of 30 to 200 km presents a natural barrier to breeding between the eastern and western populations (figure 1-6).

Loblolly pine reaches merchantable size and merchantable concentrations throughout its natural range except in south-central Georgia and the lower Coastal Plain of Florida, Mississippi, and Alabama, where it is only locally important, and along the mountain fringes of the mid-South (figure 1-6). Large-scale plantings and direct seedings have extended the commercial range throughout much of Tennessee, western Arkansas, and eastern Oklahoma. Even in southern Illinois, plantings have grown at the rate of 3.8 m^3/ha/yr over a 27-year rotation (Gilmore and Funk 1976). Figure 1-7 shows the distribution of growing-stock volume within the commercial range of the species.

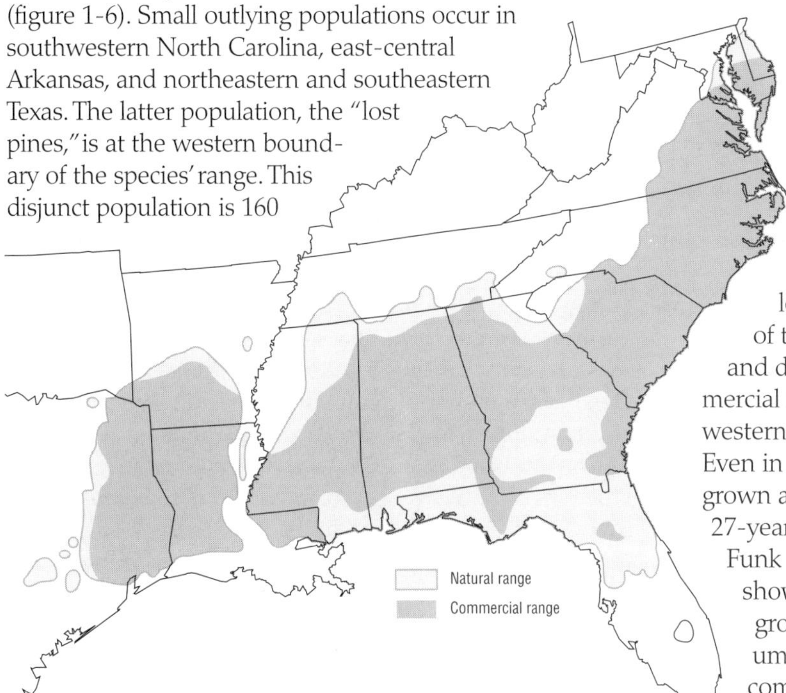

Figure 1-6—Natural and commercial ranges of loblolly pine (commercial range as shown by Goebel 1974).

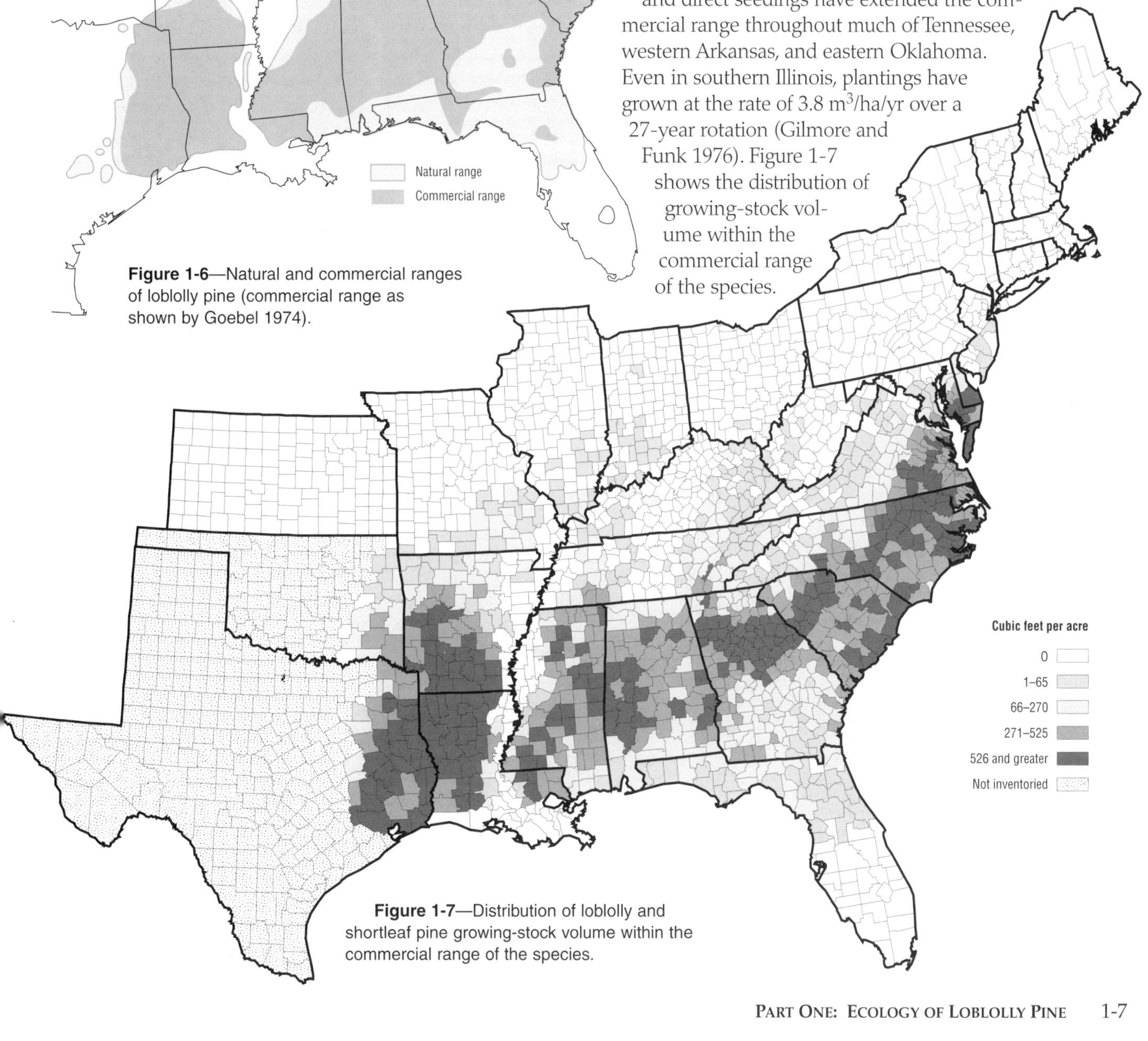

Natural range
Commercial range

Cubic feet per acre

0
1–65
66–270
271–525
526 and greater
Not inventoried

Figure 1-7—Distribution of loblolly and shortleaf pine growing-stock volume within the commercial range of the species.

Plants Associated With Loblolly Pine

Loblolly pine is an extremely versatile species capable of growing in association with numerous annual and perennial plants, including mixed hardwoods, throughout its life (Jones and others 1981, Mills and Jones 1969, Nixon and others 1987, Quarterman and Keever 1962). Plant species that compete with loblolly pine for growing space can be divided into three broad groups: trees and shrubs; pioneer herbs, grasses, and forbs; and woody vines. Deciduous trees of numerous genera (for example, *Acer, Carya,* and *Quercus*) and tolerant shrubs like waxmyrtle, *Myrica cerifera* L., and saw-palmetto, *Serenoa repens* (Bartr.) Small, can seriously compete with loblolly pine regeneration. Pioneer herbs, grasses, and forbs often compete with loblolly pine seedlings for soil moisture, nutrients, and light. Typical competing pioneer species are broomsedge, *Andropogon virginicus* L.; horseweed, *Conyza canadensis* (L.) Cronq. var. *canadensis* = *Erigeron canadensis* L.; and common ragweed, *Ambrosia artemisiifolia* L. Their populations are usually denser and their competitive effects more pronounced on better sites. Woody vines can dominate some cleared areas at the time of regeneration. Two exotics, Japanese honeysuckle, *Lonicera japonica* Thunb., and kudzu, *Pueraria lobata* (Willd.) Ohwi., can totally occupy some sites and become (or continue to be) a problem during a rotation. An extensive list of plant species that grow and compete with loblolly pine can be found in appendix A.

Grasses, herbs, and shrubs are the first competitors on disturbed areas where no hardwood rootstocks are present. Within a few years, sweetgum, *Liquidambar styraciflua* L., and red maple, *Acer rubrum* L., will often develop from seeds. Subsequently, blackgum, *Nyssa sylvatica* Marsh.; sassafras, *Sassafras albidum* (Nutt.) Nees; oaks, *Quercus* spp.; and hickories, *Carya* spp., become established. Many understory plants can be found in association with loblolly pine throughout the life of a stand (Applegate and others 1976, Krochmal and Kologiski 1974, Wolters and Schmidtling 1975). Plant associations vary by soil and site as well as by geographic location. The rate of succession from loblolly pine to a hardwood climax is faster on better sites because the hardwood understory develops more rapidly on such sites. Pines are also more abundant on light sandy soils than on heavier soils in the Piedmont, suggesting a more rapid transition to a hardwood climax on heavier soils (Nelson 1957). On old fields, where grasses and herbs predominate, succession to hardwoods is slower than in wooded areas, where hardwood sprouts grow rapidly from established root systems.

Although the use of vegetative associations as indicators of loblolly pine habitat productivity has received very little attention, muscadine grape, *Vitis rotundifolia* Michx.; red maple; and Virginia creeper, *Parthenocissus quinquefolia* (L.) Planch., seemed to be important indicators of high site quality for loblolly pine in the Alabama Piedmont (Smith 1961). Zellmer (1975) determined that hardwoods were useful in assessing site quality for loblolly pine on an Alabama Coastal Plain site, but not on a Piedmont site. It may also be feasible to predict habitat productivity on the basis of various combinations of vegetation, soils, and topography. For instance, Hodgkins (1970) was able to accurately predict longleaf pine site index in the Coastal Plain of Alabama, with a high degree of accuracy, using a combination of indicator plants, soil physical properties, and slopes.

Competing plants play an important, but generally unquantified, role in nutrient cycling and nutrient storage within the loblolly pine ecosystem. Although large numbers of small hardwoods, shrubs, and annual plants compete with the pine overstory for nutrients, many of the nutrients these plants accumulate would not be readily obtained by loblolly pines even if the competitors were absent (Cox and Van Lear 1985). The competitors also prevent the leaching loss of some minerals that would occur in a monoculture (Van Lear and others 1990). Following the death and decomposition of these plants, additional nutrients are available for loblolly pine growth. Many species of legumes that proliferate shortly after fires, notably *Lespedeza* spp., are important for nitrogen (N) fixation (see chapter 3).

Forest Cover Types in the Loblolly Pine Ecosystem

Loblolly pine grows in pure stands and in mixture with other southern pines and hardwoods throughout its range. When loblolly pine grows in pure stands or makes up the majority of the stocking, the Society of American Foresters (SAF) classifies the forest cover type as loblolly pine (SAF-81) (Eyre 1980). On well-drained sites, longleaf, shortleaf, and Virginia pines; blackjack oak, *Quercus marilandica* Muenchh.; post oak, *Q. stellata* Wangenh.; southern red oak, *Q. falcata* Michx.; white oak, *Q. alba* L.; hickories; sassafras; and persimmon, *Diospyros virginiana* L., are common associates of loblolly pine. On moderately to poorly drained sites, the species usually found in association with loblolly pine are pond pine; spruce pine, *Pinus glabra* Walt.; red

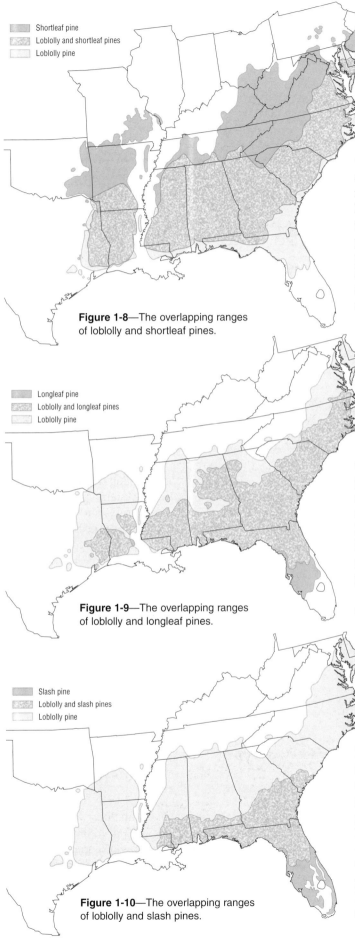

Figure 1-8—The overlapping ranges of loblolly and shortleaf pines.

- Shortleaf pine
- Loblolly and shortleaf pines
- Loblolly pine

Figure 1-9—The overlapping ranges of loblolly and longleaf pines.

- Longleaf pine
- Loblolly and longleaf pines
- Loblolly pine

Figure 1-10—The overlapping ranges of loblolly and slash pines.

- Slash pine
- Loblolly and slash pines
- Loblolly pine

maple; blackgum; black willow, *Salix nigra* Marsh.; oaks; and yellow-poplar, *Liriodendron tulipifera* L. In east Texas, loblolly pine decreases in importance along the topographic gradient from creek bottoms to uplands (Nixon and others 1987). Loblolly pine is scarce in the deep, coarse, sandy soils of the lower Gulf Coastal Plain and the Carolina sandhills.

The loblolly–shortleaf forest type (SAF-80) occurs throughout the overlapped ranges of the two pines (figure 1-8). The type extends from Delaware to east Texas and southeast Oklahoma, including much of the Piedmont, and into the southern portions of the Ouachita Mountains of Arkansas. In this type, the two species together make up a majority of the stocking, although the proportion of each varies from stand to stand. Loblolly pine is usually dominant, except on the drier sites and at higher elevations. The hardwoods identified under SAF-80 are also common associates of SAF-81. At the northwestern limits of its range, loblolly pine is usually replaced by shortleaf pine. At the northeastern limits, Virginia pine and shortleaf pine begin to predominate. In fertile, well-drained coves and along stream bottoms, especially along the Eastern Seaboard, loblolly pine often grows in association with American beech, *Fagus grandifolia* Ehrh.; Carolina ash, *Fraxinus caroliniana* Mill.; white ash, *F. americana* L.; and yellow-poplar. Within their natural ranges, longleaf, slash, and Virginia pines frequently grow with loblolly pine and shortleaf pine on well-drained sites (figures 1-9 and 1-10). Pond and spruce pines are common associates of loblolly pine on poorly drained sites. However, none of these mixtures is common enough to be given a separate forest type number. Loblolly pine occurs as a minor component of the shortleaf pine type (SAF-75), slash pine type (SAF-84), Virginia pine type (SAF-79), pond pine type (SAF-98), and longleaf pine type (SAF-70).

Loblolly pine is also a minor (but important) associate of many upland and bottomland hardwood types growing on a wide array of sites. When loblolly pine makes up at least 20% of the basal area stocking, such mixtures are classified as loblolly pine–hardwood (SAF-82). This type can be locally important. For example, Louisiana has 0.6 million ha of loblolly pine–hardwood mixtures (Mistretta and Bylin 1987). Loblolly pine will normally become established in a hardwood stand only when the hardwood canopy has been disturbed by logging, fire, or catastrophe. Once a tree has become established in a hardwood stand, it often will become part of the main canopy and complete a normal life span. On moist-to-wet sites typical of coastal areas, broadleaf evergreens—such as southern magnolia, *Magnolia grandiflora* L.; sweetbay, *M. virginiana* L.; and redbay, *Persea borbonia* (L.) Spreng.—as well as swamp tupelo, *Nyssa sylvatica* var. *biflora* (Walt.) Sarg.; red maple; and slash and pond pines are common associates. On moderately moist inland sites, the hardwood mixture is typically composed of sweetgum; white oaks—cherrybark, *Q. falcata* var. *pago-*

daefolia Ell.; water, *Q. nigra* L.; and swamp chestnut, *Q. michauxii* Nutt.—as well as white ash; pignut hickory, *C. glabra* (Mill.) Sweet; red maple; and yellow-poplar. Other occasional associates include southern magnolia, spruce pine, and sweetbay. In the Piedmont, loblolly pine often forms transitional stands with a variety of oak types. On drier sites, loblolly pine is usually found in combination with upland oaks—southern red; northern red, *Q. rubra* L.; white; post; and scarlet, *Q. coccinea* Muenchh.—and hickories—shagbark, *C. ovata* (Mill.) K. Koch; pignut; and

mockernut, *C. tomentosa* (Poir.) Nutt. Occasionally, longleaf, shortleaf, and Virginia pines will also be present.

For general resource evaluations, the forest types that include loblolly pine are lumped into several broad categories, namely loblolly–shortleaf pine (which includes all combinations from pure loblolly to pure shortleaf), longleaf–slash pine, oak–pine, oak–hickory, and bottomland hardwoods. The remainder of this chapter will emphasize these broad categories.

Commercial Forest Lands

Table 1-2—Commercial forest lands (thousands of hectares) in the loblolly pine forest (that is, loblolly pine comprises over 50% of the dominant and codominant growing stock)

State	1960*	1970*	1980	1989	State	1960*	1970*	1980	1989
Alabama	1,682.8	1,724.0	1,765.2	1,802.2	Mississippi	994.6	1,102.0	1,209.4	1,306.1
Arkansas	654.2	794.7	935.3	1,061.9	North Carolina	1,425.2	1,368.9	1,243.3	1,380.7
Delaware	50.1	36.4	31.4	29.7	Oklahoma	32.2	29.6	60.1	104.2
Florida	145.8	139.9	166.7	234.3	South Carolina	1,145.3	1,221.1	1,421.5	1,628.1
Georgia	2,021.0	2,059.5	2,068.4	2,353.9	Tennessee	NM	NM	115.2	155.4
Kentucky	NM	NM	NM	25.4	Texas	1,231.4	1,244.7	1,258.0	1,269.3
Louisiana	1,417.0	1,450.8	1,484.6	1,515.1	Virginia	635.9	615.1	653.4	736.3
Maryland	143.3	112.5	86.9	70.2	Total	11,578.8	11,899.2	12,499.3	13,672.8

All figures extrapolated from actual survey dates. Trees, up to large sawtimber size, also grow in parts of New Jersey, but hectarage figures are not available because of small volumes. NM = not measured.

* All figures for Arkansas, Louisiana, Mississippi, and Texas are extrapolated from the two most recent cycles due to differences in definitions before 1971.

There are about 74 million ha of commercial forest lands in the South. Nearly 36 million ha of these are in pine or mixed pine–hardwoods (USDA FS 1988). The area of commercial forest lands in loblolly pine has increased from about 11.6 million ha in 1960 to almost 13.7 million ha in 1989 (table 1-2).

Seventy-nine percent of the commercial forest lands in the mid-South that are classified as loblolly–shortleaf (table 1-3) are predominantly loblolly pine. Loblolly pine comprises over 50% of the dominant and codominant growing stock. The area of loblolly pine plantations in the mid-South increased from a little more than 1.1 million ha during the 1970's to 2.4 million ha in the mid-1980's (table 1-4). The area in loblolly pine plantations in both Arkansas and Texas increased threefold during that period. Most plantations are owned by industry and are less than 20 years old (Knight 1987).

Along the Atlantic Seaboard (Virginia to Florida), loblolly pine made up 43% of the southern yellow pine

Table 1-3—Commercial forest lands (thousands of hectares) in loblolly or loblolly–shortleaf in mid-South, 1989

State	Loblolly*	Loblolly–shortleaf†	Percent loblolly
Alabama	1,802.2	2,165.0	83
Arkansas	1,061.9	1,690.3	63
Louisiana	1,515.1	1,617.7	94
Mississippi	1,306.1	1,564.9	83
Oklahoma	104.2	399.1	26
Tennessee	155.4	540.2	29
Texas	1,270.0	1,550.5	82
Total	7,214.9	9,527.7	

* More than 50% of the growing stock is composed of dominant or codominant loblolly pines.

† More than 50% of the growing stock is composed of loblolly and shortleaf pines, but neither species makes up 50%.

Table 1-4—Area (thousands of hectares) in loblolly pine plantations in the mid-South

State	Survey	Plantation area
Alabama	1982	567.6
	1972	303.5
Arkansas	1988	415.2
	1978	131.6
Louisiana	1984	373.0
	1974	319.8
Mississippi	1987	450.1
	1977	272.4
Oklahoma	1986	88.2
	1980	45.3
Tennessee	1989	113.5
	1980	99.9
Texas	1986	382.4
	1975	114.1

volume and occupied 5.5 million ha in the mid-1980's. Approximately 1.5 million ha were in plantations in 1983. Loblolly pine area in these five seaboard states is almost equally divided between the Coastal Plain and the Piedmont (Kellison and Gingrich 1984, Sheffield and Knight 1983).

Growing Stock

Loblolly pine, which makes up more than half of the total southern yellow pine volume (Sheffield and Knight 1983), is the most important softwood species in the southern pine region. Loblolly pine growing stock has increased from about 0.6 billion m³ (cubic meters) in the late 1940's and early 1950's (Wahlenberg 1960) to 0.8 billion m³ in 1960, 1.1 billion m³ in 1970, 1.3 billion m³ in 1980, and 1.4 billion m³ in 1989. The steep increase of about 0.2 billion m³ per decade, from 1950 to 1980, was reduced by more than half during the 1980's, indicating a leveling-off trend (figure 1-11). Factors contributing to this decline include failure to establish loblolly pine after timber harvesting, declining forest acreage, and increased mortality in older stands on public and non-industrial private forest (NIPF) lands (Sheffield and others 1985, Williams and Gresham 1986).

Fifty-seven percent of the total loblolly pine volume in the South is in the mid-South, and 43% is in the Atlantic Coastal states (table 1-5). Of the 1.4 billion m³ of loblolly pine growing stock in 1989, 59% was in natural stands, while slightly more than 16, 17, and 7% was in plantations, mixed pine–hardwoods, and other forest types, respectively (figure 1-12). The largest concentration of loblolly pine is in central and north Louisiana, south Arkansas, and east Texas, where each of 57 con-

Table 1-5—Volume of loblolly pine growing stock (million m³) on commercial forest lands in the South

State	1960	1970	1980	1989
Alabama	153.4	155.7	167.2	179.7
Arkansas	61.8	76.6	107.2	111.3
Florida	12.3	14.3	16.4	17.3
Georgia	108.8	162.4	184.4	196.7
Louisiana	85.8	134.4	172.3	199.7
Mississippi	57.4	106.1	141.5	152.0
North Carolina	121.7	135.6	146.2	158.2
Oklahoma	1.0	1.7	2.3	3.5
South Carolina	83.7	115.4	160.1	156.9
Tennessee	1.1	5.2	7.6	10.9
Texas	87.0	126.2	144.6	145.2
Virginia	60.8	58.4	63.0	69.0
Total	834.8	1,092.0	1,312.8	1,400.4

tiguous counties and parishes has over 2.8 million m³ of growing stock. The next largest concentration is in east-central Mississippi and west-central Alabama, where each of 32 counties also has more than 2.8 million m³ of growing stock. Smaller concentrations occur in the coastal counties of South Carolina and North Carolina

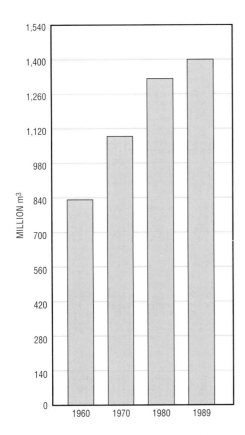

Figure 1-11—Loblolly pine growing-stock inventory by year in the Southern States.

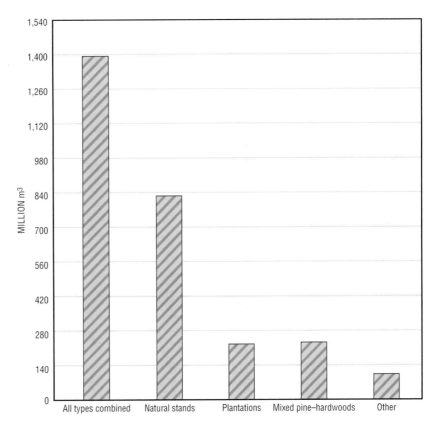

Figure 1-12—Loblolly pine growing stock by forest management type, 1989.

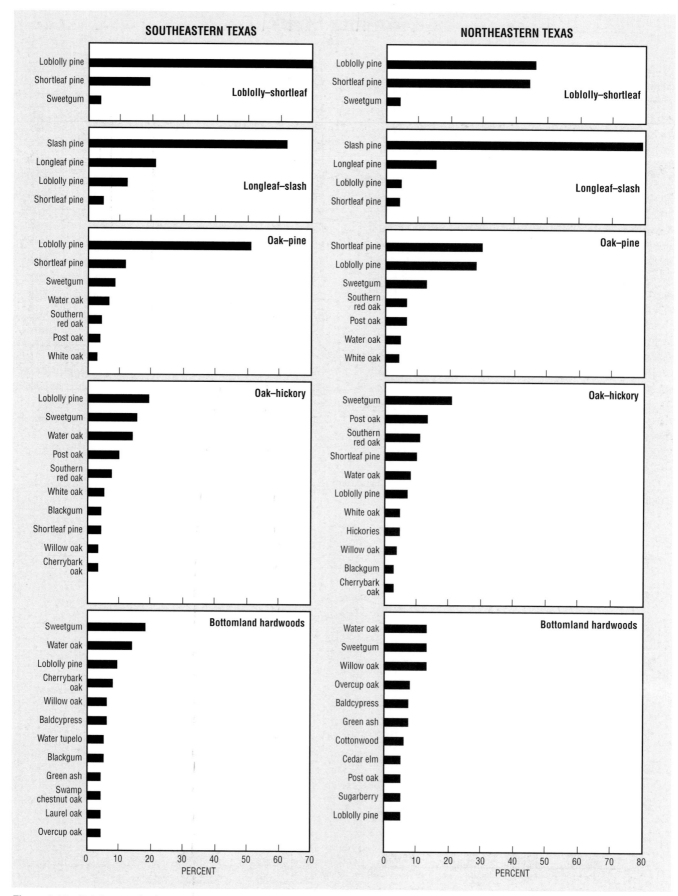

Figure 1-13—Relative species importance as a percentage of merchantable growing-stock volume by forest type in Texas, 1986 (adapted from McWilliams and Lord 1988).

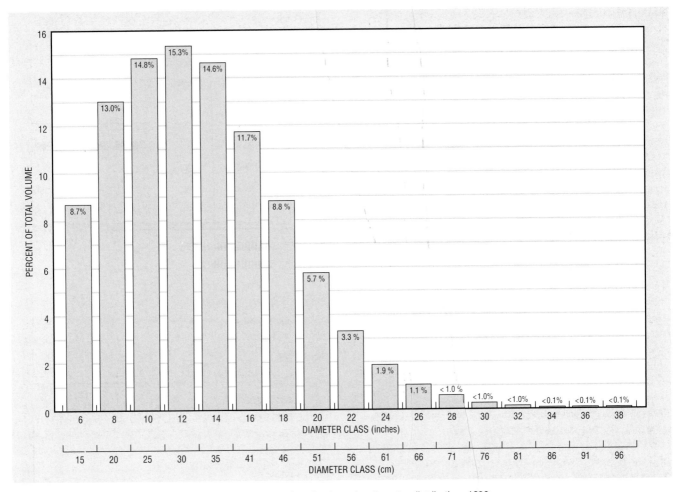

Figure 1-14—Loblolly pine growing stock as a percentage of total volume by diameter distribution, 1989.

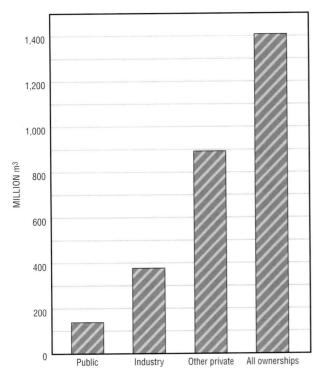

Figure 1-15—Loblolly pine inventory by ownership class in the Southern States, 1989.

(13 counties) and in extreme southeast Louisiana and southwest Mississippi (10 parishes and counties) (figure 1-7). Figure 1-13 shows the relative role of loblolly pine in the various forest types in eastern Texas. In the southeastern part of the state, loblolly pine makes up 70% of the loblolly–shortleaf growing stock and 50% of the oak-pine growing stock. In the drier northeastern part of the state, loblolly pine and shortleaf pine each make up about 45% of the loblolly–shortleaf forest type.

Of the merchantable loblolly pine growing stock—12.7 cm in diameter at breast height (dbh) and larger—in the South, 70% is in the 20- to 40-cm diameter classes (figure 1-14). About 0.9 billion m^3 (or 64%) of this growing-stock volume belong to approximately 3 million NIPF land owners, each of whom holds an average of 13 ha (Rosson and Doolittle 1987). Industry owns an additional 27% of the growing stock, and 10% is in public ownership (figure 1-15). Forest industries lease and manage or provide landowner assistance on almost 3.6 million ha of NIPF lands across the South (Meyer and others 1986, Smith 1989). Much of this land supports pure stands of loblolly pine or mixed stands in which loblolly pine is a primary or secondary species.

Seventy percent or more of all loblolly pine stands are within 0.3 km of a road (Rudis and others 1984), making access for commercial harvesting easy. Commercial harvesting is common and frequent, especially on privately owned lands. Partial cutting prevails on NIPF lands, whereas clearcutting prevails on industry holdings. In Mississippi, 47% of the pine and pine–hardwood stands on privately owned lands were harvested between 1977 and 1987, and 75% of these stands were at least 60% stocked with naturally regenerated pine following cutting (McWilliams 1988). Regeneration surveys in Louisiana and east Texas produced similar results, except that only 50% of stands in Louisiana were considered stocked after final harvest cutting (McWilliams and Frey 1986, McWilliams and Skove 1987). Southwide, between 1952 and 1985, the total area of naturally regenerated pines on NIPF holdings steadily decreased from about 36% to about 21% due to harvesting without concern for natural regeneration. Although about half of this loss was offset by planting pines (mainly loblolly), the remainder of the unstocked sites reverted to natural upland hardwoods. A similar decrease occurred on industrial holdings (a reduction from 42% to 20%); however, all of the loss was made up by planted pines (Alig and others 1986). Seventy-five percent or more of all the unstocked or poorly stocked forest lands in the South belong to NIPF owners (Birdsey and Pitcher 1986, Rosson and Doolittle 1987). Much of this land could be productively regenerated to loblolly pine.

In mixed pine-hardwood stands, the average volume of pine growing stock per hectare increases as pine stocking increases on a particular site, as long as hardwood stocking decreases so there is no change in total stocking (table 1-6). The largest volume difference should occur in the 20- to 30-year age class. As stand age increases, the difference diminishes. In the southeast Piedmont, about 2.3 million ha (or 21% of the for-

Table 1-6—Average volume of growing stock (m^3) per hectare of timberland in the southeast Piedmont, by stand-age class and percentage of pine stocking*

Stand-age class (year)	All stands	<25%	29-49%	50-74%	>75%
<10	12.6	17.1	17.9	10.4	6.4
11-20	42.5	38.1	40.6	39.5	47.5
21-30	89.7	61.5	68.3	87.5	112.2
31-40	114.5	98.8	93.6	118.2	139.0
41-50	138.7	126.4	127.9	159.6	168.3
>51	151.3	147.8	143.8	171.4	176.3

Source: Knight and Phillips (1987).

* Pine stocking as a percentage of all live tree stocking in the stand, <25%, 25–49%, 50–74%, and >75%.

est) support mixed pine–hardwood stands in which loblolly pine makes up about 58% of the pine growing stock and hardwoods make up anywhere from 25 to 75% of the total growing stock (Knight and Phillips 1987). Even pine plantations can have a substantial hardwood component. In fact, more than 0.7 million ha of pine plantations in the mid-South (Alabama and Tennessee to Texas and Oklahoma) are classified as mixed pine–hardwoods, and another 0.5 million ha are classified as hardwoods because of poor pine survival (Birdsey and McWilliams 1986).

Summary

The natural range of loblolly pine reaches from east Texas to Florida and northward to Delaware and overlaps the natural ranges of longleaf, shortleaf, slash, pitch, and Virginia pines in 14 southern and mid-Atlantic states. Of these species, only shortleaf pine has a wider geographic range than loblolly pine has.

Loblolly pine is extremely versatile, capable of growing in association with numerous annual and perennial plants, including mixed hardwoods, throughout its life. In the original forests, it was confined to moist fringes of the Coastal Plain and Piedmont, dominated by longleaf pine or mixed hardwoods, because it had limited tolerance to fire.

Intense logging of the original forests in the late 1800's and early 1900's and expanded fire control beginning in the 1930's permitted loblolly pine to become established on an array of upland sites throughout its natural range. Loblolly pine's easy and quick regeneration and rapid growth soon made it the favored forest tree species throughout the South.

Loblolly pine is now the leading timber species in the United States, predominating on 13.4 million ha. It comprises half of the total volume of southern pine growing stock (approximately 1.4 billion m^3) and has a total dry biomass in excess of 1 billion tonnes.

Literature Cited

Alig RJ, Knight HA, Birdsey RA. 1986. Recent area changes in southern forest ownerships and cover types. Res. Pap. SE-260. Asheville, NC: USDA Forest Service, Southeastern Forest Experiment Station. 10 p.

Applegate RD, Rolfe GL, Arnold LE. 1976. Common wildlife food plants in loblolly (*Pinus taeda* L.) and shortleaf pine (*P. echinata* Mill.) plantations in southern Illinois. For. Res. Rep. 76-8. Champaign/Urbana, IL: University of Illinois, Department of Forestry, Agriculture Experiment Station. 2 p.

Ashe WW. 1915. Loblolly or North Carolina pine. Bull. 24. Raleigh, NC: Edwards & Broughton Printing Co. 176 p.

Birdsey RA, McWilliams WH. 1986. Midsouth forest area trends. Res. Bull. SO-107. New Orleans: USDA Forest Service, Southern Forest Experiment Station. 17 p.

Birdsey, RA, Pitcher JA. 1986. Management options for poorly stocked stands in the south central United States. Southern Journal of Applied Forestry 10(2):73–77.

Cost ND, Howard JO, Mead B, and others. 1990. The forest biomass resource of the United States. Gen. Tech. Rep. WO-57. Washington, DC: USDA Forest Service. 21 p.

Cox SK, Van Lear DH. 1985. Biomass and nutrient accretion on Piedmont sites following clearcutting and natural regeneration of loblolly pine. In: Shoulders E, ed. Proceedings, 3rd Biennial Southern Silvicultural Research Conference; 1984 November 7–8; Atlanta, GA. Gen. Tech. Rep. SO-54. New Orleans: USDA Forest Service, Southern Forest Experiment Station: 501–506.

Critchfield WB, Little EL Jr. 1966. Geographic distribution of pines of the world. Misc. Pub. 991. Washington, DC: USDA Forest Service. 97 p.

Eyre FH, ed. 1980. Forest cover types of the United States and Canada, rev. Washington, DC: Society of American Foresters. 148 p.

Gilmore AR, Funk DT. 1976. Shortleaf and loblolly pine seed origin trials in southern Illinois: 27-year results. In: Proceedings, 10th Central States Forest Tree Improvement Conference; 1976 September 22–23; West Lafayette, IN. West Lafayette, IN: Purdue University, Department of Forestry and Natural Resources: 115–124.

Goebel NB. 1974. Growth and yield of planted loblolly pine. In: Proceedings, Symposium on Management of Young Pines; 1974 October 22–24; Alexandria, LA/December 3–5; Charleston, SC. Asheville, NC: USDA Forest Service, Southeastern Forest Experiment Station: 264–275.

Hodgkins EJ. 1970. Productivity estimation by means of plant indicators in the longleaf pine forests of Alabama. In: Tree growth and forest soils. Corvallis, OR: Oregon State University Press: 461–474.

Jones SM, Van Lear DH, Cox SK. 1981. Composition and density-diameter pattern of an old-growth forest stand of the Boiling Springs Natural Area, South Carolina. Bulletin of the Torrey Botanical Club 108(3):347–353.

Kellison RC, Gingrich S. 1984. Loblolly pine management and utilization: state of the art. Southern Journal of Applied Forestry 8(2):88–96.

Knight HA. 1987. A southwide perspective on the pine plantation resource. In: Forests, the World, and the Profession. Proceedings, 1986 National Convention of the Society of American Foresters; 1986 October 5–8; Birmingham, AL. Bethesda, MD: Society of American Foresters: 63–66.

Knight HA, Phillips DR. 1987. Silvicultural implications of mixed pine–hardwood stands in the Piedmont. In: Phillips DR, comp. Proceedings, 4th Biennial Southern Silvicultural Research Conference; 1986 November 4–6; Atlanta. Gen. Tech. Rep. SE-42. Asheville, NC: USDA Forest Service, Southeastern Forest Experiment Station: 157–161.

Koch P. 1972. Utilization of the southern pines. Agric. Handbk. 420. Washington, DC: USDA Forest Service. 1663 p. [2 vol.]

Krochmal A, Kologiski R. 1974. Understory plants in mature loblolly pine plantations in North Carolina. Res. Note SE-208. Asheville, NC: USDA Forest Service, Southeastern Forest Experiment Station. 8 p.

Little EL Jr. 1971. Atlas of United States trees. Vol. 1. Conifers and important hardwoods. Misc. Pub. 1146. Washington, DC: USDA Forest Service. 208 p.

Manogaran C. 1975. Actual evapotranspiration and the natural range of loblolly pine. Forest Science 21(4):339–340.

McWilliams WH. 1988. Status of privately owned timberland in Mississippi, 1977–87. Res. Note SO-346. New Orleans: USDA Forest Service, Southern Forest Experiment Station. 6 p.

McWilliams WH, Frey PD. 1986. Status of privately owned harvested timberland in Louisiana, 1974-84. Res. Note SO-329. New Orleans: USDA Forest Service, Southern Forest Experiment Station. 5 p.

McWilliams WH, Lord RG. 1988. Forest resources of east Texas. Resour. Bull. SO-136. New Orleans: USDA Forest Service, Southern Forest Experiment Station. 42 p.

McWilliams WH, Skove DJ. 1987. Status of privately owned harvest timberland in east Texas, 1975-1986. Res. Note SO-338. New Orleans: USDA Forest Service, Southern Forest Experiment Station. 6 p.

Meyer RD, Klemperer WD, Siegel WC. 1986. Cutting contracts and timberland leasing. Journal of Forestry 84(12):35–38.

Mills RH, Jones SB Jr. 1969. The composition of a mesic southern mixed hardwood forest in south Mississippi. Castanea 34(1):62–66.

Mistretta PA, Bylin CV. 1987. Incidence and impact of damage to Louisiana's timber, 1985. Resour. Bull. SO-117. New Orleans: USDA Forest Service, Southern Forest Experiment Station. 19 p.

Nelson TC. 1957. The original forests of the Georgia Piedmont. Ecology 38: 390–397.

Nixon ES, Matos J, Hansen RS. 1987. The response of woody vegetation to a topographic gradient in eastern Texas. Texas Journal of Science 39(4):367–375.

Quarterman E, Keever C . 1962. Southern mixed hardwood forest: climax in the southeastern Coastal Plain, U.S.A. Ecological Monographs 32(2):167–169.

Rosenzweig ML. 1968. Net primary productivity of terrestrial communities: prediction from climatological data. American Naturalist 102(923):67–74.

Rosson JF Jr, Doolittle L. 1987. Profiles of Midsouth nonindustrial private forests and owners. Resour. Bull. SO-125. New Orleans: USDA Forest Service, Southern Forest Experiment Station. 39 p.

Rudis VA, Rosson JF Jr, Kelly JF. 1984. Forest resources of Alabama. Resour. Bull. SO-98. New Orleans: USDA Forest Service, Southern Forest Experiment Station. 55 p.

Sheffield RM, Cost NE, Bechtold WA, McClure JP. 1985. Pine growth reductions in the Southeast. Resour. Bull. SE-83. Asheville, NC: USDA Forest Service, Southeastern Forest Experiment Station. 112 p.

Sheffield RM, Knight HA. 1983. Loblolly pine resource: southeast region. In: Proceedings, Symposium on the Loblolly Pine Ecosystem—East Region; 1982 December 8–10; Raleigh, NC. Raleigh, NC: North Carolina State University, School of Forest Resources: 7–24.

Smith DW. 1989. Industry-sponsored landowner assistance programs. Forest Farmer 48(5):41.

Smith OD Jr. 1961. A quantitative relationship of associated vegetation to the site index of loblolly pine on the Alabama Piedmont. Auburn University, AL: Auburn University. 55 p. Ph.D. dissertation.

USDA FS [USDA Forest Service]. 1988.   The South's fourth forest: alternatives for the future. For. Res. Rep. 24. Washington, DC: USDA Forest Service. 512 p.

Van Lear DH, Kapeluck PR, Waide JB. 1990.   Nitrogen pools and processes during natural regeneration of loblolly pine. In: Garrett S, Powers R, eds. Sustained productivity of forest soils. Proceedings, 7th North American Forest Soils Conference; 1988 July 24–28; Vancouver, BC. Vancouver, BC: University of British Columbia, Faculty of Forestry: 234–252.

Wahlenberg WG. 1960.   Loblolly pine: its use, ecology, regeneration, protection, growth and management. Durham, NC: Duke University, School of Forestry. 603 p.

Williams TM, Gresham CA. 1986.   Factors important to loblolly pine productivity on the southeastern Coastal Plain of the United States. In: Agren GI, ed. Predicting consequences of intensive forest harvesting on long-term productivity. Rep. 26. Sweden: Institutionen for Ekologi och Miljovard, Sveriges Lantbruksuniversitet: 177–186.

Wolters GL, Schmidtling RC. 1975.   Browse and herbage in intensively managed pine plantations. Journal of Wildlife Management 39(3): 557–562.

Zellmer RC. 1975.   Use of hardwood tree species as plant indicators of longleaf and loblolly pine site index in Alabama. Auburn, AL: Auburn University. 90 p. M.S. thesis.

Chapter 2

Botanical and Silvical Characteristics

Contents

Continued on next page…

Contents (cont'd)

Botanical and Silvical Characteristics

Introduction

Loblolly pine is a medium- to large-sized tree averaging 27 to 34 m in height and 61 to 76 cm in diameter at a mature age of about 80 to 100 years on average sites. It

Figure 2-1—Naturally regenerated lobolly pines, up to 200 years old and 1.3 m in dbh, growing in central Mississippi.

reaches merchantable size throughout its natural range. Trees that are 25 years old may exceed 37 m in height and 30 cm in diameter. Roots make up about 20% of the total tree biomass. Taproots reach depths of 1 to 3 m or more, and lateral roots often grow as long as a tree is tall. On the better, moist sites, loblolly pine in the South's original forests grew to 45 m in height and reached 0.9 to 1.5 m in diameter at breast height (dbh) (Rothrock 1890, Sargent 1884, Zon 1905; figure 2-1). When fully developed, loblolly pine is the largest of the southern pines, having reached a record height of 55.5 m and a dbh of 160 cm. The largest loblolly pine now living is in Virginia; it is 207.8 cm in dbh and 41 m in height, and has a crown spread of 24.4 m (AFA 1990). Another large loblolly pine, which died in 1985 at the age of 170 years, was 50 m in height and 142 cm in dbh, weighed slightly less than 13.6 tonnes (t), and had a crown spread of 19 m. The three logs cut from this tree scaled 5,664 board feet Doyle (Anonymous 1995b) or about 32 m³.

Loblolly pine is an early successional species. More tolerant hardwoods become established under developing stands of loblolly pine and ultimately form a climax stand after the mature pines are harvested or have died. Under natural conditions, 80- to 100-year-old loblolly pine stands will normally have many hardwoods in the understory and midstory. By stand age 175, only a few pines will remain, and stands will have reached the hardwood climax. Occasionally, a loblolly pine will live for 250 to 300 years. Loblolly pine rarely perpetuates itself on the same area except following disturbances such as a harvest cut or fire, hurricane, or attack by the southern pine beetle (*Dendroctonus frontalis* Zimmerman) (Harlow and Harrar 1958; Stalter 1970, 1971).

Outstanding Features

Foliage

Loblolly pine foliage is pale blue-green to yellow-green and consists of needles that are 13 to 22 cm in length and 1.2 to 1.4 mm in diameter, in fascicles of three (occasionally two and rarely four), with a weight of 0.09 to 0.21 g per fascicle. Needles are slender, generally triangular in cross section, rigid, and slightly twisted, and have basal sheaths 10 to 20 mm in length. Each needle has about 24 rows of sunken stomata, about 120 to 130 stomata/cm in each row, and 2 (rarely 2 to 4) large, medial, resin canals (Cotton and others 1975, Snyder and Hamaker 1978, Wells 1969). Both thick-walled and thin-walled fiberlike cells of needle tissue are 1.2 to 3.0 mm in length (with occasional cells as long as 5.1 mm) and are comparable to wood tracheids in length. Needle tensile strength ranges from 326 to 491 kg/cm^2, and total ash content is about 3.5% (Howard 1973). Needle moisture content is about 200% at field capacity and about 85% at the permanent wilting point (Bilan and Jan 1968). Most needles persist through two growing seasons. Needle weight increases until the summer of the second year and then decreases slowly until abscission. Needles of the first spring flush attain near-maximum length by early September of the first year (Wells and Metz 1963).

Needle form varies within the natural range of the species. Trees from inland populations generally have lower ratios of needle-length to needle-width than do trees from Atlantic or Gulf Coast populations (Wells and others 1977). Foliage form, weight, and distribution are also affected by position in the crown. Needles growing in the well-lit portions of the canopy ("sun needles") are larger and have more stomata per unit of area, than needles growing in the shaded portion of the canopy ("shade needles"). However, shade needles have more stomata per unit of dry weight (Gresham 1976, Shelton and Switzer 1984; table 2-1). Also, the thickness of various needle components is greatest in needles at the top of the crown and least in those at the lowest canopy level (table 2-2). Total needle weight per tree is discussed in chapter 11.

Strobili

Loblolly pine is monoecious: male and female "flowers" form on the same tree, but from separate buds. [Pines are not true flowering plants. Their reproductive organs are properly called "strobili," but they are often referred to as "flowers." The term "flower" is used in this book.] Flowering commonly begins between tree ages 5 and 10. Female flowers are most often borne on secondary branches that produce two to three cycles of growth in one season. Male flowers [often called "catkins"] are usually borne on tertiary branches in the lower part of the crown (Eggler 1961). Flower development, in relation to shoot growth, has been discussed in detail by Greenwood (1980).

Male flowers. The pollen-bearing catkins are morphologically modified needles and are formed on the resting bud of the preceding year's growth. Fully developed catkins range from 2.5 to 3.8 cm in length and 0.6 to 0.8 cm in diameter and are usually borne in clusters of 3 to 10, and sometimes as many as 15, below the needle fascicles on buds in the lower half of the crown. The coloration of catkins varies from light green to red or

Table 2–1—Average needle characteristics of loblolly pine at various positions within crown

Character	Top Open	Top Close	Middle Open	Middle Close	Bottom Open	Bottom Close	Coefficient of variation
Length (cm)	16.8	15.8	18.5	14.0	16.2	12.4	25
Weight (mg)	39.3	36.1	42.4	21.9	35.2	16.0	42
Surface area (mm^2)	612	573	677	451	572	358	31
No. of stomata x 10^3	57.1	52.7	57.5	34.1	48.7	25.0	15
Area/weight (mm^2/mg)	15.6	16.1	16.2	20.8	16.4	22.5	14
Stomata/weight (no./mg x 10^{-2})	14.6	14.7	13.7	15.6	13.8	15.4	12
Stomata/area (no./mm^2)	93.1	91.8	84.9	75.0	84.7	68.7	15

Source: adapted from McLaughlin and Madgwick (1968).
Open = open-grown canopy, close = close-grown canopy.

Table 2-2—Morphological features of needles by canopy for 16-year-old loblolly pine

Anatomical feature	Canopy position Top	Canopy position Middle	Canopy position Bottom
Cuticle thickness (µm)	2.9	2.6	2.1
Epidermal thickness (µm)	13.0	12.7	12.1
Hypodermal thickness (µm)	29.6	25.8	22.4
Mesophyll thickness (µm)	116.5	103.9	86.3
Length of stomata (µm)	27.8	28.2	28.6
Stomata per mm^2 (no.)	157.7	149.8	141.0

Source: adapted from Higginbotham (1974).

yellow, depending on the stage of development. Catkins are surrounded at the base by 8 to 10 scales.

Each loblolly pine pollen grain contains two air sacs, which give it great buoyancy and facilitate long-distance movement of pollen by air currents. The exterior pollen wall is composed of an extremely durable material that protects the pollen in transport and over time. Pollen grains have endured for centuries in geological deposits. Table 2-3 is a summary of detailed measurements of loblolly pine pollen grains and wings. The length of the average pollen grain for loblolly and shortleaf pines is 69 µm. For longleaf it is 62 µm, and for slash about 60 µm, indicating that there is little difference in pollen size among the southern pines.

Table 2-3—Dimensions of loblolly pine pollen (µm)

	Pollen grains ave.	Pollen grains range	Pollen wings ave.	Pollen wings range
Length	69	66–72	46	39–51
Depth	47	45–48	30	26–31
Breadth	53	50–58	58	55–62

Source: adapted from Cain (1940).

Female flowers and cones. Female flowers are generally ovoid and range from 1.0 to 1.5 cm in length. At their widest point, they are about half as wide as they are long. They vary from light green to pink or red depending on developmental stage. They are borne singly, or in whorls of two to six, as modified lateral branches on buds in the upper half of the crown, where they may be uniformly or irregularly distributed. Flowers are often located within about 10 cm of a resting vegetative bud. By the end of the first year, cones reach about 2.5 to 3.0 cm in length and 1.5 cm in diameter, have distinct bracts with sharp spines, and are uniformly brown in color. Tannin and other phenolic compounds occur in a cone throughout the cone's life. Tannin concentrations are highest when the cones are about 10 months old and lowest when cones are about 16 months old (Trembath and Askew 1987).

Mature loblolly pine cones are 5 to 15 cm in length (averaging 9 cm), about 4 cm in diameter, and light reddish brown in color. The average cone has a volume of 36 to 72 cm^3 (McLemore 1972). Cones are ovoid–cylindrical to narrowly conical, are sessile, have a flattened base, and are armed with stout sharp spines that are extremely strong and persistent (figure 2-2). The apophysis and outer scale tissue contain much oleoresin, which helps keep cones closed until they dehydrate in autumn (Kossuth and Biggs 1981). There are about 135 scales per cone, of which 40 to 110 (an average of 75) are fertile. Scales spiral from the base to the tip of a cone

according to the Fibonacci series. About half of cones spiral to the left and half to the right (Wiant 1973). The concentration of tannins in cones from a South Carolina Coastal Plain seed orchard was highest (1,832 ppm tannic acid equivalent [TAE]) at cone age 10 months and lowest (970 ppm TAE) at cone age 16 months. The high and low concentrations of phenolics were at 10 months (67 ppm TAE) and 14 months (43 ppm TAE), respectively (Trembath and Askew 1987). Cones are difficult to detach even when ripe, and some persist on trees for several years (McLemore 1974).

Seeds

Loblolly pine seeds are about 6 mm long and dark brown to black or occasionally spotted or mottled; size and color vary greatly from tree to tree. Seeds, with attached seedwings, are borne singly or in pairs at the bases of the cone scales. Seedwings are 1.9 to 2.5 cm long and are usually broadest above the center. The wings facilitate wind distribution of seeds. Individual seeds weigh 17 to 37 mg (they average about 25 mg) (Schopmeyer 1974). Seed weight can vary with cone size, position of seed in the cone, and position of the cone on the tree. About 56% of the total dry weight is in seedcoat, 37% in gametophyte, and 6% in embryo (Janick and Whipkey 1988; figure 2-3). Embryos contain a large number of uniformly distributed starch grains. In contrast, the endosperm contains relatively small amounts of starch, and the distribution of this starch is not uniform. Additionally, loblolly pine seeds contain a small amount of amylopectin and a large amount of amylose (Whetstone and others 1970). Triglycerides accumulate continuously in developing embryos and make up almost 50% of the fresh weight of a mature embryo (Feirer and others 1989).

Figure 2-3—A radiograph of a loblolly pine seed.

Figure 2-2—A loblolly pine shoot with new conelets and first- and second-year cones.

Twigs and Buds

Loblolly pine twigs are yellow-brown or reddish brown. Buds are covered with reddish brown scales except at the tips (Harlow and Harrar 1958). Winter resting buds are about 1.0 to 1.5 cm long, 0.4 to 0.6 cm wide, reddish brown, and have a smooth surface. Buds are usually set in the early fall; they expand again in late winter or early spring depending on latitude. Trees from more northerly latitudes enter dormancy before those from further south, and they enter a deeper state of dormancy (Boyer and South 1989). Volumetric changes in interphase nuclei and chromosomes in winter buds may begin as much as 2 months before the onset of visible bud growth (Taylor 1965).

Xylem

The xylem of loblolly pine cannot be visually distinguished from that of other important southern pines. Position in the stem has a greater effect than tree age on physical properties of both xylem and phloem (Stohr 1980). Thus, to accurately determine wood properties of a particular tree, samples should be taken at specified intervals throughout the merchantable length or the entire length of the tree. Nuclear magnetic resonance (NMR) imaging can provide a clear picture of the general composition of a tree stem that has not been debarked or cut into boards. This technique is based on detection of normal differences between moisture levels of different types of xylem (for example, sapwood–heartwood and earlywood–latewood) and on detection of differences between moisture levels associated with defects such as reaction wood, knots, and decay. Physical properties of loblolly pine xylem can be altered by artificially imposed environmental conditions. For example, restraining young trees from swaying in the wind can markedly reduce radial growth, the amount of compression wood, and wood specific gravity and can alter the number and diameter of tracheids (Burton and Smith 1972).

Specific gravity. Wood specific gravity is the most reliable single index of wood quality because it is closely associated with many important wood properties. It is the ratio of the weight of a sample of wood to the weight of a volume of water equal to the volume of the sample. Because specific gravity varies with wood moisture content, it must be determined on an ovendry basis so that comparisons will be consistent. Mean specific gravity across the species' range is 0.47 to 0.51 (Bendtsen

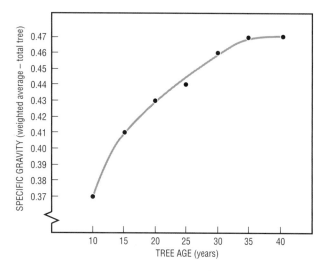

Figure 2-4—Effect of age on specific gravity of loblolly pine (adapted from Zobel and others 1972).

and Ethington 1972, Koch 1972). Specific gravity of the merchantable portion of the bole can be estimated quite accurately from increment cores taken at breast height (Christopher and Wahlgren 1964). Increment cores should be 5 mm or larger in diameter for ease of handling and to minimize breakage. A common procedure is to take two cores from the opposite sides of a tree at breast height. Cores should extend from the outer edge to the center of a tree and must be free of resin pockets, knots, and compression wood. Cores should be packaged to prevent drying and evaluated as soon as possible or frozen if delays are necessary.

There is usually very little difference between the specific gravities of stemwood or branchwood of loblolly, longleaf, shortleaf, slash, and Virginia pines of the same age that were grown on similar sites. In fact, where loblolly, longleaf, and slash pines grow together in natural stands, there are no species differences in specific gravity of wood (Cole and others 1966, Gibson and others 1986, Zobel and others 1972). Specific gravity of the sapwood of 50-year-old loblolly pine (0.54) is substantially greater than the sapwood of 50-year-old spruce pine (0.46) in south Mississippi (Snyder and Hamaker 1970).

There is no definite relationship between specific gravity and tree growth rate. Fast-growing trees can have high or low specific gravity whether young or mature (Megraw 1985, van Buijtenen 1963). Specific gravity increases directly with tree age to age 35 (figure 2-4). Specific gravity of bolewood is about 0.36 at tree ages 1 to 5, rapidly increases to about 0.45 to 0.55 from tree ages 5 to 15 (the period of "grand growth"), then remains fairly constant for merchantable wood throughout the remaining years of growth (Bendtsen and Senft 1986, Loo and others 1985, Taras and Saucier 1967, Zobel and others 1972). Mean specific gravity of oldfield loblolly pine 25.4 cm and less in dbh and less than 30 years old averaged 0.44 (with a range of 0.35 to 0.53) in Texas, Arkansas, Louisiana, and Oklahoma plantations (Lenhart and others 1977).

Specific gravity can be predicted for various tree heights and ages because it tends to decrease with tree height but increase with distance from the pith (USDA FS 1965; figure 2-5). In addition, specific gravity of unmerchantable tops (those less than 10 cm in diameter) of older trees is low, but higher than that of the topwood of young trees (Zobel and others 1972). Specific gravity of juvenile wood and topwood are comparable, but cell dimensions of topwood more closely resemble those of mature wood than those of juvenile wood (Kellison 1981). Lenhart and others (1977) developed the following equation, which predicts specific gravity (sp. gr.) for various combinations of percentage of tree height and tree age for natural stands aged 10 to 30 years:

sp. gr. = 0.44094 − 0.00125 (percentage of total tree height) + 0.00294 (tree age in years).

Site characteristics can affect the specific gravity and other physical characteristics of loblolly pine wood. Site

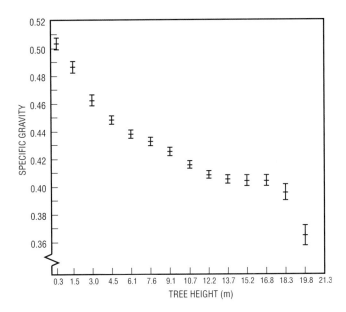

Figure 2-5—Mean specific gravity and associated standard errors as related to height of loblolly pine trees (adapted from Tauer and Loo-Dinkins 1990).

differences were associated with small but significant changes in specific gravity, lumen diameter, and cell wall thickness in loblolly pine clones in two Georgia seed orchards. Trees on the more productive site produced wood with lower specific gravity, larger mean lumen diameter, and thicker wall tracheids (Hamilton and Harris 1965). In northern Louisiana, specific gravity of the stem was about the same on wet, intermediate, and dry sites, but root specific gravity was greater on the dry site than on the other two (Gibson and others 1986).

Normal spacing intervals of 1.2 to 3.0 m in plantations had little effect on specific gravity of loblolly pines grown for 14 to 20 years in central Louisiana, Georgia, and southern Illinois (Echols 1959, Geyer and Gilmore 1965, Hamilton and Matthews 1965). Specific gravity of xylem developed shortly after thinning may increase, decrease, or fluctuate as interacting factors (such as soil moisture and crown development) promote the development of more earlywood or latewood (Paul 1958).

Generally, the specific gravity of young plantation trees is lower than that of trees of similar ages in natural stands in similar environments. Trees in a 15-year-old natural stand in the Alabama Piedmont had a specific gravity of 0.46, whereas the specific gravity of nearby planted trees was 0.42. This equates to a weight difference of 4 kg/m^3 of wood. Specific gravity patterns were the same in north Florida and south Georgia, but the differences were much smaller (Zobel and others 1972).

Fiber length and angle. The strength of wood is directly related to fiber (tracheid) length. Fiber length is significantly shorter for juvenile wood than for mature wood. Longitudinal tracheid length increases from less than 2.0 mm near the pith to 3.0 to 5.0 mm or more (average 4.3 mm) in the outer rings by tree age 10

(Jackson 1959) and then stays fairly constant for the remaining life of the tree. Wheeler and others (1966) found that average tracheid length was 3.4 mm for juvenile wood for all trees at all heights in four South Carolina natural stands and was 4.4 mm for mature wood. Average tracheid length of the fifth annual ring of planted loblolly pines in Mississippi was 3.1 mm, whereas average tracheid length for the 15th annual ring was 4.1 mm (Taylor and Moore 1981).

Fiber length also varies substantially within single annual rings in both juvenile and mature wood. In juvenile wood, first-formed earlywood cells are shorter than either last-formed earlywood or latewood tracheids (Taylor and Moore 1981). In mature wood, fibers increase in length through the earlywood to a maximum length at a distance of 50 to 65% of the ring width and then decrease in length to the end of the latewood. The amount of increase is 10 to 36%. Fiber length in slash and shortleaf pines show this same pattern of within-ring variation (Jackson and Morse 1965).

Fibril angle (the average angle between the fibers in the outer layer of the tracheid cell wall and the tracheid longitudinal axis) also influences wood strength. In normal summerwood fibers of 10- to 35-year-old loblolly pines, fibril angle can range from 2 to 51 degrees. However, fibril angle usually ranges from 20 to 35 degrees during the first 5 years of tree growth, stabilizes at about 20 degrees by tree age 12, and drops to 10 degrees for normal, high-density, mature wood in the lower bole. This pattern exists at all heights, but the angles decrease faster with increasing age at upper heights. Thus, for a given ring, fibril angles will be considerably higher at 1 m than at several meters up in a tree. Average fibril angles tend to be greater in wide annual rings than in narrow rings. The large fibril angles of wide inner rings contribute to the low strength, high longitudinal shrinkage, and lower tangential shrinkage characteristics of juvenile wood as compared to mature wood (Bendtsen and Senft 1986, Megraw 1985, Pillow and others 1953).

Fibril angle and tracheid length are highly correlated; large fibril angles are associated with short tracheid lengths, and small fibril angles are associated with long tracheid lengths. There is no constant relationship in a tree between specific gravity and desirable physical properties such as small fibril angle or long cell length. For wood of a given specific gravity, fibril angles are larger nearer the base of the tree (Megraw 1985).

Stem and branch comparisons. Cambial division is much slower in branches than in the bole. As a result, the stem is larger than any branch. In both stems and branches, the most rapid growth is in early (juvenile) years (Taylor 1979). The lower side of a branch contains a high proportion of compression wood and has wider growth increments than the upper side at all points along the branch. Thus, specific gravity of the lower side of a branch is much higher than that of the upper side

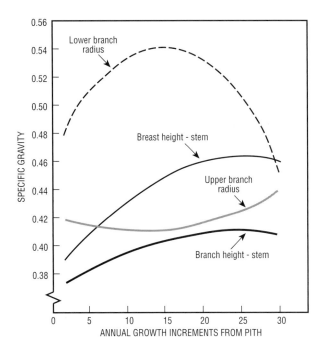

Figure 2-6—Relationship between specific gravity and age for stemwood and branchwood of loblolly pine (adapted from Taylor 1979).

or of any of the stemwood until about age 30 (figure 2-6). Tracheids in wood near the pith of branches are approximately the same length as those in stemwood. In branchwood, as in the bole, extractive materials are concentrated in the five rings nearest the pith.

Juvenile and mature wood. Wood that forms the central core of a tree is developed from immature cambium within the growing crown. This juvenile wood often has lower specific gravity and thinner cell walls, shorter tracheids, larger fibril angle, and poorer mechanical properties than mature wood (Bendtsen and Senft 1986). As the tree grows, the new wood increases in density and strength (Pearson 1986). The change from juvenile wood to mature wood with thick cell walls, long cells, and high density occurs gradually over a period of several years, and there is no specific point where juvenile wood ends and mature wood begins. The average diameter of minimum-strength juvenile wood is about 5 to 8 cm (Hallock 1968). Length of the juvenile period decreases from north to south, from about 14 years in the Piedmont to 6 to 8 years in the Gulf Coastal Plain (Clark and Saucier 1989, 1991; Clark and Schmidtling 1989). Wood near the top of an old tree is similar to that formed near the base of a young tree (figure 2-7). Mechanical strength of newly produced wood (as measured by modulus of rupture, modulus of elasticity, and specific gravity) reaches a maximum in the lower bole by about age 13, but cells may not reach maximum length until trees are about age 18 or older (Bendtsen and Senft 1986, Loo and others 1985).

The proportion of juvenile wood to mature wood in a tree and a stand can be controlled by: (1) genetic selec-

tion, (2) manipulation of stand density, and (3) control of rotation length. Stand density does not affect age of transition from juvenile to mature wood in a tree, but it does affect the diameter of the juvenile core. Planting close and thinning after trees begin producing mature wood minimizes the juvenile core (Clark and Saucier 1991). Loblolly pine stems may contain as much as 85% juvenile wood by volume at age 15. The proportion of juvenile wood decreases to about 46% at tree age 30 and to as little as 19% at age 40 to 45 (Senft and others 1985, Zobel and Blair 1976, Zobel and others 1972). These differences have numerous implications for wood processing and use. A large proportion of juvenile wood usually means lower strength and more shrinkage and warpage as well as lower yields of pulp and byproducts (Hitchings 1984, Pearson 1984, Senft and others 1985).

Earlywood and latewood. Loblolly pine growth rings are clearly delineated by distinct bands of light earlywood (springwood) and dark latewood (summerwood) produced each year. These bands can vary from less than 0.25 to more than 1.50 cm in width. Rapidly growing crowns stimulate the production of many large-diameter, thin-walled xylem cells that form wide growth rings with a high percentage of earlywood. Conversely, trees with slow-growing crowns produce small, thick-walled xylem cells and narrow growth rings with a high percentage of latewood (Beckwith and Shackelford 1976). Suppressed trees have a higher percentage of latewood than do open-grown trees (Schmidt and Horton 1961). The closer a particular cell is to the crown, the greater the influence the crown has on its development. As a result, earlywood production predominates within or near the crown, and latewood production pre-

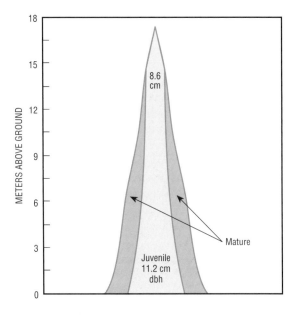

Figure 2-7—Average juvenile core of nine 17-year-old trees (adapted from Zobel and Blair 1976).

dominates near the base of the tree.

The properties of earlywood and latewood within a growth ring are somewhat similar to those of juvenile wood and mature wood. Differences between earlywood and latewood within rings laid down in the same year are fairly constant from tree to tree within a stand (Kellison 1981). The main significance of the ratio of earlywood to latewood is that specific gravity increases with increasing proportions of latewood. The differences in earlywood and latewood specific gravity, as well as the abruptness of the transition from earlywood to latewood, significantly affect the strength and machining properties of the wood (Koch 1972).

Cell wall material is deposited in the last latewood cells formed in the fall through at least March of the following year, which indicates that latewood continues to differentiate (that is, form secondary walls) throughout the winter (Nix and Villiers 1985).

Heartwood and sapwood. Sapwood is nearly white to yellowish or orange white and ranges from thin to very thick. Sapwood thickness is positively and linearly correlated with dbh (figure 2-8). Rapidly growing trees have wider zones of sapwood than do slowly growing trees. The drywood-basis ash content of sapwood ranges from about 0.25 to 0.54%. Much of the variation is associated with geographic location (Elder and Burkhart 1983, McMillan 1969, Zicherman and Thomas 1972). Highly concentrated resins and other substances impregnate cell walls and fill cell cavities as a tree ages. These substances make the heartwood much darker than the sapwood.

There is usually no distinct boundary or abrupt transition between sapwood and heartwood in loblolly pines. However, the boundary can be determined by ultraviolet scanning or color reactions to specific chemicals (diazotized benzidine dihydrochloride, 2-methoxyaniline, and fast blue) (Blanche and others 1984).

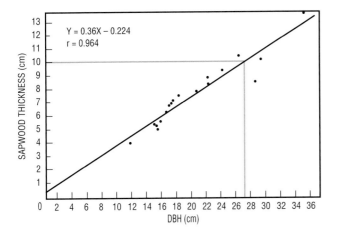

Figure 2-8—The relationship between sapwood thickness and outside bark diameter at breast height in 27-year-old loblolly pine (adapted from Blanche and others 1984).

Heartwood may begin to form at any time between tree ages 15 and 25 years, but it makes up less than 2% of total wood volume in trees less than 20 years old (Wahlenberg 1960). Heartwood formation and resin deposition in older loblolly pines increase wood specific gravity and drywood ash content. Before heartwood formation takes place, the amount of extractives deposited in bolewood is about 2 to 4% on a drywood basis. This percentage can be doubled in 40- to 50-year-old trees (Taras and Saucier 1967, Zobel and others 1972).

Knotwood and compression wood. Knotwood (branchwood) and compression wood (abnormal wood formed on the lower side of leaning trees and on the lower side of branches) can make up a significant part of loblolly pine xylem. The merchantable volume of 7- to 11-year-old plantation-grown trees (2.4- by 2.4-m spacing) included about 1% knotwood and 7% associated compression wood (von Wedel and others 1968). Widely spaced trees will have greater amounts of both knotwood and compression wood in the bole because branches of such trees grow larger. In open-grown trees, the combination of knotwood and compression wood can approach 40% of the total topwood (Zobel and others 1972). Bole straightness has a strong effect on the proportion of compression wood. Boles of trees up to 50 years of age have about 6% compression wood when straight, 9% when somewhat curved, and as much as 16% when obviously crooked or leaning (Zobel and Haught 1962). Wood from straight trees yields significantly more pulp with greater tear resistance than does wood from crooked trees (Blair and others 1974).

Rootwood. The gross structure of loblolly pine rootwood resembles that of juvenile stemwood but is more variable. Moreover, roots lack a well-defined pith and generally do not develop heartwood. Rootwood also differs from stemwood in some minute structural characteristics, but tracheid length, cell diameter, lumen diameter, and cell wall thickness are similar to those of stemwood (Kellison 1981, Koch 1972). The center of a root typically consists of primary xylem that surrounds a number of primary resin canals. In cross section, roots are often irregular in shape. Orderly structure of rootwood is often interrupted by branching. Spiral grain is common, and compression wood is sometimes present (Koch 1972).

Because rings in roots are narrow, discontinuous, and indistinct, it is difficult to estimate root age accurately. There is generally little correlation between root and stem growth patterns. Distinct bands of latewood are sometimes found, but growth increments are more often indicated only by the presence of a few rows of radically flattened cells with walls that may be no thicker than those of the earlywood. The lack of defined annual rings probably results from uninterrupted yearround root growth in many areas.

Phloem (Bark)

Loblolly pine bark is light or dark brown initially and gradually turns reddish brown or gray as the tree ages. The outer bark of loblolly pine can usually be distinguished from that of shortleaf by the absence of resin blisters, which are abundant on most shortleaf pine trees (DeVall 1945). Beneath the surface of loblolly pine bark is a slate-gray layer called the phellogen (or cork cambium). In longleaf, shortleaf, slash, and spruce pines the phellogen layer is a conspicuous ivory white. The inner bark (living phloem) of 10- to 13-cm dbh loblolly pine boles from 14- to 31-year-old trees makes up 11% of the ovendry bark weight. The other 89% consisted of dead outer bark (Pearl and Buchanan 1976).

Bark characteristics are affected by age and condition of the tree, position on the stem, and environment (Stohr 1980; figure 2-9). Bark (within about 0.3 to 0.6 m of the ground) is thin and scaly on young trees, gradually furrowing and forming a layer up to 7.5 cm thick with irregular plates or prominent ridges on mature trees. The

Table 2-4—Loblolly pine bark thickness increases linearly with tree dbh

Tree dbh (cm)	Single bark thickness (cm)	
	Ave.	Range
10	1.0	0.5–1.3
15–20	1.3	0.8–2.3
25–30	2.0	1.0–3.0
35–40	2.3	1.3–3.8
45–50	2.5	1.5–4.3
60	3.0	NA
75	3.8	NA
90	4.3	NA

Source: adapted from Ashe (1915), Burton (1962), Feduccia and Mann (1976), Judson (1964), and Minor (1953).

NA = not applicable.

thick bark of older trees provides excellent fire protection. Bark is much thicker on young thrifty trees than on slower growing older trees of the same diameter and height (Ashe 1915). Bark thickness also varies by locality. For example, the bark of trees growing in the northern part of the range can be up to 42% thicker than the bark of trees growing along the Gulf Coast and southern Atlantic Coast (Burton 1962, Minor 1953).

Bark thickness increases linearly with tree diameter (table 2-4) and gradually decreases up the bole of a tree. At stump height, bark thickness is about 0.5 cm greater than at breast height for a tree 10 cm in dbh and 1.3 cm or more greater than at breast height for trees 25 to 45 cm in dbh. A tree 25 cm in dbh will have a bark thickness of only about 0.45 cm at a top diameter of 5 cm inside bark (Phillips and Schroeder 1972). At breast height, the depth of bark fissures can range from 0.6 cm for a 10-cm tree to about 1.8 cm for a 45-cm tree.

The physical properties of bark, like those of wood, are affected more by position in the stem than by tree age. The density of ovendry bark increases with stem height, ranging from 0.35 at the groundline to 0.72 three-quarters of the way up 12-year-old trees 16 m tall. This trend is exactly opposite for the density of ovendry wood (Stohr 1980). The volume of bark is greatest near the ground, decreases to a low point about 60% of the way up the stem, and then increases sharply in the crown. This same trend occurs in other pine species (figure 2-10). The percentage of total biomass in bark decreases as tree diameter increases (Zobel and others 1972). Stohr (1980) found that bark moisture of 12-year-old loblolly pines increased linearly from about 70% at the base of a tree to 180% near the top of the crown.

Figure 2-9—The bark of a mature loblolly pine.

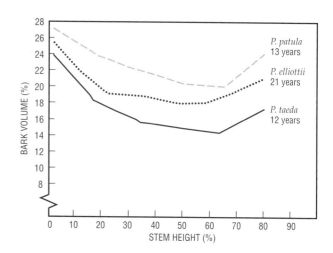

Figure 2-10—Vertical distribution of bark volume in planted *Pinus taeda*, *P. elliottii*, and *P. patula* in South Africa (adapted from Stohr 1980).

Chemical Composition of Various Tree Parts

Table 2-5—Phosphorus (P), potassium (K), calcium (Ca), and magnesium (Mg) concentrations in healthy 1-year-old loblolly pine seedlings from an Alabama nursery, averaged over a 4-year period

Tree part	Macronutrient (% of dry matter)							
	P		K		Ca		Mg	
	mean	range	mean	range	mean	range	mean	range
Needles	0.16	0.09–0.25	0.58	0.28–0.98	0.17	0.08–0.38	0.10	0.07–0.22
Stems	0.16	0.05–0.24	0.66	0.20–1.14	0.10	0.06–0.15	0.10	0.07–0.15
Roots	0.15	0.08–0.29	0.52	0.29–0.76	0.04	0.02–0.08	0.11	0.08–0.15

Source: adapted from May and others (1962).

Table 2-6—Average percentage composition of macronutrients in 7- to 21-year-old loblolly pine trees in the Piedmont of South Carolina

Tree part	Macronutrient (% of dry wt)				
	N	P	K	Ca	Mg
Needles*	1.02	0.10	0.43	0.29	0.12
Stembark	0.42	0.06	0.31	0.21	0.09
Stemwood	0.14	0.02	0.10	0.06	0.03
Branches	0.32	0.04	0.19	0.24	0.06

Source: adapted from Metz and Wells (1965).
* First and second-year needles combined.

More than half of all known elements have been found in plant tissue, so it is reasonable to assume that every element occurring in the root environment of a loblolly pine is absorbed to some extent. Of the macroelements, nitrogen (N) is most prominent in all loblolly tree parts, followed by potassium (K) or calcium (Ca), depending on tree part, then magnesium (Mg) or phosphorus (P), depending on age of tissue (tables 2-5 and 2-6). Trees accumulate nutrients most rapidly during the first 15 years (Switzer and Nelson 1972). Needles constitute a relatively small proportion of a loblolly pine's biomass (except in the case of seedlings), but they have the highest concentrations of nutrients. Nutrients are progressively less concentrated in stembark, branches, and stemwood. Macronutrient percentages remain relatively constant as these plant parts age, but total weight of each element increases as tree size increases. In mature trees most biomass is stemwood, which has the lowest concentrations of nutrients. Chung and Barnes (1977) calculated the substrate requirements to biosynthesize 1 g of biomass (table 2-7).

Needles

First-year needles consist of about 51% cell wall materials—cellulose, hemicelluloses, and lignin; 21% phenolics; 9% nitrogenous compounds (primarily proteins); 6% lipids; 8% volatile oils; 1.5% minerals; and small amounts of organic acids and soluble sugars. Alpha-pinene, beta-pinene, alpha-terpineol, and caryophyllene make up about half the total volatiles (Chung and Barnes 1977, Joye and others 1972). Needle oils contain more than 30 components, including large amounts of terpenes, terpene alcohols, and sesquiterpenes (table 2-8). Needles of loblolly, longleaf, and slash pines have very similar oil compositions and concentrations.

Young needles of loblolly pines accumulate the greatest proportion of macro- and microelements. Because of their active physiological processes, needles contain higher proportions of N and mineral elements than do any other tree component throughout the life of a tree. The relative proportions of foliar N, P, K, Ca, and Mg in 15- to 25-year-old plantation loblolly pines, growing on a wide range of sites in the Piedmont and upper Coastal Plain of the southeastern United States were 100.0/9.3/36.5/17.2/9.2 (Adams and Allen 1985). Differences between provinces were small, but the concentrations were highest in the Piedmont and lowest in the Coastal Plain.

Nutrient and starch concentrations in loblolly pine needles vary with the season of the year. Concentrations of N, P, and K in first-year needles are generally greatest (1.5, 0.2, and 1.2%, respectively) in early spring, decline

Table 2-7—Substrate requirements to biosynthesize 1 g of needle, current branch, and shoot biomass of loblolly pine

Tree part	Substrate and cosubstrate requirement (g)					Product and byproduct (g)		
	Glucose	Amino nitrogen	Sulfur oxide (SO$_4$)	Oxygen	Minerals	Biomass	Carbon dioxide	Water
Needles*	1.588	0.019	0.001	0.134	0.015	1	0.300	0.456
Current branches	1.508	0.008	NM	0.113	0.016	1	0.249	0.397
Shoots	1.574	0.017	0.001	0.130	0.016	1	0.295	0.446

Source: adapted from Chung and Barnes (1977).
NM = not measured.
* First and second-year needles combined.

Table 2-8—Composition of volatile needle oils of loblolly pine (total yield = 0.8% of dry weight of needles)

Component	Percent	Component	Percent
α-Pinene	16.4	Terpinene-4-ol	2.2
Camphene	1.8	Caryophyllene	9.4
ß-Pinene	10.2	α-Terpineol	13.6
Limonene	4.1	Borneol	0.8
ß-Phellandrene	5.9	Cadinene	1.6
p-Cymene	2.9	Unidentified	3.2
trans-Dihydro-α-terpineol	0.2	Unidentified	3.4
α-Fenchol	0.5	Unidentified	2.0
Bornyl acetate	0.8	Unidentified	9.0
ß-Terpineol	1.2	Unidentified	2.7

Source: adapted from Joye and others (1972).
* Percentage of volatiles off gas chromatography.

gradually during the growing season, and are relatively stable or fluctuate slowly during the winter. However, trends in foliar nutrient levels vary greatly among trees because individual trees can put out 2 to 4 needle cycles/year depending on site and weather conditions (Miller 1966). The concentration of N in second-year needles gradually declines from about 1% in early spring to about 0.75% by July and remains constant thereafter. Brown needles have only 0.50% N (Smith and others 1970). Foliar starch concentrations vary by season of the year. Concentrations are lowest in the winter and rise rapidly just before budbreak. They decline immediately after budbreak and remain low until photosynthesis by new needles is sufficient to meet demands. Site, temperature, and irradiance also seem to affect foliar starch concentrations (Adams and others 1986).

The total weight and concentration of nutrients in current foliage decrease with each succeeding flush for trees of all ages. In 5-year-old trees, 58% of the total current-year needle N was in the first flush, 31% in the second, 10% in the third, and less than 1% in the fourth (Smith and others 1971). At the top of the crowns of 10- to 25-year-old trees, N, P, and K concentrations can be up to 13% higher in the second and third needle flushes than in the first flush. In addition, first-flush needles at the top of the crown usually contain about 10% less N than do needles from the bottom of the crown, where only one late-developing flush usually occurs. Concentrations of essential elements vary by crown position. The percentages of Ca and Mg are greatest in the lower part of the crown, intermediate in the middle of the crown, and lowest in the top of the crown, while concentrations of K and P vary in the opposite way (figure 2-11). Because of this consistent variation, foliar sampling for comparative purposes should be carried out in the dormant season using needles from a single growth cycle, preferably the first cycle of the previous year, near the top of a tree (Wells 1969).

New needles normally have more biomass and higher concentrations of essential nutrients than do second-year needles. In a 16-year-old plantation sampled in September before major needle fall, the current year's needles made up 61% of the total needle biomass and from 48 to 72% of the macro- and micronutrients. There was a substantial reduction in N, P, K, Mg, sodium (Na), copper (Cu), and biomass from the first- to the second-year needles, but little or no change in Ca, manganese (Mn), zinc (Zn), iron (Fe), and aluminum (Al) (table 2-9). The rate and timing of translocation back into the branches and bole before needles fall vary by element. In a 5-year-old plantation, about half of the N, P, and K was translocated into the branches just before abscission. In contrast, there was no reabsorption of Ca or Mg (Wells and Metz 1963).

As a tree ages and increases in size, the weight of its foliage and the weight of each nutrient in the foliage become smaller percentages of the total weight of the tree (table 2-10). By tree age 16, the greatest total aboveground quantity of all elements, except N, is in stemwood, and the weights of Ca, Fe, Al, Na, and Cu are greater in stembark and branches than in needles (table

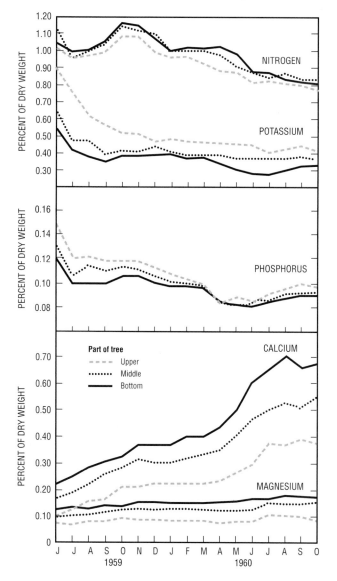

Figure 2-11—Effect of crown position on nutrient percentage in needles of 5-year-old loblolly pines during needle lifespan (adapted from Wells and Metz 1963).

Table 2-9—Relative levels (percent of ovendry weight per unit area basis) of macronutrients and micronutrients in 1- and 2-year-old needles in a 16-year-old loblolly pine plantation†

Component	Current year's needles	Previous year's needles	Component	Current year's needles	Previous year's needles
Biomass	61	39	Manganese	48	52
Nitrogen	67	33	Zinc	51	49
Phosphorus	63	37	Iron	51	49
Potassium	67	33	Aluminum	53	47
Magnesium	61	39	Sodium	72	28
Calcium	47	53	Copper	68	32

Source: adapted from Wells and others (1975).

Table 2-10—Weight of macroelements in individual components of 7- to 21-year-old loblolly pine trees growing in the Piedmont of South Carolina

Macroelements		7 yr (N=5)	8 yr (N=2)	13 yr (N=1)	21 yr (N=2)
		Wt (g)			
Nitrogen	Needles	21.5	37.3	44.9	32.7
	Stembark	3.6	8.8	14.1	15.1
	Stemwood	3.3	9.6	18.6	23.9
	Branches	4.0	8.2	17.8	23.7
Phosphorus	Needles	1.9	3.5	4.4	3.3
	Stembark	0.5	1.1	1.8	2.1
	Stemwood	0.5	1.4	2.7	4.0
	Branches	0.5	1.1	2.2	2.6
Potassium	Needles	8.0	17.3	24.1	12.9
	Stembark	2.3	6.0	7.6	9.4
	Stemwood	2.2	8.8	14.3	26.2
	Branches	2.0	5.9	10.8	12.4
Calcium	Needles	5.6	8.5	12.4	8.3
	Stembark	1.8	3.3	8.9	15.0
	Stemwood	1.6	5.7	17.4	32.1
	Branches	2.9	6.8	22.4	23.8
Magnesium	Needles	2.4	3.5	5.5	4.4
	Stembark	0.6	1.6	2.9	4.4
	Stemwood	0.6	2.1	4.8	10.3
	Branches	0.7	1.7	3.7	4.3

Source: adapted from Metz and Wells (1965).

Table 2-11—Disposition of essential macronutrients and micronutrients in the shoots and roots of 16-year-old planted loblolly pines

Tree component	Concentration (kg/ha)										
	Macronutrient				Micronutrient						
	N	P	K	Ca	Mg	Mn	Zn	Fe	Al	Na	Cu
Needles, current	55	6.3	32	8	4.8	1.2	0.2	0.3	2.2	0.3	0.0215
Needles, total*	82	10.0	48	17	7.9	2.5	0.3	0.6	4.1	0.4	0.0316
Branches, living	34	4.5	24	28	6.1	1.7	0.3	0.9	2.5	1.4	0.0637
Branches, dead	26	1.5	4	30	3.0	NM	0.3	1.3	2.9	0.3	0.0695
Stemwood	79	10.7	65	74	22.7	8.4	1.1	1.8	1.8	3.6	0.2750
Stembark	36	4.2	24	38	6.5	1.0	0.3	1.1	9.7	0.6	0.0594
Aboveground total†	257	30.9	165	187	46.2	13.7	2.4	5.8	21.0	6.3	0.4990
Roots	64	16.9	61	52	21.9	NM	NM	NM	NM	NM	NM
Total (all parts)	321	47.8	226	239	68.1						

Source: adapted from Wells and others (1975).

NM = not measured.   * Current plus older needles.   † Sum of tree parts may not equal total due to rounding.

2-11). Between tree ages 18 and 25, the total amount of N in stemwood begins to exceed that in needles.

Xylem

The chemical compositions of new shoots and new needles are very similar. However, new shoots have about 15% more carbohydrates, 6% less phenolics, and 5% less nitrogenous compounds than have new needles. Trees accumulate increasing amounts of nutrients as they increase in size (figure 2-12). There is a direct relationship between tree dbh and the total weight of nutrients in a tree. The stemwood of a tree 5 to 8 cm in dbh may contain only 10 to 15% of the total weight of mineral elements in the tree. As trees grow, this percentage increases: in a large mature tree, 5% or more of all minerals is in the stemwood. Because tree size varies greatly within tree age groups, the quantities of chemicals in trees should not be estimated on the basis of tree age (Wells and others 1975). In addition, geographic region and soil type strongly influence quantities absorbed and probably amounts stored. In general, mineral and ash contents of xylem decrease with increasing distance from the pith and are lower in latewood than in earlywood (Choong and others 1974, McMillan 1970; tables 2-12 and 2-13).

Table 2-12—Mineral composition of the xylem of 12-year-old loblolly pines produced at ages 2 to 5, 6 to 8, and 9 to 12

	Ash (%)	Elemental conc. (ppm)							
		Na	K	Ca	Mg	Mn	Fe	Zn	P
Innerwood (age 2-5)	0.45	102	399	686	260	74	37	30	53
Middlewood (age 6-8)	0.41	96	313	580	194	75	37	29	54
Outerwood (age 9-12)	0.37	72	384	489	173	57	26	21	61

Source: adapted from Choong and others (1974).

Samples are at breast height from trees grown in one north Louisiana and one south Louisiana plantation.

Table 2-13—Concentration of mineral elements in earlywood and latewood of loblolly pine innerwood, middlewood, and outerwood

	Rings from pith	Rings/ cm	Elemental conc. (ppm)						
			Mn	Ca	Na	Mg	Fe	K	P
Earlywood	0–10	3.0	134	1,267	245	398	65	148	32
	11–20	2.8	125	1,160	232	299	65	108	44
	21–30	2.8	103	997	194	194	85	93	55
Latewood	0–10	3.0	117	980	211	62	46	133	22
	11–20	2.8	106	898	42	51	49	81	32
	21–30	2.8	84	778	162	53	73	80	31

Source: adapted from McMillan (1970).

0–10 is innerwood, 11–20 is middlewood, and 21–30 is outerwood.

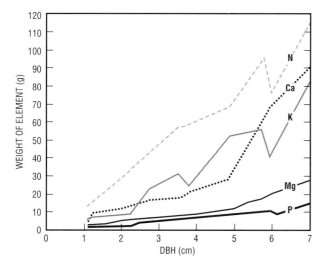

Figure 2-12—The relationship between diameter at breast height (dbh) and weight of N, P, K, Ca, and Mg in 10 loblolly pine trees (adapted from Metz and Wells 1965).

Table 2-14—Composition of resin acids and monoterpenes in xylem oleoresin of mature loblolly pines in southwest Louisiana

	Amount (mg/100 mg oleoresin)			Amount (mg/100 mg oleoresin)	
	Mean	Range		Mean	Range
Resin acids			**Monoterpenes**		
Pimaric	5.11	2.99 – 8.26	α-Pinene	16.56	9.25 – 24.76
S.C. Pimaric	1.22	0.92 – 1.56	Camphene	0.20	0.12 – 0.29
Palustric	12.18	5.80 – 18.35	Myrecene	1.56	0.47 – 4.61
Levopimaric	19.44	6.60 – 26.42	ß-Pinene	8.58	0.39 – 13.30
Isopimaric	7.15	2.48 – 14.70	Limonene	1.68	0.19 – 5.99
Abietic	8.63	5.54 – 16.53	ß-Phellandrene	1.04	0.14 – 4.62
Dehydroabietic	3.82	2.03 – 8.23	Total	29.63	NA
Neoabietic	9.49	5.64 – 14.50			
Total	67.04	64.29 – 73.78			

Source: adapted from Hodges and others (1979).

Loblolly pine xylem contains numerous resin acids and monoterpenes (table 2-14). Monoterpenes are 10-carbon compounds that form major components of the essential oils found in oleoresin. Alpha-pinene and beta-pinene make up about 90% of all monoterpenes. Small amounts of camphene, myrcene, limonene, and beta-phellandrene can also be found in most trees. Monoterpene synthesis increases as the amount of photosynthate produced exceeds that consumed in respiration (Greenwald 1972). Loblolly pine differs significantly from other southern pines in monoterpene and resin acid levels. Loblolly pine has more myrcene and limonene than does any of the other species and more beta-pinene than either slash or longleaf pine. Loblolly pine contains about twice as much levopimaric acid as slash pine. Loblolly pine also contains significantly more pimaric, but much less isopimaric resin acid, than does any other southern pine (Hodges and others 1979).

There are substantial seasonal fluctuations and year-to-year changes in the oleoresin content of loblolly pine trees (Rockwood 1972). Moisture stress decreases the proportion of resin acids relative to monoterpene hydrocarbons in oleoresin (Hodges and Lorio 1975). Gilmore

(1975) found that the concentration of alpha-pinene steadily decreased from 87% at 0.3-m stem height to 72% at 9.4-m stem height while beta-pinene increased from 4% to 19% over the same distance. This difference suggests that there may be some chemical rearranging of the two terpenes.

Loblolly pine also differs significantly from other southern pines in one or more physical properties of oleoresin (table 2-15). Loblolly pine oleoresin generally has low viscosity, moderate total yield, moderate flow rate, short flow duration, and rapid crystallization. In contrast, slash pine oleoresin is extremely viscous, crystallizes slowly, and flows slowly over a long period but has total oleoresin flow similar to that of loblolly pine. Longleaf oleoresin has moderately high viscosity, very high yield, rapid crystallization, and a high flow rate. These differences have very important implications for species susceptibility to insect attacks (see chapter 10) and for naval stores production. However, about 19% of loblolly pine trees may have oleoresin physical properties more like that of slash or longleaf than that of average loblolly pine oleoresin (Hodges and others 1977). This wide tree-to-tree variation provides opportunities for genetic modification of oleoresin properties (see chapter 7). Oleoresin exudation pressures (OEP's) as high as 15 atmospheres (atm) have been observed in the boles of mature loblolly pines. [One atmosphere is a unit of pressure equal to 101,325 newtons per square meter (N/m^2).] When OEP in one tree was followed for an entire day, OEP reached a maximum of 9 atm at 6 a.m. and gradually declined to 4 atm at 11 a.m., at which level it remained until 3 p.m. After 3 p.m., OEP gradually increased to 8 atm by 7 p.m. and to 9 atm by midnight (Hodges and Lorio 1968). A simple technique to measure OEP, using glass tubing, is available (Hodges and Lorio 1971).

Phloem

The inner bark of trees growing on different soils have different concentrations of Al, Mn, Ca, Fe, water, and ash (White and others 1972). The concentrations of Mg, Mn, Zn, Fe, water, and ash in the inner bark of mature loblolly pines also fluctuate seasonally—generally being highest in the fall and lowest in the spring. The nitrogen concentration increases rapidly in spring. Inner bark tissue should probably be sampled in late summer, when composition of such tissue is most stable (Hodges and Lorio 1969; White and others 1970, 1972).

Twenty-six free and 20 protein-bound amino acids are known to occur in the inner bark of loblolly pines (table 2-16). The number and concentration of amino acids may vary considerably with time of the year and height of tissues sampled in a tree (Hodges and others 1968). Pearl and Buchanan (1976) identified the fatty acid, resin

Table 2-15—Physical properties of the oleoresin system of major southern pines aged 27 to 94 years

Pine species		Viscosity (stokes)	Total flow (ml)	Rate of flow (ml/hr)	Flow at 8 hours (%)	Time to initial crystallization (hr)
Loblolly	Mean	18 c	12 a	1.12 c	77 c	0.98 b
	Range	7–28	2–31	0.17–2.87	54–100	0.1–3.2
Longleaf	Mean	60 b	18 b	1.55 b	66 b	0.98 b
	Range	18–142	4–46	0.33–4.42	41–88	0.1–4.0
Shortleaf	Mean	24 c	9 a	0.78 a	67 b	2.36 c
	Range	9–51	1–44	0.06–4.17	31–97	0.2–9.0
Slash	Mean	306 a	11 a	0.56 a	38 a	>48.00 a
	Range	42–580	1–32	0.01–2.18	0.1–78	

Source: adapted from Hodges and others (1977).

Numbers within a column not followed by the same letter are significantly different using Scheffe's test.

Table 2-16—Concentrations of free and protein-bound amino acids in the inner bark at the height of 8.5 to 9.5 m in an 18-m-tall loblolly pine in December

Amino acid	Free amino acids	Protein-bound amino acids
γ-Amino-*n*-butyric acid	0.10	NM
Lysine	0.11	11.49
1-Methyl histidine*	T	NM
Histidine	0.23	5.00
Ornithine	0.01	T
Arginine	0.18	7.50
Cysteic acid	0.03	0.04
Unknown 1[†]	T	NM
Unknown 2[†]	0.18	NM
Methionine sulfoxide	T	NM
Hydroxyproline*	T	T
Aspartic acid + asparagine	2.94	22.93
Threonine	0.28	11.40
Serine	1.24	14.24
Unknown 3*	T	T
Glutamic acid + glutamine	6.83	26.26
Proline	0.33	13.74
Glycine	0.69	22.82
Alanine	1.46	19.26
Half-cystine	0.06	T
Valine	0.93	16.01
Cystathionine	0.25	NM
Methionine	0.14	3.14
Unknown 4[†]	1.19	NM
Isoleucine	0.28	10.89
Leucine	0.33	16.45
Glucosamine	0.17	NM
Tyrosine	0.10	0.13
β-Alanine*	T	NM
Phenylalanine	0.10	9.04
Total	18.16	210.35
Ammonia	7.89	20.82

Conc. (µmoles/g dry wt)

Source: adapted from Hodges and others (1968).

NM = not measured; T = tentative identification.

* Found to be present by use of physiological resin; no quantitative determinations made.

† Relative concentration determination by using the integration constant for aspartic acid for those unknowns with maximum absorption at 570 nm (unknowns 1 and 2) and integration constant for proline for those at 440 nm (unknown 4).

Table 2-17—Root biomass and percentage of nitrogen (N), phosphorus (P), potassium (K), calcium (Ca), and magnesium (Mg) by root class for two 16-year-old loblolly pines

Root class		Biomass (kg/tree)	N	P	K	Ca	Mg
Taproot	Wood	10.78	0.07	0.02	0.11	0.05	0.04
	Bark	0.83	0.25	0.09	0.74	0.14	0.08
Lateral roots	>4 cm	1.54	0.10	0.02	0.06	0.05	0.02
	2-4 cm	1.17	0.19	0.05	0.24	0.09	0.05
	1-1.9 cm	0.79	0.26	0.11	0.35	0.27	0.12
	0.3-0.9 cm	0.61	0.32	0.15	0.46	0.32	0.16
	<0.3 cm	2.03	0.57	0.11	0.14	0.39	0.10

Elemental conc. (% ovendry wt)

Source: adapted from Wells and others (1975).

Table 2-18—Root starch concentrations of 8- to 9-year-old loblolly pines growing on four sites in the Coastal Plain of North Carolina

Site	Fall (9/83)	Winter (1/84)	Spring (3/84)	Fall (9/84)	Winter (1/85)
LL	55.2	71.0	142.0	91.7	69.7
HL	49.7	51.0	166.8	24.4	80.7
HH	21.9	42.4	174.1	19.2	55.4
LH	60.1	46.3	97.1	40.8	93.1

Root starch (g/kg ovendry wt)

Source: adapted from Adams and others (1986).

LL = low soil moisture, low soil fertility; HL = high soil moisture, low soil fertility; HH = high soil moisture, high soil fertility; and LH = low soil moisture, high soil fertility.

acid, glycerol, and other components in inner and outer bark. Many components appeared in both bark fractions, but their relative proportions varied considerably between inner and outer bark.

Roots

As root size increases, the concentrations of nutrients in the root xylem decrease. Taproots and roots over 4.0 cm in diameter have the lowest concentrations of all macronutrients (Pehl and others 1984; table 2-17). The percentage of N in roots less than 0.3 cm in diameter is several times higher than the percentage of N in roots over 4.0 cm in diameter. Levels of P, K, Ca, and Mg are generally highest in roots under 1.0 cm in diameter.

Nitrogen and phosphorus concentrations in 5- to 15-mm diameter roots of 10- to 11-year-old planted loblolly pines growing on four sites in the Coastal Plain of North Carolina varied with site conditions and probably with

weather conditions, but did not vary seasonally (Adams and others 1987). In contrast to nutrient concentrations, starch concentrations in the roots fluctuated seasonally on these sites. They were highest just before budbreak in the spring and lowest in the autumn. On a moist fertile site, root starch concentration was 174 g/kg of root tissue in March but only 19 g/kg in September (table 2-18).

Pollen

Loblolly pine pollen contains 7.5 to 9.0% lipids on a dry weight basis. Most of these lipids are triglycerides of oleic, linoleic, and palmitic acids. Lipids in the outer spore coat make up 1.6% of the pollen weight. Pollen of loblolly pine and other southern pines contains an array of polyphenolic compounds, including the phenolic acids *p*-hydroxybenzoic, protocatechuic, gallic, vanillic, *cis*- and *trans*-*p*-coumaric, *cis*- and *trans*-ferulic, and 4-glucosyl-oxybenzoic acid; the flavanonols dihydrokaempferol and dihydroquercetin; the flavanone naringenin; and a series of esters of *p*-coumaric acid. Vanillic acid is prominent in loblolly, longleaf, and slash pines, but lacking in shortleaf pine, suggesting a taxonomically significant difference. The types and relative amounts of phenolic acids and coumarate esters in pollen, as determined by chromotography, vary little between southern pine species. However, the flavonoid fraction from methanolic extractives and the carbonate-soluble material from ether extractives vary sufficiently between species to show promise for use in taxonomic diagnosis (Strohl and Seikel 1965).

Moisture Content of Tree Parts

The aboveground portion of the average mature loblolly pine is about 50% water, 42% dry wood, 5 to 6% dry bark, and 2% dry needles by weight. Position in the stem has the greatest effect on moisture content of both bark and wood (figure 2-13 and table 2-19). Tree age and stand and site conditions also contribute significantly to variation in moisture content (Stohr 1980). Live branches and needles have similar moisture contents. Dead branches have only about half to a third the moisture content of living material. Neither age nor position in the crown appears to affect needle moisture content. The moisture content of stembark increases as height in a tree increases, ranging from about 70% (dry weight basis) near the ground to 140 to 180% in the upper crown. The moisture content of stemwood has a similar, but much less pronounced, trend.

Stemwood moisture content varies substantially with tree age, among trees within a stand, with height in a tree, and between juvenile and mature wood of the same tree (figure 2-14 and table 2-20). Wood near the top of a tree contains a much greater proportion of moisture than does wood near the base, where the wood volume and weight are concentrated. In an African study, moisture was 138% (dry weight basis) at the tree base, 200% at 50% of tree height, and 210% at 80% of tree height in 12-year-old loblolly pines 16 m in height and 22 cm in dbh (Stohr 1980). Stemwood moisture content of young trees growing next to one another can vary by as much as 50 to 100%. Trees 35 to 45 years of age have very similar moisture contents. They often contain 20 to 30% less moisture, on a dry-weight basis, than do trees younger than age 20. Juvenile wood of young trees has 15 to 30% more moisture per unit of dry wood weight than has juvenile wood of maturing trees because most juvenile wood in the latter is heartwood, which has a relatively low moisture content. Moisture content of trees of the same age varies with geographic location, but the variation is not great (Zobel and others 1968).

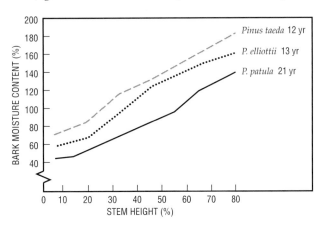

Figure 2-13—Vertical distribution of moisture content in stembark for planted Pinus taeda, P. elliottii, and P. patula growing in South Africa (adapted from Stohr 1980).

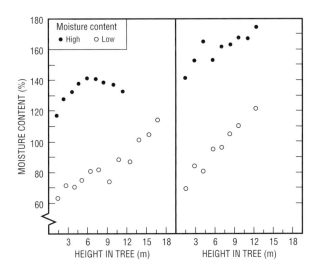

Figure 2-14—Texas loblolly pine trees with high and low stemwood moisture content (adapted from Zobel and others 1968).

Table 2-19—Average moisture content of 10 loblolly pine trees (7 to 21 years old) as a percentage of ovendry weight

Tree component	Moisture content (% OD wt)	Tree component	Moisture content (% OD wt)
Needles		Branches	
Less than 1 year old	108	Less than 1 year old	108
More than 1 year old	104	More than 1 year old	107
Average	107	Dead	49
		Average	99
Stembark			
Upper 1/3 crown	140	Stemwood	
Mid 1/3 crown	124	Upper 1/3 crown	151
Lower 1/3 crown	103	Mid 1/3 crown	149
Below crown	78	Lower 1/3 crown	145
Average	113	Below crown	131
		Average	145

Source: adapted from Metz and Wells (1965).
All averages are weighted.

Table 2-20—Moisture content of wood samples taken at various heights in loblolly pines from six locations in the United States

| Approximate tree height (m) | Moisture content (% OD wt) | | | | | |
	Georgia Upper Coastal Plain	South Carolina Piedmont	North Carolina Coastal Plain	Virginia Coastal Plain	Tennessee	Texas Coastal Plain
1.5	94	83	95	93	112	96
3.0	NA	91	108	NA	122	106
4.6	109	95	121	106	127	106
6.1	NA	99	129	NA	124	113
7.6	122	105	136	105	127	122
9.1	NA	109	145	NA	126	119
10.7	128	123	151	118	128	119
12.2	NA	126	153	NA	133	119
13.7	138	136	163	129	134	122

Source: adapted from Zobel and others (1968).
NA = not available.

Shoot Development and Growth Habits

Early Growth Patterns

The first evidence of loblolly pine seed germination is the radicle breaking through the seedcoat to form the tap root of a new tree. Shortly after the radicle breaks through, cotyledons, which are formed in the embryo, are pushed or pulled out of the ground as the shoot (hypocotyl) begins to elongate. If the seed is not buried too deeply, the seedcoat is often pulled from the duff or soil with the cotyledons and drops to the ground after the cotyledons expand fully. Newly germinated seedlings have about seven cotyledons (range of five to nine), and these average 3 cm (range of 1.3 to 3.7 cm) in length. The hyopocotyl elongates for about 18 days before it reaches a final length of about 3.9 cm, at which time it averages 0.08 cm in diameter (table 2-21). More than 90% of the hypocotyl's growth is complete in the first 8 days. Loblolly pine seedlings cannot be distinguished from slash pine or Virginia pine seedlings when in the cotyledon stage. However, they can be distinguished from newly germinated shortleaf pine seedlings, which have shorter hypocotyls and fewer and shorter cotyledons (Brown 1964; Mann 1976, 1979).

Shoot ontogeny of first-year loblolly pine seedlings grown in a greenhouse is shown in figure 2-15. Immediately after germination, cotyledons and the hypocotyl are the only photosynthetic organs. Primary (juvenile) needles soon begin to develop, and within a few weeks, the bulk of the foliage is composed of single, spirally arranged, primary needles averaging 2 cm in length. By this time, the cotyledons have died, but they often remain attached to the stem until the second year. Many of the physical characteristics of cotyledons and primary needles are quite similar (table 2-22). However, cotyledons have almost three times the volume of primary needles, and their mesophyll volume is five times as great as that of primary needles. However, primary needles have about three times as many stomata per square millimeter of surface as have cotyledons. Primary needles become scalelike at about age 2. The change usually occurs abruptly at the beginning of the second year, but it may occur gradually during the second growing season or even extend into the third year on some seedlings. If the primary bud of a young tree is damaged, shoots arising from small lateral buds sometimes bear green primary needles that resemble juvenile primary needles (Bormann 1963).

By the middle of the first growing season, secondary (permanent) needles begin to develop and become intermingled with the primary needles (table 2-23). In healthy, fast-growing seedlings, secondary needles make up about 70% of the

Table 2-21—Dimensions of cells and tissues in the basal portion of mature hypocotyls of loblolly pines, which averaged 0.08 cm in diameter

	Length (µm)	Width (µm)	No. of radial rows
Cortical cells	204 ± 13.7	24 ± 1.1	8 ± 0.4
Pith cells	497 ± 25.8	23 ± 0.6	8 ± 0.3

Source: adapted from Brown (1964).

Plants were grown in sterile sand and nutrient culture. Length and width values are means of 10 cells per plant on 15 plants of the same age, ± SEM.

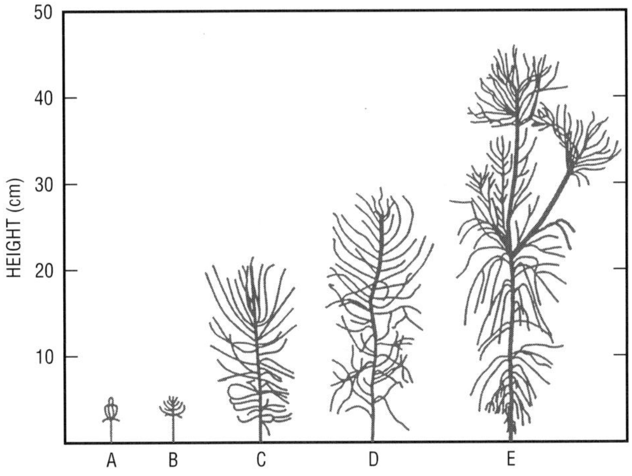

Figure 2-15—Typical shoot ontogeny of first-year loblolly pine seedlings: cotyledons emerge with seed coat attached (*A*), emerging primary needles form rosette above cotyledons (*B*), primary needles predominant, plant approaches minimum height for basal emergence of secondary needles (*C*), secondary needles emerge and budset begins after secondary needles emerge (*D*). This is the "threshold" stage; this part of the seedling will be carried as the free-growth stem axis; after first budset (*E*) cyclic growth begins. Lateral branch buds form and break, and areas of sterile cataphylls separates the cycles. Morphological description based on greenhouse observations (adapted from Williams 1987).

Table 2-22—Morphological comparison of cotyledons and primary needles of 2-month-old loblolly pine from east Texas

Morphological feature	Cotyledons	Primary needles
Dimensions		
Length (cm)	3.5	2.0
Cross section (mm²)	0.169	0.084
Volume (mm³)	5.9	1.7
Surface area (mm²)	62.5	24.8
Surface area per mm³ volume (mm²)	10.6	14.6
Number of cotyledons	6.9	
Stomatal measurements		
Stomata per cotyledon or needle	1,886.4	2,637.2
Stomata per mm² cotyledon or needle surface	30.5	107.4
Stomata per mm³ mesophyll	516.5	3,686.5
Depth of stomata (µm)	11.4	11.9
Cutinized epidermis thickness (µm)	2.3	2.4
Epidermis thickness (µm)	17.9	14.8
Cuticle thickness (µm)	1.9	1.3
Mesophyll volume (mm³)	3.7	0.7
Endodermis area in cross section (mm²)	0.032	0.030
Phloem area in cross section (µm²)	1,636.4	1,432.7
Xylem area in cross section (µm²)	1,258.6	1,661.3
Transfusion tissue, area in cross section (mm²)	0.029	0.023

Source: adapted from Knauf and Bilan (1977).

Table 2-23—Number and ovendry weight of primary and secondary needles on loblolly pine seedlings

	Seedling age		
	9 weeks	16 weeks	23 weeks
Juvenile needles			
Number	75	130	155
Dry weight (mg)	75	162	240
Secondary needles			
Number	0	26	63
Dry weight (mg)	0	56	459

Source: adapted from Ledig and others (1970).

Each number is the mean of 72 seedlings that were subjected to various light and moisture treatments.

Table 2-24—Dimensions of pith rib-meristem in apices of loblolly pine

	Days after germination			
Item	1	7	12	30
Average length of rib-meristem* longitudinal axis (μm)	90 ± 7.1	149 ± 11.2	311 ± 17.0	554 ± 19.9
Average cell number† longitudinal axis	6 ± 0.2	10 ± 0.9	15 ± 0.7	23 ± 1.1
Average cell length‡ longitudinal axis (μm)	15	15	21	24
Average width of rib-meristem§ radially (μm)	110 ± 3.7	176 ± 7.8	189 ± 4.2	221 ± 7.9
Average cell number¶ radially	6 ± 0.2	7 ± 0.1	8 ± 0.0	9 ± 0.2
Average cell width‖ radially (μm)	18	25	24	25

Source: adapted from Brown (1964).

Values are mean ± SE.

* Mean of five central vertical rows of pith rib-meristem taken from five different apices of same age.

† Mean cell counts of five vertical rows in five different apices from base of central mother cell zone to axils of cotyledons.

‡ Item 1 divided by item 2.

§ Mean of five different apices at level of axils of cotyledons.

¶ Mean cell counts at level of axils of cotyledons, five different apices.

‖ Average width of rib-meristem divided by average cell number.

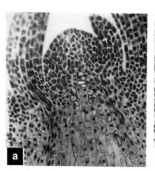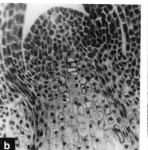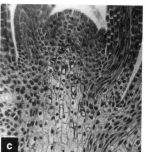

Figure 2-16—Micrographs (× 170) of median longitudinal sections of loblolly pine shoot apices: 7 days after germination (*a*), 12 days after germination (*b*), and 30 days after germination (*c*) (Brown 1964).

foliage by the end of the first growing season (Bilan and others 1977). Weak or slow-growing seedlings may develop only a few secondary needles during the first year. Secondary shoots may originate from apical meristems in needle axils, providing the seedlings with branches during the first year.

Cells and tissues change rapidly during the first 30 days after germination (figure 2-16 and table 2-24). For example, the average length of rib-meristem cells, measured along the longitudinal axis, increases by 66% during the first 7 days and by 246% during the first 12 days of a seedling's life. Dry weight of needles of 1- to 2-week-old loblolly pine seedlings is about 57% of total seedling dry weight (above and below ground). The proportion decreases to 50% by week 7, 45% by week 14, and 40% by week 21 (Ledig and Perry 1969), further showing the rapid change that occurs in seedling physiology during the first few weeks of life.

Height Growth of Juvenile Trees

Height growth in young loblolly pines occurs over a period of 180 to 210 days/year. Growth usually begins by late February in the southern part of the species' range, but may not begin until late April in the northernmost areas. Height growth is usually complete by mid-September. Growth is a complex combination of "fixed" and "free" growth throughout the crown. Fixed growth is the elongation of a winter (or resting) bud to form a spring shoot. Free growth is shoot elongation resulting from the simultaneous initiation and elongation of new stem units. During the first year, most seedlings produce a single cycle of free growth. During the second year, 1 to 3 growth cycles may occur depending on environmental conditions. The first cycle is fixed; that is, set in the previous year's resting bud.

Subsequent free-growth cycles involve recurrent formation and opening of nonresting buds during the growing season, followed by expansion of the bud contents. From about age 3 to about age 20 or 30, loblolly pines are strongly multinodal, usually producing 3 to 4 (occasionally 2 or 5) growth cycles/year. Length of the first fixed-growth cycle is primarily influenced by environmental conditions of the preceding year. In contrast, length of all of the free-growth cycles is strongly influenced by current environmental conditions. The first cycle is almost always the longest, and the last is the shortest. Two consecutive internodes on the same tree can elongate at the same time, and there may be no single, well-defined peak growth rate (Boyer and South 1989; Griffing and Elam 1971; Lanner 1976, 1978).

Growth is most rapid at the top of seedlings and saplings. The number of growth cycles, amount of secondary branching, and average shoot length decrease with increasing distance from the top (Boyer 1970, Nelson and others 1970). This is typical in conifers. Shoots on the south side of a tree grow faster than those on the north side during the early part of each growth cycle, but slower toward the cycle's end. This north–south trend is more pronounced in seedlings than in saplings.

Smith and others (1970) measured stem elongation in 7 trees during their fifth year of growth in central Mississippi. All seven trees completed four growth cycles during that year. Height growth (elongation of the leader) averaged 1.22 m and accounted for 12% of the average aggregate shoot elongation of 10.23 m (table 2-25). Eighty-six percent of the growth occurred on first-

and second-order lateral branches. Sixty-two percent of the tree height growth and 82% of the total branch elongation was completed during the first two growth cycles. Only 2% of the year's branch elongation was on third-order branches, and third-order branches completed only one growth cycle. Eighty-seven percent of the increase in dry weight accumulated during the first two growth cycles, and only 1% accumulated during the last cycle. Over half of the total weight increase was in the middle of the crown, where the greatest weight of foliage was located (table 2-26). The proportions of nitrogen accumulated by the crown portions were almost identical to the proportions of dry weight accumulated by the crown portions, showing the importance of nitrogen in foliage development. About 40% of the new wood and bark was laid down by July 1 and 100% by September 15.

Table 2-25—Elongation of loblolly pine shoot systems during a single year

Growth cycle	Elongation (cm)					
		Branch axis				
	Stem	First order	Second order	Third order	Total	Total %
1	43	218	193	23	477	47
2	33	172	136	0	341	33
3	26	80	41	0	147	14
4	20	38	0	0	58	6
Total	122	508	370	23	1,023	100
Percent	12	50	36	2	100	

Source: Smith and others (1970).

Table 2-26—Dry weight accumulation per tree in 1 year's growth cycles of 5-year-old loblolly pine

Growth cycle	Dry weight (g)					Total (%)
	Upper crown	Middle crown	Lower crown	Basal crown	Total*	
1	162	480	231	30	903	62
2	116	222	30	0	368	25
3	84	75	0	0	159	11
4	18	0	0	0	18	1
Total	380	777	261	30	1,448	100
Percent	26	54	18	2	100	

Source: Smith and others (1971).
* Column does not add to 100 due to rounding.

Table 2-27—Relation of mean diameter at breast height (dbh) to crown radius for various site indices (18 to 37 m) in normal loblolly pine stands

Mean dbh (cm)	Crown radius (m)						
	18 m	21 m	24 m	27 m	30 m	34 m	37 m
15	1.34	1.33	1.34	1.34	1.34	1.33	1.32
20	1.73	1.69	1.68	1.71	1.69	1.68	1.65
25	2.10	2.10	2.10	2.07	2.03	2.00	2.98
30		2.46	2.48	2.42	2.40	2.37	2.32
35			2.84	2.84	2.77	2.74	2.69

Source: adapted from Roberts and Ross (1965).

Crown Development

Crown density is a good indicator of tree vigor. Individual loblolly pines grow fastest when 50% or more of the tree length is in live crown. Live crown ratio decreases as crowding occurs. Trees with small crowns are generally weak and have little energy available for stem growth. The combination of dynamic changes in total needle surface area, relative dominance of first- and second-year needles, and environmental variables creates a continuous state of change within the crowns of individual trees and within the canopy of a stand. The amount of solar radiation reaching lower levels of the canopy depends on canopy density as well as on solar intensity. Reliable visual estimates of crown density for individual trees can be made using a density scale developed by Belanger and Anderson (1989).

In dense stands, loblolly pines have small narrow crowns and there is much natural pruning. Trees growing in the open have large limbs and very slow natural pruning and are often characterized as "wolf" trees because of their bushy shape (figure 2-17). Variation in crown radius for a given stem diameter is nearly independent of site index (table 2-27) and tree age (table 2-28).

Because loblolly pines commonly produce two to four growth cycles per year and retain their foliage for 2 years, the amount of foliage on an individual tree and in a stand

Figure 2-17—Large open-grown loblolly pine. Note the rough appearance and large branches due to slow natural pruning.

varies throughout the year. Needle age can vary by up to 6 months within a single year's foliage. Typical patterns of seasonal needle growth are shown in figures 2-18 and 2-19. Growth of the first cycle is well under way before the second cycle begins. Cultural treatments, such as fertilization or weed control, have no effect on needle longevity (Dalla-Tea and Jokela 1991). The ratio of foliage weight to stem weight decreases from about 1:10 at tree age 5 to 1:70 at age 55. At tree age 5, foliage weight equals branch weight, but by tree age 55, branch weight is eight times as great as foliage weight (table 2-29). Needle weight of small trees can be estimated nondestructively from root collar diameter or numbers of branches in the lower, middle, and upper thirds of the tree (Shear and Perry 1986). The weight of total foliage on large trees is closely related to tree diameter, but the length and weight of individual fascicles are independent of tree size (Rogerson 1964).

Needle surface area index in fully stocked stands ranges from 5 to 10 during the growing season (Hosker and others 1974). Second-year needles have the greatest total surface area until about July, when new needles begin to predominate. The surface area and biomass of new needles increase rapidly beginning in May. As with new branches, the vast majority of new needles are produced in the upper and middle portions of the crown (table 2-26).

During the 15th year of growth in a southeast Oklahoma plantation, the upper crown added 32% more needle area than did the middle crown and 69% more than did the lower crown (Holeman and others 1991). The total surface area and biomass of needles reach maximums just before second-year needles begin to fall in September (Wells and others 1975). About 60% of all needles on a tree in September before needlefall are from the current year (Kinerson and others 1974; figure 2-20).

Needle Surface Area

Needle area growth (A) of seedlings and saplings can be predicted accurately by the following equation:

$$A = b_0 N + b_1 \left(\sum_{}^{N} G_i L_i \right)$$

where G_i is the green length of foliated portions of individual branches, L_i is the average fascicle length for the ith fascicle cluster (where $I = 1, 2, ..., N$), and N is the number of fascicle clusters on the tree (Harms 1971). Needle surface area and needle weight of trees on poor sites are 26 to 30% lower than needle surface area and needle weight of trees on good sites.

Needle surface area can also be accurately approximated from tree diameter because weight of foliage is closely related to tree diameter over a range of sites. Fascicle weight and length are independent of tree size. Fascicle weight is a good predictor of needle surface area regardless of stand age or site class (Rogerson 1964, Shelton and Switzer 1984). Needle surface area is also linearly correlated with cross-sectional sapwood area at breast height and at the base of the crown. Sapwood area at the base of the crown is a better predictor of needle surface area than is sapwood area at breast

Table 2-28—Relation of mean diameter at breast height (dbh) to crown radius for various ages (20 to 80 years) in normal loblolly pine stands

Mean dbh (cm)	Crown radius (m)						
	20 yr	30 yr	40 yr	50 yr	60 yr	70 yr	80 yr
15	1.35	1.32					
20		1.71	1.70				
25		1.69	2.07	2.10	2.07		
30			2.38	2.42	2.48	2.44	2.44
35				2.74	2.77	2.80	2.84

Source: adapted from Roberts and Ross (1965).

Table 2-29—The ratio of foliage to branch weight and stem weight at various stages of loblolly stand development on good sites

Stand age (yr)	Dry weight ratio	
	Foliage to branches	Foliage to stems
5	1:1	1:10
25	1:2	1:20
45	1:6	1:50
55	1:8	1:70

Source: Switzer and others (1968).

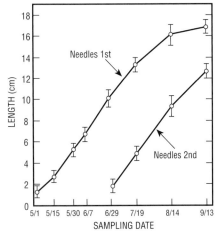

Figure 2-18 —Seasonal change in the length of current needles for two consecutive growth cycles in a stand of 15-year-old loblolly pine (adapted from Chung and Barnes 1980a).

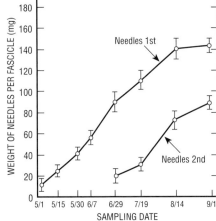

Figure 2-19—Seasonal change in dry weight of current needles for two consecutive growth cycles in a stand of 15-year-old loblolly pine (adapted from Chung and Barnes 1980a).

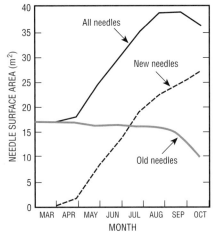

Figure 2-20—Seasonal change in needle surface area of a 5-year-old open-grown loblolly pine tree (adapted from Harms 1971).

height (Shelburne and others 1989). Additionally, the ratio of current-year or previous-year sapwood production to needle area can be used as an indicator of tree vigor (Blanche and others 1985). In a Virginia study, the cross-sectional area of seedlings at the groundline was highly correlated with needle surface area (figure 2-21). Needle surface area averaged about 0.1 m^2 for 1-year-old seedlings, 0.4 m^2 for 2-year-old seedlings, and 1.0

m^2 for 3-year-old seedlings (Johnson and others 1985).

Needle specific area (ratio of total needle surface area in square centimeters to total needle dry weight in grams) and specific gravity change with seedling and needle age (figures 2-22 and 2-23). Johnson and others (1985) found that specific area ranged from 260 cm^2/g for 1-year-old seedlings to 150 cm^2/g for 4- and 5-year-old trees. Needles of the present year have consistently higher specific areas than do needles of the previous year. Needle specific gravity increases from about 0.22 g/cm^3 at age 1 to about 0.40 g/cm^3 at ages 4 and 5. Present year needles consistently have lower specific gravities than do previous year needles (Johnson and others 1985).

Branch Surface Area

The surfaces of very small branches make up most of the branch surface area of a tree. Nearly 60% of the branch surface area of 14-year-old planted loblolly pines was in branches less than 1 cm in diameter, and only about 3% was in branches over 3 cm in diameter (figure 2-24).

Diameter Growth Periodicity

Cambial activity begins in the buds and progresses downward. Cambial activity at breast height probably begins several days to 2 weeks after initiation of cambial activity in the buds. Some trees may initially shrink in diameter. This shrinkage probably results when transpiration exceeds uptake of water from cold soil. In well-stocked, even-aged stands, trees grow rapidly in diameter during the early part of the growing season, which can begin in early February in southern and coastal habitats. Growth is slower from late May to the end of the growing season in November or December. In contrast, trees grown in the open show relatively constant diame-

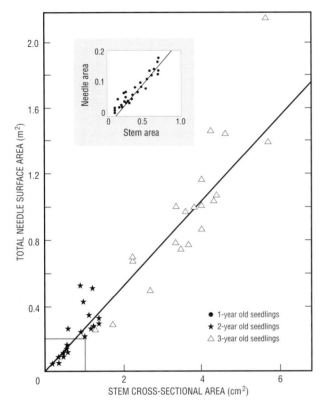

Figure 2-21—The relationship between total needle surface area and stem cross-sectional area at the groundline for 1-, 2-, and 3-year-old loblolly pine seedlings in Virginia (adapted from Johnson and others 1985).

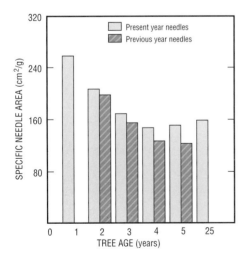

Figure 2-22—Specific needle area as influenced by seedling and needle age. No data on previous year needles available for age 25 (adapted from Johnson and others 1985).

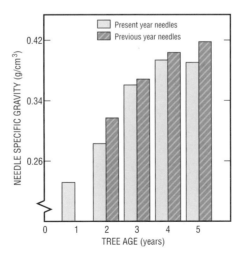

Figure 2-23—Needle specific gravity as influenced by seedling and needle age (adapted from Johnson and others 1985).

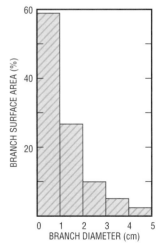

Figure 2-24—Branch surface area distribution by branch size class in a 14-year-old loblolly pine plantation (adapted from Kinerson 1975).

ter growth throughout the growing season and continue growth at least to mid-November (Harkin 1962). The average diameter growth of loblolly pines in plantations is the same as that of loblolly pines in natural stands until crown competition begins (Strub and others 1975). Once tree-to-tree competition becomes a factor, dominant trees begin growth earlier in the year, grow faster, and have a longer growing season than do trees in lower crown classes (Bassett 1966). Stand density and soil moisture conditions accentuate the growth differences between crown classes (see chapters 3 and 11).

Litterfall Patterns

During the winter, more than one-third of the total needle surface area is lost through death and shedding of second-year needles. Measurable weights of needles fall every month, but 45 to 70% of the total fall occurs during a September-to-December peak (Lockaby and Taylor-Boyd 1986, Wells and others 1972; figure 2-25 and table 2-30). Sinclair and Knoerr (1982) found 73% more needle surface area on 15-year-old loblolly pine trees in October than they found on the same trees the following winter after needlefall. In some areas, strong winds associated with local afternoon thundershowers may cause a small peak in litterfall in late spring. Many cones and dead branches also fall at that time (Gresham 1982, Nemeth 1973). Cultural treatments such as fertilization

or weed control have no effect on needlefall patterns. Needlefall quantity is strongly correlated with stand basal area (Dalla-Tea and Jokela 1991).

Natural Pruning

When insufficient solar radiation reaches the foliage of lower limbs, production of new needles ceases, mature needles drop, and branches die shortly thereafter. The length of time a dead branch remains on a tree depends on stand density, average temperature and humidity, branch angle, and the amount of wind, snow, and freezing weather. Dead branches of average size take from 4 to 11 years (average of 7 to 8) to disintegrate back to a length of 7.6 cm or less from the bole. Time required for a band of clear wood to grow over a place formerly occupied by a branch ranges from 9 to 15 years for trees 15 to 30 years old (Paul 1938, Reynolds 1967). When branches have no heartwood, there appears to be little relation between branch size and age and time required for complete healing. It also appears that the height of a limb in a tree has no effect on healing time (Reynolds 1967).

Sprouting

Loblolly pines do not sprout from adventitious buds or produce root sprouts, but seedlings, up to about age 3, may sprout from dormant buds along the lower stem if their tops are clipped off or killed by fire. Sprouting is much less common in loblolly pine than in pitch, pond, or shortleaf pine. Seedlings do not sprout if fire kills the dormant buds or if severed near the ground. As many as 90% of 1- and 2-year-old seedlings sprouted and continued to develop after their tops were cut off at about 10 cm above the ground. Although severed trees over age 3 will occasionally sprout from the root collar area, the sprouts rarely survive (Stone and Stone 1954).

Table 2-30—Monthly needle litterfall under a 14-year-old loblolly pine plantation in the Piedmont of North Carolina

	Monthly needlefall (g/m² of ground surface)											
	J	F	M	A	M	J	J	A	S	O	N	D
Maximum	14	18	16	22	31	17	58	25	62	69	162	98
Minimum	6	7	8	10	15	8	33	15	45	37	123	61
Mean	9	14	14	15	21	11	43	21	54	48	141	71

Source: Kinerson and others (1974).

Data were obtained from thirty-six 1-m² litter traps.

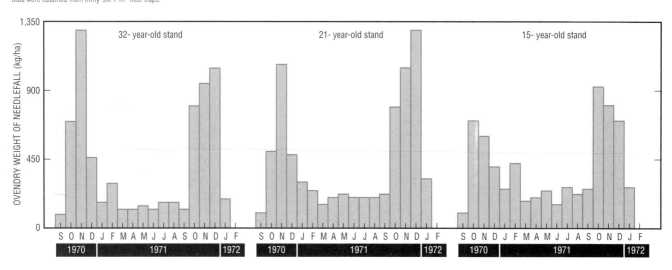

Figure 2-25—Distribution and quantity of needlefall in three unthinned loblolly pine plantations in the Piedmont of South Carolina (adapted from Van Lear and Goebel 1976).

Root Growth Habits

Loblolly pine trees have sturdy taproots and extensive lateral root systems, both of which are fixed by heredity. However, the form and extent of both the lateral and taproot systems are strongly influenced by tree age, soil, water table level, and microenvironment. Trees with more roots grow better than those with fewer roots. Computer-assisted tomography (CAT scan) can be used to examine root growth and development on a continuous basis, without disturbing the root system (Weiss 1987).

Early Rooting

After breaking through the seedcoat, the taproot of a new tree usually penetrates vertically into the soil. The elongation rate increases gradually, reaching a maximum just before the appearance of secondary needles about 10 to 12 weeks after germination, then decreases until the end of the first growing season (Bilan 1965). Lateral roots arise from the stele of the main root and form a network of feeder roots throughout the surface 30 cm of soil all around the new tree. The first laterals appear about 3 weeks after seed germination. Main root tissue must be at least 1 week old before it can produce lateral roots (Bilan 1965). Even though the root system of a young seedling is very fibrous, the slender taproot is prominent (figure 2-26). Although the extent of branching and rebranching is very rapid for trees growing with little or no competition (tables 2-31 and 2-32), 6-month-old flowering dogwood,

Cornus florida L., seedlings have 3½ times more roots, with a 13-fold greater root length than 6-month-old loblolly pines. In forests, 1-year-old white oaks have 30% more roots and 2½ times more root length than have loblolly pines of the same age (Kozlowski and Scholtes 1948). The lack of an extensive root system limits the capacity of loblolly pine seedlings to compete with tolerant hardwoods under forest cover.

Taproot

Loblolly pines usually have a single taproot. Of 116 three- to eight-year-old trees grown from seeds, 79% had a single taproot, 12% had more than 1 major root with a downward orientation, 5% had no taproot, and 4% had a J-shaped or disfigured taproot. There was no difference between taproot characteristics on Highland and Coastal Plain sites, and root orientation was unrelated to tree survival or stability (Harrington and others 1987). Functions of the taproot include water and nutrient absorption and physical support. The taproot of a growing, maturing tree can form any of a wide array of configurations depending on the texture of the soil, presence or absence of spodic horizons, and water table level (Ashe 1915). In fact, the taproots of two trees growing within 2 m of each other can grow totally differently depending on the characteristics of the soil directly beneath each tree.

Taproots normally grow to a depth of 1 to 2 m and

Table 2-31—Extent of the root system of a 6-month-old loblolly pine growing without competition

Root order		No. of Roots	Root length (cm)
Taproot		1	32.2
Lateral roots	First	71	187.5
	Second	496	146.1
	Third	199	21.2
Total		767	387.0

Source: adapted from Kozlowski and Scholtes (1948).

Table 2-32—Extent of the root systems of 8-month-old east Texas loblolly pines (N=10) growing in a nursery bed at 30- by 30-cm spacing

Root order		Ave. no. of roots	Ave. root length (cm)
Taproot		1.0	41.4 ± 6.9
Lateral roots	First	99.2 ± 24.9	230.5 ± 60.5
	Second	564.0 ± 173.7	233.4 ± 101.6
	Third	503.5 ± 286.5	115.8 ± 117.8
	Fourth	145.3 ± 141.5	25.1 ± 28.2
	Fifth	16.4 ± 23.3	2.4 ± 3.7
Total		1,328.4 ± 556.6	648.6 ± 280.6

Source: adapted from Bilan and others (1978).

Figure 2-26—Fibrous root systems of young loblolly pine seedlings with prominent taproots.

often reach 30 to 45 cm in diameter. Loblolly pines adapt to droughty conditions by early development of large, deep, and heavily branched root systems that absorb moisture efficiently (van Buijtenen and others 1976). If a taproot encounters a rock, hard claypan, or spodic horizon, it often turns and grows laterally until it encounters softer material, whereupon it may grow downward again. If the tree's site has a fluctuating water table, the taproot often divides into numerous short fingers with a proliferation of small feeder roots that die when covered by a high water table and regenerate when the water table recedes. On very wet soils, the taproot may be extremely short and provide little if any support to the tree. On dry soils, the taproot can penetrate to a depth greater than 3 m.

Loblolly pine sinker roots regularly descend from major lateral roots at points 2 m or more from the taproot (Carlson and others 1988). Sinker roots can penetrate deep into the soil, providing additional support to the tree and increasing soil volume accessible for water and nutrient absorption. The depth of penetration of sinker roots can be predicted from the diameters of sinker roots 1 cm away from their origin on lateral roots, using the equation:

$$y = 125 \ [1 - \exp(-0.2x)]$$

where y = sinker root depth (in centimeters) and x = sinker root diameter (in millimeters) (Carlson and others 1988).

Lateral Root System

The major supporting and absorbing tissues are long-lived, perennial, lateral roots growing in all directions from the taproot, usually within 15 to 30 cm of the soil surface (figure 2-27). Young trees develop several major lateral roots that are longer than the tree is tall. Three to ten or more first-order superficial lateral roots, growing within 15 cm of the soil surface, live for the entire life of a tree. In addition, 10 or more first-order lateral roots often grow from the taproot, at depths of 15 to 100 cm, depending on soil texture and aeration. Three- to nine-year-old loblolly pines in Arkansas, Oklahoma, and

Texas had 14 to 58 (average of 28) first-order lateral roots per tree (Carlson and Harrington 1987).

Lateral root length and spread increase with a tree's competitive position and age up to maturity. Mature loblolly pines have extensive lateral root systems, with some roots two to three or more times as long as the crown is wide. Individual roots can be longer than a mature tree is tall. Branching and rebranching of roots can result in an almost continuous mat of fine roots at the soil–forest floor interface. Young trees often have difficulty in getting established, even in open stands, because of severe root competition with large trees. There was about 754 m of root length per cubic meter of soil in the A horizon under a 19-year-old loblolly stand (Roberts 1948). A 100-year-old pine tree in Finland had a total root system length of 50,000 m and 5 million root tips (Kalela 1954).

Unsuberized and suberized roots.　Roberts (1948) found that growing root tips accounted for 1.35% of the total root length of 19-year-old loblolly pines. New and growing root tips remain white and unsuberized (that is, cell walls are thin and not impregnated with suberin) for a period of several days to several weeks. Gradually, the cortical tissue of the older portions of root tips turns brown and degenerates, and the remaining outer cells undergo suberization (that is, cell walls are converted into thick corky tissue by infiltration with suberin, a waxy polyester complex of hydroxy fatty acids and phenolic acids). As a tree ages, an increasing proportion of the root system undergoes secondary (woody) growth and suberization. Depending on the time of the year, 94 to 99% of the root surface area of a mature loblolly is suberized (Kramer and Bullock 1966).

Root hairs.　Root hairs are an important part of the root absorption system. They are single-celled, thin-walled, highly vacuolated protuberances up to 10 mm long that arise from the epidermis, or from cortical cells one or two layers beneath the epidermis, just behind the zone of most active meristematic development in the root tips. Root hairs live only for a few weeks, until secondary growth occurs in the maturing root tip cells. Root hairs begin developing on the radicle shortly after seed germination. Seven-week-old trees have as much surface area in root hairs as in roots. Approximately 217 root hairs are required to form 1 cm^2 of surface area (table 2-33). New root hairs continue to develop as long as root tips continue growing. Small feeder roots elongate slowly, bear few root hairs, and do not have secondary growth.

Figure 2-27—The lateral root system of a 22-year-old loblolly pine growing on a poorly drained flatwoods site in northern Florida.

Table 2-33—Development of roots and root hairs of 7-week-old loblolly pine seedlings

Surface	Root length (cm)	Root surface area (cm²)	No. of root hairs	Root hair area (cm²)
Primary	6.45	1.73	215	0.80
Secondary	5.93	0.97	371	2.08
Total	12.38	2.70	586*	2.87

Source: adapted from Kozlowski and Scholtes (1948).
* Equivalent to 217 roots hairs per cm² of root surface.

Mycorrhizae. Loblolly pine root systems are greatly modified by the presence of mycorrhizae. These nutrient-absorbing structures, formed when a fungus infects the living primary cortical cells of a short root, are symbiotic associations between nonpathogenic fungi and living root cells. At least 200, and possibly 1,000, species of fungi form mycorrhizal associations with loblolly pine. Many mycorrhizal fungi are not aggressive invaders so they are often crowded out by other microorganisms. Loblolly mycorrhizae are ectotrophic; that is, the fungal mycelia form a feltlike covering over the root surface and extend into the soil for several centimeters. This covering greatly increases the root surface that is in direct contact with soil particles. Hyphae enter short roots through natural openings between root cap cells, between degenerating epidermal or cortical cells, and between living cortical cells of the root tissue (Warrington and others 1981, 1982). This produces marked hypertrophy and extensive dichotomous branching of roots. Mycorrhizae add about 1.4% to the total root length of a mature loblolly pine and account for 0.5 to 6.1% (an average of about 2.7%) of the total root surface area during the year (Kramer and Bullock 1966, Roberts 1948). Mycorrhizae enable trees to absorb and accumulate ions more selectively, and this promotes increased photosynthesis and growth. Their role in plant development is well documented (Dixon and Marx 1987, Kramer 1969, Melin 1962).

Rapidly growing long roots typically do not have mycorrhizal associations but often have mycorrhizal branches a short distance back from the growing tip. Branches from the long roots are the primary mycorrhizal roots. They grow relatively slowly and produce few root hairs. Once infected with a mycorrhizal fungus, short roots are quickly colonized. Four weeks after inoculation with *Pisolithus tinctorius*, 9% of all short roots of 2-month-old seedlings were mycorrhizal. By seedling ages 4 months and 10 months, 40% and 73% of all roots, respectively, were mycorrhizal. At seedling age 10 months, mycor-

rhizal seedlings were also substantially larger than nonmycorrhizal seedlings (Reid and others 1983).

Mycorrhizal fungi can help protect trees by acting as a physical barrier to disease entry, utilizing excess carbohydrates, secreting fungistatic substances, and favoring protective organisms of the rhizosphere. Other benefits of ectomycorrhizae include keeping short roots alive longer and increasing tree tolerance to inorganic and organic soil toxins, extremes of soil acidity, and high soil temperatures (Marx 1969, 1975; Zak 1964). Mycorrhizae can be shared by two or more loblolly pine trees. Under such conditions there is potential for interroot transfer of substances (Reid 1971). The extent and significance of this phenomenon are unknown.

Root Surface Area and Root Weight Relationships

Most of the surface area of loblolly pine lateral roots is in small roots, but most of the weight is usually in large roots (figure 2-28). The weight of growing tips and mycorrhizae is minuscule in comparison with that of suberized roots, except in newly germinated seedlings. Although 50 to 65% of the root biomass in 15-year-old plantations is in the taproot, 10% of the total root biomass can be in roots 1 cm in diameter or smaller (Kinerson and others 1977, Wells and others 1975). Of the 9.7 tonnes(t)/ha of lateral roots in a 25-year-old plantation, equal amounts (38%) were in roots less than 0.5 cm in diameter or greater than 2 cm in diameter. The remaining biomass was in roots of intermediate size (Pehl and others 1984). A 34-year-old stand had 93.5 to 99.4% of its total root surface area in suberized roots throughout the year; unsuberized, growing root tips accounted for 0.1 to 0.5% of root surface area most of the year (maximum of 1.4% during a period of rapid growth) with mycorrhizae making up the rest. Roots less than 2 mm in diameter made up half of the total root surface area in this stand (Kramer and Bullock 1966).

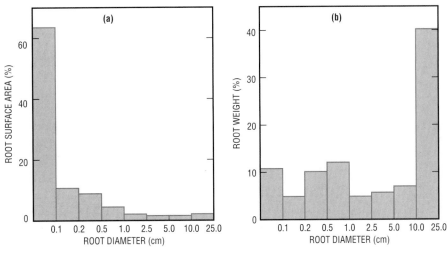

Figure 2-28—Thirteen-year-old planted loblolly pine: root surface area distribution by root diameter class (**a**) and root weight distribution by root diameter class (**b**) (adapted from Kinerson 1975).

Distribution of Roots in the Soil

More than 95% of the root biomass of loblolly pine is in the surface 60 cm of soil whether the site is dry or wet (Brewer and Linnartz 1978, Harris and others 1977). Usually about 70 to 80% of the biomass of both small and large lateral roots is in the surface 20 cm of soil (Box 1968; table 2-34). However, Kinerson and others (1977) found that only 37% of the lateral root biomass in a 14-year-old plantation was in the top 20 cm of a sandy loam Piedmont soil. Most short, branched, absorbing roots are in the surface 15 cm of soil, regardless of soil type or tree age. Absorbing roots are most concentrated within the dripline of the crown. This concentration of roots near the soil surface permits good access to moisture and associated nutrients from even small rain showers and promotes rapid utilization of minerals from decomposing organic matter. A second concentration of small feeder roots can usually be found near the normal water table or in and around a spodic horizon (zone of mineral deposition). In dry soils, lateral roots may be distributed from near the soil surface to depths of 1 m or

more. Taproots may grow deeper than 3 m in dry, sandy soils, but reach less than half that depth in wet or heavy soils (Brewer and Linnartz 1978; table 2-35).

Loblolly pine roots can penetrate deep into rather heavy subsoils if aeration is adequate. Soil bulk density above 1.4 g/cm^3 reduces the number of new roots, limits root elongation, and causes root tips to be misshapen (Mitchell and others 1981). The water table level has a strong influence on both short- and long-term root development and on location of root concentrations. Root biomass and aboveground tree growth is greatest when the water table stays fairly constant throughout the year. When the water table fluctuates from at or near the ground surface during wet periods to 1 m or more below ground during dry periods, roots are constantly dying and regenerating (White and others 1971).

Primary laterals, with fine absorbing rootlets, approach the soil surface a short distance from the base of a tree and become less dense with increasing distance from the tree. As a result, total root surface area is usually 2 to 3 times higher within 1 m of a tree bole than at greater distances from a bole (Schultz 1972b). In a 7-year-old Georgia Piedmont plantation, roots were concentrated within 1.2 m of the bole and at the maximum distance at which roots were studied (4.9 m) (figure 2-29). Surface concentration of roots was highest but subsurface concentration of roots was lowest 1.2 m from the bole.

Seasonal variation in root activity. Roots grow throughout the year, and length of primary lateral roots increases by 10 to 30 mm/week when conditions are favorable (Bilan 1967). Most root growth occurs in the spring, and the least occurs in the winter. About 80% of the root growth of 6-year-old loblolly pines occurs during the shoot growth period (Reed 1939). Growth in the summer is restricted during periods of low soil moisture. Seedling roots cease to elongate when needle moisture content falls below about 150% (needle moisture content at field capacity is about 200 to 250%) (Bilan and Jan 1968, Pharis and Kramer 1964). Dry or cold conditions can cause root growth to cease at any time, but roots are never truly dormant. During the winter, the periods of slowest root growth coincide with low soil temperatures. Whenever the soil warms, roots resume growth. The most favorable temperatures for root growth are between 20 and 30 °C. Seedling roots can grow more than 5 mm/day when the soil temperature is 25 °C, but growth slows to less than 0.2 mm/day at 5 °C, and no growth occurs below 0 °C. Growth continues at soil temperatures as high as 35 °C, but it is very slow (Barney 1951, Kramer and Kozlowski 1979, Perry 1971a, Wahlenberg 1960).

There is substantial seasonal variation in glycolytic enzyme activity in roots. Sung and oth-

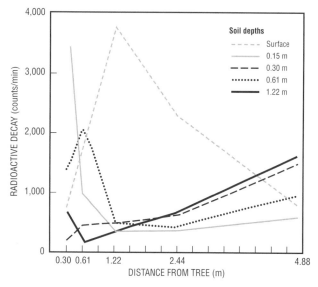

Table 2-34—Distribution of lateral roots in a 15-year-old plantation growing on a typic Hapludult in the Piedmont of North Carolina ▼

Soil depth (cm)	< 1 cm roots		> 1 cm roots	
	(kg/ha)	(%)	(kg/ha)	(%)
0-10	1,980	46.0	2,145	33.0
10-20	1,075	25.0	2,990	46.0
20-30	430	10.0	715	11.0
30-40	390	9.0	520	8.0
40-50	170	4.0	65	1.0
50-60	130	3.0	30	0.5
60-70	130	3.0	30	0.5
Total	4,305	100.0	6,495	100.0

Source: Harris and others (1977).

▲ **Figure 2-29**—Root concentration in a 7-year-old loblolly pine plantation as determined by measurement of radioactive decay (adapted from Walker and Arnold 1963).

Table 2-35—Length of mature loblolly pine taproots on various sites in northern Louisiana ▼

	Length* (m)		
Site	Average	Range	Plantation age (yr)
Dry	2.0	1.3–2.8	26
Intermediate	1.3	0.9–1.7	27
Wet	1.1	0.8–1.5	25

Source: adapted from Gibson and others (1986).
* Average length from groundline to taproot tip.

ers (1988) reported that the highest rate of sucrose synthase activity (up to 177 nanomoles per minute per milligram of protein) occurs during periods of active growth while the lowest rate (50 nmol/min/mg of protein) occurs during the winter. PPi-dependent phosphofructokinase activity decreases by about 50% in the winter, but acid invertase, alkaline invertase, UDPglucose pyrophosphorylase, fructokinase, glucokinase, NTP-dependent phosphofructokinase, and phosphoglucomutase activities are relatively constant throughout the year.

Roots die throughout the year and during all stages of tree growth. Small feeder roots usually live less than 1 year because of unfavorable environmental conditions (including cold weather and poor aeration) and attacks by insects, fungi, and other organisms. Older and larger primary roots also die back periodically as a result of moisture stress and pathogenic invasion. In a 25-year-old plantation in southern Illinois, 47% of the total annual root production of 3,500 kg/ha died and decomposed the same year (Fisher and others 1975).

Although flooding stresses roots, roots in flooded soils can continue to develop slowly by means of anaerobic metabolism (DeBell and others 1984). Fluctuation in environmental conditions is greatest near the soil surface and at considerable depths. For this reason, root death or dormancy is most frequent near the surface or among very deep roots. Healthy trees easily make up these losses in the spring or during other periods when conditions favor growth.

Root grafting.   Both intraspecific grafting (between roots of two or more trees) and self-grafting (between roots of the same tree) are common in loblolly pine. The factor that most strongly affects the amount of intraspecific root grafting is distance between trees. This is true for both plantations and natural stands. The closer together two trees are, the more often their roots make contact and ultimately fuse (figure 2-30). In stands of typical pole-sized loblolly pines, from 5 to 25% of all trees are root grafted to one or more neighboring trees (Schultz and Woods 1967). However, most root contacts do not form grafts.

Taproots of seedlings less than 1 year old growing in nursery beds will occasionally graft. There is a high probability that a young tree growing under the drip line of a mature tree will graft with the overtopping tree one or more times, even if the ages of the trees differ by 50 years or more. As a stand ages, grafts become more common because of extended root systems and enlarged roots. In most fully stocked stands, trees are no more than about 3 to 6 m apart. When trees are this close together, it is quite possible that any individual tree may be root grafted to one or more of its neighbors. Trees growing very close together often form numerous root grafts. Occasionally, five or more trees form an interconnected root system.

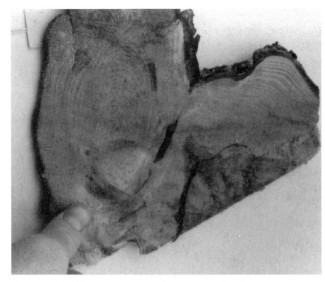

Figure 2-30—The cross section of a root-graft showing vascular continuity and included bark at the initial point of contact (Schultz 1965).

Overtopped trees that persist for a decade or longer under a dense canopy are usually root grafted to the nearest dominant or codominant tree. A firm graft at or near the root collar of one loblolly pine can support the entire stump and root system of a cut neighbor (figure 2-31).

Although grafting permits the movement of water and nutrients between two trees or between a living tree and the root system of a recently cut tree, there is no evidence to suggest that this exchange significantly aids or detracts from individual tree growth (Miller and Woods 1965, Schultz and Woods 1967). Self-grafting probably has no meaningful effect on tree growth. However, the annosum root-rot fungus—*Heterobasidion annosum* (Fr.:Fr.) Bref. = *Fomes annosus* (Fr.:fr.) Cooke—can be transferred from one tree to another through root grafts.

Figure 2-31—A dominant loblolly pine supporting an entire stump and root system through a large collar graft (Schultz 1972a).

After one tree of a grafted pair is cut, the stump may callus over during a period of 1 to 5 years (figure 2-32). Living stumps more than 30 years old can often be found in healthy thinned stands. Callus tissue on living stumps consists of swirled and twisted fibers that are usually separated from the old stump xylem by a thin resinous layer (figure 2-33). The amount of callusing depends on the extent of the grafting and on the distance of the graft or grafts from both the living tree and the stump. Callus tissue is normally about 0.6 to 1.3 cm thick, but varies in thickness even on a single stump. Callus tissue often extends several centimeters above the cut surface of a stump and is thicker on the side of the stump facing the donor tree because a graft will normally be directly between the donor and the living stump. Usually, only one root and a small portion of the connected stump are alive 5 years after the grafted tree is felled, and translocation of water, nutrients, or photosynthate occurs only during times of high moisture

stress. The stump and root system probably creates a minor net deficit to the living tree.

Effects of nutrients on root development. The availability of nutrients in the soil strongly affects both the growth rate and distribution of loblolly pine roots. Soil acidity and soil moisture content together determine the availability of nutrients. Although loblolly pine is relatively tolerant of acidic soil conditions, root development is inhibited in low-pH soils as a result of toxicity of the hydrogen ion, or more frequently as a result of Al toxicity. Aluminum becomes more soluble as soil acidity increases (Pritchett 1979). High levels of Al adversely affect the mitotic cycle, seem to cause premature cell maturation and senescence, and reduce primary root elongation (Tepper and others 1989). Fertilization stimulates root growth when soils are poor in nutrients. For example, dry weight of seedling roots doubled, following P fertilization, in lower Coastal Plain soils (typic Ochraquults) deficient in P. Mycorrhizal development was also increased by adding P. Adding large amounts of N to these soils reduced shoot, root, and mycorrhizal development (Pritchett 1973). Effects of fertilizer additions on overall tree growth is discussed in chapter 11.

Relationships Between Shoots and Roots

The roots and shoots of loblolly pines depend on each other in numerous ways. If one structure is modified, the other is usually affected. Because the soil protects the roots, extremes of air temperature affect root growth less adversely than they affect shoot growth (Greenwald 1972).

It is a common nursery practice to undercut (prune) the roots when lifting seedlings from a nursery in preparation for outplanting (see chapter 6). Under favorable conditions, loblolly pines can rapidly regenerate roots lost as a result of nursery lifting or other disturbances. However, severe root breakage or pruning can result in a seedling that is unable to supply enough water to offset transpiration from the needles after planting. An inadequate water supply can result in stomatal closure, wilting, and ultimately death of the seedling even during relatively short dry spells.

Cross-sectional seedling stem area is a good predictor of seedling root volume. One-year-old seedlings with a cross-sectional stem area of 0.4 cm^2 have a root volume of

Figure 2-32—Tangential section of a living stump. Callus has formed around the periphery, over the cut surface, and down into the rotted central portion of the stump. A thick layer of resin separates the callus from the decaying old xylem, and there are several large resin pockets in the callus tissue (Schultz 1965).

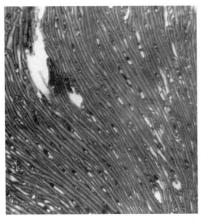

Figure 2-33—Irregular growth of callus tissue around the stump of a recently cut loblolly pine tree: **left**, × 75; **right**, × ⅔ (adapted from Schultz and Woods 1967).

about 4.0 cm³. At age 2, the average tree has a cross-sectional stem area of about 1 cm² and a root volume of 10 cm³. A 3-year-old tree with a cross-sectional stem area of 4 cm² has a root volume of 45 to 60 cm³ (figure 2-34). In 3- to 9-year-old trees, the cross-sectional stem area at the groundline is equal to the cross-sectional area of all first-order lateral roots at their origin (Carlson and Harrington 1987).

The ratio of loblolly pine root weight to shoot weight is commonly about 0.20 to 0.25 except in very young trees, where it exceeds 0.80. Monk (1966) reported root-to-shoot ratios ranging from 0.83 for a tree approximately 1.0 m tall to 0.20 for a tree approximately 6.5 m tall. He also noted a high correlation between the dry weight of roots and the dry weight of stems or needles or shoots (stems and needles) for trees up to about 12.7 cm in dbh growing on two South Carolina soils. Root biomass of 11- and 12-year-old trees in the North Carolina Coastal Plain was about 2% of the biomass of the stems plus live branches and about 21% of the combined biomass of the stems, live branches, and foliage (Nemeth 1972). The root-to-shoot ratio of 13- to 16-year-old planted loblolly pines in the North Carolina Piedmont was 0.22 to 0.25 when the shoot weight included the weights of stems, branches, and foliage (Kinerson and others 1977, Ralston and others 1972, Wells and others 1975).

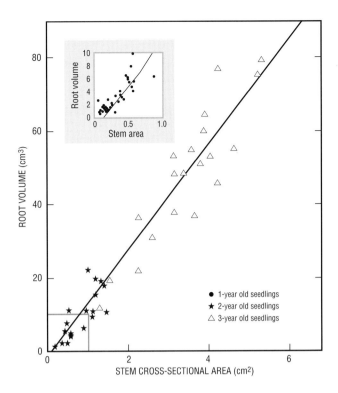

Figure 2-34—Linear relationship between stem cross-sectional area at the groundline and root volume of 1- to 3-year-old loblolly pine seedlings in Virginia (adapted from Johnson and others 1985).

Sexual Reproduction

Flower and Cone Development

Some seedlings produce isolated cones when they are only 3 to 5 years old. At these tree ages, female flowering is 2 to 3 times more frequent than male flowering (Greene and Porterfield 1962, Greenwood and Gladstone 1978, Schmidtling 1971). Male strobili steadily increase in number beginning at tree age 5. Substantial numbers of female flowers usually form beginning about tree ages 10 to 15 in open stands and somewhat later in closed stands. About 2.5 years elapse between formation of female flower primordia and seed release. Abundant flowering is a prerequisite for a plentiful cone crop but does not necessarily ensure it. In loblolly pine, good flower crops are much more frequent than good cone crops. During the long maturation period for female reproductive structures, physiological changes, insect problems, and environmental events such as high temperatures, fire, freezes, and ice storms destroy flowers, new cones, and even maturing cones. During a 6-year period in south Arkansas, an average of 55% (range, 36 to 73%) of the strobili that reached the flower stage matured to cones (Grano 1973). Male flowers (catkins) and pollen are produced in only 7 to 9 months, reducing the likelihood that they will be destroyed.

Formation of catkins. Male primordia begin to form in twig buds in late June or early July. Growth continues throughout the summer, and the catkins appear as small knobs around the base of vegetative buds from mid-September to November (Dorman and Zobel 1973, Greenwood 1980). By mid-December, the pollen sacs are filled with well-defined microspore mother cells. Growth slows during the coldest winter periods, but the catkins develop rapidly as the temperature rises in late winter and early spring. Periods of low temperature in the spring do not slow development of male flowers (Dorman 1976). Huge quantities of pollen are present in each catkin; the number has been estimated to range from 0.4 to 1.5 million pollen grains for some pines and spruces (Fechner 1979).

Pollen grains are released and disseminated by wind from February to April, depending on latitude and yearly climatic conditions (Fowells 1965, Mergen and others 1963). Loblolly pine pollen is shed from an individual catkin over a 2- to 3-week period, but very small amounts are released during the first week (Grano 1973). During a 6-year period in southwest Alabama, peak pollen shed occurred within a 23-day period. In 4 of the 6 years, the peak occurred within the same week in mid-March (Boyer 1978). In a 7-year period in south Arkansas, all pollen was shed between March 14 and April 13. Peak pollen shed occurred between April 1 and 8 in 6 of the 7 years and occurred 1 week earlier in the other year. In southern Mississippi, pollen was shed as early as February 11 to 21 and as late as March 19 to April 10 during a 9-year period (Mergen and others 1963). Female flower receptivity of surrounding trees normally peaks during periods of heaviest pollen shed (Grano 1973).

Pollen ripening is strongly related to latitude. Ripening begins on about the first day of February at latitude 29% N. Ripening occurs about 10 to 15 days later for each 2-degree increase in latitude above latitude 29% N. Pollen ripens over a period of about 2 weeks at a particular latitude, but length of the ripening period at a given latitude is influenced by elevation and proximity to the seacoast. Time of peak pollen shed can be calculated within about 4 days by accumulating temperatures in degree-days above a base temperature for the area of interest (table 2-36). Some trees may shed pollen 200 to 300 degree-days ahead of the average for a stand. Most pollen is deposited within 100 m of the point where it was released, but some is carried many kilometers on updrafts and wind currents. Loblolly pine pollen, and that of many other North American pines, has been found in fossil beds from the Lower Miocene Epoch at Landes, France—showing that there is some worldwide movement of pollen (Sivak and Caratini 1973). After pollen is shed, catkins dry up quickly and most fall from the tree within a few weeks.

Table 2-36—Peak pollen shed in four southern pines in southern Alabama based on heat sums

Pine species	Base temperature (°F)	Starting date for heat sums	Average heat sums to peak pollen shed (deg-days)
Slash	55	Dec. 5	735
Longleaf	50	Dec. 31	1,208
Shortleaf	55	Jan. 31	1,140
Loblolly	55	Feb. 1	636*

Source: adapted from Boyer (1978)

* Beginning on Feb. 1, add positive differences between the daily high temperature and 55 °F. Once a sum of 636 is reached, loblolly pine should be at peak pollen shed.

Formation of cones. Primordia of female flowers do not become apparent until August, which indicates that such tissues are initiated after male flowers (Mergen and Koerting 1957). The first evidence of a flower bud is a swelling on the apex of a vegetative bud in late fall or winter. Flower primordia, which are enclosed by protective bud scales, develop rapidly when the temperature begins to rise in late February and early March. Developing flowers emerge from the bud scales in an erect position at the tips of new shoots. Female flowers are composed of many soft, fleshy scales spirally attached at right angles to a central axis. Pairs of ovules originate as small protuberances at the bases of scales. Only those scales in the central region have the potential to produce ovules. These scales are called fertile

scales. The lower scales and those at the tip are infertile and will not produce seeds.

Pollination occurs when pollen grains, carried from the catkins by wind, contact a female flower. Three patterns of airflow are typically generated around female strobili that are ready to be pollinated. The movement of air over the flower, with its many protrusions, gives rise to significant turbulence on the leeward (downwind) side of the flower. Also, air passing over each scale drops toward the scale's base and swirls chaotically near the micropyles. Finally, air circling the cone axis washes over the upper (ovule-bearing) surfaces (Niklas 1987). These diverse air movements ensure that pollen-laden air is transported over most micropyles.

Pollination typically occurs from February to April. Because the flowers of a single tree usually develop almost synchronously, pollination of all flowers of a tree often is completed in 5 to 7 days, but may require up to 10 to 14 days. Flowers of different trees can develop at substantially different rates, so pollination within a single stand can extend over a period of several weeks. A mature loblolly pine can produce 10 times as many female flowers one year as it produces in another. This shows that environmental conditions have a tremendous impact on reproduction (Grano 1973).

Pollination in loblolly pine is a two-step process. In the first step, pollen is accumulated on the micropylar horns. In the second, the grains are transferred to the nucellus by rain or the pollen drop. Three to seven pollen grains commonly reach the mycropylar arm of each ovule (March and others 1986). All pollen grains reaching the micropylar horns, whether they arrive early or late, have an equal chance of reaching the nucellus and presumably germinating (Greenwood and Rucker 1985). For 16 months following pollination, the pollen tube grows slowly downward through the tissue of the nucellus while the egg cell develops. During the first 12 months, the ovule remains only a fraction of the size of a fully developed seed, and the female flower (now called a conelet) grows very little—remaining about 2 cm long.

Once spring vegetative growth begins, the cones and the ovules within them expand rapidly so that both are full sized at the time of fertilization. Fertilization takes place in late spring or early summer of the year after pollination, when pollen tubes have grown far enough into an ovule to reach specialized structures (archegonia) containing egg cells (March and others 1986). Loblolly pine gametophytes have several archegonia containing egg cells, so multiple fertilizations are possible. Thus, in the same ovule, a self-fertilized egg cell usually fails to grow, whereas another embryo in the same ovule, if fertilized by pollen from a different tree, usually develops and produces a filled seed (Bridgwater and Bramlett 1982).

Following fertilization, both seeds and cones continue to mature until late summer or fall. In the southern coastal areas, cone ripening is usually complete by mid-October. Farther north and in the Piedmont, ripening is often not

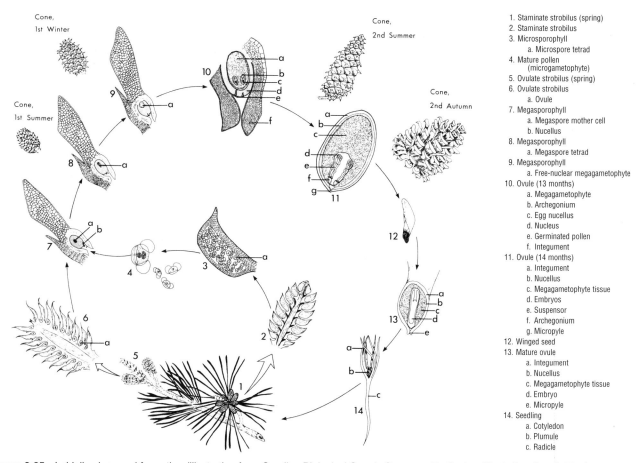

1. Staminate strobilus (spring)
2. Staminate strobilus
3. Microsporophyll
    a. Microspore tetrad
4. Mature pollen
    (microgametophyte)
5. Ovulate strobilus (spring)
6. Ovulate strobilus
    a. Ovule
7. Megasporophyll
    a. Megaspore mother cell
    b. Nucellus
8. Megasporophyll
    a. Megaspore tetrad
9. Megasporophyll
    a. Free-nuclear megagametophyte
10. Ovule (13 months)
    a. Megagametophyte
    b. Archegonium
    c. Egg nucellus
    d. Nucleus
    e. Germinated pollen
    f. Integument
11. Ovule (14 months)
    a. Integument
    b. Nucellus
    c. Megagametophyte tissue
    d. Embryos
    e. Suspensor
    f. Archegonium
    g. Micropyle
12. Winged seed
13. Mature ovule
    a. Integument
    b. Nucellus
    c. Megagametophyte tissue
    d. Embryo
    e. Micropyle
14. Seedling
    a. Cotyledon
    b. Plumule
    c. Radicle

Figure 2-35--Loblolly pine seed formation (illustration from Carolina Biological Supply Company, Burlington, North Carolina © 1975).

complete until late October or November. The mature, fully developed seed has an embryo composed of immature needles (cotyledons), an immature stem (hypocotyl), and an immature root (radicle). The embryo is enveloped by gametophyte tissue that provides food reserves for germination and a hard outer protective layer (seedcoat) (figure 2-3). The entire process of loblolly pine seed formation takes 2 years (figure 2-35). Cones are ready for collection when their specific gravity has decreased to about 0.88 and the cone moisture content is about 112% (see chapter 6). Biochemical indications of cone maturity include reduced sugar content of seeds at 0.14% or less, and crude fat content of seeds in excess of 20% (Barnett 1979).

Weather conditions affect female flower development more than they affect male flower development. The timing of rainfall can alter the amount of flowering and the time of peak flowering. Abundant spring rainfall or irrigation (in April to June) and a relatively dry summer (in July to September) during the year preceding flowering can significantly increase female flower production (Dewers and Moehring 1970, Grano 1973, Shoulders 1973, Wenger 1957). Both newly formed female flower buds and first-year flowers become dormant in the fall. A chilling period is necessary for the buds to resume growth. If strobilus maturation is to be hastened, this period must be broken artificially. Low temperatures in the spring slow development of female flowers (Dorman 1976). If the develop-

ment of female flowers is greatly retarded, the chance of fertilization by other southern pines is increased. Normally, the timing of pollen ripening and female flower receptivity differs enough from species to species to prevent hybridization. However, unusual weather conditions can result in pollination of loblolly pine by shortleaf pine, which usually blooms later than loblolly pine. Similarly, slash pine can be pollinated by loblolly pine if weather delays female flowering in slash. In both cases, hybrids can be produced (se chapter 9).

Cross-pollination and cross-fertilization predominate in loblolly pine, primarily because (1) the volume of pollen from surrounding trees overwhelms that of an individual tree, (2) male flowers tend to mature before female flowers on the same tree, and (3) most catkins are borne on branches in the lower crown, and pollen is usually carried away from the mother tree before it is lifted on wind currents. In combination, these factors promote pollination by surrounding trees. However, open-grown trees with large crowns commonly have both male and female flowers intermingled in the middle part of the crown and occasionally have female flowers on lower branches. This tends to promote limited self-fertilization (see chapter 7).

Simple polyembryony (the fertilization of more than one egg in a gametophyte) or cleavage polyembryony (splitting of a single egg after a single fertilization) can occur in loblolly pines. However, two or more viable embryos in a single seed occur only occasionally because of competition among developing embryos. Ordinarily, one seedling is large and apparently normal and the other quite small and imperfectly developed. Generally, twin embryos are oriented in the same direction in the seed, and their radicles emerge from the seed at the same place. On rare occasions, the embryos are inverted (Dorman 1976).

Depending on the severity of injury, partial girdling, or strangling, putting tightly wrapped bands on a tree can increase, reduce, or have no effect on cone and seed production. In a Louisiana study, partial stem girdling of loblolly pine trees, 25 cm in dbh and larger, more than doubled the number of cones per tree, but both cone size and seed size were reduced and there were detrimental effects to some trees (table 2-37). Conversely, banding suppressed cone production in both released and unreleased 21-year-old loblolly pines in the North Carolina Piedmont. It also reduced by half the number of viable seeds per cone in released trees (Bilan 1960). Partial girdling and strangling of trees 8 to 38 cm in dbh had no significant effect on cone production over a 6-year period in southeast Arkansas (Grano 1960). Because all types of injury usually reduce diameter growth and live crown ratio, purposeful injury to promote seed production is not recommended.

Seed Production

Seed production of individual trees increases with tree age, tree size, and freedom from crown competition. With good cultural care, seed orchard trees can be in full seed production by about age 15 (see chapter 7). In forest stands of widely spaced loblolly pines, trees may produce enough seeds by age 25 to regenerate an area. However, 40-year-old trees generally produce three to five times more seeds than do 25-year-old trees. A large open-grown tree can produce up to 40,000 seeds in a bumper year, but the average mature tree yields about 9,000 to 15,000 seeds in a good year (Wahlenberg 1960). When the seed crop is large, the percentage of sound seeds is usually 60% or greater (Campbell 1967, Grano 1973), and the proportion of sound seeds lost to insects or other users is reduced. Seed production per hectare varies widely over time within a stand and between forest stands (see chapter 5).

The average cone has the potential to produce about 155 seeds. Often only 20 to 25% of this number actually develop, primarily because of the combination of insufficient pollen and insect damage (Bramlett 1986). Insect damage is discussed in chapter 10. Almost half of the potential loblolly pine seeds can be lost in first-year abortion due to lack of viable pollen (Bramlett 1974). Inbreeding (see chapter 7) also results in some abortion of first-year conelets. Early abortions can result in the loss of entire first-year cones or more commonly in the loss of individual ovules that are not pollinated. The conelet usually aborts if the whole flower is not pollinated. However, a few cones survive to maturity even without seeds. These cones contain aborted ovules and seed wings and are smaller than pollinated cones (McLemore 1977). Increasing the pollen supply increases the chance that most ovules will be pollinated. Because pollen is rarely 100% viable, multiple pollinations increase the probability that each ovule will contain at least one pollen grain that will germinate, fertilize a female gametophyte, and produce a seed.

The number of second-year cones can be accurately estimated by early summer (see chapter 5). The number of seeds per cone can be estimated early in the fall by taking sample cones from a number of trees, slicing them longitudinally through the middle, and counting the number of sound seeds on each face. This number can then be projected to total sound seeds per cone (Dierauf and Wasser 1975; figure 2-36). Cones collected should be typical in shape and size and from the upper or middle part of the crown. About 5 to 10 cones from each of 20 to 30 trees in a stand can provide a good data base for developing a localized regression equation (Asher 1964, McLemore 1962). If cones are collected in an orchard, a sample consisting of one representative cone from each tree should provide a satisfactory estimate of sound seeds in the orchard.

There is no visual method for forecasting good seed crops more than a few months before seedfall. Early in

Table 2-37—Partial stem girdling alters loblolly pine cone size and number, and tree diameter growth

Treatment	No of. cones 100 L	No of. cones Tree	Weight of seeds (g) 100 L	Weight of seeds (g) Tree	% seed viability	% germination energy	Diameter growth (cm) 1956-60	% tree survival
Girdling	1,180	931	477	380	85	80	5.6	90
No girdling	1,007	428	880	394	84	78	8.6	98

Source: adapted from Hansbrough and Merrifield (1963).

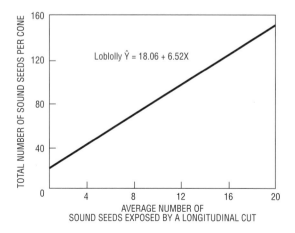

Loblolly $\hat{Y} = 18.06 + 6.52X$

Figure 2-36— Relationship between number of sound seeds exposed by a longitudinal cut and number of sound seeds per cone for loblolly pines in central Louisiana (adapted from McLemore 1962).

the spring, there is a short period when first-year cones can be counted before they are obscured by new needle growth. The absence of first-year conelets is a sure sign of a poor seed crop the following year, but the presence of many conelets does not necessarily ensure a good crop. Various causes can result in losses of cones, and seeds within them, during the following 18 months of development (see chapter 7).

Mature cones always contain empty seeds. The number of viable seeds per cone can vary from 3 or 4 to more than 200. A cone of average size usually has 30 to 40 filled seeds but can have as many as 89 seeds (Dorman and Zobel 1973, VanHaverbeke and Barber 1964). [The actual viability and germination rate strongly depend on the environmental conditions to which the seeds are subjected.] In seed orchards that are managed well, cones may contain an average of 100 or more filled seeds each year. Although the proportion of sound seeds to all seeds collected can range from less than 10 to more than 80%, it is generally 40 to 60% (Bramlett 1974, Franklin 1970; table 2-38). Research to undertand and improve this istuation would be helpful.

Table 2-38—Seed production per hectare in well-stocked and poorly stocked 70-year-old mixed loblolly–shortleaf pine stands

| | No. of seeds falling to ground (thousands) | | | | | |
| | Well stocked (closed canopy) | | | Poorly stocked (open canopy) | | |
Seed year	Total	Sound	% sound	Total	Sound	% sound
1	1,596	1,136	71	1,344	808	60
2	388	165	42	1,593	1,052	61
3	30	10	30	168	44	27
4	141	59	43	561	314	56
5	526	282	54	417	178	42
Total	2,677	1,652	62	4,085	2,356	59

Source: adapted from Campbell (1967).

Seed Dissemination

Normally, cones ripen on the tree and seeds fall to the ground within about 30 m of the crown. Depending on wind speed, wind direction, and air turbulence, some seeds can be carried long distances from the mother tree. However, downwind seeding is usually not effective more than about 90 m from the mother tree.

Seeds are disseminated gradually over a period of several months. Seedfall usually begins in October, and 30 to 35% of seeds are shed by the end of October, 60 to 75% by the end of November, and 80 to 90% by the end of December (Grano 1973; figure 2-37). Small numbers of seeds fall from January to May, but this late seedfall is erratic and of little consequence. Sound seeds are generally dispersed slightly faster than unfilled seeds. Cone opening and seedfall are hastened by warm, dry, windy weather and retarded by cool, wet weather. Viability is generally uniformly good for seeds shed during the peak period of October, November, and December (Grano

1973, Lotti 1956). Viability of the few seeds shed in late winter or early spring may be reduced, but such a reduction does not affect the seed crop significantly.

Seed Germination

Loblolly pine seeds are relatively dormant in comparison with seeds of other southern pines. An individual seedlot usually germinates over an extended period unless exposed to about 30 to 60 days of moist prechilling at about 3 °C. Dormancy in loblolly pine is a complex phenomenon controlled by several factors. The seedcoat, which restricts water absorption by limiting swelling of the megagametophyte and embryo, seems to be a primary cause of delayed germination. Moisture content of seeds does not exceed about 36% until the seedcoat cracks and germination begins. Low-temperature dormancy stimulates metabolic activity, which decreases the dry weight of the megagametophyte, increases the dry weight of the embryo, and seems to stimulate embryonic growth (Barnett 1972a, 1976; Carpita and others 1983). Following prechilling, about 90% of the sound seeds will germinate within 2 weeks under conditions of 10 to 30% moisture content and about 16 hours of light per day (Campbell 1982, also see chapter 6).

Larger, heavier seeds germinate more quickly and produce larger seedlings than do small seeds. However, seed size appears to have no effect on ultimate tree size (Dunlap and Barnett 1983). Germinating seeds contain less protein than do dormant seeds (Whetstone and others 1970). Germinating seedlings release small amounts of volatile compounds that are apparently formed during metabolism of stored substances (Vancura and Stotzky 1976). The release of methanol, acetaldehyde, ethanol, and formic acid is greatest during the first 24 to 48 hours of germination and precedes the appearance of the radicle. Liberation of the volatile compounds may attract and influence the growth of fungal spores and hyphae.

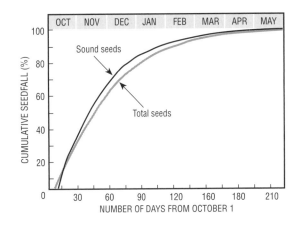

Figure 2-37—Cumulative seedfall averaged over a 5-year period during October through May from two mixed loblolly–shortleaf pine (75% loblolly pine) stands in north Louisiana (adapted from Campbell 1967).

Physiological Processes

In loblolly pine, physiological activities such as absorption, photosynthesis, respiration, and transpiration continue throughout the year but are slowed during the winter months.

Absorption of Water and Nutrients

Most absorption is through roots. However, small amounts of water are absorbed through needles and twigs of seedlings (Kramer and Kozlowski 1979). Water absorbed above ground may make the difference between survival and death during critically dry periods. Although there is no direct experimental evidence, it appears that small amounts of rainwater or dew deposited on needles and small branches are absorbed by loblolly pines of all sizes.

Absorption Through Roots

Water and nutrients are absorbed through roots in all stages of development—from newly formed, delicate root tips to large, old roots covered with rough bark. Water and solutes can be absorbed rapidly. For example, a small amount of ^{14}C applied to a culture medium moved into the roots of 55- and 155-day-old seedlings within 1 hour. Water, and ions in water, are absorbed much more readily and in much greater quantity by dead roots that are attached to the tree than by living roots because dead roots offer no active resistance to ion movement. In living roots, new root tips are the more permeable and efficient absorbers, while suberized roots are less permeable and less efficient (Woods and others 1962). The cortical tissue collapses during the process of suberization, reducing the ability of cells to absorb materials. However, the suberized portion of the root is still quite permeable to both water and solutes (Kramer and Bullock 1966). Although root pressure is often slow to develop in fully suberized apical roots, total exudation from suberized roots is about ½ times higher than from unsuberized root tips (O'Leary and Kramer 1964). Hydraulic conductance of suberized roots is estimated to be 7.55×10^{-7} cm/sec/bar, while that of unsuberized root tips is about 1.95×10^{-6} cm/sec/bar regardless of the amount of mycorrhizal infection (Sands and others 1982). [A bar is a unit of pressure equal to 100,000 newtons per square meter (N/m^2) or about 0.98697 standard atmosphere (atm).]

Even though the permeability rate of suberized roots is low, such roots accounted for 60 to 96% of total absorption in mature trees depending on the season of the year (Kramer and Bullock 1966). Absorption occurs through cracks or wounds in the bark, fissures between bark plates, lenticels, and crevices around branch roots of suberized portions of root systems. Uptake of water and radioactive P by seedlings with entirely suberized roots was 71 and 58%, respectively, of that absorbed by

seedlings having 40 to 50% unsuberized roots. Thus, absorption through suberized roots is important even in seedlings (Chung and Kramer 1975). Absorption by suberized roots should be relatively more important during periods of lower moisture availability (Kramer and Bullock 1966). However, if soil dries to the point that the roots separate from it, absorption through suberized roots will normally be extremely limited.

Even though the major function of roots is water and nutrient conduction, as much as 65% of the volume of slash pine roots is filled with air (Anonymous 1985a). For both slash and loblolly pines there may be sufficient transfer of oxygen from the stem to permit some normal root functioning under anaerobic conditions.

Absorption Through Root Hairs and Mycorrhizae

Root hairs absorb water and nutrient solutions very effectively during their few weeks of life. In large numbers, they can multiply the absorptive capacity of a root system many times.

Mycorrhizae multiply the absorbing surface area and absorbing capacity of individual roots several times. Short mycorrhizal roots usually function effectively for about 1 year, which is much longer than the effective absorbing life of the unsuberized region of a nonmycorrhizal root. Mycorrhizal roots appear to be just as effective as growing root tips in absorbing water and many times more effective than suberized roots. On average, 22% of the total root absorption occurs through mycorrhizae that make up less than 3% of the total absorbing surface area.

Ions absorbed by fungal hyphae, which extend several centimeters into the soil, are quickly transferred to the root on which the fungus is growing. Absorption by hyphae greatly increases the ability of a tree to obtain and utilize scarce nutrients. In one study, 2- to 10-month-old loblolly pine seedlings with mycorrhizal roots always had more foliar N and P than did seedlings without mycorrhizae (table 2-39). Mycorrhizae also absorb and accumulate ions more selectively than do roots without mycorrhizae (figure 2-38). In turn, the trees supply fungi with carbohydrates and other metabolites important to fungal growth. Mycorrhizae are most abundant on trees that grow in nutrient-deficient soils. On very harsh sites, this symbiosis can mean the difference between life and death for a tree. Sihanonth and Todd (1977) found significant differences between levels of several critical elements in mycorrhizal and in nonmycorrhizal roots of young seedlings growing under conditions of low nutrition (table 2-40). They also found that the concentrations of most elements were substantially higher in the mantle sheath and Hartig net than in the epidermis, cortex, or stele of mycorrhizal roots, indicating that a substantial nutrient pool is captured by the fungal biomass. In very fertile soils, mycorrhizae do not effectively aid tree growth because adequate nutrients are readily available through normal root absorption.

Translocation

Water and solutes in the xylem move upward in a clockwise spiral, primarily in the outermost growth rings. The translocation rate is controlled mostly by the rate of transpiration and can be extremely rapid. For example, ^{14}C moved from the roots to the needles of 55- and 155-day-old seedlings within 5 hours (Werner 1973). Werner (1971) injected the bases of 9.8- to 11.3-m planted loblolly pines with a dye in mid-October when oleoresin pressure was relatively low. The dye usually moved throughout the stem and branches within 2 days after injection. Although dye moved up the stem in a spiral, dye movement in branches was parallel to the branch axis.

Transpiration

Transpiration is the vaporization of water from living cells of plant tissues. On an annual basis, loblolly pines transpire more water than do hardwoods because loblolly pines retain foliage throughout the year and have greater foliar surface area (Swank and Douglass 1974). Yu and Cruise (1982) estimated that an average of 1.5% of the total soil moisture under a loblolly pine stand is lost each day through the combination of transpiration and evaporation.

Stomata are the chief regulators of water loss, and light largely determines the daily trend of stomatal resistance in loblolly pines if the level of soil moisture is not very low and if air temperature is above 10 °C. Stomatal opening can be initiated below 0.04 cal/cm^2/min, and minimal resistance occurs by 0.50 cal/cm^2/min (Strain and Higginbotham 1976). Stomatal resistance decreases sharply just after sunrise and remains relatively low during the morning and early afternoon (figure 2-39). Re-

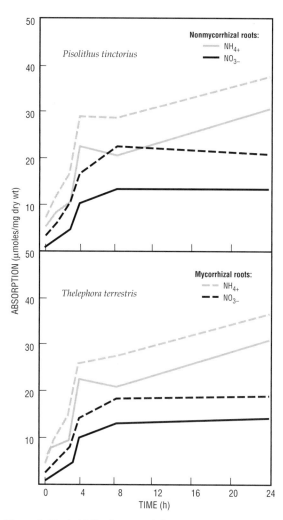

Figure 2-38—Loblolly pine roots infected with the mycorrhizal fungus *Pisolithus tinctorius* absorb greater amounts of nitrogen than do nonmycorrhizal roots. These absorption trends are only slightly lower when the mycorrhizal fungus is *Thelephora terrestris* (adapted from France and Reid 1979).

Table 2-39—Foliar nutrient concentration of nitrogen and phosphorus for loblolly pine seedlings

Seedling age (mon)	Nitrogen (%)		Phosphorus (%)		% Mycorrhizal roots
	Mycorrhizal	Nonmycorrhizal	Mycorrhizal	Nonmycorrhizal	Short roots*
2	1.1	0.8†	0.09	0.08	9
3	1.3	0.9	0.10	0.07	17
4	1.7	1.1	0.12	0.09	41
6	2.1	1.4	0.16	0.10	52
8	2.4	1.5	0.15	0.07	61
10	2.2	1.2	0.18	0.08	78

Source: adapted from Reid and others (1983).
* Visual estimation of the percentage of all short roots that are mycorrhizal.
† Each foliar concentration represents the average of 4 to 6 seedlings at each age.

Table 2-40—Distribution of magnesium (Mg), phosphorus (P), sulfur (S), potassium (K), and calcium (Ca) in mycorrhizal and nonmycorrhizal roots of loblolly pine

Location	Symbiont	Elemental conc. (μg/g tissue)				
		Mg	P	S	K	Ca
Epidermis	U	158	90	402	927	191
	P	277*	109	487	3,370*	234*
	C	352*	373*	881*	2,560*	223*
Cortex	U	421	733	902	1,640	250
	P	487	1,030	1,040	2,450*	316*
	C	447	1,130*	1,170*	2,260*	321*
Stele	U	294	741	867	1,370	211
	P	650*	1,090*	1,220*	3,670*	371
	C	647*	1,340*	1,270*	3,870*	380*
Fungal mantle	P	1,360	2,000	2,150	6,840	513
	C	1,330	1,400	1,310	5,000	725
Hartig net	P	693	1,220	1,540	4,810	465
	C	666	966	2,180	4,140	584

Source: adapted from Sihanonth and Todd (1977).
U = uninfected root, P = infected with *Pisolithus tinctorius*, C = infected with *Cenococcum graniforme*.
* Significantly greater than uninfected root at the 95% probability level.

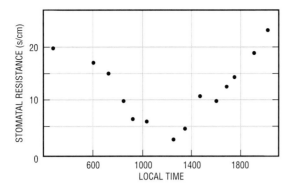

Figure 2-39—Diurnal pattern of stomatal resistance in new foliage in the lower canopy of a 16-year-old loblolly pine plantation. Each point represents an average of several days during the growing season (adapted from Gresham and others 1975).

sistance increases abruptly during late afternoon, and the stomata close shortly after sunset.

Moisture stress decreases needle moisture content and results in stomatal closure. In a controlled greenhouse study with 1-year-old loblolly pine seedlings from east Texas, moisture content of needles averaged 224% on a dry weight basis and 23% of the stomata were open 1 day after watering. Three days after watering, needle moisture content had dropped to 219% and 17% of the stomata were open. By 7 days after watering, needle moisture was 193% and only 5% of the stomata were open. The rate of transpiration was 11.0 mg/min/cm^2 on the first day, but only 1.8 on the seventh day (Bilan and others 1977).

Transpiration, especially in seedlings, can be reduced by moisture stress conditioning or by foliage reduction. One to 3 days after watering, seedlings mildly stressed for 8 weeks had 30% less transpiration on a needle dry weight basis than had unstressed seedlings (Seiler and Johnson 1985). Abscission of 1-year-old needle fascicles of loblolly pine seedlings has been induced by the application of ethephon, a chemical that releases ethylene gas into plant tissue (Griffing and Ursic 1977).

Photosynthesis

In loblolly pines, photosynthesis occurs throughout the year (Perry 1971b), but rates fluctuate depending on the physiological condition of the tree and environmental conditions. Physiological factors that strongly influence photosynthesis are age and structure of needles, number and response of stomata, chlorophyll content, internal water deficits, and carbohydrate utilization and accumulation. The environmental factors that most affect photosynthesis include light, temperature, carbon dioxide (CO_2) concentration in the air, water availability, soil fertility, and season of the year (Kramer and Kozlowski 1979). Net photosynthesis (P_n) and stomatal conductance are linearly related under a wide range of humidity and air temperature conditions, water deficits, irradiance, and CO_2 concentrations. Photosynthesis is limited mainly by the direct action of light, water deficit, and ambient CO_2 concentrations within the mesophyll cells and not by the rate of diffusion of CO_2 through stomata (Teskey and others 1986).

Over the long term, the best measurement of photosynthesis is the increase in dry matter in a tree or stand. It is impractical to measure short-term growth increases, so CO_2 uptake is used to estimate photosynthesis. The rate of photosynthesis in loblolly pine seedlings is sharply reduced when the atmospheric CO_2 concentration drops below 0.06%. No photosynthesis occurs when the CO_2 level is below 0.01% (figure 2-40).

Cotyledonary needles are the most efficient photosynthetic structures; secondary needles are the least efficient. Primary needles are more photosynthetically efficient and less self-shading than secondary needles. Thus, seedlings having only juvenile (primary) needles or a mixture of juvenile and first-formed, immature, secondary needles photosynthesize more rapidly than do seedlings with fully developed secondary needles. During the second year, photosynthetic rates of seedlings are less than half those of seedlings in the first year, but

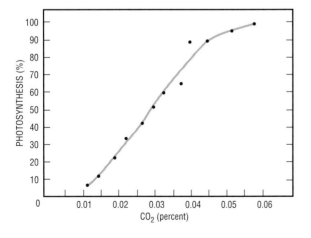

Figure 2-40—The rate of photosynthesis of loblolly pine as a function of carbon dioxide concentration in the atmosphere (adapted from Brix 1962).

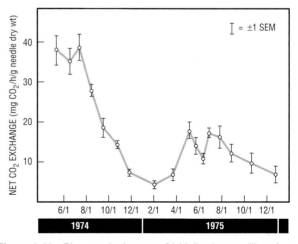

Figure 2-41—Photosynthetic rates of loblolly pine seedlings from 30 days after germination through two growing seasons (adapted from Drew and Ledig 1981).

high rates of photosynthesis coincide with periods of rapid growth during both years (Bormann 1956, 1958; Ledig and Perry 1967; figure 2-41).

Photosynthetic mesophyll tissue in juvenile needles is covered only by a thin layer of cutin and a layer of relatively thin-walled epidermal tissue with no hypodermis. In mature needles, the mesophyll is buried under a thick cuticle, thick-walled epidermal tissue, and one to several layers of thick-walled hypodermal tissue, making energy exchange more difficult. Thus, young loblolly pine seedlings, with mostly primary needles, reach maximum rates of photosynthesis at relatively low light intensities, as do hardwood seedlings, and can survive under a heavy overstory.

Photosynthate production, consumption, and surplus vary with age of needles on a branch. Chung and Barnes (1980b) found that, within a 1-year-old branch unit in the upper crown of a 15-year-old tree, 63% of the photosynthate production was supplied by the two growth flushes of the previous year. Growth of the current year's shoot consumed 66% of the total photosynthate consumed in the branch. Changes in the rates of photosynthate production, consumption, and surplus are depicted in figures 2-42, 2-43, and 2-44. The relative daily rates of photosynthate production of different growth cycles change during the growing season (figure 2-42). Previous years' needles dominate production early in the growing season, but production by the first cycle of current needles surpasses production by 1-year-old needles by mid-June. The net photosynthetic rate of stomatal surface area is higher in old needles than in new needles throughout the year, but the number of new needles exceeds the number of old needles by mid-June (Higginbotham 1974).

The first cycle of current growth consumes most photosynthate until about mid-July (figure 2-43). The second cycle of the current year utilizes little photosynthate until late June, when the needles become visible beyond the fascicle sheaths. Consumption by second-cycle needles does not exceed that by first-cycle needles until September. Photosynthate surplus, or the difference between production and consumption, is shown in figure 2-44. About 38% of the photosynthate is surplus (available for translocation from the branch), and most of this surplus is produced by needles of the previous year.

Shading and photosynthetic efficiency. Loblolly pine seedlings can survive through the first growing season in dense shade, but little or no growth will occur. The limited photosynthesis severely curtails root development, and the ratio of transpiring surface to absorbing surface (shoot-to-root ratio) decreases quickly. The shoot-to-root ratios of 23-week-old seedlings ranged from 1.0/1.11, for seedlings in full sunlight, to 1.0/0.86, for those in two-thirds full sunlight, to 1.0/0.69, for those in one-third full sunlight (Ledig and others

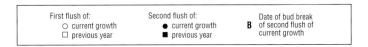

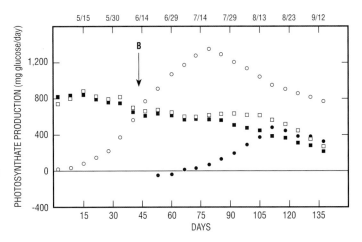

Figure 2-42—Changes in rates of photosynthate production of different growth cycles (adapted from Chung and Barnes 1980b).

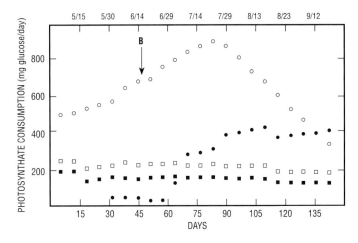

Figure 2-43—Changes in rates of photosynthate consumption of different growth cycles (adapted from Chung and Barnes 1980b).

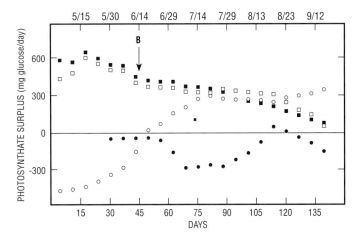

Figure 2-44—Changes in amounts of surplus photosynthate produced by different growth cycles (adapted from Chung and Barnes 1980b).

1970). Because they are relatively intolerant to shade, loblolly pines compete poorly with the many hardwoods that can survive even when light is limited severely (Teskey and Shrestha 1985).

Because of shading, photosynthetic efficiency varies greatly between needles on a branch. Needles are generally more shaded and less efficient the farther they are from the tip of the branch. Even the needles of a single fascicle shade each other. Needles that are spread out and fully exposed to light are nearly as efficient as leaves of northern red oak, and the needles and leaves of the two species become light saturated at approximately 26,900 lumens per square meter (lm/m^2). However, entire loblolly pine seedlings require 100,100 lm/m^2 of light to reach the level of photosynthesis that oak seedlings reach at 26,900 lm/m^2 (Kramer and Clark 1947).

Older trees may have sun-adapted needles in the upper canopy and shade-adapted needles in the lower canopy. The metabolic rate of large sun needles is higher than that of shade needles. This arrangement results in the availability of more carbohydrates for translocation and tree growth. Maximum rates of net photosynthesis during the summer for 15-year-old loblolly pines ranged from 6 $mg/dm^2/h$ of CO_2 for sun needles to 3.5 $mg/dm^2/h$ of CO_2 for shade needles. During the winter, maximum photosynthesis is approximately 3 $mg/dm^2/h$ at all canopy levels. Branches bearing only sun needles are not photosynthetically light saturated even at radiation levels exceeding

full sunlight. In contrast, branches containing only shade needles are light saturated at about half of full sunlight (Higginbotham and Strain 1973). The effect of canopy position on CO_2 uptake is just as dramatic. The upper one-third of the canopy contains 29% of the total leaf surface of a tree but is responsible for about 38% of the total CO_2 uptake. The middle one-third of the canopy contains 44% of the leaf surface area and absorbs about 44% of the CO_2. The lowest third of the canopy contains 27% of the leaf surface area and absorbs about 18% of the CO_2.

By the time secondary needles are 2 months old, their daily net photosynthesis should exceed their daily demand for photosynthate. Only needles that can carry out CO_2 exchange above the compensation point, on a long-term basis, can survive. Thus, the lower limit of the live crown of a tree occurs where the intensity of radiation is insufficient to permit needles to carry out compensatory photosynthesis. The peak capacity for CO_2 uptake by needles occurs during the second spring and summer of needle life. The efficiency of second-year needles declines rapidly during the late summer and fall, just before the needles are shed (Higginbotham 1974).

Effects of water stress and temperature on photosynthesis. When the water stress of loblolly pine seedlings (expressed as diffusion pressure deficit, or DPD, of needles) exceeds 12 atm, photosynthesis ceases (figure 2-45). However, seedlings are extremely hardy

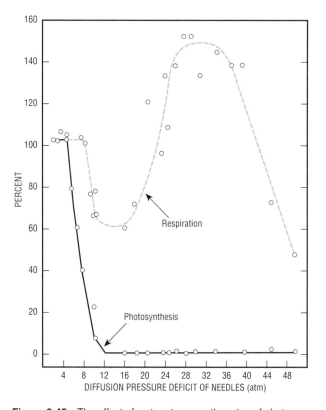

Figure 2-45—The effect of water stress on the rates of photosynthesis and respiration in loblolly pine seedlings. Rates of photosynthesis and respiration are given as a percentage of the rates with the soil moisture at field capacity (adapted from Brix 1962).

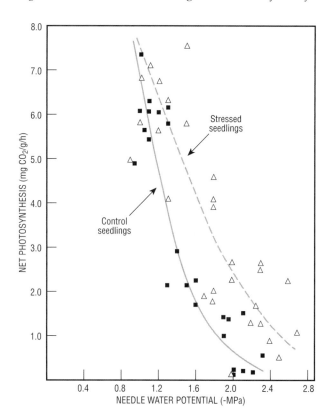

Figure 2-46—Moisture stress conditioning increases net photosynthesis of loblolly pine seedlings (adapted from Seiler and Johnson 1985).

and can survive severe water stress for longer than 1 month. Subjecting seedlings to water stress can increase the seedlings' ability to photosynthesize under stress at a later time. For example, 1-year-old seedlings that had been exposed to mild water stress for 8 weeks subsequently could photosynthesize at much lower needle water potentials than could trees that had not been so conditioned (figure 2-46).

Seasonal temperature can also greatly influence the temperature at which maximum P_n occurs in loblolly pines. If temperatures are relatively low (day, 17 °C and night, 11 °C), maximum P_n in seedlings will occur at about 10 °C. If temperatures are high (day 32 °C, night 26 °C), maximum P_n will occur at about 25 °C (Strain and others 1976). Thus, metabolic relationships generated under one set of environmental conditions cannot be used to predict behavior under different conditions.

Seasonal trends in photosynthesis. Loblolly pines exhibit distinct seasonal trends in photosynthesis. Net photosynthesis per seedling peaks once in late October. In contrast, P_n per unit of leaf area peaks twice, once in midsummer and once in late October. Patterns of P_n in trees from different parts of loblolly pine's range show the same trends, but vary considerably, both in P_n

per seedling and P_n per unit leaf area (figures 2-47 and 2-48). When loblolly pine seedlings were grown under laboratory conditions of 25 °C and 43,040 lm/m² of light, P_n per seedling was first detectable in February, reached a peak in September, and then declined rapidly but still exceeded 20 mg of CO_2 per hour in January (McGregor and Kramer 1963). The spring increase began before new needles emerged, and the fall decrease occurred before appreciable loss of foliage. A significant excess of photosynthesis over respiration does not occur until April, and it is small even during that month. After April, P_n increases rapidly and reaches high levels from July until mid-November. Because the growing season is long in most of loblolly pine's range, much of the current photosynthesis is used for height growth. It is unclear whether seasonal changes in the level of photosynthesis are related to initiation and cessation of growth, but Perry and Baldwin (1966) suggest that winter cold breaks down chloroplasts and disrupts the photosynthetic process and that the general color of needles is not a reliable index of the degree of disruption.

Effects of mycorrhizal fungi on photosynthesis. Net photosynthesis is directly related to the degree of mycorrhizal development in loblolly pine seedlings

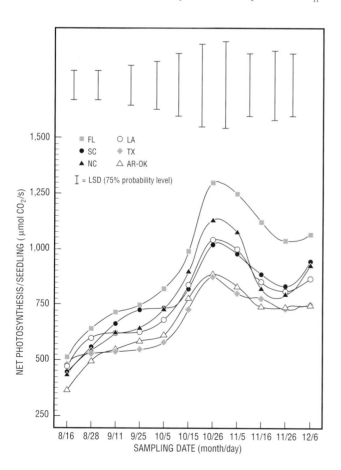

Figure 2-47—Seasonal trends in net photosynthesis per seedling for six provenances of loblolly pine (adapted from Boltz and others 1986).

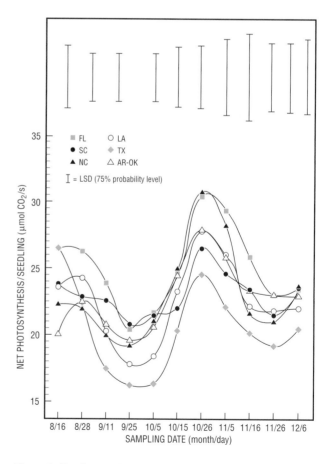

Figure 2-48—Seasonal trends in net photosynthesis per unit of leaf area for seedlings from six provenances of loblolly pine (adapted from Boltz and others 1986).

(Reid and others 1983). In one study, P_n of 4-month-old seedlings inoculated with a mycorrhizal fungus was twice that of nonmycorrhizal seedlings, and the difference continued to increase through seedling age 10 months (figure 2-49). In addition, the average dry weights of mycorrhizal seedlings were about 63 and 58% greater than the average dry weights of nonmycorrhizal seedlings at ages 4 months and 10 months.

Carbon Cycling and Respiration

Carbon dioxide uptake in loblolly pines is high in the morning, rises to a maximum by early afternoon, and declines as the afternoon progresses. In a South Carolina plantation of rapidly growing 12-year-old loblolly pines, maximum uptake rates of CO_2 during the day exceeded 2.0 mg per square meter of needle surface per second (mg/m²/sec). At night, up to 0.16 mg/m²/s was released. Net annual CO_2 uptake is 10.5 t/ha, biomass accumulation is 4.5 t/ha, and the efficiency of conversion of CO_2 to biomass is 43% (Murphy 1985).

The carbon content of needles, twigs, branches, and bark of 12- to 16-year-old planted loblolly pines in the Piedmont of North Carolina averaged 49% (range, 45 to 54%) and was similar for all plant parts (Kinerson and others 1977). The total standing tree crop at age 16 was 7,062 g of carbon/m², and net primary production was 2,056 g/m²/yr. Heterotrophic respiration from litter decomposition was 694 g/m²/yr, resulting in a net ecosystem production of 1,362 g/m²/yr. Autotrophic respiration from CO_2 evolution of intact tissue was 2,068 g of carbon/m²/yr.

Respiration is the oxidation of food in living cells and results in the release of energy. Respiration consumes most food produced by a tree and supplies energy to all living tissues, especially meristems and needles. The ratio of photosynthetic tissue to respiring tissue decreases as trees get larger. After about tree age 10, the lower amount of energy available for growth results in a gradual reduc-

tion in growth rate for the remainder of the tree's life. Kinerson (1975) estimated that 58% of the photosynthate produced by a stand of pole-sized loblolly pines was used in respiration. Needles constitute only about 4% of stand dry weight but account for about 32% of total respiration—as little as 24 to 28% in vigorous trees or as much as 38% in suppressed trees of low vigor. Twigs and branches use about 8% of the available photosynthates. Roots make up about 19% of the dry matter, use about 9% of the carbohydrates produced, and account for 3% of the respiration. The remaining 65% of the respiration occurs in stems and branches. In older trees, about 1% of available photosynthate is required for seed production (Clason 1982, Kinerson and others 1977).

Seasonal variations in respiration rates of aboveground tissues are substantial and increases are directly related to temperature increases. The rate of respiration of stems of 14-year-old loblolly pines increased fourfold when air temperature was increased from 10 to 20 °C (figure 2-50). Respiration increases are especially large following initiation of cambial activity in the spring

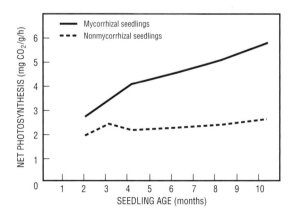

Figure 2-49—Net photosynthesis (P_n) of mycorrhizal and nonmycorrhizal loblolly pine seedlings at monthly intervals from ages 2 to 10 months. Net photosynthesis of mycorrhizal seedlings is significantly greater at the 95% probability level than P_n of nonmycorrhizal seedlings at all ages except 3 months (adapted from Reid and others 1983).

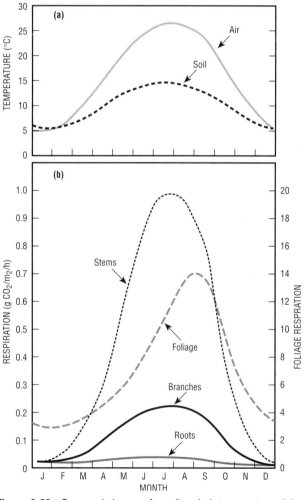

Figure 2-50—Seasonal changes for soil and air temperatures (**a**) and respiration of stems, foliage, branches, and roots of loblolly pines (**b**) in a 14-year-old plantation. Branch and root respiration rates were determined by studying excised tissue. Note that the scale for foliage is 20 times that for the other organs (adapted from Kinerson 1975).

(Drew and Ledig 1981; figure 2-51). Rates of respiration are high in summer, when trees are in periods of rapid photosynthesis and rapid growth. Patterns of dark respiration in shoots are similar to patterns of photosynthesis, but periods of peak dark respiration and photosynthesis differ somewhat.

The rate of respiration is also influenced by water stress. Low water stress (2 to 8 atm) has no adverse effects on respiration, but intermediate water stress (10 to 14 atm) reduces respiration by 30 to 40%. If needles are severely dehydrated, respiration increases temporarily and then decreases rapidly (figure 2-45).

Respiration in loblolly pine roots is strongly influenced by age, size, and mycorrhizal condition of roots. Unsuberized root tips respire more rapidly than suberized roots. Roots with vigorous, active mycorrhizae respire more than twice as fast as nonmycorrhizal roots or mycorrhizal roots of low vigor (Barnard and Jorgensen 1977). The loss of C during both root and shoot respiration is significantly greater in mycorrhizal than in nonmycorrhizal seedlings (figure 2-52). The rate of root

respiration is substantially altered by soil temperature changes, and rates of respiration change most in fine roots with active mycorrhizae (figure 2-53). Boyer and others (1971) found that oxygen (O_2) utilization in excised root segments increased by 69% when the temperature of air-saturated water was raised from 17 to 28 °C in the late winter and increased by 31% with a similar temperature increase in the spring.

Excess soil water alters root respiration and limits growth of loblolly pines on many lowland sites in the Atlantic and Gulf Coastal Plain. DeBell and others (1984) found that loblolly pine seedlings, growing under continuously flooded conditions for 2 years, had root weights only 15% as great as those of trees grown under seasonally flooded conditions. Root tips of seedlings grown under flooded conditions contained 2 to 3 times as much CO_2 and malate, which are products of anaerobic metabolism, as seasonally flooded seedlings contained.

Photorespiration is a transitory acceleration of CO_2 production that accompanies photosynthesis. Photorespiration by loblolly pine seedlings can double when the temperature increases from 15 to 25 °C and triple when the temperature increases from 15 to 35 °C. Photorespiration is also higher in well-watered seedlings than in those that are mildly or severely water stressed and is higher in seedlings from slow-growing seed sources than in those from fast-growing sources (Samuelson and Teskey 1987).

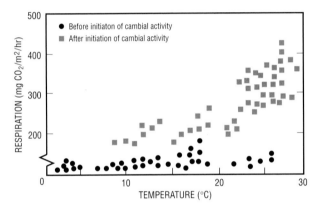

Figure 2-51—Respiration of loblolly pine stems at various temperatures before and after the initiation of cambial activity (adapted from Kinerson 1975).

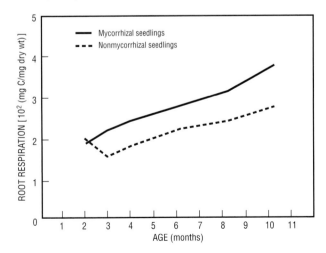

Figure 2-52—Total root respiration ($^{12}CO_2$ + $^{14}CO_2$) of mycorrhizal and nonmycorrhizal loblolly pine seedlings. Differences are statistically significant at the 95% probability level at all ages except 2 months (adapted from Reid and others 1983).

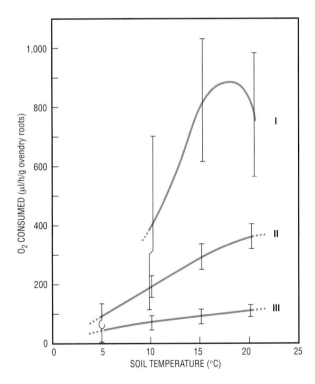

Figure 2-53—The relationship between respiration and soil temperature for three groups of loblolly pine roots: (I) fine roots with active mycorrhizae, (II) fine roots that are nonmycorrhizal or with moribund mycorrhizae, and (III) roots greater than 1 mm but less than 5 mm in diameter. Vertical lines represent 95% probability levels about the regressions (adapted from Barnard and Jorgensen 1977).

Summary

Loblolly pine grows to about 30 m in height and 70 cm in diameter at maturity (80 to 100 years) on average sites. Roots make up about 20% of the total biomass of the tree. Loblolly pine commonly produces 2 to 4 growth cycles (flushes) per year from age 3 to age 30. New growth is greatest at the top of rapidly growing trees and declines with increasing distance from the terminal. Needles are 13 to 22 cm long and usually three to a fascicle. Needles are retained for 2 years. Within a single year's foliage, needle age can vary by up to 6 months. The ratio of foliage weight to stem weight decreases from 1/1 at tree age 7 weeks to 1/10 at tree age 5 years to 1/70 at tree age 55 years.

Flowering commonly begins between tree ages 5 and 10. Most female "flowers" are borne on secondary branches in the upper and middle parts of the crown. Most male "flowers" are borne on tertiary branches in the lower part of the crown. Mature cones average 9.0 cm in length and 4.0 cm in diameter. They are sessile and have stout, sharp, persistent spines. Individual seeds are about 0.6 cm in length and weigh 17 to 37 mg.

Xylem of loblolly pines closely resembles that of other southern pines. Position in the stem has a greater effect on physical properties of the xylem than has tree age. Mean specific gravity of xylem is 0.47 to 0.51 on a dry weight basis. There is no relationship between specific gravity and tree growth rate. Fibers of juvenile wood are shorter than those of mature wood. The change from juvenile wood (thin cell walls, short cells, and low density) to mature wood (thick cell walls, long cells, and high density) takes place gradually over a period of several years. Length of the juvenile period increases from 6 to 8 years in the Gulf Coastal Plain to 14 years in the Piedmont. Growth rings are distinct. A pronounced band of light earlywood and dark latewood is produced each year.

Heartwood may begin to form any time between tree ages 15 and 25, but there is usually no distinct boundary between heartwood and sapwood. Boles of trees up to 50 years old contain about 6% compression wood (abnormal wood) when straight, 9% when somewhat curved, and as much as 16% when obviously crooked or leaning. Rootwood is similar to stemwood in important physical characteristics such as tracheid length, cell diameter, lumen diameter, and cell wall thickness.

Phloem (bark) characteristics are affected by age and condition of the tree, position on the stem, and environment. Bark thickness increases linearly with tree diameter and gradually decreases up the bole of a tree. The physical properties of phloem, like those of xylem, are affected more by position in the stem than by tree age. The chemical composition of inner bark, which contains at least 46 amino acids, is very complex and varies seasonally with height in the tree and with soil type.

Nitrogen is the most abundant element in loblolly pines, followed in order by K, Ca, Mg, and P. Concentrations of nutrients are lowest in stemwood and highest in needles. Concentrations of nutrients in root xylem decrease as root size increases. First-year needles are 51.0% celluloses and lignin, 21.0% phenolics, 9.0% nitrogenous compounds, 6.0% lipids, 8.0% volatile oils, and 1.5% minerals, with small amounts of organic acids and sugars. The chemical compositions of new shoots and of new needles are very similar, but levels of carbohydrates are about 15% higher, and levels of phenolic and nitrogenous compounds are 6% and 5% lower in new shoots. Stem xylem contains numerous resin acids and monoterpenes. Both the physical and chemical properties of loblolly pine oleoresin differ significantly from those of other southern pines.

The aboveground portion of a mature tree is 50% water, 42% dry xylem, 6% dry phloem, and 2% dry needles. Moisture content varies with tree age and height in the tree. Moisture content of juvenile wood differs from that of mature wood.

In trees less than 30 years old, height growth takes place over a period of 180 to 210 days/year and is a combination of fixed (elongation of winter buds) and free (elongation of new stem units) growth. The rate of new growth is greatest at the top of seedlings and saplings.

Crown density is a good indicator of tree vigor. Growth is greatest when 50% or more of the tree is in live crown. Total needle surface area of a tree can be predicted accurately from tree diameter. Needles fall every month of the year, but 45 to 70% of the total needlefall takes place from September to December.

Loblolly pines have sturdy taproots and extensive lateral roots. However, the form and extent of the taproot and lateral roots are strongly influenced by tree age, soil physical characteristics, water table level, and microenvironment. The shoot-to-root ratio is usually about 4:1 to 5:1, except in very young trees, where it approaches 1:1. Over 95% of the root biomass is in the surface 60 cm of soil, whether the soil is dry or wet. The availability of nutrients in the soil is the primary factor affecting both the growth rate and distribution of roots. Taproots normally grow to a depth of 1 to 2 m but can grow much deeper in dry soils. Numerous sinker roots, growing down from major lateral roots, provide additional support and water and nutrient absorption at lower soil levels away from the base of a tree. Trees have 15 to 60 first-order lateral roots that extend many meters beyond the taproot. Some of them are as long as the tree is tall. Most of the surface area of lateral roots is in roots less than 1 cm in diameter, but most of the biomass is in roots over 5 cm in diameter. The taproot usually makes up over 50% of the root biomass. Root tips account for only about 1% of the total root length of trees beyond the sapling stage.

Roots grow throughout the year, but most growth

takes place in the spring. Length of primary lateral roots increases about 10 to 30 mm/wk when conditions are favorable. Roots die throughout the year and during all stages of tree growth. As much as 50% of the annual root production dies and decomposes annually.

Both intraspecific grafting (between roots of two or more loblolly trees) and self-grafting (between roots of the same tree) are common. The closer together trees are located, the more often their roots make contact and graft. As stands age, grafts become more common because roots and root systems of older trees are larger than those of younger trees. In typical stands of pole-sized loblolly pines, 5 to 25% of all trees are root grafted to one or more neighboring trees. Occasionally, five or more trees form an interconnected root system. If grafted to an interconected root system, the stump and part of the root system of a cut tree can live and grow for 30 years or longer. Water, nutrients, and/or photosynthate are translocated between a living tree and a stump only during times of high moisture stress. There is probably more translocation from the living tree to the stump root system than from the stump root system to the living tree.

Production of flowers, cones, and seeds by individual trees increases with increasing tree age, increasing tree size, and freedom from competition. Substantial production begins at about tree age 10 to 15 in open stands and somewhat later in closed stands. In forest stands of widely spaced trees, loblolly pines may produce enough seeds to regenerate areas by age 25. However, 40-year-old trees generally produce 3 to 5 times as many seeds as do 25-year-old trees.

Loblolly pine trees require 2 years from the initiation of female flower primordia to produce viable seeds in ripe cones. An average cone has the potential to produce 155 seeds, but only 20 to 25% of that number normally develop. When cones ripen on a tree, seeds usually fall within 30 m of the crown. Where there is substantial wind, seeds fall within 90 m of the crown. Seeds are relatively dormant and do not germinate unless exposed to 30 to 60 days of moist prechilling at about 3 °C. Although large seeds germinate more quickly and produce larger seedlings than do small seeds, seed size has no effect on ultimate tree size.

Physiological activities, such as absorption, translocation, transpiration, photosynthesis, and respiration, continue throughout the year but proceed at slower rates during winter. Most absorption is through roots. Root tips, mycorrhizal roots, and root hairs are very highly permeable. However, their surface area is small, and they account for only about 25% of absorption in mature trees. Suberized roots account for the remaining 75% of absorption by roots.

Translocation is controlled mostly by the rate of transpiration. Transpiration occurs throughout the year. An average of 1.5% of the total soil moisture under a loblolly pine stand is lost through transpiration and evaporation each day.

Photosynthesis takes place throughout the year, but rates vary with the physical condition of the tree and environmental conditions. Environmental factors that most affect photosynthesis include light, temperature, CO_2 concentration in the air, water availability, soil fertility, and season of the year. The best long-term measurement of photosynthesis is the increase in tree or stand dry matter. Uptake of CO_2 can be used to estimate photosynthesis.

Carbon dioxide exchange in rapidly growing loblolly pines is high in the morning, rises to a maximum by early afternoon, and then declines. This daily pattern can yield a net annual CO_2 uptake of 10.5 t/ha, a biomass of 4.5 t/ha/yr, and a 43% conversion efficiency of CO_2 to biomass.

Respiration, crown and root growth, seed production, and maintenance of vascular tissues have physiological priority over cellulose (wood) production. The ratio of photosynthetic tissue to respiring tissue decreases as a tree gets larger. After about tree age 10, the amount of energy available for growth declines, and the tree's growth slows. Twenty-four to thirty-eight percent of the carbohydrates produced by a pole-sized tree go to needle growth, 8% to twigs and branches, 9% to root development, and the remainder to cellulose production. In pure even-aged plantations, the dry weight's of foliage, current branches, and stembark become relatively constant between tree ages 20 and 30. Subsequent weight increases result chiefly from growth of older branches and stemwood. This relative constancy in foliage, current branches, and stembark may occur somewhat after age 30 in natural stands if stand density is low. In large trees, all but the outer 2 to 5 cm of the bole is composed of dead cells that provide structural support but have little direct involvement in the growth process.

Literature Cited

Adams MB, Allen HL. 1985. Nutrient proportions in foliage of semi-mature loblolly pine. Plant and Soil 86(1):27–34.

Adams MB, Allen HL, Davey CB. 1986. Accumulation of starch in roots and foliage of loblolly pine: effects of season, site and fertilization. Tree Physiology 2(1/3):35–46.

AFA [American Forestry Association]. 1990. National register of big trees. American Forests 96(1/2):30.

Allen RM, McGregor WHD. 1962. Seedling growth of three southern pine species under long and short days. Silvae Genetica 11(2):43–45.

Anonymous. 1985a. Pine root ventilation. In: Cooperative research in forest fertilization (CRIFF), 1985 annual report. Gainesville, FL: University of Florida, School of Forest Resources and Conservation: 17–21.

Anonymous. 1985b. SPB kills national champion tree. Louisiana Forestry Association News 28(3): [not paged].

Ashe WW. 1915. Loblolly or North Carolina pine. Bull. 24. Raleigh, NC: Edwards & Broughton Printing Company. 176 p.

Asher WC. 1964. A formula for estimating slash pine and yields. Journal of Forestry 62(1):37–39.

Barnard EL, Jorgensen JR. 1977. Respiration of field-grown loblolly pine roots as influenced by temperature and root type. Canadian Journal of Botany 55(6):740–743.

Barnett JP. 1972a. Seedcoat influences dormancy of loblolly pine seeds. Canadian Journal of Forest Research 2(1):7–10.

Barnett JP. 1976. Delayed germination of southern pine seeds related to seed coat constraint. Canadian Journal of Forest Research 6(4):504–510.

Barnett JP. 1979. Maturation of tree seeds. In: Proceedings, Symposium on Flowering and Seed Development in Trees; 1978 May 15–18; Mississippi State, MS. Washington, DC: USDA Forest Service: 206–217.

Barney CW. 1951. Effects of soil temperature and light intensity on root growth of loblolly pine seedlings. Plant Physiology 26:146–163.

Bassett JR. 1966. Seasonal diameter growth of loblolly pines. Journal of Forestry 64(10):674–676.

Beckwith JR III, Shackelford LS. 1976. Relationship between crown growth and annual xylem sheath development in loblolly pine saplings. Forest Science 22(3):247–260.

Belanger RP, Anderson RL. 1989. A guide for visually assessing crown densities of loblolly and shortleaf pines. Res. Note SE-352. Asheville, NC: USDA Forest Service, Southeastern Forest Experiment Station. 2 p.

Bendtsen BA, Ethington RL. 1972. Properties of major southern pines: 2. Structural properties and specific gravity. Res. Pap. FPL-177. Madison, WI: USDA Forest Service, Forest Products Laboratory. 10 p.

Bendtsen BA, Senft J. 1986. Mechanical and anatomical properties in individual growth rings of plantation-grown eastern cottonwood and loblolly pine. Wood and Fiber Science 18(1):23–38.

Bilan MV. 1960. Stimulation of cone and seed production in pole-size loblolly pine. Forest Science 6(3):207–220.

Bilan MV. 1965. Initial root growth in loblolly pine. Ecology Society of America Bulletin 46(3):94.

Bilan MV. 1967. Effect of low temperature on root elongation in loblolly pine seedlings. In: Proceedings, 14th Congress of IUFRO: part 4, section 23; 1967; Munich. [Place of publication and publisher unknown]: 74–82.

Bilan MV, Hogan CT, Carter HB. 1977. Stomatal opening, transpiration, and needle moisture in loblolly pine seedlings from two Texas seed sources. Forest Science 23(4):457–462.

Bilan MV, Jan SW. 1968. Needle moisture content as indicator of cessation of root elongation in loblolly pine seedlings. Ecology Society of America Bulletin 49(3):109.

Bilan MV, Leach JHJr, Davies G. 1978. Root development in loblolly pine (Pinus taeda L.) from two Texas seed sources. In: Proceedings, Symposium on Root Form of Planted Trees; 1978 May 16–19; Victoria, BC. Victoria, BC: British Columbia Ministry of Forestry; Environment Canada, Forestry Service, 8:17–22.

Blair RB, Zobel BJ, Franklin EC, and others. 1974. The effect of tree form and rust infection on wood and pulp properties of loblolly pine. TAPPI Journal 57(7):46–50.

Blanche CA, Hodges JD, Nebeker TE. 1985. A leaf area to sapwood area ratio developed to rate loblolly pine tree vigor. Canadian Journal of Forestry 15(6):1181–1184.

Blanche CA, Nebeker TE, Schmitt JJ, Hodges JD. 1984. Techniques for distinguishing the sapwood–heartwood boundary in living loblolly pine. Forest Science 30(3):756–760.

Boltz BA, Bongarten BC, Teskey RO. 1986. Seasonal patterns of net photosynthesis of loblolly pine from diverse origins. Canadian Journal of Forest Research 16(5):1063–1068.

Bormann FH. 1956. Ecological implications of changes in the photosynthetic response of Pinus taeda seedlings during ontogeny. Ecology 37(1):70–75.

Bormann FH. 1958. The relationships of ontogenetic development and environmental modification to photosynthesis in Pinus taeda seedlings. In: Thimann KV, ed. The physiology of forest trees. New York: Ronald Press: 197–215.

Bormann FH. 1963. Ontogenetic relationships of the primary leaf of Pinus taeda L. and P. echinata Mill. Bulletin of the Torrey Botanical Club 90(5):320–332.

Box BH. 1968. A study of root extension and biomass in a six-year-old pine plantation in southeastern Louisiana. Dissertation Abstracts International 28B(9):3545–3546.

Boyer JN, South DB. 1989. Seasonal changes in intensity of bud dormancy in loblolly pine seedlings. Tree Physiology 5(3):379–385.

Boyer WD. 1970. Shoot growth patterns of young loblolly pine. Forest Science 16(4):472–482.

Boyer WD. 1978. Heat accumulation: an easy way to anticipate the flowering of southern pines. Journal of Forestry 76(1):20–23.

Boyer WD, Romancier RM, Ralston CW. 1971. Root respiration rates of four tree species grown in the field. Forest Science 17(4):492–493.

Bramlett DL, Belcher EW Jr, DeBarr GL, and others. 1977. Cone analysis of southern pines: a guidebook. Gen. Tech. Rep. SE-13. Asheville, NC: USDA Forest Service, Southeastern Forest Experiment Station. 28 p.

Bramlett DL. 1974. Seed potential and seed efficiency. In: Kraus J, ed. Seed yield from southern pine seed orchards. Proceedings of a colloquium; 1974 April 2–3; Macon, GA. Macon, GA: Georgia Forest Research Council: 1–7.

Bramlett DL. 1986. Potential and actual seed yields from a southern pine seed orchard. In: Shearer RC, comp. Proceedings, Conifer Tree Seed in the Inland Mountain West Symposium; 1985 August 5–6; Missoula, MT. Gen. Tech. Rep. INT-203. Ogden, UT: USDA Forest Service, Intermountain Research Station: 162–165.

Brewer CW, Linnartz NE. 1978. Soil moisture utilization by mature loblolly pine stands in the Coastal Plain of southeastern Louisiana. In: Balmer WE, ed. Proceedings, Soil Moisture…Site Productivity Symposium; 1977 November 1–3; Myrtle Beach, SC. Atlanta: USDA Forest Service, Southeastern Area, State and Private Forestry: 296–306.

Bridgwater FE, Bramlett DL. 1982. Supplemental mass pollination to increase seed yields in loblolly pine seed orchards. Southern Journal of Applied Forestry 6(2):100–103.

Brix H. 1962. The effect of water stress on the rates of photosynthesis and respiration in tomato plants and loblolly pine seedlings. Physiologia Plantarum 15(1):10–20.

Brown CL. 1964. The seedling habit of longleaf pine. GA For. Res. Rep. 10. Athens, GA: Georgia Forest Research Council; University of Georgia, School of Forestry. 68 p.

Burton JD, Smith DM. 1972. Guying to prevent wind sway influences loblolly pine growth and wood properties. Res. Pap. SO-80. New Orleans: USDA Forest Service, Southern Forest Experiment Station. 8 p.

Burton JD. 1962. Bark thickness in Tennessee loblolly plantations. In: SO For. Notes 142. New Orleans: USDA Forest Service, Southern Forest Experiment Station: [not paged].

Cain SA. 1940. The identification of species in fossil pollen of Pinus by size-frequency determinations. American Journal of Botany 27:301–347.

Campbell TE. 1967. Loblolly–shortleaf pine seedfall in Louisiana. Journal of Forestry 65(12):89–895.

Campbell TE. 1982. Imbibition, desiccation, and reimbibition effects on light requirements for germinating southern pine seeds. Forest Science 28(3):539–543.

Carlson WC, Harrington CA. 1987. Cross-sectional area relationships in root systems of loblolly and shortleaf pine. Canadian Journal of Forest Research 17(6):556–558.

Carlson WC, Harrington CA, Farnum P, Hallgren SW. 1988. Effects of root severing treatments on loblolly pine. Canadian Journal of Forest Research 18(11):1376–1385.

Carpita NC, Skaria A, Barnett JP, Dunlap JR. 1983. Cold stratification and growth of radicles of loblolly pine embryos. Physiologia Plantarum 59:601–606.

Choong ET, Chang BY, Kowalczuk J. 1974. Mineral composition in loblolly pine wood after fertilization. Wood Util. Notes 26. Baton Rouge, LA: Louisiana State University and A&M College, Agricultural Experiment Station. 5 p.

Christopher JF, Wahlgren HE. 1964. Estimating specific gravity of south Arkansas pine. Res. Pap. SO-14. New Orleans: USDA Forest Service, Southern Forest Experiment Station. 10 p.

Chung HH, Barnes RL. 1977. Photosynthate allocation in *Pinus taeda*: 1. Substrate requirements for synthesis of shoot biomass. Canadian Journal of Forest Research 7(1):106–111.

Chung HH, Barnes RL. 1980a. Photosynthate allocation in *Pinus taeda*: 2. Seasonal aspects of photosynthate allocation to different biochemical fractions in shoots. Canadian Journal of Forest Research 10(3):338–347.

Chung HH, Barnes RL. 1980b. Photosynthate allocation in *Pinus taeda*: 3. Photosynthate economy: its production, consumption and balance in shoots during the growing season. Canadian Journal of Forest Research 10(3):348–356.

Chung HH, Kramer PJ. 1975. Absorption of water and ^{32}P through suberized and unsuberized roots of loblolly pine. Canadian Journal of Forest Research 5(2):229–235.

Clark A III, Saucier JR. 1989. Influence of initial planting density, geographic location, and species on juvenile wood formation in southern pine. Forest Products Journal 39(78):42–48.

Clark A III, Saucier JR. 1991. Influence of initial planting density, geographic location, and species on juvenile wood formation in southern pine. GA For. Res. Pap. 85. Macon, GA: Georgia Forestry Commission, Georgia Forest Research Council. 13 p.

Clark A III, Schmidtling RC. 1989. Effect of intensive culture on juvenile wood formation and wood properties of loblolly, slash, and longleaf pine. In: Miller JP, comp. Proceedings, 5th Biennial Southern Silvicultural Research Conference; 1988 November 1–3; Memphis, TN. Gen. Tech. Rep. SO-74. New Orleans: USDA Forest Service, Southern Forest Experiment Station: 211–217.

Clason TR. 1982. Thinning influences on individual tree growth and development in a loblolly pine plantation. In: Stephenson EH, ed. Proceedings, Workshop on Thinning Southern Pine Plantations; 1982 May 24–26; Long Beach, MS. Long Beach, MS: Forestry and Harvesting Training Center: 56–67.

Cole DE, Zobel BJ, Roberds JH. 1966. Slash, loblolly, and longleaf pine in a mixed natural stand; a comparison of their wood properties, pulp yields, and paper properties. TAPPI Journal 49(4):161–166.

Cotton MH, Hicks RR Jr, Flake RH. 1975. Morphological variability among loblolly and shortleaf pines in east Texas with reference to natural hybridization. Castanea 40(4):309–319.

Dalla-Tea F, Jokela EJ. 1991. Needlefall, canopy light interception, and productivity of young intensively managed slash and loblolly pine stands. Forest Science 37(5):1298–1313.

DeBell DS, Hook DD, McKee WH Jr, Askew JL. 1984. Growth and physiology of loblolly pine roots under various water table level and phosphorus treatments. Forest Science 30(3): 705–714.

DeVall WB. 1945. A bark character for the identification of certain Florida pines. 1944 Proceedings of the Florida Academy of Science 7(2/3):101–103.

Dewers RS, Moehring DM. 1970. Effect of soil water stress on initiation of ovulate primordia in loblolly pine. Forest Science 16(2):219–221.

Dierauf TS, Wasser RG. 1975. Predicting number of sound seeds per cone from a cone cutting study in a 12 year old loblolly orchard. Occas. Rep. 46. Charlottesville, VA: Virginia Division of Forestry, Department of Conservation and Economic Development. 5 p.

Dixon RK, Marx DH. 1987. Mycorrhizae. In: Durzan DJ, Bonga JM, eds. Tissue culture methods in forestry. Vol. 2. Dordrecht, The Netherlands: Martinus Nijhoff: 336–350.

Dorman KW. 1976. The genetics and breeding of southern pines. Agric. Handbk. 471. Washington, DC: USDA Forest Service. 407 p.

Dorman KW, Zobel BJ. 1973. Genetics of loblolly pine. Res. Pap. WO-19. Washington, DC: USDA Forest Service. 21 p.

Drew AP, Ledig FT. 1981. Seasonal patterns of CO_2 exchange in the shoot and root of loblolly pine seedlings. Botanical Gazette 142(2):200–205.

Dunlap JR, Barnett JP. 1983. Influence of seed size on germination and early development of loblolly pine germinants. Canadian Journal of Forest Research 13(1):40–44.

Echols RM. 1959. Evaluating trees and stands from large increment cores. In: Proceedings, Annual Meeting of the Society of American Foresters; 1958; [Location unknown]. Bethesda, MD: Society of American Foresters: 145–148.

Eggler WA. 1961. Stem elongation and time of cone initiation in southern pines. Forest Science 7(2):149–158.

Elder TJ, Burkhart LF. 1983. Chemical comparison of two ecotypes of loblolly pine. Society of Wood Science and Technology 15(3):245–250.

Fechne, GH. 1979. The biology of flowering and fertilization. In: Bonner FT, ed. Proceedings, Symposium on Flowering and Seed Development in Trees; 1978 May 15–18; Mississippi State, MS. Washington, DC: USDA Forest Service: 1–24.

Feduccia DP, Mann WF Jr. 1976. Bark thickness of 17-year-old loblolly pine planted at different spacings. Res. Note SO-210. New Orleans: USDA Forest Service, Southern Forest Experiment Station. 2 p.

Feirer RP, Conkey JH, Verhagen SA. 1989. Triglycerides in embryogenic conifer calli: a comparison with zygotic embryos. Plant Cell Reports 8(4):207–209.

Fisher RF, Rolfe GL, Eastburn RP. 1975. Productivity and organic matter distribution in a pine plantation and an adjacent, old field. For. Res. Rep. 75-1. Champaign/Urbana, IL: University of Illinois, Department of Forestry, Agricultural Experiment Station. 3 p.

Fowells HA, comp. 1965. Silvics of forest trees of the United States. Agric. Handb. 271. Washington, DC: USDA Forest Service. 762 p.

France RC, Reid CP. 1979. Absorption of ammonium and nitrate by mycorrhizal and non-mycorrhizal roots of pine. In: Riedacker A, Gagnaire-Michard J, eds. Root physiology and symbiosis: Proceedings, IUFRO Symposium, S2-01-13; 1978 September 11–15; Nancy, France. [Place of publication unknown]: [Publisher unknown]: 336–345.

Franklin EC. 1970. Survey of mutant forms and inbreeding depression in species of the family Pinaceae. Res. Pap. SE-61. Asheville, NC: USDA Forest Service, Southeastern Forest Experiment Station. 21 p.

Geyer WA, Gilmore AR. 1965. Effect of spacing on wood specific gravity in loblolly pine in southern Illinois. For. Note 113. Champaign/Urbana, IL: University of Illinois, Department of Forestry, Agricultural Experiment Station. 5 p.

Gibson MD, McMillin CW, Shoulders E. 1986. Moisture content and specific gravity of the four major southern pines under the same age and site conditions. Wood and Fiber Science 18(3):428–435.

Gilmore AR. 1975. Composition of monoterpenes in loblolly pine at different stem heights. Transactions of the Illinois State Academy of Science 68(1):26–28.

Grano CX. 1960. Strangling and girdling effects on cone production and growth of loblolly pine. Journal of Forestry 58:897–898.

Grano CX. 1973. Loblolly pine fecundity in south Arkansas. Res. Note SO-159. New Orleans: USDA Forest Service, Southern Forest Experiment Station. 7 p.

Greene JT, Porterfield HD. 1962. Selection and progeny testing. In: Proceedings, Forest Genetics Workshop; 1962 October 25–27; Macon, GA. Macon, GA: Southern Forest Tree Improvement Committee, 22: 9–10.

Greenwald SM Sr. 1972. Some environmental effects on the growth and monoterpene production of *Pinus taeda* L. and *Ocimum basilicum* L. Durham, NC: Duke University. 85 p. Ph.D. dissertation.

Greenwood MS. 1980. Reproductive development in loblolly pine: 1. The early development of male and female strobili in relation to long shoot growth behavior. American Journal of Botany 67(10):1,414–1,422.

Greenwood MS, Gladstone WT. 1978. Topworking loblolly pine for precocious flowering. Tech. Rep. 042-3004/78/80. Hot Springs, AR: Weyerhaeuser Corporation, Technical Information Center. 8 p.

Greenwood MS, Rucker T. 1985. Estimating pollen contamination in loblolly pine seed orchards by pollen trapping. In: Proceedings, 18th Southern Forest Tree Improvement Conference; 1985 May 21–23; Long Beach, MS. Macon, GA: USDA Forest Service, Eastern Tree Seed Laboratory: 179–186.

Gresham CA. 1976. Stomatal resistance in a loblolly pine plantation. Dissertation Abstracts International 36B(7):3140.

Gresham CA. 1982. Litterfall patterns in mature loblolly and longleaf pine stands in coastal South Carolina. Forest Science 28(2):223–41.

Gresham CA, Sinclair TR, Wuenscher JE. 1975. A ventilated diffusion porometer for measurement of the stomatal resistance of pine fascicles. Photosynthetica 9(1):72–77.

Griffing CG, Elam WW. 1971. Height growth patterns of loblolly pine samplings. Forest Science 17(1):52–54.

Griffing CG, Ursic SJ. 1977. Ethephon advances loblolly pine needle cast. Forest Science 23(3):351–354.

Hallock H. 1968. Observations on form of juvenile core in loblolly pine. Res. Note FPL-0188. Madison, WI: USDA Forest Service, Forest Products Laboratory. 6 p.

Hamilton JR, Harris JB. 1965. Influence of site on specific gravity and dimensions of tracheids in clones of *Pinus elliottii* Engelm. and *Pinus taeda* L. TAPPI Journal 48(6):330–333.

Hamilton JR, Matthews RM. 1965. Wood characteristics of planted loblolly and shortleaf pine. GA For. Res. Pap. 27. Macon, GA: Georgia Forestry Commission, Georgia Forest Research Council. 5 p.

Hansbrough T; Merrifield RG. 1963. The influence of partial girdling on cone and seed production of loblolly pine. LSU For. Res. Note 52. Baton Rouge, LA: Louisiana State University and A&M College, School of Forestry and Wildlife Management, Agricultural Experiment Station. 2 p.

Harkin DA. 1962. Diameter growth periodicity of several tree species in the South Carolina Coastal Plain. Forest Science 8(4):363–370.

Harlow WM, Harrar ES. 1958. Textbook of dendrology. 4th ed. York, PA: Maple Press. 561 p.

Harms WR. 1971. Estimating leaf-area growth in pine. Ecology 52(5):931–934.

Harrington CA, Carlson WC, Brissette JC. 1987. Relationships between height growth and root system orientation in planted and seeded loblolly and shortleaf pines. In: Phillips DR, ed. Proceedings, 4th Biennial Southern Silvicultural Research Conference; 1986 November 4–6; Atlanta, GA. Gen. Tech. Rep. SE-42. Asheville, NC: USDA Forest Service, Southeastern Forest Experiment Station: 53–60.

Harris WF, Kinerson RS Jr, Edwards NT. 1977. Comparison of belowground biomass of natural deciduous forest and loblolly pine plantations. Pedobiologia 17:369–381.

Higginbotham KO. 1974. The influence of canopy position and the age of leaf tissue on growth and photosynthesis in loblolly pine. Durham, NC: Duke University. 267 p. Ph.D. dissertation.

Higginbotham KO, Strain BR. 1973. The influence of canopy osition on net photosynthesis in loblolly pine. American Journal of Botany 60(4)(Suppl.):24–25.

Hitchings RG. 1984. The effect of juvenile wood of loblolly pine on the kraft pulp yield. In: Proceedings, Symposium on Utilization of the Changing Wood Resource in the Southern United States; 1984 June 12–14; [Location unknown]. [Place of publication and publisher unknown]: 147–159.

Hodges JD, Barras SJ, Mauldin JK. 1968. Free and protein-bound amino acids in inner bark of loblolly pine. Forest Science 14(3):330–333.

Hodges JD, Elam WW, Watson WF. 1977. Physical properties of the oleoresin system of the four major southern pines. Canadian Journal of Forest Research 7(3):520–525.

Hodges JD, Elam WW, Watson WF, Nebeker TE. 1979. Oleoresin characteristics and susceptibility of four southern pines to southern pine beetle attacks. Canadian Entomology 111:889–896.

Hodges JD, Lorio PL Jr. 1968. Measurement of oleoresin exudation pressure in loblolly pine. Forest Science 14(10):75–76.

Hodges JD, Lorio PL Jr. 1969. Carbohydrate and nitrogen fractions of the inner bark of loblolly pines under moisture stress. Canadian Journal of Botany 47:1651–1657.

Hodges JD, Lorio PL Jr. 1971. Comparison of field techniques for measuring moisture stress in large loblolly pines. Forest Science 17(2):220–223.

Hodges JD, Lorio PL Jr. 1975. Moisture stress and composition of xylem oleoresin in loblolly pine. Forest Science 21(3):283–290.

Holeman R, Hennessey T, Dougherty P. 1991. Shoot and foliage phenology of main branch terminals of 15-year-old loblolly pine. In: Abstracts, 6th Southern Silvicultural Research Conference; 1990 October 30–31; Memphis, TN. Asheville, NC: USDA Forest Service, Southeastern Forest Experiment Station: 52.

Hosker RP Jr, Nappo CJ Jr, Hanna SR. 1974. Diurnal variation of vertical thermal structure in a pine plantation. Agricultural Meteorology 13(2):259–265.

Howard ET. 1973. Properties of southern pine needles. Wood Science 5(4):281–286.

Jackson LWR. 1959. Loblolly pine tracheid length in relation to position in tree. Journal of Forestry 57(5):366–367.

Jackson LWR, Morse WE. 1965. Tracheid length variation in single rings of loblolly, slash, and shortleaf pine. Journal of Forestry 63(2):110–112.

Janick J, Whipkey A. 1988. Fatty acid accumulation in loblolly pine seed (*Pinus taeda* L.). In: Proceedings, 85th Annual Meeting of the American Society for Horticultural Science and 33rd Annual Meeting of the Canadian Society for Horticultural Science; 1988 August 6–11; East Lansing, MI. HortScience 23(3):734.

Johnson JD, Zedaker SM, Hairston AB. 1985. Foliage, stem, and root interrelations in young loblolly pine. Forest Science 31(4):891–898.

Joye NM Jr, Proveaux AT, Lawrence RV. 1972. Composition of pine needle oil. Journal of Chromatographic Science 10(9):590–592.

Judson GM. 1964. Inexpensive and accurate form class estimates. Res. Pap. SO-11. New Orleans: USDA Forest Service, Southern Forest Experiment Station. 6 p.

Kalela E. 1954. Mantysiemenpuiden japuustojen juurisuhteista [On root relations of seed-trees]. Acta Forest Fennica 61(28):1–17.

Kellison RC. 1981. Characteristics affecting quality of timber from plantations, their determination and scope for modification. In: Proceedings, 17th World Congress of IUFRO; 1981; [Location unknown]. [Place of publication and publisher unknown]: 77–88.

Kinerson RS. 1975. Relationships between plant surface area and respiration in loblolly pine. Journal of Applied Ecology 12:965–971.

Kinerson RS, Higginbotham KO, Chapman RC. 1974. The dynamics of foliage distribution within a forest canopy. Journal of Applied Ecology 11(1):347–353.

Kinerson RS, Ralston CW, Wells CG. 1977. Carbon cycling in a loblolly pine plantation. Oecologia 29(1):1–10.

Knauf TA, Bilan MV. 1977. Cotyledon and primary needle variation in loblolly pine from mesic and xeric seed sources. Forest Science 23(1):33–36.

Koch P. 1972. Utilization of southern pines, Vol. 1. Agric. Handbk. 420. Washington, DC: USDA Forest Service. 734 p.

Kossuth SV, Biggs RH. 1981. Role of apophysis and outer scale tissue in pine cone opening. Forest Science 27(4):828–836.

Kozlowski TT, Scholtes WH. 1948. Growth of roots and root hairs of pine and hardwood seedlings in the Piedmont. Journal of Forestry 46:750–754.

Kramer PJ. 1969. Plant and soil water relationships: a modern synthesis. New York: McGraw-Hill. 482 p.

Kramer PJ, Bullock HC. 1966. Seasonal variations in the proportions of suberized and unsuberized roots of trees in relation to the absorption of water. American Journal of Botany 53(2):200–204.

Kramer PJ, Clark WS. 1947. A comparison of photosynthesis in individual pine needles and entire seedlings at various light intensities. Plant Physiology 22:51–57.

Kramer PJ, Kozlowski TT. 1979. Physiology of woody plants. Orlando, FL: Academic Press. 811 p.

Lanner RM. 1976. Patterns of shoot development in *Pinus* and their relationship to growth potential. In: Cannell MGR, Last FT, eds. Tree physiology and yield improvement. New York: Academic Press: 224–243.

Lanner RM. 1978. Development of the terminal bud and shoot of slash pine saplings. Forest Science 24(2):167–179.

Ledig FT, Bormann FH, Wenger KF. 1970. The distribution of dry matter growth between shoot and roots in loblolly pine. Botanical Gazette 131(4):349–359.

Ledig FT, Perry TO. 1967. Variation in photosynthesis and respiration among loblolly pine progenies. In: Proceedings, 9th Southern Forest Tree Improvement Conference; 1967 June 8–9; Knoxville, TN. Macon, GA: Southern Forest Tree Improvement Committee 28: 120–128.

Ledig FT, Perry TO. 1969. Net asssimilation rate and growth in loblolly pine seedlings. Forest Science 15(4):431–438.

Lenhart JD, Shinn KH, Cutter BE. 1977. Specific gravity at various positions along the stem of planted loblolly pine trees. Forest Products Journal 27(9):43–44.

Lockaby BG, Taylor-Boyd JE. 1986. Nutrient dynamics in the litter fall and forest floor of an 18-year-old loblolly pine plantation. Canadian Journal of Forest Research 16(5):1109–1112.

Loo JA, Tauer CG, McNew RW. 1985. Genetic variation in the time of transition from juvenile to mature wood in loblolly pine. Silvae Genetica 34(1):14–19.

Lotti T. 1956. Good seed production from a young stand of loblolly pine. Res. Note 97. Asheville, NC: USDA Forest Service, Southeastern Forest Experiment Station. 2 p.

Mann WF Jr. 1976. Some characteristics of newly germinated seedlings of four major southern pines. Tree Planters' Notes 27(4):23–34.

Mann WF Jr. 1979. Relationships of seed size, number of cotyledons, and initial growth of southern pines. Tree Planters' Notes 30(2):22–23, 26.

March RA, Bramlett DL, Dashek WV, Mayfield JE. 1986. Timing of fertilization in *Pinus taeda*. In: Proceedings, International Conference on Biotechnology and Ecology of Pollen; 1985 July 9–11; Amherst, MA. New York: Springer-Verlag: 505–506.

Marx DH. 1969. The influence of ectotrophic mycorrhizal fungi on the resistance of pine roots to pathogenic infection: 1. Antagonism of mycorrhizal fungi to root pathogenic fungi and soil bacteria. Phytopathology 59:153–163.

Marx DH. 1975. Mycorrhizae of forest nursery seedlings. In: Peterson GW, Smith RS Jr, tech. coords. Forest nursery diseases of the United States. Agric. Handbk. 470. Washington, DC: USDA Forest Service: 35–40.

May JT, Johnson HH, Gilmore AR. 1962. Chemical composition of southern pine seedlings. Georgia For. Res. Pap. 10. Macon, GA: Georgia Forestry Commission, Georgia Forest Research Council. 11 p.

McGregor WHD, Kramer PJ. 1963. Seasonal trends in rates of photosynthesis and respiration of loblolly pine and white pine seedlings. American Journal of Botany 50(8):760–765.

McLaughlin SB, Madgwick HA. 1968. The effects of position in crown on the morphology of needles of loblolly pine. American Midland Naturalist 80(2):547–550.

McLemore BF. 1962. Predicting seed yields of southern pine cones. Journal of Forestry 60(9):639–641.

McLemore BF. 1972. Determining numbers of southern pine cones per bushel. Journal of Forestry 70(1):35–36.

McLemore BF. 1974. Anatomical characteristics of loblolly and slash pine cone stalks. Forest Science 20(1):41–46.

McLemore BF. 1977. Cone influences maturation of unpollinated strobili in southern pines. Silvae Genetica 26(4):134–135.

McMillan CW. 1970. Mineral content of loblolly pine wood as related to specific gravity, growth rate, and distance from pith. Holzforschung 24(5):152–157.

McMillan CW. 1969. Ash content of loblolly pine wood as related to specific gravity, growth rate, and distance from pith. Wood Science. Madison, WI: Forest Products Research Society 2(1):26–30.

Megraw RA. 1985.Wood quality factors in loblolly pine: the influence of tree age, position in tree, and cultural practice on wood specific gravity, fiber length, and fibril angle. Atlanta: TAPPI Press. 96 p.

Melin E. 1962. Physiological aspects of mycorrhizae of forest trees. In: Kozlowski TT, ed. Tree growth. New York: Ronald Press: 247–263.

Mergen F, Koerting LE. 1957. Initiation and development of flower primordia in slash pine. Forest Science 3(2):145–155.

Mergen F, Stairs GR, Snyder EB. 1963. Microsporogenesis in *Pinus echinata* and *Pinus taeda*. Silvae Genetica 12(4):127–129.

Metz LJ, Wells CG. 1965. Weight and nutrient content of the aboveground parts of some loblolly pines. Res. Pap. SE-17. Asheville, NC: USDA Forest Service, Southeastern Forest Experiment Station. 20 p.

Miller L, Woods FW. 1965. Root-grafting in loblolly pine. Botanical Gazette 126(4):12–14.

Miller WF. 1966. Annual changes in foliar nitrogen, phosphorus, and potassium levels of loblolly pine with site, and weather factors. Plant and Soil 24(3):369–378.

Minor CO. 1953. Loblolly pine bark thickness. LSU For. Note 1. Baton Rouge, LA: Louisiana State University and A&M College, School of Forestry and Wildlife Management, Agricultural Experiment Station. 2 p.

Mitchell ML, Hassan AE Davey CB, Gregory JD. 1981. Effect of soil compaction on root development and seedling establishment. ASAE Pap. 81-1040. St. Joseph, MI: American Society of Agricultural Engineers. 20 p.

Monk CD. 1966. Root-shoot dry weights in loblolly pine. Botanical Gazette 127(4):246–248.

Murphy CE Jr. 1985. Carbon dioxide exchange and growth of a pine plantation. Forest Ecology Management 11(3):203–224.

Nelson LE, Switzer GL, Smith WH. 1970. Dry matter and nutrient accumulation in young loblolly pine. In: Youngberg CT, Davey CB, eds. Tree growth and forest soils: Proceedings, 3rd North American Forest Soils Conference; 1968 August; Raleigh, NC. Corvallis, OR: Oregon State University Press: 261–273.

Nemeth JC. 1972. Dry matter production in young loblolly and slash pine plantations. Raleigh, NC: North Carolina State University. 75 p. Ph.D. dissertation.

Nemeth JC. 1973. Dry matter production in young loblolly and slash plantations. Ecological Monographs 43(1):21–41.

Niklas KJ. 1987. Aerodynamics of wind pollination. Scientific American 257(1):90–95.

Nix LE, Villiers K. 1985. Tracheid differentiation in southern pines during the dormant season. Wood and Fiber Science 17(3): 397–403.

O'Leary JW, Kramer PJ. 1964. Root pressure in conifers. Science 145(3629):284–285.

Paul BH. 1938. Knots in second-growth pine and the desirability of pruning. Misc. Publ. 307. Washington, DC: USDA Forest Service. 23 p.

Paul BH. 1958. Specific gravity changes in southern pines after release. Southern Lumberman 1958 (December):122–124.

Pearl IA, Buchanan MA. 1976. A study of the inner and outer barks of loblolly pine. TAPPI Journal 59(2):136–139.

Pearson RG. 1984. Characteristics of structural importance of clear wood and lumber from fast-grown loblolly pine stands. In: Proceedings, Symposium on Utilization of the Changing Wood Resource in the Southern United States; 1984 June 12–14; Raleigh, NC. Raleigh, NC: North Carolina State University: 66–70.

Pearson RG. 1986. Effect of the changing wood resource on solid wood products. In: Proceedings, 1986 Research and Development Conference; 1986 September 28–October 1; Raleigh, NC. Atlanta: TAPPI Press: 35–37.

Pehl CE, Tuttle CL, Houser JN, Moehring DM. 1984. Total biomass and nutrients of 25-year-old loblolly pines. Forest Ecology Management 9(3):155–160.

Perry TO. 1971a. Dormancy of trees in winter. Science 171:29–36.

Perry TO. 1971b. Winter-season photosynthesis and respiration by twigs and seedlings of deciduous and evergreen trees. Forest Science 17(1):41–43.

Perry TO, Baldwin GW. 1966. Winter breakdown of the photosynthetic apparatus of evergreen species. Forest Science 12(3):298–300.

Pharis RP, Kramer PJ. 1964. The effects of nitrogen and drought on loblolly pine seedlings: 1. Growth and composition. Forest Science 10(2):143–150.

Phillips DR, Schroeder JG. 1972. Some physical characteristics of bark from plantation-grown slash and loblolly pine. Forest Products Journal 22(10):30–33.

Pillow MY, Terrell BZ, Hiller CH. 1953. Patterns of variation in fibril angles in loblolly pine. Rep. D1935. Madison, WI: USDA Forest Service, Forest Products Laboratory. 10 p.

Pritchett WL. 1973. The effect of nitrogen and phosphorus fertilizers on the growth and composition of loblolly and slash pine seedlings in pots. Proceedings of the Soil and Crop Science Society of Florida 32:161–165.

Pritchett WL. 1979. Properties and management of forest soils. New York: John Wiley and Sons. 500 p.

Ralston CW, Chapman RC, Kinerson RS Jr. 1972. Biomass distribution in a loblolly pine plantation: Oakridge Laboratory 1972 annual report. Oakridge, TN: U.S. Atomic Energy Commission. 10 p.

Reed JF. 1939. Root and shoot growth of shortleaf and loblolly pines in relation to certain environmental conditions. Bull. 4. Durham, NC: Duke University School of Forestry. 52 p.

Reid CPP. 1971. Transport of carbon-1 labeled substances in mycelial strands of thelephora-terrestris. In: Hacskaylo E, ed. Mycorrhizae: Proceedings, 1st North American Conference on Mycorrhizae; 1969 April 1–3; Champaign/Urbana, IL. Misc. Publ. 1189. Washington, DC: USDA Forest Service: 222–227.

Reid CPP, Kidd FA, Ekwebelam SA. 1983. Nitrogen nutrition, photosynthesis and carbon allocation in ectomycorrhizal pine. Plant and Soil 71:415–431.

Reynolds RR. 1967. Natural pruning. Forest Farmer 26(6):8–9, 18.

Roberts EG, Ross RD. 1965. Crown area of free-growing loblolly pine and its apparent independence of age and site. Journal of Forestry 63(6):462–463.

Roberts FL. 1948. Study of the absorbing surfaces of the roots of loblolly pine. Durham, NC: Duke University. 28 p. M.S. thesis.

Rockwood DL. 1972. Aspects of monoterpene composition in loblolly pine. Raleigh, NC: North Carolina State University. 128 p. Ph.D. dissertation.

Rogerson TL. 1964. Estimating foliage on loblolly pine. Res. Note SO-16. New Orleans: USDA Forest Service, Southern Forest Experiment Station. 3 p.

Sands R, Fiscus EL, Reid CPP. 1982. Hydraulic properties of pine and bean roots with varying degrees of suberization, vascular differentiation and mycorrhizal infection. Australian Journal of Plant Physiology 9:559–569.

Sargent CS. 1884. Report on the forests of North America (exclusive of Mexico). Washington, DC: Government Printing Office. 612 p.

Schmidt JD, Horton IF. 1961. A study of the relationship between width of growth ring and percentage of latewood in suppressed stems of plantation-grown *Pinus elliottii* Engelm. var. *elliottii* and *Pinus taeda* L.: Project QTP 2-2, experiment 1, lab report 5. Brisbane, Australia: Queensland Forest Service. 8 p.

Schmidtling RC. 1971. Cultivating and fertilizing stimulate precocious flowering in a loblolly pine seed orchard. Silvae Genetica 20(5-6):220–221.

Schopmeyer CS, tech. coord. 1974. Seeds of woody plants in the United States. Agric. Handbk. 450. Washington, DC: USDA Forest Service. 883 p.

Schultz RP. 1972a. Intraspecific root grafting in slash pine. Botanical Gazette 133(1):26–29.

Schultz RP. 1972b. Root development of intensively cultivated slash pine. Soil Science Society of America Proceedings 36(1):158–162.

Schultz RP, Woods FW. 1967. The frequency and implications of intraspecific root-grafting in loblolly pine. Forest Science 13(3):226–239.

Schultz RP. 1965. The frequency and implications of intraspecific root-grafting in loblolly pine (*Pinus taeda* L.). Durham, NC: Duke University. 139 p. Ph.D. dissertation.

Seiler JR, Johnson JD. 1985. Photosynthesis and transpiration of loblolly pine seedlings as influenced by moisture-stress conditioning. Forest Science 31(3):742–749.

Senft JF, Bendtsen BA, Galligan WL. 1985. Weak wood: fast-grown trees make problem lumber. Journal of Forestry 83(8):477–484.

Shear TH, Perry TO. 1986. Nondestructive estimation of the needle weight and stem weight of small loblolly pine trees. Canadian Journal of Forest Research 16(2):403–405.

Shelburne VB, Hedden RL, Allen RM. 1989. The relationship of leaf area to sapwood area in loblolly pine as affected by site, stand basal area, and sapwood permeability. In: Miller JH, comp. Proceedings, 5th Biennial Southern Silvicultural Research Conference; 1988 November 1–3; Memphis, TN. Gen. Tech. Rep. SO-74. New Orleans: USDA Forest Service, Southern Forest Experiment Station: 75–80.

Shelton MG, Switzer GL. 1984. Variation in the surface area relationships of loblolly pine fascicles. Forest Science 30(2):355–363.

Shoulders E. 1973. Rainfall influences female flowering of slash pine. Res. Note SO-150. New Orleans: USDA Forest Service, Southern Forest Experiment Station. 7 p.

Sihanonth P, Todd RL. 1977. Transfer of nutrients from ectomycorrhizal fungi to plant roots. Ecological Bulletin 25:392–397.

Sinclair TR, Knoerr KR. 1982. Distribution of photosynthetically active radiation in the canopy of a loblolly pine plantation. Journal of Applied Ecology 19(1):183–191.

Sivak J, Caratini C. 1973. Determination of American *Pinus* pollen in the lower Miocene of Landes, France, according to the ectexine structure of their air sacs. Grana 13(1):1–17.

Smith WH, Nelson LE, Switzer GL. 1971. Development of the shoot system of young loblolly pine: 2. Dry matter and nitrogen accumulation. Forest Science 17(1):55–62.

Smith WH, Switzer GL, Nelson LE. 1970. Development of the shoot system of young loblolly pine: 1. Apical growth and nitrogen concentration. Forest Science 16(4):483–490.

Snyder EB, Hamaker JM. 1970. Specific gravity and fiber length of loblolly and spruce pines on the same site. Res. Note SO-103. New Orleans: USDA Forest Service, Southern Forest Experiment Station. 3 p.

Snyder EB, Hamaker JM. 1978. Needle characteristics of hybrids of some species of southern pine. Silvae Genetica 27(5):184–188.

Stalter R. 1971. Age of a mature pine (*Pinus taeda*) stand in South Carolina. Ecology 52(3):532–533.

Stalter RA. 1970. Mature stand of *Pinus taeda* near Columbia, South Carolina. Plant Science Bulletin 16(2):4–5.

Stohr HP. 1980. Initial moisture content and density and drying rate of three pine species growing in the Natal midlands: 1. Moisture content and density of standing trees. South African Forestry Journal 114:49–57.

Stone EL Jr, Stone MH. 1954. Root collar sprouts in pine. Journal of Forestry 52(7):487–491.

Strain Br, Higginbotham KO, Mulroy J.C. 1976. Temperature pre-conditioning and photosynthetic capacity of *Pinus taeda* L. Photosynthetica 10(1):47–53.

Strain BR, Higginbotham KO. 1976. A summary of gas exchange studies on trees undertaken in the U.S. IBP (International Biological Program) eastern deciduous forest biome. In: Proceedings, 16th World Congress of IUFRO, division 2; 1976 [dates unknown]; Oslo, Norway. N-1432 As-NLH. [Place of publication unknown]: Norwegian IUFRO Congress Committee, Norwegian Forest Research Institute: 99–101.

Strohl MJ, Seikel MK. 1965. Polyphenols of pine pollens: a survey. Phytochemistry 4(3):383–399.

Strub MR, Vasey RB, Burkhart HE. 1975. Comparison of diameter growth and crown competition factor in loblolly pine plantations. Forest Science 21(4):427–431.

Sung SS, Xu DP, Kormanik PP, Black CC. 1988. Seasonal patterns of gylcolytic [sic] enzyme activities in tree roots. In: Proceedings, Annual Meeting of the American Society of Plant Physiologists; 1988 July 10–14; Reno, NV. Plant Physiology 86:36.

Swank WT, Douglass JE. 1974. Streamflow greatly reduced by converting deciduous hardwood stands to pine. Science 185:857–859.

Switzer GL, Nelson LE. 1972. Nutrient accumulation and cycling in loblolly pine plantation ecosystems: the first twenty years. Soil Science Society of America Proceedings 36(1):143–147.

Switzer GL, Nelson LE, Smith WH. 1968. The mineral cycle in forest stands. In: Bengston GW, ed. Forest fertilization: theory and practice. Muscle Shoals, AL: Tennessee Valley Authority: 1–19.

Taras MA, Saucier JR. 1967. Influence of extractives on specific gravity of southern pine. Forest Products Journal 17(9):97–99.

Tauer CG, Loo-Dinkins JA. 1990. Seed source variation in specific gravity of loblolly pine grown in a common environment in Arkansas. Forest Science 36(4):1133–1145.

Taylor FG Jr. 1965. Nuclear volume changes in southeastern tree species before spring growth. Radiation Botany 5(1):61–64.

Taylor FW. 1979. Variation of specific gravity and fiber length in loblolly pine branches. Journal of the Institute of Wood Science 8(4):171–175.

Taylor FW, Moore JS. 1981. A comparison of earlywood and latewood tracheid lengths of loblolly pine. Wood and Fiber 13(3):159–165.

Tepper HB, Yang CS, Schaedle M. 1989. Effect of aluminum on growth of root tips of honey locust and loblolly pine. Environmental and Experimental Botany 29(2):165–173.

Teskey RO. 1987. Photorespiration in loblolly pine. Plant Physiology 83(4)(Suppl.): 33

Teskey RO, Fites JA, Samuelson LJ, Bongarten BC. 1986. Stomatal and nonstomatal limitations to net photosynthesis in *Pinus taeda* L. under different environmental conditions. Tree Physiology 2(1/3):131–142.

Teskey RO, Shrestha RB. 1985. A relationship between carbon dioxide, photosynthetic efficiency and shade tolerance. Physiologia Plantarum 63(1):126–132.

Trembath TN, Askew GR. 1987. Clonal variation of tannic and phenolic concentrations of cones from a selected population of loblolly pine. In: Proceedings, 19th Southern Forest Tree Improvement Conference; 1987 June 16–18; College Station, TX. Springfield, VA: National Technical Information Service: 223–231.

USDA FS [U.S. Department of Agriculture, Forest Service]. 1965. Southern wood density survey: 1965 status report. Res. Pap. 26. Madison, WI: USDA Forest Service, Forest Products Laboratory. 38 p.

van Buijtenen JP. 1963. Heritability of wood properties and their relation to growth rate in *Pinus taeda*. In: World consultation on forest genetics and tree improvement; 1963 August 23–30; Stockholm, Sweden. FAO/FORGEN 63-7/2. Rome: FAO. 13 p.

van Buijtenen JP, Bilan MV, Zimmerman RH. 1976. Morpho-physiological characteristics related to drought resistance in *Pinus taeda*. In: Cannell MGR, Last FT, eds. Tree physiology and yield improvement. New York: Academic Press: 349–359.

Vancura V, Stotzky G. 1976. Gaseous and volatile exudates from germinating seeds and seedlings. Canadian Journal of Botany 54:518–532.

VanHaverbeke DF, Barber JC. 1964. Seed crop estimation in a loblolly pine seed production area. GA For. Res. Pap. 21. Macon, GA: Georgia Forestry Commission, Georgia Forest Research Council. 5 p.

Van Lear DH, Goebel NB. 1976. Leaf fall and forest floor characteristics in loblolly pine plantations in the South Carolina Piedmont soil. Soil Science Society of America Journal 40:116–119.

von Wedel KW, Zobel BJ, Shelbourne CJA. 1968. Prevalence and effects of knots in young loblolly pine. Forest Products Journal 18(9):97–103.

Wahlenberg WG. 1960. Loblolly pine: its use, ecology, regeneration, protection, growth and management. Durham, NC: Duke University School of Forestry; Washington, DC: USDA Forest Service. 603 p.

Walker LC, Arnold CJ. 1963. Detecting tree feeding roots with radioactive phosphorus. Advancing Frontiers of Plant Science 4:179–188.

Warrington SJ, Black HD, Coons LB. 1981. Entry of *Pisolithus tinctorius* hyphae into *Pinus taeda* roots. Canadian Journal of Botany 59(11):2135–2139.

Warrington SJ, Black HD, Coons LB. 1982. Early stages of ectomycorrhiza formation between *Pisolithus tinctorius* hyphae and *Pinus taeda* short roots. In: Proceedings, 1982 TAPPI Research and Development Conferences; 1982 August 29–September 1; Asheville, NC. Atlanta: TAPPI Press: 335–340.

Weiss R. 1987. You say tomato, they say tomography. Science News 132(11):164.

Wells C, Whigham D, Leith H. 1972. Investigation of mineral nutrient cycling in upland Piedmont forest. Journal of the Elisha Mitchell Scientific Society 88(2):66–78.

Wells CG. 1969. Foliage sampling guides for loblolly pine. Res. Note SE-113. Asheville, NC: USDA Forest Service, Southeastern Forest Experiment Station. 3 p.

Wells CG, Jorgensen JR, Burnette CE. 1975. Biomass and mineral elements in a thinned loblolly pine plantation at age 16. Res. Pap. SE-126. Asheville, NC: USDA Forest Service, Southeastern Forest Experiment Station. 10 p.

Wells CG, Metz LJ. 1963. Variation in nutrient content of loblolly pine needles with season, age, soil and position on the crown.

Soil Science Society of America Proceedings 27(1):90–93.

Wells OO, Nance WL, Thielges BA. 1977. Variation in needle traits in provenance tests of *Pinus taeda* and *P. echinata.* Silvae Genetica 26(4):125–130.

Wenger KF. 1957. Annual variation in the seed crops of loblolly pine. Journal of Forestry. 55(8):567–569.

Werner RA. 1971. Clockwise spiral ascent of dye in southern pines. Forest Science 17(1):44–45.

Werner RA. 1973. Absorption, translocation, and metabolism of root-absorbed 14C-monitor in loblolly pine seedlings. Journal of Economic Entomology 66(4):867–8 72.

Wheeler EY, Zobel BJ, Weeks DL. 1966. Tracheid length and diameter variation in the bole of loblolly pine. TAPPI Journal 49(11):484–490.

Whetstone R, Paul KB, Payne BR, Biswas PK. 1970. Mechanism of tree seed dormancy: 2. Histochemical studies on dormant and germinating seeds of selected tree species. HortScience 5(5):321.

White EH, Pritchett WL, Robertson WK. 1971. Slash pine root biomass and nutrient concentrations. In: Forest biomass studies: Proceedings, 15th IUFRO Conference; 1971 [dates unknown]; Gainesville, FL. [Place of publication and publisher unknown]: 165–176.

White JD, Alexander LT, Clark EW. 1972. Fluctuations in the inorganic constituents of inner bark of loblolly pine with season and soil series. Canadian Journal of Botany 50(6):1287–1293.

White JD, Wells CG, Clark EW. 1970. Variations in the inorganic composition of inner bark and needles of loblolly pine with tree height and soil series. Canadian Journal of Botany 48(6):1079–1084.

Wiant HV Jr. 1973. Relation of southern pine cone spirals to the Fibonacci series. Creation Research Society Quarterly 9(4):218–219.

Williams CG. 1987. The influence of shoot ontogeny on juvenile-mature correlations in loblolly pine. Forest Science 33(2):411–422.

Woods FW, Ferrill MD, McCormack ML. 1962. Methyl bromide for increasing I[131] uptake by pine trees. Radiation Botany 2(3/4):273–277.

Yu SL, Cruise JF. 1982. Time series analysis of soil moisture data. In: El-Shaarawi AH, Esterly SR, eds. Time series methods in hydrosciences. Amsterdam: Elsevier Scientific Publishing: 600–606.

Zak B. 1964. Role of mycorrhizae in root disease. Annual Review of Phytopathology 2:377–392.

Zicherman JB, Thomas RJ. 1972. Analysis of loblolly pine ash materials. Holzforschung 26(4):150–152.

Zobel B, Blair, R. 1976. Wood and pulp properties of juvenile wood and topwood of the southern pines. Applied Polymer Symposium 28:421–433.

Zobel BJ, Haught AE Jr. 1962. Effect of bole straightness on compression wood of loblolly pine. Tech. Rep. 15. Raleigh, NC: North Carolina State College, School of Forestry. 5 p.

Zobel BJ, Kellison RC, Matthias MF, Hatcher AV. 1972. Wood density of the southern pines. Tech. Bull. 208. St. Paul, MN: USDA Forest Service, North Central Forest Experiment Station. 56 p.

Zobel BJ, Matthias M, Roberds JH, Kellison RC. 1968. Moisture content of southern pine trees. Tech. Rep. 37. Raleigh, NC: North Carolina State University, School of Forestry, Cooperative Tree Improvement Program. 44 p.

Zon R. 1905. Loblolly pine in eastern Texas, with special reference to the production of cross-ties. Bull. 64. Washington, DC: USDA Forest Service. 53 p.

Chapter 3

Habitat

Contents

Habitat

Introduction

Loblolly pine grows in diverse habitats that can be described in terms of physiography, climate and length of growing season, past agricultural uses, and physical and chemical properties of soils. Loblolly pine's range extends from the flat lower Atlantic and Gulf Coastal Plain to the rolling and dissected Piedmont province and includes the mountains and deeply dissected Appalachian Highlands of the Carolinas and southern Virginia and the Cumberland Mountains of Tennessee. Approximately 36% of loblolly pine's range is lowlands or smooth plains, 49% is irregular or rolling plains, and 15% is hilly or mountainous land (Hammond 1964, Switzer and others 1978). Soils supporting loblolly pine

vary from wet organics to heavy clays to dry sands and from very fertile to infertile. Loblolly pine can grow vigorously right up to the streambanks in the Coastal Plain, the Piedmont, and Interior Upland physiographic regions (figure 3-1).

Large areas of loblolly pine forests, primarily in the Piedmont but also on well-drained Coastal Plain soils, developed from retired farmlands during the early part of the 20th century. Most of these farmlands had been cropped for long periods without chemical amendments or control of water and erosion (Trimble 1974). The soil of wornout farms was often highly eroded and usually was depleted of available nutrients.

Figure 3-1—A mixed loblolly pine–hardwood stand growing along a streambank in the Piedmont of North Carolina.

At the southern limit of the species' range in central Florida, the average monthly temperature variation is only 10 °C throughout the year, whereas average monthly temperature variation reaches 25 °C at the northern limit in Delaware. In addition, average monthly rainfall varies from as little as 25 mm in Oklahoma and Texas to more than 200 mm in Florida. Clearly, loblolly pine is well adapted to prosper in a wide range of environments. However, if carbon dioxide (CO_2) levels and temperatures continue to rise, both the northern and southern limits of loblolly pine's range could shift northward substantially (Miller and others 1987).

Physiographic Provinces of the Loblolly Pine Ecosystem

The general physiography of the loblolly pine ecosystem is outlined in figure 3-2. Loblolly pine is productive on all but a few land types (e.g., the Mississippi Alluvial Floodplain and Gulf and Atlantic Coast marshes) within its range. The parent material is unconsolidated Pleistocene sediments in the Coastal Plain, crystalline rocks in the Piedmont, and sandstones and limestones in the Appalachian Highlands (table 3-1).

The Coastal Plain

About three-quarters of the loblolly pine ecosystem is in the Atlantic Coast and Gulf Coastal Plain. Loblolly pine grows in the Coastal Plain from the Delmarva Peninsula along the Middle Atlantic Coast south to Florida and west from Florida to east Texas with only a narrow interruption at the Mississippi River Delta. Loblolly pine's natural range extends about 80 km into Tennessee on Coastal Plain soils between the Mississippi and Tennessee Rivers.

The Coastal Plain is about 240 km wide along most of the Atlantic Coast and about 240 to 640 km wide along the Gulf Coast. With minor exceptions, the Coastal Plain is less than 150 m above sea level in elevation, and more than half is less than 30 m in elevation. However, the region is extremely diverse in both topography and soils, so that there are numerous local exceptions to generalized trends. In the Atlantic Coastal Plain, elevations increase from sea level westward, and the topography progresses from flat to undulating to hilly

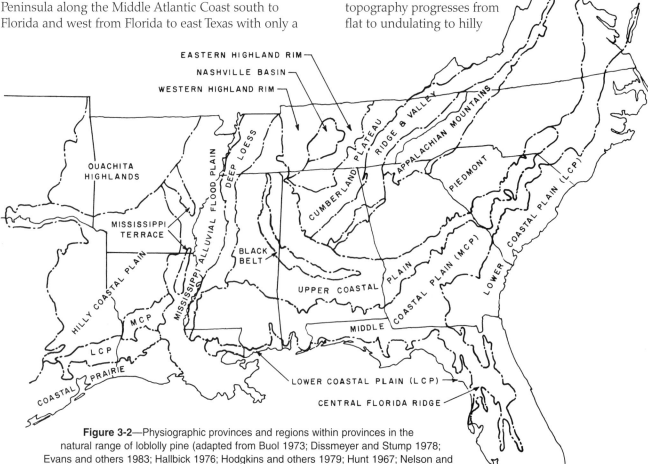

Figure 3-2—Physiographic provinces and regions within provinces in the natural range of loblolly pine (adapted from Buol 1973; Dissmeyer and Stump 1978; Evans and others 1983; Hallbick 1976; Hodgkins and others 1979; Hunt 1967; Nelson and Zillgitt 1969; Pehl and Brim 1985; Smalley 1979, 1980, 1982, 1983, 1984; Thornbury 1965).

on a series of well-developed terraces, which are discontinuously marked by seaward-facing scarps.

Topography of the Gulf Coastal Plain is more complex and diverse than that of the Atlantic Coastal Plain (Hunt 1967). The Gulf Coastal Plain is underlain by relatively unconsolidated sediments ranging in age from early Cretaceous to recent. Because the underlying Cretaceous, Tertiary, and marine Quaternary Period rocks differ greatly in resistance to erosion, erosion has produced complex and ill-defined coastal terraces and an inner region of belted topography punctuated by prominent landward-facing scarps. Cretaceous parent material forms an inland belt, Tertiary material an intermediate belt, and Quaternary material a coastal belt (figure 3-3). The Cretaceous and Tertiary formations in both the East and West Gulf Coastal Plains are thicker, more folded, and have more fault zones than do Atlantic Coastal Plain formations of the same periods. The east bluff of the Mississippi River Valley is covered with loess (wind-deposited silt) to depths up to several meters. The loess thins rapidly to the east, where the emerged edges of a series of gently dipping strata give the landscape a belted character (Buol 1973, Hunt 1967, Murray 1961, Thornbury 1965).

The Coastal Plain can be divided into lower, middle, and upper Coastal Plain regions (table 3-1). Topography of the lower Coastal Plain is level to gently rolling. Up to six marine terraces lie roughly parallel to the coast and rise from sea level to elevations of about 15 to 30 m. The province is crossed by many broad, shallow valleys with

Table 3-1—Characteristics of the physiographic regions within the range of loblolly pine

Principal physiographic region	Topography	Elevation	Parent material
Lower Coastal Plain	Level to gently rolling	Below 30 m	Quaternary Period: marine deposits of sands, sandy limestones, and clays
Middle and Upper Coastal Plain	Level to hilly or undulating	30–150 m	Quaternary Period: marine sediments of sands, sandy limestones, and clays
Piedmont Plateau	Rolling uplands with ridges and deep, wide valleys	180–610 m	Precambrian and Paleozoic Eras: granite, schist, mica, slate, and basic rock
Valley and Ridge	Hilly to steep ridges and broad intervening valleys	Valley: 180–240 m Ridge: 300–610 m	Paleozoic Era: shales, limestone, sandstone, and dolomite
Highland Rim	Deeply dissected plateaus and sandstone barrens	210–340 m	Cretaceous and Tertiary Periods: limestone, sandstone, shale, and loess
Cumberland Plateau	High, narrow, flat-topped ridges bordered by steep mountain slopes	490–610 m	Paleozoic Era and Cretaceous Period: interbedded sandstone, shales, and quartzite

Sources: Adapted from May (1965) and Smalley (1979, 1982).

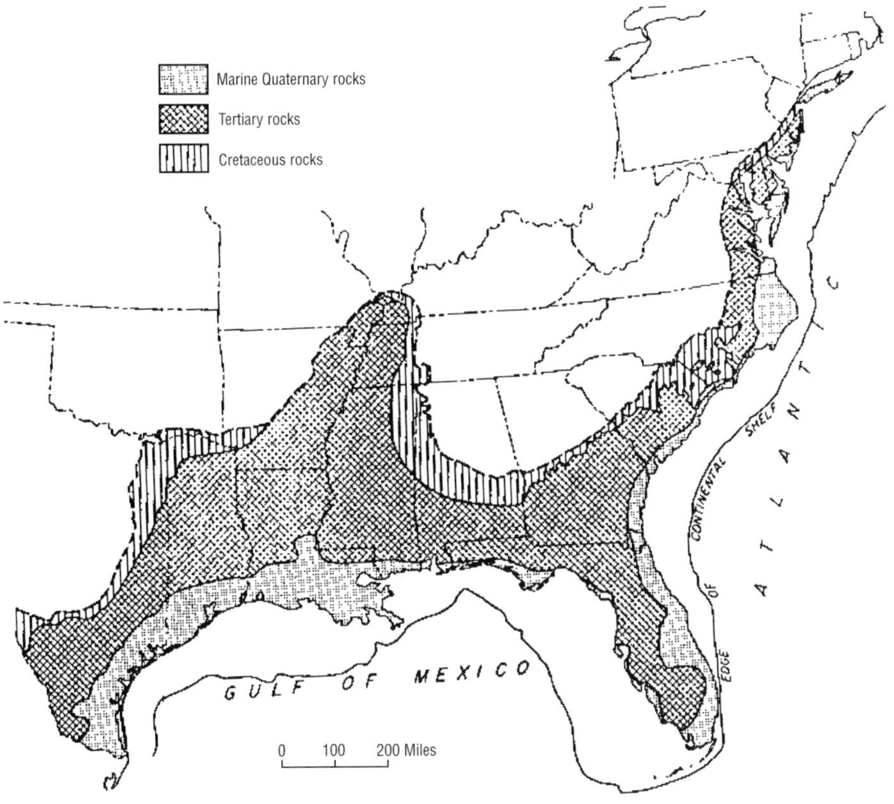

widely meandering stream channels that terminate in estuaries along the coast. The lower lying flat terraces have ill-defined drainage systems, and runoff moves slowly through sloughs and slow-moving streams to the Atlantic Ocean and the Gulf of Mexico.

Forest soils of the lower Coastal Plain are primarily well-drained sands (Ultisols and Alfisols), organic soils (Spodosols and Histosols), or alluvial soils and deep sands (Entisols). Ground-Water Podzols with organic spodic horizons (Spodosols) dominate extensive areas of imperfectly to poorly drained sands of Georgia and Florida and have local importance elsewhere. A common name given to much of the wet lower Coastal Plain, dominated by Spodosols, is "flatwoods." Pine–shrub bogs on clay soils that do not have distinct drainage patterns are called "pocosins." Pocosins are found on all terraces of the lower Coastal Plain in the Carolinas and Georgia. Erosion of most lower Coastal Plain soils is slight, and inherent fertility is low because of extensive leaching (Ralston 1978, Thornbury 1965). Because of the wide range in topography, drainage, and soil nutrition, loblolly pine growth in the lower

Marine Quaternary rocks

Tertiary rocks

Cretaceous rocks

GULF OF MEXICO

0   100   200 Miles

Figure 3-3—The Coastal Plain with ages of underlying rocks (adapted from Monroe 1953).

Coastal Plain can range from excellent to very poor even within the same hectare.

Both the middle and upper Coastal Plains have gently rolling to hilly topography, well-developed natural drainages, and extremely diverse soils. Sandy to sandy loam surface soils with friable, kaolinitic, clay subsoils (Ultisols) predominate in both parts of the region and support fine stands of loblolly pine. Loess-derived upland soils (Alfisols) most suitable for loblolly pine are subject to erosion, particularly where thin layers cover sandy sediments. Logging compaction can severely reduce soil aeration in these soils. Alfisols derived from phosphatic limestones, especially in north-central Florida, also support good mixed stands of loblolly pine and hardwoods. Soils that are generally unsuitable for loblolly pine include calcareous Vertisols, which have shrinking and swelling clays, and associated Alfisols in the Black Prairies of Alabama, Mississippi, and east Texas, and Carolina bay soils (Histosols) from Virginia to Georgia (Buol 1973, Ralston 1978).

The Piedmont

At the boundary of the Piedmont and the Coastal Plain, that is, the fall line, metamorphic rocks of Paleozoic Era extend under the Cretaceous formations. The Piedmont Plateau is a weathered peneplain created by erosion of the older Appalachian Plateau and Blue Ridge Mountains. The topography is conspicuously hilly, and landscapes are finely dissected by numerous rivers, streams, and small branch bottoms. The Piedmont Plateau forms a continuum between the mountains and the Coastal Plain, and continues to furnish sediments to the Atlantic Coastal Plain. The Piedmont Plateau extends southwesterly from New Jersey to Alabama and widens toward the south. It is about 16 km wide at its narrowest point and about 200 km wide near the Virginia–North Carolina border. It ends abruptly at the southern terminus of the newer Appalachians in east-central Alabama (Thornbury 1965; figure 3-2). The dominant parent rocks are gneiss and schist, with some marble and quartzite, which were derived by metamorphism of older sedimentary and volcanic rocks (Hunt 1967). Extensive acid igneous intrusions occur in southern and eastern areas. Fine-textured volcanic material of the Carolina slate belt occurs from Virginia to mid-Georgia. Sandstones and shales are of local importance in the Triassic basins of North Carolina and Virginia. Basic intrusions are found throughout the region (Ralston 1978).

In the Piedmont, general slopes are to the east and north and average roughly 4 m/km. Elevations range from about 30 to 150 m at the northeastern extreme of the loblolly pine range. To the south, elevations range from about 150 m along the fall line to between 300 and 550 m at the foot of the Appalachians. The principal upland soils of the Piedmont are moderately productive Ultisols that are characterized by red and yellow, friable,

kaolinitic, clay subsoils (Ralston 1978). The region also contains significant areas of Alfisols with brown or mottled plastic montmorillonite clay subsoils as well as highly productive alluvial Entisols.

The Interior Highlands

The natural range of loblolly pine extends into the Ridge and Valley province of northern Georgia, northern Alabama, and southeastern Tennessee and into the Cumberland Plateau and the Highland Rim of northern Alabama and south-central Tennessee. The topography and soils of these Interior Highlands are extremely variable, and the boundary between the Highlands and the upper Coastal Plain is indistinct and irregular.

The Ridge and Valley province ranges from about 65 to 160 km wide and separates the Cumberland Plateau from the Blue Ridge Mountains. Its topography is characterized by a series of valley floors intermixed with long, narrow, zigzagging ridges. Elevations range from about 180 m in the valley bottoms to about 600 m along the ridgetops. The Cumberland Plateau is just west of the Ridge and Valley province. It extends from northern Alabama to eastern Kentucky, is underlain by massive sandstone layers, and has a topography characterized by winding, narrow-crested ridges and narrow valleys. In some places, variable sandstone weathering has produced upland flats and mesalike knobs. Elevations range from an average of about 180 m in the southern portion of the Ridge and Valley province and along the valley floors to about 460 m along the ridgetops in northern Alabama and more than 600 m in Tennessee. The Highland Rim encircles the Nashville Basin and has ridgetops about 240 to 335 m above sea level and local relief of about 60 to 120 m. Northern Alabama and east-central Tennessee are in the eastern Highland Rim region. The western Highland Rim region includes extreme northwest Alabama and central Tennessee. The Highland Rim is generally underlain by a series of Mississippian Period limestones of varying coarseness, purity, and solubility. Unconsolidated Cretaceous Period sands and gravels cover the uplands in almost all of the Rim (Smalley 1979, 1980, 1982, 1983, 1984).

Unique Areas

The lost pines population of loblolly pines grows in the Texas counties of Caldwell, Fayette, and Bastrop, more than 160 km west of the main range of the species (see chapter 1, figure 1-2). Rainfall in this area averages only one-half to two-thirds of that in the pine belt of east Texas, and July and August are the driest months. Loblolly pine also occupies special niches along the tops of ridges on the Atlantic Coast barrier islands. The distribution of loblolly pine on these islands is strongly controlled by tidal immersion, wave exposure, salt spray exposure, and catastrophic events such as hurricanes and fires (Willis and Zaneveld 1971). Disturbances such as logging, livestock grazing, and surface fires increase the proportion of loblolly pine at the expense of evergreen oaks (Bratton and Davison 1987). However, crown fires destroy loblolly pines, whereas the hardwoods sprout after crown fires (Davison and Bratton 1988). Little is known about the range of salt tolerance among loblolly pine genotypes.

Physiographic Site Classification

Sound management of loblolly pine begins with a thorough understanding of the physiographic, biotic, climatic, and edaphic factors associated with the diverse habitats in which the species grows. Techniques of site classification must be flexible enough so that sites growing loblolly pine and sites supporting no vegetation or only undesirable species can be classified consistently and in the same terms. Furthermore, a practical system must be economical, applicable to stands of all sizes and to all classes of ownership, and easy to use. The diversity of environments on which loblolly pine grows makes it difficult to construct such a system. The character of a Coastal Plain site can change drastically within a few meters due to a slight rise or fall in elevation. Similarly, on an upland site, a short distance can separate a slope from a river bottom or a ridgetop. Not all of the South's forest soils have been surveyed, so soil maps are not always available to assist managers in evaluating site quality. Even when survey information is available, site quality can vary widely within soil mapping units.

The growth potential of a particular area or forest site is usually determined by measuring or estimating heights of dominant and codominant trees. However, this procedure can be applied only where there are adequate numbers of trees at least 10 years old. Where reliable height growth information is not available, growth potential can be predicted by reference to one or more environmental variables. For example, landform is a practical basis for rapid and accurate classification of loblolly pine sites and for projections of yields in many parts of the South. Landform classifications are based on easily recognized topographic features and geologic differences. Topography exerts an indirect effect on growth by modifying local climates and soils and, particularly, by modifying moisture and temperature regimes.

Many organizations with substantial forest land holdings now rely on classification systems that combine landform and topographic variables, soil drainage differences, soil taxonomic units, and other holistic factors to predict loblolly pine growth (Broerman 1978, Campbell 1978, Wiggins 1978). Because different positions on a landscape support distinctive plant communities, vegetation can be used to supplement data on topography and soils in the delineation of sites (Van Lear and Jones 1987).

Physiographic site classifications, based on satellite imagery and ancillary soils data, are available for the states of Louisiana and Mississippi, which have only Coastal Plain sites, and for the Coastal Plain, Piedmont, and Highlands of Alabama and South Carolina. Within these 4 states, more than 60 loblolly pine habitat regions have been identified and described. Loblolly pine grows extensively in six of the eight physiographic regions of Louisiana (table 3-2). It is absent only from the Coastal

Table 3-2—Loblolly pine forest site classification in Louisiana

Region and land type	Area (thousands of ha)	% of state	Loblolly pine site index* (m)
Upper Coastal Plain	2,592	21.7	
Lower loam hills	2,333	19.5	22–27
Interior flatwoods	259	2.2	21–26
Middle Coastal plain	1,256	10.6	
Southern loam hills, rugged topography	637	5.3	<20–28
Southern loam hills, gentle topography	68	0.6	26–28
Fragipan loam hills	368	3.1	24–29
Southern loessial loam hills, gentle topography	57	0.5	26–32
Central interior flatwoods	127	1.1	27–28
Lower Coastal Plain	1,076	8.9	
Southwest flatwoods	766	6.4	24–26
Southeast flatwoods	161	1.3	26–28
Terrace flatwoods	149	1.2	26–30
Deep loess hill and bluff	41	0.4	27–32
Alluvial floodplains	274	2.3	27–30
Mississippi terrace	710	6.0	
Baton Rouge terrace	101	0.8	20–30
Opelousas ridge	271	2.3	26–32
Macon ridge	269	2.3	26–29
Bastrop	68	5.5	26–27
Coastal prairie	658	5.5	25–27

Source: Adapted from Evans and others (1983).

* Base age 50 years.

Table 3-3—Loblolly pine forest site classifications in Alabama and Mississippi

Region and land type	Loblolly pine site index*(m)
Highland†	
Limestone	20–26
Chert hills	20–26
Sandstone	18–24
Shale	17–23
Mixed sandstone-shale	18–24
Old alluvium	21–27
Mountain colluvium	23–27
Highland‡	
Quartzite ridge	17–23
Slate-phyllite ridge	18–24
Schist hills	18–24
Piedmont	
Granite-gneiss	20–27
Chlorite schist plains	18–24
Upper Coastal Plain	
Chalk (clay soils)	23–26
Clay plains	21–30§
Clay hills (shallow topsoils)	23–26
Clay hills (deep loamy topsoils)	24–27
Loam hills and plains	21–32
Sand hills and plains (deep sands)	20–23
Sand hills and plains (loamy)	24–26
Middle Coastal Plain	
Clay hills	23–26
Loam hills and plains	21–32
Sand hills and plans (deep sands)	20–23
Sand hills and plans (loamy)	24–26
Lower Coastal Plain	
Loam hills and bluffs	21–32
Old sand dunes	21–26
Deep loess	
Loess hills and bluffs	21–32
Loess plains	21–26
All regions	
Large floodplain	26–35
Small floodplain	26–35

Source: adapted from Hodgkins and others (1979).
* Base age 50 years.
† Limestone Plateau, Cumberland Plateau, Great Appalachian Valley.
‡ Blue Ridge, Talladega Mountains, Piedmont.
§ 21 to 26 m on clays, 24 to 27 m on silts, and 26 to 30 m on floodplains.

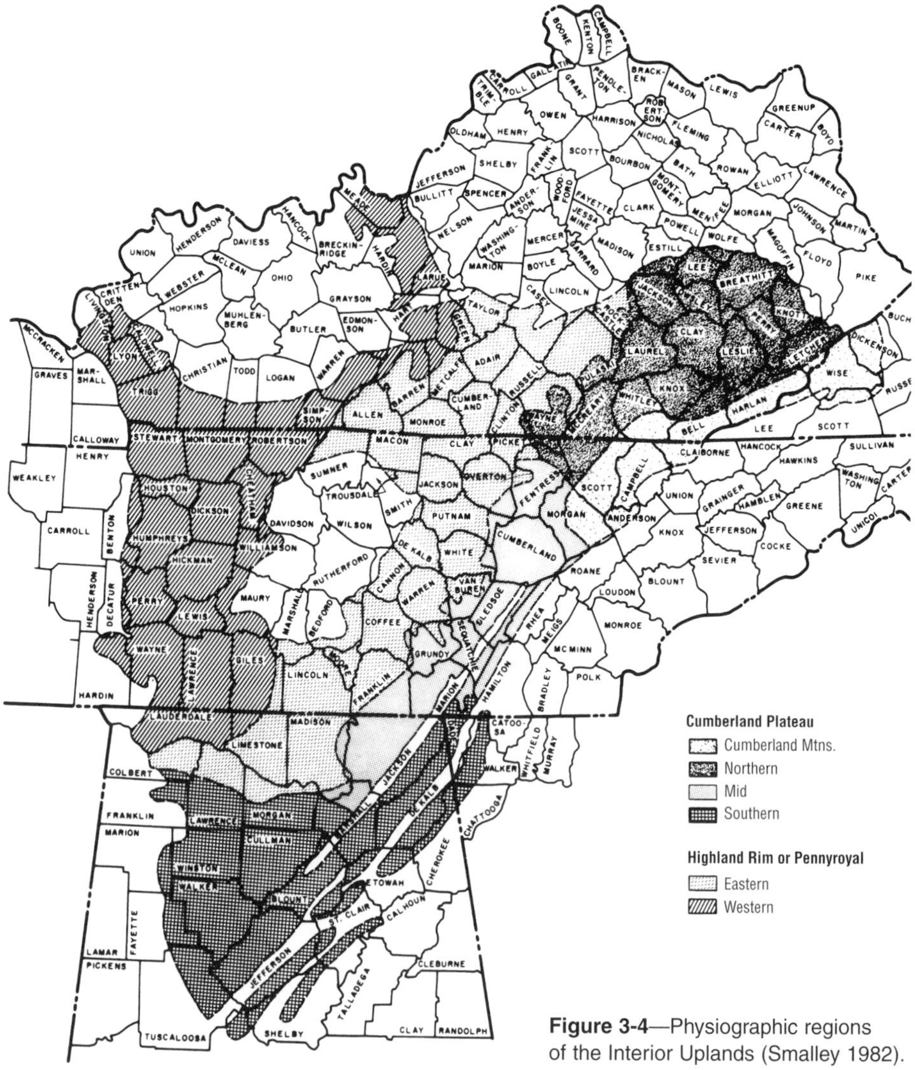

Figure 3-4—Physiographic regions of the Interior Uplands (Smalley 1982).

Marsh region and has limited representation in the Alluvial Floodplain region (figure 3–2 and table 3-2). Loblolly pine grows well on most land types in Mississippi, Alabama, and South Carolina (tables 3-3 and 3-4).

A comprehensive forest site classification system based on landforms is available for the Cumberland Plateau and Highland Rim physiographic regions of Alabama, Georgia, Kentucky, and Tennessee (figure 3-4). Of the 21 land types in the southern Cumberland Plateau region, 17 support natural stands of loblolly pine, and loblolly pine is among the most desirable forest species on 20 land types (Smalley 1979). Of the 21 land types in the mid-Cumberland Plateau region, 16 support natural loblolly pine stands, and loblolly pine is a pre-

ferred species on 13 land types. The generally high average elevation of 450 to 600 m above sea level, versus 300 to 365 m for the southern Cumberland Plateau, is the primary factor reducing the presence of loblolly pine in the mid-Cumberland Plateau (Smalley 1982). Loblolly pine is not native to the northern Cumberland Plateau, and plantings are not recommended (Smalley 1986). Loblolly pine occurs naturally in 30 of the 49 forest types on the western Highland Rim and is among the most desirable species for 28 of the 30 forest types (Smalley 1980). Loblolly pine has been planted successfully in western Kentucky. It grows naturally on 33 of the 49 land types on the eastern Highland Rim and is a preferred species for forest management on all land types except major river bottoms and sites that are transitions to the Kentucky Bluegrass region (Smalley 1983). Plantings have extended the range of loblolly pine throughout the Highland Rim region and well above its natural elevational limit of 335 m. Although trees will grow at elevations up to 640 m, glaze storms occasionally do severe damage, and periods of subzero weather result in needle desiccation and browning.

Table 3-4—Loblolly pine forest site classifications in South Carolina

Region and land type	Area (thousands of ha)	% of state	Loblolly pine site index* (m)	Region and land type	Area (thousands of ha)	% of state	Loblolly pine site index* (m)	Region and land type	Area (thousands of ha)	% of state	Loblolly pine site index* (m)
Blue Ridge	133	1.7		Upper Coastal Plain	941	12.0		Lower Coastal Plain	2,191	27.9	
Blue Ridge	91	1.2	NA	Sandhills	694	8.8	21–26	Upper terraces	1,264	16.1	26–27
Chauga Ridges	42	0.5	NA	Upper loam hills, gentle top	52	0.7	23–27	Lower terraces	848	10.8	27
				Upper loam hills, moderate top	180	2.3	24–26	Recent beach ridges	79	1.0	26–27
Piedmont	2,653	33.9		Redhills	15	0.2	24–27				
Upper foothills	44	0.6	NA					Floodplains and terraces	656	8.4	
Lower foothills	170	2.2	21–24	Middle Coastal Plain	816	10.4		Alluvial floodplains	293	3.7	29–30
Interior plateau	770	9.8	15–30	Southwestern loam hills	385	4.9	24–27	River terraces	116	1.5	26–27
Charlotte belt	1,079	13.8	24–30	Clay hills	15	0.2	23–26	Blackwater River floodplains	247	3.2	NA
Carolina slate belt	462	5.9	15–21	Northeastern loam plains	416	5.3	24–27	Coastal marsh and islands	324	4.1	24–27
Southern Piedmont hills	69	0.9	21–26					Area in large reservoirs	123	1.6	
Kings Mountain	59	0.7	24–30					Total	7,837	100.0	

Source: adapted from Myers and others (1986).   NA = not applicable.   * Base age 50 years.

Climatic and Atmospheric Factors Affecting Tree Growth

The average length of the growing season or frost-free period ranges from about 180 days at the northern end of the Coastal Plain to more than 300 days along the Florida Gulf Coast (Hunt 1967). The climate throughout loblolly pine's range is predominantly humid with long, hot summers and mild winters.

Conditions known to substantially influence loblolly pine growth and reproduction include air temperature, precipitation (especially summer rainfall and winter glaze or ice storms), summer soil water deficits, and the solar radiation budget. All but the solar radiation budget are most favorable for tree growth near the Gulf and southern Atlantic Coasts and least favorable at the northern and western limits of the species' range. Warm, moist, tropical air masses originate over the Gulf of Mexico and the South Atlantic and produce more total rainfall, fewer days of inadequate soil moisture, and more moderate temperatures along the coast than in the interior. Although the northern part of the range is relatively moist, severe weather conditions (for example, winter glaze or ice storms) can heavily damage trees and reduce overall growth (see chapter 10).

Temperature

Mean annual soil temperatures range from 15 °C in the North to 21 °C in the South (figure 3-5). Mean annual air temperatures range from 13 °C along the mid-Atlantic Seaboard to 21 °C in north Florida (figure 3-5). Mean daily temperatures for each month of the year are available for many locations across the range of the species (US Department of Commerce 1968). Temperatures average more than 24 °C and frequently exceed 38 °C in the midsummer. Midwinter temperatures average 2 to 17 °C and occasionally drop to –23 °C in the northern and western part of the range (Fowells 1965). Winter temperatures appear to be the primary factor limiting the northern range of loblolly pine. Extremely cold periods during the spring adversely affect seed germination, survival of newly germinated or.newly planted seedlings, both root and shoot elongation of trees, and flower and subsequent cone production. Friend and Hafley (1989) found that high cumulative mean monthly temperatures from March to May were positively related with rapid tree diameter growth in North Carolina.

The temperature in and around the canopy of a stand varies considerably on a diurnal basis. The air is coolest near the forest floor during the entire day. On clear days, there are very unstable temperature gradients just

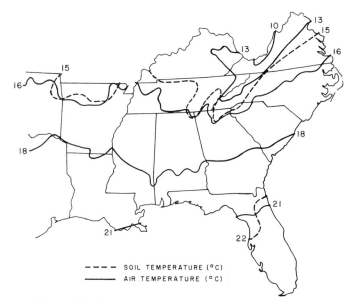

Figure 3-5—Mean annual air and soil temperatures for the range of loblolly pine (USDA 1941).

Table 3-5—Effect of CO_2 concentration on total thickness and on thickness of epidermis, mesophyll, and endodermis-transfusion tissue-vascular bundle (E-TT-VB) zones of needles from 1-year-old loblolly pines

CO_2 treatment* (ppm)	Needle thickness by zone (µm)			
	Epidermis	Mesophyll	E-TT-VB	Total needle
340A	56	274	337	666
340	57	278	328	663
520	55	252	322	629
718	56	264	355	675
910	56	305	365	726
LSD 0.05	6	26	21	39

Source: adapted from Thomas and Harvey (1983).

* The value 340A is ambient plot (no chamber); other values are from controlled environment chambers.

above the crowns, and a strong inversion of about 8 °C develops below the crowns. At night, the air just above the trees stabilizes, whereas the air just below the crown becomes unstable. On rainy days, the temperature inversion beneath the tree crowns is less than 1 °C (Hosker and others 1974).

If there is no severe soil moisture deficit, high ambient air temperature is the environmental condition that most strongly promotes spring shoot growth of seedlings and saplings (Boyer 1970). However, spring growth in one tree can begin as much as 3 weeks before spring growth begins in a neighboring tree, suggesting that individual trees have different temperature accumulation thresholds for growth (Boyer 1976).

Carbon Dioxide Enrichment

Short- and long-term carbon dioxide enrichment, from the ambient level of 340 ppm to about 500 ppm, seems to consistently promote seedling growth. Trees may (Fetcher and others 1988, Rogers and others 1983, Sionit and others 1985) or may not (Tolley and Strain 1984a, 1984b) respond to levels above 500 ppm, or the response may be reduced. For example, increasing CO_2 from 350 ppm to 500 or 650 ppm over three growing seasons significantly increased cellulose production. The greatest response occurred between 350 and 500 ppm (Doyle 1986). Variability in response to CO_2 above 500 ppm may partially be the result of differences in soil moisture. Tolley and Strain (1984a, 1984b) found that 14 days of water stress seemed to promote the positive effect of an elevated CO_2 level on seedlings. Total needle thickness of 1-year-old loblolly pines grown in an atmosphere containing 910 ppm of CO_2 was 9% greater than that of loblolly pines grown at 340 ppm of CO_2. All areas of the needles showed an increase except the epidermis (table 3-5). Greater cell expansion at high CO_2 levels was attributed to increased osmotic potential of cells having high total carbohydrate content (Thomas and Harvey 1983).

Precipitation

Annual gross precipitation in most of the loblolly pine ecosystem ranges from 122 to 163 cm. It is 142 to 163 cm along the Gulf Coast and 122 to 142 cm along the Atlantic Coast, but declines to less than 102 cm at the semiarid western extreme of the species' range (Bilan and others 1977; figure 3-6). Snowfall accounts for a small percentage of the total precipitation in the more northerly portions of the range. Precipitation is generally adequate for tree growth throughout the species' range, except along the western extreme in Texas and Oklahoma. The patterns of mean annual precipitation and potential evapotranspiration for east Gulf Coast and inland areas are depicted in figure 3-7. In coastal areas, monthly averages for mean annual precipitation range from a low of about 7 cm in October to a high of 16 to 18 cm in midsummer. Inland areas have the least precipitation in October and the most in winter.

The pattern of rainfall varies by location and significantly affects growth periodicity. The South Atlantic region tends to have more rainfall during the growing season than during the dormant season, whereas the mid-South states of Arkansas, Louisiana, Mississippi, and Texas tend to have more rain in the dormant season than in the growing season (figure 3-8). In Texas, tree diameter growth is positively affected by the number of rain days during the current year and the total summer rainfall during the previous year (Chang and Aguilar 1980). In general, adequate growing season rainfall (April to September) minimizes soil-water deficits and increases site productivity and tree growth. Loblolly pine growth and development in Louisiana and southern Mississippi is greatest if the growing-season rainfall is about 61 cm/yr, the cool-season rainfall is about 79 cm/yr, and the available soil moisture in the subsoil is about 7% (Shoulders and Tiarks 1980). Early growing-

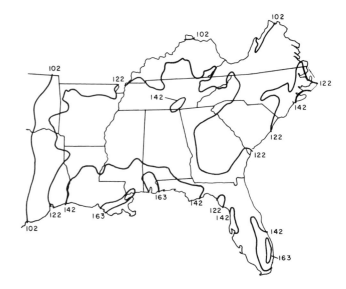

Figure 3-6—Normal annual gross precipitation over the range of loblolly pine (adapted from US Department of Commerce 1968).

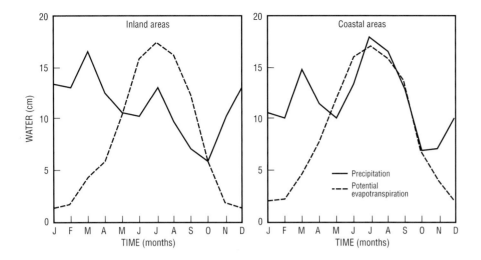

Figure 3-7—Pattern of mean annual precipitation and potential evapotranspiration in representative coastal and inland portions of the loblolly pine range (adapted from Switzer and others 1978).

season (April to June) rainfall is critical to natural regeneration in eastern Virginia. If rainfall during this period exceeds 25 cm, newly germinated seedlings are able to develop extensive root and shoot systems that effectively withstand subsequent moisture fluctuations during the first growing season (Trousdell and Wenger 1963).

Interception, Evaporation, and Evapotranspiration

"Interception" is a term applied to moisture that lands on vegetation or litter but never reaches the ground. Almost all of it is returned to the atmosphere by evaporation. Interception of rainfall and subsequent evaporation from crowns, stems, and surface litter accounts for 10 to 22% of the total rainfall in stands with closed canopies. Dense stands intercept from 10 to 25% more rainfall, depending on the intensity of the rain, than do sparse stands. Interception is greatest during the growing season, when quantities of foliage and evapotranspiration are greatest (Swank and others 1972, Switzer and others 1988). Without thinning or severe mortality, the crown density of loblolly pine stands increases

until about stand age 20 (Switzer and others 1968). Loss of precipitation through interception and evaporation appears to stabilize at about 25 cm/yr in fully stocked stands. A litter interception loss of about 5 cm/yr is included in this total (table 3-6). Although interception and evaporation play important roles in the effectiveness of gross annual precipitation, they are least significant when a large amount of rain falls in a single storm.

Interception by hardwood stands in the Piedmont of South Carolina, although highly variable, averages about 15 cm/yr or about 11% of annual precipitation. This is about 10 cm less than interception by loblolly pines (Swank and others 1972). Thus, conversion of Piedmont hardwood stands to loblolly pine could lower streamflow by 25% just as a result of increased interception and evaporation losses. Douglass (1974) estimated that planting about 12 million ha of southern hardwood sites to pine could reduce water yield by an amount equal to the annual water requirements of about 30 million people.

Evapotranspiration (ETS) is transpiration from trees and other vegetation and evaporation from the forest floor and soil surfaces. Potential ETS ranges from 1 to 2 cm/mo in December and January to about 17 cm/mo in midsummer (figure 3-7). In coastal areas, precipitation normally exceeds ETS except during hot and dry periods. In inland areas, ETS normally exceeds precipitation by several centimeters per month throughout the summer and early fall.

Table 3-6—Annual loss of rainfall by interception and evaporation in five South Carolina stands

Stand type	Stand age (yrs)	Average basal area (m²/ha)	Annual interception (cm)	
			Loss from litter	Total loss*
Loblolly	5	14.9	NM	18.5
Loblolly	10	25.3	5.3	29.7
Loblolly	20	31.7	5.6	24.4
Loblolly	30	34.9	6.1	24.4
Mixed shortleaf/hardwood	Mature	21.6	4.6	23.6

Source: adapted from Swank and others (1972).

NM = not measured.

* Including loss from litter; precipitation averaged 137 cm/yr during the study period; long-term average for the area is 130 cm/yr.

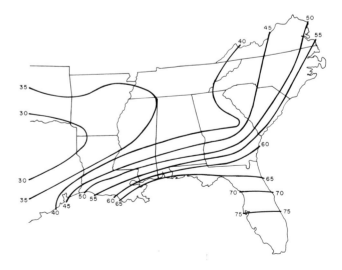

Figure 3-8—June through September rainfall in centimeters for the loblolly pine ecosystem (adapted from US Department of Commerce 1968).

Throughfall and Stemflow

Rainfall that lands on trees but does not evaporate reaches the forest floor either as throughfall or as stemflow. Throughfall (rainfall that reaches the ground by passing directly through holes in the canopy or by dripping off needles and branches) decreases as crown cover and basal area increase. Throughfall in a well-stocked loblolly pine stand is usually about 70 to 85% of gross precipitation and can reach 95% of gross precipitation if canopy density is very low. In an 11-year-old southeast Oklahoma plantation, throughfall during the growing season, increased by approximately 3% of total rainfall for every 4 m²/ha of reduction in basal area (Stogsdill and others 1989). Throughfall is usually greater in an old, thinned stand than in a young dense stand because the former has more openings in the canopy. However, the frequency, duration, and rate of rainfall or the spatial distribution of the canopy, or both, may be more important than stand density or tree size in determining the amount of precipitation reaching the forest floor as throughfall. When rain is intense, a greater proportion of the total reaches the forest floor. Also, more rainfall reaches the forest floor once the canopy is thoroughly wet (Rogerson 1967, Swank and others 1972, Switzer and others 1988).

A small but important portion of the total precipitation reaches the forest floor as stemflow. Stemflow is moisture that leaches through the canopy and finally reaches the ground by running down tree stems. It increases with increasing tree size. Stemflow accounts for about 9 to 18% of the gross annual precipitation in unthinned plantations from 5 through 23 years of age. This moisture, and the heavy load of nutrients the moisture carries, are deposited on only about 25% of the total ground surface area (Swank and others 1972, Switzer and others 1988). When storms are of short duration or of low intensity, there often is no stemflow because the rough bark absorbs all the moisture as it moves down the boles. However, stemflow cannot be ignored when studying the moisture budget without running the risk of significantly overestimating interception loss (Swank and others 1972). Nutrient concentrations in precipitation increase with passage through the canopy. Thus, concentrations in stemflow are equal to or greater than concentrations in throughfall, and concentrations in throughfall are greater than or equal to concentrations in rainfall.

The Solar Radiation Budget

Overhead light is essential for prompt and adequate regeneration of loblolly pine. Light is also the factor that most strongly controls seedling growth and development. Four-year-old planted trees growing in the Georgia Piedmont required 125 to 150 langleys/day [1 langley is a unit of solar radiation equivalent to 1 gram-calorie

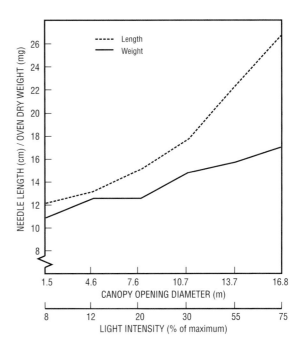

Figure 3-9—Relationship of light intensity (canopy opening size) to length and ovendry weight of needles of loblolly pine seedlings (adapted from Jackson 1962).

per square centimeter of irradiated surface] to survive (March and Skeen 1976). In general, the longer the photoperiod, the more rapidly loblolly pines grow, even when the added light is of exceedingly low intensity. Growth of the juvenile stem (from the cotyledonary node to the first terminal bud) and of primary needles is greatest at photoperiods of 12 to 14 hours. Seedling height growth can be doubled by increasing day length from 10 to 15 hours. Stem, branch, and secondary needle growth of seedlings is greatest when day length is at least 16 hours. However, the response to day length is controlled genetically. Trees from more northerly locations, such as northern Georgia, grow 20 to 40% slower than do trees from more southerly locations, such as northern Florida, whether days are long or short (see chapter 7). The kind of light also affects tree growth. For example, supplementary incandescent light promotes more growth than does supplementary fluorescent light (Allen and McGregor 1962, Downs and Piringer 1958).

There can be substantial differences in needle length, needle weight, specific gravity, and tracheid length of seedlings growing under different light intensities during the first 5 years of life (figures 3-9 and 3-10). When available sunlight was 75% of maximum (canopy opening approximately 17 m in diameter), needles grew to 27 cm in length. Needle length was only 12 cm when 8% of maximum sunlight was available. Needle width and diameter vary with the amount of available light, but not as much as needle length. In one study, needle width increased from 0.94 to 1.26 mm, and needle thickness increased from 0.47 to 0.68 mm with increasing light intensity (Jackson 1962).

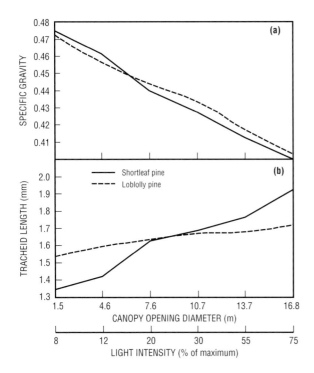

Figure 3-10—Relationship of light intensity (canopy opening size) to specific gravity (**a**) and tracheid length (**b**) of the stems of short-leaf and loblolly pine seedlings (adapted from Jackson 1962).

Loblolly pines significantly modify incoming radiation and greatly influence radiation exchange at the forest floor. Very young trees absorb very little of the total incoming radiation. As trees grow and their crowns spread, more of the incoming radiation is absorbed and less reaches the forest floor. Because the tops of crowns do not meet, radiation is randomly intercepted by the entire live crown of each tree. Trees tend to grow needles to fill gaps deep in their crowns (Sinclair and Knoerr 1982).

Table 3-7—Role of the canopy of a 32-year old loblolly pine plantation* in modifying the radiation exchange at the forest floor.

	Radiation (langleys)					
	Spring			Fall		
	Short-wave	Long-wave	All-wave	Short-wave	Long-wave	All-wave
Above the canopy						
Downward	652	753	1,405	390	594	984
Upward	–70	–960	–1,030	–50	–814	–864
Net change	582	–207	375	340	–220	120
Beneath the canopy						
Downward	208	855	1,063	64	714	778
Upward	–51	–895	–946	–14	–754	–768
Net change	157	–40	117	50	–40	10

Source: adapted from Gay and Knoerr (1975).

* The plantation averaged 752 trees/ha and a basal area of 37.7 m²/ha; trees averaged 23.4 m tall.

Seasonal change in solar zenith angle and concentration of needles results in seasonal variation in canopy absorptive efficiency (table 3-7). Gay and Knoerr (1975) determined the fall and spring radiation budget for a 32-year-old loblolly pine plantation in the Piedmont of North Carolina. On clear days in early May, about one-third of the daily total incoming solar radiation was transmitted to the forest floor. Thickening of the canopy with new needles during the summer, combined with an expanded solar zenith angle, resulted in only 8% of the daily total incoming solar radiation reaching the forest floor during late October and early November. Crown cover was estimated to be 0.35 in the spring and 0.50 in the fall after canopy growth had ceased. The season of the year also affects the radiant energy supply. The canopy greatly reduces both the amount of shortwave energy absorbed and the net loss of longwave energy at the forest floor.

The Forest Floor

The forest floor protects the soil surface by modifying moisture movement and ameliorating the effects of climate. The forest floor is composed of newly fallen needles and other litter (the L layer), partially decomposed material with recognizable needles (the fermentation or F layer), and mostly decomposed litter (the humus or H layer).

The composition of the forest floor is directly related to the combined overstory and understory vegetation. Physical and chemical properties of the forest floor and the soil surface change during succession from herbaceous dominance to loblolly pine dominance to mixed-hardwood dominance. As much as 20% of the litter under 1- and 2-year-old loblolly pine stands is herbaceous, but the proportion of herbaceous litter decreases to 1% by stand age 4 and is negligible thereafter. By

stand age 10, needles in various stages of decomposition make up about 70 to 90% of the forest floor. Branches, cones, and bark make up the remainder (Jorgensen and others 1980, Van Lear and Goebel 1976). Even when loblolly pine basal area is as high as 31 m²/ha, as much as 20% of litter comes from the hardwood understory (Lockaby and Taylor-Boyd 1986).

Switzer and others (1979) traced the progress of succession as a mixed loblolly-shortleaf pine stand in the small-pole stage developed through maturity and was replaced by a mixture of oaks, hickories, and pines over the course of 175 years. Pine litter made up 98% of the L layer under the stand of pole-sized pines but only 12% of the L layer under the stand of mature oaks, hickories, and pines (table 3-8).

Table 3-8—Composition of the litter layer of the forest floor by stage of succession and period of development

Stage of succession	Period of development	% Composition of the L layer*	
		Coniferous	Deciduous
Early	Small pole	98 a	2 e
	Large pole	86 b	14 d
Middle	Standard	77 b	23 c
	Veteran	49 c	51 b
Late	Oak–hickory–pine	12 d	88 a

Source: adapted from Switzer and others (1979).

* Within a column, numbers not followed by a common letter differ significantly at the 95% probability level according to Duncan's new multiple range test.

Table 3-9—Ovendry weight of the forest floor under loblolly pine stands

Location	Stand age (yr)	Basal area (m²/ha)	Annual litterfall (t/ha)	Total litter (t/ha)	Reference
North MS	1	NM	1.5	1.5	McClurkin (1971))
NC Coastal Plain	1	NM	0.8	3.7	Nemeth (1972)
NC Coastal Plain	4	NM	3.6	5.8	Nemeth (1972)
MS Coastal Plain	5	NM	4.5	2.0	Switzer and Nelson (1972)
SC Piedmont	10	23.7	7.7	NM	Metz (1952)
SC Piedmont	10	23.2	4.0	NM	Swank and others (1972)
NC Piedmont	11–15	49.2	4.2	29.0	Wells and Jorgensen (1975)
SC Piedmont	15–17	34.9	4.4	20.8	Van Lear and Goebel (1976)
North MS	16	NM	NM	19.5	McClurkin (1971)
VA Piedmont	16	38.3	NM	24.7	Metz and others (1970)
SC Piedmont	12–17	46.5	NM	36.3	Kodama and Van Lear (1980)
North LA	18–20	31.0	7.2	11.0	Lockaby and Taylor-Boyd (1986)
SC Piedmont	19	NM	NM	25.9	Jorgensen and Wells (1986)
MS Coastal Plain	20	31.7	4.4	NM	Swank and others (1972)
NC Piedmont	20	NM	NM	17.0	Switzer and Nelson (1972)
South IL	20	NM	4.5	37.0	Gilmore and Boggess (1976)
SC Piedmont	21–22	43.1	4.1	NM	Van Lear and Goebel (1976)
SC Piedmont	20–25	23.4	6.3	NM	Metz (1952)
NC Piedmont	24–27	33.8	5.1	NM	Wells and Jorgensen (1975)
SC Piedmont	30	34.9	5.1	NM	Swank and others (1972)
NC Piedmont	31–39	31.6	6.0	NM	Wells and Jorgensen (1975)
SC Piedmont	32–33	39.9	4.2	NM	Van Lear and Goebel (1976)
NC Piedmont	32–40	34	4.2–7.5	32.9	Jorgensen and others (1980)
NC Piedmont	40	NM	NM	29.3	Jorgensen and Wells (1986)
SC Piedmont	62	22.0	4.6*	NM	Wells and others (1972)
SC Coastal Pine	90–100†	25.7	7.8	NM	Gresham (1982)

NM = not measured.

* Seventy-one percent was pine litter, remainder was mixed hardwood litter.

† Stand has 20-year-old loblolly pine understory.

Litter production and total weight of the forest floor are positively correlated to age and basal area stocking of loblolly pine stands. Litter production increases rapidly during early succession, producing considerable forest floor biomass well before crown closure. For very young stands, annual litter production may be only 1 to 2 tonnes per hectare (t/ha). It may take 4 years before a measurable forest floor develops under a plantation (Switzer and Nelson 1972). On good sites, the forest floor can weigh as much as 30 t/ha by stand age 10. In well-stocked pole stands, annual litter production averages 4 to 9 t/ha, depending on site quality. However, weather conditions can cause large variations in annual production of litter. By stand age 15 to 20, the forest floor under a well-stocked stand in the Coastal Plain equilibrates at about 30 to 35 t/ha, and annual litterfall is about 4 to 7 t/ha, depending on site quality. On average Piedmont sites, forest floor weight for plantations and natural stands increases steadily to about 18 t/ha by stand age 23 and reaches equilibrium at approximately 19 t/ha at about stand age 35 (Brender and others 1976, Jorgensen and others 1980). Litter thickness can range from as little as 0.23 cm under 1-year-old stands on eroded sites to 10 cm under rapidly growing 20- to 25-year-old planted stands. In older stands, the litter is also thickest near the trunks of trees where bark sloughing off from trunks mixes with needles. Because loblolly pine grows faster than shortleaf pine, Virginia pine, and eastern redcedar (*Juniperus virginiana* L.), it usually forms a heavier and thicker forest floor with more nutrients than do these other species (McClurkin 1971, Metz and others 1970, Miceli and others 1975). Figure 3-11 and table 3-9 summarize litterfall and accumulation of litter under stands from inception to maturity.

Removal of all or part of a loblolly pine stand causes rapid reductions in both weight and thickness of the forest floor. Thinning a 23-year-old north Mississippi plantation from 29.8 to 17.2 m² of basal area/ha resulted

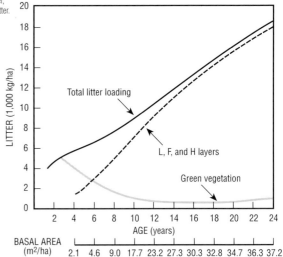

Figure 3-11—Forest floor accumulation in average loblolly pine plantations from 1 to 24 years of age (adapted from Brender and others 1976).

in a 46% decrease in the weight of the forest floor (from 23.3 to 12.5 t/ha) in 2 years. Clearcutting reduced the weight of the forest floor by 59% in 2 years (Dickerson 1972). Three years after clearcutting, weight of the forest floor was still only about 50% of the preharvest weight. By the third year after thinning, weight of the forest floor was 67% of the preharvest weight.

The Soil Resource

Soil type is a key determinant of loblolly pine growth even though the species will grow successfully on soils ranging from flat, poorly drained Spodosols of the lower Coastal Plain to rolling Piedmont and Plateau Ultisols (figure 3-12). Loblolly pines usually grow most rapidly when the topsoil is at least 15 cm deep and there is a very friable, well-drained subsoil to promote rooting. The least productive soils have thin topsoil, impervious layers in the rooting zone, or plastic subsoils. The underlying parent material strongly influences the soil properties and suitability of a soil for loblolly pines.

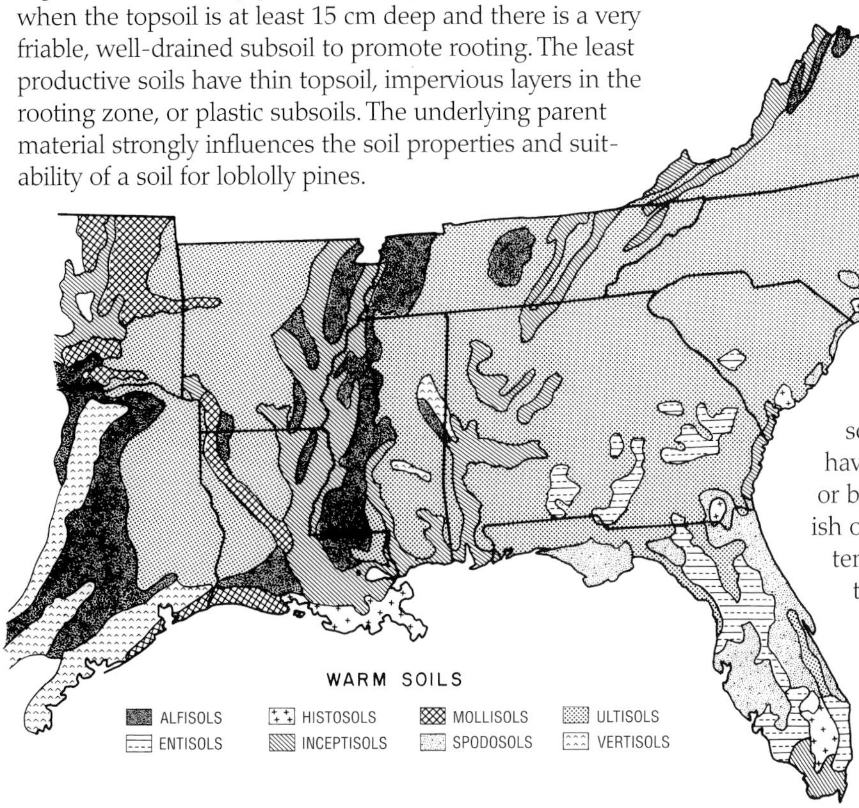

formed, for the most part, in quartz-rich sands having a fluctuating level of ground water. The characteristic feature of Spodosols is a spodic horizon, an accumulation of an amorphous mixture of organic matter and aluminum (Al). A spodic horizon may or may not contain iron (Fe). It is normally within 1.0 m of the soil surface and is often no more than 0.5 m from the surface. Entisols are mineral soils with little or no horizon development.

Westward from Alabama, the broad soil orders are less continuous, but Ultisols, Inceptisols (suborder Aquepts), and Alfisols (suborder Udalfs) predominate. Inceptisols are mineral soils that have altered horizons that have lost bases or Fe and Al but retain some weatherable materials. Inceptisols may have horizons in which translocated silica, Fe, or bases have accumulated. Alfisols are brownish or reddish, freely drained, mineral soils that tend to have a dry period during 3 months of the growing season and may have zones of deposition. Alfisols predominate in central and western Tennessee and along the western fringe of the loblolly pine ecosystem.

WARM SOILS

▨ ALFISOLS	⊡ HISTOSOLS	▩ MOLLISOLS	▦ ULTISOLS
⊟ ENTISOLS	▨ INCEPTISOLS	⊡ SPODOSOLS	⊡ VERTISOLS

Figure 3-12—Soils of the South (adapted from USDA SCS 1975).

Seventy-five percent of the soils on which loblolly pines grow are Ultisols, 11% are Alfisols, 7% are Entisols, and 3% are Spodosols. Only about 1% of the area supporting loblolly pines is in each of the other four soil orders (Buol 1973, Switzer and others 1978).

Most soils of the Atlantic Coastal Plain and of the Piedmont from Georgia to Maryland are Ultisols. Udults and Aquults are the principal suborders. Ultisols are mineral soils derived from a wide variety of parent materials, and their properties are extremely variable. They usually contain an argillic (silicate clay) horizon that is deficient in calcium (Ca). Udults are more or less freely drained, humus-poor Ultisols. Most have light-colored upper horizons that rest on a yellowish-brown to reddish argillic horizon. Aquults are saturated with water at some time of the year (usually in winter and early spring) or are artificially drained. They are typically gray or olive in color (USDA 1975).

In Florida, Spodosols (suborder Aquods), Entisols (suborder Psamments), and Ultisols (suborder Udults) are about equally important. Spodosols are mineral soils

Soil Physical Properties

Predictions of tree growth potential can be improved greatly if soil physical properties are considered. In general, loblolly pines will attain greater heights and dry weights on soils that are loamy throughout the profile than on soils that are predominantly coarse or fine textured (DeBell and others 1982, McKee 1977, Shoulders and Walker 1979; table 3-10). Growth is also limited on deep, excessively drained soils with a deep water table. However, if the water table is accessible to tree roots, loblolly pines can grow well on upland sandy soils. The least productive soils are badly eroded ones with very plastic subsoils (Fowells 1965, Ralston 1978). The

Table 3-10—Loblolly pine seedlings had significantly greater shoot and root dry weights following 1 year of growth in loamy soils than in clay soils

	Components (%)			Shoot height (m)	Dry weight (g)		Shoot-to-root ratio
Soil type	Sand	Clay	Loam		Shoot	Root	
Loamy sand	84	8	8	0.47	5.61	3.42	1.64
Sandy loam	61	20	18	0.47	5.61	2.62	2.14
Clay	24	20	56	0.44	4.33	2.23	1.94

Source: adapted from Stransky and Wilson (1967).

amount of organic matter present in the topsoil is an especially important index to loblolly pine productivity because it largely determines the quantity of nitrogen (N) available for tree growth. High levels of organic matter, especially in the surface of wet clays, improve soil structure, increase soil aeration, and consequently increase tree growth. Depth of the A horizon and the silt-plus-clay content of topsoil are positively correlated with growth in the Alabama Coastal Plain (Goggans and Schultz 1958). When the A horizon is absent, tree growth is normally very poor.

Soil bulk density is closely related to microporosity, macroporosity, moisture-holding capacity (figure 3-13), and hydraulic conductivity. It is affected by soil texture, soil structure, and organic matter content and can be increased by machine compaction during harvesting and regeneration operations. Bulk density averages about 1.2 to 1.5 g/cm^3 for near-surface soil under established loblolly pine stands. It ranges from less than 0.9 g/cm^3 on recently cultivated sites to more than 2.0 g/cm^3 on severely degraded or compacted sites. Bulk density of some soils can be relatively uniform throughout the soil profile. However, other soil profiles vary extensively in bulk density, primarily due to the presence of clay lenses, spodic horizons, or other zones of relative impermeability, which substantially affect soil water relationships (table 3-11).

Microsites and Slopes

Microsite conditions can cause trees only a couple of meters apart to grow and develop differently. Typical microsites are minor changes in topography, such as small, wet depressions or small mounds, or specific soil changes, such as rocky outcrops that create distinctive environmental conditions. Microsite differences often are the cause of superior or inferior growth of specific trees within a stand. Previous agricultural activity can cause microenvironmental differences, but these (for example, a plow line) usually have well-delineated boundaries.

Low "pimple mounds" occupy as much as 30% of the total surface area of some wet sites in southwest Louisiana. These mounds are usually less than 15.0 m in diameter and 0.6 m in height, but trees growing on them have improved health and greater longevity. Although the aboveground features on mounds and flats appear similar, trees on the wet, flat sites have fewer fine roots and mycorrhizae than do their neighbors on mounds, and the usually high water level seems to favor the development and distribution of root pathogens that are more destructive to the root tips of trees growing on the

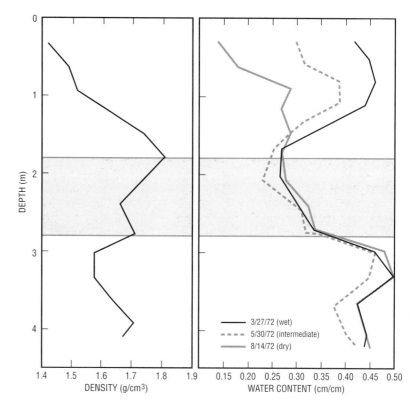

Figure 3-13—Dry soil density profile and water content profiles during wet, intermediate, and dry conditions. The soil is a Guyton silt loam (fine-silty, thermic, typic Glossaqualf) in southwest Louisiana. The argillic horizon is marked by horizontal lines at 1.8 and 2.8 m (adapted from Lorio 1977).

Table 3-11—Soil texture and bulk density throughout the profiles of well drained and poorly drained soils supporting mature loblolly pines in southeast Louisiana

Soil designation	Soil depth (m)	Mechanical analysis (%)			Texture class	Bulk density (g/cm^3)
		Sand	Silt	Clay		
Ruston	0.3	53.1	32.5	14.4	SL	1.59
(Typic Paleudult)	0.6	73.7	17.5	8.8	SL	1.71
located on a flat ridgetop,	0.9	81.2	13.8	5.0	LS	1.68
well drained	1.2	75.6	18.8	5.6	LS–SL	1.63
	1.5	71.3	10.6	18.1	SL	1.75
	1.8	73.8	10.0	16.2	SL	1.76
	2.1	75.0	9.4	15.6	SL	1.72
Myatt-Mashulaville	0.3	74.4	20.0	5.6	LS–SL	1.42
complex	0.6	85.0	5.0	10.0	LS	1.63
(no classification given)	0.9	85.0	7.5	7.5	LS	1.69
located on a flat stream	1.2	72.5	13.1	14.4	SL	1.68
terrace, poorly drained	1.5	93.7	1.9	4.4	S	1.52
	1.8	91.3	3.7	5.0	S	NM
	2.1	95.6	1.9	2.5	S	1.51

Source: adapted from Brewer and Linnartz (1978).

SL = sandy loam, LS = loamy sand, S = sand, NM = not measured.

wetter microsites. When severe droughts do occur, trees on flats have lower average oleoresin exudation pressure. In combination, these factors result in a gradual decline in health of maturing trees growing on the flats, which makes them good hosts for endemic populations of bark beetles and probably other pathogens (Lorio and Hodges 1968, 1971; Lorio and others 1972; also see chapter 10).

Gentle slopes may improve loblolly pine growth, but growth usually declines when slopes are greater than

4%. A slope of 1 to 2% is optimal for tree growth on azonal soils (those without distinct horizons), but a 0% slope is no better than a well-drained, 4% slope. On zonal soils, tree height decreases as slope increases from 1 to 15%. Loss of potential soil moisture through runoff may be the cause of reduced growth on slopes (Shoulders and Walker 1979, Zahner 1958b).

Soil Acidity

Loblolly pines generally grow most rapidly when the pH of the surface soil is between 4.5 and 6.0. They can grow at a reasonably good rate when the pH is as low as 4.0 or as high as 6.7 (Jain and others 1989), especially when other vegetation is controlled. However, mycorrhizal development at pH 6.7 is usually less than a fourth of that at pH 5.8 (Marx 1990). Growing trees can change the soil pH, especially in poorly buffered soils (Binkley and others 1989). Soil pH under the crown declines as soon as a significant quantity of litter accumulates—usually beginning about stand age 4. Leachate from needles and other litter is the principal cause of the lower surface soil pH. Soil pH is lower around a tree's trunk than at the drip line of the crown (table 3-12) because of the high level and mineral concentration of water that runs down the tree's main stem.

Soil Organic Matter

Organic matter concentration in the soil is the single most important indicator of soil quality because organic matter affects the physical and chemical properties of soil and is a storage pool for nutrients. Studies in the loess-covered hills of northern Mississippi and the Coastal Plain of southern Illinois indicate that stands of pole-sized and larger loblolly pines can increase the concentration of organic matter in the surface soil by 20 to more than 100%, compared to nearby unvegetated old fields or surrounding natural stands of hardwoods (Gilmore 1980, Watson and others 1974). Shortleaf pine stands produce even more soil organic matter than loblolly pine at all ages (Gilmore and Rolfe 1980).

Stocking level probably has little effect on organic matter concentration in the surface 15 cm of soil under mature loblolly pines, when initial stocking is between 1,480 and 6,670 trees/ha. However, initial stocking of fewer than about 1,100 trees/ha has been found to produce a measurably lower level of surface soil organic matter during a rotation (Gilmore and Rolfe 1980).

Flora and Fauna on Trees and in Litter and Soil

Numerous plants and animals live directly on trees or in the forest floor or soil. For example, at least 19 species of lichens, including 8 species of *Parmelia*, inhabit the bark of loblolly pines in the Coastal Plain of North Carolina (Culberson 1958). Microbiological populations are extremely variable, depending on soil and site conditions, but numbers of microbes decrease rapidly with increasing soil depth (Lane 1974). High concentrations of meso- and microfauna and microflora, and generally moist and humid conditions, promote the rapid decomposition of organic matter and the recycling of nutrients (Fisher and others 1975, McBrayer and others 1977, Watson and others 1974). There were approximately 5×10^4 fungal colonies/g of dry soil under a 25-year-old loblolly pine plantation in southern Illinois. These colonies decomposed 3,500 kg of roots/ha/yr, or 47% of the annual root production (Fisher and others 1975). Loblolly pine stembark is highly resistant to decomposition by many species of soil- and root-inhabiting fungi (Kuhlman 1970). This is one reason why pine bark makes a good mulch.

The decomposition process in loblolly pine needles begins even before the needles are fully developed. Soon after they begin to grow, new needles are colonized by several fungal species, principally *Alternaria alternata* (Fr.:Fr.) Keissl., *Sclerophoma pythiophila* (Corda) Hoehn., and *Cladosporium* spp. Usually one species dominates at any particular time. The concentration of these fungi is relatively high during the growing season but is drastically reduced during the winter months. Freezing temperatures or ice or both kill the surface-colonizing fungi. First-year needles do not seem to be colonized internally. Internal colonization takes place during the second year, and fungal hyphae are in the stomata and epithelial cells lining the resin canals by the end of the second year (Katz and Lieth 1980). Twenty-nine species of active fungi were found on living and dead needles attached to trees in northern Mississippi (Watson and others 1974).

The litter contains many more microflora (fungi, bacteria, and actinomycetes) than does the soil below it (table 3-13). At least 20 species of fungi were found in the litter and soil layers under a loblolly pine plantation in South Carolina. Ten species were in

Table 3-12—The pH of the surface 15 cm of air-dried mineral soil taken from under southern pine stands of various ages (1–50 yrs)

Sample position	Surface soil pH				
	1 yr	4 yrs	12 yrs	24 yrs	50 yrs
Near tree trunk	5.49	5.29	4.72	4.66	4.82
Crown extremity	5.51	5.37	5.37	5.19	5.39

Source: adapted from Lane (1964).

Table 3-13—Soil microflora in surface organic matter and soil under a South Carolina loblolly pine stand

Litter or soil layer	Fungi (millions)		Bacteria + actinomycetes (millions)	
	per g	per cm²	per g	per cm²
F + H	1.51	0.64	51.5	21.53
0–5 cm	0.13	NM	4.1	NM
13–18 cm	0.03	NM	1.3	NM

Source: adapted from Jorgensen and Hodges (1970).

NM = not measured; F + H = fermentation plus humus layers of litter.

the F and H layers of litter, 12 at 0 to 5 cm in the soil layer, and 14 at 13 to 18 cm in the soil layer (Jorgensen and Hodges 1970). Sixty-two species of fungi, including 29 that were also found in needles attached to trees, were isolated from litter in northern Mississippi. The fungal class Deuteromycetes predominated in the L layer, whereas Ascomycetes were the second most important organisms decomposing the L layer. The classes Deuteromycetes, Phycomycetes, Ascomycetes, and Basidiomycetes were all represented in the F layer. Basidiomycetes dominated the H layer (Watson and others 1974). The types and quantities of decomposers are directly related to the composition of litter and surface soil organic matter as well as to the moisture conditions of the microenvironment. Deciduous litter and pine needles support separate but overlapping faunal communities, so that decomposition takes place at different rates in mixed stands depending on species composition.

The soil mesofauna, which are up to 1.0 cm in length, are a prominent component of the soil animal population. In the lower Coastal Plain of South Carolina, they consist mainly of mites (Acarina), 83%; springtails (Collembola), 11%; and other insects, small spiders, and centipedes (6%). Eighty-five percent of these animals are in the forest floor and upper 3 cm of mineral soil, and about 50% of them are in the H layer of the forest floor. Periodic fires that do not consume the F and H layers of the forest floor do not substantially alter the numbers or distribution of soil mesofauna if there is sufficient time between burns to permit development and decomposition of an L layer. Annual burning that substantially reduces the forest floor drastically reduces the number of individuals per species, but not the total number of mesofaunal species (Metz and Farrier 1973).

Many arthropods, especially springtails, herbivorous mites, and predaceous mites, thrive in the soil under planted loblolly pines in southern Illinois (table 3-14). Their spring and summer populations did not differ. In the same area, there were about 1.5×10^6 bacteria and 0.9×10^6 actinomycetes/g of dry soil, the nematode population was insignificant, and the earthworm population weighed 128 g/m^3 in the spring and 80 g/m^3 in the summer (Fisher and others 1975).

In the lower Coastal Plain of South Carolina, seasonal density of decomposing microarthropods in the litter and surface 3 cm of soil under mature loblolly pines that were protected from fire was quite stable (10.0 to 14.0 × 10^4/m^2) during most of the year but fluctuated greatly during the late summer and fall (6.2 to 26.5 × 10^4/m^2). Moisture undoubtedly plays an important role in regulating the population of invertebrate decomposers. For example, the level of oribatid mites reached an annual low of approximately 4.0 × 10^4/m^2 in October when moisture was low in partially

decomposed litter (L and H layers) and a high of 16.0 × 10^4/m^2 about 3 weeks later after litter moisture was recharged. This South Carolina stand included a substantial number of understory hardwoods, and the quantity of deciduous litter gradually increased over time causing the kinds and levels of decomposing fauna to change (McBrayer and others 1977).

Silvicultural treatments such as prescribed burning and the application of herbicides seem to have no serious effect on soil microfaunal populations. Neither periodic nor annual winter prescribed burns altered the composition of saprophytic spore-forming microfungi or reduced the number of bacteria and actinomycetes enough to impair soil metabolic processes on a Coastal Plain soil. Annual burning did, however, reduce the combined weights of the F and H layers by two-thirds and consequently reduced the numbers of bacteria and actinomycetes in these layers from 51 million to 28 million/g of dry organic matter. When burns were 8 years apart, the number of these organisms increased to 71 million/g (Jorgensen and Hodges 1970). The microbiological population of South Carolina Piedmont sites was not changed significantly when unwanted hardwoods were killed with chemicals and loblolly pines were planted, largely because the soil was protected continuously by a layer of litter (Lane 1975).

Soil Moisture and Soil Aeration

Available soil moisture is the most important single factor affecting the growth and natural distribution of loblolly pine. The wet–dry cycles in the moisture content of southern soils can be very erratic. In 1 year, total rainfall at a site in the lower Coastal Plain of South Carolina was 188 cm. The wettest month had 48 cm of rainfall, and the driest month had only about 1 cm. Total annual rainfall was 63.5 cm above average, but there was severe moisture stress during parts of the year (Lane 1974). Such extremes are common in much of loblolly pine's range. In much of the lower Coastal Plain, excess soil moisture limits tree growth for long periods during the growing season. In the rest of loblolly pine's range, excess moisture is rarely a problem for longer than 1 week at a time except in stream bottoms or minor depressions.

Rates of change in soil moisture also affect the growth of loblolly pines. Even when soil moisture levels exceeded 60%, rapid short-term decreases to moisture levels of 15 to 25% caused 35- to 40-year-old trees growing on silt loams in northeast Louisiana to cease growing (Moehring and Ralston 1967). Growth stops under such conditions because moisture loss at the soil–root interface cannot be replenished rapidly enough to eliminate internal tree moisture stress.

Table 3-14—Soil arthropods in a 25-year old loblolly pine plantation in southern Illinois

Arthropod group	Organisms/m^2 in the upper 5 cm of soil
Springtails	5,830
Protura	1,610
Herbivorous mites	6,450
Predaceous mites	6,690
Insect larvae	600

Source: adapted from Fisher and others (1975).

The oxygen (O_2) content in soil air varies with the season of the year, slope, and soil moisture content. As moisture content in the soil increases, the O_2 content decreases. Oxygen also decreases with increasing soil depth, especially during winter and early spring on wet sites. Soil O_2 content decreases sharply immediately above a rising water table. It also decreases progressively from the top to the bottom of a slope, probably because of drainage (Hu and Linnartz 1972).

Moisture stress. Moisture stress results from a lack of available soil moisture. It causes physiological changes in trees and, if prolonged, can slow or interrupt tree growth (primarily diameter growth). Moisture stress usually occurs one or more times during the summer and fall growing season in much of loblolly pine's range. With adequate moisture, trees grow at near maximum rates from late March to late August and continue to grow more slowly until the first of October. If the spring and summer are dry, radial growth still begins in March but slows by May and may cease as early as the middle of June, resulting in reduced volume. For example, available soil moisture in the surface 30 cm of loess soils accounted for 95 to 97% of the variation in merchantable volume growth of an uneven-aged pole and sawtimber stand (mostly 30- to 50-year-old trees) of mixed loblolly and shortleaf pines during 21 growing seasons in southeast Arkansas. The number of days per year of no tree growth ranged from 0 to 88. Merchantable volume growth was 3 times greater in years when trees grew every day than in years when there was no growth for 88 days (Bassett 1964).

Moisture depletion during the summer months is much more severe on well-drained sites than on nearby poorly drained sites. This results in much more deeply distributed root systems on well-drained sites but higher site indexes on poorly drained sites. Where 36-year-old loblolly pines grew on a poorly drained site in southeast Louisiana, there was always more than 50 cm of total soil moisture in the 0- to 2.1-m soil profile. In contrast, there was always less than 50 cm of total soil moisture in well-drained soil. Moisture depletion was most severe in the surface 30 cm of the well-drained soil, where 61% of the roots were located, but extended into the 30- to 60-cm layer, where 35% of the roots were located. In the wet soil, almost all moisture depletion was in the surface 30 cm—primarily because 92% of the roots were in that zone (Brewer and Linnartz 1978).

Many of a loblolly pine's fine feeder roots grow in the partially decomposed litter. Moisture in the 20 to 30 or more tonnes of litter/ha under loblolly pine stands can be an important source of water for tree growth and development. Metz (1958) determined the moisture content of litter under a 12-year-old loblolly pine plantation during wetting and drying cycles. Water content of litter reached a maximum of 220% of the ovendry litter weight immediately after prolonged rains, but evaporation

rapidly reduced the amount of available water (figure 3-14). Saturated litter loses about 77% of its water during the first 4 days of drying. The moisture content of litter reaches equilibrium within 11 days (that is, no more moisture is lost through evaporation after 11 days).

Loblolly pines should not be planted on excessively drained sandy soils because there is a high probability of moisture stress on such soils (Burns 1968). Trees are most susceptible to prolonged drought during the first few years after stand establishment. A tree will not recover after 75% of its crown turns brown as a result of drought stress (Yeiser and Burnett 1982). Seedlings subjected to severe water stress tend to produce sugars rather than starch or structural compounds. These sugars tend to stay in source leaves and are not transported to other parts of the tree (Kuhns and Gjerstad 1988). In large trees, moisture stress alters the relative proportions of resin acids and monoterpenes and alters the concentrations of various monoterpenes (Gilmore 1977, Hodges and Lorio 1975). Moisture stress also reduces resin flow, and reduced resin flow makes trees more susceptible to beetle attack (Lorio and Hodges 1971, see chapter 10). A pressure chamber can measure plant moisture stress rapidly and accurately (McGilvray and Barnett 1988). Computer programs can simulate the day-by-day impact of drought on forest stand and site health and can provide estimates of the daily response of trees to current soil moisture availability (Zahner and Myers 1987).

Summer droughts are most common in the northern and western portions of loblolly pine's range. These droughts often result in large soil water deficits during the growing season, especially in coarse soils, and such deficits reduce tree growth (McClurkin and Covell 1965,

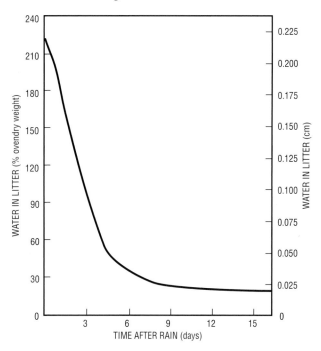

Figure 3-14—Drying of litter in a 12-year-old loblolly pine plantation (adapted from Metz 1958).

Shoulders and Tiarks 1980; figure 3-15). Even mature trees react to these moisture deficits (figure 3-15). The frequency and severity of summer droughts are the main factors limiting loblolly pine's western range.

Avoidance mechanisms help young loblolly pines tolerate drought. These mechanisms, in apparent order of importance, are stomatal control (drought-hardy trees appear to transpire rapidly when water is available and to conserve water under stress), increased root system (drought-hardy trees have deeper roots and wider ranging lateral roots), and adapted needle anatomy (drought-hardy trees may have somewhat smaller needles with deeper stomatal pits than have drought-susceptible trees and drought-hardy trees have fewer stomata per square millimeter in rows somewhat farther apart) (Knauf and Bilan 1977, van Buijtenen and others 1976).

Stomatal apertures decrease markedly as soil water stress increases (figure 3-16). Fourteen hours after watering, about 70% of the stomata of seedlings growing in warm/moist conditions were open, whereas only about 30% of the stomata of seedlings growing in warm/dry conditions were open. By 62 hours after watering, the proportions of open stomata on seedlings growing under warm/moist, warm/dry, and cool/dry conditions were very similar (about 30%). Only

seedlings growing in cool/moist conditions had significantly higher percentages of open stomata. Loblolly pines appear to have cellular mechanisms for increased tolerance to drought or desiccation, but these mechanisms are not understood (Newton and others 1987). Genetic differences undoubtedly affect the ability of individual trees, and even tree needles, to withstand moisture deficiency.

When evaluating the effects of low soil moisture tension on the development of loblolly pines, three things must be kept in mind. First, the ultimate criterion for evaluating drought resistance is not the death of a single organ but the ability of the tree as a whole to resume normal functioning after severe dehydration (Brix 1960). Second, the average moisture stress in a volume of soil is not a measurement of the moisture stress at root–soil interfaces. Although both moisture stresses are variable, stress at the root–soil interfaces is considerably greater than that elsewhere in the soil. And finally, the magnitude of water stress in the soil differs from the magnitude of water stress in tree tissues, and stresses in various tree tissues are unequal. The water potential of loblolly pine roots is lower than that of soil except at very low soil water potentials, and the water potential of shoots is lower than that of roots (Kaufmann 1968). Although internal moisture tension may result from soil moisture tension, the former can occur even when soil moisture is at field capacity if transpiration rates are high. When the soil is moist and transpiration is rapid, moisture absorption by roots can lag behind the loss of water through the needles because root cells are somewhat resistant to rapid water movement. Stress is normally alleviated at night, when absorption exceeds transpiration. Therefore, rapid daytime transpiration should have much less of an adverse impact on tree growth

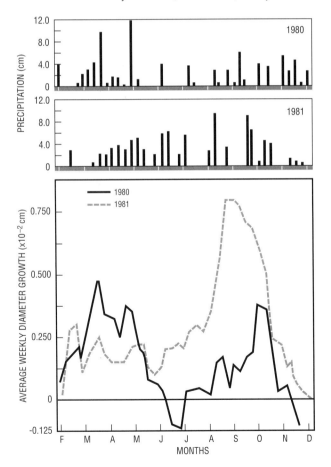

Figure 3-15—Effect of precipitation on diameter growth at breast height of 70- to 80-year-old, open-grown loblolly pine trees in east Texas (adapted from Amonett 1982).

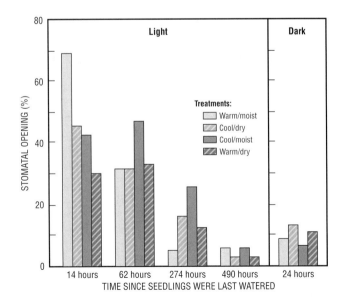

Figure 3-16—Stomatal opening as related to time after last watering of 10-month-old loblolly pine seedlings (adapted from Heth and Kramer 1975).

than stress caused by soil moisture deficiency. However, nightly watering of potted seedlings to field capacity—soil moisture tension of about 0.5 atmosphere [an atmosphere (atm) is a unit of pressure equal to 101,325 newtons per square meter (N/m^2)]—yielded average needle water potentials of less than −5.0 atm, a water stress considerably greater than that implied by the soil water tension (Miller 1965).

Tree survival and growth. The ability of loblolly pine seedlings to withstand moisture stress under a wide range of conditions is critical to seedling survival. During dry periods, survival of seedlings and even individual needles is closely related to air temperature and relative humidity. Survival time is longest when the environment is cool and moist and shortest under dry and warm conditions (Heth and Kramer 1975). Tree survival is increased by eliminating competing vegetation, especially during dry seasons (see chapter 8). Much of this improved survival is attributable to soil moisture conservation. For example, elimination of all vegetation within 1.5 m of 5-year-old loblolly pine trees on Piedmont and upper Coastal Plain sites significantly lowered

tree moisture stress when compared with no vegetation elimination (Carter and others 1984). Elimination of only tree competition reduced water stress by one-half to two-thirds as much as did removal of all competing vegetation. In southern Arkansas, removal of understory hardwoods in well-stocked, even-aged, 50-year-old, loblolly–shortleaf stands increased available midsummer moisture by 50%. Soil moisture was increased more where hardwoods were killed by chemical treatments than where hardwoods were killed by burning (Zahner 1958a). However, hardwood removal does not affect evapotranspiration when the soil is moist, and understory hardwood control may not improve pine growth where midsummer rainfall is plentiful (Klawitter 1966, Russell 1961, Williston 1978).

Tree growth is reduced whenever spring or summer soil moisture becomes limiting. Height growth is inhibited by soil moisture tensions as low as 2.0 atm. Shoot elongation ceases and needle moisture content begins to decline as tensions approach 3.5 atm (figure 3-17). New growth wilts visibly when soil moisture tension reaches about 5.0 atm. All seedlings die when the soil moisture tension reaches 15.0 atm, the estimated permanent wilting point. Soil moisture availability is most critical to growth during May through July, when trees are actively growing in height. However, dry spring weather has little effect on the first cycle of height growth because the length of this cycle is determined in the overwintering terminal bud (see chapter 2). Since first-cycle growth accounts for 50% or more of the seasonal total, the impact of growing-season moisture shortages on height growth is highly buffered, even though later cycles may be reduced in length, delayed, or even omitted. During September through November, height growth is very limited, but rates of root and stem diameter growth are still high and can be reduced by moisture stress (Kaufmann 1968; table 3-15).

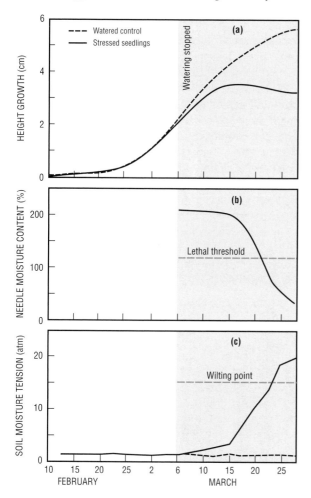

Figure 3-17—Loblolly pine: height growth (**a**) and needle moisture content (**b**) as affected by soil moisture tension(**c**) in a drying soil and in a well-watered soil (adapted from Stransky and Wilson 1964).

Table 3-15—Terminal and radial growth of loblolly pine saplings as affected by growing season drought

Growth		Pretreatment 3rd ring		Treatment period			
				4th ring		5th ring	
		Wet	Dry	Wet	Dry	Wet	Dry
Number of terminal cycles (internodes)		3	3	4	2	4	2
Length of internodes (cm)	1st	33	24	38	37	40	32
	2nd	18	29	25	7	26	14
	3rd	12	19	14	NTM	22	NTM
	4th	NTM	NTM	10	NTM	15	NTM
Total annual height growth (cm*)		63±6	72±9	87±7	44±4	103±11	46±7
Average annual radial ring width (mm)		3.6	3.7	8.8	4.5	7.6	4.6

Source: adapted from Zahner (1962).

NTM = no terminal growth. Pretreatment = 3rd growing season under natural rainfall conditions. Treatment = 4th and 5th growing seasons. Wet treatment consisted of irrigating containers throughout the year by surface watering to field capacity whenever moisture dropped to 80% of field capacity. Dry treatment maintained the soil near field capacity during winter and early spring but no water was added from May 1 through October 31.

* Deviations are full extremes of observations.

Table 3-16—Average growth responses of transplanted 1+0 loblolly seedlings with varying watering intervals

Watering interval	Shoot height (m)	Dry weight (g)				Shoot-to-root ratio
		Stem	Foliage	Shoot	Root	
3 days	0.41	2.31	2.81	5.12	6.09	0.84
1 week	0.43	2.71	3.33	6.04	5.73	1.05
2 weeks	0.42	2.56	4.26	6.82	4.69	1.45
3 weeks	0.40	1.84	3.56	5.40	3.27	1.65

Source: adapted from Stransky and Wilson (1967).

Seedling shoot elongation is twice as great in soils allowed to dry to 60% available water before rewatering than in soils allowed to dry to 20% available water before rewatering. Also, seedlings growing in soils maintained near field capacity elongated three times more than seedlings growing in soils that dried to 20% available water before rewatering (Wenger 1952). Seedlings watered at weekly or biweekly intervals can grow more than seedlings watered at 3-day or 3-week intervals even when soil moisture declines to 6.4% during 2-week watering intervals (table 3-16). Long watering intervals cause larger reductions in root weight than in stem weight.

Other growth characteristics directly affected by soil moisture conditions include width of annual rings, relative amounts of earlywood and latewood production, tracheid diameter, and cell wall thickness. In years of abundant rainfall, earlywood and latewood growth patterns are accentuated in loblolly pines. Radial growth in mature trees may be 20 to 30% less in years with drier growing seasons than in years with wetter growing seasons. Also, radial growth is more uniform throughout trees in years with drier growing seasons. Latewood growth decreases with decreasing soil moisture, especially in August and September, and the percentage of latewood increases basipetally. Earlywood growth is much less affected by soil moisture levels (DeBrunner 1968, Hiller and Brown 1967, USDA FS 1963). The average diameter of earlywood cells formed during a year of adequate moisture is smaller than that of those formed during a drought year. The opposite is true for latewood cells. Also, latewood cell walls formed during a drought year are thinner than those formed during a moist year (Hiller and Brown 1967). Buckingham and Woods (1969)

concluded that the effect of moisture deficiency on latewood production in loblolly pines during the trees' 15th to 40th years was greatest when moisture deficits were small (−8 to −24%). Increasing moisture deficits reduced latewood growth further, but at progressively smaller rates per unit of moisture deficit.

Relationship between crown class and tree moisture stress. Trees in all crown classes grow well during the first 3 months of the growing season, when soil moisture is high. Because they are in a strong competitive position, dominant trees are affected less by low soil moisture than are trees with smaller crowns. When growing-season rainfall in southeast Arkansas was 30 cm below the normal 84 cm, dominant loblolly pines grew during 58% of the growing season and intermediates grew during 28% of the growing season (table 3-17). When growing-season rainfall was 20 cm above normal, the dominant and intermediate trees grew during 96 and 79% of the growing season, respectively. Over the 4 years of the study, dominant trees grew during 80% of the sum of the growth periods, whereas codominants and intermediates grew during 70 and 53% of the sum of the growth periods, respectively.

Needle growth and development. Although soil moisture stress decreases needle growth and development, needle moisture content is not closely correlated with soil moisture tension or tree height growth. The normal needle moisture content of turgid needles of loblolly pine seedlings is about 200 to 250%. Height growth ceases when needles lose as little as 15% of their turgid moisture content. Some seedlings die when needle moisture content falls below about 105%. All seedlings die once needle moisture content falls below about 65% (figure 3-18); however, there is no clear-cut lethal level for individual needles or seedlings (Heth and Kramer 1975, Stransky 1963, Ursic 1961). Bilan and Stransky (1966) found that the moisture content of seedling needles declined from about 250 to 50% as available soil moisture declined from 100 to 1%. Needle moisture did

Table 3-17—Affect of soil moisture on the percentage of growth period that natural loblolly pines grew in diameter in southeast Arkansas

Crown class	% of growth period				During wettest year (1961)	During driest year (1963)
	1960-64 inclusive					
	3/1-5/31	6/1-8/16	8/16-10/31	3/1-10/31		
Dominant	96	79	66	80	96	58
Codominant	90	66	53	70	92	46
Intermediate	77	43	38	53	79	28
Suppressed	51	15	17	28	49	8

Source: adapted from Bassett (1966).

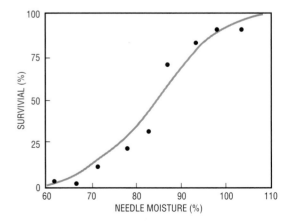

Figure 3-18—Loblolly pine seedling survival in the critical range of needle moisture content (adapted from Stransky 1963).

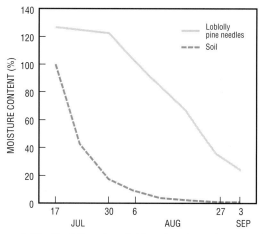

Figure 3-19—Depletion of available soil moisture in an east Texas forest soil (Magnolia fine sandy loam) and the corresponding decline in needle moisture content of loblolly pine seedlings (adapted from Bilan and Stransky 1966).

not fall below 100% until about 90% of the available soil moisture had been depleted. Needle moisture fell below 50% only when available soil moisture declined to below 1% (figure 3-19).

If soil moisture is kept near field capacity, needles grow about 1.0 mm/day until they reach about 70% of their maximum length. Growth then slows to 0.8 mm/day (figure 3-20). During soil drying cycles, needles grow about 0.4 to 0.6 mm/day until maximum length is achieved. The elongation of young needles of loblolly pine seedlings is directly correlated with needle water potential. Total 30-day elongation of needles at – 10.2 atm of water potential was less than half that at – 3.6 atm (figure 3-21). The water stress appeared to cause no permanent damage because needles of both stressed and unstressed seedlings elongated to the same length during 60 days of watering after stress (Miller 1965).

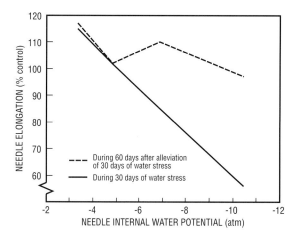

Figure 3-21—The relationship between needle internal water potential and needle elongation of loblolly pine seedlings growing under water stress for 30 days (**lower line**); total needle elongation for the same seedlings during 90 days (30 days of stress and 60 days following rewatering) (**upper line**). Points are the average water potentials of needles measured periodically at midday (adapted from Zahner 1968).

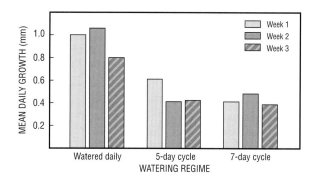

Figure 3-20—Mean daily needle growth of loblolly pine seedlings subjected to daily watering and 5- and 7-day drying cycles (adapted from Kaufmann 1968).

Environmental conditions in forests do not usually cause needle curling. However, needle curling may occur if seedlings are subjected to moisture stress in greenhouses or other confined places. Needles may curl if the relative humidity is maintained at less than 30% and the photoperiod is long (Seiler and Johnson 1984) or if soil moisture is very low when secondary needles emerge from fascicle sheaths (Jackson 1948). Needle tip curling is significantly more common in seedlings from some seed sources than in seedlings from others (Seiler and Johnson 1984). Thus, environmental conditions may not always be the problem.

Soil moisture's effect on root growth. Moisture stress strongly influences root growth and the rate of water absorption by roots. As soil dries, water becomes progressively less available to roots. The ratio of root dry weight to stem dry weight is larger in seedlings growing in dry conditions and smaller in those growing in moist conditions. This probably is true for larger trees also. When roots are subjected to severe moisture stress, they mature toward the tips and eventually become dormant until the soil moisture content rises or until the tree dies (Bongarten and Teskey 1987, Kaufmann 1968, Stransky and Wilson 1967). When rains occur at 5- to 7-day intervals, root growth decreases substantially during each drying cycle (figure 3-22).

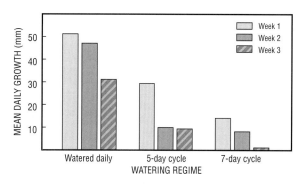

Figure 3-22—Mean daily root growth of loblolly pine seedlings subjected to daily watering and 5- and 7-day drying cycles (adapted from Kaufmann 1968).

Stress adaptations by the lost pines of east Texas.
Special physical and chemical adaptations in needles, roots, and stem xylem seem to be mechanisms for drought tolerance in trees that evolved in this area of low rainfall. Both primary and secondary needles of lost pines seedlings have thicker protective layers, smaller cross-sectional areas, and fewer and more deeply recessed stomata. Even cotyledons have some of these characteristics (Bilan and others 1977; Knauf and Bilan 1974, 1977; Thames 1963; Van Buijtenen and others 1976). Root adaptations include very extensive early development for rapid utilization of available moisture (van Buijtenen and others 1976) and a potassium–calcium adenosine triphosphatase (ATPase) activator system in the nuclear fraction of the root tips. This potassium–calcium system is completely different from the sodium–magnesium ATPase system found in loblolly pines in the rest of the species' range (McClurkin and others 1971). Earlywood xylem of trees from the lost pines has significantly lower levels of holocellulose and α-cellulose and has higher levels of potassium (K) and magnesium (Mg) than has xylem of loblolly pines from the rest of the species' range (Elder and Burkhart 1983). Potassium is important in controlling guard cell action, which regulates stomatal opening and transpiration, and high levels of K may be critical to the survival of lost pines.

Excess moisture. Loblolly pines appear to be quite tolerant to low levels of soil O_2 associated with flooding, especially in the winter and spring. One-year-old potted seedlings will survive up to 12 days of total submersion during the growing season. About 50% will survive 21 days, but almost all will die after 1 month of submersion. However, most seedlings can survive as much as 1 month of total submersion during the dormant season (Williston 1962). Seedlings whose roots are under water for extended periods of each winter will be shorter than unflooded seedlings. Much of the immediate damage caused by flooding results from the lack of O_2 in roots and not from the buildup of phytotoxins or soil nutrient imbalances (Topa and McLeod 1986c).

When the soil is flooded, large open spaces may develop throughout the length of seedling roots. This internal aeration system permits diffusion of O_2 from the stem into the root system and limits the need for air from the soil. Root anatomy changes associated with this phenomenon include the development of aerenchyma tissue within the stele between the xylem poles, extending from the phloem outward to the pericycle, and the formation of large intercellular spaces in the pericyclic parenchyma within the phellogen (McKevlin and others 1987a). Loblolly pines show genetic variation in waterlogging tolerance and physiological response to waterlogging (Shear and Hook 1987). Anaerobic condi-

tions significantly reduce root volume, taproot length, and lateral root development of young loblolly pines. These conditions can also induce a proliferation of lenticels around the root collar. Adventitious first-order lateral roots can subsequently emerge through these taproot lenticels. The stem and root-collar lenticels are the major sites of atmospheric O_2 entry for submerged roots (Topa and McLeod 1986b, 1986c, 1986d).

Rapidly transpiring trees help to increase soil O_2 levels by reducing soil moisture during wet periods. However, soil CO_2 levels can exceed 1% in areas that remain wet throughout the year (Jorgensen 1974). Such high soil CO_2 can severely limit height and diameter growth, dry weight increment, needle development, and flowering. Poor aeration also limits root development, and reduced root development can result in severe moisture deficiency during subsequent dry periods, which usually occur at least once each year even on normally wet loblolly pine sites (Zahner 1958b).

Flooding concentrates Fe and phosphorus (P) in the roots of seedlings, drastically reduces the movement of nutrients from roots to shoots, and retards shoot growth. Iron is concentrated on the epidermal surface, in and between cortical cell walls, in and between precursor phloem cells, and elsewhere in flooded roots. Iron accumulation may result from the diffusion of O_2 through the stressed root system. The Fe probably immobilizes much of the absorbed P, preventing its translocation to shoots. If P is available in large quantities, enough to permit good shoot growth may still be translocated to the bole. Thus, soil-applied P fertilizers may reduce the need for drainage on wet sites (McKee and others 1984; McKevlin and others 1987a, 1987b; Topa and McLeod 1986a).

Pocosin soils of the lower Coastal Plain often have various combinations of high water table, poor internal drainage, poor aeration, P deficiency, and high acidity.

Table 3-18—Average height growth and evapotranspiration of 1-year-old loblolly pine seedlings growing on different soil types normally watered during the first growth cycle and then either watered through a second cycle or not watered until death

	First growth cycle		Second growth cycle				
	Normally watered		Normally watered		Water withheld		
Soil type†	Height growth (cm)	ET (kg)	Height growth (cm)	ET (kg)	Height growth (cm)	ET (kg)	Days until death
Ruston sandy clay	11	1.70	3	1.98	1	0.86	42
Swift sandy loam	13	1.94	4	2.14	1	0.70	38
Sacul sandy loam	12	1.78	2	1.94	1	0.65	37
Shubuta loamy sand	12	1.84	3	2.08	1	0.72	37
Eustis-A loamy sand	13	1.97	2	2.09	1	0.66	35
Troup loamy sand	10	1.20	1	1.00	0	0.23	32
Troup-A sand	10	1.11	0	0.89	0	0.27	31
Eustis loamy sand	11	1.13	0	0.87	0	0.25	30
D*	3	0.30	1	0.21	1	0.21	4

Source: adapted from Eneim and Watterston (1970).

ET = evapotranspiration.

* Differences > D are significant at the 95% probability level.

† Soil types marked A are from Anderson County, Texas; others are from Nacogdoches County, Texas.

Loblolly pine is a preferred species on some of these soils, but P fertilization, improved drainage, and liming to reduce acidity may be necessary for good tree growth (MacCarthy and Davey 1976).

The Interrelationship of Soil Texture, Moisture Retention, and Tree Growth

The survival, growth, and evapotranspiration of loblolly pine seedlings are positively related to soil moisture retention capability. There is more readily available water in fine-textured than in coarse-textured soils. When water was not limiting, seedlings in Texas grew more in height on sandy loam soils than on soils that contained more clay or more sand. Under conditions of moisture stress, seedlings in soils with low moisture retention (sand or loamy sand) generally survived for significantly shorter periods than those in soils with high moisture retention (sandy clay and sandy loam) (table 3-18). The sandy clay and sandy loam soils were at least 40% silt and clay, had soil moisture levels of about 20 to 25% at field capacity, and generally had moisture levels of 10% or more even at the permanent wilting point (15.0 atm of tension). In contrast, the loamy sand and sandy soils, which were at least 75% sand, usually had soil moisture levels of 10% or less at field capacity and below 5% at the permanent wilting point.

The Loblolly Pine Nutrient Budget

Loblolly pine can grow on infertile sites partly because it requires smaller amounts of nutrients than do many other species. Loblolly pine is an extremely efficient species; it conserves essential nutrients by minimizing surface erosion or leaching losses to deeper soil layers or to the atmosphere by collecting additional nutrients made available through soil weathering and atmospheric deposition, by recycling nutrients within a tree and between trees, by using mycorrhizae efficiently, and by capturing N from N-fixing legumes and from free-living soil organisms.

Nutrient Retention Following Disturbance

Microbial uptake of N during the decomposition of residual organic matter is the process most responsible for retaining N in the forest ecosystem (Vitousek and Matson 1984). Uptake and accumulation of nutrients in herbaceous plants are major factors in the early recovery of cut-over loblolly pine sites (Van Lear and others 1989). Two years after mature loblolly pines were harvested on two sites in the South Carolina Piedmont, legumes and other herbs accounted for 85 to 88% of the total aboveground biomass and added 40 to 65 kg/ha of N, 2 to 4 kg/ha of P, 47 to 72 kg/ha of K, and 23 to 38 kg/ha of Ca to the available nutrient pool (table 3-19). By the fifth year, most of the biomass and nutrients were tied up in loblolly pines and competing hardwoods.

Nutrient Losses

Nutrients are lost through leaching and erosion even in well-stocked stands with a thick forest floor. In undisturbed mature Piedmont plantations, losses of NO_3–N, NH_4–N, and PO_4–P in runoff water averaged 0.028, 0.036, and 0.004 kg/ha/yr, respectively. Cation losses ranged from 0.32 kg/ha/yr for Mg to 0.70 kg/ha/yr for K (Douglass and

Table 3-19—Biomass and nutrient accretion in regrowth 1, 2, and 5 years after harvest of mature loblolly pines on two sites in the South Carolina Piedmont

Vegetative component	Accretion (kg/ha)					
	Whole tree harvest			Conventional harvest		
	1 yr	2 yr	5 yr	1 yr	2 yr	5 yr
Biomass						
Legumes	130	925	120	92	415	158
Other herbaceous vegetation	2,532	3,986	1,182	2,035	2,663	991
Hardwoods	459	753	3,726	324	359	1,804
Pines	9	146	11,037	5	73	17,822
Total	3,130	5,800	16,065	2,456	3,510	20,775
Nitrogen						
Legumes	1.82	12.95	2.75	1.29	5.81	3.62
Other herbaceous vegetation	32.92	51.82	11.12	26.46	34.62	9.33
Hardwoods	1.44	6.85	31.82	2.95	3.27	14.81
Pines	0.09	1.46	90.45	0.05	0.73	128.51
Total	36.27	73.08	136.14	30.75	44.43	156.27
Phosphorus						
Legumes	0.09	0.65	0.13	0.06	0.29	0.17
Other herbaceous vegetation	2.03	3.19	1.11	1.63	2.13	0.93
Hardwoods	0.42	0.45	3.10	0.19	0.22	1.45
Pines	0.01	0.12	3.10	0.19	0.22	1.45
Total	2.55	4.41	12.38	1.88	2.70	14.33
Potassium						
Legumes	1.25	8.88	0.88	0.88	3.98	1.16
Other herbaceous vegetation	40.15	63.78	10.01	32.56	42.61	8.39
Hardwoods	4.04	6.63	16.87	2.85	3.16	7.86
Pines	0.07	1.21	40.14	0.04	0.61	59.21
Total	45.87	80.50	67.90	36.39	50.36	76.62
Calcium						
Legumes	1.26	8.97	0.85	0.89	4.03	1.12
Other herbaceous vegetation	18.23	28.70	7.10	14.65	19.17	5.96
Hardwoods	8.86	14.53	44.70	6.25	6.93	21.08
Pines	0.02	0.38	30.16	0.01	0.19	46.41
Total	28.38	52.58	82.81	21.80	30.32	74.57

Source: adapted from Cox and Van Lear (1985).

Table 3-20—Nutrient losses over a 41-year rotation from two loblolly pine watersheds in the South Carolina Piedmont

| | Nutrient loss (kg/ha/41 yr) | | | | | | | |
| | Whole-tree harvest | | | | Conventional harvest | | | |
Output	N	P	K	Ca	N	P	K	Ca
Final harvest	151	13	68	134	63	5	36	70
Burning	160	1	4	15	94	1	4	10
Thinning (stems only)	16	1	9	18	16	1	9	18
Stormflow	11	1	17	18	33	1	97	68
Leaching	27	2	72	175	15	2	49	125
Total output	365	18	170	360	221	10	195	291

Source: adapted from Van Lear and others (1983).

Van Lear 1983). Stormflow and leaching removed 38 to 48 kg/ha of N, 89 to 146 kg/ha of K, and 193 kg/ha of Ca from two South Carolina Piedmont watersheds over a 41-year rotation (table 3-20). The annual solution losses by stormflow and deep seepage under plantations in the loessial hills of north Mississippi were estimated to be 3.0, 0.06, and 4.5 kg/ha of N, P, and K, respectively (Duffy 1985). Nutrient losses increase with rainfall temperature (Duffy and Schreiber 1990). For a given amount of rainfall, chemical leaching generally increases with decreasing rainfall intensity, probably because of longer contact time between rainwater and forest floor materials (Schreiber and others 1990). These low losses demonstrate the tightness of nutrient cycles in mature loblolly pine forests.

Practices that reduce the amount of organic matter on the forest floor lead to elevated losses of N and other essential nutrients. Significant nutrient losses occur when logs or whole trees are removed from forest sites. Removals of N, P, K, and Ca resulting from whole-tree harvesting in a 41-year-old plantation on a poor site in the upper Piedmont of South Carolina were twice as great as those resulting from conventional harvesting (table 3-20). Removal of whole trees from 40-year-old stands on good sites in Mississippi resulted in N, P, K, and Ca losses that were 22, 43, 18, and 14% greater than those resulting from conventional harvesting. Similarly, complete tree utilization during two 20-year rotations removed more nutrients than conventional logging removed during the same 40-year period (table 3-21). Fire can also reduce organic matter and affect nutrient levels (see chapter 8).

Table 3-21—Nutrient losses from natural stands of loblolly pines growing on good sites as affected by degree of utilization and rotation length

| | Nutrient loss (kg/ha) | | | | | | | |
| | One 40-year rotation | | | | Two 20-year rotations | | | |
Degree of utilization	N	P	K	Ca	N	P	K	Ca
Partial-tree removal	464	28	292	304	584	34	336	356
Complete-tree removal	568	40	344	348	768	54	424	408

Source: adapted from Switzer and Nelson (1974).

Nutrient Additions to the Loblolly Pine Ecosystem

Nutrients are added to the loblolly pine ecosystem naturally by biological N fixation, weathering of underlying soil material, and deposition of dry gases, solid particles, and materials dissolved in rainwater, snow, or fog. In undisturbed ecosystems, inputs of nutrients in precipitation generally exceed losses in surface runoff and leaching. Microbial actions and precipitation are especially important in replacing N lost from soil through leaching, fire, and absorption by plants. Drainage of submerged soils also promotes the mineralization of organic matter to forms that are available to trees (Bhangoo and others 1976).

Nitrogen fixation. Nitrogen fixation is the combining of atmospheric N with other elements for use in plants. Loblolly pines benefit from the N-fixing ability of many legumes, some nonlegumes such as waxmyrtle, and saprophytic bacteria and blue-green algae (Bond 1963, Kramer and Kozlowski 1979). Waxmyrtle, a woody pioneer species that occurs as an understory associate of loblolly pine in many areas of the South, adds as much as 11 kg/ha of N to a forest site annually (Permar and Fisher 1983). Generally, bacteria and algae (e.g., lichens) contribute less than 1.1 kg of N/ha annually because of their small numbers in most soils. Their activity is limited by low soil pH, availability of nutrients, and energy sources (Jorgensen and Wells 1986). Mycorrhizae do not fix N. Although N fixation from all sources probably does not exceed a few kilograms per hectare per year in soils under loblolly pine stands, except where legumes or nonleguminous N fixers are abundant, it can vary greatly depending on specific environmental conditions. For example, rates of N fixation are higher on burned than on unburned sites and are higher at high than at low temperatures. On poorly to very poorly drained South Carolina Coastal Plain soils, fixation in the surface 4 cm of soil was about 0.04 kg/ha/yr without burning and 0.95 kg/ha/yr with burning (Jorgensen and Wells 1971). Also, fixation may be as much as 40% greater when soil moisture content is at field capacity than when soil is drier, primarily because the number of N-fixing bacteria is directly related to soil wetness (Jorgensen 1975). Di Stefano (1984) estimated rates of N fixation by free-living organisms at about 2 to 3 kg of N/ha/yr in the surface 16.5 cm of poorly drained, acid soils in north Florida. Fixation rates greater than 10 kg/ha/yr have been reported for swamp sites (Jorgensen 1975). In the Piedmont, fixation rates averaged about 1.84 kg/ha/yr in the surface 30 cm of an eroded, xeric soil supporting a mature loblolly pine plantation (Van Lear and others 1989). However, rates of fixation averaged only 0.002 kg/ha/yr in the forest floor and surface 4 cm of soil under a variety of other loblolly pine or hardwood forest types (Grant and Binkley 1987). Nitrogen fixation by free-living organisms is not great enough to compensate for losses caused by forest management or natural processes on loblolly pine sites.

Weathering and wet and dry atmospheric deposition. Weathering is the release of nutrients from primary and secondary soil minerals by geochemical and biogeochemical processes. Older and more deeply weathered soils generally have less potential to release nutrients than do younger soils. Weathering of an eroded Pacolet fine sandy loam (typic Hapludult, kaolinitic, thermic) in the South Carolina Piedmont added 0.25 and 0.33 kg/ha/yr of K and Ca, respectively, to a loblolly pine forest over a 41-year period. The amounts added are only about 5% of the amounts removed during a harvest (Van Lear and others 1983). Atmospheric deposition, and not weathering, supplies the greatest quantities of new nutrients to highly weathered soils (Jorgensen and Wells 1986).

Precipitation (mainly rain and snow) adds significant quantities of nutrients to the loblolly pine ecosystem, but inputs of nutrients vary substantially from location to location. Average annual nutrient contribution of precipitation, throughout the species range, is 6.0 kg of N, 0.4 kg of P, 1.7 kg of K, 7.2 kg of Ca, and 1.7 kg of Mg (Jorgensen and Wells 1986). Atmospheric inputs of N, P, and K to a north Mississippi site with average annual rainfall of 135 cm were 8.2, 0.1, and 2.7 kg/ha, respectively. Atmospheric inputs of N and P exceeded losses of N and P in stormflow and deep seepage, so there was a net accumulation of these two elements (Duffy 1985). Areas with high rainfall and many electrical storms generally receive greater inputs of atmospheric nutrients than do those with low rainfall and few electrical storms. Input of minerals in dust and aerosols is probably insignificant in most of loblolly pine's range, but areas near the ocean can receive marine aerosols that are high in sodium (Na), Mg, chloride, and sulfate. Trees near urban or industrial areas are exposed to varying concentrations of particulate pollutants and gaseous pollutants such as sulfate sulfur, nitrates, and ammonium N depending on wind direction and the concentration of pollutants at the point of release (Torrenueva 1975). Other dry atmospheric depositions include insect and animal droppings, which are deposited on the soil surface or in parts of the tree canopy, and water-soluble gases, which are absorbed by leaves. Sulfur dioxide and gaseous ammonia can be absorbed directly from the air by soil or plants.

Particulate additions can range from minor to very important levels depending on specific conditions (Lindberg and Garten 1988).

Nutrient Fluxes Associated With Precipitation

The amount of nutrients cycled through a loblolly pine stand depends not only on the amount of precipitation but also on the way in which water moves through the system. Rainfall tends to be enriched with minerals as it passes through the canopy as throughfall (the part that actually comes into contact with the crown before falling to the ground) and as stemflow (table 3-22). In a 34-year-old Georgia plantation, K levels in throughfall during large storms were more than five times as great as those in direct precipitation (Torrenueva 1975).

Stemflow receives minerals in raindrops, in leachate from bark, and in contamination from lichens, mosses, and other microorganisms on the tree bole. Leachate from the foliage, twigs, and branches, which is funneled down the stem, can also add to this total. The bark of loblolly pines, and especially that of older trees, has broad, flat, scaly plates that tend to disperse stemflow around the entire bole of a tree.

Stemflow accounts for only a small percentage of the total annual input of nutrients in precipitation (Wells and others 1972). However, some nutrients are much more concentrated in stemflow than in precipitation that filters through the forest canopy or does not touch the canopy (Kaul and Billings 1965, Switzer and others 1988, Torrenueva 1975). Even though the volume of water and nutrients in stemflow is small relative to the ecosystem budgets, stemflow's localized distribution and high nutrient content increase its relative importance. The annual addition of nutrients by precipitation and foliar and bark leaching was similar to the addition by needlefall for Ca, Mg, P, and N and higher than the addition by needlefall for K in a 20-year-old loblolly pine plantation in southern Illinois (Rolfe and others 1976).

Gross precipitation is generally less enriched chemically than stemflow or throughfall. However, total nutrient returns in gross precipitation can be much greater than those in stemflow or throughfall when a relatively large volume of water reaches the soil without touching foliage. This is especially true in young stands before crown closure and in older stands of low density (Switzer and others 1988; tables 3-22 and 3-23). Switzer and Nelson (1972) found that, in a 20-year-old stand, most sulfur

Table 3-22—Effects of throughfall and stemflow on cation movement into the soil under a 34-year-old loblolly pine plantation following 855 mm of rainfall in 18 storms over a 6-month period

	Cation movement (kg/ha)		
Nutrient	Rainfall	Throughfall	Stemflow
K	0.75	4.13	1.02
Ca	1.40	2.02	3.08
Mg	0.20	0.39	1.68
Na	3.20	3.74	1.41

Source: adapted from Torrenueva (1975).

Table 3-23—Total annual nutrient inputs from rainfall, throughfall, and stemflow in a 17-year-old loblolly pine plantation and a 21- to 23-year-old loblolly pine stand with a hardwood understory in northeast Texas

	Nutrient inputs (kg/ha)			
		Throughfall gain*		Stemflow
Nutrient	Rainfall	Pine-hardwood	Pine plantation	Pine plantation
Ca	5.0	2.7	2.5	0.3
Mg	1.1	1.6	1.3	0.1
N	4.1	2.1	3.1	0.2
K	3.3	10.8	7.6	0.3
Na	9.9	2.0	2.3	0.2

Source: adapted from Pehl and Ray (1983).

* Throughfall gain equals total throughfall input minus incident precipitation.

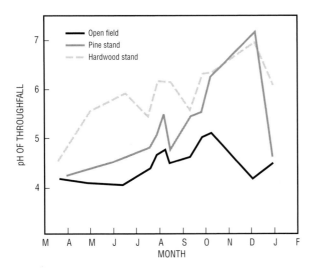

Figure 3-23—Throughfall pH in a loblolly pine stand, a mixed hardwood stand, and a nearby field in the North Carolina Piedmont (adapted from Wells and others 1972).

(S) came directly from gross precipitation, and that half of the K came from throughfall (table 3-24). The pH of throughfall water is also altered by the tissues the water contacts. Hardwood leaves increase the pH of throughfall more than do loblolly pine needles (figure 3-23).

Seventy percent of the annual rainfall reached the forest floor as throughfall in a well-stocked, 22-year-old loblolly pine plantation in southern Illinois. Fifty-two percent of this throughfall was subsequently lost as evaporation. A comparable shortleaf plantation had 84% throughfall, but only 30% evaporation because of a less dense canopy and a thinner, but denser, litter layer. The loblolly pine plantation also had a higher stemflow (10% of total rainfall) than did the shortleaf pine plantation (6%). The result of these differences is that less water and fewer nutrients reach the forest floor as throughfall, and more are channeled to the soil as stemflow in a loblolly pine stand than in a shortleaf pine stand (Miceli and others 1975).

Rainfall also promotes the rapid recycling of nutrients in surface litter by washing and leaching this material. Nutrients are also made available for absorption by surface roots through the washing and leaching of litter on the ground. Loss of nutrients from litter peaks at the beginning of a rain, when dust is washed from the litter. Leaching of nutrients from litter is relatively constant thereafter and is affected only by the amount of litter. Intensity of rainfall has little effect on the rate of nutrient leaching from litter. Ions deposited directly on surface soil are readily available for recycling through surface roots (Duffy and others 1985).

Nutrients in the Forest Floor

The forest floor is a very important source of nutrients for loblolly pines except in the case of newly established trees on cleared or site-prepared areas. The supply of nutrients generally increases as a stand ages. However, nutrient content of the forest floor under established stands can vary greatly depending on the climate and specific soil. For example, the forest floor of a 15-year-old plantation in Mississippi had only one-third as much N and P, half as much K, and two-thirds as much Ca and Mg as did the forest floor of a 16-year-old plantation in North Carolina. The forest floors of five 15-year-old plantations in Virginia contained slightly less N, P, K, and Mg but more Ca than did the forest floor of the North Carolina plantation (Jorgensen and Wells 1986). The nutrient content of the forest floor of a 17-year-old plantation on a poor site is described in table 3-25. Plantation-to-plantation differences in nutrient content probably reflect the influences of stand density and soil characteristics on initial needle composition and the effects of stand density, soil characteristics, and precipitation on the rate of needle decomposition (Jorgensen and Wells 1986).

Forest soil nutrients are replenished continuously by decomposition of the forest floor. Although nutrients in the forest floor are in relatively available forms, the

Table 3-24—The relative contribution of nutrient sources to the 20th-year requirements of a loblolly pine plantation ecosystem

Nutrient Source	% contribution					
	N	P	K	Ca	Mg	S
Litter decomposition	40	23	16	54	38	60
Throughfall	5	9	50	24	16	0
Precipitation	16	6	12	39	16	88
Internal transfer	39	60	22	0	24	22
Soil	0	2	0	0	6	0
Total	100	100	100	117*	100	170*

Source: adapted from Switzer and Nelson (1972).

* Values greater than 100 indicate soil accretions if root requirements and leaching losses are less than the excess indicated.

Table 3-25—Nutrient concentration as a percentage of total weight and accumulation in the forest floor of a 17-year-old, unthinned loblolly pine plantation growing on a poor site in the Piedmont of South Carolina

Forest floor component	Weight (kg/ha)	N		P		K		Ca		Mg	
		%	kg/ha	%	kg/ha	%	kg/ha	%	kg/ha	%	kg/ha
Needles											
L layer	4,539	0.60	27.3	0.08	3.6	0.07	3.1	0.37	16.8	0.07	3.1
F layer	14,311	0.94	134.5	0.12	17.2	0.08	11.5	0.30	42.9	0.06	8.5
Coarse twigs	1,198	0.42	5.0	0.03	0.3	0.07	0.8	0.18	2.1	0.02	0.2
Fine twigs	569	0.57	3.2	0.03	0.2	0.06	0.3	0.27	1.6	0.04	0.2
Bark	105	0.49	0.6	0.02	NA	0.05	NA	0.25	0.2	0.03	NA
Cones	35	0.54	0.2	0.02	NA	0.07	NA	0.06	NA	0.04	NA
Miscellaneous	67	0.82	0.6	0.04	NA	0.13	0.1	0.25	0.2	0.04	NA
Total	20,824		171.4		21.3		15.8		63.8		12.0

Source: adapted from Van Lear and Goebel (1976).

NA = negligible amounts, < 0.1 kg/ha.

organic matrix must decompose before plants can use the nutrients. The epidermis of newly fallen needles initially impedes the leaching of water-soluble substances. Once biological and physical decomposition begins, the rate of leaching increases (Godeas 1987). Needles can decompose completely in as little as 2 to 3 years under ideal conditions, but decomposition time increases if conditions are cooler or drier than optimum. Although hardwood leaves decompose more rapidly than do needles, the rate of decomposition of needles is not changed if needles are mixed with hardwood leaves. In North Carolina and Tennessee, needles took more than 8 years to decompose (Jorgensen and others 1980). They decomposed at a uniform rate during the first year after

falling to the ground, losing about 30 to 45% of their weight in North Carolina and Tennessee field plots. During the first year, about 30% of the organic matter and carbon, 10% of the N, 50% of the P, 70% of the K, 25% of the Ca, and 57% of the Mg were released and available for tree growth or microbial uptake. Coarse litter releases N at a slower rate than does fine litter (figure 3-24). After 4 years, the needles retained less than 50% of each element other than N (about 80% of N was retained). Even after 8 years, 77% of the N was retained in needles. Faunal decomposition of the litter is primarily by springtails, mites, flies (Diptera), and ants (Hymenoptera) (Thomas 1968). Fungi are the primary decomposing flora (Jorgensen and others 1980, Thomas 1968).

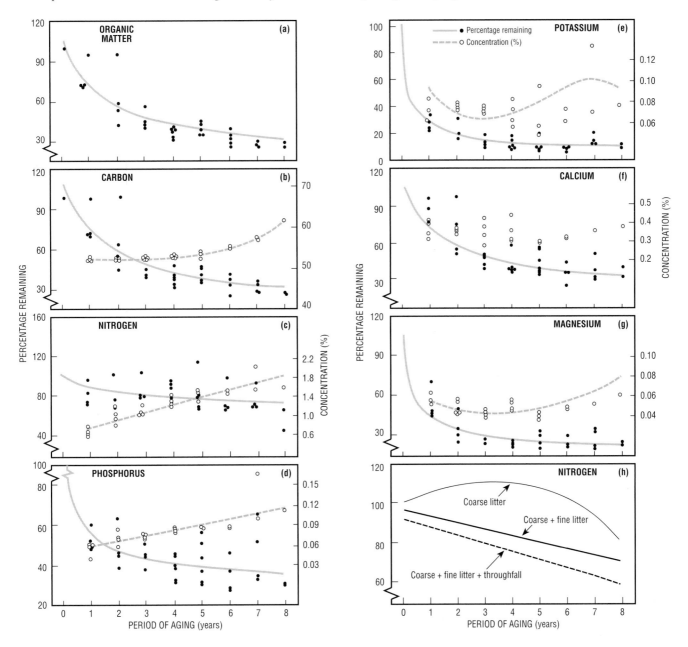

Figure 3-24—Percentages of initial quantities of organic matter and macronutrients in the forest floor during 8 years of needle decomposition under two plantations in the North Carolina Piedmont: organic matter (**a**), carbon (**b**), nitrogen (**c**), phosphorus (**d**), potassium (**e**) calcium (**f**), magnesium (**g**), and nitrogen (**h**) in different types of litter (adapted from Jorgensen and others 1980).

Nutrient concentrations in litter-fall vary with the season of the year (figure 3-25). Needles that fall from October to December have the lowest levels of N and P. Needles that fall during the rest of the year contain high concentrations of these elements. In contrast, concentrations of Ca and Mg are lowest in needles that fall from March to May but are relatively high in the fall, when needle drop peaks. Newly fallen needles in 10- to 20-year-old plantations throughout the Piedmont and Coastal Plain contained only 47, 36, and 20% as much N, P, and K as live needles contained. However, the Ca level was about twice as high in newly fallen needles as in living needles (Lea and Ballard 1982).

Nutrients are also released from woody tissue at variable rates. In one case, 76% of the K, 56% of the Mg, and 47% of the Ca were released from woody slash during the first 5 to 6 years after harvesting. However, almost no N or P had been released even after 7 years. Logging slash that is in contact with the soil decomposes about 50% faster than slash not in contact with the soil (Barber and Van Lear 1984).

Although considerable quantities of all elements, except N, are released from litter during the early stages of decomposition, the forest floor functions as an important reserve of or "sink" for nutrients throughout the life of a stand (Jorgensen and others 1980; table 3-24). In one loblolly stand, 2% of the standing biomass pool was deposited as litter during the stand's 20th year. This litter contained about 6, 17, 8, 20, and 25% of the standing pool of N, P, K, Ca, and Mg, respectively (Rolfe and others 1976). Even at stand age 34, litterfall accounted for 48, 55, and 57% of the total K, Ca, and Mg fluxes in a Georgia Piedmont plantation (Torrenueva 1975). As a stand ages, the litter layer gradually comes into equilibrium in which nutrients are released from old litter and deposited in new litter at approximately equal rates (figures 3-26 and 3-27). Equilibrium is reached at about the time when humus and mineral soil show evidence of substantial mixing.

The chemical composition of soils and litter is not the same under all southern pines. Schmidtling (1984) found more P, K, Mg, zinc (Zn), and organic matter, but less S and copper (Cu) under loblolly pines than under longleaf pines.

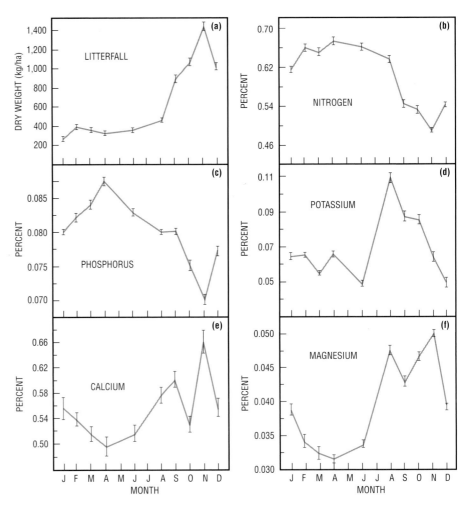

Figure 3-25—Mean monthly litterfall dry weight and the concentrations of macronutrients under an unthinned, 18-year-old loblolly pine plantation in north Louisiana: litterfall dry weight (**a**), nitrogen (**b**), phosphorus (**c**), potassium (**d**), calcium (**e**), and magnesium (**f**). Bars at each point represent standard deviations from the mean (adapted from Lockaby and Taylor-Boyd 1986).

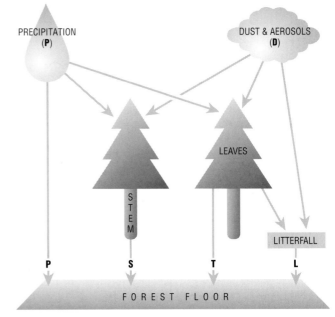

Figure 3-26—Flow of minerals to the forest floor. Nutrient sources include precipitation (**P**), stemflow (**S**), throughfall (**T**), litterfall (**L**), and dust and aerosols (**D**) (adapted from Torrenueva 1975).

Nutrients in the Mineral Soil

Concentrations of soil nutrients in the loblolly pine ecosystem vary enormously. For example, total N in the rooting zone can range from less than 2,000 to more than 10,000 kg/ha. Similarly, levels of soil P, K, Ca, and Mg can vary by factors of two to four. Concentrations of various minerals in the foliage, inner bark, and probably other parts of loblolly pine trees of all ages also vary from soil to soil and site to site (Wells 1965, White and others 1972). Some of the variation in soil nutrients results from differences in overstory composition. On Piedmont soils, the rate of nitrate production was lowest under a mature loblolly pine stand with a hardwood understory, intermediate under a 120- to 180-year-old oak–hickory stand, and highest under a 6- to 8-year-old natural loblolly–sweetgum stand on an old field. Adding ammonium fertilizer generally stimulated nitrate production regardless of overstory (Montes and Christensen 1979).

During the first few years of tree growth, mineral soil must provide almost all the nutrients loblolly pines need, especially when there is little or no surface organic matter. Planted trees decrease N levels in all soil horizons in which roots develop until about tree age 15. The surface 60 cm of mineral soil under a 5-year-old plantation in South Carolina contained 2,392 kg of N/ha, but the same layer of soil contained only 2,010 kg of N/ha 10 years later. During this same 10-year period, exchangeable K, exchangeable Ca, and exchangeable Mg in the mineral soil decreased by 15, 18, and 29%, respectively (Wells and Jorgensen 1977).

Loblolly pine roots often reach deeper than 2 m in soils that do not have restrictive horizons or shallow water tables. It is reasonable to infer that roots that penetrate deeply into soils absorb nutrients as well as moisture from the subsoil. When moisture stress in the surface soil is severe, the importance of subsoil for nutrient uptake may be critical. Even if the subsoil supplies only small quantities of specific nutrients to a tree, these additions could make the difference between average and poor tree growth. About 13% of P absorbed by 7-year-old loblolly pines in the surface 1.2 m of a sandy clay soil occurred right at the 1.2-m depth (Walker and Arnold 1963).

Changes in soil characteristics are associated with succession from herbaceous cover to loblolly pine to climax oak–hickory. These changes are the result, and not the cause, of successional change in the dominant species. In a greenhouse study, loblolly pine seedlings grew equally well in soil taken from abandoned fields, in soil from 10- to 20-year-old Virginia pine stands on old fields, in soil from 50- to 70-year-old Virginia pine stands on abandoned farmland, and in soil from climax oak–hickory stands. However, the lack of mycorrhizae in oldfield soils can initially limit tree growth (Hosner and Graney 1970).

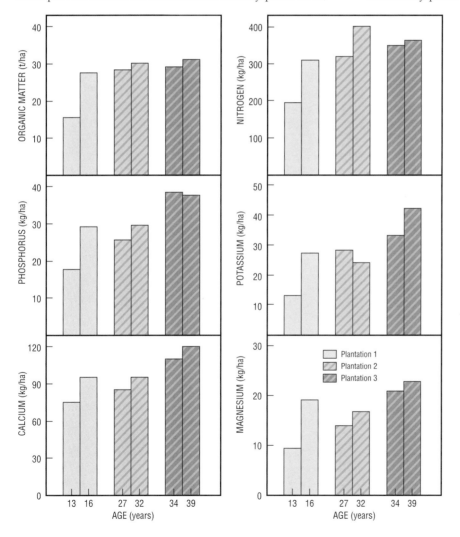

Figure 3-27—Accumulation of organic matter, N, P, K, Ca, and Mg in the forest floor of three North Carolina Piedmont plantations of different ages (adapted from Wells and Jorgensen 1975).

Accumulation of Biomass and Nutrients in Trees

Newly regenerated loblolly pines have small crowns and small root systems. Competing grasses, shrubs, and mixed hardwoods grow fast and can accumulate large quantities of some essential elements. At about loblolly pine stand age 5, the N tied up in aboveground biomass of competing species ranges from about 72 to 108 kg/ha (Switzer and Nelson 1972, White and Pritchett 1970). In

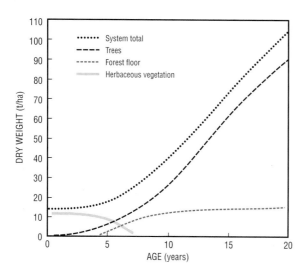

Figure 3-28—Biomass accumulation in a young loblolly pine plantation (adapted from Switzer and Nelson 1972).

Table 3-26—Mean quantities of nutrients in the boles of 19-year-old loblolly pines growing on diverse soils

Soil group	Tissue	Nutrient (Kg/ha)				
		N	P	K	Ca	Na
Coastal Plain (poorly drained)	Wood	105	11	69	83	14
	Bark	51	7	21	34	2
	Entire bole	156 a	18	90	117 a	16
Coastal Plain (well drained)	Wood	82	9	53	86	12
	Bark	40	3	15	52	2
	Entire bole	122 a,b	12 a	68 a	138 b	14 a
Loess (well drained)	Wood	74	8	52	77	13
	Bark	37	4	13	48	1
	Entire bole	111 b	12 a	65 a	125 a,b	14 a
Loess (poorly drained)	Wood	94	9	49	58	10
	Bark	30	2	10	18	1
	Entire bole	124 a,b	11 a	59 a	76	11
Average (poorly drained)	Wood	89	9	56	76	12
	Bark	39	4	14	38	2
	Entire bole	128	13	70	114	14

Source: adapted from Ku and Barton (1973).

Means in the same column not having the same letters are significantly different at the 95% probability level.

one young plantation in the Piedmont of North Carolina, aboveground herbaceous vegetation contained 75, 8, 10, 23, and 8 kg/ha of N, P, K, Ca, and Mg, respectively (Jorgensen and Wells 1986). Loblolly pine crowns usually close and shade out most competing vegetation by stand age 8 (figure 3-28). The dead vegetation and small quantities of loblolly pine needles form a forest floor rich in essential nutrients.

The amounts of nutrients in various tree components and the nutrient transfer rates change with tree size, tree age, and changing environmental conditions. During a 60-year stand life, N, Ca, K, Mg, P, and S are accumulated in descending order of quantity. Nitrogen, K, and Ca accumulate rapidly during the first 30 years. Nitrogen accumulates most rapidly in the first 10 years of stand life; P and K accumulate most rapidly in the second decade; and Ca and Mg accumulate most rapidly in the third decade. By stand age 45, nutrition is a matter of recycling nutrients already in the trees. Different macronutrients cycle at different rates. Rates of uptake of N, P, and K closely follow the rate of canopy development, and rates of uptake of Ca, Mg, and S follow the rate of stem dry matter accumulation (Switzer and others 1968). The pattern of nutrient accumulation for an entire stand differs from that for an individual dominant or codominant tree. For example, N accumulates in the foliage of a stand most rapidly after crown closure but before tree-to-tree competition causes much crown loss. The total amount of N in stems and branches of a stand rises rapidly until about stand age 40, when the rate of N accumulation begins to decrease slowly. In contrast, N accumulation in the stems, branches, and foliage of individual dominant or codominant trees continues unchecked through tree age 60, with no evidence that an equilibrium is reached.

Soil characteristics also affect the quantities of nutrients in loblolly pine stands. For example, trees growing on poorly drained Coastal Plain soil in southeastern Arkansas had significantly higher levels of tissue N, P, and K than

did trees on well-drained Coastal Plain soils (table 3-26).

A substantial part of the total nutrient fund in the aboveground portion of a loblolly pine stand is cycled every year. Switzer and Nelson (1972) determined that the percentages of N, P, K, Ca, Mg, and S cycled during the 20th year of a plantation were 23, 19, 28, 7, 15, and 17%, respectively.

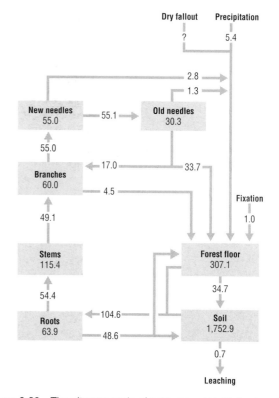

Figure 3-29—The nitrogen cycle of a 16-year-old loblolly pine plantation in the Piedmont of North Carolina. Values in boxes indicate nitrogen storage in individual components; values outside boxes indicate annual nitrogen transfer. All values are in kilograms per hectare (adapted from Jorgensen and Wells 1986).

The nitrogen cycle. Diagrams of the N cycle have been developed for plantations of pole-sized loblolly pines in the Piedmont of North Carolina (figure 3-29) and in the Coastal Plain of Mississippi (Switzer and others 1968). In the former plantations, the forest floor contained 307 kg of N/ha, and annual input of N from the atmosphere, leaching, fixation, and litterfall was 49 kg/ha. Roots in the forest floor and mineral soil provided an additional 49 kg of N/ha, bringing the total input of N to the forest floor and mineral soil to 97.6 kg/ha. Nitrogen absorbed by the pine trees totaled 105 kg/ha. Thus, there was a net loss of 7 kg of N/ha from the soil and forest floor. About half the N absorbed by roots was translocated to aboveground portions of trees. The remainder was recycled between the roots and the forest floor–soil complex. Of the 54.4 kg of N translocated up trees, 5.3 kg were bound in the stem biomass and the remainder moved into branches. Older needles translocated 17 kg of N/ha back to branches just before falling. Of the 66.1 kg of new N in branches, 4.5 kg were lost to branch death, 6.6 kg were used to form new branches, and 55.0 kg were used to produce new needles. The 17 kg of N/ha translocated from old needles prior to abscission were important to the formation of new needles. In summary, 14% of the available N was tied up by trees and an additional 13% was bound in the forest floor (Jorgensen and Wells 1986). The fact that 27% of the 2,382 kg of available N/ha was already tied up partially

explains why fertilization with N often promotes growth in stands of pole-sized loblolly pines.

The phosphorus cycle. The amount of P available for tree growth at any time is a small proportion of the total in the mineral soil and the forest floor. The surface 70 cm of mineral soil supporting a 16-year-old North Carolina plantation contained 371 kg of P/ha. The mineral soil gained 3.8 kg/ha/yr of P from the forest floor but lost a net 10 kg/ha/yr to the roots (figure 3-30). About 50% of the P in newly fallen needles is released and is available for root absorption.

The potassium cycle. Potassium is cycled more rapidly than any other major nutrient because it is not a structural part of organic matter. About three-fourths of the K in loblolly pine needles is transferred back to the stem before needlefall. Large quantities of K are leached from living needles by rainfall (figure 3-31). Up to 80% of the K in newly fallen needles is leached by precipitation in the first year and is readily available for reabsorption by tree roots (figure 3-24e). The quantity of K in the forest floor is about twice the quantity of K in annual litterfall.

Within-tree nutrient cycling. Nutrients move continuously in actively growing trees. The amounts of nutrients in various tree components and the transfer rates vary according to tree size, tree age, and environ-

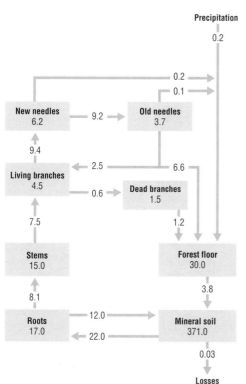

Figure 3-30—The phosphorus cycle of a 16-year-old loblolly pine plantation growing in the Piedmont of North Carolina. Values in boxes indicate stored components; values outside boxes indicate annual phosphorus transfer. All values are in kilograms per hectare (adapted from Wells 1976).

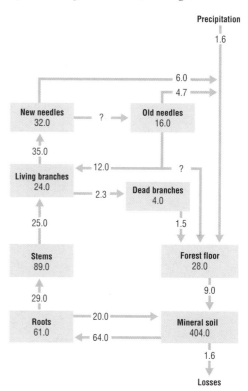

Figure 3-31—Potassium cycle of a 16-year-old loblolly pine plantation growing in the Piedmont of North Carolina. Values in boxes indicate potassium storage in individual components; values outside boxes indicate annual potassium transfer. All values are in kilograms per hectare (adapted from Wells 1976).

mental conditions. Large percentages of the N, P, and K in a tree are apparently translocated throughout the tree, while much of the Ca, Mg, and S is immobilized in the tree's woody parts (Switzer and others 1968). Virtually all of the Ca required by 20-year-old loblolly pines had to come from sources outside the trees, whereas 60% of the P and 22% of the K required was supplied by within-tree transfers. Foliage is the tissue most involved in the internal recycling process, and much of the nutrient exchange takes place just prior to needlefall. Translocation of key elements from foliage to branches conserves

nutrients effectively. It is probable that nutrients are translocated from roots and branches to the central portion of the tree when roots and branches die. Because stands approaching maturity grow little, their loss of new nutrients to stem biomass is minimal. Nutrient pools in the mineral soil and the forest floor can be recharged gradually during the late part of the stand growth cycle. At the same time, uptake of nutrients by late-successional understory plants becomes significant.

Summary

Loblolly pines grow well in various habitats, under wide-ranging environmental conditions, and with numerous annual and perennial plant associates. About three-quarters of the loblolly pine ecosystem is in the Atlantic and Gulf Coastal Plain. Loblolly pines also grow well on the Piedmont Plateau and in parts of the Interior Highlands. Loblolly pine's extensive natural range—from Delaware to Florida, Tennessee, Arkansas, and Texas—indicates the great adaptability of the species.

The climate in the loblolly pine ecosystem is humid with long, hot summers and mild winters. Temperatures average over 24 °C, and frequently exceed 38 °C in midsummer. Midwinter temperatures average 2 to 17 °C and occasionally drop to – 23 °C in the northern and western portions of the species' range. Annual precipitation ranges from 120 to 160 cm and consists mostly of rainfall. Snowfall makes up a small percentage of total precipitation in the northern half of the range. Loss of rainfall to crown interception can reach 25 cm/yr in a fully stocked stand. Throughfall in well-stocked stands is about 70 to 85% of total precipitation. Potential evapotranspiration ranges from 1 to 2 cm/mo in midwinter to about 17 cm/mo in midsummer. Overhead light is essential for prompt and adequate regeneration and good tree growth.

Loblolly pines are an excellent choice for regeneration of disturbed areas and severely eroded soils because they can rapidly generate a litter layer and can quickly increase soil fertility. The thickness and nutrient content of the forest floor generally increase as stand age increases up to about age 35. Weight of the forest floor increases from 1 to 4 t/ha under new stands to more than 30 t/ha under stands more than 20 years old. The composition of this material is directly related to the loblolly pine overstory and associated understory vegetation. In a fully stocked stand, needles make up about 70 to 90% of the forest floor.

Twenty-five-year site index can vary by as much as 12 m on individual soil series. About 75% of the soils in loblolly pine's range are Ultisols. Trees grow best on soils

with loamy textures throughout the profile. Loblolly pine generally outperforms all other southern pines on moderately well- to well-drained soils. It grows reasonably well even on poorly drained flatwoods sites, but liming, P fertilization, and improved drainage may be necessary for good tree growth. Loblolly pines should not be planted on excessively drained sandy soils. However, if the water table is accessible to tree roots, trees can grow well on upland sandy soils. Best growth occurs when soil acidity is between pH 4.5 and 6.0.

The loblolly pine nutrient cycle consists of nutrient inputs from soil weathering, precipitation, dry fallout, biological N fixation, transfers within the plant–soil complex, and losses from the system through leaching. During the first few years of tree growth, mineral soil must provide almost all the nutrients a loblolly pine needs, especially where there is little or no surface organic matter. Rainfall promotes rapid recycling of nutrients by washing and leaching the canopy, tree boles, and litter on the ground. Precipitation and decomposition of the forest floor are the principal sources of nutrients for established trees. Although it may take 8 years for needles to decompose completely, over half the total P, K, Ca, and Mg in fallen needles are available to trees in the second year after needlefall. However, even after 4 years, only about 20% of the N in fallen needles is available. Most nutrients are released from woody tissue and from decomposing needles at similar rates. However, P is held as tightly as N in woody material, and woody material decomposes 50% faster when in contact with the ground than when not in contact with the ground. As a stand ages, the litter layer matures toward an equilibrium in which nutrients are released and deposited at approximately equal rates. By stand age 45, tree nutrition is accomplished almost entirely through the recycling of nutrients already present in trees.

Both the amounts of nutrients in various tree components and nutrient transfer rates change with tree size, tree age, and environmental conditions. Cycling of each nutrient within trees is unique in terms of quantity and transfer rate, but the basic processes are similar to each other. Foliage is the tissue most involved in nutrient recycling within trees, and much of the nutrient exchange takes place just before needlefall. The concen-

trations of nutrients in falling needles vary seasonally. Nitrogen and K levels are lowest in needles that fall from October through December, but concentrations of Ca and Mg are highest in those needles.

Literature Cited

Allen RM, McGregor WHD. 1962. Seedling growth of three southern pine species under long and short days. Silvae Genetica 11(2):43–45.

Amonett CO. 1982. Relationships between weekly radial growth of mature loblolly pines and selected climatic variables in east Texas. Nacogdoches, TX: Stephen F. Austin State University. 115 p. M.S. thesis.

Barber BL, Van Lear DH. 1984. Weight loss and nutrient dynamics in decomposing woody loblolly pine logging slash. Soil Science Society of America Journal 48(4):906–910.

Bassett JR. 1966. Seasonal diameter growth of loblolly pines. Journal of Forestry 64(10):674–676.

Bassett JR. 1964. Tree growth as affected by soil moisture availability. Soil Science Society of America Proceedings 28(3):436–438.

Bhangoo MS, Albritton DJ, Shoulders E. 1976. Aeration, phosphorus, and lime affect nitrogen mineralization in imperfectly drained forest soils. In: Proceedings, Arkansas Academy of Science; [date unknown]; [Place of publication unknown]: 30:16–18.

Bilan MV, Hotan CT, Carter HB. 1977. Stomatal opening, transpiration, and needle moisture in loblolly pine seedlings from two Texas seed sources. Forest Science 23(4):457–462.

Bilan MV, Stransky JJ. 1966. Pine seedling survival and growth response to soils of the Texas post-oak belt. FS Bull. 12. Nacogdoches, TX: Stephen F. Austin State College: 5–21.

Binkley D, Valentine D, Wells C, Valentine U. 1989. An empirical analysis of the factors contributing to 20-year decrease in soil pH in an old-field plantation of loblolly pine. Biogeochemistry 8(1):39–54.

Bond G. 1963. The root nodules of nonleguminous angiosperms. Symposium of the Society of General Microbiology 13:72–91.

Bongarten BC, Teskey RO. 1987. Dry weight partitioning and its relationship to productivity in loblolly pine seedlings from seven sources. Forest Science 33(2):255–267.

Boyer WD. 1970. Shoot growth patterns of young loblolly pine. Forest Science 16(4):472–482.

Boyer WD. 1976. Thermal efficiency: a possible determinant of height growth potential in young loblolly pines. Forest Science 22(3):279–282.

Bratton SP, Davison K. 1987. Disturbance and succession in Buxton Woods, Cape Hatteras, NC. Castanea 52(3):166–179.

Brender EV, McNab WH, Williams S. 1976. Fuel accumulations in Piedmont loblolly pine plantations. Res. Note SE-233. Asheville, NC: USDA Forest Service, Southeastern Forest Experiment Station. 4 p.

Brewer CW, Linnartz NE. 1978. Soil moisture utilization by mature loblolly pine stands in the Coastal Plain of southeastern Louisiana. In: Balmer WE, ed. Proceedings, Soil Moisture ... Site Productivity Symposium; 1977 November 1–3; Myrtle Beach, SC. Atlanta: USDA Forest Service, Southeastern Area, State and Private Forestry: 296–306.

Brix H. 1960. Determination of viability of loblolly pine seedlings after wilting. Botanical Gazette 121(4):220–223.

Broerman FS. 1978. Site classification—Union Camp Corporation. In: Balmer WE, ed. Proceedings, Soil Moisture ... Site Productivity Symposium; 1977 November 1–3; Myrtle Beach, SC. Atlanta: USDA Forest Service, Southeastern Area, State and Private Forestry: 64–73.

Buckingham FM, Woods FW. 1969. Loblolly pine (Pinus taeda L.) as influenced by soil moisture and other environmental factors. Journal of Applied Ecology 6(1):47–59.

Buol SW, ed. 1973. Soils of the southern states and Puerto Rico. SO Coop. Series Bull. 174. Auburn, AL: Auburn University, Alabama Agricultural Experiment Station. 105 p.

Burns RM. 1968. Sand pine: a tree for west Florida's sandhills. Journal of Forestry 66(7):561–562.

Campbell RG. 1978. The Weyerhaeuser land classification system. In: Balmer WE, ed. Proceedings, Soil Moisture ... Site Productivity Symposium; 1977 November 1–3; Myrtle Beach, SC. Atlanta: USDA Forest Service, Southeastern Area, State and Private Forestry: 74–82.

Carter CA, Miller JH, Davis DE, Patterson RM. 1984. Effect of vegetative competition on the moisture and nutrient status of loblolly pine. Canadian Journal of Forest Research 14(1):1–9.

Chang M, Aguilar GJR. 1980. Effects of climate and soil on the radial growth of loblolly pine (Pinus taeda L.) in a humid environment of southeastern U.S.A. Forest Ecology and Management 3(2):141–150.

Chen MY, Hodgkins EJ, Watson WJ. 1977. Alternative fire and herbicide systems for managing hardwood understory in a southern pine forest. Circ. 236. Auburn, AL: Auburn University, Alabama Agricultural Experiment Station. 19 p.

Cox SK, Van Lear DH. 1985. Biomass and nutrient accretion on Piedmont sites following clearcutting and natural regeneration of loblolly pine. In: Shoulders E, ed. Proceedings, 3rd Biennial Southern Silvicultural Research Conference; 1984 November 7–8; Atlanta, GA. Gen. Tech. Rep. SO-54. New Orleans: USDA Forest Service, Southern Forest Experiment Station: 501–506.

Culberson WL. 1958. Variation in the pine-inhabiting vegetation of North Carolina. Ecology 39(1):23–28.

Davison KL, Bratton SP. 1988. Vegetation response and regrowth after fire on Cumberland Island National Seashore, Georgia. Castanea 53(1):47–65.

DeBell DS, Askew GR, Hook DD, Owens EG. 1982. Species suitability on a lowland site altered by drainage. Southern Journal of Applied Forestry 6(1):2–9.

DeBrunner LE. 1968. The evaluation of certain climate related factors to diameter growth of loblolly pine (Pinus taeda L.) and Virginia pine (Pinus virginiana Mill.) in the Duke (NC) forest. Dissertation Abstracts International 28B(9):3547–3548.

Dickerson BP. 1972. Changes in the forest floor under upland oak stands and managed loblolly pine plantations. Journal of Forestry 70(9):560–562.

Dissmeyer GE, Stump RF. 1978. Predicted erosion rates for forest management activities in the Southeast. Atlanta: USDA Forest Service, Southeastern Area, State and Private Forestry. 26 p.

Di Stefano J. 1984. Nitrogen mineralization and non-symbiotic nitrogen fixation in an age sequence of slash pine plantations in North Florida. Gainesville, FL: University of Florida. 219 p. Ph.D. dissertation.

Douglass JE. 1974. Watershed values-important in land use planning on southern forests. Journal of Forestry 72:617–621.

Douglass JE, Van Lear DH. 1983. Prescribed burning and water quality of ephemeral streams in the Piedmont of South Carolina. Forest Science 29(1):181–189.

Downs RJ, Piringer AA Jr. 1958. Effects of photoperiod and kind of supplemental light on vegetative growth of pines. Forest Science 4(3):185–195.

Doyle TW. 1986. Seedling response to CO_2 enrichment under stressed and non-stressed conditions. In: Proceedings, International Symposium on Ecological Aspects of Tree-Ring Analysis; 1986 August 17–21; Tarrytown, NY. Washington, DC: U.S. Department of Energy: 501–510.

Duffy PD. 1985. Nutrient gains and losses for loblolly pine plantations. In: Forestry and water quality: Proceedings of a Midsouth symposium; 1985 May 8–9; Little Rock, AR. Fayetteville, AR: University of Arkansas: 42–54.

Duffy PD, Schreiber JD. 1990. Nutrient leaching of a loblolly pine forest floor by simulated rainfall: 2. Environmental factors. Forest Science 36(3):777–789.

Duffy PD, Schreiber JD, McDowell LL. 1985. Leaching of nitrogen, phosphorus, and total organic carbon from loblolly pine litter by simulated rainfall. Forest Science 31(3):750–759.

Elder TJ, Burkart LF. 1983. Chemical comparison of two ecotypes of loblolly pine. Society of Wood Science and Technology 15(3):245–250.

Eneim RC, Watterston KG. 1970. Pine seedling survival and growth related to moisture retention of eight Texas forest soils. Tree Planters' Notes 21(1):12, 17–20.

Evans DL, Burns PY, Linnartz NE, Robinson CJ. 1983. Forest habitat regions of Louisiana. LSU For. Res. Rep. 1. Baton Rouge, LA: Louisiana State University and A&M College, School of Forestry and Wildlife Management, Agricultural Experiment Station. 23 p.

Fetcher N, Jaeger CH, Strain BR, Sisnet N. 1988. Long-term elevation of atmospheric CO_2 concentration and the carbon exchange rates of saplings of *Pinus taeda* L. and *Liquidambar styraciflua* L. Tree Physiology 4:255–262.

Fisher RF, Rolfe GL, Eastburn RP. 1975. Productivity and organic matter distribution in a pine plantation and an adjacent, old field. For. Res. Rep. 75-1. Champaign/Urbana, IL: University of Illinois at Champaign/Urbana, Department of Forestry, Agricultural Experiment Station. 3 p.

Fowells HA, comp. 1965. Silvics of forest trees of the United States. Agric. Handbk. 271. Washington, DC: USDA Forest Service. 762 p.

Friend AL, Hafley WL. 1989. Climatic limitations to growth in loblolly and shortleaf pine (*Pinus taeda* and *P. echinata*): a dendroclimatological approach. Forest Ecology and Management 26(2):113–122.

Gay LW, Knoerr KR. 1975. The forest radiation budget. Bull. 19. Durham, NC: Duke University, School of Forestry and Environmental Studies. 165 p.

Gilmore AR. 1977. More on the effects of soil moisture stress on monoterpenes in loblolly pine. For. Res. Rep. 77-2. Champaign/Urbana, IL: University of Illinois at Champaign/Urbana, Department of Forestry, Agricultural Experiment Station. 2 p.

Gilmore AR. 1980. Changes in a reforested soil associated with tree species and time: 4. Soil organic content and pH in pine plantations after 24 years. For. Res. Rep. 80-3. Champaign/Urbana, IL: University of Illinois, Department of Forestry, Agricultural Experiment Station. 3 p.

Gilmore AR, Boggess WR. 1976. Changes in reforested soil associated with tree species and time: 1. Soil organic content and pH in pine plantations. For. Res. Rep. 76-4. Champaign/Urbana, IL: University of Illinois, Department of Forestry, Agricultural Experiment Station. 5 p.

Gilmore AR, Rolfe GL. 1980. Variation in soil organic matter in shortleaf pine and loblolly pine plantations at different tree spacings. For. Res. Rep. 80-2. Champaign/Urbana, IL: University of Illinois, Department of Forestry, Agricultural Experiment Station. 4 p.

Godeas AM. 1987. Decomposition studies of *Pinus taeda* forest: 2. Decomposition of leaf litter. Pedobiologia 30:323–331.

Goggans JF, Schultz EF. 1958. Growth of pine plantations in Alabama's Coastal Plain. Bull. 313. Auburn, AL: Alabama Polytechnic Institute, Agricultural Experiment Station. 19 p.

Grano CX. 1967. Growing loblolly and shortleaf pine in the Midsouth. Farmers Bull. 2102. Washington, DC: USDA. 27 p.

Grant D, Binkley D. 1987. Rates of free-living nitrogen fixation in some Piedmont forest types. Forest Science 33(2):548–551.

Gresham CA. 1982. Litterfall patterns in mature loblolly and longleaf pine stands in coastal South Carolina. Forest Science 28(2):223–241.

Hallbick DC. 1976. Classification of the soils in the Atlantic Coastal Plain. In: Proceedings, 6th Southern Forest Soils Workshop; 1976 October 19–21; Charleston, SC. [Place of publication unknown]: Forest Soils Council: [page numbers unknown].

Hammond EH. 1964. Classes of land surface form in the forty-eight states. In: United States of America. Annual of American Geographers 54:11–19 [Map supplement 4; national atlas sheet 62].

Heth D, Kramer PJ. 1975. Drought tolerance of pine seedlings under various climatic conditions. Forest Science 21(1):72–82.

Hiller CH, Brown RS. 1967. Comparison of dimensions and fibril angles of loblolly pine tracheids formed in wet or dry growing seasons. American Journal of Botany 54(4):453–460.

Hodges JD, Lorio PL Jr. 1975. Moisture stress and composition of xylem oleoresin in loblolly pine. Forest Science 21(3):283–290.

Hodgkins EJ, Golden MS, Miller WF. 1979. Forest habitat regions and types on a photomorphic–physiographic basis: a guide to forest site classification in Alabama–Mississippi. SO Coop. Series 210. Auburn, AL: Auburn University, Alabama Agricultural Experiment Station. 64 p.

Hosker RP Jr, Nappo CJ Jr, Hanna SR. 1974. Diurnal variation of vertical thermal structure in a pine plantation. Agricultural Meteorology 13(2):259–265.

Hosner JF, Graney, D.L. 1970. The relative growth of three forest tree species on soils associated with different successional states in Virginia. American Midland Naturalist 84(2): 418–427.

Hu SC, Linnartz NE. 1972. Variations in oxygen content of forest soils under mature loblolly pine stands. Sta. Bull. 668. Baton Rouge, LA: Louisiana Agriculture Experiment Station. 27 p.

Hunt CB. 1967. Physiography of the United States. San Francisco: W.H. Freeman. 480 p.

Jackson LWR. 1948. "Needle curl" of shortleaf pine seedlings. Phytopathological Notes 38(12):1028–1029.

Jackson LWR. 1962. Effect of size of forest openings on morphology of pine seedlings. Ecology 43(4):768–770.

Jain RK, Lockaby BG, Caulfield JP. 1989. Nutrition of loblolly pine on calcareous soils in western Alabama. Communications in Soil Science and Plant Analysis 20(3/4):421–437.

Jorgensen JR. 1974. A simple apparatus for obtaining multiple soil atmosphere samples from a single bore hole. Soil Science Society of America Proceedings 38(3):540–541.

Jorgensen JR. 1975. Nitrogen fixation in forested Coastal Plain soils. Res. Pap. SE-130. Asheville, NC: USDA Forest Service, Southeastern Forest Experiment Station. 16 p.

Jorgensen JR, Hodges CS Jr. 1970. Microbial characteristics of a forest soil after twenty years of prescribed burning. Mycologia 62(4):721–726.

Jorgensen JR, Wells CG. 1986. Foresters' primer in nutrient cycling—a loblolly pine management guide. Gen. Tech. Rep. SE-37. Asheville, NC: USDA Forest Service, Southeastern Forest Experiment Station. 42 p.

Jorgensen JR, Wells CG, Metz LJ. 1980. Nutrient changes in decomposing loblolly pine forest floor. Soil Science Society of America Journal 44(6):1307–1314.

Kaloyereas SA. 1958. A new method of determining drought resistance. Plant Physiology 33(3):232–233.

Katz B, Lieth HH. 1980. Fungi associated with loblolly pine needles: 2. Phenology and vertical distribution of fungi in the canopy and first year litter. International Journal of Biometeorology

24(3):179–197.

Kaufmann MR. 1968. Water relations of pine seedlings in relation to root and shoot growth. Plant Physiology 43(2):281–288.

Kaul ON, Billings WD. 1965. Cation content of stemflow in some forest trees in North Carolina. Indian Forester 91(6) 367–370.

Kinerson RS, Higginbotham KO, Chapman RC. 1974. The dynamics of foliage distribution within a forest canopy. Journal of Applied Ecology 11:347–353.

Klawitter RA. 1966. Diameter growth of mature loblolly pine unaffected by under-story control. Southern Lumberman 213(2656): 154–155.

Knauf TA, Bilan MV. 1974. Needle variation in loblolly pine from mesic and xeric seed sources. Forest Science 20(1):88–90.

Knauf TA, Bilan MV. 1977.Cotyledon and primary needle variation in loblolly pine from mesic and xeric seed sources. Forest Science 23(1):33–36.

Kodama HE, Van Lear DH. 1980. Prescribed burning and nutrient cycling relationships in young loblolly pine plantations. Southern Journal of Applied Forestry 4(3):118–121.

Kramer PJ, Kozlowski TT. 1979. Physiology of woody plants. Orlando, FL: Academic Press. 811 p.

Ku TT, Burton JD. 1973. Dry matter and minerals in loblolly pine plantations on four Arkansas soils. Proceedings of the Arkansas Academy of Science 27:21–25.

Kuhlman EG. 1970. Decomposition of loblolly pine bark by soil- and root-inhabiting fungi. Canadian Journal of Botany 48(10): 1787–1793.

Kuhns MR, Gjerstad DH. 1988. Photosynthate allocation in loblolly pine (Pinus taeda) seedlings as affected by moisture stress. Canadian Journal of Forest Research 18(3):285–291.

Lane CL. 1964. Soil acidity changes in pine stands. Journal of Forestry 62(4):263–264.

Lane CL. 1974. The chemical, physical, and microbiological properties of the soils of the Hobcaw Barony, Georgetown, South Carolina. For. Res. Series 30. Clemson, SC: Clemson University, Department of Forestry: 1–12.

Lane CL. 1975. Forest stand conversion from hardwoods to pines: effects on soil nutrients, microorganisms and forest floor weight during the first seven years. Forest Science 21(2):155–159.

Lea R, Ballard R. 1982. Relative effectiveness of nutrient concentrations in living foliage and needle fall at predicting response of loblolly pine to N and P fertilization. Canadian Journal of Forest Research 12:713–717.

Lockaby BG, Taylor-Boyd JD. 1986. Nutrient dynamics in the litter fall and forest floor of an 18-year-old loblolly pine plantation. Canadian Journal of Forestry Research. 16(5):1109–1112.

Lorio PL Jr. 1977. Groundwater levels and soil characteristics in a forested Typic Glossaqualf. Res. Note SO-225. New Orleans: USDA Forest Service, Southern Forest Experiment Station.

Lorio PL Jr, Hodges JD. 1968. Microsite effects on oleoresin exudation pressure of large loblolly pines. Ecology 49(6):1207–1210.

Lorio PL Jr, Hodges JD. 1971. Microrelief, soil water regime, and loblolly pine growth on a wet, mounded site. Soil Science Society of America Proceedings 35(5):795–800.

Lorio PL Jr, Howe VK, Martin CN. 1972. Loblolly pine rooting varies with microrelief on wet sites. Ecology 53(6):1134–1140.

MacCarthy R, Davey CB. 1976. Nutritional problems of the Pinus taeda L. (loblolly pine) growing on pocosin soil. Soil Science Society of America Journal 40(4):582–585.

March WJ, Skeen JN. 1976. Global radiation beneath the canopy and in a clearing of a suburban hardwood forest. Agricultural Meteorology 16(3):321–327.

Marx DH. 1990. Soil pH and nitrogen influence Pisolithus ectomycorrhizal development and growth of loblolly pine seedlings. Forest Science 36(2):224–245.

May JT. 1965. Site evaluation and species selection. In: Wahlenberg WG, ed. A guide to loblolly and slash pine plantation management in southeastern USA. GA For. Res. Rep. 14.

Macon, GA: Georgia Forestry Commission, Georgia Forest Research Council: 10–21.

McBrayer JF, Ferris JM, Metz LJ, and others. 1977. Decomposer invertebrate populations in U.S. forest biomass. Pedobiologia. 17(2):89–96.

McClurkin DC. 1971. Site rehabilitation under planted red cedar and pine. In: Youngberg CT, Davey CB, eds. Tree growth and forest soils. Proceedings, 3rd North American Forest Soils Conference; 1968 August; Raleigh, NC. Corvallis, OR: Oregon State University Press: 339–345.

McClurkin DC, Covell RR. 1965. Site index predictions for pines in Mississippi. Res. Pap. SO-15. New Orleans: USDA Forest Service, Southern Forest Experiment Station. 9 p.

McClurkin DC, McClurkin IT, Culpepper TJ. 1971. Cytochemical and tissue homogenate analysis of adenosine triphosphatase in root tips of Texas "lost pines." Forest Science 17(4):446–451.

McGilvray JM, Barnett JP. 1988. Increasing speed, accuracy, and safety of pressure chamber determinations of plant moisture stress. Tree Planters' Notes 39(3):3–4.

McKee WH. 1977. Soil–site relationships for loblolly pine on selected soils. In: Proceedings, 6th Southern Forest Soils Workshop; 1976 October 19–21; Charleston, SC. [Place of publication unknown]: Southern Forest Soils Council: 115–120.

McKee WH, Hook DD, DeBell DS, Askew JL. 1984. Growth and nutrient status of loblolly pine seedlings in relation to flooding and phosphorus. Soil Science Society of America Journal 48(6): 1438–1442.

McKevlin MR, Hood DD, McKee WH, and others. 1987a. Loblolly pine seedling root anatomy and iron accumulation as affected by soil waterlogging. Canadian Journal of Forest Research 17: 1257–1264.

McKevlin MR, Hook DD, McKee WH, and others. 1987b. Phosphorus allocation in flooded loblolly pine seedlings in relation to ion uptake. Canadian Journal of Forest Research 17:1572–1576.

Metz LJ. 1958. Moisture held in pine litter. Journal of Forestry 56(1):36.

Metz LJ. 1952. Weight and nitrogen and calcium content of the annual litter fall of forests in the South Carolina Piedmont. Proceedings of the Soil Science Society of America 16(1):38–41.

Metz LJ, Farrier MH. 1973. Prescribed burning and populations of soil mesofauna. Environmental Entomology 2(3) 433–440.

Metz LJ, Wells CG, Kormanik PP. 1970. Comparing the forest floor and surface soil beneath four pine species in the Virginia Piedmont. Res. Pap. SE-55. Asheville, NC: USDA Forest Service, Southeastern Forest Experiment Station. 8 p.

Miceli JC, Rolfe GL, Arnold LE, Boggess WR. 1975. A preliminary study of the role of precipitation in nutrient cycling in loblolly and shortleaf pine plantations. For. Res. Rep. 75-5. Champaign/Urbana, IL: University of Illinois, Department of Forestry, Agriculture Experiment Station. 4 p.

Miller LN. 1965. Changes in radiosensitivity of pine seedlings subjected to water stress during chronic gamma irradiation. Health Physics 11:1653–1662.

Miller WF, Dougherty PM, Switzer GL. 1987. Effect of rising carbon dioxide and potential climate change on loblolly pine distribution, growth, survival, and productivity. In: Shands WE, Hoffman JS, eds. The greenhouse effect, climate change, and U.S. forests. Washington, DC: Conservation Foundation: 157–187.

Moehring DM, Ralston CW. 1967. Diameter growth of loblolly pine related to available soil moisture and rate of soil moisture loss. Soil Science Society of America Proceedings 31(4):560–562.

Monroe WH. 1953. General geologic features of the Atlantic and Gulf Coastal Plain. In: McGrain P, ed. Techniques of mineral resources exploration and evaluation. Proceedings, Southeastern Mineral Symposium, 1950. Spec. Publ. 1-950, Series 9. Lexington, KY: University of Kentucky: 5–16.

Montes RA, Christensen NL. 1979. Nitrification and succession in the Piedmont of North Carolina. Forest Science 25(2):281–297.

Murray GE. 1961. Geology of the Atlantic and Gulf Coastal Province of North America. New York: Harper & Brothers. 692 p.

Myers RK, Zohner R, Jones SM. 1986. Forest habitat regions of South Carolina from Landsat imagery. For. Res. Sec. 42. Clemson, SC: College of Forest and Recreation Resources, Clemson University. 31 p.

Nelson TC, Zillgitt WM. 1969. A forest atlas of the South. New Orleans: USDA Forest Service, Southern Forest Experiment Station. 27 p.

Nemeth JC. 1972. Dry-matter production in young loblolly (Pinus taeda L.) and slash pine (Pinus elliottii Engelm.) plantations. Dissertation Abstracts International 32B(7):3896–3897.

Newton RJ, Sen S, Puryear JD. 1987. Free proline in water-stressed pine callus. TAPPI Journal 70(6):141–144.

Pehl CE, Brim RL. 1985. Forest habitat regions of Georgia: Landsat IV imagery. Spec. Publ. 31. Athens, GA: University of Georgia, College of Agriculture, Georgia Agriculture Experiment Station. 12 p.

Pehl CE, Ray KF. 1983. Atmospheric nutrient inputs to three forest types in east Texas. Forest Ecology and Management 7:11–18.

Permar TA, Fisher RF. 1983. Nitrogen fixation and accretion by wax myrtle (Myrica cerifera) in slash pine (Pinus elliottii) plantations. Forest Ecology and Management 5(1):3946.

Ralston CW. 1978. The southern pinery: forests, physiography, and soils. In: Proceedings, Symposium on Principles of Maintaining Productivity on Prepared Sites; 1978 March 21–22; [Location unknown]. [Place of publication and publisher unknown]: 6–11.

Rogers HH, Bingham GE, Cure JD, and others. 1983. Responses of selected plant species to elevated carbon dioxide in the field. Journal of Environmental Quality 12(4):569–574.

Rogerson TL. 1967. Throughfall in pole-sized loblolly pine as affected by stand density. In: Sopper WE, Lull HW, eds. Forest hydrology. Proceedings, National Science Foundation Advanced Science Seminar; 1965 August 29–September 10; University Park, PA. New York: Pergamon Press: 187–190.

Rolfe GL, Miceli JC, Arnold LE, Boggess WR. 1976. Biomass and nutrient pools in loblolly and shortleaf pine in southern Illinois. In: Fralish JS, Weaver GT, Schlesinger RC, eds. Proceedings, Central Hardwood Forest Conference; 1976 October 17–19; Carbondale, IL. [Place of publication and publisher unknown]: 363–375.

Russell TE. 1961. Control of understory hardwood fails to speed growth of pole-size loblolly. Sta. Note 131. New Orleans: USDA Forest Service, Southern Forest Experiment Station. 4 p.

Schmidtling RC. 1984. Early intensive culture affects long-term growth of loblolly pine trees. Forest Science 30(2):491–498.

Schreiber JD, Duffy PD, McDowell LL. 1990. Nutrient leaching of loblolly pine forest floor by simulated rainfall: 1. Intensity effects. Forest Science 36(3):765–776.

Seiler JR, Johnson JD. 1984. Abnormal needle morphology in loblolly pine induced by low humidity. HortScience 19(4):521–522.

Seiler JR, Johnson JD. 1985. Photosynthesis and transpiration of loblolly pine seedlings as influenced by moisture-stress conditioning. Forest Science 31(3):742–749.

Seiler JR, Johnson JD. 1985. Moisture stress conditioning of containerized loblolly pine. In: Lantz CW, comp. Proceedings, 1984 Southern Nursery Conferences; 1984 June 11–14; Alexandria, LA/July 24–27; Asheville, NC. Atlanta: USDA Forest Service, Southern Region: 60–65.

Shear TH, Hook DD. 1988. Interspecific genetic variation of loblolly pine tolerance to soil waterlogging. In: Hook DD, McKee WH Jr, Smith JG, and others, eds. The ecology and management of wetlands. Vol. 1, Ecology of wetlands. Portland, OR: Timber Press: 489–493.

Shoulders E, Tiarks A. 1980. Predicting height and relative performance of major southern pines from rainfall, slope, and available soil moisture. Forest Science 26(3):437–447.

Shoulders E, Walker FV. 1979. Soil, slope, and rainfall affect height and yield in 15-year-old southern pine plantations. Res. Pap. SO-153. New Orleans: USDA Forest Service, Southern Forest Experiment Station. 52 p.

Sinclair TR, Knoerr KR. 1982. Distribution of photosynthetically active radiation in the canopy of a loblolly pine plantation. Journal of Applied Ecology 19(1):183–191.

Sionit N, Strain BR, Hellmers H, and others. 1985. Long-term atmospheric CO_2 enrichment affects the growth and development of Liquidambar styraciflua and Pinus taeda seedlings. Canadian Journal of Forest Research 15:468–471.

Smalley GW. 1979. Classification and evaluation of forest sites on the Southern Cumberland Plateau. Gen. Tech. Rep. SO-23. New Orleans: USDA Forest Service, Southern Forest Experiment Station. 59 p.

Smalley GW. 1980. Classification and evaluation of forest sites on the Western Highland Rim and Pennyroyal. Gen. Tech. Rep. SO-30. New Orleans: USDA Forest Service, Southern Forest Experiment Station. 120 p.

Smalley GW. 1982. Classification and evaluation of forest sites on Mid-Cumberland Plateau. Gen. Tech. Rep. SO-38. New Orleans: USDA Forest Service, Southern Forest Experiment Station. 58 p.

Smalley GW. 1983. Classification and evaluation of forest sites on the Eastern Highland Rim and Pennyroyal. Gen. Tech. Rep. SO-43. New Orleans: USDA Forest Service, Southern Forest Experiment Station. 123 p.

Smalley GW. 1984. Landforms: a practical basis for classifying forest sites in the interior uplands. In: Proceedings, 12th Annual Hardwood Symposium; 1984 May 8–11; Cashiers, NC. Asheville, NC: Hardwood Research Council: 92–112.

Smalley GW. 1986. Classification and evaluation of forest sites on the northern Cumberland Plateau. Gen. Tech. Rep. SO-60. New Orleans: USDA Forest Service, Southern Forest Experiment Station. 74 p.

Stogsdill WR Jr, Wittwer RF, Hennessy TC, Dougherty PM. 1989. Relationship between throughfall and stand density in a Pinus taeda plantation. Forest Ecology and Management 29(1/2):105–113.

Stransky JJ. 1963. Needle moisture as mortality index for southern pine seedlings. Botanical Gazette 124(3):178–179.

Stransky JJ, Wilson DR. 1964. Terminal elongation of loblolly and shortleaf pine seedlings under soil moisture stress. Soil Science Society of America Proceedings 28(3):439–440.

Stransky JJ, Wilson DR. 1967. Soil moisture and texture affect root and shoot weights of transplanted pine seedlings. Res. Note SO-62. New Orleans: USDA Forest Service, Southern Forest Experiment Station. 3 p.

Swank WT, Goebel NB, Helvey JD. 1972. Interception loss in loblolly pine stands of the South Carolina Piedmont. Journal of Soil Water Conservation 27(4):160–164.

Switzer GL, Nelson LE. 1972. Nutrient accumulation and cycling in loblolly pine (Pinus taeda L.) plantation ecosystems: the first twenty years. Soil Science Society of America Proceedings 36(1):143–147.

Switzer GL, Nelson, LE. 1974. Maintenance of productivity under short rotations. In: FAO/IUFRO International Symposium on Forest Fertilization; 1973 December 3–7; Paris. Paris: Ministry of Agriculture: 365–389.

Switzer GL, Moehring DM, Terry TA. 1978. Clearcutting vs. alternative timber harvesting stand regeneration systems: effects on soils and environment of the south. In: Youngberg CT, ed. Forest soils and land use: Proceedings, 5th North American Forest Soils Conference; 1978 August; Fort Collins, CO. Fort Collins, CO: Colorado State University, Department of Forest and Wood Sciences: 477–515.

Switzer GL, Nelson LE, Shelton MG. 1988. Influence of the canopy of loblolly pine plantations on the disposition and chemistry of precipitation. Tech. Bull. 154. Mississippi State, MS: Mississippi Agricultural and Forestry Experiment Station. 32 p.

Switzer GL, Nelson LE, Smith WH. 1968. The mineral cycle in forest stands. In: Forest fertilization. Muscle Shoals, AL: Tennessee Valley Authority. 9 p.

Switzer GL, Shelton MG, Nelson LE. 1979. Successional development of the forest floor and soil surface on upland sites of the East Gulf Coastal Plain. Ecology 60(6):1162–1171.

Thames JL. 1963. Needle variation in loblolly pine from four geographic seed sources. Ecology 44(1):16–169.

Thomas JF, Harvey CN. 1983. Leaf anatomy of four species grown under continuous CO_2 enrichment. Botanical Gazette 114(3):303–309.

Thomas WA. 1968. Decomposition of loblolly pine needles with and without addition of dogwood leaves. Ecology 49(3):568–571.

Thornbury WD. 1965. Regional geomorphology of the United States. New York: John Wiley and Sons. 609 p.

Tolley LC, Strain BR. 1984a. Effects of CO_2 enrichment and water stress on growth of *Liquidambar styraciflua* and *Pinus taeda* seedlings. Canadian Journal of Botany 62(10):2135–2139.

Tolley LC, Strain BR. 1984b. Effects of CO_2 enrichment on growth of *Liquidambar styraciflua* and *Pinus taeda* seedlings under different irradiance levels. Canadian Journal of Forest Research 14(3):343–350.

Topa MA, McLeod KW. 1986a. Effects of anaerobic growth conditions on phosphorus tissue concentrations and absorption rates of southern pine seedlings. Tree Physiology 2(13):327–340.

Topa MA, McLeod KW. 1986b. Aerenchyma and lenticel formation in pine seedlings: a possible avoidance mechanism to anaerobic growth conditions. Physiologia Plantarum 68(3):540–550.

Topa MA, McLeod KW. 1986c. Responses of *Pinus clausa*, *Pinus serotina* and *Pinus taeda* seedlings to anaerobic solution culture: 1. Changes in growth and root morphology. Physiologia Plantarum 68(3):523–539.

Topa MA, McLeod KW. 1986d. Responses of *Pinus clausa*, *Pinus serotina* and *Pinus taeda* seedlings to anaerobic solution culture: 2. Changes in tissue nutrient concentration and net acquisition. Physiologia Plantarum 68(3):532–539.

Torrenueva AL. 1975. Variation in mineral flux to the forest floors of a pine and a hardwood stand in the Georgia Piedmont. Athens, GA: University of Georgia. 110 p. Ph.D. dissertation.

Trimble SW. 1974. Man-induced soil erosion on the southern Piedmont 1700–1970. [Place of publication unknown]: Soil Conservation Society of America. 130 p.

Trousdell KB, Wenger KF. 1963. Some factors of climate and soil affecting establishment of loblolly pine stands. Forest Science 9(2):130–136.

USDA [U.S. Department of Agriculture]. 1941. Yearbook of agriculture: climate and man. Washington, DC: USDA.

USDA SCS [U.S. Department of Agriculture]. 1975. Soil taxonomy. Agric. Handbk. 436. Washington, DC: USDA Soil Conservation Service. 754 p.

USDA FS [U.S. Department of Agriculture, Forest Service]. 1963. Quality of standing timber: wood density surveys: specific gravity of slash, loblolly and longleaf pine in Georgia and Florida. Madison, WI: USDA Forest Service, Forest Products Laboratory; 1962 annual report. 8 p.

U.S. Department of Commerce. 1968. Climatic atlas of the United States. Washington, DC: USDC.

Ursic SJ. 1961. Tolerance of loblolly pine seedlings to soil moisture stress. Ecology 42:823–825.

van Buijtenen JP, Bilan MV, Zimmerman RH. 1976. Morphophysiological characteristics related to drought resistance in *Pinus taeda*. In: Cannell MG, Last FT, eds. Tree physiology and yield improvement. New York: Academic Press: 349–359.

Van Lear DH, Goebel NB. 1976. Leaf fall and forest floor characteristics in loblolly pine plantations in the South Carolina Piedmont. Soil Science Society of America Journal. 40(1):116–119.

Van Lear DH, Jones SM. 1987. An example of site classification in the southeastern coastal plain based on vegetation and land type. Southern Journal of Applied Forestry 11(1):23–28.

Van Lear DH, Swank WT, Douglass JE, Waide JB. 1983. Forest management practices and the nutrient status of a loblolly pine plantation. In: Ballard R, Gessel SP, tech. eds. IUFRO Symposium on Forest Site and Continuous Productivity; 1982 August 22–28; Seattle, WA. Gen. Tech. Rep. PNW-163. Portland, OR: USDA Forest Service, Pacific Northwest Forest and Range Experiment Station: 252–258.

Van Lear DH, Kapeluck PR, Waide JB. 1989. Nitrogen pools and processes during natural regeneration of loblolly pine. In: Garrett S, Powers R, eds. Proceedings, 7th North American Forest Soils Conference; 1988 July 24–28; Vancouver, BC. [Place of publication and publisher unknown]: [page numbers unknown].

Vitousek PM, Matson PA. 1984. Mechanisms of nitrogen retention in forest ecosystems: a field experiment. Science 225(4657): 51–52.

Walker LC, Arnold JC. 1963. Detecting tree feeding roots with radioactive phosphorus. Advancing Frontiers of Plant Science 4:179–188.

Watson ES, McClurkin DC, Huneycutt MB. 1974. Fungal succession on loblolly pine and upland hardwood foliage and litter in north Mississippi. Ecology 55(5):1128–1134.

Wells CG. 1965. Nutrient relationship between soils and needles of loblolly pine (*Pinus taeda*). Soil Science Society America Proceedings 29(5):612–614.

Wells CG. 1971. Effects of prescribed burning on soil chemical properties and nutrient availability. In: Proceedings, Prescribed Burning Symposium; 1971 April 14–16; Charleston, SC. Georgetown, SC: The Belle W. Baruch Research Institute: 86–99.

Wells CG. 1976. Nutrient cycling and its relationship to fertilization. In: Proceedings, 6th Southern Forest Soils Workshop; 1976 October 19–21; Charleston, SC: [Place of publication unknown]: Southern Forest Soils Council: 78–87.

Wells CG, Jorgensen JR. 1975. Nutrient cycling in loblolly pine plantations. In: Bernier B, Winget CH, eds. Soils and forest land management. Quebec: Laval University Press: 137–158.

Wells CG, Jorgensen JR. 1977. Nutrient cycling in loblolly pine: silvicultural implications. In: 1977 TAPPI Forest Biology Wood Chemistry Conference; 1977 June 20–22; Madison, WI. Atlanta: TAPPI Press: 8993.

Wells C, Whigham D, Lieth H. 1972. Investigation of site of mineral nutrient cycling in Upland Piedmont forest. Journal of the Mitchell Society 88(2):66–78.

Wenger KF. 1952. Effect of moisture supply and soil texture on the growth of sweetgum and pine seedlings. Journal of Forestry 50(11):862–864.

White EH, Pritchett WL. 1970. Water table control and fertilization for pine production in the flatwoods. Tech. Bull. 743. Gainesville, FL: University of Florida, Agricultural Experiment Station. 41 p.

White JD, Alexander LT, Clark EW. 1972. Fluctuations in the inorganic constituents of inner bark of loblolly pine with season and soil series. Canadian Journal of Botany 50(6):1287–1293.

Wiggins JE Jr. 1978. Soil-tree growth correlation and site classification. In: Proceedings, Soil Moisture … Site Productivity Symposium; 1977 November 1–3; Myrtle Beach, SC. Atlanta: USDA Forest Service, Southeastern Area, State and Private Forestry: 87–92.

Willis WM, Zaneveld JS. 1971. Vegetation composition and distribution on a barrier island of Virginia's eastern shore. Virginia Journal of Science 22(3):103.

Williston HL. 1962. Loblolly seedlings survive twelve days' submergence. Journal of Forestry 60 412.

Williston HL. 1978.   The case for understory hardwood control to improve soil moisture availability. In: Proceedings, Soil Moisture … Site Productivity Symposium; 1977 November 1–3; Myrtle Beach, SC. Atlanta: USDA Forest Service, Southeastern Area, State and Private Forestry: 359–362.

Yeiser JL, Burnett F. 1982.   Fate of forest trees stressed by heat and drought in southeastern Arkansas. Southern Journal of Applied Forestry 6(4):194–195.

Zahner R. 1968.   Water deficits and growth of trees. In: Kozlowski TT, ed. Water deficits and plant growth. Vol. 2, Plant water consumption and response. New York: Academic Press: 191–244.

Zahner R. 1958a.   Hardwood understory depletes soil water in pine stands. Forest Science 4(3):178–184.

Zahner R. 1958b.   Site-quality relationships of pine forests in southern Arkansas and northern Louisiana. Forest Science 4(2):163–176.

Zahner R, Myers RK. 1987.   Assessing the impact of drought on forest health. In: Forests, the world, and the profession: Proceedings, 1986 National Convention of the Society of American Foresters; 1986 October 5–8; Birmingham, AL. Bethesda, MD: Society of American Foresters: 227–234.

Part 2

··

Management Of Loblolly Pine

Chapter 4

Site Preparation

Contents

Site Preparation

Introduction

Loblolly pines grow best on sites with moist, friable, nutrient-rich soils and full sunlight. Where site conditions are not optimum, tree survival and growth can be increased by limiting the development of other vegetation and by improving the physical and chemical properties of microsites. Maintaining the quality of the A and B horizons is especially important if tree growth is to be promoted (McKee 1977). Shrubs and trees are the most important competitors in about 62% of the loblolly pine

ecosystem. Herbaceous weeds are the most serious competitors on 23% of the area, and vines cause the greatest problems on about 6% (Fitzgerald and others 1973). Loblolly pine seedlings and saplings usually grow most rapidly if all other vegetation is removed prior to regeneration operations. However, controlling all vegetation associated with loblolly pines generally is both very expensive and ecologically undesirable.

Site Preparation Techniques

Site preparation for tree planting can remove obstructions to planting, control competing plants, and improve the microsite for each seedling. Factors to be considered when determining the method of site preparation include soil type, soil moisture, slope of terrain, harvesting residue, climate and weather patterns, availability of equipment, intensity of management, pollution control standards, and cost. Between 400,000 and 600,000 ha of land are site prepared for loblolly pine planting each year. Effective techniques for vegetation control and site manipulation include prescribed burning, mechanical scarification, and herbicide treatment; these can be used singly or in various combinations. Widely used combinations of site preparation treatments include

- Burning and herbicide application(s) (injection or spray)
- Shearing and burning
- Burning and disking
- Shearing, burning, and disking
- Burning and chopping
- Shearing, chopping, and burning
- Chopping and bedding
- Shearing, chopping, and bedding
- Disking and bedding
- Shearing, chopping, burning, and bedding

Disking along the contour, chopping up and down slopes, or chemical control on fragile soils minimize erosion during heavy rains and help maintain the quality of sites where some form of vegetation control is necessary. About 50 to 70% of the managed land in pine undergoes some form of mechanical site preparation. Twenty-five to thirty percent receives chemical preparation treatments, and 10 to 30% is burned (Blackburn and others 1978, Fitzgerald and others 1973). Well-planned harvesting that removes all or most of the aboveground biomass and scarifies the soil can make planting or seeding much easier and more successful.

Prescribed Burning

Fire has long been a mainstay in the regeneration of loblolly pines (Rothkugel 1907). Since the 1940's, winter and summer controlled burns have been used to deaden small hardwoods and prepare seedbeds for artificial and natural regeneration of loblolly pine throughout its range. Prescribed burning must be planned so that enough unburned surface organic matter is left to protect the site, and fire lines must be placed so that they do not cause severe erosion. The kinds of fires and effects of fuel on fire intensity are discussed in chapter 8.

Under favorable conditions, a single prescribed fire can reduce hardwood cover by two-thirds or more. No other preparatory treatment may be needed if seedlings are planted soon after burning and can capture a site before hardwood sprouts become severe competitors (table 4-1). Some state governments assist landowners in burning their property to prepare sites for regeneration (Pennock 1978).

Table 4-1—Stocking and height of loblolly pines 4 years after burning

Treatment	Stocking (%)		Average height (m)	
	All trees	Free growing	All trees	Free growing
Planted in open	78	78	2.2	2.2
Burned and planted	74	43	1.6	1.8
Not burned, planted in moderately dense cover	67	28	1.3	1.6
Not burned, planted in dense hardwood cover	70	0	0.9	0.0

Source: adapted from Walker and Brender (1959).

Burning to prepare sites for natural or artificial regeneration can be done before or after harvesting. Regular burning during a rotation can kill almost all competing hardwoods and can make site preparation for the next rotation easy. Burning shortly before harvesting is a very effective method of preparing seedbeds for natural loblolly pine regeneration because it reduces the duff layer and minimizes the number of small hardwoods (figure 4-1). In fact, young hardwoods are easier to kill before harvest than after harvest because shaded plants usually have less vigor and smaller reserves of stored carbohydrates than do plants that grow in the open. Preharvest burning also makes harvesting easier by clearing under-

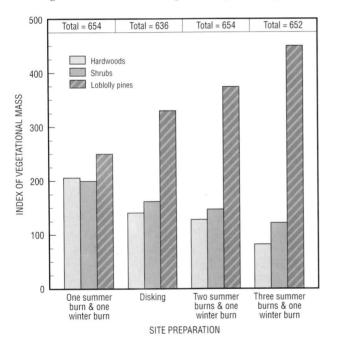

Figure 4-1— Control of hardwood and shrub competition increases the growth of loblolly pines in the Virginia Coastal Plain. The totals above each site preparation treatment are the total accumulated indices of vegetational mass at 6 years, indicating that total mass values produced after the various treatments were nearly equal (adapted from Trousdell and Langdon 1970).

brush. Similarly, both preharvest and postharvest burns can make mechanical site preparation easier.

Prescribed burning shortly after harvesting is especially effective in creating a favorable seedbed for loblolly pine regeneration because harvesting increases the amount of fuel available and so makes for a hotter fire. The impact of fire depends on vegetation type, landform, soil type, slope percentage, aspect, fire intensity, and a host of environmental factors. If properly controlled, postharvest burns can consume competing vegetation and logging slash and damage or kill superficial roots of competing plants while consuming only 30 to 50% of the litter layer. The effectiveness of burning can be increased by chain-saw felling of standing residual trees in the spring, when they are almost in full leaf; permitting 6 to 8 weeks of drying before burning; running a high-intensity fire over a moist fuel bed; and planting during the next planting season.

The fell-and-burn technique has produced excellent loblolly pine stands at low cost in the southern uplands (Sims 1989). In the Piedmont and upper Coastal Plain, where hardwood competition is intense, fire is often most effective as a preplanting treatment applied to vegetation that has been chopped or crushed.

On the Umbric and Humic soil groups of the lower Coastal Plain, which have an abundance of organic matter, and on Histosols, which are almost entirely organic, burning is desirable and often essential to reduce logging slash and other undecomposed organic matter before forest renewal. On some Histosols, burning up to 0.3 m of the root mat will substantially aid loblolly pine regeneration by destroying much of the native vegetation. However, destruction of the root mat severely limits vehicle trafficability and rules out machine planting on these areas (Maki 1977). On many other lower Coastal Plain sites, postharvest prescribed burning is most often used to reduce logging slash and consume dense ground cover such as saw-palmetto, *Serenoa repens* (*Bartr.*) Small; gallberry, *Ilex glabra* (L.) Gray; and small hardwoods.

The most favorable conditions for loblolly pine establishment are created when hot fires destroy competing vegetation late in the growing season (late summer and early fall), just before seedfall or planting. Under such conditions, loblolly pine seedlings begin growth on a relatively equal footing with most vegetation, except sprouting hardwoods that already have well-developed root systems. Conditions are least favorable following surface fires in the dormant season because many hardwood species sprout promptly and more numerously at the beginning of the new growing season. Fire intensity-fuel relationships are discussed in detail in chapter 8.

Controlled fires for site preparation can be initiated from the ground or from the air. The preferred technique for initiating prescribed fires from the ground is to walk along a cleared strip (fire line) with a backpack flame sprayer or drip torch that drops burning fuel in an almost continuous line. Large areas of debris can be burned quickly by dropping ignited petroleum from a torch slung under a helicopter. Where loblolly pines have not yet been harvested, site preparation or hazard reduction fires can be set quickly, safely, and economically by dropping potassium permanganate balls injected with ethylene glycol from a helicopter (Roten 1981).

The greatest advantages of fire as a site preparation measure are low cost (except on very small areas), limited site disturbance, and ease of integration with chemical or mechanical treatments. Low-intensity prescribed fires that do not destroy the litter layer cause little sedimentation and have little adverse effect on water quality. However, even prescribed fire can increase erosion if it destroys most of the litter layer or if fire lines are constructed poorly (Richter and others 1982, Van Lear and others 1985). The main disadvantages of fire for site preparation are that it seldom provides lasting benefits when used alone because advanced hardwood regeneration is not deadened, and that large pieces of debris and high stumps are rarely consumed, thus making machine planting difficult. Other disadvantages include variable effectiveness on sites with sparse fuel, site damage and reduced loblolly pine growth associated with annual or intense fires, safety problems, air pollution (see chapter 10), and soil nitrogen (N) reduction. About 50 to 150 kg of N/ha are usually lost when logging debris is burned during site preparation (Vitousek and others 1983).

Mechanical Site Preparation

Mechanical site preparation is normally accomplished with tractor-drawn equipment and is designed to subdue competing vegetation, clear logging debris, reduce fire hazards, improve soil properties, and facilitate regeneration. Standard farm implements can be used on old fields and open, cut-over areas with few stumps. Crawler tractors or heavy-duty, rubber-tired vehicles and sturdy attachments are needed on forest sites with undesirable trees, many stumps, or much logging debris or brush. The most damaging effects of mechanical site preparation are physical displacement of organic matter and surface soil, compaction of surface soil, and erosion.

Equipment. Machines are available that (1) knock down standing trees by bulldozing, chaining, tree crushing, and chopping; (2) sever standing shrubs by bush hogging and mowing (not widely used for loblolly regeneration though); (3) incorporate living or dead surface vegetation into the topsoil by disking, bedding, chopping, and tree crushing; (4) remove vegetation from the site to be regenerated by whole-tree chipping, then shearing and piling with a shearing or KG blade, and then rootraking; (5) push the duff and some surface soil away from narrow strips by furrowing and scalping; and (6) loosen compacted soil layers by ripping or subsoiling with a heavy, metal plow that tills soil 30 to 90 cm below

the soil surface. These techniques, used singly or in various combinations, can be highly beneficial where soil properties (that is, aeration, moisture-holding capacity, and bulk density) or vegetative competition would reduce tree survival and growth. Treatments that damage or destroy surface roots of competing vegetation are especially effective in promoting the growth of loblolly pine seedlings (Lockaby and others 1988).

There are many different types of site preparation equipment (Larson and Hallman 1980, McKenzie and Miller 1978):

Bulldozer blade. A standard (2.4-m-wide) blade attached to the front of a bulldozer. When set 0.3 to 0.6 m above the ground, such a blade knocks all large vegetation to the ground. The blade can be used to windrow or pile surface debris. It can be used alone or accompanied by another implement pulled by the prime mover.

Shearing blade (KG blade). A modified bulldozer blade with a sharp cutting blade along its bottom edge. It severs stumps and trees at the groundline, simplifying subsequent site preparation and regeneration activities. A stinger, or stump splitter, is located on the blade's lower leading edge, and the blade is mounted at a 30% angle to the longitudinal axis of the prime mover. The angle increases the slicing and shearing capability of the blade. The blade can be tilted for more effective stump removal. Shearing blades are 4.6 to 7.0 m long with a cutting width of 2.7 to 4.3 m. They weigh from 0.9 to 5.4 tonnes (t).

V-blade. Essentially two dozer blades joined at a narrow angle (less than 90%) and mounted with the apex forward. Serrated cutting blades along the bottom edge have a sawing and shearing effect. A stinger, or splitter, protrudes 0.6 to 1.2 m in front of the leading edge in the center of the blade. The unit can weigh from 0.4 to 5.4 t, and the cutting width can range up to 4.6 m.

Rootrake. A modified bulldozer blade 2.4 to 4.9 m wide and weighing up to 3.6 t. The base of the blade bears tines 30 to 66 cm long at 15- to 56-cm intervals. As the name implies, the implement is designed to rake tree stems, roots, and other large objects over the soil surface without displacing large portions of the forest floor or surface soil.

Disk-harrow. One or two gangs of angled or offset disks 66 to 96 cm in diameter. Disks are spaced from 30 to 43 cm apart and churn soil, roots, and surface debris to depths that can exceed 20 cm in swaths that can exceed 3.7 m wide. Eight- to 12-disk units weigh from 1.6 to 2.2 t. The harrow can be pulled by a crawler tractor or a rubber-tired skidder depending on terrain and physical conditions of a site.

Bedding harrow. Often, two disk gangs positioned to cut toward each other, pulling the surface soil into long parallel ridges 1.8 to 2.4 m apart and 20 to 45 cm above the normal groundline. A unit commonly has six disks from 70 to 90 cm in diameter. An hourglass weight or roller can be pulled behind the unit to pack down the mounded soil. A thin metal flange is usually mounted on the middle of the packer to keep the unit rolling along the top of the newly constructed bed. Intermittent mounds can be constructed with a bulldozer blade or other implement that pushes soil and organic matter into piles.

Roller chopper. A metal cylinder 1.8 to 4.9 m long and about 1.2 to 1.8 m in diameter. From 8 to 16 longitudinal cutting blades are spaced at 46-cm intervals around the drum. Blades can be straight or V-shaped and project 15 to 25 cm from the drum surface. A unit 1.5 m in diameter and 2.4 m in length weighs about 4.5 t when empty and 10.0 to 13.6 t when the cylinder is filled with water. One or two drums can be pulled behind a crawler tractor to knock down and break trees and other vegetation, forcing the broken material into the surface soil. Two drums can be offset so that surface debris is torn as they roll along.

Tree crusher. A self-propelled, three-drum chopper that rolls over and flattens all vegetation on a site. Heavy-duty cutting blades on each drum break tree parts into 0.6-m lengths and push them into the soil surface as the crusher moves along. A unit can weigh from 34.5 to 60.0 t and can be from 4.9 to 7.3 m in width. The two front rollers turn like steerable wheels to give the machine maximum mobility.

Chain. Anchor chains (of the kind used by large ships) pulled between two large crawler tractors. These knock over most trees and brush and scarify the soil surface. The chain can weigh from 34 to 164 kg/m and can be as long as 90 m. The chain should be pulled in a U- or J-shaped pattern, with the chain length two to three times the distance between the tractors. Because most vegetation is left scattered over the ground, regeneration is difficult in the absence of additional treatments.

Furrowing or fire line plows. Usually, a single 51- to 76-cm coulter followed by a V-shaped share and then a pair of disks that force surface vegetation and the upper 5 to 15 cm of soil to either side of the furrow. Such plows can be used to construct continuous shallow furrows or intermittent scalped spots. These plows can be pulled behind crawler tractors or rubber-tired machines.

Scalper. A small V-blade mounted on the front of a tractor that pulls a planting machine. The scalper clears debris from strips to facilitate planting. It can be adjusted to remove only surface material or various amounts of soil from the planting row.

Mower or bush hog. Covered rotary blade, which severs surface vegetation, can be mounted either in front of or behind a rubber-tired vehicle. Mowers rapidly cut 2.1- to 2.4-m swaths through brush and small trees up to 15 cm in dbh.

Subsoiler or ripper. A single plow blade that can break up sandstone, shale layers, or compacted surface or subsurface soil to depths exceeding 0.9 m. It is pulled behind a crawler tractor and leaves only a narrow groove of disturbed material at the surface as it is pulled through the soil. Flanges can be added to the base of the blade to expand the zone of soil shattering where penetration is deepest.

Mixing of soil and organic matter. Mixing organic matter on or near the soil surface with topsoil increases the rate of decomposition, improves soil tilth, and makes mechanical planting easier and more successful. This mixing can be done in several ways.

Disking (harrowing). Disking is the technique most often used to mix mineral soil and organic matter. Disking breaks up the aboveground portions of small trees, shrubs, and grasses and incorporates this material into the surface soil. It can also break up the dense root mats formed just under the soil surface by species, such as runner oak, *Quercus pumila* Walt.; gallberry; saw-palmetto; and wiregrass, *Aristida stricta* Michx. Combining the litter layer, surface vegetation, and roots with the upper 15 to 20 cm of soil quickly improves soil chemical and physical properties, and increases soil moisture holding capacity. On sloping or hilly land, disking should be along the contour so that the small berms created reduce overland flow of rainwater (figure 4-2). On slopes greater than 10%, disked and undisked alternating strips along contours provide better protection against erosion than does complete disking (Balmer and Little 1978). Disking is also very effective in ameliorating surface soil that has been compacted during harvesting operations (for example, skid trails and log landings). However, if compaction extends more than 20 to 25 cm deep, normal disking treatments will not rectify the problem.

Disking breaks up or damages stems and roots and promotes sprouting, especially of small hardwoods. The sprouts that develop after disking can be more numerous and more competitive with a new pine stand than those that develop in the absence of disking. On some sites where competition is intense, a second disking about 6 weeks after the first and run at right angles to the first keeps competing vegetation in check until loblolly pine seedlings are firmly established. Time of

Figure 4-2—Contour disking on sloping soils (Dissmeyer and Foster 1980).

Figure 4-3—Chopping an upland scrub hardwood site with dual, offset, 10-t choppers pulled by a D-8 tractor.

disking can influence response. In the Georgia Piedmont, loblolly pine survival was greatest and hardwood competition was least when disking was done in August. Results were poorest when disking was done in March and were intermediate when disking was done in May (Shelton and others 1989).

Chopping. Chopping mixes soil and organic matter. Chopping treatments knock down standing vegetation, breaking most small material into short lengths and pushing some into the surface soil with only local soil movement (figure 4-3). Most material is concentrated near the soil surface, facilitating burning and decomposition of organic matter. Double chopping at right angles with an appropriate interval between passes (usually 6 weeks to 6 months) is generally much more effective than single chopping. However, chopping does not remedy soil damage caused by harvesting operations and may increase soil compaction if done during wet periods (Gent and others 1984).

To minimize erosion, run choppers straight up and down slopes wherever possible so that depressions created by penetrating blades follow the contour. Because of irregular slope directions, this is not easy to accomplish on a continuous basis. If the cutting blades penetrate across the contour, erosion is promoted.

Tree crushing. Tree crushing, like chopping, is intended to flatten and break up all material. A heavy crusher forces some organic material into the surface soil and speeds the rate of decomposition. Tree crushing is usually conducted when surface vegetation is large or dense or both; therefore, sites where crushers have operated are often difficult to traverse unless subsequent treatments such as burning or windrowing eliminate or congregate the downed material. A tree crusher should be run up and down slopes so that the depressions made follow the contour and erosion is minimized. This practice can increase retention storage of water by 127 m³/ha and potentially keep up to 152 t of soil/ha from moving down a slope (Ursic 1974). Both crushing and chopping

treatments are most effective if applied from the time hardwoods have fully leafed out in the spring until about October. If these treatments are applied later in the fall, it is difficult to make satisfactory broadcast burns before spring planting. Tree crushing, like chopping, will not remedy soil damage caused by logging operations.

Bedding. Bedding both mixes and moves soil, although soil is moved only a short distance (figure 4-4). The treatment consists of disking and moving topsoil and surface organic matter onto adjacent topsoil in long continuous strips and of forming furrows on both sides of these strips. Organic matter and nutrients are taken from furrows and concentrated in beds. Beds can be compacted with a rolling, water-filled drum or left to settle through normal weathering. Beds are about 2 m wide at the base, and after settling, their tops are usually 12 to 20 cm above the normal ground surface (figure 4-5). Bedding generally lowers the bulk density of surface soil by increasing the thickness of surface horizons and increasing the amount of organic matter (Terry and others 1981). However, bedding may not be adequate to improve the physical condition of skid trails, landing areas, or other compacted areas. A bedding harrow does not disk all the soil. Rather it throws loose soil on compacted soil, and the compacted soil may restrict future rooting (Gent and others 1983).

Figure 4-4—Bedding a forest site with a crawler tractor and bedding harrow. Because the beds are not being packed, the soil should be allowed to settle for at least 6 months before planting bareroot seedlings.

Figure 4-5—Contour of soil surface following bedding showing berm, furrows, and nonbedded surface.

Bedding has been most successful on somewhat poorly to poorly drained soils of the coastal flatwoods, on flat areas of fine-textured soil, on relatively poorly drained soils in the rolling Coastal Plains, and on alluvial soils where flooding is not severe (Shoulders and Terry 1978). These poorly drained soils are most often bedded to raise the surface soil above the water level and provide a deeper rooting zone with improved aeration. Bedding on the contour may also be useful in some upland situations because more moisture can be trapped and maintained in the beds throughout the year (Tuttle and others 1985b). However, it is difficult to construct beds on the contour on steep, stump-covered areas, and erosion of beds may promote the creation of gullies (Beasley 1979).

Shearing. Trees and shrubs can be severed just above the groundline without removing vegetation or soil from the microsites. The advantages of shearing are low cost and limited site disturbance. However, hand planting may be necessary because shearing produces much surface debris. Also, shearing is often followed by intense hardwood sprouting, and mixed pine-hardwood stands often develop even on planted areas. If shearing is followed by disking so that debris is incorporated into the surface soil, the combined treatments can substantially increase soil organic matter and nutrients (table 4-2), reduce hardwood sprouting, and make planting easier. Bedding also increases soil organic matter and nutrients. Disking and bedding treatments are effective only if most surface vegetation is less than 10 cm in diameter. Shearing operations can fill in logging ruts, helping restore productivity to these microsites (Tiarks 1990).

Displacement of soil and organic matter.

Mounding, furrowing, or scalping treatments may displace surface soil and organic matter by a few centimeters to a few meters, whereas windrowing may displace these materials 30 m or more.

Mounding. Mounds are small discontinuous areas raised 15 to 60 cm above the general groundlevel with a bulldozer. Although the technique is rarely used, mounding is effective for regenerating depressions up to a few hectares in size around ponds or other wet areas. An operator forms a mound by using a bulldozer blade to scalp a 4- to 14-m^2 area to a depth of 15 to 30 cm and to deposit the scalped material in an adjacent pile. Several trees can be established on the crest of each mound by seeding or planting. Even during wet periods, some well-aerated rooting space is usually available to trees growing on mounds.

Table 4-2—Biomass and phosphorus (P) content in vegetation, forest floor, and surface soil of three loblolly pine plantations during the third growing season in the Virginia Piedmont

System component	Treatment	Biomass (kg/ha)	P content (kg/ha)
Planted pines	Shear, rake, disk	928	0.7
	Chop, burn	659	0.5
	Shear-disk	327	0.3
Native vegetation	Shear, rake, disk	5,901	5.3
	Chop, burn	5,496	4.8
	Shear-disk	9,885	10.3
Forest floor	Shear, rake, disk	10,345	5.2
	Chop, burn	14,579	2.8
	Shear-disk	39,597	19.1
Surface 15 cm of mineral soil	Shear, rake, disk	NA	762.7
	Chop, burn	NA	565.2
	Shear-disk	NA	849.9
Total	Shear, rake, disk	17,174	774.9
	Chop, burn	20,734	573.3
	Shear-disk	49,809	879.6

Source: adapted from Paganelli and others (1987).
NA = not applicable.

Furrowing. Furrowing cuts a trough about 5 to 8 cm deep and 25 to 40 cm wide in the surface soil. Trees are planted in the cleared strip. Furrowing can greatly increase early survival of newly regenerated loblolly pines during dry periods because more moisture is available in the immediate rooting zone due to reduced competition. In Texas, survival of planted loblolly pines in furrows 35 cm wide and 8 cm deep was 94% after 1 year. Survival of trees planted in sod was only 65% (Stransky 1962). Within 1 or 2 years, roots of young pines spread into surrounding, unaltered soil, indicating that the minor displacement of organic matter and nutrients did not inhibit tree growth.

Scalping. Scalping is more drastic than furrowing. Although the principal objective in scalping is to clear a planting row of logging debris and reduce undesirable vegetation, the treatment usually creates a planting trough 1.2 to 2.0 m wide as sod, topsoil, and organic matter are cast to the sides. Soil is displaced by a V-blade mounted on the front of a tractor pulling a planting machine. On very dry sites or where grasses are a severe problem, scalping can increase early survival of newly planted seedlings 20 to 90% without adversely affecting height growth (Ferguson 1959, Posey and Walker 1969, Stransky 1964, Stransky and Wilson 1966). Hand scalping a small area around each planted seedling can also increase early survival by as much as 18% (Shoulders 1957).

Unfortunately, scalping can have long-lasting, negative, environmental effects. Ten years after four sandy east Texas sites were scalped, organic matter in the surface 15 cm of soil near the bases of planted loblolly pines averaged 1.5%, whereas organic matter in the berms on each side of the planting row averaged 1.9% (Ezell and Arbour 1985).

Shearing and windrowing. This treatment consists of severing all stumps and remaining trees near the groundline and then raking all material into long rows of debris. Thirty to seventy tonnes of logging residue per hectare may be deposited in windrows depending on utilization at harvesting, degree of site clearing, and distance between windrows. Windrows should not be pushed against adjacent timber, and regularly spaced openings should be left in each windrow to provide access, especially for firefighting equipment.

Windrows (or piles if the accumulations are not continuous) can occupy more than 10% of a planting area. Spacing varies depending on the amount of debris, but windrows are often about 30 to 70 m apart. Windrows are about 4.0 to 7.0 m wide and range from 0.5 to over 2.0 m in height. Their cross-sectional area varies from 2 to 7 m^2. On a north

Figure 4-6—Shearing and windrowing a flatwoods site in north Florida. When properly done, little topsoil is moved.

Figure 4-7—An example of excessive soil removal during shearing and windrowing a flatwoods site in north Florida.

Florida site, about 150 m of windrows were formed per hectare. These windrows had an average width of 4.2 m and an average cross-sectional area of 2.5 m², and occupied about 6% of the total ground area (Morris and others 1983). Equations based on size of windrows and wood pieces can predict the weight of woody material in windrows (McNab 1981, Morris and others 1983).

Windrows may be burned to speed the process of decomposition and then disked and planted or seeded. If windrows are left for a year before they are burned, much of the soil they contain washes down and burning is more effective. When burned windrows are planted, seedling roots must be placed in soil below the ashes. Burned windrows are excellent microsites for tree growth. In the Georgia Piedmont, 2-year-old loblolly pine seedlings growing in ash piles averaged 1.4 m tall, whereas those growing outside the ash zone averaged 0.6 m tall. Survival was equally good on the two types of microsites (McNab and Ach 1977).

Careful windrowing moves very little topsoil (figure 4-6). When windrowing is done poorly (figure 4-7), more than 600 t of topsoil/ha (or up to 8 cm of topsoil) are displaced (Glass 1976, Morris and others 1983, Pye and Vitousek 1985, Tuttle and others 1985a). Such displacements can cause serious reductions in levels of organic matter and nutrients between windrows, where most trees are planted (figure 4-7). These reductions contrast sharply with chopping, burning, and herbicide treatments, which raise N levels (Neary and others 1983, Stransky and others 1983). A total of 373 kg of N/ha was transferred into windrows in the pine flatwoods of Florida (Morris and others 1983). On a Piedmont site, the organic matter and slash in windrows contained 254 kg of N and 6 kg of phosphorus (P)/ha (Pye and Vitousek 1985). When the uppermost 5 cm of surface soil and litter were incorporated into windrows on a North Carolina Piedmont site, the concentrations of P, calcium (Ca), and organic matter in windrows were increased by as

much as 1,400%, 540%, and 36%, respectively (Glass 1976). Losses of N resulting from windrowing may represent 15 to 20% of the total N capital of a site to a depth of 50 cm and can be equivalent to the amount of N removed in six conventional harvests (Pye and Vitousek 1985, Tew and others 1984, Vitousek and others 1983). Even 15 years after Piedmont sites were windrowed, N loss was 35% with careful windrowing and 45% with careless windrowing (figure 4-8).

Care must be taken when evaluating the effect of windrowing because early tree survival often occurs due to limited vegetative competition in completely cleared

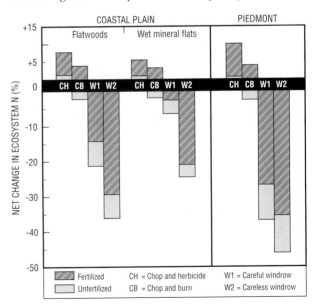

Figure 4-8—Net change in ecosystem nitrogen (N) 15 years after site preparation on Coastal Plain and Piedmont sites. The nutrients displaced by windrows are considered unavailable (adapted from Neary and others 1983).

areas. For example, removing 2.5 to 7.6 cm of top-soil during site preparation in the Piedmont and upper Coastal Plain of Alabama increased first-year loblolly pine survival from 65 to about 80% (Tuttle and others 1983). In east Texas, using a shearing blade and then windrowing sites increased loblolly pine survival by 30% (from 57 to 87%) over untreated forest sites. However, chopping increased survival just as much (Stransky 1981).

When organic matter and soil are moved many meters into windrows or piles, only trees planted on the piled material or along each side of it can capture the displaced nutrients for the first several years. If windrows are close together, more trees can eventually use the displaced minerals, but more of the area is also in windrows and access and planting opportunities are reduced. Because windrowed soil remains on the site, it eventually contributes to total site productivity. However, natural mechanisms that disperse soil across a site operate very slowly.

Early tree growth may also be better on windrowed sites than on disked or chopped sites because of less competition on the windrowed sites. However, because the quantities of organic matter and nutrients available to most trees are reduced when only 2.5 cm of topsoil are removed (table 4-3), there is a high potential that the final productivity of trees growing between windrows (and unable to access nutrients in windrows) will be less than for treatments that do not move organic matter from the rooting zone (see chapter 11).

When soils have inherently high fertility, single windrowing operations that displace only small amounts of surface soil and organic matter usually have little adverse effect on soil nutrition or long-term tree growth. Furthermore, if stands are managed properly during the first rotation after intensive land clearing, there should be limited hardwood competition at harvest time and

Figure 4-9—Effect of a spodic horizon in a flatwoods soil on pine taproot growth.

regeneration to pine should not require intensive site preparation. However, hardwoods develop extremely well in windrows and can be expected to provide competition for neighboring pines. At the very least, some form of management will be required for hardwood trees in windrows when the pines are harvested.

Ameliorating compacted subsoil. Treatments that loosen compacted subsoil can facilitate correct planting of loblolly pine seedlings with large root systems, increase root penetration, and increase the amount of soil moisture available during dry seasons. Subsoiling can also improve productivity in borrow pits, eroded areas, log landings, and on abandoned roads. Treatment costs range from $37 to $136/ha (Dennington 1989). Breaking up sandstone, shale, and stony colluvium in the Ouachita Mountains of Oklahoma and Arkansas, to a depth of 45 cm, increased soil moisture 2.5% by weight during the growing season and increased early height growth of loblolly pines 10% (Wittwer and others 1986). Similarly, subsoiling eroded Piedmont sites loosened compacted soil, increased water penetration into lower horizons, and facilitated planting, root development, and aboveground growth of loblolly pines. Roots grew to the bottom of subsoiled trenches up to 1 m deep within 2 years, but only to a depth of 15 cm in compacted soils that were disked but not subsoiled (Berry 1987, 1988). For maximum benefit, subsoil only on specific problem sites. Subsoil on the contour and to a depth of 45 to 60 cm when the soil is dry, about 2 to 3 months before planting. The spacing of rips should conform to the spacing of planting rows. Seedlings must be planted in the rips. Subsoiling thick and continuous spodic horizons (hardpans) that are close to the surface will also increase tree growth. Spodic horizons are common throughout much of the Florida pine lands. Because

Table 4-3—Effect of soil removal on soil nutrient concentrations and organic matter in the upper 30 cm of soil at the end of the third growing season

Soil removal treatment	Soil nutrients per hectare (kg/ha)						Soil organic matter %
	Ca	Mg	K	Mn	P	N	
Piedmont old field							
Control	1,970 a	575 a	242 a	119 a	6 a	3,423 a	1.85 a
2.5 cm removed	1,874 ab	543 ab	197 a	91 b	3 ab	2,079 b	1.25 ab
7.6 cm removed	1,639 b	483 b	207 a	84 b	2 b	1,546 b	0.89 b
Coastal Plain old field							
Control	1,398 a	172 a	224 a	71 a	32 a	2,748 a	1.58 a
2.5 cm removed	748 b	93 b	187 a	58 a	27 a	1,520 b	0.87 b
7.6 cm removed	893 b	96 b	176 a	50 a	28 a	1,285 b	0.60 b
Coastal Plain cut-over							
Control	371 a	45 a	103 a	21 a	12 a	1,510 a	1.40 a
2.5 cm removed	226 b	35 b	67 b	17 a	9 a	1,131 b	0.59 b
7.6 cm removed	187 b	35 b	64 b	15 a	7 a	920 b	0.50 b

Source: adapted from Tuttle and others (1987).

Means within a soil removal treatment followed by the same letter are not significantly different at the 95% probability level.

Figure 4-10—A disked and bedded site in North Carolina completely covered with grass 2 years after site preparation.

spodic horizons vary in thickness and consistency, penetration by roots is variable (figure 4-9).

Exposure and recovery of mechanically prepared sites. Undisturbed forest land normally has only about 1 to 5% of its surface soil exposed. Mechanical site preparation dramatically increases soil exposure. Low-intensity treatments, like furrowing or chopping and burning, increase soil exposure to about 15 to 35%. Either shearing, windrowing, and burning or scalping alone can expose from 50 to 60% of the surface soil. Either chopping, windrowing, and bedding; shearing, windrowing, and bedding; or disking and bedding can expose 70 to 90% (Beasley

1979, Blackburn and others 1986; table 4-4 and figure 4-4). The period that soil remains bare can vary by 2 to 3 years, depending on the site and intensity of culture. On some sites, vegetation can completely cover a site-prepared area in as little as 2 years (figure 4-10). However, Dissmeyer and Stump (1978) estimate that it takes 4 years for most sites to become fully revegetated following intensive site preparation (table 4-5). On a sheared and windrowed area in the southern Piedmont of Alabama, 48% of the soil surface was bare 1 year after treatment and 16%was bare after 2 years. Thirty-two percent of the soil surface was bare 1 year after chopping, and 7% was bare after 2 years. Trees and shrubs made up 55% of the vegetation on chopped areas after 2 years, while trees and shrubs made up 32% of vegetation 2 years after shearing and windrowing (Miller 1980). On upper Coastal Plain sites, 57% of the soil surface remained bare 2 years after shearing, windrowing, and bedding (Tuttle and others 1985a; table 4-4).

The type of site preparation affects the density of hardwood vegetation in the new pine stand. Eight years after an interior flatwoods site in Mississippi was sheared, piled, bedded, and planted, loblolly pines made up 83% of total basal area. Where tree crushing was the site preparation treatment, loblolly pines accounted for 46% of total basal area after 8 years. Pine basal area was intermediate on plots that were sheared and piled (table 4-6). Regardless of the intensity of site preparation, hardwoods will not be totally eliminated and will gradually become more prevalent during a loblolly pine rotation unless action is taken to reduce their numbers.

Treatments like subsoiling or furrowing, which disturb only a small percentage of the soil surface, have only short-term effects on competing vegetation. Soil is quickly washed back into the denuded areas, and new herbaceous plants and sprouts of surrounding vegetation soon occupy these microsites. If furrows are less than 5 cm deep, erosion will

Table 4-4—Effect of site preparation on soil cover and number of hardwood stems on three upper Coastal Plain sites in Alabama

Site preparation treatment	Litter cover %	Bare soil %	No. hardwood stems/ha
Pretreatment			
Shear/burn	80 a	8 a	7,975 a
Shear/chop/burn	76 a	9 a	8,073 a
Shear/windrow/bed	78 a	5 a	6,789 a
Shortly after treatment			
Shear/burn	55 a	33 b	1,072 a
Shear/chop/burn	57 a	32 b	116 b
Shear/windrow/bed	6 b	92 a	445 b
1 year after treatment			
Shear/burn	45 a	30 b	18,825 a
Shear/chop/burn	44 a	34 b	21,074 a
Shear/windrow/bed	21 b	61 a	10,433 b
2 years after treatment			
Shear/burn	32 a	25 b	27,165 a
Shear/chop/burn	36 a	25 b	28,304 a
Shear/windrow/bed	16 b	57 a	14,056 b

Source: adapted from Tuttle and others (1985a).

For each time category, means followed by the same letter are not significantly different at the 95% probability level.

Table 4-5—Recovery period and average erosion rates following site preparation on common loblolly pine sites

Location and site prep. treatment	Recovery period (yr)	Erosion rates (t/ha/yr)		
		Low	Average	High
Atlantic Coast flatwoods (1–2% slope)				
Burn	2	0.00	0.11	0.69
Chop	3	0.00	0.11	1.61
Shear	4	0.11	0.45	1.93
Bed	4	0.04	0.45	6.50
Gulf Coast flatwoods (1–2% slope)				
Bed	4	0.07	0.54	8.06
Middle and upper Coastal Plain (Texas to Virginia) (1–61% slope)				
Burn	2	0.00	0.38	31.36
Chop	3	0.00	0.54	79.52
Shear	4	0.07	1.43	101.47
Disk	4	0.16	5.89	≥224.00
Bed	4	0.09	1.46	≥224.00
Southern Piedmont (Alabama to central Virginia) (1–63% slope)				
Burn	2	0.00	0.31	15.90
Chop	3	0.00	0.49	23.30
Shear	4	0.04	4.03	99.68
Disk	4	0.13	9.18	≥224.00

Source: adapted from Dissmeyer and Stump (1978).

Table 4-6—Effect of 3 site treatments on the basal area of hardwood sprout competition 8 years after planting loblolly pines

Component	Basal area (m²/ha)		
	Tree crush	Shear/ pile	Shear/ pile/bed
Pine	4.7 a	7.8 b	9.4 b
Hardwood	5.6 a	2.3 b	1.9 b
Total	10.3	10.1	11.3

Source: adapted from Dewitt and Terry (1983).

Means on the same line followed by different letters are significantly different at the 95% probability level.

obliterate them within a few years.

Mechanical site preparation equipment can compact soil and decrease productivity. Machines typically weigh 9 t or more, and the ground pressure exerted by prime movers may exceed 0.6 kg/cm^2 for tracked vehicles and 1.1 kg/cm^2 for rubber-tired vehicles. Under such weights, both micropore and macropore space are reduced, and bulk density is increased. Infiltration, soil aeration, and soil porosity decrease, and site productivity is degraded. The whole process is exacerbated by removal of surface soil (Augspurger and others 1985; Gent and others 1983, 1984; Slay and others 1987; Tuttle and others 1985b) and by high soil moisture content. During wet periods that are most common in winter, heavy machines can puddle soils high in silt and clay and can increase bulk density by 25 to 75%. When soil moisture is at or near field capacity, one pass by a heavy crawler tractor can increase bulk density by 10% (Simmons and Ezell 1983). Even disking and bedding treatments, which normally till the soil and reduce bulk density, should not be applied on wet clay soils.

If site preparation work is done under relatively dry conditions, increases in bulk density can usually be kept to less than 10%. Shearing, raking, and burning well- to moderately well-drained east Texas pine sites with sandy or sandy loam surface soils increased bulk density by 9% at 10 cm below the soil surface, while chopping and burning increased bulk density by 3%. There was little recovery over the 3-year study period (table 4-7). Shearing and piling somewhat poorly drained interior flatwoods in Mississippi significantly increased bulk density in the surface 0 to 8 cm of soil by 7% over tree crushing, 9% over shearing, piling, and bedding, and 19% over a nearby untreated natural stand (Dewit and Terry 1983). Windrowing a northwest Louisiana site having Vertic Paleudalf and Glossaquic Paleudalf soils increased bulk density in the surface 0 to 8 cm from 0.88 g/cm^3 to 1.03 g/cm^3, a level at which root growth is not impaired (Slay and others 1987). Under normal circumstances, bulk density is gradually ameliorated over time by tree root growth, animal digging, and a building organic layer. Even though

bulk density is often increased by mechanical site preparation, young loblolly pines grow more rapidly on mechanically prepared sites than on unprepared ones because preparation decreases competition (Dewit and Terry 1983, Stransky 1981).

Erosion resulting from the interaction of mechanical site preparation and rainfall. Some natural soil erosion occurs from all but perfectly flat soils. Erosion typically removes fine organic, silt, and clay particles and is greatest during periods of heavy rainfall, on the steepest slopes, and on areas that have the least vegetative cover. The percentage of ground cover is the single most important factor determining the amount of erosion from forest land (Douglass and Goodwin 1980). On forested sites, most erosion results from streambed scouring during heavy rains. Erosion is generally greatest during the summer rainy season and especially during peak rainfall periods. Even on a fragile loess soil in the Coastal Plain of northern Mississippi, sediment loss from a forested watershed over a 2-year period was only 0.7 t/ha, and 77% of this was caused by stream scouring during a single storm (table 4-8). Erosion from Piedmont loblolly pine stands with slopes of 8 to 14% and with more than 80% ground cover is typically less than 11 kg/100 m^3 of runoff (Douglass and Goodwin 1980).

Mechanical site preparation commonly results in short-term increases in water yield, including peakflow and stormflow. Stormflow volumes can be increased up to eighteenfold, depending on the particular practice involved (Douglass and others 1983). In the Gulf Coastal Plain of Arkansas, stormflow was 14.1 cm in the first year after clearcutting, 5.7 cm after selection cutting, and only 1.6 cm without cutting (Beasley and Granillo 1983). In the upper Coastal Plain of northern Mississippi, total stormflows for chopped, sheared, bedded, and undisturbed watersheds were 34, 28, 24, and 3 cm, respectively, in the first year after treatment, when precipitation was 122 cm (Beasley 1979). The cumulative effects of clearcutting, chopping, and planting on a Piedmont watershed more than doubled small stormflows and peakflows, but had much less influence on large, flood-producing flows (Hewlett 1979).

Unless there is careful planning, rates of erosion will be very high for 1 to several years following harvesting and site preparation on sloping sites throughout the range of loblolly pine (Douglass and Goodwin 1980, Hunt and Miller 1976; figures 4-11 and 4-12, tables 4-5

Table 4-7—Soil bulk density 10 cm below the soil surface 1 and 3 years after various site preparation treatments on well- to moderately well-drained pine sites in east Texas (each value is the mean of soils from three sites)

Years after site preparation	Bulk density (g/cm^3)			
	Control	Burn	Chop and burn	Shear, rake, and burn
1	1.29 a	1.28 a	1.33 b	1.40 b
3	1.26 a	1.27 a	1.33 b	1.36 b

Source: adapted from Stransky (1981).

Values within each row followed by the same letter are not significantly different at the 95% probability level.

Table 4-8—First- and second-year sediment losses and sediment concentrations following clearcutting and site preparation treatments on fragile loess soil in the Coastal Plain of northern Mississippi

Site treatment	% exposure	Sediment loss (t/ha)		Sediment concentration (mg/l runoff)	
		1st yr	2nd yr	1st yr	2nd yr
No disturbance	NA	0.6	0.1	2,127	393
Chop and burn	37	12.5	2.3	2,471	670
Shear, windrow, and burn	53	12.8	2.2	2,837	794
Shear, windrow, burn, and bed	69	14.2	5.5	2,808	2,346

Source: adapted from Beasley (1979).

NA = not applicable.

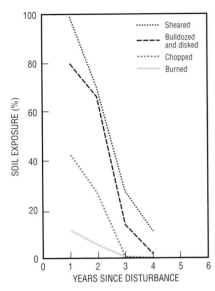

Figure 4-11—Average soil exposure rates of recovery over 4 years following logging and site preparation on southern Coastal Plain soils (adapted from Dissmeyer 1976).

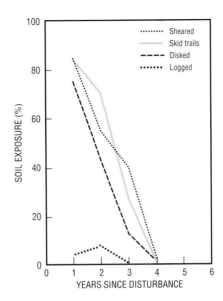

Figure 4-12—Average soil exposure rates of recovery over 4 years following logging and site preparation on southern Piedmont soils (adapted from Dissmeyer 1976).

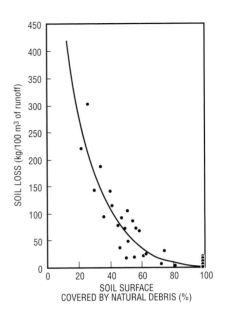

Figure 4-13—The effect of ground cover on soil loss in Piedmont watersheds (adapted from Douglass and Goodwin 1980).

and 4-8). Erosion is positively related to the amount of surface soil that is exposed to the impact of direct rain and to the amount of overland water flow. Duration of soil exposure also affects the amount of erosion. Rapid reestablishment of sprouts and new seedlings reduces the amounts of bare soil and soil loss significantly by the second year after site disturbance. However, it normally takes 3 years on coastal flatwoods and 4 to 5 years on rolling sites for vegetation to cover all exposed soil after intensive site preparation and planting to loblolly pines. Although erosion rates during this period normally average less than 4.5 t/ha/yr, they can be held to as little as 0.2 t/ha/yr (Hewlett 1979). Conversely, from 31 to more than 224 t/ha/yr can be lost to erosion (table 4-5), depending on slope, ground cover, and the season in which site preparation is performed. Such losses can severely reduce site productivity on slopes with thin surface soil. Where severe erosion has created deep gullies, brush dams can be built to trap sediment. Loblolly pine seedlings can then be planted to further stabilize the trapped soil (Rains 1977).

Erosion can be minimized if (1) clearing measures are not used on lands with slopes greater than 5%, (2) windrows and disking treatments are along contours, (3) natural debris is left on more than 50% of the soil surface (figure 4-13), and (4) regeneration is completed soon after site preparation so that followup vegetation control treatments are not needed (Douglass and Goodwin 1980, Pye and Vitousek 1985). If these precautions are taken, most erosion that does occur moves material only from one microsite to another nearby microsite and does not transport material offsite. If herbicides are applied 1 or 2 years after mechanical site preparation, the time required for complete revegetation may be increased, and losses of soil and nutrients may again increase.

Vegetation changes associated with mechanical site preparation. A mature, well-stocked pine or pine–hardwood stand has an understory that contains few herbaceous or shrub species and little competing vegetation above 1.5 m tall. The herbaceous and shrub plants in such stands have a relatively low combined dry weight. Removing the overstory and preparing the site for a new pine rotation causes extensive changes in understory species composition, frequencies, and dry weights (Schultz 1976, Schultz and Wilhite 1974). Land-clearing treatments such as rootraking and windrowing remove most standing hardwoods and many of their roots and seeds, and promote the establishment of early successional grasses and forbs from seeds (Lantagne and Burger 1987, Miller 1980, Nusser and Wentworth 1987).

Once a new pine overstory begins to dominate a site, most understory species are shaded out or decline to preharvest densities. For example, the understory of an uncut loblolly–shortleaf–hardwood stand in east Texas contained 16 herbaceous species. One year after clearcutting with no further site preparation, the number of herbaceous species had increased to 40. Clearcutting plus chopping increased the number of species to 58 in 1 year. It took 2 years for the number of species to reach 40 following combined shearing, windrowing, and burning. As planted pines increased in size, the less tolerant understory species were shaded out. By plantation age 10, the number of herbaceous species in the understory returned to pretreatment levels (figure 4-14). The net annual production of the herbaceous community increased more than thirteenfold, from an average of 50 kg/ha before harvest to an average of 679 kg/ha immediately after clearcutting. Clearcutting followed by burning, chopping, or windrowing resulted in further increases in the net annual production of herbs (to 1,803 kg/ha, 2,555

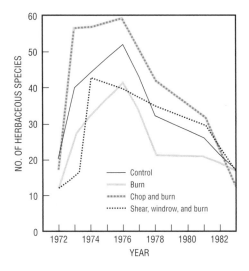

Figure 4-14—Number of herbaceous plant species in a loblolly-shortleaf pine-hardwood forest in east Texas before (1972) and after (1973) clearcutting, and for 8 growing seasons after site preparation. No site preparation was applied to the control plots after clearcutting (adapted from Stransky and others 1986).

kg/ha, and 2,411 kg/ha, respectively) 1 year after treatment. Ten years after treatment, the net annual production of herbs had receded to pretreatment levels (figure 4-15).

Because of their tremendous sprouting capacity, many hardwood and shrub species may be inhibited only for a short period—even with the most intensive site preparation treatments. One year after a Piedmont site was sheared and windrowed, 24% of the ovendry weight of new vegetation was in tree and shrub sprouts. Two years after shearing and windrowing, 32% of the ovendry weight was in tree and shrub sprouts. One year after chopping, 39% of the dry weight was in tree and shrub sprouts. Two years after chopping, 55% of the dry weight was in tree and shrub sprouts (table 4-9). Windrowed areas had about 86,000 sprouts/ha and chopped areas about 116,000 sprouts/ha 2 years after treatment (Miller 1980). On a moist site on Maryland's Eastern Shore, knocking over all vegetation by blading and then disking one or two times reduced the average size of hardwood stems but increased the number of stems twofold to fourfold 1 year after treatment. The number of red maple stems increased more than fiftyfold (from 550 to 30,200 stems/ha) but changes in the size and number of oaks; blackgum, *Nyssa sylvatic* Marsh.; sweetgum, *Liquidambar styraciflua* L.; American holly, *Ilex opaca* Ait.; and sweetbay, *Magnolia virginiana* L., were relatively inconsequential (Little and Mohr 1964).

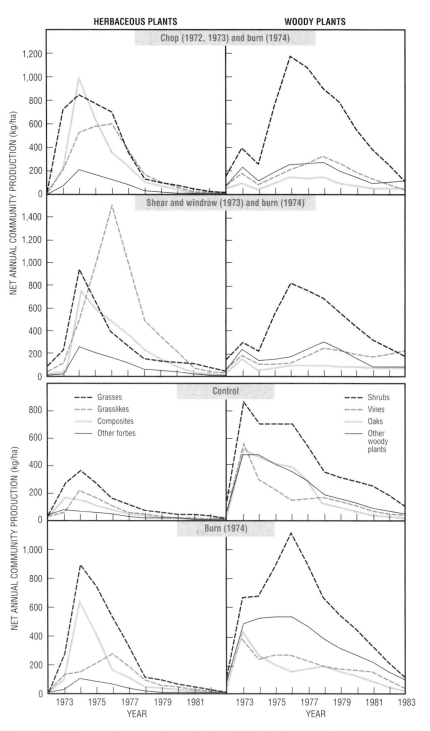

Figure 4-15—Net annual community production of herb-shrub stratum (vegetation no taller than 1.5 m) of a loblolly-shortleaf pine-hardwood forest in east Texas before (1972) and after (1973) clearcutting, and for 10 growing seasons after site preparation. No site preparation was applied to the control plots after clearcutting (adapted from Stransky and others 1986).

When a loblolly pine stand is managed by clearcutting followed by planting or direct seeding, long-suppressed pine saplings that are too small for use must be removed because they grow slowly and interfere with the development of new pine seedlings within a radius of at lease 3 m from their boles. In the Georgia Piedmont, seedlings planted within 1.5 m of suppressed saplings

Table 4-9—Ovendry weight of new vegetation following site preparation on a Piedmont site

Classes of vegetation	Uncut stand	Weight of new vegetation (t/ha)			
		First year		Second year	
		Chopped	Windrowed*	Chopped	Windrowed*
Trees and shrubs	0.61†	0.95	0.37	2.29	0.99
Vines	0.07	0.09	0.01	0.27	0.15
Grass and grasslike species	0.05	0.40	0.37	0.74	1.02
Composites	0.01	0.89	0.70	0.63	0.61
Legumes	0.002	0.02	0.06	0.18	0.22
Other forbs	0.001	0.10	0.04	0.07	0.07
Total	0.743	2.45	1.55	4.18	3.06

Source: adapted from Miller (1980).
* Sheared and windrowed with a KG blade.
† Understory trees only.

were 26% shorter than seedlings 3.7 to 4.6 m from suppressed saplings (Brender 1961).

Chemical Site Preparation

Environmentally safe and cost-effective herbicides are available for use in preparing sites for artificial and natural establishment of loblolly pines (Golden 1987, Mitchell 1987). They are a low-cost means of suppressing unwanted trees, shrubs, and herbaceous vegetation on both poor and moderately productive Piedmont and Coastal Plain sites that are to be converted to loblolly pines and are especially cost-effective when used on small areas. Chemical site preparation causes little if any soil erosion and may control herbaceous vegetation more effectively than does mechanical preparation (Yeiser and others 1987). Use of herbicides may be especially appropriate on steep slopes and highly erodible soils. Use of herbicides leaves the forest floor intact and thus reduces the severity of surface soil freezing, lessens surface soil drying, and limits seedling desiccation during the first few months after planting. Consequently, some chemically prepared areas can be regenerated when mechanically prepared areas are frozen or too dry to plant. Chemical site preparation is the primary method of preparing cut-over sites on southern forest industry lands.

Chemicals commonly used to prepare sites for loblolly pines are picloram + 2,4-D(amine) (Tordon® 101) and diclorprop (Weedone® 2,4-DP). On drier sites, hexazinone (Velpar® L) is often more effective. Hexazinone is particularly effective in controlling oaks (Mitchell 1987). Triclopyr (ester) (Garlon® 4) will kill most gallberry, saw-palmetto, vacciniums, waxmyrtle, and sweetbay stems. More than 25 herbicides are registered

Table 4-10—Herbicides registered for site preparation in the South

Common name	Trade name	Approved application method			
		Foliar	Soil	Tree injection	Bark spray
Glyphosate	Accord®	■		■	
Imazapyr	Arsenal®	■		■	
Dichlorprop + 2, 4-D (ester) +dicamba	Acme Super Brush Killer®	■		■	■
Dicamba + 2, 4-D (amine)	Banvel® 720	■		■	
Dicamba + 2, 4-D (ester)	Banvel® 520				■
Dicamba	Banvel® CST				
Triclopyr (amine)	Garlon® 3A	■		■	
Triclopyr (ester)	Garlon® 4	■			■
Fosamine ammonium	Krenite®	■			
Fosamine ammonium	Krenite® S	■			
Hexazinone	Pronone® 5G		■		
Hexazinone	Pronone® 10G		■		
Glyphosate	Roundup®	■		■	
MSMA*	Riverside® 912	■			
Picloram	Tordon® K	■			
Picloram + 2, 4-D (amine)	Tordon® 101 mixture	■		■	
RTU Picloram + 2,4-D (amine)	Tordon® 101R			■	
MSMA†	Trans-Vert® (additive)	■			
Hexazinone	Velpar ULW®		■		
Hexazinone	Velpar® L	■	■	■	
Dichlorprop	Weedone® 2, 4-DP	■			
Dichlorprop + 2, 4-D (ester)	Weedone® 170	■		■	■

Source: adapted from Mitchell (1987).
* Registered under FIFRA Section 24-C in Alabama and Mississippi.
† Registered for use only as a tank mix with Weedone 170.

for site preparation use in the South (table 4-10), and many guides to their use are available (for example, Miller 1984). Both liquid and granular herbicides are effective, and each has special advantages. Some liquid herbicides can be mixed together for improved control of a range of herbaceous weeds, shrubs, and hardwood trees.

Application methods and rates. Herbicides can be broadcast, applied in strips along planting rows, applied to the soil around each tree to be removed (basal spot), or applied to plants as foliar sprays, basal bark sprays, stem injections, or stump sprays. Transport mechanisms include backpack sprayers, ground machines, airplanes, and helicopters. Broadcast application rates commonly range from 9 to 28 liters of active ingredient (ai) per hectare (table 4-11).

Advances in aerial spray technology for forestry applications have reduced drift and increased the coverage of broadcast foliar sprays, making such sprays safer and more effective than previously. Granules can be dispensed from aircraft safely and without drifting to unintended targets. Both liquid and granular chemicals are usually most

Table 4-11—Effective application rates for commonly used site preparation chemicals

Herbicide	Rate/ha
Tordon® 101 mixture + Garlon® 4	14.0 + 4.7 liters
Pronone 10G®	11 – 45 kg
Roundup®	9.4 liters
Velpar L®	14 – 28 liters
Tordon® 101 mixture + Weedone® 2, 4-DP	19 + 9 liters
Tordon® 101 mixture	19 – 28 liters

Source: adapted from Mitchell (1987).

efficient and economical when large areas are treated by helicopter or fixed-wing aircraft (Balmer and Little 1978). Ground machines can also broadcast herbicide sprays efficiently and effectively, especially on open tracts, or apply materials in bands. Sprayers can apply both foliar and soil-active herbicides that dissolve or disperse when contacted by water. Spreaders disperse granular herbicides by means of a spinning disc or a forced-air blower. Mist-blowing with tractor-mounted machines is also effective, but this technique should be used only in isolated areas because herbicide drift can damage nontarget vegetation for more than 0.8 km downwind.

Liquid herbicides can be injected directly into the stems of unwanted trees before or after loblolly pine regeneration. Injections can be made with a tubular tree injector (for example, Jim-Gem®, Cranco®), with a Hypo-Hatchet® (hatchet with an attachment that automatically injects a small amount of a chemical into each frill cut around a tree), or by the hack-and-squirt method (a hatchet is used to make frills around a stem and a chemical is squirted into the openings). In each of these methods, 1.0 ml of herbicide is applied to each of the incisions, which are systematically spaced around the lower boles of larger trees. The hack-and-squirt treatment is as fast and effective as the tree injector treatment and has the added advantages of being adaptable for use in treating small trees, permitting greater maneuverability in dense stands of small hardwoods, and being less expensive and less tiring (McLemore and Yeiser 1987). Although injection is labor intensive, it can kill 50 to 90% of trees of most hardwood species with limited exposure of the surrounding environment to chemicals.

Some herbicides kill trees less than about 15 cm in dbh when mixed with oil and sprayed onto the entire lower 30 to 50 cm of the stem. Stems less than 5 cm in dbh can be killed if one side of the stem is wet thoroughly; the herbicide–oil mixture usually flows all around the stem as it runs downward. Basal spraying of individual trees is slow but kills much of the target vegetation.

Hardwood stumps can be treated with herbicide to inhibit sprouting. Freshly cut stumps should be treated immediately. The cambial region and outer 2.5 cm of xylem should be thoroughly sprayed with herbicides such as dichlorprop or triclopyr amine (Troth and others 1986). If the herbicide is applied more than 2 hours after a tree is cut down, efficacy can be reduced substantially. However, a mixture of 20% triclopyr ester, 10% Cide-Kick® II, and 70% diesel fuel controls sprouting fairly well for up to 5 months (Williamson and Miller 1988). A backpack sprayer is commonly used for this application.

Both liquid and granular herbicides, when applied to the ground surface in a grid or banded pattern, can control hardwoods such as black cherry (*Prunus serotina* Ehrh.), green ash (*Fraxinus pennsylvanica* Marsh.), sweetgum, white ash, hickories, and oaks as well as blackberry (*Rubus* spp.), honeysuckle (*Lonicera* spp.), sumac (*Rhus* spp.), and many herbaceous weeds. Hexazinone is partic-

ularly effective in controlling oaks; it should be applied from March to early June and must be activated by rain. A metered amount of herbicide applied at 1- by 1-m intervals throughout a stand kills small hardwoods or a combination of small and large trees. If most unwanted trees are 15 to 20 cm in dbh, a 1.8- by 1.8-m grid pattern is satisfactory. Another effective spot treatment is to place the herbicide at intervals of equal distance around the base of a tree and within 1 m of the bole (Edwards 1987, Mitchell 1987, Williamson and Miller 1988). Hexazinone herbicides should be applied at different rates depending on soil texture and soil organic matter content. More herbicide is needed as the soil texture goes from sand to silty clay or as organic matter content increases. Hexazinone is not recommended on any clay soils. Applying hexazinone both before and just after planting can increase seedling growth significantly more than can preplant injections or broadcast applications alone (Clason and Atkins 1986).

Season of application. The season of application strongly affects the effectiveness of herbicides as site preparation tools (Fitzgerald and Fortson 1981). Both injection and broadcast applications seem to be most effective if made in the late spring or early summer when plants are growing vigorously. Application at this time allows a herbicide to work for a full growing season before winter planting. Heavy flows of sap during early spring sometimes wash herbicides out of injection wounds. Some plants with waxy leaves (for example, gallberry, vacciniums, and sawpalmetto) are most susceptible to summer or fall applications of herbicides such as triclopyr ester (Minogue and Zutter 1986). In the Piedmont of central Georgia, picloram-triclopyr ester combinations applied in the spring and glyphosate applied in the fall kill a broad array of hardwood species (Knowe and others 1987). Even winter injection should give from 50 to 80% kill of all hardwood species except red maple (Campbell 1984, Kidd and others 1985, Kossuth and others 1980, McLemore 1984).

Special considerations relating to herbicide use. Herbicides are especially effective in controlling scattered blackberry; Japanese honeysuckle; multiflora rose, *Rosa multiflora* Thunb.; privet, *Ligustrum* spp.; switch cane, *Arundinaria tecta* (Walt.) Muhl.; trumpet creeper, *Campsis radicans* (L.) Seem.; wisteria, *Wisteria sinensis* (Sims) Sweet. (Miller 1984), and even kudzu, which is extremely difficult to suppress. Kudzu, a perennial leguminous vine, is now a severe competitor of loblolly pine on several million hectares throughout the South. Kudzu grows very rapidly (up to 30 m/year) and forms dense mats of vegetation that make forest regeneration almost impossible. It can smother trees as tall as 25 m. Because the species sprouts readily and because its taproots can reach a depth of 4 m, kudzu is not controlled by mechanical site preparation methods. Soil-active herbicides containing picloram or dicamba and applied in two right-angle passes provide the best control. More than a dozen herbicides have been registered for kudzu control (Michael 1986, Miller and Edwards 1983), and new herbicides show promise in screening tests (Miller 1988). Followup treatments are necessary with all chemicals because kudzu regenerates quickly if even a few roots survive.

Herbicide treatments are relatively ineffective where site indexes are high and resistant hardwoods or understory competitors, such as saw-palmetto, switch cane, or wiregrass, are abundant. Mechanical site preparation combined with prescribed burning provides more consistent topkill and initial competition control for regeneration under these conditions (Nelson 1978). Also, herbicide treatments do not remove surface debris, so burning may be required after vegetation has dried out, especially on areas to be machine planted.

Combining Prescribed Burning, Mechanical Site Preparation, and Chemical Site Preparation

Various combinations of prescribed burning, mechanical site preparation, and chemical site preparation usually suppress unwanted vegetation on both upland and wetland sites. When a herbicide treatment is combined with burning on Coastal Plain or Piedmont sites, undesirable woody vegetation is usually reduced more than it is when either treatment is applied alone. Chemical treatment can precede or follow prescribed burning. If chemicals are broadcast first, followup burning reduces debris substantially, especially where there are numerous small trees and shrubs or where there is much surface organic matter. A prescribed burn 4 to 6 weeks after herbicide treatment also kills new hardwood sprouts. When sufficient fuel is present, it may be preferable to burn first and then apply herbicide with a spot gun when top-killed vegetation is almost fully refoliated (Golden 1987). When the treatments are applied in this way, it is easier for the applicator to move through the area. Also, a smaller quantity of chemical is needed because some vegetation is killed by the fire, there is less nontarget material to absorb the herbicide, and surviving plants are weakened and have smaller food reserves. Burning in the spring will probably give the best results, but burning during other seasons should also be effective. Another advantage of combining herbicides with fire is that dried vegetation burns more quickly and completely and with less smoke. The combination of aerially applied chemicals and subsequent aerial ignition of prescribed fires can prepare large areas at relatively low cost. Fire may be more effective than herbicides in top-killing some hardwood species. Under many conditions, the use of fire on a regular basis is more cost effective and environmentally sound than the use of herbicides (Chen and others 1977).

Prescribed burning can also be very effective in reducing debris and killing sprouts following mechanical site preparation treatments such as roller chopping, crushing, or shearing. Disking or chopping after a herbicide treatment effectively incorporates organic matter into surface soil and improves a site for planting. Mechanical site preparation can also be followed by varying intensities of herbicide application to kill sprouting hardwoods and annual vegetation. For example, ripping (subsoiling) stony Ouachita Mountain sites to a depth of about 45 cm, combined with banded spraying of hexazinone increased 2-year height growth of newly planted loblolly pines by 50% (Wittwer and others 1986).

Intensive site preparation can remove so much organic matter that microbial N uptake and uptake of N by new vegetation are relatively insignificant. When this is the case, losses of N to the atmosphere (denitrification) and through leaching can be substantial. Nitrate N is rarely detectable in soil or soil solutions of undisturbed loblolly pine stands. However, the surface soil of a cleared North Carolina Piedmont forest site that had been sheared, piled, disked, and treated with herbicide contained more than 25 kg of easily lost nitrate N/ha at 7 months after treatment (figure 4-16). In the Alabama

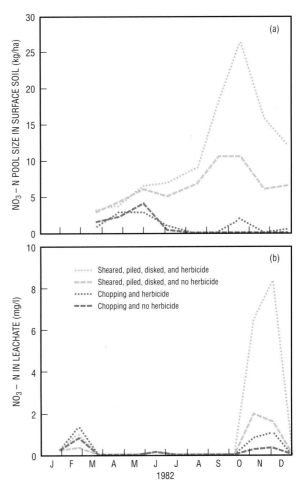

Figure 4-16—Amounts of **(a)**, nitrate N pool sizes in the surface soil to a depth of 15 cm; and **(b)**, nitrate N concentrations in leachate solutions extracted from a depth of 70 cm during the first growing season after site preparation of a North Carolina Piedmont forest site. Each point is the mean of six plots. Three unharvested plots were also sampled but nitrate was rarely detectable in soil or soil solutions (adapted from Vitousek and Matson 1984).

Piedmont, whole-tree chipping followed by herbicidal control of sprouts resulted in significant leaching losses over a 5-month period (table 4-12).

Water Management on Poorly Drained Sites

In parts of the lower Coastal Plain, a continuous high water table limits loblolly pine growth. In very wet areas, ditches, canals, and water barriers can regulate water table depth as well as improve soil aeration and nutrient availability (figure 4-17). Trees apparently grow fastest when the water table is kept at least 60 cm below the soil surface during the growing season. Drainage has modified more than 800,000 ha of southeastern Coastal Plain land since about 1950 and has substantially increased loblolly pine growth on some sites (Carpenter 1978, DeBell and others 1982, Klawitter 1978, Miller and Maki 1957).

Major wetland types where drainage can promote the establishment and growth of loblolly pines include moist oak hammocks, savannas, gum–cypress wetlands, and pocosins (figure 4-18). However, ditching does not drain all wetland sites effectively. For example, ditching has little effect beyond about 30 m in colloidal mucks in pocosins because these soils have very low hydraulic conductivity. Moreover, oxidation of organic matter and changes in vegetation may have long-term adverse environmental impacts (Campbell 1977, Debell and others 1982, Maki 1977, Ralston 1965). Recent wetland protection laws and regulations limit conversion of wetlands to pine forests (Cubbage and Harris 1988, Siegel 1989).

Proper drainage requires skillful engineering, especially if pumping systems are required. Primary drainage ditches often need to be 1.5 m or more deep and 1.5 to 3.0 m wide. Where pumping is unnecessary, a ditch slope of about 20 cm/km is usually satisfactory. A road system can be

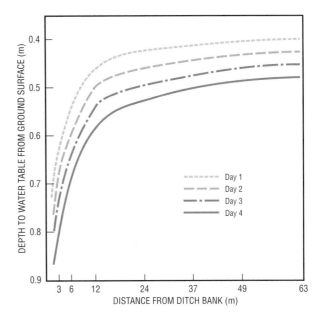

Figure 4-17— Daily trend of drawdown in water table on a North Carolina pocosin ditched to a depth of 0.9 m during a 4-day rain-free period (adapted from Maki 1977).

constructed with spoil material. If wet Coastal Plain sites are ditched carefully, there is very little change in sediment or chemical levels in drainage water. The principal sources of sediment are roads and other disturbed sites immediately adjacent to drainage ditches. Any initial effects of disturbance decrease rapidly as a drainage system stabilizes. The environmental impact of draining and developing a large area is reduced if the work is done in phases separated by recovery periods. Once a drained

Table 4-12—Leaching losses of eight nutrients over a 5-month period after site preparation of a completely harvested mixed loblolly–shortleaf stand in the Alabama Piedmont

	Nutrient loss (g/ha)		
Nutrient	Unharvested check	Whole-tree chipping	Whole-tree chipping and herbicide treated
Ca	58	826	1,355
Mg	46	574	786
K	83	732	846
Na	220	1,670	2,495
NO_3-N	60	1,161	2,363
PO_4-P	0	15	16
SO_4-S	9	834	2,225
HCO_3-C	400	3,719	4,696

Source: adapted from Gorden and others (1981).

Figure 4-18—Ditching a wet site along the North Carolina coast to lower the water table and improve growth of loblolly pines.

area is stabilized, concentrations of suspended sediment are not appreciably increased by logging or site preparation if the drainage ditches are not disturbed (Askew and Williams 1984, 1986).

Bedding can also improve drainage. If beds are constructed up and down slopes on gently sloping wetlands, they promote overland flow during very wet periods. Where lateral drainage is very poor, it can be beneficial to construct both beds and ditches. Beds can raise root systems a few critical centimeters above the normal soil surface and provide some well-aerated soil even when the water table is at the normal soil surface. Mounds constructed at regular or irregular intervals can provide the benefits of continuous beds without disrupting drainage.

It is especially difficult to prepare sites with organic soils. Such sites are usually dry enough to be worked only during a short period each year. Even when drained, they cannot withstand the weight of heavy machinery during much of the year. Surface organic matter is not important to tree growth, especially in the pocosins. However, operations that decrease elevation by even a few centimeters may affect tree growth adversely if the water table is near the surface. Site preparation should always be kept to a minimum when new pine stands are being established. This reduces costs and minimizes environmental degradation on poorly drained sites.

Microenvironmental Changes Resulting From Site Preparation

All site preparation treatments cause microenvironmental changes. Some of these changes are of short duration; others are long lasting. Fire blackens the soil surface, resulting in elevated temperatures at the soil surface until rainfall, leaching, and the growth of new vegetation eliminate the blackening. Most mechanical site preparation treatments tend to make the microenvironment more uniform by eliminating small potholes or mounds developed through soil weathering or windfalls and by eliminating the protective influences of downed timber, stumps, or tree tops. Treatments that expose the soil surface increase the temperature, the amount of light, and wind movement near the ground, and these changes promote rapid drying of surface soil. Combined burning, disking, and bedding can increase the maximum temperatures 2.5 cm below ground 5 °C more than burn and disk treatments and as much as 10 °C more than no site preparation. Temperatures may be increased by 2 to 5 °C for as long as 3 years after treatment (Schultz 1976). Similarly, combined shearing, piling, and disking can increase the maximum temperature 15 cm below ground 2 to 5 °C more than chopping increases it (Vitousek and Matson 1985).

Windrowing, piling, and bedding treatments cause long-term changes in the surface soil configuration and thus change surface water flow and microenvironments within a stand. Changes increase as the amount of soil deposited in windrows and beds increase. When beds are spaced every 3.7 m, they occupy 36% of the site, 29% of the site is in furrows, and the remaining 35% is unaffected by the treatment. The depressions on either side of each bed are slower to revegetate because they have been stripped of surface soil and generally remain wetter than surrounding areas. Although furrows appear to remain bare for the first 2 years, many small *Xyris* spp. plants quickly occupy new furrows on flatwoods soils. Environmental characteristics around beds are more variable than those of sites that are left relatively flat (Schultz 1976, Schultz and Wilhite 1974).

Energy Efficiency and Cost Efficiency of Site Preparation Practices

Mechanical site preparation and planting require three to six times as much fuel energy as do burning and planting or burning, direct seeding, and thinning (table 4-13). However, site preparation and planting increase yield enough to make the higher energy use cost effective.

The costs of site preparation treatments can be substantial, and they continue to rise. Prescribed burning is the least expensive treatment. Its cost in the early 1980's ranged from $5 to $25/ha (Guldin 1984) and depended on the size of the burn, the topography, and the proximity to roads or human habitation. The 1980 per-hectare cost of mechanical site preparation in the Coastal Plain

Table 4-13—Fuel consumption rates per hectare for establishment of loblolly pine stands

Operation		Fuel consumption	
		liters	thousand BTU's
Plant	Burn, plant	20.2	754
	Chop, burn, plant	62.0	2,305
	Shear, burn, plant	73.6	2,738
	Shear, chop, burn, plant	115.4	4,292
	Shear, pile, plant	132.8	4,940
Direct seed	Burn, seed, thin precommercially	21.7	808
	Burn, disk, seed, thin precommercially	35.9	1,337

Source: adapted from Frazier and others (1981).

1 British thermal unit (BTU) = 1,056 joules (J).

averaged $109 for a single chop, $42 for bedding, and $225 for shearing and raking (Guldin 1983). In 1984, the average costs of these treatments, across the South, were about $136, $72, and $235, respectively (Straka and Watson 1985). The base cost of mechanical site preparation increased by 6.4% annually between 1952 and 1982. With inflation, the annual increase was 10.8%. At these rates, costs double every 7 years (Moak and others 1983). Costs of intensive mechanical site preparation in the early 1990's averaged $370 to $480/ha but could exceed $740/ha. One small consolation is that the cost of planting decreases as the intensity of site preparation increases. The costs of chemical treatments in the mid 1980's ranged from about $136 to more than $395/ha, depending on the type and amount of chemical used (Mitchell 1987). If chemicals are used selectively (for example, in individual tree or strip treatments) and seedlings are planted by hand, the total cost of regeneration can be 50% less than the total cost of regeneration with mechanical site preparation.

Expensive site preparation treatments are economically justifiable only if they result in substantial increases in yield. For example, the combination of P fertilization, bedding, and planting provides the greatest total cubic volume and after-tax net present value on many poorly drained lower Coastal Plain sites (Gent and others 1986b). There is evidence that costly intensive site preparation provides no more long-term hardwood control than do chopping-and-burning or herbicide-and-burn-

ing treatments (Needham and others 1987). On some P-deficient sites in the lower Coastal Plain, P fertilization or P fertilization-and-bedding treatments can make costly drainage unnecessary. Low-cost treatments that produce a significant portion of the total yield produced by expensive treatments are often more cost effective than high-cost, high-yield treatments.

It is expensive to transport and set up large drum choppers, tree crushers, and other heavy machines. For this reason, it is usually uneconomical to use intensive mechanical site preparation methods on sites smaller than about 15 ha. However, if two or more small tracts are near each other, they can sometimes be treated economically.

Aerial application of herbicide may also be impractical on small tracts for economic reasons and because aerially applied spray cannot be confined within such tracts. Conversely, individual-tree injection or basal spraying are very economical and effective on small areas. Hypo-Hatchet, basal injector, and stem spray treatments are especially useful to nonindustrial private forest landowners who want to establish loblolly pine stands or eliminate competing trees in young loblolly pine stands. One person can treat a few hectares at little expense and with little chance of environmental damage or personal injury. Another labor-intensive technique that can be practical on small holdings is felling unwanted trees of any size and treating the cut surfaces with liquid or granular chemicals to prevent sprouting.

· **Summary** ·

Site preparation controls competing plants, improves microsite conditions for new seedlings, removes obstructions, and ultimately increases tree growth. Methods include harvesting only, prescribed burning, herbicide treatments, mechanical scarification, or various combinations of these treatments, and drainage or bedding, or both, to remove excess water from a regeneration site.

The minimum amount of disturbance (for example, herbicide and burning, or chopping and burning) to ensure a satisfactorily stocked plantation is usually the most cost effective treatment over a complete rotation. When done properly, site preparation promotes early tree survival and growth with little site damage. Site preparation can affect nutrient availability for at least 15 years after treatment and probably throughout an entire rotation. Chemical treatments and mechanical treatments that mix soil and organic matter (for example, chopping, disking, and bedding) raise N levels. In contrast, intensive mechanical site preparation treatments (for example, combined rootraking and windrowing) usually remove most vegetation from planting sites. These treatments are costly, often esthetically undesir-

able, and can reduce site productivity by physically damaging soil, by removing up to 67 t of soil/ha, and by causing nutrient losses and nonpoint source air or water pollution. In addition, such intensive treatments may not provide any more long-term hardwood control than do less expensive treatments such as combined herbicide and burning or chopping and burning.

Soil type, site quality, and topography strongly influence site preparation and equipment requirements. Seedling survival and subsequent tree growth are reduced by the loss of any organic matter or topsoil from dry sites, which are generally of lower quality. Chemical site preparation is usually best on dry sites, whereas shearing, raking, and windrowing are most detrimental. If hardwood brush is a problem, chopping is usually the preferred mechanical site preparation treatment. If logging debris is very heavy, piling in windrows may be necessary to permit access and mechanical planting. Prescribed burning is a valuable and inexpensive method for controlling understory vegetation and litter before or following mechanical treatments. However, burning logging debris during site preparation commonly removes about 50 to 150 kg/ha of N. Sites that are more fertile support greater amounts and more kinds of competing vegetation. On such sites, improved fiber utilization and chopping, crushing, or herbicide application provide the greatest long-term benefits. Prescribed burning before or after chopping or crushing may make planting faster and easier if there is a great deal of vegetation to dispose of, but it does not increase tree survival or growth. However, fires can produce unacceptable amounts of air pollution if they are not managed carefully. Whole-tree chipping reduces the need for fire and intense mechanical site preparation, but large quantities of nutrients are lost if the chips are removed from the

site. On sites that are eroded easily, it is better to use tree chopping or crushing equipment (directly up or down slopes to minimize erosion) than to use machines that remove surface debris and loosen or expose mineral soil. Soil erosion and nutrient loss increase in direct proportion to the amount of exposed ground surface. Fire should be used with care on sloping sites because substantial erosion can occur in and around fire lines. Bedding, after chopping or disking, usually improves growing conditions for young trees on sites that are wet periodically. Area drainage may be necessary on very wet pocosin sites, but environmental laws and regulations control forestry practices in wetlands.

Research Needs

■ Better understanding of how loblolly pine interacts with other plant species on numerous, diverse sites throughout the species range are needed to project the lowest cost method of vegetation control that is also environmentally safe.

■ Definitive long-term studies are needed to fully assess the fate of herbicides used for vegetation control.

■ More data are needed to fully understand the role of prescribed fire in site preparation and to identify when prescribed fire is detrimental to forest productivity.

■ The relative effects of mechanical versus chemical site preparation on long-term site productivity need critical evaluation on a wide range of important timber-producing sites.

Literature Cited

Askew GR, Williams TM. 1984. Sediment concentrations from intensively prepared wetland sites. Southern Journal of Applied Forestry 8(3):152–157.

Askew GR, Williams TM. 1986. Water quality changes due to site conversion in coastal South Carolina. Southern Journal of Applied Forestry 10(3):134–136.

Augspurger MK, Kellogg GR, McDade WD, Van Lear DH. 1985. Microsite variation and height of loblolly pine seedlings within the South Carolina Piedmont. In: Shoulders E, ed. Proceedings, 3rd Biennial Southern Silvicultural Research Conference; 1984 November 7–8; Atlanta, GA. Gen. Tech. Rep. SO-54: New Orleans: USDA Forest Service, Southern Forest Experiment Station: 337–339.

Balmer WE, Little NG. 1978. Site preparation methods. In: Tippin T, ed. Proceedings, Symposium on Pinciples of Mintaining Productivity on Prepared Sites; 1978 March 21–22; Mississippi State, MS. Atlanta: USDA Forest Service, Southeastern Area, State and Private Forestry: 60–64.

Beasley RS. 1979. Intensive site preparation and sediment losses on steep watersheds in the Gulf Coastal Plain. Soil Science Society of America Journal 43(2):412–417.

Beasley RS, Granillo AB. 1983. Sediment losses from forest practices in the Gulf Coastal Plain of Arkansas. In: Jones EP, ed. Proceedings, 2nd Biennial Southern Silvicultural Research Conference; 1982 November 4–5; Atlanta, GA. Gen. Tech. Rep. SE-24. Asheville, NC: USDA Forest Service, Southeastern Forest Experiment Station: 461–467.

Berry CR. 1987. Subsoiling improves growth of trees on a variety

of sites. In: Phillips DR, comp. Proceedings, 4th Biennial Southern Silvicultural Research Conference; 1986 November 4–6; Atlanta, GA. Gen. Tech. Rep. SE-42. Asheville, NC: USDA Forest Service, Southeastern Forest Experiment Station: 360–367.

Berry CR. 1988. Use of municipal sewage sludge for improvement of forest sites in the southeast. Res. Pap. SE-266. Asheville, NC: USDA Forest Service, Southern Forest Experiment Station. 33 p.

Blackburn WH, Hickman CA, deSteiguer JE, and others, 1978. Silvicultural activities in relation to water quality in Texas: an assessment of potential problems and solutions. Tech. Rep. 97. College Station, TX: Texas A&M University, Texas Water Resources Institute. 266 p.

Blackburn WH, Wood JC, Welchert AT, and others. 1986. The impact of harvesting and site preparation on stormflow and water quality in east Texas. Final Proj. Rep. College Station, TX: Texas A&M University; Texas Agricultural Experiment Station. 174 p.

Brender EV. 1961. Residual saplings in clearcut and planted stands. GA For. Res. Pap. 4. Macon, GA: Georgia Forestry Commission, Georgia Forest Research Council. 4 p.

Campbell RG. 1977. Drainage of lower Coastal Plain soils. In: Proceedings, 6th Southern Forest Soils Workshop; 1976 October 19–21; Charleston, SC. Atlanta: USDA Forest Service, Southeastern Area, State and Private Forestry: 17–27.

Campbell TE. 1984. Two tree injectors compared at widely spaced incisions. In: Biotechnology and weed science: Proceedings of the Southern Weed Science Society 37:168–172.

Carpenter RL. 1978. Site preparation with fertilizers/drainage. In: Proceedings, Site Preparation Workshop—East; 1977 November

8–9; Raleigh, NC. [Place of publication and publisher unknown]: 39–42.

Chen MY, Hodgkins EJ, Watson WJ. 1977. Alternative fire and herbicide systems for managing hardwood understory in a hilly southern pine forest. Circ. 236. Auburn University, AL: Auburn University, Alabama Agricultural Experiment Station. 19 p.

Clason TR, Atkins RL Jr. 1986. Split-application chemical site preparation for loblolly pine plantations. Proceedings of the Southern Weed Science Society 39:229–235.

Cubbage F, Harris T Jr. 1988. Wetlands protection and regulation: federal law and history. TOPS [Georgia Forestry Association] 22(1):18–23, 26.

DeBell DS, Askew GR, Hook DD, Owens EG. 1982. Species suitability on a lowland site altered by drainage. Southern Journal of Applied Forestry 6(1):2–9.

Dennington RW. 1989. Ripping can improve tree planting success. R8-MB 31. Atlanta: USDA Forest Service, Southern Region, Cooperative Forestry. 2 p.

DeWit JN, Terry TA. 1983. Site preparation effects on early loblolly pine growth, hardwood competition, and soil physical properties. In: Jones EP Jr, ed. Proceedings, 2nd Biennial Southern Silvicultural Research Conference; 1982 November 4–5; Atlanta, GA. Gen. Tech. Rep. SE-24. Asheville, NC: USDA Forest Service, Southeastern Forest Experiment Station: 40–47.

Dissmeyer GE. 1976. Erosion and sediment from forest land uses, management practices and disturbances in the Southeastern United States. In: Proceedings, 3rd Federal Inter-Agency Sedimentation Conference; 1976 March 22–25; Denver, CO. Denver: Sedimentation Committee Water Resources Council: 140–148.

Dissmeyer GE, Foster GR. 1980. A guide for predicting sheet and rill erosion on forest land. SA-TP 11. Atlanta: USDA Forest Service, Southeastern Area, State and Private Forestry. 40 p.

Dissmeyer GE, Stump RF. 1978. Predicted erosion rates for forest management activities and conditions sampled in the southeast. Atlanta: USDA Forest Service, Southeastern Area. 27 p.

Douglass JE, Goodwin OC. 1980. Runoff and soil erosion from forest site preparation practices. In: What course in the 80's: an analysis of environmental and economical issues: Proceedings, U.S. Forestry and Water Quality; 1980 June 19–20; Richmond, VA. [Place of publication and publisher unknown]: 50–74.

Douglass JE, Van Lear DH, Valverde C. 1983. Stormflow changes after prescribed burning and clearcutting pine stands in the South Carolina Piedmont. In: Jones EP Jr, ed. Proceedings, 2nd Biennial Southern Silvicultural Research Conference; 1982 November 4–5; Atlanta, GA. Gen. Tech. Rep. SE-24. Asheville, NC: USDA Forest Service, Southeastern Forest Experiment Station: 454–460.

Edwards MB. 1987. Application of pelleted and granular herbicides with hand-operated broadcast spreaders. In: Miller JH, Mitchell RJ, eds. A manual on ground applications of forestry herbicides: Proceedings, workshop on ground applications of forestry herbicides; 1987 June 10–12; Natchez, MS. R8-MB 21. Atlanta: USDA Forest Service, Southern Region: 25–32.

Ezell AW, Arbour SJ. 1985. Long-term effects of scalping on organic matter content of sandy forest soils. Tree Planters' Notes 36(3):13–15.

Ferguson ER. 1959. Furrowing increases first-year survival of planted pine in Texas. SO For. Notes 124. New Orleans: USDA Forest Service, Southern Forest Experiment Station. [Not paged].

Fitzgerald CH, Fortson JC. 1981. Application time effect of hexazinone for forest site preparation. Proceedings of the Southern Weed Science Society 34:197–202.

Fitzgerald CH, Peevy FA, Fender DE. 1973. The southern region. Journal of Forestry 71(3):148–153.

Frazier JR, Burkhart HE, McMinn JW. 1981. Energy output/input relationships for loblolly pine stands. Journal of Forestry 79(10):670–673.

Gent JA, Allen HL, Campbell RG. 1986. Phosphorus and nitrogen plus phosphorus fertilization in loblolly pine Pinus-taeda stands at establishment. Southern Journal of Applied Forestry 10(2):114–117.

Gent JA Jr, Ballard R, Hassan AE. 1983. The impact of harvesting and site preparation on the physical properties of Lower Coastal Plain forest soils. Soil Science Society of America Journal 47(3):595–598.

Gent JA Jr, Ballard R, Hassan AE, Cassel DK. 1984. Impact of harvesting and site preparation on physical properties of Piedmont forest soils. Soil Science Society of America Journal 48(1):173–177.

Glass GG Jr. 1976. The effects from rootraking on an upland Piedmont loblolly pine (Pinus taeda L.) site. Tech. Rep. 56. Raleigh, NC: North Carolina State University, School of Forest Resources. 44 p.

Golden MS. 1987. Development and evaluation of low-cost systems for artificial regeneration of pines. GA For. Res. Pap. 71. Macon, GA: Georgia Forestry Commission, Georgia Forest Research Council. 12 p.

Gorden R, Miller JH, Brewer C. 1981. Site preparation treatments and nutrient loss following complete harvest using the Nicholson-Koch Mobile Chipper. In: Barnett JP, ed. Proceedings, 1st Biennial Southern Silvicultural Research Conference; 1980 November 6–7; Atlanta, GA. Gen. Tech. Rep. SO-34. New Orleans: USDA Forest Service, Southern Forest Experiment Station: 79–84.

Guldin RW. 1983. Site preparation costs in the Southern Coastal Plain: an update. Res. Note SO-292. New Orleans: USDA Forest Service, Southern Forest Experiment Station. 3 p.

Guldin RW. 1984. Site characteristics and preparation practices influence costs of hand-planting southern pine. Journal of Forestry 82(2):97–100.

Hewlett JD. 1979. Forest water quality: an experiment in harvesting and regenerating Piedmont forest. Res. Pap. Athens, GA: University of Georgia, School of Forest Resources. 22 p.

Hunt EV Jr, Miller EL. 1976. Plant cover and soil erosion following site preparation and planting in east Texas. TX For. Pap. 29. Nacogdoches, TX: Stephen F. Austin State University, School of Forestry. 5 p.

Kidd FA, Kline WN III, Hern KL. 1985. Fall site prep with TORDON® and GARLON® herbicides. Proceedings of the Southern Weed Science Society 38: 206–212.

Klawitter RA. 1978. Growing pine on wet sites in the southeastern coastal plain. In: Proceedings, Soil Moisture ... Site Productivity Symposium; 1977 November 1–3; Myrtle Beach, SC. Atlanta: USDA Forest Service, Southeastern Area, State and Private Forestry: 49–62.

Knowe SA, Kline WN, Shiver BD. 1987. First-year comparisons of mechanical and chemical site preparation treatments in the Georgia Piedmont. Proceedings of the Southern Weed Science Society 40:146–155.

Kossuth SV, Young JF, Voeller JE, Holt HA. 1980. Year-round hardwood control using the hypo-hatchet injector. Southern Journal of Applied Forestry 4(2):73–76.

Lantagne DO, Burger JA. 1987. Comparison of site preparation methods for weed control in loblolly pine. Weed Science 35(4):590–593.

Larson J, Hallman R, comps. 1980. Equipment for reforestation and timber stand improvement. Missoula, MT: USDA Forest Service, Equipment Development Center. 254 p.

Little S, Mohr JJ. 1964. Disking to convert hardwood-loblolly pine stands to pine in eastern Maryland. Res. Pap. NE-20. Upper Darby, PA: USDA Forest Service, Northeastern Forest Experiment Station. 17 p.

Lockaby BG, Slay JM, Adams JC, Vidrine CG. 1988. Site preparation influences on below ground competing vegetation and loblolly pine seedling growth. New Forests 2:131–138.

Maki TE. 1977. Impact of site manipulation on the Atlantic Coastal Plain. In: Proceedings, 6th Southern Forest Soils Workshop; 1976 October 19–21; Charleston, SC. Atlanta: USDA Forest Service, Southeastern Area, State and Private Forestry: 108–114.

McKee WH. 1977. Soil-site relationships for loblolly pine on selected soils. In: Proceedings, 6th Southern Forest Soils Workshop; 1976 October 19–21; Charleston, SC. Atlanta: USDA Forest Service, Southeastern Area, State and Private Forestry: 115–120.

McKenzie DW, Miller M. 1978. Field equipment for precommercial thinning and slash treatment. Proj. Rec. 7824-1203. San Dimas, CA: USDA Forest Service, Equipment Development Center. p. 14–19.

McLemore BF. 1984. A comparison of herbicide for tree injection. Proceedings of the Southern Weed Science Society 37:161–167.

McLemore BF, Yeiser JL. 1987. Use of a hatchet and squirt bottle for killing unwanted hardwoods. Arkansas Farm Research 36(1):10.

McNab WH. 1981. Inventorying windrowed logging residues. In: Barnett JP, ed. Proceedings, 1st Biennial Southern Silvicultural Research Conference; 1980 November 6–7; Atlanta, GA. Gen. Tech. Rep. SO-34. New Orleans: USDA Forest Service, Southern Forest Experiment Station: 234–237.

McNab WH, Ach EE. 1977. Slash burning increases survival and growth of planted loblolly pine in the Piedmont. Tree Planters' Notes 28(2):22–24.

Michael JL. 1986. Pine regeneration with simultaneous control of kudzu. Proceedings of the Southern Weed Science Society 39:282–288.

Miller JH. 1980. Competition after windrowing or single-roller chopping for site preparation in the southern Piedmont. Proceedings of the Southern Weed Science Society 33:139–145.

Miller JH. 1984. Where herbicides fit into forest management schemes. In: Herbicides: prescription and application. Proceedings, 4th Annual Forestry Forum; 1984 March 21; Clemson, SC. Clemson, SC: Clemson University, Department of Forestry, Cooperative Extension Service: 113.

Miller JH. 1988. Kudzu eradication trials with new herbicides. Proceedings of the Southern Weed Science Society 41:220–225.

Miller JH, Edwards MB. 1983. Kudzu: where did it come from? And how can we stop it? Southern Journal of Applied Forestry 7(3):165–169.

Miller WD, Maki TE. 1957. Planting pines in pocosins. Journal of Forestry 55:659–663.

Minogue PS, Zutter BR. 1986. Second-year results of herbicide screening trials for forest site preparation in the flatwoods. Proceedings of the Southern Weed Science Society 39:219.

Mitchell RJ. 1987. Herbicide alternatives for the private forest landowner. Alabama's Treasured Forests 6(2):18–21.

Moak JE, Watson WF, Watson MS. 1983. Costs of forestry practices in the South. Forest Farmer 42(5):26–32.

Morris LA, Pritchett WL, Swindel BF. 1983. Displacement of nutrients into windrows during site preparation of a flatwood forest. Soil Science Society of America Journal 47:591–594.

Neary DG, Morris LA, Swindel BF. 1983. Site preparation and nutrient management in southern pine forests. In: Stone EL, ed. Forest soils and treatment impacts. Proceedings, 6th North American Forest Soils Conference; 1983 June; Knoxville, TN. Knoxville, TN: University of Tennessee, Department of Forestry, Wildlife and Fisheries: 121–144.

Needham T, Burger JA, Stafford CW. 1987. Competition in loblolly pine plantations four years after regeneration using seven different site preparation methods. In: Phillips DR, ed. Proceedings, 4th Biennial Southern Silvicultural Research Conference; 1986 November 4–6; Atlanta, GA. Gen. Tech. Rep. SE-42. Asheville, NC: USDA Forest Service, Southeastern Forest Experiment Station: 351–355.

Nelson LR. 1978. Major brush and weed control methods for even age pine management in the South. In: Proceedings, Soil Moisture … Site Productivity Symposium; 1977 November 1–3; Myrtle Beach, SC. Atlanta: USDA Forest Service, Southeastern Area, State and Private Forestry: 211–220.

Nusser SM, Wentworth TR. 1987. Relationships among first-year loblolly pine seedling performance, vegetation regrowth, environmental conditions, and plantation management practices. In:

Phillips DR, ed. Proceedings, 4th Biennial Southern Silvicultural Research Conference; 1986 November 4–6; Atlanta, GA. Gen. Tech. Rep. SE-42. Asheville, NC: USDA Forest Service, Southeastern Forest Experiment Station: 565–575.

Paganelli DJ, Hockman JN, Burger JA. 1987. Phosphorus distribution in three loblolly pine plantations after different site preparation. In: Phillips DR, ed. Proceedings, 4th Biennial Southern Silvicultural Research Conference; 1986 November 4–6; Atlanta, GA. Gen. Tech. Rep. SE-42. Asheville, NC: USDA Forest Service, Southeastern Forest Experiment Station: 384–387.

Pennock CM Jr. 1978. Prescribed burning for site preparation. In: Proceedings, Site Preparation Workshop—East; 1977 November 8–9; Raleigh, NC. [Place of publication and publisher unknown]: 4–13.

Posey CE, Walker R. 1969. Scalping improves growth and survival of loblolly pine seedlings during drought. Tree Planters' Notes 19(4):25–28.

Pye JM, Vitousek PM. 1985. Soil and nutrient removals by erosion and windrowing at a southeastern USA Piedmont site. Forest Ecology Management 11(3):145–155.

Rains MT. 1977. Brush dams reduce sediment production and create favorable planting sites. Southern Journal of Applied Forestry 1(4):4–7.

Ralston CW. 1965. Forest drainage. In: Wahlenberg WG, ed. A guide to loblolly and slash pine plantation management in southeastern USA. GA For. Res. Rep. 14. Macon, GA: Georgia Forestry Commission, Georgia Forest Research Council: 298–320.

Richter DD, Ralston CW, Harms WR. 1982. Prescribed fire: effects on water quality and forest nutrient cycling. Science 285(5):661–662.

Roten D. 1981. Prescribed burning by aerial ignition. In: Barnett JP, ed. Proceedings, 1st Biennial Southern Silvicultural Research Conference; 1980 November 6–7; Atlanta, GA. Gen. Tech. Rep. SO-34. New Orleans: USDA Forest Service, Southern Forest Experiment Station: 54–56.

Rothkugel M. 1907. Forest management in southern pines. Forestry Quarterly 5(1):1–10.

Schultz RP. 1976. Environmental change after site preparation and slash pine planting on a flatwoods site. Res. Pap. SE-156. Asheville, NC: USDA Forest Service, Southeastern Forest Experiment Station. 20 p.

Schultz RP, Wilhite LP. 1974. Changes in a flatwoods site following intensive preparation. Forest Science 20(3):230–237.

Shelton LW, Cathey TN, Helm DB. 1989. Survival and competition response from seasonal variation in disking treatments. In: Miller JH. comp. Proceedings, 5th Biennial Southern Silvicultural Research Conference; 1988 November 13; Memphis, TN. Gen. Tech. Rep. SO-74. New Orleans: USDA Forest Service, Southern Forest Experiment Station: 129–32.

Shoulders E. 1957. Scalping boosts planting survival. SO For. Notes 110. New Orleans: USDA Forest Service, Southern Forest Experiment Station: 3.

Shoulders E, Terry TA. 1978. Dealing with site disturbances from harvesting and site preparation in the lower Coastal Plain. In: Tippin T, ed. Proceedings, symposium on principles of maintaining productivity on prepared sites; 1978 March 21–22; Mississippi State, MS. New Orleans: USDA Forest Service, Southern Forest Experiment Station: 85–97.

Siegel WC. 1989. State water quality laws and programs to control nonpoint source pollution from forest land in the eastern United States. In: Nonpoint water quality concerns—legal and regulatory aspects: Proceedings, 1989 National Symposium; 1989 December 11–12; New Orleans, LA. St. Joseph, MI: American Society of Agricultural Engineers: 131–140.

Simmons GL, Ezell AW. 1983. Root development of loblolly pine seedlings in compacted soils. In: Jones EP Jr, ed. Proceedings, 2nd Biennial Southern Silvicultural Research Conference; 1982 November 4–5; Atlanta, GA. Gen. Tech. Rep. SE-24. Asheville,

NC: USDA Forest Service, Southeastern Forest Experiment Station: 26–29.

Sims DH. 1989. Low cost site preparation: fell and burn. R8-MB 32. Atlanta: USDA Forest Service, Southern Region, Cooperative Forestry. 2 p.

Slay JM, Lockaby BG, Adams JC, Vidrine CG. 1987. Effects of site preparation on soil physical properties, growth of loblolly pine, and competing vegetation. Southern Journal of Applied Forestry 11(2):83–86.

Straka TJ, Watson WF. 1985. Costs of forestry practices. Forest Farmer 44(5):16–22.

Stransky JJ. 1962. Furrows aid pine survival during drought. Tree Planters' Notes 53:23–24.

Stransky JJ. 1964. Site preparation effects on early growth of loblolly pine. Tree Planters' Notes 64:4–6.

Stransky JJ. 1981. Site preparation effects on soil bulk density and pine seedling growth. Southern Journal of Applied Forestry 5(4):176–179.

Stransky JJ, Wilson DR. 1966. Pine seedling survival under simulated drought. Res. Note SO-30. New Orleans: USDA Forest Service, Southern Forest Experiment Station. 2 p.

Stransky JJ, Halls LK, Watterston KG. 1983. Soil response to clearcutting and site preparation in east Texas. In: Jones EP Jr, ed. Proceedings, 2nd Biennial Southern Silvicultural Research Conference; 1982 November 4–5; Atlanta, GA. Gen. Tech. Rep. SE-24. Asheville, NC: USDA Forest Service, Southeastern Forest Experiment Station: 54–58.

Stransky JJ, Huntley JC, Risner WJ. 1986. Net community production dynamics in the herb-strub stratum of a loblolly pine–hardwood forest: effects of clearcutting and site preparation. Gen. Tech. Rep. SO-61. New Orleans: USDA Forest Service, Southern Forest Experiment Station. 11 p.

Terry TA, Cassel DK, Wollum AG II. 1981. Effects of soil sample size and included root and wood on bulk density in forested soils. Soil Science Society of America Journal 45(1):135–138.

Tew T, Morris LA, Allen HL, Wells CG. 1984. Estimates of nutrient removal and displacement resulting from harvest and site preparation of a P. taeda plantation in the Piedmont of North Carolina. Site Productivity Study Rep. 2. Raleigh, NC: North Carolina State University, School of Forest Resources, Southern Forest Research Center. 15 p.

Tiarks AE. 1990. Growth of slash pine planted in soil disturbed by wet-weather logging. Journal of Soil and Water Conservation 45(3):405–408.

Troth JL, Lowery RF, Fallis FG. 1986. Herbicides as cut-stump treatments during precommercial thinning. Proceedings of the Southern Weed Science Society 39:297–304.

Trousdell KB, Langdon OG. 1970. Disking and prescribed burning: sixth-year residual effects on loblolly pine and competing vegetation. Res. Note SE-133. Asheville, NC: USDA Forest Service, Southeastern Forest Experiment Station. 6 p.

Tuttle CL, Golden MS, Meldahl RS. 1983. Effects of surface soil removal on selected soil properties and loblolly pine seedlings after the first growing season. Gen. Tech. Rep. SE-24. Asheville, NC: USDA Forest Service, Southeastern Forest Experiment Station: 18–22.

Tuttle CL, Golden MS, Meldahl RS. 1985a. Site preparation effects on selected soil properties and early loblolly pine seedling growth. In: Shoulders E, ed. Proceedings, 3rd Biennial Southern Silvicultural Research Conference; 1984 November 7–8; Atlanta, GA. Gen. Tech. Rep. SO-54: New Orleans: USDA Forest Service, Southern Forest Experiment Station: 45–52.

Tuttle CL, Golden MS, Meldahl RS. 1985b. Surface soil removal and herbicide treatment effects on soil properties and loblolly pine early growth. Soil Science Society of America Journal 49(6):1558–1562.

Tuttle CL, Golden MS, Meldahl RS. 1987. Effect of soil removal and herbicide treatment on soil properties and early loblolly pine growth. Bull. 588. Auburn University, AL: Auburn University, Alabama Agricultural Experiment Station: 3–22.

Ursic SJ. 1974. Pine management influences the southern water resource. In: Proceedings, Symposium on Management of Young Pines; 1974 October 22–24; Alexandria, LA/December 3–5; Charleston, SC. Atlanta: USDA Forest Service, Southeastern Area, State and Private Forestry: 42–48.

Van Lear DH, Douglass JE, Cox SK, Augspurger MK. 1985. Nutrient export in runoff from burned and harvested pine watersheds in the South Carolina Piedmont. Journal of Environmental Quality 14(2):169–174.

Vitousek PM, Matson PA. 1984. Mechanisms of nitrogen retention in forest ecosystems: a field experiment. Science 225(4657):51–52.

Vitousek PM, Matson PA. 1985. Disturbance, nitrogen availability, and nitrogen losses in an intensively managed loblolly pine plantation. Ecology 66(4):1360–1376.

Vitousek PM, Allen HL, Matson PA. 1983. Impacts of management practices on soil nitrogen status. In: Proceedings, 1st Regional Technical Conference on Maintaining Forest Site Productivity; 1983; Clemson, SC. Clemson, SC: Society of American Foresters, Appalachian Chapter: 25–39.

Walker LC, Brender EV. 1959. Planting following prescribed fire. Journal of Forestry 57(2):123–124.

Williamson M, Miller JH. 1988. Crew applications of forestry herbicides. In: Miller JH, Mitchell RJ, eds. A manual on ground applications of forestry herbicides: Proceedings, Workshop on Ground Applications of Forestry Herbicides; 1987 June 10–12; Natchez, MS. R8-MB 21. Atlanta: USDA Forest Service, Southern Region: 5–14.

Wittwer RF, Dougherty PM, Cosby D. 1986. Effects of ripping and herbicide site preparation treatments on loblolly pine seedling growth and survival. Southern Journal of Applied Forestry 10(4):253–257.

Yeiser JL, Sundell E, Boyd JW. 1987. Preplant and postplant treatments for weed control in newly planted pine. Bull. 902. Monticello, AR: University of Arkansas, Forest Resources Department, Arkansas Agricultural Experiment Station. 10 p.

Chapter 5

Natural Regeneration

· · · · · · · · · · **Contents** ·

Natural Regeneration

Introduction

Figure 5-1—A 50-year-old naturally regenerated, even-aged loblolly pine stand growing on an abandoned cotton field.

Loblolly pine is well suited for natural regeneration. The species is aggressive and opportunistic, and quickly establishes itself after destructive fires, heavy logging, or the abandonment of agricultural land (figure 5-1). Besides growing in pure stands, loblolly pine competes successfully in mixed pine and mixed pine–hardwood forests throughout its range when it has the opportunity to become established. Natural stand management is often practiced throughout the South on small tracts (2 to 15 ha), but more than 1.2 million ha of highly productive industrial and federal lands in the Western Gulf Coastal Plain are managed under natural regeneration systems in tracts of 15 to more than 200 ha. Managers can create conditions that favor natural reestablishment of the species by applying simple, inexpensive manipulations that have little adverse ecological impact. Natural regeneration of loblolly pine is often accidental and not part of a management scheme. Unfortunately, as the human population increases and as more land is reserved for non-timber uses, accidental natural regeneration will not produce adequate supplies of loblolly pine.

Natural stands now make up about 75% of the area in loblolly pine. That percentage is expected to remain constant in the future. Natural stand management does not produce unsightly clearcuts and permits flexible thinning, timber stand improvement, and controlled burning schedules. For these reasons, stand management with natural regeneration is often compatible with the desires of owners and the general public. Also, growing trees for market is not a high priority for many non-industrial private forest (NIPF) landowners in the South. When NIPF landowners do want to practice forest management, large amounts of capital often are not available.

There is an expanding social demand for mixed forest stands in the South. It is feasible to grow hardwoods in mixture with naturally regenerated loblolly pines (figure 5-2). Management costs are greater and pine growth is less than in pure pine stands (see chapter 11), but the overall result may be an acceptable compromise, especially at the highly visible interface between rural and urban areas.

Figure 5-2—Naturally regenerated loblolly pines growing with mixed hardwoods in the Piedmont of North Carolina.

Successional Trends

When southern forests are destroyed by fires, hurricanes, harvesting, or land clearing, natural succession usually proceeds through an early burst of annual forbs and grasses to pines or mixed pine–hardwoods and finally to a hardwood climax forest. More subtle changes, such as the deaths of individual dominant trees, also provide opportunities for loblolly pine establishment. Loblolly pines usually seed into a newly disturbed area during the first autumn. Some additional seeding may take place for the next several years, depending on the density of early stocking. Even-aged stands are usually well established by the fifth year after disturbance. Under exceptional conditions, new seedlings can become established over a period of 20 or more years and can form a stand of many ages and sizes (figures 5-3 and 5-4) if hardwood competition is light. The key to loblolly pine development in this successional sequence is site disturbance. Sites with exposed mineral soil and full sunlight provide the best conditions for establishment and rapid tree growth.

Loblolly pine, with its rapid juvenile height growth and capacity for long-distance seed dispersal, can even invade bottomland areas and form a significant component of the main canopy. Twenty-two years after a highly productive bottomland hardwood site in central Mississippi was clearcut, loblolly and spruce pines made up only 2% of the trees but 10% of the basal area. Loblolly pine was a dominant species despite its infrequent occurrence on this hardwood site (Bowling and Kellison 1983). However, harvesting mature bottomland hardwood stands usually results in new hardwood stands.

Although loblolly pine is classified as shade intolerant, established seedlings compete successfully with annual plants, shrubs, sprouts of destroyed trees, and seedlings of some light-demanding hardwood species (such as sweetgum). Loblolly pines usually outperform Virginia or shortleaf pines established at the same time on both moist and dry sites. A dominant loblolly pine stand emerges within 10 to 30 years if enough seedlings were established initially. From age 30 to 150 or more, loblolly pines may dominate a site. Shade-tolerant hardwoods gradually form a secondary canopy beneath the pine overstory. By the time a loblolly pine stand reaches age 35, hardwoods can form a conspicuous midstory canopy (Harrington 1987, Little and Escheman 1976, Stalter 1971).

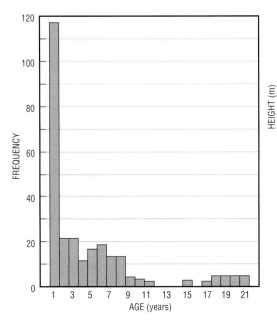

Figure 5-3—The number of loblolly pine trees, by age class, established in a single old field over a period of 21 years, as determined from line transects (adapted from Spring and others 1974).

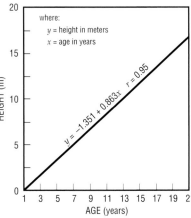

Figure 5-4—The relationship between tree height and age of individual loblolly pines shown in figure 5-3 (adapted from Spring and others 1974).

Naturally or artificially created openings in mixed stands of loblolly pine and southern hardwoods promote early and rapid loblolly regeneration. Time strongly affects subsequent successional trends and height stratification. For example, on a north Georgia Piedmont site, newly established loblolly pine seedlings outgrew all other trees except yellow-poplar for about the first 4 years after a storm opened a 15- by 25-m hole in the canopy of a mature hardwood forest. The relative density of loblolly pines decreased from 40% at age 5 to only 20% at age 6 as a result of severe competition with hardwoods (Skeen 1981).

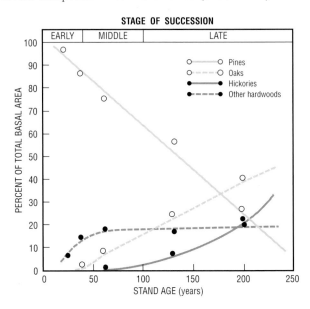

Figure 5-5—The general relationship of loblolly pine–mixed hardwood stand composition to stand age and stage of succession (adapted from Switzer and others 1979).

As loblolly pine trees die as a result of lightning strikes, insect and disease attacks, or old age, individual understory hardwoods replace pines in the main canopy of formerly pure loblolly pine stands. Over a 50- to 100-year period, hardwoods totally supplant loblolly pines and form mixed stands containing few or no loblolly pine trees (figure 5-5). The general successional sequence is for various herbaceous taxa to be replaced by fast-growing loblolly pines, which in turn are succeeded by climax hardwood types as long as fire is not frequent enough to keep the hardwoods from asserting dominance. Another catastrophe can renew the cycle, but the species mixture and interactions are never the same (Nicholson and Monk 1974).

Site Conditions Favoring Natural Regeneration

Loblolly pine can regenerate naturally on almost any site that is near a seed source. Natural regeneration is especially easy on excellent sites if other vegetation is controlled but is also appropriate for managing loblolly pine on adverse sites. Throughout the Piedmont and Interior Highlands, there are disjunct rocky areas where planting is difficult at best and where root deformity resulting from poor planting would likely be severe. Additionally, there are many short, steep slopes with thin and highly erodible soils that make site preparation and planting risky in terms of soil compaction, displacement, and erosion. These conditions often occur very near oldfield stands that can provide adequate seeds for new regeneration. On these fragile soils, natural stand management provides many long-term biological and socioeconomic benefits.

In coastal portions of loblolly pine's range, large areas are extremely wet, and the water table is kept below the soil surface primarily by transpiration. Maintaining a shelterwood overstory can keep the water table low enough to permit the establishment of a new loblolly pine stand, whereas establishing a stand following clearcutting might require expensive ditching or bedding treatments. Additionally, during good seed years, seedlings become established on most of the hummocks and other high microsites where growth is best.

A site's aspect, degree of slope, and slope position affect natural regeneration of loblolly pine. In the lower Piedmont, the most favorable conditions for regeneration are on gentle upper slopes that face southwest or northeast (figure 5-6). However, loblolly pine can usually be perpetuated without hardwood control on all gentle upper slopes and on moderate upper slopes with a southwest exposure. Loblolly pine can be established only with hardwood control on moderate and steep upper slopes with a northeastern exposure.

Small loblolly pine plantations that are surrounded by seed-producing loblolly pine stands often contain many volunteer seedlings. These volunteers can greatly alter stand density and growth rate, and can partially negate the spacing and stocking control benefits of planting. Conversion of small, overstocked plantations to naturally managed stands can be a realistic, cost-effective alternative to plantation management.

Soil moisture in the spring is the most important single factor affecting seed germination and survival of newly germinated seedlings (Trousdell and Wenger 1963). If rainfall from March 15 to May 1 totals 5 cm, only about 1 seed in 55 will become an established seedling at the end of 1 year. If rainfall between March 15 and May 1 totals 12 cm, more than 1 seed in 10 will become a seedling (figure 5-7). In the Georgia Piedmont, few seedlings were

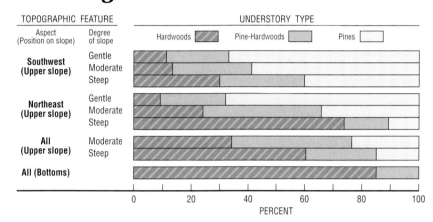

Figure 5-6—The distribution of understory types beneath loblolly pine sawtimber stands in the lower Piedmont of Georgia (adapted from Brender and Davis 1959).

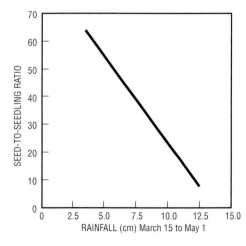

Figure 5-7—The effect of March 15 to May 1 rainfall on the number of loblolly pine seeds required to produce one seedling (seed-to-seedling ratio) in South Carolina and Virginia (adapted from Langdon 1979).

established in a good seed year with little rainfall, whereas natural regeneration was plentiful in years with both good seed crops and good rainfall (Brender 1958). Local rainfall records are a good indicator of probable field germination.

On sites subject to extreme weather, loblolly pines occur as scattered trees in protected or secluded locations or as dwarf trees on adverse sites. The only loblolly pines to survive on the Outer Banks of North Carolina during the severe hurricanes of the 1950's were those

that were stunted. During good weather in the 1960's and early 1970's, stands of well-developed loblolly pines were produced (Burk 1974).

Loblolly pine can regenerate naturally under less than optimum conditions even outside its native range. Loblolly pines planted 370 km northwest of their native range in Oklahoma (where rainfall averages only about 75 cm/yr), produced abundant natural regeneration at age 25 years (Posey 1967).

Advantages and Disadvantages of Natural Regeneration

Natural regeneration has many advantages:

1. Establishment costs are low.

2. Little labor and heavy equipment are required.

3. Little site disturbance or soil movement is needed.

4. Seeds are usually of local origin.

5. There is no dependence on availability of nursery-grown seedlings or processed seeds.

6. Good root systems develop early.

7. Insect and disease damage is minimal.

8. Selection management minimizes visual impact, reduces the economic effect of loss of young trees to wildfire, and yields timber income at short intervals even if tracts are small.

Natural regeneration also has many disadvantages:

1. Natural regeneration does not permit complete species conversion.

2. Genetically improved stock cannot be used.

3. There is little control over spacing and initial stocking.

4. The lengths of regeneration periods are variable.

5. It may be necessary to increase rotation lengths in order to obtain volumes equal to those produced in plantations.

6. Precommercial thinnings are often needed to remedy overstocking.

7. There is risk of seed tree loss.

8. Income is lost if seed trees are not harvested with the main stand.

9. Pulpwood rotations are impractical because young trees produce few seeds.

10. When young stands are very dense, access for fire equipment is reduced, and harvesting is more difficult.

11. A number of preharvest operations may be required to ensure regeneration.

The choice of whether to use natural regeneration or to direct seed depends on a number of factors, the most important being the availability of seeds at the time regeneration. A south Louisiana study showed no clear advantage for using either the direct seeding, seed tree, or shelterwood methods of regeneration in terms of stocking and tree height during the first 9 years (Brewer and Linnartz 1974).

Tailoring Natural Regeneration to Site Characteristics

Natural stand management would be much easier and more successful if stocking of free-to-grow loblolly pine seedlings could be predicted accurately from the amount of seeds and various environmental conditions. The abundance of new regeneration is determined by weather, type of harvesting, time since harvest cutting, competing vegetation, and soil conditions. In the North Carolina Coastal Plain, the number of 1-year-old, naturally regenerated, loblolly pine seedlings

was directly related to the number of sound seeds and the amount of April through June rainfall (Trousdell and Wenger 1963). The number of seedlings increased rapidly as rainfall increased to 25 cm, but more slowly from then on (figure 5-8). This pattern was especially pronounced when seedfall was high. With high seedfall, the number of established seedlings more than doubled as rainfall increased from 20 to 25 cm. The strong effect of April through June rainfall on seedling

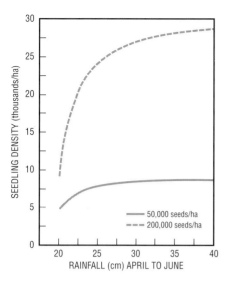

Figure 5-8—The effect of April through June rainfall and seeds sown per hectare on loblolly pine seedling establishment on a coastal North Carolina site with heavy-textured soil (adapted from Trousdell and Wenger 1963).

Table 5-1—Predicted, free-to-grow, stocking percentage for loblolly pine at age 3 for four site preparation treatments, with and without control of hardwood basal areas of 4.6 m²/ha

Sound seed first year (thousands/ha)	Logged only (hardwoods not controlled)	Hardwoods controlled by frilling and poisoning		
		Logged only	Burned after logging	Disked before logging
Light-textured soils				
50	36	49	52	61
100	42	58	66	70
150	46	64	73	75
200	49	68	78	79
Heavy-textured soils				
50	52	67	75	79
100	56	74	83	86
150	60	78	88	90
200	62	82	92	93

Source: adapted from Trousdell (1963).

establishment indicates that seedlings that survive this period are able to withstand subsequent environmental stresses quite well.

Most heavy-textured (clayey) soils seem to provide a better seedbed than do light-textured (sandy) soils. Trousdell (1963) found that 50,000 sound seeds/ha provided 67% stocking on heavy soils that had been logged and on which the hardwoods had been controlled by frilling and poisoning, and that it took nearly 200,000 seeds/ha to do the same on light soils with the same site preparation treatment (table 5-1). However, when heavy clay soils are dry, rates of seed germination can be low.

Managing for Natural Regeneration

Whatever reproduction cutting method is used, the following basic conditions must be met to ensure successful natural regeneration (Baker 1987):

- An adequate seed source.

- Site preparation and competition control to maintain adequate moisture and light.

- Early stocking control to reduce competition among pine trees.

- Protection of reproduction from wildfire, insects, and diseases.

A high level in one of these conditions can at least partially compensate for a low level of one or more of the other conditions. If the seed supply is marginal, more intense site preparation can improve the seedbed and reduce competition, increasing germination and early survival. If site preparation is to be minimal, the seed supply must be increased. The moisture level can be estimated from long-term weather records and adjusted by altering the level of root competition.

Seed Source

If natural regeneration is to succeed, there must be an adequate source of high-quality seeds on or adjacent to the area to be regenerated. Seeding characteristics vary with physiographic regions, climatic factors, tree condi-

tions, and stand conditions. Even though year-to-year cone and seed production is affected by both genetic and environmental factors, loblolly pines usually produce some cones and viable seeds each year, and good seed crops normally occur every 3 to 6 years. Wenger (1957) suggested that a light seed crop can be predicted 3 years in advance because a heavy seed crop is usually followed by a light crop 2 years later unless environmental or stand conditions are altered favorably. With 3 years of lead time, managers could select and release seed trees in order to stimulate seed production in a subsequent poor year.

Evidence of seed crop size is normally apparent by early summer; therefore, seedbed preparation can be planned and completed well before seeds begin to drop in late fall. Seed crop size can be predicted quite accurately by counting second-year cones in a forest stand as soon as they have enlarged enough to be distinguished from persistent old cones by their bright green color (old cones are brown). A binocular count of all currently maturing cones on a single tree, as seen from a single point on the ground, is made from a distance approximately equal to the height of that tree. A correction factor based on cone counts from a sample of felled trees is then applied and the total number of cones per tree estimated (Wenger 1953). This technique also works in seed production areas. Doubling the binocular count for 50 loblolly pines closely approximated the actual number of cones (VanHaverbeke and Barber 1964). The number of seeds per cone can also be estimated once cones near maturity. It may be necessary to adjust estimates for the size of the cone crop, because the proportion of sound seeds to total seeds may increase as the size of the seed crop increases. In the Virginia Coastal Plain, excellent seed crops (843,000 to 2,056,000 seeds/ha) produced by mature stands contained 76% sound seeds one year, whereas the next year, average crops (124,000 to 351,000 seeds/ha) contained only 27% sound seeds (Trousdell 1950a).

When conditions are exceptionally favorable, loblolly pines can produce more than 2.5 million sound seeds/ha. A partially cut, 35- to 45-year-old stand in coastal South Carolina produced 3.5 million seeds/ha (Lotti 1956). A crop of more than 500,000 sound seeds/ha is considered excellent. A crop of 200,000 to 500,000 sound seeds is good, and a crop of 75,000 to 200,000 is fair. A crop of fewer than 75,000 sound seeds/ha is considered a failure because it will not satisfactorily regenerate an area unless seedbed characteristics and weather are exceptionally good (Baker 1982, Brender and McNab 1972). In the South Carolina Coastal Plain, 49,000 to 91,000 seeds/ha were sufficient to regenerate an area of undisturbed mineral soil. From 99,000 to 148,000 seeds/ha were needed on a burned seedbed, and 247,000 to 371,000 on an undisturbed seedbed (Trousdell 1950b).

Numerous factors play a role in seed production. Natural regeneration is generally impractical when rotations are shorter than 30 years. Even widely spaced trees seldom produce enough seeds for stand regeneration before age 25 (Baker and Balmer 1983). Individual tree size, crown ratio, and crown density strongly affect cone production. Potential cone production increases with increasing stem diameter and crown density. Trees in the 36-cm diameter class can produce four times as many cones as can those in the 20-cm diameter class (figure 5-9).

Seed production varies by physiographic region. In the lower Coastal Plain, loblolly pine is generally a prolific and consistent seed producer. Seed production decreases and is more variable in the upper Coastal Plain and is often even lower and more erratic in the Piedmont and at the western extremity of the species' range. Consequently, more seed trees are usually needed in the upper Coastal Plain and the Piedmont than in the lower Coastal Plain to produce adequate numbers of seeds.

An individual stand or area can produce an exceptionally large seed crop in one year and an insignificant number of seeds the next year. In the Coastal Plain of South Carolina during one 27-year period, there was one crop failure and three crops of more than 2.5 million sound seeds/ha, and 23 years of intermediate seed crops (Baker and Langdon 1990). There was adequate to excellent seedfall in each of 8 consecutive years in coastal North Carolina (Wenger and Trousdell 1958). There was excellent seedfall in a South Carolina Coastal Plain old-field stand in 9 of 10 years (figure 5-10). During an 8-year period, yields ranged from 4,900 to 504,000 sound seeds/ha in the middle Coastal Plain of Virginia. These included three good seed crops, two fair crops, and three crop failures (Stewart 1965). In south Arkansas, production ranged from 35,600 to 668,700 sound seeds/ha during a 7-year period. More than 341,000 seeds/ha were produced during 4 of the 7 years (Grano 1973).

Although mature loblolly pines can produce large numbers of seeds and seedlings over a wide range of stocking levels, stand density affects seed production significantly. Four-year seed yield in the Coastal Plain of southeast Arkansas increased from about 1.1 million viable seeds/ha at 2.2 to 4.6 m² of basal area to almost 2 million at 13.8 to 16.1 m² of basal area/ha (figure 5-11). In another southeast Arkansas study, an 80-year-old

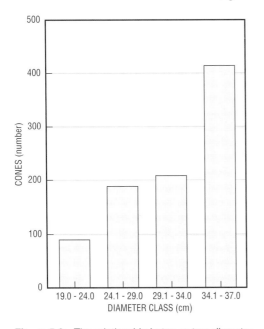

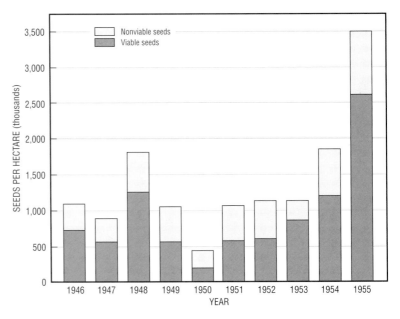

Figure 5-9—The relationship between tree diameter and cone production (adapted from Grano 1957b).

Figure 5-10—A 10-year record of loblolly pine seedfall in a 35- to 45-year-old stand in the South Carolina Coastal Plain (adapted from Lotti 1956).

Table 5-2—Sound seeds produced during 10 consecutive years in the Georgia Piedmont for four types of stands in which loblolly pine constituted an average of 85% of the sawtimber volume and the remainder consisted of shortleaf pine

| | No. of sound seeds (ha) | | | |
Year	Mature and well stocked	Immature and open grown	Seed tree	Shelterwood
1	59,120	75,240	17,200	182,730
2	19,350	17,200	30,095	23,650
3	6,450	3,225	4,300	4,300
4	6,450	4,300	6,450	0
5	26,340	2,150	32,245*	111,790*
6	342,890	197,780	180,575	752,420
7	1,075	4,250	21,520	17,220
8	5,375	0	15,048	32,245
9	529,920	321,390	455,750	1,100,680
10	5,375	0	2,150	21,520

Source: adapted from Brender (1958).

* Amounts for years 5 through 10 under the seed tree and shelterwood types are from a different stand than those for years 1 through 4 because of scheduled cutting operations in the original stands.

Table 5-3—Frequency of loblolly pine seed crops in seed tree and shelterwood stands over a 22-year period in the Georgia Piedmont

| Seed crop quality* | Seed tree stands[†] | | Shelterwood stands[†] | |
	No.	%	No.	%
Failure	10	53	6	34
Fair	5	26	3	16
Good	3	16	4	22
Excellent	1	5	5	28
Total	19	100	18	100

Source: adapted from Brender and McNab (1972).

* Failure is less than 75,000 seeds/ha; fair is 75,000 to 245,000 seeds/ha; good is 250,000 to 500,000 seeds/ha; excellent "bumper" is more than 500,000 seeds/ha.

[†] Stands released for less than 2 years were omitted.

show why the shelterwood method is often preferred to the seed tree method for reproduction cutting (table 5-3).

Viable seeds in contact with mineral soil germinate within 20 days, whereas less than half of all seeds on litter germinate within 40 days. Under natural conditions, most loblolly pine seeds that do not germinate decay during the summer after seedfall. Probably less than 0.1% of the seeds remain viable and have the potential to germinate during the second year after seedfall (Little and Somes 1959).

Seedbed Preparation and Cultural Treatments

Loblolly pines do not require exposed mineral soil for seed germination and seedling establishment; therefore, adequate reproduction can be obtained during abundant seed crop years regardless of seedbed or site conditions. Even when the seed crop is light, natural regeneration can be good to excellent without special seedbed preparation if the logging operation causes substantial site disturbance. In fact, the main concern when loblolly pines are regenerated naturally is that stocking may be too high. Careful control of the type or amount of site preparation can limit stocking during bumper seed years and increase stocking when seed crops are smaller. If loblolly seedfall is expected to exceed 200,000 seeds/ha and there is little understory competition, only minimal soil disturbance is usually needed. Logging operations at the time of the reproduction cut [a term that is interchangeable with "harvest cut" because most timber is removed] usually create a receptive seedbed, particularly if prescribed burning precedes the logging by less than 2 years. If cutting and followup site preparation take place in winter or spring, competing species may grow enough before loblolly seedfall to greatly reduce loblolly germination and survival.

Natural regeneration works reliably only if vegetation control and seedbed preparation measures are applied before peak seedfall. The type of vegetation present is usually a good indicator of the degree of control needed. Some species reduce the growth of loblolly pine more than others do. If kudzu is present, a several-step program is usually required to ensure complete control (Miller 1988). Disking reduces the problems caused by Japanese honeysuckle and greatly increases stocking of natural seedlings. Mowing does not promote natural regeneration (McLemore 1985). Preharvest hardwood control can increase the amount of new regeneration and subsequent growth, regardless of the reproduction

stand with a basal area of 16.1 m^2/ha produced 2.5 million seeds/ha, which resulted in at least 70% stocking after 3 years (Cain 1988b). In good seed years, shelterwood stands in the Piedmont can produce three times as many seeds as seed tree stands can and twice as many seeds as fully stocked stands can produce (table 5-2). However, stand density has little effect on seed production during poor seed years. In the Georgia Piedmont, seed crop failures occur about half of the time in seed tree stands (which have approximately 2.2 m^2 of basal area/ha) and a third of the time in shelterwood stands (which have about 5.7 m^2 of basal area/ha). These results

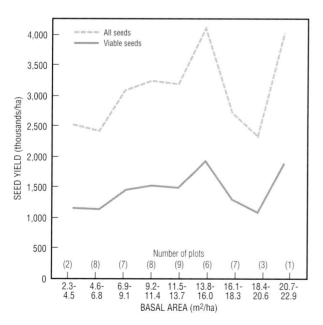

Figure 5-11—Four-year per-hectare seed yield of loblolly pines in relation to stand basal area (adapted from Grano 1970).

cutting method (Cain 1988b). In some instances, herbaceous vegetation inhibits pine growth more than hardwoods do. When this is the case, treatments that control herbaceous vegetation can be more beneficial than those that control hardwoods (Cain 1988a).

More intensive brush control is usually required on highly productive moist sites than on less-productive, drier sites. Inadequate control of competing vegetation, particularly midstory and overstory hardwoods, probably causes most loblolly pine regeneration failures. Prescribed burning treatments and broadcast chemical treatments are the most effective single treatments promoting new seedling establishment. Tree injection is most effective in releasing pines from overtopping hardwoods. If hardwood competition is moderate, two or more annual burns before the reproduction cut usually control undesirable vegetation and create a good seedbed. A single burn after the reproduction cut does the same, but some seed trees may be damaged or destroyed if they are near dense logging slash. Burning at this time is also favorable for improving wildlife habitat (see chapter 9). Applications of soil-active herbicides and basal-bark chemical sprays are as effective as tree injection and usually less labor intensive. Treatments with lightweight mechanical equipment or handtools, alone or in various combinations with fire and chemicals, also promote seedling establishment (Baker 1987, Cain 1987, Loyd and others 1978; table 5-1). Conditions that are unfavorable for germination (for example, undisturbed or slash-covered areas) are also unfavorable for seedling survival and growth (table 5-4).

Because prescribed fire is inexpensive and effective for seedbed preparation, it is used throughout the South. If there has been no regular prescribed burning during stand management, burning should begin 3 to 5 years before the harvest (or regeneration) cut. Burning in the winter will reduce fuel accumulation; then one or more hot summer burns will topkill small hardwoods and expose mineral soil (Crow and Shilling 1980, Trousdell and Langdon 1967). Burning at 3-year intervals is more effective than burning annually (Jones 1989). Seed catch

is maximized if a hot fire destroys competing vegetation and much of the surface organic matter just before seedfall. Burning should not follow seedfall in poor or average seed years because too many seeds will be destroyed. A late winter burn in southeast Arkansas destroyed so many seeds that an average of 15 seeds, rather than 5, had to fall for 1 seedling to be produced (Cain 1986). It is much more difficult to get adequate natural regeneration in the Piedmont than in the Coastal Plain. However, prescribed burning can greatly increase the likelihood that natural regeneration will succeed in the Piedmont. On a lower Piedmont site, burning just before seedfall resulted in a seedfall-to-seedling ratio of 55 to 1 after 1 year. Without burning, the ratio was 111 to 1. Stocking was significantly increased by burning (59 versus 46%), and hardwood competition was significantly reduced by burning (23 versus 37%) (McNab and Ach 1967).

The number and distribution of seedlings vary directly with the proportion of mineral soil exposed; therefore, burning is better than no treatment and disking is better than burning, especially when the seed supply is limited (Grano 1971, Wenger and Trousdell 1958; table 5-1). Any seedbed preparation should increase in intensity with distance from the seed source to encourage uniform stocking (Baker 1987). However, disking is relatively expensive and may not be as cost effective as burning (Trousdell and Langdon 1967). In a Coastal Plain study, the seedfall-to-seedling ratio was 9 to 1 the first year after harvesting and site disturbance. Three years after harvest without site disturbance, the ratio was 427 to 1 (table 5-5).

Soil compaction can adversely affect seedling establishment and early growth. Tuttle and others (1988) concluded that natural regeneration is most successful and seedling growth most rapid when bulk density is 1.3 mg/m^3 for sandy soils and 1.4 mg/m^3 for loamy sands.

Fertilizing new loblolly pine reproduction does not increase survival of seedlings. Supplying modest amounts of nitrogen (N), phosphorus (P), and potassium (K) to 2-year-old seedlings under a shelterwood stand in the Georgia flatwoods had no effect on seedling survival, but seedling growth did increase when fertilizers were combined with adequate amounts of water (Walker and Leiser 1965).

Precommercial Thinning

Too much reproduction is often obtained with naturally regenerating loblolly pine, particularly under even-aged management, when a good seed crop follows intensive seedbed preparation. If a new stand contains more than 12,400 stems/ha at 3 to 5 years, it should be thinned precommercially to accelerate growth of potential crop

Table 5-4—Effects of site disturbance on loblolly pine seedling establishment in the Virginia Coastal Plain 1 year after a seed crop of 212,500 sound seeds/ha

| Surface condition | Seedling distribution | |
	No./ha	Stocking %
Bare soil	29,916	100
Some disturbance	21,735	100
Severe burn	20,667	100
Intermediate burn	14,534	94
Light burn	17,487	100
Undisturbed	6,425	80
Slash covered	2,624	56

Source: adapted from Pomeroy and Trousdell (1948).

Table 5-5—Number of sound seeds needed to establish one loblolly pine seedling by condition and age of seedbed (1 to 3 years) in the North Carolina Coastal Plain

| Initial condition of seedbed | No. sound seeds/seedling | | |
	1 yr	2 yr	3 yr
Disturbed*	9	36	126
Burned	15	47	134
Undisturbed	46	NM	427

Source: adapted from Wenger and Trousdell (1958).

NM = not measured.

* Litter disturbed and mineral soil exposed by logging or seedbed preparation.

trees. Occasional dense patches of reproduction can occur in uneven-aged stands, but precommercial thinning does not increase the rate of growth of the released saplings or the overstory crop trees (Cain and others 1987). There is no information on how precommercial thinning might affect immature overstory trees. (Precommercial thinning is also discussed in chapter 8.)

Protection

Newly regenerated stands must be protected from insects, diseases, and especially from wildfires. Loblolly pines are particularly susceptible to fire until they are about 4.6 m tall (figure 5-12). If a new stand is destroyed by fire after the seed trees have been removed, artificial regeneration must be used. However, if the seed trees or a few shelterwood trees are left standing until the first pulpwood thinning, a second attempt at natural regeneration is usually possible.

Insect and disease problems are usually not severe in naturally regenerated stands. Insects that occasionally affect loblolly pine include seedling debarking weevils (*Hylobius* spp. and *Pachylobius* spp.) and pine tip moths (*Rhyacionia* spp.). Weevils affect young natural regeneration near the stumps of recently felled trees whereas tip moths damage young seedlings growing in open areas.

Figure 5-12—A young stand of row-seeded loblolly pines completely destroyed by fire.

The fusiform rust fungus—*Cronartium quercuum* (Berk.) Miyabe ex Shirai f. sp. *fusiforme* Burdsall and Snow—can damage loblolly pines, especially in high rust-hazard areas. The ecology of and management options to control these pathogens are discussed in detail in chapter 10.

Reproduction Cutting Methods

There are several methods of regenerating loblolly pine or loblolly–shortleaf pine forest types naturally. Even-aged or uneven-aged stands can be developed, depending on the particular objectives of a land manager. Cutover stands with as little as 1.15 m²/ha of pine basal area or stocking levels of just 15 to 25% may be acceptable for rehabilitating degraded lands (Baker 1989).

Even-aged management alternatives. Clearcutting, seed tree, and shelterwood methods are all effective ways to establish fully stocked even-aged stands by natural regeneration. All long-suppressed pine saplings should be removed when any even-aged regeneration cycle is started. Any new seedlings growing within 3 m of old, stunted residuals will be suppressed, and the residuals themselves usually develop too slowly to be of economic value in even-aged systems (Brender 1961).

Clearcutting. There are three methods of regenerating loblolly pines naturally with clearcutting. These are clearcutting strips or small blocks, seed-in-place, and seedling-in-place. When clearcutting strips or small blocks, a prescribed burn after logging disposes of slash, prepares the seedbed, and controls small hardwoods. If the seed-in-place or seedling-in-place method is employed, postharvest burning should not be used because it destroys many of the seeds or seedlings.

Natural regeneration with clearcutting has several advantages. Management areas are easily defined and treated. All high-value trees are removed. Harvesting and cultural operations are concentrated in time and space. Little technical skill or supervision is needed except for the seed- and seedling-in-place methods. Wildlife that is dependent on early successional vegetation will benefit.

There are a number of disadvantages also. There may be much logging debris. Appearance of the site may be esthetically undesirable for a short period. All trees in the new stand pass through the same developmental stages simultaneously, so all are equally susceptible to the same hazards at the same times. No merchantable material can be harvested from a new stand for a relatively long period. Wildlife that depend on mature trees may be displaced. Regeneration may be distributed irregularly and be quite variable in density.

Clearcutting in strips or small blocks. Natural regeneration of narrow strips or blocks of 2 ha or less commonly occurs if there are adequate seed sources adjacent to the openings. The long axis of an irregular strip or patch should be perpendicular to the direction of the prevailing autumn winds so that seeds will be dispersed throughout the area. Strips should be at least as wide as 2 to 3 times the height of adjacent trees to permit adequate light to reach the ground. Strips or patches are commonly 60 to 90 m wide. Width must be less than 120 m to ensure adequate seed dispersal throughout the area to be regenerated. Eighty-five percent of seeds fall within 60 m downwind of a loblolly pine stand. An additional 8% can be expected to fall between 60 and 90 m of the stand (Baker 1987, Pomeroy 1949, Wenger and Trousdell 1958).

Contour clearcutting of 20-m-wide strips separated by 10-m-wide leave tree strips can be used to regenerate loblolly pine on fragile loessial soils with little erosion and only a slight, short-lived impairment of water quality. Twelve years after plantations established on abandoned farmland in west Tennessee were harvested, natural loblolly pine regeneration averaged 2,063 stems/ha and stocking was 44% (Ursic and Duffy 1987).

Planning is important if strip or patch clearcutting is to be perpetuated throughout a forest property. Some mature stands must be retained until newly regenerated trees in neighboring strips are old enough to produce substantial quantities of seeds. Strip or patch clearcutting creates even-aged blocks, but the forest as a whole is uneven-aged. It is possible to combine strip or patch clearcutting with other natural regeneration techniques.

Stocking can be very high for 2 to 3 years following cutting, but most seedlings die by age 10. In east Texas, strip clearcutting of a mixed shortleaf-loblolly pine stand on fine sandy loam resulted in 27,900 seedlings/ha with a stocking of 70% at 6 months after timber removal. Thirty-three months after cutting, seedling density was 7,400 stems/ha and stocking was 52% (Taylor and Bilan 1973). Injecting the hardwoods before seedfall, or burning and injection before seedfall, had similar effects on density and stocking.

Seed-in-place and seedling-in-place. Coastal Plain or Piedmont areas of any size can be effectively regenerated by clearcutting, using either the seed- or seedling-in-place technique (Lotti 1961, Van Lear and others 1983). The techniques require several steps. First, the large unmerchantable hardwoods are deadened with chemicals or cut down. A prescribed fire is then used to control small hardwoods and prepare a seedbed. After 75,000 to 125,000 seeds/ha have fallen, the pine overstory is clearcut. If clearcutting takes place after peak seedfall but before seed germination (November 15 through March 31), the method is called "seed-in-place." If clearcutting is delayed until after seed ger-

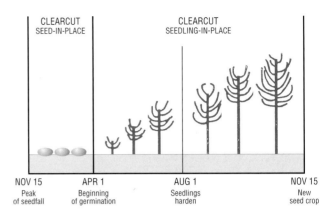

Figure 5-13—Regeneration by clearcutting with seed-in-place and seedling-in-place methods (adapted from Lotti 1961).

mination (April 1 through November 15), the technique is called "seedling-in-place" (figure 5-13).

Ample seeding is essential to the success of either method, so stands must be examined carefully for potential seed crops before beginning the process. Once the overstory is removed, there is no opportunity to increase stocking by natural seeding. There is less risk with the seedling-in-place technique because young trees are relatively easy to find. In contrast, it is difficult to find seeds among surface debris, so seeding estimates must be predicted from the cone crop. A disadvantage of the seed-in-place method, especially following a bumper seed crop, is that it may result in an extremely dense stand of young trees.

The entire overstory should be harvested during the dormant season (soon after seedfall) to promote maximum regeneration (table 5-6) and minimize hardwood sprouting (Sims and McMinn 1990). Seed germination can be delayed for several weeks in the spring if a full overstory is present. Such delay can result in substantial seed predation by birds and rodents (Langdon 1981). Thus, harvesting must be completed before April for best results. A common way to apply the seed-in-place technique is to clearcut a stand after the cones have reached maturity but before the cones open. The mature cones that are scattered in the logging slash will then open, and some seeds will fall on bare soil. A disadvantage of this technique is that seeds from any one cone are concentrated in a small area, especially if the cone

Table 5-6—Density and stocking of loblolly pine seedlings in the upper Piedmont of Georgia 2 years after whole tree harvesting of hardwoods and pines in the winter and summer. The initial stand was 75% mixed hardwoods and 25% loblolly pines, with 23 m² of basal area/ha

Harvest season	Pine seedling development			
	Diameter limit (cm)	Density* (stems/ha)	Stocking† (%)	Height (cm)
Winter	10.2	741	60	25
	2.5	3,122	97	41
Summer‡	10.2	14	3	10
	2.5	7	2	5

Source: adapted from McMinn (1985).

* Densities after winter harvests are significantly different at the 95% probability level.
† Stocking after winter harvests are significantly different at the 99% probability level.
‡ Insufficient number of observations to conduct analyses of variance on data after summer harvests.

Table 5-7—Regeneration of loblolly pine by the seed- and seedling-in-place methods in South Carolina

Regeneration method	Date logged	Seedlings per hectare	Stocking* (%)	Tallest tree† (m)
Seed-in-place	Jan–Feb	25,950	91	1.1
Seedling-in-place	May–Jun	4,450	49	0.9
Seedling-in-place	Aug–Sep	3,700	51	0.8

Source: adapted from Langdon (1979).

* Percentage of area having free-to-grow seedlings.
† Average height of tallest seedlings measured.

Table 5-8—Clearcutting schedule for natural regeneration of a hypothetical, fully stocked, 50-year-old, even-aged loblolly pine stand having some midstory and overstory hardwoods and no previous hardwood control activities

Treatment or activity	Schedule
1. First hardwood control burn	6 years before clearcutting
2. Second hardwood control burn	3 years before clearcutting
3. Site preparation burn	Spring in year of clearcutting
4. Treat nonmerchantable hardwoods with herbicide*	Spring in year of clearcutting
5. Harvest all merchantable pines and hardwoods	Before September†, or September through March‡, or fall§, 1 year after a good seed year
6. Evaluate stocking	Winter 2 years after clearcutting
7. Evaluate need for pine release and/or precommercial thinning	3 to 5 years after clearcutting

Source: Baker (1987).

* May use foliar or basal spray, cut-surface treatment, or soil-applied herbicide. Treatment will depend on size and number of hardwood stems.

† If area is to seed from trees in adjacent stands.
‡ If seed-in-place technique is used.
§ If seedling-in-place technique is used.

Table 5-9—Minimum number and size of loblolly pines recommended for regeneration by the seed tree method

Dbh (cm)	Number of trees/ha	Basal area (m²/ha)	Cones/ tree	Seeds/ ha
25	30	1.5	190	123,500
30	20	1.4	210	123,500
35	15	1.5	410	123,500
>40	10	1.3	NM	123,500

Source: adapted from Baker (1987), Grano (1957b), Williston and others (1982).

NM = not measured.

is knocked to the ground during the felling process. However, seeds are not buried in the soil or in logging debris, as so often happens when logging follows seedfall.

The degree of overstory removal affects success of the seed-in-place method, but only if overstory removal takes place shortly after seedfall. In the upper Piedmont of Georgia, winter harvesting to a 2.5-cm diameter limit resulted in four times as many seedlings as did harvesting to a 10-cm diameter limit because of the more complete hardwood control. Summer harvesting resulted in very few new seedlings no matter how much overstory competition was removed (table 5-6).

Both the seed- and seedling-in-place methods gave excellent results in tests in Virginia and South Carolina. The seed-in-place method was particularly effective (table 5-7). Treatment differences in stocking and number of seedlings resulted largely from logging damage. About two-thirds of the seedlings-in-place were destroyed by logging, but enough well-distributed seedlings survived to ensure fully stocked stands. The extent of destruction of seedlings-in-place depends on the number and size of overstory trees removed and on the method of removal. Seedling destruction during logging can be reduced by in-woods bucking of logs to practical lengths and by the use of well-planned skid trails (Edwards 1987b). If stocking is inadequate after the first year, later seed crops may supplement a stand.

Table 5-8 is a schedule of clearcutting activities to obtain natural regeneration in a hypothetical, fully stocked, 50-year-old, even-aged loblolly pine stand with some midstory and overstory hardwoods and no previous hardwood control. Stands growing under different conditions may not need all of these treatments. For example, stands in which hardwoods had been controlled effectively during stand development probably would not need treatments 1, 2, or 4.

Seed tree method. The seed tree method regenerates loblolly pine effectively and inexpensively in the Coastal Plain, where seed crops are consistently heavy. However, the risk of failure is greater in the Piedmont,

where seed production is erratic and seedbeds are usually not favorable for germination of loblolly seeds. Burning and other site modification treatments improve seedbeds and usually increase stocking if seeds are produced.

The seed tree technique requires cutting all but 10 to 30 well-spaced, seed-bearing trees/ha (figure 5-14). Seed trees should be 30 or more years of age for best cone production. They should also be at least 25 cm and preferably 30 to 40 cm in diameter at breast height (dbh) (table 5-9). In Arkansas, 35-cm loblolly pines produced

Figure 5-14—Natural regeneration resulting from a seed tree cut in an even-aged loblolly pine stand.

Table 5-10—Seedling success following natural regeneration in central Louisiana and east Texas from seed trees of loblolly pine

Test began*	No. seed trees/ha	First-year sound seed production/ha	First-year Seedlings/ha	First-year Stocking (%)	Third-year† Seedlings/ha	Third-year† Stocking (%)
1960	17	149,500	48,700	NA	44,000	100
1961	NS	Failure	NA	NA	4,400	56
1962	12	74,000 to 99,000	3,500	47	6,400	63
1962	12	11,100	3,700	34	8,200	69
1963	NS	16,300	9,600	94	4,000	66
1965	15	21,300	2,200	40	3,000	60
1966	17	Failure	600	NA	1,600	43
1966	17	Failure	NA	NA	120	5

Source: adapted from Campbell and Mann (1973).

NA = not available, NS = not stated, but no stand had more than 30 seed trees/ha.

* Seed tree cuttings were made 2 years earlier.

† Combination of survivors from the first year plus new seedlings from seeds falling during the second and third years.

more than 400 cones/tree/year, while 25-cm trees produced about 190/tree (Grano 1957b). The best trees should be kept as seed trees because they supply the best quality seeds for the next stand. They should be from the dominant crown class, of good quality (straight, clean bole, small limbs, and appear to be disease resistant), have dense, full crowns, and show indications of previous and present fruitfulness. Table 5-10 gives examples of first- and third-year stocking after seed tree cuttings made over a 7-year period in central Louisiana and east Texas.

Released seed trees normally produce some seeds during the first year after the reproduction cut because some trees will already be bearing cones. Releasing trees can stimulate seed production during the second year because the released trees may produce more sound seeds per cone. However, because it takes 2 years to produce cones, greatly increased cone and seed production generally does not occur until the third year after cutting. Release cuttings should be completed by the first of May, and preferably during the dormant season, to get increased seedfall within 3 calendar years (Stewart 1965). As many as 6 years may be required to get a good seed crop during periods of poor seed yield. The Virginia Seed Law requires that seed trees be kept uncut for 3 years after harvesting to provide a good opportunity for an adequate seed crop (Graff and Kaiser 1986).

To ensure adequate production of seeds immediately following the regeneration cut, seed trees should be released by thinning 2 to 4 years before the regeneration cut. This lead time is especially important if the stand is overstocked and the tree crowns are small. The preparatory cut should reduce the loblolly basal area to about 14 m²/ha and the best formed trees should be retained for possible later selection as seed trees.

The number of seed trees needed depends on many factors, including tree sizes, crown density, probable

seed crop, possible seed tree loss, and site conditions. Trees with dense crowns grow faster in diameter, height, crown length, and crown width than do trees with average or sparse crowns (Grano 1957a) and thus are more likely to produce good seed crops. The taller the tree, the farther the seed will drift or be blown, further increasing the chances of well-distributed seeds. Seed trees are particularly vulnerable to wind, lightning, insects, and disease, so probable losses from these causes should be considered when determining the number of trees to leave. More seeds and thus more seed trees are necessary to ensure adequate seedling survival under conditions of drought or severe competition.

Seed trees can be left in small groups or strips rather than uniformly scattered over a regeneration area (Wahlenberg 1960). Seed trees provide more protection to one another and are more easily harvested when in groups. However, seed distribution is less uniform when seed trees are grouped. Wind transports loblolly pine pollen effectively only about 90 m downwind and as little as 23 m upwind, so the closer the spacing between seed trees, the better the chances of pollination and a high number of viable seeds per cone. However, spacing should be of less concern than tree quality.

In seed tree regeneration, loblolly pine seedlings established before the main harvest cut cannot be relied upon to form part of the new stand unless care is taken to preserve those seedlings (see earlier discussion of seedling-in-place). These seedlings survive only where the forest floor is not disturbed by harvesting, fire, or other seedbed treatments and where little or no slash is deposited (Little and Mohr 1963).

Once seed trees develop an adequate cone crop, fire or other site preparation treatments are needed to reduce the litter level to improve the chances of germination. Mechanical site preparation for seed tree regeneration usually results in excessive stocking. Occasionally, where there is a dearth of seed trees and hardwood competition is intense, chopping combined with fire or chemicals may be practical. Following a good seed crop in southeast Arkansas, the number of loblolly seedlings (right) was at its greatest just after the litter was totally destroyed and generally decreased as litter depth increased (Grano 1949).

Litter depth (cm)	No. of seedlings
0.0–1.3	64,700
1.4–2.5	34,100
2.6–3.8	24,200
3.9–5.1	9,000
5.2–6.3	9,900
6.4–7.6	2,000
7.7–8.9	4,000

Seed trees are usually removed within 5 to 10 years after an adequate stand has been established (approximately 2,500 to 3,700 well-distributed seedlings/ha). The best time for seed tree removal depends on both biological and economic conditions for each stand. The over-

Table 5-11—Loblolly pine seed tree growth by crown density class over a 7-year period

Crown density class	Tree diameter (cm)		Tree height (m)		Crown length (m)		Crown width (m)	
	Original size	Annual increase	Original size	Annual increase	Original size	Annual increase	Original size	Annual increase
Dense	31.7	1.63	21.0	0.27	10.7	0.21	6.7	0.12
Average	29.7	1.30	20.4	0.30	9.5	0.18	5.8	0.12
Sparse	30.0	1.27	21.0	0.27	10.1	0.18	5.5	0.12

Source: adapted from Grano (1957a).

story should be removed as soon as a new stand is fully stocked and relatively safe from fire. However, from a practical standpoint, seed trees may have to be held for 1 year or more before they can be logged. Fortunately, loss of reproduction during harvesting is usually minimal because the seed tree basal area is so low.

If seed trees are few and it is uneconomical to harvest them, they can be left in place and removed during the first pulpwood thinning. Such reserve seed trees increase in value because they grow rapidly with little competition. Trees with dense canopies grow fastest in diameter (table 5-11). Reserved seed trees can produce a replacement seed crop if the first is destroyed. There are several disadvantages of leaving seed trees for an extended period: some trees may be killed by lightning, windthrow, or other causes; seedlings near the seed trees may show reduced growth; and continuous seedling establishment may result in overstocking. When 32 trees/ha were held for 20 years after a reproduction cut in southeast Arkansas, harvesting the overstory and thinning the understory yielded 16,897 board feet/ha (about 98 m^3 of sawn lumber/ha), and there was little damage to the residual stand (Grano 1961).

Shelterwood method. The shelterwood method is similar to seed tree regeneration except that more high-quality trees are left to produce and disseminate seeds. Seed-producing trees constitute about 4.6 to 6.9 m^2 of basal/ha; the minimum number of trees per hectare depends on tree size and site conditions (table 5-12). As with seed tree regeneration, the shelterwood method works best when overstory trees are more than 30 years old and in their prime period of seed production potential. A two-cut shelterwood is normally recommended for regeneration of loblolly–shortleaf pine stands, but a preparatory cut is not needed unless there is overstocking. Hardwood competition should be controlled by harvesting, fire, or chemicals before seed fall or by chemicals after seed fall. The leave trees respond to reduced competition by growing more rapidly.

It normally takes 3 to 6 years for adequate loblolly pine regeneration to become established after a shelterwood reproduction cut. Seed trees are removed subsequently. Logging damage can be minimized or expanded intentionally

to maintain or reduce stocking depending on the density of regeneration. Careful extraction—felling trees on one another, bucking before skidding, planning skid trails well—can limit losses of reproduction to 15% or less (table 5-13). Use of random skid trails and whole tree removal can kill 50% or more of the seedlings present.

Shelterwood cutting has advantages over clearcutting and seed tree techniques for natural regeneration. The shelterwood trees are numerous enough to retard the development of competing hardwoods. They may also aid newly germinated loblolly pine seedlings, especially on drier sites, by shading the ground and lowering soil surface temperatures. The added overstory also provides more visual appeal, and the quantity of logging slash is reduced. Another advantage is that the loblolly seedlings developing slowly under partial shade are not as susceptible to fusiform rust as are open-grown seedlings. However, shelterwood cutting often produces excessive reproduction, does much logging damage to residual trees, impedes harvesting and site preparation operations and increases their costs, and slows early height growth of new stands.

Gradations between seed tree and shelterwood reproduction cuts. These two methods of reproduction do not have to be mutually exclusive of one another. Under some circumstances, a manager might judge that a stocking of between 1.4 and 4.6 m^2 of overstory basal area would be most appropriate to regenerate a particular area. In some circumstances, it might be best to leave only a few seed trees on certain kinds of microsites and to leave many more on other microsites, depending on slope, soil, drainage, or other environmental conditions within a stand.

Uneven-aged management alternatives. Well-stocked, uneven-aged loblolly pine or mixed loblolly–shortleaf pine stands are developed and maintained by removing financially mature trees (usually the largest) and poorer trees from all diameter classes, either singly or in small groups, at relatively short intervals. Trees are harvested throughout a stand and new seedlings are

Table 5-12—Recommended stocking for loblolly pine shelterwood stands

Average dbh (cm)	Trees/ha	
	Lower limit	Upper limit
25	91	180
30	62	126
35	44	91
40	37	72
45	35	57
50	27	44

Source: adapted from Dennington and Larson (1984) and Tankersley (1985).

Table 5-13—Loblolly–shortleaf pine reproduction destroyed by removing 7.1 to 9.6 m^2 of overstory basal area/ha from a southeast Arkansas stand

Plot	Basal area* (m^2/ha)	Stocking lost (%)
A	7.1	9.6
B	8.0	15.4
C	9.6	16.3
Mean	8.6	13.8

Source: adapted from Grano (1961).
* Of felled trees ≥25 cm in dbh.

Figure 5-15—An uneven-aged stand of loblolly pines (USDA Forest Service Collection, National Agricultural Library).

tive exponential probability density function (reverse J-shaped curve) (Farrar 1981). Fully stocked, uneven-aged stands have 14 to 17 m^2 of merchantable basal area/ha, with two-thirds to three-fourths of the basal area in sawlogs. A fully stocked, uneven-aged stand has considerably less basal area than does a fully stocked, even-aged stand. In uneven-aged stands, harvest volumes should approximate growth for the cutting period. If stands are not fully stocked, only a portion of the growth is harvested until stocking reaches the desired level. For a 5-year cutting cycle, overstory density should generally be reduced to about 14 m^2 of loblolly pine/ha, in trees with dbh values equal to or greater than 9 cm.

established in the resulting openings (figure 5-15). However, it is not unusual to find young pines growing in small openings in mature stands or even under the crowns of larger trees. If given growing space, such young trees can grow to maturity, making it unnecessary to rely on new seedlings. Fifteen- to forty-year-old over-topped trees more than 5 cm in diameter at the base of the crown and having more than 20% live crowns usual-ly recover quickly enough after release to develop into crop trees (figure 5-16). Of course, the greater the crown ratio, the more successful and rapid the recovery (McLemore 1987).

Periodic cuttings (every 5 to 10 years) are repeated indefinitely to reduce overstory density enough to permit regular establishment of natural reproduction. However, the overstory is never cut completely. The overall objectives are to maintain seedlings, saplings, poles, and small and large sawtimber throughout a stand and to harvest at relatively short intervals to provide continuous income. A regulated, uneven-aged forest can contain as few as three distinct age (size) classes, or it can be in a balanced condition in which all diameter classes are represented and are distributed according to a nega-

To reliably regenerate loblolly pine under a pine overstory, stand density must be carefully controlled. Any midstory and overstory hardwoods should be eliminated or reduced drastically, and aggressive hardwoods should be controlled periodically with chemicals. Fire normally should not be used because it destroys pine regeneration along with young hardwoods. Selection stands should not be permitted to exceed 18.5 m^2 of basal area/

Figure 5-16—A 30-year-old loblolly pine tree, 13 cm in dbh at the time of release (**left**) and 23 cm in dbh 5 years later (**right**) (McLemore 1987).

ha before harvesting. The life expectancy of newly germinated seedlings in the Georgia Piedmont ranges from 20 years when overstory basal area is 16 m²/ha to only 4 years when basal area is 30 to 32 m²/ha (table 5-14).

The longevity of newly germinated loblolly pines under uneven-aged management also depends on the amount of hardwood overstory. For example, in southeast Arkansas, a hardwood cover of 90% resulted in no pine seedlings surviving more than 4 years, while 55% of the young seedlings survived more than 4 years under 90% pine cover (Wahlenberg 1960). Root competition is a major factor in this mortality.

Uneven-aged management can be accomplished through single-tree selection, group selection, or a combination of the two techniques, provided that new seedlings are established during at least 1 year in every 10. Single-tree selection is the removal of individual scattered trees from throughout a stand. Esthetically, this is the best method for maintaining an uneven-aged stand because disturbed areas are almost imperceptible. Reproduction usually develops following single-tree harvesting, if selection reduces overstory density to 10 to 14 m² of basal area/ha and if site conditions are favorable. If the overstory basal area is not reduced sufficiently, then single-tree selection is least likely to provide new regeneration because removal of individual trees creates small holes in the canopy and the amount of light that reaches the forest floor through these holes may be very limited. In a southeast Louisiana stand, single-tree selection produced 54% stocking of new seedlings 4 years after treatment. There were free-to-grow seedlings in 25% of the stand (table 5-15). However, the success of single-tree selection cannot be judged until the new trees have reached pole size.

Harvesting and site preparation are more efficient when small patches are cut throughout a stand than when single trees are selected. Small patch cuts provide settings for good to excellent natural regeneration without serious visual degradation. In stands having more than 16 m² of basal area/ha, openings of at least 0.04 ha, and preferably 0.1 to 0.2 ha, are needed to admit enough light for good seedling germination, establishment, and growth. Appropriate site preparation must precede seedfall if there is significant competing vegetation. In southeastern Arkansas, disking of small clearcut patches infested with Japanese honeysuckle, when followed by seedfall of 158,000 seeds/ha, resulted in 100% stocking. There were 29,000 and 10,200 seedlings/ha after the first and second years, respectively. Where comparable

Table 5-14—The life expectancy of newly germinated loblolly pine seedlings in the Georgia Piedmont for various overstory basal areas

Overstory basal area (m²/ha)	Expected seedling life (yr)
16	20
18	10
21	7
23	6
25	5
28	5
30	4
32	4

Source: adapted from Wahlenberg (1960).

patches were mowed with a bush hog to control the honeysuckle vines, stocking of pine seedlings was only 22% after the second year (McLemore 1985). In another study, small hardwood-infested openings in uneven-aged pine stands were site-prepared with various combinations of mechanical equipment, prescribed fire, herbicides, and hand-tools. All treatments facilitated establishment of pine regeneration. The least intensive and least expensive treatment, logging followed by injection of hardwoods with herbicides, resulted in 31,216 seedlings/ha and 84% stocking 3 years after treatment. Untreated control plots had only 1,154 seedlings/ha and 21% stocking after 3 years (Cain 1987).

Various combinations of group and single-tree selection can be used to increase or decrease regeneration during a particular cut. Single-tree selection can be employed along roadways and stream corridors, and larger patches of trees can be removed in the interior of a stand.

Managing for natural regeneration by selection cutting has numerous advantages for multiple-use forestry. A stand can be rapidly upgraded by favoring high-quality trees. The method creates a diverse habitat suitable for many animals and birds and is esthetically pleasing. Vulnerability to complete destruction by fire, bad weather, or biotic agents is less than with even-aged management. Income scheduling is regulated by the landowner, and is flexible and unhampered by interruptions for stand regeneration.

However, selection management requires more skill and supervision and harvesting is usually more difficult and expensive than with even-aged management. Also, management costs may be higher because large-scale efficiencies related to burning or chemical treatments are difficult to realize.

It is important to understand that successful selection management depends on two key factors: aggressive control of competing vegetation and periodic harvesting to reduce overstory density enough for seedling establishment and development.

Table 5-15—Fourth-year inventory of loblolly pine seedlings by four regeneration methods in southeast Louisiana

Rating factor	Clearcutting and hand planting	Seed tree	Shelter-wood	Single-tree selection
Total seedlings/hectare (no.)	4,324	5,560	6,672	5,466
Average height of free-to-grow seedlings (m)	3.6	2.4	2.3	0.6
Average diameter of free-to-grow seedlings (cm)	5.8	3.6	3.3	<1.3
Total area stocked with seedlings (%)	65	74	68	54
Total area stocked with free-to-grow seedlings (%)	48	56	47	25
Total area stocked with overtopped seedlings (%)	17	18	21	29

Source: adapted from Hu (1983).

Table 5-16—Loblolly pine stocking in the lower Piedmont of Georgia for 3 years following harvesting to promote natural regeneration

Treatment	Seedlings/ha		
	1984	1985	1986
Clearcut	990 a	4,570 c	3,090 b
Clearcut and burn	990 a	7,660 c	6,300 b
Shelterwood	1,610 a	14,580 ab	11,609 b
Shelterwood and burn	1,360 a	23,100 a	26,930 a
Seed tree	1,360 a	12,110 bc	9,640 b
Seed tree and burn	490 a	17,170 ab	12,350 b

Source: adapted from Edwards (1987a).

Means for each year followed by the same letter are not significantly different at the 95% probability level.

Table 5-17—Loblolly pine management guidelines for natural regeneration

Situation	Procedure
1. Well-stocked stand in a forest to be managed in even-aged units while making frequent periodic cuts.	Use clearcut method. Starting at the leeward side of a stand or management unit, clearcut strips approximately 60 to 90 m wide or patches of approximately 2 to 3 ha. Burn uncut areas after fuel has dried but before seedfall. Treat midstory and overstory hardwoods greater than 2.5 cm in dbh with herbicides. Precommercially thin stand if there are more than 12,400 stems/ha at age 3 to 5.
2. Well-stocked stands to be managed in even-aged units. Periodic cuts not required in immediate future or the stand is mature and growing slowly.	Use seed tree, shelterwood, or clearcutting method with seed- or seedling-in-place. Prescribe burn about 1 year before reproduction cut. Following reproduction cut, treat hardwoods greater than 2.5 cm in dbh with herbicides.
3. Well-stocked stand in a forest to be managed with all-aged units and with periodic cutting.	Selectively harvest single trees or groups of trees at periodic (5- to 10-yr) intervals to create openings for regeneration. Prescribed burning for seedbed preparation possible in some cases, but fire and uneven-aged management are usually incompatible. Treat hardwood brush with herbicides as needed to free young pines from competition.
4. Mature, slow-growing, or sparse pine stand with seed-bearing trees.	Use seed tree method. Control brush chemically or mechanically, then burn in August or September before good seedfall. Remove seed trees when young pines are 1 to 3 years old.
5. Understocked or cutover stand (less than 7 m² of merchantable basal area/ha) with some seed-bearing trees.	Use seed tree selection cutting methods described above. Control hardwoods as necessary.
6. Understocked or cutover pine stand with no seed-bearing trees.	Attempt to rehabilitate stand with selection cutting and hardwood control if some pines will become seed producers within 3 to 5 years; otherwise, regenerate area artificially.
7. Scattered sawlog trees with heavy understory of hardwood brush.	Control brush mechanically or with chemicals, then burn in late August or early September.

Source: Williston and Balmer (1974) and Williston and others (1982).

Comparing reproduction under various cutting methods. Good reproduction can usually be obtained using any of the natural reproduction cutting methods if adequate seed sources are developed and hardwood and vine competition is suppressed. Five years after regeneration cutting in southeast Arkansas, clearcuts, seed tree cuts, and selection cuts all had at least 84% stocking and from 6,200 to 9,400 new seedlings/ha (Grano 1954). In the lower Piedmont of Georgia, pine regeneration was inadequate during the year following treatment because few seeds were produced (table 5-16). However, all cutting methods produced adequate regeneration within 3 years. In each case, burning increased seedling density during the second and third years. Patience is an important part of natural stand management.

In southeast Louisiana, seed tree (15 leave trees/ha) and shelterwood cutting (50 leave trees/ha) produced stocking as good as that produced by clearcutting and planting 4 years after treatment (table 5-15). After 3 years, all three treatments produced stocking greater than 40%, the minimum recommended by Campbell and Mann (1973). Although selection cutting and the other natural regeneration methods yielded similar numbers of seedlings, fewer of the seedlings produced by the selec-

tion method were free to grow, and they averaged only about one-fourth the height of the seed tree and shelterwood seedlings.

Guide to natural regeneration methods. Guidelines for management alternatives in stand situations common in the loblolly pine ecosystem are listed in table 5-17 (Baker 1982, Williston and Balmer 1974, Williston and others 1982). They are also applicable to the management of loblolly–shortleaf pine stands. Depending on specific circumstances and stand conditions, various combinations of these procedures may be appropriate.

Summary

About 75% of the loblolly pine forest type consists of naturally regenerated stands. Growth and development characteristics of loblolly pine make the species a good choice for planned natural regeneration and management. Natural regeneration offers landowners low capital investment, periodic revenue, and multiple-use options. However, it is usually more complicated than artificial regeneration because competition control, site disturbance, and a good seed crop must all come together in sequence during a short period to make the system work effectively. A good understanding of the silvics of loblolly pine and of the species' role in diverse ecosystems, as well as patience and the ability to act quickly as opportunities arise, are required to naturally regenerate loblolly pines on a regular basis under diverse site, stand, and environmental conditions.

Successful natural regeneration can be achieved through a variety of reproduction cutting methods. Clearcutting, seed tree, and shelterwood methods promote even-aged stands, whereas selection cutting produces all-aged or uneven-aged stands. Each of these methods can successfully maintain fully stocked stands if certain management principles are followed. Competition control and site preparation are usually needed, but the intensity of these treatments is often dictated by abundance of the seed crop, site productivity, moisture availability, and present stand conditions. For best results, overstory and midstory hardwoods should be eliminated, a receptive seedbed should be available, and understory vegetation should be controlled. Usually, minimal vegetation control and seedbed preparation are required if a good seed crop is expected.

Prescribed burning is the most economical method for creating a good seedbed in even-aged stands and is often the only treatment needed. The most favorable conditions for loblolly pine establishment are created when a hot fire destroys competing vegetation and much of the surface organic matter late in the growing season and just before seedfall. Newly fallen seeds germinate rapidly, and seedlings begin growth on a relatively equal footing with most vegetation except sprouting hardwoods, which already have well-developed root systems. The conditions least favorable for regeneration occur after a surface fire during the dormant season because only a small amount of the surface organic matter is consumed, and many hardwood species sprout promptly and more numerously at the beginning of a new growing season.

If the seed crop is sparse, more intensive cultural treatments, such as disking, are usually required to get a good stand established. Whatever the amount of competition control or the intensity of seedbed preparation, treatments should be completed before seeds begin to fall in October.

Planned natural regeneration often produces too many, rather than too few, seedlings. Many die within the first 3 years, but regular monitoring of stocking and competition, for intermediate stand treatments, must be incorporated into the management schedule if natural regeneration is to be successful.

Varying numbers and various species of hardwoods are usually associated with natural loblolly pine stands. However, stand mixture usually occurs by happenstance. There is an expanding social demand for more mixed pine–hardwood stands throughout the loblolly pine range. It is feasible to grow mixed stands by culturing appropriate numbers of various hardwoods in the understory and in the overstory. The cost of producing pine timber in mixed stands is greater than the cost of producing it in pure stands, but mixed stands may be an acceptable environmental compromise, especially at the rural–urban interface.

Research Needs

■ Reliable methods are needed to predict poor seed crops before conelet development so sufficient lead time is available to stimulate flower and seed production.

■ Sound ecological and economic evaluations are needed for growing various combinations of pine–hardwood mixtures from regeneration to maturity to expand multiple-use options for forest lands. These evaluations should include alternative herbaceous weed control and selective hardwood control measures to promote the best species combinations for various sites and environmental conditions.

Literature Cited

Baker JB. 1982. Natural regeneration of loblolly/shortleaf pine. In: Proceedings, Low Cost Alternatives for Regeneration of Southern Pines; 1982 June 16–17; Athens, GA. Athens, GA: Georgia Center for Continuing Education: 31–50.

Baker JB. 1987. Silvicultural systems and natural regeneration methods for southern pines in the United States. In: Proceedings, Seminar on Forest Productivity and Site Evaluation; 1987 November 10–11; Taipei, Taiwan. Taipei: Council of Agriculture: 175–191.

Baker JB. 1989. Recovery and development of understocked loblolly–shortleaf pine stands. Southern Journal of Applied Forestry 13(3):132–139.

Baker JB, Balmer WE. 1983. Loblolly pine. In: Burns RM, comp. Silvicultural systems for the major forest types of the United States. Agric. Handbk. 445, rev. Washington, DC: USDA Forest Service: 148–152.

Baker JB, Barnett JB. 1991. Regeneration methods. In: Duryea ML, Dougherty PM, eds. Forest regeneration manual. Dordrecht, The Netherlands: Kluwer Academic Publishers: 35–50.

Baker JB, Langdon OG. 1990. *Pinus taeda* L., Loblolly pine: Pinaceae, Pine family. In: Burns RM, Honkala BH, tech. coords. Silvics of North America: Vol. 2. Conifers. Agric. Handbk. 654. Washington, DC: USDA Forest Service: 497–512.

Bowling DR, Kellison RC. 1983. Bottomland hardwood stand development following clearcutting. Southern Journal of Applied Forestry 7(3):110–116.

Brender EV. 1958. A 10-year record of pine seed production on the Hitchiti Experimental Forest [Georgia]. Journal of Forestry 56(6):408–410.

Brender EV. 1961. Residual saplings in clearcut and planted stands. GA For. Res. Pap. 4. Macon, GA: Georgia Forestry Commission, Georgia Forest Research Council. 4 p.

Brender EV, Davis LS 1959. Influence of topography on the future composition of lower Piedmont forests. Journal of Forestry 57(1):33–34.

Brender EV, McNab WH. 1972. Loblolly pine seed production in the lower Piedmont under various harvesting methods. Journal of Forestry 70(6):345–349.

Brewer CW, Linnartz NE. 1974. Regenerating loblolly pine by direct seeding, seed trees, and shelterwood. LSU For. Note 111. Baton Rouge, LA: Louisiana State University and A&M College, Agricultural Experiment Station. 3 p.

Burk CJ. 1974. The vegetation of Portsmouth Island, North Carolina: fourteen years of change [abstract]. Associated Southeast Biology Bulletin 21(2):44.

Cain MD. 1986. Late-winter prescribed burns to prepare seedbeds for natural loblolly-shortleaf pine regeneration: are they prudent? Fire Management Notes 47(2):36–39.

Cain MD. 1987. Site-preparation techniques for establishing natural pine regeneration on small forest properties. Southern Journal of Applied Forestry 11(1):41–45.

Cain MD. 1988a. Competition impacts on growth of naturally regenerated loblolly pine seedlings. Res. Note SO-345. New Orleans: USDA Forest Service, Southern Forest Experiment Station. 5 p.

Cain MD. 1988b. Hardwood control before harvest improves natural pine regeneration. Res. Pap. SO-249. New Orleans: USDA Forest Service, Southern Forest Experiment Station. 6 p.

Cain MD, Baker JB, Murphy PA. 1987. Precommercial thinning of pine regeneration in uneven-aged stands. In: Phillips DR, ed. Proceedings, 4th Biennial Southern Silvicultural Research Conference; 1986 November 4–6; Atlanta, GA. Gen. Tech. Rep. SE-42. Asheville, NC: USDA Forest Service, Southeastern Forest Experiment Station: 419–424.

Campbell TE, Mann WF Jr. 1973. Regenerating loblolly pine by direct seeding, natural seeding, and planting. Res. Pap. SO-84. New Orleans: USDA Forest Service, Southern Forest Experiment Station. 9 p.

Crow AB, Shilling CL. 1980. Use of prescribed burning to enhance southern pine timber production. Southern Journal of Applied Forestry 4(1):15–18.

Dennington RW, Larson LK. 1984. Natural regeneration methods for loblolly pine. In: Proceedings, Symposium on the Loblolly Pine Ecosystem—West Region; 1984 March 20–22; Jackson, MS. Mississippi State, MS: Mississippi State University: 61–69.

Edwards MB. 1987a. A comparison of natural regeneration alternatives for a loblolly pine forest in the lower Piedmont of Georgia. In: Phillips DR, ed. Proceedings, 4th Biennial Southern Silvicultural Research Conference; 1986 November 4–6; Atlanta, GA. Gen. Tech. Rep. SE-42. Asheville, NC: USDA Forest Service, Southeastern Forest Experiment Station: 84–86.

Edwards MB. 1987b. Natural regeneration of loblolly pine. Gen. Tech. Rep. SE-47. Asheville, NC: USDA Forest Service, Southeastern Forest Experiment Station. 17 p.

Farrar RM. 1981. Regulation of uneven-aged loblolly–shortleaf pine forests. In: Barnett JP, ed. Proceedings, 1st Biennial Southern Silvicultural Research Conference; 1980 November 6–7; Atlanta, GA. Gen. Tech. Rep. SO-34. New Orleans: USDA Forest Service, Southern Forest Experiment Station: 294–304.

Graff J, Kaiser F. 1986. Area foresters and Virginia seed tree law effectiveness. Southern Journal of Applied Forestry 10(1):42–44.

Grano CX. 1949. Is litter a barrier to the initial establishment of shortleaf pine reproduction? Journal of Forestry 47(7):554–548.

Grano CX. 1954. Re-establishment of shortleaf–loblolly pine under four cutting methods. Journal of Forestry 52:132–133.

Grano CX. 1957a. Growth of loblolly pine seed trees in relation to crown density. Journal of Forestry 55(11):852.

Grano CX. 1957b. Indices to potential cone production of loblolly pine. Journal of Forestry 55(12):890–891.

Grano CX. 1961. Shortleaf–loblolly reproduction losses moderate following seed tree felling. Journal of Forestry 59(1):24–25.

Grano CX. 1967. Growing loblolly and shortleaf pine in the Midsouth. Farmers Bull. 2102. Rev. Washington, DC: USDA Forest Service. 27 p.

Grano CX. 1970. Seed yields in loblolly–shortleaf pine selection stands. Res. Note SO-109. New Orleans, LA. USDA Forest Service, Southern Forest Experiment Station. 4 p.

Grano CX. 1971. Conditioning loessial soils for natural loblolly and shortleaf pine seedling. Res. Note SO-116. New Orleans: USDA Forest Service, Southern Forest Experiment Station. 4 p.

Grano CX. 1973. Loblolly pine fecundity in south Arkansas. Res. Note 159. New Orleans: USDA Forest Service, Southern Forest Experiment Station. 7 p.

Harrington CA. 1987. Site-index comparisons for naturally seeded loblolly pine and shortleaf pine. Southern Journal of Applied Forestry 11(2):86–91.

Hu SC. 1983. Regenerating loblolly pine by natural seeding and by planting in southeastern Louisiana. In: Jones EP Jr, ed. Proceedings, 2nd Biennial Southern Silvicultural Research Conference; 1982 November 4–5; Atlanta, GA. Gen. Tech. Rep. SE-24. Asheville, NC: USDA Forest Service, Southeastern Forest Experiment Station: 94–95.

Jones EP. 1989. Changes in vegetation under four burning regimes. In: Miller JH, comp. Proceedings, 5th Biennial Southern Silvicultural Research Conference; 1988 November 1–3; Memphis, TN. Gen. Tech. Rep. SO-74. New Orleans: USDA Forest Service, Southern Forest Experiment Station: 389–393.

Langdon OG. 1979. Natural regeneration of loblolly pine. In: Proceedings, 1979 National Silviculture Workshop; 1979 September 17–21; Charleston, SC. Washington, DC: USDA Forest Service: 101–116.

Langdon OG. 1981. Natural regeneration of loblolly pine: a sound strategy for many forest landowners. Southern Journal of Applied Forestry 5(4):170–176.

Little S, Escheman RT. 1976. Nineteen-year changes in the composition of a stand of Pinus taeda in eastern Maryland. Bulletin of the Torrey Botanical Club 103(2):57–66.

Little S, Mohr JJ. 1963. Conditioning loblolly pine stands in eastern Maryland for regeneration. Res. Pap. NE-9. Broomall, PA: USDA Forest Service, Northeastern Forest Experiment Station. 21 p.

Little S, Somes HA. 1959. Viability of loblolly pine seed stored in the forest floor. Journal of Forestry 57(11):848–849.

Lotti T. 1956. Good seed production from a young stand of loblolly pine. Res. Note 97. Asheville, NC: USDA Forest Service, Southeastern Forest Experiment Station. 2 p.

Lotti T. 1961. The case for natural regeneration. In: Crow AB, ed. Advances in management of southern pine. Baton Rouge, LA: Louisiana State University Press: 16–25.

Loyd RA, Thayer AG, Lowry GL. 1978. Pine growth and regeneration following three hardwood control treatments. Southern Journal of Applied Forestry 2(1):25–27.

McLemore BF. 1985. Comparison of three methods for regenerating honeysuckle-infested openings in uneven-aged loblolly pine stands. In: Shoulders E, ed. Proceedings, 3rd Biennial Southern Silvicultural Research Conference; 1984 November 7–8; Atlanta, GA. Gen. Tech. Rep. SO-54: New Orleans: USDA Forest Service, Southern Forest Experiment Station: 97–99.

McLemore BF. 1987. Development of intermediate and suppressed loblolly pines following release. In: Phillips DR, ed. Proceedings, 4th Biennial Southern Silvicultural Research Conference; 1986 November 4–6; Atlanta, GA. Gen. Tech. Rep. SE-42. Asheville, NC: USDA Forest Service, Southeastern Forest Experiment Station: 439–444.

McMinn JW. 1985. Whole-tree harvesting affects pine regeneration and hardwood competition. Southern Journal of Applied Forestry 9(2):81–84.

McNab WH, Ach EE. 1967. Prescribed burning improves Piedmont loblolly pine seedbeds. Res. Note SE-76. Asheville, NC: USDA Forest Service, Southeastern Forest Experiment Station. 2 p.

Miller JH. 1988. Guidelines for kudzu eradication treatments. In: Miller JH, Mitchell RJ, eds. A manual on ground applications of forestry herbicides. Proceedings, Workshop on Ground Applications of Forestry Herbicides; 1987 June 10–12; Natchez, MS. R8-MB 21. Atlanta: USDA Forest Service, Southern Region: 33–38.

Murphy PA, Guldin RW. 1987. Financial maturity of trees in selection stands revisited. Res. Pap. SO-242. New Orleans: USDA Forest Service, Southern Forest Experiment Station. 7 p.

Nicholson SA, Monk CD. 1974. Plant species diversity in old-field succession on a Georgia Piedmont. Ecology 55(95):1075–1085.

Pomeroy KB. 1949. Loblolly pine seed trees: selection, fruitfullness, and mortality. Res. Pap. 5. Asheville, NC: USDA Forest Service, Southeastern Forest Experiment Station. 17 p.

Pomeroy KB, Trousdell KB. 1948. The importance of seed-bed preparation in loblolly pine management. Southern Lumberman 177(2225):143–144.

Posey CE. 1965. The effect of fertilization upon some wood properties of loblolly pine. Dissertation Abstracts International 26B(2):598–599.

Posey CE. 1967. Natural regeneration of loblolly pine 230 miles northwest of its native range. Journal of Forestry 65(10):732.

Sims DH, McMinn JW. 1990. Season and intensity of harvest influence natural pine and hardwood regeneration in the Piedmont. R8-MB 44. Atlanta: USDA Forest Service, Southern Region. 2 p.

Skeen JN. 1981. The pattern of natural regeneration and height stratification within a naturally-created opening in an all-aged Piedmont deciduous forest. In: Barnett JP, ed. Proceeding, 1st Biennial Southern Silvicultural Research Conference; 1980 November 6–7; Atlanta, GA. Gen. Tech. Rep. SO-34. New Orleans: USDA Forest Service, Southern Forest Experiment Station: 259–268.

Spring PE, Brewer ML, Brown JR, Fanning ME. 1974. Population ecology of loblolly pine in an old field community. Oikos 25(1):1–6.

Stalter R. 1971. Age of a mature pine (Pinus taeda) stand in South Carolina. Ecology 52(3):532–533.

Stewart JT. 1965. Regenerating loblolly pine with four seed trees. Virginia Forests 29(2):14–15.

Switzer GL, Shelton MG, Nelson LE. 1979. Successional development of the forest floor and soil surface on upland sites of the east gulf Coastal Plain. Ecology 60(6):1162–1171.

Tankersley L. 1985. Don't cut yourself out of the timber business. Leaflet 380. Athens, GA: University of Georgia, Cooperative Extension Service. 6 p.

Taylor DR, Bilan MV. 1973. Strip clear cutting to regenerate east Texas pines. TX For. Pap. 20. Nacogdoches, TX: Stephen F. Austin State University. 6 p.

Trousdell KB. 1950a. A method of forecasting annual variations in seed crop for loblolly pine. Journal of Forestry 48(5):345–348.

Trousdell KB. 1950b. Seed and seedbed requirements to regenerate loblolly pine. Sta. Pap. 8. Asheville, NC: USDA Forest Service, Southeastern Forest Experiment Station. 13 p.

Trousdell KB. 1963. Loblolly pine regeneration from seed: what do site preparation and cultural measures buy? Journal of Forestry 61(6):441–444.

Trousdell KB, Langdon OG. 1967. Disking and prescribed burning for loblolly pine regeneration. Journal of Forestry 65(8):548–551.

Trousdell KB, Wenger KF. 1963. Some factors of climate and soil affecting establishment of loblolly pine stands. Forest Science 9(2):130–136.

Tuttle CL, Golden M., Meldahl RS. 1988. Soil compaction effects on Pinus taeda establishment from seed and early growth. Canadian Journal of Forest Research 18(5):628–632.

Ursic SJ, Duffy PD. 1987. Strip cutting to regenerate erosion-control plantations of loblolly pine. In: Phillips DR, ed. Proceedings, 4th Biennial Southern Silvicultural Research Conference; 1986 November 4–6; Atlanta, GA. Gen. Tech. Rep. SE-42. Asheville, NC: USDA Forest Service, Southeastern Forest Experiment Station: 326–30.

VanHaverbeke DF, Barber JC. 1964. Seed crop estimation in a loblolly pine seed production area. GA For. Res. Pap. 21. Macon, GA: Georgia Forestry Commission, Georgia Forest Research Council. 5 p.

Van Lear DH, Douglass JE, Cox SK, and others. 1983. Regeneration of loblolly pine plantations in the Piedmont by clearcutting with seed in place. In: Jones EP Jr, ed. Proceedings, 2nd Biennial Southern Silvicultural Research Conference; 1982 November 4–5; Atlanta, GA. Gen. Tech. Rep. SE-24. Asheville, NC: USDA Forest Service, Southeastern Forest Experiment Station: 87–93.

Wahlenberg WG. 1960. Loblolly pine: its use, ecology, regeneration, protection, growth and management. Durham, NC: Duke University, School of Forestry. 603 p.

Walker LC, Leiser A. 1965. Fertilizers applied to natural regeneration. Castanea 30(4):231–237.

Wenger KF. 1953. How to estimate the number of cones in standing loblolly pine trees (Pinus taeda). Res. Note 44. Asheville, NC: USDA Forest Service, Southeastern Forest Experiment Station. 2 p.

Wenger KF. 1954. The stimulation of loblolly pine seed trees by preharvest release. Journal of Forestry 52:115–118.

Wenger KF. 1957. Annual variation in the seed crops of loblolly pine. Journal of Forestry 55(8):56–569.

Wenger KF, Trousdell KB. 1958. Natural regeneration of loblolly pine in the south Atlantic Coastal Plain. Prod. Res. Rep. 13. Asheville, NC: USDA Forest Service, Southeastern Forest Experiment Station. 78 p.

Williston HL, Balmer WE, eds. 1974. Proceedings, symposium on management of young pines; 1974 October 22–24; Alexandria, LA/December 3–5; Charleston, SC. Asheville, NC: USDA Forest Service, Southeastern Forest Experiment Station. 349 p.

Williston HL, Balmer WE, Sims DH. 1982. Managing the family forest in the South. Gen. Rep. SA-GR 22. Atlanta: USDA Forest Service, Southern Region, State and Private Forestry. 89 p.

Chapter 6

Artificial Regeneration

Contents

Continued on next page…

Contents (cont'd)

Artificial Regeneration

Introduction

Forty years of intense pine harvesting before 1930 destroyed 90% of the original 48.6 million ha of southern pine forests and left 25% of the entire southern pine region without natural reproduction or seed trees (Mann 1969). Artificial regeneration by planting or direct seeding was the only way to restore pine production on this land. A 1.2-ha tract of loblolly pines planted near the Savannah River in 1873 is still growing. A few other small plantations were established before 1900 using young wildings lifted from the woods, but these plantations totaled less than 200 ha. Between 1920 and 1926, the Great Southern Lumber Company of Bogalusa, Louisiana, planted about 4,900 ha of loblolly and other southern pines on a commercial basis (Wakeley 1954). The Clarke–McNary Act of 1924 provided funding for cooperative Federal and State Government establishment of state nurseries. This program and the establishment of small industrial nurseries made it possible to increase the area of southern pine plantations to 30,000 ha by 1931. Large-scale seedling production began in the mid-1930's, when the U.S. Department of Agriculture, Forest Service, began operating its Ashe Nursery in southern Mississippi. During the Great Depression of the 1930's, the newly formed Civilian Conservation Corps planted more than 200,000 ha to pines during a 7-year period. These early nursery operations and outplantings proved that loblolly pines could be regenerated artificially on a large scale and that they would grow rapidly on a variety of sites. The early successes, together with favorable markets for softwood products, state and federal incentive programs, and industry's commitment to short-rotation, high-fiber yield forestry and tree improvement programs resulted in an exponential increase in production of loblolly pine seedlings during the mid- to late-1900's. About 1.5 billion loblolly seedlings are now produced and planted annually (Lantz 1988).

Advantages and Disadvantages of Artificial Regeneration

The choice between natural and artificial regeneration methods should be made only after detailed economic and environmental analyses are performed. Artificial regeneration may not always be the better option, but it has several distinct advantages over natural regeneration:

- With artificial regeneration, it is easy to define and treat management areas, especially in new clearcuts.

- Harvesting, cultural operations, and regeneration are concentrated in time and space.

- Relatively little technical skill and supervision are required.

- Wildlife species that depend on early successional vegetation benefit.

- Species conversion is possible, and genetically improved planting stock can be used.

- Spacing and initial stocking are controlled.

- There is no dependence on natural seed crops.

However, artificial regeneration, especially by planting, also has the following disadvantages:

- Establishment costs are higher than with natural regeneration.

- The heavy equipment generally used can cause environmental degradation.

- Because there is a single age class and a lack of species variability, plantations are more susceptible to severe insect and disease problems.

- The site's appearance may be degraded for a few years.

- Some wildlife species that depend on mature trees are displaced.

Species–Site Relationships

Loblolly pine performs best on fertile and moist sites but can be grown successfully on all but the very driest sites in the South. It should be the favored species for pine regeneration throughout most of its natural range (Balmer and Williston 1974, Kellison and others 1979, Lantz 1987; table 6-1). Slash pine usually outperforms loblolly on wet flats and savannas of the lower Coastal Plain from Louisiana to South Carolina and especially in central and northern Florida, where fusiform rust can damage loblolly severely. However, loblolly grows as well as or better than slash on intermediate or drier sites where clay is 75 cm or more beneath the soil surface (Cole 1973, Shoulders 1982; table 6-1). Also, loblolly outgrows slash on bedded wet flats in South Carolina (Crutchfield D. 1989. personal communication). Longleaf and sand pines, *Pinus clausa* (Chapm. ex Engelm.) Vasey ex Sarg., outperform loblolly on deep sandy sites. Shortleaf and Virginia pines generally do better than loblolly

on harsh upland sites. These general rules should be supplemented with local knowledge of past growth trends and risks (Caulfield and others 1989). For instance, loblolly competes well with both shortleaf and Virginia pines on diverse sites in the southern Cumberland and mid-Cumberland Plateau (Smalley 1979, 1982), in the eastern Highland Rim and Pennyroyal (Smalley 1983), and in the western Highland Rim and Pennyroyal of Tennessee (Smalley 1980).

Table 6-1—Species-site guide for specific soil groups in the southern Coastal Plain

Drainage class	Diagnostic horizon	Soil subgroup	Representative series	Order of preferred species
Very poorly to somewhat poorly drained	No spodic horizon; argillic within 50 cm	Typic & Plinthic Aqults	Portsmouth-Bladen	Loblolly*/slash
	No spodic horizon; argillic below 50	Arenic & Grossarenic Aqults, Aquents, & Aquepts	Rutledge-Plummer	Slash/loblolly*
	Spodic & argillic horizons present	Ultic Aquods & Humods (Spodosols)	Mascotte-Sapelo	Loblolly*/slash/longleaf
Poorly to moderately well drained	Spodic but no argillic horizons present	Typic, Aeric, & Arenic Aquods & Humods (Spodosols)	Ridgeland-Leon	Slash/loblolly/longleaf
Moderately well to well drained	No spodic horizon; argillic within 50 cm	Typic & Plinthic Udults	Goldsboro-Norfolk	Loblolly/slash/longleaf
	No spodic horizon; argillic below 50 cm	Arenic & Grossarenic Udults, Umbrepts, & Ochrepts	Blanton-Orsino	Slash/loblolly/longleaf
Somewhat excessively to excessively drained	No spodic horizon; argillic may or may not be present	Psamments	Lakeland-Eustis	Longleaf/sand
Very poorly to poorly drained	Organic surface >50 cm thick	Medisaprists & Histic Humaquepts	Kingsland-Pettigrew	Loblolly*/slash

Source: adapted from Fisher (1981).

* Loblolly should be used only if adequate phosphorus is available or supplied.

Artificial Regeneration by Planting

Either bareroot or container seedlings can be planted. Seed handling and seedling planting techniques are very similar for both, but nursery production methods and materials for bareroot seedlings are quite different from those for container seedlings.

Producing Bareroot Loblolly Pine Seedlings

Between 1974 and 1980, annual production of loblolly pine seedlings tripled from 337 million (Abbott and Fitch 1977) to almost 1 billion, and 60% of all nursery stock produced in the United States and 75% of that produced in the South was loblolly pine (table 6-2). Between 1985 and 1990, annual Southwide production and planting of bareroot loblolly pine seedlings ranged from 1.2 to 1.5 billion, and loblolly accounted for about 80% of all pine seedlings planted in the southern United States. Fifty-five to sixty percent of all loblolly seedlings were grown in Alabama, Arkansas,

Georgia, and South Carolina (McDonald and Krugman 1985; table 6-3). Between 550 and 590 million of these seedlings were grown in state nurseries annually (USDA FS 1985), and more than 85% were from genetically improved seeds (Lantz 1988). Effective seed collection and storage techniques, production of high-quality seedlings, and ad-

Table 6-2—Production of bareroot forest tree nursery stock in the United States in 1980

	Bareroot production	
	No.	%
Loblolly pine	965,620,000	59.9
Other pines	283,921,000	17.6
Other species	34,766,000	2.1
Total raised in the South	1,284,307,000	79.6
Total raised outside the South	328,686,000	20.4
Grand total in the United States	1,612,993,000	100.0

Source: adapted from Boyer and South (1984a).

Table 6-3—Estimated nursery production of loblolly pines by state

	Estimated production (millions of seedlings)		Percent of total southern pine nursery production*
	1988-89*	1989-90	
Alabama	225	183	79
Arkansas	148	139	100
Florida	26	20	18
Georgia	199	110	63
Kentucky	9	10	100
Louisiana	78	49	80
Mississippi	89	73	92
North Carolina	86	76	93
Oklahoma	75	73	100
South Carolina	189	228	96
Tennessee	12	6	100
Texas	25	149	94
Virginia	77	76	100
Total	1,238	1,192	78

Source: adapted from Mangold and others (1991).

* Lantz CW. 1990. Unpublished data. Atlanta, GA: USDA Forest Service, Cooperative Forestry.

† Based on percentage produced in state nurseries during 1987-89.

Table 6-4—Characteristics of loblolly pine cones and seeds after various collection dates and storage periods

Collection date (1969) and storage period (weeks)	Cone specific gravity	% Cone moisture content	No. seeds/ cone	% Germination*
September 15	0.99	129.3	NA	NA
1			0*	96
3			14	98
5			38	98
Average			17	97
September 22	0.93	119.9	NA	NA
1			22	95
3			27	97
5			28	98
Average			26	97
September 29	0.88	112.1	NA	NA
1			1*	98
3			40	98
5			65	98
Average			35	98
October 6	0.82	103.6	NA	NA
1			35	98
3			45	98
5			38	98
Average			39	98
October 13	0.80	84.3	NA	NA
1			47	99
3			52	99
5			44	99
Average			48	99

Source: adapted from Barnett (1976).

NA = not applicable.

* Germination was determined from seeds that were removed from unopened cones.

vanced methods of seedling care and handling have made it possible to establish large plantations in which survival rates are high and early tree development is vigorous.

Cone and seed collection and handling. The first step in artificial regeneration is cone collection. Carefully controlled cone collection, cone and seed processing, and storage can greatly increase the viability of loblolly pine seeds. Unfavorable conditions during any of these steps can cause secondary seed dormancy, reduced storability, or loss of viability. A wide variety of equipment for collecting, processing, storing, and testing of forest tree seeds is available (Bonner 1977).

Because loblolly pine cones are firmly attached to limbs, they must usually be picked by hand from ladders, platforms, hydraulic lifts, or other devices that reach all levels of a tree's crown (Dooley and Fridley 1981). Such handpicking is slow and costly but is presently the only practical method of collecting loblolly cones. Because it takes about 20 kg of force to detach a loblolly cone from a branch, as opposed to only about 2 kg for slash pine (McLemore 1973), brief mechanical shaking of a tree dislodges few loblolly cones. Extended mechanical shaking does dislodge many cones but it also breaks branches and damages roots and therefore is not recommended. Chemicals such as ethrel, ascorbic acid, and indoleacetic acid, which induce abscission in fruit trees, are not effective in breaking the firm attachment of cone to branch.

The ends of limbs bear ripe cones, the next year's cones, and the primordia for the following year. Therefore, care must be taken not to break branches. However, rough handling of cones is not harmful and does not affect the rate or percentage of seed germination (Lyle and Gilmore 1958). An alternative to picking

cones is letting them open on the tree and collecting fallen seeds in nets placed on the ground. This is usually practical only in seed orchards (see chapter 7).

Cone moisture content and ripeness are most quickly determined by measuring cone specific gravity (sp. gr.). Cones are fully mature and begin to open on trees when their specific gravity decreases to about 0.70. However, seeds mature 2 to 3 weeks before cones mature fully, so cones can be picked when moisture content decreases to 70% (0.88 sp. gr.) (Barnett 1979a, Belcher and McKinney 1981). The earliest indication of seed ripeness is when cone specific gravity drops to 1.0 and cone moisture content is about 130% on a dry weight basis (Barnett and McLemore 1970; table 6-4). If cones are picked at this time, seed quality and the germination rate are increased as long as the cones are stored for 3 to 7 weeks before being opened, apparently because seeds continue to mature during the storage period. If cones are more mature when picked, the storage period can be shortened (Barnett 1979b; Bonner 1987a, 1987b). It is important to know just how long it takes seeds to mature during cone storage because not all cones can be picked when fully ripe. If early picked cones are not allowed to complete maturation in storage, some seeds may have to be extracted by hand, and seed immaturity may result in up to 20% abnormal germination (McLemore and Barnett 1966a, 1966b).

A fast and accurate field measurement of specific gravity can be made by immersing a cone in a graduated cylinder partially filled with water, according to the following procedure (Barnett 1979a):

1. Record the initial water level in milliliters.

2. Place the cone in the cylinder. If the cone sinks, its specific gravity is greater than 1.0 and the cone is not ripe. If the cone floats, record the difference between the initial water level and the water level when the cone is floating. This difference is the volume of the floating portion of the cone. For example, if the water level is 500 ml before the cone is added and 650 ml after the cone is added, the volume of the floating portion of the cone is 150 ml.

3. Use a wire or small stick to submerge the cone, and record the new water level. The difference between the original water level and the new water level is the total cone volume. For example, if the water level is now 670 ml, the total cone volume is 670 ml – 500 ml, or 170 ml.

4. Compute the cone's specific gravity by dividing floating cone volume by total cone volume: sp. gr. = 150 ml ÷ 170 ml = 0.88.

Because cone maturity can vary greatly from tree to tree, the specific gravity of several freshly picked cones from different trees should be measured before extensive collections are made. If the specific gravity of 19 of 20 randomly picked cones has reached the appropriate level, cones are ready for collection. If collections are being made in an orchard, the manager can determine how quickly cones are ripening on individual trees or clones and use this information to design a more systematic cone collection schedule for the future.

Cone storage, cone drying, and seed extraction.
After-ripening techniques can extend the cone collection season and increase the number of viable seeds per cone. Newly picked cones are commonly left to dry naturally on screens or packed loosely in containers that permit air movement and unimpeded opening of drying cones. Cones are commonly dried outdoors under partial shade but can be dried in a shed or unheated building. Good containers for outdoor storage include burlap bags and wooden crates filled no more than half full. Drying trays or open paper sacks are suitable indoor storage containers. Natural drying takes 3 weeks to 2 months, depending on environmental conditions and on storage conditions (under shelter or in the open). Cones can be stored up to 11 weeks without reduction in seed viability (Bonner 1991a). Cones must be dried to about 10% moisture content for successful seed removal. Once cones open, many seeds fall out and others can be shaken out by hand. Extraction of seeds appears to be more complete following unprotected outdoor drying than when cones are dried indoors, apparently as a result of naturally alternating wet and dry conditions outdoors. If rain is infrequent, cones should be wet thoroughly at least once a week. Although considerable amounts of external mold often develop on cones in the center of larger boxes, this mold

does not reduce seed quality (Barnett 1976a, Bonner 1987b, Lantz 1979, McLemore 1975, Waldrip 1970).

In large operations, seeds are most efficiently extracted by kiln drying after cones have been air dried to a moisture content of 35 to 50%. Cones dry rapidly if subjected to uniform heat with continuous air circulation in a building or forced draft kiln. Small lots of cones can be dried in portable kilns. Tray kilns are the most widely used drying and seed extraction equipment. Wire trays with mesh bottoms and measuring 1.2 by 2.4 by 0.4 m and filled with 0.2 m^3 of cones can be stacked up to 6 trays high. Heated air is blown up through the stacks. The optimum temperature depends on initial cone moisture content, relative humidity of the air, and the number of cones in the kiln. Initial kiln temperatures should be about 30 to 35 °C if cone moisture is about 50%. As cones dry, temperatures can be increased to a maximum of about 46 °C. Cones usually dry and open in less than 48 hours. If cones are dried too quickly, they do not open well. High kiln temperatures may injure seeds and will increase energy costs. As cones open, seeds fall to the screen. Tray kiln systems are suitable for large or small batch processing because seeds can be kept separate by tray. The kiln drying process can increase the normal germination percentage for seeds collected early by about 10% if done properly. Drying cones from 50% (0.81 sp. gr.) to 10% moisture content results in the removal of about 26 kg of water/m^3 of cones (Bonner 1984, Easley 1966, McLemore and Barnett 1966a).

If many cones do not open completely during the first kiln drying cycle, a second cycle may increase the number of seeds released by 4 to 9%. Cones should be soaked in or sprayed with water until completely closed and then returned to the kiln. The second drying can produce more seeds than the first drying if many cones are mildly case-hardened. Although seeds released by the second drying are usually of reduced quality, it may still be desirable to recover those of valuable genotypes (Karrfalt 1979).

Solar drying, microwave drying, dehumidifying, and vacuum drying also dry cones effectively. Microwave drying can open green cones with 0.90 sp. gr. in 75 to 125 min, and the energy used is only 10 to 33% of that required for conventional drying (Barnett 1979a, 1982a; Belcher and McKinney 1981). However, because kiln and open-air drying are easy and inexpensive, no other drying treatments are now used operationally.

Dewinging, cleaning, and sizing seeds. After seeds are extracted from cones, they should be separated from their wings and other debris, separated by size classes, and dried. Seed wings can be removed by tumbling seeds slowly in a drum or cylinder that is lined with soft rubber to minimize abrasion (Lowman 1975). Dewinging is hastened if slowly tumbling seeds are moistened with a fine water spray. The wings absorb moisture quickly and are broken off by rubbing against other seeds. Wet dewinging usually raises seed moisture content to about 12 to 14%. This can greatly increase fungal growth, so seeds should be redried to 10% as soon as possible. Redrying requires little heat (Belcher 1984, Bonner 1991c) and can be accomplished by any method that forces air through the seeds. After they have been dewinged, seeds can quickly be cleaned and sized. Various combinations of screens and air systems do this job in a single pass or in separate operations. Sound seeds sink in water, so empty seeds and large debris can easily be removed by flotation. However, seeds must be redried after flotation cleaning. Empty and partially filled seeds can also be removed by specific gravity separation (promoted by vibration and blowing air) or with a fractionating aspirator, which is now preferred over gravity table separation. Bonner (1977) presents a detailed listing of equipment available for cleaning seeds.

Seeds can be sized by screening followed by gravity separation. Gravity sizing must be preceded by screening because a gravity sizer cannot separate by physical size and density at the same time (Belcher and others 1984). Large-mesh screens (0.45 cm) yield about 32,200 seeds/kg; medium mesh (0.25 by 1.90 cm), 39,700 seeds/kg; and small mesh (0.20 cm), about 52,900 seed/kg (Darby 1962).

Viable seeds of all sizes should be used. Sorting seeds by size class facilitates mechanical sowing and reduces the cull percentage by making emergence in the seedbed more uniform. However, sorting does not result in any consistent increase in germination, early outplanting survival, or early growth of loblolly pine seedlings (Barnett and Dunlap 1982, Hodgson 1980; table 6-5).

Seed testing.   Accurate seed testing begins with the selection of representative samples from a seedlot. Samples are taken with a "trier"—a hollow, slotted brass tube inside a slotted outer shell (Bonner 1981). If a seedlot is held in several containers, samples should be taken from the top, middle, and bottom of each container and mixed into a single composite sample (Belcher 1984).

No matter how good seeds look, it is preferable to germinate samples under controlled laboratory conditions to ascertain germinability in order to determine accurately how many seeds to sow to get an acceptable number of seedlings (Barnett and McLemore 1984). The most reliable test is to germinate random replicates from pure seedlots. The Association of Official Seed Analysts recommends

two specific germination tests for loblolly pine seeds (table 6-6). Both speed and completeness of germination are needed to accurately measure seed quality and, ultimately, seedling yields. Speed and completeness of germination can be incorporated into a numerical rating called the germination value (Czabator 1962):

$$\text{germination value} =$$
$$\text{mean daily germination (MDG)} \times \text{peak value (PV)}$$

where MDG = percentage of full-seed germination at the end of the test divided by the number of days to the end of the test and PV = MDG of the most vigorous component of the seedlot. Larger germination values imply faster and more complete germination.

Purity tests determine the proportion of seeds to other material. Good seed processing should yield seeds with purity of at least 95% (Bonner 1991c). On the average, there are about 40,100 (range of 27,100 to 58,200) clean seeds/kg (AOSA 1987). Seed weight is determined from the pure seed fraction obtained in the purity test and includes empty or broken seeds, if they occur in the sample. Five samples of 100 seeds each, randomly drawn and weighed to 3 significant digits, give a good estimate of average seed weight if none of the replicate weights varies from the mean weight by more than 10%. If variation is greater, more samples must be used.

Several indirect methods, such as cutting, tetrazolium staining, leachate conductivity testing, or x-raying, can be used to estimate seed viability quickly when time constraints make the standard 28-day laboratory tests impractical. Cutting tests are simplest and are quite reliable for fresh seeds. However, they are not suitable for stored seeds because they may not reveal loss of seed quality in storage and may lead workers to overestimate seed quality. Seeds should be cut in half along the length of the embryonic cavity. Good seeds typically have fully grown, firm, undamaged tissue with a characteristic creamy white color (Bonner 1991c).

Tetrazolium stains live tissue pink to red. Tetrazolium staining takes only 18 to 24 hours and requires little equipment. Unfortunately, the test is subjective, hard to standardize (because it is affected by the pH of the solution used, temperature, and light), and very labor inten-

Table 6-5—Survival and growth of loblolly pines in Georgia as affected by seed size

| Seed size | Seedling size | Age 3 years | | Age 13-15 years | | | % volume increase over lower grade |
		Survival %	Height (m)	Survival %	Height (m)	Volume (m³/ha)	
Medium	Select	75 a	2.4 a	62 a	15.0 a	145 a	26.9
Medium	Average	52 b	2.2 a	47 a	14.3 ab	114 c	—
Large	Select	64 ab	2.4 a	55 a	14.1 ab	137 ab	13.6
Large	Average	63 ab	2.3 a	54 a	13.7 bc	121 bc	—
Mean		64	2.3	55	14.3	129	

Source: adapted from Sluder (1979).

Values in rows followed by the same letter are not significantly different at the 95% probability level according to Duncan's new multiple range test.

Table 6-6—Testing methods for laboratory germination of loblolly pine seeds

Minimum weight of seeds for purity analysis	Substrata	Temp. (°C)	Test duration (days)	Additional directions
60	TB, P	22–30	28	Paired tests; prechill 28 days
60	P	22	28	Paired tests; prechill 28 days; use16-hr light

Source: adapted from AOSA (1987).

TB = top of blotter; P = covered petri dishes with seeds placed on (a) two layers of blotters, (b) three thicknesses of filter paper, or (c) top of sand or soil.

sive (Belcher 1984, Bonner 1991c).

Leachate conductivity testing provides quick estimates of seed quality. Seeds are leached for 24 hours in de-ionized water at 25 to 27 °C. Electrical conductivity of the leachate is then measured. As seeds deteriorate or are damaged, their membranes lose electrolytes and other cellular substances. Increased leaching results in increased electrical conductivity, which is related to decreased seed quality. The technique has predicted laboratory germination of loblolly pine seeds to within 6.5 to 9.0%. Additional research should improve the accuracy of this test (Bonner 1991b, Vozzo and Bonner 1985). X-ray images (radiographs) can be used to identify empty seeds, insect damage, some advanced disease damage, incompletely developed or abnormal embryos, and some mechanical damage, such as bruising and cracking (Belcher and Vozzo 1979, Bonner 1991c). X-raying is quick, nondestructive, and provides a permanent record for future study. However, x-raying requires expensive equipment, and radiographs can be hard to interpret.

Other laboratory tests for seed quality (for example, oxygen uptake, glutamic acid decarboxylase activity [GADA], and carbohydrate leakage) are too time consuming and sensitive to external factors to be useful in loblolly pine seed testing. The dark seedling growth test is impractical because of fungal problems. Seedling growth in an incubator or greenhouse may eventually be practical if the influences of pathogens, insects, and water and heat conditions can be controlled (Bonner 1986).

Seed prechilling (stratification). Under natural conditions, loblolly pine seeds disperse in the fall, over-winter for about 3 to 4 months on the forest floor, and germinate in the spring. The long exposure to cold, moist conditions breaks the seeds' inherent dormancy. Seeds collected and stored without a natural overwintering period develop a dormancy that inhibits germination. Of the major southern pines, only loblolly commonly exhibits a high level of dormancy (Pawuk and Barnett 1979). Prechilling [also called "stratification," a term derived from the early practice of storing seeds and a moist substrate in alternate layers in outdoor pits; the term "prechilling" is more descriptive of present treatments and is used throughout this book] overcomes this dormancy, makes germination rapid and uniform, and promotes survival and uniform seedling development. Holding moist seeds at a low temperature may speed germination by stimulating growth within the embryonic axis, which overcomes the mechanical restraint of the seed coat (Carpita and others 1983).

Loblolly pines show considerable genetic variation in dormancy and the need for prechilling. Seeds of some families are practically nondormant; prechilling has no effect on their germination or may even reduce it slightly (Barnett and McLemore 1984). Paired tests (four replicates with prechilling and four without) are recommended to identify seed source differences and to support prechilling and germination schedules (Bonner 1991a).

Fresh or stored seeds that are to be prechilled should be soaked in tap water for at least 24 hours, then drained and put in watertight 4-mil (0.01-mm) polyethylene bags or other sealed containers that permit limited air movement in order to prevent overheating. Containers of seeds should be kept in a room cooled to 1 to 5 °C for 30 to 60 days. Seeds are generally packed without media, but they can be mixed with moist vermiculite, damp moss, or other material to maintain a uniform moisture content. Sixty days of prechilling is recommended if rapid and uniform germination is desired in the early spring, when soil temperatures are low and days are short. If temperatures fall below freezing during prechilling, seeds may be injured. If temperatures rise above 5 °C, germination may occur. After prechilling, the moisture content of seeds ranges from about 26 to 34% of the ovendry weight (Belcher 1984, Bonner 1991c, Jones 1965).

Seeds can also be prechilled by soaking in 3 to 4 °C aerated water for about 14 to 30 days. Water aeration is easy, inexpensive, and eliminates the dangers of heating and molding that can occur during prechilling in sealed containers (Barnett and McLemore 1967, Pasztor 1962).

After seeds have been prechilled, they can be treated with a bird repellent and a chemical fungicide to minimize predation and *Fusarium* spp. infection and subsequent damping-off of newly germinated seedlings. Numerous chemicals are acceptable for this purpose. Adhesives can be used to increase the amount of fungicide that sticks to seeds. Chemical additives do not reduce rapid and vigorous germination (Pawuk and Barnett 1979).

Germination. Seeds that germinate fastest produce seedlings with the lowest mortality rates and the largest diameters at lifting and produces fewest culls. The last seeds to germinate will be the smallest and weakest seedlings (Barnett and McLemore 1984; Boyer and others

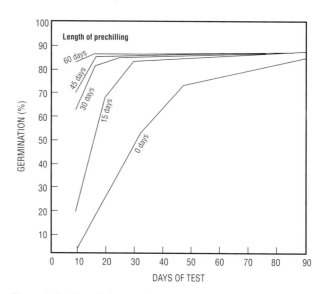

Figure 6-1—Cumulative germination (average of 29 lots) following 5 different periods of prechilling. Tests after 0, 15, 30, 45, and 60 days' prechilling were terminated at 90, 90, 75, 60, and 45 days, respectively (adapted from McLemore and Czabator 1961).

1985, 1987; Mexal 1980; Mexal and Fisher 1987). This fact is especially significant when one is dealing with seedlots of different families. Optimum prechilling treatments should be determined for each family (Boyer and others 1987). Germination of loblolly pine seeds, like that of many other plants, follows a sigmoidal pattern character-ized by a lag period, slow initial germination, a rapid rise, and finally a plateauing as the last small percentage of seeds completes germination.

Prechilling has a great effect on speed of germination (figure 6–1). In one study, at least 80% of the seeds prechilled 30 days or longer germinated within 15 days of sowing. Without prechilling it took 45 days for 75% of the seeds to germinate. Barnett and McLemore (1984) showed that the germination value for prechilled seeds was more than twice the germination value for seeds that were not prechilled. Such differences can be critical in direct-seed-ing operations, in which early germination minimizes seed predation, and cool spring weather and high soil moisture at sowing promote early survival of seedlings.

Effects of light, moisture, and temperature on seed germination. Several environmental factors strongly af-fect both the speed and completeness of loblolly pine seed germination. Exposure of seeds to light shortens the prechilling period required for rapid germination. In light, seedlots that are not prechilled often take 30 days to reach 80 to 90% germination. In contrast, 80 to 90% of prechilled, imbibed seeds germinate in 10 days or less. Imbibition is the taking up of fluids through colloidal processes and results in seed swelling. Seeds with high moisture content that are kept in darkness germinate more slowly and have lower germination percentages than do seeds that are exposed to light during imbibition (table 6-7). The light requirement for germination of seeds can be extremely small and is normal-ly satisfied by routine handling procedures that interrupt darkness. Five minutes' exposure to light every 4 days dur-ing a 32-day prechilling period increased germination in the dark (Campbell 1982c). Photoperiods of 0.001 to 0.002 sec resulted in 40 to 55% germination of seeds after 15 days, whereas only 9 to 14% of seeds that were not exposed to light germinated (Woods and Mollish 1963). The germina-tion process in prechilled seeds is promoted by red light (580 to 695 nm) and halted by far-red light (695 to 790 nm) (Toole and others 1962). Irradiating seeds with fluorescent light (high in red light) during prechilling can increase later germination in the darkness (McLemore 1964).

Seed moisture is critical in both storage and germina-tion of loblolly pine seeds. Seeds normally should not be dried to a moisture content lower than about 5%. However, moisture content less than 5% may not be detrimental if drying is done slowly so that internal structures are not damaged (Belcher 1984, Schoorel 1960). Detailed guidelines for measuring and managing seed moisture were reported by Bonner (1981).

Seeds should be sown in moist soil, or other moist me-dia, to promote imbibition. If sufficient moisture is avail-able, seeds absorb 80% or more of the moisture necessary

Table 6-7—Germination data for loblolly pine seeds under two light regimes

% Moisture content*	% Total germination		Days to reach 90% of total germination		Germination value§	
	Light†	Dark‡	Light	Dark	Light	Dark
30	92	82	12	16	22.6 a	14.5 a
25	89	83	12	15	20.1 a	14.9 a
20	96	84	12	16	22.6 a	14.4 a
15	87	81	12	17	19.4 a	13.1 a
10	89	79	13	19	17.9 a	10.0 b
Means¶	91 a	82 b	12 a	17 b	20.5 a	13.4 b

Source: adapted from Campbell (1982c).

* Moisture content responses by light regimes for germination value not followed by the same letter are significantly different at the 95% probability level. There were no differences between moisture levels for the other parameters.

† Exposure to 1,300 lumen/m^2 of light in a 16- to 8-hour light/dark cycle not in light proof bags.

‡ Exposure to 1,300 lumen/m^2 of light in a 16- to 8-hour light/dark cycle in light proof bags.

§ Germination value is an index combining both speed and completeness of seed germination.

¶ Combined moisture content means by light regime for each of the three major measurement parameters not followed by the same letter are significantly different at the 95% probability level.

for germination within 24 hours. When seed moisture content reaches about 36% (on a dry-weight basis), loblol-ly pine seedcoats rupture and germination begins (Barnett 1976a). Any level of moisture stress decreases the rate of germination, and ultimately reduces total germination (Dunlap and Barnett 1984a). However, drying and wetting prechilled seeds a number of times has little effect on total germination (Adams 1975, Adams and Feret 1976).

Air and water temperatures during imbibition affect germination. High water temperature increases absorp-tion of moisture by seeds during the first 24 hours of up-take. However, after 48 hours of absorption, germination percentages are the same at water temperatures from 9 to 29 °C (Barnett 1981). Germination percentage is reduced only slightly even at a water temperature of 36 °C (table 6-8). Germination of seeds that have not been prechilled is promoted when nighttime temperatures are from 18 to 21 °C and daytime temperatures are 28 to 32 °C. Prechill-

Table 6-8—Germination percentages and values of loblolly pine seeds after treatments with varying water temperatures and light regimes for 48 hours

Water temperature (°C)	Light condition*	% Germination	Germination value†
9	Light	92 a	17.2 c
	Dark	93 a	17.5 cd
16	Light	94 a	20.7 a
	Dark	96 a	18.7 b
21	Light	94 a	18.0 bc
	Dark	86 c	14.5 f
29	Light	92 a	16.5 e
	Dark	94 a	17.9 bc
36	Light	91 b	16.4 de
	Dark	90 b	15.9 e

Source: adapted from Barnett (1981).

Numbers in the same column not followed by the same letter are significantly different at the 95% confidence level.

* Light during absorption was 1,300 lumen/m^2 from cool-white fluorescent bulb; dark was total darkness in lightproof bags.

† Germination value is an index combining both speed and completeness of seed germination.

ed seeds germinate rapidly and completely at constant temperatures of 25 to 28 °C. Prechilling widens the range of temperatures that will give satisfactory germination (Barnett 1979b, Bonner 1983).

Special techniques for promoting germination. Some seeds may be difficult to germinate even after prechilling. Chemical treatments may solve this problem. Rinsing with 1% nitric acid can cause some recalcitrant seeds to germinate (Hare 1981). Soaking seeds for several days in 100- to 10,000-ppm solutions of citric acid following prechilling can also increase the germination percentage (Cotrufo 1963). Under certain conditions, other chemical treatments (for example, application of gibberellic acid, kinetin, potassium nitrate, or thiourea) promote germination of seeds that have been prechilled for less than the recommended period (Biswas and others 1972). Electromagnetic radiation of seeds does not increase seed germination, alter seedling development or disease resistance, or affect field performance of trees (Barnett and Krugman 1989). Osmotic priming has been shown to promote loblolly pine seed germination rate and rapidity of germination in the laboratory. This technique may be useful for germinating seeds that have not been prechilled or seeds that cannot be prechilled fully because of time constraints (Hallgren 1989).

Seed storage. Because loblolly pines do not produce large seed crops every year, seeds produced in good years must be stored to provide for seed failures or to supplement poor seed crops. Tree age does not affect seed viability or seed storage capability, so any sound seeds can be stored for future use (Barnett and McLemore 1961, Wakeley 1954). However, both seed moisture content and temperature of the environment strongly affect seed storage (especially long-term storage). Drying seeds below 5% moisture content is not recommended; it requires a great deal of heat and subsequent germination is not increased. In fact, such drying can increase prechilling requirements and increase mortality (Karrfalt R. 1989, personal communication). When seed moisture content exceeds 8 to 9%, insects become active and begin reproduction. When seed moisture exceeds 14%, fungi can grow on the interior and exterior of seeds. When seed moisture exceeds 18 to 20%, seed respiration can cause excess heating.

Seeds with moisture content above 18% should not be stored at subfreezing temperatures. If stored at – 17 °C, viability of seeds can be maintained with up to 18% moisture content, but it is safer to store seeds at a lower moisture content. Prechilled or unchilled seeds that have been treated with repellents can be stored for up to 60 days at room temperature (Jones 1963). When seeds are to be stored for 1 year at 1 °C, seed moisture content should be 10% or less. Seeds can be stored for 2 to 3 years at 1 °C if moisture content is 8% or below. For best long-term storage (4 to 8 years, viability above 90%, no deep dormancy), seeds should be dried to a moisture content of 6 to 10% and stored at subfreezing temperatures (Barnett 1974a,

Barnett and McLemore 1970, Bonner 1990, Donald and Jacobs 1990). However, seeds with moisture contents between 6 and 14% can maintain an 85 to 90% germination rate for at least 6 to 8 years even when stored at 2 to 4 °C (Bonner 1990). Loblolly pine seedlots of 68 to 227 kg have been stored for 18 to 26 years and have yielded 70 to 90% germination (Belcher and Karrfalt 1976). Seventy percent of slash pine seeds stored in an airtight container at 1 to 3 °C for 40 years germinated (Barnett 1972). Loblolly seeds will probably have a similar germination rate if stored under these same conditions.

Seed dormancy increases during storage, but the increase is smaller in dry than in moist seeds. For example, seeds stored for 1 to 5 years at moisture levels between 10 and 18% are more dormant than seeds stored for 1 to 5 years at moisture levels below 10%. Seeds are least dormant if their moisture content is above 20%, provided that the temperature is kept near or below freezing (Barnett and McLemore 1970, McLemore and Barnett 1968).

Seeds that are ready for germination can be stored from several weeks to 1 year without drying. Drying makes long-term storage safer but necessitates a second prechilling, which is risky with large quantities of repellent-coated seeds (McLemore and Barnett 1966b). Seeds soaked or dressed with the fungicide triadimefon to control fusiform rust can be stored for at least 3 weeks without diminishing the effectiveness of the chemical (Kelley 1988). Belcher (1968) reported that repellent-coated seeds are more dormant after storage than are uncoated seeds and that repellent-coated seeds germinate much better if prechilled for about 30 days in polyethylene bags containing moist moss. Repellent-coated seeds should not be soaked in water. Soaking causes the seeds to absorb the chemicals, and these may injure the seeds. High-quality seeds should be stored for short periods as follows (Barnett 1972; Barnett and McLemore 1966, 1970; Belcher 1982):

- Repellent-coated, prechilled seeds should be stored at –4 °C without drying. A second prechilling is not needed.

- Prechilled seeds that have not been coated with repellent should be dried to 10% moisture content and stored at –4 °C. They should be prechilled again before use. Prechilled seeds can also be dried to 21 to 26% moisture content and stored at 3 °C. Drying prechilled seeds for storage reinduces a slight secondary dormancy, which increases with time and both prolongs the germination period and reduces the number of seeds that germinate.

- Seeds with moisture content above 25% should not be stored at temperatures below –4 °C.

Low-quality seeds do not keep as well as high-quality seeds but can usually be stored up to 90 days at –4 °C without drying and a second prechilling.

Loblolly pine seeds should always be stored in moisture-proof, sealed containers to prevent moisture uptake. Metal or fiberboard drums with plastic liners make excellent containers for large seedlots. For small lots, rigid plastic bottles with good screw-top lids work well.

Because they are breakable, glass containers are usually not used. Plastic bags thinner than 4 mils are ineffective moisture barriers and are easily torn, so they should not be used (Bonner 1991c). Care must be taken to prevent spontaneous heating and destruction of seeds when large lots of moist seeds (moisture content above 20%) are stored in sealed containers (Belcher 1982).

Nursery management. In 1986, loblolly pine seedling production reached 1.5 billion in 96 nurseries (37 forest industry, 36 state, 22 private, 1 federal) in the South (Lantz 1988). Small nurseries may produce fewer than 1 million loblolly pine seedlings each year, whereas large nurseries may grow from 20 to 35 million seedlings/year (AAN 1987). More than 99% of all loblolly seedlings produced each year are 1+0 bareroot stock. More than 90% of the seedlings now growing in nurseries are genetically improved (Lantz 1988).

Nursery production of loblolly seedlings has several important components. The management of nursery soil is especially complex. Seed and seedling mortality in southern forest tree nurseries is about 12%, but more than 40% of the seeds used can be lost if site and soil management practices are poor.

Efficient nursery production requires careful control of capital and production costs. In the early 1980's, the production cost of sowing, growing, lifting, and packing 20 to 30 million bareroot seedlings averaged $16 to $27/ 1,000 seedlings. A new bareroot nursery must produce about 15 million seedlings/year to be economical (Guldin 1983b). During the 1987–88 growing season, production cost in state nurseries generally ranged from $20 to $30/ 1,000 trees (Anonymous 1987). Because production is labor intensive, costs continue to rise rapidly. The cost of seeds constitutes from 5 to 30% of total production cost, depending on whether improved or unimproved seeds are used (Guldin 1983b, Mills and South 1984). The number of frost-free days per year does not affect the cost of growing bareroot seedlings (figure 6-2). Seed efficiency is the ratio of plantable seedlings in a nursery bed at time of lifting to the number of viable seeds sown, expressed as a percentage (South and Larsen 1986). Increasing nursery seed efficiency by 10% can reduce annual costs by more than $20,000 in a nursery producing 25 million seedlings/year. This 10% increase could also result in outplanting more than 1,400 ha with improved trees and providing a present value of over $90,000/year (Boyer and South 1984a, South 1987a).

Site, facilities, and equipment. A good nursery site and modern cultural practices are keys to the production of vigorous seedlings. The best nursery sites have well-drained, fine-sand to sandy-loam soils with bulk densities of 1.4 or less. These sites are not subject to flooding, have an average slope of less than 2%, and have a source of good-quality water for irrigation. In addition, the subsoil should be quite permeable. These conditions promote good tillage, drainage, and fumigation. If the site must be

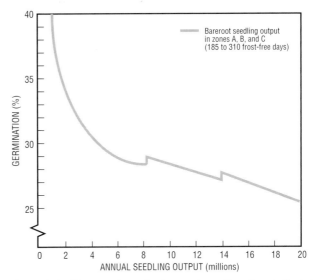

Figure 6-2—The cost of growing bareroot seedlings is not affected by the number of frost-free days. The cost of seedling production is the same for zone A (260 to 310 frost-free days), zone B (215 to 245 frost-free days), and zone C (185 to 215 frost-free days) (adapted from Guldin 1981).

leveled, the topsoil must be stripped and stored, the subsoil graded, and the topsoil returned. Nurseries also need road and irrigation systems; buildings for offices, equipment maintenance, and storage; space for packaging seedlings; refrigerated storage for seedlings; and a freezer for seed storage. Wells or surface water sources must be able to supply at least 2.5 cm of water to the seedbeds each week. A secondary water source should be connected to the primary source for emergency purposes. Morby (1984) provides a comprehensive discussion of site-selection factors that should be evaluated.

At large nurseries, all operations from initial site preparation to final seedling removal are highly mechanized. Specialized equipment is available for seedbed preparation, fertilization, mulching, precision seeding, chemical pest control, lifting, optical seedling sorting, bundling, and other specific needs (Dooley and Fridley 1981, Hassan 1983, Lowman and McLaren 1976). How-

Figure 6-3—Typical 1.2-m-wide nursery beds, with 8 rows of seedlings, separated by 0.6-m-wide wheel tracks.

ever, there is still a considerable need to develop inexpensive and fast equipment that has low soil compaction and causes little damage to seedlings. In addition, 1.2-m-wide nursery beds use only two-thirds of the available nursery area (figure 6-3). Most of the remainder is used for tractor wheel paths.

Seedbed preparation. In the fall or winter (October to January), composite soil samples are taken and analyzed to identify nutrient and organic matter deficiencies or undesirable pH levels. Area control and standard sampling procedures should be maintained so that year-to-year results apply to specific locations within a nursery (South and Davey 1983). Necessary liming, fertilization, and organic matter additions are generally made and soil fumigation completed before seedbeds are prepared. Fertilizers can be mixed with the soil as the nursery beds are formed.

Nursery beds can be fumigated with various chemicals. Methyl bromide (scheduled to be withdrawn from use in 2002) is commonly applied at rates of 120 to 160 kg/ha to control soil-borne pathogenic fungi, insects, nematodes, and weed seeds and to increase the availability of some nutrients; other fumigants are also used. Liquid or gas fumigants may be incorporated into the soil by injection, applied to the soil in a drench, or applied to the soil and incorporated by cultivation. Special equipment is available to apply the fumigant and to lay a sealed, plastic film over a treated area. After about 1 week, the covering is removed and the soil allowed to aerate for a minimum of 72 hours. Although fumigation destroys or retards the development of many organisms, including important fungi, it does not kill all organisms (Danielson and Davey 1969). Depth of chemical application, soil moisture level, or soil organic content can influence the effectiveness of fumigation, but pathogenic organisms can be controlled to a depth of 30 cm with the proper fumigant (May 1985a). Depending on the severity of pest problems, fumigation is done prior to each seedling crop or once for every two to three seedling crops. Fumigation is most effective when soil, target organism, and chemical factors are considered together.

Seedbed formation is the last step before sowing seeds and ectomycorrhizal inoculation. The soil should be disked to break up any coarse material a few days before bed preparation. If irrigation lines are needed, they are installed next. Unframed beds 1.2 m wide and about 7.5 to 15 cm high, depending on soil texture, are then prepared with farm equipment or specialized bed shapers. Bed length is commonly 180 m but can vary depending on the shape of the nursery. Beds should be prepared when the soil is moist but not wet, so there will be no puddling or compaction. For best seedling growth, bulk density should be about 1.3 g/cm^3 for sandy clay loam and 1.4 g/cm^3 for loamy sand. Higher or lower densities affect seedling growth adversely (Tuttle and others 1988b). Erosion is minimized if nursery beds do not slope from end to end or from side to side and if their upper surface is slightly concave.

If seedlings are grown in the same nursery bed in 2 consecutive years, there is often very little time between lifting the first crop and preparing and fumigating the seedbed before sowing the next crop. The beds may have to lie fallow for 3 to 4 weeks before the fumigant level is low enough so that seeds can be sown. If beds are fallow for 1 or 2 years between seedling crops, fumigation can be done in the fall. Fall fumigation increases the time available for seedbed preparation in the spring.

Sowing seeds. Seeds are almost always sown mechanically. Vacuum seeders can place seeds at precise intervals within rows and can space rows very uniformly (Barnett 1983a).

Depending on location and environmental conditions, spring nursery sowing can begin as early as late February or as late as early June (Boyer and South 1988). Timing is important. Sowing as soon as conditions are favorable can increase seedling caliper (basal stem diameter) and biomass but may necessitate undercutting of roots in the summer or fall to limit height growth. If sowing is done too early in the spring, the germination period may be extended. A long germination period can result in excessive variation in seedling size and can reduce the yield of plantable seedlings. Also, the cold moist soil conditions characteristic of early spring favor fungi (*Pythium* spp. and *Phytophthora* spp.) that cause damping-off of germinating seedlings. Delaying spring sowing until soils warm usually prevents this problem. However, seedlings that germinate late in the spring can also be affected adversely by soil pathogens and by heat. Late sowing usually results in smaller seedlings of lower quality.

Although not normally done, loblolly pine seeds can be sown in the fall (between October 15 and November 30) to produce larger seedlings. Seeds sown at this time do not require prechilling because contact with moist soil over the winter provides natural chilling. When the soil warms in the spring, seeds normally germinate promptly and uniformly, and have the benefit of a long growing season. This technique should only be used where there is little likelihood of spring freezes, because newly germinated seedlings are often killed by a freeze.

Seeds are normally placed on the surface of the soil or in shallow grooves and then pressed into the soil by a roller, but are not buried. Seeds covered with more than about 1 cm of soil germinate slowly, but 50 to 70% of seeds sown 2.5 cm deep may eventually germinate (Dierauf and Apgar 1988). If heavy rains are expected during the first month after sowing, seeds in outer rows can be covered with up to 0.6 cm of soil to help prevent the seeds from washing away (Rowan 1982). After loblolly seeds have germinated, a preemergence herbicide is often applied to the seedbed to prevent the seeds of unwanted plants from germinating.

Separation of seeds by size results in more uniform germination and more uniform seedling density in the seedbed (Belcher 1984). Sowing prechilled seeds of similar size on a uniform seedbed is most likely to result in uniformly good germination and seedling growth. Seedlings grown from small seeds are smaller and more delicate at germination than those grown from larger seeds. If the larger and smaller seedlings are managed separately in the nursery, all of the seedlings can be brought to about equal in size and quality by outplanting time (table 6-9).

Table 6-9—Average top height, root length, and stem diameter for loblolly seedlings, grown from large, medium, and small seeds*

Month	Top height (cm)			Root length (cm)			Stem diameter (mm)		
	Large	Medium	Small	Large	Medium	Small	Large	Medium	Small
May	8.9	7.6	4.4	8.9	7.6	7.6	1.6	1.6	0.8
June	9.5	10.3	7.6	8.9	11.4	8.9	1.6	1.6	0.8
July	11.4	14.6	9.8	12.4	13.3	9.5	3.2	2.4	2.4
August	17.9	17.8	15.2	16.5	17.1	15.2	3.2	3.2	3.2
September†	22.9	22.9	20.3	17.8	19.0	22.2	4.0	4.0	4.0
October	23.2	22.9	21.6	19.0	19.0	19.0	4.8	4.8	4.8
November	23.2	22.9	21.6	19.0	19.0	19.0	6.3	6.3	6.3

Source: adapted from Darby (1962).

* Seeds were sown on April 13, 1960, and grown at Morgan Memorial Nursery, Byron, GA. Measurements were taken on the 15th of each month.

† Stock was root pruned in beds.

Nursery seedbed density. Seedbed density significantly influences the growth and development of young seedlings. As density increases, average seedling dry weight rapidly decreases. Needle weight and surface area, needle length and thickness, root absorption surface, average seedling grade, tree survival, and early growth on droughty sites also decrease as seedling density increases (Nebgen and Meyer 1985; figure 6-4).

Seedling density depends primarily on the rate at which seeds are sown. Prechilled seeds with known germination potentials are usually machine sown in rows or broadcast at rates calculated to produce 260 to 320 seedlings/m^2 of bed space (with an average of 300/m^2) (Boyer and South 1984a, Caulfield and others 1987; figure 6-3). There is no one best sowing density for nursery seedling production because cultural conditions and treatments such as fertility, irrigation, and undercutting affect production. For example, high levels of nutrients, and especially of nitrogen (N), can partially offset the negative effect of high density on seedling size. The proportion of high-quality seedlings decreases as nursery bed density increases, so it is crucial to keep the number of seedlings per unit area within prescribed limits (Boyer and South 1985, 1987, 1988; Brissette and Carlson 1987; South and others 1985; Switzer and Nelson 1967). A greater percentage of large, high-quality seedlings that survive better and grow faster is produced when seedling density is less than 260 seedlings/m^2 (Rowan 1985). Mexal (1981) suggested that a density of 200 seedlings/m^2 optimized the balance between individual seedling biomass and total biomass. However, as many as 430 well-developed seedlings can be grown per square meter of nursery bed (Shoulders 1961, Switzer and Nelson 1963).

The effect of sowing density on the quality of seedlings produced is depicted in figure 6-5. When seedling density is high, competition between individual seedlings is also high. Such competition reduces seedling growth and vigor and increases susceptibility to pathogenic fungi, nematodes, and insects. When sowing density is 320 seeds/m^2 of nursery bed, 79% of the seedlings are plantable grades 1 and 2. When 240 seeds/m^2 of bed are sown, 84% of the seedlings are plantable. Assuming equal germination, site fertility, and management practices, sow-

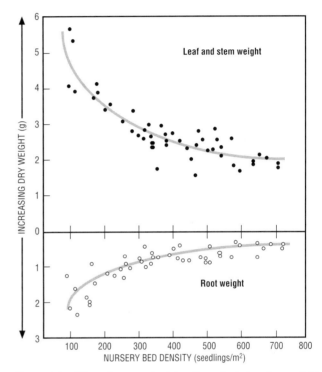

Figure 6-4—Effect of nursery bed density on leaf plus stem weight and root weight of loblolly pine seedlings (adapted from Harms and Langdon 1977).

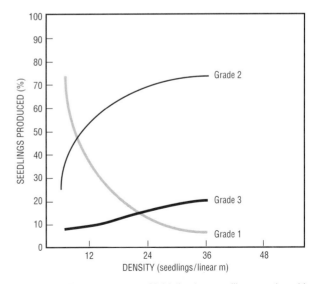

Figure 6-5—The percentage of loblolly pine seedlings produced in each grade is a function of nursery sowing density (adapted from Caulfield and others 1987).

ing at the higher density requires 33% more seeds but yields 25% more plantable seedlings (Caulfield and others 1987). When less than 200 seeds/m² of bed are sown, the soil will probably be underutilized and seedling production uneconomical (Barnett 1986). The appropriate seeding density is ultimately determined by comparing the cost of seeds with the value of plantable seedlings and, ultimately, with final product yields.

Mulching seedbeds. Seedbeds must be covered to prevent the displacement of seeds by wind, rain, or irrigation water. Normally, a layer of chopped or partially rotted pine needles, sawdust, bark, or wood fiber (hydromulch) or shredded paper is spread over seeded beds. This amounts to about 1,800 to 2,250 kg of hydromulch/ ha of bed. The covering must be thin enough to permit water, air, and some light to reach the seeds, or it can inhibit germination. Hydromulch is clean, uniform, and free of weed seeds or plant pathogens. If pine bark is used, it should be screened to remove large particles. Germinating seedlings can develop basal crooks as they grow around such particles. Shredded grain straw (rye, wheat, or oat) is a good mulch, but frequent early herbicide applications are usually needed to kill germinating grain seeds, which are usually present in the straw. Mulch material may contain pathogenic fungi and should be fumigated before being placed on beds.

The choice of mulching material should be at least partially dictated by expectations of rainfall during the first month after sowing. If heavy rains are expected, pine straw is more effective than hydromulch in minimizing damage to beds and reducing seed loss (Rowan 1982). An emulsified polyethylene adhesive has also proven to be effective in stabilizing nursery beds by polymerizing the surface 0.2 to 0.4 cm of soil. In an Arkansas nursery, this polymer increased seedling yield by 15% (Carlson and others 1987).

Mulching keeps soil moisture high and thus promotes germination. In the absence of mulching, the soil surface often bakes into a hard crust. Early germination is usually more rapid with dark mulches, probably because such mulches promote heating of the soil surface (Summerville 1985). Mulches positively influence seedlings from germination to lifting by maintaining good surface moisture and temperature conditions (figure 6-6).

Water management. Early, heavy rains are the greatest single factor contributing to seedling mortality (Boyer and South 1984a). Excessive moisture reduces soil aeration and can weaken or even kill roots, increasing the possibility of damage by soil-borne nematodes and pathogenic fungi, such as *Pythium* spp. and *Phytophthora* spp. Raising seedbeds often corrects minor drainage problems, but subsoiling and the installation of drainage tiles may be necessary on nursery sites that have chronic drainage problems.

Correctly regulated irrigation is important to the development of quality seedlings. Three phases of seedling development require different irrigation regimes. They are the seed germination phase, maximum seedling development phase, and hardening off. Hardening off is the preparation of seedlings for lifting and outplanting by forcing growth to cease. In the seed germination phase, soil moisture should be maintained at a high level by frequent irrigation in small amounts (May 1985c). Because drought is most damaging to seedlings at the time of germination and during the cotyledonary stage, it is especially important that irrigation be applied whenever needed during this phase. Drought and heat injury frequently occur together and are most serious on coarse-textured soils.

Once germination is complete, irrigation schedules are gradually adjusted to incorporate longer, less frequent waterings. The amount of moisture needed during seedling development depends on the water-holding capacity of the soil, the air temperature, and the humidity. After taproots reach 15 cm in length, regular watering to maintain surface moisture is not needed and is probably a waste of money. Soaking irrigation treatments, when needed, are most effective. Seedlings that are moderately water stressed in the nursery show greater root regeneration after outplanting in cold soils than do seedlings that are well watered in the nursery. Moderately waterstressed seedlings also have an increased capacity to maintain turgor over a range of water potentials, and this capacity probably increases their ability to grow in areas subject to summer droughts (Hennessey and Dougherty 1984).

Withholding irrigation after September helps harden off seedlings on many soils (Johnson and others 1985). However, fall irrigation can increase the number of plantable seedlings and greatly increase the percentage of grade 1 seedlings on sandy sites (South and others 1988b, 1989a; Williams and others 1988b). For example, fall irrigation of a sandy nursery in Florida increased the average root collar diameter of seedlings by 10% (Boyer and South 1987).

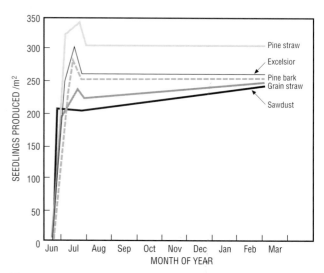

Figure 6-6—Effect of mulch type on seedling production (adapted from Summerville 1985).

Systematic monitoring of plant moisture status or soil moisture tension in the rooting zone indicates when it is time to irrigate. Plant moisture stress can be determined with a simple pressure chamber (McGilvray and Barnett 1988). Soil moisture can be determined with tensiometers or electrical probes. If soil tensiometers are used, beginning irrigation when soil tension is 30 kPa [1 kilopascal = 1 centibar] for sandy soils to 50 kPa for silt loam soils will help ensure adequate soil aeration without excess irrigation (Retzlaff and South 1985a). If the environment around seedling roots is constantly wet (mean soil moisture tension less than about 10 kPa), root growth and seedling development can be reduced (Retzlaff and South 1985b). Watering (figure 6-7) can be done either during the day or at night. Because wind speeds are usually lower at night, night watering usually provides more uniform water distribution. However, it is more difficult to locate nonfunctioning sprinklers or identify other problems in the dark.

Minerals in irrigation water can have important effects on soil and seedlings. Some salt in the water is acceptable if calcium is the source, because calcium is important to tree growth. However, high levels of sodium in the water can affect soil structure adversely and can cause osmotic stress in seedlings. Good quality irrigation water in reasonable amounts and good soil drainage prevent the accumulation of excess salts in the soil (Davey 1972).

Temperature control. Seedlings grow best when the daytime temperature is about 23 °C and the nighttime temperature is about 10 to 17 °C (figure 6-8). However, seedlings can grow well at a constant temperature of 17 °C, which indicates that loblolly pine is not thermoperiodic (Greenwald 1972, Kramer 1957, Perry 1962). Changes in daytime temperature can affect some seed sources differently. For instance, seedlings from Tennessee grew faster than seedlings from Texas when daytime temperatures were below 28 °C and grew slower than Texas seedlings at higher daytime temperatures (Perry 1962).

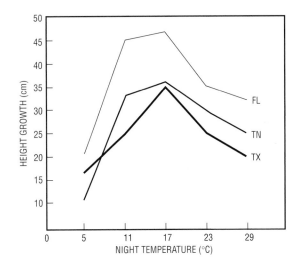

Figure 6-8—Height growth of three provenances of loblolly pine between 3 weeks and 9 months of age at 23 °C day temperature and various night temperatures (adapted from Greenwald 1972).

Loblolly pine seedlings are most vulnerable to heat during the first few weeks after germination. Irrigation applied to reduce surface soil temperature can reduce seedling mortality. Irrigating during the hottest part of the day can lower soil temperature by as much as 11 °C. Such irrigation may prevent extensive injury or seedling loss if begun at the first sign of injury or when air temperatures are high early in the season (May 1985a). Irrigation for cooling is usually applied for short durations and has little effect on soil moisture levels.

Weeds and weed control. Many weed species are troublesome in nurseries (table 6-10). Controlling weeds increases the size and quality of seedlings, which then grow more rapidly after outplanting (Mitchell and others 1988). Crabgrass (*Digitaria* spp.) and nutsedge (*Cyperus* spp.) are by far the most common nursery weeds. In the past, hand weeding often accounted for 20 to 40% of the cost of producing loblolly pine seedlings. Today, hand weeding makes up only 2 to 4% of seedling production costs but is still

Figure 6-7—Irrigation of loblolly pine seedlings at the Ashe Nursery, near Gulfport, Mississippi.

Table 6-10—Troublesome weed species occurring in 47 southern nurseries

Common name*	Nurseries where weed is a problem		Common name*	Nurseries where weed is a problem	
	No.	%		No.	%
Crabgrass	30	64	Clover	3	6
Nutsedge	29	62	Barnyard grass	3	6
Bermudagrass	17	36	Florida pusley	2	4
Purslane	14	30	Broomsedge	2	4
Morning-glory	13	28	Cocklebur	2	4
Sicklepod	11	23	Crowfootgrass	2	4
Goose grass	11	23	Flathead sedge	2	4
Carpet-weed	8	27	Spurge	1	2
Fennel	6	13	Others	19	40

Source: adapted from Boyer and South (1984a).

* Scientific names are given in Appendix A.

Table 6-11—Common, trade, and chemical names of selected herbicides used in southern forest nurseries

Common name	Trade name	Chemical name
Bifenox	Modown®	Methyl 5-2,4-dichlorophenoxyl)-2-nitrobenzoate
Diphenamid	Enide®	N,N-dimethyl - a-phenyl benzeneacetamide
EPTC	Eptam Genept®	S-ethyl dipropyl carbamothioate
Fluasifop-butyl	Fusilade®	(±)-butyl 2-[4-[(5-(trifluoromethyl) -2-pyridinyl)oxy]phenoxy]-propanoate
Glyphosate	Roundup®	N-(phosphonomethyl)glycine
Napropamide	Devrinol®	N,N-diethyl-2-(1-napthalenyloxy)propanamide
Oxadiazon	Ronstar®	3-[2,4-dichloro-5-(1-methylethoxy)phenyl]-5- (1,1-dimethylethyl-1,3,4-oxadiazol-2-(3H)-one
Oxyfluorfen	Goal®	2-chloro-1-(3-ethoxy-4-nitrophenoxy) -4-(trifluoromethyl)benzene
Prometryn	Caparol Prometryn®	N,N¹-bis(1-methylethyl)-6-(methylthio) -1,3,5-triazine-2,4-diamine
Sethoxydim	Poast®	2-[1-(ethoxyamino)-butyl]-5-[2-(ethylthio) propyl]-3-hydroxy-2-cyclohexene 1-one
Trifluralin	Treflan®	2,6-dinitro-N,N-dipropyl-4- (trifluoromethyl)benzenamide

Source: adapted from South (1986).

an important supplemental method of weed control on localized areas. Chemicals are the primary means of weed control in all southern nurseries (Boyer and South 1984a; South 1988; tables 6–11 and 6–12). Other pest management practices in nurseries will be discussed in chapter 10.

Soil fertility. Growing seedlings at high densities on short rotations rapidly depletes the organic matter and nutrients in nursery soils. During the 9- to 10-month nursery growing season, about 1,730,000 to 1,980,000 plantable seedlings are produced per hectare of nursery bed. As each seedling has an ovendry weight of 1.1 to 6.6 g (May 1985a), somewhere between 1.9 and 13.1 t of dry matter are removed from each hectare in each seedling crop.

Because soil nutrient concentrations vary from nursery to nursery, standard fertilizer treatments may not create optimum growing conditions for seedlings. Fertilizers other than N should be added on the basis of detailed soil analyses. Chemical analyses for pH, organic matter, and essential elements—especially phosphorus (P), potassium (K), calcium (Ca), and magnesium (Mg)— should be performed every year. Fall or early winter is the

Table 6-12—Estimated effectiveness of herbicides on selected troublesome weeds

Time of application and herbicide	Formu-lation	Rate (kg ai/ha)	No. of applica-tions	Surfac-tant type	Surfactant rate (vol/vol)	Site of uptake	Mode of action	Estimated half-life of parent compound in soil (months)	Injury on pines	Crab-grass	Bermuda-grass	Flathead sedge	Yellow nutsedge	Purple nutsedge	Sicklepod	Smallflower morning-glory	Prostrate spurge
Incorporated before sowing pine seeds																	
EPTC	7 EC	6.8	1	—	—	root	?	0.25	1	G	F	G	G	G	P-F	P-F	P
Trifluralin	4 EC	0.6	1	—	—	root	ICD	1–2	1–3	G-E	P	P	N	N	N	P	N
Preemergence of seedlings																	
Bifenox	4 F	3.4	1	—	—	shoot	DCM	0.25–0.5	1–2	P	N	G	N	N	P	F	P
Diphenamid	90 WP	4.5	1	—	—	root	?	1	1	F	N	N	N	N	N	N	N
Napropamide	50 WP	1.1	1	—	—	root	?	2–3	1–3	E	P	G	P	P	P	P	F
Oxyfluorfen	1.6 EC	0.6	1	—	—	shoot	DCM	1–1.5	1–2	G	P	G	N	N	P	F	G
Trifluralin	4 EC	1.1	1	—	—	root	IDC	0.5–1	1–2	F	P	P	N	N	N	P	N
Postemergence of seedlings and preemergence of weeds																	
Bifenox	4 F	0.6	8–14	—	—	shoot	DCM	0.25–0.5	1	P	N	G	N	N	P	F	P
Bifenox	4 F	2.2	2–3	—	—	shoot	DCM	0.25–0.5	1	P	N	G	N	N	P	F	G
Diphenamid	90 WP	4.5	1	—	—	root	?	1	F	N	N	N	N	N	N	G	N
Napropamide	50 WP	1.1	1	—	—	root	DCM	2–3	1	E	P	G	P	P	P	P	F
Oxadiazon	2 G	1.1	1	—	—	shoot	DCM	?	1	E	P	E	P	P	P	G	P
Oxyfluorfen	1.6 EC	0.14	8–14	—	—	shoot	DCM	1–1.5	1	G	P	G	N	N	P	F	G
Oxyfluorfen	1.6 EC	0.6	2–3	—	—	shoot	DCM	1–1.5	1	G	P	G	N	N	P	F	G
Prometryn	80 WP	1.1	1	—	—	root & shoot	PI	1–3	2	G	P	G	N	N	F	F	P
Trifluralin	4 EC	1.1	1	—	—	shoot	ICD	0.5–1	0	F	P	P	N	N	N	P	N
Postemergence of seedlings and postemergence of weeds																	
Bifenox	4 F	0.6	8–14	COS	0.25%	shoot	DCM	0.25–0.5	1	P	N	P	N	N	P	P	N
Bifenox	4 F	2.2	2–3	COS	1%	shoot	DCM	0.24–0.5	1	P	N	P	N	N	P	P	N
Fluazifop-butyl	4 EC	0.28	1–2	NI	0.25%	shoot	?	0.25	0	E	G	N	N	N	N	N	N
Glyphosate	4 S	5.6	1–4	—	—	shoot	IAAS	0.02	4	E	E	E	G	E	E	E	E
Oxyfluorfen	1.6 EC	0.14	2–3	COS	0.25%	shoot	DCM	1–1.5	1	G	P	P	P	P	P	F	N
Oxyfluorfen	1.6 EC	0.6	2–3	COS	1%	shoot	DCM	1–1.5	1	G	P	P	P	P	P	F	N
Prometryn	80 WP	1.1	1	NI	0.5%	root & shoot	PI	1–3	2	G	P	G	N	N	F	F	P
Sethoxydim	1.5 EC	0.21	1–2	COS	1%	shoot	?	0.17–0.5	0	E	G	N	N	N	N	N	N

Source: adapted from South (1986).

COS = crop oil and nonionic surfactant blend, NI = nonionic surfactant; ? = unknown mode of action, ICD = inhibits cell division, DCM = disrupts cell membranes, PI = photosynthetic inhibitor, IAAS = inhibits amino acid synthesis, 0 = no apparent injury; 1 = slight injury; 2 = moderate injury; 3 = severe injury; 4 = complete crop destruction; E = excellent control, G = good control, F = fair control, P = poor control, N = no control; Blank fields indicate no surfactant used.

best time to sample soil nutrients. Nitrogen fertilization involves determining the amount of N in a sample of lifted seedlings, multiplying this amount by the total number of seedlings removed, and applying 1.5 times the product to the soil for the next seedling crop (Davey 1972, May 1985a).

Each nursery block should be sampled separately. Also, any area that differs visibly from the rest of a block and any area where seedlings regularly grow better or worse than the average should be sampled separately. Approximately 20 to 25 soil subsamples should be mixed thoroughly to provide a composite sample. Subsamples should be taken with a sampling tube. They should be taken from the surface 15 cm of soil in a criss-cross or W-shaped pattern so that soil throughout the sampling block is represented. Samples should be sent to the same testing service every year so that results are based on the same kinds of analyses each time. Recommended soil nutrient levels are summarized in table 6-13.

Keeping the level of organic matter high (about 2% on a soil dry weight basis) may be the most difficult task in loblolly pine nursery management. With careful management, annual pine seedling cropping can produce high yields and high-quality seedlings for 3 to 5 years (Switzer and Nelson 1967). Even 10 to 24 years of continuous cropping may not have apparent undesirable consequences on sandy soil if organic matter and inorganic fertilizers are applied (Dierauf 1985, May 1985a). However, unless exceptional care is taken, continuous cropping usually results in the production of reduced-quality stock. Cover crops or exogenous organic materials or both are commonly used to maintain soil organic matter levels and to protect nursery soils from erosion. Common summer cover crops include sorghum-sudan (*Sorghum* spp.) and millet (*Panicum ramosum* L.); rye (*Lolium* spp.) is considered the most effective winter cover crop, but wheat (*Triticum* spp.) and oats (*Avena* spp.) are also popular in some areas. There does not seem to be one best crop rotation program, but most nursery blocks are in cover crops for as many years as they are in seedling production. Various rotations—1:1, 1:2, 2:2, 2:3, and 3:1 in years in seedbed to years in cover crop—have all been used successfully for extended periods (Boyer

and South 1984b, Davey 1982, Nelson and Switzer 1985).

Amendments such as sawdust, bark, ground cones, or peat are commonly used to increase soil organic matter levels. At least 50% of organic matter added in the form of sawdust, cones, or peat decomposes within 18 months (Munson 1983). Milled pine bark may be superior to other amendments because it decomposes slowly and appears to suppress certain soil-borne plant pathogens (Pokorny 1983). Sewage sludge has also proven effective in adding organic matter and nutrients to nursery sites (Berry 1985a, 1985b, 1985c). It is critical that amendments to nursery beds be balanced to maintain optimum seedling growth. Patchy summer chlorosis can result from excessively heavy mulching in parts of a nursery bed. Such mulching reduces N availability and the concentration of N in seedlings (Carter 1964). It is often best to add nutrients and compost to sawdust or other undecomposed organic matter before applying them to the soil. The addition of such supplements prevents reduction in N availability during the decomposition of organic matter (Davey 1972).

Fertilization corrects nutritional problems, accelerates seedling growth, and increases the number of plantable seedlings (May 1985a). In one case, the addition of small amounts of N, P, and K (84, 25, and 69 kg/ha, respectively) resulted in 226 plantable seedlings/m^2 of nursery bed when 646 seeds/m^2 were sown. Heavy fertilization with N, P, and K (336, 99, and 279 kg/ha, respectively) more than doubled the yield to 517 plantable seedlings/m^2 (Switzer and Nelson 1967). Additions of N and K are commonly needed in sandy nurseries with low organic matter. Either rapidly soluble or slowly soluble sources of N can be used on most soils (Zarger 1964). Ammonium nitrate is usually the best source of N. When pH is below 5.0, calcium nitrate is recommended; when pH is above 6.0, ammonium sulfate is recommended. Table 6-14 lists the principal sources of N for use in loblolly pine nurseries.

Phosphorus from fertilizer is rapidly tied up in insoluble compounds of iron (Fe), aluminum (Al), manganese (Mn), Ca, and Mg, and little is lost by leaching in the soil solution. Fertilizers commonly worked into the soil before planting or covercropping include ordinary super-

Table 6-13—Range of pH and nutrient levels recommended for pine nursery soils

Soil Texture	% Organic matter	% N	pH	P	K	Ca	Mg
Sands & light loamy sands	1.5	0.07	5.3 to 5.8	55 to 110	80 to 140	450 to 670	55 to 65
Loamy sands & sandy loams	2.0	0.10	5.3 to 5.8	85 to 110	140 to 200	670 to 1,010	67 to 100
Loams, silt loams & clay loams	>3.0	0.15	5.3 to 5.8	85 to 140	170 to 280	>1,010	>100

The "Conc. (kg/ha)" heading spans the P, K, Ca, and Mg columns.

Source: adapted from May (1985b).

Table 6-14—Sources of nitrogen for loblolly pine nurseries

Compound	Formula	% Nitrogen
Ammonium nitrate	NH_4NO_3	33
Ammonium sulfate	$(NH_4)2SO_4$	21
Diammonium phosphate	$(NH_4)2HPO_4$	16–21
Anhydrous ammonium	Liquid NH_3	82
Urea	$CO(NH_2)2$	46
Calcium nitrate	$Ca(NO_3)2$	15
Mixed fertilizers	10-10-10	10

Source: adapted from May (1985b).

phosphate (0-20-0) and triple superphosphate (0-46-0). Water-soluble diammonium and monoammonium phosphates are among the better P fertilizers available as top dressings for seedlings during the growing season. These water-soluble P compounds can be applied through irrigation systems or with conventional spreaders.

Many nurseries have sufficient soil K to grow loblolly pines without fertilization, but K can become limiting near the end of the growing season, especially in sandy soils. This limitation results from heavy utilization by seedlings and extensive leaching in rain and irrigation water. A top dressing of K as muriate of potash in mid- to late August can prevent K deficiency (Rowan 1987). All K fertilizer salts are soluble in water, and the K is readily available to plants. No one K fertilizer appears to be superior to others. Common K fertilizers for loblolly pine nurseries are listed in table 6-15.

Magnesium sulfate ($MgSO_4 \cdot 7H_2O$) contains 16% MgO and is used to correct deficiencies in soil Mg. It can be broadcast and worked into the soil or applied through an irrigation system (May 1985b).

The use of concentrated relatively pure N, P, or K fertilizer can result in deficiencies of other essential elements— and especially micronutrients. Application of fertilizers that include both macro- and micronutrients is recommended to minimize the possibility of nutrient deficiencies and subsequent seedling damage. Standard micronutrient combinations that provide elemental Fe, zinc (Zn), copper (Cu), and Mn are available. Chlorosis resulting from Fe deficiency is common in many nurseries. Iron deficiency can usually be corrected by foliar treatments with chelated Fe at rates as high as 7 to 11 kg/ha. Several years of application of diammonium phosphate ($(NH_4) \cdot 2HPO_4$), can result in sulfur (S) deficiency chlorosis. Chlorosis resulting from S deficiency may also occur following several years of using concentrated fertilizers low in S. Treatments with ammonium sulfate, sodium sulfate, or superphosphate (which contains 40 to 50% calcium sulfate) at rates of 56 to 84 kg/ha correct S deficiencies (Lyle and Pearce 1968, May 1985b). Boron (B) deficiency can damage or kill buds and shoot tips (Stone and others 1982). If not corrected, micronutrient deficiencies can severely retard the growth of seedlings and increase mortality following outplanting. Once the cause of a fertility problem has been pinpointed, proper treatment usually corrects the situation within 10 days.

Nutrient content of nursery-grown seedlings. Most visible symptoms of nutrient deficiency appear in needles. Relying solely on visual symptoms, such as chlorosis, is normally unacceptable because seedling health is affected before corrective measures can be taken. Tissue analyses, when combined with soil analyses and a continuous review of past fertilizer treatments, provide objective information about the nutritional health of nursery seedlings before obvious problems occur. Tissue analysis also provides a basis for projection of nutrient removals and fertilization needed for the next seedling crop. Acceptable tissue nutrient levels, based on data from 21

Table 6-15—Common potassium fertilizers for loblolly pine nurseries

Compound	Formula	% Potassium
Potassium chloride (muriate of potash)	KCL	39–60
Potassium sulfate	K_2SO_4	39–49
Potassium sulfate (magnesium sulfate)	$K_2SO_4(Mg_2SO_4)$	21–25
Potassium nitrate	KNO_3	36

Source: adapted from May (1985b).

Table 6-16—Macro- and micronutrient concentrations and content in foliage, stems, and roots of loblolly pine seedlings

Tissue	Nutrient concentration										Amount/seedling (mg)									
	N %	P %	K %	Mg %	Ca %	S %	Na %	B (ppm)	Cu (ppm)	Zn (ppm)	N	P	K	Mg	Ca	S	Na	B	Cu	Zn
Foliage																				
Minimum	0.92	0.12	0.82	0.03	0.22	0.05	0.01	10	2	30	12.0	1.3	6.6	0.3	2.3	0.5	0.1	0.01	0.00	0.03
Median	1.64	0.21	1.12	0.10	0.30	0.08	0.02	17	6	55	21.6	2.7	14.5	1.2	4.3	1.0	0.2	0.03	0.01	0.07
Maximum	2.24	0.30	1.47	0.23	0.66	0.16	0.12	65	10	87	30.7	4.5	26.2	3.1	7.3	2.4	1.5	0.08	0.02	0.14
Stems																				
Minimum	0.45	0.10	0.82	0.05	0.14	0.02	0.01	8	2	32	1.7	0.5	2.0	0.2	0.6	0.1	0.0	0.00	0.00	0.01
Median	0.95	0.20	1.12	0.11	0.22	0.06	0.02	16	8	59	6.4	1.2	7.3	0.6	1.4	0.4	0.1	0.01	0.01	0.04
Maximum	1.79	0.37	1.46	0.16	0.33	0.19	0.13	33	24	97	12.5	2.5	12.2	1.4	3.0	1.2	0.9	0.03	0.02	0.06
Roots																				
Minimum	0.52	0.12	0.87	0.03	0.10	0.04	0.01	13	3	26	1.2	0.3	1.5	0.1	0.3	0.1	0.0	0.00	0.00	0.01
Median	0.85	0.20	1.14	0.10	0.20	0.08	0.03	23	9	47	4.5	0.9	5.4	0.5	1.0	0.4	0.2	0.01	0.00	0.02
Maximum	1.66	0.39	1.53	0.16	0.31	0.49	0.22	47	26	94	7.9	2.4	11.6	1.7	2.6	2.3	1.2	0.03	0.02	0.06
Total																				
Minimum											16.2	2.6	10.1	0.7	3.7	0.7	0.2	0.02	0.00	0.06
Median											32.5	4.9	27.1	2.3	6.7	1.9	0.5	0.05	0.02	0.13
Maximum											50.4	9.2	49.2	5.2	12.0	4.4	3.4	0.14	0.06	0.25

Source: adapted from Boyer and South (1985).

nurseries, are listed in table 6-16. Foliar N content of 1.7 to 2.2% at the time of outplanting is associated with rapid seedling growth for the first 3 years after outplanting (Fowells and Krauss 1959, Larsen and others 1988).

Adjusting soil pH. Soil pH levels below 5.0 are lower than optimum for good seedling growth, whereas pH levels above 6.0 promote damping-off problems. Calcium carbonate (limestone) is generally applied to raise soil pH. Raising pH by 0.5 to 1.0 unit usually requires 2.2 to 4.5 t of limestone/ha for sandy soils and 4.5 to 9.0 t/ha for fine-textured soils. If more than 2 t/ha are needed, the limestone should be added in two applications, and the second application should not be made until the effects of the first have been observed.

Additions of Fe or Al sulfates, sulfuric acid, or elemental S lower soil pH. The sulfates and sulfuric acid cause rapid changes, whereas elemental S acidifies the soil slowly over a period of about 1 year. None of these materials is effective in high-lime soils. The lime in such soils must be neutralized and then removed by drainage before any significant change in soil acidity can occur. Acidifying material should be applied only after soil testing and consultation with an expert. Acidifying materials are generally very costly, and some, such as aluminum sulfate, can be toxic to seedlings (May 1985b).

Promoting development of mycorrhizae. Mycorrhizal fungi are important to the growth of loblolly pine seedlings, especially under conditions of low nutrition. Nursery soil fumigation destroys mycorrhizal fungi and many other desirable soil organisms in the surface 20 cm of soil. Nurseries usually rely on airborne spores or on microbial recolonization from inoculum that survives fumigation to reestablish ectomycorrhizae. Although natural recolonization may be satisfactory in many nurseries, inoculation of fumigated nursery soil may be desirable if the source of natural inoculum is limiting or if the natural re-infection process is unacceptably slow. Inoculation may be especially important when seedbeds are formed on new ground (South and others 1988a). Soil or litter from forest or old nursery sites can be used as mycorrhizal inoculum, but these materials can introduce weed seeds into nursery beds. It is much more practical to directly inoculate nursery soil with basidiospores or mycelia of desirable mycorrhizae such as *Pisolithus tinctorius* (Pt) or *Thelephora terrestris* (Tt) or to encapsulate seeds with basidiospores of such fungi. Pure cultures of the fungi can form abundant mycorrhizal associations with loblolly seedlings in fumigated soils and can stimulate seedling growth significantly. Generally, where nutrient levels are very high, whether in the nursery, the greenhouse, or the field, mycorrhizal infection is reduced and root systems have smaller surface areas. Under conditions of low to good fertility, mycorrhizal development is accelerated and mycorrihizae increase tree growth most on such sites (table 6-17; Cordell and others 1981; Marx and Artman 1978; Marx and Bell 1985; Marx and others 1976, 1977b, 1978, 1979, 1984a, 1984b, 1988, 1989a, 1989b; Torbert and others 1986).

Thelephora terrestris is a common, naturally occurring fungus and forms ectomycorrhizae on loblolly pine seedlings in nurseries. It colonizes recently fumigated nursery soil by means of wind-disseminated basidiospores produced under trees near nurseries. In contrast, Pt rarely occurs naturally in nurseries but can be found in great abundance on pines and oaks growing on disturbed and adverse sites throughout the South (Marx 1977, Marx and Bell 1985). In the absence of fumigation, competing organisms severely restrict the development of Pt. Thus, soil fumigation must precede successful artificial soil inoculation with Pt basidiospores or vegetative material (Marx and others 1976, 1978). When Pt spores mixed in a hydromulch were applied immediately after sowing, mycorrhizae developed on almost 75% of the seedlings, and the number of plantable seedlings was increased by 15% (Marx and others 1979). Basidiospore inoculum of Pt is effective in forming mycorrhizal relationships when mixed with a physical carrier such as peat moss before soil inoculation, suspended in water and drenched onto soil, injected in row drills, dusted onto soil, pelletized and broadcast onto soil, or encapsulated on pine seeds (Beckjord and others 1984; Cordell and others 1981; Marx and Bell 1985; Marx and others 1984a, 1984b).

Ectomycorrhizae may be visible on feeder roots within 6 to 10 weeks after seed germination (Marx and Bryan 1975). Seedbed density does not appear to affect the proportion of mycorrihizal to nonmycorrhizal roots formed (Rowan 1985). A mosaic pattern of yellow and green seedlings in a nursery bed can indicate nutrient deficiency associated with patchy distribution of mycorrhizae (South and others 1989b). The systemic fungicide triadimefon, which is used to control fusiform rust infection on nursery seedlings, suppresses ectomycorrhizal development and may cause chlorosis at some dosages (Marx and Cordell 1987, Marx and others 1986). Three or four 170-g applications of triadimefon to a nursery bed in the spring do not reduce overall mycorrhizal development or result in chemical buildup in the soil (Kelley 1987).

Table 6-17—Growth of 7-month-old loblolly pine seedlings with and without *Pisolithus tinctorius* in nursery microplots

Measurement	Artificial soil infestation with *Pisolithus tinctorius*	Soil infestation by airborne spores of naturally occurring fungi
Height (cm)	36.0*	26.0
Stem diameter (mm)	8.2*	6.0
Foliar-stem dry weight (g)	8.9*	4.2
Root dry weight (g)	2.6*	1.4
Ectomycorrhizal development (%)	92	49
Number of fungal symbionts in ectomycorrhizae[†]	1	2 or more[‡]

Source: adapted from Marx and Bryan (1975).

* Artificial treatments means are significantly greater than natural infestation at the 99% probability level.
† Only *P. Tinctorius*.
‡ *Thelephora terrestris* and unidentified species; *P. Tinctorius* not observed.

Conditioning seedlings. Loblolly pine seedling size, shoot-to-root ratio, and physiological adaptability can be altered in the nursery by various cultural practices to increase survival after outplanting and to promote early growth. Practices that help control growth and development and harden off seedlings in the nursery include root and top pruning during the summer and early fall (May 1985a). Altering the moisture regime can also help condition seedlings.

Taproot pruning. Taproots are usually undercut (figure 6-9) to stimulate the development of compact root systems, increase the number of lateral roots, reduce seedling growth, decrease seedling shoot-to-root ratios, and create repeated mild water stress in seedlings. Undercutting increases the rate of survival of seedlings planted on difficult sites (Nebgen and Meyer 1985). Undercutting also increases soil aeration in the nursery bed (Miller and others 1985). It is normally accomplished with a thin (0.25-cm) and narrow (2.50-cm) horizontal blade that is fixed or that oscillates at a rate of about 100 revolutions/min as it cuts through the soil and taproots at a set level (usually about 15 cm below the groundline). This treatment may be administered once or several times during the growing season. It can be followed by or replaced by a "wrenching" treatment, which causes a more extensive disruption of the soil. Wrenching loosens the soil and severs roots. A wrenching blade, which is thicker (0.5 to 1.3 cm) and wider (6.0 to 13.0 cm) than an undercutting blade, can be fixed or vibrating and can be tilted at an angle of 20 to 30% (Tanaka and others 1976). Undercutting and wrenching should not be done when the soil is dry because they can cause soil clods to fracture, exposing and injuring many lateral roots. Because taproot pruning increases seedling stress, nursery beds should be irrigated well shortly after treatment (Shoulders 1965).

Root pruning substantially reduces taproot length and can have varying effects on aboveground seedling morphology and growth depending on the timing and frequency of treatments. Frequent undercuttings reduce root-collar diameter and shoot and root growth of seedlings at all seedbed densities (Dierauf 1988, Feret and Kreh 1986,

Mexal and Fisher 1985, Miller and others 1985, Tanaka and others 1976, Venator and Mexal 1981, Walstad and others 1977). Hammer and others (1985) concluded that wrenching is not a beneficial nursery treatment for loblolly pine. However, most research indicates that the growth loss caused by undercutting conditions seedlings to water stress. The combination of this conditioning, an increase in the number of fibrous roots, and the ease of planting smaller seedlings with straight roots increase both seedling quality and outplanting survival (Johnson and others 1985, Tanaka and others 1976). Seedlings with poorly developed root systems may respond better to nursery root pruning and replace severed roots more abundantly than those with good root systems. The presence of mycorrhizae may decrease moisture stress in root-pruned seedlings.

Lateral or side root pruning. Cutting lateral roots, which grow between the rows of seedlings, effectively stimulates the development of a more fibrous root system (new laterals and more second- and third-order laterals) without reducing height growth (Dierauf and Olinger 1982). It also separates the rows of seedlings, lessening the root damage that results from entanglement at lifting. Side root pruning is usually done with sharp rolling disks. It is most effective when done late in the growing season. Because few new seedlings develop extensive root systems by the end of July, pruning side roots in June or July substantially affects only 10 to 15% of seedlings. However, secondary growth of pruned roots is stimulated. By August, side pruning affects most seedlings, and those pruned on two sides respond better, in terms of new root formation, than those pruned on one side only. Pruning lateral roots 2 to 3 months before lifting is better than pruning immediately before lifting. This early pruning stimulates new lateral root development between pruning and lifting, and increases first-year seedling survival after outplanting (May 1985a). The more fibrous root systems resulting from lateral root pruning, undercutting, or wrenching support more short roots, which are colonized by mycorrhizal fungi (Ruehle 1980).

Loblolly pines can survive and grow rapidly even after severe root damage. Moderate to severe pruning of roots of large seedlings (all laterals removed and all taproots severed 7.5 or 15 cm below the ground) just before planting reduced survival by only 4 to 8%, and surviving trees were just as large as unpruned trees 3 years after outplanting. Small seedlings were affected even less by severe pruning (Dierauf and Garner 1978).

Top pruning. Near the end of the growing season, height dominance may be evident in nursery beds. Tops of seedlings can be pruned with rotary mowers or other machines to obtain seedlings of uniform height. Pruning may improve field survival, especially of large seedlings (Dierauf 1976b, Dierauf and Olinger 1982). It reduces diameter growth and stops height growth for about 3 weeks while new fascicle buds form just below the cut. However, families differ in their responses to top pruning. Some overcome the injury quickly, while others respond more slowly.

Figure 6-9—Undercutting loblolly pine seedlings at Ashe Nursery, near Gulfport, Mississippi.

When the new buds begin to elongate, height growth resumes. Top pruning should be limited to the succulent portion of the shoot. Even if it is, it may reduce foliage biomass significantly. Mexal and Fisher (1985) estimated that top pruning that removes 20% of the shoot length reduces the biomass of secondary needles by 45%. Top pruning does not appear to alter the size of seedling root systems and does not usually result in forking. Individual seedlings may develop multiple leaders following pruning, but one leader dominates within the first 1 or 2 years after outplanting (Dierauf 1976b). Top pruning may (Dierauf 1976b) or may not (Mexal and Fisher 1985) release small, unpruned seedlings growing beside clipped seedlings. However, top pruning results in the production of more seedlings in the average diameter and height classes, a decreased shoot-to-root ratio, and fewer culls. Packing and storing are easier when seedlings are of uniform size (Davey 1982, Dierauf 1976b). Top pruning should not be done late in the growing season because it can delay dormancy, cause poor budset at dormancy, or even result in succulent growth during the lifting season—all of which can make seedlings less tolerant to lifting, storage, and outplanting (Hennessey and Dougherty 1984, Thames 1962).

Top pruning generally corrects management shortcomings rather than problems inherent in loblolly pine seedling growth. More effort should be devoted to improving nursery management than to top pruning. Options include longer seed prechilling to promote rapid and uniform germination, sowing during the optimal period, sowing by clone or seedlot to reduce growth differences, and providing optimum irrigation and fertilization. The development of loblolly pine seedlings from germination to lifting from the nursery bed is summarized in figure 6-10.

Nursery lifting. Lifting and planting must be synchronized if the best possible seedlings are to be available for all planting requirements. The lifting date affects seedling quality and the speed of budbreak. Ideally, seedlings should not be removed from the nursery beds until they become fully dormant, especially if they are to be stored for more than a few days prior to planting. The optimum lifting window is December 1 through March 1, but lifting can begin earlier or continue later depending on storage procedures and local environmental conditions. Survival of seedlings lifted and planted in October is often poor, probably because the planting sites are normally dry at that time. Trees lifted in November survive best if they are planted within a few days of lifting (Dierauf 1976a, Garber and Mexal 1980). Gagnon and Johnson (1988a) found that lifting in mid-December maximized height growth and the proportion of seedlings growing in midspring. Seedlings should be lifted before height growth begins in the spring.

Although height growth may stop and buds may set as early as October, seedling shoot weight may increase by as much as 70%, and root weight may double during the late fall and winter. These increases indicate that dormancy is not continuous even when night temperatures

dip below –5 °C (Garner and Dierauf 1976, Munson and Stone 1985, Perry 1971). However, periods of low temperature can quickly halt growth (Brissette and Roberts 1984, Carlson 1986, DeWald and Feret 1987, Larsen and others 1986, Venator and Barnett 1985). Physiological changes in seedlings can also continue without visible signs of seedling growth. Once buds are set in the fall, seedlings must be exposed to chilling temperatures before normal budbreak will occur the next spring (Garber 1983). The normal chilling requirement can be satisfied by late December in the nursery (Garber 1978) but can also be met by cold storage (Carlson 1985). At the Ashe Nursery in southern Mississippi, root growth potential in the nursery bed and in cold storage peaks at about 600 hours of accumulated chilling (0 to 8 °C) and then declines gradually (Brissette and others 1988).

Weather conditions at the nursery are important to the success of lifting operations. Conditions are most favorable when the air temperature is between 2 and 24 °C, relative humidity is 50% or more, wind speed is less than 16 km/h, and soil moisture is 75 to 100% of field capacity (Jeffries 1983). From the moment seedlings are lifted until they are planted on a forest site, they are subjected to varying temperature, light, and moisture conditions. Throughout this period, care must be taken to minimize exposure of roots to direct sunlight and desiccating winds, which can kill them quickly. Careful protection of seedlings greatly increases early survival even on poorly prepared sites.

The first step in lifting is undercutting the nursery bed with a flat blade. A tractor-drawn lifter blade or conveyer then uproots seedlings 1, 2, or 8 rows at a time. The soil is

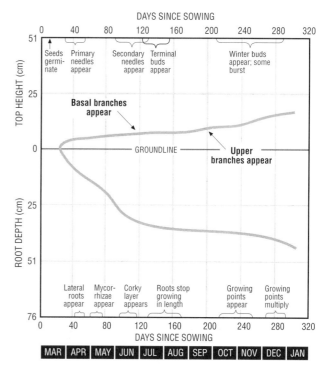

Figure 6-10—The normal development regent sequence of loblolly pine seedlings (adapted from Wakeley 1954).

gently shaken from the seedlings' roots by hand or machine, and the seedlings are loosely placed in tubs or boxes for transportation to a packing shed. Seedling roots should not be exposed for more than 3 minutes during the lifting process (that is, while they are being field packed or secured for transportation to packing facilities).

Most of the finer, more efficient, absorbing roots of bareroot nursery seedlings are lost or damaged between lifting and planting. This is usually not a serious problem because healthy seedlings rapidly regenerate small roots when outplanted properly. The probability of root loss is greater with machine lifting than with careful hand lifting. If nursery soil is very wet or sticky, machine lifting can result in a serious loss of lateral roots and mycorrhizae. Whatever technique is used, a great deal of care must be exercised.

In most nurseries, seedlings are brought into covered sheds for sorting and bundling. However, they can be packed on the lifting machine, and this procedure greatly reduces handling. Seedlings with long, coarse roots are difficult to pack and plant, so such roots should be trimmed during the packing process. This trimming reduces exposure and damage during planting and also prevents the development of misshapen root systems. If seedlings are undercut and side pruned in the nursery, roots normally do not need further pruning.

Grading seedlings. Morphological grades for loblolly pine seedlings are based on stem characteristics that indicate seedling quality (table 6-18). Seedlings with widely varying stem characteristics can be planted successfully. Ideal physical characteristics for a seedling include (Brissette and Lantz 1983, May 1985a):

- A balanced shoot-to-root ratio (about 2:1).

- Stem height 18 to 30 cm (depending on the intended planting site and planting method).

- Root collar diameter 3 to 10 mm.

- Fibrous root system (30 or more first-order laterals) about 15 cm long with abundant mycorrhizae.

- Winter buds present, indicating a low state of physiological activity in the stem (but seedling size is more important than the presence of a well-formed terminal bud) (Williams and others 1988a).

- Some secondary needles and a stiff woody stem with bark.

- No diseases or injuries.

Counting seedlings. Planning for lifting and outplanting requires accurate estimates of the number of seedlings in a nursery or in nursery beds. Nursery seedbed inventory can be determined easily and accurately using 3-P (probability proportional to prediction) sampling. This system is more reliable than conventional counting and is less time consuming and expensive (Conn and Watson 1985). Standard systematic or random sampling procedures can also be used to approximate the number of seedlings per unit area (Karrfalt and Hall 1983).

After seedlings have been lifted, their numbers can be determined in several ways. They can be counted in groups of 10 during culling. More commonly, estimates are based on weights of samples taken from each lot of trees during the packing process. Weight counts are accurate only if seedling size is uniform. Weighing is less tedious than counting and almost as accurate. Estimation by weighing is better than counting in that root exposure is minimized, and both handling time and cost are decreased. If regular checks are made, weight counts will be within 5% of actual bag counts (Eliason and Carlson 1962, King 1976, Simms 1983, Wynens 1964). An electronic beam can also be used to give fast and accurate counts of seedlings moving along a conveyor belt. If beam width, beam intensity, and belt speed are regulated carefully, seedling counts can consistently have 95% accuracy (Wynens 1983). Such a beam system may also be practical for inventorying seedlings in nursery beds.

In many industrial nurseries, loblolly pine seedlings are neither graded nor counted at the nursery. As soon as seedlings are lifted, they are placed in polyethylene-lined kraft bags or similar containers, which are immediately stitched or strapped closed. The number of seedlings per bag is estimated based on a bed inventory (for example, 1,000 seedlings/3 m of linear nursery bed). Cull seedlings (oversized, undersized, damaged, etc.) are discarded during planting (Davey 1982). This system works effectively only if planting crews are well trained and efficient.

Packing and root protection. Once grading and counting are complete, seedlings are packed. Traditionally, seedlings have been grouped in bales of 1,000 with roots at the center and tops exposed on both ends (figure 6-11). Seedlings can be placed in polyethylene-lined kraft bags (figure 6-12). An advantage of bagging is that no additive (for example, moss) is needed if the roots are moist when the seedlings are packed and if the seedlings are kept cool (Williston 1965). Another technique is to roll seedlings in a long section of packing paper ("jelly roll") and secure the roll with metal straps. The jelly roll is unrolled progressively during outplanting, so the roots of only a few seedlings are exposed at one time. Packing seedlings in rolls is slow and more expensive than the other two methods. Normally, each of these methods gives excellent seedling survival.

Table 6-18—Morphological grades of loblolly pine seedlings

Grade	Stem length (cm)	Thickness of stem at groundline (mm)	Nature of stem	Bark of stem	Needles	Winter buds	No. first order lateral roots	Shoot/ root ratio
1	23–30	5–8	Stiff, woody	Usually on entire stem	Almost all in fasicles	Usually present	>30	2.5:1
2	15–25	3–5	Stiff, woody	All over part of stem	Partly in fasicles	Occasionally present	>20	2.5:1–3:1
3	8–30	< 3	Weak, often succulent	Often lacking	Some in fasicles	Rarely present	< 15	> 3:1

Source: adapted from May (1985a) and Wakeley (1954).

Usually, additional steps are taken to protect seedlings' roots and to keep them moist. Roots are dipped in a kaolinite clay slurry before the seedlings are packed, or seedlings are packaged with wet moss, wet wood fiber, or starch gel around the roots. Some superabsorbent artificial materials (which absorb up to 300 times their weight in water) are as effective as clay slurry in keeping bareroot seedlings moist (Stangle and Venator 1985, Venator and Brissette 1983). Root-dipping loblolly pine seedlings in a 1% solution of alginate (b-D-mannurono-pyranose) was found to increase seedling survival (Miller and Reines 1974).

Clay slurry is the substance most commonly used to protect loblolly pine roots. The treatment is easily adapted to mechanization. The slurry provides a uniform moist environment that protects seedling roots before and after planting and reduces the amount of watering required for stored bales (May 1985c, Williston 1967). Also, a systemic insecticide or fungicide can be incorporated into a clay slurry to protect seedlings after outplanting. Clay treatment can increase early seedling survival by as much as 10% if roots are exposed for 30 to 90 minutes during the handling and planting process (Dierauf and Marler 1971). However, if roots will not be exposed for more

Figure 6-11—Bales of loblolly pine seedlings with roots to the center and tops exposed at both ends.

Figure 6-12—Baling loblolly pine seedlings in polyethylene-lined kraft bags that are strapped closed.

than a few minutes, clay slurry is no more effective than keeping roots moist in bales or bags with peat moss (Venator and Brissette 1985).

Storing bareroot seedlings. From the time of packing at the nursery until outplanting, tree seedlings are subjected to environmental conditions that can reduce survival and growth. The best procedure is to transport seedlings to the field immediately after packing and to outplant them within 2 to 3 days. Such a rapid progression is often not possible, so storage for varying periods of time is necessary in many cases. Loblolly seedlings do not store well unless they are fully dormant. Dormant seedlings properly stored in bales or bags under refrigerated or ambient conditions for up to 30 days survive and grow after outplanting just as well as seedlings planted immediately after lifting (Venator and Brissette 1985). Survival gradually decreases as storage time increases. Seedlings lifted in the spring, after dormancy has been broken, should be planted as soon as possible. They have already used some of their food reserves, and this may reduce their storability and subsequent outplanting survival (Garber and Mexal 1980). However, such physiologically active seedlings can be stored for as long as 2 months if care is taken to ensure that they do not overheat (Dierauf 1974).

Adding benomyl to the packing medium or to clay slurry root coating significantly increases survival of seedlings stored longer than 3 weeks, apparently because the treatment controls pathogenic microorganisms that reduce seedling quality during storage. This treatment is especially beneficial for seedlings that are lifted late (Barnett and others 1988; Barnett and Brissette 1987, 1988).

Seedlings should be protected from freezing and from excess heating. Storage temperatures above 5 °C can result in accelerated respiration and mold growth. Bundled seedlings can usually withstand temperatures of –7 to 0 °C for 2 to 3 days without adverse effects (Byrd and Peevy 1963, May 1985a). Lower temperatures may (Bean 1963) or may not kill the seedlings (Garner and Dierauf 1974). The physiological quality of seedlings appears to have a great effect on the length of time stored seedlings can resist the effects of freezing. Because of this variability, it is safest to store seedlings at temperatures between 1 and 5 °C.

Stored seedlings produce ethylene on a cyclical basis. Ethylene produced in sealed storage bags can reduce seedling survival by about 5% during a 3- to 6-week storage period. A high ethylene concentration (5%) in containers can also reduce height growth after outplanting. Adding ethylene-absorbent material to the packing medium can significantly increase root growth potential and may control ethylene buildup satisfactorily (Barnett 1983b, Barnett and others 1985, Garrett-Kraus and others 1985, Johnson and Stumpff 1985).

Nonrefrigerated storage. Dormant seedlings in bags or bales can be stored successfully for 1 to 2 months in unheated buildings during the winter (Dierauf and Marler 1971). Freezing for short periods does not reduce survival (Garner and Dierauf 1974). However, nonrefrigerated storage is risky if intermittent warm periods occur in the winter, and it is not acceptable when weather begins to warm in the spring. Storage time should be kept as short as possible, and trees should be protected from direct sunlight and extreme temperatures. Packages of seedlings should be placed on the floor or ground and should be separated enough to permit good air movement. If stacking is required, 5- by 5-cm spacers should be placed between bundles. Containers should not be stacked more than three high (Dierauf 1982). Regular watering of bales is essential. Temperatures inside containers should be monitored at several locations; they can rise to damaging levels if packages are too close together. Time–temperature monitors (TTM's) that change color irreversibly when a preset time–temperature is exceeded are available, but there are few sound data on the effects of combinations of storage times and temperatures on field performance (Taylor and Barnett 1985a, 1985b).

Refrigerated storage. Newly bundled or bagged seedlings should be moved to coolers quickly and stored at temperatures of about 1 to 4 °C and with good air circulation around each container. In this temperature range, seedling health can be maintained for 2 months with only a small decrease in outplanting survival. Seedlings can be stored for 3 months, but some reduction in survival will occur (Dierauf 1974, Dierauf and Marler 1969). Cold storage should not reduce seedling root growth potential (DeWald and Feret 1988). If seedling mortality is to be minimized, a favorable water status must be maintained during storage of bundles. The walls and floor of the storage facility should be wet down periodically to keep relative humidity at about 90%. Bales packed with moss or similar materials should be watered at 2- to 3-day intervals depending on relative humidity and results of visual inspection. When waterproof sealed bags are used, watering and precise humidity control are not necessary (Dierauf 1982, May 1985a). Trees should be planted as soon as possible after removal from cold storage.

Seedlings respire even in cold storage, and this respiration depletes food reserves and decreases survival. Thus, early outplanting is normally preferred to long storage. However, severe weather along the northern part of the range often kills newly planted seedlings, so cold storage during the coldest months (usually January and February) may result in higher survival than does outplanting immediately after lifting. Exposure to low-intensity light during cold storage accelerates bud activity and growth through the first year after outplanting (Johnson 1983). Root pruning does not reduce the viability of seedlings even after 3 months in cold storage (Dierauf 1984).

Transporting seedlings to the field. It is best to transport seedlings in refrigerated trucks with shelves or racks. Slat-sided trucks with racks and tarpaulin tops are also satisfactory if there is free air movement around each bundle and if the bundles are protected from wind and sun. Completely open trucks or trailers should not

be used to transport seedlings, except for very short distances. Use of open vehicles promotes excessive drying of baled seedlings and heating of bagged seedlings.

It is important to control temperature, even during transport, because seedlings killed by high or low temperatures usually do not show signs of physical damage at the time of planting. When the outside temperature is below freezing, seedlings in exposed packages may be killed (Hodges 1961). It is important that internal bag or bale temperature does not exceed 30 °C (Barnett and others 1984). On warm days, exposure to the sun may kill the most exposed seedlings. At the very least, respiration rates are increased. It is advisable to transport seedlings early in the morning or late in the evening during warm weather. If bundles are exposed for several hours, they should be watered as soon as they reach the storage or planting area. Bales or bags should not be piled more than two deep for transportation because such piling results in compaction and reduced air flow.

Planting Bareroot Seedlings

Seedlings can be planted either by hand or by machine. The art of planting is easily learned, but planting is tedious, and so it is frequently done incorrectly. Incorrect planting results in poor survival or misshapen root systems. The cost of planting bareroot seedlings is influenced by intensity of site preparation, size and shape of the regeneration area, site topography, type of planting method, and risk of damage by insects, diseases, and environmental variables. The less vegetation there is on a site, the easier it is to plant, either by machine or by hand. Guldin (1983a) determined that each additional mechanical site preparation treatment reduced the cost of contract hand planting by $9.27/ha. Regeneration alternatives also vary by size and type of ownership of the land to be planted, availability of wood products markets, and availability of expert advice. For example, when holdings are too small for elaborate site preparation, an owner may be better off spot seeding or hand planting his own property. Per-hectare regeneration costs are greatest when small, scattered blocks are being regenerated because the cost of moving people and equipment is disproportionately high in such cases. Hand planting is less costly than machine planting on very small areas. Nevertheless, costs should always be analyzed carefully, because hand planting is sometimes the least expensive method on large areas (Guldin 1983b).

Planting time. The planting season coincides roughly with the dormant period of the seedlings. This is usually from about December 1 to March 1, although local and yearly environmental conditions can alter dormancy. In actual practice, the beginning and ending of a planting season is determined primarily by the amount of moisture in the ground during late fall and early winter and by spring temperatures. Conditions at planting time can affect results significantly. Planting should be preceded by 5 to 7.5 cm of accumulated rainfall to ensure adequate soil moisture, and it should be suspended during extended periods of drought. Planting should not be done when the soil is frozen, hard, dry, or extremely wet or sticky because planting under these conditions results in misplanted seedlings, decreased survival, and reduced growth. The best time to plant seedlings is in the late winter and early spring, after soil temperatures have warmed to about 5 °C, so that roots can begin growing immediately. This is especially true along the northern extremes of the range where severe winter weather and soil freezing are a problem. When trees are outplanted too early, they are just stored in the ground and exposed to increased risk of frost or animal damage. Survival can be increased by 2 to 13% if seedlings are planted after mid-January north of latitude 33% N (Ursic and others 1966). Where winters are mild and the soil remains warm, midwinter planting permits seedlings to start growing early in the spring. This early establishment increases growth and reduces the possibility of mortality due to early summer drought.

Initial planting density. Next to choice of species, choice of initial spacing is probably the most important decision a land manager makes when establishing a plantation. Initial spacing affects all subsequent activities in the plantation. Site quality, tree survival rate, and growth rate as well as management objectives and financial policies must be considered in determining initial spacing. Close spacings generally offer the greatest opportunity to maximize total volume or to select the best trees for final harvest. Close spacings are more appropriate on good sites, whereas wider spacings are best on inferior sites. However, if survival is a severe problem on poor sites, it is imperative that initial spacing be close enough to ensure adequate stocking after early mortality (Mann and Dell 1971). Both the distance between seedlings and the spacing between rows can vary greatly depending on management objectives, available equipment, site quality, and expected early survival. For many years the standard spacing was 1.8 by 1.8 m or 2,990 trees/ha. Under most conditions, precommercial thinning is necessary to optimize growth when loblolly pines are planted at this density. Planting about 1,730 trees/ha, in various configurations, probably provides a manager with the best variety of management options, both economically and ecologically. Spacing and its implications for multiple use and wood yields are discussed in subsequent chapters.

Care of seedlings at the planting site. Seedlings should be planted promptly unless adequate storage facilities are available. Refrigerated vans used for transport make excellent field storage units. If refrigerated storage is not available, both bags and bales should be kept shaded, off the ground, and separated for ventilation. Seedlings can be damaged when bundles or bags are exposed to direct sunlight. Short-term exposure is inconsequential, but exposure

lasting longer than 1 hour usually causes some damage. During March and April planting in Virginia, 6 hours of exposure reduced seedling survival by 11 to 28%, depending on temperature conditions (Dierauf and Garner 1974).

Bags or bales of seedlings should be protected from wind, sun, and temperature extremes. Only one bag should be opened at a time, seedlings should be transferred to planting containers quickly, and the bag should be resealed until needed again. Soaking bundles for a short time just prior to planting may increase survival of seedlings that have been stored without refrigeration for longer than 1 month (Dierauf and Edwards 1985). At the end of the day, all unplanted seedlings should be watered well and packed back into bales for protection. Alternatively, seedlings can be placed in a trench, and their roots covered with soil. This practice is commonly called "heeling in."

Hand planting. Hand planting has been a well-established technique since the 1940's. Numerous publications demonstrating handling and planting techniques are available (for example, USDA FS 1989, Wakeley 1954). Hand planting provides the following advantages over machine planting, especially for the nonindustrial private forest landowner:

- Capital outlay is small.

- Survival rates of seedlings hand planted by personnel with only a little training is as good or better than that of machine-planted seedlings.

- The technique can be used to regenerate small, rough, hard-to-reach areas or unprepared sites.

- Hand planters can select the best microsites and adjust planting depth for each seedling.

- There is little chance that planting spots will be missed.

However, hand planting has the following disadvantages:

- Spacing is imprecise.

- Roots can dry out during handling and before planting.

- Physical demands on planters are great.

- Few seedlings are planted per unit of time.

- Planters cannot carry large numbers of container seedlings.

The primary tool for hand planting is the dibble or planting bar. The standard dibble has a 25-cm, wedge-shaped blade that makes an opening large enough to accept a seedling root system with very little friction. Larger blades should be used for seedlings with extremely large root systems. Mattocks, hoedads, shovels, or other tools can also be used (Larson and Milodragovich 1982).

Careless handling of seedlings by planters causes seedling mortality. Planters can carry seedlings in canvas bags, baskets, or trays as long as roots are well protected by packing media. Kaolin clay root dip or spray treatments provide only slight protection against drying during planting (Dierauf and Marler 1971). Seedlings should not be carried in a pail of water because immersion washes clay slurry from the roots and because long root immersion increases mortality. Care must be taken to expose the roots of only one seedling at a time to sunlight during planting; this exposure should last only a few seconds—the time it takes to remove the seedling from the planting bag and insert it into the soil. Carrying large numbers of seedlings in the hand with roots exposed is a common cause of mortality.

Choosing the planting spot. On cut-over and site-prepared areas, planters can increase seedling survival by choosing planting spots carefully. This may result in somewhat irregular spacing, but hand planting is not precise anyway. It is a good practice to plant on high spots or hummocks in areas subjected to periodic high water; this keeps roots in well-aerated soil as much as possible. Seedlings should not be planted on microsites where there are unusually thick accumulations of litter or duff, which prevent roots from being packed in soil; where there are loose clods of soil, which usually dry out rapidly; in small depressions on wet sites, where water may stand after rains; on small mounds on droughty sites; in compacted areas such as wheel tracks; or close to hardwood stumps that may sprout.

Planting techniques. Regardless of the implement used, a hole should be made straight down into the mineral soil, deep and wide enough so that the entire root system can be inserted easily. The seedling should be inserted slightly deeper than planting depth and then lifted enough to straighten its roots before packing the soil. This minimizes the potential for malformed roots (J- or U-shaped or balled roots), which commonly occur when seedlings are planted in holes that are too shallow. Proper root placement permits the taproot to begin growing downward immediately rather than growing parallel to the surface or toward the surface before turning downward. Soil should be packed firmly around the root system so that the roots can begin absorbing moisture immediately. A small air pocket in a planting hole may not harm a seedling, but the fewer the roots that contact the soil, the greater the chance of early seedling desiccation.

Depth of planting should be adjusted to the site and soil type. Seedlings should never be set so that roots are exposed. Shallow planting can cause mortality, especially when water stress occurs shortly after outplanting (Brissette and Barnett 1989). On poorly drained and wet sites, seedlings should be planted at the level at which they grew in the nursery. On sites where water stands through the winter and into the spring, burying half or more of the stem can decrease first-season survival from 15 to 60%, depending on soil characteristics (Dierauf 1982, Switzer 1960) and affects tree growth adversely (Bilan 1987, Koshi 1960, Slocum 1951, Slocum and Maki 1956). However, planting seedlings 5 to 10 cm deeper than normal can improve survival on eroded (Williston and Ursic 1979), normally dry, or well-drained sites (Brissette and Barnett 1989, Dierauf 1984, Stransky 1962). This deep planting does not affect root development ad-

versely. It may stimulate early height growth but does not increase total tree height. On average to dry sites, burying some green needles does not reduce survival or growth and may increase sprouting if exposed tops are killed by frost or clipped by animals (Dierauf 1982).

Machine planting. The vast majority of loblolly pine plantings are done with machines. Machine planting involves setting seedlings in continuous slits or intermittent holes punched in the ground. One or two rows of seedlings can be planted in a continuous motion by either method. Seedlings can be inserted in the ground mechanically or pneumatically with acceptable planting quality (Haddock and Hassan 1981). On large areas that are adequately cleared and site prepared, machine planting is both efficient and effective. Site preparation and planting can be combined in some cases, reducing costs substantially. Machine planting generally requires more skill than does hand planting. The planter needs a good sense of timing. The tractor's speed should be constant, the ground should be relatively smooth, and the seedlings should be relatively uniform in size. If planting density must be changed during the day, it is best to change the spacing between rows without altering within-row spacing. This procedure changes planting density but does not force the planter to vary his or her timing. Machine planting permits precise spacing of seedlings, easy adjustment of planting depth, adjustment of planting speed, easy adaptation to container seedlings, and good protection of roots.

Machine planting has several disadvantages, however. It requires a fairly well-prepared site. The planter has no opportunity to select microsites where trees might grow the best. Planting spots may be missed, and many seedlings may be planted incorrectly if coulter depth and packing wheels are not checked carefully at regular intervals.

Seedling roots are usually in the form of an "L" if the root system is dragged during the machine-planting process. Roots are in the form of a "J" or are balled if the planting slit or hole is not deep enough. Moving from one soil to another with a different consistency may require mechanical adjustments to maintain proper planting.

Some root deformation usually occurs during planting. Unfortunately, the effects of root deformation on tree survival and growth are not understood clearly. A recent controlled greenhouse study showed that J-rooted seedlings, when planted to the normal root collar or planted shallow, had both lower survival and less new growth after 12 weeks than seedlings planted with their roots straight (Brissette and Barnett 1989). Three- to eight-year-old trees with J-roots also grew slower than trees with straight roots (Harrington and others 1987). However, there is considerable evidence that seedlings with roots deformed at planting survive and grow to maturity about as well as properly planted seedlings (Cabrera and Woods 1975, Hunter and Maki 1980, Mexal and Burton 1978, Schultz 1973, Trousdell 1959, Woods 1980). Even when roots are distorted badly in planting, they are soon overgrown by the expanding taproot and lateral roots (Little 1973). Hay and Woods (1974) found that larger trees in North Carolina Piedmont plantations were frequently supported by deformed root systems and that small trees of the same age had normal root systems. Poor planting seems to promote lateral root growth over taproot growth, and increased growth of lateral roots may be the reason seedlings with deformed root systems often compete successfully with well-planted seedlings (Hay and Woods 1975, 1978). Unfortunately, even if roots are planted relatively straight, they are compressed into a single plane and grow mainly in two opposite directions for many years (figure 6-13). This development pattern can make planted trees less windfirm than naturally regenerated trees, especially during the seedling and sapling stages.

Survival and early growth of seedlings.　Most successful plantings are made during December, January, and February. From 85 to 95% of all trees planted on prepared sites may survive if environmental conditions are good and planting is supervised carefully (Branan and Porterfield 1971, Muller 1983). However, most plantings are much less successful. A study of 25-year records for 101,200 ha of plantings (mostly machine plantings) throughout the South indicated that average first-year survival for loblolly and slash pines was 71% (Schultz 1975). Between 1979 and 1981, first-year survival of machine-planted loblolly pines in Georgia averaged 61% (Rowan 1987). Conservation reserve plantings on old fields in Georgia during 1986 to 1989 had survival rates of 65 to 76% (Steinbeck 1990). Survival is about the same on Coastal Plain, Piedmont, and mountain sites if planting conditions are good (Jones and Thacker 1965). According to Baldwin (1989), 60 to 70% of both hand- and machine-planted seedlings can be expected to survive and become established. Unless special care is taken and seedlings are planted under ideal conditions, a sufficient number of trees should be planted to absorb an average first-year loss of 30%. Most mortality occurs during

the spring and summer following outplanting. Barring a catastrophic event, 90 to 95% of the trees that survive the first growing season can be expected to survive until stand competition or fusiform rust begin to take their toll (Jones and Thacker 1965, Xydias 1983).

Seedling survival and early growth after outplanting are strongly affected by seedling quality (especially root surface area and needle moisture content), planting date, and microenvironment (especially soil moisture conditions and competing vegetation). Sixteen to 28% of seedlings with only 50% of their feeder root mass intact die during the first year after outplanting, and mortality is 45% or more if 75% of root mass is lost (Rowan 1983). Moisture content of healthy, turgid needles is about 200% of the needle dry weight. When needle moisture content drops below 100%, seedlings begin to die. Half of all seedlings die by the time needle moisture drops to 85%, and all die at 65% (Stransky 1963). Theoretically, water loss and moisture stress desiccation might be reduced by coating needles with materials that block stomata or inhibit metabolism. However, coating needles of seedlings with the metabolic inhibitors decenyl succinic acid (DSA) and phenylmercuric acetate (PMA) at varying concentrations did not increase seedling survival during droughts lasting up to 6 weeks (McClurkin 1974).

There is a clear relationship between lifting and planting dates and field survival (figure 6-14). Survival is greatest for plantings made between late October and mid-March. Late lifting and planting is often the primary cause of first-year mortality (Bilan 1987, Venator 1985). However, poor seedling quality, poor planting technique, and adverse microenvironment can each cause 3 to 6% mortality during the first year (Godbee and others 1983). Fumigating the planting site does not increase survival, whether seedlings are nursery fumigated or not (Hansbrough and others 1964, Shepard 1973). Seedlings with low vigor (chlorotic, small branches or no branches, short secondary needles, and a small terminal bud) during the first year after planting will probably become the suppressed trees in

Figure 6-13—Most superficial lateral roots of 5-year-old loblolly pine trees that were planted with a dibble on beds grow at right angles to the direction of the beds due to compression into a single plane at planting.

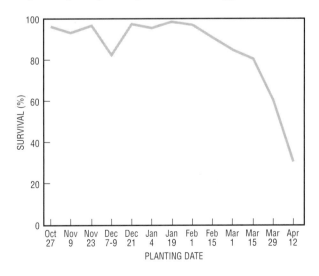

Figure 6-14—Effect of planting date on first-year survival of loblolly pines (adapted from Wakeley 1954).

maturing plantations (Venator 1983b).

Survival in a new plantation is most often estimated by counting living seedlings in randomly sampled plots. Rapid estimates of survival in large areas can be obtained by means of 35-mm color infrared aerial photography (Campbell and Mead 1981). For example, more than 95% of the 1-year-old planted loblolly pines growing on site-prepared areas in the Virginia Coastal Plain could be detected on film at a scale of 1:297 (Smith and others 1986). Mortality within a plantation is often not random; therefore, careful stratification is needed to identify areas of high or low survival. Once areas of low survival have been delineated, managers can assess the benefits of replanting (Matney and Hodges 1985).

Effects of seedling quality on survival and early growth. No true test of seedling quality has been developed, primarily because both environmental conditions and the physiological state of seedlings are critical to survival and early growth. Root growth potential (RGP) is presently the best comprehensive indicator of seedling quality because it measures the ability of a seedling to initiate and elongate new roots when held in an environment favorable for root growth (Brissette and Ballenger 1985, Brissette and Roberts 1984). Neither root length nor root weight is an acceptable measurement of RGP. Root growth potential is affected by nursery practices and cold storage and seems to be linked closely to bud dormancy (Ritchie and Dunlap 1980). Root growth potential of plantable seedlings increases from a low in autumn to a peak in early March, then decreases rapidly (Feret and others 1985a). Root growth potential is normally highest for large seedlings and lowest for small seedlings (figure 6-15). However, seedlings with similar morphology can have very different RGP's, as can seedlings produced at

Table 6-19—Survival and growth of loblolly pines planted on sites in Louisiana as affected by seedling size

Seedling grade*	Age 3 years		Age 13–15 years		
	Survival %	Height (m)	Survival %	Height (m)	Volume (m³/ha)
Grade 1	95 a	2.8 a	90 a	17.8 a	401 a
Grade 2	95 a	2.4 a	85 a	17.3 b	341 b
Grade 3	90 b	1.9 b	78 b	17.0 b	322 b

Source: adapted from South and others (1985).

Values in columns followed by the same letter are not significantly different at the 95% probability level according to Duncan's new multiple range test.

* Each grade is an average of six sources.

Table 6-20—Seedling size and survival data of 1+0 and 2+0 top-pruned loblolly pine seedlings

Measurements	1+0 seedlings	2+0 seedlings
Root collar diameter when planted (mm)	3.9	5.3
Height when planted (cm)	12	13
1st-year survival (%)	96	76
1st-year height (cm)	28	19
2nd-year survival (%)	95	72
2nd-year height (cm)	55	42

Source: adapted from McLemore (1982).

different nurseries (Larsen and Boyer 1986).

The number and length of new roots seem to be good predictors of survival. For example, 70 to 90% of seedlings outplanted with 30 to 40 new root tips were alive after 1 year. In contrast, only half of those with 20 new root tips survived (Barden and others 1987, Larsen and others 1986). New root length may be an even better predictor of field growth performance than number of new roots (Feret and others 1985a, 1985b, 1985c; Freyman and Feret 1987).

Low nursery bed density increases seedling size and increases the growth of trees after outplanting (Shipman 1964). Large, bushy 1-year-old seedlings with much root biomass (grade 1 seedlings) have the best chance of survival following outplanting (tables 6-19 and 6-20). Small seedlings tend to have a small amount of foliage and usually have poor survival rates. However, any seedling with a low shoot-to-root ratio has an excellent chance of survival (Rowan 1987). Root collar diameter is the best easily measured indicator of the potential of seedlings for survival and future growth (South 1987b, Wakeley 1954; figure 6–16). Seedlings with root collar diameters of 3.2 to 4.8 mm had survival rates 15 to 20% higher than those of seedlings with root collar diameters of 1.6 to 2.4 mm in both the Coastal Plain and Piedmont during 1 planting year (Dierauf and Garner 1970). Stem length is less im-

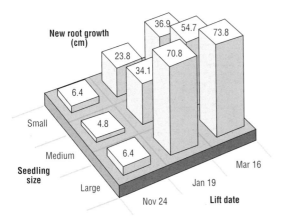

Figure 6-15—Root growth potential of graded loblolly pine seedlings averaged for two nurseries for three lifting dates in 1981-82 (adapted from Brissette and Roberts 1984).

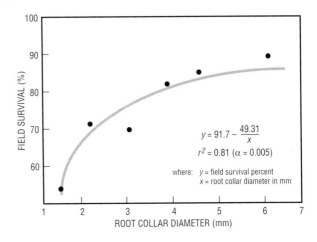

$$y = 91.7 - \frac{49.31}{x}$$

$$r^2 = 0.81 \ (\alpha = 0.005)$$

where: y = field survival percent
x = root collar diameter in mm

Figure 6-16—The relationship between seedling root collar diameter at lifting and field survival (adapted from South and Mexal 1984).

portant than root collar diameter or root length, but trees taller than 30 cm and having shoot-to-root ratios greater than 2.5 to 1.0 tend to have lower rates of survival on droughty or other adverse sites than do seedlings of average height (18 to 25 cm) (Boyer and South 1987, Tuttle and others 1988a). On good sites, however, tall seedlings may survive as well as or better than seedlings of average height (Barber and VanHaverbeke 1961, Hatchell and others 1972, Hunt and Gilmore 1967, Tuttle and others 1987).

This interaction between site and tree height may partially explain why survival rates of grade 2 seedlings are sometimes higher than those of taller, grade 1 seedlings (Venator 1983a).

In newly planted seedlings, some root growth can occur throughout the first winter (Bilan and Ferguson 1985). This growth reduces the shoot-to-root ratio and increases potential for survival. In east Texas, measurable elongation of lateral roots in seedlings planted in mid-November began in early February, 10 weeks after planting. By mid-April, new root growth averaged 200 cm/seedling. Root regeneration begins on laterals close to the root collar and proceeds downward. The taproot is usually the last root to begin elongation (Bilan and Ferguson 1985). When the aboveground portion of a seedling is dormant, new root growth is primarily through elongation of existing roots. Periods of low temperature can quickly halt root and shoot growth of newly outplanted seedlings (DeWald and Feret 1987, Larsen and others 1986, Venator and Barnett 1985). From just before bud burst and thereafter, new root growth results both from elongation of existing roots and from initiation of new roots.

High-quality seedlings grow more rapidly than those of lower quality, especially on good sites. This growth difference may continue throughout a rotation. There are genetic differences in loblolly pine seedling sizes, shoot-to-root ratios, rooting habits, and root regeneration poten-

tials. All of these characteristics are correlated with transplanting success (Beineke and Perry 1966). However, traits that enable some progeny to survive well at one time of the year may not increase survival during other periods.

Effects of environmental conditions on survival and early growth. Low temperature is the main factor limiting root growth until about the end of February. After that time, soil moisture is the most significant controlling factor (Bilan 1962). It is best to plant trees in moist soil. However, the amount of soil moisture available at planting time is not critical if soil moisture is above the wilting point and rain is expected soon. If a drought begins shortly after planting and the site is already low in moisture, considerable mortality will probably occur, especially on a sandy site. Droughts early in the growing season (April to May) are usually more lethal than summer droughts. Droughts lasting 3 weeks or longer usually reduce survival greatly (McClurkin 1966). Seedlings that have optimum foliar N concentrations (about 2.5% on a dry weight basis) under normal moisture conditions are the most drought resistant (Pharis and Kramer 1964).

Compacted soil makes seedling establishment difficult and reduces the growth rate by 50% or more, depending on the amount of root growth restriction and the net increase in soil density. Reductions occur in both shoot and root growth and are measurable within 7 weeks of establishment (Perry 1964; figures 6-17, 6-18, and 6-19). Even a small increase in bulk density (for example, from 1.28 to 1.42) can decrease growth significantly (Simmons and Ezell 1983). Roots may be unable to penetrate compacted sands with bulk densities of 1.75 or clays with bulk densities exceeding 1.55 (Pritchett 1979). Twenty-six-year-old loblolly pines growing on compacted soil had aboveground volume only 46% as great as that of nearby trees on soil that was not compacted (Perry 1964).

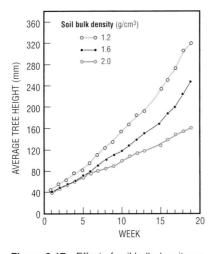

Figure 6-17—Effect of soil bulk density on average height of seedlings during 19 weeks of growth for three bulk density treatments. Curves are significantly different from each other at the 95% probability level (adapted from Mitchell and others 1982).

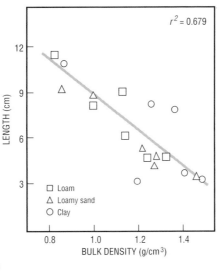

Figure 6-18—The relationship between root length and soil density. Points shown are averages of three replications (adapted from Foil and Ralston 1967).

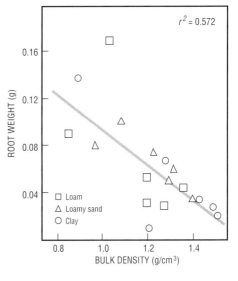

Figure 6-19—Effect of soil density on root weight, one growing season after seed germination (adapted from Foil and Ralston 1967).

Various cultural treatments can promote seedling survival as well as height, diameter, and root growth (Dougherty 1990, Lockaby and others 1988, South and Barnett 1986). Reduction or removal of competing vegetation may be required to reduce moisture stress, which is one of the major causes of seedling mortality (South and Barnett 1986). Vegetation control measures may be necessary before planting (see chapter 4) and for 1 or 2 years after planting (see chapter 8). Herbicides can even be applied in bands along each side of the planting row with sprayers attached to the planting machine (Miller 1990). The advantage of intensive site preparation before planting is that most native vegetation is killed back to the groundline, allowing newly planted seedlings to establish and grow rapidly before competition becomes severe (Nusser and Wentworth 1987). On a Louisiana flatwoods site, survival was 74% at 2 years after burning and planting, but was 88% at 2 years after burning, disking, and planting. At plantation age 13, the difference between survival rates was still 11% (Haywood 1983). Herbaceous weed control in the first year can increase the growth of loblolly pine. On an upland Piedmont site in northern Georgia, the most economical and effective treatment for increasing seedling survival was to apply 343 ml of Oust®/ha in spots 1.8 m in diameter (Dougherty 1990). The application of fertilizers during planting does not increase survival (Bilan 1966, Hammond 1976, Pope and Voeller 1976).

Chemical applications can stimulate the growth of newly planted seedlings. Planting site fumigation can stimulate seedling height growth. Fumigation immediately stimulated height growth of outplanted loblolly seedlings in north Louisiana, and fumigation had increased volume by at least 32% by age 14 (Hansbrough and others 1964, Shepard 1973). Spraying an ethylene-releasing growth regulator on nursery seedlings can affect dormancy and promote height growth of outplanted seedlings (Gagnon and Johnson 1988b). Fertilization just before, during, or just after planting can promote growth of newly planted seedlings. On P-deficient sites, application of N and P can double seedling growth by age 3 (Hammond 1976). Effects of fertilizers on long-term growth are discussed in chapter 11.

Effects of mycorrhizae on survival and growth of newly planted seedlings.

Mycorrhizae increase the root surface area and speed the regeneration of new roots, and thus increase early survival, nutrient absorption, and tree growth on sites where conditions are less than optimum (Hatchell and Marx 1987, Marx and Hatchell 1986, Shoulders and Jorgensen 1969). Seedlings having high, medium, or low percentages of root infection at the time of outplanting have similar rates of survival and of growth (Barnett 1987). When soil fertility and soil moisture are optimum, the presence of mycorrhizae does not increase seedling survival or early growth. High N fertilization can greatly reduce the number of mycorrhizae on loblolly seedlings (table 6-21). An N-to-P ratio of less than 20:1 in the shoots may be necessary for extensive mycorrhizal development (Pritchett 1973).

Table 6-21—Influence of nitrogen (N) additions on the number of mycorrhizae per loblolly pine seedling grown in Bladen fine sandy loam from southeast Georgia

N treatment (ppm)	No. of mycorrhizae/seedling			
	Simple forked	Multiple forked	Cluster	Total
0	200	232	34	466
80	161	16	2	179
320	34	0	0	34

Source: adapted from Pritchett (1973).

Root tips formed after outplanting are soon inoculated as a result of interactions between growing roots and numerous fungal species present on any forest site (Tainter and Walstad 1977, Woods and Martin 1973). When loblolly pine was planted in Arkansas, 160 km north of its native range and 24 km from the nearest shortleaf pine stand, 30% of all seedling root tips were infected with mycorrhizal fungi within 5 months (Tainter and Walstad 1977).

Both survival and growth of seedlings can be increased by Pt on sites with good to poor fertility. However, seedlings inoculated with Pt probably will not survive or grow better than seedlings naturally infected with other ectomycorrhizal fungi (Leach and Gresham 1983, Marx and others 1977a). Because more than 1,000 fungal species form mycorrhizal associations with plants, it is probable that other effective associations between loblolly pine and mycorrhizal fungi will be identified in the future.

Planting actively growing, bareroot seedlings.

Seedlings that break dormancy either in the nursery or in bales during the regular planting season can be planted successfully under some environmental conditions. Although new leaders may die, the seedlings usually recover quickly (McClurkin 1962). Although not a recommended practice, loblolly seedlings lifted from the nursery during active height growth may survive satisfactorily if planted within a few days of lifting and if soil moisture conditions are favorable. This conclusion is based on the fact that slash pines weighing as little as 1.3 g, with shoot-to-root ratios of 6:1 and few secondary needles, survived and grew well in Florida when planted from June to September. In this study, average first-year survival was 71%, and only two dry-site plantings had survival less than 53%. These plantings succeeded because the soil was well prepared, settled, and moist; the seedlings were planted deep (half of the stem buried); and no more than 2 days elapsed between lifting and planting (Schultz and Wilhite 1967). However, summer planting of even the hardiest southern pines on dry, sandy sites normally results in total failure (Wilhite and Schultz 1969).

Preserving surplus nursery stock.

Nurseries occasionally have unused seedlings. Top-pruned, 2-year-old loblolly seedlings can be outplanted with satisfactory survival and growth (Lyle and others 1958; table 6-20).

Replacement planting or interplanting. No information on interplanting or replacement planting with bareroot seedlings can be found for loblolly pine. Interplanting midway between rows of slash pine 1 year after initial planting in rows 3.7 to 5.8 m apart was a total failure in a Georgia study. Only 1% of the interplants were in the dominant crown class at age 16, while 64% were suppressed (Schultz 1965). Although loblolly pine is more shade tolerant than slash pine, neither interplanting nor replacement planting with bareroot loblolly stock is recommended. However, replanting first-year fail spots with potted loblolly seedlings the same age as those in the ground increases stocking (Schmidtling 1972). It may prove efficient to replant fail spots, with container stock having superior height growth characteristics, in the fall as soon as adequate moisture is available. If the number of surviving trees at ages 1 to 3 is considered inadequate and potted trees are unavailable, the stand should be destroyed and the area replanted.

Planting loblolly with other species. Loblolly pine out-competes or competes well with other southern pines when planted in mixtures. Loblolly has also been planted with hardwoods. Such planting increases forest diversity, enhances stand use by wildlife, improves stand visual appearance, and still provides satisfactory biomass productivity. Loblolly out-competes sweetgum and yellow-poplar when planted with these species (Bruner and Reamer 1966, Buckner and Maki 1977). Five years after sweetgum and loblolly were planted in alternate rows on an old field, sweetgum averaged only 0.8 m tall and loblolly pine averaged 3.4 m tall (Burns 1962). However, naturally regenerated sweetgum gradually dominates fail spots in pine plantations where adequate light is available and forms mixed stands with loblolly.

If loblolly seedlings are planted beneath a hardwood overstory, immediate release is necessary for best survival and early growth. In a central Louisiana study, survival averaged 86% for seedlings released immediately after establishment and 46% for those released later or not at all. At tree age 7 years, heights of released trees were also as much as 2 m greater than heights of trees that were not released. Even if loblolly seedlings are planted in small openings, survival and height growth are reduced by surrounding hardwood competition (Shoulders 1955).

Producing and Planting Container Seedlings

Planting container-grown loblolly pines came into commercial use in the 1970's. As many as 10 million container seedlings are now planted each year. Use of container seedlings has several advantages over use of bareroot seedlings. A crop of container seedlings can be produced at any time of the year on short notice. Production of container seedlings makes more efficient use of limited numbers of seeds, and seedling growth is increased. Use of container seedlings extends the planting season, often improves growth on adverse sites, and makes it easier to automate planting.

Growing container seedlings also has several disadvantages. It takes more care to grow container seedlings than to grow bareroot seedlings; container seedlings are smaller than bareroot seedlings; container seedlings are bulky; and per-seedling production costs are often higher for container seedlings than for bareroot seedlings (Barnett and Brissett 1986, Brissette and others 1991).

The root morphology of container seedlings differs from that of bareroot seedlings, and the two types of seedlings are in different physiological states when outplanted, so regeneration processes and techniques must be modified when container stock is used.

Growing container seedlings in small numbers is more expensive than expanding production of bareroot seedlings in an established nursery. However, if new nurseries must be established, the cost of producing container seedlings is about the same as the cost of producing bareroot seedlings if at least 3 million container seedlings are grown per year. In 1980, the cost of producing 25 million loblolly seedlings in Styroblocks® in a timber-truss greenhouse nursery in the Coastal Plain was $30.20/1,000, and the cost of producing bareroot seedlings in a new nursery was $35.66/1,000 (Guldin 1981, 1982a, 1983a, 1983c). Container nurseries can be established on land too poor to support bareroot nurseries, require one-third less irrigation water than do bareroot nurseries, and have lower construction costs than do bareroot nurseries. Also, maximum seedling production can begin in less than 1 year in a new container seedling nursery but cannot begin for almost 3 years in a new bareroot nursery (Guldin 1982a, 1982b). Container type is the variable that most strongly affects the cost of production in container nurseries. Figure 6-20 indicates that seedlings can be grown in Styroblocks at lower cost than bareroot stock can be grown up to an annual output of about 14 to 19 million seedlings depending on the number of frost-free days. However, because there is very little competition

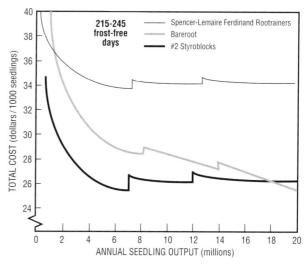

Figure 6-20—Cost of growing bareroot and containerized seedlings in 1980 as affected by annual seedling output (adapted from Guldin 1981).

among growers of container seedlings, bareroot stock is usually much less expensive than container stock.

Types of containers and growing media. Containers can be divided into two general categories: containers planted with seedlings and containers that are removed before outplanting (figure 6-21). Paper pots, wood fiber containers, and biodegradable plastic containers are outplanted with the seedlings as a unit when the seedlings are of sufficient size. Most containers are sturdy enough to withstand mechanical planting. Wood fiber containers planted with seedlings make direct contact with the soil, so root development is not restricted (Barnett 1975). Seedlings in paper pots have less restricted root growth than do those in plastic containers because of the rapid degradation of the container (Barnett and Brisette 1986, Barnett and McGilvray 1981).

Seedlings removed from their containers before outplanting are called "plugs." After roots have developed sufficiently to bind the growing medium into a cohesive unit, the seedling and growing medium are removed from the container as one unit and planted. Plug seedlings grow to plantable size in about 3 to 5 months, depending on container size. If they are handled properly, newly outplanted plug seedlings have all their roots intact, so roots can begin growing into the surrounding soil immediately. Many varieties of this type of container, made from a variety of substances (Styrofoam® and hard plastics) in different arrangements (tubes in racks, Styroblocks with holes for the plugs) can produce excellent seedlings (Barnett and McGilvray 1981, Landis and others 1990b).

Larger seedlings can be produced in larger containers if seedlings are kept long enough in the nursery. Appropriate container size depends on container type and growing conditions. Containers with volumes of from 40 to 165 cm^3 are easy to handle and plant. A container length of about 13 cm will permit the development of quality seedlings for most planting conditions. Slightly shorter lengths are advantageous on moist, prepared sites,

Figure 6-21—Loblolly pine seedlings grown in three type of containers: biodegradable plastic tube (**A**), peat-moss–vermiculite molded block (**B**), and Styroblock plug (**C**) (Barnett and McGilvray 1981).

and longer lengths are superior on dry or unprepared sites (Barnett 1974b).

Soil, artificial media, and combinations of the two will grow high-quality container seedlings. If topsoil is used, it should be fumigated or sterilized to promote germination and seedling growth. Fiber blocks can be made of many combinations of sphagnum peat moss, vermiculite, wood cellulose, and nutrients. A mixture of sphagnum and vermiculite at a ratio of 1:1 or 2:1 is the commonest growing medium for container seedlings. Sphagnum has good water-holding capacity, low pH, good buffering capacity, and a high cation-exchange capacity. Mixing sphagnum with vermiculite increases pore space and aeration (Barnett and Brissette 1986). A wetting agent is normally added to sphagnum mixtures to increase the uniformity and rate of moisture movement. Wetting agents should be used at very low rates. Even manufacturers' recommended rates can reduce seed germination (Barnett 1977). Milled pine bark, alone or mixed with other materials, is also a satisfactory growth medium; it is lightweight and porous, may inhibit the development of disease organisms (Pawuk 1981), and is generally free of toxic materials that interfere with mycorrhizal development (Ruehle and Marx 1977).

Facilities. Various kinds of structures, from glass greenhouses to pole shadehouses, can be used to grow container stock (figure 6-22).

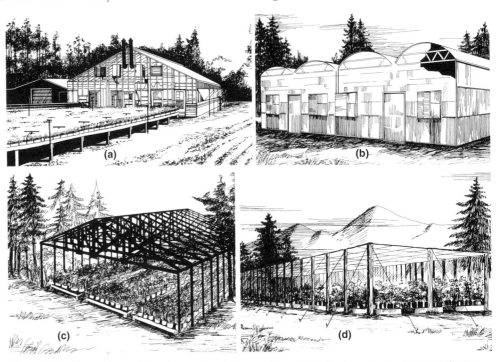

Figure 6-22—Several types of structures adequate for growing containerized seedlings: glass greenhouse with outdoor hardening bench (**a**), two fiberglass greenhouses with a common sidewall (**b**), timber truss greenhouse (**c**), and pole shadehouse (**d**) (Guldin 1983c).

Because the growing medium for each container seedling is predetermined and premixed and because the seedlings are raised in controlled facilities, production is not affected by local topographic or soil characteristics. Important considerations include road and utility access, labor supply, quantity and quality of irrigation water, climate, and access to outplanting areas. If seedlings are to be raised during cold periods, heated structures are needed. Special care must be taken to prevent air pollution and disease problems in greenhouses (see chapter 10). There are many opportunities to mechanize the growing of container seedlings, but such mechanization presents numerous technical challenges. Practical guidelines for developing a container nursery program are described by Landis and others (1995).

Seed handling and sowing. The high-quality seeds necessary for efficient production of container seedlings require carefully controlled processing and storage. Seed treatments are essentially the same as those used in bareroot nurseries. The best seed processing techniques (including soaking seeds overnight and monitoring temperatures carefully) should be rigorously followed to maximize the proportion of full containers and minimize seedling costs (Pawuk and Barnett 1979).

Vacuum sowing, which is efficient and accurate, is the sowing method most often employed. Sowing can also be done by hand. One or more seeds are placed in each container, depending on expected germination (Balmer and Space 1976). Alternatively, 1, 2, or 3 seeds can be sown in specific numbers of the containers based on prediction equations (Pepper and Barnett 1981a, Pepper and Hodge 1982) or on linear programming analysis (Pepper and Barnett 1981b). For example, 50% of the containers might receive 1 seed, 30%, 2 seeds, and 20%, 3 seeds. Sowing more than 1 seed/container increases seed requirements and also necessitates the removal of excess seedlings before outplanting. An alternative is to sow only 1 seed/container and to germinate additional seeds in trays for transplanting. After a reasonable period, pregerminated seeds can be planted in empty containers. This technique requires careful timing to minimize suppression of young trees. The transplanting process is labor intensive and expensive, but transplanting ensures that almost all containers are filled. Another option is to sow single seeds in enough containers to offset expected germination failures. Barnett and Brissette (1986) recommend that additional containers be sown if germination is expected to be less than 85%.

Growing container seedlings.

Greenhouse densities up to 1,810 seedlings/m² yield stock with acceptable out-

planting survival and early field growth. However, for best field performance of seedlings, densities should not exceed 1,075 seedlings/m² (Barnett 1980). The key to growing high-quality container seedlings in a reasonable length of time is rigid control of moisture, temperature, and fertility (Barnett 1984a, 1984b; Barnett and Brissette 1986). Because loblolly pines do not require high light intensity for germination, supplemental light is not normally needed in greenhouses or shadehouses. Moisture content of the potting medium should be kept near field capacity throughout the developmental phase of young seedlings. The need for water varies by rooting medium, environmental condition, and seedling developmental stage. Usually, germination is most rapid and complete when seeds are on top of the rooting medium and seeds are watered frequently by a mist system. When seeds are watered less frequently, covering them with a small amount of medium (0.6 cm or less) helps germination (Barnett 1978). Seedlings grow fastest in dry weight when the moisture content of peat–vermiculite mixtures is about 300 to 400%. The shoot-to-root ratio increases as medium moisture content increases to about 400% (figure 6-23). Seedling dry weight decreases steadily as medium moisture content increases past 400%. Excess moisture (that is, poor aeration) is often indicated by needle chlorosis and results in stunted shoot and root growth. The water content of containers is easily monitored by random weighing once the relationship between moisture level and container weight has been determined for a specific medium. The time to rewater is when the container weight decreases to about 75 to 80% of the saturated weight, depending on container type (Barnett and Brissette 1986).

Peak germination of loblolly pine seeds that have not been prechilled occurs when the air and the growing medium are about 24 °C. Prechilling broadens the germination temperature range, permitting superior germination from about 18 to 30 °C. Germination may be substantially reduced if temperatures are kept above 30 °C (figure 6-24).

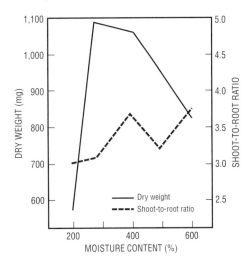

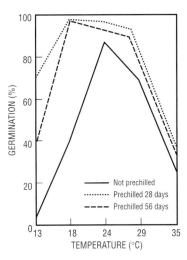

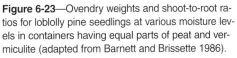

Figure 6-23—Ovendry weights and shoot-to-root ratios for loblolly pine seedlings at various moisture levels in containers having equal parts of peat and vermiculite (adapted from Barnett and Brissette 1986).

Figure 6-24—Effect of temperature on loblolly pine seed germination with and without prechilling (adapted from Barnett 1979b).

Excessively high temperatures affect prechilled seeds more adversely than they affect seeds that are not prechilled (table 6-22). However, exposing seeds to temperatures of 35 °C for part of a day can speed germination without adversely affecting total germination (Dunlap and Barnett 1984b). Container seedlings grow well at day/ night temperature regimes of 23/17 °C, 26/20 °C, and 29/23 °C (Bates 1976). As seedlings mature, moisture and nutrient regimes need to be altered to promote rapid growth, and it is probable that seedling growth could be increased by altering temperature regimes as seedlings mature.

Container seedlings are usually grown in commercial potting mixtures that include balanced combinations of fertilizers. Nutrition can be altered to fit particular needs by blending nutrients with the potting medium or by fertilizing through the irrigation system during seedling growth (Landis and others 1989). When water supply and mineral nutrients are optimal, an increase in carbon dioxide (CO_2) concentration usually produces at least a temporary increase in height, diameter, and dry weight growth without reducing field survival. Enriching the CO_2 levels from ambient concentrations (about 175 ppm) to about 1,000 ppm can increase seedling dry weight by 60% (Kramer 1981, Retzlaff and others 1987).

Mycorrhizae. Container seedlings with mycorrhizae survive and grow better after outplanting than container seedlings without mycorrhizae (table 6-23). There is less mycorrhizal development when container seedlings are fertilized heavily. Although mycorrhizae are most beneficial when container seedlings are grown in the field under conditions of low fertility, even under conditions of high fertility, some strains of mycorrhizae may be particularly effective in increasing survival and early growth (Ruehle and Wells 1984).

Successful inoculation with vegetative mycelium or basidiospores can be accomplished either in the greenhouse or at the planting site. The best inoculation time is at or shortly after seed germination if it is desirable that a specific species or strain of mycorrhiza predominate. In the greenhouse, inoculation can be accomplished by adding duff, humus, infected soil, crushed sporophores, or excised mycorrhizal roots to the growing medium (Ruehle 1980). However, inocula in these forms may not contain the most desirable fungi for loblolly pines or for the planting site, and some may even contain harmful microorganisms and noxious weeds. Container seedlings can be inoculated with pure culture vegetative mycelium or with basidiospores of special strains of mycorrhizal fungi (Marx and others 1982, 1989a, 1989b). For mass production, basidiospores can be blown onto the soil surface, or autoclaved inoculum can be mixed into the rooting medium. Soaking containers and their growth medium in benomyl promotes the development of Pt, probably because benomyl inhibits the growth of fungi antagonistic to Pt (Pawuk and Barnett 1981). During outplanting, thin wafers of peat moss or other materials containing pure culture basidiospores can be inserted in the soil with the containers (Beckjord and others 1984). However, root tips of container seedlings generally become mycorrhizal as they grow into undisturbed soil around the planting hole.

Root development of container seedlings. Root development in most biodegradable containers is satisfactory if reasonable precautions are taken during growing and outplanting. Root constriction is minimized if seedlings are not grown in containers for longer than about 12 to 15 weeks (Barnett 1982b, Barnett and McGilvray 1981). Rigid tube containers severely restrict root development and seedling growth, resulting in lateral roots that often spiral around the taproot or are diverted downward once they reach the sides of a rigid container (Dickerson and McClurkin 1980; figure 6-25). Root spiraling can be prevented by proper container selection or by coating the insides of containers with cupric carbonate ($CuCO_3$). This treatment prevents most first-order lateral roots from growing down the walls of the containers but does not inhibit root growth or mycorrhizal development (Ruehle 1985a). Root growth outside containers is usually controlled naturally by air pruning (that is, growing tips dry and fall off) if air can circulate around the containers. Roots can also be constrained physically. When container seedlings are grown on a copper screen, the copper prevents roots from growing through the drainage holes in the bottoms of containers. This constraint stimulates lateral growth of roots within the container and improved outplanting survival (Barnett and McGilvray 1974).

For the first few months after outplanting, about 75% of lateral root development is from the lower third and about 9% is from the middle third of the root system (Ruehle 1983). Young

Table 6-22—Germination of loblolly pine seeds at various temperature regimes

Seed	% Germination		
	Constant 24 °C	24-35 °C*	Constant 35 °C
Prechilled	88 a	89 a	27 b
Not prechilled	97 a	96 a	46 b

Source: adapted from Barnett and Brissette (1986).

Means within prechilling treatments (across rows) followed by the same letter are not significantly different at the 95% probability level.

* 18 hours at 24 °C and 6 hours at 35 °C.

Table 6-23—Height, root collar diameter, and volume index of container-grown loblolly pine seedlings planted with the ectomycorrhizae *Pisolithus tinctorius* (Pt), *Thelephora terrestris* (Tt), or no ectomycorrhizae (control)

	Treatment = Pt				Treatment = Tt				Treatment = control		
Year	Height (cm)	Root collar diameter (cm)	Volume index* (cm³)	Year	Height (cm)	Root collar diameter (cm)	Volume index* (cm³)	Year	Height (cm)	Root collar diameter (cm)	Volume index* (cm³)
0	12.6	0.20	0.5	0	12.8	0.21	0.6	0	8.1	0.12	0.1
1	22.5	3.50	3.6	1	25.0	4.20	5.4	1	11.5	2.00	0.6
2	55.2	11.30	100.1	2	61.0	12.30	126.6	2	39.6	6.26	23.5
3	107.3	27.20	911.2	3	107.6	26.40	714.4	3	77.3[†]	16.60[†]	251.1[†]

Source: adapted from Ruehle (1982). * Diameter squared times height. † Control means are significantly lower than the Pt or Tt means at the 95% probability level.

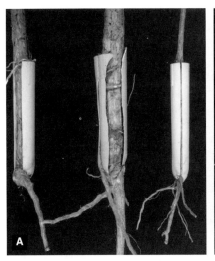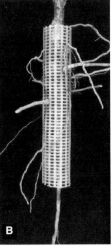

Figure 6-25—Root development of loblolly pines 3 years after outplanting in plastic bullets (**A**) and mesh containers (**B**) (Barnett and Brisette 1986).

bareroot seedlings produce significantly more new laterals, especially from the middle part of the original root system, than container seedlings produce. New roots of bareroot seedlings grow faster, extend farther from the original root system, and have more ectomycorrhizae on egressed laterals than do new roots of container seedlings. Also, the mycorrhizae associated with bareroot seedlings extend to greater distances from the taproot than do those associated with container seedlings (Ruehle 1985b, Tainter and Walstad 1977).

Although it is not now practical to fumigate soil at the planting site, such fumigation can increase both root

growth and the rate and amount of mycorrhizal development on roots of outplanted container seedlings. In one trial, fumigation tripled the number of lateral roots with Pt and increased the total length of lateral roots by 70% after 16 weeks (table 6-24).

Acclimating seedlings for outplanting. Successful establishment of container loblolly pines depends on matching the physiological state of the seedlings to the physical environment. Rapidly growing seedlings normally have succulent shoots. Excessively tall, spindly, actively growing seedlings are very susceptible to moisture or temperature stress following outplanting. Managers can reduce such susceptibility by reducing the photoperiod, moisture, and fertilization where the seedlings are being grown. Most seedlings respond to these changes by ceasing height growth, setting a bud, and beginning stem lignification (Barnett and Brissette 1986). Container stock for late fall or winter outplantings should be conditioned by exposure to natural temperatures and natural day lengths and by cessation of fertilization and irrigation. Lengthening the exposure to natural conditions increases cold hardiness, survival, and growth following outplanting (table 6-25). Water stressing container seedlings for 2 to 3 months before outplanting also reduces shoot and root development and may increase early survival and growth after outplanting (Seiler and Johnson 1985).

Container seedlings grown in greenhouses are taller, more slender, less branched, have poorer root systems, and are generally of lower quality than those grown outdoors (tables 6-26 and 6-27). Variation in amount of wind disturbance and quantity and quality of light causes most

Table 6-24—Development of *Pisolithus tinctorius* (Pt) ectomycorrhizae on lateral roots of container loblolly pine seedlings after 16 weeks in fumigated and nonfumigated soils

Soil Treatment	No. of lateral roots with Pt and total no. of lateral roots	Lateral roots with Pt (%)	Total length lateral roots (cm)	Total no. of Pt ectomycorrhizae	Pt ectomycorrhizae/cm of lateral root*
Fumigated	27.0/28.8	94.3 ± 2.6	936.9 ± 77.5	1,041 ± 24	1.2 ± 0.2
Nonfumigated	9.5/22.6	42.8 ± 14.6	551.4 ± 164.1	131 ± 100	0.5 ± 0.2

Source: adapted from Ruehle (1983).

* Only those lateral roots with Pt ectomycorrhizae were used to calculate this ratio. Values are means and standard deviations based on summation of 4 seedlings per plot for each of 5 replicates.

Table 6-25—Cold hardiness, first-year survival, and height growth of containerized loblolly pines after different lengths of exposure to natural conditions

Weeks of exposure to natural conditions	Cold hardiness (LT_{50})	First-year field survival (%)	Height growth (cm)
0	−4.3 °C	28	3.9
2	−6.4 °C	52	10.1
6	−13.6 °C	76	18.2

Source: adapted from Mexal and Carlson (1982).

All values are significantly different at the 95% probability level according to Duncan's multiple range test.

LT_{50} = temperature at which 50% of the seedlings were killed.

Table 6-26—Morphological characteristics of loblolly pine seedlings from two seed sources grown from seeds for 12 weeks inside a greenhouse or for 12 weeks outdoors

Seed source	Treatment	Stem length (mm)	Stem diameter (mm)	Length-to-diameter ratio	No. lateral branches/tree
Southeastern Georgia	Inside	69.8	1.42	49.0	0.23
	Outdoors	37.4	1.78	21.0	2.62
Southeastern Virginia	Inside	73.7	1.48	49.7	0.11
	Outdoors	41.7	1.85	22.5	2.80

Source: adapted from Boyer and South (1984b).

Each number represents a mean of 100 seedlings. All differences between locations are significant at the 99.99% probability level.

Table 6-27—Effects of shade and full sunlight on development of loblolly pine container seedlings

Developmental characteristic		Seedling age			
		8 wk	12 wk	16 wk	20 wk
Stem diameter (mm)	Shade	1.6	2.2	2.4	2.7
	Sun	2.0	2.5	2.8	3.2
	Percent increase	25.0	14.0	14.0	19.0
Top weight (mg)	Shade	323	716	1,158	1,499
	Sun	451	1,040	1,589	2,043
	Percent increase	40	45	37	36
Root weight (mg)	Shade	76	161	241	282
	Sun	166	337	469	505
	Percent increase	118	109	94	79

Source: adapted from Barnett (1989a).

of these differences. Growing container seedlings outdoors in full sunlight also reduces production costs compared to growing seedlings under partial shade in a lathhouse or other shelter.

Morphological and physiological features of acceptable planting stock. For optimum survival and growth after outplanting, container seedlings should be about 15 to 20 cm tall, with a groundline diameter of about 2.5 mm. In addition, seedlings should have some woody tissue and some secondary needles at planting (Barnett and Brissette 1986). Seedling height is the best single indicator of the quality of container seedlings. It is best not to top prune seedlings to limit their size because such pruning can reduce height growth after outplanting. If top pruning is absolutely necessary, it should be done early. Physiological characteristics (for example, levels of lipids, sugars, N, and chlorophyll) can also be used to identify good planting stock (table 6-28).

Storage and transport of container seedlings.
Seedlings are normally extracted from their containers and boxed at the nursery to reduce weight and save shipping and storage space. Once seedlings have been extracted, both their shoots and roots can be graded. Extracted seedlings can be cold stored using the same procedures as for bareroot stock. However, storage and handling can seriously impair stock quality if extracted seedlings are not completely dormant and cold hardy. If seedlings are to be planted over an extended season, they should not be extracted from their containers until just before shipment. Seedlings can be transported by nonrefrigerated trucks fitted with racks if the planting site is within 1 day's drive. In hot weather, seedlings should be hauled at night. Covered, stake-bodied trucks with air holes for ventilation have been successfully used to move seedlings that were not hardened-off up to 1,000 km. Use of refrigerated trucks is very effective and economical when 500,000 or more seedlings are moved at a time, provided racks are used to protect stacked boxes (Barnett and Brissette 1986, Gates 1974). Storage of seedlings between the nursery and the planting site should be avoided or kept to very short periods, especially if the seedlings are growing actively. If temporary storage is necessary, refrigerated storage is best.

However, seedlings can be stored successfully for short periods in unheated buildings or any shady spot if air circulation is not restricted (Brissette and others 1991).

Outplanting container seedlings. Although container stock is bulkier than bareroot seedlings, the uniform shape of the containers makes hand and machine planting relatively easy. The tools and machines used to plant container seedlings, and the operation of that equipment, are described in detail in Lowman and others (1992). Container seedlings can be hand planted with conventional planting tools such as dibbles or mattocks. Tools specifically designed for planting containers can greatly speed planting, but their effectiveness varies with soil characteristics. These tools force open a space in the soil equal to the size of the container. They work well in loams, sandy loams, and silt loams. However, very sandy soils often cave in before the container can be inserted. In clay soils, the walls of the opening can be compacted, and this compaction can inhibit root penetration. Therefore, it is better to remove soil cores before planting containers in clay soils. Core removal usually increases container seedling growth in soils with bulk densities equal to or greater than 1.6 g/cm^3 (Barnett and Brissette 1986). Table 6-29 gives survival rates for dibble- and core-planted container seedlings.

Most continuous or intermittent machine planters used to plant bareroot seedlings can be used to plant containers with minor modifications in operator technique or seedling holding mechanisms. Self-propelled machines capable of automatically planting various kinds of containers have been developed. They can scarify planting spots while planting 2 to 3 seedlings simultaneously at rates of 1,200 to 3,000 seedlings/hour with 90% correct planting (Kohonen 1982, Pease 1980, Walters and Silversides 1979).

Both machine-planted and hand-planted seedlings should be planted deep enough so that the container top is covered with about 1 cm of soil. Planting at this depth eliminates rapid drying in the rooting zone caused by wicking from the container. It should also prevent frost heaving of containers planted in the fall (Walker and Johnson 1980). As with bareroot seedlings, container stock should not be set deeper than half the height of the seedlings (see discussion under bareroot planting techniques).

Table 6-28—Ranges of physiological and morphological characteristics associated with acceptable field success of container grown loblolly pines

Physiological characteristic – Shoot –		Physiological characteristic – Root –		Morphological characteristic	
Characteristic	Range	Characteristic	Range	Characteristic	Range
Lipids (%)	8.6 – 12.6	Lipids (%)	4.2 – 4.9	Height (mm)	90 – 318
Total sugars (%)	1.5 – 2.2	Total sugars (%)	1.9 – 2.7	Shoot diameter (mm)	1.5 – 3.0
Reducing sugars (%)	0.9 – 1.6	Reducing sugars (%)	0.8 – 1.4	Shoot weight (mg)	228 – 1,244
Nitrogen (%)	2.3 – 3.3	Nitrogen (%)	1.9 – 2.4	Root weight (mg)	90 – 189
Chlorophyll (mg/g)	0.9 – 1.7			Shoot/root ratio	2.0 – 6.7

Source: adapted from Barnett (1984a).

Table 6-29—Survival of dibble- and core-planted loblolly pine container seedlings on three soils

Soil type		% Survival	
		At 2 months	At 18 months
Beauregard series (silt loam)	Dibbled	86 ab	74 ab
	Cored	90 ab	76 a
Wrightsville series (heavy silt loam)	Dibbled	85 ab	64 b
	Cored	93 a	80 a
Ruston series (sandy loam)	Dibbled	83 bc	73 ac
	Cored	70 c	63 b

Source: adapted from Barnett and Brissette (1986).

Numbers within columns followed by the same letter are not significantly different at the 95% confidence level.

Planting time. Container seedlings can be planted year-round throughout most of loblolly pine's natural range. From a practical standpoint, commercial planting is quite feasible during 9 to 10 months of the year, particularly if summer rains are frequent. Planting should not be done during droughts or hard freezes. Seeds can be sown on demand to produce acceptable planting stock at any time of the year. Thus, if a bareroot or container planting is unsuccessful, an area can be replanted with container seedlings within 3 months, rather than having to wait an entire year, which often requires that the site be prepared again to destroy new competing vegetation.

Survival and early growth of seedlings. Container seedlings survive and grow well on a wide range of sites throughout the South when planted in any season. However, field performance is affected by type of container and type of growing medium, degree of site preparation prior to outplanting, and site quality (Barnett 1989b). Growing seedlings in a peat or peat-vermiculite medium produces stock capable of good survival and growth during the first few years after outplanting. Survival of 8- to 16-week-old container seedlings is generally as good as or better than that of 1 + 0 bareroot stock even though the container seedlings are more juvenile than the bareroot seedlings. Even container seedlings as short as 5 cm or taller than 45 cm can survive when outplanted during most periods of the year (Anderson and others 1984, Dickerson 1974, Goodwin 1974). Trees can grow to 2.4 m in height within 2 years after summer planting (Aycock 1974). Early growth of container stock is generally faster than that of bareroot seedlings (table 6-30). In the first year, container seedlings planted in the late spring or early summer can grow to sizes comparable to those at-

Table 6-30—Survival and growth comparison of 11-week-old, loblolly pine, container seedlings planted in July and 1+0 bareroot seedlings planted the following winter

Type of stock	First season		Second season		Third season	
	Survival %	Height (m)	Survival %	Height (m)	Survival %	Height (m)
11-week container seedlings	87	0.5	85	1.3	85	2.6
1+0 seedlings	89	0.4	89	1.1	89	2.3

Source: adapted from Goodwin (1976).

Values are for the end of the seasons.

tained by bareroot seedlings planted during the preceding winter (Barnett and Brissette 1986).

Container stock is often reserved for the toughest planting sites (for example, droughty, wet, and sticky clay soils), which are hard to plant with bareroot stock or where survival of bareroot seedlings is generally low. Even container stock should not be planted in excessively wet soils. However, survival of container seedlings may be up to 20% greater than that of bareroot seedlings on flatwoods or floodplain sites once the water table recedes. Such an increase in survival could make replanting unnecessary, and so justify use of container stock (Yeiser and Paschke 1987). Under droughty conditions, or when soil moisture at planting time is less than 13% (on a dry weight basis), container stock survives and grows better than bareroot stock (Amidon and others 1982, South and Barnett 1986). The availability of container stock gives managers the flexibility to plant throughout the year, on short notice, and on a wide variety of sites.

Artificial Regeneration of Loblolly Pine by Direct Seeding

Direct seeding is the oldest method of artificial regeneration. It is a versatile technique that can be used on many sites, but it is most valuable where a suitable natural seed source is not available or where access, terrain, or soil conditions make planting difficult and expensive (Mann 1966). Direct seeding is a practical way to convert low-grade hardwood stands to loblolly pine, even on the Cumberland Plateau and Highland Rim of Tennessee and northern Alabama (Russell and Mignery 1968). Since 1920, more than 2 million ha in the South have been successfully regenerated with southern pines by direct seeding (Campbell 1976, Mergen and others 1981). During the two planting seasons between 1958 and 1960, more than 50,000 ha of loblolly and slash pines were direct seeded in Louisiana alone (Mann 1960). In one case, more than 6,500 ha in central Louisiana were successfully seeded to loblolly (Mann and Burkhalter 1961).

Although direct seeding is simple and easy, it may fail to produce an acceptable stand of seedlings. The greatest environmental obstacle to successful regeneration is dry weather during the first year after germination, which may result in as little as 20 to 30% seedling survival. Poor judgment is usually the overriding cause of direct-seeding failures. Some of the most common mistakes are inadequately preparing sites, sowing poor-quality seeds, sowing too few seeds, sowing too early or too late in the year, and seeding sites where plantings have failed repeatedly (Campbell 1982a, 1982b). Hazel and others (1989) found the cost of direct seeding North Carolina Piedmont sites (exclusive of site prepartion) to be $25/ha for hand-casting and $44/ha for mechanical sowing. Direct seeding can cost only half as much as planting, but direct seeding can be more expensive than planting if the site has to be seeded a second time.

Site Selection

Possible seeding sites should be evaluated individually. Most areas can be seeded successfully, but seeding is inappropriate on the following kinds of sites (Campbell 1982a, 1982b):

- Areas subjected to heavy grazing, unless they can be protected for 2 to 3 years during seedling establishment.

- Low, poorly drained sites that are likely to be covered with standing water for 1 or more weeks between February and April.

- Deep, upland sands that dry out too rapidly to permit germination (these soils may also crust over, preventing penetration by the radicle even when seeds germinate).

- Highly erodible soils and steep slopes where seeds are likely to be displaced by water movement.

Seedbed Preparation

Seeds must be in contact with mineral soil for effective germination and seedling establishment. Materials such as ground litter, grass, or sod hinder germination. Open grasslands, low brush, overstory hardwoods, and combinations of brush and overstory hardwoods are common conditions that must be altered prior to direct seeding. Prescribed burning can prepare an excellent environment for direct seeding in cut-over areas. For direct seeding to be successful following burning, only sites where planting would be highly successful should be seeded (Williston and Cox 1969). Burning should be done as soon after harvest as possible. Many grasslands can easily be site-prepared by burning, preferably in midsummer. Burning often destroys enough of the accumulated duff so that germinating seeds can reach mineral soil. Although growing-season burning is best, even dormant-season burns are helpful. In the lower Piedmont of Georgia, stocking was almost doubled when burning was done 1 year after harvesting rather than 2 years after harvesting (McNab 1976).

Fire can effectively prepare some areas covered with standing hardwoods. However, burning usually must be combined with overstory removal and/or with various mechanical or chemical treatments to expose enough mineral soil for adequate seed germination. For example, a site with dense, low brush and herbaceous vegetation that was aerially sprayed with herbicide in May, then burned in September and direct seeded in February, produced an excellent stand of loblolly pine (Campbell 1986). Heavy sod, such as that formed by carpetgrass (*Axonopus affinis* Chase), does not burn sufficiently to expose mineral soil, so sites with heavy sod must be disked or furrowed before seeds are sown. Disking a site once before sowing seeds can be expected to increase stocking and early height growth of seedlings whether fire is used or not (Derr and Mann 1971, Lohrey 1974). The cost of disking is reduced if disking is in strips 1.8 to 2.4 m wide and spaced 2.4 m apart. Soil can also be disked into beds to increase drainage on wet areas. Disked soils should be permitted to settle somewhat before seeds are sown, so that seeds are not covered by excess settling soil. In addition, seeding 6 months after seedbed preparation usually permits adequate regrowth of native vegetation to hide some seeds from predators and shade new germinants.

Seed Handling Before Direct Seeding

For direct seeding to be successful, sound seeds should be stored properly, prechilled, and treated with repellents. Seeds are a relatively inexpensive part of the regeneration process, so it is cost effective to use the best available. Seedlots should be 95% pure and have a germination capacity of 80% or more. Prechilling usually increases both total germination and speed of germination under a wide range of environmental conditions (table 6-31). Sowing prechilled seeds in the spring minimizes the time of exposure to predators, maximizes germination during optimum weather conditions, and permits seedlings to grow sufficiently long so that they develop good root systems before hot, dry, summer weather begins.

Chemical treatments can provide seeds with a high degree of protection from most seed-eating birds, small mammals, and troublesome insects. Seeds are coated with a mixture of the bird repellent thiram, the insect repellent endrin, and a latex sticker. Aluminum powder is added as a final ingredient to hasten drying. Normally, seeds are treated with repellents just before sowing to avoid any risk of loss of viability. Repellent-treated seeds weigh about 35% more than untreated seeds (Derr 1963, Mann and Derr 1966, Royall and Ferguson 1962). About 20 to 50% of treated seeds can be expected to germinate and grow. Seedings are rarely successful without this critical chemical protection (Derr and Mann 1971).

Table 6-31—Initial stocking of seedlings from prechilled and unchilled loblolly pine seeds sown at the rate of 1.1 kg/ha

Seedbed condition	Seed treatment	No. seedlings/ha	Increase due to prechilling (%)
Heavy grass	Prechilled	1,280	367
	Unchilled	274	
Light grass	Prechilled	9,059	22
	Unchilled	7,413	
Disked	Prechilled	3,845	460
	Unchilled	687	
Burned and disked	Prechilled	5,765	75
	Unchilled	3,296	
All seedbeds	Prechilled	4,986	71
	Unchilled	2,918	

Source: adapted from Derr and Mann (1971).

Placing Seeds

Seeds can be broadcast or placed in rows or spots by hand or with various kinds of equipment (Larson and Hallman 1980). Broadcast seeding is designed to spread seeds uniformly throughout the seeding area. When small areas are being seeded, it is usually most efficient and economical to use hand-operated broadcast seeders. On very small and irregular areas, seeds can be scattered efficiently by hand. One person using a cyclone seeder can seed up to 5 ha/day on a relatively level site (Campbell 1982a, 1982b). Mechanical broadcast seeders permit rapid seeding of wide strips on sites accessible to ground vehicles. They can be mounted on crawler tractors for seeding during site preparation even on rough terrain. Other vehicles that can pull seeding machines include rubber-tired skidders, trucks, and all-terrain vehicles. It is often most efficient to seed blocks of 200 ha or more by helicopter or with fixed-wing aircraft (Derr and Mann 1971). One aircraft can seed as many as 1,200 ha at one time. Even blocks as small as 15 ha can be direct seeded effectively by air (Campbell 1986). The combination of carefully flagged lines and well-calibrated seeders can result in excellent and uniform distribution of seeds.

Row seeding may be preferred over broadcast seeding because it uses a limited quantity of seeds efficiently, achieves more precise spacing, and facilitates subsequent mechanical harvesting. On well-prepared sites, seeds can be dropped by hand while walking along furrows or planned courses. For best results, seeds should be spaced 30 to 60 cm apart within the rows. The standard for between-row spacing is 3 m, but it may vary depending upon objectives. Row seeding requires fewer seeds than broadcast seeding and helps offset the higher application costs of row seeding.

Several types of precision mechanical seeders are available to speed row seeding. Seeds can be dropped in rows on previously prepared ground, or seedbed preparation (disking narrow strips, plowing shallow furrows, or building low beds) and seeding can be combined. Furrow seeders can seed about 6 ha/day and are effective on light- to medium-textured soils with good internal drainage. Furrow seeders should not be used on sites with poor surface drainage because furrowing increases the probability of prolonged flooding (Lohrey and Jones 1983). Row seeders with rotating disks that throw up seedbeds 7 to 15 cm high are effective on low, poorly drained sites because the slightly elevated seedbed provides better aeration than the surrounding soil (Derr and Mann 1971).

Aerial row seeding is feasible, but generally not practical or economical. An aerial, multiple-row seeder, operating from a helicopter at an altitude of 8 m, seeded relatively straight rows without reducing germination. Seeds were coated with clay (to make their shape uniform and to improve their aerodynamics) and ejected with an initial downward velocity of 100 km/h (Barnett and Chappell 1975).

Spot seeding is the slowest and most labor-intensive method of direct seeding but is appropriate for owners of small tracts because it requires little in the way of tools or equipment. Where sod or surface litter occupies the drop site, a spot should be cleared with the foot, a hoe, or other implement. Deep hardwood leaf litter should be pushed far away so that it will not blow back onto the spot. Once mineral soil is exposed, 5 to 8 seeds are dropped in a cluster and are pressed gently into the surface soil with the foot. This technique requires 7 to 15 person-hours/ha, depending on site conditions and spacing requirements (Garner 1974). Seeding 2,500 spots/ha produces an acceptable stand under average conditions. When moisture is not severely limiting, spot seeding under hardwoods may be successful. Hardwood overstories seem to improve germination by retarding evaporation from surface soil (Campbell 1974).

Whether the seeds are placed by hand or by machine, they should be pressed lightly into the soil surface. On sloping, sandy, or dry sites, germination is promoted by covering seeds with about 0.5 cm of soil. Germination of seeds covered with more than 1.3 cm of soil is much lower than that of lightly covered seeds or of seeds pressed into the surface soil. Germination of seeds left on the surface is generally somewhat reduced (Campbell 1982a, 1982b; table 6-32).

Table 6-32—Effect of soil type and depth of soil cover on loblolly pine seeding success 1 year after sowing in December

Sowing treatment	Percentage of seeds that became live seedlings			
	Norfolk FSL	Lakeland LS	Red Bay SL	All sites
Placed on soil surface	3.9	1.4	9.3	4.60
Pressed into surface	16.1	7.9	16.4	14.10
0.6 cm deep	5.7	2.1	12.5	6.50
1.3 cm deep	3.8	2.5	1.4	2.90
1.9 cm deep	0.8	0.7	0.5	0.70
2.5 cm deep	0.2	0.4	0.5	0.30
5.1 cm deep	0.0	0.0	0.2	0.04

Source: adapted from Hodgkins (1966).

FSL = fine, sandy loam, LS = loamy sand, SL = sandy loam.

Prechilled, repellent-coated seeds should be sown in late winter or early spring. Predation of fall-sown seeds may be greater due to erosion of their repellent coating over time. Fall germinants may also suffer some freeze damage. The best time for sowing varies by latitude. Sowing is earliest in the South or along the eastern seaboard and latest inland or farther north. In the lower Piedmont of Georgia, February or March sowing of prechilled seeds resulted in the most prompt germination. Seeds that were not prechilled germinated well only when sown in February, while germination was zero for April or May sowings (Hatchell 1966).

Acceptable sowing rates can vary from fewer than 3,700 to 62,000 seeds/ha depending on site characteristics, environmental conditions, and dispersal methods. Regular checks must be made if the sowing rate is based on seed weight, because the number of seeds per kilogram can vary from 27,000 to 59,000, depending on year and seedlot. If seed weight is not accounted for, conservative seeding rates of 1.12 kg/ha for broadcast seeding, 0.70 kg/ha for strip disk seeding, 0.44 kg/ha for row seeding (1.8 m apart), and 0.36 kg/ha for spot seeding have been suggested (Derr and Mann 1971). Other options are listed in table 6-33.

Table 6-33—Recommended sowing rates for loblolly pine, assuming 100%-sound, prechilled, and repellent-coated seeds

Seeding method	Seeding rate	
	No. of seeds/ha	kg/ha
Broadcast	29,520	0.84
Rows 3 m apart, 0.6-m spacing between rows	5,300	0.16
Spots spaced 1.8 by 3.0 m, 5 seeds/spot	9,000	0.26

Source: adapted from Campbell (1982b).

Even under drought conditions, 20 to 30% of the germinants usually survive, indicating how hardy these new trees are. If adverse weather is anticipated, it is best to sow enough seeds to establish a stand even if 80% of the seedlings are lost in the first year (Mann 1968). Increased seeding rates cannot substitute for site preparation, coating seeds with repellents, or high seed quality. Nevertheless, if there is any doubt about the seeding rate, it is better to err on the high side and to produce an excess of seedlings than to risk failure through understocking.

Estimating Seedling Establishment and Early Survival

Because seeds and newly germinated seedlings are small, it is necessary to examine systematic sample plots carefully to accurately determine regeneration success following direct seeding. A cursory examination can easily lead to an erroneous conclusion that a seeding failed. Unnecessary reseeding is costly and can result in serious overstocking.

At least two seedling inventories should be made during the first year. One should take place at the beginning of summer when germination is completed, and a second, at the end of the first growing season when danger of mortality from drought is past. The difference between the two inventories indicates losses during the first summer (Derr and Mann 1971). Campbell (1982a, 1982b) recommends four inventories for careful evaluation of seed germination and seedling development during the first critical year. The first inventory, which should be made about 1 week after sowing, determines how successfully the seed repellent is for controlling predators. If predation is high, adjustments should be made in the repellent coating for other seedings, and reseeding should be considered. A second inventory late in the germination period and a third inventory after germination is complete provide early notice of failure caused by extreme weather or loss of new germinants to predators such as ants, crickets, or rabbits (see chapter 10). Finally, a detailed inventory of seedling establishment is made after one complete growing season. Losses after the

first year are usually low (Derr and Mann 1971). Few, if any, viable ungerminated loblolly pine seeds survive longer than one growing season (Barnett and McGilvray 1991).

Each sowing method requires a different inventorying technique, but a minimum of 25 sample plots should be checked and projected to a per-hectare basis, even if only a few hectares were seeded. Circular plots are best for evaluating broadcast seeding. Row seeding is inventoried by examining segments of rows and projecting to a per-hectare basis. Spot seeding is inventoried by examining a specific number of spots for live seedlings and projecting to a per-hectare basis (Derr and Mann 1971).

It is desirable that there be at least 2,500 seedlings/ha on broadcast-seeded areas after one growing season and that at least 60% of sample plots be stocked at that time. Row-stocked areas should have 3,700 seedlings/ha and 50% stocking. In spot-seeded areas, a minimum of 1,360 spots/ha should have 1 or more seedlings (Campbell 1982a, 1982b). Spot-seeded trees can be expected to grow well, express height dominance early, and form acceptable stands without precommercial thinning. Sowing 5 to 7 seeds per spot normally results in 3 or fewer trees/spot at age 5. There is no need to thin spots to a single loblolly pine seedling unless 5 or more trees are growing in a clump at age 5. Once a dominant tree attains a height advantage of at least 30 cm, it maintains its superiority. However, diameter growth of even the largest tree can be reduced when there are several trees on a spot (Campbell 1981, Lohrey 1970, Russell 1974). Seeded loblolly pines should be released from overtopping hardwoods early in the first growing season if maximum growth is to be obtained. According to Hatchell (1964), however, release can be delayed for as long as 4 years without seriously affecting stocking.

The most important factor in seedling establishment is root growth and development. Soil texture affects root development significantly. Taproots of direct-seeded loblolly pines can grow to more than 25 cm during the first 100 days, depending on soil texture (table 6-34). Total root length is about twice the taproot length. By the time seedlings are 2 months old, all have some native mycorrhizal fungi.

Table 6-34—Average taproot length, total root length, and number of lateral roots for loblolly seedlings 30, 60, and 100 days old for soils with three different textures

Seedling age (days)	Soil texture	Taproot length (cm)	Total root length (cm)	No. of lateral roots
30	Sand	7.1	8.1	0.8
	Loam	11.7	21.3	6.2
	Clay	7.4	20.1	7.5
60	Sand	16.0	26.9	5.9
	Loam	14.7	35.1	13.0
	Clay	14.2	38.9	12.7
100	Sand	19.6	33.0	10.7
	Loam	23.6	52.3	17.4
	Clay	25.9	54.6	20.0

Source: adapted from Jorgensen (1968).

Comparison of Direct Seeding and Planting

Under favorable conditions, stocking percentage in direct-seeded stands is about the same as that in planted stands. Where moisture is deficient and competition with herbaceous vegetation is substantial, direct seeding yields lower stocking than does planting (Little 1973). Because planted seedlings are 1 year old when outplanted, they are 1 year's growth larger than seedlings produced by direct seeding for at least the first several years in the field (Campbell and Mann 1973, Dierauf and others 1971, Lohrey 1973). On the Highland Rim of Tennessee and the Piedmont of Virginia, seeded trees were as much as 1 to 1.5 m shorter than planted trees by ages 5 to 8. This difference equates to about 2 years of lost growth (Dierauf 1975, Thor and Huffman 1969). Fifty-seven percent of the trees in a 9-year-old planted stand in central Louisiana were 10 cm or greater in dbh. In contrast, only 6% of the trees in a direct-seeded stand were that large (table 6-35). However, dominant, well-spaced, direct-seeded trees averaged 5.9 m in height and 8.9 cm in dbh.

The early growth loss associated with direct seeding does not necessarily imply reduced yield at rotation age. After 20 years of growth on the lower Coastal Plain of Louisiana, the total volumes of planted and direct-seeded loblolly pines were not significantly different. However, planted trees were fewer in number, larger in average diameter, and more uniformly spaced (Campbell 1985).

Direct-seeded seedlings, like those naturally regenerated, do not have the distorted taproots, intertwined lateral roots, and single-plane root development characteristic of planted seedlings (Harrington and others 1987, Little and Somes 1964). Planted trees also have fewer small first-order lateral roots than do trees grown from seeds, and they exhibit greater spiraling and bending of large first-order lateral roots. In addition, the uppermost lateral roots of planted trees are deeper than those of trees grown from seeds (Harrington and others 1989). The effect that root distortion may have on the relative growth rates of planted versus seeded trees is unknown. However, young trees grown from seeds have superior root distribution and thus are more windfirm than young planted trees.

Table 6-35—Number of trees per hectare in 9-year-old strip-seeded and 9-year-old planted loblolly pine stands in central Louisiana

Dbh class (cm)	Stocking (no./ha)	
	Seeded	Planted
< 2.5	1,211	0
2.5	2,644	27
5.0	2,528	240
7.5	1,762	665
10.0	445	904
12.5	57	311
15.0	7	12
Total	8,654	2,031

Source: adapted from Hatchell (1961).

Establishing Loblolly Pine in Tension Zones

Loblolly pine is an extremely diverse species capable of being artificially regenerated and of growing rapidly on a wide range of sites—from wet to dry, warm to cold, and fertile to infertile—outside of its natural range. For example, survival and height growth of 6-year-old loblolly seedlings planted on 8 Florida sites south of the natural range of the species were as good as that of other native and exotic pines (Bethune 1963). At other extremes, loblolly pines survive and grow well on Coastal Plain sites as far north as southern Illinois and at elevations up to 520 m in northern Arkansas.

In Oklahoma, loblolly pine is native only to Coastal Plain sites in the extreme southeastern corner of the state. If adequate moisture is available during the first growing season, stands can be established successfully in much of the 2.5-million-ha hilly Cross Timbers region of eastern Oklahoma. First-year survival of planted 1+0 stock was 97% during a year when precipitation was about 25 cm greater than normal and was 67% when rainfall was normal. Removal of competing vegetation (primarily post and blackjack oaks) is essential to good survival. Once established, seedlings are quite resistant to poor moisture conditions. Planted loblolly pines perform best on sites that are level to gently sloping, have coarse-textured soil, and have a fairly deep A horizon (Lantz 1975, Osterhaus and Lantz 1978, Woods and others 1988).

Loblolly pines have also survived and grown on both droughty and wet sites in the northern post oak belt of Texas, which lies between the pine–mixed hardwood forest type to the east and the blackland prairie soils to the west. Climatic and edaphic factors, relating directly or indirectly to the amount of available moisture, account for only about 17% of height growth variation (Hansen and Bilan 1989).

Many low-quality hardwood stands of the Alabama, Tennessee, and Georgia highlands have been converted to loblolly pines. Conversion has been reasonably successful on most medium and good sites. Best results are achieved where hardwoods are controlled completely and where there is intensive site preparation. Where utilization of hardwoods is almost complete, as in shearing and whole-tree chipping, loblolly can be introduced at very low cost (McGee 1980). On poor sites, increased growth may not offset the cost of site preparation, but on good sites, only very intensive preparation prevents new hardwood sprouts from retarding pine growth seriously (McGee 1982).

Summary

Successful artificial regeneration of loblolly pines requires systematic planning and a great deal of organization. Nursery and field procedures must be coordinated to provide an environment conducive to rapid seedling development. Seed collection, seed processing, nursery activities, and outplanting or direct seeding must fit into a careful scheme that includes evaluation of site quality, site preparation options, and matching seedlings to a specific environment. Monetary benefits to society from past investments in loblolly pine regeneration have been substantial. Foster (1982) estimated that for every $100 of public monies spent to regenerate pines, society will benefit from a $3,800 reduction in the total price of the wood products it consumes in the year 2020—a compound rate of return that exceeds 10% after inflation. However, regeneration costs and investment schedules must be carefully analyzed over an entire rotation based on site productivity and expected product values. The best sites should be regenerated first because they are most likely to generate sufficient revenue to offset the high costs of management (Anderson and Guttenberg 1971, Weaver and Osterhaus 1976).

Over 95% of the more than 1.2 billion loblolly seedlings produced annually are grown in bareroot nurseries. Seed preparation and the nursery sowing process are the most important aspects of loblolly seedling production. Loblolly seeds need presowing treatments to stimulate germination and to protect them from birds and rodents. Seeds should be sown systematically in nurseries and should be in contact with mineral soil. They should be covered with a nonphytotoxic mulch that promotes germination and protects both the seeds and germinating seedlings. The timing of nursery sowing is critical; it affects germination, incidence of disease, and possible losses from bad weather. The entire operation must be completed within about 5 working days. Sowing the correct number of seeds per unit area of seedbed requires precise information about seed quality and a knowledge of many site and environmental factors, including soils, pests, and climatic conditions. To be economical, a bareroot nursery must produce at least 15 million seedlings/year.

The combination of lower seedbed density and an earlier sowing date results in larger, heavier seedlings of higher quality. Uniformity of seed emergence, fertilization, concentration of mycorrhizae, irrigation, and pruning can also substantially affect the production of high-quality seedlings. Stems of nursery seedlings should be 20 to 25 cm long by early September. Mycorrhizal development should be noticeable by midsummer, and fruiting bodies should appear in late fall. Some seedlings may develop terminal buds in August, others during the fall, and some may not have set buds even by lifting time. Root and top pruning retard growth and can be employed to develop uniform seedlings. Tops should be pruned only when all other treatments fail to maintain appropriate shoot growth. Root growth potential (potential for early, rapid root growth after outplanting) is the best comprehensive measurement of seedling quality.

Loblolly seedlings are normally packaged in bales or polyethylene-lined kraft paper bags at a rate of 500 to 2,000/container. Frequently used packing media include moss, wood fiber, and wood shavings. Treating root systems with clay slurry can provide superior field survival and is easily mechanized. For best survival, seedlings should be planted shortly after lifting unless weather conditions are severe. If seedlings must be stored, they should be kept at a temperature of 1 to 4 °C. Refrigerated storage is effective for up to 4 months. Without refrigeration, seedlings can usually be stored satisfactorily for 2 to 3 weeks. Freezing or heating of packaged seedlings usually reduces seedling survival.

Planting can be done manually or by machine. Survival can be excellent if seedlings are of high quality and if the roots are firmly packed in moist soil. Planting during dry periods increases mortality and greatly increases the probability of plantation failure. Planting permits the efficient use of genetically improved stock and good control of initial stocking. It also makes thinning and harvesting easier and minimizes the need for precommercial thinning.

Growing container seedlings in small numbers is more expensive than expanding production of bareroot seedlings in an established nursery. However, if new nurseries must be established, the cost of producing container stock is similar to the cost of producing bareroot stock when seedlings are produced in quantities of 3 million or more. Container seedlings can be produced at any time of the year to meet unexpected demands or to extend the planting season so that dry sites and wetlands can be regenerated during optimum periods. Survival rates of container seedlings are often higher than those of bareroot seedlings.

Direct seeding is much less expensive than planting and is a quick and reliable method of regenerating large areas following wildfire or where terrain is difficult to plant. Failures of regeneration are more common with direct seeding than with planting, but direct seeding may be the best or only viable option for regenerating areas of rough mine spoils, very rocky sites, or other inhospitable places.

Research Needs

▓ Improved techniques for rapid, nondestructive cone collection.

▓ Cost-effective technology to improve nursery management and seedling vigor, including

1. Better equipment for nursery site preparation, bed construction, cultural treatment, and seedling lifting to minimize soil compaction and damage to growing seedlings.

2. Improved techniques for separate management of seedlings grown from different size seeds.

3. Improved precision seeders.

4. Machinery for box-pruning to provide each seedling with equal growing space.

5. Wide-bed (15 m or more) management to maximize nursery space and new technology and to minimize labor.

6. A completely mechanized lifting and baling system.

7. Minimum chemical use.

8. Improved hygroscopic or other root protective substances to provide greater latitude for handling seedlings without excess mortality.

9. Better information on seedling storage time/temperature relationships and lifting date/storability relationships and their effects on field performance.

10. Better assessment of the economical significance of ethylene production in storage containers on outplanting success of seedlings.

▓ An accurate test of seedling quality to enhance artificial regeneration.

▓ Quantification of the effects of root deformation at planting on early survival and on long-term growth.

▓ Better understanding of the potential of mycorrhizal associations, including nitrogen–carbohydrate interactions, growth factors stimulating attraction and invasion of mycorrhizal fungi, and genetic manipulation of fungi.

▓ Detailed computerized comparisons of nursery practices and field performance to selectively use genetically improved seedlings to the best advantages.

▓ Techniques to successfully interplant poorly stocked stands, especially with superior container stock, as soon as possible after plantation failures are known.

▓ Techniques to grow planted loblolly pines mixed with artificially regenerated, or naturally regenerated, hardwoods.

▓ Techniques to optimize the different stages of container seedling development under controlled conditions by integrating temperature, moisture, and nutrient regimes.

Literature Cited

Abbott H, Fitch SD. 1977. Forest nursery practices in the United States. Journal of Forestry 75(3):141–145.

Adams RE. 1975. Effect of repeated drying and rewetting on laboratory germination of stratified loblolly pine seed. Forest Science 21(1):61–62.

Adams RE, Feret PP. 1976. Effect of desiccation on germination of stratified loblolly pine seeds. Virginia Journal of Science 27(2):53.

AAN [American Association of Nurserymen]. 1987. Directory of forest tree nurseries in the United States. [Place of publication unknown]: American Association of Nurserymen. 35 p.

Amidon TE, Barnett JP, Gallagher HP, McGilvray JM. 1982. A field test of containerized seedlings under drought conditions. In: Proceedings, Southern Containerized Forest Tree Seedling Conference; 1981 August 25–27; Savannah, GA. Gen. Tech. Rep. SO-37. New Orleans:U.S. Department of Agriculture,

Forest Service, Southern Forest Experiment Station: 139–144.

Anderson RL, Knighten JL, Powers HR Jr. 1984. Field survival of loblolly and slash pine seedlings grown in trays and Ray Leach containers. Tree Planters' Notes 35(2):3–4.

Anderson WC, Guttenberg S. 1971. Investor's guide to converting southern oak–pine types. Res. Pap. SO-72. New Orleans: USDA Forest Service, Southern Forest Experiment Station. 10 p.

Anonymous. 1987. Seedlings available from state nurseries. Forest Farmer 47(1):19–23.

AOSA [Association of Official Seed Analysts]. 1987. Rules for testing seeds. Journal of Seed Technology 6(2):114.

Aycock O. 1974. Field performance of containerized seedlings in the Southern Region, USDA Forest Service. In: Proceedings, North American Containerized Forest Tree Seedling Symposium; 1974 August 2629; Denver, CO. Denver, CO: Great Plains

Agricultural Council: (68): 321–323.

Baldwin BL. 1989. Making every tree count, secrets of seedling survival. In: Proceedings, 5th Biennial Southern Silvicultural Research Conference; 1988 November 1–3; Memphis, TN. Gen. Tech. Rep. SO-74. New Orleans: USDA Forest Service, Southern Forest Experiment Station: 187–189.

Balmer WE, Space JC. 1976. Probability tables for containerized seedlings. Atlanta: USDA Forest Service, Southern Region, State & Private Forestry. 27 p.

Balmer WE, Williston HL. 1974. Guide for planting southern pines. Atlanta: USDA Forest Service, Southern Area, State and Private Forestry. 17 p.

Barber JC, VanHaverbeke DF. 1961. Growth of outstanding nursery of seedlings of *Pinus elliottii* Engelm. and *Pinus taeda* L. Sta. Pap. 126. Asheville, NC: USDA Forest Service, Southeastern Forest Experiment Station. 12 p.

Barden CJ, Feret PP, Kreh RE. 1987. Root growth potential and outplanting performance of loblolly pine seedlings raised at 2 nurseries. In: Proceedings, 4th Biennial Southern Silvicultural Research Conference; 1986 November 4–6; Atlanta, GA. Gen. Tech. Rep. SE-42. Asheville, NC: USDA Forest Service, Southeastern Forest Experiment Station: 237–244.

Barnett JP. 1972. Southern pine seeds germinate after forty years' storage. Journal Forestry 70(10):629.

Barnett JP. 1974a. Low temperatures reduce storability of loblolly pine seeds at high moisture contents. Tree Planters' Notes 25(2): 28-29.

Barnett JP. 1974b. Growing containerized southern pines. In: Proceedings, North American Containerized Forest Tree Seedling Symposium; 1974 August 26–29; Denver, CO. [Place of publication unknown]: Great Plains Agricultural Council Publication. 68:124–128.

Barnett JP. 1975. Containerized pine seedlings thrive in wood-fiber blocks. Tree Planters' Notes 26(2):13, 20–21.

Barnett JP. 1976. Collecting and processing methods affect pine seed germinability. In: Lantz CW, ed. Proceedings, Southeastern Nurserymen's Conference; 1976 August 17–19; Mobile, AL. Atlanta: USDA Forest Service, Southern Region, State and Private Forestry: 70–72.

Barnett JP. 1977. Effects of soil wetting agent concentration on southern pine seed germination. Southern Journal of Applied Forestry 1(3):14–15.

Barnett JP. 1978. Covering affects container germination of southern pine seeds. Tree Planters' Notes 29(2):13–15.

Barnett JP. 1979a. An easy way to measure cone specific gravity. In: Proceedings, seed collection workshop; 1979 May 16–18; [Location unknown]. Tech. Pub. SA-TP 8. Atlanta: USDA Forest Service, Southern Region, State and Private Forestry: 21–23.

Barnett JP. 1979b. Germination temperatures for container culture of southern pines. Southern Journal of Applied Forestry 3(1):13–14.

Barnett JP. 1980. Density and age affect performance of containerized loblolly pine seedlings. Res. Note SO-256. New Orleans: USDA Forest Service, Southern Forest Experiment Station. 5 p.

Barnett JP. 1981. Imbibition temperatures affect seed moisture uptake, germination, and seedling development. In: Proceedings, 1st Biennial Southern Silvicultural Research Conference; 1980 November 6–7; Atlanta, GA. Gen. Tech. Rep. SO-34. New Orleans: USDA Forest Service, Southern Forest Experiment Station: 41–45.

Barnett JP. 1982a. Freeze- and kiln-drying of slash pine cones and seeds. In: Proceedings, 2nd Biennial Southern Silvicultural Research Conference; 1982 November 4–5; Atlanta, GA. Gen. Tech. Rep. SE-24. Asheville, NC: USDA Forest Service, Southeastern Forest Experiment Station: 387–389.

Barnett JP. 1982b. Producing plantable containerized seedlings — a status report. In: Proceedings, Workshop on Regeneration

of Southern Pines; 1982 October 19–21; Woodworth, LA. Long Beach, MS: Forestry and Harvesting Training Center, University of Mississippi, Gulf Park: 103–149.

Barnett JP. 1983a. Optimizing nursery germination by fluid drilling and other techniques. In: Proceedings, 1982 Southern Nursery Conferences; 1982 August 9–12; Oklahoma City, OK/1982 July 12–15; Savannah, GA. Tech. Pub. R8-TP4. Atlanta: USDA Forest Service, Southern Region: 88–91.

Barnett JP. 1983b. Ethylene: a problem in seedling storage. Tree Planters' Notes 34(1):28–29.

Barnett JP. 1984a. Relating seedling morphology and physiology of container-grown southern pines to field success. In: Proceedings, 1983 Convention of the Society of American Foresters; 1983 October 16–20; Portland, OR. Bethesda, MD: Society of American Foresters: 405–409.

Barnett JP. 1984b. Relating seedling physiology to survival and growth in container-grown southern pines. In: Proceedings, 1983 Convention of the Society of American Foresters, Physiology working group technical session; 1983 October 16–20; Portland, OR. Bethesda, MD: Society of American Foresters: 62–74.

Barnett JP. 1986. Principles of sowing southern pine seeds. In: Proceedings, Southern Forest Nursery Association; 1986 July 22–24; Pensacola, FL. Tallahassee, FL: Florida Department of Agricultural and Consumer Services: 22–31.

Barnett JP. 1987. Influence of mycorrhizae and nursery on survival and growthof loblolly pine seedlings. Final Rep. Sum. FS-SO-4101-3.38, problem 2. [On file with USDA Forest Service, Southern Forest Experiment Station, New Orleans.]

Barnett JP. 1989a. Shading reduces growth of longleaf and loblolly pine seedlings in containers. Tree Planter's Notes 40(1):23–26.

Barnett JP. 1989b. Site preparation, containers, and soil types affect field performance of loblolly and longleaf pine seedlings. In: Proceedings, 5th Biennial Southern Silvicultural Research Conference; 1988 November 1–3; Memphis, TN. Gen. Tech. Rep. SO-74. New Orleans: USDA Forest Service, Southern Forest Experiment Station: 155–158.

Barnett JP, Brissette JC. 1986. Producing southern pine seedlings in containers. Gen. Tech. Rep. SO-59. New Orleans: USDA Forest Service, Southern Forest Experiment Station. 71 p.

Barnett JP, Brissette JC. 1987. Improving outplanting survival of stored southern pine seedlings by addition of benomyl to the packing medium. In: Meeting the challenge of the nineties: Proceedings, Intermountain Forest Nursery Association; 1987 August 10–14; Oklahoma City, OK. Gen. Tech. Rep. RM-151. Fort Collins, CO: USDA Forest Service, Rocky Mountain Forest and Range Experiment Station: 43–45.

Barnett JP, Brissette JC. 1988. Using benomyl to improve performance of stored southern pine seedlings. In: Proceedings, Southern Forest Nursery Association; 1988 July 25–28; Charleston, SC. Columbia, SC: Southern Forest Nursery Association: 8–12.

Barnett JP, Chappell TW. 1975. Viability of seeds sown with an aerial multiple-row seeder. Tree Planters' Notes 26(2):1–2.

Barnett JP, Dunlap JR. 1982. Sorting loblolly pine orchard seeds by size for containerized seedling production. Southern Journal of Applied Forestry 6(2):112–115.

Barnett JP, Krugman SL. 1989. Electromagnetic treatment of loblolly pine seeds. Res. Note SO-356. New Orleans: USDA Forest Service, Southern Forest Experiment Station. 7 p.

Barnett JP, McGilvray JM. 1974. Copper screen controls root growth and increases survival of containerized southern pine seedlings. Tree Planters' Notes 25(2):11–12.

Barnett JP, McGilvray JM. 1981. Container planting systems for the South. Res. Pap. SO-167. New Orleans:USDA Forest Service, Southern Forest Experiment Station. 18 p.

Barnett JP, McGilvray JM. 1991. Carry-over of loblolly pine seeds on cutover forest sites. Tree Planters' Notes 42(4):17–18.

Barnett JP, McLemore BF. 1961. Tree age unimportant in longleaf seed viability. SO For. Notes. 135. New Orleans: USDA Forest Service, Southern Forest Experiment Station: 2–3.

Barnett JP, McLemore BF. 1966. Repellent-coated pine seed can be stored. Forest Farmer 15(9):14.

Barnett JP, McLemore BF. 1967. Germination of loblolly pine seed hastened by soakings in aerated cold water. Tree Planters' Notes 18(2):1–2.

Barnett JP, McLemore BF. 1970. Storing southern pine seeds. Journal of Forestry 68(1):24–27.

Barnett JP, McLemore BF. 1984. Germination speed as a predictor of nursery seedling performance. Southern Journal of Applied Forestry 8(3):157–162.

Barnett JP, Brissette JC, Kais AG, Jones JP. 1988. Improving field performance of southern pine seedlings by treating with fungicides before storage. Southern Journal of Applied Forestry 12(4):281–285.

Barnett JP, Campbell TE, Dougherty PM. 1984. Seedling establishment: artificial methods. In: Proceedings, Symposium on the Loblolly Pine Ecosystem—West Region; 1984 March 20–22; Jackson, MS. New Orleans: USDA Forest Service, Southern Forest Experiment Station: 109–125.

Barnett JP, Johnson JD, Stumpff NJ. 1985. Effects of ethylene on development and field performance of loblolly pine seedlings. In: Proceedings, Intermountain Nurseryman's Association Meeting; 1985 August 13–15; [Location unknown]: Fort Collins, CO: USDA Forest Service, Rocky Mountain Forest and Range Experiment Station: 48–53.

Bates ME. 1976. Growth responses of containerized southern pine seedlings to temperature and light in controlled-environment greenhouses. Durham, NC: Duke University. 280 p. Ph.D. dissertation.

Bean SD. 1963. Can bundled seedlings survive freezing? Tree Planters' Notes 58(1):20–21.

Beckjord PR, McIntosh MS, Hacskaylo E, Melhuish JH Jr. 1984. Inoculation of loblolly pine seedlings at planting with basidiospores of ectomycorrhizal fungi in chip form. Res. Note NE-324. Broomall, PA: USDA Forest Service, Northeastern Forest Experiment Station. 4 p.

Beineke WF, Perry TO. 1966. Genetic variation in ability to withstand transplanting shock. In: Proceedings, 8th Southern Conference on Forest Tree Improvement; 1965 June 16–7; Savannah, GA. Publication 24. Macon, GA: Georgia Forest Research Council, Committee on Southern Forest Tree Improvement: 106–109.

Belcher EW. 1968. Repellent-coated seed of loblolly pine can be stratified. Tree Planters' Notes 19(2):10–12.

Belcher EW. 1982. Storing stratified seed for extended periods. Tree Planters' Notes 33(4):23–25.

Belcher EW Jr. 1984. Seed handling. In: Lantz CW, ed. Southern pine nursery handbook. Atlanta: USDA Forest Service, Southern Region: 1–29.

Belcher EW, Karrfalt RP. 1976. Twentieth laboratory report: fiscal years 1975 and 1976. Macon, GA: USDA Forest Service, Eastern Tree Seed Laboratory. 37 p.

Belcher EW, McKinney HF. 1981. Low-energy drying of pine cones. Tree Planters' Notes 32(4):19–21.

Belcher E, Vozzo JA. 1979. Radiographic analysis of agricultural and forest tree seeds. In: The handbook on seed testing. [Place of publication unknown]: Association of Official Seed Analysts. 29 p.

Belcher EW, Leach GN, Gresham HH. 1984. Sizing slash pine seeds as a nursery procedure. Tree Planters' Notes 35(2):5–10.

Berry CR. 1985a. Growth and heavy metal accumulation in pine seedlings grown with sewage sludge. Journal Environmental Quality 14(3):415–419.

Berry CR. 1985b. Growth of loblolly pine seedlings in a nursery soil amended with different municipal sewage sludges. In: Lantz CW, comp. Proceedings, 1984 Southern Nursery Conferences; 1984 June 11–14; Alexandria, LA/1984 July 24–27; Asheville, NC. Atlanta: USDA Forest Service, Southern Region: 145–151.

Berry CR. 1985c. Subsoiling and sewage sludge aid loblolly pine establishment on adverse sites. Reclamation and Revegetation Research 3:301–311.

Bethune JE. 1963. Introduction of loblolly pine south of its natural range in Florida. Journal of Forestry 61(10):782–784.

Bilan MV. 1962. Effect of planting date on regeneration and development of roots of loblolly pine seedlings. In: Proceedings, 13th IUFRO Congress; 1961 [dates unknown]; Vienna, Austria. [Place of publication and publisher unknown]: Pt. 2(1), Sect. 22–15: 5.

Bilan MV. 1966. Calphos stimulates growth of newly planted loblolly pines. Tree Planters' Notes (79):28–29.

Bilan MV. 1987. Effect of time and depth of planting on survival and growth of loblolly pine (Pinus taeda L.) seedlings in Texas. In: Proceedings, 4th Biennial Southern Silvicultural Research Conference; 1986 November 4–6; Atlanta, GA. Gen. Tech. Rep. SE-42. Asheville, NC: USDA Forest Service, Southeastern Forest Experiment Station: 67–72.

Bilan MV, Ferguson ER. 1985. Root regeneration in out-planted loblolly pine (Pinus taeda L.) seedlings. In: South DB, ed. Proceedings, International Symposium on Nursery Management Practices for the Southern Pines; 1985 August 4–9; Montgomery, AL. Auburn University, AL: Auburn University, Department of Research Information: 329–341.

Biswas PK, Bonamy PA, Paul KB. 1972. Germination promotion of loblolly pine and baldcypress seeds by stratification and chemical treatments. Physiologia Plantarum 27(1):71–76.

Bonner FT. 1977. Equipment and supplies for collecting, processing, storing, and testing forest tree seed. Gen. Tech. Rep. SO-13. New Orleans: USDA Forest Service, Southern Forest Experiment Station. 35 p.

Bonner FT. 1981. Measurement and management of tree seed moisture. Res. Pap. SO-177. New Orleans: USDA Forest Service, Southern Forest Experiment Station. 11 p.

Bonner FT. 1983. Germination response of loblolly pine to temperature differentials on a two-way thermogradient plate. Journal of Seed Technology (8)1:6–14.

Bonner FT. 1984. New forests from better seeds: the role of seed physiology. In: Seedling physiology and reforestation success. Dordrecht, The Netherlands: Martinus Nijhoff/Dr. W. Junk Publishers: 37–59.

Bonner FT. 1986. Measurement of seed vigor for loblolly—Pinus taeda and slash pines—Pinus elliottii. Forest Science 32(1):170–178.

Bonner FT. 1987a. Cone storage and seed quality in longleaf pine. Res. Note SO-341. New Orleans: USDA Forest Service, Southern Forest Experiment Station. 4 p.

Bonner FT. 1987b. Effect of storage of loblolly and slash pine cones on seed quality. Southern Journal of Applied Forestry 11(1):59–65.

Bonner FT. 1990. Long-term storage of seeds of major "orthodox" species. Progress report FS-SO-4103-3.2. 6 p.[On file with USDA Forest Service, Southern Forest Experiment Station, New Orleans.]

Bonner FT. 1991a. Effect of cone storage on pine seed storage potential. Southern Journal of Applied Forestry 15(4):216–221.

Bonner FT. 1991b. Estimating seed quality of southern pines by leachate conductivity. Res. Pap. SO–263. New Orleans: USDA Forest Service, Southern Forest Experiment Station. 4 p.

Bonner FT. 1991c. Seed management. In: Duryea ML, Dougherty PM, comps. Forest regeneration manual. Dordrecht, The Netherlands: Kluwer Academic Publishers: 51–73.

Boyer JN, South DB. 1984a. Forest nursery practices in the South. Southern Journal of Applied Forestry 8(2):67–75.

Boyer JN, South DB. 1984b. A morphological comparison of greenhouse-grown loblolly pine seedlings with seedlings grown outdoors. Tree Planters' Notes 35(3):15–18.

Boyer JN, South DB. 1985. Nutrient content of nursery-grown loblolly pine seedlings. Circ. 282. [Auburn, AL]: Alabama Agricultural Experiment Station. 28 p.

Boyer JN, South DB. 1987. Excessive seedling height, high shoot-to-root ratio, and benomyl root dip reduce survival of stored loblolly pine seedlings. Tree Planters' Notes 38(4):19–22.

Boyer JN, South DB. 1988. Loblolly pine seedling morphology and production at 53 southern forest nurseries. Tree Planters' Notes 39(3):13–16.

Boyer JN, Duba SE, South DB. 1987. Emergence timing affects root-collar diameter and mortality in loblolly pine seedbeds. New Forests 1(2):135–140.

Boyer JN, South DB, Muller C, and others. 1985. Speed of germination affects diameter at lifting of nursery-grown loblolly pine seedlings. Southern Journal Applied Forestry 9(4):243–247.

Branan JR, Porterfield EJ. 1971. A comparison of six species of southern pines planted in the Piedmont of South Carolina. Res. Note SE-171. Asheville, NC: USDA Forest Service, Southeastern Forest Experiment Station. 3 p.

Brissette JC, Ballenger L. 1985. Using root growth potential for comparing the quality of loblolly pine seedlings from two nurseries in Arkansas. In: Proceedings, Northeast Area Nursery Supervisor's Conference; 1985 August 6–9; Dover, DE. Dover, DE: Delaware Forest Service.

Brissette JC, Barnett JP. 1989. Depth of planting and J-rooting affect loblolly pine seedlings under stress. In: Proceedings, 5th Biennial Southern Silvicultural Research Conference; 1988 November 1–3; Memphis, TN. Gen. Tech. Rep. SO-74. New Orleans: USDA Forest Service, Southern Forest Experiment Station: 169–175.

Brissette JC, Carlson WC. 1987. Effects of nursery bed density and fertilization on the morphology, nutrient status, and root growth potential of shortleaf pine seedlings. In: Proceedings, 4th Biennial Southern Silvicultural Research Conference; 1986 November 4–6; Atlanta, GA. Gen. Tech. Rep. SE-42. Asheville, NC: USDA Forest Service, Southeastern Forest Experiment Station: 198–205.

Brissette JC, Lantz CW. 1983. Seedling quality: summary of a workshop. In: Proceedings, 1982 Southern Nursery Conferences; 1982 August 9–12; Oklahoma City, OK; 1982 July 12–15; Savannah, GA. R8-TP4. Atlanta: USDA Forest Service, Southern Region: 303–305.

Brissette JC, Roberts TC. 1984. Seedling size and lifting date effects on root growth potential of loblolly pine from two Arkansas nurseries. Tree Planters' Notes 35(1):34–38.

Brissette JC, Barnett JP, Gramling CL. 1988. Root growth potential of southern pine seedlings grown at the W.W. Ashe Nursery. In: Proceedings, Southern Forest Nursery Association; 1988 July 25–28; Charleston, SC. Columbia, SC: Southern Forest Nursery Association: 173–183.

Brissette JC, Barnett JP, Landis TD. 1991. Container seedlings. In: Duryea ML, Dougherty PM, comps. Forest regeneration manual. Dordrecht, The Netherlands: Kluwer Academic Publishers: 117–141.

Bruner MH, Reamer LD. 1966. Loblolly pine or yellow-poplar on upland Piedmont sites? Journal of Forestry 64(4):251–252.

Buckner E, Maki T. 1977. Seven-year growth of fertilized and irrigated yellow-poplar, sweetgum, northern red oak, and loblolly pine planted on two sites. Forest Science 23(4):402–410.

Burns RM. 1962. Southern pines and sweetgums do not mix. SO For. Notes. 141. New Orleans: USDA Forest Service, Southern Forest Experiment Station: 4.

Byrd RR, Peevy CE. 1963. Freezing temperatures affect survival of planted loblolly and slash pine seedlings. Tree Planters' Notes 58:18–19.

Cabrera H, Woods FW. 1975. Effects of root deformation upon early growth of loblolly pine (Pinus taeda L.). Tennessee Farm and Home Science (93):28 –30.

Campbell TE. 1974. Direct seeding loblolly pine beneath hardwoods on dry sands. Tree Planters' Notes 25(3):2–24.

Campbell TE. 1976. The nation's oldest industrial direct seeding. Forest and People (Third Quarter):22–24.

Campbell TE. 1981. Spot seeding is effective and inexpensive. In: Proceedings, 1st Biennial Southern Silvicultural Research Conference; 1980 November 6–7; Atlanta, GA. Gen. Tech. Rep. SO-34. New Orleans: USDA Forest Service, Southern Forest Experiment Station: 50–53.

Campbell TE. 1982a. Direct seeding may present attractive option for pine regeneration on smaller tracts. Forest Farmer 42(2):8–10.

Campbell TE. 1982b. Guidelines for direct seeding. In: How to help landowners with forest regeneration. Jackson, MS: Mississippi Forestry Commission; and Atlanta: USDA Forest Service, Southern Region, State and Private Forestry: 20–26.

Campbell TE. 1982c. Imbibition, desiccation, and reimbibition effects on light requirements for germinating southern pine seeds. Forest Science 28(3):539–543.

Campbell TE. 1985. Development of direct-seeded and planted loblolly and slash pines through age 20. Southern Journal of Applied Forestry 9(4):205–211.

Campbell TE. 1986. Herbicides, fire, and direct seeding for regenerating loblolly pine. In: Proceedings of the Southern Weed Science Society 39:197–201.

Campbell TE, Mann WF Jr. 1973. Regenerating loblolly pine by direct seeding natural seeding and planting. Res. Pap. SO-84. New Orleans: USDA Forest Service, Southern Forest Experiment Station. 9 p.

Campbell TE, Mead RA. 1981. Seedling survival estimates using 35mm aerial photography. In: Proceedings, 1st Biennial Southern Silvicultural Research Conference; 1980 November 6–7; Atlanta, GA. Gen. Tech. Rep. SO-34. New Orleans: USDA Forest Service, Southern Forest Experiment Station: 188–191.

Carlson WC. 1985. Effects of natural chilling and cold storage on budbreak and root growth potential of loblolly pine (Pinus taeda L.). Canadian Journal of Forest Research 15:651–656.

Carlson WC. 1986. Root system considerations in the quality of loblolly pine seedlings. Southern Journal of Applied Forestry 10(2):87–92.

Carlson WC, Anthony JG, Plyler RP. 1987. Polymeric nursery bed stabilization to reduce seed losses in forest nurseries. Southern Journal of Applied Forestry 11(2):116–119.

Carpita NC, Skaria A, Barnett JP, Dunlap JR. 1983. Cold stratification and growth of radicles of loblolly pine (Pinus taeda) embryos. Physiologia Plantarum 59:601–606.

Carter MC. 1964. Nitrogen and "summer chlorosis" in loblolly pine. Tree Planters' Notes 64:18–19.

Caulfield JP, Shoulders E, Lockaby BG. 1989. Risk-efficient species-site selection decisions for southern pines. Canadian Journal of Forest Research 19(6):743–753.

Caulfield JP, South DB, Boyer JN. 1987. Nursery seedbed density is determined by short-term or long-term objectives. Southern Journal of Applied Forestry 11(1):9–14.

Cole CE. 1973. Comparisons within and between populations of planted slash and loblolly pine: a seed source study. In: Proceedings, 12th Southern Forest Tree Improvement Conference; 1973 June 12–13; Baton Rouge, LA. Baton Rouge, LA: Louisiana State University, Division of continuing Education: 277–292.

Conn JP, Watson EE. 1985. Operational test of 3-P sampling for seedling inventory at the Carolina nursery. In: Lantz CW, comp. Proceedings, 1984 Southern Nursery Conferences; 1984 June 11–14; Alexandria, LA/1984 July 24–27; Asheville, NC. Atlanta: USDA Forest Service, Southern Region: 46–52.

Cordell CE, Marx DH, Lott JR, Kenney DS. 1981. The practical application of Pisolithus tinctorius ectomycorrhizal inoculum in forest tree nurseries. In: Forest regeneration. Proceedings, Symposium on Engineering Systems for Forest Regeneration; 1981 March 2–6; Raleigh, NC. St. Joseph, MI: American Society of Agricultural Engineers: 39–42.

Cotrufo C. 1963. Citric acid stimulates seed germination [Abstract]. Plant Physiology 38.

Czabator FJ. 1962. Germination value: an index combining speed and completeness of pine seed germination. Forest Science 8(4):386–396.

Danielson RM, Davey CB. 1969. Microbial recolonization of a fumigated nursery soil. Forest Science 15(4):368–380.

Darby SP Jr. 1962. Intensified nursery practices: the key to high-quality, custom-grown field-graded forest tree seedlings. Tree Planters' Notes 52:7–11.

Davey CB. 1972. Nursery soil management. In: Proceedings, Southeastern Area Forest Tree Nurserymen's Conference; 1972 July 24–26; Greenville, MS/1972 August 7–10; Wilmington, NC. [Place of publication unknown]: Southeastern Area Forest Tree Nurserymen's Association: 182–187.

Davey CB. 1982. Loblolly pine seedling production. In: Proceedings, Symposium on the Loblolly Pine Ecosystem—East Region; 1982 December 8–10; Raleigh, NC. Raleigh, NC: North Carolina State University: 115–123.

Derr HJ. 1963. Better repellent for direct seeding. Tree Planters' Notes 61:26–30.

Derr HJ, Mann WF Jr. 1971. Direct-seeding pines in the South. Agric. Handbk. 391. Washington, DC: USDA Forest Service. 68 p.

DeWald LE, Feret PP. 1987. Changes in loblolly pine root growth potential from September to April. Canadian Journal of Forest Research 17(7):635–643.

DeWald LE, Feret PP. 1988. Changes in loblolly pine seedling root growth potential, dry weight, and dormancy during cold storage. Forest Science 34(1):41–54.

Dickerson BP. 1974. Seedling age influences survival of containerized loblolly pines. Res. Note SO-171. New Orleans: USDA Forest Service, Southern Forest Experiment Station. 4 p.

Dickerson BP, McClurkin DC. 1980. A field trial of year-round planting of "bullet" seedlings. Tree Planters' Notes 32(2):21–22.

Dierauf TA. 1974. Effect of time of lifting and length of time in cold storage. Occas. Rep. 43. Charlottesville, VA: Virginia Division of Forestry, Department of Conservation and Economic Development. 5 p.

Dierauf TA. 1975. Height growth of planted and direct seeded loblolly pine. Occas. Rep. 48. Charlottesville, VA: Virginia Division of Forestry, Department of Conservation and Economic Development. 3 p.

Dierauf TA. 1976a. Fall planting and storage using non-dormant seedlings. In: Lantz CW, ed. Proceedings, Southeastern Nurserymen's Conference; 1976 August 17–19; Mobile, AL. Atlanta: USDA Forest Service, Southern Region, State and Private Forestry: 30–36.

Dierauf TA. 1976b. Top clipping in the nursery bed. In: Lantz CW, ed. Proceedings, Southeastern Nurserymen's Conference; 1976 August 17–19; Mobile, AL. Atlanta: USDA Forest Service, Southern Region, State and Private Forestry: 37–43.

Dierauf TA. 1982. Planting loblolly pine. In: Proceedings, Symposium on the Loblolly Pine Ecosystem—East Region; 1982 December 8–10; Raleigh, NC. Raleigh, NC: North Carolina State University: 124–135.

Dierauf TA. 1984. Survival of root pruned loblolly after long-term storage. Occas. Rep. 64. Charlottesville, VA: Virginia Division of Forestry, Department of Conservation and Economic Development. 2 p.

Dierauf TA. 1985. Continuous cropping at New Kent. In: South DB, ed. Proceedings, International Symposium on Nursery Management Practices for the Southern Pines; 1985 August 4–9; Montgomery, AL. Auburn University, AL: Auburn University, Department of Research Information: 237–243.

Dierauf TA. 1988. An undercutting study in loblolly pine seedbeds. Occas. Rep. 72. Charlottesville, VA: Virginia Division of Forestry, Department of Conservation and Economic Development. 7 p.

Dierauf TA, Apgar LJ. 1988. A two-year study comparing five sowing depths for loblolly pine seed. Occas. Rep. 73. Charlottesville, VA: Virginia Division of Forestry, Department of Conservation and Economic Development. 10 p.

Dierauf TA, Edwards LC. 1985. A three-year study of immersing stored loblolly pine seedlings in water before planting. Occas. Rep. 66. Charlottesville, VA: Virginia Division of Forestry, Department of Conservation and Economic Development. 7 p.

Dierauf TA, Garner JW. 1970. First year results of 1970 loblolly pine seedling grade study. Res. Notes 4. Charlottesville, VA: Virginia Division of Forestry, Department of Conservation and Economic Development. 3 p.

Dierauf TA, Garner JW. 1974. Survival of loblolly pine seedlings packed in kraft paper bags compared to conventional packaging. Occas. Rep. 45. Charlottesville, VA: Virginia Division of Forestry, Department of Conservation and Economic Development. 6 p.

Dierauf TA, Garner JW. 1978. Root pruning loblolly pine seedlings effect on survival and growth. Occas. Rep. 52. Charlottesville, VA: Virginia Division of Forestry, Department of Conservation and Economic Development. 4 p.

Dierauf TA, Marler RL. 1969. Loblolly pine cold-storage planting study. Occas. Rep. 31. Charlottesville, VA: Virginia Division of Forestry, Department of Conservation and Economic Development. 10 p.

Dierauf TA, Marler RL. 1971. Effect of exposure, clay treatment, and storage on survival and growth of loblolly pine seedlings. Occas. Rep. 34. Charlottesville, VA: Virginia Division of Forestry, Department of Conservation and Economic Development. 10 p.

Dierauf TA, Olinger HL. 1982. A study of undercutting, lateral root pruning and top clipping in loblolly pine nursery beds. Occas. Rep. 58. Charlottesville, VA: Virginia Division of Forestry, Department of Conservation and Economic Development. 6 p.

Dierauf TA, Garner JW, Marler R. 1971. Direct seeding and planting Virginia and loblolly pine on sites prepared by burning. Occas. Rep. 37. Charlottesville, VA: Virginia Division of Forestry, Department of Conservation and Economic Development. 4 p.

Donald DGM, Jacobs C. 1990. The effect of storage time, temperature and container on the viability of the seed of four pine species. South African Forestry Journal (154):41–46.

Dooley JH, Fridley RB. 1981. Equipment development for forest nurseries. In: Proceedings, Symposium on Engineering Systems for Forest Regeneration; 1981 March 2–6; Raleigh, NC. St. Joseph, MI: American Society of Agricultural Engineers: 43–45.

Dougherty PM. 1990. Survival and growth responses of loblolly pine to a range of competition control. GA For. Res. Pap. 81. Macon, GA: Georgia Forestry Commission, Research Division. 5 p.

Dunlap JR, Barnett JP. 1984a. Manipulating loblolly pine (Pinus taeda L.) seed germination with simulated moisture and temperature stress. In: Duryea ML, Brown GN, comp. Proceedings, Physiology Working Group Technical Session—Seedling Physiology and Reforestation Success; 1983 October 16–20; Portland, OR. Bethesda, MD: Society of American Foresters: 62–74.

Dunlap JR, Barnett JP. 1984b. Stress induced distortions of seed germination patterns in Pinus taeda (L.). In: New forests for a changing world: Proceedings, 1983 Convention of the Society of American Foresters; 1983 October 16–20; Portland, OR. Bethesda, MD: Society of American Foresters: 392–397.

Easley LT. 1966. Westvaco cone kiln. Tree Planters' Notes 77:6–9.

Eliason EJ, Carlson D. 1962. Tests with tree packing materials. Tree Planters' Notes (54):17–18.

Feret PP, Kreh RE. 1986. Effect of undercutting on loblolly pine–Pinus taeda seedling size and its relation to root growth potential. Southern Journal Applied Forestry 10(1):24–27.

Feret PP, Freyman RC, Kreh RE. 1985a. Variation in root growth potential of loblolly pine from seven nurseries. In: South DB, ed. Proceedings, International Symposium on Nursery Management Practices for the Southern Pines; 1985 August 4–9; Montgomery, AL. Auburn University, AL: Auburn University, Department of Research Information: 317–328.

Feret PP, Kreh RE, DeWald LE. 1985b. Root growth potential of stored loblolly pine seedlings. In: Proceedings, 3rd Biennial Southern Silvicultural Research Conference; 1984 November

7–8; Atlanta, GA. Gen. Tech. Rep. SO-54. New Orleans: USDA Forest Service, Southern Forest Experiment Station: 18–24.

Feret PP, Kreh RE, Mulligan C . 1985c.   Effects of air drying on survival, height, and root growth potential of loblolly pine seedlings. Southern Journal of Applied Forestry 9(2):125–128.

Fisher RF. 1981.   Soils interpretations for silviculture in the southeastern Coastal Plain. In: Proceedings, 1st Biennial Southern Silvicultural Research Conference; 1980 November 6–7; Atlanta, GA. Gen. Tech. Rep. SO-34. New Orleans: USDA Forest Service, Southern Forest Experiment Station: 323–330.

Foil RR, Ralston C. 1967. The establishment and growth of loblolly pine seedlings on compacted soils. Soil Science Society of America Journal 31(4):565–568.

Foster BB. 1982.   Taxpayers gain from southern pine regeneration programs. Southern Journal of Applied Forestry 6(4):188–193.

Fowells HA, Krauss RW. 1959.   The inorganic nutrition of loblolly pine and Virginia pine with special reference to nitrogen and phosphorus. Forest Science 5(1):95–112.

Freyman RC, Feret PP. 1987.   A 15 day hydroponic system for measuring root growth potential: measurement and sample size for loblolly pine. In: Proceeding, 4th Biennial Southern Silvicultural Research Conference; 1986 November 4–6; Atlanta, GA. Gen. Tech. Rep. SE-42. Asheville, NC: USDA Forest Service, Southeastern Forest Experiment Station: 230–236.

Gagnon KG, Johnson JD. 1988a.   Bud development and dormancy in slash and loblolly pine: 1. speed of budbreak and second year height as related to lifting date. New Forests. 2(4):26–268.

Gagnon KG, Johnson JD. 1988b.   Bud development and dormancy in slash and loblolly pine: 2. effects of ethephon applications. New Forests 2(4):269–274.

Garber MP. 1978.   Dormancy of vegetative growth of loblolly pine seedlings. In: Greenhouse technology—South. For. Res. Tech. Rep. 042-2010/78/87. Hot Springs, AR: Weyerhaeuser Corporation. 11 p.

Garber MP. 1983.   Effects of chilling and photoperiod on dormancy release of container-grown loblolly pine seedlings. Canadian Journal of Forest Research 13(6):1265–1270.

Garber MP, Mexal JG. 1980.   Lift and storage practices: their impact on successful establishment of southern pine plantations. New Zealand Journal of Forestry Science 10(1):72–82.

Garner JW Jr. 1974.   Operational spot-seeding of loblolly pine. Res. Notes 12. Charlottesville, VA: Virginia Division of Forestry, Department of Conservation and Economic Development. 2 p.

Garner JW, Dierauf TA. 1974.   Effect of freezing on survival of loblolly pine seedlings. Occas. Rep. 44. Charlottesville, VA: Virginia Division of Forestry, Department of Conservation and Economic Development. 4 p.

Garner JW, Dierauf TA. 1976.   Changes in loblolly pine seedling dry weight and top to root ratio between October and March. Occas. Rep. 50. Charlottesville, VA: Virginia Division of Forestry, Department of Conservation and Economic Development. 3 p.

Garrett-Kraus K, Blanche CA, Elam WW. 1985.   Ethylene production by stored pine seedlings and its relation to root regeneration and survival. In: South DB, ed. Proceedings, International Symposium on Nursery Management Practices for Southern Pines; 1985 August 4–9; Montgomery, AL. [Place of publication and publisher unknown]: 363–371.

Gates JE. 1974.   Handling and shipping containerized southern pines. In: Proceedings, North American Containerized Forest Tree Seedling Symposium; 1974 August 26–69; Denver, CO. Denver, CO: Great Plains Agricultural Council. 68: 144–145.

Godbee JF Jr, Rakestraw JL, Boreman F. 1983.   Pine plantation survival: a corporate look at the problem. In: Proceedings, 1982 Southern Nursery Conferences; 1982 August 9–12; Oklahoma City, OK/1982 July 12–15; Savannah, GA. R8-TP4. Atlanta: USDA Forest Service, Southern Region: 21–26.

Goodwin OC. 1974.   Field performance of containerized seedlings in North Carolina (Pinus taeda, Pinus palustris). In:

Proceedings, North American Containerized Forest Tree Seedlings Symposium; 1974 August 26–29; Denver, CO. Denver, CO: Great Plains Agricultural Council: 324–328.

Goodwin OC. 1976.   Summer-planted loblolly and longleaf pine tubelings outgrow 1-0 nursery seedlings in North Carolina. Journal of Forestry 74(8): 515–516.

Greenwald SM Sr. 1972.   Some environmental effects on the growth and monoterpene production of Pinus taeda L. and Ocimum basilicum L. Durham, NC: Duke University. 85 p. Ph.D. dissertation.

Guldin RW. 1981.   Capital intensity and economies-of-scale for different types of nurseries. In: Proceedings, Southern Containerized Forest Tree Seedling Conference; 1981 August 25–27; Savannah, GA. New Orleans: USDA Forest Service, Southern Forest Experiment Station: 87–95.

Guldin RW. 1982a.   Nursery costs and benefits of container-grown southern pine seedlings. Southern Journal of Applied Forestry 6(2):93–99.

Guldin RW. 1982b.   What does it cost to grow seedlings in containers? Tree Planters' Notes 33(1):34–37.

Guldin RW. 1983a.   Economies-of-scale for newly constructed southern pine nurseries. In: Proceedings, 1982 Southern Nursery Conferences; 1982 August 9–12; Oklahoma City, OK/1982 July 12–15; Savannah, GA. R8-TP4. Atlanta: USDA Forest Service, Southern Region: 49–65.

Guldin RW. 1983b.   Regeneration costs for industrial landowners using hand vs. machine planting. Southern Journal of Applied Forestry 7(2):104–108.

Guldin RW. 1983c.   Regeneration costs using container-grown southern pine seedlings. Res. Pap. SO-187. New Orleans: USDA Forest Service, Southern Forest Experiment Station. 29 p.

Haddock WH, Hassan AE. 1981.   Pneumatic conveyance of seedlings. In: Forest regeneration. Proceedings, Symposium on Engineering Systems for Forest Regeneration; 1981 March 2–6; Raleigh, NC. ASAE Pub. 10-81. St. Joseph, MI: American Society of Agricultural Engineers: 178–185.

Hallgren SW. 1989.   Effects of osmotic priming using aerated solutions of polyethylene glycol on germination of pine seeds. Annals of Scientific Forestry 46(1):31–38.

Hammer MF, Ray KF, Miller AE. 1985.   An evaluation of root-wrenched and stored loblolly pine seedlings. In: South DB, ed. Proceedings, International Symposium on Nursery Management Practices for the Southern pines; 1985 August 4–9; Montgomery, AL. Auburn, AL: Auburn University, Department of Research Information: 351–362.

Hammond WJ. 1976.   Application of N&P at planting. In: Proceedings, 6th Southern Forest Soils Workshop; 1976 October 1921; Charleston, SC. [Place of publication and publisher unknown]: 127129.

Hansbrough T, Hollis JP, Merrifield RG, Foil RR. 1964.   Fumigation of loblolly pine planting sites. Plant Disease Reporter 48(12):986–989.

Hansen RS, Bilan MV. 1989.   Height growth of loblolly and slash pine plantations in the northern post-oak belt of Texas. Southern Journal of Applied Forestry 13(1):5–8.

Hare RC. 1981.   Nitric acid promotes pine seed germination. Res. Note SO-281. New Orleans: USDA Forest Service, Southern Forest Experiment Station. 2 p.

Harms WR, Langdon OG. 1977.   Competition-density effects in a loblolly pine seedling stand. Res. Pap. SE-161. Asheville, NC: USDA Forest Service, Southeastern Forest Experiment Station. 8 p.

Harrington CA, Brissette JC, Carlson WC. 1989.   Root system structure in planted and seeded loblolly and shortleaf pine. Forest Science 35(2):469–480.

Harrington CA, Carlson WC, Brissette JC. 1987.   Relationships between height growth and root system orientation in planted and seeded loblolly and shortleaf pines. In: Proceedings, 4th Biennial

Southern Silvicultural Research Conference; 1986 November 4–6; Atlanta, GA. Gen. Tech. Rep. SE-42. Asheville, NC: USDA Forest Service, Southeastern Forest Experiment Station: 53–60.

Hassan AE. 1983. Nursery equipment development for automatic feeding of bareroot seedlings. In: Proceedings, 1982 Southern Nursery Conferences; 1982 July 12–15; Savannah, GA. [Place of publication and publisher unknown]: 246–266.

Hatchell GE. 1961. A look at 9-year-old seeded loblolly pine. Forests and People 11(3):25, 44–45.

Hatchell GE. 1964. Immediate release needed for maximum growth of seeded loblolly pine. Tree Planters' Notes 66:19–22.

Hatchell GE. 1966. Loblolly pine direct seeding in the lower Piedmont of Georgia. GA For. Res. Pap. 40. Macon, GA: Georgia Forest Research Council. 4 p.

Hatchell GE, Marx DH. 1987. Response of longleaf, sand, and loblolly pines to Pisolithus ectomycorrhizae and fertilizer on a sandhills site in South Carolina. Forest Science 33(2):301–315.

Hatchell GE, Dorman KW, Langdon OG. 1972. Performance of loblolly and slash pine nursery selections. Forest Science 18(4): 308–313.

Hay RL, Woods FW. 1974. Shape of root systems influences survival and growth of loblolly seedlings. Tree Planters' Notes 25(3):1–2.

Hay RL, Woods FW. 1975. Distribution of carbohydrates in deformed seedling root systems. Forest Science 21(3):263–267.

Hay RL, Woods FW. 1978. Carbohydrate relationships in root systems of planted loblolly pine seedlings. In: Proceedings, Symposium on the Root Form of Planted Trees; 1978 May 16–19; Victoria, BC; Victoria, BC: British Columbia Ministry of Forests/Canadian Forestry Service: 73–84.

Haywood JD. 1983. Response of planted to site preparation on a Beauregard–Caddo soil. In: Proceedings, 2d Biennial Southern Silvicultural Research Conference; 1982 November 4–5; Atlanta, GA. Gen. Tech. Rep. SE-24. Asheville, NC: USDAForest Service, Southeastern Forest Experiment Station: 14–17.

Hazel DW, Smith MD, Franklin C. 1989. Direct-seeding of loblolly pine in the North Carolina Piedmont: four-year results. Southern Journal of Applied Forestry 13(2):91–93.

Hennessey TC, Dougherty PM. 1984. Characterization of the internal water relations of loblolly pine seedlings in response to nursery cultural treatments: implications for reforestation success. In: Duryea ML, Brown GN, eds. Seedlings physiology and reforestation success. Dordrecht, The Netherlands: Martinus Nijhoff Publishers: 225–243.

Hodges CS. 1961. Freezing lowers survival of three species of southern pines. Tree Planters' Notes 47:23–24.

Hodgkins EJ. 1966. A study of direct seeding depth for loblolly pine. Journal of Forestry 64(5):317–319.

Hodgson TJ. 1980. Pine seed grading: the implication for orchard seed. South African Forestry Journal (112):10–14.

Hunt EV Jr, Gilmore G. 1967. Taller loblolly pine seedlings grow faster in a Texas plantation. Tree Planters' Notes 18(2):25–28.

Hunter SC, Maki TE. 1980. The effects of root-curling on loblolly pine. Southern Journal of Applied Forestry 4(1):45–49.

Jeffries KF. 1983. Operational guidelines for handling seedlings. In: Proceedings, 1982 Southern Nursery Conferences; 1982 August 9–12/Oklahoma City, OK; 1982 July 12–15; Savannah, GA. R8-TP4. Atlanta: USDA Forest Service, Southern Region: 212–223.

Johnson JD. 1983. The effect of photoperiod during cold storage of the survival and growth of loblolly pine seedlings. In: Proceedings, 2nd Biennial Southern Silvicultural Research Conference; 1982 November 4–5; Atlanta, GA. Gen. Tech. Rep. SE-24. Asheville, NC: USDA Forest Service, Southeastern Forest Experiment Station: 401–408.

Johnson JD, Stumpff NJ. 1985. Loblolly pine seedling performance is affected by ethylene. In: Lantz CW, comp. Proceedings, 1984 Southern Nursery Conferences; 1984 June 11–14; Alexandria, LA/1984 July 24–27; Asheville, NC. Atlanta: USDA Forest Service, Southern Region: 169–173.

Johnson JD, Seiler JR McNabb KL. 1985. Manipulation of pine seedling physiology by water stress conditioning. In: South DB, ed. Proceedings, International Symposium on Nursery Management Practices for the Southern Pines; 1985 August 4–9; Montgomery, AL. Auburn University, AL: Auburn University, Department of Research Information: 290–302.

Jones L. 1963. Germination of repellent-treated southern pine seed before and after storage. Res. Note 15. Asheville, NC: USDA Forest Service, Southeastern Forest Experiment Station. 4 p.

Jones L. 1965. Water content and cost of stratified seed related. Tree Planters' Notes 71:17.

Jones L, Thacker S. 1965. Survival. In: Wahlenberg WG, ed. A guide to loblolly and slash pine plantation management in southeastern U.S.A. GA For. Rep. 14. Macon, GA: Georgia Forest Research Council: 68–73.

Jorgensen JR. 1968. Root growth of direct-seeded southern pine seedlings. Res. Note SO-79. New Orleans: USDAForest Service, Southern Forest Experiment Station. 7 p.

Karrfalt RP, Hall O. 1983. Nursery inventory workshop. In: Proceedings, 1982 Southern Nursery Conferences; 1982 August 9–12; Oklahoma City, OK/1982 July 12–15; Savannah, GA. R8-TP4. Atlanta: USDA Forest Service, Southern Region: 285–300.

Karrfalt RP. 1979. The quality of unextracted pine seed. In: Proceedings, 1978 Southern Nursery Conferences; 1978 July 24–27; Hot Springs, AR/1978 August 7–10; Williamsburg, VA. SA-TP6. Atlanta: USDA Forest Service, Southern Region, State and Private Forestry: 126–130.

Kelley WD. 1987. Effect of triadimefon on development of mycorrhizae from natural inoculum in loblolly pine nursery beds. Southern Journal of Applied Forestry 11(1):49–52.

Kelley WD. 1988. Effect of short-term storage of triadimefon-treated loblolly pine seed on incidence of fusiform rust. Southern Journal of Applied Forestry 12(1):18–20.

Kellison RC, Slichter TK, Frederick DJ. 1979. Matching species to site for increased wood production. TAPPI Journal 62(8):77–79.

King GW. 1976. Grading, packing and storage of forest tree seedlings in the Southeast. In: Lantz CW, ed. Proceedings, Southeastern Nurserymen's Conference; 1976 August 17–19; Mobile, AL. Atlanta: USDAForest Service, Southern Region, State and Private Forestry: [page numbers unknown].

Kohonen M. 1982. Site preparation and automatic machine planting of containerized stock. In: Proceedings, Canadian Containerized Tree Seedling Symposium; 1981 September 14–16; Toronto, Ontario, Canada. Saulte Ste. Marie, ON, Canada: Department of the Environment, Canadian Forestry Service, Great Lakes Forest Service Research Center: 287–290.

Koshi PT. 1960. Deep planting has little effect in a wet year. Tree Planters' Notes 40:7.

Kramer PJ. 1957. Some effects of various combinations of day and night temperatures and photoperiod on the height growth of loblolly pine seedlings. Forest Science 3(1):45–55.

Kramer P. 1981. Carbon dioxide concentration, photosynthesis, and dry matter production. BioScience 31(1):29–33.

Landis TD, Tinus RW, McDonald SE, Barnett JP. 1989. The container tree nursery manual. Vol. 4. Seedling nutrition and irrigation. Agric. Handbk. 674. Washington, DC: USDA Forest Service. 119 p.

Landis TD, Tinus RW, McDonald SE, Barnett JP. 1990. The container tree nursery manual. Vol. 2. Containers and growing media. Vol. 2. Agric. Handbk. 674. Washington, DC: USDA Forest Service. 87 p.

Landis TD, Tinus RW, McDonald SE, Barnett JP. 1995. The container tree nursery manual. Vol. 1. Nursery planning, development, and management. Agric. Handbk. 674. Washington, DC: USDA Forest Service. 188 p.

Lantz CW. 1975. Tree improvement on marginal sites. In: Proceedings, 13th Southern Forest Tree Improvement Conference; 1975 June 10–11; Raleigh, NC. Macon, GA: USDA Forest Service, Eastern Tree Seed Laboratory 35: 45–51.

Lantz CW. 1979. Artificial ripening techniques for loblolly pine cones. In: Proceedings, seed collection workshop; 1979 May 16–18; Macon, GA. SA-TP-8. Atlanta: USDA Forest Service, Southern Region, State and Private Forestry: 53–58.

Lantz CW. 1987. Which southern pine species is best for your site? Forest Farmer (October):11–12.

Lantz CW. 1988. Overview of southern regeneration. In: Proceedings, 1988 Southern Forest Nursery Association; 1988 July 25–28; Charleston, SC. [Place of publication unknown]: Southern Forest Nursery Association: 1–7.

Larsen HS, Boyer JN. 1986. Root growth potential of loblolly pine (Pinus taeda L.) seedlings from twenty southern nurseries. Circ. 286. Auburn, AL: Alabama Agricultural Experiment Station. 16 p.

Larsen HS, South DB, Boyer JM. 1986. Root growth potential, seedling morphology and bud dormancy correlate with survival of loblolly pine seedlings planted in December in Alabama. Tree Physiology 1(3):253–263.

Larsen HS, South DB, Boyer JN. 1988. Foliar nitrogen content at lifting correlates with early growth of loblolly pine seedlings from 20 nurseries. Southern Journal of Applied Forestry 12(3):181–185.

Larson J, Hallman R. 1980. Planting. In: Equipment for reforestation and timber stand improvement. Missoula, MT: USDA Forest Service, Equipment Development Center: 117–151.

Larson J, Milodragovich E. 1982. Catalog for hand planting tools. No. 8224-2501 (Project 9123). Missoula, MT: USDA Forest Service, Equipment Development Center. 33 p.

Leach GN, Gresham HH. 1983. Early field performance of loblolly pine seedlings with Pisolithus tinctorius ectomycorrhizae on two lower Coastal Plain sites. Southern Journal of Applied Forestry 7(3):149–153.

Little S. 1973. Survival, growth of loblolly, pitch, shortleaf pines established by different methods in New Jersey. Tree Planters' Notes 24(4):1–5.

Little S, Somes HA. 1964. Root systems of direct-seeded and variously planted loblolly, shortleaf, and pitch pines. Res. Pap. NE-26. Upper Darby, PA: USDA Forest Service, Northeastern Forest Experiment Station. 13 p.

Lockaby BG, Slay JM, Adams JC, Vidrine CG. 1988. Site preparation influences on below ground competing vegetation and loblolly pine seedling growth. New Forests 2:131–138.

Lohrey RE. 1970. Spot seeding slash and loblolly pines. Forest Farmer 29(12):12–18.

Lohrey RE. 1973. Planted pines grow better than seeded pines on hardwood-dominated site. Tree Planters' Notes 24(2):12–13.

Lohrey RE. 1974. Site preparation improves survival and growth of direct-seeded pines. Res. Note SO-185. New Orleans: USDA Forest Service, Southern Forest Experiment Station. 4 p.

Lohrey RE, Jones EP Jr. 1983. Natural regeneration and direct seeding. In: Proceedings of the managed slash pine ecosystem symposium; 1981 June 9–11; Gainesville, FL. Gainesville, FL: University of Florida, School of Forest Resources and Conservation: 183–193.

Lowman BJ. 1975. Equipment for processing small seed lots. Catalog No. 7524-2505. Missoula, MT: USDAForest Service. Equipment Development Center. 57 p.

Lowman BJ, McLaren J. 1976. Nursery equipment catalog. Catalog 7624-2501. Missoula, MT: USDA Forest Service, Equipment Development Center. 111 p.

Lowman BJ, and others. 1992. Bareroot nursery equipment catalog. Missoula, MT: USDA Forest Service, Equipment Development Center: 126–130.

Lyle ES, Gilmore AR. 1958. The effect of rough handling of loblolly pine cones seed germination. Journal of Forestry 56(8):595.

Lyle ES, Pearce ND. 1968. Sulfur deficiency in nursery seedlings may be caused by concentrated fertilizers. Tree Planters' Notes 19(1):9–10.

Lyle ES Jr, Gilmore AR, May JT. 1958. Survival and growth of 2-0 longleaf and loblolly seedlings in the field. Tree Planters' Notes 33:26–28.

Mangold RD, Moulton RJ, Snellgrove JD. 1991. Tree planting in the United States 1990. Washington, DC: USDA Forest Service, State and Private Forestry, Cooperative Forestry. 18 p.

Mann WF Jr. 1960. Direct-seeding comes to the South. In: Proceedings, Meeting of the Society of American Foresters; 1960; [Location unknown]. Washington, DC: Society of American Foresters: 15–18.

Mann WF Jr. 1966. Guides for direct-seeding the southern pines. Forest Farmer 25(7):99–103.

Mann WF Jr. 1968. Ten years' experience with direct-seeding in the South. Journal of Forestry 66(11):828–833.

Mann WF Jr. 1969. Techniques and progress in regenerating southern pines. Forest Products Journal 19(8):10–16.

Mann WF Jr, Burkhalter HD. 1961. The South's largest successful direct-seeding. Journal of Forestry 59(2):83–87.

Mann WF Jr, Dell TR. 1971. Yields of 17-year-old loblolly pine planted on a cutover site at various spacings. Res. Pap. SO-70. New Orleans: USDA Forest Service, Southern Forest Experiment Station. 9 p.

Mann WF Jr, Derr HJ. 1966. Guidelines for direct-seeding loblolly pine. Occ. Pap. 188. New Orleans: USDA Forest Service, Southern Forest Experiment Station. 23 p.

Marx DH. 1977. Manipulation of selected mycorrhizal fungi to increase forest biomass. In: 1977 TAPPI Forest Biology Wood Chemistry Cconference; 1977 June 20–22; Madison, WI. Atlanta: TAPPI Press: 139–149.

Marx DH, Artman JD. 1978. Growth and ectomycorrhizal development of loblolly pine seedlings in nursery soil infested with Pisolithus tinctorius and Thelephora terrestris in Virginia. Res. Note SE-256. Asheville, NC: USDA Forest Service, Southeastern Forest Experiment Station. 4 p.

Marx DH, Bell W. 1985. Formation of Pisolithus ectomycorrhizae on loblolly pine seedlings with spore pellet inoculum applied at different times. Res. Pap. SE-249. Asheville, NC: USDA Forest Service, Southeastern Forest Experiment Station. 6 p.

Marx DH, Bryan WC. 1975. The significance of mycorrhizae to forest trees. In: Forest soils and forest land management. Quebec City, Quebec: Les Presses de l'Universite Laval: 107–117.

Marx DH, Cordell CE. 1987. Triadimefon affects Pisolithus ectomycorrhizal development, fusiform rust, and growth of loblolly and slash pines in nurseries. Res. Pap. SE-267. Asheville, NC: USDA Forest Service, Southeastern Forest Experiment Station. 14 p.

Marx DH, Hatchell GE. 1986. Root stripping of ectomycorrhizae decreases field performance of loblolly and longleaf pine seedlings. Southern Journal of Applied Forestry 10(3):173–179.

Marx DH, Bryan WC, Cordell CE. 1976. Growth and ectomycorrhizal development of pine seedlings in nursery soils infested with the fungal symbiont Pisolithus tinctorius. Forest Science 22(1):91–99.

Marx DH, Bryan WC, Cordell CE. 1977a. Survival and growth of pine seedlings with Pisolithus ectomycorrhizae after two years on reforestation sites in North Carolina and Florida. Forest Science 23(3):363–373.

Marx DH, Cordell CE, Clark A III. 1988. Eight-year performance of loblolly pine with Pisolithus ectomycorrhizae on a good-quality forest site. Southern Journal of Applied Forestry 12(4):275–280.

Marx DH, Cordell CE, France RC. 1986. Effects of triadimefon on growth and ectomycorrhizal development of loblolly and slash pines in nurseries. Phytopathology 76(8):824–831.

Marx DH, Cordell CE, Kenney DS, and others. 1984a. Commercial vegetative inoculum of Pisolithus tinctorius and inoculation techniques for development of ectomycorrhizae on bare-root tree seedlings. Monogr. 25. Forest Science 30(3):101.

Marx DH, Cordell CE, Maul SB, Ruehle JL. 1989a. Ectomycorrhizal development on pine by Pisolithus tinctorius in bare-root and container seedling nurseries: 1. Efficacy of various vegetative inoculum formulations. New Forests 3:45–56.

Marx DH, Cordell CE, Maul SB, Ruehle JL. 1989b. Ectomycorrhizal development on pine by *Pisolithus tinctorius* in bare-root and container seedling nurseries: 2. Efficacy of various vegetative and spore inocula. New Forests 3:57–66.

Marx DH, Hatch AB, Mendicino JF. 1977b. High soil fertility decreases sucrose content and susceptibility of loblolly pine roots to ectomycorrhizal infection by *Pisolithus tinctorius*. Canadian Journal of Botany 55(12):1569–1574.

Marx DH, Jarl K, Ruehle JL, Bell W. 1984b. Development of *Pisolithus tinctorius* ectomycorrhizae on pine seedlings using basidiospore-encapsulated seeds. Forest Science 30(4):897–907.

Marx DH, Mexal JG, Morris WG. 1979. Inoculation of nursery seedbeds with *Pisolithus tinctorius* spores mixed with hydromulch increases ectomycorrhizae and growth of loblolly pines. Southern Journal of Applied Forestry 3(4):175–178.

Marx DH, Morris WG, Mexal JG. 1978. Growth and ectomycorrhizal development of loblolly pine seedlings in fumigated and nonfumigated nursery soil infested with different fungal symbionts. Forest Science 24(2):193–203.

Marx DH, Ruehle JL, Riffle JW, and others. 1982. Commercial vegetative inoculum of *Pisolithus tinctorius* and inoculation techniques for development of ectomycorrhizae on container-grown tree seedlings. Forest Science 28(2):373–400.

Matney TG, Hodges JD. 1985. A method for evaluating survival adequacy in young plantations. In: Proceedings, 3rd Biennial Southern Silvicultural Research Conference; 1984 November 7–8; Atlanta, GA. Gen. Tech. Rep. SO-54. New Orleans: USDA Forest Service, Southern Forest Experiment Station: 110–116.

May JT. 1985a. Basic concepts of soil management. In: Lantz CW, ed. Southern pine nursery handbook. Atlanta: USDA Forest Service, Southern Region, Cooperative Forestry: 1-1-1-25.

May JT. 1985b. Nutrients and Fertilization. In: Lantz CW, ed. Southern pine nursery handbook. Atlanta: USDA Forest Service, Southern Region, Cooperative Forestry: 12-1-12-41.

May JT. 1985c. Soil moisture. In: Lantz CW, ed. Southern pine nursery handbook. Atlanta: USDA Forest Service, Southern Region, Cooperative Forestry: 11- 1-11-19.

McClurkin DC. 1962. Good survival of nondormant loblolly pine seedlings. Tree Planters' Notes 51:10.

McClurkin DC. 1966. Survival of planted loblolly pine seedlings: moisture, temperature, and soil as influences. Journal of Forestry 64(11):731–734.

McClurkin DC. 1974. Survival, dry matter accumulation, and water use of loblolly pine seedlings treated with chemical antitranspirants. Forest Science 20(4):372–374.

McDonald S, Krugman SL. 1985. Worldwide planting of southern pines. In: South DB, ed. Proceedings, International Symposium on Nursery Management Practices for the Southern Pines; 1985 August 4–9; Montgomery, AL. Auburn University, AL: Auburn University, Department of Research Information: 1–19.

McGee CE. 1980. Expanding options for reforestation of the Cumberland Plateau. Southern Journal of Applied Forestry 4(4):158–162.

McGee CE. 1982. Low-quality hardwood stands. Opportunities for management in the interior uplands. Gen. Tech. Rep. SO-40. New Orleans: USDA Forest Service, Southern Forest Experiment Station. 6 p.

McGilvray JM, Barnett JP. 1988. Increasing speed, accuracy, and safety of pressure chamber determinations of plant moisture stress. Tree Planters' Notes 39(3):3–4.

McLemore BF. 1964. Light during stratification hastens dark-germination of loblolly pine seed. Forest Science 10(3):348–349.

McLemore BF. 1973. Chemicals fail to induce abscission of loblolly and slash pine cones. Res. Note SO-155. New Orleans: USDA Forest Service, Southern Forest Experiment Station. 3 p.

McLemore BF. 1975. Collection date, cone-storage period affect southern pine seed yields, viability. Tree Planters' Notes 26(1): 24–26.

McLemore BF. 1982. Comparison of 1-0 and 2-0 loblolly pine seedlings. Tree Planters' Notes 33(2):22–23.

McLemore BF, Barnett JP. 1966a. Loblolly seed dormancy influenced by cone and seed handling procedures and parent tree. Res. Note SO-41. New Orleans: USDA Forest Service, Southern Forest Experiment Station. 4 p.

McLemore BF, Barnett JP. 1966b. Storing repellent-coated southern pine seed. Journal of Forestry 64(9):619–621.

McLemore BF, Barnett JP. 1968. Moisture content influences dormancy of stored loblolly pine seed. Forest Science 14(2):219–221.

McLemore BF, Czabator FJ. 1961. Length of stratification and germination of loblolly pine seed. Journal of Forestry 59(4):267–269.

McNab WH. 1976. Prescribed burning and direct-seeding old clearcuts in the Piedmont. Res. Note SE-229. Asheville, NC: USDA Forest Service, Southeastern Forest Experiment Station. 4 p.

Mergen F, Abbot HG, Mann WF Jr, and others. 1981. Sowing forests from the air. Washington, DC: National Academy Press. 61 p.

Mexal JG. 1980. Growth of loblolly pine seedlings: 1. morphological variability related to day of emergence. For. Res. Tech. Rep. 045830 Hot Springs, AR: Weyerhaeuser Corp. 9 p.

Mexal JG. 1981. Seedling bed density influence seedling yield and performance. In: Proceedings, 1980 Southern Nursery Conference; 1980 September 2–4; Lake Barkley, KY. [Place of publication and publisher unknown]: 89–95.

Mexal JG, Burton S. 1978. Root development of planted loblolly pine seedlings. In: Proceedings, Root Form of Planted Trees Symposium; 1978 May 16–19; Victoria, BC: British Columbia Ministry of Forests, Canadian Forestry Service. 8: 85–90.

Mexal JG, Carlson WC. 1982. Dormancy and cold-hardiness of containerized loblolly pine seedlings. In: Guldin RW, Barnett JP, comp. Proceedings, Southern Containerized Forest Tree Seedling Conference; 1981 August 25–27; Savannah, GA. Gen. Tech. Rep. SO-37. New Orleans: USDA Forest Service, Southern Forest Experiment Station: 59–63.

Mexal JG, Fisher JT. 1985. Pruning loblolly pine seedlings. In: Lantz CW, comp. Proceedings, 1984 Southern Nursery Conferences; 1984 June 11–14; Alexandria, LA/1984 July 24–27; Asheville, NC. Atlanta: USDA Forest Service, Southern Region: 75–83.

Mexal JG, Fisher JT. 1987. Size hierarchy in conifer seedbeds. 1: Time of emergence. New Forests 1(3):187–196.

Miller AE, Rose RW, Ray KF. 1985. Root wrenching and top pruning effects on loblolly pine nursery seedling development. In: Proceedings, 3rd Biennial Southern Silvicultural Research Conference; 1984 November 7–8; Atlanta, GA. Gen. Tech. Rep. SO-54. New Orleans: USDA Forest Service, Southern Forest Experiment Station: 11–7.

Miller AE, Reines M. 1974. Survival and water relations in loblolly pine seedlings after root immersion in alginate solution. Forest Science 20(2):192–194.

Miller JH. 1990. Effectiveness of banded herbicide applications at the time of planting. Final report summary FS-SO-4105-2.26, problem 2. 1 p. [On file with USDA Forest Service, Southern Forest Experiment Station, Auburn, AL.]

Mills WL Jr, South DB. 1984. Production costs in southern bare-root nurseries. Tree Planters' Notes 35(3):19–22.

Mitchell ML, Hassan AE, Davey CB, Gregory JD. 1982. Loblolly pine growth in compacted greenhouse soils. Transactions of the American Society of Agricultural Engineers 25(2):304–307, 312.

Mitchell RJ, Zutter BR, South DB. 1988. Interaction between weed control and loblolly pine, *Pinus taeda*, seedling quality. Weed Technology 2:191–195.

Morby FE. 1984. Nursery site selection, layout, and development. In: Duryea ML, Landis TD, eds. Forest nursery manual: production of bareroot seedlings. Boston: Kluwer Academic Publishers: 9–15.

Muller CA. 1983. Loblolly pine seedling survival study, 1979–80 and 1980–81 planting seasons. In: Proceedings, 1982 Southern Nursery Conferences; 1982 August 9–12; Oklahoma City,

OK/1982 July 12–15; Savannah, GA. R8-TP4. Atlanta: USDA Forest Service, Southern Region: 27–39.

Munson KR. 1983. Decomposition and effect on pH of various organic soil amendments. In: Proceedings, 1982 Southern Nursery Conferences; 1982 August 9–12; Oklahoma City, OK/1982 July 12–15; Savannah, GA. R8-TP4. Atlanta: USDA Forest Service, Southern Region: 121–130.

Munson KR, Stone EL. 1985. Seedling and soil nutrient status during the lifetime period in a north Florida nursery. In: Lantz CW, comp. Proceedings, 1984 Southern Nursery Conferences; 1984 June 11–14; Alexandria, LA/1984 July 24–27; Asheville, NC. Atlanta: USDA Forest Service, Southern Region: 152–157.

Nebgen RJ, Meyer JF. 1985. Seed bed density, undercutting, and lateral root pruning effects on loblolly seedling morphology, field survival, and growth. In: South DB, ed. Proceedings, International Symposium on Nursery Management Practices for the Southern Pines; 1985 August 4–9; Montgomery, AL. Auburn University, AL: Auburn University, Department of Research Information: 136–147.

Nelson L, Switzer GL. 1985. Trends in the maintenence of soil fertility in Mississippi nurseries. In: South DB, ed. Proceedings, International Symposium on Nursery Management Practices for the Southern Pines; 1985 August 4–9; Montgomery, AL. Auburn, AL: Auburn University, Department of Research Information: 222–236.

Nusser SM, Wentworth TR. 1987. Relationships among first-year loblolly pine seedling performance, vegetation regrowth, environmental conditions and plantation management practices. In: Proceedings, 4th Biennial Southern Silvicultural Research Conference; 1986 November 4–6; Atlanta, GA. Gen. Tech. Rep. SE-42. Asheville, NC: USDA Forest Service, Southeastern Forest Experiment Station: 565–75.

Osterhaus CA, Lantz CW. 1978. Pine plantations on the cross timbers area of Oklahoma. Southern Journal of Applied Forestry 2(3):90–93.

Pásztor de Castro YP. 1962. Soaking at low temperature as a substitute for stratification of seed of *Pinus elliottii* and *P. taeda*. Silvicultura em São Paulo 1(1):39–60.

Pawuk WH. 1981. Potting media affect growth and disease development of container-grown southern pines. Res. Note SO-268. New Orleans: USDA Forest Service, Southern Forest Experiment Station. 4 p.

Pawuk WH, Barnett JP. 1979. Seed handling practices for southern pines grown in containers. Southern Journal of Applied Forestry 3(1):19–22.

Pawuk WH, Barnett JP. 1981. Benomyl stimulates ectomycorrhizal development by *Pisolithus tinctorius* on shortleaf pine pine grown in containers. Res. Note SO- 267. New Orleans: USDA Forest Service, Southern Forest Experiment Station. 3 p.

Pease DA. 1980. Prototype tree planter undergoes refinement. Forest Industries 107(12):42–43.

Pepper WD, Barnett JP. 1981a. Choosing sowing strategies for containerized seedling operations. Canadian Journal of Forest Research 11(3):682–688.

Pepper WD, Barnett JP. 1981b. Predicting seed germination and seedling establishment in containers. Canadian Journal of Forest Research 11(3):677–681.

Pepper WD, Hodge WD. 1982. Computer can choose sowing strategies for containerized seedlings. Gen. Tech. Rep. SO-39. New Orleans: USDA Forest Service, Southern Forest Experiment Station. 12 p.

Perry TO. 1962. Racial variation in the day and night temperature requirements of red maple and loblolly pine. Forest Science 8(4):336–344.

Perry TO. 1964. Soil compaction and loblolly pine growth. Tree Planters' Notes 67:9.

Perry TO. 1971. Dormancy of trees in winter. Science 171:29–36.

Pharis RP, Kramer PJ. 1964. The effects of nitrogen and drought on loblolly pine seedlings. Forest Science 10(2):143–150.

Pokorny FA. 1983. Pine bark as a soil amendment. In: Proceed-

ings, 1982 Southern Nursery Conferences; 1982 August 9–12; Oklahoma City, OK/1982 July 12–15; Savannah, GA. R8-TP4. Atlanta: USDA Forest Service, Southern Region: 131–139.

Pritchett WL. 1973. The effect of nitrogen and phosphorus fertilizers on the growth and composition of loblolly and slash pine seedlings in pots. Proceedings of the Soil and Crop Science Society of Florida 32:161–165.

Pritchett WL. 1979. Properties and management of forest soils. New York: Wiley. 500 p.

Retzlaff WA, South DB. 1985a. High soil moisture levels in the nursery can advers[e]ly affect loblolly pine seedling morphology. In: Lantz CW, comp. Proceedings, 1984 Southern Nursery Conferences; 1984 June 11–14; Alexandria, LA/1984 July 24–27; Asheville, NC. Atlanta: USDA Forest Service, Southern Region: 158–167.

Retzlaff WA, South DB. 1985b. Variation in seedbed moisture correlated with growth of *Pinus taeda* seedlings. South African Forestry Journal 133:2–5.

Retzlaff WA, Miller AE, Toler JE. 1987. Effection of carbon dioxide enrichment on growth and field survival of container-grown *Pinus taeda* L. seedlings. In: Proceedings, 4th Biennial Southern Silvicultural Research Conference; 1986 November 4–6; Atlanta, GA. Gen. Tech. Rep. SE-42. Asheville, NC: USDA Forest Service, Southeastern Forest Experiment Station: 212–216.

Ritchie GA, Dunlap JR. 1980. Root growth potential: its development and expression in forest tree seedlings. Journal of Forest Science 10(1):218–248.

Rowan SJ. 1982. Effects of rate and kind of seedbed mulch and sowing depth on germination of southern pine seed. Tree Planters' Notes 33(2):19–21.

Rowan SJ. 1983. Loss of feeder roots lowers seedling survival more than severe black root rot. Tree Planters' Notes 34(1):18–20.

Rowan SJ. 1985a. Growth, survival, and ectomycorrhizal development of slash pine seedlings inoculated with *Pisolithus tinctorius* and sprayed with Ferbam and Bayleton fungicides. In: Lantz CW, comp. Proceedings, 1984 Southern Nursery Conferences; 1984 June 11–14; Alexandria, LA/1984 July 24–27; Asheville, NC. Atlanta: USDA Forest Service, Southern Region: 91–98.

Rowan SJ. 1985b. Seedbed density affects performance of slash and loblolly pine in Georgia. In: South DB, ed. Proceedings, International Symposium on Nursery Management Practices for the Southern Pines; 1985 August 4–9; Montgomery, AL. Auburn University, AL: Auburn University, Department of Research Information: 126–135.

Rowan SJ. 1987. Nursery seedling quality affects growth and survival in outplantings. GA For. Res. Pap. No. 70. Macon, GA: Georgia Forestry Commission, Research Division. 13 p.

Royall WC Jr, Ferguson ER. 1962. Controlling bird and mammal damage in direct seeding loblolly pine in east Texas. Journal of Forestry 60(1):37–39.

Ruehle JL. 1980. Inoculation of containerized loblolly pine seedlings with basidiospores of *Pisolithus tinctorius*. Res. Note SE-291. Asheville, NC: USDA Forest Service, Southeastern Forest Experiment Station. 4 p.

Ruehle JL. 1982. Field performance of container-grown loblolly pine seedlings with specific ectomycorrhizae on a reforestation site in South Carolina. Southern Journal of Applied Forestry 6(1):30–33.

Ruehle JL. 1983. The relationship between lateral-root development and spread of *Pisolithus tinctorius* ectomycorrhizae after planting of container-grown loblolly pine seedlings. Forest Science 29(3):519–526.

Ruehle JL. 1985a. The effect of cupric carbonate on root morphology of containerized mycorrhizal pine seedlings. Canadian Journal Forest Research 15(3):586–592.

Ruehle JL. 1985b. Lateral-root development and spread of *Pisolithus tinctorius* ectomycorrhizae on bare-root and container-grown loblolly pine seedlings after planting. Forest

Science 31(1):220–225.

Ruehle JL, Marx DH. 1977. Developing ectomycorrhizae on containerized pine seedlings. Res. Note SE-242. Asheville, NC: USDA Forest Service, Southeastern Forest Experiment Station. 8 p.

Ruehle JL, Wells CG. 1984. Development of *Pisolithus tinctorius* ectomycorrhizae on container-grown pine seedlings as affected by fertility. Forest Science 30(4):1010–1016.

Russell TE. 1974. Broadcast and spot-seeded pines grow equally well in central Tennessee. Tree Planters' Notes 25(3):20–22.

Russell TE, Mignery AL. 1968. Direct-seeding pine in Tennessee's highlands. Res. Pap. SO-31. New Orleans: USDA Forest Service, Southern Forest Experiment Station. 22 p.

Schmidtling RC. 1972. Replacement planting with potted southern pines on research plots. Res. Note SO-146. New Orleans: USDA Forest Service Southern Forest Experiment Station. 4 p.

Schoorel AF. 1960. The influence of extreme temperatures and desiccation on the germination of seeds. Proceedings of the International Seed Testing Association 25(1): 573–579.

Schultz AJ. 1965. Replacement planting. In: A guide to loblolly and slash pine plantation management in southeastern USA. Rep. 14: Macon, GA: Georgia Forest Research Council: 75–82.

Schultz RP. 1973. Site treatment and planting method alter root development of slash pine. Res. Pap. SE-109. Asheville, NC: USDA Forest Service, Southeastern Forest Experiment Station. 11 p.

Schultz RP. 1975. Intensive culture of southern pines: maximum yields on short rotations. Iowa State Journal of Research 49(3/2):325–327.

Schultz RP, Wilhite LP. 1967. Operational summer planting of slash pine. Res. Note SE-80. Asheville, NC: USDA Forest Service, Southeastern Forest Experiment Station. 3 p.

Seiler JR, Johnson JD. 1985. Moisture stress conditioning of containerized loblolly pine. In: Lantz, C.W., comp. Proceedings, 1984 Southern Nursery Conferences; 1984 June 11–14; Alexandria, LA/1984 July 24–27; Asheville, NC. Atlanta: USDA Forest Service, Southern Region: 60–65.

Shepard RK. 1973. The effect of soil fumigation on the growth and development of loblolly pine. LSU Forest Res. Rep. Baton Rouge: Louisiana State University, North Louisiana Hill Farm Experiment Station: 42–48.

Shipman RD. 1964. Low seedbed densities can improve early height growth of planted slash and loblolly pine seedlings. Journal of Forestry 62(11):814–817.

Shoulders E. 1955. Release underplanted loblolly early. Res. Note 100. New Orleans:USDA Forest Service, Southern Forest Experiment Station. 1 p.

Shoulders E. 1961. Effect of nursery bed density on loblolly and slash pine seedlings. Journal of Forestry 59(8):576–579.

Shoulders E. 1965. Root pruning in southern pine nurseries. Tree Planters' Notes 70:12–15.

Shoulders E. 1982. Comparison of growth and yield of four southern pines on uniform sites in the Gulf Coastal Plain. In: Predicting growth and yield in the mid-South: Proceedings, 31st Annual Forestry Symposium; [dates unknown]: [Location unknown]. Baton Rouge, LA: Louisiana State University, Division of Continuing Education: 75–100.

Shoulders E, Jorgensen JR. 1969. Mycorrhizae increase field survival of planted loblolly pine. Tree Planters' Notes 20(1):14–17.

Simmons GL, Ezell AW. 1983. Root development of loblolly pine seedlings in compacted soils. In: Proceedings, 2nd Biennial Southern Silvicultural Research Conference; 1982 November 4–5; Atlanta, GA. Gen. Tech. Rep. SE-24. Asheville, NC: USDA Forest Service, Southeastern Forest Experiment Station: 26–29.

Simms DA. 1983. Field packing of southern pine seedlings at the Columbia nursery. In: Proceedings, 1982 Southern Nursery Conferences; 1982 August 9–12; Oklahoma City, OK/1982 July 12–15; Savannah, GA. R8-TP4. Atlanta: USDA Forest Service, Southern Region: 229–232.

Slocum GK. 1951. Survival of loblolly pine seedlings as influenced by depth of planting. Journal of Forestry 49(7):51.

Slocum GK, Maki TE. 1956. Some effects of depth of planting upon loblolly pine in the North Carolina Piedmont. Journal of Forestry 54(1):21–25.

Sluder ER. 1979. The effects of seed and seedling size on survival and growth of loblolly pine. Tree Planters' Notes 30(4):2–28.

Smalley GW. 1979. Classification and evaluation of forest sites on southern Cumberland Plateau. Gen. Tech. Rep. SO-23. New Orleans: USDA Forest Service, Southern Forest Experiment Station. 59 p.

Smalley GW. 1980. Classification and evaluation of forest sites on the Western Highland Rim and Pennyroyal. Gen. Tech. Rep. SO-30. New Orleans: USDA Forest Service, Southern Forest Experiment Station. 120 p.

Smalley GW. 1982. Classification and evaluation of forest sites on mid-Cumberland Plateau. Gen. Tech. Rep. SO-38. New Orleans: USDA Forest Service, Southern Forest Experiment Station. 58 p.

Smalley GW. 1983. Classification and evaluation of forest sites on Eastern Highland Rim and Pennyroyal. Gen. Tech. Rep. SO-43. New Orleans: USDA Forest Service, Southern Forest Experiment Station. 123 p.

Smith JL, Campbell CD, Mead RA. 1986. Imaging and identifying loblolly pine seedlings after the first growing season on 35mm aerial photography. Canadian Journal of Remote Sensing 12(1):19–27.

South DB. 1986. Herbicides for southern pine seedbeds. Southern Journal of Applied Forestry 10(3):152–161.

South DB. 1987a. Economic aspects of nursery seed efficiency. Southern Journal of Applied Forestry 11(2):106–109.

South DB. 1987b. A re-evaluation of Wakeley's "critical tests" of morphological grades of southern pine nursery stock. South African Forestry Journal (142):56–59.

South DB. 1988. Diphenylether herbicides used on southern pine seedlings in the United States. Aspects of Applied Biology (16):215–221.

South DB, Barnett JP. 1986. Herbicides and planting date affect early performance of container-grown and bare-root loblolly pine seedlings in Alabama. New Forests 1(1):17–27.

South DB, Larsen HS. 1986. Seed efficiency in southern pine nurseries. Highlights of Agricultural Research [Alabama Agricultural Experiment Station] 33(2):5.

South DB, Davey CB. 1983. The southern forest nursery soil testing program. In: Proceedings, 1982 Southern Nursery Conferences; 1982 August 9–12; Oklahoma City, OK/1982 July 12–15; Savannah, GA. R8-TP4. Atlanta: USDA Forest Service, Southern Region: 140–170.

South DB, Mexal JG. 1984. Growing the "best" seedling for reforestation success. For. Ser. 12. Auburn, AL: Alabama Agricultural Experiment Station: 4–11.

South DB, Boyer JN, Bosch L. 1985. Survival and growth of loblolly pine as influenced by seedling grade: 13-year results. Southern Journal of Applied Forestry 9(2):76–81.

South DB, Kelley WD, Chapman W. 1989b. "Fall mosaic" of loblolly pine in a forest tree nursery. Tree Planters' Notes 40(1):19–22.

South DB, Mitchell RJ, Dixon RK, Vedder M. 1988a. New-ground syndrome: an ectomycorrhizal deficiency in pine nurseries. Southern Journal of Applied Forestry 12(4):234–239.

South DB, Williams HM, Webb A. 1988b. Should fall irrigation be applied at nurseries located on sands? Southern Journal of Applied Forestry 12(4):273–274.

South DB, Williams HM, Webb A. 1989a. Costs and benefits from fall irrigation at a sandy loblolly pine nursery. Applied Agricultural Research 4(4):275–279.

Stangle CM, Venator CR. 1985. Testing superabsorbent treatments for loblolly pine seedlings. In: Lantz CW, comp. Proceedings, 1984 Southern Nursery Conferences; 1984 June 11–14; Alexandria, LA/1984 July 24–27; Asheville, NC. Atlanta: USDA Forest Service, Southern Region: 174–177.

Steinbeck K. 1990. Pine seedling mortality in conservation reserve planting in Georgia. GA For. Res. Pap. 82. Macon, GA: Georgia Forestry Commision. 7 p.

Stone EL, Hollis CA, Barnard EL. 1982. Boron deficiency in a southern pine nursery. Southern Journal of Applied Forestry 9(2):108–112.

Stransky JJ. 1962. Furrows aid pine survival. Tree Planters' Notes 53:23–24.

Stransky JJ. 1963. Needle moisture as mortality index for southern pine seedlings. Botanical Gazette 124(3):178–179.

Summerville KO. 1985. Another look at nursery bed mulches and stickers. In: Lantz CW, comp. Proceedings, 1984 Southern Nursery Conferences; 1984 June 11–14; Alexandria, LA/1984 July 24–27; Asheville, NC. Atlanta: USDA Forest Service, Southern Region: 66–74.

Switzer GL. 1960. Exposure and planting depth effects on loblolly pine planting stock on poorly drained sites. Journal of Forestry 58(5):390–391.

Switzer GL, Nelson LE. 1963. Effects of nursery fertility and density on seedling characteristics, yield, and field performance of loblolly pine. Soil Science Society of America Journal 27(4):461–464.

Switzer GL, Nelson LE. 1967. Seedling quality strongly influenced by nursery soil management, Mississippi study shows. Tree Planters' Notes 18(3):5–14.

Tainter FH, Walstad JD. 1977. Colonization of outplanted loblolly pines by native ectomycorrhizal fungi. Forest Science 23(1):77–79.

Tanaka Y, Walstad JD, Borrecco JE. 1976. The effect of wrenching on morphology and field performance of Douglas fir and loblolly pine seedlings. Canadian Journal of Forest Research 6(4):453–458.

Taylor R, Barnett,JP. 1985a. Evaluation of time-temperature monitors for control of seedling storage. Tree Planters' Notes 36(1):19–20.

Taylor R, Barnett JP. 1985b. Use of time-temperature monitors for controlling seedling quality in storage. In: Lantz CW, comp. Proceedings, 1984 Southern Nursery Conferences; 1984 June 11–14; Alexandria, LA/1984 July 24–27; Asheville, NC. Atlanta: USDA Forest Service, Southern Region: 178–183.

Thames JL. 1962. Seedling size and soil moisture affect survival of loblolly pine sprouts. Tree Planters' Notes 55:27–29.

Thor E, Huffman PJ. 1969. Direct seeding and planting of loblolly pine on the highland rim in Tennessee. Tree Planters' Notes 20(2):19–22.

Toole VK, Toole EH, Borthwick HA, Snow AG Jr. 1962. Responses of seeds of *Pinus taeda* and *P. strobus* to light. Plant Physiology 37(2):228–233.

Torbert JL, Burger JA, Kreh RE. 1986. Nutrient concentration effects on *Pisolithus tinctorius* development on containerized loblolly pine (*Pinus taeda* L.) seedlings. Tree Planters' Notes 37(3):17–22.

Trousdell KB. 1959. Site treatment reduces need for planting at loblolly harvest time. Res. Pap. 102. Asheville, NC: USDA Forest Service, Southeastern Forest Experiment Station. 11 p.

Tuttle CL, Golden MS, South DB, Meldahl RS. 1987. Survival of loblolly pine seedlings on adverse sites is influenced by initial height. Highlights of Agricultural Research [Alabama Agricultural Experiment Station] 34(4):15.

Tuttle CL, Golden MS, South DB, Meldahl RS. 1988a. Soil compaction effects on *Pinus taeda* establishment from seed and early growth. Canadian Journal of Forest Research 18(5):628–632.

Tuttle CL, South DB, Golden MS, Meldahl RS. 1988b. Initial *Pinus taeda* seedling height relationships with early survival and growth. Canadian Journal of Forest Research 18(7):867–871.

USDA FS [U.S. Department of Agriculture, Forest Service]. 1985. National Forest System reforestation and timber stand improvement report for fiscal year 1984. 2490 Records and reports. 4 p. [On file with USDA Forest Service, Washington, DC.]

USDA FS [U.S. Department of Agriculture, Forest Service]. 1989. A guide to care and planting of southern pine seedlings. R8-MB39. Atlanta: USDA Forest Service, Southern Region. 44 p.

Ursic SJ, Williston HL, Burns RM. 1966. Late planting improves loblolly survival. Res. Pap. SO-24. New Orleans: USDA Forest Service, Southern Forest Experiment Station. 12 p.

Venator CR. 1983a. First-year survival of morphologically graded loblolly pine seedlings in central Louisiana. Tree Planters' Notes 34(3):34–36.

Venator CR. 1983b. Is it possible to detect cull trees within 1 year after planting? Tree Planters' Notes 34(2):26–27.

Venator CR. 1983c. A systems approach to forest tree seedling production: a new concept. In: Proceedings, 1982 Southern Nursery Conferences—Western Session; 1982 August 9–12; Oklahoma City, OK. Eastern Session; 1982 July 12–15; Savannah, GA. R8-TP4. Atlanta: USDA Forest Service, Southern Region: 267–278.

Venator CR. 1985. Evidence of the presence of a lifting window for loblolly pine nursery seedlings. In: Lantz CW, comp. Proceedings, 1984 Southern Nursery Conferences; 1984 June 11–14; Alexandria, LA/1984 July 24–27; Asheville, NC. Atlanta: USDA Forest Service, Southern Region: 184–191.

Venator CR, Barnett JP. 1985. Relating root growth potential to survival and growth of loblolly pine seedlings. In: Proceedings, 3rd Biennial Southern Silvicultural Research Conference; 1984 November 7–8; Atlanta, GA. Gen. Tech. Rep. SO-54. New Orleans: USDA Forest Service, Southern Forest Experiment Station: 125–126.

Venator CR, Brissette JC. 1983. The effectiveness of superabsorbent materials for maintaining southern pine seedlings during cold storage. In: Proceedings, 1982 Southern Nursery Conferences; 1982 August 9–12; Oklahoma City, OK/1982 July 12–15; Savannah, GA. R8-TP4. Atlanta: USDA Forest Service, Southern Region: 240–245.

Venator CR, Brissette JC. 1985. Survival and height growth of loblolly pine seedlings as influenced by packing, storage, and drought. In: Lantz CW, comp. Proceedings, 1984 Southern Nursery Conferences; 1984 June 11–14; Alexandria, LA/1984 July 24–27; Asheville, NC. Atlanta: USDA Forest Service, Southern Region: 192–198.

Venator CR, Mexal JG. 1981. The effect of wrenching and planting date on the survival of loblolly seedlings. In: Proceedings, 1st Biennial Southern Silvicultural Research Conference; 1980 November 6–7; Atlanta, GA. Gen. Tech. Rep. SO-34. New Orleans: USDA Forest Service, Southern Forest Experiment Station: 20–24.

Vozzo JA, Bonner FT. 1985. Quality of pine seed collected from the net retrieval system. In: Lantz CW, comp. Proceedings, 1984 Southern Nursery Conferences; 1984 June 11–14; Alexandria, LA/1984 July 24–27; Asheville, NC. Atlanta: USDA Forest Service, Southern Region: 121–126.

Wakeley PC. 1954. Planting the southern pines. Agric. Mono. 18. Washington, DC: USDA Forest Service. 233 p.

Waldrip BT Jr. 1970. Artificial ripening of loblolly pine cones and seed. In: Proceedings, 1970 Southeastern Nurserymen's Conference; [dates and location unknown]. [Place of publication and publisher unknown]: 82–91.

Walker NR, Johnson HJ. 1980. Containerized conifer seedling field performance in Alberta and the northwest territories. Info. Rep. NOR-X-218. Edmonton, AB: Canadian Forestry Service, Northern Forest Research Centre. 32 p.

Walstad JD, Breland JH, Mexal JG. 1977. Application of wrenching and later pruning in loblolly pine nurseries. For. Res. Tech. Rep. 74-17. Hot Springs, AR: Weyerhaeuser Corp. 7 p.

Walters J, Silversides R. 1979. Injection planting of containerized tree seedlings. Info. Rep. FMR-X-120. Ottowa, Canada: Forest Management Institute. 27 p.

Weaver GH, Osterhaus CA. 1976. Economic analysis of planting costs in loblolly pine management. Journal of Forestry 74(4):217–219.

Wilhite LP, Schultz RP. 1969. Summer plantings of sand and longleaf pines fail. Tree Planters' Notes 20(1):7.

Williams HM, South DB, Glover GR. 1988a. Effect of bud status on seedling biomass on root growth potential of loblolly pine. Canadian Journal of Forest Research 18(12):1635–1640.

Williams HM, South DB, Webb A. 1988b. Effects of fall irrigation on morphology and root growth potential of lobloly pine seedlings growing in sand. South African Forestry Journal (147):1–5.

Williston HL. 1965. Moss not needed in kraft-polyethylene bags during loblolly pine seedling transport and cold storage. Tree Planters' Notes 72:10.

Williston HL. 1967. Clay slurry root dip impairs survival of loblolly pine seedlings in Mississippi. Tree Planters' Notes 18(4):28–30.

Williston HL, Cox RG. 1969. Direct seeding of loblolly pine in north Mississippi. Tree Planters' Notes 20(3):28–30.

Williston HL, Ursic SJ. 1979. Planting loblolly pine for erosion control: a review. Tree Planters' Notes 30(2):1–18.

Woods ED, and others. 1988. Influence of site factors on growth of loblolly and shortleaf pine in Oklahoma. Res. Rep. P-900. Oklahoma State, OK: Oklahoma Agricultural Experiment Station. 25 p.

Woods FW. 1980. Growth of loblolly pine with roots planted in five configurations. Southern Journal of Applied Forestry 4(2):70–73.

Woods F, Martin R. 1973. Loblolly pine mycorrhizae in east Tennessee. Tree Planters' Notes 24(4):27.

Woods F, Mollish AP. 1963. Light requirements for germination of imbibed loblolly pine seed. Tree Planters' Notes 58:26–28.

Wynens JC. 1964. Baling tree seedlings by weight. In: Proceedings, Region 8 Forest Nurserymen's Conferences; 1964 August 19–20; Morganton, NC/1964 September 16–17; Oklahoma City, OK. Atlanta: USDA Forest Service, Southern Region: 62–64.

Wynens JC. 1983. Electronic counter use in forest tree nurseries. In: Proceedings, 1982 Southern Nursery Conferences; 1982 August 9–12; Oklahoma City, OK/1982 July 12–15; Savannah, GA. R8-TP4. Atlanta: USDA Forest Service, Southern Region: 279–284.

Xydias GK. 1983. Factors influencing survival and early stocking trends in plantation of loblolly pine. In: Proceedings, 2nd Biennial Southern Silvicultural Research Conference; 1982 November 4–5; Atlanta, GA. Gen. Tech. Rep. SE-24. Asheville, NC: USDA Forest Service, Southeastern Forest Experiment Station: 101–108.

Yeiser JL, Paschke JL. 1987. Regenerating wet sites with bareroot and containerized loblolly pine seedlings. Southern Journal of Applied Forestry 11(1):52–56.

Zarger TG. 1964. Comparison of slowly and rapidly available nitrogen fertilizers for nursery production of pine seedlings. Tree Planters' Notes 66:8–10.

Chapter 7

Genetics and Tree Improvement

Contents

Continued on next page…

Contents (cont'd)

Genetics and Tree Improvement

Introduction

Every stage in the life of a tree is controlled by genes. Tree improvement programs have provided the most exciting area for increasing the quantity and quality of loblolly pine growth and development in the 20th century. Beginning about 1951, great strides were made in finding loblolly trees that exhibited rapid growth, good form, and desirable wood properties. Intensity of selection varied, but as few as 1 tree in 100,000 examined was selected as superior based on appearance (Kellison and Weir 1980; figure 7-1). Nothing was known of the ability of the selected trees to pass on desired properties to their progeny. Both clonal and seedling seed orchards were produced from these selections.

Genetic gains from planting first-generation, improved loblolly pines include more rapid volume growth on both good and poor sites, increased specific gravity, and increased resistance to fusiform rust (table 7-1). The value gained over a 25-year rotation may be as much as 32%

Table 7-1—Estimated gain and correlated response obtained from one generation by selection for specific traits in loblolly pine

Trait and source of genetic variation	Estimated gain obtainable	Correlated response expected if other traits are not controlled*
Volume (geographic variation)	2 m³/ha/yr	Decrease in wood specific gravity; decrease in straightness
Volume (stand-to-stand variation)	2 m³/ha/yr	Decrease in wood specific gravity; decrease in straightness
Volume (within-stand variation)	2 m³/ha/yr	Decrease in wood specific gravity; decrease in straightness
Mature wood specific gravity (within-stand variation)	0.04 g/cm³	Increase in straightness; decrease in volume
Juvenile wood specific gravity (within-stand variation)	0.03 g/cm³	Increase in straightness; decrease in volume
Rust resistance (geographic variation)	50%†	Uncertain
Rust resistance (within-stand variation)	20%‡	Uncertain
Straightness (within-stand variation)	Substantial, but no quantitative data available	Decrease in volume; increase in wood specific gravity

Source: adapted from Van Buijtenen (1985).

* If traits are positively correlated, gains can be additive or even greater. If traits are negatively correlated, one trait may have to be traded for another, or a reasonable compromise arrived at.

† This is a 50% reduction in rust infection; i.e., from 70% to 20% infection.

‡ This is a 20% reduction in rust infection; i.e., from 70% to 50% infection.

Figure 7-1— A superior, 50-year-old loblolly pine. Note the straight, clear bole, small crown, and disease-free condition.

(Talbert and others 1985). There are opportunities to breed loblolly for resistance to diseases other than fusiform rust. For example, susceptibility of loblolly xylem to decay is heritable and is inversely related to specific gravity, diameter growth, and the proportion of summerwood. Thus, breeding for high specific gravity will also decrease susceptibility to decay (Schmidtling and Amburgey 1982). Resistance to hard pine gray blight, *Hypoderma lethale* Dearn., is another strongly inherited character in loblolly (Kraus and Hunt 1971). Preliminary results suggest that susceptibility of loblolly to the annosus root-rot fungus may also vary by genotype (Artman 1974).

Almost all of the 1.5 billion loblolly pine seedlings presently produced each year are reported to have some superior characteristics (Lantz 1988). Many breeding programs are now into the second generation, and some are into the third generation. Advanced-generation gains are expected to exceed initial gains substantially (especially gains in disease resistance) and to far outweigh costs. Genetic engineering (or custom designing of trees) may further increase gains made through tree breeding if specific morphological or physiological changes in a tree can be made in a reasonable period of time. However, isolating genes will not be easy because

each pine cell has 174 times more DNA than a fruit fly (Pearce 1986). Nevertheless, artificial inoculation of *Agrobacterium tumefaciens* into two wild strains of loblolly has produced galls and has transformed pine tissue. The fact that bacterial genes can be transferred into and expressed in loblolly indicates that DNA transfer into the species may be possible (Sederoff and others 1986), and such transfer could revolutionize tree development.

The three major sources of variation available for selective breeding include geographic variation, stand-to-stand variation, and tree-to-tree variation.

Geographic Variation

Geographic variation is probably the most substantial source of genetic variation in loblolly pine. Sixty years of provenance testing has clearly demonstrated the presence and value of geographic variation in the growth rate of the species (Wakeley and Bercaw 1965, Wells 1983). Because loblolly occurs over a wide range of latitudes and longitudes with widely differing climates and photoperiods, geographic variation in the species is substantial. Six general seed source regions differentiate much of the major geographic variation in loblolly (figure 7-2).

Geographic Variation in Morphology

Loblolly pine has adapted physically to varied ecological conditions across its broad range. The following are examples of physical differences associated with regional or local adaptations:

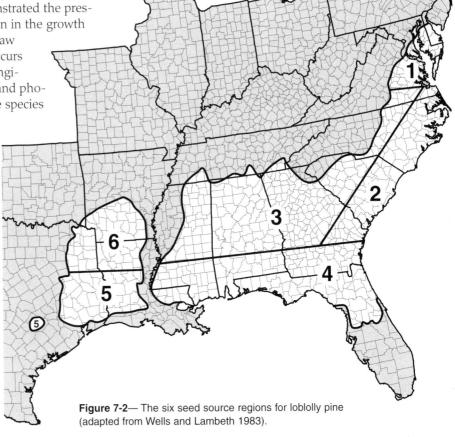

Figure 7-2— The six seed source regions for loblolly pine (adapted from Wells and Lambeth 1983).

1. Trees from the southern part of the range may produce as many as seven branch whorls per growing season, whereas trees from northern areas produce as few as two whorls even when growing in southern locations. However, exposure to prolonged photoperiods can stimulate trees from as far north as Maryland to produce as many as four whorls (Perry and others 1966).
2. Trees from southern areas such as Florida or Georgia may have as much as 10 cm of bud enlargement during winter months, whereas those from northern areas such as Maryland have negligible winter bud growth (Perry and others 1966).

3. Trees from western provenances have more cotyledons, shorter needles, and shorter needle sheaths than do trees from eastern sources (table 7-2). Needle cross-section perimeter as well as the number of hypodermal cells and the thickness of epidermal cells in needles of young trees also vary by seed source. In one 4-source comparison, these factors were highest for trees from the lost pines area of Texas; intermediate for those from Cherokee County, Texas, and north

Table 7-2—Morphological characteristics of 50 rangewide seed sources of loblolly pine

Characteristic	Eastern provenances	Western provenances
Needle length (cm)	17.2	13.3
Sheath length (cm)	1.0	0.7
Needles per fascicle	3.2	3.0
Cotyledons	6.9	7.4
Seedcoat thickness (mm)	0.33	0.28
Seed weight (mg)	27.3	26.0

Source: adapted from Hare and Switzer (1969).

Georgia; and lowest for those from the Crossett, Arkansas, area (Thames 1963; table 7-3). Phenolic compounds in loblolly foliage have a high degree of heritability, and some could be correlated with disease resistance. Most of the phenolics found in grafted trees can also be found in selfed progenies (Chen and van Buijtenen 1980).

4. Seed size, seed weight, and seedcoat thickness vary by region of the South and affect seedling growth. Seed size decreases from east to west (Belcher and Karrfalt 1976). A greenhouse test comparing early growth of loblolly from 7 seed sources (North Carolina, South Carolina, Georgia, Florida, Louisiana, Arkansas, and Texas) indicated that seed size was the factor that most strongly affected seedling growth rate. Seeds and seedlings from Florida were largest, and those from Texas and Arkansas were smallest. Seedcoat thickness of loblolly from eastern sources was 16% greater than that of loblolly from western sources, and seed weight of loblolly from eastern

Table 7-3—Variation in needle characteristics of 2-year-old loblolly pines from various sources grown on droughty sands near Oxford, Mississippi

	Seed source			
Needle characteristic	Lost pines of Texas	Cherokee County, Texas	Northwest Georgia	Crossett, Arkansas
Length (cm)	17.6	16.0	16.5	16.9
Cross-sectional perimeter* (mm)	1.94	1.76	1.72	1.67
Cross-sectional area† (mm²)	0.201	0.167	0.171	0.141
Ratio of perimeter to cross section	1:0.104	1:0.095	1:0.099	1:0.084
Stomatal rows	22	20	22	23
Stomata per mm of row*	12.2	12.9	13.3	13.1
Stomata per mm of needle	268	258	293	301
Stomata per mm² of surface	138	147	170	180
Stomata per mm³ of volume	1,333	1,545	1,713	2,135
Hypodermal cells in needle cross section*	165	142	142	103
Thickness of epidermal cells* (µm)	11.2	10.0	10.4	9.4

Source: adapted from Thames (1963).

* Significant difference between seed sources at the 99% probability level.

† Significant difference between seed sources at the 95% probability level.

sources averaged 5% greater than that of loblolly from western sources (table 7-2).

5. Some wood and oleoresin traits vary geographically. Environmental conditions where a tree grows strongly affect the specific gravity of mature xylem. In general, specific gravity decreases from the southern to the northern part of the species range, from the coast to the Piedmont, and from east to west (Byram and Lowe 1988, Gilmore 1967, Gilmore and others 1966, Talbert and Jett 1981). When trees from the same families are grown in different locations, they have significantly different moduli of elasticity and xylem crushing strengths (Pearson 1988). Concentrations of the monoterpenes alpha-pinene, myrcene, and limonene in cortical oleoresin have a strong east-to-west clinal trend. Alpha-pinene concentrations are highest along the Atlantic and Gulf Coastal Plains. If used in conjunction with other traits, such as seed morphology, monoterpene variation may be useful in determining the geographic origin of unknown seed sources (Gilmore 1971, McRae and Thor 1982, Squillace and Wells 1981). Generally, there is little geographic variation in wood properties within small geographic areas such as a part of a state. Evidence of such trends should be interpreted with caution. Similarly, gain estimates and gain predictions from progeny tests at single locations or with small numbers of families should be used with caution because they may not be valid over broad areas (Barker 1973, Choong and others 1986, Chuntanaparb 1973). Byram and Lowe (1988) found that environmental and genetic patterns of variation in specific gravity among western Gulf Coast seed sources did not agree. This finding led them to conclude that decisions about seed movement should not be based on *in situ* studies of regional specific gravities.

6. There are regional differences in bark thickness, which is one of the most strongly inherited tree characteristics. For example, 10-year-old loblolly in South Carolina had bark volume to wood volume ratios of about 0.31 to 1 on the Coastal Plain and 0.52 to 1 on the Piedmont (Pederick 1970). Because bark thickness is closely associated with tree diameter (Matziris and Zobel 1973), comparisons should be made using similar-sized trees.

7. Provenances can vary greatly in survival, height, diameter, tree volume, and needle surface area. Bongarten and Teskey (1986, 1987) concluded that variations in rates of growth of different plant organs may partially account for growth rate differences between provenances.

8. Tree form varies geographically. Variation in stem crook is normally greater between provenances than within a provenance. In Georgia, 60% of the total variation in crook was attributable to differences between flatwood, Coastal Plain, and Piedmont sources and 4% to differences between mother trees within any provenance

(LaFarge 1974). Stand origin, seed source, and family differences in stem taper also have been identified (Amateis and Burkhart 1987, Pederick 1970, Schmidtling and Clark 1989), but the extent of this variation and its overall effect on volume is not known.

There are a number of morphological characteristics that do not appear to vary geographically. For example, the specific gravity of juvenile wood (the inner 9 to 10 rings) is very stable (about 0.41 to 0.42) throughout the range of the species (Talbert and Jett 1981). There is no apparent geographic trend in tracheid length (Jackson and Strickland 1962).

Geographic Variation in Fusiform Rust Infection

Rangewide provenance tests have demonstrated that genetic resistance to fusiform rust is substantial in the Florida parishes of southeast Louisiana and neighboring counties of southwest Mississippi, on the Eastern Shore of Maryland, and in much of the range west of the Mississippi River and south of Arkansas. In fact, trees from Livingston Parish, Louisiana, have up to 50% less fusiform rust infection than many susceptible sources in the Southeast, and, with a few limited exceptions, they exhibit resistance and good growth when planted as far north as central Alabama and as far east as Dooly County in the Coastal Plain of Georgia. During the 1970's, industry planted more than 120,000 ha from south Arkansas to north Florida and southeast South Carolina with Livingston Parish loblolly pines (Henry 1959, Powers and Kraus 1986, Powers and Matthews 1987, Wells 1985, Wells and Switzer 1971, Wells and Wakeley 1966, Wells and others 1991).

Geographic Movement of Seed Sources

Geographic variation is substantial in loblolly pine, and provenance testing has been an excellent means of capturing a wide array of valuable genetic traits. The first loblolly racial variation trial was installed in 1926 in southeast Louisiana (Wakeley and Bercaw 1965). By age 15, trees from the local source were obviously the largest. By age 35, total volume of trees from the local source was almost twice that of trees from the next best source (table 7-4). Since this classic study, loblolly provenance tests have been made in almost all of the southern states. A 19-plantation Southwide test was installed in 10 states from Maryland to Texas in 1953, and a 6-state test was installed during 1954 to 1956 (Dorman 1976, Kraus and others 1984). Tests that have been more localized have also been made (LaFarge 1974). The most important finding from these studies is that trees from introduced seed sources can grow substantially faster than trees from native sources. However, it usually takes detailed long-term research to establish whether it is advantageous to grow loblolly from one seed source in another area. The use of a few seed sources as representative of an entire state or region may be misleading because inherent variability can be masked. Also, early survival and growth results may be misleading because excessive mortality or drastic growth reductions can occur late in a rotation. For example, in a Georgia Piedmont planting, Livingston Parish loblolly trees were the tallest of those from 6 seed sources for the first 15 years, but by age 25, they were the shortest at 16.8 m, whereas trees from the best source averaged 19.8 m tall (figure 7-3). Progeny tests must cover at least one rotation to show that trees from outside seed sources will adapt to a different environment and do better than those from local sources. If poorly adapted trees from an outside seed source are grown, yield at harvest can be 30% less than yield from the local source (Kraus and Sluder 1984).

The importance of local seed sources. In Maryland, Delaware, tidewater Virginia, the Piedmont and Coastal Plain of North and South Carolina, the Piedmont of Georgia and Alabama, and northern Mississippi, trees grown from local seeds from stands with average or better stem form and growth perform best (Kraus and Sluder 1984, Wells 1983). After 15 years of growth, trees from local Maryland sources had 10% more volume than those from the next

Table 7-4—Growth and yield of loblolly pine seed from 4 sources 15 to 35 years after planting in southeastern Louisiana

Trait	15 yrs	22 yrs	28 yrs	35 yrs
Height (m)				
Louisiana	9.8	14.0	18.0	19.6
Texas	8.9	12.5	15.4	16.9
Georgia	8.0	11.6	15.1	16.6
Arkansas	7.7	11.0	12.8	13.2
Dbh (cm)				
Louisiana	12.7	17.0	20.6	25.1
Texas	10.7	13.2	17.0	20.3
Georgia	10.2	13.2	15.7	18.3
Arkansas	9.7	11.9	13.2	14.0
Volume (m³/ha)				
Louisiana	94.2	253.3	319.3	445.2
Texas	59.4	139.0	146.1	250.5
Georgia	48.2	111.1	142.3	189.8
Arkansas	42.9	98.8	80.0	89.8

Source: adapted from Kraus and others (1984).

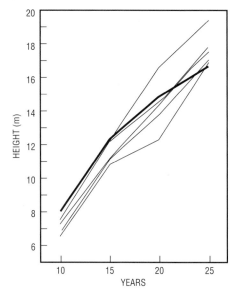

Figure 7-3— Height of dominant and codominant loblolly pines for 6 seed sources in a Spalding County, Georgia, planting. The dark line is a Livingston Parish, Louisiana, seed source (adapted from Wells 1985).

best source (Arkansas) and more than twice as much volume as those from a Livingston Parish, Louisiana, seed source (Little 1969). Similarly, trees from local sources in east Texas and west Louisiana produced an average of 20% more volume than trees from sources in 6 other southern states produced. There was also more plantation-to-plantation variation in volume production with trees from nonlocal sources (Long 1980).

Moving eastern seed sources west.   The Mississippi River disjunction and related environmental differences have influenced the genetic evolution of loblolly pine significantly (Florence and Rink 1979). The populations from west of the Mississippi River (regions 5 and 6 in figure 7-2) are generally slower growing, more resistant to infection by fusiform rust, and more drought resistant than those from the East wherever they are planted (Florence 1981, Wells 1983). In fact, loblolly pine shows a great deal of regional variability in drought resistance. When trees from outside sources are planted at the dry western fringe of loblolly's range, they are much more likely to be desiccated and killed during periods of severe drought than are local sources. Survival under drought conditions is poor for trees from Gulf Coast sources, poor to moderate for those from East Coast sources, moderate for those from northeastern and interior sources, but excellent for those from both southwestern and northwestern sources (Grigsby 1977, Lambeth and others 1984b, Wells and Wakeley 1966).

Moving coastal North and South Carolina loblolly pines to Arkansas and Oklahoma can result in volume gains of up to 25% if the trees are planted on moist sites (Lambeth and others 1984a, Schmidtling 1987, Wells and Lambeth 1983). Over a 25-year rotation, a 1.2- to 3.0-m gain in height of dominant and codominant trees and corresponding increases in volume and product value can be obtained by using trees from east of the Mississippi River in plantations in Arkansas and east Oklahoma (Sprinz and others 1989; figure 7-4). However, if long sawlog rotations are used, trees from western sources may ultimately grow as tall as trees from eastern sources (Sprinz and others 1989). There is also some risk that fast early growth may predispose trees from eastern sources to damage from ice and southern pine beetles if plantations are not managed well (Kraus and Sluder 1984) or if they are established on poor sites. Finally, the effects of extended drought on survival, growth, and beetle damage to older trees from East Coast sources growing in Arkansas and Oklahoma is not known.

Under ideal conditions, the growth rate potential of loblolly pine seedlings planted west of the Mississippi is excellent for Gulf Coast and East Coast sources; moderate for northeastern, interior, and southwestern sources; and poor for northwestern sources (Lambeth and others 1984b). Even if eastern trees grow larger than local trees in far-western plantings, their specific gravities can be lower than those of local trees, negating some or all of the

growth gain. In a southwest Arkansas provenance study, cellulose yields at tree age 29 did not differ for northwestern, northeastern, and East Coast sources, but the specific gravities of the sources differed by 15% (Szymanski and Tauer 1991, Tauer and Loo-Dinkins 1990). Similarly, when trees from west Gulf Coast seed sources were planted throughout the region, trees from southern Arkansas always had the highest specific gravities, and trees from Livingston Parish, Louisiana, always had the lowest. This trend toward low specific gravity negates some of the growth advantage south Louisiana loblolly pine seems to have over other sources (Byram and Lowe 1988).

Moving seed sources north or inland.   Trees from coastal sources generally grow faster and produce significantly more dry weight than those from interior sources even when planted on interior sites (Bongarten and Teskey 1987, LaFarge 1974, Lantz and Hofmann 1969, Robinson and others 1984, Wells 1975).

Low temperature is probably the factor that most limits the northern range of loblolly pine (Parker 1965). Genetic variation in cold tolerance may be more pronounced among nursery seedlings than among older trees in the field (Kolb and Steiner 1985). The average freeze-free period across loblolly's range varies from about 270 days along the central Gulf Coast to about 210

Figure 7-4— At 25 years, South Carolina Coastal Plain loblolly pine trees **(right)** averaged 21.3 m tall compared to 19.2 m for loblolly pine trees from Oklahoma **(left)** when planted in southern Arkansas (Wells and Lambeth 1983).

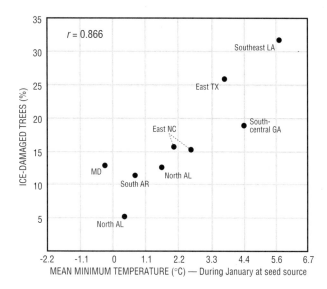

Figure 7-5—Ice damage to loblolly pine trees planted in south-central Georgia is significantly correlated (99% level of probability) with the mean minimum temperature during January at the seed source location (adapted from Jones and Wells 1969).

Table 7-5—Survival and growth of loblolly pines by seed source 15 years after planting on an old field in the Ozark Mountains of Arkansas

Seed source	Survival/ha		Average tree dbh (cm)	Average tree height (m)	Merchantable volume (m³/ha)
	%	no. of trees			
Tennessee	90	1,515	18.5	11.9	120
Georgia	81	1,364	19.0	12.2	145
North Mississippi	73	1,228	18.3	11.9	107
East Mississippi	69	1,161	19.0	11.9	113
South Alabama	69	1,161	18.0	11.9	76
North Alabama	65	1,095	19.6	12.2	120
Virginia	58	976	18.8	12.2	82
Maryland	56	941	18.5	11.9	94

Source: adapted from Maple (1966).

days at the northern and inland extremes of the range. Trees from Gulf Coast sources have been grown successfully in areas that have up to 40 additional freezing days/year (about 240 km inland). Trees from northern sources can probably be grown farther north or inland, where there are about 20 additional freezing days/year (Kraus and others 1984). Even though ice storms and heavy snowfall break the limbs and tops of trees from coastal sources more frequently than they break those of trees from inland sources (figure 7-5), few if any trees die as a direct result of ice or snow damage. Although volume loss resulting from ice or snow damage is greater for coastal sources than for inland sources, the rapid growth of coastal sources more than offsets such losses (Gilmore and Funk 1976, Jones and Wells 1969).

It is probably more advantageous to plant trees a short distance to the north of their seed source than to plant trees south of their seed source when a local seed source is not available. For example, trees from southern Arkansas and southeastern Oklahoma seed sources perform well in northern Arkansas (AFC 1989). Better than average growth has been obtained by moving southern Alabama seed sources to central Alabama and by moving trees from central Alabama to northern Alabama

(Duba and others 1984). Similarly, seedlings from Virginia should perform well in Maryland and Delaware (Kraus and Sluder 1984).

In the absence of information that justifies another course of action, it is best to use trees from the nearest seed source of acceptable quality when regenerating loblolly pine outside its natural range. However, judicious selection of seed source can result in considerable gains in survival and growth when loblolly is planted north of its natural range (Gilmore and Funk 1976, Kolb and others 1985, McKeand and others 1989, Rink and Thor 1971; table 7-5). For western Tennessee, western Kentucky, and southern Illinois, the preferred seed sources, in descending order of preference, are: north Mississippi, north Alabama, or northwest Georgia; central Arkansas; and eastern Virginia, northeastern North Carolina, or the Eastern Shore of Virginia and Maryland (Lantz and Kraus 1987).

Using seeds from foreign sources. Loblolly pine progenies from the southeastern United States have been growing for many years in South Africa (see chapter 12). Seeds from selected seed orchard clones in South Africa have recently been brought back to the United States and compared with Georgia seed orchard progeny. Several of these selections showed greater 5-year growth than did open-pollinated seed orchard progeny. This finding suggests that the gene pool of trees from foreign countries may strengthen breeding programs in the United States (Kraus and Sluder 1981).

Stand-to-Stand Variation

There is very little scientific information on the genetic component of stand-to-stand variation in loblolly pine. In a Texas study, growth differences between stands within local seed sources were as great as 3 m³/ha/yr over 20 years of plantation growth

(table 7-6). The size of these differences indicates that substantial gains can be made. In fact, among-stand differences in rust resistance may be several times as great as within-stand differences (LaFarge 1974, Wells and Switzer 1971).

Resistance to fusiform rust is under moderate additive genetic control (Barker 1973). Also, there is evidence linking monoterpene composition and resistance

Table 7-6—Twenty-year average growth rates of local seed source plantings in three counties of Texas

Plantation within seed source	Growth rate (m³/ha/yr)		
	Leon County seed source	Fayette County seed source	Bastrop County seed source
1	5.5	7.5	7.0
2	8.3	9.3	7.5
3	8.5	7.2	9.8
4	—	7.5	8.3
5	—	—	10.0
Average	7.4	7.9	8.5

Source: adapted from Long (1980).

to fusiform rust (Rockwood 1973, Squillace and Wells 1981, Squillace and others 1985). Seventeen percent of Livingston Parish, Louisiana, loblolly pines that had grown on high rust hazard sites on the Georgia Piedmont for 10 years were infected with rust, whereas 86% of local trees of commercial size were rust infected. Growth rates for trees from the two sources were nearly identical (Powers 1986). Highly significant differences in rust resistance occur even between flatwoods, upper Coastal Plain, and Piedmont provenances of Georgia (LaFarge 1974). This selective resistance may be related to long-term introgression with shortleaf or longleaf pine. Electrophoretic patterns of seed proteins and similarities in morphological characteristics of needles and seeds support the hypothesis that there is shortleaf pine introgression.

Tree-to-Tree Variation

There can be considerable genetic variation between neighboring loblolly pine trees within a stand. For example, individual trees have very different levels of monoterpenes, indicating that both the quantity and quality of monoterpenes are under relatively strong genetic control (Rockwood 1972). Growth studies of young and old loblolly stands show that there is much unexplained variation between individual trees on uniform sites (Langdon and others 1970, Nelson 1964). These studies prove that there is substantial genetic variation in fecundity, survival, growth, form, and resistance to insects and diseases among individual loblolly trees.

Tree-to-tree differences in growth and development were first exploited through rogueing of mature stands for seed production areas. Removing inferior phenotypes increased the growth of the next generation of trees by 10 to 30% (Easley 1963). Rigidly controlled progeny tests identified volume growth or specific gravity differences of 30% or more between selected families as early as age 4 to 7 years (Dorman and Zobel 1973, Zobel and others 1969). This natural tree-to-tree variation is a renewable resource in the sense that specific traits of individual trees can be continually combined to develop families having desirable properties (LaFarge 1974).

Variation in Flower, Cone, and Seed Production

Family-to-family differences in both male and female fruitfulness can be large in loblolly pine. Generally, fewer than 20% of the clones in a seed orchard less than 10 years old produce 50 to 80% of all flowers, cones, and seeds. Also, some clones characteristically form many female flowers at each bud, whereas others develop only single or double flowers (Bergman 1968). In a south Mississippi study, more than 50% of the variation in female flowering, cone production, and seed production and about 40% of the variation in male flowering was attributable to genetic differences (Schmidtling 1983a). Webster (1974) found a strong clonal effect in loblolly fruitfulness in a southeast Virginia seed orchard. Inherently fruitful trees usually respond better to flower-inducing treatments than do unfruitful trees (Schmidtling 1975).

Identifying the least fruitful clones at an early age is not a straightforward process. Clones that are fruitful early in their lives tend to continue to be fruitful, but some clones that exhibit little reproductive activity in early years become fruitful later. Moreover, clonal flower production varies from year to year, making it necessary to assess male and female fruitfulness over several years for best results (Schmidtling 1983a).

There are large clone-to-clone differences in seed properties that are primarily maternally influenced. For example, there are such differences in total seed weight, seedcoat thickness, seedcoat weight, lipid weight, polyembryony, and pretreatment requirements. Most of the clone-to-clone variation in seedling height at the end of the first growing season and as much as 45 to 80% of clone-to-clone variation in tree height through the first 4 to 8 years of growth can be attributed to these maternally influenced factors. However, there is no simple relationship between factors such as gross seed weight and seedling performance. Storing and growing seeds by clone should result in greater uniformity in seedling size. Even grading of bulked seeds can result in partial separation of families because seed size varies between families (Brown and Goddard 1959, Perry 1975, Shear 1985). Loblolly pine also shows genetic variability in susceptibility to damage by cone and seed insects (Askew and others 1985, Sartor and Neel 1971).

Variation in Tree Development

Tree-to-tree variation in growth can be substantial. Single-tree experimental plots are best for making growth comparisons as long as final measurements are completed prior to about age 5, when trees begin to show the effects of intensive competition. Multiple-tree plots are as efficient as single-tree plots for trees 8 to 12 years old (Conkle 1963). Crowding affects early growth of some families differently than it affects early growth of others. Thus care must be taken when studying and ranking progeny development, whether trees are grown in family groups or grown as randomly mixed individuals from numerous families (Adams and others 1973). However, even when trees are grown at close spacing, young loblolly pine progeny tests can accurately predict patterns of additive genetic variation in height, diameter, and volume growth of competing seed sources (table 7-7). Mortality can be as low as 10% after 5 years when each seedling had as little as 100 cm² of growing space (Franklin 1983).

Competitiveness can also vary from trait to trait: family patterns of early diameter growth and dry weight growth can be unlike family patterns of height growth. Such intergenotypic interactions should only be compared for a specific trait unless supporting data are available (Adams and others 1973).

Clonal testing of loblolly pine can be substituted for, or can supplement, progeny testing in seedling seed orchards because similarities between progeny and clonal parents are greater than those between progeny and mature parent trees (Corriveau 1976).

Survival and early growth. Tree survival is closely related to early root development. Even within a specific portion of the range, there is great variability in survival and feeder root development between the progenies of individual trees. Feeder root development has an important regulating effect on formation of ectomycorrhizae in seedlings (Long 1973). Families that grow faster may avoid water stress on better drained sites by developing more extensive root systems than other families—that is, they tend to have relatively higher root-to-shoot growth rates (Cannell and others 1978, van Buijtenen 1966a). Differences in needle anatomy, and especially in the number of stomata (see chapter 4) are also important factors in drought resistance. Knauf and Bilan (1977) estimated that breeders could immediately obtain a 10% increase in survival by selecting the most drought-resis-

tant 25% of open-pollinated progenies.

The ability of bareroot seedlings to regenerate new roots (root growth potential) significantly affects early height growth of outplanted seedlings. Root growth potential is genetically controlled. In a planting of 15 half-sib families, first-year height growth averaged 15 cm for seedlings with 14 new roots and 21 cm for seedlings with 24 new roots (figure 7-6). This root growth/height growth trend continued through the second year (DeWald and others 1985).

There is substantial genetic variation in shoot growth patterns of loblolly pine (Ledig and Perry 1966). External, easily measurable characteristics of trees (for example, height and diameter) are normally the first to be evaluated when determining superiority. Trees that excel in growth are given the highest marks. However, growth changes with age—that is, seedlings, saplings, and mature trees exhibit different patterns of shoot elongation (see chapter 2). This factor, combined with growth variation caused by environment and genetic × environment (G × E) interactions, can make long-term growth projections based on data from young trees uncertain. Even so, shoot lengths of seedlings only 18 months old can show significant correlations with 8-year height, indicating that juvenile-mature correlations can be useful (Williams 1987). Variable shoot elongation patterns of juvenile trees during the growing season may also indicate mature performance. Leader elongation patterns include those in which most stem elongation occurs in the first (fixed growth) and second (first summer shoot) growth cycles, and those in which more cycles of summer shoot growth occur and elongation continues later in the season (figure 7-7).

Nursery selections. Height growth, especially during the first 5 to 10 years after outplanting, often can be improved by selecting the tallest, most vigorous trees in nursery beds (Barber and VanHaverbeke 1961, Grigsby 1975, Hunt 1967, Langdon and others 1968, Robinson and others 1984, Waxler and van Buijtenen 1981, Zarger 1965, Zobel and others 1957; figure 7-8). Unfortunately,

Table 7-7—Estimated number of growing months for 35 loblolly pine families at 33- to 100-cm spacings to reach maximum heritability in a short-term progeny test

	No. of growing months			
Trait	33 cm	50 cm	67 cm	100 cm
Height	15	15	15	30*
Diameter	23	23	23	23
Volume†	21	23	23	23

Source: adapted from Franklin (1983).

* In the 100-cm spacing, a sharp, distinct peak occurred at 15 months, but a rounded, less distinct peak that was 0.5 unit higher occurred at 30 months.

† Volume index based on diameter squared x height.

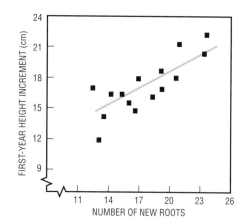

Figure 7-6—First-year field performance of loblolly pine half-sib families lifted and outplanted on the Virginia Piedmont Plateau (adapted from DeWald and others 1985).

fast-growing nursery selections often have "wolf tree" characteristics (Dorman 1976), and they are probably of limited genetic value (LaFarge 1975). To be certain of the value of the progeny, field plantations should be established regardless of nursery performance. Wakeley (1971) determined that trees that are superior at age 30 can be identified with a high degree of certainty at age 20 and in some instances at age 15, but not at earlier ages.

Stem form.   Loblolly pine stem form is highly heritable. Selection from natural stands is particularly valuable in improving this characteristic (Goddard and Strickland 1964, Talbert and others 1983). Perry (1960) found that more than 88% of the offspring produced by crossing crooked parent trees were crooked at age 3. When straight parents were crossed, only 4% of their progeny were as crooked as the average individual produced by crossing crooked parents. Goddard and Strickland (1964) reported good agreement between crookedness evaluations made when trees are 2 and 7 years of age, and this agreement indicates that early evaluations are practical. Bridgwater (1984) estimated that a 13% increase in lumber length plus a 2% increase in the amount of lumber could be obtained by selecting trees in unrogued, first-generation seed orchards for stem straightness. However, results of progeny tests with small numbers of families are generally of little value when estimating the heritability of stem straightness (Chuntanaparb 1973).

Wood and bark chemical properties.   McCullough (1976) found a positive relationship between the concentrations of calcium (Ca) and potassium (K) in the wood of 1-year-old, half-sib seedlings and volume production at age 15. This finding suggests that some degree of

genetic control may operate for nutrient concentrations. There are also important genetic differences among loblolly pine families in both turpentine and extractive yields from xylem, and both genetic and phenotypic correlations can be relatively large (Franklin 1975). Among-tree variation in stem and branch monoterpenes can be extremely large (table 7-8). For example, alpha-pinene can range from 47 to 97% of the total monoterpenes in stem xylem and from 10 to 87% in branch cortex, whereas the concentration of myrcene or limonene can range from 0 to about 10% in stem xylem and from 0 to about 60% in branch cortex. In contrast, branch cortex monoterpenes are excellent for within-tree comparative studies because the variation is minimal and remarkably consistent throughout an individual tree (Rockwood 1973). Bole straightness has no important effect on yields of turpentine and extractives, but trees with large limbs produce more of both than do trees with small limbs (Franklin 1975).

There is a great deal of tree-to-tree variation in the physical properties of oleoresin in loblolly pine, indicating that there are substantial opportunities to modify oleoresin quality and quantity. For example, trees growing on similar sites in Louisiana had initial oleoresin crystallization times ranging from 0.1 to 3.2 hours. The rate of oleoresin flow in these trees varied from 0.17 to 2.87 ml/hour (Hodges and others 1977). These differences might be exploited to increase tree resistance to southern pine beetles, in developing mating systems, and in the production of preferred raw materials. Mutant forms of slash pine produce yellow or pale-yellow oleoresin that is useful as a genetic marker in studies of mating systems, population structures, and biochemical pathways. Yellow oleoresin also occurs in some loblolly phenotypes (Griggs and Squillace 1982). Oleoresin composition might be a good biological marker for loblolly pine, but this

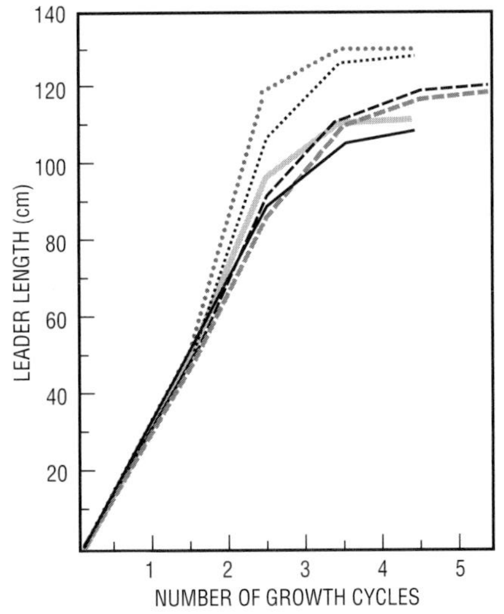

Table 7-8—Among-tree variation in monoterpenes of 5- to 6-year-old loblolly pines

Type of monoterpene	% of total monoterpenes		
	Mean	Standard deviation	Range
Stem xylem monoterpenes (346 five-year-old trees)			
α-pinene	70.3	10.7	47–97
β-pinene	25.1	10.8	1–48
myrcene	1.9	1.0	0–8
limonene	1.1	1.5	0–13
Branch cortex monoterpenes (357 six-year-old trees)			
α-pinene	48.3	16.5	10–87
β-pinene	19.0	9.5	2–42
myrcene	17.5	14.3	0–63
limonene	6.4	11.3	0–61
β-phellandrene	7.9	7.6	0–33

Source: adapted from Rockwood (1973).

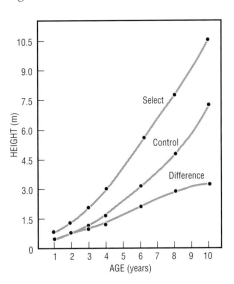

Figure 7-7—Average cumulative leader length for 6-year-old half-sib families growing on a somewhat poorly drained Coxville fine sandy loam (clayey, kaolinitic, thermic Typic Paleaquult) in North Carolina. Each line represents a different family (adapted from Bridgwater and others 1985).

Figure 7-8—Pattern of height growth behavior of trees selected for rapid height growth in the nursery bed and control loblolly pines for 10 years following planting (adapted from Hatchell and others 1972).

supposition must be tested experimentally.

Loblolly pine trees differ significantly in the yield of chemicals (for example, petroleum ether, ether, ethanol, and ethyl acetate) from their bark, suggesting that tree improvement could be directed to increasing the amounts or concentrations of specific chemicals (Labosky 1979, Pearl 1975).

Needle length. Future performance of trees might be predicted by analyses of needle length-tree height growth relationships. Analysis of data for open-pollinated progeny of 30- to 40-year-old, second-growth loblolly pines in south Alabama 2 years after outplanting showed very strong heritability for needle length and tree height (Cech and others 1963).

Genetic Testing

The objectives of genetic testing include (1) progeny testing, (2) estimating variance components and heritability, (3) producing base populations for subsequent generations of selection and breeding, and (4) demonstrating or estimating genetic gain. To accurately assess progress in a tree improvement program, breeders must compare performance of improved and unimproved trees in the same test (Zobel and Talbert 1984). Numerous mating designs, experimental designs, and statistical analyses are available to serious tree breeders who wish to conduct tests and determine genetic gain (Lowe and van Buijtenen 1989, Zobel and Talbert 1984). Uniform stock for progeny tests can be grown in containers. This method makes best use of available seeds and permits breeders to control shoot and root morphology so that they can produce stock adapted for outplanting under specific conditions (Barnett 1988). Loblolly pine breeding programs are now in their second and third generations; clonal stock produced following controlled crossing of seed orchard parents is now in use.

Gene Arrangement

Loblolly pine has 12 chromosomes. The length of haploid chromosomes obtained from root tip meristems is shown in table 7-9. Gene arrangement is highly conservative, and it appears that many loci are associated. Linked loci have a consistent gene order that may be a basis for the mapping and manipulation of genetically controlled phenotypic traits (Conkle 1981). The three loci that control cortical concentrations of myrcene, limonene, and beta-phellandrene in loblolly are closely linked. There are methods for detecting linkages and estimating rates of recombination (Squillace and Swindel 1986). Foreign genes can be transferred into loblolly, and they can create changes that might not occur in nature (Stomp and others 1988).

There appears to be a pattern of peroxidase isozyme inheritance in loblolly pine. Electrophoretic studies of needles from control-pollinated progeny of loblolly and longleaf pines isolated 11 peroxidase bands (isozymes), 9 of which were common to both species. Two of these isozymes (numbers 10 and 11) were recommended as genetic markers for identification of loblolly ramets, popula-

tions, or hybrids (Snyder and Hamaker 1978a). An examination of gametophytes and embryos of wind-pollinated and control-crossed families from seed orchard clones showed that allozyme variants in 10 enzyme systems are encoded by at least 17 loci (Adams and Joly 1980a).

Selection and Breeding Criteria

To maximize gains from tree improvement, tree breeders should select superior loblolly pine trees on the basis of several traits. Although fast growth is usually the primary criterion for selection, other traits such as bole straightness and specific gravity can be important. Even though aggregate gains in yield or quality, based on selection for two or more traits, are greater than gains from single-trait selection, the economic value of such gains may be small (Bridgwater and Stonecypher 1979, Wilcox and Smith 1973).

Breeding to accelerate physiological activities. Although little work has been done in the area of breeding to accelerate physiological activities in loblolly pine, physiological activities vary by seed source (Bongarten and others 1985, Greenwald 1972), and loblolly selections can be crossed to increase the rate of physiological activity in the progeny. For example, progenies of select

Table 7-9—Length of somatic chromosomes in loblolly pine

Haploid chromosome	Length (µm)			Relative length	Order of increasing length
	Short arm	Long arm	Total		
1	7.45	8.27	15.72	100	1
2	6.98	7.18	14.16	90	2
3	6.73	7.18	13.91	89	3
4	6.45	6.82	13.27	84	6
5	6.36	7.27	13.63	87	4
6	6.27	7.27	13.54	86	5
7	6.18	6.82	13.00	83	7
8	6.18	6.26	12.44	80	9
9	5.82	6.91	12.73	81	8
10	5.64	6.18	11.82	75	10
11	5.45	5.73	11.18	71	11
12	3.55	5.45	9.00	57	12

Source: adapted from Kim (1963).

trees had more photosynthetic activity (micrograms of CO_2 per hour per milligram of needle) than progenies from random matings when rates of photosynthesis were compared near their seasonal peak (Ledig and Perry 1967). Ledig and Perry (1969) also found that three progenies had substantially different net assimilation rates, which affected total dry weights during a 24-week growth period (figure 7-9).

Greenwald (1972) identified temperature-related germination and growth differences among loblolly pines from different seed sources (table 7-10). Seedlings grown under short-day (9.5 hours) and long-day (15 hours) conditions respond in direct relation to the latitude of their origin. Under both short- and long-day conditions, trees from the southernmost latitude studied grew tallest, whereas those from the northernmost latitude grew least (figure 7-10). Physiological differences are probably the main reason that loblolly from some seed sources are more resistant to fusiform rust than others. Although extremely complex and not always effective (Bongarten and others 1985, Seiler and Johnson 1988), tree physiology × genetic interactions probably can provide important breakthroughs in science.

Selection and breeding to reduce initial flowering age. Although most loblolly pines begin to produce female strobili at about 8 to 10 years of age (see chapter 2), they are capable of flowering and fruiting as early as age 3 to 4 (Greene 1966, Greene and Porterfield 1962). Most young trees fail to flower because their normal growth behavior does not permit strobilus buds to develop. That is, they grow vegetatively much longer than mature trees do and set a quiescent bud relatively late in the growing season, when there may not be sufficient time for flower bud initiation and formation (Greenwood 1978a, Griffing and Elam 1971). If breeders are to promote consistently high levels of male and female flowering in young trees, they must develop new techniques.

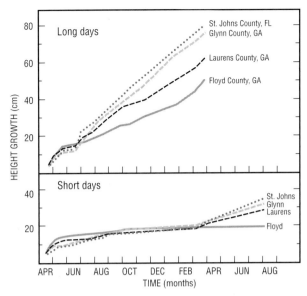

Figure 7-10—Height growth of loblolly pine seedlings from four geographical seed sources grown under short (9.5-hour) and long (15-hour) days (adapted from Allen and McGregor 1962).

In traditional breeding schemes, loblolly pines are selected at about age 8, and the breeding period from grafting to test establishment lasts at least 12 years. Thus, generation turnover is at least 20 years (Greenwood 1983). Early testing and accelerated breeding can reduce the cycle to 10 years (if selections are made at tree age 5, which requires flower stimulation, and if the breeding period is 5 years). Ultimately, a 6- or 7-year breeding cycle may be practical if processes are refined further (Greene 1966, Lambeth 1983).

In loblolly pine, female flower production tends to begin several years before pollen catkin production (Greenwood and Schmidtling 1981). In a 5-year-old Arkansas plantation, female flowers were present on 9% of the trees, but male flowers were present on only 3% (Greenwood and Gladstone 1978). Similarly, female flowering was 2 to 3 times more frequent than male flowering on 4-year-old loblolly in southern Mississippi (Schmidtling 1975). Female strobili also occur more frequently than male strobili on young, grafted ramets even when mature scionwood is used as

Table 7-10—Effect of prechilling at 3 °C on the germination of loblolly pine seeds from three seed sources*

Length of prechilling (wk)	% Germination		
	Florida	Tennessee	Texas
0	90	10	12
1	67	35	38
2	50	75	73
3	30	92	94

Source: adapted from Greenwald (1972).
* The values for each week within each source are significantly different at the 95% probability level.

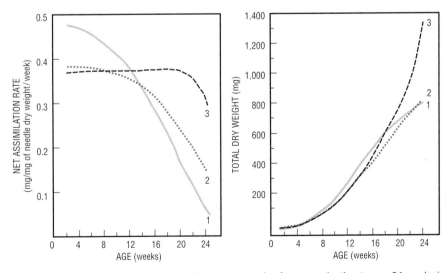

Figure 7-9—Variation among three loblolly pine progenies from germination to age 24 weeks in the net assimilation rate (**left**) and total dry weight (**right**) (adapted from Ledig and Perry 1969).

graft material (Greenwood and Gladstone 1978; Greenwood and Schmidtling 1981; Schmidtling 1971, 1979).

Both male and female strobili may be induced repeatedly on juvenile loblolly pines depending on the vegetative growth behavior of the terminal bud. In one study, breeders induced male and female strobili on 3-, 5-, and 7-year-old scions, taken from trees grown from seed and grafted on young rootstock, by prolonging vegetative growth through the winter and then forcing bud set in the early spring by lowering the temperature and shortening the photoperiod. Thirty-eight percent of the ramets grown under these controlled conditions produced female strobili and 66% produced male strobili. When grown under natural conditions outdoors, only 1 of 76 clones produced female strobili and 2 of 76 produced male strobili (table 7-11). Pruning tops of scions as young as 3 years old from seeds also induces both male and female flowering, but at lower frequencies (Greenwood 1978a).

Table 7-11—Number of ramets of young loblolly pines producing male and female strobili

Scion age (yrs)	Grown indoors			Grown outdoors		
	Total ramets	Producing		Total ramets	Producing	
		Females	Males		Females	Males
3	15	2	8	15	0	1
5	12	5	8	14	0	0
7	46	21	32	47	1	1
Total	73	28	48	76	1	2

Source: adapted from Greenwood (1978a).

The production of both male and female strobili can be accelerated on scions of seedlings by grafting the scions into crowns of large seed orchard trees. Within 2 to 3 years after grafting, 50% or more of the surviving grafts produce male strobili, which is about 20 times more than their expected frequency without grafting. Female strobili appear less frequently than male strobili but still occur on about 20% of the scions, which is double their expected frequency (Greenwood and Gladstone 1978).

Flowers of some clones become receptive earlier than do flowers of others. In Virginia seed orchards, 5- to 7-year-old grafts showed a single-year variation of as much as 10 days in early pollen receptivity when growing in the Piedmont and 7 days when growing in the Coastal Plain (Wasser 1967). Date of cone opening in the fall also varies substantially by clone. Clonal orchard blocks can increase genetic gain and improve seed yields because mandatory artificial pollination will produce desirable matings and minimize negative effects of fertilization by background pollen. Also, addition of fertilizers, insect control, roguing, and cone harvest should all be more efficient in clonal orchard blocks (Greenwood 1983).

Breeding to increase tree growth and quality.

Heritability estimates indicate that dry weight, volume, and diameter are under moderate to strong genetic control (Barker 1973). One-half of the rotation age

seems to be a safe point for making accurate projections of the growth behavior of progeny (Franklin 1979, Kung 1989, Wakeley 1971). LaFarge (1973) concluded that height at tree age 15 cannot be predicted reliably from height at age 3 or 5. However, there is considerable evidence that the best phenotypes in genetic tests can be selected as early as ages 4 to 8 (Barnes 1987, Foster 1986, Lambeth and others 1983, McKeand 1988). Even first-year seedling growth characteristics have been positively correlated with mean heights or volumes of specific families after 8 to 12 years (Bailian and others 1989, Cannell and others 1978). Accelerating juvenile growth with supplemental light and fertilizer does not improve juvenile/mature correlations (Williams 1988). Some selections based on early height have been as effective as those based on early volume in identifying families that produce large volumes at rotation (Lambeth and others 1983, Miller 1982). A large number of first-order lateral roots on nursery seedlings may also indicate superior growth (Kormanik and Ruehle 1989). Although progeny tests provide indications of expected growth increases, the true test of superiority will come only when improved trees are grown on a commercial scale under normal forest conditions (including a wide variety of sites and some noncommercial areas) for complete rotations. Data for these conditions are not yet available. For the present, growth models can be used to estimate genetic gain on an area basis (Knowe and Foster 1989).

Increased survival and accelerated growth.

Genetic selection is usually for superior growth (see chapter 11); however, loblolly can be selected for superior survival. Superior trees planted throughout Tennessee had 94% survival 3 years after planting, wheras 3-year survival of wild stock was 81% (Cox 1985). The Texas Forest Service developed genetically improved "drought hardy" loblolly pines with a survival rate 7.2% higher than that of "woods run" stock (Nebgen and Meyer 1985). Normally, if good nursery management and handling practices are used (see chapter 6), survival is adequate in most areas without special genetic manipulation.

Crossing trees from widely separated areas with diverse environmental conditions may have genetic benefits. When planted in North Carolina, crosses from distant locations had an average heterosis of 8%. Heterosis seems to be stable over a range of environments; that is, it may be as effective to select trees in good environments as to select them in less favorable environments (Owino and Zobel 1977). When loblolly pines from the Coastal Plain of North Carolina and Georgia were crossed with Piedmont sources from Mississippi to North Carolina and with a Texas source, the results suggested that desirable new genetic combinations can be produced—even if juvenile growth is the same (Woessner 1972a). Offspring of south Louisiana female and selected male trees from the Carolinas and Florida had heights equal to those of south Louisiana trees and some of the rust resistance characteristics of south Louisiana trees (Schmidtling 1989).

Shoot weight or total dry weight is probably a better predictor of field performance of a family than total height or height-growth increment. This is especially true when dealing with small, early test trees in greenhouses or under other controlled conditions (Duke and Lambeth 1982, Waxler and van Buijtenen 1981). The tendency of individual trees to halt height growth and set a resting bud, even when the environment is held constant, contributes to the inaccuracy of height increment as a predictor. However, even when a tree has a resting bud, it can grow a great deal in biomass if the environment is favorable (Lambeth 1983).

Improved tree form.   Loblolly pines commonly have poor form, large limbs, and a large crown. Selection of only straight trees with little taper and fine crowns has minimized these problems. Corriveau (1976) projected gains of 20% in straightness and 9% in crown form in addition to an 11% increase in mean annual height growth for loblolly following selection at an intensity of 1 in 100 in wild forest stands and designed roguing of 50% of the grafted clones. Ramicorn branching appears to be under partial genetic control because some families exhibit high levels of this characteristic. The genetics of forking is unknown at this time. Natural pruning is also quite variable in loblolly, so selection to maintain the high crown efficiency necessary for rapid growth seems feasible (Dorman and Zobel 1973). Breeders should carefully evaluate the relative importance of crown and branch traits to the economic value of trees that will yield various products before making final genetic selections. For example, large knots may degrade logs, but substantial growth increases associated with large limbs may more than offset the reduction in grade (Busby 1983).

Altered wood properties.   Wood physical properties should be considered in the selection process. There are significant family-to-family differences in fibril angle, specific gravity, tracheid length, latewood cell wall thickness, latewood cell lumen width, and moisture content (Choong and others 1986, Jackson and Morse 1965, Matziris and Zobel 1973). Fibril angle is significantly correlated with that of the female parent and is subject to genetic manipulation. Fibril angle and tracheid length are highly correlated, but an increase in specific gravity does not necessarily result in a proportionate increase in cell length or decrease in fibril angle (Megraw 1985). Heritability estimates indicate that specific gravity of juvenile and mature wood and wood moisture content are under strong genetic control, whereas tracheid length is under moderate to strong genetic control (Barker 1973, Loo and others 1984). There were strong negative correlations between specific gravity and wood moisture con-

tent in 7- and 11-year-old plantations (Chuntanaparb 1973). Branchwood can be used for testing bole specific gravity variation and to estimate fibril angle variation among parents and their progeny (Jackson and Morse 1965, Jackson and Warren 1962).

Tree improvement can reduce the differences between juvenile and mature wood properties and between earlywood and latewood. For example, tree improvement can raise juvenile wood specific gravities to the range of 0.50 to 0.60. In addition, the specific gravity of trees at age 25 can be predicted reliably from the specific gravity of 2-year-old trees (Loo and others 1985). The result is a substantial increase in xylem density of young loblolly pines and thus increased pulp yield and greater strength. All of this increases the utility of short-rotation plantation management (Blair and others 1976, Jett and Talbert 1982, Stonecypher and Zobel 1966, van Buijtenen 1986, Zobel 1972). A single cycle of selection for high specific gravity may increase the weight of solid wood by as much as 10 to 20% (Zobel 1970). Unfortunately, selection for high specific gravity in juvenile trees (ages 6 to 10) may result in a significant reduction in both height and diameter growth by age 20 (Loo and others 1985, McKinley and others 1982, Talbert and others 1982).

There is conflicting information on the ease of changing tracheid length by breeding. Early studies indicated that although there is geographical variation in tracheid length, heredity probably exerts the dominant influence on this characteristic in loblolly pine (Gilmore 1969, Goggans 1962, Jackson and Greene 1958, Matziris and Zobel 1973, Zobel and others 1960). Matziris and Zobel (1973) noted that families with high specific gravities may have either long or short tracheids, making it possible to breed for specific gravity while maintaining a desired tracheid length. Recent research indicates that tracheid length probably cannot be changed easily by genetic selection. Loo and others (1984) concluded that the length of tracheids in juvenile wood is not a genetic predictor of tracheid length in mature wood or in the entire tree core and that phenotypic correlations mostly reflect environmental relationships. Choong and others (1986) found no significant differences in tracheid length among five Louisiana seed sources and concluded that tracheid length is controlled more strongly by environmental factors than by genetics. They suggested that selection of individual trees rather than seed sources would be a more efficient means of obtaining genetic gain in tracheid length.

Altered resistance to fusiform rust.   Resistance to fusiform rust infection is under moderate additive genetic control (Barker 1973). The importance of genetics to rust resistance was initially determined through geographic differences. Controlled crosses among orchard-grown loblolly pines from a fast-growing central Florida source, a fast-growing and cold-tolerant coastal Carolina source, and a rust-resistant Livingston Parish, Louisiana, source produced wide-cross hybrids that were intermediate to the parent populations in rust resistance and growth. This work indicates that rust resistance can be transferred to susceptible but fast-growing and cold-tolerant pines (Schmidtling 1987).

Within a local population, there are wide differences that can be captured through tree breeding. Even within a highly adapted seed source, inherent variation is large enough to justify selection for resistance to fusiform rust (Barber 1966, Blair and Zobel 1971, Lowerts 1986). In a Georgia test, superior trees were 8% more rust-free than average forest-grown trees (Kraus and LaFarge 1982). Selection to reduce the number of galls per tree may produce substantial gains in resistance (Sluder 1989). Second-generation selection for fusiform rust resistance may reduce the fusiform rust problem to a tolerable level except on the most severe sites.

Genotype ×
Environment Interactions

Overall, genotype × environment effects on stands within a population are not nearly as great or conspicuous as are the genetic differences between trees from widely divergent seed sources. It is usually unnecessary to test families over environmental extremes to determine breeding values because family performance on good sites is highly correlated with family performance on poor sites (Li and McKeand 1989). Nevertheless, there are some genotypes, or families, which may vary in growth and resistance to pests under different environmental conditions (Duba and others 1985; Dunlap and Barnett 1984; Hook and Denslow 1987; Ledig and Perry 1967; Roberds and others 1976; Seiler and Johnson 1988; Shear and Hook 1988; Woessner 1972a, 1972b; Woessner and others 1975; Yeiser and others 1981). Thus, testing over environmental extremes may identify a few families that excel under special environmental conditions. Selections should be based on overall performance at several locations, even if performance at one location happens to be below average. Such selection should not diminish genetic gain appreciably (LaFarge and Kraus 1981, 1984). As a general practice, it may be most profitable to plant the best available families on the best sites and to propagate genotypes that are broadly adapted to a wide range of conditions so that costly cultural treatments are not needed to get superior growth (Duzan and Williams 1988, Matziris 1975, Owino 1977).

Genotype × fertilizer interactions are quite common in loblolly pines (Schmidtling 1973, Zobel and Roberds 1970). It is probable that response to fertilizer is expressed in many traits and that these change as a tree ages. For example, there are substantial clonal differences in flowering response to nitrogen (N) and to sources of N fertilizer (Greenwood 1977a, Schmidtling 1975, Webster 1974). Factors that may play a role in these responses include genetic differences in mycorrhizal development and net assimilation rate (Dixon and others 1987). Genotypes selected for good growth and form under nonfertilized conditions generally perform well with fertilizers. Goddard and others (1976) summarized the results of numerous tests in the first 8 years of growth as follows:

1. All families respond to fertilizer application when there is a significant overall response on a site.

2. Families that grow rapidly without fertilizers also grow better with fertilizers. There are occasional major exceptions that suggest genotype × fertilizer interactions.

3. Fertilizer response of faster growing families is generally less than that of slower growing families.

Future fertilizer treatment strategies in plantation management should be planned around tree-breeding strategies. Progeny tests should be carried out both with and without fertilization to minimize inadvertent movement toward the creation of fertilizer-dependent populations. Availability and cost of nutrient amendments must also be factored into this interrelationship. Care must be taken not to promote families that grow rapidly only when intensively cultured if progeny will not be provided similar culture after outplanting. Where plantations will not be fertilized, the most desirable genotypes may be those that can extract nutrients effectively from deficient soils or those that have small nutrient needs.

Hybridization With Other Southern Pines

The natural range of loblolly pine overlaps the natural ranges of longleaf, slash, pitch, Virginia, and pond pines. Completely mixed stands occur in many areas, and natural hybridization is relatively common. Time of flowering is an important factor inhibiting crossing between species. In spite of the hybridization that does occur, loblolly and the other southern pines maintain their individual integrities in sympatric populations (Smouse and Saylor 1973).

Hybrids of loblolly pine with other southern pines do not exhibit any evidence of hybrid vigor, but rather tend to be intermediate between the parent species in growth. Seed yield per cone from crosses between loblolly and other southern pine species are lower than for intraspecific fertilization of loblolly (Snyder and Squillace 1966).

The ability of loblolly to cross with other southern pines also varies greatly between male and female parents. When loblolly was the male parent, mature seeds per cone following crosses with shortleaf, slash, longleaf, and Sonderegger pines ranged from 11 to 34. In contrast, only 2 to 3 seeds/cone matured when loblolly was the female parent (table 7-12).

Many needle characteristics (needle length, fascicle sheath length, numbers of needles per fascicle, numbers of stomata per centimeter of needle length, and number of resin canals) are useful in identifying hybrids between loblolly pine and other southern pines. For any one hybrid, only certain needle traits are efficient indicators of hybridity (Florence 1973, Hicks 1973, Mergen 1958, Schmidtling and Scarbrough 1968, Snyder and Hamaker 1978b). Other potential indicators of hybrids include stem color, stem form, variation in needle form, variation in terminal elongation of nursery seedlings (Bilan 1966), and fusiform rust resistance.

Loblolly × Shortleaf Pine Hybrids

Loblolly and shortleaf pines have a large shared range (figure 7-11). Considerable evidence shows that flowering and pollen release of the two species overlap and that natural hybridization occurs wherever the species grow together (Dorman and Barber 1956; Florence 1973; Hicks 1973, 1974; Mergen and others 1965; Smouse and Saylor 1973). Loblolly normally flowers before shortleaf, but early conelets of shortleaf may become receptive while loblolly pollen is still being cast. Loblolly flowering may occasionally be retarded by cold weather, so that loblolly conelets are receptive when shortleaf starts pollinating. One study found that 10% of shortleaf pines produced pollen simultaneously with more than half of the loblolly (Hicks and others 1972). Although natural hybridization is not uncommon, hybrids constitute a relatively small proportion of the combined population. In general, loblolly × shortleaf hybrids grow on the more xeric sites with shortleaf (Florence and Hicks 1980).

Viable hybrid progeny were produced from artificial shortleaf × loblolly pine crosses as early as 1933 (Little and Righter 1965). Artificial crosses between the two species exceed loblolly pine in fusiform rust resistance, resistance to frost damage, and survival on dry sites. Height and diameter growth rates of hybrids generally exceed those of shortleaf pine, suggesting that it might be reasonable to plant the hybrids rather than shortleaf on some sites (Benson and others 1982, Mergen and others 1965, Minckler 1952, Schoenike and others 1977, Sluder 1970). Backcrossing the progeny of selected

Table 7-12—Mean cone survival and seed yield from interspecific, controlled pollination

Male parent	Station years	No. of seed parents*	No. of flowers	% Cone survival	No. of seeds Per flower	No. of seeds Per cone
Loblolly pine female parent						
Slash	13	47	1,689	20	0.5	2.6
Longleaf	10	42	1,461	16	0.3	1.8
Shortleaf	3	8	345	9	0.2	1.8
Sonderegger	4	20	601	50	7.8	15.6
Loblolly (controlled)	10	105	7,193	36	6.6	18.2
Sonderegger pine female parent						
Slash	4	9	182	46	13.9	30.2
Longleaf	6	15	375	31	12.0	23.4
Loblolly	6	17	443	57	19.4	34.0
Shortleaf	3	4	40	30	5.2	17.3
Sonderegger (controlled)	5	16	309	63	23.8	37.5
Wind-pollinated	1	4	—	20	—	25.6
Self-pollinated	4	13	305	60	3.1	5.1
Slash pine female parent						
Loblolly	7	39	732	37	4.1	11.2
Sonderegger	5	12	249	26	0.4	1.6
Longleaf pine female parent†						
Loblolly	12	41	990	4	0.6	14.4
Sonderegger	5	13	220	26	10.0	38.1
Shortleaf pine female parent†						
Loblolly	10	32	1,874	36	5.6	15.8
Sonderegger	2	5	98	28	0.1	0.2

Source: adapted from Snyder and Squillace (1966).
Blank fields indicate no data available.

† Crosses were made in Florida, Georgia, Mississippi, Arkansas, and Louisiana.

* Sum of trees per year pollinated by one or more pollens. In many cases, some of the same trees were used from year to year.

Shortleaf pine
Loblolly and shortleaf pines
Loblolly pine

Figure 7-11—The distributions of loblolly and shortleaf pines (adapted from Wells and others 1977).

F_2 hybrids with loblolly can produce offspring that are rust resistant, grow as rapidly as loblolly, and are morphologically indistinguishable from loblolly. Similarly, F_1 hybrids, progeny of open-pollinated F_2 hybrids, and F_3 hybrids can grow as fast as loblolly, and are almost as resistant as shortleaf to fusiform rust (Kraus 1986, LaFarge and Kraus 1980). The end result can be a rust-resistant strain of loblolly pine that excels in growth.

When breeding for loblolly × shortleaf pine hybrids, it is most convenient to use shortleaf or shortleaf × loblolly trees as the female parents because fresh pollen is available from the earlier flowering loblolly trees. If loblolly is used as the mother tree, it is usually necessary to use shortleaf or hybrid pollen stored since the previous year, generally with some loss in pollen viability (LaFarge and Hunt 1980).

The following morphological characteristics of loblolly × shortleaf hybrids were identified by Little and Righter (1965):

Bark rough, thick, furrowed into long scaly plates, grey. Spring shoots multinodal. Twigs glabrous, glaucous when young, light yellow-green and shiny the first year, becoming light reddish brown the second year. Buds acuminate, light reddish brown, resinous. Leaves 3, sometimes mostly 3 and less frequently 2, in a fascicle, slightly stout and stiff, 7–12 cm long, acute-acuminate, serrulate, green; stomatal rows 9–15 dorsal and 5–7 on each ventral surface or 10–12 on ventral surface of leaves in 2's. Needle anatomy in cross section: Hypodermis usually biform with 2 (rarely 3) layers of cells, sometimes uni-

form with 1 layer, the inner border straight; endodermis of thin-walled cells; resin canals medial, sometimes medial and internal, 2 large medial at angles and often 1–4 additional, about 0.04–0.08 mm in diameter.

Male strobili (dry) 10–18 mm long, 3–5 mm in diameter, orange brown. Cones single or paired, sometimes in whorls of 3 or 4, almost sessile, ovoid conic, symmetrical, 6–8 cm long, 4.5–7 cm across when open, often persistent for several years on old branches; apophyses dull pale fulvous brown, elevated along a transverse keel, the nut-brown umbo forming a sharp stout curved prickle or spine about 3 mm long. Winged seeds 17–27 mm. long, the detachable wing nut-brown, body ovoid, 5–6 mm long, blackish.

Loblolly pine traits dominate in vegetative characteristics and flowering phenology of the hybrid, whereas shortleaf traits dominate in the morphology of reproductive characteristics. Length of male strobili is outstandingly discriminative; male strobili of the hybrid are about twice as long as those of shortleaf and half as long as those of loblolly. Needle length and needle sheath length are also excellent discriminators, with the hybrid having intermediate lengths (Snyder and Hamaker 1978b; figure 7-12a and b):

	Average needle length (cm)	Average sheath length (mm)
Loblolly	17.32	11.16
Hybrid	12.81	6.34
Shortleaf	9.24	4.02

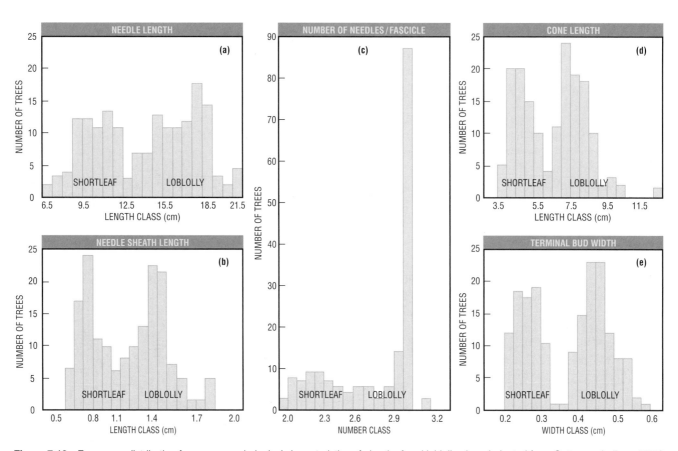

Figure 7-12—Frequency distribution for some morphological characteristics of shortleaf and loblolly pines (adapted from Cotton and others 1975).

Other characteristics well suited for taxonomic classification of loblolly, shortleaf, and the interspecific hybrids are number of needles per fascicle (hybrids have two and three needles to a fascicle, whereas loblolly uniformly have three and shortleaf normally have two) (figure 7-12c), terminal bud width, cone length (figure 7-12d and e), and seed weight. The hybrid is also intermediate in cone and bud size. Other intermediate characteristics include twig color and length-to-width ratio of the axillary scale (Hicks 1973, Mergen and others 1965). Rows of stomata are consistently more numerous in the hybrid than in either of the parent species. A combination of flower, cone, seed, needle, and twig measurements provides the most meaningful evidence of hybridization across a range of sites (Keng and Little 1961). Starch-gel electrophoresis can be used to accurately and precisely differentiate between first-generation loblolly × shortleaf hybrids and the two parent species (Huneycutt and Askew 1989).

Loblolly × Longleaf Pine Hybrids

Sonderegger pine, *Pinus × sondereggeri* H. H. Chapm., is a naturally occurring cross between a longleaf female parent and a loblolly pollen parent. These crosses are common in nature because loblolly and longleaf pines flower at about the same time. There are indications that the reciprocal cross also occurs naturally. As a female parent, Sonderegger pine crosses well with both of the parents

Table 7-13—Thirteen traits in 20-year-old Sonderegger and loblolly pines growing in 2 South Carolina plantations

Trait	Mean values	
	Sonderegger	Loblolly
Dbh (cm)	29.2	29.5
Height (m)	17.7	18.0
Crown width (m)	9.1	9.5
Live crown (%)	60.3	63.0
Branch diameter (cm)	5.6	5.3
Branch angle (degrees from horizontal)	22.6*	27.8*
Bark thickness (cm)	7.0*	6.6*
Girard form class	73.9	73.8
Bole form index[†]	3.9	4.0
Cone productivity index[‡]	2.4	2.2
Volume (m³, diameter outside bark)	0.459	0.465
Bole rust damage class[§]	3.0	3.2
Branch rust damage class[§]	3.6	3.7

Source: adapted from Henderson and Schoenike (1981).
* Significant difference at the 95% probability level.
[†] Visual evaluation with a scale of 1 to 5 (1 = fork, 2 = sweep, 3 = crook, 4 = normal or typical loblolly form, 5 = straight).
[‡] Ratings based on a scale of 1 to 4 (1 = none, 2 = light, 3 = intermediate, 4 = heavy).
[§] On a scale of 1 to 5 (1 = most severe).

from which it is derived (longleaf and loblolly). As a male parent, Sonderegger generally crosses well with both parents, but pollen of some Sonderegger F$_1$ hybrids is highly fertile on loblolly flowers and completely infertile on longleaf. Backcrosses to Sonderegger and Sonderegger × Sonderegger crosses are generally not very successful. Introgression is skewed toward the loblolly parent (Brown 1964, Snyder and Squillace 1966).

Sonderegger pines can be easily identified in longleaf pine nursery beds because they lack the typical grass stage of longleaf. As hybrid trees mature, characteristics of both species are expressed. These include long needles and heavy, long branches typical of longleaf; and persistent, armed cones and a brown, striped bud characteristic of loblolly. Loblolly and Sonderegger differ little in growth, development, and susceptibility to fusiform rust (table 7-13). Unfortunately, the resistance of longleaf to tip moth is not transmitted to Sonderegger (Grigsby 1959). Some physical characteristics of Sonderegger are intermediate between those of the two species. Such characteristics include cone and seed size, hypocotyl growth, seedling (figure 7-13) and sapling growth, bole form, and branch angle (Schoenike and others 1975). Within 48 hours of germination, loblolly pine hypocotyls are longer than mature hypocotyls of either longleaf or Sonderegger. Cell multiplication continues in loblolly hypocotyls until about the 16th day, but is essentially complete in Sonderegger by the end of the 10th day and in longleaf by the

Figure 7-13—Two-year-old pine seedlings: loblolly (*a*), longleaf × loblolly hybrid, called Sonderegger pine (*b*), and longleaf (*c*).

Table 7-14—Dimensions of cells and tissues in the basal portion of mature hypocotyls of loblolly and longleaf pines and their F$_1$ cross*

Species	Cortical cells[†]			Pith cells[†]			Overall width of hypocotyl[‡] (mm)
	Length[‡] (µm)	Width[‡] (µm)	No. of radial rows	Length[‡] (µm)	Width[‡] (µm)	No. of radial rows	
Longleaf	179±10.9[§]	25±0.78	14±0.36	319±20.7	27±1.10	16±0.51	1.30
Longleaf × loblolly[ǁ]	189±15.1	30±0.91	12±0.60	357±21.2	27±0.63	12±0.48	1.20
Loblolly × longleaf	176±14.1	27±0.84	9±0.41	320±20.1	25±0.60	8±0.29	0.90
Loblolly	204±13.7	24±1.10	8±0.38	497±25.8	23±0.61	8±0.31	0.80

Source: adapted from Brown (1964).
* All plants grown under comparable greenhouse conditions in sterile sand, nutrient cultures.
[†] Counts made on 15 different plants of same age.
[‡] Mean of 10 cells per plant (total 150 measurements).
[§] Standard error of the mean.
[ǁ] Sonderegger pine.

5th day. Differences in cortical cells, pith cells, and hypocotyl widths are listed in table 7-14. These differences clearly demonstrate the strong genetic control over physiological processes during early growth and development.

Loblolly × Slash Pine Hybrids

Loblolly and slash pines grow together naturally along the Atlantic and Gulf Coasts from South Carolina to Louisiana. Although their flowering periods are staggered, there are occasional opportunities for natural hybridization. Best results seem to occur between the slash pine female and the loblolly pine male.

Little and Righter (1965) described the following basic morphological characteristics of loblolly × slash hybrids and the reciprocal cross:

Bark rough, thick, furrowed into scaly plates, blackish gray with brown exposed in deep furrows. Spring shoots multinodal. Twigs glabrous, glaucous when young, light yellow-green the first year, becoming brown the second year. Buds reddish brown, the scales whitish fringed. Leaves 3 and 2 in a fascicle, stout, stiff, 10–19 cm long, acuminate, serrulate, green; stomatal rows of leaves in 3's 7–12 dorsal and 4–8 on each ventral surface, of leaves in 2's 12-14 dorsal and 9–10 ventral. Needle anatomy in cross section: Hypodermis biform, of 2, sometimes 3, layers of cells, the inner border straight; endodermis of thin-walled cells; resin canals medial, internal and medial, or partly subinternal, 2–7, 2 large usually medial at angles and often 1–5 additional smaller.

Cones 1–4 at a node, almost sessile, ovoid conic, symmetrical, 7–11 cm long, 5–7 cm across when open at maturity, persistent 1 year or more; apophyses dull nut brown, elevated along a transverse keel, umbo raised and about 3 mm high including the sharp spine....

The occurrence of leaves partly in 2's is similar to *Pinus elliottii*, as *P. taeda* has needles uniformly 3 in a fascicle. Parents have similar needle anatomy except that resin canals are mostly medial in *P. taeda*, mostly internal in *P. elliottii*, and intermediate in the hybrid. Hybrid cones are intermediate between the small cone with stout spines in *P. taeda* and the large cone with smaller prickles in *P. elliottii*. Cones of *P. taeda* and the hybrid are dull nut brown, while those of *P. elliottii* are shiny reddish brown.

Most physical characteristics of hybrids of loblolly and slash pines are intermediate between those of the two species. Traits that most clearly identify hybrids are the number of stomata per centimeter of needle length and proportion of internal resin canals touching the needle endodermis (Mergen 1958, Snyder and Hamaker 1978b). Loblolly has 50% more stomata per unit of needle length than does slash pine. The number of stomata on the hybrid's needles is median between the two species. Also, the number of rows of stomata and the number of teeth on needles of the hybrid is intermediate between slash pine, which is low, and loblolly pine, which is high (figure 7-14). Tracheid length in hybrids ranges from 1.13 to 1.33 mm, whereas tracheid length ranges from 1.09 to 1.57 mm in the parent trees (Jackson and Greene 1958). Wood specific gravity of hybrids tends to be closer to that of the female parent than to that of the male parent (Jackson and Warren 1962).

Artificial crosses between loblolly and slash pines are relatively easy to make. However, the crosses have not yet proven to be of value, primarily because many economically important traits are involved and because it is difficult to obtain large numbers of hybrid seeds. Rust incidence seems to be higher for the hybrid than for either species. Also, when both parents are adapted to a particular area and have good growth characteristics, hybrid intermediacy is of little practical consequence (Schmitt 1968a, 1968b).

Loblolly × Pond Pine Hybrids

Loblolly and pond pines have overlapping ranges along the East Coast from Virginia to Florida (Wenger 1958a, 1958b). Natural hybrids and natural introgressive hybrids between these species (*P. serotina × taeda*) occur widely. They are quite common throughout southern Delaware and appear to be more common than typical loblolly. They are also prevalent in Maryland (Little and others 1967) and in the Piedmont and Coastal Plain of North Carolina (Saylor and Kang 1973). Hybrids are not restricted to wet areas but are found on a wide variety of soils and sites. Morphological characteristics of the parents and the hybrids are well documented (Little and others 1967).

Characteristics of cones, seeds (table 7-15), and oleoresin terpenes can be used to identify mature hybrids. Seedlings are most reliably distinguished on the basis of hypocotyl length, hypocotyl color, and seed germination rate. Gene movement is predominantly from pond pine to loblolly. Backcrosses of the intermediates to loblolly appear to be common, but backcrosses to pond have not been found. It is probable, however, that there is some gene flow back to pond pine.

The hybrids are usually located in open areas along road cuts or at the edges of stands, suggesting that hybrids are unable to compete in a normal forest environment. Where hybridization is prevalent, natural loblolly seeds can be collected with few intergrades if cone collections are limited to large cones with stout prickles from trees that have few cones older than 1 year and have nonresinous buds, and relatively long, flexible needles (Little and others 1967).

Loblolly × Pitch Pine Hybrids

Natural hybrids and intergrades between loblolly and pitch pines occur in New Jersey, Delaware, and Maryland where the ranges of loblolly and pitch overlap. Because the species have little common range, their hybrids are not of widespread occurrence (Little and others 1967). Many of the cone and seed characteristics of the hybrids are gradational between those of the two species (table 7-15). However, pitch pine produces cones at an earlier age than does loblolly, and most cones on hybrid saplings exhibit the short crooks that are characteristic of pitch pine. Crosses of these species yield as many as 40 seeds/cone (Ledig and Fryer 1974).

There appears to be no substantial barrier to artificial crossing of loblolly and pitch pines. The first control-pollinated hybrid was produced in 1933. Hybrid progeny have higher rates of survival and more vigor than either parental type on some sites (Little and Trew 1977). Hybrids from

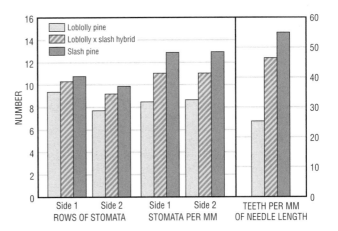

Figure 7-14—Relationships between loblolly, slash, and the loblolly × slash pine hybrid in number of rows of stomata, stomata per millimeter of needle length, and teeth per millimeter of needle length (adapted from Mergen 1958).

individual parental combinations have varied in height in the seedbed by as much as 40%, and this variation indicates the potential value of careful genetic selection (Hyun and others 1971). Pitch × loblolly hybrids (*P. × rigitaeda*) are produced in large quantities for commercial plantings in South Korea (Hyun and Ahn 1959) (see chapter 12).

Table 7-15—Comparison of characteristics of pond, pond × loblolly hybrid, loblolly, pitch, and pitch × loblolly hybrid pines

	Characteristic	Pond pine	Pond × loblolly hybrid pine	Loblolly pine	Pitch pine	Pitch × loblolly hybrid pine
Trunk	Leaves on short twigs	Present	Usually absent (I)	Absent	Present	Usually absent (I)
	Buds	Usually resinous	Usually resinous (PO)	Usually nonresinous, shiny	Usually resinous	Resinous (PI)
Needles	Length	11–20 cm	12–21 cm	12–22 cm	6–14 cm	10–19 cm (I)
	Width	1.6–1.8 mm	1.4–1.6 mm (I)	1.1–1.3 mm	1.1–1.6 mm	1.1–1.5 mm
	Stiffness	Slightly stiff	Flexible to slightly stiff (I)	Flexible	Slightly stiff	Slightly stiff (PI)
	Marginal teeth	Stout	Fine (L)	Fine	Fine	Fine
	Resin canals	3–9, mostly small	4–5, mostly small (I)	2–4, large and small	2–6, small	2 large and 0–2 small (I)
Cones	Length	4.5–6 cm	7–9 cm (I)	7–11 cm	4–7 cm	5–6 cm (PI)
	Width closed	4–5 cm	3.5–4.5 cm (I)	3.5 cm	2.5–3.5 cm	3.2–3.5 cm
	Width open	5.6–7 cm	5.5–6 cm	6–7.5 cm	4.5–5.5 cm	4.5–6 cm (I)
	Shape closed	Ovoid to subglobose	Conic or narrowly ovoid (I)	Conic	Narrowly ovoid	Conic (L)
	Shape open	Nearly hemispherical, broader than long, broadest at flat base formed by reflexed scales	Ovoid, broadest below middle, flattened at base (I)	Ovoid, broadest below middle, not flat at base	Ovoid, mostly longer than broad, broadest below middle, flattened at base	Ovoid, flattened at base (PI)
	Dehiscence	Late (serotinous) to early	Early to late (I)	Early	Early or late	Early
	Persistence	Persistent	Partly persistent (I)	Usually deciduous	Persistent	Persistent (PI)
	Phyllotaxy	High order, many scales	Intermediate (I)	Normal	Normal	Normal
Cone scales	Width	6–10 mm	9–13 mm (I)	12–15 mm	7–10 mm	8–13 mm (I)
	Keel	Weak on basal scales	Weak on basal scales (PO)	Prominent	Prominent	Prominent
	Prickle	About 1 mm long or less, small, slender, weak, often deciduous	About 2-3 mm long or less, small, slender, sharp, persistent (I)	About 2-3 mm long, including broad umbo, large, stout, persistent	About 2 mm long, small, sharp, persistent	About 2 mm long, small, slender, sharp persistent (PI)
	Prickle on basal scales	Smaller than pitch or loblolly	Smaller (PO)	Almost same size as pitch	Almost same size as loblolly	Almost same size as pitch and loblolly
	Color of apophysis	Tawny yellow, slightly shiny	Tawny yellow, dull (I)	Nut brown, dull	Tawny yellow, slightly shiny or dull	Tawny yellow, slightly shiny or dull (PI)
Seeds	Length with wing	21–24 mm	24–27 mm (I)	27–28 mm	15–21 mm	21–22 mm (I)
	Length of body	5 mm	6–7 mm (L)	6–7 mm	4–5 mm	4.5–6 mm (I)
	Shape of body	3-angled or ovoid	Rhomboid or ovoid (L)	Rhomboid	3-angled	3-angled (PI)
Summary (number of characteristics of each hybrid in each category)		3 PI, 15 I, 3 L				8 PO, 7 I, 1 L

Source: adapted from Little and others (1967).

I = the characteristic is intermediate; PO = the characteristic is more like pond pine; PI = the characteristic is more like pitch pine; L = the characteristic is more like loblolly pine.

The hybrid is intermediate between loblolly and pitch pines in needle characteristics (length, width, fascicle sheath length, and color), speed of germination, and cold hardiness. No single morphological characteristic identifies hybrid seedlings. Little and Righter (1965) described an artificial pitch pine × loblolly pine hybrid as follows:

Bark rough, thick, furrowed into scaly plates, blackish gray, the trunk sometimes bearing short twigs with needles. Spring shoots multinodal. Twigs glabrous, light yellow green and shiny the first year, becoming light brown the second year. Buds acute, reddish brown, resinous. Leaves 3 in a fascicle, stout and stiff, 10–20 cm long, acute-acuminate, serrulate, green; stomatal rows 10–15 dorsal and 5–8 on each ventral surface. Needle anatomy in cross section: Hypodermis biform, of 2–5 layers of cells, the inner border often angled; endodermis of thin-walled cells; resin canals medial (rarely also internal), 2 (rarely 3), about 0.04–0.08 mm. in diameter; a line of thick-walled cells often outside phloem in transfusion tissue.

Male strobili (old and dry) 17–25 mm long, 4–5 mm in diameter, orange brown. Cones 3, 2, or 1 at a node, almost sessile, ovoid-conic, symmetrical, 7–8 cm long, 4–4.5 cm in diameter closed, serotinous, opening after 1 or more years, long persistent in quantity for several years; apophyses pale fulvous brown or tawny yellow, dull or slightly shiny, elevated along a transverse keel, the nut-brown umbo forming a sharp stout prickle or spine about 3 mm long. Winged seeds about 25 mm long, the detachable wing nut-brown, body ovoid, 5 mm long, blackish....

In needle anatomy the hybrid and both parents are similar. The hybrid is like *Pinus taeda* in the large resin canals, while *P. rigida* has diameters of about 0.02–0.04 mm. Needle length is intermediate. The intermediate cones have the larger, stout prickles of *P. taeda* and the slightly serotinous habit of *P. rigida* in this variation from southern New Jersey.

Pitch pine is cold hardy but slow growing. It has significantly shorter needles and a more compact crown than has loblolly, and these characteristics reduce the opportunity for heavy snow or ice accumulation and subsequent crown damage. Hybrids of pitch and loblolly pines exhibit the rapid growth characteristic of loblolly and the cold hardiness and resistance to damage by wet snow and ice characteristic of pitch pine. Breeding for this superior combination has produced well-formed, rapid-growing, winter-hardy trees that have been established in more than 50 plantations in 9 Northeastern and Midwestern States (Knezick and others 1985a, Little and Trew 1979a). Where growing seasons are short or where other conditions are unfavorable near the northern extremes of loblolly's range, the best pitch × loblolly hybrids should outgrow pitch pine

by appreciable amounts (Little and Trew 1977, 1979a, 1979b). Herrick (1981) estimated that growing the hybrid is economically beneficial when interest rates are less than 9%. Nevertheless, loblolly should be favored over pitch or intergrades near or slightly beyond the natural range of loblolly if the sites are not excessively harsh and if loblolly from northern sources are used (Little and others 1967).

Many chromosomal similarities between loblolly and pitch pines have been identified (Kim 1963) showing why hybridization is relatively easy. Kim (1963) summarized the chromosomal similarities of loblolly and pitch × loblolly hybrids:

- When the chromosomes are arranged in order of the length of full chromosome as well as in the order of the short arm, many chromosomes of the two species at the same position are the same in the centromere position.

- The mean length of long and short arm chromosomes are similar in the two species.

- In the shortest chromosomes, the ratios: the short arm to the long arm, length of short arm to the width and the short arm to the full length are similar in the two species.

Mass pollinating (mistblowing) a multiclonal pitch pine orchard with loblolly pollen can be expected to produce about 11% hybrid seeds, but individual clones may produce from near zero to 32% hybrid seeds. Isolated single clones of pitch pine are sufficiently self-sterile so that mass pollination can be used to produce much higher percentages of hybrids. Mass pollination may be adaptable to producing loblolly hybrids with other southern pines also (Joly and Adams 1983; Knezick and others 1985a, 1985b).

Hybridization between loblolly and the pitch pine–pond pine complex (*P. rigida* ssp. *rigida* and *P. rigida* ssp. *serotina*) is also common, and there is genetic exchange in both directions. Smouse and Saylor (1973) concluded that loblolly pine has made a pervasive (but minor) contribution to the gene pool of this transitional type, but that little reverse genetic infiltration has occurred.

Loblolly × Sand Pine Hybrids

The few crosses made between loblolly and sand (*P. clausa*) pines have produced only seedlings that died soon after germination. These results suggest hybrid inviability (Critchfield 1963).

Seed Orchards

When loblolly pines were first regenerated by artificial means, seeds were obtained from any easily accessible tree with numerous cones. It was quickly realized that this practice perpetuated many undesirable traits. Subsequent selection of seeds from good individual

trees and good stands still provided limited genetic improvement because only one parent was known and the heritability for growth was low (Zobel and Talbert 1984). The next step in genetic improvement of loblolly was to establish seed production areas by isolating specific stands, roguing undesirable phenotypes, and growing large numbers of cones on the best trees in specific areas. This technique permitted the production of large numbers of seeds within 2 to 5 years after a seed production area was established (Cole 1963), but it provided very limited control over the genetic quality of seeds produced. To maximize control over the genetic composition of the progeny, breeders now plant trees with desirable characteristics in orchards, control-pollinate them, and culture them for seed production. The theory behind the use of seed orchards as a means of producing genetically superior seeds is well documented (Dorman 1976, Dorman and Zobel 1973). Advances in pollen management are discussed in detail in a recent agriculture handbook (Bramlett and others 1993).

Seed Orchard Development

Seed orchards are plantations consisting of clones or seedlings from selected trees. They are isolated to reduce pollination from outside sources, rogued of undesirable individuals, and cultured for early and abundant production of seeds. Loblolly pines are well suited to orchard culture and the rapid development of genetically improved planting stock. Small loblolly orchards for the production of superior seeds were first established in the early 1960's (Johnson 1973, Kitchens 1985). Since that time, the number of orchards and the total area in seed orchards have steadily increased. The decision to enter into a seed orchard program should be based on careful economic analysis. The investment in a mature orchard can be hundreds of thousands of dollars per hectare (Robbins and others 1985).

Seed orchard development begins with the selection of trees that appear to be fast growing, straight stemmed, and free of visible disease and insect infection. Candidate trees should also show some ability to produce cones and have satisfactory wood specific gravities. To minimize the problem of relatedness and inbreeding, breeders should not select candidate trees growing less than 0.4 km apart in natural stands (USDA FS 1988). The U.S. Department of Agriculture, Forest Service, has minimum wood specific gravity limits for select loblolly pines: Alabama and northern Mississippi, 0.440; Georgia, 0.450; southern Mississippi, 0.480; South Carolina Coastal Plain, 0.470; and other southern states and sources, 0.490.

At moderate heritability levels ($h^2 = 0.15$), offspring selection (selecting the best trees from the best families) yields higher genetic gain than parent selection. [Parent selection is a strategy in which individuals are selected on the basis of the performance of their progeny. In offspring selection, the selected individuals are the best members of the progeny family.] However, orchards established with juvenile scion material may not reach commercial flower production as soon as orchards established with scion material from older parents. Even a 1-year delay in full production can make offspring selection less profitable than parent selection (Hodge 1985).

Orchard location. Numerous environmental and economic factors must be considered when planning a new orchard. The most efficient orchards are located near the center of the area in which plantations are to be established and are close to nursery operations. However, consideration must be given to future development of the area. Condemnation of a 15-year-old orchard for construction of a new highway or urban development can be a major setback to a tree improvement program. When orchards are small and scattered, there is less risk of total loss from a tornado or other catastrophe, but such orchards are more expensive to establish and operate. If all clones are concentrated in a single orchard, a separate clone bank should be established and maintained at another location as insurance against a catastrophe. It is not necessary to locate an orchard where the ortets originate, but no orchard should ever be placed in a harsher environment than the one in which its ortets originated. Loblolly pine seed orchards in the southern part of loblolly's range produce more cones and seeds than do northern orchards (figure 7-15).

Growing loblolly pine seed orchards south of loblolly's native range may have practical benefits (especially at young orchard ages), but available data are limited. Fruitfulness of a

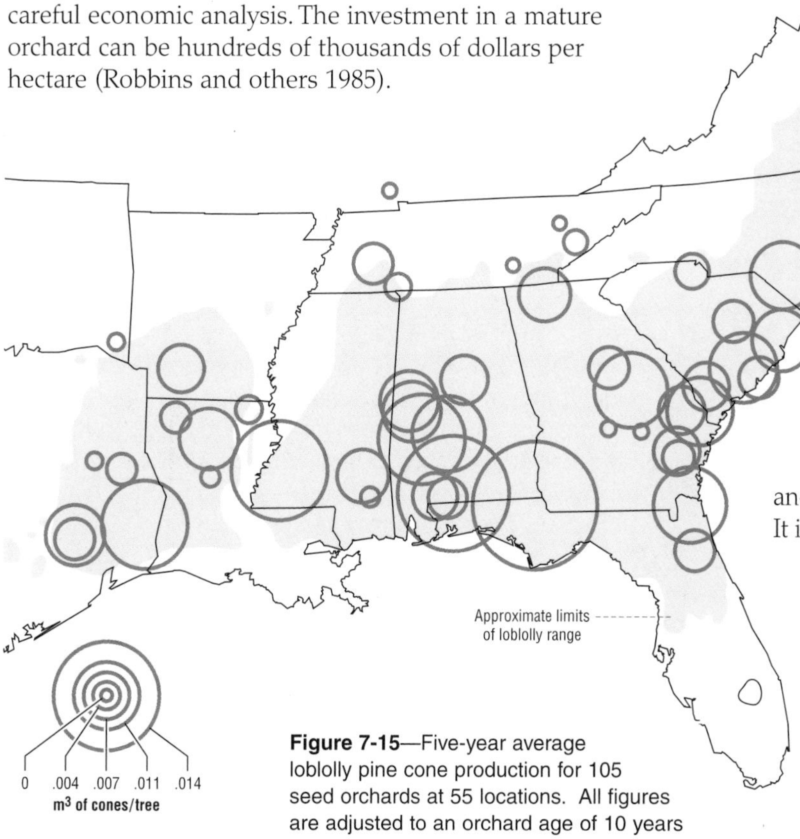

Approximate limits of loblolly range

Figure 7-15—Five-year average loblolly pine cone production for 105 seed orchards at 55 locations. All figures are adjusted to an orchard age of 10 years (adapted from Schmidtling 1979).

0   .004   .007   .011   .014
m³ of cones/tree

Table 7-16—Comparison of loblolly pine flowering in seed orchards established in 1976–77 in the lower Rio Grande Valley of south Texas and in south Arkansas and measured from 1979 to 1982

Location		Orchard age (yrs)	No. of ramets	% Ramets with flowers	No. of flowers/ramet
South Texas	1979	3	164	63.4	4.96
	1980	4	146	77.4	15.06
	1981	5	138	83.3	17.26
	1982	6	132	97.7	51.23
South Arkansas	1979	3	464*	23.7	1.03
	1980	4	464	9.5	0.30
	1981	5	464	33.0	2.12
	1982	6	464	29.3	3.14

Source: adapted from Richmond and McKinley (1986).

* 20% sample.

young orchard in south Florida, well south of the natural range of loblolly, was greater than that of orchards in north Florida, south Mississippi, or north Mississippi for the first 5 years (Schmidtling 1983b). More than half of the ramets in a Texas orchard 640 km south of loblolly's natural range were flowering by age 3 while only about one-fourth of the ramets in an Arkansas orchard were flowering by age 3 (table 7-16). However, within a few years, cone production and the number of seeds per cone at the south Texas orchard were no longer greater than in many orchards within loblolly's range. At orchard age 8, 53% of the female strobili formed cones in southern Texas, but only 22 seeds developed per cone. Supplemental mass pollination increased the number of flowers maturing to cones by 15%, but the number of seeds per cone did not exceed 26 (Byram and others 1986b). In addition to more extensive early flowering, an isolated southern orchard receives little extraneous pollen, so pollen contamination is minimal.

Orchards outside the natural range of loblolly pine will probably require special management. For example, the south Texas loblolly orchard required windbreaks and trickle irrigation to offset the effects of strong prevailing winds and special treatments to ameliorate alkaline soil with a high salt content (Byram and others 1986b).

Orchard sites. Abandoned cropland, especially in the lower and middle Coastal Plain, can make very desirable sites for loblolly pine seed orchards. Such land normally requires little clearing, is relatively level, has good drainage and fertility, and is easily accessible. Gently sloping terrain reduces the likelihood that soils will be water logged during the early part of the year when reproductive primordia are initiated. Topography must permit the use of motorized vehicles, and microclimatic variation must be minimal to limit losses from frost or wind. Former homesites should not be used for orchards because they often contain mixtures of building products, such as concrete, or refuse that can cause extreme tree-to-tree variation in growth (Bengtson and Goddard 1966). Sites close to concentrations of oaks or other alternate hosts of cone rust (*Cronartium strobilinum* Hedgc. &

Hahn.) should not be used if other options are available.

Soil properties, to a depth of at least 0.5 m, should be evaluated carefully before orchard sites are selected. Soil types should be mapped, water-holding capacity and nutritional levels determined, and areas of uniform growth potential identified. A sandy loam or loam A horizon, 20 to 30 cm thick, is best for manipulation of soil moisture to increase cone production and for year-round vehicle trafficability (Gallegos 1979). It is extremely important to evaluate soil acidity in potential seed orchard sites. Soil pH directly affects soil reactions, the behavior of soil organisms, and the growth and health of tree roots. A pH range of 5.5 to 6.0 is generally optimum for loblolly pine seed orchards.

Orchard size. Individual seed orchards can range from as few as 8 ha to as many as 150 ha and still be economical. The size of an orchard is determined by anticipating the number of seedlings needed for future plantings. To reach this figure, an estimate must be made of the number of cones that can be produced per tree and the number of viable seeds that can be produced per cone. These figures are determined by orchard location and intensity of management. Before attempting to establish an orchard, the expected costs should be compared to the cost and availability of seeds from other sources. When outplantings total less than about 2,000 ha/yr, it is usually more economical to purchase improved seeds or seedlings from State or private orchards than to install and maintain a seed orchard.

Orchard design. There are many planting designs that can be used, depending on the number of clones or families involved (Giertych 1971). Layouts can favor crossing between specific trees, but designers usually attempt to maximize random pollination within an orchard. Orchard design should facilitate cross-pollination among orchard trees and establish clonal patterns that minimize inbreeding. Clonal seed orchards usually contain similar numbers of trees of each clone. Additional genetic gains may be realized if the better clones are used in higher proportions. Algorithms are available to project this relationship (Lindgren and Matheson 1986).

Orchards should also be designed to reduce edge effect and minimize contamination by outside pollen. In areas where there is a steady prevailing wind, edge effect can be reduced by making the orchard rectangular and by orienting the orchard's long axis with wind direction at the time of pollen dispersal (Dyson and Freeman 1968). Installation of a buffer zone devoid of pollen-bearing loblolly pines and at least 120 m wide greatly increases the probability that most pollination will be by male parents of selected orchard trees. Buffer strips (pollen dilution zones) should always be maintained between orchards of trees from different physiographic regions and between advanced-generation and early-generation orchards (Zobel and Talbert 1984).

It is important that seed orchard managers estimate the level of unwanted pollen and reduce it if it is excessive. Inexpensive pollen traps can be placed in and around an orchard to estimate background contamination (Greenwood and Rucker 1985). Unfortunately, even with a wide pollen dilution zone, gene flow caused by foreign pollen can be a problem, especially when a small orchard (4 to 6 ha) is surrounded by concentrated stands of loblolly pines (Friedman and Adams 1985a). Estimates of pollen contamination range from 3% to near 90% depending on orchard location and age. In one orchard, background pollen made up 88% of the pollen pool at orchard age 10 and 68% of the pool at age 11. In another orchard, background pollen constituted 32% of the pollen pool at orchard age 24 and 31% of the pool at age 25 (Greenwood and Rucker 1985). Friedman and Adams (1981) estimated that outside pollen contamination of a 16-year-old loblolly orchard was 28%. This amount of contamination could reduce genetic gain by 15%.

Pollen contamination can be reduced in the following ways (Squillace and Long 1981):

1. Increase the size of the isolation zone.

2. Increase orchard size to increase the level of orchard pollen relative to the level of background pollen.

3. Avoid using clones that are exceptionally early or late in either male or female flowering.

4. Establish approximately equal numbers of ramets per clone to increase the number of compatible matings in an orchard.

5. Increase pollen production through cultural treatments.

6. Apply pollen artificially from collections made within the orchard or from other superior clones.

7. Establish orchards in areas outside the loblolly pine range, in areas where the species is scarce, or where flower phenology of orchard trees will differ from that of native trees.

8. Avoid collecting cones from orchards until orchard pollen production is abundant.

Wide spacing is important for maximum growth and crown development in a seed orchard. As an orchard gets older, wider spacings are needed to maintain vigorous crowns. Spacing is best adjusted by roguing. A spacing of 9- by 9-m increased seed production at least threefold over a 6- by 6-m spacing through age 9 in a Texas study (van Buijtenen 1966b). In producing stands, 12- by 12-m spacing may be ideal for cone production.

Seedling Seed Orchards

Loblolly pine seed orchards can be established with seedling stock of known parentage, but grafting is the preferred approach (van Buijtenen H. 1989. Personal communication). The greatest advantage of seedling seed orchards is that some of the trees will have favorable recombinations of desirable characteristics and should be genetically superior to their parents. Another advantage is that the grafting process is avoided, saving labor and eliminating the problem of graft incompatibility. Establishing an orchard with seedlings from controlled crosses has disadvantages, however. The process is usually more difficult and time consuming than grafting, and seedling seed orchards normally combine breeding method, progeny testing, and seed production in one operation, which greatly impairs their seed production efficiency in early years (Barber and Dorman 1964).

If the desired progenies have been determined, seedling seed orchards can be planted at a wide spacing and managed intensively for seed production. More often, these orchards are planted at high initial densities to evaluate the development of individual progenies and are then converted into seed orchards using one or more tree feature(s) as selection criteria. As trees develop, families that grow slowly, have high incidences of disease or insect problems, or exhibit many crown or stem defects are removed. Thinnings must begin early and

must be done frequently to allow full crown and root development of the better families. Trees normally begin producing flowers between ages 5 and 10, so progeny tests should be rogued by age 10. Combining progeny testing with seed orchard development reduces crown development and delays cone and seed production. However, with proper cultural treatments, flowering of trees in seedling seed orchards should be comparable with that of trees in clonal orchards of the same age within a few years after final roguing (Goddard 1964). Progeny testing can be separated, to some degree, from seed orchard development by simultaneously establishing several tests of the same families. One test is managed for eventual seed production through wide spacing and intensive culture, whereas the others are used strictly to assess family performance. The seedling seed orchard is then rogued of poor families based upon their performances in the other tests designed for that purpose (Zobel and Talbert 1984).

Grafted Clonal Orchards

The regeneration cycle is much shorter when stock is propagated vegetatively than when seedlings must be produced and developed. The most common way of bringing together the best loblolly pine trees is through clonal seed orchards composed of mixtures of grafted trees originating from trees selected from many locations. It is technically feasible to establish clonal orchards from plantlets developed from organs, tissues, or individual cells of mature trees selected for specific phenotypic characteristics. Somatic cell propagation is also feasible for loblolly and may ultimately be a superior technique for seed orchard establishment.

A distinct advantage of clonal orchards is that clonal material can be reproduced, grafts made, and orchards started as soon as selections are made. Scion production from seed orchard or clone bank trees can be maximized by clipping lateral branches. Trees do not need to be hedged (McKeand and others 1988). Another advantage of clonal orchards is that flowers and seeds are produced much sooner than on trees grown from seeds. Because the scion is physiologically mature, a grafted tree generally starts flowering and producing substantial quantities of seeds 6 to 10 years earlier than a tree originating from a seed. Seed orchards can be established by grafting in three ways (Wynens 1966).

- **Nursery bed grafting**—Grafting is done in the nursery on 1+0 nursery stock that has been thinned to about 30 by 30 cm, root pruned, and fertilized. Scions should be approximately the same diameter as the rootstock. This is a good method for mass production; it concentrates efforts at one location where there is close supervision and environmental control, and it is relatively inexpensive. Nursery treatments and pruning of rootstock limbs at outplanting greatly reduces fusiform rust infection. Enough grafts must be made to offset mortality during grafting and transplanting.

- **Grafting on potted or container stock**—Selected genetic material is grafted to desirable rootstock previously established in containers. If done with care, this technique can be highly successful, but the number of plants established in the field is limited by physical facilities available for propagation. Postplanting problems related to root-to-shoot ratio occur in varying degrees. This method is more expensive than nursery bed grafting because it involves intensive cultural and handling practices.

- **Field grafting on planted stock**—Rootstock is established at the desired orchard spacing, so there is no movement after grafting. Grafting is best accomplished in the early spring (especially in the more southern climates), and success is highly dependent on weather conditions. For greatest success, place three seedlings about 0.9 m apart at each site. The best two seedlings should be grafted, and the best one of the two should be retained to form part of the orchard. Field grafting is the preferred technique (van Buijtenen H. 1989. Personal communication).

Grafting techniques.   Several types of grafts (cleft, bottle, veneer, and inarch) are effective in propagating loblolly pines (Dorman 1976, Mergen and Rossoll 1954). Ortets of different ages provide scions of different physiological capabilities, even though scion sizes may be the same. Generally, grafting success is greater with the younger ortets (Greenwood 1984). Commonly, twigs of select trees are grafted onto young seedlings within 60 cm of the ground. Grafting within 60 cm of the ground is not a problem with small nursery bed or potted seedlings, but if field grafts do not take the first time, rootstock can grow quite tall before subsequent grafts are made. When grafts are high in the seedling, the understocks must be pruned extensively, and the trees that are produced are usually poorly formed. A skilled technician can make about 50 grafts/day (van Buijtenen H. 1989. Personal communication). Successful grafting requires clean, sharp instruments and much skill. The success rate can exceed 90% if grafting is done properly with compatible tissues. Paraffin wax is the preferred protective covering for grafts. It is less expensive than other materials and can be applied much more quickly than and protects as well as aluminum foil, polyethylene, or kraft bag wrappers. Technicians using wax grafting methods can graft succulent summer shoots to rootstock with 85% success, as long as water stress of grafted trees is low (McKeand and others 1987, White and others 1983, Wynens 1966).

Clone incompatibility.   Grafting success of loblolly pines varies widely by clone. Most clones graft easily, but as many as 90% of the ramets of some clones die from incompatibility during the first year after grafting. In a regionwide study, 169 of 770 clones were incompatible (table 7-17). Incompatibility in loblolly pine is similar to incompatibility in pond, slash, shortleaf, and Virginia pines, suggesting that the primary cause of incompatibility is the genetic difference between stock and scion (Lantz 1973). When a 1- or 2-year-old grafted loblolly pine produces abundant male flowers, its ramets are usually incompatible with each other (Zobel and Talbert 1984).

Table 7-17—Compatibility of loblolly pine clones in 31 seed orchards by state and province

State	Province	No. of orchards	Total clones grafted	Incompatible clones No.	Incompatible clones Range of %	Mean % Incompatible Province	Mean % Incompatible State
Virginia	Coastal Plain	4	134	35	11–43	26	24
	Piedmont	2	64	12	13–29	19	
North Carolina	Coastal Plain	6	169	32	13–33	19	16
	Piedmont	5	116	14	10–18	12	
South Carolina	Coastal Plain	3	56	15	6–48	27	30
	Piedmont	2	43	15	21–46	35	
Georgia	Coastal Plain	2	38	8	15–28	21	26
	Piedmont	2	42	13	28–33	31	—
Tennessee	Mountain	2	41	8	20–21	20	—
Alabama	Piedmont	2	67	17	24–28	25	—
	Total	30	770	169	6–48	22	—
Combined*	Coastal Plain	15	397	90	6–48	23	—
	Piedmont	11	265	54	10–46	20	—

Source: adapted from Lantz (1973).

* Virginia, North Carolina, South Carolina, and Georgia

Blank fields indicate no data available.

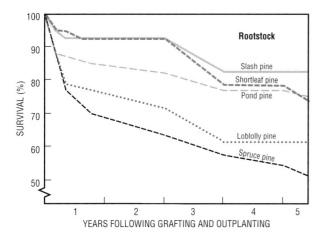

Figure 7-16—Survival percentage of three loblolly pine clones grafted on five southern pine rootstocks (adapted from Schmidtling 1973).

Effect of rootstock species. Rootstock can significantly influence the survival, growth, and fruitfulness of grafts. Loblolly pine scions generally survive and grow best when grafted to loblolly rootstock, but they also can do well when grafted to Japanese red, *Pinus densiflora* Sieb. and Zucc.; pond; shortleaf; and slash pine rootstock (Allen 1967, Hashizume 1979, Schmidtling 1983c; figure 7-16). Loblolly pine rootstock seems to be better than rootstock of other southern pines for grafting shortleaf scions (Schmidtling 1969a), and it is a good rootstock for grafting slash pine (Schmidtling 1988). Rootstock does not alter the

cortical monoterpene composition of loblolly scion material (Schmidtling 1974).

Indoor Potted Breeding Orchards

Potted, grafted ramets of loblolly pines grown indoors can be stimulated to flower more profusely than the same material grown outdoors. Use of indoor potted breeding orchards permits the completion of a breeding cycle within about 5 years from the time when selections are made (Greenwood and others 1979; figure 7-17). Trees can be grown for a decade or more in domed greenhouses, if pruned judiciously and individual branches are treated mechanically or chemically to stimulate either male or female flowering. Several hundred clones can be grown in a complex of greenhouses. The use of these indoor orchards gives breeders excellent control of environmental factors and pathogens.

Figure 7-17—A 2-year-old, potted, indoor-grown loblolly pine seedling with 1-year-old cones.

Seed Orchard Management

During a seed orchard's establishment phase, cultural practices such as fertilization, weed control (figure 7-18), irrigation, and tip moth control are used to encourage rapid early tree growth. During the seed production phase, cultural treatments are changed to promote flowering (for example, different fertilizer regimes or subsoiling) and control of cone and seed insects becomes critical. Number of cones per tree, number of seeds per cone, and seed vigor can all be influenced by cultural practices.

Although flowering is erratic until about orchard age 10, average orchards produce 2.2 kg of seeds/ha/year by age 6. Annual production should increase by about 2.2 kg to about 56 to 67 kg of seeds/ha/year. Seed yields vary greatly from year to year, but a well-tended orchard can produce up to 112 kg of seeds/ha/year under ideal conditions. Sixty-seven kilograms of seeds can produce enough seedlings to establish about 325 ha of plantations (Kellison and Weir 1980). Cones of seed orchard trees can produce twice as many seeds per cone as can cones of trees in natural stands (Summerville 1987).

Both female and male flowering capabilities are highly heritable, but production by a single clone can vary greatly

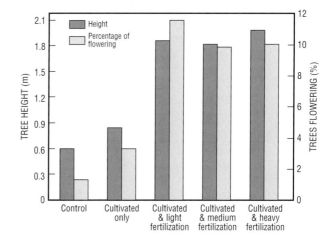

Figure 7-18—Effects of cultural treatments on height and percentage of flowering of 4-year-old loblolly pines (adapted from Schmidtling 1969b).

from year to year. Also, male flowering and female flowering of an individual tree or clone are not well correlated; they are initiated at different times, and environment plays a large role in flower development (see chapter 2).

Although cultural treatments and water stress can promote both male and female flower formation, treatment timing is critical if significant changes are to be obtained (Greenwood and Schmidtling 1981). Soil pH is probably the single soil attribute that most affects flowering because it directly affects many reactions in the soil, the behavior of soil organisms, and plant roots. A soil pH of 5.5 to 6.0 is optimum for loblolly pine flowering. When soil pH drops below 5.1, lime should be added to raise the pH. When pH rises above 6.5, acid-forming fertilizers such as ammonium sulfate, ammonium nitrate, or elemental sulfur should be added to reduce the pH (Davey 1981).

Fertilization

Good soil fertility is essential for the establishment and maintenance of a healthy, vigorous seed orchard, and fertilization is usually the best way to increase cone production in loblolly pine orchards. However, trees that are not producing cones cannot be expected to begin producing them as a result of fertilization. The differences among seed orchards make it impossible to recommend standard rates of fertilization for all orchards. Amounts of fertilizer and lime should be functions of tree age, geographical location, and soil type. Clones and provenances also differ in efficiency of nutrient use and fertilizer requirements. Usually N, phosphorus (P), and K (and other specific macro- and micronutrients) are needed to promote rapid vegetative growth when the trees are young. When trees become fruitful, applying ammonium nitrate in the summer usually promotes flowering.

Soil amendments should be added based on data from soil and foliar analyses. Each microsite that appears different in topography, soil, native vegetation, or drainage should be sampled separately. The following minimum soil fertility standards can be used as a general guide (Davey 1981): Ca, 450 kg/ha; magnesium (Mg), 55 kg/ha; K, 90 kg/ha; P, 45 kg/ha; and pH, 5.5.

Nitrogen fertilizers are most effective in promoting female flowering (figure 7-19). Nitrogen sources that can increase flower development include nitrate of soda ($NaNO_3$), ammonium sulfate ($[NH_4]_2SO_4$), calcium nitrate ($CaNO_3$), potassium nitrate (KNO_3), and ammonium nitrate (NH_4NO_3). The combined N source (NH_4NO_3) seems to be the best fertilizer for increasing flowering in young grafted orchards. A loblolly pine orchard in east Texas fertilized with more than 2,950 kg of N (as $CaNO_3$)/ha in a split application (April and July) produced 8,542 sound seeds/tree at age 6 and 24,874 sound seeds/tree at age 7. Without fertilizer treatment, production was 5,628 sound seeds/tree at age 6 and 16,419 sound seeds/tree at age 7 (Robinson 1979). May (1977) stated that moderately high levels of N (224 to 364 kg/ha) and P (97 to 158 kg/ha) generally gave the best yields of cones in five seed orchards from Arkansas to South Carolina. Low levels of N (84 kg/ha), P (37 kg/ha), and K (70 kg/ha) did not stimulate production. High levels of P (195 kg/ha) and K (373 kg/ha) tended to reduce cone production. Webster (1974) recommended annual fertilization of Piedmont and coastal Virginia clones with 135 to 180 kg/ha of N and 45 to 90 kg/ha of P to stimulate both female and male flower production. He found that rates of flower production with heavy fertilization were consistently superior to rates of flower production with light fertilization, and no one combination of N and P gave consistently superior results. However, monthly applications of ammonium nitrate can reduce male flowering.

Timing of fertilization may also be important for best results, but the importance of timing may hinge on the amount of N used and on the overall fertilizer regime applied to an orchard from its inception. Schmidtling (1975, 1983d) found that male flowering in coastal Mississippi and South Carolina was stimulated most when fertilizer was applied in early summer. Female flowering was stimulated most (increased by more than 300%) when N

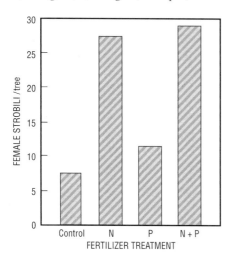

Figure 7-19—Effects of different fertilizer treatments on flowering of 5- to 6-year-old loblolly pine grafts (adapted from Schmidtling 1975).

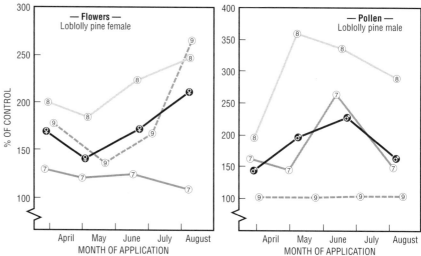

Figure 7-20—Loblolly pine female and male flowering response to different dates of application of NPK fertilizers (7 = flowering in 1977, 8 = flowering in 1978, 9 = flowering in 1979, ♀ = average female flowering, and ♂ = average male flowering) (adapted from Schmidtling 1983d).

or mixed fertilizer was applied in mid-August to holes around the drip line of grafted orchard trees that had not been fertilized for at least several years (figure 7-20). In another Coastal Plain site, flowering was not affected by the timing of summer applications of ammonium nitrate, probably because the orchard had been fertilized frequently and heavily (Greenwood 1977a).

Application of nitrapyrin, 2-chloro-6-(trichloromethyl)-pyridine, which inhibits nitrification, may stimulate male and female cone production in loblolly pines. In one instance, soil application of 1.5 to 2.0 g of nitrapyrin/tree was as effective as application of 150 g of elemental N per tree in stimulating cone production (table 7-18).

Table 7-18—Percentage of branches with male or female cone buds* following application of nitrogen fertilizer[†] and nitrapyrin[‡] to loblolly pine grafted propagules

Sex of cone buds	Tree age (yrs)	Percentage of branches			
		No fertilizer		NH$_4$NO$_3$	
		No nitrapyrin	Nitrapyrin	No nitrapyrin	Nitrapyrin
Male	12	33 a[§]	53 ab	66 b	93 c
	13	60 a	75 b	61 a	59 a
	14	46 a	89 b	86 b	85 b
Female	12	26 a	41 a	40 a	41 a
	13	38 a	59 b	63 b	46 ab
	14	26 a	63 b	64 b	66 b

Source: adapted from Hare (1984a).
* Based on the average percentage of 20 branches in each of 10 trees showing male or female strobili.
† Calculated to supply 150 g N/tree.
‡ Dosage: 1.5 to 2.0 g N-serve/tree.
§ Different letters within a row or sex indicate significant differences at the 95% probability level.

Irrigation

The effect of irrigation on cone and seed production is not well understood, probably because it is masked by variability in natural precipitation. Irrigation of young orchards usually increases tree growth and may increase production of male flowers, but it can decrease female flowering significantly (Jett 1983). Once an orchard is well established, it should be irrigated to promote vegetative growth only in the spring and early summer, before female flower initiation. During this period, the total amount of water from irrigation and rainfall should be at least 25 mm/week. A condition of water stress should then be created during the mid- and late summer to promote both male and female flowering (Dewers and Moehring 1970, Greenwood and Schmidtling 1981, Gregory and others 1982, Harcharik 1983). Because both irrigation early in the growing season and moisture stress late in the growing season are important in promotion of flowering, orchards should be established on sites that are well drained and moderately droughty, in areas where summer drought occurs, where late season moisture stress can be induced, and where water is available for irrigation.

During the first 1 to 2 years, an orchard can be irrigated with water from portable tanks. Long-term irrigation sys-

tems can consist of risers and sprinkler heads, trickle or drip irrigation equipment, or furrow application where the soil slopes. Underground water lines should be placed at least 1 m deep if subsoiling is contemplated at any time during the life of the orchard (Robbins and others 1985). A distinct advantage of the trickle irrigation system is that it can be used to tailor water application to the needs of individual clones. For example, some clones produce more female flowers without early season irrigation. With a trickle system, water can be withheld from such clones, and total female flower production in an orchard can be increased (Harcharik 1983). However, trickle systems may not supply enough water for mature trees.

Irrigation is highly profitable if it is used to increase graft survival, increase tree vigor, increase seed production, and minimize cone harvesting costs by concentrating seed production in relatively small areas. However, if irrigation is used only to increase seed yield, it may be more economical to increase orchard size than to irrigate (Harcharik 1983).

Irrigation plus fertilization with NPK may increase flower and cone production under some conditions, but the increase may not be significantly greater than if the orchard is irrigated but not fertilized (Gregory and others 1982). Water-soluble fertilizers can be applied through irrigation systems. However, P is not recommended for application through trickle equipment; it is not completely soluble in water and may clog emitters (O'Loughlin 1979).

Ground Cover

In many orchards, it is necessary to establish a ground cover to minimize erosion, limit unwanted vegetative competition, and facilitate equipment movement. The appropriate cover crop depends on soil and drainage conditions, the seed harvesting method, and other local characteristics. Commonly used species include bermudagrass, *Cynodon dactylon* (L.) Pers.; tall fescue, *Festuca arundinacea* Schreb.; weeping lovegrass, *Eragrostis curvula* (Schrad.) Nees; browntop millet, *Brachiaria ramosa* (L.) Stapf.; sudan, *Sorghum* spp.; and some clovers, *Trifolium* spp., and lespedezas, *Lespedeza* spp. (May 1977). No one species is best for all sites. In most instances, a single grass or a combination of grasses provides an adequate cover (Long and others 1974). Bahiagrass, *Paspalum notatum* Fluegge, should not be used; it is hard to mow, promotes the accumulation of potential fuel, and crowds out most other grasses (van Buijtenen H. 1989. Personal communication).

Subsoiling

Continued use of machines in orchards during all types of weather results in soil compaction. Subsoiling, to depths of 30 to 90 cm, may be necessary to eliminate soil compaction and enhance tree vigor, especially on heavier soils. Subsoiling also promotes the entry of water and nutrients into the soil. It should be considered before establishment of a new orchard and should be mandatory on land that was formerly cultivated or in pasture, where compaction or a plow pan is likely. Subsoiling prior to planting should be done in a grid pattern corresponding to planting sites for orchard trees. Subsoiling in an established orchard should be done only on a prescription basis and not as a regular treatment because it prunes roots as it loosens soil. Excessive root pruning can reduce tree growth and affect flower production. Subsoiling should be done only on one or two sides of a tree in any one year. Most lateral roots grow in the surface 15 cm of soil, and even shallow subsoiling can be expected to sever at least 75 to 80 roots/tree in a mature orchard. The actual number of roots cut varies greatly depending on tree size, depth of subsoiling, and closeness of subsoiling to a tree. Subsoiling should not be done within 1.2 m of young orchard trees or within 1.8 m of mature trees. It is essential that a subsoiler be preceded by a rolling coulter, designed to cut the roots so that large surface roots are not torn away from a tree. A root severed in the subsoiling process may produce from two to five new roots near the cut end. Some of these new roots may grow along the original root track, but others may grow along the slit or as sinkers down the slit.

Subsoiling can result in minor increases in flowering for 1 or 2 years after treatment; such increases are probably the consequence of physiological stimulation associated with root pruning (Gregory and Davey 1977). Subsoiling should take place prior to floral initiation. In one case, single passes of a subsoiler on opposite sides of and 1.2 m away from 8-year-old orchard trees increased cone production significantly (from 97 to 117 cones/tree). Three parallel cuts on opposite sides of trees increased cone production to 143 cones/tree. The number of sound seeds per cone and the number of small, medium, and large sound seeds per cone were slightly but not significantly increased by subsoiling (table 7-19). However, the effect of subsoiling can vary greatly from clone to clone (Struve and others 1989).

Table 7-19—Seed production for 10 loblolly pine clones in a seed orchard 3 years after subsoiling treatments

Subsoiling treatment	Total seeds	Ave. no. of seeds/cone				% Sound seeds/cone
		Sound seeds				
		Total	Small	Medium	Large	
Control	76 a*	51 a	1.6 a	37.2 a	11.7 a	67 a
Single rip†	85 ab	56 a	3.5 a	40.4 a	12.9 a	66 a
Multiple rip‡	92 b	62 a	6.5 a	42.0 a	13.7 a	67 a

Source: adapted from Struve and others (1989).

* Different letters following values within a column indicate significant differences at the 95% probability level using the Waller-Duncan test.

† One cut to a depth of 45 cm, 1.3 m from the trunk, on opposite sides of each tree.

‡ Three parallel cuts to a depth of 45 cm, 1.3 m, 2.6 m, and 3.9 m from the trunk, on opposite sides of each tree.

Mowing and Disking

Mowing is a common treatment in loblolly pine seed orchards. Frequent mowing develops healthy sod that can withstand vehicle traffic. Healthy sod also increases the benefits of fertilizers and water for trees by minimizing growth of undesirable vegetation. Regular mowing reduces the probability of fire, which can severely damage grafted trees.

Disking is a very effective and inexpensive means of maintaining control of understory vegetation and promoting rapid growth of orchard trees. However, the loose soil created by disking can hinder vehicle movement. If an orchard is on a sloping site, disking must be done on the contour to minimize erosion. Root pruning caused by disking can stress trees severely, depending on the time and extent of the treatment. This stress generally increases female flowering and subsequent seed production (Greenwood 1978b). In a 6- to 9-year-old orchard in east Texas, disking increased seed production 5 to 6 times more than mowing increased it.

Roots cut by subsoiling, disking, or any other treatment are subject to colonization by soil-borne microorganisms, so root decline might be a problem under certain circumstances.

Stem Manipulation

Wire girdling of the main stem or branches promotes male flowering in loblolly pine, but usually kills the branch and sometimes the tree (Greenwood and Schmidtling 1981, Hare 1979a, White and Wright 1987). Such flower stimulating treatments are useful only in young orchards because flower production of most clones is adequate by the time trees reach 8 to 10 years of age. Branch girdling did not increase flowering of 3-year-old, field-grown, grafted ramets of sexually mature trees (Ross and Greenwood 1979). Overlapping saw-cut girdles on the main stem significantly increased female, but not male, flower production in a 10-year-old Georgia orchard (Wheeler and Bramlett 1991). More rigorous studies relating flowering to tree condition, stem mutilation treatment, and timing of treatments are needed to decrease the probability of branch or tree death.

Pruning the tops of orchard trees to make cones more accessible generally reduces flower and cone production by 30 to 50% (Gerwig 1987, Greenwood and Bramlett 1989, McLemore 1979). Indiscriminant annual pruning of branch tips can reduce cone production by 90% (Long and others 1974, van Buijtenen and Brown 1963). Some flower and cone loss associated with upper crown pruning can be eliminated if branches are cut in midsummer. Top pruning should be done above the first flush that bears the current conelet crop. Pruning should be done late enough in the growing season to remove the maximum amount of new growth but early enough so that the cut terminals can develop resting buds and flower primordia for the next flower crop (Gerwig 1987).

Pruning low limbs reduces pollen production because most male strobili are on the lower limbs. Pruning of lower limbs may also increase cone production slightly. On balance, it is worthwhile to prune low limbs in producing orchards because such pruning facilitates mowing, vehicle access, and cone collection with little loss in cone production (Long and others 1974).

Forcing main branches into a horizontal position does not increase cone production (McLemore 1979). In a South African study, loblolly pine trees that were bent to facilitate hand pollination produced only half as many cones as free-growing trees produced (van der Sijde 1969).

Chemical Stimulation of Flowers

Giberellic acid (GA) treatments seem to promote both male and female flowering. Greenwood (1977b) found that GA stimulated dormant female strobili of young grafted and potted stock to grow within 7 weeks of treatment. When ramets were grown in pots, treated with GA, and subjected to water stress, the number of clones producing female cones was four times the number of clones producing female cones when trees were field grown. The number of pot-grown ramets with female flowers was 20 times the number of field-grown ramets with female flowers. Production of cones and seeds by field-grown grafted ramets was increased twelvefold by biweekly applications of 500 mg of GA/branch from May to September (Ross and Greenwood 1979).

Biweekly topical application and injection into the main stem are both effective ways to apply the chemical (Greenwood 1982, Wheeler and Bramlett 1991). In studies with 7- to 14-year-old loblolly and slash pines, male flowering was increased tenfold or more by branch girdling and GA treatment. July-to-August chemical applications were most effective in promoting formation of male cone buds (Hare 1979a, 1984b). In Japan, applications of GA_4 and $GA_{4/7}$ promoted formation of both male and female strobili of loblolly (Hashizume 1985). Giberellic acid can probably be used to stimulate flowering on a large scale, but much more research on concentrations, timing, and environmental relationships is needed.

Pollen Management

It takes 1 to 2 weeks to collect and extract loblolly pine pollen, so controlled pollinations cannot always be made during the year of pollen collection. Therefore, careful planning, pollen handling, and extended protection of viable pollen are important aspects of many tree improvement programs.

Pollen collection. Ideally, pollen should be collected just as it is being released. However, a loblolly pine tree often sheds all of its pollen during a 1- to 2-day period, or even in a few hours during ideal weather conditions. Consequently, it is preferable to collect catkins somewhat earlier—after they have turned yellow and when they produce very little liquid when squeezed between the fingers (Beers and others 1981).

Almost-mature catkins can be nursed into shedding. Branches bearing catkins that are almost ready to shed can be removed from trees and stored in a warm place for a few days with their stems in water. The ripening of immature pollen can also be accelerated by covering male strobili with plastic bags at the same time female strobili are isolated for pollination (if heat buildup is a problem, reflective colored paint can be applied to the outside of the plastic bags). This method is effective in catching pollen produced by early-maturing strobili on trees growing in areas far from the center of operations (Snyder 1961, Snyder and Clausen 1974).

There are many techniques for harvesting catkins (Beers and others 1981). Catkins should be collected in clusters to allow for maximum aeration during shipment. Sprague and Johnson (1977) recommend that freshly picked catkin clusters be placed in paper bags lined with paper towels to absorb moisture. Bags should then be packed loosely in well-aerated containers and transported rapidly to a heated building and spread out to dry in paper-lined racks or trays.

Pollen extraction, drying, and cleaning The condition of catkins significantly affects pollen extraction, yield, and viability. Unripened catkins shed very little pollen, regardless of the duration of extraction. Catkins should not be harvested when they are wet from rain or dew because moisture prolongs the extraction period, contributes to low pollen yield, and may cause molding. Catkins should be dried in warm, dry, moving air (21 to 27 °C and 20 to 40% relative humidity) to increase speed of extraction and for maximum yield of viable pollen. Strobili (in layers 1 to 2 strobili thick) can be dried in a variety of containers that do not impede the movement of forced air. In damp, cold weather, circulating air should be heated artificially and dehumidified (Sprague and Snyder 1981). Vacuum drying is recommended for long-term storage of loblolly pine pollen. Once extracted, pollen should be sieved through a fine mesh screen to remove insect larvae and other debris.

Short-term pollen storage. Freshly extracted pollen is highly resistant to temperatures as great as 50°C for as long as 24 hours (Bramlett and Matthews 1991). Day-to-day storage of viable pollen to be used during the season of collection should be handled as follows (Matthews and Kraus 1981):

1. Place fresh pollen in glass containers having a volume no greater than 100 ml. Containers should be plugged with cotton to prevent spillage and contamination but permit gas exchange.

2. Keep containers in a sealed desiccator containing easily handled drying agents, such as calcium chloride or granular anhydrous lithium chloride, that can maintain a 0% relative humidity in the desiccator.

3. If pollen is used daily, keep the desiccator in a cool room away from heaters and sunlight. If pollen will not be used for several days, refrigerate the desiccator at about 4°C.

4. If cold-stored, bring the desiccator and its contents back to room temperature (before pollen is removed from the desiccator) by removing the desiccator from the refrigerator the night before pollen is to be used.

Long-term pollen storage. The key to successful long-term pollen storage is early cold storage of pollen that has been kept dry at all times. Pollination success and seed yield with properly dried, cleaned, and refrigerated stored pollen are as good as pollination success and seed yield with fresh pollen (Kraus and Hunt 1970, Matthews and Bramlett 1983, Sprague and Johnson 1977). The simplest form of long-term desiccator storage is similar to short-term storage and keeps pollen viable for 1 year (Bramlett and Matthews 1991). The treatment is as follows: (1) clean the fresh, viable pollen and dry it to 9% moisture content, (2) place the pollen in loosely covered 100-ml glass containers, (3) store the pollen in a desiccator at a constant temperature of 4 °C (self-defrosting refrigerator units are unsatisfactory because they do not maintain constant temperatures), (4) remove the desiccator from the refrigerator in time to permit its contents to reach room temperature before any pollen is removed, and (5) reseal the desiccator as soon as needed pollen is removed and then return it to cold storage immediately.

For storage from 1 to 3 years, dried pollen should be placed in tightly closed glass or plastic bottles and held at – 20 °C. Vacuum drying (2 to 3% moisture content) and storage in small, evacuated ampules at 3 °C keeps pollen viable for 10 years or longer because the technique creates conditions that keep pollen metabolic activity extremely low (Bramlett and Matthews 1991). Fiveash and McConnell (1989) demonstrate an easy-to-use pollen storage technique using a freeze-dryer and a vacuum-sealing system. Frozen pollen should be rewarmed slowly, first in a refrigerator, then at room temperature under desiccation to minimize damage from moisture condensation.

Testing pollen for viability. Pollen must be rehydrated before testing. Viability of pollen can be determined in as little as 45 minutes by assessing ultraviolet absorbance or conductivity of pollen leachate (Foster and Bridgwater 1979). Several other simple procedures are available, but they generally require 48 to 72 hours. Pollen germinates in distilled water and on agar with or without additives. Commonly used additives include sucrose, honey, or boron. Pollen sprinkled on a dry glass slide germinates if the slide is placed where humidity is high and kept at room temperature so that moisture condenses on the slide. Pollen also germinates in small vials of distilled water at about 29 °C (Goddard and Matthews 1981). Another technique is to germinate pollen in a 0.01% sucrose solution for 48 hours at approximately 21 °C (Sprague and Johnson 1977). Germination percentage is based on the number of germinated pollen grains (tube length equal to or greater than the width of the pollen grain) from a random sample of at least 200 grains.

Pollination and Fertilization

Most orchard pollen is released during mid- to late morning (9 to 11 a.m.), after catkins have dried out and when the wind is sufficiently strong to move branches. Small amounts of pollen from the orchard and background sources are airborne throughout the day and night (Greenwood and Rucker 1985).

Controlled pollination. Many thousands of controlled pollinations are made in loblolly pine orchards each year, and proper timing is critical to the success of this operation. The largest seed yields are produced when strong conelet-bearing branches in the upper part of the crown (each growing in a relatively upright position) are used. These strong branches can carry heavy cones to maturity. Pollination bags should be installed when conelets are at stage 2 (figure 7-21 and table 7-20) and supported with a piece of wire or wood. Early bagging can speed flower development so greatly that flowers become receptive before fresh pollen is available.

The optimum time for breeding is when cone scales

Figure 7-21—Stages of pine conelet development: early stage 1—small flower buds, the bud on the right has female strobili that are barely visible (*a*); two females at stage 1 (*b*); stage 2—large flower buds (*c*); stage 3—flower emerges from the bud scales (*d*); stage

form right angles with the cone axis and there are large openings between cone scales (flower developmental stage 5). Pollination success is very near maximum for 48 hours before and 48 hours after this point of maximum receptivity. Pollination droplets emerge on unpollinated strobili as the strobili approach full maturity. Droplets reemerge throughout the receptive period, primarily during the early morning or evening until pollination occurs, after which they do not emerge again. Droplet reemergence for a given ovule is independent of the condition of other ovules on the same strobilus. The rate at which strobili pass through the developmental stages is accelerated by hot and sunny conditions and slowed by cool and wet conditions. Multiple pollinations may increase fertilization success if flowers within a bag are at different stages of maturity or if pollinations are not made at the period of maximum receptivity (Bramlett and Matthews 1983, Bramlett and O'Gwynn 1981, Brown and Bridgwater 1987).

The pollination bags used normally consist of viscose sausage-casing material, but paper or cloth bags are also suitable. Larger quantities of pollen are normally dispensed by means of air delivery devices such as syringes with rubber bulbs, ear syringes, wash bottles, or

Table 7-20—Stages of pine conelet development

Stage	Description
1	Buds small
2	Buds large
3	Buds opening
4	Flowers partly open
5	Flowers maximum
6	Flowers closed
7	Cones enlarging

Source: adapted from Wakeley and Campbell (1954).

Table 7-21—Effect of pollen germination rate on usefulness of loblolly pine pollen for control pollinations

Pollen germination (%)	Rating	Utility for control pollinations
≥35	Excellent	Use
20–34	Good	Use
10–19	Fair	Use only if fresh pollen is unavailable
1–9	Poor	Do not use

Source: adapted from Sprague and Johnson (1977).

cyclone pollinators. When only small amounts of pollen are available, a camel's hair brush can be used to apply pollen directly to individual flowers. When a brush is used, a large hole must be cut into the bag or the bag must be removed. Either of these actions increases the probability of contamination by undesirable pollen (Bramlett and O'Gwynn 1981).

Pollen viability largely determines the success of controlled pollinations (Matthews and Bramlett 1986; figure 7-22 and table 7-21), so viability should always be tested before pollen is used. If viability is 30%, the maximum number of seeds per cone is about 70; if pollen viability increases to 70%, the maximim number of seeds per cone increases to about 110. This very large increase in seed production per cone (more than 50%) can be realized at very little cost. It is much more expensive to increase total seed production by the same amount by pollinating greater numbers of flowers.

Adequate quantities of pollen should be used and should be distributed uniformly within the bags. However, increasing the quantity of pollen applied to each bag results in only minor increases in seed yield when pollen viability is less than about 50%. To compensate for low viability of pollen, the number of flowers pollinated should be increased rather than adding

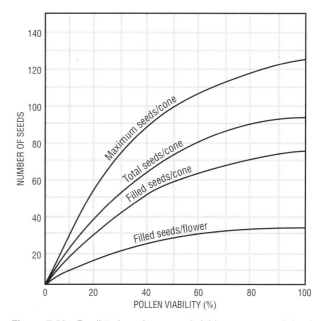

Figure 7-22—Predicted maximum seed yield per cone, total developed seeds per cone, filled seeds per cone, and filled seeds per flower for controlled pollinations in loblolly pine. The predicted values are generated from a model with 2.0 pollen grains/ovule and a seed potential of 160 ovules/cone and are shown for varying pollen viabilities (adapted from Bramlett and others 1985).

5—receptive scales open (**e**); stage 6—scales are closed (**f**); beyond stage 6—a young conelet (**g**); conelets beginning their second year (**h**) (photos by Ron Schmidtling, USDA Forest Service, Southern Forest Experiment Station, Gulfport, MS).

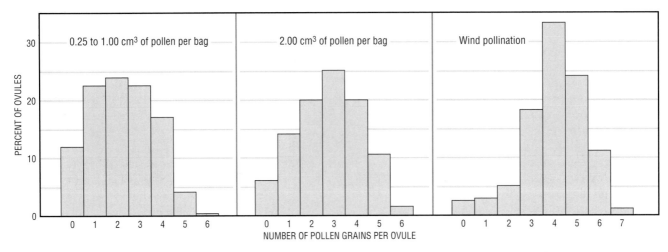

Figure 7-23—Number of pollen grains per ovule following controlled and wind pollination of 3 loblolly pine clones in Georgia (adapted from Bramlett and others 1985).

more pollen to each bag (Matthews and Bramlett 1986; figure 7-23) because about 10% of the ovules of a flower will receive no pollen grains regardless of whether 0.25, 0.50, 1.00, or 2.00 cm^3 of pollen are applied to each pollination bag. If pollen viability is only 25%, about 40% of the ovules receive no viable pollen grains. Ovules receive more pollen grains when naturally wind pollinated than when control pollinated. Also, about 10% of wind-pollinated ovules and about 50% of control-pollinated ovules receive fewer than three pollen grains. It appears that loblolly pine ovules seldom receive more than five pollen grains. Bags should be removed from artificially pollinated flowers as soon as growth has completely closed the openings between scales (stage 6). This usually occurs about 7 to 10 days after stage 5 begins.

Supplemental mass pollination. Supplemental mass pollination (SMP) is the broadcast application of pollen to conelets that are not isolated or protected from airborne pollen. It can be used to produce specific genetic combinations in seed orchards or to greatly increase the probability that receptive conelets in young orchards will be pollinated when little viable local pollen is present. It can also be used to pollinate trees where freezing weather prior to pollen shedding has destroyed the viability of orchard pollen (Bridgwater and Bramlett 1982, Bridgwater and Trew 1981, Bridgwater and others 1987). Supplemental mass pollination also seems to be an effective method of making controlled cross pollinations between loblolly and pitch pines (Hyun 1969).

Timing is critical in SMP because the first pollen applied to strobili have the best chance of producing seeds. It is best to apply pollen when the receptivity of flowers is greatest (Bridgwater and Williams 1983). A pollination success rate of 70% may be operationally practical for SMP if each tree is saturated with viable pollen at peak receptivity (Blush 1987). However, increases in seed production may not justify investments

in SMP in all instances. Supplemental mass pollination increased the cone crop in a south Texas orchard by 15% but increased the number of seeds per cone only from 22 to 26 (Byram and others 1986b). Supplemental mass pollination with selected superior pollen has the potential to produce specific genetic combinations and provide genetic gains in loblolly pine orchards. Each pollen parent has an equal probability of mating when equal amounts of pollen from a number of trees are combined for SMP or for pollination of individual flowers (Wiselogel and van Buijtenen 1988).

Supplemental mass pollination with a mist blower is rapid and can increase seed yield by about 25% in operational orchards (Brown 1987). A pole duster with a compressed air supply efficiently mass pollinates individual clusters of female strobili even at heights greater than 15 m (Bridgwater and others 1987).

Selfing. Selfing generally results in a high level of inbreeding depression and does not appear to be a practical way of improving loblolly pines. The frequency of natural self-fertilization in an oldfield plantation in

Table 7-22—Loblolly pine seed and seedling comparisons following self- and cross-pollination

Characteristic	Self-pollination	Cross-pollination
Total seeds/cone	33	37
Filled seeds/cone	5	27
Germinable seeds/cone	4	23
Germination %	73	85
Living seedlings/cone 6 weeks after outplanting	3	23
Survival 1 year after outplanting 1+0 stock (%)	66	79
Height 1 year after outplanting 1+0 stock (m)	0.34	0.37

Source: adapted from Franklin (1969).

North Carolina was estimated to be about 7% in upper crowns and 34% in the lower crowns (Franklin 1971). Self-fertilization usually produces less than 20% as many filled seeds as cross-fertilization produces, and many of the filled seeds fail to germinate. Also, seedling survival is substantially lower for selfs (table 7-22). Snyder (1968) found that (1) 80% of slash pine trees produce less than 1 seedling/self-pollinated flower, (2) self-pollination yields only 10% as many seedlings as wind pollination yields on a per-cone basis, (3) parents that produce high seed yields when self-pollinated also tend to produce high yields when wind pollinated, and (4) although selfed seedlings are generally shorter than wind-pollinated seedlings, the differences are not great enough to differentiate selfs from crosses. These characteristics probably hold for loblolly pine because of the numerous similarities between the two species.

Self-pollination can result in numerous mutant forms such as cotyledons with chlorophyll deficiency, abnormally colored hypocotyls, abnormally colored primary and secondary foliage, and morphological abnormalities including fused cotyledons, dwarfing, and crinkly needles, or combinations of these abnormalities. Some of these mutant forms are useful as genetic markers (Franklin 1969).

If care is taken in establishing clonal seed orchards, self-fertilization and inbreeding should not be major problems, even when natural fertilization is permitted. Studies using unique markers show that about 98% of all pollinations are cross-pollinations even when only about 25 clones are represented (Adams and Joly 1980b; Friedman and Adams 1981, 1985b). Seeds from unrelated parents can be assured in advanced generation orchards by dividing a desired population into breeding groups and only crossing individuals contained within that breeding group using planned mating designs (van Buijtenen and Lowe 1979).

Cone and Seed Collection

Only a few clones produce most of the cone crop early in the life of an orchard (ages 5 to 10). As an orchard matures, more clones begin production, and eventually about 60% of the clones produce about 90% of the cone crop. Rankings of clones as cone producers frequently change from year to year (Byram and others 1986a). Good seed crops are usually produced every 2 to 4 years (Kucera 1973).

Genetic and environmental variation significantly affects harvesting of orchard seeds. Cones produced by some clones may ripen as much as 2 months earlier than those produced by other clones. Cones of early-ripening clones may take up to 3 weeks to open, whereas those of clones that ripen later may take only half as long to open. Weather conditions can change the ripening date by as much as 3 weeks (Zoerb 1969). Seed orchard cones have been collected as early as August 29th and yielded satis-

factory quantities of seeds as long as they were given a postharvest air-drying treatment (Cobb and others 1984).

As an alternative to picking cones, seeds can be left to fall onto polypropylene netting that has been spread on the ground. This method is most practical in seed orchards where the ground is relatively clean and smooth. Cones open naturally, and many seeds drop by December or January. A mechanical tree shaker is then used to complete seed removal. Following seed drop, the netting is rolled up, and the materials on the netting are processed to separate seeds from debris (Brooks 1975, Edwards and McConnell 1982, Major 1983). Mechanical retrieval and cleaning associated with the net system does not appear to damage seeds (Vozzo and Bonner 1984).

Advantages of the net retrieval system are that (1) judgment of cone maturity is unnecessary; (2) potential damage to seeds in extraction and dewinging operations is avoided (because seeds are dewinged naturally); (3) in good cone production years, collection costs per kilogram of seeds are lower than with handpicking; (4) purchase or lease of hydraulic bucket trucks is unnecessary; and (5) less vehicle traffic reduces soil compaction in the orchard (Bonner 1991; Edwards 1985; McConnell and Edwards 1985, 1986). However, use of nets precludes collection of seeds from individual clones and exposes valuable orchard seeds to predation by birds and rodents for as long as 3 months (table 7-23).

Table 7-23—Estimated seed loss from unopened cones and predators at four seed orchards during the 1983-84 seed year

Orchard	Location	Collection date	Seeds left in cones* (%)	Predator loss† (%)
Stuart	Kisatchie National Forest, Louisiana	December 14	43	20
Erambert	Desoto National Forest, Mississippi	January 10	16	64
Francis-Marion	Francis-Marion National Forest, South Carolina	January 3	25	18
Ouachita	Ouachita National Forest, Arkansas	January 17	11	78

Source: adapted from Vozzo and Bonner (1984).

* Data represent seeds collected from 5 cones from each of 20 trees.

† Data represent 100 seeds at each of 20 locations within an orchard.

Other problems inherent to the net retrieval system include high collection costs in poor seed years, the need for specialized equipment, and difficulty cleaning seeds because of a large amount of weed seeds and inert materials (including broken seeds and seed wings, branches, needles, cones, and bark). In one study, seed loss caused by predators ranged up to 78% when collection was delayed to January 17th; however, the number of seeds left in cones was the least of the four collection dates (table 7-23). Even with the potential for severe problems, the net retrieval system is a valuable method for collecting seeds from orchards.

Evaluation of Seed Orchard Performance

There were about 2,835 ha of loblolly pine seed orchards across the South in the mid-1980's. First-generation loblolly seed orchards produced about 1.9 m³ of cones/ha over their 25-year operational lifespan. Very young superior trees—whether they are control- or open-pollinated—can produce a wide range in numbers of seeds per cone and plantable seedlings. Cones collected from 4-year-old seedlings contained 24 to 109 seeds/cone, and these seeds produced from 1 to 71% plantable seedlings depending on the family (Greene 1966). Ten- to fifteen-year-old orchards in the west Gulf Coast area have produced an average of 12.8 kg of seeds/m³ of cones, with a range of 0.3 to 25.3 kg/m³. At age 15, 33 loblolly orchards yielded an average of 16.2 kg of seeds/m³ of cones (Byram and others 1986b). Yield of sound viable seeds varies greatly by year and region (Belcher and Hitt 1973).

Although average families produce 40 to 60 seeds/cone, potential seed production exceeds 150 seeds per cone. During the 18-month development period, environmental, physiological, and pathological factors can greatly reduce the level of seed production (see chapter 2). Although the reasons for losses are often hard to determine, the lack of initial seed development caused by poor pollination and selfing can be much more significant than insect damage. In a 2-year evaluation of 25 orchards in 9 states, only 30% of the potential 150 seeds/cone were sound and viable. More than 60% of the potential 150 seeds/cone were never produced. Only about 3 to 5% of the potential seeds per cone were lost due to insect damage (Bramlett 1979).

Seed production can be evaluated by estimating the efficiency of cone, seed, and seedling development. Cone efficiency (CE) is the ratio of mature cones to the initial flower crop. Seed efficiency (SE) is the ratio of filled seeds per cone to the seed potential. Extraction efficiency (EE) is the ratio of extracted seeds per cone to total seeds per cone. Germination efficiency (GE) is the ratio of germinated seeds per cone to filled seeds per cone. Biological efficiency, the product of these four values, is a measurement of seed orchard to nursery efficiency. With excellent seed orchard management and protection, values of 75% are possible for CE and SE and 90% for EE and GE. When these efficiencies are achieved, biological efficiency is 45% ($0.75 \times 0.75 \times 0.90 \times 0.90$). When biological efficiency is less than 45%, it is likely that management improvements can be made (Bramlett 1979).

Because large quantities of superior seeds have been available since the late 1970's, more than 40% of all planted loblolly pine trees now in the field are superior in one or more characteristics (Harris 1985, Lantz 1979). Twenty-thousand hectares of southern national forest lands are being planted with superior trees (mostly loblolly pines) on an annual basis (Kitchens 1985).

Second-generation seed orchards are assembled by selecting the best trees in the best families from progenies of the first-generation seed orchard trees. Because stringent family selection is employed, second-generation orchards should provide much greater genetic gains than first-generation orchards provide (Kraus and LaFarge 1982).

Vegetative Propagation

Because vegetative propagation produces uniform copies of a tree, it is a valuable tool for increasing genetic gain and increasing the uniformity of trees (Libby and Rauter 1984). Both micropropagation and macropropagation techniques can be used for this purpose. Mass production of selected material by vegetative propagation has the potential to eliminate the need for seed orchards and to greatly accelerate the widespread use of superior stock. However, there are dangers inherent in large-scale clonal forestry of loblolly pines. No further genetic gain can be made once a clone is selected. Propagating only a few outstanding clones on selected areas could severely limit the genetic base of a forest and make the forest more susceptible to a biotic disaster. Combining clonal propagation with continued selection and tree improvement will provide both rapid reproduction of a desired genetic base and opportunities for progressive improvement.

Tissue Culture

Trees can be developed from tissues that have various origins and that are maintained in a stable diploid condition (stable nuclear DNA). Loblolly pines can now be propagated by 3 tissue culture methods: (1) cotyledon system propagation, (2) axillary or fascicular shoot micropropagation, and (3) cellular cloning (embryogenesis).

In cotyledon system propagation, cotyledon or embryo explants are surgically removed from seeds, grown in a culture medium to promote shoot and root development, transferred to greenhouse soil for development, and outplanted. Adding ascorbic acid to the culture medium seems to increase shoot morphogenesis. Rooting response is sporadic and unpredictable with this system, and genotypic variation is considerable (Brown and Sommer 1977; Mott and Amerson 1984;

Renfroe and Berlyn 1984; Sen and others 1987, 1989). Axillary and fascicular shoot *in vitro* micropropagation techniques work with juvenile or mature tree explants. Juvenile-appearing shoots from hedged trees can be induced to multiply by chemical treatment. Plant regeneration by somatic embryogenesis and somatic polyembryogenesis techniques makes use of embryonal-suspensor masses of developing seeds. These have preformed roots and shoots (Becwar and others 1988; Durzan 1988; Gupta and Durzan 1987a, 1987b).

Preliminary results suggest that embryogenic cell lines can be stored for several years in liquid N. Such storage will greatly increase the flexibility of long-term progeny testing (Gupta and others 1987). Also, it now seems feasible to produce embryoids by cell culture and to encapsulate them to produce artificial seeds with high clonal fidelity (Libby 1986).

Substantial time and cost savings in mass vegetative propagation will be achieved if plantlets can be developed reliably in soil (Gupta and Durzan 1987a). It will then be possible to produce large numbers of propagules within 1 to 2 years after a selection is made. Another advantage of propagation by tissue culture is that it can be done anytime of the year. Greenhouse and field trials show that tissue culture plantlets (somaclones) and seedlings differ in growth, morphology, and possibly physiology, and that seedlings grow more rapidly than do plantlets. Root pruning increases the maturity of plantlets (in terms of bud length, bud diameter, needle length, and needle dry weight). Plantlets with dark-green, healthy needles and vigorous apical growth are more likely to grow as rapidly as seedlings than are plantlets of lower shoot quality. Under field conditions, tissue culture plantlets equal, or nearly equal, seedling growth for the first several years where soils are very fertile but grow more slowly than seedlings under less favorable conditions (Frampton and Isik 1987; Frampton and others 1985; Wisniewski and others 1986, 1987). Five-year results suggest that the wood specific gravity of trees grown from tissue culture plantlets may be one-fourth less variable than that of the progeny of open-pollinated trees (Frampton and Jett 1989).

Part of the growth differences between plantlets and seedlings may be because plantlets rapidly develop growth and morphological characteristics of mature trees even when they originate from juvenile embryonic tissues (McKeand 1985). Plantlet growth is probably adversely affected by tissue culture techniques. One possible cause is that plantlets have fewer fibrous secondary lateral roots near the soil surface than do seedlings. There is no indication that plantlet roots are less efficient than seedling roots in absorbing and transferring nutrients (Amerson and others 1985, Frampton and Isik 1987, McKeand and Allen 1984, McKeand and Frampton 1984, McKeand and Wisniewski 1983).

Rooting of Cuttings

New loblolly trees can be mass-produced from branch tips removed from trees and grown in a controlled environment that promotes root development. Rooted cuttings can be produced from branch tips collected at any time of the year, but branch tips collected during the period of dormancy usually demonstrate maximum rooting ability. Nonsucculent shoot material taken from young seedlings seems to root best in February (Frampton and Hodges 1989). Succulent material cut in the spring and summer may be difficult to root (Grigsby 1962a, Marino 1982, Reines and Bamping 1962). The cost of producing rooted cuttings now exceeds the cost of producing bareroot seedlings, but the possibility of mass-producing planting stock more rapidly by rooting than by sexual propagation makes rooting a promising option for artificial regeneration (Frampton and Hodges 1989).

The hormone indolebutyric acid (IBA) induces rooting in loblolly pine cuttings. An application of 0.8% IBA in powdered form to the cut end is effective in most cases. Concentrations of 2,000 to 7,500 ppm of IBA are best for quick dips before potting. Soaking the base of cuttings for 3 to 24 hours in 100-ppm solutions of IBA is effective also. Different rooting treatments may be appropriate at different times of the year (Grigsby 1962a, Mahalovich and others 1987).

Maximum rooting ability is closely associated with juvenile conditions. Cuttings from 1-year-old trees are rooted more successfully than cuttings of any other age. Rooting success can exceed 60% when cuttings from trees not more than 4 years old undergo dip treatments and receive low levels of intermittent misting while developing under controlled conditions. However, excessive misting is detrimental to rooting (Greenwood and others 1980). Unless moisture level and other environmental conditions are controlled carefully, the amount of rooting cannot be predicted accurately for cuttings from trees of any age.

The genetic makeup and age of a tree can also affect rooting. Some clones root easily, whereas others root with varying degrees of difficulty. The older a donor gets, the more difficult it is to root its branch tissue. However, more than 40% rooting success can be obtained using cuttings from trees 25 years old when environmental conditions are controlled carefully (Grigsby 1962a). The stage of maturation is transmitted from the ortet to its ramets. Hence, older cuttings that do root may also grow more slowly than cuttings from young trees. This result could partially negate the genetic gain expected from clonal selection. Juvenile clones should be used during testing and operational propagation wherever possible (Foster and others 1987). Cuttings from older trees occasionally grow abnormally, but this is not a common problem. Old trees that lack a genetic propensity to root can be almost impossible to root.

Air Layering

Clonal propagation can also be accomplished by air layering, which promotes rooting by branches that are still attached to trees. Branches suitable for air layering are straight, healthy, and located in the upper part of the crown. Such a branch should be girdled by removing a ring of bark 1.2 to 2.5 cm wide, about 25 to 30 cm from the tip of the branch. A rooting compound that contains IBA is applied to the girdled area, and damp moss or an artificial rooting medium is wrapped around the wound, covered with transparent plastic or other film, and wrapped tightly to maintain a moist environment for rooting (Dorman 1976, Hare 1979b). Air layers can be made in the spring on tissue of the previous season, or in late summer on hardened shoots of the current year's growth. Hare (1979b) reported more than 60% rooting of air layers made in early June on terminal branches in the lower crowns of 8-year-old trees. Wood older than 1 year can be used, but rooting success will be lower. As with rooted cuttings, the success of air layering in loblolly pines is highly sensitive to tree age.

When air layered in the spring, loblolly pines begin to produce roots in 6 to 10 weeks. After about 12 weeks, rooted branches can be removed; however, it is generally best not to remove and pot rooted branches until the fall when the tree becomes dormant. Branches should be cut 10 to 13 cm below the girdle, and the sphagnum moss should not be removed from the girdled area. Because most airlayers have small and tender root systems, they must be potted carefully and watered frequently for several weeks. Their tops should be trimmed if the root-to-shoot ratio is in great imbalance. A potting mixture consisting of equal parts of sand, vermiculite, and peat is suitable. Fertilization with water-soluble fertilizers promotes root growth. If they are handled properly, trees air layered during one spring can be outplanted to their permanent location in the following spring (Dorman 1976, Grigsby 1962b).

Air-layered slash pine trees generally have from one to three or more large roots that arch from the tree base—each functioning like a taproot. Root distribution is similar to that of a tree grown from seed (Schultz 1972). Loblolly pine air layers probably develop in the same manner. Loblolly pine ramets obtained by air layering and by grafting have similar shoot form and shoot growth at early ages (Hare 1985).

Rooting of Needle Bundles

Bundles of loblolly pine needles are capable of rooting. Peak rooting occurs in material collected during the winter months (Reines and Bamping 1964). Pinching off branch tips forces fascicle buds into active growth. Multiple adventitious buds have been induced in the region where needles join in a fascicle (Metra-Pacta and others 1977). If these juvenile buds can be cultured practically, new tissue could be regenerated from old trees, making rooting much easier. Although there has been little success in getting these buds to root even with a hormone and mist treatment (Hare 1965), this type of rejuvenation deserves closer study because it has broad practical implications.

Nelson and others (1992) studied a method of vegetatively propagating loblolly, slash, and longleaf pines from needle fascicles. In their experiment, the rooting phase was completed in a water-based medium, and not in a solid medium such as peat–perlite–sand, as in similar experiments in the United States (Hare 1965, Metra-Pacta and others 1977, Mergen and Simpson 1964, Reines and Bamping 1964). The experiment showed that it is possible to propagate loblolly pines by water-based, needle fascicle, culture methods.

· **Summary** ·

Loblolly pine tree improvement is having a major impact on southern forestry. Vast areas of superior trees are now established across the South, and the use of superior stock is expected to increase volume at rotation age by 7 to 13%. Significant gains in wood density, tree form, wood quality, and fusiform rust resistance have been made during the first generation of genetic improvement. Use of progeny of rogued, first-generation orchards may result in stand value gains of 18 to 32% at harvest time depending on site quality, management type, rotation age, and product marketed. Unless improved seedlings are specifically designed to excel with vegetative competition or other adverse conditions, some soil or vegetative manipulation must still be carried out to obtain the best growth rates.

There is substantial geographic variation in loblolly pines. Provenance trials have shown that loblolly pines from east of the Mississippi River grow faster than loblolly from west of the river, but the eastern trees are more susceptible to fusiform rust. Trees from the Atlantic and Gulf Coast provenances grow faster but are more cold and drought susceptible than trees from interior provenances. Faster growing trees from Atlantic Coast provenances can be moved north and west to northern Alabama, northern Mississippi, central and southern Arkansas, and eastern Oklahoma, but survival can be poor. High-quality trees from local sources should be planted in Maryland, Delaware, Tidewater Virginia, the

Piedmont and Coastal Plain of North and South Carolina, the Piedmont of Georgia, Alabama, and northern Mississippi as well as east Texas and west Louisiana. When loblolly is planted outside its natural range in western Tennessee, western Kentucky, and southern Illinois, trees from northern Mississippi, northern Alabama, or northwestern Georgia are preferred.

Some genotypes are better adapted to specific sites and grow faster on them than other genotypes. Visible characteristics that make a superior loblolly pine, growing in the woods, easy to identify include rapid and straight growth and a small crown. Difficult to identify, but very important characteristics that must also be included in superior tree selections, include resistance to disease and desirable wood physical characteristics such as high specific gravity. These genetically controlled characteristics can be captured by direct breeding but are most often obtained by grafting small branches onto rootstock of similar diameters, growing the new trees in seed orchards under intensive culture, then cross-breeding the new trees in controlled environments. Both clonal and seedling seed orchards will be important indefinitely as significant sources of genetically improved loblolly pine seeds and germplasm.

Future challenges and opportunities are now concentrated in second- and third-generation selections and in advanced cloning techniques that employ tissue and individual cell propagation to greatly speed the process of genetic improvement. Breeders can create hybrids of loblolly and other southern pines for improved growth under specific environmental conditions. The environment in which hybrids will be used will probably dictate the crossing strategy employed.

Research Needs

■ Traditionally, clonal seed orchards were established using a similar number of trees of each clone. Additional genetic gains may be realized by using the better clones in higher proportions. This concept, combined with improved techniques to optimize the number of clones in an orchard, deserves expanded emphasis in the near future.

■ More research should be done on low-cost seed orchard establishment via rooted cuttings or plantlets developed from organs, tissues, or individual cells of mature trees selected for specific phenotypic characteristics. Propagation from somatic cells or needle bundles has proven to be feasible for loblolly pine, and, with improved technology, could be a superior technique for clonal propagation and seed orchard establishment. Associated with this technique is the need to develop technology that would permit an unbiased evaluation of the growth potential of rooted plants so comparisons with seedlings can be made.

■ Improved techniques are needed to promote consistently high levels of both male and female flower production in young trees (5 to 15 years old) to shorten breeding cycles and increase early production in seed orchards. Stem girdling and/or chemicals, such as GA, may be effective approaches, but more research is needed on effective concentrations, timing of applications, long-term tree growth, and environmental relationships.

■ Ways to increase the number of sound seeds per cone in mature orchards are needed.

■ Improved measures are needed to accurately predict long-term tree growth and resistance to pathogens under normal forest conditions from young experimental stock. Presently available information on significant physical and chemical differences between young trees (for example, oleoresin physical and chemical properties, needle characteristics, root growth potential, and physiological activity) suggests that such indicators may well be within the genome of each tree.

■ More research is needed on genetic selection for early natural pruning without reducing crown efficiency or rapid stem growth.

■ Basic research is needed to determine how genetic information is used by trees so that genes that improve growth or reproduction can be isolated and transferred or manipulated.

■ More research and development is needed to refine vegetative propagation from needle fascicles.

Literature Cited

Adams WT, Joly RJ. 1980a. Allozyme studies in loblolly pine seed orchards: clonal variation and frequency of progeny due to self-fertilization. Silvae Genetica 29(1):1–4.

Adams WT, Joly RJ. 1980b. Genetics of allozyme variants in loblolly pine. Journal of Heredity 71:33–40.

Adams WT, Roberds JH, Zobel BJ. 1973. Intergenotypic interactions among families of loblolly pine. Theoretical and Applied Genetics 43(7):319–322.

AFA [Arkansas Forestry Commission]. 1989. Letter to author.

Allen RM, McGregor WHD. 1962. Seedling growth of three southern pine species under long and short days. Silvae Genetica 11(2):43–45.

Allen RM. 1967. Influence of the root system on height growth of three southern pines. Forest Science 13(3):253–257.

Amateis RL, Burkhart HE. 1987. Tree volume and taper of loblolly pine varies by stand origin. Southern Journal of Applied Forestry 11(4):185–189.

Amerson HW, Frampton LJ Jr, McKeand SE, and others. 1985. Loblolly pine tissue culture: laboratory, greenhouse, and field studies. In: Henke RR, and others, eds. Tissue culture in forestry and agriculture. Proceedings, 3rd Tennessee Symposium on Plant Cell and Tissue Culture; 1984 September 9–13; Knoxville, TN. New York: Plenum Press: 271–287.

Artman JD. 1974. Greenhouse screening of loblolly pine of known parentage for resistance to *Fomes annosus*. Plant Disease Reporter 58(5):409–411.

Askew GR, Hedden RL, DeBarr G. 1985. Selection potential for coneworm and seed bug resistance in loblolly pine seed orchards. In: Proceedings, 18th Southern Forest Tree Improvement Conference; 1985 May 21–23; Long Beach, MS. Springfield, VA: National Technical Information Service: 221–225.

Bailian L, McKeand SE, Allen HL. 1989. Early selection of loblolly pine families based on seedling shoot elongation characters. In: Proceedings, 20th Southern Forest Tree Improvement Conference; 1989 June 26–30; Charleston, SC. Charleston, SC: Charleston Forest Tree Improvement Committee. Sponsored by: Westvaco Corp., Clemson 42: 228–234.

Barber JC. 1966. Variation among half-sib families from three loblolly pine stands in Georgia. Res. Pap. 37. Macon, GA: Georgia Forest Research Council. 5 p.

Barber JC, Dorman KW. 1964. Clonal or seedling seed orchards? Silvae Genetica 13(3):11–17.

Barber JC. VanHaverbeke DF. 1961. Growth of outstanding nursery of *Pinus elliottii* Engelm. and *Pinus taeda* L. Res. Pap. SE-126. Asheville, NC: USDA Forest Service, Southeastern Forest Experiment Station. 12 p.

Barker JA. 1973. Location differences and their influence on heritability estimates and gain predictions for ten-year-old loblolly pine. In: Proceedings, 12th Southern Forest Tree Improvement Conference; 1973 June 12–13; Baton Rouge, LA. Baton Rouge, LA: Louisiana State University, Division of Continuing Education: 38–45.

Barnes RD. 1987. The breeding seedling orchard in a multiple population breeding strategy for tropical trees. In: Proceedings, Simposio Sobre Silvicultura y Mejoramiento Genetico de Especies Forestales; 1987 April 6–10; Buenos Aires, Argentina. [Place of publication and publisher unknown]: 1–18.

Barnett JP. 1988. Container production of seedlings for progeny tests. In: Proceedings, WGFTIP tree improvement short course; 1988 August 2–4; Magnolia, AR. Magnolia, AR: Western Gulf Forest Tree Improvement Program: 113–131.

Becwar MR, Wann SR, Johnson MA, and others. 1988. Development and characterization of *in vitro* embryogenic systems in conifers. In: Ahuj MR, ed. Proceedings, IUFRO Working Party-S2. 04-07; Somatic cell genetics of woody plants; 1987 August 10–13; Grosshansdorf, Germany. Dordrecht, The

Netherlands: Kluwer Academic Publishers: 1–18.

Beers WL Jr, Bivens J, Mocha JE. 1981. Pollen collection. In: Franklin EC, ed. Pollen management handbook. Agric. Handbk. 587. Washington, DC: USDA Forest Service: 30.

Belcher EW Jr, Hitt RG. 1973. Observations on two-year results of the seed orchard survey (S.O.S.). In: Proceedings, 12th Southern Forest Tree Improvement Conference; 1973 June 12–13; Baton Rouge, LA. Baton Rouge, LA: Louisiana State University, Division of Continuing Education: 55–53.

Belcher EW, Karrfalt RP. 1976. Cooperative approach to better tree seed. 20th Lab Rep. Macon GA: USDA Forest Service, Eastern Tree Seed Laboratory. 37 p.

Bengtson GW, Goddard RE. 1966. Establishment, culture, and protection of slash and loblolly pine seed orchards: some tentative recommendations. In: Proceedings, Southeastern Area Forest Nurserymen Conferences; 1966 August 23–24; Columbia, SC/August 30–31; Hot Springs, AR. Asheville, NC: USDA Forest Service, Southeastern Forest Experiment Station: 47–63.

Benson JD, Schoenike RE, Van Lear DH. 1982. Early growth and survival of loblolly, shortleaf, and putative hybrid pines on little-leaf sites in the Piedmont of South Carolina. Southern Journal of Applied Forestry 6(4):218–221.

Bergman A. 1968. Variation in flowering and its effect on seed cost. Raleigh, NC: North Carolina State University, School of Forest Resources, Cooperative Programs. 62 p.

Bilan MV. 1966. Some morphological variations among loblolly pine seedlings. In: Proceedings, 8th Southern Conference on Forest Tree Improvement; 1965 June 16–17; Savannah, GA. Macon, GA: USDA Forest Service, Eastern Tree Seed Laboratory: 124–125.

Blair RL, Zobel BJ. 1971. Predictions of expected gains in resistance to fusiform rust in loblolly pine. In: Proceedings, 11th Southern Forest Tree Improvement Conference; 1971 June 15–16; Atlanta, GA. Macon, GA: USDA Forest Service, Eastern Tree Seed Laboratory: 52–67.

Blair R, Zobel B, Hitchings RG, Jett JB. 1976. Pulp yield and physical properties of young loblolly pine with high density juvenile wood. In: 28th Applied Polymer Symposium. New York: John Wiley & Sons: 435–444.

Blush TD. 1987. An operational trial of supplemental mass pollination in a loblolly pine seed orchard. In: Proceedings, 19th Southern Forest Tree Improvement Conference; 1987 June 16–18; College Station, TX. College Station, TX: Texas Forest Service and Texas A&M University: 240–246.

Bongarten BC, Teskey RO. 1986. Water relations of loblolly pine seedlings from diverse geographic origins. Tree Physiology 1(3):265–276.

Bongarten BC, Teskey RO. 1987. Dry weight partitioning and its relationship to productivity in loblolly pine seedlings from seven sources. Forest Science 33(2):255–267.

Bongarten BC, Teskey RO, Boltz BA. 1985. Comparative physiology of loblolly pine seedlings from seven geographic sources as related to growth rate. In: Proceedings, 18th Southern Forest Tree Improvement Conference; 1985 May 21–23; Long Beach, MS. Springfield, VA: National Technical Information Service: 321–33.

Bonner F. 1991. Seed management. In: Duryea ML, Dougherty PM, eds. Forest regeneration manual. Dordrecht, The Netherlands: Kluwer Academic Publishers: 51–73.

Bramlett DL, Bridgwater FE, Jett JB, Matthews FR. 1985. Theoretical impact of pollen viability and distribution on the number of strobili to use for controlled pollinations in loblolly pine. In: Proceedings, 18th Southern Forest Tree Improvement Conference; 1985 May 21–23; Long Beach, MS. Springfield, VA:

National Technical Information Service: 194–203.

Bramlett DL. 1979. Efficiency of seed production in southern pine seed orchards. In: Proceedings, 13th Lake States Forest Tree Improvement Conference; 1977 August 17–19; St. Paul, MN. Gen. Tech. Rep. NC-50. St. Paul, MN: USDA Forest Service, North Central Forest Experiment Station: 17–25.

Bramlett DL, Matthews FR. 1983. Pollination success in relation to female flower development in loblolly pine. In: Proceedings, 17th Southern Forest Tree Improvement Conference; 1983 June 6–9; Charleston, SC. Macon, GA: USDA Forest Service, Eastern Tree Seed Laboratory: 84–88.

Bramlett DL, Matthews FR. 1991. Storing loblolly pine pollen. Southern Journal of Applied Forestry 15(3):153–157.

Bramlett DL, O'Gwynn CH. 1981. Controlled pollination. In: Franklin EC, ed. Pollen management handbook. Agric. Handbk. 587. Washington, DC: USDA Forest Service: 44–50.

Bramlett DL, Askew GR, Blush TD, and others. 1993. Advances in pollen management. Agric. Handbk. 698. Washington, DC: USDA Forest Service. 101 p.

Bridgwater FE. 1984. The impact of genetic improvement of stem straightness on yield and value of lumber. In: Proceedings, Symposium on Utilization of the Changing Wood Resource in the Southern United States; 1984 June 12–14; Raleigh, NC. Raleigh, NC: North Carolina State University: 80–87.

Bridgwater FE, Bramlett DL. 1982. Supplemental mass pollination to increase seed yields in loblolly pine seed orchards. Southern Journal of Applied Forestry 6(2):100–104.

Bridgwater FE, Stonecypher RW. 1979. Index selection for volume and straightness in a loblolly pine population. In: Proceedings, 15th Southern Forest Tree Improvement Conference; 1979 June 19–21; Mississippi State, MS. Macon, GA: USDA Forest Service, Eastern Tree Seed Laboratory: 132–139.

Bridgwater FE, Trew IF. 1981. Supplemental mass pollination. In: Franklin EC, ed. Pollen management handbook. Agric. Handbk. 587. Washington, DC: USDA Forest Service: 52–56.

Bridgwater FE, Williams CG. 1983. Feasibility of supplemental mass pollination to increase genetic gains from seed orchards. In: Proceedings, 17th Southern Forest Tree Improvement Conference; 1983 June 6–9; Charleston, SC. Macon, GA: USDA Forest Service, Eastern Tree Seed Laboratory: 78–83.

Bridgwater FE, Bramlett DL, Matthews FR. 1987. Supplemental mass pollination is feasible on an operational scale. In: Proceedings, 19th Southern Forest Tree Improvement Conference; 1987 June 16–18; College Station, TX. Springfield, VA: National Technical Information Service: 216–222.

Bridgwater FE, Williams CG, Campbell RG. 1985. Patterns of leader elongation in loblolly pine Pinus taeda families. Forest Science 31(4):933–944.

Brooks TL. 1975. Georgia Forestry Commission loblolly (Pinus taeda) seed collection technique. In: Proceedings, Southeastern Nurserymen's Conferences—Eastern and Western Sessions; 1974 August 6–8; Gainesville, FL/July 17–18; Nacogdoches, TX. Atlanta: USDA Forest Service, Southern Region, State and Private Forestry: 186–189.

Brown AG. 1964. The seedling habit of longleaf pine. GA Res. Rep. 10. Athens, GA: University of Georgia, School of Forestry. 68 p.

Brown CL, Goddard RE. 1959. Variation in nursery grown seedlings from individual mother trees in a seed production area. In: Proceedings, 5th Southern Forest Tree Improvement Conference; 1959 June 11–12; Raleigh, NC. Raleigh, NC: North Carolina State University, School of Forestry: 68–76.

Brown CL, Sommer HE. 1977. Bud and root differentiation in conifer cultures. In: TAPPI Forest Biology Wood Chemistry Conference; 1977 June 20–22; Madison, WI. Atlanta: TAPPI Press: 1–3.

Brown RA. 1987. Increased seed yields with a mist blower that distributes pollen in loblolly pine seed orchards. Tree Planters' Notes 38(4):3–5.

Brown SD, Bridgwater FE. 1987. Observations on pollination in loblolly pine. Canadian Journal of Forest Research 17(4):299–303.

Busby CL. 1983. Crown-quality assessment and the relative economic importance of growth and crown characters in mature loblolly pine. In: Proceedings, 17th Southern Forest Tree Improvement Conference; 1983 June 6–9; Charleston, SC. Macon, GA: USDA Forest Service, Eastern Tree Seed Laboratory: 121–130.

Byram TD, Lowe WJ. 1988. Specific gravity variation in a loblolly pine seed source study in the Western Gulf Region. Forest Science 34(3):789–803.

Byram TD, Lowe WJ, McGriff JA. 1986a. Clonal and annual variation in cone production in loblolly pine seed orchards. Forest Science 32(4):1067–1073.

Byram TD, Lowe WJ, McKinley CR, and others. 1986b. 34th progress report of the cooperative forest tree improvement program. Circ. 273. College Station, TX: Texas Forest Service, Texas A&M University. 23 p.

Cannell MGR, Bridgwater FE, Greenwood MS. 1978. Seedling growth rates water stress responses and root-shoot relationships related to eight-year volumes among families of Pinus taeda L. Silvae Genetica 27(6):237–248.

Cech FC, Stonecypher R, Zobel B. 1963. Early results from the cooperative loblolly pine heritability study. In: Proceedings, Forest Genetics Workshop; 1962 October 25–27; Macon, GA. Macon, GA: Southern Forest Tree Improvement Committee 22: 64–68.

Chen CC, van Buijtenen JP. 1980. Chemogenetic study of phenolic compounds extracted from loblolly pine (Pinus taeda L.) needles. Silvae Genetica 29(5–6):205–208.

Choong ET, Zabala NQ, Thielges BA, Fogg PJ. 1986. Variations in growth and certain wood properties of loblolly pine seed sources in Louisiana. LSU Res. Rep. 9. Baton Rouge, LA: Louisiana Agricultural Experiment Station, Louisiana State University, School of Forestry, Wildlife, and Fisheries. 160 p.

Chuntanaparb L. 1973. Inheritance of wood and growth characteristics and their relationships in loblolly pine (Pinus taeda L.). Raleigh, NC: North Carolina State University. [number of pages unknown]. Ph.D. dissertation.

Cobb SW, Astriab TD, Schoenike RE. 1984. Early cone collection and postharvest treatment comparisons in a South Carolina loblolly pine seed orchard. Tree Planters' Notes 35(3):12–14.

Cole DE. 1963. Management of pine seed production areas. In: Proceedings, 7th Southern Forest Tree Improvement Conference; 1963 June 26–27; Gulfport, MS. New Orleans: USDA Forest Service, Southern Forest Experiment Station: 44–49.

Conkle MT. 1963. The determination of experimental plot size and shape in loblolly and slash pines. Tech. Rep. 17. Raleigh, NC: North Carolina State, College School of Forestry. 51 p.

Conkle MT. 1981. Isozyme variation and linkage in six conifer species. In: Proceedings, symposium on isozymes of North American forest trees and forest insects; 1979 July 27; Berkeley, CA. Gen. Tech. Rep. PSW-48. Berkeley, CA: USDA Forest Service, Pacific Southwest Forest and Range Experiment Station: 11–17.

Corriveau AG. 1976. The clonal test: an aid to progeny testing and a way to speed up genetic gains. In: Proceedings, 12th Lake States Forest Tree Improvement Conference; 1975 August 18–22; Chalk River, ON. Gen. Tech. Rep. NC-26. St. Paul, MN: USDA Forest Service, North Central Forest Experiment Station: 167–180.

Cotton MH, Hicks RR Jr, Flake RH. 1975. Morphological variability among loblolly and shortleaf pines of east Texas with reference to natural hybridization. Castanea 40(4):309–319.

Cox R. 1985. Forest genetics: the case of the loblolly pine. Tennessee Conservationist 51(3):14–15.

Critchfield WB. 1963. Hybridization of the southern pines in California. In: Proceedings, Forest Genetics Workshop; 1962 October 25–27; Macon, GA. Macon, GA: Southern Forest Tree Improvement Committee: 40–48.

Davey CB. 1981.   Seed orchard soil management. In: Tree improvement short course. Raleigh, NC: North Carolina State University, Industry Cooperative Tree Improvement Program, School of Forest Resources: 90–95.

DeWald LE, Feret PP, Kreh RE. 1985.   Genetic variation in loblolly pine root growth potential. In: Proceeding, 18th Southern Forest Tree Improvement Conference; 1985 May 21–23; Long Beach, MS. Springfield, VA: National Technical Information Service: 155–162.

Dewers RS, Moehring DM. 1970.   Effect of soil water stress on initiation of ovulate primordia in loblolly pine. Forest Science 16(2):219–221.

Dixon RK, Garrett HE, Stelzer HE. 1987.   Growth and ectomycor-rhizal development of loblolly pine progenies inoculated with three isolates of Pisolithus tinctorius. Silvae Genetica 36(5/6): 240–245.

Dorman KW, Barber JC. 1956.   Time of flowering and seed ripen-ing in southern pines. Res. Pap. SE-72. Asheville, NC: USDA Forest Service, Southeastern Forest Experiment Station. 15 p.

Dorman KW, Zobel BJ. 1973.   Genetics of loblolly pine. Res. Pap. WO-19. Washington, DC: USDA Forest Service. 21 p.

Dorman KW. 1976.   The genetics and breeding of southern pines. Agric. Handbk. 471. Washington, DC: USDA Forest Service. 407 p.

Duba SE, Goggans JF, Patterson RM. 1984.   Seed source testing of Alabama loblolly pine: implications for seed movements and tree improvement programs. Southern Journal of Applied Forestry 8(4):189–193.

Duba SE, Nelson LR, Gjerstad DH. 1985.   Interaction of genotype and vegetation control on loblolly pine seedling performance. In: Proceedings, 3rd Biennial Southern Silvicultural Research Conference; 1984 November 7–8; Atlanta, GA. Gen. Tech. Rep. SO-54: New Orleans: USDA Forest Service, Southern Forest Experiment Station: 305–308.

Duke SD, Lambeth CC. 1982.   Early screening of loblolly pine families in an artificial environment. Tech. Note 050-1204/2. Hot Springs, AR: Weyerhaeuser Technical Information Center. 5 p.

Dunlap JR, Barnett JP. 1984.   Manipulating loblolly pine (Pinus taeda L.) seed germination with simulated moisture and temper-ature stress. In: Duryea ML, Brown GN, eds. Seedling physiolo-gy and reforestation success. Dordrecht, The Netherlands: Martinus Nijhoff Publishers: 61–74.

Durzan DJ. 1988.   Rooting in woody perennials: problems and opportunities with somatic embryos and artificial seeds. Acta Horticulturae (227):121–125.

Duzan WH Jr, Williams CG. 1988.   Matching loblolly pine families to regeneration sites. Southern Journal of Applied Forestry 12(3):166–169.

Dyson WG, Freeman GH. 1968.   Seed orchard designs for sites with constant prevailing wind. Silvae Genetica 17(1):12–15.

Easley LT. 1963.   Growth of loblolly pine from seed produced in a seed production area vs. nursery run stock. Journal of Forestry 61(5):388–389.

Edwards JL. 1985.   Orchard pine seed harvesting system. In: Proceedings, 1985 Winter Meeting of the American Society of Agricultural Engineers; 1985 December 17–20; Chicago, IL. ASAE Pap. 85-1603. St. Joseph, MI: American Society of Agricultural Engineers. 3 p.

Edwards JL, McConnell JL. 1982.   Forest tree seed harvesting system for loblolly pine. In: ASAE Pap. 82-1589. Proceedings, 1982 Winter Meeting of the American Society of Agricultural Engineers; 1982 December 14–17; Chicago, IL. St. Joseph, MI: American Society of Agricultural Engineers: 10 p.

Fiveash J, McConnell JL. 1989.   A storage method for pollen using freeze drying. Tree Planters' Notes 40(4):18–19.

Florence LZ, Hicks RR Jr. 1980.   Further evidence for introgres-sion on Pinus taeda with P. echinata: electrophoretic variability and variation in resistance to Cronartium fusiforme. Silvae Genetica 29(2):41–43.

Florence LZ. 1973.   Prospects for using natural loblolly × shortleaf hybrids for resistance to fusiform rust. In: Proceedings, 12th Southern Forest Tree Improvement Conference; 1973 June 12–13; Baton Rouge, LA. Baton Rouge, LA: Louisiana State University, Division of Continuing Education: 302–309.

Florence LZ, Rink G. 1979.   Geographic patterns of allozymic vari-ation in loblolly pine. In: Proceedings, 15th Southern Forest Tree Improvement Conference; 1979 June 19–21; Mississippi State, MS. Macon, GA: USDA Forest Service, Eastern Tree Seed Laboratory: 33–41.

Florence LZ. 1981.   Allozymic variation and population structure in loblolly pine. Nacogdoches, TX: Stephen F. Austin State University. Ph.D. dissertation. 188 p.

Foster GS, Lambeth CC, Greenwood MS. 1987.   Growth of loblolly pine rooted cuttings compared with seedlings. Canadian Journal of Forest Research 17(2):157–164.

Foster GS 1986.   Trends in genetic parameters with stand devel-opment and their influence on early selection for volume growth in loblolly pine. Forest Science 32(4):944–959.

Foster GS, Bridgwater F. 1979.   Viability tests to evaluate pollen reliability in loblolly pine controlled pollinations. Forest Science 25(2):270–274.

Foster LJ Jr, Hodges JF. 1989.   Nursery rooting of cuttings from seedlings of slash and loblolly pine. Southern Journal of Applied Forestry 13(3):127–132.

Frampton LJ Jr, Jett JB. 1989.   Juvenile wood specific gravity of loblolly pine tissue culture plantlets and seedlings. Canadian Journal of Forest Research 19(10):1347–1350.

Frampton LJ, Mott RL, Amerson HV. 1985.   Field performance of loblolly pine tissue culture plantlets. In: Proceedings, 18th Southern Forest Tree Improvement Conference; 1985 May 21–23; Long Beach, MS. Springfield, VA: National Technical Information Service: 136–144.

Frampton LJ Jr, Isik K. 1987.   Comparison of field growth among loblolly pine seedlings and three plant types produced in vitro. TAPPI Journal 70(7):119–123.

Franklin EC. 1969.   Inbreeding as a means of genetic improvement of loblolly pine. In: Proceedings, 10th Southern Forest Tree Improvement Conference; 1969 June 17–19; Houston, TX. College Station, TX: Texas Forest Service, Texas A&M University: 107–115.

Franklin E C. 1971.   Estimating frequency of natural selfing based on segregating mutant forms. Silvae Genetica 20(5/6):193–194.

Franklin EC. 1975.   Phenotypic and genetic variation of sulfate naval stores yields in loblolly pine. In: Proceedings, 1974 Forest Biology Conference; 1974 September 18–20; Seattle, WA. Atlanta: TAPPI: 99–102.

Franklin EC. 1979.   Model relating levels of genetic variance to stand development of four North American conifers. Silvae Genetica 28(5/6):207–212.

Franklin EC. 1983.   Patterns of genetic and environmental vari-ance in a short-term progeny test of loblolly pine. In: Proceed-ings, 17th Southern Forest Tree Improvement Conference; 1983 June 6–9; Charleston, SC. Macon, GA: USDA Forest Service, Eastern Tree Seed Laboratory: 332–343.

Friedman ST, Adams WT. 1981.   Genetic efficiency in loblolly pine seed orchards. In: Proceedings, 16th Southern Forest Tree Improvement Conference; 1981 May 27–28; Blacksburg, VA. Athens, GA: USDA Forest Service, Southeastern Forest Experiment Station: 213–224.

Friedman ST, Adams WT. 1985a.   Estimation of gene flow into two seed orchards of loblolly pine (Pinus taeda). Theoretical and Applied Genetics 69:609–615.

Friedman ST, Adams WT. 1985b.   Levels of outcrossing in two loblolly pine seed orchards. Silvae Genetica 34(4/5):157–162.

Gallegos CM. 1979.   Criteria for selecting loblolly pine (Pinus taeda L.) seed orchard sites in the southeastern United States. In: Proceedings, A Symposium on Flowering and Seed Develop-ment in Trees; 1978 May 15–18; Mississippi State, MS. Starkville,

MS: USDA Forest Service, Southern Forest Experiment Station: 163–176.

Gerwig DM. 1987. Annual top pruning as a crown management technique in a young loblolly pine seed orchard to reduce height and still produce flowers. In: Proceedings, 19th Southern Forest Tree Improvement Conference; 1987 June 16–18; College Station, TX. Springfield, VA: National Technical Information Service: 208–215.

Giertych M. 1971. Systematic layouts for seed orchards. Silvae Genetica 20(1-2):137–138.

Gilmore AR. 1967. Specific gravity of loblolly pine in the middle Mississippi Valley. Journal of Forestry 65(9):631.

Gilmore AR. 1969. Soil moisture stress and tracheid length in loblolly pine. In: Proceedings, 10th Southern Forest Tree Improvement Conference; 1969 June 17–19; Houston, TX. College Station, TX: Texas A&M University, Texas Forest Service: 205–207.

Gilmore AR. 1971. Variation in monoterpene composition of loblolly pine as related to geographic source of seed. In: Proceedings, 11th Southern Forest Tree Improvement Conference; 1971 June 15–16; Atlanta, GA. Macon, GA: USDA Forest Service, Eastern Tree Seed Laboratory: 128–132.

Gilmore AR, Boyce SG, Ryker RA. 1966. The relationship of specific gravity of loblolly pine to environmental factors in southern Illinois. Forest Science 12(4):399–405.

Gilmore AR, Funk DT. 1976. Shortleaf and loblolly pine seed origin trials in southern Illinois: 27-year results. In: Proceedings, 10th Central States Forest Tree Improvement Conference; 1976 September 22–23; West Lafayette, IN. West Lafayette, IN: Purdue University, Department of Forestry and Natural Resources: 115–124.

Goddard RE. 1964. Tree distribution in a seedling seed orchard following between and within family selection. Silvae Genetica 13(3):17–21.

Goddard RE, Zobel BJ, Hollis CA. 1976. Responses of Pinus taeda and Pinus elliottii to varied nutrition. Gainesville, FL: University of Florida, School of Forest Resources and Conservation: 449–462.

Goddard RE, Matthews FR. 1981. Pollen testing. In: Franklin EC, ed. Pollen management handbook. Agric. Handbk. 587. Washington, DC: USDA Forest Service: 40–42.

Goddard RE, Strickland RK. 1964. Crooked stem form in loblolly pine. Silvae Genetica 13(5):155–157.

Goggans JF. 1962. The correlation, variation, and inheritance of wood properties in loblolly pine (Pinus taeda L.). Tech. Rep. 14. Raleigh, NC: North Carolina State College, School of Forestry, Forest Tree Improvement Program. 155 p.

Greene JT. 1966. Seed yield and plantable seedlings from controlled-and open-pollinated four-and five-year-old seedlings of loblolly and shortleaf pine. In: Proceedings, 8th Southern Conference on Forest Tree Improvement; 1965 June 16–17; Savannah, GA. Macon, GA: USDA Forest Service, Eastern Tree Seed Laboratory: 155–157.

Greene JT, Porterfield HD. 1962. Early cone production in loblolly pine through selection and control-pollination. Acad. Science Bull. 20. Athens, GA: University of Georgia: 6.

Greenwald SM. 1972. Some environmental effects on the growth and monoterpene production of Pinus taeda L. and Ocimum basilicum L. Raleigh, NC: Duke University. 85 p. Ph.D. dissertation.

Greenwood MS. 1977a. The role of dormancy in the development of male and female strobili of loblolly pine. Forest Science 23(3): 373–375.

Greenwood MS. 1977b. Seed orchard fertilization: optimizing time and rate of ammonium nitrate application for grafted loblolly pine (Pinus taeda L.). In: Proceedings, 14th Southern Forest Tree Improvement Conference; 1977 June 14–16; [Location unknown]. Macon, GA: USDA Forest Service, Eastern Tree Seed Laboratory: 16–41.

Greenwood MS. 1978a. Flower stimulation techniques for loblolly pine (Pinus taeda L.). In: Proceedings, 3rd World Consultation on Forest Tree Breeding; 1977 March 21–26; Canberra, Australia. [Place of publication unknown]: IUFRO: 1031–1042.

Greenwood MS. 1978b. Flowering induced on young loblolly pine grafts by out-of-phase dormancy. Science 201(4354):443–444.

Greenwood MS. 1982. Rate, timing, and mode of gibberellin application of female strobilus production by grafted loblolly pine. Canadian Journal of Forest Research 12(4):998–1002.

Greenwood MS. 1983. Maximizing genetic gain in loblolly pine by application of accelerated breeding methods and new concepts. In: Proceedings, 17th Southern Forest Tree Improvement Conference; 1983 June 5–9; Charleston, SC. Macon, GA: USDA Forest Service, Eastern Tree Seed Laboratory: 290–295.

Greenwood MS. 1984. Phase change in loblolly pine: shoot development as a function of age. Physiologia Plantarum 61:518–522.

Greenwood MS, Bramlett DL. 1989. Effects of crown pruning on height and cone production by loblolly pine after 6 years. In: Proceedings, 20th Southern Forest Tree Improvement Conference; 1989 June 26–30; Charleston, SC. Springfield, VA: National Technical Information Service: 130–134.

Greenwood MS, Gladstone WT. 1978. Topworking loblolly pine for precocious flowering. Tech. Rep. 042-3004/78/80. Hot Springs, AR: Weyerhaeuser Technical Information Center. 8 p.

Greenwood MS, Rucker T. 1985. Estimating pollen contamination in loblolly pine seed orchards by pollen trapping. In: Proceedings, 18th Southern Forest Tree Improvement Conference; 1985 May 21–23; Long Beach, MS. Springfield, VA: National Technical Information Service: 179–186.

Greenwood MS, Schmidtling RC. 1981. Regulation of catkin production. In: Franklin EC, ed. Pollen management handbook. Agric. Handbk. 587. Washington, DC: USDA Forest Service: 20–25.

Greenwood MS, Marino TM, Meier RD, Shahan KW. 1980. The role of mist and chemical treatments in rooting loblolly and shortleaf pine cuttings. Forest Science 26(4):651–655.

Greenwood MS, O'Gwynn CH, Wallace PG. 1979. Management of an indoor, potted loblolly pine breeding orchard. In: Proceedings, 15th Southern Forest Tree Improvement Conference; 1979 June 19–21; Mississippi State, MS. Macon, GA: USDA Forest Service, Eastern Tree Seed Laboratory: 94–98.

Gregory JD, Davey CB. 1977. Subsoiling to stimulate flowering and cone production in loblolly pine seed orchard. Southern Journal of Applied Forestry 1(2):20–23.

Gregory JD, Guinness WM, Davey CB. 1982. Fertilization and irrigation stimulate flowering and cone production in a loblolly pine seed orchard. Southern Journal of Applied Forestry 6(1):44–48.

Griffing CG, Elam WW. 1971. Height growth patterns of loblolly pine saplings. Forest Science 17(1):52–54.

Griggs MM, Squillace AE. 1982. Inheritance of yellow oleoresin in shortleaf and slash pine. Journal of Heredity 73(6):405–407.

Grigsby HC. 1959. Two promising pine hybrids for the mid-South. Southern Lumberman 198(2466):32–33.

Grigsby HC. 1962a. How to propagate plants by air layering. Forests and People 12(3):22–23

Grigsby HC. 1962b. Propagation of loblolly pine by cuttings. Plant Propagators Society Proceedings 1961:33–35.

Grigsby HC. 1975. Performance of large loblolly and shortleaf pine seedlings after 9 to 12 years. Res. Note SO-196. New Orleans: USDA Forest Service, Southern Forest Experiment Station. 4 p.

Grigsby HC. 1977. A 16-year provenance test of loblolly pine in southern Arkansas. In: Proceedings, 14th Southern Forest Tree Improvement Conference; 1977 June 14–16; Gainesville, FL. Macon, GA: USDA Forest Service, Eastern Tree Seed Laboratory: 261–268.

Gupta PK, Durzan DJ. 1987a. Biotechnology of somatic polyembryogenesis and plantlet regeneration in loblolly pine. Bio/Technology 5(2):147–151.

Gupta PK, Durzan DJ. 1987b.   Somatic embryos from protoplasts of loblolly pine proembryonal cells. Bio/Technology 5(7):710–712.

Gupta PK, Durzan DJ, Finkle BJ. 1987.   Somatic polyembryogenesis in embryogenic cell masses of *Picea abies* (Norway spruce) and *Pinus taeda* (loblolly pine) after thawing from liquid nitrogen. Canadian Journal of Forest Research 17(9):1130–1134.

Harcharik DA. 1983.   The timing and economics of irrigation in loblolly pine seed orchards. Raleigh, NC: North Carolina State University. 125 p. Ph.D. dissertation.

Hare RC. 1965.   Breaking and rooting of fascicle buds in southern pines. Journal of Forestry 63(7):544–546.

Hare RC. 1979a.   Promoting flowering in loblolly and slash pine with branch, bud and fertilizer treatments. In: Proceedings, Symposium on Flowering and Seed Development in Trees; 1978 May 15–19; Gulfport, MS. Starkville, MS: USDA Forest Service, Southern Forest Experiment Station: 112–121.

Hare RC. 1979b.   Modular air-layering and chemical treatments improve rooting of loblolly pine. International Plant Propagators' Society Combined Proceedings 29:446–454.

Hare RC. 1984a.   Nitrapyrin (2-chloro-6-trichloromethyl-pyridine), a nitrification inhibitor, may replace fertilizers for promoting cone bud production in southern pine seed orchards. Canadian Journal of Forest Research 14(2):206–208.

Hare RC. 1984b.   Application method and timing of gibberellin $A_{4/7}$ treatments for increasing pollen conebud production in southern pines. Canadian Journal of Forest Research 14(1):128–131.

Hare RC. 1985.   A comparison of survival, growth, and flowering of loblolly and slash pine ramets obtained by grafting and rooting. Prog. Rep. 3. Gulfport, MS: USDA Forest Service, Southern Forest Experiment Station. 1 p.

Hare RC, Switzer GL. 1969.   Introgression with shortleaf pine may explain rust resistance in western loblolly pine. Res. Note SO-88. New Orleans: USDA Forest Service, Southern Forest Experiment Station. 2 p.

Harris GH. 1985.   The North Carolina division of forest resources regeneration program. In: Proceedings, 1984 Southern Nursery Conferences—Western Session; 1984 June 11–14; Alexandria, LA/1984 July 24–27; Asheville, NC. Atlanta: USDA Forest Service, Southern Region: 204–208.

Hashizume H. 1979.   Flowering of slash pine and loblolly pine grafted onto Japanese red pine rootstocks. Journal of the Japanese Forestry Society 61(10):372–375.

Hashizume H. 1985.   Effect of gibberellins on the promotion of flowering in Pinaceae species. Bulletin of the Faculty of Agriculture, Tottori University 37:80–87.

Hatchell GE, Dorman KW, Langdon OG. 1972.   Performance of loblolly and slash pine nursery selections. Forest Science 18(4):308–313.

Henderson LT Jr, Schoenike RE. 1981.   How good is Sonderegger pine? Southern Journal of Applied Forestry 5(4):183–186.

Henry BW. 1959.   Diseases and insects in the Southwide pine seed source study plantations during the first five years. In: Proceedings, 5th Southern Forest Tree Improvement Conference; 1959 June 11–12; Raleigh, NC. Raleigh, NC: North Carolina State University, School of Forestry: 12–17.

Herrick OW. 1981.   Economics of pitch × loblolly pine hybrids. Silvae Genetica 30(1):1–7.

Hicks RR Jr. 1973.   Evaluation of morphological characters for use in shortleaf hybrids. Castanea 38(2):182–189.

Hicks RR Jr. 1974.   Comparisons of seedlings from east Texas loblolly, shortleaf and suspected hybrid pines. TX For. Pap. 24. Nacogdoches, TX: Stephen F. Austin State University, School of Forestry. 6 p.

Hicks RR Jr, Jones JC. 1972.   Pollen development and release in loblolly and shortleaf pine near Nacogdoches, Texas. TX For. Pap. 13. Nacogdoches, TX: Stephen F. Austin State University, School of Forestry. 4 p.

Hodge GR. 1985.   Parent vs. offspring selection: a case study. In: Proceedings, 18th Southern Forest Tree Improvement Conference; 1985 May 21–23; Long Beach, MS. Springfield, VA: National Technical Information Service: 145–154.

Hodges JD, Elam WW, Watson WF. 1977.   Physical properties of the oleoresin system of the four major southern pines. Canadian Journal of Forest Research 7:520–525.

Hook DD, Denslow S. 1987.   Metabolic responses of four families of loblolly pine to two flood regimes. In: Crawford RMM, ed. Plant life in aquatic and amphibious habitats. Oxford: Blackwell Scientific Publications: 281–292.

Huneycutt M, Askew GR. 1989.   Electrophoretic identification of loblolly pine-shortleaf pine hybrids. Silvae Genetica 38(3-4):95–96.

Hunt DL. 1967.   Ninth-year performance of slash and loblolly pine nursery selections in Georgia. In: Proceedings, 9th Southern Forest Tree Improvement Conference; 1967 June 8–9; Knoxville, TN. Macon, GA: USDA Forest Service, Eastern Tree Seed Laboratory: 92–94.

Hyun SK. 1969.   Mass controlled pollination. In: Proceedings, 2nd World Consultation on Forest Tree Breeding; 1969 August 7–16; Washington, DC. [Place of publication and publisher unknown]: 10 p.

Hyun SK, Ahn KY. 1959.   Mass production of pitch-loblolly hybrid pine ((*Pinus rigitaeda*) seed. Res. Rep. 1. Suwon, Korea: Institute of Forest Genetics, Office of Forestry: 11–24.

Hyun SK, Ahn KY, Hong SH. 1971.   Developing advanced generation breeding population for a hybrid breeding program. Res. Rep. 9. Suwon, Korea: Institute of Forest Genetics, Office of Forestry: 1–8.

Jackson LWR, Greene JT. 1958.   Tracheid length variation and inheritance in slash and loblolly pine. Forest Science 4(4):316–318.

Jackson LWR, Morse WE. 1965.   Variation in fibril angle of slash and loblolly pine. GA For. Res. Pap. 34. Macon, GA: Georgia Forest Research Council. 5 p.

Jackson LWR, Strickland RK. 1962.   Geographic variation in tracheid length and wood density of loblolly pine. GA For. Res. Pap. 8. Macon, GA: Georgia Forest Research Council. 4 p.

Jackson LWR, Warren BJ. 1962.   Variation and inheritance in specific gravity of slash and loblolly pine progeny. GA For. Res. Pap. 14. Macon, GA: Georgia Forest Research Council. 4 p.

Jett JB. 1983.   The impact of irrigation and supplemental nitrogen fertilization on the development of a young loblolly pine seed orchard. Raleigh, NC: North Carolina State University. 42 p. Ph.D. dissertation.

Jett JB, Talbert JT. 1982.   Place of wood specific gravity in the development of advanced-generation seed orchards and breeding programs. Southern Journal of Applied Forestry 6(3):177–180.

Johnson H. 1973.   Tree improvement in International Paper Company's delta region. In: Proceedings, 12th Southern Forest Tree Improvement Conference; 1973 June 12–13; Baton Rouge, LA. Baton Rouge, LA: Louisiana State University, Division of Continuing Education: 74–78.

Joly RJ, Adams WT. 1983.   Allozyme analysis of pitch × loblolly pine hybrids produced by supplemental mass-pollination. Forest Science 29(2):423–432.

Jones EP, Wells OO. 1969.   Ice damage in a Georgia planting of loblolly pine from different seed sources. Res. Note SE-126. Asheville, NC: USDA Forest Service, Southeastern Forest Experiment Station. 4 p.

Kellison RC, Weir RJ. 1980.   How forest genetics is helping grow better trees for tomorrow. Tappi Journal 63(2):57–62.

Keng H, Little EL Jr. 1961.   Needle characteristics of hybrid pines. Silvae Genetica 10(5):131–146.

Kim CS. 1963.   The karyotype analysis in *Pinus rigida* Mill., *Pinus taeda* L. and their F_1 hybrid. Res. Rep. 3. Suwon, Korea: Institute of Forest Genetics, Office of Forestry: 21–28.

Kitchens RN. 1985.   One-quarter century of tree improvement in the southern region. In: Proceedings, National Silviculture

Workshop; 1985 May 13–16; Rapid City, SD. Washington, DC: USDA Forest Service, Division of Timber Management: 284–288.

Knauf TA, Bilan MV. 1977. Cotyledon and primary needle variation in loblolly pine from mesic and xeric seed sources. Forest Science 23(1):33–36.

Knezick DR, Kuser JE, Sacalis JN. 1985a. Single clone orchard production of pitch × loblolly hybrids. In: Proceedings, Northeastern Forest Tree Improvement Conference; 1984; Durham, NH. [Place of publication and publisher unknown]: 23–31.

Knezick DR, Kuser JE, Garrett PW. 1985b. Supplemental mass pollination of single clone orchards for the production of southern pine hybrids. In: Proceedings, 18th Southern Forest Tree Improvement Conference; 1985 May 21–23; Long Beach, MS. Springfield, VA: National Technical Information Service: 187–193.

Knowe SA, Foster GS. 1989. Application of growth models for simulating genetic gain of loblolly pine. Forest Science 35(1):211–228.

Kolb TE, Steiner KC. 1985. Cold tolerance variation in loblolly pine needles from different branch types, families, and environments. In: Proceedings, 18th Southern Forest Tree Improvement Conference; 1985 May 21–23; Long Beach, MS. Springfield, VA: National Technical Information Service: 358–367.

Kolb TE, Steiner KC, Barbour HF. 1985. Seasonal and genetic variations in loblolly pine cold tolerance. Forest Science 31(4):926–932.

Kormanik PP, Ruehle JL. 1989. First-order lateral root development: something to consider in mother tree and progeny assessment. In: Proceedings, 20th Southern Forest Tree Improvement Conference; 1989 June 26–30; Charleston, SC. Springfield, VA: National Technical Information Service: 220–227.

Kraus JF, Sluder ER. 1984. Guide for the selection and use of imporved loblolly pine planting stock. Unpublished report. [On file with the USDA Forest Service, National Tree Seed Laboratory, Dry Branch, GA.]

Kraus JF. 1986. Breeding shortleaf × loblolly pine hybrids for the development of fusiform rust-resistant loblolly pine. Southern Journal of Applied Forestry 10(4):195–197.

Kraus JF, Hunt DL. 1970. Fresh and stored pollen from slash pine-G and loblolly pine-G compared for seed yields. Res. Note SE-143. Asheville, NC: USDA Forest Service, Southeastern Forest Experiment Station. 5 p.

Kraus JF, Hunt DL. 1971. Inherent variation of resistance to hypodermalethale in slash and loblolly pines. Forest Science 17(1):143–144.

Kraus JF, LaFarge T. 1982. Georgia's seed orchard trees: a report on the first-generation selections. GA For. Res. Pap. 37. Macon, GA: Georgia Forest Research Council. 10 p.

Kraus JF, Sluder ER. 1981. Fifth-year performance of progenies of selected South African slash and loblolly pine clones. Southern Journal of Applied Forestry 5(2):62–65.

Kraus JF, Wells OO, Sluder ER. 1984. Review of provenance variation in loblolly pine in the southern United States. In: Proceedings, Joint Working Conference of IUFRO on Provenance and Genetic Improvement Strategies in Tropical Forest Trees; 1984 April 9–14; Mutare, Zimbabwe. Harare, Zimbabwe: University of Oxford, Commonwealth Forestry Institute, Department of Forestry, Zimbabwe Forestry Commission: 281–317.

Kucera DR. 1973. Cone and seed losses in loblolly pine. Dissertation Abstracts International 33(11):5327.

Kung FH. 1989. Optimal age for selecting loblolly pine seed sources. In: Proceedings, 20th Southern Forest Tree Improvement Conference; 1989 June 26–30; Charleston, SC. Springfield, VA: National Technical Information Service: 302–308.

Labosky P Jr. 1979. Chemical constituents of four southern pine barks. Wood Science 12(2):80–85.

LaFarge T. 1973. Relationships among third-, fifth-, and fifteenth-year measurements in a study of stand variation of loblolly pine in Georgia. In: Proceedings, IUFRO Working Party on Progeny

Testing. 1972; [Location unknown]. Macon, GA: Georgia Forest Research Council: 1–16.

LaFarge T. 1974. Genetic variation among and within three loblolly pine stands in Georgia. Forest Science 20(3):272–275.

LaFarge T. 1975. Correlations between nursery and plantation height growth in slash and loblolly pine. Forest Science 21(2):197–200.

LaFarge T, Hunt DL. 1980. Direction of pollination affects seed productivity in (shortleaf × loblolly) × loblolly hybrids. Res. Note SE-294. Asheville, NC: USDA Forest Service, Southeastern Forest Experiment Station. 4 p.

LaFarge T, Kraus JF. 1980. A progeny test of (shortleaf × loblolly) × loblolly hybrids to produce rapid-growing hybrids resistant to fusiform rust. Silvae Genetica 29(5/6):197–200.

LaFarge T, Kraus JF. 1981. Genotype × environment interactions of loblolly pine families in Georgia. Silvae Genetica 30(4/5):156–162.

LaFarge T, Kraus JF. 1984. Genotype × environment interactions of 14 loblolly pine parents at three locations. Progr. Rep. Summary 4. [On file with USDA Forest Service, National Tree Seed Laboratory, Dry Branch, GA.]

Lambeth CC, Dougherty WT, Gladstone RB, and others. 1984a. Large-scale planting of North Carolina loblolly pine in Arkansas and Oklahoma: a case of gain versus risk. Journal of Forestry 82(12):736–741.

Lambeth CC, McCullough RB, Wells OO. 1984b. Seed source movement and tree improvement in the western Gulf region. In: Proceedings, Symposium on the Loblolly Pine Ecosystem—Western Region; 1984 March 20–22; Jackson, MS. Mississippi State, MS: Mississippi Cooperative Extension Service, Extension Forestry Department: 71–86.

Lambeth CC, van Buijtenen JP, Duke SD, McCullough RB. 1983. Early selection is effective in 20-yr-old genetic tests of loblolly pine. Silvae Genetica 32(5/6):210–215.

Lambeth CC. 1983. Early testing: an overview with emphasis on loblolly pine. In: Proceeding, 17th Southern Forest Tree Improvement Conference; 1983 June 6–9; Charleston, SC. Macon, GA: USDA Forest Service, Eastern Tree Seed Laboratory: 297–311.

Langdon OG, Hatchell GE, LeGrande WP. 1968. Can you top this loblolly pine growth? Southern Lumberman 217(2704):197.

Langdon OG, Hatchell GE, LeGrande WP. 1970. Loblolly pine growth topped! Southern Lumberman 221(2752):126–127.

Lantz CW. 1973. Survey of graft incompatibility in loblolly pine. In: Proceedings, 12th Southern Forest Tree Improvement Conference; 1973 June 12–13; Baton Rouge, LA. Baton Rouge, LA: Louisiana State University, Division of Continuing Education: 79–85.

Lantz CW. 1979. Progress report: improved seedling production in the South. In: Proceedings, 15th Southern Forest Tree Improvement Conference; 1979 June 19–21; Mississippi State, MS. Macon, GA: USDA Forest Service, Eastern Tree Seed Laboratory: 115–119.

Lantz CW. 1988. Overview of southern regeneration. In: Proceedings, Southern Forest Nursery Association; 1988 July 25–28; Charleston, SC. Atlanta: USDA Forest Service, southern Region: 1–7.

Lantz CW, Hofmann JG. 1969. Geographic variation in growth and wood quality of loblolly pine in North Carolina. In: Proceedings, 10th Southern Forest Tree Improvement Conference; 1969 June 17–19; Houston, TX. College Station, TX: Texas Forest Service, Texas A&M University: 175–188.

Lantz CW, Kraus JF. 1987. A guide to southern pine seed sources. Gen. Tech. Rep. SE-43. Asheville, NC: USDA Forest Service, Southeastern Forest Experiment Station. 34 p.

Ledig FT, Fryer JH. 1974. Genetics of pitch pine. Res. Pap. WO-27. Washington, DC: USDA Forest Service. 14 p.

Ledig FT, Perry TO. 1966. Physiological genetics of the shoot-root ratio. In: Proceedings, Society of American Foresters Meeting;

1965; [Location unknown]. Washington, DC: Society of American Foresters: 39–43.

Ledig FT, Perry TO. 1967. Variation in photosynthesis and respiration among loblolly pine progenies. In: Proceedings, 9th Southern Forest Tree Improvement Conference; 1967 June 8–9; Knoxville, TN. Macon, GA: USDA Forest Service, Eastern Tree Seed Laboratory: 120–128.

Ledig FT, Perry TO. 1969. Net assimilation rate and growth in loblolly pine seedlings. Forest Science 15(4):431–438.

Li B, McKeand SE. 1989. Stability of loblolly pine families in the southeastern U.S. Silvae Genetica 38(3/4):96–101.

Li B, McKeand SE, Allen HL. 1989. Early selection of loblolly pine families based on seedling shoot elongation characters. In: Proceedings, 20th Southern Forest Tree Improvement Conference; 1989 June 26–30; Charleston, SC. Charleston, SC: The Southern Forest Tree Improvement Committee. Springfield, VA: National Technical Information Service: 228–234.

Libby WJ. 1986. Clonal propagation: the clones are coming! Journal of Forestry 84(1):37–39.

Libby WJ, Rauter RM. 1984. Advantages of clonal forestry. Forestry Chronicle 60(3):145–149.

Lindgren D, Matheson AC. 1986. An algorithm for increasing the genetic quality of seed from seed orchards by using the better clones in higher proportions. Silvae Genetica 35(5/6):173–177.

Little EL Jr, Little S, Doolittle WT. 1967. Natural hybrids among pond, loblolly, and pitch pines. Res. Pap. NE-67. Upper Darby, PA: USDA Forest Service, Northeastern Forest Experiment Station. 22 p.

Little EL, Righter F. 1965. Botanical descriptions of forty artificial pine hybrids. Tech. Bull. No. 1345. Washington, DC: USDA Forest Service. 47 p.

Little S. 1969. Local seed sources recommended for loblolly pine in Maryland and shortleaf pine in New Jersey and Pennsylvania. Res. Pap. NE-134. Upper Darby, PA: USDA Forest Service, Northeastern Forest Experiment Station. 6 p.

Little S, Trew IF. 1977. Progress report on testing pitch × loblolly pine hybrids and on providing hybrid seed for mass plantings. In: Proceedings, 24th Northeastern Forest Tree Improvement Conference; 1976 July 26–29; Pennington, NJ. Durham, NH: USDA Forest Service, Northeastern Forest Experiment Station: 14–28.

Little S, Trew IF. 1979. Pitch × loblolly pine hybrids: loblollies for the north? Journal of Forestry 77(11):709–713, 716.

Long AJ. 1973. Genotype and ectomycorrhizal fungi as factors in feeder root development and patterns of growth in four and one-half-month-old loblolly pine (Pinus taeda L.) seedlings. Raleigh, NC: North Carolina State University. Ph.D. dissertation. 133 p.

Long EM. 1980. Texas and Louisiana loblolly pine study confirms importance of local seed sources. Southern Journal of Applied Forestry 4(3):127–132.

Long EM, van Buijtenen JP, Robinson JF. 1974. Cultural practices in southern pine seed orchards. In: Proceedings of a colloquium: seed yield from southern pine seed orchards; 1974 April 2–3; Macon, GA. Macon, GA: Georgia Forest Research Council: 73–85.

Loo JA, Tauer CG, McNew RW. 1985. Genetic variation in the time of transition from juvenile to mature wood in loblolly pine (Pinus taeda L.). Silvae Genetica 34(1):14–19.

Loo JA, Tauer CG, van Buijtenen JP. 1984. Juvenile-mature relationships and heritability estimates of several traits in loblolly pine (Pinus taeda). Canadian Journal of Forest Research 14(6):822–825.

Lowe WJ, van Buijtenen JP. 1989. The incorporation of early testing procedures into an operational tree improvement program. Silvae Genetica 38(5/6):243–250.

Lowerts GA. 1986. Realized genetic gain from loblolly and slash pine first generation seed orchards. In: Proceeding, IUFRO Joint Meeting of Working Parties on Breeding Theory, Progeny Testing, Seed Orchards; 1986 October 13–17; Williamsburg, VA. [Place of publication unknown]: IUFRO: 142–149.

Mahalovich MF, McKeand SE, Jett JB. 1987. Seasonal rooting response of 6-year-old loblolly pine clones to different concentrations of indole-3-butyric acid and dimethyl sulfoxide. In: Proceedings, 19th Southern Forest Tree Improvement Conference; 1987 June 16–18; College Station, TX. Springfield, VA: National Technical Information Service: 125–131.

Major RE. 1983. Net retrieval system for pine seed collection. In: Proceedings, 1982 Southern Nursery Conferences; 1982 August 9–12; Oklahoma City, OK/July 12–15; Savannah, GA. R8-TP4. Atlanta: USDA Forest Service, Southern Region: 109–112.

Maple WR. 1966. Appalachian loblolly grows well in Arkansas Ozarks. Res. Note SO-33. New Orleans: USDA Forest Service, Southern Forest Experiment Station. 2 p.

Marino TM. 1982. Propagation of southern pines by cuttings. Proceedings of the International Plant Propagators' Society 31:581–527.

Matthews FR, Kraus JF. 1981. Pollen storage. In: Franklin EC, ed. Pollen management handbook. Agric. Handbk. 587. Washington, DC: USDA Forest Service: 37–39. Chapter 8.

Matthews FR, Bramlett DL. 1983. Pollen storage methods influence filled seed yields in controlled pollinations of loblolly pine. In: Proceedings, 2nd Biennial Southern Silvicultural Research Conference; 1982 November 4–5; Atlanta, GA. Gen. Tech. Rep. SE-24. Asheville, NC: USDA Forest Service, Southeastern Forest Experiment Station: 441–445.

Matthews FR, Bramlett DL. 1986. Pollen quantity and viability affect seed yields from controlled pollinations of loblolly pine. Southern Journal of Applied Forestry 10(2):78–80.

Matziris DI, Zobel BJ. 1973. Inheritance and correlations of juvenile characteristics in loblolly pine (Pinus taeda L.). Silvae Genetica 22(1/2):38–45.

Matziris DI. 1975. Predicted versus realized gain in loblolly pine (Pinus taeda L.) improvement. Dissertation Abstracts International 35(11):5218.

May JT. 1977. Effects of fertilization on seed orchards. In: Proceedings, 14th Southern Forest Tree Improvement Conference; 1977 June 14–16; Gainesville, FL. Macon, GA: Eastern Tree Seed Laboratory: 152–164.

McConnell JL, Edwards JL. 1985. The net retrieval seed collection system in the southern region seed orchards: an economy study. In: Proceedings, 3rd Biennial Southern Silvicultural Research Conference; 1984 November 7–8; Atlanta, GA. Gen. Tech. Rep. SO-54: New Orleans: USDA Forest Service, Southern Forest Experiment Station: 252–254.

McConnell JL, Edwards JL. 1986. Net retrieval seed collection. Gen. Tech. Rep. INT-203. Ogden, UT: USDA Forest Service, Intermountain Forest and Range Experiment Station: 125–128.

McCullough RB. 1976. Elemental concentrations as a means of early evaluation of open-pollinated families of loblolly pine. Dissertation Abstracts International 36(12):5882–5883.

McKeand SE. 1985. Expression of mature characteristics by tissue culture plantlets derived from embryos of loblolly pine. Journal of the American Society for Horticultural Science 110(5):619–623.

McKeand SE. 1988. Optimum age for family selection for growth in genetic tests of loblolly pine. Forest Science 34(2):400–411.

McKeand SE, Allen HL. 1984. Nutritional and root development factors affecting growth of tissue culture plantlets of loblolly pine. Physiologia Plantarum 61:523–528.

McKeand SE, Frampton LJ Jr. 1984. Performance of tissue culture plantlets of loblolly pine in vivo. In: Proceedings, International Symposium of Recent Advances in Forest Biotechnology; 1984 June 10–13; Traverse City, MI. East Lansing, MI: Michigan Biotechnology Institute: 82–91.

McKeand SE, Wisniewski LA. 1983. Root morphology of loblolly pine tissue culture plantlets. In: Proceedings, North American Forest Biology Workshop; 1982 July 26–28; Lexington, KY. Lexington, KY: University of Kentucky: 214–219.

McKeand SE, Jett JB, Sprague JR, Todhunter MN. 1987. Summer wax grafting of loblolly pine. Southern Journal of Applied Forestry 11(2):96–99.

McKeand SE, Sprague JR, Jett JB. 1988. Management of loblolly pine clone banks for scion production. Southern Journal of Applied Forestry 12(4):231–234.

McKeand SE, Weir RJ, Hatcher AV. 1989. Performance of diverse provenances of loblolly pine throughout the southeastern United States. Southern Journal of Applied Forestry 13(1):46–51.

McKinley CR, Lowe WJ, van Buijtenen JP. 1982. Genetic improvement of wood specific gravity in loblolly pine (Pinus taeda L.) and its relation to other traits. In: Proceedings, TAPPI Research and Development Division Conference; 1982 August 29–September 1; Asheville, NC. Atlanta: TAPPI Press: 153–158.

McLemore BF. 1979. Top pruning and bending branches fail to aid collection and production of loblolly cones. Tree Planters' Notes 30(2):27–30.

McRae J, Thor E. 1982. Cortical monoterpene variation in 12 loblolly pine provenances planted in Tennessee. Forest Science 28(4):732–736.

Megraw RA. 1985. Specific gravity. In: Wood quality factors in loblolly pine: the influence of tree age, position in tree, and cultural practice on wood specific gravity, fiber length, and fibril angle. Atlanta: TAPPI Press. 96 p.

Mehra-Palta A, Smeltzer RH, Mott RL. 1977. Hormonal control of induced organogenesis from excised plant parts of loblolly pine (Pinus taeda L.). In: Proceedings, TAPPI Forest Biology Wood Chemistry Conference; 1977 June 20–22; Madison, WI. Atlanta: TAPPI Press: 15–19.

Mergen F. 1958. Genetic variation in needle characteristics of slash pine and in some of its hybrids. Silvae Genetica 7(1):1–9.

Mergen F, Rossoll H. 1954. How to root and graft slash pine. Res. Pap. SE-46. Asheville, NC: USDA Forest Service, Southeastern Forest Experiment Station. 22 p.

Mergen F, Simpson BA. 1964. Asexual propagation of Pinus by rooting needle fascicles. Silvae Genetica 13(5):133–139.

Mergen F, Stairs GR, Snyder EB. 1965. Natural and controlled loblolly × shortleaf pine hybrids in Mississippi. Forest Science 11(3):306–314.

Miller DE. 1982. Early selection of loblolly pine based on genotype × fertilizer interaction of seedlings. College Station, TX: Texas A&M University. 51 p. M.S. thesis.

Minckler LS. 1952. Loblolly pine seed source and hybrid tests in southern Illinois. Tech. Pap. 128. Columbus, OH: USDA Forest Service, Central States Forest Experiment Station. 8 p.

Mott RL, Amerson HV. 1984. Role of tissue culture in loblolly pine improvement. In: Proceeding, International Symposium on Recent Advances in Forest Biotechnology; 1984 June 10–13; Traverse City, MI. East Lansing, MI: Michigan Biotechnology Institute: 24–36.

Nebgen RJ, Meyer JF. 1985. Seed bed density, undercutting, and lateral root pruning effects on loblolly seedling morphology, field survival, and growth. In: South DB, ed. Proceedings, International Symposium on Nursery Management Practices for Southern Pines; 1985 August 4–9; Montgomery, AL. Auburn, AL: Auburn University Department of Research Information: 136–147.

Nelson CD, Linghai Z, Hamaker JM. 1992. Propagation of loblolly, slash, and longleaf pine from needle fascicles. Tree Planters' Notes 43(3):67–71.

Nelson TC. 1964. Diameter distribution and growth of loblolly pine. Forest Science 10(1):105–114.

Nichols CR. 1974. Interrelation of tree improvement and management objectives: small ownerships. In: Proceedings, Symposium on Management of Young Pines; 1974 October 22–24; Alexandria, LA/1974 December 3–5; Charleston, SC. Asheville, NC: U.S. Department of Agriculture, Forest Service, Southeastern Forest Experiment Station: 175–179.

O'Loughlin TC. 1979. Trickle irrigation for seed orchards. In:

Proceedings, 15th Southern Forest Tree Improvement Conference; 1979 June 19–21; Mississippi State, MS. Macon, GA: USDA Forest Service, Eastern Tree Seed Laboratory: 86–91.

Owino F. 1977. Genotype × environment interaction and genotypic stability in loblolly pine: 2. Genotypic stability comparisons. Silvae Genetica 26(1): 21-26.

Owino F, Zobel B. 1977. Genotype × environment interaction and genotypic stability in loblolly pine: 3. Heterosis and heterosis × environment interaction. Silvae Genetica 26(2/3):114–116.

Parker J. 1965. The ability of warm-climate pines to become cold hardy. Pakistan Journal of Forestry 15(2):156–160.

Pearce RB. 1986. Genetic engineering comes to forestry. Forestry Research West [Washington, DC: USDA Forest Service]: 1–6.

Pearl IA. 1975. Variations of loblolly and slash pine bark extractive components and wood turpentine components on a monthly basis. TAPPI Journal 58(10):146–149.

Pearson RG. 1988. Compressive properties of clear and knotty loblolly pine juvenile wood. Forest Products Journal 38(7/8): 15–22.

Pederick LA. 1970. Variation and inheritance of stem form and bark thickness in young loblolly pine. Tech. Rep. 31. Raleigh, NC: North Carolina State University, School of Forest Resources. 44 p.

Perry TO. 1960. The inheritance of crooked stem from in loblolly pine (Pinus taeda L.). Journal of Forestry 58(12):943–947.

Perry TO. 1975. Maternal effects on the early performance of tree progenies. In: Cannell MGR, Fast FT, eds. Tree physiology and yield improvement—mineral nutrition. London: Academic Press: 473–481.

Perry TO, Wang CW, Schmitt D. 1966. Height growth for loblolly pine provenances in relation to photoperiod and growing season. Silvae Genetica 15(3):61–64.

Powers HR Jr. 1986. Performance of Livingston Parish loblolly pine in the Georgia Piedmont. Southern Journal of Applied Forestry 10(2):84–87.

Powers HR Jr, Kraus JF. 1986. A comparison of fusiform rust-resistant loblolly pine seed sources. Southern Journal of Applied Forestry 10(4):230–232.

Powers HR Jr, Matthews FR. 1987. Five fusiform rust-resistant seed sources in coastal South Carolina: a field comparison. Southern Journal of Applied Forestry 11(4):198–201.

Reines M, Bamping JH. 1962. Carbohydrates and seasonal rootings of cuttings. GA For. Res. Pap. 9. Macon, GA: Georgia Forest Research Council. 8 p.

Reines M, Bamping JH. 1964. Rooting of needle bunches. Journal of Forestry 62(3):181–182.

Renfroe MH, Berlyn GP. 1984. Stability of nuclear DNA content during adventitious shoot formation in Pinus taeda L. tissue culture. American Journal of Botany 71(2):268–272.

Richmond GB, McKinley CR. 1986. An experimental seed orchard in south Texas. Journal of Forestry 84(7):19, 43.

Rink G, Thor E. 1971. Results from ten loblolly pine provenance tests in Tennessee. In: Proceedings, 11th Southern Forest Tree Improvement Conference; 1971 June 15–16; Atlanta, GA. Macon, GA: USDA Forest Service, Eastern Tree Seed Laboratory: 158–164.

Robbins JWD, Coleman SW, McMahone DW. 1985. Drip systems for pine tree seed orchards. In: Drip/trickle irrigation in action: Proceedings, 3rd International Drip/Trickle Irrigation Congress; 1985 November 18–21; Fresno, CA. St. Joseph, MI: American Society of Agricultural Engineers: 101–104.

Roberds JH, Namkoong G, Davey CB. 1976. Family variation in growth response of loblolly pine to fertilizing with urea. Forest Science 22(3):291–299.

Robinson JF. 1979. Response to nitrate and ammonium fertilizers—flowers, cones and seed in a loblolly pine seed orchard. In: Proceedings, 15th Southern Forest Tree Improvement Conference; 1979 June 19–21; Mississippi State, MS. Macon, GA: USDA Forest Service, Eastern Tree Seed Laboratory: 78–85.

Robinson JF, van Buijtenen JP, Long EM. 1984. Traits measured on seedlings can be used to select for later volume of loblolly pine. Southern Journal of Applied Forestry 8(1):59–63.

Rockwood DL. 1973. Variation in the monoterpene composition of two oleoresin systems of loblolly pine. Forest Science 19(2):147–153.

Rockwood DL. 1972. Aspects of monoterpene composition in loblolly pine. Dissertation Abstracts International 33(3):976.

Ross SD, Greenwood MS. 1979. Promotion of flowering in the Pinaceae by gibberellins: 2. Grafts of mature and immature *Pinus taeda*. Physiologia Plantarum 45(2):207–210.

Sartor CF, Neel WW. 1971. Impact of *Dioryctria amatella* on seed yields on maturing slash and loblolly pine cones in Mississippi seed orchards. Journal of Economic Entomology 64(1):28–30.

Saylor LC, Kang KW. 1973. A study of sympatric populations of *Pinus taeda* L. and *Pinus serotina* Michx. in North Carolina. Journal of the Elisha Mitchell Scientific Society 89(1/2):101–110.

Schmidtling RC. 1969a. Influence of rootstock on flowering in shortleaf pine. In: Proceedings, 10th Southern Forest Tree Improvement Conference; 1969 June 17–19; Houston, TX. College Station, TX: Texas Forest Service and Texas A&M University: 229–230.

Schmidtling RC. 1969b. Reproductive maturity related to height of loblolly pine. Res. Note SO-94. New Orleans: USDA Forest Service, Southern Forest Experiment Station. 2 p.

Schmidtling RC. 1971. Cultivating and fertilizing stimulate precocious flowering in a loblolly pine seed orchard. Silvae Genetica 20(5-6):220–221.

Schmidtling RC. 1973. Rootstock influences early fruitfulness, growth, and survival in loblolly pine grafts. In: Proceedings, 12th Southern Forest Tree Improvement Conference; 1973 June 12–13; Baton Rouge, LA. Baton Rouge, LA: Louisiana State University, Division of Continuing Education: 86–90.

Schmidtling RC. 1974. Rootstock does not affect cortical monoterpene composition in loblolly pine. Forest Science 20(4):375–376.

Schmidtling RC. 1975. Fertilizer timing and formulation affect flowering in a loblolly pine seed orchard. In: Proceedings, 13th Southern Forest Tree Improvement Conference; 1975 June 10–11; Raleigh, NC. Macon, GA: USDA Forest Service, Eastern Tree Seed Laboratory: 153–160.

Schmidtling RC. 1979. Southern loblolly pine seed orchards produce more cone and seed than do northern orchards. In: Report of the southern forest tree improvement committee's subcommittee on seed orchard yields. Gulfport, MS: USDA Forest Service, Southern Forest Experiment Station: 177–186.

Schmidtling RC. 1983a. Genetic variation in fruitfulness in a loblolly pine (*Pinus taeda* L.) seed orchard. Silvae Genetica 32(3/4):76–80.

Schmidtling RC. 1983b. Influence of interstock on flowering and growth of loblolly pine grafts. Tree Planters' Notes 34(1):30–32.

Schmidtling RC. 1983c. Timing of fertilizer application important for management of southern pine seed orchards. Southern Journal of Applied Forestry 7(2):76–81.

Schmidtling RC. 1983d. Geographic location affects flowering of loblolly pines. In: Proceedings, 17th Southern Forest Tree Improvement Conference; 1983 June 6–9; Charleston, SC. Macon, GA: USDA Forest Service, Eastern Tree Seed Laboratory: 42–48.

Schmidtling RC. 1987. Wide crossing in loblolly pines: incorporating rust resistance into fast growing provenances [abstract]. In: Proceedings, Southwide Forest Disease Workshop; 1987 January; Athens, GA. [Place of publication and publisher unknown]. 1 p.

Schmidtling RC. 1988. Genetic contribution of the roots to reproduction, survival, and growth of loblolly and slash pine grafts. Final Rep. Summary FS-SO=4108.21.37, problem 2. [On file with USDA Forest Service, Southern Forest Experiment Sation, New Orleans.]

Schmidtling RC. 1989. Wide crossing in loblolly pine: crossing Livingston Parish with Atlantic Coast and central Florida populations [abstract]. In: Proceedings, 20th Southern Forest Tree Improvement Conference; 1989 June 26–30; Charleston, SC. Pub. 42. Charleston, SC: Southern Forest Tree Improvement Committee.

Schmidtling RC, Clark A III. 1989. Loblolly pine seed sources differ in stem form. In: Proceedings, 5th Biennial Southern Silvicultural Research Conference; 1988 November 1–3; Memphis, TN. Gen. Tech. Rep. SO-74. New Orleans: USDA Forest Service, Southern Forest Experiment Station: 421–425.

Schmidtling RC, Scarbrough NM. 1968. Graphic analysis of Erambert's hybrid. Res. Note SO-80. New Orleans: USDA Forest Service, Southern Forest Experiment Station. 3 p.

Schmidtling RC, Amburgey TL. 1982. Genetic variation in decay susceptibility and its relationship to growth and specific gravity in loblolly pine. Holzforschung 36:159–161.

Schmitt D. 1968a. Crossing the southern pines. Southern Lumberman 217(2704):–107.

Schmitt D. 1968b. Performance of southern pine hybrids in south Mississippi. Res. Pap. SO-36. New Orleans: USDA Forest Service, Southern Forest Experiment Station. 14 p.

Schoenike RE, Hart JD, Gibson MD. 1975. Growth of a nine-year-old Sonderegger pine plantation in South Carolina. Silvae Genetica 24(1):10–11.

Schoenike RE, Van Lear DH, Benson JD. 1977. Comparison of shortleaf, loblolly, and putative hybrid pines in the Piedmont of South Carolina. Silvae Genetica 26(5/6):182–184.

Schultz RP. 1972. Root development of intensively cultivated slash pine. Soil Science Society of America Journal 36(1):158–162.

Sederoff R, Stomp AM, Chilton WS, Moore LW. 1986. Gene transfer into loblolly pine by *Agrobacterium tumefaciens*. Biotechnology 4(7):647–649.

Seiler JR, Johnson JD. 1988. Physiological and morphological responses of three half-sib families of loblolly pine to water-stress conditioning. Forest Science 34(2):487–495.

Sen S, Newton RJ, Fong F. 1987. Abscisic acid: a role in pine shoot induction. Plant Physiology 83(4):75.

Sen S, Newton RJ, Fong F, Neuman P. 1989. Abscisic acid: a role in shoot enhancement from loblolly pine (*Pinus taeda* L.) cotyledon explants. Plant Cell Reports 8(4):191–194.

Shear TH, Hook, DD. 1988. Interspecific genetic variation of loblolly pine tolerance to soil waterlogging. In: Hook DD and others, eds. The ecology and management of wetlands. Ecology of wetlands. Portland, OR: Timber Press: 489–93. Vol. 1.

Shear TH. 1985. Seed properties of loblolly pine (*Pinus taeda* L.): genetic variability and effects on seedling establishment and performance. Raleigh, NC: North Carolina State University. 61 p. Ph.D. dissertation.

Sluder ER. 1970. Shortleaf × loblolly pine hybrids do well in central Georgia. GA For. Res. Pap. 64. Macon, GA: Georgia Forest Research Council. 4 p.

Sluder ER. 1989. Fusiform rust in crosses among resistant and susceptible lobolly and slash pines. Southern Journal of Applied Forestry 13(4):174–177.

Smouse PE, Saylor LC. 1973. Studies of the *Pinus rigida–serotina* complex: 2. Natural hybridization among the *Pinus rigida-serotina* complex, *Pinus taeda* and *Pinus echinata*. Annuals of the Missouri Botanical Garden 60(2):129–203.

Snyder EB. 1968. Seed yield and nursery performance of self-pollinated slash pines. Forest Science 14(1):69–74.

Snyder EB, Clausen KE. 1974. Pollen handling. In: Schopmeyer CS, tech. Coord. Seeds of woody plants in the United States. Agric. Handbk. 450. Washington, DC: USDA Forest Service: 45–92.

Snyder EB, Hamaker JM. 1978a. Inheritance of peroxidase isozymes in needles of loblolly and longleaf pines. Silvae Genetica 27(3/4):125–129.

Snyder EB, Hamaker JM. 1978b. Needle characteristics of hybrids of some species of southern pine. Silvae Genetica 27(5):184–188.

Snyder EB, Squillace AE. 1966. Cone and seed yields from controlled breeding of southern pines. Res. Pap. SO-22. New Orleans: USDA Forest Service, Southern Forest Experiment Station. 7 p.

Snyder EB. 1961. Extracting, processing, and storing southern pine pollen. Occas. Pap. 191. New Orleans: USDA Forest Service, Southern Forest Experiment Station. 14 p.

Sprague JR, Johnson VW. 1977. Extraction and storage of loblolly pine (Pinus taeda) pollen. In: Proceedings, 14th Southern Forest Tree Improvement Conference; 1977 June 14–16; Gainesville, FL. Macon, GA: USDA Forest Service, Eastern Tree Seed Laboratory: 20–27.

Sprague JR, Snyder EB. 1981. Extracting and drying pine pollen. In: Franklin EC, ed. Pollen management handbook. Agric. Handbk. 587. Washington, DC: USDA Forest Service: 33–36.

Sprinz PT, Talbert CB, Strub MR. 1989. Height–age trends from an Arkansas seed source study. Forest Science 35(3):677–691.

Squillace AE, Long EM. 1981. Proportion of pollen from nonorchard sources. In: Franklin, E. Carlyle, ed. Pollen management handbook. Agric. Handbk. 587. Washington, DC: USDA Forest Service: 15–19.

Squillace AE, Powers HR Jr, Kossuth SV. 1984. Monoterpene phenotypes in loblolly pine populations: natual selection, trends and implications. In: Proceedings, 18th Southern Forest Tree Improvement Conference; 1984 May 21–23; Long Beach, MS. Springfield, VA: National Technical Information Service: 299–307.

Squillace AE, Swindel BF. 1986. Linkage among genes controlling monoterpene constituent levels in loblolly pine. Forest Science 32(1):97–112.

Squillace AE, Wells OO. 1981. Geographic variation of monoterpenes in cortical oleoresin of loblolly pine. Silvae Genetica 30(4/5):127–135.

Stomp AM, Sederoff RR, Chilton WS, Moore LW. 1988. Transformation of pine cells by Agrobacterium tumefaciens [abstract]. In: Valentine FA, ed. Colloquium on Forest and Crop Biotechnology: Progress and Prospects; 1985 April 18–20; Syracuse, NY. New York: Springer-Verlag: 427.

Stonecypher RW, Zobel BJ. 1966. Inheritance of specific gravity in five-year-old seedlings of loblolly pine. TAPPI Journal 49(7):303–305.

Struve DK, Jett JB, McKeand SE, Cannon GP. 1989. Subsoiling in an loblolly pine seed orchard: effects on seed quality. Canadian Journal of Forestry 19(4):505–508.

Summerville KO. 1987. Seed yields per bushel: orchard vs natural stands. In: Proceedings, 19th Southern Forest Tree Improvement Conference; 1987 June 16–18; College Station, TX. Springfield, VA: National Technical Information Service: 190–194.

Szymanski MB, Tauer CG. 1991. Loblolly pine provenance variation in age of transition from juvenile to mature wood specific gravity. Forest Science 37(1):160–174.

Talbert JT, Jett JB. 1981. Regional specific gravity values for plantation-grown loblolly pine in the southeastern United States. Forest Science 27(4):801–807.

Talbert JT, Weir RJ, Arnold RD. 1983. Loblolly pine tree improvement: an attractive forestry investment. In: Proceedings, Southern Forest Economics Workshop; 1983 April 7–8; Mobile, AL. Raleigh, NC: North Carolina State University. 16 p.

Talbert JT, Weir RJ, Arnold RD. 1985. Costs and benefits of a mature first generation loblolly pine tree improvement program. Journal of Forestry 83(3):162–166.

Talbert JT, Bridgwater FE, Jett JB, Jahromi S. 1982. Genetic parameters of wood specific gravity in a control pollinated loblolly pine genetic test. In: Proceedings, TAPPI Research and Development Division Conference; 1982 August 29–September 1; Asheville, NC. Atlanta: TAPPI Press: 179–182.

Tauer CG, Loo-Dinkins JA. 1990. Seed source variation in specific gravity of loblolly pine grown in a common environment in Arkansas. Forest Science 36(4):1133–1145.

Thames JL. 1963. Needle variation in loblolly pine from four geographic seed sources. Ecology 44(1):168–169.

USDA FS [USDA Forest Service]. 1988. Tree improvement handbook. Amendment 16. Atlanta: USDA Forest Service: 440.4-2–440.4-7.

United States Department of Agriculture. 1965. Southern wood density survey: 1965 status report. Res. Pap. FPL-26. Madison, WI: USDA Forest Service, Forest Products Laboratory. 38 p.

van Buijtenen JP. 1966a. The effect of spacing, fertilization, and cultivation on flowering and seed production in loblolly pine. In: Proceedings, 8th Southern Forest Tree Improvement Conference; 1965 June 16–17; Savannah, GA. Macon, GA: Georgia Forest Research Council: 141–145.

van Buijtenen JP. 1966b. Testing loblolly pines for drought resistance. Tech. Rep. 13. College Station, TX: Texas Forest Service, Texas A&M University. 15 p.

van Buijtenen JP. 1985. Increasing forest productivity and value by breeding for outstanding combinations of desirable characteristics. In: Proceedings, Forest Potentials—Productivity and Value; 1984 August 20–24; Tacoma, WA. Centralia, WA: Weyerhaeuser Co.: 233–251.

van Buijtenen JP. 1986. Computer simulation of the effect of wood specific gravity and rotation age on the production of linearboard and multiwall sack paper. In: Proceedings, TAPPI Research and Development Division Conference; 1986 September 28–October 1; Raleigh, NC. Atlanta: TAPPI Press: 49–53.

van Buijtenen JP, Brown CL. 1963. The effect of crown pruning on strobili production of loblolly pine. In: Proceedings, Forest Genetics Workshop; 1962 October 25–27; Macon, GA. Macon, GA: Southern Forest Tree Improvement Committee: 88–93.

van Buijtenen JP, Lowe WJ. 1979. The use of breeding groups in advanced generation breeding. In: Proceedings, 15th Southern Forest Tree Improvement Conference; 1979 June 19–21; Mississippi State, MS. Macon, GA: USDA Forest Service, Eastern Tree Seed Laboratory: 59–65.

van der Sijde HA. 1969. Bending of trees as a standard practice in pine seed orchard management in South Africa. In: Proceedings, 2nd FAO/IUFRO World Consultation on Forest Tree Breeding—FAO-FTB-69-11/9; 1969; Washington, DC. Rome: FAO: 1373–1379.

Vozzo JA, Bonner FT. 1984. Quality of pine seed collected from the net retrieval system. In: Proceedings, Southern Nursery Conferences; 1984 June 11–14; Alexandria, LA/July 24–27; Asheville, NC. Atlanta: USDA Forest Service, Southern Region: 121–126.

Wakeley PC. 1971. Relation of 30th year to earlier dimensions of southern pines-G. Forest Science 17(2):200–209.

Wakeley PC, Bercaw TE. 1965. Loblolly pine provenance test at age 35. Journal of Forestry 63(3):168–174.

Wakeley PC, Campbell TE. 1954. Some new pine pollination techniques. Occas. Pap. 136. New Orleans: USDA Forest Service, Southern Forest Experiment Station. 13 p.

Wasser RG. 1967. A shortleaf and loblolly pine flowering phenology study. Occas. Rep. 28. Charlottesville, VA: Virginia Division of Forestry, Department of Conservation and Economic Development. 16 p.

Waxler MS, van Buijtenen JP. 1981. Early genetic evaluation of loblolly pine. Canadian Journal of Forest Research 11(2):351–355.

Webster SR. 1974. Nutrition of seed orchard pine in Virginia. Dissertation Abstracts International 36(2):512.

Wells OO. 1975. Geographic variation in southern tree species. In: Thielges BA, ed. Forest tree improvement: the third decade. Baton Rouge, LA: Louisiana State University, Division of Continuing Education: 19–31.

Wells OO. 1983. Southwide pine seed source study: loblolly pine at 25 years. Southern Journal of Applied Forestry 7(2):63–71.

Wells OO. 1985. Use of Livingston Parish, Louisiana loblolly pine by forest products industries in the southeast. Southern Journal of Applied Forestry 9(3):180–185.

Wells OO, Lambeth CC. 1983.   Loblolly pine provenance test in Southern Arkansas. Southern Journal of Applied Forestry 7(2):71–75.

Wells OO, Nance WL, Thielges BA. 1977.   Variation in needle traits in provenance tests of *Pinus taeda* and *P. echinata*. Silvae Genetica 26(4):125–130.

Wells OO, Switzer GL. 1971.   Variation in rust resistance in Mississippi loblolly pine. In: Proceedings, 11th Southern Forest Tree Improvement Conference; 1971 June 15–16; Atlanta, GA. Macon, GA: USDA Forest Service, Eastern Tree Seed Laboratory: 25–30.

Wells OO, Switzer GL, Schmidtling RC. 1991.   Geographic variation in Mississippi loblolly pine and sweetgum. Silvae Genetica 40(3/4):105–119.

Wells OO, Wakeley PC. 1966.   Geographic variation in survival, growth, and fusiform-rust infection of planted loblolly pine. Forest Science Monograph 11:1–40.

Wenger KF. 1958a.   Silvical characteristics of loblolly pine. Sta. Pap. 98. Asheville, NC: USDA Forest Service, Southeastern Forest Experiment Station. 32 p.

Wenger KF. 1958b.   Silvical characteristics of pond pine. Sta. Pap. 91. Asheville, NC: USDA Forest Service, Southeastern Forest Experiment Station. 13 p.

Wheeler NC, Bramlett DL. 1991.   Flower stimulation treatments in a loblolly pine seed orchard. Southern Journal of Applied Forestry 15(1):44–50.

White G, Lowe, William J, Wright J. 1983.   Paraffin grafting for loblolly pine. Southern Journal of Applied Forestry 7(3):116–118.

White G. Wright JA. 1987.   Wire girdles increase male flower production on young loblolly pine grafts. Tree Planters' Notes 38(3):33–35.

Wilcox MD, Smith HD. 1973.   Selection indices for wood quality in loblolly pine. In: Proceedings, 12th Southern Forest Tree Improvement Conference; 1973 June 12–13; Baton Rouge, LA. Baton Rouge, LA: Louisiana State University, Division of Continuing Education: 322–342.

Williams CG. 1987.   The influence of shoot ontogeny on juvenile-mature correlations in loblolly pine. Forest Science 33(2):411–422.

Williams CG. 1988.   Accelerated short-term genetic testing for loblolly pine families. Canadian Journal of Forest Research 18(8):1085–1089.

Wiselogel AE, van Buijtenen JP. 1988.   Probability of equal mating in polymix pollinations of loblolly pine (*Pinus taeda* L.). Silvae Genetica 37(5/6):184–187.

Wisniewski LA, Frampton LJ Jr, McKeand SE. 1986.   Early shoot and root quality effects on nursery and field development of tissue-cultured loblolly pine. Horticultural Science 21(5):1185–1186.

Wisniewski LA, McKeand SE, Amerson HV. 1987.   The effect of root pruning on the maturation of loblolly pine (*Pinus taeda*) tissue culture plantlets [abstract]. Plant Physiology 83(4):125.

Woessner RA. 1972a.   Crossing among loblolly pines indigenous to different areas as a means of genetic improvement. Silvae Genetica 21(1/2):35–39.

Woessner RA. 1972b.   Growth patterns of one-year-old loblolly pine seed sources and inter-provenance crosses under contrasting edaphic conditions. Forest Science 18(3):205–210.

Woessner RA, Davey CB, Crabtree BE, Gregory JD. 1975.   Nutrient content of the aboveground tissues of 12-week-old loblolly pine intraprovenance and interprovenance crosses. Canadian Journal of Forest Research 5:592–598.

Wynens JC. 1966.   Large scale seedbed grafting and seed orchard development. In: Proceedings, 8th Southern Forest Tree Improvement Conference; 1965 June 16–17; Savannah, GA. Macon, GA: Georgia Forest Research Council: 148–152.

Yeiser JL, van Buijtenen JP, Lowe W. 1981.   Genotype × environment interactions and seed movements for loblolly pine in the western Gulf region. Silvae Genetica 30(6):196–200.

Zarger TG. 1965.   Performance of loblolly, shortleaf, and eastern white pine superseedlings. Silvae Genetica 14:182–186.

Zobel B. 1972.   Three rings-per-inch, dense southern pine: can it be developed? Journal of Forestry 70(6):333–336.

Zobel B, Kellison R, Matthias M. 1969.   Genetic improvement in forest trees: growth rate and wood characteristics in young loblolly pine. In: Proceedings, 10th Southern Forest Tree Improvement Conference; 1969 June 17–19; Houston, TX. College Station, TX: Texas Forest Service, Texas A&M University: 59–75.

Zobel B, Talbert J. 1984.   Applied forest tree improvement. New York: John Wiley & Sons. 505 p.

Zobel B, Thorbjornsen E, Henson F. 1960.   Geographic, site and individual tree variation in wood properties of loblolly pine. Silvae Genetica 9(6):149–158.

Zobel BJ, Goddard RE, Cech FC. 1957.   Outstanding nursery seedlings. Res. Note 18. College Station, TX: Texas Forest Service, Texas A&M College; 1957. 14 p.

Zobel B. 1970.   Developing trees in the southeastern United States with wood qualities most desirable for paper. Journal of the Technical Association Pulp and Paper Industry 53(12):2320–2325.

Zobel B, Roberds JH. 1970.   Differential genetic response to fertilizers within tree species [abstract]. In: 1st North American Forest Biology Workshop; 1970 August 5–7; East Lansing, MI. East Lansing, MI: Michigan State University. 2 p.

Zoerb MH. 1969.   Clonal variation in time of cone ripening in loblolly pine. Woodl. Res. Note 22. Savannah, GA: Union Camp Corporation, Woodlands Research Department. 3 p.

Chapter 8

Stand Management

· · · · · · · · · · · **Contents** ·

Stand Management

Introduction

Loblolly pines can be managed successfully in pure natural stands or pure plantations, or mixed with short-leaf pines, other southern pines, or various hardwoods. Rotations of 25 to at least 120 years are practical, depending on management objectives. On moist, fertile sites where high-quality hardwoods can be grown successfully, conversion to pines is generally difficult, and costs frequently exceed the gain in value obtained by growing only pines. On such sites, it may be desirable to grow 250 to 500 well-spaced loblolly/ha with high-quality hardwoods.

Under optimum conditions, loblolly pines grow about 1.5 m in height per year between ages 5 and 10, which is the period of "grand growth." Height growth slows to about 0.9 m/yr between tree ages 10 and 15 and usually drops to about 0.6 m/yr between tree ages 15 and 35 (Kellison and Gingrich 1984). Thus, if stand culture does not begin until after a stand reaches age 10, the best opportunity to increase growth is lost. Earlywood of selected genotypes can have high density and adequate strength properties, and latewood of fast-growing trees can be as strong as that of slow-growing trees. For these reasons, managers should emphasize early and fast growth of the best trees.

Crown condition and tree vigor should always be assessed when evaluating stands for silvicultural treatment. Crown condition can be estimated visually, determined as a proportion of biomass weight in the crown (Newbold 1984), or determined through leaf area estimates (Zedaker 1983). Crown condition reflects the effect of environmental influences and competitive relations on branch and shoot development and on the number, length, and retention of needles and is a good general indicator of tree and stand vigor. A sparse crown usually means poor growth. Rates of height and diameter growth are also good indicators of present vigor and can usually be determined quickly in young stands.

Equipment needs for stand management depend on the condition of the stand, difficulty of site access, and maneuverability on the terrain. Most available equipment has evolved from agricultural or forest harvesting machines. Generally, equipment must be stable on slopes, sturdy enough to traverse stumps and rocks, and narrow enough to pass between rows of planted trees without damaging them. It must have low ground pressure so that it can operate in wet areas without causing excessive soil compaction or puddling. The prime mover should be inexpensive and capable of traveling on roads.

Competition Control

Growth of loblolly pines from seedling stage to maturity, in naturally or artificially regenerated stands, is usually affected by competing vegetation. Competition from other vegetation increases with decreases in pine stocking. Some competition helps loblolly maintain good form and keeps branches small, but too much competition affects growth negatively. The greatest reduction in growth usually occurs where young stands of loblolly are in severe competition with other plant species. Although loblolly responds in both diameter and height growth when competing vegetation is controlled, diameter growth increases most. Competition occurs when the immediate supply of light, water, and/or nutrients is less than demand. Competition can occur below ground,

above ground, or both. Belowground competition, especially for moisture, has the greatest impact on seedling growth during the first 2 years (Carter and others 1984, Morris and Moss 1989, Zutter and others 1986).

For maximum biological benefit, cultural treatments should begin as soon as competition begins to slow loblolly pine height growth. This may be as early as seedling germination for direct-seeded or naturally regenerated trees (Hatchell 1964). A stand of at least 1,000 well-spaced pines/ha after the third growing season is satisfactorily stocked for most purposes. Early and total elimination of all competing vegetation (herbaceous and woody) provides the best conditions for survival and growth of young loblolly pines. However, par-

Figure 8-1—Bole damage to loblolly pine by grape vines.

forest site. There are problems with competing vegetation in about 53 to 60% of the loblolly and mixed pine–hardwood stands during the intermediate growth period (Fitzgerald and others 1973). Controlling this vegetation is difficult because of the diversity of species and plant cover present. Herbaceous vegetation constitutes the severest competition in many newly established stands. However, shrubs and unwanted trees are the major competitors for most of the life cycle of loblolly. Vines usually present the least serious problem, but they can degrade individual trees severely (figure 8-1). Vines are generally most severe in mixed pine-hardwood stands because they usually grow on moist and more fertile sites. The success of vegetation management depends on identifying, evaluating, and selectively controlling only those species providing substantial competition to loblolly crop trees.

Controlling Herbaceous Vegetation

Herbaceous vegetation has its greatest negative effect on loblolly pines during the first few years in the life of a stand (Cain 1988, Miller and others 1987, Morris and Moss 1989). Grasses and forbs reduce the early growth of loblolly more than do juvenile hardwoods (Ayers and others 1987, Cain 1988, Miller and others 1987). Herbaceous competition reaches a peak about 3 to 4 years after a stand has been established, then it gradually diminishes as the pine canopy closes. Depending on the concentration of vegetation, vegetation control can increase loblolly survival by 10 to 30% and increase height and volume growth by as much as 100% during the first 5 years of loblolly's life (Fitzgerald and others 1973, Hansen and Johnson 1974, Knowe and others 1985, Smith and Schmidtling 1970, Tiarks and Haywood 1986). Complete herbaceous weed control is not necessary to promote excellent growth of loblolly (Haywood 1988).

Although herbaceous weed control can promote tree growth if done during the first 5 years of a stand, this growth advantage may not last for an entire rotation. Cultivation (disking and mowing) for the first 5 years in a south Mississippi plantation significantly increased tree growth up to tree age 9, but the advantage had disappeared by tree age 17 (Schmidtling 1985, 1987). Fertilization can promote the development of heavy herbaceous competition and thus retard rather than accelerate the growth of young loblolly pines. Rodent predation of young seedlings and the hazard of grass fires also increase as the level of herbaceous competition increases.

Herbaceous weed control can be especially important in newly regenerated natural stands where density and stocking of loblolly seedlings are inadequate or only marginally adequate. Temporarily controlling herbaceous competition can permit further seedling establishment if an adequate seed source is available. Where the seed source has been removed and additional natural regeneration is not possible, a marginally stocked natural

tial competition control can be as effective as complete control (Bacon and Zedaker 1985, 1987).

The early development, stocking, and competitive status of new plantations should be evaluated by the end of the third growing season. Visual estimates are unsatisfactory, but aerial photographs may reduce the amount of field work needed (Smith and others 1989). Competition control at the end of the second growing season increases loblolly pine growth more than does competition control at age 3 (Bacon and Zedaker 1986). Thus, if there is a reasonable assurance that good survival at age 2 will continue, competition control should be done at this time. Normally, competition control treatments should not be applied at the end of the first growing season; severe drought or weevil damage can substantially reduce stocking and even destroy a stand during the second or third growing season. In the case of natural regeneration, new seedlings often become established over a 3- to 5-year period, so it may not be possible to evaluate the need for competition control until 5 years have passed. After about age 4 to 5, a well-stocked loblolly stand begins inhibiting competition from below. By age 7, loblolly usually dominates a site.

It is nearly impossible, and is normally neither environmentally nor economically feasible, to eradicate all competing vegetation, especially hardwood trees, on a

Table 8-1—Number of competing plants by predominant species group and type of treatment following annual hardwood control from plantation age 1 through 6 on a north Louisiana site

Predominant species group	Stems/ha		
	No control	Top control*	Top and root control†
Hardwood trees			
Sweetgum (*Liquidambar styraciflua*)	2,928	5,491	823
Oaks (*Quercus* spp.)	1,922	2,380	1,463
Others (*Acer rubrum, Carya* spp., *Cornus florida, Diospyros virginiana, Nyssa sylvatica, Sassafras albidum*)	4,025	3,020	1,463
Subtotal	8,876	10,890	3,749
Hardwood shrubs			
Shining sumac (*Rhus copillina*)	9,427	9,518	2,928
American beautyberry (*Callicarpa americana*)	3,020	6,133	2,197
Others (*Crataegus* spp., *Ilex vomitoria, Myrica cerifera, Vaccinium* spp.)	6,042	5,582	4,574
Subtotal	18,488	21,233	9,699
Vinelike vegetation			
Vines (*Gelsemium sempervirens, Lonicera japonica, Vitis* spp.)	13,605	27,823	22,424
Briars (*Rubus* spp., *Smilax* spp.)	11,349	19,677	27,732
Subtotal	24,955	47,500	50,156
Total	52,318	79,623	63,604

Source: adapted from Cain and Mann (1980).

* All woody stems were cut 15 cm above the ground with handtools during six successive summers.

† Hardwood tops were cut as in top control treatment and fresh-cut stumps were brushed with undiluted 2, 4-D amine the first year. During the next three summers, tops were cut and part of the roots were removed by grubbing. In the summer of the sixth growing season, a mixture of 2, 4-D and 2, 4, 5-T in water was sprayed at a rate of 5.6 kg/ha to nonselectively reduce regrowth of all competing vegetation. No pines were killed by this treatment.

stand of 500 to 750 fairly well spaced trees/ha can be satisfactory if herbaceous competition is quickly removed to minimize pine seedling mortality (Cain 1988).

Controlling Woody Vegetation

Loblolly pines often must compete with a wide variety of hardwoods and shrubs before crown closure, especially when there has been no vegetation control before regeneration. Plantations frequently contain 12,500 or more woody stems/ha at 3 to 5 years after establishment on cleared, cultivated sites. Growth of young loblolly is inversely related to the amount of this competition (Glover and Creighton 1985, Langdon and Trousdell 1974, Williston 1962). Large hardwoods provide more aboveground and belowground competition than an equal basal area of small hardwoods. The kind and number of control treatments necessary to suppress these competitors depend on the site and on the species, which vary in their ability to sprout. The most common competitors include sweetgum; blackgum; flowering dogwood, *Cornus florida* L.; red maple; American holly; sourwood, *Oxydendrum arboreum* (L.) DC.; most oaks; waxmyrtle; gallberry; fetterbush, *Lyonia lucida* (Lam.) K. Koch; blueberry, *Vaccinium* spp.; blackberry; and sweet pepperbush, *Clethra alnifolia* L. Many of these competitors sprout prolifically from basal dormant buds or roots when top-killed (table 8-1). They must be top-killed repeatedly before their numbers and size decline substantially (figure 8-2). Trying to eliminate all woody plants is economically impractical and ecologically unsound. However, annual summer burning for 10 or more years kills most woody plants (Brender and Cooper 1968, Langdon 1981, Lotti and others 1960, Waldrop and others 1987). Hardwood shrubs can severely retard growth of young loblolly pines even at densities as low as 5 stems/m^2 (Neary 1988).

To be most effective, hardwood control should begin soon after planting or natural regeneration so that pine mortality is minimized and young trees do not lose their potential for rapid early growth (Grano 1965). Treatment expense is also least at this time. Young pines usually can be visually categorized as (1) free to grow without hardwood competition; (2) free to grow but receiving side shade from hardwood com-

Figure 8-2—Burning at 3- to 5-year intervals has kept this 40- to 50-year-old naturally regenerated loblolly pine stand nearly free of hardwood competition.

petition; (3) having questionable growth potential; and (4) not free to grow based on their size and vigor and the size, vigor, and species of nearby hardwoods (or other pines). Control prescriptions should provide for repeated treatments as necessary so that young pines can maintain a height advantage and dominate the site. Removing competing vegetation stimulates pine growth more on good sites than on poor sites. It may not be economical to release trees growing on some low-quality sites (Guldin 1985).

Understory hardwoods can constitute an important component of loblolly pine stands more than 40 years old. Understory hardwood biomass can range from less than 10 to more than 50 tonnes per hectare (t/ha) depending on the intensity of management. Control of understory hardwoods may (Cain and Yaussy 1984, Grano 1970a) or may not (Cain 1985b, Klawitter 1966, McClay 1955, Russell 1961) increase growth of maturing or mature trees depending on stand age and stocking, level of competition, and site and environmental conditions. Hardwoods under mature stands should be controlled to increase pine growth only on sites where there is clear evidence that economic gains can be expected.

On dry sites, there is little difficulty in maintaining the dominance of loblolly pine, even though establishment is difficult. On sites where soil moisture is less limiting, competition from hardwoods, shrubs, and annual plants normally begins early in a rotation and continues to intensify. Removal of understory vegetation increases evaporation from the litter and soil surface under loblolly stands, but this loss is more than compensated for by reduced transpiration. Boyer (1987) suggests that understory hardwoods below a site-dependent threshold density (2.3 to 6.9 m^2 of basal area/ha) may have no discernible effect on growth of the pine overstory. Burkhart and Sprinz (1984) developed a model for predicting hardwood competition effects on yields of loblolly plantations on cutover and oldfield sites across the range of the species. The model predicts a distinct reduction in average tree size as hardwood basal area increases from 20 to 40% of the stand total (figure 8-3).

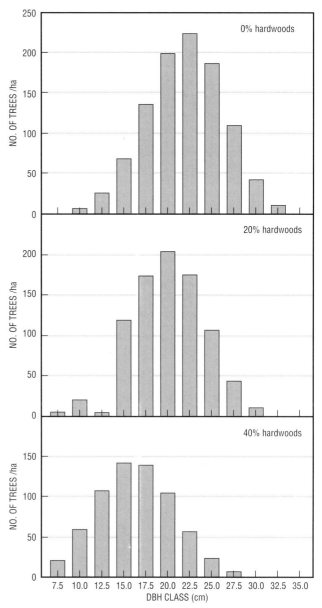

Figure 8-3—Diameter breast height (dbh) distribution of 30-year-old planted loblolly pines with 1,975 trees/ha planted on site index 18 m (base age 25 years) with varying levels of hardwood basal area (adapted from Burkhart and Sprinz 1984).

Vegetation Control Techniques

Unwanted vegetation can be controlled with machines, handtools, fire, or herbicides. Herbicides are usually the most effective in the long run because sprouting is limited when they are used. Fire is usually the cheapest method of controlling vegetation, but it is also effective for the shortest length of time. Mechanical treatments are especially effective in young natural stands because they improve spacing and create accessibility for equipment into the stand.

Hand or Mechanical Pine Release

Removal of unwanted vegetation with handtools is very effective on small tracts, especially if the landowner does not regard personal labor as a cost. Mechanical treatments include disking, chopping, and mowing in one or two directions between plantation rows. In young natural stands, mechanical vegetation control treatments can be used in conjunction with precommercial thinning.

Large unwanted hardwoods that survive site preparation can be girdled or felled depending on species, tree age, and season of the year. Unwanted trees are least likely to sprout if girdled or felled in summer.

Removal of hardwood trees and shrubs when pines are about 2 to 5 years old can increase average loblolly pine size by as much as 40 to 80% during the first 10 to 20 years of stand life. Manual and mechanical vegetation control treatments often increase the numbers of competing stems by inducing vigorous stump and root sprouting. However, if treatments are timed properly, loblolly can often stay ahead of this regrowth. Growth of shrubs and vines is also promoted by mechanical or manual hardwood control (Cain and Mann 1980; Dierauf 1986a, 1986b, 1986c, 1986d; Haywood 1986). If mechanical hardwood control is not done under very wet conditions, it results in little or no environmental degradation. However, it is often very costly, and injury to pine crop trees can increase fusiform rust incidence in young stands by 150 to 300% (Hunt and Cleveland 1978).

Pine Release With Fire

Wildfire has always played an important role in perpetuating loblolly pines. Controlled fires can effect some of the same changes as wildfire without extensive site or environmental damage. As many as 1 million ha of established pine stands are burned annually (primarily in the Coastal Plain) to control understory hardwood, shrub, and herbaceous species (figure 8-4); reduce the hazard of wildfire; and improve wildlife habitat (Mobley and Balmer 1981). Properly conducted prescribed burning inexpensively and effectively maintains loblolly as a dominant species throughout much of its range, without eliminating hardwoods or other plant species important to the ecological diversity of southern forests. Well-managed winter or summer prescribed fire does not increase

or decrease the growth of a loblolly stand (Grano 1970b, Waldrop and others 1987, Wenger and Trousdell 1958). However, very intense prescribed fires may reduce growth, possibly by physically damaging surface soil.

Controlled burns at 3- to 5-year intervals throughout a rotation keep the amount of combustible material at a low level. This limits the annual probability of destructive wildfire to less than 0.2%, as opposed to 7.0% when fuel accumulates for more than 5 years (Wade and Lunsford 1989). Also, prescribed burning can kill shrubs and hardwood trees up to 7.5 cm in diameter at breast height (dbh), thus modifying the composition, amount, and size of understory vegetation and improving stand access, which makes thinnings and final harvesting easier and more economical. The effect of prescribed burning on loblolly pine succession depends on the frequency, intensity, and season of burning and on the type and amount of vegetative competition. Because loblolly grows well on a wide range of sites and grows in association with many hardwood trees and shrubs, the use of fire in pine stands must be tempered by local environmental conditions. Proven methods of prescription burning in established pine stands include backfiring (burning into the wind), strip-head firing (line fire), spot firing, and flank firing (Johansen 1987, Wade and Lunsford 1989).

Loblolly pines less than 5 years old can be killed even by low-intensity fires if their crowns are scorched severely or if their thin bark does not protect their cortical tissues. As saplings increase in height and diameter, they quickly develop resistance to fire. By the time trees reach 3 to 5 m in height and about 7 cm in dbh, their crowns are above the reach of low surface fires, and they have developed bark thick enough to insulate them from heat that kills associated hardwoods of the same size. Extreme caution must be taken when first burning young stands; accumulations of dead needles in the tops of shrubs and small trees and on lower branches of crop trees can form

Figure 8-4—A loblolly pine stand before (**a**) and after (**b**) thinning and release with fire (USDA Forest Service Collection, National Agricultural Library).

Figure 8-5—Fire can quickly destroy entire stands of trees if crowns are totally consumed (USDA Forest Service Collection, National Agricultural Library).

a ladder that conducts fire into the crowns of crop trees (figure 8-5). However, even trees less than 4 m tall and with groundline diameters less than 5 cm can survive low-intensity backfires if their crowns are not scorched severely (Cain 1983, Greene and Shilling 1987, Waldrop and Lloyd 1987). Initially, a low-intensity winter backfire should be used in both plantations and natural stands to reduce fuel levels. If the first fire does not reduce fuel loads to safe levels, it may be necessary to apply a second backfire the following year. Once the fuel level has been reduced to an acceptable level, head fires can be used successfully in plantations averaging 7.5 m or more in height and 9 cm or more in diameter, with crown closure of 75% (Jackson 1974). Alternatively, backfires can be applied at regular 3- to 5-year intervals. Repeat burning generally should be withheld until just before the largest hardwood sprouts that originated after the previous fire become too large to be top-killed by fire (Chen and others 1975). This should give a 2- to 4-year burning interval that also provides sufficient time for the litter layer to build enough to support an acceptably hot and uniform fire. Burning to control less than about 2.3 m² of hardwood basal area/ha usually cannot be justified.

Good prescribed backfires under a loblolly pine stand are dependent on a uniform pine needle litter or grass understory for fuel and very specific environmental conditions. The wind speed inside the stand should be 1.5 to 5 km/hr (measured at eye level) for most fuel and topographic situations, and the wind should be expected to persist for the duration of the burn. The temperature should be below 16 °C, relative humidity between 30 and 55%, fine-fuel moisture between 10 and 20%, and the lower duff and soil moist from a recent soaking rain (Wade and Lunsford 1989). Topography strongly influences wind movement, especially in mountainous areas. Upslope fires generally burn as head fires, whereas downslope fires burn as backfires (York and Buckner

1983). Fuel should be ignited on the tops of ridges, and fires should be permitted to "back" down the slopes. Times required to burn a particular area can differ by a factor of 8, depending on the type of burn, fuel, slope percentage, and wind speed (de Bruyn and Buckner 1981).

Newly established stands can be protected from wildfire for the first 8 to 10 years by surrounding them with older stands in a checkerboard fashion. The older stands are prescribe-burned regularly, and thus provide a fuel-depleted buffer around all sides of a young stand. Regular maintenance of fire lines is also important and is often critical along roadsides, where many wildfires start.

Effects of prescribed fire. If continued for a decade or longer, regular burning can kill 60 to 95% of trees of most hardwood species under a loblolly pine overstory. Annual summer burns produce results fastest (figures 8-6, 8-7, and 8-8). The few individual trees that are not killed by regular summer fires (mainly sweetgum, but also blackgum and oaks) survive only as stems less than 2.5 cm in dbh (Waldrop and others 1987). Although less effective than summer burns, winter burns at annual or other regular intervals keep most hardwood sprouts and shrubs small (Lewis and Harshbarger 1976). Fewer unwanted trees will be killed by fire as they increase in size.

Figure 8-6—Few competing plants under a loblolly–shortleaf pine stand remain after nine annual burns (Grano 1970b).

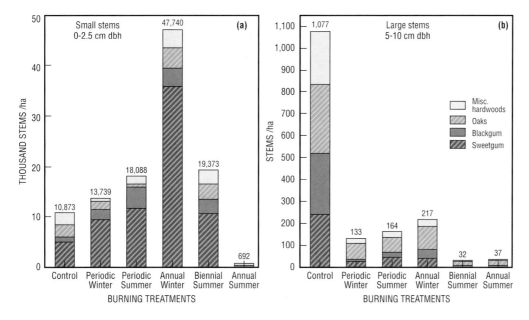

Figure 8-7—Effects of 30 years of fire treatments in a South Carolina Coastal Plain loblolly pine plantation on the numbers of small (**a**) and large (**b**) hardwood trees (adapted from Langdon 1981).

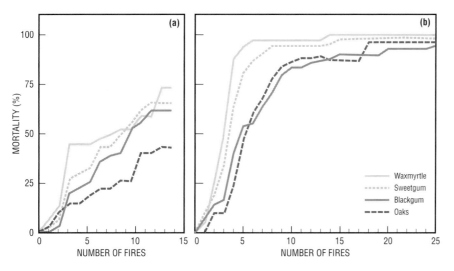

Figure 8-8—Relationship between mortality of species competing with loblolly pines and number of biennial (**a**) and annual (**b**) fires (adapted from Langdon 1981).

Fire intensity. Duration and intensity of the fire are critical factors when burning. Plant tissue is killed when specific time-temperature combinations are reached. More small hardwoods and other vegetation are likely to be killed as fire intensity increases. The susceptibility of loblolly pines to fire also varies with fire intensity. Fire intensity is the rate of energy release per unit length of fire front per unit of time (kJ/m/s) (Byram 1959, Rothermel and Deeming 1980). Flame height is estimated visually. In relatively young stands, fire intensity can be estimated indirectly by measuring the height of stem-bark char, height of crown scorch, and subsequent needle cast (Cain 1984, McNab 1977, Waldrop and Van Lear 1984). Fire intensity can be predicted before a fire by estimating aboveground fuel weight (Reeves and Lenhart 1988). Loblolly

pines with groundline diameters of 30 to 40 mm can tolerate a backfire with an intensity less than 80 kJ/m/s. Trees with groundline diameters of at least 50 mm can tolerate a backfire with an intensity less than 98 kJ/m/s (Greene and Shilling 1987).

Crown scorch is the principal cause of loblolly pine mortality following fire, especially when trees are less than 2.4 m tall. Mortality results when flames are concentrated around the live crown or when convection increases temperatures in the crown to at least 60 °C. Because ambient temperatures are higher in the summer than in other seasons, a lethal temperature is produced much more easily in the summer (Wade 1985, Wade and Lunsford 1989). Needles that are yellow or bronze immediately after a fire have been killed. Charring or partial consumption of needles shows that an ignition temperature of about 232 °C was reached. Saplings defoliated at any time of the year, without other injury, refoliate and may even grow while totally defoliated (table 8-2). Tree mortality results when buds, twigs, and needles are killed. Crown scorch during the growing season is generally more damaging than crown scorch during the dormant season, at least partly because growing season scorch kills developing buds and growing tips as well as needles.

Growth loss and mortality of trees (ages 1 to 9) can be predicted within a few days after fire, based on the

Table 8-2—Three-month growth response in diameter at breast height (dbh) and height of 4-year-old, planted loblolly pines by location and level of defoliation (0 to 100%) during early April

Location	dbh (%)*					Height (%)*				
	0%	33%	66%	95%	100%	0%	33%	66%	95%	100%
Bainbridge, GA	100	79	70	47	34	100	100	94	67	53
Branchville, SC	100	82	65	40	32	100	102	77	59	38

Source: adapted from Wade and Johansen (1987).

* Expressed as a percentage of the growth of trees with no defoliation.

amount of crown scorch and needle consumption and the terminal leader condition. Scorching that affects no more than 60% of the crown has little effect on the survival of young trees. Only about half of the trees with 90% crown scorch survive. Very little of the foliage is actually consumed until about 90% of the crown is scorched. Once foliage consumption exceeds 40%, there is only a 20% chance that a tree will live (Waldrop and Lloyd 1988; figures 8-9 and 8-10). Diameter growth and height growth of saplings are negatively correlated with intensity of crown scorch for the first year after burning (Cain 1985c). Young loblolly pines rarely sprout from the root collar once their tops have been deadened by fire.

Trees 20 cm in dbh and larger can probably have as much as 60% severe crown scorch with less than 10% mortality. When crown scorch is 90% or more, about 20% of dominants and codominants and 35% of intermediate trees are killed (Allen 1960, Mann and Gunter 1960, Villarrubia and Chambers 1978, Waldrop and Van Lear 1984). If crown scorch does not exceed one-third of the live crown of a healthy tree, growth loss is negligible. When 80% or more of the crown of a large tree is scorched, diameter growth is reduced for the following 2 to 4 years (Lilieholm and Hu 1987, Tew and others 1989).

Death of the cambium at the base of the tree is the second commonest cause of pine mortality following fire (Mann and Gunter 1960, Wade 1985). Summer burns, which move through stands slowly, are more likely than winter burns to create temperatures high enough to damage bole tissue (Hodgkins and Whipple 1963). Also, if there is a large amount of debris around the base of a tree, fire can result in high temperatures for long periods at any time of the year, and tree death or severe damage can occur. Mortality is highest for loblolly pines having groundline diameters less than 5 cm (Cain 1985c). Trees larger than 10 cm in dbh usually are not killed by the heat of backfires or small head fires (Cooper and Altobellis 1969).

The height of bark char is an indirect indication of fire intensity in sapling and pole stands (figure 8-11). Fire intensity is low if height of bark char is 1 m or less, medium if char height is 1.2 to 1.8 m, and high if char height is greater than 1.8 m. If the base of the live crown is within 7.5 m of the ground, a fire that chars bark

to a height of 2.4 to 2.7 m can be expected to consume many needles and to cause a 5- to 10% reduction in growth the following year. However, if the height of bole char is not more than about 2.1 m and if crown scorch does not exceed one-third of the live crown, tree mortality should be nearly zero and growth loss negligible (Waldrop and Van Lear 1984). Indirectly estimating fire intensity by bark char is not useful in older stands because crowns are too high to be affected by most fires, and bark char often lasts for several years, making accurate measurements of the most recent char difficult (Cain 1984).

Effects of fire on the forest floor and surface soil. Low-intensity prescribed burning for hazard reduction and vegetation control does not consume all the forest floor under a pine stand and does not have a negative impact on the soil or nutritional level of a forest site or on the growth of loblolly pines even when continued for 30 to 65 years (McKee 1987, Waldrop and others 1987). Controlled fires reduce organic matter in the forest floor (primarily in the litter, or L, layer) by 10 to 50% while increasing organic matter in the surface 15 cm of soil (Jorgensen and Wells 1986; figure 8-12 and table 8-3). Organic matter consistently builds up faster in mineral soil on burned areas than in mineral soil on unburned areas (Jorgensen and Wells 1986; McKee 1982, 1987; McKee and Lewis 1983; Moehring and others 1966). The protective mat of unburned litter on the forest floor reduces the effect of raindrop impact and minimizes soil erosion and plugging of soil macropores (Waldrop and others 1987). As fire intensity increases, a larger portion of the forest floor is consumed. Generally, smaller percentages

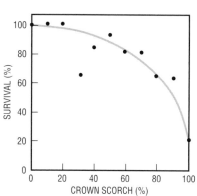

Figure 8-9—Survival of young, planted loblolly pines as a function of crown scorch (adapted from Wade 1985).

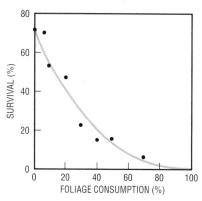

Figure 8-10—Relationship of foliage consumption to first postfire growing-season survival of 1- to 8-year-old, plantation-grown loblolly pines (adapted from Wade 1985).

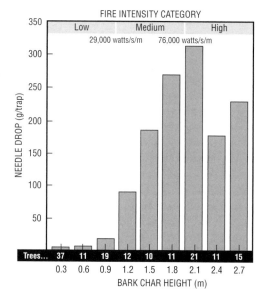

Figure 8-11—Bark char height and fire intensity relationship to needle drop 3 weeks after burning. Number of trees indicates the sample size for each bark char height (adapted from Waldrop and Van Lear 1984).

Table 8-3—Average weights of forest floor component in 12- to 17-year-old loblolly pine plantations before and after a single, prescribed, strip head fire

Forest floor component	Weight (kg/ha)		
	Preburn	Postburn*	Reduction
L layer	8,875	3,581	5,294[†]
F+H layer	24,745	23,350	1,396
Branches and miscellaneous debris	2,636	2,481	156
Total	36,257	29,411	6,845

Source: adapted from Kodama and Van Lear (1980).

* Postburn values are from paired samples taken adjacent to preburn samples.

[†] Significant difference at the 95% probability level.

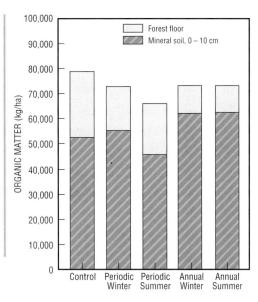

Figure 8-12—Organic matter in the forest floor and mineral soil after 30 years of prescribed burning under natural loblolly pines in the South Carolina Coastal Plain (adapted from McKee 1982, figure was redrawn by Waldrop and others 1987).

Table 8-4—Quantities of nutrients in forest floor layers of four 12- to 17-year-old South Carolina loblolly pine plantations before and after a single prescribed fire

Nutrient and time sample was taken	L layer		F+H layer	
	Amt. (kg/ha)	Change (%)	Amt. (kg/ha)	Change (%)
Nitrogen				
Preburn	56.9		294.0	
Postburn	31.0	–45*	275.0	–6
Phosphorus				
Preburn	7.1		19.0	
Postburn	3.0	–57*	20.9	+10
Potassium				
Preburn	18.0		42.0	
Postburn	7.1	–61*	41.0	–2
Calcium				
Preburn	38.0		89.9	
Postburn	17.0	–55*	99.0	+10
Magnesium				
Preburn	15.0		26.0	
Postburn	5.0	–66*	26.9	+3

Source: adapted from Kodama and Van Lear (1980).

* Significant difference at the 95% probability level.

of the forest floor are consumed by fire as the ratio of hardwood litter to pine litter increases because hardwood leaves form compacted layers that restrict air movement and remain wet longer than do layers of pine litter (Brender and Cooper 1968).

Burning results in changes in the surface soil pH and movement of available nutrients from the organic layer into the surface soil. Regular prescribed burning retards soil weathering and increases pH in the surface 10 to 15 cm of soil by up to 0.9 units. It also increases the amounts of available phosphorus (P), calcium (Ca), and magnesium (Mg) in the surface soil by factors of 2 to 20. In the absence of burning, up to 60% of the total Ca in the forest floor can be immobilized, leading to nutrient imbalance and accelerated soil weathering over the long term (Binkley 1986, Lewis 1974, Linnartz and others 1984, McKee 1982, McKee and Lewis 1983, McKevlin and McKee 1986, Waldrop and others 1987, Wells 1971).

Partial consumption of the forest floor and understory plants by fire volatilizes significant amounts of nitrogen (N) and can immobilize some of the remaining N if the ratio of carbon (C) to N is increased. Nitrogen losses have been estimated to range from 20 to 112 kg/ha (Bell and Binkley 1989, Van Lear and others 1983, Wells 1971). In one case, the percentage of nutrients lost from the L layer (60%) was approximately the same as the percentage of litter consumed by fire (table 8-4). The amount of volatilization increases as fire intensity increases (Jorgensen and Wells 1986, Lewis 1974, Wells 1971). Burning can convert a small amount of organic N to ammonia, which in turn can be absorbed by the soil. Increases in symbiotic and nonsymbiotic N fixation following prescribed burning may partially or totally offset the loss to volatilization. The amount of N fixed by legumes and other higher plants can range from a few to more than 110 kg/ha/yr, depending on plant density and growth environment. Fixation of N by free-living soil microorganisms ranges from about 1.1 to 14 kg/ha/yr in burned

areas and is less than 0.6 kg/ha/yr in unburned areas (Jorgensen and Wells 1986). Decomposition of the forest floor after a burn may release some N, in effect fertilizing a stand (Schoch and Binkley 1986). Prescribed burning does not reduce the effectiveness of fertilizer treatments applied as late as 6 months before burning (Mollitor and others 1983).

Prescribed burning can cause secondary losses of nutrients from the L layer. Air currents can remove ash, erosion can be increased, and leaching of more available or more soluble forms of elements can be increased. Where sites are good to excellent, the quantities lost do not appear to be significant if only a portion of the L layer and none of the fermentation (F) and humus (H) layers are consumed (Brender and Cooper 1968, Cushwa and others 1971, Lewis 1974, Ralston and Hatchell 1971, Richter and others 1982, Wells 1971). However, on marginal sites where inherent fertility may limit productivity, repeated burning at intervals of less than 5 years might eventually result in decreased productivity (Kodama and Van Lear 1980). Very steep slopes with thin topsoil are generally too fragile to tolerate burning, and any loss of soil through erosion can seriously degrade these sites.

Controlled burning causes little heating of the surface soil and has little effect on soil physical properties (Moehring and others 1966, Ralston and others 1983). Minor increases in bulk density and reduced surface soil aggregation disappear within 4 years (Bower 1966). Burning has little if any effect on populations of soil microorganisms, but annual burning can reduce the numbers of bacteria and actinomycetes in the F and H layers (Berry 1970, Jorgensen and Hodges 1970). Under some conditions, fire can promote the development of the parasitic weed *Seymeria cassioides* (J.F. Gmel.) Blake, which reduces the growth of, and sometimes kills, loblolly and other southern pines (see chapter 10).

Pine Release With Herbicides

The use of herbicides to reduce competing vegetation in loblolly pine stands can be very cost effective, and treatment results can usually be quantified within a few years. Herbicides are usually very effective in controlling large and small hardwood competitors, herbaceous weeds, and scattered infestations of pests such as privet, kudzu, and Japanese honeysuckle (Cain 1985a, Edwards and Gonzalez 1986, McLemore 1981, Micheal 1984). Many of the herbicide formulations appropriate for site preparation (see chapter 4) are also effective for pine release. In the late 1980's, glyphosate (Roundup® and Accord®), hexazinone (Velpar® and Pronone®), dichlorprop (Weedone®), triclopyr (Garlon®) (Edwards and Miller 1988), and imazapyr (Arsenal® AC) herbicides were labeled for forestry use in all states. Application of these herbicides on loblolly more than 2 years old results in only minor needle damage (Campbell 1985a, Fitzgerald and others 1980, Fitzgerald and Griswold 1984). If they are used repeatedly and in large quantities, chemicals can markedly reduce plant species diversity (Swindel and others 1989). However, once chemicals are discontinued, both the number and diversity of hardwood species will increase under pine stands (Cain and Yaussy 1983, 1984).

Any release herbicide can kill loblolly pines or stunt their growth if applied at rates or in concentrations that are too high. However, controlled-release formulations can be applied at rates that are higher than normal to extend the effective life of herbicides without being excessively phytotoxic to loblolly. The tolerance of loblolly to herbicides is also influenced by uniformity of herbicide application, season of the year, soil texture, and tree age, condition, vigor, and stage of growth (Minogue and others 1985). For example, the probability that a herbicide will kill loblolly increases as temperature increases. Similarly, dry conditions following application can delay or minimize effects of granular herbicides because chemical action cannot begin until rain dissolves the granules and material is absorbed by the target vegetation. For all of these reasons, effects on target species are inconsistent and nontarget species are often killed or injured.

A disadvantage of some herbicides is that application just before planting can injure or kill seedlings. Even the correct application may be toxic to seedlings initially (Haywood 1980). However, delaying planting for 2 months after herbicide treatment can eliminate this problem (McLemore 1988).

Herbaceous weed control. Competing weeds and grasses can be controlled and pine survival and growth increased by broadcast, spot, or band spraying selected herbicide mixtures around or directly over the tops of young loblolly pines. Growth increases are proportional to the size of the area treated with herbicide when spot treatments are used (Dougherty and Lowery 1991). Spot sprays should be applied in a circular area 1.2 to 1.5 m across with a pine in the center. The best time of application is usually March through June— before weeds are 15 cm tall. Resulting growth increases in young loblolly can be attributed to increased availability of water for use in physiological processes (Zutter and others 1986). At the western limit of loblolly's range, competition control may be the only means of maintaining satisfactory stands of young loblolly when drought stress is severe or on sites with well-established herbaceous cover (Voth 1987). Commonly used herbicides and

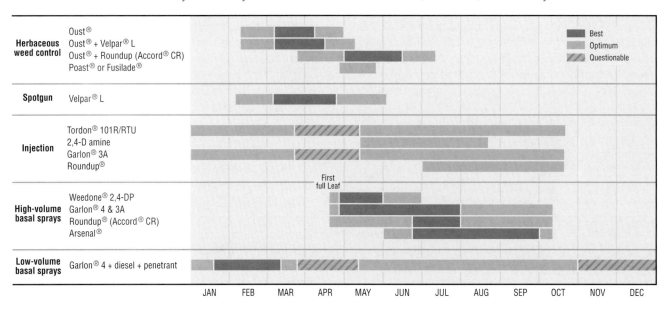

Figure 8-13—Approximate optimum time periods for herbicide applications for the upper Coastal Plain (adapted from Miller and Bishop 1989). Going from the Coastal Plain to the mountains, spring periods of application will be later (a shift to the right) because of later frost in the mountains and fall dates will be earlier (a shift to the left) because of earlier frost.

application periods are listed in figure 8-13.

Treatments for controlling herbaceous weeds should reduce competition to a level that economically improves survival and growth of young stands, while preserving enough vegetative cover to prevent significant soil erosion and to provide adequate food and cover for wildlife (see chapter 9).

Woody vegetation control.   Tree injection, basal bark spray, foliar spray, and soil applications of chemicals are all effective ways to kill hardwoods without damaging loblolly pines severely. Application is the same as for site preparation (see chapter 4) except that rates for soil spot application are much lower for vegetation control than for site preparation. Herbicides seem to affect hardwoods more when there is little moisture stress and when wind velocity is low. High-volume basal bark spray treatments with chemicals such as dichlorprop or triclopyr top-kill more than 95% of oaks, sweetgum, dogwood, and red maple throughout the year (Yeiser and McLemore 1986). Controlling hardwoods with mistblown herbicides during the pine sapling stage can increase loblolly volume by up to 90% at rotation age depending on the severity of hardwood competition and on site conditions (Dierauf 1986a, 1986b, 1986c, 1986d). However, because environmental contamination is possible, mistblown herbicides must be used carefully.

Spraying the foliage of competing hardwoods and other woody vegetation is effective in releasing 1- and 2-year-old loblolly pines (Yeiser and others 1987, Zutter and others 1988). Liquid herbicides are most effective when applied with a backpack sprayer. When low herbicide concentrations (0.3 to 2.0%) are used, the growing tips as well as the foliage of target vegetation should be sprayed. More concentrated mixtures (3.0 to 4.0%) generally require less wetting and coverage to be effective. Established loblolly seedlings and saplings are tolerant to aerial sprays of glyphosate at rates up to 1.7 kg of active ingredient (ai)/ha (Larsen and others 1983). They tolerate broadcast or banded hexazinone at rates up to 3 kg ai/ha (Fitzgerald and others 1976, Griswold 1981). Currently recommended herbicides, spray mixtures, and preferred application periods for release of young pines by directed foliar spray are listed in table 8-5.

Table 8-5—Application rate and time period for pine release herbicides

Herbicide	Application rate in water (%)	Time of application
Imazapyr (Arsenal® AC)	0.5	June–October
Trichlopyr amine (Garlon® 3A)	2–5	April–October
Trichlopyr ester (Garlon® 4)	2–4	April–October
Glyphosate (Roundup® or Accord® CR)	1–2	August–October
Dichlorprop (Weedone® 2,4-DP)	4–5	April–early June

Source: adapted from Edwards and Miller (1988).

Banded applications of liquid or granular herbicides are especially effective for controlling hardwood brush in plantations on a wide variety of sites because the herbicide is concentrated on only about 10 to 20% of the total ground area near the trees that require release (Griswold and Gonzalez 1985, Miller and Andrews 1985, Yeiser and others 1987). However, soil-applied hexazinone inhibits photosynthesis in loblolly pines and kills some pines, especially when the chemical is applied within 8 cm of newly planted seedlings (Griswold 1981, Karr and Janzen 1985, Sung and others 1982). Once pines become well established, mortality caused by nearness to banded herbicide is greatly reduced (Campbell 1981).

Density Control

Because loblolly pine expresses dominance, natural thinning eventually occurs in both naturally and artificially regenerated stands. Self-thinning begins when a stand occupies its growing space completely. This usually occurs when crown closure is complete and branches at the base of the crown of even the largest trees begin to die from lack of light. At this point, the smallest and weakest trees begin to die because they are no longer able to obtain sufficient amounts of light, moisture, and nutrients for growth and survival. The released root and crown space is quickly occupied by the remaining trees. Tree growth, competition, and mortality form a continuous cycle that controls the development of the stand. Even a plantation with as few as 1,580 trees/ha at age 10 can be expected to lose about 620 trees/ha by age 20 through self-thinning (Xydias and others 1983). However, the process is usually slow and erratic and results in considerable loss of growth by potential crop trees. No single constant adequately predicts self-thinning over a range of environmental conditions (Zeide 1987).

Artificial thinning efficiently promotes vigorous diameter growth of selected trees within 1 to 2 years after treatment by reducing competition for light, moisture, and nutrients. The need for thinning varies by site, stand density, and uniformity of tree heights. Stands on poor sites are more likely to need treatment than those on good sites, but trees on good sites grow faster when released. Thinning can slow or prevent succession from loblolly pine to climax hardwoods if unwanted species are removed in thinning (Little and Escheman 1976).

Because thinnings have both biological and economic ramifications, they should be part of an overall plan for long-term management. If stands are initiated at close spacing for high pulpwood volume production and then shifted at intermediate ages into long-term management for high-quality products, growth of the final crop trees is reduced and management costs are increased. Computer simulation techniques are available for evaluating the many complex factors involved in thinning alternatives (Arthaud and Klemperer 1986, 1988; Reisinger 1985).

Precommercial thinning. Precommercial thinning is most useful in managing natural stands of even-aged loblolly pines to regulate spacing and stocking where new reproduction is dense. Large seed crops give rise to natural stands with densities that can reach 125,000 to 250,000 stems/ha. When the density of 3- to 5-year-old stands exceeds 12,000 pine stems/ha, precommercial thinning is needed to promote diameter and height growth, especially where site index is below average (less than 23 m at base age 50). Stands of 3,700 to 12,000 trees/ha should not be thinned precommercially unless the live crown ratios of dominants and codominants are expected to be less than 35% at the time of first commercial thinning. Precommercial thinning can rarely be justified in natural stands having less than 3,700 stems/ha.

Precommercial thinning should be done between stand ages 2 and 6 to minimize costs and prevent reduction in live crowns. Maximum tree growth normally results when thinning is done at age 2. If thinning is delayed until ages 4 to 6, mechanical thinning is easier, and cut swaths are less likely to fill in with prolific regrowth of hardwood sprouts, vines, and unwanted pines. Stocking should be reduced to 1,250 to 1,850 well-spaced stems/ha to promote rapid diameter growth of crop trees without reducing volume production. Trees should be cut less than 15 cm from the groundline in late summer to minimize pine sprouting or growth from low live limbs (Balmer and Williston 1973, Brender and McNab 1978, Campbell 1985b, Mann and Lohrey 1974, Williams 1974).

Precommercial thinning is occasionally practiced in young plantations with more than 2,500 stems/ha. It is used to select the best crop trees early and to promote their development by maintaining a high crown ratio during the period of maximum height growth (ages 5 to 15). However, precommercial thinning of plantations is not cost effective. Precommercial thinning is probably of no value in natural uneven-aged stands either, because dense reproduction does not affect the growth of overstory trees, and regular harvesting, prescribed burning, and other management practices can be expected to kill many of the new seedlings that do not succumb to overstory competition (Cain and others 1987). Where precommercial thinning is used, it shortens rotation lengths, creates machine access for fire protection and commercial thinning, and stimulates production of wildlife food and livestock herbage.

Precommercial thinning can be accomplished mechanically, by hand, with herbicides (Paschke 1988), with fire, or with fertilizers. Grano (1969) concluded that to be most profitable, precommercial thinning should be done by machine at age 2 or 3 to at least a 2.4- by 2.4-m spacing. In dense stands, precommercial thinning should be combined with hardwood control to produce greatest early growth (Clason 1979, 1984).

Mechanical strip thinning. Mechanical strip thinning is commonly employed in dense natural loblolly pine stands because it can be applied precisely and the quality of the remaining trees is nearly as good as selecting individual stems for cutting. Swaths should be 2.4 to 3.0 m wide and should leave very narrow strips of trees. If sawtimber production is the goal, swaths can be cut in two directions, leaving small patches of trees on 2.4- to 3.0-m centers. If hand labor is available, each of these patches can be reduced to the single best tree. Early thinning permits the use of relatively small machines, greatly improves visibility, and minimizes the risk of *Ips* spp. attack or infection by the annosus root-rot fungus (see chapter 10). Drum choppers or rotary mowers are effective for thinning stands where trees are at least 1.5 m tall, but have an average diameter of less than 7.5 cm. If a site is relatively free of high stumps and slash, using a tractor-drawn rotary mower is usually less expensive than chopping. If saplings in very dense stands average more than 7.5 cm in diameter, it is probably too late to thin precommercially. Mechanical strip thinning of dense loblolly stands often results in a high fuel hazard level. A skillful prescribed burn reduces the hazard and can also kill the smaller trees left in the leave strips, providing a good stand for future development.

Hand thinning. Thinning can be done with small rotary saws, brush hooks, or other handtools. The main advantage of hand thinning over machine thinning is that it permits the selection of individual trees on the basis of both form and spacing. Although too costly to be practical on most large properties, it is a very reasonable alternative for the nonindustrial private forest (NIPF) landowner of a small woodlot.

Prescribed burning. Controlled backfires can be used to thin large, dense, very young stands inexpensively. A winter backfire reduced the density of a 4-year-old natural stand from 16,800 to 7,040 stems/ha and increased the average tree diameter by killing mostly small trees (Waldrop and Lloyd 1988). A winter burn in an 8-year-old natural stand killed all trees less than 1.4 m tall, 80% of the trees from 1.5 to 2.9 m tall, but only 8% of trees taller than 3 m. In total, the fire killed half of the trees and increased average tree height

Table 8-6—Changes in the composition of an 8-year-old loblolly pine stand as a result of a single winter backfire

Variable		≤1.4 m	1.5 to 2.9 m	≥3 m	Total	Weighted means
Density (stems/ha)	Preburn	8,478	6,726	14,243	29,447	NA
	Postburn	0	1,408	13,111	14,520	NA
Total height (m)	Preburn	0.7	2.2	4.9	NA	3.3
	Postburn	NA	2.4	5.4	NA	5.1
Dbh (cm)	Preburn	NA	0.69	4.17	NA	3.15
	Postburn	NA	1.07	4.52	NA	4.22

(Height class spans the ≤1.4 m, 1.5 to 2.9 m, and ≥3 m columns.)

Source: adapted from Cain (1983).

NA = no data available.

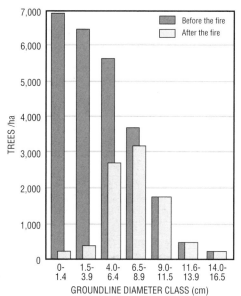

Figure 8-14—Number of loblolly pines per hectare by groundline diameter class before and after thinning an overcrowded natural loblolly pine stand with fire (adapted from McNab 1977).

Table 8-7—Mean total height of the tallest 40% of the trees in a plantation by age and 5 different spacings*

	Height (m)				
Age	1.2 x 1.2 (m)	1.8 x 1.8 (m)	1.8 x 2.4 (m)	2.4 x 2.4 (m)	3.0 x 3.0 (m)
13	11.8	12.5	12.5	12.9	13.5
18	14.9	15.5	15.6	15.7	17.9
21	16.8	18.3	18.3	18.4	20.4
22	17.1	18.5	18.6	18.6	21.2
25	19.3	21.0	20.9	20.5	23.5
28	19.8	21.7	21.9	21.5	24.3
29	20.7	22.5	22.5	21.9	25.1
33	21.6	24.0	24.5	23.4	26.6

Source: adapted from Ayers and others (1987).

* Values shown are averages of 2 blocks for the 1.2 x 1.2 m spacing, 1.8 x 1.8 m, 1.8 x 2.4 m, and 2.4 x 2.4 m; the 3 x 3 m spacing had only 1 block.

by 1.8 m and average diameter by 1 cm (table 8-6). Backfire in a stand having more than 25,000 stems/ha and in which tree age averaged 17 years reduced stocking by 65% by killing almost all trees with diameters less than 4 cm. No pines with groundline diameters larger than 10 cm were killed (figure 8-14).

Although inexpensive and effective, prescribed burning is an imprecise method of thinning. Weather, amount of combustible ground fuel, size and density of the pines being thinned, and state burning laws must be considered when burning. Diameter growth during the first year after burning usually is not affected greatly, but height growth can be reduced by as much as one-third of the previous year's growth, depending on crown scorch (Waldrop and Lloyd 1987).

Other precommercial thinning techniques. Fully stocked or overstocked sapling and pole stands can be thinned by fertilizing them with 225 to 335 kg of N/ha. This treatment accelerates mortality in the lower crown classes (Windsor and Reines 1973). However, the value gain obtained is probably not large enough to make the treatment economical. For example, a single application of N (260 kg/ha) to a 19-year-old loblolly pine stand containing 8,800 trees/ha increased mortality of intermediate and suppressed trees during the following 3 years by approximately 15% over no fertilization. Mortality was slower (but continuous) without fertilization. Within 7 years after treatment, cumulative mortality in fertilized stands was only about 7% greater than that in nonfertilized stands (Brender and McNab 1978). However, without fertilization, volume losses associated with slowly dying trees in lower diameter classes offset volume gains in the larger diameter classes for a longer period of time.

Some herbicide formulations can be used to thin overstocked loblolly pine stands precommercially (Fitzgerald and Fortson 1979b, Keister and McGriff 1974, Whipple and Moeck 1968). Strip applications of sprays or granules may provide results similar to those of strip mechanical thinning.

Commercial thinning. Commercial thinning in even-aged stands is the removal of some of the salable trees that would normally die before rotation age to provide revenue and additional growing space for the remaining trees. The goal is to keep crop trees growing at near maximum potential rates for greatest value at rotation age. Lower crown shade needles can increase their photosynthetic rate immediately after thinning because of increased light (Ginn and others 1989).

Regular harvesting of merchantable trees of all sizes in uneven-aged stands serves the same purpose as thinning in even-aged stands. When the selection system is employed, low-vigor trees (those growing at a rate of no more than 0.5 cm in diameter per year) should be cut when they reach minimum sawlog size (25 cm in dbh). Medium-vigor trees (those growing 0.8 cm/yr) should be cut at 40 cm in dbh High-vigor trees (those growing 1.0 cm or more per year) should be harvested at 51 to 58 cm in dbh (Murphy and Guldin 1987).

Management plans for wood products typically include at least one thinning and specify a rotation age of about 30 years (Hotvedt and Straka 1987). Most thinnings are performed in stands 13 to 27 years of age (Feduccia 1983, Gardner 1985, Pienaar and others 1984, Siegel 1961). Thirty-six percent of the total loblolly pine growing stock is presently in the 15- to 25-cm diameter classes, where first thinning is most appropriate. Thinning will not significantly affect the age of xylem transition from juvenile to mature wood (Gibson and Clason 1991).

Although thinning normally reduces the total volume produced by a stand, volume of higher value products is increased if thinning is performed before about age 25 on average or better sites (Schultz 1975). Stands on good to excellent sites should be thinned to a basal area (BA) of about 18 m^2/ha when density reaches BA of about 25 to 28 m^2/ha. A BA of 34 m^2/ha or higher is usually too high for maximum growth. Stands on poor sites should be thinned to about 16 m^2/ha when density reaches about 21 m^2/ha. Both tree height (table 8-7) and diameter are negatively correlated with stand density. However, stand density's greatest effect is on tree diameter (Lohrey and Nesmith 1988a, 1988b; Sprinz and others 1979).

Figure 8-15—Selection harvesting between corridors with a thinner/harvester equipped with a long articulating arm.

Commercial thinnings are normally accomplished by systematically removing specific rows in plantations or corridors in natural stands, by selecting individual trees based on size and quality criteria, or by a combination of the two systems (figure 8-15). Normally, loblolly pines should be thinned from below to release higher quality trees, favor uniformity of stocking, and eliminate trees that are poor risks. Crop trees can be identified when the dominant trees are as small as 18 cm in dbh. Although the best formed dominant and codominant trees are favored, healthy intermediate trees may be retained at the expense of larger trees that have insect or disease problems. Intermediate trees may also be retained to promote good spacing if they are deemed to have a good chance of growing faster after release. Even 40-year-old suppressed trees with small, thin crowns can recover and grow satisfactorily following release if they have at least 20% live crown and if the diameter at the base of the crown is 5 cm or greater (see chapter 5, figure 5-16). However, dominant and codominant trees should be kept for the final crop whenever possible.

Commercial forestry machines are well adapted for systematic thinning. Mechanical thinning of rows in plantations or of corridors in natural stands is not selective, but it can be combined with selection thinning to remove poor-quality trees. If every fifth or seventh row in a plantation is removed, or if 3-m straight or meandering corridors are cut at 12- to 15-m intervals in a natural stand, well-trained machine operators can use small, mobile machines or articulated cutting arms attached to large machines to remove individual trees from areas between cut rows or corridors. Evaluations of the physical capabilities and costs of many common machines are available (Granskog 1982, Stokes and Lanford 1982).

Other thinning techniques sometimes used with loblolly pine include crown thinning (or thinning from above), diameter-limit thinning, and D+6 thinning. Crown thinning removes upper canopy trees but still favors the most promising dominant and codominant trees. Trees from the lower canopy and others that may not live until the next thinning are also cut at this time. Crown thinning, practiced on a regular basis, should be discouraged because it removes many or most of the best stems and is detrimental to the health of the stand. However, it can be used on a one-time basis to increase the number of high-quality poles when stand density is kept between 12.5 and 30 m^2/ha. Burton (1977) found that initially thinning a 20-year-old, second-growth, loblolly–shortleaf stand from above and then thinning trees in the lower crown classes produced more poles, while initial thinning from below resulted in longer poles and higher pole values.

Diameter-limit thinning periodically removes all trees larger than a specific minimum diameter. If a small diameter limit is adopted, all large trees are removed, and much of the subsequent growth occurs on unmerchantable trees. The method simplifies cutting, but does not allow for continued growth of high-quality seed trees or production of large valuable sawlogs. Diameter-limit thinning is not recommended unless a diameter limit of at least 40 cm is set, all trees at or above that limit are cut regardless of quality, and hardwood competition is controlled regularly.

The D+6 method of thinning, which is designed to promote uniformity of spacing, can be applied by thinning from below, by crown thinning, or by selection thinning. According to this rule for spacing, 6-inch (15-cm) trees should be left 12 ft (3.7 m) apart. For each additional inch (2.5 cm) in average diameter of stems reserved, an additional foot (0.3 m) is allowed between trees (Brender 1965).

Any thinning method other than the D+6 method can be applied at intensities ranging from light to heavy. The amounts to be removed and to remain can be measured and expressed in terms of volume (cords, board feet, or cubic measurement), number of stems, or basal area.

Thinning has both biological and economic risks. Biological risks include physical damage to the residual trees and to the site, and predisposition of residual trees to subsequent insect or disease attacks. Felling and removal can break crowns and roots, scar boles and roots of residual trees, and compact soil. Damage can be minimized by proper timing of harvesting, operator training, and equipment selection. Long-term implications of thinning damage are often hard to evaluate at the time of treatment. Trees in a stand grow with mutual support, and removing 25 to 35% of the stems can be like removing some supports from a bridge. If strong winds, heavy glaze, or snow occurs shortly after a thinning, many stems can be damaged or lost. The risk diminishes gradually as remaining trees expand their crowns and root systems. Depending on local risks of post-thinning damage, it may be best to thin two or three times over 10 to 15 years rather than once. The following financial risks are associated with thinning:

1. **Uncertain economic projection**—Thinnings are done to increase tree growth and normally to increase the total value of a stand. However, final results may not be available for 10 to 20 years after treatment, so it is difficult to project the economic outcome.

2. **High administration cost**—Expenses, such as marking trees to cut or leave, preparing the area (for example, controlled burning), cleaning up the area, and overseeing the operation raise the cost of producing wood by thinning.

3. **Low yield and high cost-per-unit-product and per-unit- time**—The need for care in felling, coupled with the small product size and relatively low weight of juvenile wood, makes thinning costs much higher than clear-felling costs.

Thinning also has distinct economic advantages:

1. **An early return on investment**—Early removal of some wood helps pay for stand establishment and early management.

2. **Increased size, quality, and unit value of products at rotation age**.

3. **Increased resistance of thrifty stands to damage by bark beetles and diseases**—Although difficult to quantify, this factor should be considered in any cost and benefit analysis.

Burton (1982) discussed the rapid development of loblolly pine sawlogs with small knotty cores through early, heavy thinning, pruning of green limbs, and understory control. A severe thinning at age 9 reduced stocking from 2,720 to 250 trees/ha. Four subsequent thinnings reduced stocking to only 100 trees/ha at age 30. Another area was thinned to a basal area of 20 m^2/ha every 3 years between stand ages 12 and 30. At age 33, the 100 trees in the heavily thinned area had an average dbh of more than 45 cm. The 100 largest trees in the more lightly thinned area had an average dbh of less than 35 cm. Almost two-thirds of the 11-cm growth difference occurred between ages 9 and 15, when height growth of loblolly pines is typically 1.2 to

1.5 m/yr. The heavy thinning positioned the best trees for exceptional growth for several years without adversely affecting form class, whereas trees in the more lightly thinned plots suffered from competition and crown reduction. Total volume growth was greatest with light thinning, but it was distributed over many trees of small diameter.

Pruning

When grown close together, loblolly pines quickly loose lower limbs and develop clear stems (see chapter 2). This self-pruning, when combined with judicious thinning from below and removal of poor self-pruners in the upper canopy, can produce high-quality stands. In contrast, widely spaced trees grow rapidly in diameter but are of poor quality because crown closure occurs late in life, if at all. Late crown closure results in development of large lower limbs and rapid bole taper. If a stand contains only 350 to 500 trees/ha, crown closure does not occur until trees are about age 20, and trees have knotty 25- to 40-cm cores in the first log. Artificial pruning can limit diameter of the knotty core to no more than 18 cm (Brender 1961). Most forest stands are kept at a close spacing to promote self-pruning because artificial pruning is costly. Most pruning is confined to seed orchards or other stands in which trees are spaced far apart for improved machine access. Pruning does not affect the age of xylem transition from juvenile to mature wood (Gibson and Clason 1991). If green limb pruning is done, it should be confined to the best 250 to 300 well-spaced trees/ha, and at least half the tree's length should be left in the crown. Pruning should be done in two steps, beginning at about age 6, when trees are 7.5 to 13 cm in dbh and 4.6 to 7.6 m in height. The first pruning should be to 2.5 m or to half of the tree's height. The second pruning, at about age 11, should be to 5.2 m to provide one clear 5-m log. Removal of the lower live limbs at a young age promotes maximum growth of knot-free, high-quality wood in the lower bole. Pruning also slows diameter growth at the base of the tree and speeds diameter growth near the base of the crown, making the stem more cylindrical and increasing its volume. Small, pruned limbs cut flush with the bole heal fastest—taking about 3 to 4 years depending on the diameter growth of the bole adjacent to the wound. Pruning scars heal more rapidly from the sides than from top or bottom (Garin 1965). Although pruning of dry limbs has no effect on growth, it can improve stem quality. Unpruned trees may take 11 years or longer to envelop the stubs of limbs that die naturally, depending on the size and condition of the stub and the growth rate of the tree (Grano 1961).

Saws are the best tools for pruning. Motorized saws are available for rapid pruning of any sized limbs (Dahlin 1981). A handsaw that has coarse, incurved teeth is frequently used to prune the lower 2.4 m of a tree bole. Long-handled saws can be used to prune upper sections of butt logs from a ground position. Axes should never be used for pruning because they usually tear part of the limb from the bole, increasing wound size and slowing the healing process. Also, missed strokes can scar tree boles. Pruning can be done at any

time of the year. There is less resin production during the dormant season, so pruning at that time should minimize the development of pitch pockets in the wood. Severed branches should be pulled away from the base of crop trees to reduce or avoid fire damage.

Harvesting

Loblolly pine and associated hardwood stands are harvested to yield (1) shortwood pulp, (2) product-length logs, or (3) tree-length logs. Shortwood pulp and product-length logs are always moved to processing or distribution centers without change. Tree-length material can be chipped on site or transported to a processing center for chipping or merchandizing.

All harvesting methods include at least four phases—felling, limbing and bucking, loading, and hauling. Normally, skidding is required also except in highly mechanized shortwood systems in which trees are felled, cut to length, and stacked on forwarders. Felling, limbing, and bucking can be accomplished either manually or by machine. In tree-length harvesting, bucking merely cuts the tops off trees at a specified length.

Regeneration Opportunities Immediately After Harvesting

Traditional logging disturbs varying amounts of the organic surface layer and, if done properly, may permit adequate loblolly pine regeneration. In some instances, unmerchantable standing trees, slash lying on the ground, numerous sprouts from coppicing hardwoods, and a thick litter layer must be reduced before an area can be artificially regenerated to loblolly. The presence of a large number of big pine and hardwood tops can severely impede regeneration. The unused crown of a typical 25-cm-dbh pine weighs about 45 kg on an ovendry basis. The discarded top of a 45-cm-dbh pine may weigh more than 180 kg.

Loblolly pines can be cut and chipped in the same operation. Although such whole-stand chipping is not a site preparation method, it can leave an area sufficiently clean and disturbed to permit artificial or natural regeneration. Unfortunately, because whole-stand chipping can result in rapid hardwood sprout growth and some soil compaction, followup site preparation may be necessary. For example, complete harvesting of all standing trees with a mobile chipper left 54% of an Alabama site undisturbed or only slightly disturbed. However, a third of the surface soil was compacted an average of 12%, and 7% of the surface area was covered by piles of chips or other debris (Gorden and others 1981). In addition, more than 17,000 new hardwood stems/ha were grow-

ing vigorously on the area 1 year after chipping.

Whole-tree removal is a slightly less intensive harvesting treatment than whole-tree chipping but it can also prepare a site for regeneration. In a mixed pine-hardwood stand in the upper Piedmont, whole-tree removal of trees with dbh's greater than 10 cm exposed mineral soil on 32.5% of the site's surface area. When removal was to a dbh limit of 2.5 cm, the proportion of soil exposed increased to 66% (McMinn 1983).

Environmental Concerns in Harvesting

Clearcutting. Clearcutting followed by removal of logs or whole trees invariably creates some site damage by removing litter from the soil surface, compacting soil, and reducing infiltration rates. Extensive site disturbance associated with harvesting can usually be attributed to improper harvesting techniques, the use of improper equipment, or both. Piedmont and upper Coastal Plain sites with loessial soils are particularly susceptible to site degradation and productivity declines if trees are not harvested carefully. Harvest method (conventional stem removal or removal of whole trees) from a Piedmont site had no effect on the erosion rate during the following year (Pye and Vitousek 1985).

Careful logging can disturb as little at 8 to 10% of a site. If main drainages are left undisturbed, haul roads and landings kept outside cutting areas, and slash left on the site, clearcutting and planting can be accomplished without excessive negative effects even on some of the most fragile soils (McClurkin and others 1985).

Careless logging can disturb 40% or more of an area and greatly increase overland flow of water. Skidding has the greatest potential for adversely affecting a site and the quality of water coming from it. Logs should not be skidded across stream channels, because such skidding can destroy the channels, nor straight uphill, because such skidding creates new channels for gully erosion. Stream channels should not be left littered with debris.

Leaving forested buffer strips along streams is a very effective way to minimize streambank damage and to filter out eroded soil before it reaches the stream channel. Integrity of buffer strips must be maintained by felling trees away from them and limiting machine access. The use of buffer strips is not a cure-all; the strips are effective only if the volume of eroded material does not exceed their absorption capacity or if sediment transferred from degraded slopes into buffer strips moves into stream channels very slowly over a period of many years (Blackburn and others 1986).

Buffer strips can be harvested if 50% canopy cover is left to shade fishable streams and if trees are removed by cable skidding. Tractors, log decks, mechanical site preparation, and fires should be excluded and roads allowed only at designated stream crossings (Dissmeyer 1978).

Careful harvesting causes only brief and minimal increases in sedimentation, even on erosive sites. Harvesting has the potential to increase sedimentation primarily because canopy removal exposes the forest floor to the direct impact of raindrops and because soil moisture increases and soils reach saturation more quickly when the transpirational and evaporational losses associated with tree stands are eliminated. Even felling of trees increases onsite soil movement, but felling has little effect on soil loss. Skid trails and spur roads can occupy 10% or more of logged areas on very hilly or steep sites, and they are invariably the chief sources of sediment moving into streams (Dissmeyer 1976).

Harvesting during or before periods when rainfall is normally low is a good way to minimize erosion provided some new vegetation can be established quickly. Other simple but effective techniques for minimizing erosion include

1. Felling trees parallel to skidding direction with the butt toward the landing to minimize skidding damage.

2. Using natural topographic features when laying out skid trails, and disturbing steep gradients only as a last resort.

3. Water-barring, seeding, and mulching skid trails immediately following logging.

4. Using culverts at temporary stream crossings and removing them upon completion of work.

When these precautions are taken, most sediment is trapped by logging debris, by ground cover (in lower areas within a stand) or by adjacent uncut forest areas, especially if slopes are less than 20%. If harvesting is planned well and executed properly, most of the litter layer remains intact, soils do not become compacted so infiltration rates remain high, and overland flow occurs only during high-intensity storms.

The litter layer developed by a fully stocked loblolly pine stand deteriorates rapidly following harvesting. On very erosive sites, soil movement can be expected within 2 years after clearcutting unless a new stand of loblolly is established. Within 3 years after a loblolly plantation in northern Mississippi was clearcut, weight of the forest floor had decreased to 12.8 t/ha, which was 5.6 t/ha less than where there was no cutting. Even reducing basal area from 30 to 17 m^2/ha caused a decline of 3.4 t/ha in forest floor weight and reduced annual litterfall by 18% (Dickerson 1972).

It can take a long time to rebuild a litter layer destroyed by harvesting and delayed regeneration. Planted loblolly pines take from 3 to as much as 10 years to develop a significant litter layer, depending on growth rate. In that time, the forest floor can decline to a level at which excessive erosion occurs on some sites. Young loblolly yield more litter for a given tree height than shortleaf (Thames 1962).

Regeneration of clearcuts. Even where soils are fragile, it can be environmentally sound to combine prescribed burning and natural regeneration. The combination of preharvest burning, harvesting of mature loblolly pine stands, and natural regeneration on erosive South Carolina Piedmont soils caused very little soil loss or degradation of water quality. Low-intensity burns had little effect on water quality or water flow. Elevations in sediment concentrations and sediment export after harvesting were small and of short duration (Douglass and others 1983, Van Lear and others 1985).

Salvage cutting. Land managers can minimize timber losses by harvesting trees killed or damaged by hurricanes, fusiform rust, southern pine beetles, or other causes. The need for salvage depends on the extent, severity, and kind of damage. Stand conditions and site factors determine how a salvage is carried out. The success of salvage cutting is based on anticipation of the death of merchantable trees before the end of a rotation and quick removal of dead or severely damaged trees. Large salvage operations can be handled much like clearcutting. Salvage work in small plots or salvage of scattered dead trees is similar to thinning. Salvage operations of all sizes must be conducted with the same care given to thinning or final harvesting. If insufficient care is taken to protect the site and the remaining trees, the eventual cost of the salvage operation may exceed the value of the material removed.

Logging roads. Erosion from roads is the biggest water quality problem in forested areas. Dissmeyer (1976) estimated that spur road surfaces in the South contribute from 22 to more than 100 t/yr of sediment/ha of road surface for 3 years after logging. Poorly developed access roads and poor streamside management caused 7.2 t/ha/yr of sediment export for 2 years after road construction and machine planting on a rolling Piedmont site in Georgia (Hewlett 1979). Soil compaction related to skidding or hauling of logs can each reduce the growth of loblolly pines. Twenty-six-year-old trees planted in old road ruts were 6.1 cm smaller in diameter and 2.4 m shorter, and produced only 46% as much cubic volume as trees planted in a surrounding field (Perry 1964).

Figure 8-16— Newly planted loblolly pines on an eroded logging road. Within 3 years, this site will be stabilized.

Because roads can be so damaging to soil and water resources, the following precautions should be taken (Kochenderfer 1970, Jackson and others 1981):

1. Keep roads to an absolute minimum and out of harvesting areas if possible.
2. Locate roads on stable soils away from streams, marshes, wet fields, and natural drainage channels.
3. Do not use right-of-way debris in roadbeds or fills.
4. Construct roads with dips and wing ditches to reduce surface water velocity.
5. Where necessary, use large aggregate material to stabilize road surfaces.
6. Use bridges or culverts at stream crossings and install them at right angles to the stream channel. Crossings should not constrict clearly defined stream channels.
7. Do not deposit excess soil below the high water mark of a stream.
8. Where all vegetation must be removed, reestablish vegetation by seeding and mulching or planting (figure 8-16).
9. Do not build roads with grades greater than 7%.
10. When roads are to be taken out of service, close them to nonessential traffic, then construct water-bars and sow grass on steeper slopes and near streams.

<table style="text-align:center">......................... **Fertilization** ....</table>

Only about 10,700 ha of loblolly pine received fertilizer treatments before 1970. About 85% of the area treated was fertilized at or within 2 years after establishment (Allen and Ballard 1983). During the 1970's and early 1980's, a total of about 354,000 ha of loblolly pine were fertilized, divided about equally between newly planted stands and established stands (Allen and Ballard 1983, Wells and Allen 1985). Even though intensive forest management activities, including short rotations and intensive utilization, accelerate the loss of nutrients (table 8-8), fertilization may not increase growth where soils are very fertile. Even if growth is increased, the additional yield may not offset the expense of fertilizer application. Yields associated with fertilization are described in chapter 11.

Phosphorus Fertilization

Phosphorus is usually the most limiting nutrient on very poorly and poorly drained lower Coastal Plain sites. Consequently, applications of P at planting or as soon as

Table 8-8—The effect of intensity of utilization and length of rotation on the mean annual nutrient demands of natural loblolly pine stands on good sites in the southeastern United States

	Mean annual nutrient demands (kg/ha/yr)			
	Partial utilization		Complete utilization	
Nutrient	20-yr rotation	40-yr rotation	20-yr rotation	40-yr rotation
Nitrogen	14.60	11.60	19.20	14.20
Phosphorus	0.84	0.69	1.35	1.01
Potassium	8.40	7.30	10.60	8.60
Calcium	8.90	7.60	10.20	8.70

Source: adapted from Switzer and Nelson (1974).

possible thereafter often accelerate net photosynthesis (Rousseau and Reid 1990) and result in substantial and long-lasting growth increases. A single application of about 40 to 80 kg of P/ha is generally adequate for an entire rotation—often increasing site index (base age 25) by 2.4 to 5.2 m. Aboveground biomass can be doubled without increasing fine root biomass or density (Adams and others 1989). Even as little as 25 kg of P/ha can produce responses that last 13 to 20 years. Adding 50 kg of N/ha with P increases young tree growth more than P fertilization alone on moist to wet Coastal Plain soils (Comerford and others 1983). However, application of N without P on P-deficient sites does not increase growth and may reduce it (Buford and McKee 1987). On some very poorly drained clay soils, trees may not respond to any fertilizer treatment (Gent and others 1986a). Loblolly pines are not likely to respond to phosphate fertilization on Piedmont sites (Torbert and Burger 1984). This subject is further discussed in chapter 11.

Several kinds of P materials are available for large-scale fertilization. They include triple superphosphate (TSP), diammonium phosphate (DAP), and fine ground rock phosphate (GRP) (table 8-9). The last of these is slowly soluble, and the first two are highly soluble. The effectiveness of water-insoluble phosphates such as GRP generally increases as particle size is reduced. Triple superphosphate and GRP seem to be about equally effective. Where GRP is available locally, it usually costs less per kilogram than TSP. However, the cost of treating with GRP is usually greater than the cost of treating with TSP. Ground rock phosphate must be applied at higher rates than TSP and is harder to spread than TSP. Diammonium phosphate contains both N and P. On stands 3 years old or older, DAP can be used if N deficiency is suspected. Diammonium phosphate generally costs only a little more than TSP, so the N is applied

Table 8-9—Common nitrogen (N) and phosphorus (P_2O_5) fertilizers used to promote loblolly pine growth

Fertilizer	N (%)	P_2O_5 (%)	Fertilizer	N (%)	P_2O_5 (%)
Ammonium nitrate	33	0	Urea ammonium phosphate	28	28
Ordinary superphosphate	0	20	Ammonium polyphosphate	11	55
Triple superphosphate	0	46	Sulfurcoated urea	36	0
Diammonium phosphate	16–21	46	Urea	46	0
Urea ammonium polyphosphate	35	17	Ground rock phosphate	0	28–35

inexpensively when DAP is used.

Both N and P fertilizers can be applied to new or thinned stands from the air or ground. Cost usually determines how they are applied, but finely ground rock phosphate can only be spread practically from the ground. Because it is bulky, lime is usually broadcast from ground vehicles. Placing fertilizers in the immediate rooting zone of young pines permits earlier and more efficient use of limiting nutrients, especially those that are highly soluble. However, placement close to the roots of a tree does not guarantee fertilizer uptake. Physical and chemical characteristics of the soil and root distribution influence fertilizer uptake and contribute to the effectiveness of specific placement systems (Bengtson 1970, Bilan and Gillespie 1985, Brendemuehl 1970).

Nitrogen Fertilization

Nitrogen is the element most often deficient in pole and sawtimber stands, especially on old fields throughout the range of loblolly pine (Dippon and Shelton 1983, Pritchett and Smith 1975, Simmons 1974). Consequently, pole and sawtimber trees usually respond most to N fertilization, but they sometimes respond more to fertilization with N plus P (Haines and others 1977). There are no simple indices to predict response to N, which can vary considerably by site and stocking level (Ballard and Lea 1986, Hart and others 1986, Lea and Ballard 1982a). Leaf area index (LAI) can be increased by up to 60% by N fertilization on N-deficient sites (Vose and Allen 1988). Recommended fertilization rates for stemwood growth increases are 100 to 200 kg N/ha or 100 to 200 kg N plus 45 to 55 kg P/ha, unless specific conditions dictate otherwise. Fertilization with more N may increase growth further, but the additional growth may not justify the added cost (Ballard 1981a, Brender and McNab 1978, Comerford and others 1983, Fisher and Garbett 1980, Wells and Allen 1985). For greatest efficiency, late-rotation N fertilization should be combined with stocking control. Nitrogen fertilization can also stimulate residual pine growth, especially diameter growth in recently thinned loblolly pine stands (see chapter 11). The following are general guidelines for fertilizing various sites with N (Wells and Allen 1985):

1. Very responsive sites are those where nutrients are limiting but moisture availability and other site factors are favorable. These include most upland Piedmont clay soils, poorly to moderately drained sandy Coastal Plain soils, and moderately well-drained soils with relatively deep spodic horizons.

2. Moderately responsive sites are those with moderately well-drained to well-drained upland loamy soils that are typically droughty for some portions of the year. The droughty character of such soils may restrict fertilizer availability.

3. Weakly responsive sites are those where nutrient limitations are typically overshadowed by gross deficiencies in other environmental variables such as moisture, soil volume, or soil concentration (rocky or concreted soils) or sites that already have sufficient available nutrients. Overstocked, stagnated, natural stands are unlikely to respond well to N fertilization until after they are thinned.

Once responsive sites have been identified, the following guidelines should be used to select specific stands for treatment:

1. The stand should be moderately to fully stocked (basal area of 16 to 28 m²/ha).

2. The site index at age 25 should be between 15 and 23 m.

3. The N concentration of ovendried sample needles should be less than 1.2% and the P concentration less than 0.12%.

4. Stands should be on soils where moisture (excesses or deficits) does not limit growth.

Less than 25% of the added N may be absorbed by loblolly pines, but these increases are maintained in tree tissues for 6 to 11 years (Cotrufo 1983; table 8-10). Another 25% of added N is captured on the site by soil or other plants, and the remaining 50% is lost by leaching and volatilization. Thus 2 to 4 kg of N must be added to a site to balance the loss of 1 kg (Jorgensen and Wells 1986, Neary and others 1984).

Fertilizer can also substantially alter the composition of other vegetation, as well as speed up the development of an organic layer, increase soil aeration, and rapidly diminish erosion on steep sites. For example, plants such as fireweed, *Erechtites hieracifolia* (L.) Raf., and other herbs can dominate fertilized sites for the first 1 or 2 years and slow the growth of young loblolly pines (Haines and Haines 1979, Moschler and others 1970). Therefore, when N is added early in the life of a stand, some herbaceous weed control is usually needed to make the fertilization treatment most effective (Swindel and others 1988). Loblolly pine crown cover can exceed 70% in 5-year-old plantations in which competition is controlled and where fertilizer is applied repeatedly. Crown cover can be as low as 11% in 5-year-old plantations that are not fertilized and in which competition is not controlled (Swindel and others 1989).

Urea and ammonium nitrate are the nitrogen fertilizers most often applied to loblolly pines (Wells and Allen 1985). These fertilizers are equally effective, so choice can be based on local cost. A single application of N in the spring probably benefits trees more than several smaller applications during the growing season if the total amounts applied are the same (Johnson and Todd 1988). Nitrogen fertilizers are usually most effective when applied in the spring or fall partly because volatilization losses of N (especially as NH_3 gas from urea fertilizer) are greater during dry conditions at high temperatures. Also, significant amounts of N from both urea and ammonium nitrate can be leached from the rooting zone if heavy rains closely follow application or if the ground is waterlogged when the fertilizer is applied (Craig and Wollum 1982, Lucier 1985). Loblolly pines are likely to use more of the N, if it is applied in a slow-release form or is applied to the foliage.

Fertilization With Other Macronutrients and Micronutrients

The addition of potassium (K), Ca, or Mg rarely increases loblolly pine's growth or changes its wood properties, although fertilization may increase foliar concentrations of these elements. These elements seem to be supplied adequately through nutrient uptake from soil reserves or nutrient cycling (Carter and Lyle 1966, Posey 1965, Shoulders and McKee 1973, Switzer and Nelson 1972, Wells 1970). However, Bengtson (1976) suggested that K deficiency limits growth potential of loblolly on intensively prepared and excessively well-drained sandhills in west Florida. Young trees affected by K deficiency have dormant season foliage K concentrations below 0.30%. Fisher (1981) reported that critical foliar concentrations for Ca and Mg are 0.10% and 0.06%, respectively.

Loblolly pines grow fastest when soil pH is between about 4.5 and 6.0. Addition of lime (Ca and Mg) raises the pH of acidic Coastal Plain and Piedmont soils. The disadvantage of lime is that it may take 5 to 6 t of lime/ha to raise soil pH one-half of one unit. Calphos—a lime–phosphate–kaolin mixture containing about 8% P, 17% Ca, and lesser amounts of 18 other elements—can raise soil pH by 1 unit when applied at 1 t/ha (Bilan and Gillespie 1985, MacCarthy and Davey 1976). The elevation in pH caused by liming may persist for one or more rotations. Liming low-pH Piedmont soils may not increase tree growth (Torbert and Burger 1984). Liming may even reduce survival and tree growth on some soils by causing increased weed competition (Gilmore 1980).

Most micronutrients probably remain in plant biomass or soil and contribute to tree growth for at least one rotation (Jorgensen and Wells 1986).

Soil-Improving Plants

Soil N can be increased by seeding N-fixing plants such as winter annual subterranean clovers and summer annual and perennial lespedezas into newly established loblolly pine plantations. Legume litter, which is high in N, may speed up forest floor decomposition, thereby hastening nutrient release and cycling in young stands. On P-deficient sites, combining P fertilization with service lespedeza, *Lespedeza cuneata* (Dumont) G. Don, and *L. thunbergii* (D.C. Naki), adds N to the soil and increases wood volume for 7 to 11 years, compared to using P fertilizer alone (Jorgensen and Craig 1984, Jorgensen and

Table 8-10—Aboveground recovery of nitrogen (N) by loblolly pine trees following application of N to the soil surface

Age of trees at application (yr)	Rate of application* (kg/ha)	Time after application (yr)	N recovery in trees %	N recovery in trees kg/ha	Source
3	112	2	13	15	Baker and others (1974)
3	224	2	9	20	Baker and others (1974)
4	224	2	3	6	Baker and others (1974)
4	224	2	5	12	Baker and others (1974)
11	168	10	8	13	Strader (1982)
11	336	10	9	30	Strader (1982)
20	112	11	21	24	Strader (1982)
20	224	11	13	29	Strader (1982)
20	672	11	5	31	Strader (1982)

* Ammonium nitrate was applied to the 3-, 4-, and 11-year-old trees; urea was applied to the 20-year-old trees.

Wells 1986, Schoeneberger and Jorgensen 1989). However, most legumes will not grow suitably under well-stocked loblolly pine stands with a closed canopy, and tree growth is rarely stimulated by their presence. Maintaining a good stand of legumes under a 25-year-old loblolly stand thinned to 250 stems/ha did not increase pine growth or affect soil nutrient content, showing that legumes may not justify their cost on some sites (Clason 1987, Jorgensen 1981). For legumes to be effective during the middle or near the end of a rotation, legume species that are very shade tolerant need to be developed.

Organic Fertilizers

Forest lands offer an environmentally acceptable way of recycling some wastes (Sopper and Kardos 1973). Properly handled organic wastes can improve soil used to grow loblolly pines. Opportunities in this area are great and could be expanded substantially in the future. Waste materials are most easily applied by ground equipment during the site preparation and planting process, but they can be applied at any time during the life of a stand if tree spacing and stand terrain permit machine access and maneuverability.

Solid or liquid municipal and animal wastes cause no damage to trees if applied at reasonable rates and can be sources of N, P, and other elements that promote tree growth (Berry 1987, Hegg and others 1984, Lane and Shade 1982; table 8-11). Other wastes, such as composted garbage and fly ash from coal-burning electric facilities, may be most effective in improving the physical properties of soils rather than as effective fertilizers. Applications of industrial wastes with high concentrations of heavy metals can increase concentrations of those metals in soil and affect tree growth adversely (Berry 1985).

Table 8-11—Soil characteristics after 5 years on nonirrigated and municipal-irrigated sites

| Site | pH | Nutrient content (kg/ha) | | | |
		Phosphorus	Potassium	Magnesium	Calcium
No irrigation	5.3	54	18	32	291
Municipal effluent irrigation	6.5	72	59	47	864

Source: Lane and Shade (1982).

Waste treatments are most effective in promoting tree growth in stands from about age 8, when crowns close, to rotation age. However, the added nutrients stimulate weed competition in young stands, and this competition may reduce tree survival and growth for the first several years in newly regenerated stands. Heavy applications of sludge greatly increase weed competition. Applications of sludge probably stimulate loblolly pine growth for many years, because sludge releases nutrients for extended periods (Berry 1977, 1987; Fiskell and others 1982; McKee and others 1987; McLeod and others 1987; Wells and others 1984).

Waste materials can affect soil mesofauna populations. The addition of well-decomposed sludge with a low solids content reduces the total number of mesofauna, while the addition of less decomposed sludge with a higher solids content increases the number of mesofauna (MacConnell and others 1987).

Effects of Fertilization on Tree and Site Characteristics

Fertilization with inorganic supplements of N and P or with waste materials increases the amount of loblolly pine foliage and darkens its green color. The increase in amount of foliage is usually in the size and weight of individual needle fascicles and occurs primarily in the middle and lower crown. Needle weight can be increased by up to 30% per fascicle, needle length by up to 15%, and the proportion of fascicles with more than 3 needles by up to 15% (Ridgeway and others 1987, Vose 1988, Wells 1970, Wells and others 1975). Needles of modestly fertilized trees may persist on the tree 6 to 8 months longer than needles of unfertilized trees (Zahner 1959). However, very heavy N fertilization can cause needles to fall early (McKee W. 1991. Personal communication). Fertilization of unthinned pole and sawtimber stands may result in a short-term improvement in stem form, but little significant net change in form will be apparent 5 years after treatment (Jack and others 1988).

The effect of fertilization on mineral cycling is greatest during the first 3 years after treatment. Wells and others (1975) found that litterfall and throughfall during the first year after fertilization contained about 5% of the N and 10% of the K that had been applied. During the second year after fertilization, increased litterfall and increased concentrations of N and K in litterfall and throughfall amounted to 10% of the N and K that had been applied.

Nitrogen fertilization in loblolly pine stands reduces populations of mycorrhizal fungi by 10 to 20% for a short time. However, as the level of soil N decreases, the number of basidiocarps of all fungal species begins to increase. Phosphorus fertilization alone does not increase or decrease the population of mycorrhizal fungi on a site (Menge and Grand 1978, Menge and others 1977).

Estimating Plant and Soil Nutrient Levels and Deficiencies

Foliar analyses and soil tests are important ways to identify sites that require fertilization. Total P concentration in ovendried needles is the best indicator of P deficiency (Wells and others 1973, 1986). Foliage should be collected from a random sample of dominant trees, codominant trees, or both in an area of relatively homogeneous soil and uniform tree growth. The sample should be a composite one collected from at least 15 trees. Composite samples should consist of at least 200 fascicles that are free of soil and other contaminants. Sampling requirements include (Lea and Ballard 1982b, Wells 1969, Wells and Allen 1985):

1. Samples should be representative of a tree crown. Needles should be fully mature, in their second growing season, attached to primary branches in the upper half of the crown, and free from competition for light. First-flush needles are preferred. Samples should be collected during the winter from December through March.

2. Samples should be largely free of insect and disease damage.

3. Samples must be refrigerated, stored on ice, or placed in a drier within 12 hours of collection. Dried samples are preferable for transporting to the laboratory. Drying is done best in a forced-air oven at a temperature of 60 to 70 °C for 24 to 48 hours.

Guidelines for P fertilization based on foliar P concentrations are listed in table 8-12. Growth response to P fertilization increases as the needle P content, without fertilization, decreases from 0.10 to 0.06%.

Stand variables, such as stocking level, site index, and environmental conditions including drainage and soil pH, must be considered when evaluating the results of foliar analyses and predicting growth responses (Ballard and Lea 1986, McNeil and others 1988, Wells and Allen 1985, Wells and others 1986). For example, growth response to P fertilization tends to increase as pH decreases (Wells and others 1986). Stands growing on poorly drained clays and sands (Aqualfs, Aquents, and Aquepts) in the lower Coastal Plain are generally the most consistent responders to additions of P.

Forest soils are very heterogeneous, making it difficult to determine general nutrient levels and weakening the relationship between soil nutrient analyses and tree growth responses. However, there is a high probability that loblolly pines will respond to P fertilization when growing on soils where extractable soil P levels are below 3 to 6 ppm, depending on the test used (Allen and Ballard 1983, Lea and others 1980, Wells and others 1973). Each soil sample should consist of a composite of at least 15 subsamples from an area fairly uniform in topography and vegetation. All surface organic matter must be removed from these soil samples. Generally,

Table 8-12—Guidelines for phosphorus (P) fertilization based on concentration of P in needles

Concentration in needles (%)	Interpretation
<0.08*	Severe deficiency. Five-year height growth increase of 50 to 140% can be expected in the lower Coastal Plain by fertilizing young stands with 50 kg P/ha.
0.08–0.10	Site is deficient, and there is a high probability of tree response. In the lower Coastal Plain, height growth response should be between 15 and 50%.
0.10–0.12	Trees will usually respond to P in combination with nitrogen.
>0.12	Trees will generally not respond to P fertilization.

Source: adapted from Ballard and Lea (1986) and Wells and Allen (1985).

* Under very poor drainage conditions, even fertilization will not raise foliar P according to Dr. William McKee. 1990. Charleston, SC: USDA Forest Service, Southeastern Forest Experiment Station. Personal communication.

soil samples are confined to specific depths, such as 0 to 5 cm or 15 to 30 cm, to minimize sample variability. The forest floor may retain greater quantities of nutrients than the mineral soil retains, especially if the soils are sandy and have a very low cation-exchange capacity.

There are numerous other potential ways to estimate tree nutrient levels. For example, freshly fallen needles can be analyzed, but there is greater within-site variability in nutrient levels in freshly fallen needles than in living ones. Although more samples may be required, the ease and safety of collection on the ground justify additional research on the potential value of this residue for predicting tree nutrient status (Lea and Ballard 1982a). Xylem and twigs may also characterize the N status in loblolly pine trees, but diagnostic techniques are not yet available. It may be possible to develop a test to determine N status from increment cores (Cotrufo 1983). The arginine ($C_6H_{14}N_4O_2$) N content in freshly fallen twigs and needles may be another possible technique for assaying N in loblolly pines (Cotrufo 1985).

Remote sensing might be used to detect nutrient deficiencies and fertilizer responses in loblolly pines as well as locations or periods of loblolly pine stress. Winter yellowing of loblolly needles, especially in interior upland plantations, is related to foliar N and possibly P and Mg levels. Loblolly pine genotypes that show foliar color shifts in the winter might serve as indicators of the need for supplemental nutrients in plantations (Blinn and Buckner 1987, Lyons and Buckner 1981).

Symptoms of Nutrient Deficiencies

A proper balance of nutrients is critical to good form and rapid growth in loblolly pine. Deficiency symptoms include reduced growth, unusual morphology of various tree parts, reduced flower and cone production, and unusual coloration of needles, buds, or other parts. The most common and obvious symptom is color change,

especially in needles. Yellowing of needles usually indicates a shortage of N, but may also indicate a lack of Mg, sulfur (S), or iron (Fe). Nitrogen-deficient loblolly pine needles contain less than 1.2% N. Visual and physical symptoms of N deficiency include yellowish-green coloration and short stiff needles. Phosphorus deficiency causes a reddish-purple coloration of needles. Needles deficient in P contain less than 0.1% P, and early abscission may occur. Potassium deficiency is indicated by reddish-colored needles that tend to form spirals around buds. Severe K deficiency in young seedlings causes a purpling or browning of the tips of primary needles, reduced development of secondary needles, and eventual top dieback. These symptoms occur when needles contain 0.16 to 0.26% K on a dry weight basis. Magnesium-deficient seedlings (those with needles that contain less than 0.08% Mg on a dry weight basis) are characterized by yellowing of needles, reduced growth, and in severe cases top dieback. Calcium and boron (B) deficiencies result in degeneration of buds and secretion of resin from surrounding tissues. Needles that contain less than 0.03% Ca on a dry weight basis are deficient in Ca. Exudation of resin from the buds, first on branches and then on the terminal leader, is an early indication of deficiency. Later, needles become mottled yellow-green, mainly at the tops of seedlings. Other symptoms of Ca deficiency include reductions in numbers of needles; needles that are thicker, wider, and shorter than normal; terminal buds that are smaller and shorter than normal and bear dead, brown scales; and root tips that are blunt and covered with dead, partially decomposed cells. Copper (Cu)-deficient seedlings produce needles that are normal in shape but have tan and greenish-yellow bands. Seedlings that are deficient in manganese (Mn) produce single needles and few three-needle bundles. Molybdenum (Mo) deficiency has no apparent visible symptoms (Blinn and Buckner 1987, Davis 1949, Fowells and Krauss 1959, Lyle 1970, Sucoff 1961).

The following dichotomous key can be used to identify deficiencies in essential elements in greenhouse-grown loblolly pine seedlings (Lyle 1969).

I. Resin exudation from needles and/or buds
  A. Needles 10.0 Y 5/4 with splotches or 5.0 YR 5/6. Exudation from buds and needles. (Ca)
  B. Needles 7.5 GY 4/4 or 3/4. Exudation from buds. (B)

II. No resin exudation
  A. Needle color 7.5 GY
    1. Needles 7.5 GY 4/4 or 4/6 and short, thick, and twisted (zinc = Zn)
    2. Needles not short, thick, and twisted.
      a. Some dead needles 5.0 RP 3/4. Dead needle tips 7.5 YR.

(1) Some dead needles 5.0 RP 3/4. Dead needle tips 7.5 YR 7/4. (P)
(2) Some dead needles 10.0 R or 5.0 R.
  (a) Some dead needles 10.0 R 4/2. Needles spiral about terminals and present tufted appearance. (K)
  (b) Live needles 7.5 GY 7/8 or 6/6 with some dead needles 5.0 R 6/6. Poor secondary needle development. (Mn)
      b. No dead needles RP or R but dead needle ends 5.0 YR 5/4, 6/4, or 5/6 with bands at intervals around the dead portions. (Cu)
  B. Needle color 2.5 GY
    1. Large portions of needles vary in color.
      a. Needles 2.5 GY 7/6. Ends of needles YR or R but never Y. (N)
      b. Needles 2.5 GY 8/6. Ends of needles 5.0 Y 8/8 before YR and R stages. (Mg)
    2. Needles tend to have uniform color from tip to base.
      a. Needles 2.5 GY 8/6, 8/8, 8/10. Base of some needles become 10.0 Y 8/6 as deficiency progresses. (Fe)
      b. Needles 2.5 GY 6/6 or 5/6. No part of needle becomes Y. (S)

Foliage color is determined using Munsel color charts. Notations are written with a symbol for hue followed by a fraction. The symbols for hue are: 7.5 GY = green, 2.5 GY = yellowish green, 7.5 YR = brownish yellow, 5.0 YR = reddish brown, 10.0 Y = greenish yellow, 5.0 Y = yellow, 10.0 R = brownish red, 5.0 R = red, and 5.0 RP = reddish purple. The fraction (for example, 5/4) includes a value (the numerator) between white and black and a chroma (the denominator), which is the strength of the color in relation to a neutral grey of the value under consideration.

Relying on visual symptoms to ascertain chemical deficiencies can be misleading because different chemical deficiencies result in similar visual symptoms and because multiple chemical deficiencies can mask individual deficiencies. In addition, moisture stress can affect needle color. During dehydration, foliage normally turns from dark greenish yellow to light greenish yellow. The moisture content of healthy, dark greenish yellow (7.5 GY) needles can range from 70 to more than 200%. The moisture content of light greenish yellow (2.5 GY) needles can range from 40% to about 180%. Yellowish red (5 YR) needles never have more than 60% moisture content and are usually dead (Stransky 1963).

Water Management

On wet sites, tree height and diameter growth increase as the level of the water table declines. Loblolly pine do not grow very well at any age on wet sites even if the water table remains at the soil surface only during the winter and the soil is well aerated during the growing season (Tiarks and Shoulders 1982). Loblolly pines usually grow best where average water table depth is 45 to 72 cm (Campbell 1977, Debell and others 1982, Gresham and Williams 1978). During the first 5 years of growth on a Florida flatwoods site, average height and diameter of loblolly were about 80% greater when depth to the water table was artificially maintained at 46 cm than when depth to the water table was allowed to fluctuate throughout the growing season. Water control was also superior to fertilization as a single treatment (White and Pritchett 1970). Height growth of 14- to 31-year-old loblolly in natural stands in the South Carolina Coastal Plain was greatest when the average depth to water was 64 cm. However, maximum diameter growth occurred when the average depth to water was 72 cm (Gresham and Williams 1978).

Stands of pole and sawtimber loblolly pines often keep the water table well below ground level in wet areas by removing 90 to 100 cm of water/year through evapotranspiration. Once these stands are cut, the water table usually climbs to the soil surface and makes regeneration difficult and spotty. Uneven-aged management may permit continuous good growth without costly drainage treatments on some wet sites.

Stand density also affects moisture-nutrient interactions on dry sites. Soil moisture can be significantly increased by reducing stocking (Lilieholm and Hu 1985), and water can be rationed by selecting genotypes that grow well under conditions of low soil moisture. These actions can effectively lengthen the growing season and increase the growth of loblolly pines on dry sites. Although few data are available, combining stocking control with loblolly genotypes that require less water may offer alternatives for loblolly management on dry sites.

Economics of Forest Management

The economics of loblolly pine management must be evaluated on a case-by-case basis because the profitability of growing trees varies by tract size, site, and management regime and is extremely sensitive to the interest rate or cost of capital used. For example, long rotations are normally more profitable than short rotations for owners of small woodlots, especially on good sites when discount rates are low. Also, average costs are significantly greater for tracts less than about 30 ha, and mechanized operations are often uneconomical where tracts are small (Cubbage 1983). Where loblolly and shortleaf grow together, it is more profitable to grow loblolly.

Cultural treatments are economically justified only if their cost is less than the expected returns in the form of salable products or long-term benefits. For example, removal of undesirable hardwoods is usually economically advantageous. The most cost-effective method of hardwood control is prescribed burning (Franklin 1985). Kline and Kidd (1986) estimated that under conservative economic assumptions, on land with a site index of 21 m, at base age 25, and with a 30-year rotation, a 10% change in hardwood basal area yields an average change of $260/ha in the net present value of a loblolly pine plantation. Similarly, Bullard and Karr (1986) projected that up to $50/ha spent to control hardwoods in a new stand of loblolly on land with a site index of 21 m and a base age of 25 would provide double-digit returns at stand age 25. Control of only large hardwoods can double pine production and increase financial returns by more than 200% (Balmer and others 1978). Herbaceous weed control in new plantations can be economically advantageous even if rotation length is reduced by only 1 year (Busby 1989). However, it is generally not cost effective to spend as much money controlling herbaceous weeds as controlling woody weeds (Dangerfield and Merck 1989).

In plantation management, returns are maximized when initial stocking is moderate to low and when moderate to heavy thinning is done when commercially feasible (Franklin 1987). The internal rate of return (IRR) obtained by planting and growing loblolly pines under various intensive culture regimes for 29 years on a north Louisiana oldfield site ranged from 17 to 22%. However, untreated plantings provided a very respectable IRR of 16.4% (Hotvedt 1983). The use of genetically improved trees is a good investment wherever silvicultural practices are sufficiently intense to ensure good early survival and growth (Smith 1983).

Natural stand management may often be more cost effective than plantation management (table 8-13), and it definitely gives NIPF landowners more low-cost alternatives. The relative economy of even-aged versus uneven-aged natural stand management seems to depend on whether or not the zero-age volume for an uneven-aged stand is considered a cost (Guldin and Guldin 1990). Regeneration costs for natural stands of loblolly pines can range from zero to $370/ha. On the Coastal Plain, the average regeneration cost of seed tree, shelterwood, and clearcutting treatments ranges from $75 to $150/ha. Regeneration costs for selection management range from $50 to $75/ha at every 5- to 10-year harvest cycle. Any delay in regeneration is costly because it extends the

Table 8-13—Economic parameters for four loblolly pine management systems with a 50-year management period and a 7% discount rate

Management system	Net present value ($/ha)	Benefit-to-cost ratio	Cost efficiency*	
			m^3/$	fbm/$
Uneven-aged (HS)	998	3.71	1.1	142.6
Uneven-aged (LS)	776	3.11	0.8	118.2
Even-aged (natural)	1,337	5.40	1.8	133.4
Even-aged (plantation)	1,218	3.13	1.0	90.7

Source: adapted from Baker (1987).

fbm = foot board measure in the English system; HS = high stocking; LS = low stocking.

* Cost efficiency = total production ÷ total discounted cost.

time until the next harvest and because it usually entails the additional cost of controlling competing vegetation that is more extensive, or larger, or both.

From a financial standpoint, hardwood control and precommercial thinning are the most important treatments in managing natural loblolly pines. Because timber stand improvement does not affect normal annual ownership costs or overhead charges, it can provide

earning rates of 25 to 30% if it is done at key times and if the products are sold (Anderson 1975). Guldin (1984) calculated that it is economical for a landowner to spend as much as $130/ha to release a natural loblolly-short-leaf stand at age 3 if the stand can be thinned at age 15, a chip-and-saw market exists, and the alternative rate of return is 10%.

Summary

It is practical to manage loblolly pines over rotations of 25 to at least 120 years, depending on management objectives. Stand management has many components. In the early stages of stand development, vegetation control is important, but it is never necessary to eradicate any indigenous plant species. If competing hardwood trees, shrubs, vines, and herbaceous plants are not controlled during the first several growing seasons, young loblolly may not be able to compete for growing space or may not dominate a forest site. Competition with grasses and forbs for surface soil moisture is more likely to slow loblolly seedling growth for the first 1 to 3 years than is competition with hardwood sprouts or new shrubs. By stand age 4 to 5, hardwood sprouts begin to compete destructively with young pines, especially where there are more than about 7,400 hardwood sprouts/ha. It is best to perform hardwood control during the first or second year of pine growth because control is easiest and cheapest while hardwoods are small. When loblolly is to be the only crop species, dominant and codominant hardwoods should be treated (as necessary) to enable young pines to maintain a height advantage over all hardwood competition. However, if adequate numbers of pines are free to grow, competition control may not be profitable even at young tree ages and especially on poor sites. Loblolly eventually dominates the site if a good stand has been established. The value of competition control diminishes after crown closure. Once loblolly reaches about age 40, growth increases associated with any kind of competition control are usually small, and competition control treatments uneconomical.

Precommercial thinning of dense natural stands, coupled with hardwood control, can be cost effective if done before stand age 6. Where loblolly pines are more than 3 m tall, low intensity winter backfires can be applied every 3 to 5 years to reduce the thickness of the organic layer by 10 to 20% and to kill the aboveground portion of most young understory hardwoods. Such fires cause only minor pollution, result in little nutrient loss, and probably promote N fixation by free-living microorganisms and N-fixing plants. Tree injection, basal bark, foliar, or soil applications of chemicals are all effective

ways to kill competing hardwoods and promote loblolly growth. Basal bark spraying can be very effective throughout the year. Broadcast, spot, and band spraying of chemicals are the most practical ways of controlling herbaceous competition.

Periodic thinnings are necessary to accelerate growth of crop trees and to maximize yields, except when rotations are very short. Stocking control treatments should be regulated by guidelines that specify (1) the number of trees that should remain after thinning, (2) the proper spacing for crop trees, (3) the kinds of defects that can be tolerated in a stand, and (4) the priorities for removal of defective trees. Competition promotes crown differentiation in a stand and directs growth potential toward dominant and codominant trees. Stocking control can eliminate all but the final crop trees early or over time through several thinnings. Selection thinning is more effective than row or corridor thinning in stimulating stand growth because remaining trees are of larger size and better quality. However, row thinning is much easier and much less costly. Selection thinning is clearly advantageous where high-value products are in demand. Row thinning is preferred in large forests of closely spaced stands that have to be thinned in a short time. Selection and row thinnings can be combined when a stand contains many high-risk and low-quality trees. Crown ratios should be kept close to 50%, especially during the early years of rapid growth (through about age 15). Close plantation spacing is normally a commitment to early and frequent thinning of small material to minimize losses to mortality and to maximize returns per tree planted. Conversely, wide spacing is an equally strong commitment to delayed thinning, reduced site productivity potential, and larger trees of lower quality unless pruning is accomplished early. Neither spacing, thinning, nor pruning significantly affects age of xylem transformation from juvenile to mature wood.

Fertilization, alone or combined with thinning, can greatly increase the growth of loblolly pine stands, especially if applied at critical times and in the proper sequence or combination. The value of fertilization is very site specific, depending on nutrient availability, nutrient reserves, and a host of environmental factors including rainfall patterns, soil physical and chemical properties, and competing vegetation. Effects of rainfall are most noticeable in the West Gulf area, where evapotranspiration exceeds rainfall in summer and where severe competition for moisture reduces or negates the potential value of fertilizer. From the time of planting, P fertilization dramatically increases loblolly growth on many wet soils of the lower Coastal Plain. Loblolly would probably benefit from P or N+P fertilization shortly before or soon after regeneration on about two-thirds of all Coastal Plain sites. Established stands are often responsive to N and N+P fertilizers, but growth improvement varies considerably. The effect of N applications is rather short lived (5 to 10 years), but a single application of P may increase growth throughout a rotation. Fertilization increases both diameter and height growth of dominant and codominant trees much more than it increases the growth of intermediate or over-topped trees. Thus, fertilization makes trees in lower crown classes less competitive and so increases or accelerates mortality. Fertilization accelerates tree growth most when combined with weed control.

The season of fertilizer application makes no difference except in the case of N, which should be applied in the spring or fall. The earlier the application of deficient nutrients in a particular year, the greater the tree growth. The direct benefit of fertilizer is primarily to the trees. The site benefits indirectly from rapid tree growth and greater levels of litter accumulation because trees and abundant litter provide excellent early protection for eroded soils.

The commonest symptom of nutrient deficiency is yellowing of needles. Yellowing usually indicates an N deficiency but can be caused by a deficiency of Mg, S, or Fe. Reddish-purple needles indicate P deficiency. Potassium deficiency is indicated by reddish-colored needles that tend to form spirals around buds.

Research Needs

- Reliable and inexpensive estimates of both commodity and noncommodity values of forest stands are needed for even-aged and uneven-aged management alternatives, and for both large- and small-scale operations.

- Better criteria are needed to equitably compare the cost efficiency of various natural stand management methods and to compare natural stand management with plantation management.

- To maintain a combination of excellent pine growth and maximum biological diversity, detailed information is needed on how individual plant species compete with loblolly pine. Then, specific techniques should be developed to selectively control only those plant species that provide the most competition to loblolly pine.

- Improved, safer, and less expensive methods are needed to estimate the nutrient status of trees. For example, getting reliable results from freshly fallen needles or twigs or new xylem from the tree base would greatly improve the safety and cost of tissue sampling.

- More effective systems are needed to ameliorate nutrient deficiencies through the manipulation of fertilizer sources, and rates, frequency, and methods of application.

- Better understanding is needed of the interaction between nutrition, moisture, light, and genetic potential to effectively relate cultural treatments (such as thinning, fertilizing, and water control) to tree growth potential.

- Our understanding of the role optimum nutrition plays in minimizing stand susceptibility to diseases, insects, and adverse climatic conditions needs to be improved.

Literature Cited

Adams MB, Pennell KD, Campbell RG. 1989. Fine root distribution in a young loblolly pine (*Pinus taeda* L.) stand: effects of preplant phosphorus fertilization. Plant and Soil 113(2):275–278.

Allen HL, Ballard R. 1983. Forest fertilization of loblolly pine. In: Proceedings, Symposium on the Loblolly Pine Ecosystem—East Region; 1982 December 8–10; Raleigh, NC. Raleigh, NC: North Carolina State University, School of Forest Resources: 163–181.

Allen PH. 1960. Scorch and mortality after a summer burn in loblolly pine. Res. Note 144. Asheville, NC: USDA Forest Service, Southeastern Forest Experiment Station. 2 p.

Anderson WC. 1975. Timber stand improvement. Journal of Forestry 73(4):222–223.

Arthaud GJ, Klemperer WD. 1986. An economic approach to thinning in loblolly pine plantations. In: Forest economics—

gumbo New Orleans style: Proceedings of the 1986 Southern Forest Economics Workshop; 1986 April 16–18; New Orleans, LA. Raleigh, NC: North Carolina State University: 93–100.

Arthaud GJ, Klemperer WD. 1988. Optimizing high and low thinnings in loblolly pine with dynamic programming. Canadian Journal of Forest Research 18(9):1118–1122.

Ayers GD, Clason TR, Smith WD. 1987. Impact of intensive competition management on dominant stand height. In: Proceedings, 4th Biennial Southern Silvicultural Research Conference; 1986 November 4–6; Atlanta, GA. Gen. Tech. Rep. SE-42. Asheville, NC: USDA Forest Service, Southeastern Forest Experiment Station: 576–580.

Bacon CG, Zedaker SM. 1985. First year growth response of young loblolly pine (Pinus taeda L.) to competition control on the Virginia Piedmont. In: Proceedings, 3rd Biennial Southern Silvicultural Research Conference; 1984 November 7–8; Atlanta, GA. Gen. Tech. Rep. SO-54: New Orleans: USDA Forest Service, Southern Forest Experiment Station: 309–314.

Bacon CG, Zedaker SM. 1986. Competition control in young loblolly pine plantations of Virginia Piedmont. Proceedings of the Southern Weed Science Society 39:196.

Baker JB, Switzer GL, Nelson LE. 1974. Biomass production and nitrogen recovery after fertilization of young loblolly pines. Soil Science Society of America Proceedings 38(6):958–961.

Baker JB. 1987. Production and financial comparisons of uneven-aged and even-aged management of loblolly pine. In: Proceedings, 4th Biennial Southern Silvicultural Research Conference; 1986 November 4–6; Atlanta, GA. Gen. Tech. Rep. SE-42. Asheville, NC: USDA Forest Service, Southeastern Forest Experiment Station: 267–273.

Ballard R. 1981a. Optimum nitrogen rates for fertilization of loblolly pine plantations. Southern Journal of Applied Forestry 5(4):212–216.

Ballard R. 1981b. Urea and ammonium nitrate as nitrogen sources for southern pine plantations. Southern Journal of Applied Forestry 5(3):105–108.

Ballard R, Lea R. 1986. Foliar analysis for predicting quantitative fertilizer response: the importance of stand and site variables to the interpretation. Forestry Sciences 20:163–170.

Ballard R, Duzan HW Jr, Kane MB. 1981. Thinning and fertilization of loblolly pine plantations. In: Proceedings, 1st Biennial Southern Silvicultural Research Conference; 1980 November 6–7; Atlanta, GA. Gen. Tech. Rep. SO-34. New Orleans: USDA Forest Service, Southern Forest Experiment Station: 100–104.

Balmer WE, Utz KA, Langdon OG. 1978. Financial returns from cultural work in natural loblolly pine stands. Southern Journal of Applied Forestry 2(4):111–17.

Balmer WE, Williston HL. 1973. The need for precommercial thinning. For. Mgmt. Bull. Atlanta: USDA Forest Service, Southeastern Area, State and Private Forestry. 6 p.

Bell RL, Binkley D. 1989. Soil nitrogen mineralization and immobilization in response to periodic prescribed fire in a loblolly pine plantation. Canadian Journal of Forest Research 19(6):816–820.

Bengtson GW. 1976. Comparative response of four southern pine species to fertilization: effects of P, NP, and NPKMgS applied at planting. Forest Science 22(4):487–494.

Bengtson GW. 1970. Placement influences the effectiveness of phosphates for pine seedlings. In: Tree growth and forest soils. Proceedings, 3rd North American Soils Conference; 1968 August; Raleigh, NC. Corvallis, OR: Oregon State University Press: 51–63.

Berry CR. 1985. Growth and heavy metal accumulation in pine seedlings grown with sewage sludge. Journal of Environmental Quality 14(3):415–419.

Berry CR. 1977. Initial response of pine seedlings and weeds to dried sewage sludge in rehabilitation of an eroded forest site. Res. Note SE-249. Asheville, NC: USDA Forest Service, Southeastern Forest Experiment Station. 8 p.

Berry CR. 1987. Use of municipal sewage sludge for improvement of forest sites in the Southwest. Res. Pap. SE-266. Asheville, NC: USDA Forest Service, Southeastern Forest Experiment Station. 33 p.

Berry CW. 1970. Enumeration and identification of the microbial populations from burned and unburned pine forest soil. Ruston, LA: Louisiana Tech University. 44 p. M.S. thesis.

Bilan MV, Gillespie MA. 1985. Long term response of loblolly pine to colloidal phosphate. In: Proceedings, 3rd Biennial Southern Silvicultural Research Conference; 1984 November 7–8; Atlanta, GA. Gen. Tech. Rep. SO-54: New Orleans: USDA Forest Service, Southern Forest Experiment Station: 341–345.

Binkley D. 1986. Soil acidity in loblolly pine stands with interval burning. Soil Science Society of America Journal 50(6):1590–1594.

Blackburn WH, Wood JC, DeHaven MG. 1986. Storm flow and sediment losses from site-prepared forestland in east Texas. Water Resources Research 22(5):776–784.

Blinn CR, Buckner ER. 1987. Foliage color and nutrient levels: for loblolly pine, indicator trees might serve as a guide to forest fertilization. Journal of Forestry 85(5):48–49.

Bower DR. 1966. Surface soil recovers quickly after burn. Res. Note SO-46. New Orleans: USDA Forest Service, Southern Forest Experiment Station. 2 p.

Boyer WD. 1987. Role of competing vegetation in forest health. In: Forests, the World, & the Profession: Proceedings, 1986 Society of American Foresters National Convention; 1986 October 5–8; Birmingham, AL. Bethesda, MD: Society of American Foresters: 235–239.

Brendemuehl RH. 1970. The phosphorus placement problem in forest fertilization. In: Tree growth and forest soils: Proceedings, 3rd North American Soils Conference; 1968 August; Raleigh, NC. Corvallis, OR: Oregon State University Press: 43–50.

Brender EV. 1961. Pruning open-grown loblolly pine. Southern Lumberman 123(2537):134–136.

Brender EV. 1965. Thinning loblolly pine. In: Wahlenberg WG, ed. A guide to loblolly and slash pine plantation management in southeastern USA. Rep. 14. Macon, GA: Georgia Forest Research Council: 99–110.

Brender EV, Cooper RW. 1968. Prescribed burning in Georgia's Piedmont loblolly pine stands. Journal of Forestry 66(1):31–36.

Brender EV, McNab WH. 1978. Precommercial thinning of loblolly pine by fertilization. Res. Pap. 90. Macon, GA: Georgia Forest Research Council. 8 p.

Bruner MH, Reamer LD. 1966. Loblolly pine or yellow poplar on upland Piedmont sites? Journal of Forestry 64(4):251–252.

Buford MA, McKee WH Jr. 1987. Effects of site preparation, fertilization and genotype on loblolly pine growth and stand structure—results at age 15. In: Proceedings, 4th Biennial Southern Silvicultural Research Conference; 1986 November 4–6; Atlanta, GA. Gen. Tech. Rep. SE-42. Asheville, NC: USDA Forest Service, Southeastern Forest Experiment Station: 378–383.

Bullard SH, Karr BL. 1986. Rates of return on silvicultural practices. Proceedings of the Southern Weed Science Society 39:318–323.

Burkhart HE, Sprinz PT. 1984. A model for assessing hardwood competition effects on yields of loblolly pine plantations. Publ. FWS-3-84. Blacksburg, VA: Virginia Polytechnic Institute and State University, School of Forestry and Wildlife Resources. 55 p.

Burton JD. 1982. Sawtimber by prescription—the sudden sawlog story through age 33. Res. Pap. SO-179. New Orleans: USDA Forest Service, Southern Forest Experiment Station. 9 p.

Burton JD. 1977. Managing for high-value poles in the loblolly–shortleaf belt. Southern Journal of Applied Forestry 1(1):11–15.

Busby RL. 1989. Economic returns using sulfometuron methyl (Oust) for herbaceous weed control in southern pine plantations. In: Proceedings, 5th Biennial Southern Silvicultural Research Conference; 1988 November 1–3; Memphis, TN. Gen. Tech. Rep. SO-74. New Orleans: USDA Forest Service, Southern Forest Experiment Station: 359–364.

Byram GM. 1959. Combustion of forest fuels. In: Davis KP, ed. Forest fires: control and use. New York: McGraw-Hill Book Company: 61–89.

Cain MD. 1983. Precommercial thinning for the private, nonindustrial landowner. In: Proceedings, 2nd Biennial Southern Silvicultural Research Conference; 1982 November 4–5; Atlanta, GA. Gen. Tech. Rep. SE-24. Asheville, NC: USDA Forest Service, Southeastern Forest Experiment Station: 200–205.

Cain MD. 1984. Height of stem-bark char underestimates flame length in prescribed burns. Fire Management Notes 45(1):17–21.

Cain MD. 1985a. Japanese honesuckle and associated ground cover inhibit establishment and growth of pine seedlings in all-aged stands. In: Proceedings, 3rd Biennial Southern Silvicultural Research Conference; 1984 November 7–8; Atlanta, GA. Gen. Tech. Rep. SO-54: New Orleans: USDA Forest Service, Southern Forest Experiment Station: 300–304.

Cain MD. 1985b. Long-term impact of hardwood control treatments in mature pine. Res. Pap. SO-214. New Orleans: USDA Forest Service, Southern Forest Experiment Station. 8 p.

Cain MD. 1985c. Prescribed winter burns can reduce the growth of nine-year-old loblolly pines. Res. Note SO-312. New Orleans: USDA Forest Service, Southern Forest Experiment Station. 4 p.

Cain MD. 1988. Competition impacts on growth of naturally regenerated loblolly pine seedlings. Res. Note SO-345. New Orleans: USDA Forest Service, Southern Forest Experiment Station. 5 p.

Cain MD, Mann WF Jr. 1980. Annual brush control increases early growth of loblolly pine. Southern Journal of Applied Forestry 4(2):67–70.

Cain MD, Yaussy DA. 1983. Reinvasion of hardwoods following eradication in an uneven-aged pine stand. Res. Pap. SO-188. New Orleans: USDA Forest Service, Southern Forest Experiment Station. 8 p.

Cain MD, Yaussy DA. 1984. Can hardwoods be eradicated from pine sites? Southern Journal of Applied Forestry 8(1):7–13.

Cain MD, Baker JB, Murphy PA. 1987. Precommercial thinning of pine regeneration in uneven-aged stands. In: Proceedings, 4th Biennial Southern Silvicultural Research Conference; 1986 November 4–6; Atlanta, GA. Gen. Tech. Rep. SE-42. Asheville, NC: USDA Forest Service, Southeastern Forest Experiment Station: 419–424.

Campbell RG. 1977. Drainage of lower Coastal Plain soils. In: Proceedings, 6th Southern Forest Soils Workshop; 1976 October 19–21; Charleston, SC. Atlanta: USDA Forest Service, Southeastern Area, State and Private Forestry: 17–27.

Campbell TE. 1981. Evaluating Velpar gridball for pine release. Proceedings of the Southern Weed Science Society 34:159–164.

Campbell TE. 1985a. Herbicide sprays tested for loblolly pine tolerance. Proceedings of the Southern Weed Science Society 38:176–180.

Campbell TE. 1985b. Sprouting of slash, loblolly and shortleaf pines following a simulated precommerical thinning. Res. Note SO-320. New Orleans: USDA Forest Service, Southern Forest Experiment Station. 3 p.

Carter GA, Miller JH, Davis DE, Patterson RM. 1984. Effect of vegetative competition on the moisture and nutrient status of loblolly pine. Canadian Journal of Forest Research 14:1–9.

Carter MC, Lyle ES Jr. 1966. Fertilization of loblolly pine on two Alabama soils: effects on growth and foliar mineral content. Bull. 370. Auburn, AL: Auburn University, Alabama Agricultural Experiment Station. 18 p.

Chen MY, Hodgkins EJ, Watson WJ. 1975. Prescribed burning for improved pine production and wildlife habitat in the Hilly Coastal Plain of Alabama. Bull. 473. Auburn, AL: Auburn University, Alabama Agricultural Experiment Station. 20 p.

Clason TR. 1979. Removal of hardwood vegetation increased growth and yield of a young loblolly pine stand. Fors. Res. Rep. 1979. Homer, LA: North Louisiana Hill Farm Experiment Station: 43–48.

Clason TR. 1984. Hardwood eradication improves productivity of thinned loblolly pine stands. Southern Journal of Applied Forestry 8(4):194–197.

Clason TR. 1987. Effect of legumes on pine growth in thinned loblolly pine plantations. In: Proceedings, 4th Biennial Southern Silvicultural Research Conference; 1986 November 4–6; Atlanta, GA. Gen. Tech. Rep. SE-42. Asheville, NC: USDA Forest Service, Southeastern Forest Experiment Station: 429–432.

Comerford NB, Fisher RF, Pritchell WL. 1983. Advances in forest fertilization on the Southeastern Coastal Plain. In: IUFRO Symposium on Forest Site and Continuous Productivity; 1982 August 22–28; Seattle, WA. Gen. Tech. Rep. PNW-163. Portland, OR: USDA Forest Service, Pacific Northwest Forest and Range Experiment Station: 370–378.

Cooper RW, Altobellis AT. 1969. Fire kill in young loblolly pine. Fire Control Notes 30(4):14–15.

Cotrufo C. 1983. Xylem nitrogen as a possible diagnostic nitrogen test for loblolly pine. Canadian Journal of Forest Research 13(2):355–357.

Cotrufo C. 1985. Progress in tissue analysis to determine the response of loblolly pine to nitrogen fertilization. In: Proceedings, 3rd Biennial Southern Silvicultural Research Conference; 1984 November 7–8; Atlanta, GA. Gen. Tech. Rep. SO-54: New Orleans: USDA Forest Service, Southern Forest Experiment Station: 385–388.

Craig JR, Wollum AG II. 1982. Ammonia volatilization and soil nitrogen changes after urea and ammonium nitrate fertilization of *Pinus taeda* L. Soil Science Society of America Journal 46(2):409–414.

Cubbage F. 1983. Economics of forest tract size: theory and literature. Gen. Tech. Rep. SO-41. New Orleans: USDA Forest Service, Southern Forest Experiment Station. 21 p.

Cushwa CT, Hopkins M, McGinnes BS. 1971. Soil movement in established gullies after a single prescribed burn in the South Carolina Piedmont. Res. Note SE-153. Asheville, NC: USDA Forest Service, Southeastern Forest Experiment Station. 4 p.

Dahlin B. 1981. New equipment for pruning in young stands. In: Forest regeneration: Proceedings, Symposium on Engineering Systems for Forest Regeneration; 1981 March 2–6; Raleigh, NC. ASAE Publ. 10-81. St. Joseph, MI: American Society of Agricultural Engineers: 362–367.

Dangerfield CW, Merck HL. 1989. Economics of herbaceous and woody weed control in loblolly pine plantations. In: Proceedings, 5th Biennial Southern Silvicultural Research Conference; 1988 November 1–3; Memphis, TN. Gen. Tech. Rep. SO-74. New Orleans: USDA Forest Service, Southern Forest Experiment Station: 365–370.

Davis DE. 1949. Some effects of calcium deficiency on the anatomy of *Pinus taeda*. American Journal of Botany 36:276–282.

DeBell DS, Askew GR, Hook DD, and others. 1982. Species suitability on a lowland site altered by drainage. Southern Journal of Applied Forestry 6(1): 2–9.

de Bruyn P, Buckner E. 1981. Prescribed fire on sloping terrain in west Tennessee to maintain loblolly pine (*Pinus taeda* L.). In: Proceedings, 1st Biennial Southern Silvicultural Research Conference; 1980 November 6–7; Atlanta, GA. Gen. Tech. Rep. SO-34. New Orleans: USDA Forest Service, Southern Forest Experiment Station: 67–69.

Dickerson, B.P. 1972. Changes in the forest floor under upland oak stands and managed loblolly pine plantations. Journal of Forestry 70(9):560–562.

Dierauf TA. 1986a. Loblolly pine release report no. 3. Occas. Rep. 67. Charlottesville, VA: Virginia Division of Forestry, Department of Conservation and Economic Development. 11 p.

Dierauf TA. 1986b. Loblolly pine release report no. 4. Occas. Rep. 68. Charlottesville, VA: Virginia Division of Forestry, Department of Conservation and Economic Development. 7 p.

Dierauf TA. 1986c. Loblolly pine release report no. 5. Occas. Rep. 69. Charlottesville, VA: Virginia Division of Forestry,

Department of Conservation and Economic Development. 9 p.

Dierauf TA. 1986d. Loblolly pine release report no. 6. Occas. Rep. 70. Charlottesville, VA: Virginia Division of Forestry, Department of Conservation and Economic Development. 12 p.

Dippon DR, Shelton JT. 1983. Rate of return from fertilization of semimature slash pine plantations. In: Proceedings, 2nd Biennial Southern Silvicultural Research Conference; 1982 November 4–5; Atlanta, GA. Gen. Tech. Rep. SE-24. Asheville, NC: USDA Forest Service, Southeastern Forest Experiment Station: 302–311.

Dissmeyer GE. 1976. Erosion and sediment from forest land uses, management practices, and disturbances in the southeastern United States. In: Proceedings, 3rd Federal Interagency Sedimentation Conference; 1976 March 22-25; Denver, CO. [Place of publication unknown]: Sedimentation Committee Water Resources Council: 1-140–1-148.

Dissmeyer GE. 1978. Forest management principles revealed by recent water quality studies. In: Proceedings, Soil Moisture ... Site Productivity Symposium; 1977 November 1–3; Myrtle Beach, SC. Asheville, NC: USDA Forest Service, Southern Region, State and Private Forestry: 97–110.

Dougherty PM, Lowery RF. 1991. Spot-size of herbaceous control impacts loblolly pine seedling survival and growth. Southern Journal of Applied Forestry 15(4):193–199.

Douglass JE, Van Lear DH, Valverde C. 1983. Stormflow changes after prescribed burning and clearcutting pine stands in the South Carolina Piedmont. In: Proceedings, 2nd Biennial Southern Silvicultural Research Conference; 1982 November 4–5; Atlanta, GA. Gen. Tech. Rep. SE-24. Asheville, NC: USDA Forest Service, Southeastern Forest Experiment Station: 454–460.

Edwards MB, Gonzalez FE. 1986. Forestry herbicide control of kudzu and Japanese honeysuckle in loblolly pine sites in central Georgia. Proceedings of the Southern Weed Science Society 39:272–275.

Edwards MB, Miller JH. 1988. Please release me, let me grow! Forest Farmer 47(6):17–19.

Feduccia DP. 1983. Thinning pine plantations. Forest Farmer 42(10):10–11.

Fisher RF. 1981. Soils interpretations for silviculture in the southeastern Coastal Plain. In: Proceedings, 1st Biennial Southern Silvicultural Research Conference; 1980 November 6–7; Atlanta, GA. Gen. Tech. Rep. SO-34. New Orleans: USDA Forest Service, Southern Forest Experiment Station: 323–330.

Fisher RF, Garbett WS. 1980. Response of semimature slash and loblolly pine plantations to fertilization with nitrogen and phosphorus. Soil Science of America Journal 44(4):850–854.

Fiskell JGA, Martin FG, Pritchett WL, Maftoun M. 1982. Effects of cadmium levels and sludges on loblolly pine seedlings. Proceedings of the Soil and Crop Science Society of Florida 41:163–168.

Fitzgerald CH, Fortson JC. 1979a. Herbaceous weed control with hexazinone in loblolly pine (Pinus taeda) plantations. Weed Science 27(6):593–588.

Fitzgerald CH, Fortson JC. 1979b. Release and precommercial thinning of natural loblolly pine seedlings with bromacil. Proceedings of the Southern Weed Science Society 32:212.

Fitzgerald CH, Golden JK, Fortson JC. 1976. Postemergence effects of Velpar in a Piedmont pine plantation [Abstract]. Proceedings of the Southern Weed Science Society 29:299.

Fitzgerald CH, Griswold HC. 1984. Chemical loblolly pine release with aerial triclopyr applications. Proceedings of the Southern Weed Science Society 37:218–222.

Fitzgerald CH, Newbold RA, Fortson JC. 1980. Loblolly pine release with triclopyr and glyphosate [abstract]. Proceedings of the Southern Weed Science Society 33:119.

Fitzgerald CH, Peevy FA, Fender DE. 1973. The southern region. Journal of Forestry 71(3):148–153.

Fowells HA, Krauss RW. 1959. The inorganic nutrition of loblolly pine and Virginia pine with special reference to nitrogen and phosphorus. Forest Science 5(1):95–111.

Franklin EC. 1985. How to manage your woodlands profitably. Forest Farmer 44(5):14–15.

Franklin EC. 1987. Economics of forest management options: influence on wood properties. TAPPI Journal 70(1):85–88.

Gardner WE. 1985. Thin your pines for periodic income and better stands. Forest Farmer 44(5):36–39.

Garin GI. 1965. Pruning. In: Wahlenberg WG, ed. A guide to loblolly and slash pine plantation management in southeastern USA. Rep. 14. Macon, GA: Georgia Forest Research Council: 84–98.

Gent JA Jr, Allen HL, Campbell RG. 1986. Phosphorus and nitrogen plus phosphorus fertilization in loblolly pine stands at establishment. Southern Journal of Applied Forestry 10(2):114–117.

Gibson MD, Clason TR. 1991. Effect of pruning, spacing, and thinning on juvenile wood formation in loblolly pine. In: Proceedings, 6th Biennial Southern Silvicultural Research Conference; 1990 October 30–November 1; Memphis, TN. Gen. Tech. Rep. SE-70. Asheville, NC: USDA Forest Service, Southeastern Forest Experiment Station: 769–785.

Gilmore AR. 1980. Changes in a reforested soil associated with tree species and time. 4: Soil organic content and pH in pine plantations after 24 years. Fors. Res. Rep. 80-3. Urbana-Champaign, IL: University of Illinois, Department of Forestry. 3 p.

Ginn SE, Seiler JR, Cazell BH, Kreh RF. 1989. Physiological responses to thinning in eight-year-old loblolly pine stands on the Virginia Piedmont. In: Proceedings, 5th Biennial Southern Silvicultural Research Conference; 1988 November 1–3; Memphis, TN. Gen. Tech. Rep. SO-74. New Orleans: USDA Forest Service, Southern Forest Experiment Station: 67–73.

Glover GR, Creighton JL. 1985. Effects of hardwoods on pine yield, summary of data [abstract]. Proceedings of the Southern Weed Science Society 38:256 .

Gorden R, Miller JH, Brewer C. 1981. Site preparation treatments and nutrient loss following complete harvest using the Nicholson-Koch Mobile Chipper. In: Barnett JP, ed. Proceedings, 1st Biennial Southern Silvicultural Research Conference; 1980 November 6–7; Atlanta, GA. Gen. Tech. Rep. SO-34. New Orleans: USDA Forest Service, Southern Forest Experiment Station: 79–84.

Grano CX. 1961. Does pruning pay off? Forest Farmer 20(12):10–11.

Grano CX. 1965. Mortality of planted loblolly pine from hardwood overtopping. Journal of Forestry 63(12):938–939.

Grano CX. 1969. Precommercial thinning of loblolly pine. Journal of Forestry 67(11):825–827.

Grano CX. 1970a. Small hardwoods reduce growth of pine overstory. Res. Pap SO-55. New Orleans: USDA Forest Service, Southern Forest Experiment Station. 9 p.

Grano CX. 1970b. Eradicating understory hardwoods by repeated prescribed burning. Res. Pap. SO-56. New Orleans: USDA Forest Service, Southern Forest Experiment Station. 11 p.

Granskog JE. 1982. Performance of four row thinning systems using three types of harvesters. In: Stephenson EH, ed. Proceedings, Workshop on Thinning Southern Pine Plantations; 1982 May 24–26; Long Beach, MS. [Place of publication and publisher unknown]: 82–104.

Greene TA, Shilling CL. 1987. Predicting girdling probability for pine and hardwood saplings in low-intensity backfires. Forest Science 33(4):1010–1021.

Gresham CA, Williams TM. 1978. Water table depth and growth of young loblolly pine. In: Proceedings, Soil Moisture ... Site Productivity Symposium; 1977 November 1–3; Myrtle Beach, SC. Atlanta: USDA Forest Service, Southeastern Area, State and Private Forestry: 371–376.

Griswold HC. 1981. Application of Velpar herbicide by banding in newly established pine plantations. Proceedings of the Southern Weed Science Society 34:165–173.

Griswold HC, Gonzalez EI. 1985. Band applications of liquid hexazinone in newly established pine plantations for brush control. Proceedings of the Southern Weed Science Society 38:226–229.

Guldin JM, Guldin RW. 1990. Economic assessments of even-aged and uneven-aged loblolly–shortleaf pine stands. In: Proceedings, Southern Forest Economics Workshop on Evaluating Even and All-aged Timber Management Options for Southern Forest Lands; 1990 March 29–30; Monroe, LA. Gen. Tech. Rep. SO-79. New Orleans: USDA Forest Service, Southern Forest Experiment Station: 55–64.

Guldin RW. 1984. Economic returns from spraying to release loblolly pine. Proceedings of the Southern Weed Science Society 37:248–254.

Guldin RW. 1985. Pine release in unevenly stocked stands on droughty soils may be uneconomical. Res. Pap. SO-216. New Orleans: USDA Forest Service, Southern Forest Experiment Station. 5 p.

Haines LW, Haines SG. 1979. Fertilization increases growth of loblolly pine and ground cover vegetation on a Cecil soil. Forest Science 25(1):169–174.

Haines LW, Haines SG, Allen VH Jr. 1977. Fertilizing established loblolly pine stands. In: Proceedings, 6th Southern Forest Soils Workshop; 1976 October 19–21; Charleston, SC. Atlanta: USDA Forest Service, Southeastern Area, State and Private Forestry: 57–77.

Hansen RA, Johnson NE. 1974. Culture of the growing forest. Journal of Forestry 72(11):686–691.

Hart SC, Binkley D, Campbell RG. 1986. Predicting loblolly pine current growth and growth response to fertilization. Soil Science Society of America Journal 50(1):230–233.

Hatchell GE. 1964. Immediate release needed for maximum growth of seeded loblolly pine. Tree Planters' Notes 66:19–22.

Haywood JD. 1980. Charcoal fails to protect planted loblolly pine from soil herbicides. Tree Planters' Notes 31(2):14–16.

Haywood JD. 1986. Response of planted *Pinus taeda* L. to brush control in northern Louisiana. Forest Ecology and Management 15(2):129–134.

Haywood JD. 1988. Loblolly pine (*Pinus taeda*) response to weed control in central Louisiana. Weed Technology 2(4):490–494.

Hegg RO, Shearin AT, Handlin DL, Grimes LW. 1984. Irrigation of swine lagoon effluent onto pine and hardwood forests. Transactions of the American Society of Agricultural Engineers 27(5):1411–1418.

Hewlett JD. 1979. Forest water quality: an experiment in harvesting and regenerating Piedmont forest. Athens, GA: University of Georgia, School of Forest Resources. 22 p.

Hodgkins EJ, Whipple SD. 1963. Changes in stand structure following prescribed burning in a loblolly–shortleaf pine forest. Journal of Forestry 61(7):498–502.

Hotvedt JE. 1983. Economic returns from a 29-year-old loblolly pine plantation. Louisiana Agriculture 27(2):12–13, 16.

Hotvedt JE, Straka TJ. 1987. Using residual values to analyze the economics of southern pine thinning. Southern Journal of Applied Forestry 11(2):99–106.

Hunt R, Cleveland G. 1978. Cultural treatments affect growth, volume, and survival of sweetgum, sycamore, and loblolly pine. Southern Journal of Applied Forestry 2(2):55–59.

Jack SB, Stone EL, Swindel BF. 1988. Stem form changes in unthinned slash and loblolly pine stands following midrotation fertilization. Southern Journal of Applied Forestry 12(2):90–97.

Jackson BD, Hickman CD, Blackburn WH, Walterscheidt MJ. 1981. Water quality guidelines for east Texas timber producers. College Station, TX: Texas A&M University, Texas Agricultural Extension Service. [not paged].

Jackson RS. 1974. Fire as a tool in young pine management. In: Proceedings, Symposium on Management of Young Pines; 1974 October 22–24; Alexandria, LA/December 3–5; Charleston, SC. Asheville, NC: USDAForest Service, Southeastern Forest Experiment Station: 65–70.

Johansen RW. 1987. Ignition patterns and prescribed fire behavior in southern pine stands. Georgia For. Res. Pap. 72. Macon, GA: Georgia Forestry Commission, Research Division. 5 p.

Johnson DW, Todd DE. 1988. Nitrogen fertilization of young yellow poplar and loblolly pine plantations at differing frequencies. Soil Science Society of America Journal 52: 1468–1477.

Jorgensen JR, Craig JR. 1984. Influence of lespedeza and phosphorus on loblolly pine growth and site nutrients [abstract]. In: Forest soils and treatment impacts: Proceedings, 6th North American Forest Soils Conference; 1983 June; Knoxville, TN. SAF Publ. 84-10. Bethesda, MD: Society of American Foresters: 444.

Jorgensen JR, Hodges CS Jr. 1970. Microbial characteristics of a forest soil after twenty years of prescribed burning. Mycologia 62(4):721–726.

Jorgensen JR. 1981. Use of legumes in southeastern forestry research. In: Proceedings, 1st Biennial Southern Silvicultural Research Conference; 1980 November 6–7; Atlanta, GA. Gen. Tech. Rep. SO-34. New Orleans: USDA Forest Service, Southern Forest Experiment Station: 205–211.

Jorgensen JR, Wells CG. 1986. Foresters' primer in nutrient cycling. Gen. Tech. Rep. SE-37. Asheville, NC: USDA Forest Service, Southeastern Forest Experiment Station. 42 p.

Karr BL, Janzen GC. 1985. Loblolly pine response to hexazinone. Proceedings of the Southern Weed Science Society 38:191–196.

Keister TD, McGriff JA. 1974. Thinning dense young loblolly pine stands with a granular herbicide. LSU Forestry Notes 107. Baton Rouge, LA: Louisiana State University and A&M College, Louisiana Agricultural Experiment Station, School of Forestry and Wildlife Management. 4 p.

Kellison RC, Gingrich S. 1984. Loblolly pine management and utilization: state of the art. Southern Journal of Applied Forestry 8(2):88–96.

Klawitter RA. 1966. Diameter growth of mature loblolly pine unaffected by under-story control. Southern Lumberman 213(2656):154–155.

Kline WN, Kidd FA. 1986. Economics of brush control in loblolly pine plantations: weed science and risk assessment. Proceedings of the Southern Weed Science Society 39:324–334.

Knowe SA, Nelson LR, Gjerstad DH, and others. 1985. Four-year growth and development of planted loblolly pine on sites with competition control. Southern Journal of Applied Forestry 9(1):11–15.

Kochenderfer JN. 1970. Erosion control on logging roads in the Appalachians. Res. Pap. NE-158. Upper Darby, PA: USDA Forest Service, Northeastern Forest Experiment Station. 28 p.

Kodama HE, Van Lear DH. 1980. Prescribed burning and nutrient cycling relationships in young loblolly pine plantations. Southern Journal of Applied Forestry 4(3):118–121.

Lane CL, Shade HI. 1982. Irrigation of effluents to forested soils in South Carolina. In: Proceedings, Specialty Conference on Environmentally Sound Water and Soil Management; 1982; Clemson, SC. New York: American Society of Civil Engineers: 42–48.

Langdon OG. 1981. Some effects of prescribed fire on understory vegetation in loblolly pine stands. In: Proceedings, Prescribed Fire and Wildlife in Southern Forests; 1981 April 6–8; Myrtle Beach, SC. Georgetown SC: Clemson University, Belle W. Baruch Forest Science Institute: 143–153.

Langdon OG, Trousdell KB. 1974. Increasing growth and yield of natural loblolly pine by young stand management. In: Proceedings, Symposium on Management of Young Pines; 1974 October 22–24; Alexandria, LA/December 3–5; Charleston, SC. Asheville, NC: USDA Forest Service, Southeastern Forest Experiment Station: 288–296.

Larsen TE, Gnegy JD, Olinger HL. 1983. Glyphosate for release of loblolly pine. Proceedings of the Southern Weed Science Society 36:235–238.

Lea R, Ballard R. 1982a. Predicting loblolly pine growth response from N fertilizer using soil-N availability indices. Soil Science Society of America Journal 46(5):1096–1099.

Lea R, Ballard R. 1982b. Relative effectiveness of nutrient concentrations in living foliage and needle fall at predicting response of loblolly pine to N and P fertilization. Canadian Journal of Forest Research 12(3):713–717.

Lea R, Ballard R, Wells CG. 1980. Amounts of nutrients removed from forest soils by two extractants and their relationship to *Pinus taeda* foliage concentrations. Communications in Soil Science and Plant Analysis 11(10):957–967.

Lewis CE, Harshbarger TJ. 1976. Shrub and herbaceous vegetation after 20 years of prescribed burning in the South Carolina Coastal Plain. Journal of Range Management 29(1):13–18.

Lewis WM Jr. 1974. Effects of fire on nutrient movement in a South Carolina pine forest. Ecology 55:1120–1127.

Lilieholm RJ, Hu SC. 1985. Effect of thinning young loblolly pine on soil moisture in southeastern Louisiana. In: Proceedings, 3rd Biennial Southern Silvicultural Research Conference; 1984 November 7–8; Atlanta, GA. Gen. Tech. Rep. SO-54. New Orleans: USDA Forest Service, Southern Forest Experiment Station: 550–554.

Lilieholm RJ, Hu SC. 1987. Effect of crown scorch on mortality and diameter growth of 19-year-old loblolly pine. Southern Journal of Applied Forestry 11(4):209–211.

Linnartz NE, Hu SC, Langston HW. 1984. The effects of prescribed burning on some chemical properties of forest soils in southeastern Louisiana. LSU Forestry Notes 141. Baton Rouge: Louisiana State University and A&M College, Louisiana Agricultural Experiment Station, School of Forestry and Wildlife Management, Agricultural Center. 2 p.

Little S, Escheman RT. 1976. 19-year change in the composition of a stand of *Pinus taeda* in eastern Maryland. Bulletin of the Torrey Botanical Club 103(2):57–66.

Lohrey RE, Nesmith OW. 1988a. Spacing in row-seeded loblolly pine on a good site. Progress Rep. Summary FS-SO-4101-3.25. 1 p. [On file with USDA Forest Service, Southern Forest Experiment Station, Pineville, LA.]

Lohrey RE, Nesmith OW. 1988b. Sapcing in row-seeded loblolly pine ona medius ite. Progress Report Summary FS-SO-4101-3.23, 1 p. [On file with USDA Forest Service, Southern Forest Experiment Station, Pineville, LA.]

Lotti T. 1956. Growing loblolly pine in the south Atlantic States. Farmers' Bull. 2097. Washington, DC: USDA Forest Service. 33 p.

Lucier AA. 1985. Transformations and movement of urea and ammonium nitrate in a Piedmont forest soil. Forestry Abstracts 46(10):655–656.

Lyle ES Jr. 1969. Mineral deficiency systems in loblolly pine seedlings. Agronomy Journal 61:395–398.

Lyle ES Jr. 1970. Mineral deficiency systems in loblolly pine seedlings. Highlights of Agricultural Research 17(3):–15.

Lyons A, Buckner E. 1981. Color aerial photography as a guide to foliar nutrient levels and site index in loblolly pine plantations. In: Color aerial photography in the plant sciences and related fields: Proceedings, 8th Biennial Workshop on Color Aerial Photography in the Plant Sciences; 1981 April 21–23; Luray, VA. Falls Church, VA: American Society of Photogrammetry: 53–58.

MacCarthy R, Davey CB. 1976. Nutritional problems of *Pinus taeda* L. (loblolly pine) growing on Pocosin soil. Soil Science Society of America Journal 40(4):582–585.

MacConnell GS, Wells CG, Metz LJ. 1987. Influence of municipal sludge on forest soil mesofauna. In: The forest alternative for treatment and utilization of municipal and industrial wastes. Seattle, WA: University of Washington Press: 177–187. Chapter 17.

Mann WF Jr, Gunter ER. 1960. Predicting the fate of fire-damaged pines. Forest and People 43: 26–27.

Mann WF Jr, Lohrey RE. 1974. Precommercial thinning of southern pines. Journal of Forestry 72(9):557–560.

McClay TA. 1955. Loblolly pine growth as affected by removal of understory hardwoods and shrubs. Res. Notes 73. Asheville, NC: USDA Forest Service, Southeastern Forest Experiment Station. 2 p.

McClurkin DC, Duffy PD, Ursic SJ, Nelson NS. 1985. Water quality effects of clearcutting upper coastal Plain loblolly pine plantations. Journal of Environmental Quality 14(3):329–332.

McKee WH Jr, McLeod KW, Davis CE, and others. 1987. Growth response of loblolly pine to municipal and industrial sewage sludge applied at four ages on Upper Coastal Plain sites. In: The forest alternative for treatment and utilization of municipal and industrial wastes. Seattle, WA: University of Washington Press: 272–281.

McKee WH Jr. 1982. Changes in soil fertility following prescribed burning on Coastal Plain pine sites. Res. Pap. SE-234. Asheville, NC: USDA Forest Service, Southeastern Forest Experiment Station. 23 p.

McKee WH Jr. 1987. Impacts of prescribed burning on Coastal Plain soils. In: Forests, the world, & the profession. Proceedings, 1986 Society of American Foresters National Convention; 1986 October 5–8; Birmingham, AL. Bethesda, MD: Society of American Foresters: 107–111.

McKee WH Jr, Lewis CE. 1983. Influence of burning and grazing on soil nutrient properties and tree growth on a Georgia Coastal Plain site after 40 years. In: Proceedings, 2nd Biennial Southern Silvicultural Research Conference; 1982 November 4–5; Atlanta, GA. Gen. Tech. Rep. SE-24. Asheville, NC: USDA Forest Service, Southeastern Forest Experiment Station: 79–86.

McKevlin MR, McKee WH Jr. 1986. Long-term prescribed burning increases nutrient uptake and growth of loblolly pine seedlings. Forest Ecology and Management 17:245–252.

McLemore BF. 1981. Evaluation of chemicals for controlling Japanese honeysuckle. Proceedings of the Southern Weed Science Society 34:208–210.

McLemore BF. 1988. Survival of loblolly pine seedlings planted on areas fall-sprayed with soil-active herbicides. Tree Planters' Notes 39(2):10–12.

McLeod KW, Davis CE, Sherrod KC, Wells CG. 1987. Understory response to sewage sludge fertilization of loblolly pine plantations. In: The forest alternative for treatment and utilization of municipal and industrial wastes. Seattle, WA: University of Washington Press: 308–323.

McMinn JW. 1983. Intensive whole-tree harvesting as a site preparation technique. In: Jones EP Jr, ed. Proceedings, 2nd Biennial Southern Silvicultural Research Conference; 1982 November 4–5; Atlanta, GA. Gen Tech. Rep. SE-24. Asheville, NC: USDA Forest Service, Southeastern Forest Experiment Station: 59–61.

McNab WH. 1977. An overcrowded loblolly pine stand thinned with fire. Southern Journal of Applied Forestry 1(1):24–26.

McNeil RC, Lea R, Ballard R, Allen HL 1988. Predicting fertilizer response of loblolly pine using foliar and needle-fall nutrients sampled in different seasons. Forest Science 34(3):698–707.

Menge JA, Grand LF. 1978. Effect of fertilization on production of epigeous basidiocarps by mycorrhizal fungi in loblolly pine plantations. Canadian Journal of Botany 56(19):2357–2362.

Menge JA, Grand LF, Haines LW. 1977. The effect of fertilization on growth and mycorrhizae numbers in 11-year-old loblolly pine. Forest Science 23(1):37–44.

Michael JL. 1984. Impacts of rate of hexazinone application on survival and growth of the loblolly pine. Proceedings of the Southern Weed Science Society 37:210–213.

Miller JH, Andrews GW. 1985. Banded herbicides can be as effective as windrowing. Proceedings of the Southern Weed Science Society 38:216–225.

Miller JH, Bishop LM. 1989. Optimum timing for ground-applied forestry herbicides in the South. Manag. Bull. R8-MB 28. Atlanta: USDA Forest Service, Southern Region, Cooperative Forestry. 2 p.

Miller JH, Zutter B, Zedaker SM, and others. 1987. A region-wide study of loblolly pine seedling growth relative to four competition levels after two growing seasons. In: Proceedings, 4th Biennial Ssouthern Silvicultural Research Conference; 1986 November 4–6; Atlanta, GA. Gen. Tech. Rep. SE-42. Asheville, NC: USDA Forest Service, Southeastern Forest Experiment Station: 581–592.

Minogue PJ, Zutter BR, Gjerstad DH. 1985. Comparison of liquid and solid hexazinone formulations for pine release. In: Proceedings, 3rd Biennial Southern Silvicultural Research Conference; 1984 November 7–8; Atlanta, GA. Gen. Tech. Rep. SO-54. New Orleans: USDA Forest Service, Southern Forest Experiment Station: 292–298.

Mobley HE, Balmer WE. 1981. Current purposes, extent, and environmental effects of prescribed fire in the South. In: Proceedings, Prescribed Fire and Wildlife in Southern Forests; 1981 April 6–8; Myrtle Beach, SC. Georgetown, SC: Clemson University, Belle W. Baruch Forest Science Institute: 15–21.

Moehring DM, Grano CX, Bassett JR. 1966. Properties of forested loess soils after repeated prescribed burns. Res. Note SO-40. New Orleans: USDA Forest Service, Southern Forest Experiment Station. 4 p.

Mollitor AV, Comerford NB, Fisher RF. 1983. Prescribed burning and nitrogen fertilization of slash pine plantations. In: Proceedings, 2nd Biennial Southern Silvicultural Research Conference; 1982 November 4–5; Atlanta, GA. Gen. Tech. Rep. SE-24. Asheville, NC: USDA Forest Service, Southeastern Forest Experiment Station: 66–69.

Morris LA, Moss SA. 1989. Effects of six weed conditions on loblolly pine growth. Proceedings of the Southern Weed Science Society 42:217–221.

Moschler WW, Jones GD, Adams RE. 1970. Effects of loblolly pine fertilization on a Piedmont soil: growth, foliar composition, and soil nutrients 10 years after establishment. Soil Science Society of America Journal 34(4):683–685.

Murphy PA, Guldin RW. 1987. Financial maturity of trees in selection stands revisited. Res. Pap. SO-242. New Orleans: USDA Forest Service, Southern Forest Experiment Station. 7 p.

Neary DG. 1988. Effect of gallberry on early slash and loblolly pine growth. Proceedings of the Southern Weed Science Society 41:251–255.

Neary DG, Morris LA, Swindel BF. 1984. Site preparation and nutrient management in southern pine forests. In: Forest soils and treatment impacts: Proceedings, 6th North American Forest Soils Conference; 1983 June; Knoxville, TN. SAF Publ. 84-10. Bethesda, MD: Society of American Foresters: 121–144.

Newbold RA. 1984. Tree crown response as a measure of successful pine release. Proceedings of the Southern Weed Science Society 37:245–247.

Paschke J. 1988. Injected HOE-38866 for precommercial pine thinning. Proceedings of the Southern Weed Science Society 41:151–154.

Perry TO. 1964. Soil compaction and loblolly pine growth. Tree Planters' Notes 67:9.

Pienaar LV, Bailey RL, Clutter ML. 1984. Pine plantation thinning practices. Georgia Forestry Res. Pap. 51. Macon, GA: Georgia Forestry Commission, Research Division. 5 p.

Posey CE. 1965. The effects of fertilization upon some wood properties of loblolly pine (Pinus taeda L.). Dissertation Abstracts 26(2):598–599.

Pritchett WL, Smith WH. 1975. Forest fertilization in the U.S. Southeast. In: Proceedings, 4th North American Forest Soils Conference; 1973 August; Université Laval, Quebec. Quebec: Laval University Press: 467–476.

Pye JM, Vitousek PM. 1985. Soil and nutrient removals by erosion and windrowing at a southeastern USA Piedmont site. Forest Ecology Management 11(3):145–155.

Ralston CW, McKee WH Jr, Langdon OG, Harms WR. 1983. Prescribed burning: uses and effects. In: Proceedings, Symposium on the Loblolly Pine Ecosystem—East Region; 1982 December 8–10; Raleigh, NC. Raleigh: North Carolina State University, School of Forest Resources: 154–162.

Ralston CW, Hatchell GE. 1971. Effects of prescribed burning on physical properties of soil. In: Prescribed burning symposium proceedings; 1971 April 14–16; Charleston, SC. Clemson, SC: Clemson University, Belle W. Baruch Research Institute in Forestry, Wildlife Science, and Marine Biology: 68–85.

Reeves HC, Lenhart JD. 1988. Fuel weight predictions equations for understory woody plants in eastern Texas. Texas Journal of Science 40(1):49–54.

Reisinger TW. 1985. A simulation-based approach to evaluating commercial thinning decisions in loblolly pine plantations. Southern Journal of Applied Forestry 9(4):211–216.

Richter DD, Ralston CW, Harms WR. 1982. Prescribed fire: effects on water quality and forest nutrient cycling. Science 215(5):661–663.

Ridgeway GL, Donova LA, McLeod KW. 1987. Response of loblolly pine to sewage sludge application: water relations. In: The forest alternative for treatment and utilization of municipal and industrial wastes. Seattle, WA: University of Washington Press: 301–307.

Rothermel RC, Deeming JE. 1980. Measuring and interpreting fire behavior for correlation with fire effects. General Tech. Rep. INT-93. Ogden, UT: USDA Forest Service, Intermountain Forest and Range Experiment Station. 4 p.

Rousseau JVD, Reid CPP. 1990. Effects of phosphorus and ectomycorrhizas on the carbon balance of loblolly pine seedlings. Forest Science 36(1):101–112.

Russell TE. 1961. Control of understory hardwoods fails to speed growth of pole-size loblolly. In: Southern Forestry Notes 131. New Orleans: USDA Forest Service, Southern Forest Experiment Station. 2 p.

Schmidtling RC. 1985. Species and cultural effects on soil chemistry in a southern pine plantation after 24 years. In: Proceedings, 3rd Biennial Southern Silvicultural Research Conference; 1984 November 7–8; Atlanta, GA. Gen. Tech. Rep. SO-54. New Orleans: USDA Forest Service, Southern Forest Experiment Station: 573–577.

Schmidtling RC. 1987. Relative performance of longleaf compared to loblolly and slash pines under different levels of intensive culture. In: Proceedings, 4th Biennial Southern Silvicultural Research Conference; 1986 November 4–6; Atlanta, GA. Gen. Tech. Rep. SE-42. Asheville, NC: USDA Forest Service, Southeastern Forest Experiment Station: 395–400.

Schoch P, Binkley D. 1986. Prescribed burning increased nitrogen availability in a mature loblolly pine stand. Forest Ecology and Management 14(1):13–22.

Schoeneberger MM, Jorgensen JR. 1989. Long-term benefit of lespedeza on loblolly pine growth. In: Proceedings, 5th Biennial Southern Silvicultural Research Conference; 1988 November 1–3; Memphis, TN. Gen. Tech. Rep. SO-74. New Orleans: USDA Forest Service, Southern Forest Experiment Station: 477–481.

Schultz RP. 1975. Intensive culture of southern pines: maximum yields on short rotations. Iowa State Journal of Research 49(3):325–337.

Shoulders E, McKee WH Jr. 1973. Pine nutrition in the West Gulf Coastal Plain: a status report. Gen. Tech. Rep. SO-2. New Orleans: USDA Forest Service, Southern Forest Experiment Station. 25 p.

Siegel WC. 1961. Loblolly planters thin early. Southern Forestry Notes 135. New Orleans: USDA Forest Service, Southern Forest Experiment Station. 2 p.

Simmons DW. 1974. The economics of late rotation fertilization of loblolly pine pulpwood stands. Tech. Rep. 51. Raleigh, NC: North Carolina State University, School of Forest Resources. 44 p.

Smith HD. 1983. Economics of intensive forestry. In: Proceeding, Symposium on the Loblolly Pine Ecosystem—East Region; 1982 December 8–10; Raleigh, NC. Raleigh, NC: North Carolina State University, School of Forest Resources: 246–254.

Smith JL, Zedaker SM, Heer RC. 1989. Estimating pine density and competition condition in young pine plantations using 35mm aerial photography. Southern Journal of Applied Forestry 13(3):107–112.

Smith LF, Schmidtling RC. 1970. Cultivation and fertilization speed early growth of planted southern pines. Tree Planters' Notes 21(1):1–3.

Sopper WE, Kardos LT. 1973. Vegetation responses to irrigation with treated municipal wastewater. In: Recycling treated municipal wastewater and sludge through forest and cropland. University Park, PA: Pennsylvania State University Press: 271–294.

Sprinz P, Clason T, Bower D. 1979. Spacing and thinning effects on the growth and development of a loblolly pine plantation. Fors. Res. Rep. 1979. Homer, LA: North Louisiana Hill Farm Experiment Station. 42 p.

Stokes B, Lanford BL. 1982. Patterns and equipment for selective thinning. In: Stephenson, Everett H., ed., Proceedings, Workshop on Thinning Southern Pine Plantations; 1982 May 24–26; Long Beach, MS. [Place of publication and publisher unknown]: 105–118.

Strader RH Jr. 1982. Nitrogen fertilization of two loblolly pine plantations: biomass production and nitrogen recovery and distribution after 10 and 11 years. Raleigh, NC: North Carolina State University. 40 p. M.S. thesis.

Stransky JJ. 1963. Needle moisture as mortality index for southern pine seedlings. Botanical Gazette 124(3):178–179.

Sucoff EI. 1961. Potassium, magnesium, and calcium deficiency symptoms of loblolly and Virginia pine seedlings. Sta. Note 164. Broomall, PA: USDA Forest Service, Northeastern Forest Experiment Station. 18 p.

Swindel BF, Neary DG, Comerford NB, and others. 1988. Fertilization and competition control accelerate early southern pine growth on flatwoods. Southern Journal of Applied Forestry 12(2):116–121.

Swindel BF, Smith JE, Neary DG, Comerford NB. 1989. Recent research indicates plant community responses to intensive treatment including chemical amendments. Southern Journal of Applied Forestry 13(3):152–156.

Switzer GL, Nelson LE. 1972. Nutrient accumulation and cycling in loblolly pine (Pinus taeda L.) plantation ecosystems: the first twenty years. Soil Science Society of America Journal 36(1):143–147.

Switzer GL, Nelson LE. 1974. Maintenance of productivity under short rotations. In: Proceedings, FAO/IUFRO International Symposium on Forest Fertilization; 1973 December; Paris. Paris: Ministère de l'Agriculteur, Services de Forêt: 355–381.

Tew DT, Jervis LG, Steensen DHJ. 1989. The effect of varying degrees of crown scorching on growth and mortality of a young Piedmont loblolly pine plantation. In: Proceedings, 5th Biennial Southern Silvicultural Research Conference; 1988 November 1–3; Memphis, TN. Gen. Tech. Rep. SO-74. New Orleans: USDA Forest Service, Southern Forest Experiment Station: 395–400.

Tiarks AE, Haywood JD. 1986. Pinus taeda L. response to fertilization, herbaceous plant control, and woody plant control. Forest Ecology and Management 14:103–112.

Tiarks AE, Shoulders E. 1982. Effects of shallow water tables on height growth and phosphorus uptake by loblolly and slash pines. Res. Note SO-285. New Orleans: USDA Forest Service, Southern Forest Experiment Station. 5 p.

Torbert JL Jr, Burger JA. 1984. Long-term availability of applied phosphorus to loblolly pine on a Piedmont soil. Soil Science Society of America Journal 48(5):1174–1178.

Van Lear DH, Douglas JE, Cox SK, Auspurger MK. 1985. Sediment and nutrient export in runoff from burned and harvested watersheds in the South Carolina Piedmont. Journal of Environmental Quality 14(2):169–174.

Van Lear DH, Swank WT, Douglass JE, Waide JB. 1983. Forest management practices and the nutrient status of a loblolly pine plantation. In: IUFRO Symposium on Forest Site and Continuous Productivity; 1982 August 22–28; Seattle, WA. Gen. Tech. Rep. PNW-163. Portland, OR: USDA Forest Service, Pacific Northwest Forest and Range Experiment Station: 252–258.

Villarrubia CR, Chambers JL. 1978. Fire: its effects on growth and survival of loblolly pine, Pinus taeda L. Proceedings of the Louisiana Academy of Sciences 41:85–93.

Vose JM, Allen HL. 1988. Leaf area stemwood growth and nutrition relationships in loblolly pine. Forest Science 34(3):547–563.

Vose JE. 1988. Patterns of leaf area distribution within crowns of nitrogen-and phosphorus-fertilized loblolly pine trees. Forest Science 34(3):564–573.

Voth RD. 1987. Pine responses to Glyphosate plus sulfometuron methyl treatments. Proceedings of the Southern Weed Science Society 40:167–174.

Wade DD. 1985. Survival in young loblolly pine plantations following wildfire. In: Weather—The Drive Train Connecting the Solar Engine to Forest Ecosystems: Proceedings, 8th Conference on Fire and Forest Meterology; 1985 April 29–May 2; Detroit, MI. Bethesda, MD: Society of American Foresters: 52–57.

Wade DD, Johansen RW. 1987. Relating wildland fire to defoliation and mortality in pine. In: Proceedings, 4th Biennial Southern Silvicultural Research Conference; 1986 November 4–6; Atlanta, GA. Gen. Tech. Rep. SE-42. Asheville, NC: USDA Forest Service, Southeastern Forest Experiment Station: 107–110.

Wade DD, Lunsford JD. 1989. A guide for prescribed fire in southern forests. Rev. ed. Tech. Publ. R8-TP 11. Atlanta: USDA Forest Service, Southern Region. 56 p.

Waldrop TA, Lloyd FT. 1987. Prescribed fire for precommercial thinning in a four-year-old loblolly pine stand. In: Proceedings, 4th Biennial Southern Silvicultural Research conference; 1986 November 4–6; Atlanta, GA. Gen. Tech. Rep. SE-42. Asheville, NC: USDA Forest Service, Southeastern Forest Experiment Station: 97–102.

Waldrop TA, Lloyd FT. 1988. Precommercial thinning a sapling-sized loblolly pine stand with fire. Southern Journal of Applied Forestry 12(3):203–207.

Waldrop TA, Van Lear DH. 1984. Effect of crown scorch on survival and growth of young loblolly pine. Southern Journal of Applied Forestry 8(1):35–40.

Waldrop TA, Van Lear DH, Lloyd FT, Harms WR. 1987. Long-term studies of prescribed burning in loblolly pine forests of the Southeastern Coastal Plain. Gen. Tech. Rep. SE-45. Asheville, NC: USDA Forest Service, Southeastern Forest Experiment Station. 23 p.

Wells CG. 1969. Foliage sampling guides for loblolly pine. Res. Note SE-113. Asheville, NC: USDA Forest Service, Southeastern Forest Experiment Station. 3 p.

Wells CG. 1970. Nitrogen and potassium fertilization of loblolly pine on a South Carolina Piedmont soil. Forest Science 16(2):172–176.

Wells CG. 1971. Effects of prescribed burning on soil chemical properties and nutrient availability. In: Proceedings, Prescribed Burning Symposium; 1971 April 14–16; Charleston, SC. Georgetown, SC: Clemson University, Belle W. Baruch Research Institute: 87–99.

Wells CG, Allen L. 1985. When and where to apply fertilizer. Gen. Tech. Rep. SE-36. Asheville, NC: USDA Forest Service, Southeastern Forest Experiment Station. 23 p.

Wells CG, Craig JR, Kane MB, Allen HL. 1986. Foliar and soil tests for the prediction of phosphorus response in loblolly pine. Soil Science Society of America Journal 50(5):1330–1335.

Wells CG, Crutchfield DM, Berenyi NM, Davey CB. 1973. Soil and foliar guidelines for phosphorus fertilization of loblolly pine. Res. Pap. SE-110. Asheville, NC: USDA Forest Service, Southeastern Forest Experiment Station. 15 p.

Wells CG, McLeod KW, Murphy CE, and others. 1984. Response of loblolly pine plantations to two sources of sewage sludge. In: Proceedings of the TAPPI 1984 Research and Development Conference; 1984 September 30–October 3; Appleton, WI. Atlanta: TAPPI Press: 85–94.

Wells CG, Nicholas AK, Buol SW. 1975. Some effects of fertilization on mineral cycling in loblolly pine. In: Proceedings, Mineral Cycling in Southeastern Ecosystems; 1974 May 1–3; Augusta, GA. CONF-740513. Springfield, VA: National Technical Information Service: 754–764.

Wenger KF, Trousdell KB. 1958. Natural regeneration of loblolly pine in the south Atlantic Coastal Plain. Prod. Res. Rep. 13. Washington, DC: USDA Forest Service. 78 p.

Whipple SD. 1970. Improving mixed hardwood stands. Bull. 410. Auburn, AL: Auburn University, Alabama Agricultural Experiment Station. 3–12.

Whipple SD, Moeck KP. 1968. Potential uses of Tordon 10K pellets in forest management. Down to Earth 24(1):13–17.

White EH, Pritchett WL. 1970. Water table control and fertilization for pine production in the flatwoods. Tech. Bull. 743. Gainesville, FL: University of Florida, Agricultural Experiment Station. 41 p.

Williams RA. 1974. Precommercial thinning. In: Proceedings, Symposium on Management of Young Pines; 1974 October 22–24; Alexandria, LA/December 3–5; Charleston, SC. Asheville, NC: USDA Forest Service, Southeastern Forest Experiment Station: 72–76.

Williston HL. 1962. Conifers for conversion planting in north Mississippi. Tree Planters' Notes 54:5–7.

Windsor CL Jr, Reines M. 1973. Diameter growth in loblolly pine after fertilization. Journal of Forestry 71(10):659–661.

Xydias GK, Gregory AH, Sprinz PT. 1983. Ten-year results from thinning an eleven-year-old stand of loblolly pine on an excellent site. In: Proceedings, 2nd Biennial Southern Silvicultural Research Conference; 1982 November 4–5; Atlanta, GA. Gen. Tech. Rep. SE-24. Asheville, NC: USDA Forest Service, Southeastern Forest Experiment Station: 193–200.

Yeiser JL, McLemore BF. 1986. Basal bark sprays evaluated for efficacy and season of application. Arkansas Farm Research November–December:10.

Yeiser JL, Sundell E, Boyd JW. 1987. Preplant and postplant treatments for weed control in newly planted pine. Arkansas Experiment Station Bulletin 902. 10 p.

York M, Buckner E. 1983. Prescribed fire for hardwood control and fuel reduction in pine plantations on the Cumberland Plateau. In: Proceeding, 2nd Biennial Southern Silvicultural Research Conference; 1982 November 4–5; Atlanta, GA. Gen. Tech. Rep. SE-24. Asheville, NC: USDA Forest Service, Southeastern Forest Experiment Station: 74–77.

Zahner R. 1959. Fertilizer trials with loblolly pine in southern Arkansas. Journal of Forestry 57(11):812–815.

Zedaker SM. 1983. The competition-release enigma: adding apples and oranges and coming up with lemons. In: Proceedings, 2nd Biennial Southern Silvicultural Research Conference; 1982 November 4–5; Atlanta, GA. Gen. Tech. Rep. SE-24. Asheville, NC: USDA Forest Service, Southeastern Forest Experiment Station: 357–364.

Zeide B. 1987. Analysis of the 3/2 power law of self-thinning. Forest Science 33(2):517–537.

Zutter BR, Glover GR, Gjerstad DH. 1986. Effects of herbaceous weed control using herbicides on a young loblolly pine plantation. Forest Science 32(4):882–899.

Zutter BR, Minogue PJ, Gjerstad DH. 1988. Response following aerial applications of glyphosate for release of loblolly pine in the Virginia Piedmont. Southern Journal of Applied Forestry 12(1):54–58.

Chapter 9

Multiple-Use Management of Loblolly Pine Forest Resources

• • • • • • • • • • • • • **Contents** •

Multiple-Use Management of Loblolly Pine Forest Resources

Introduction

Most of the South's loblolly pine forests are intermixed with varying amounts of upland and bottomland hardwoods and other pines. Typically, an area of 1,000 or more hectares includes a variety of soils and topography and supports combinations of sawtimber, poles, saplings, and seedlings (Reed and Noble 1987) and an array of animal and understory plant species. Loblolly pine forests provide valuable wildlife habitat, grazing range, and watershed protection. They have esthetic value and provide opportunities for agroforestry and many types of recreation (for example, hunting, camping, hiking, sightseeing, and birdwatching). Loblolly pines are also valuable for use in reclamation and reha-

bilitation of severely degraded lands including surface mines and mine spoils, borrow pits, eroded loess soils, and clay slopes and spoils throughout the South.

More than half of all Americans participate in some form of forest-related outdoor recreation each year. Most forest stands are within 0.4 km of a road, and this easy access is an important inducement to wide-scale human use (Rudis 1988a, 1988b). Recreational use of loblolly pine forests will continue to rise rapidly in the future because of an ever-expanding southern population, more disposable income, and more leisure time. Leasing of forest land for hunting can even make wildlife management profitable.

Wildlife Associated With Loblolly Pine

Loblolly pine management and wildlife management are closely related. Actions taken to promote tree growth affect wildlife by altering food, water, and vegetative cover. Extensive unbroken tracts of pure loblolly, or any other single species, are not good habitats for wildlife (Johnson 1987). Habitats that provide conditions suitable for an array of wildlife species include stand openings and stands in all stages of development. Maintaining forest structural diversity and diverse habitats increases game populations and land values because few animals, particularly larger game species, fulfill their life requirements in a single stand or even in a single forest type (Buckner and Perkins 1975, Halls 1975). The general impact of conversion from mixed stands to loblolly plantations is negative for many wildlife species but positive for others that are pine specialists. Natural site differences and silvicultural treatments also affect the mixture of plant species and the habitat for wildlife. Over the long term, it is necessary to coordinate wildlife habitat management and loblolly pine timber management, especially to promote nongame wildlife species.

More than 400 species of vertebrates occur in the forests of the Southeast. These include approximately 100 species of amphibians and reptiles, 250 species of birds, and 50 species of mammals. Loblolly pines and associat-

ed grass, herb, shrub, and tree species are important to the well-being of many of these vertebrates. All the important upland game mammals and birds such as eastern cottontail rabbit, *Sylvilagus floridanus*; fox squirrel, *Sciurus niger* (figure 9-1); gray squirrel, *S. carolinensis*; white-tailed deer, *Odocoileus virginianus*; bobwhite quail, *Colinus virginianus* (L.); mourning dove, *Zenaida macroura* (L.); and wild turkey, *Meleagris gallopavo* L., are common or abundant in loblolly pine or loblolly pine–hardwood stands.

Figure 9-1—A fox squirrel in a loblolly pine forest of east Texas.

Table 9-1—Amphibians inhabiting mixed loblolly–shortleaf–hardwood stands in central Louisiana and eastern Texas

Species	Abundance*				Species	Abundance*			
	Seedling stands	Sapling stands	Pole stands	Sawtimber Stands		Seedling stands	Sapling stands	Pole stands	Sawtimber Stands
Ambystoma opacum (Gravenhorst) marbled salamander	rare	rare	rare	abundant	*Hyla cinerea* (Schneider) green treefrog	absent	absent	absent	rare
A. talpoideum (Holbrook) mole salamander	abundant	absent	absent	rare	*H. chrysoscelis* Cope Cope's gray treefrog	absent	absent	absent	rare
Eurycea quadridigitata (Holbrook) dwarf salamander	rare	common	abundant	common	*H. versicolor* LeConte southern gray treefrog	abundant	abundant	abundant	common
Bufo valliceps valliceps Wiegmann Gulf Coast toad	rare	absent	absent	absent	*Pseudacris crucifer crucifer* (Wied-Neuwied) northern spring peeper	abundant	common	absent	abundant
B. woodhousii Girard Woodhouse's toad	rare	rare	common	common	*P. feriarum feriarum* (Baird) upland chorus frog	common	rare	rare	abundant
Scaphiopus holbrookii hurterii Strecker Hurter's spadefoot	common	abundant	rare	rare	*Rana clamitans clamitans* Latreille bronze frog	common	absent	absent	absent
Gastrophryne carolinensis (Holbrook) eastern narrowmouth toad	common	common	common	common	*R. catesbeiana* Shaw bullfrog	rare	absent	absent	absent
Acris crepitans crepitans Baird northern cricket frog	common	rare	absent	rare	*R. utricularia utricularia* Harlan southern leopard frog	abundant	common	common	common

Source: adapted from Whiting and others (1987) and Williams and Mullin (1987).

* Amphibian abundance in various forest stands based on number of individuals encountered in a stand are: absent = not encountered, rare = 1 or 2 individuals encountered, common = 3 to 10 individuals encountered, and abundant = 11 or more individuals encountered.

Table 9-2—Reptiles inhabiting mixed loblolly–shortleaf–hardwood stands in central Louisiana and eastern Texas

Species	Abundance*				Species	Abundance*			
	Seedling stands	Sapling stands	Pole stands	Sawtimber stands		Seedling stands	Sapling stands	Pole stands	Sawtimber stands
Turtles					**Snakes (continued)**				
Terrapene carolina triunguis (Agassiz) three-toed box turtle	rare	common	common	common	*Nerodia erythrogaster flavigaster* (Conant) yellow-bellied water snake	rare	absent	rare	absent
T. ornata ornata (Agassiz) ornate box turtle	rare	rare	rare	absent	*Diadophis punctatus* (L.) ringneck snake	absent	absent	absent	rare
Lizards					*Elaphe obsoleta* (Say) rat snake	absent	rare	rare	rare
Anolis carolinensis (Voigt) green anole	common	abundant	abundant	abundant	*Elaphe obsoleta lindheimerii* (Baird & Girard) Texas rat snake	rare	rare	absent	rare
Eumeces laticeps (Schneider) broadhead skink	absent	absent	common	common	*Masticophis flagellum flagellum* (Shaw) eastern coachwhip	rare	absent	absent	rare
E. fasciatus (L.) five-lined skink	absent	common	common	abundant	*Opheodrys aestivus* (L.) rough green snake	absent	rare	rare	absent
E. anthracinus pluvialis Cope southern coal skink	rare	abundant	common	rare	*Thamnophis proximus proximus* (Say) western ribbon snake	common	absent	absent	absent
Sceloporus undulatus hyacinthinus (Green) northern fence lizard	abundant	abundant	rare	absent	*T. sirtalis sirtalis* (L.) eastern garter snake	absent	rare	absent	absent
Scincella lateralis (Say) ground skink	common	abundant	abundant	abundant	*Storeria dekayi* (Holbrook) brown snake	absent	rare	rare	common
Cnemidophorus sexlineatus sexlineatus (L.) six-lined racerunner	abundant	rare	absent	absent	*Heterodon platirhinos* Latreille eastern hognosed snake	common	abundant	rare	common
Snakes					*Regina grahamii* Baird & Girard Graham's crayfish snake	absent	absent	absent	rare
Coluber constrictor anthicus (Cope) buttermilk snake	abundant	common	common	absent	*Agkistrodon contortrix contortrix* (L.) southern copperhead	rare	abundant	abundant	abundant
C. constrictor priapus Dunn & Wood southern black racer	rare	rare	rare	absent	*A. piscivorus leucostoma* (Troost) western cottonmouth	absent	absent	rare	absent
Lampropeltis calligaster calligaster (Harlan) prairie kingsnake	common	absent	absent	absent	*Sistrurus miliarius* (L.) pigmy rattlesnake	absent	absent	rare	rare
L. getula (L.) common kingsnake	absent	rare	absent	absent	*Micrurus fulvius* (L.) eastern coral snake	common	common	common	rare
L. getula holbrooki Stejneger speckled kingsnake	rare	absent	absent	absent					

Source: adapted from Whiting and others (1987) and Williams and Mullin (1987).

* Reptile abundance in various forest stands based on number of individuals encountered are: absent = not encountered, rare = 1 or 2 individuals encountered, common = 3 to 10 individuals encountered, and abundant = 11 or more individuals encountered.

Table 9-3—Avian species and their relative abundance in loblolly–shortleaf–hardwood stands of central Louisiana. The table is a summary of data gathered from 3,238 ha of which approximately 56% was sawtimber, 23% poletimber, 13% saplings, 4% seedlings, and 3% unstocked. Species are listed in order of relative abundance in each category. For example, northern cardinal is most abundant; the last 19 species in the rare category (third column and bottom of second column) were sighted only once

Abundant*	Common*		Uncommon*	Rare*		
Northern cardinal *Cardinalis cardinalis* (L.)	Northern bobwhite *Colinus virginianus* (L.)	Eastern wood-pewee *Contopus virens* (L.)	Common grackle *Quiscalus quiscula* (L.)	Eastern phoebe *Sayornis phoebe* Latham	Song sparrow *Melospiza melodia* (Wilson)	Eastern kingbird *Tyrannus tyrannus* (L.)
Blue jay *Cyanocitta cristata* (L.)	Kentucky warbler *Oporornis formosus* (Wilson)	American robin *Turdus migratorius* (L.)	White-throated sparrow *Zonotrichia albicollis* (Gmelin)	Dark-eyed junco *Junco hyemalis* (L.)	Field sparrow *Spizella pusilla* (Wilson)	Green-backed heron *Butorides striatus* (L.)
Carolina wren *Thryothorus ludovicianus* (Latham)	Summer tanager *Piranga rubra* (L.)	Mourning dove *Zenaida macroura* (L.)	Downy woodpecker *Picoides pubescens* (L.)	Gray catbird *Dumetella carolinensis* (L.)	White-crowned sparrow *Zonotrichia leucophrys* (Forster)	Lark sparrow *Chondestes grammacus* (Say)
White-eyed vireo *Vireo griseus* (Boddaert)	Black-and-white warbler *Mniotilta varia* (L.)	Great crested flycatcher *Myiarchus crinitus* (L.)	Red-headed woodpecker *Melanerpes erythrocephalus* (L.)	Hairy woodpecker *Picoides villosus* (L.)	American kestrel *Falco sparverius* (L.)	Little blue heron *Egretta caerulea* (L.)
Tufted titmouse *Parus bicolor* (L.)	Rufous-sided towhee *Pipilo erythrophthalmus* (L.)	Brown thrasher *Toxostoma rufum* (L.)	Fish crow *Corvus ossifragus* Wilson	Barred owl *Strix varia* Barton	Blue grosbeak *Guiraca caerulea* (L.)	Loggerhead shrike *Lanius ludovicianus* (L.)
Pine warbler *Dendroica pinus* (Wilson)	Wood thrush *Hylocichla mustelina* (Gmelin)	Hermit thrush *Catharus guttatus* (Pallas)	Cattle egret *Bubulcus ibis* (L.)	Cedar waxwing *Bombycilla cedrorum* Vieillot	Chimney swift *Chaetura pelagica* (L.)	Northern parula *Parula americana* (L.)
Hooded warbler *Wilsonia citrina* (Boddaert)	Ruby-crowned kinglet *Regulus calendula* (L.)	Brown-headed nuthatch *Sitta pusilla* Lathum	Prairie warbler *Dendroica discolor* (Vieillot)	Chipping sparrow *Spizella passerina* (Bechstein)	Cooper's hawk *Accipiter cooperii* (Bonaparte)	Painted bunting *Passerina ciris* (L.)
Carolina chickadee *Parus carolinensis* Audubon	Blue-gray gnatcatcher *Polioptila caerulea* (L.)	Red-breasted nuthatch *Sitta canadensis* (L.)	Common yellowthroat *Geothlypis trichas* (L.)	Fox sparrow *Passerella iliaca* (Merrem)	Northern oriole *Icterus galbula* (L.)	Scarlet tanager *Piranga olivacea* (Gmelin)
Red-eyed vireo *Vireo olivaceus* (L.)	Yellow-rumped warbler *Dendroica coronata* (L.)	Worm-eating warbler *Helmitheros vermivorus* (Gmelin)	Brown creeper *Certhia americana* (Bonaparte)	Sharp-shinned hawk *Accipiter striatus* Vieillot	Prothonotary warbler *Protonotaria citrea* (Boddaert)	Snow goose *Chen caerulescens* (L.)
Red-bellied woodpecker *Melanerpes carolinus* (L.)	Pileated woodpecker *Dryocopus pileatus* (L.)	Brown-headed cowbird *Molothrus ater* (Boddaert)	Broad-winged hawk *Buteo platypterus* (Vieillot)	American woodcock *Scolopax minor* Gmelin	Purple finch *Carpodacus purpureus* (Gmelin)	Solitary vireo *Vireo solitarius* (Wilson)
Acadian flycatcher *Empidonax virescens* (Vieillot)	Yellow-throated vireo *Vireo flavifrons* Vieillot	Indigo bunting *Passerina cyanea* (L.)	Northern mockingbird *Mimus polyglottos* (L.)	Black vulture *Coragyps atratus* (Bechstein)	Mississippi kite *Ictinia mississippiensis* (Wilson)	Swainson's warbler *Limnothlypis swainsonii* (Audubon)
Yellow-breasted chat *Icteria virens* (L.)	Northern flicker *Colaptes auratus* (L.)	Yellow-bellied sapsucker *Sphyrapicus varius* (L.)	Turkey vulture *Carthartes aura* (L.)	Orchard oriole *Icterus spurius* (L.)	Red-winged blackbird *Agelaius phoeniceus* (L.)	Eastern bluebird *Sialia sialis* (L.)
American (common) crow *Corvus brachyrhynchos* Brehm	Yellow-billed cuckoo *Coccyzus americanus* (L.)	Golden-crowned kinglet *Regulus satrapa* Lichtenstein		Red-shouldered hawk *Buteo lineatus* (Gmelin)	White-fronted goose *Anser albifrons* (Scopoli)	Great horned owl *Bubo virginianus* (Gmelin)
				Chuck-will's-widow *Caprimulgus carolinensis* Gmelin	Winter wren *Troglodytes troglodytes* (L.)	Eastern screech-owl *Otus asio* (L.)
				American goldfinch *Carduelis tristis* (L.)	Wood duck *Aix sponsa* (L.)	Swamp sparrow *Melospiza georgiana* (Latham)
				Bachman's sparrow *Aimophila aestivalis* (Lichtenstein)	Yellow-crowned night-heron *Nycticorax violaceus* (L.)	Wild turkey *Meleagris gallopavo* (L.)
				Orange-crowned warbler *Vermivora celata* (Say)		House wren *Troglodytes aedon* Vieillot
				Red-tailed hawk *Buteo jamaicensis* (Gmelin)		
				Ruby-throated hummingbird *Archilochus colubris* (L.)		

Source: Hamilton and Lester (1987).

* Abundant = 196 to 771 sightings, common = 37 - 128 sightings, uncommon = 10 - 27 sightings, and rare = 1 to 9 sightings.

However, the vast majority of mammal species are non-game, and there is very little information about the effects of loblolly pine management on their populations. Species of amphibians and reptiles associated with loblolly pine stands are listed in tables 9-1 and 9-2. These shy animals are important food sources for some wildlife species, and they compete with others for habitat. Amphibians such as the Hurter's spadefoot, *Scaphiopus holbrookii hurterii* Strecker; northern spring peeper, *Pseudacris crucifer crucifer* (Wied-Neuwied); and southern leopard frog, *Rana utricularia utricularia* Harlan are most abundant in the winter in seedling and sapling stands. Winter amphibians (especially frogs and toads) are more common where there are ponds suitable for breeding nearby. Reptiles (primarily snakes and lizards) are most abundant in the spring and in seedling stands but can be found in significant numbers in stands of all ages (table 9-2). Some species of lizards, such as northern fence lizard, *Sceloporus undulatus hyacinthinus* (Green), and six-lined racerunner, *Cnemidophorus sexlineatus sexlineatus* L., adapt more readily to seedling stands, whereas others, such as broadhead skink, *Eumeces laticeps* (Schneider); five-lined skink, E. *fasciatus* (L.); green anole, *Anolis carolinensis* (Voigt); and ground skink, *Scincella lateralis* (Say), have higher repre-

sentation in older stands (Whiting and others 1987). The northern fence lizard seems to be the only reptile that is active during brief warm periods in winter—usually in seedling and sapling stands where the soil surface is exposed.

Dickson and others (1980) summarized the relative abundance of breeding birds in young, intermediate, and mature loblolly–shortleaf stands throughout the Southeast. They found that 8 species were common or abundant in mature stands, 3 in intermediate stands, and 2 in young stands. Only the northern cardinal, *Cardinalis cardinalis* L., was common or abundant in stands in all three age classes. Avian species occurring in loblolly–shortleaf–hardwood stands of central Louisiana and their relative abundance in those stands are listed in table 9-3. Thirty mammal species were also identified as

Table 9-4—Mammals inhabiting loblolly–shortleaf–hardwood stands of varying ages in central Louisiana

Species	Relative abundance	Species	Relative abundance	Species	Relative abundance	Species	Relative abundance
Opossum *Didelphis virginiana*	common	Eastern cottontail *Sylvilagus floridanus*	abundant	White-footed mouse *Peromyscus leucopus*	common	American black bear *Procyon lotor*	abundant
Eastern pipistrelle *Pipistrellus subflavus*	abundant	Swamp rabbit *S. aquaticus*	abundant	Cotton mouse *P. gossypinus*	abundant	North American mink *Mustela vison*	common
Red bat *Lasiurus borealis*	abundant	Gray squirrel *Sciurus carolinensis*	abundant	Golden mouse *Ochrotomys nuttalli*	abundant	Striped skunk *Mephitis mephitis*	common
Evening bat *Nycticeius humeralis*	common	Fox squirrel *S. niger*	abundant	Cotton rat *Sigmodon hispidus*	rare	Bobcat *Lynx rufus*	common
Eastern mole *Scalopus aquaticus*	common	Southern flying squirrel *Glaucomys volans*	common	Nutria *Myocastor coypus*	rare	White-tailed deer *Odocoileus virginianus*	abundant
Short-tailed shrew *Blarina brevicauda*	abundant	Plains pocket gopher *Geomys bursarius*	common	Coyote *Canis latrans*	abundant	Feral hog *Sus scrofa*	common
Least shrew *Cryptotis parva*	rare	American beaver *Castor canadensis*	rare	Gray fox *Urocyon cinereoargentatus*	abundant		
Armadillo *Dasypus novemcinctus*	abundant	Fulvous harvest mouse *Reithrodontomys fulvescens*	common	Red fox *Vulpes fulva*	common		

Source: adapted from Hamilton and others (1987).

inhabitants of these central Louisiana stands (table 9-4). In east Texas, the cotton mouse, *Peromyscus gossypinus*; eastern woodrat, *Neotoma floridana*; and short-tailed shrew, *Blarina brevicauda* were the predominant small mammals under mature pine–hardwood stands. In an adjacent 6-year-old loblolly pine plantation, the hispid cotton rat, *Sigmodon hispidus*; fulvous harvest mouse, *Reithrodontomys fulvescens*; golden mouse, *O. nuttalli*; and eastern wood rat were the most common small mammals (Fleet and Dickson 1984).

Wildlife Food in Loblolly Pine Stands

Seeds produced by trees in older stands are especially important to rodents and birds during the fall. Seed predation may be so heavy that it jeopardizes natural and artificial regeneration. Pine seeds remain an important source of food throughout the winter (Kennamer and others 1980). Southern wildlife sometimes forage on newly germinated or newly planted seedlings but rarely consume needles or shoots of more mature loblolly pines. However, deer may eat such needles and shoots when preferred foods are scarce (Blair and Brunett 1980, Furrh and Ezell 1983).

About 100 woody plant species growing in association with natural or planted loblolly pines produce fruit or other plant parts used by wildlife (Halls 1977, Krochmal and Kologiski 1974). Bobwhite quail used 79 plant or animal species as food in 1- to 4-year-old loblolly pine plantations. *Panicum* spp. were the most important to quail (Sweeney and others 1981). Mushrooms are an important source of readily accessible nutrition (especially protein and phosphorus) for many mammal species. Other common wildlife foods in loblolly forests include (right):

Common name	Scientific name
Blackberries	*Rubus* spp.
Greenbrier	*Smilax rotundifolia* L.
Japanese honeysuckle	*Lonicera japonica* Thunb.
Poison-ivy	*Rhus radicans* L.
Pokeweed	*Phytolacca americana* L.
Saw greenbrier	*Smilax bona-nox* L.
Tickclover, beggarticks	*Desmodium* spp.
Trumpet creeper	*Campsis radicans* (L.) Seem.
Virginia creeper	*Parthenocissus quinquefolia* (L.) Planch.
Wild grape	*Vitis* spp.

Most information about food plants relates to deer. Important deer browse species are listed in table 9-5. About 55 to 70% of the plant species in loblolly–shortleaf and oak–pine stands are fair to good deer browse. In contrast, only about 20% of the vegetation in the longleaf–slash pine ecosystem provides fair or good deer browse (Pearson and Sternitzke 1976, Wolters and others 1977). Although deer browse many woody species, most of their browse diet comprises only a few species. Deer generally prefer green leaves to twigs. Browse plants grown in the open usually contain more crude protein and phosphorus but less crude fiber and calcium than plants grown beneath stands (Halls and Epps 1969). Browse makes up at least 20% of white-tailed deer diet during all seasons where half of the land area accessible to deer is composed of young loblolly pine plantations or mixed pine–hardwood stands (figure 9-2). Forbs are important dietary constituents in May, mushrooms in July, and acorns in autumn (Short 1971).

Wild turkeys occur throughout most of the loblolly pine range (Dickson 1992). Loblolly pine stands contain many important turkey foods throughout the year. These foods include grass seeds, insects, and berries in young stands from spring to fall, and pine seeds, acorns, and insects in older pine and mixed pine–hardwood stands from fall to winter (Kennamer and others 1980).

Integrating Wildlife Management and Timber Management

Regardless of the silvicultural system used, large numbers of animals of many wildlife species can be accommodated in pure loblolly or mixed pine–hardwood stands, with little sacrifice in timber yield, if individual stands are kept relatively small and age classes are well interspersed.

A wide variety of wildlife commonly forage and nest in loblolly pine stands of all ages. However, some bird species occur only in pure loblolly pine stands of certain ages (table 9-6). In pure stands, numbers of bird and small mammal species and individuals generally are greatest shortly after regeneration takes place. The diversity of lesser vegetation within a single young loblolly plantation may satisfy all of the needs of some songbirds. Such birds flourish for about the first 5 years and gradually leave as plant succession progresses, both in plantations and second-growth pine–hardwood forests (Childers and others 1986). Clusters of dense vegetation are primary roosting sites for doves (Grand and Mirarchi 1988). In contrast, some birds, such as Bachman's sparrow, *Aimophila aestivalis* (Lichtenstein); brown-headed nuthatch, *Sitta pusilla* Latham; pine warbler, *Dendroica pinus* (Wilson); and red-cockaded woodpecker, *Picoides borealis* (Vieillot), fare best in mature, open pine stands.

Mixed pine–hardwood stands provide good habitat for more bird species than do pure pine or pure hardwood stands. Mixed pine–hardwood stands also support larger overall populations of wintering and breeding birds than do pure pine stands of any age primarily because there is vertical layering of diverse vegetation (especially numerous hardwood species) in most mixed stands (Dickson and Segelquist 1979). Of the 146 forest bird species in Louisiana, 72 species occur mostly in pine–hardwood forests, 11 are most abundant in pine forests, and 63 reach their greatest density in hardwood forests (Noble and others 1980). If managed properly, mixed pine–hardwood stands can also be excellent habitat for most game species. Primary deer food in these stands consists of suc-

Table 9-5—Important deer browse species of trees, shrubs, and vines (by common and scientific names) commonly associated with loblolly pine forest types in central Louisiana

Desirable	
American beautyberry *Callicarpa americana* L.	Possum-haw *Ilex decidua* Walt.
Bigleaf snowbell *Styrax grandifolius* Ait.	St. Andrew's cross *Ascyrum hypercoides* (L.) Crantz
Saw greenbrier *Smilax bona-nox* L.	Sassafras *Sassafras albidum* (Nutt.) Nees
Elliott's blueberry *Vaccinium elliottii* Chapm.	Downy serviceberry *Amelanchier arborea* (Michx. f.) Fern.
Fringetree *Chionanthus virginicus* L.	Strawberry bush *Euonymus americana* L.
Common greenbrier *Smilax rotundifolia* L.	Grape vines *Vitis* spp.
Japanese honeysuckle *Lonicera japonica* Thunb.	

Moderately desirable	
Alabama supply jack or rattan vine *Berchemia scandens* (Hill) K. Koch.	Rusty blackhaw *Virburnum rufidulum* Raf.
Blackberries *Rubus* spp.	Sawbrier, cat greenbrier *Smilax glauca* Walt.
Blackgum *Nyssa sylvatica* Marsh.	Southern arrowwood *Viburnum dentatum* L.
Carolina yellow jessamine *Gelsemium sempervirens* (L.) Ait. f.	Southern crab apple *Malus angustifolia* (Ait.) Michx.
Cockspur hawthorn *Crateagus crus-galli* L.	White ash *Fraxinus americana* L.
Mexican plum or big tree plum *Prunus mexicana* Wats.	Wild azalea *Rhododendron canescens* (Michx.)
Parsley hawthorn *Crataegus marshallii* Eggl.	Winged elm *Ulmus alata* Michx.
Red mulberry *Morus rubra* L.	Yaupon *Ilex vomitoria* Ait.

Source: adapted from Blair and Brunett (1980).

culent new leaves and stems of woody species, forbs, fungi (especially mushrooms), and fruits. To increase the deer carrying-capacity of mixed pine–hardwood stands significantly, selection harvests must be made at 5-year intervals. Harvesting must remove enough pines and hardwoods to admit significant amounts of light to the herb and shrub layers (Blair and Brunett 1976).

Yields of herbage and browse peak within 2 years after selection logging in mixed pine–hardwood stands. These habitats should be able to support 1 deer for every 5 to 7 ha for up to 4 years after logging. Carrying-capacity declines rapidly after that time as overstory competition increases and the supply of preferred foods diminishes. Browse can be expected to comprise 75% or more of the annual forage production. Deer carrying-capacities of habitats managed primarily for loblolly pine and habitats where hardwoods make up to 25% of the total tree basal area differ little because mast yield in a pine–hardwood forest may not be sufficient to improve deer health and productivity noticeably (Blair and Brunett 1977, Halls and Boyd 1982).

Figure 9-2—White-tailed deer browsing in a loblolly pine stand opening in east Texas.

Table 9-6—Winter and breeding season bird populations in 6- and 20-year-old loblolly pine plantations, a 46-year-old natural loblolly stand, and

Bird species	Wintering January–March 1975				Breeding May–June 1974				Bird species	Wintering January–March 1975				Breeding May–June 1974			
	6 yr	20 yr	46 yr	mixed pine–hdwd*	6 yr	20 yr	46 yr	mixed pine–hdwd*		6 yr	20 yr	46 yr	mixed pine–hdwd*	6 yr	20 yr	46 yr	mixed pine–hdwd*
Yellow-rumped warbler *Dendroica coronata* (L.)	50	9	5	124					American woodcock *Scolopax minor* Gmelin	1							
Swamp sparrow *Melospiza georgiana* (Latham)	49		2						Orange-crowned warbler *Vermivora celata* (Say)	1	1		5				
Short-billed marsh wren *Cistothorus platensis* (Latham)	32								Field sparrow *Spizella pusilla* (Wilson)	1							
Ruby-crowned kinglet *Regulus calendula* (L.)	26	34	10	92					American bittern *Botaurus lentiginosus* (Rackett)	1							
Carolina wren *Thryothorus ludovicianus* (Latham)	24	7	4	21	9	14	14	60	Turkey vulture *Cathartes aura* (L.)	1			1				
Northern cardinal *Cardinalis cardinalis* (L.)	22	4	2	48	40	34	20	200	Black vulture *Coragyps atratus* (Bechstein)	1							
Rufous-sided towhee *Pipilo erythrophthalmus* (L.)	18			1	26	6	14	2	Red-shouldered hawk *Buteo lineatus* (Gmelin)	1	1		9				4
Blue jay *Cyanocitta cristata* (L.)	11	15	10	60		6	6	6	Carolina chickadee *Parus carolinensis* Audubon	1	5		24		14		14
American robin *Turdus migratorius* L.	10	4	1	87					Long-billed marsh wren *Cistothorus palustris* (Wilson)	1							
Song sparrow *Melospiza melodia* (Wilson)	6								Eastern bluebird *Sialia sialis* (L.)		1		8	2		4	
Northern mockingbird *Mimus polyglottos* (L.)	5				4				Dark-eyed junco *Junco hyemalis* (L.)	1		2					
White-throated sparrow *Zonotrichia albicollis* (Gmelin)	4	2	2	32					Pine warbler *Dendroica pinus* (Wilson)		25	55	36		20	46	4
Common flicker *Colaptes auratus* (L.)	4		1	7					Hermit thrush *Catharus guttatus* (Pallas)		14	2	28				
Winter wren *Troglodytes troglodytes* (L.)	3								Red-bellied woodpecker *Melanerpes carolinus* (L.)		9	7	24			14	14
White-eyed vireo *Vireo griseus* (Boddaert)	3			2	14	14		240	Golden-crowned kinglet *Regulus satrapa* (Lichtenstein)		6		14				
Common yellowthroat *Geothlypis trichas* (L.)	3				20				Pileated woodpecker *Dryocopus pileatus* (L.)		4		3				6
Mourning Dove *Zenaida macroura* (L.)	2								Solitary vireo *Vireo solitarius* (Wilson)		4		3				
House wren *Troglodytes aedon* Vieillot	2		3	1					Downy woodpecker *Picoides pubescens* (L.)		3	2	5			6	2
American goldfinch *Carduelis tristis* (L.)	2	2	5	3					Eastern phoebe *Sayornis phoebe* (Latham)		2	2	4				2
Tufted titmouse *Parus bicolor* (L.)	2		1	13	4	4		14	Barred owl *Strix varia* Barton		2	2	4				2

Source: adapted from Nobel and Hamilton (1976).

* The mixed–pine–hardwood stand was uneven-aged and mature to overmature.

Effects of clearcutting on wildlife. Of all the timber-harvesting systems, clearcutting has the greatest impact on wildlife populations because it normally causes a drastic change in forest structure, plant species composition, stand density, and vegetation growth rates. Habitat for most wildlife species can be protected even when stands are clearcut if the size, amount of edge, distribution of cutting units, and timing of cuts are arranged to provide birds and mammals with easy access to a wide diversity of food and cover (Meyers and Johnson 1978). In fact, habitat requirements of many wildlife species can be met only in areas where early successional plant spec-ies thrive. Of 35 plant species or groups of species considered important as food for songbirds in east Texas, 28 were more abundant 15 months after a mature loblolly–shortleaf pine stand was cut than in adjacent pine forests (Stransky and others 1976). Clearcuts of modest size (20 to 40 ha) provide a variety of wildlife food and cover. Clearcutting can, however, add the risk of replacing uncommon wildlife species with a greater number of common species (Harris and Smith 1978). Extremely small clearcuts may not improve habitat because little or no vegetative reproduction will follow.

Both the numbers of species and the densities of birds and small mammals, and raptors that prey on them, are generally greater on an area 1 or 2 years after clearcut-

an uneven-aged mature to overmature mixed pine–hardwood stand in southeast Louisiana; populations are expressed as number of birds/40 ha

Bird species	Wintering January–March 1975				Breeding May–June 1974			
	6 yr	20 yr	46 yr	mixed pine–hdwd*	6 yr	20 yr	46 yr	mixed pine–hdwd*
Common crow *Corvus brachyrhynchos* Brehm	1							
Brown-headed nuthatch *Sitta pusilla* Latham			10				26	
Bachman's sparrow *Aimophila aestivalis* (Lichtenstein)		1				14		
American kestrel *Falco sparverius* (L.)			1					
Henslow's sparrow *Ammodramus henslowii* (Audubon)		1						
Brown thrasher *Toxostoma rufum* (L.)			25					
Yellow-bellied sapsucker *Sphyrapicus varius* (L.)			7					
Hairy woodpecker *Picoides villosus* (L.)			1				2	2
Fox sparrow *Passerella iliaca* (Merrem)			1					
Cedar waxwing *Bombycilla cedrorum* Vieillot			1					
Yellow-breasted chat *Icteria virens* (L.)					74			
Prairie warbler *Dendroica discolor* (Vieillot)					54		14	
Painted bunting *Passerina ciris* (L.)					20			
Northern bobwhite *Colinus virginianus* (L.)					14			
Orchard oriole *Icterus spurius* (L.)					4			
Indigo bunting *Passerina cyanea* (L.)					4		6	
Acadian flycatcher *Empidonax virescens* (Vieillot)						20	6	18
Great crested flycatcher *Myiarchus crinitus* (L.)						20	2	2
Red-headed woodpecker *Melanerpes erythrocephalus* (L.)					14			
Eastern wood-pewee *Contopus virens* (L.)								14

Bird species	Wintering January–March 1975				Breeding May–June 1974			
	6 yr	20 yr	46 yr	mixed pine–hdwd*	6 yr	20 yr	46 yr	mixed pine–hdwd*
Yellow-throated vireo *Vireo flavifrons* Vieillot							14	20
Summer tanager *Piranga rubra* (L.)							6	2
Ruby-throated hummingbird *Archilochus colubris* (L.)							2	
Red-cockaded woodpecker *Picoides borealis* (Vieillot)							2	
American redstart *Setophaga ruticilla* (L.)								414
Red-eyed vireo *Vireo olivaceus* (L.)								214
Northern parula *Parula americana* (L.)								120
Yellow-billed cuckoo *Coccyzus americanus* (L.)					2			40
Prothonotary warbler *Protonotaria citrea* (Boddaert)								34
Hooded warbler *Wilsonia citrina* (Boddaert)								32
Swainson's warbler *Limnothlypis swainsonii* (Audubon)								26
Worm-eating warbler *Helmitheros vermivorus* (Gmelin)							26	
Louisiana waterthrush *Seiurus motacilla* (Vieillot)								20
Blue-gray gnatcatcher *Polioptila caerulea* (L.)								14
Wood thrush *Hylocichla mustelina* (Gmelin)								6
Black-and-white warbler *Mniotilta varia* (L.)								6
Kentucky warbler *Oporornis formosus* (Wilson)								4
Green-backed heron *Butorides striatus* (L.)								2
Yellow-crowned night heron *Nyctanassa violacea* (L.)								2
Total	289	154	139	686	282	154	250	1,572
Total species	31	21	24	31	13	13	22	33

ting than before clearcutting (Conner and others 1981). For example, occurrence of early successional birds such as the northern cardinal; prairie warbler, *Dendroica discolor* (Vieillot); white-eyed vireo, *Vireo griseus* (Boddaert); and yellow-breasted chat, *Icteria virens* (L.), is positively associated with increasing density of shrub stems, number of shrub species, foliage volume at 1 to 3 m aboveground, and percentage of sapling pines. The same bird species are negatively associated with increasing vegetation height, canopy closure, and number of pole-sized trees (Conner and others 1983). If bird species such as these are to be maintained in a forest, there must be disturbances at various places and at regular intervals to provide a constant cycle of successional stages. Ages of

adjacent even-aged stands should differ by at least 7 years to optimize benefits for these birds.

The number and diversity of birds in the woods along the edge of a clearcut are about three times as great as in the interior woods or in adjacent clearcuts (Strelke and Dickson 1980). During the winter and the prenesting period, turkeys spend a considerable amount of time in edges (Holbrook and others 1987). The edge effect diminishes rapidly as distance into the woods interior increases. The edge-to-area ratio for clearcuts can be enhanced by keeping cutting areas small and narrow and by creating irregularly shaped boundaries. Round or square cutting blocks provide the least amount of edge for habitat diversity. An irregular, 20-ha clearcut can

Figure 9-3—Streamside management zones in east Texas on a loblolly pine forest that was recently logged.

mouse, *Peromyscus leucopus*) may use mature forest streamside management zones as narrow as 25 m (Dickson and Williamson 1988).

Streamside zones can greatly improve the appearance of clearcuts by making them look smaller and less uniform. Furthermore, they are valuable as sediment filters and, if wide and dense, can improve warmwater fish habitat by shading the water surface and maintaining moderate summer water temperatures. In the Georgia Piedmont, clearcutting a loblolly pine stand and leaving only a 12-m-wide, low-density streamside zone of trees increased maximum summer water temperature from 20 to 26° C (Hewlett 1979).

Diversity of bird species can be increased by leaving standing snags in clearcuts. For best results, 12 or more large, dead, hardwood trees/ha should be left. Similarly, it may be desirable to retain some snags or cull trees in streamside zones. These provide dens and insects for pecking birds and perching sites for raptors, and are essential for maintenance of primary or secondary cavity nesters, as well as overwintering cavity users (Conner 1978, Dickson and Conner 1982, Dickson and others 1983). Similarly, if lower Coastal Plain cypress–bay ponds that occur in moist flatwoods are left intact during clearcutting operations, indigenous birds can use them as refuges while repopulating adjacent growing plantations (Rowse and Marion 1981).

Managers often leave strips of pines up to 30 m wide between roads and areas that are being harvested. Such strips reduce the visual harshness of clearcuts but can pose a safety hazard for animals and automobiles. These strips are used as easy travel zones, especially by larger animals such as deer, when recent clearcuts are choked with dense vegetation. Unfortunately, increased animal travel along well-used roads increases road-kills (Lalo 1987). Road-killed animals attract scavengers that may in turn be killed by vehicles.

have a few hundred meters of edge per hectare depending on its shape. A square clearcut of the same size has only about 36 m of edge/ha. A square 200-ha clearcut has only about 11 m of edge/ha of clearcut.

Edge effect and habitat diversity can be increased by maintaining permanent openings, especially where loblolly pine stands of one age class occupy large areas. Occasional plantings of small seed crops such as corn, *Zea mays* L.; cowpeas, *Vigna unguiculata* (L.) Walp. Subsp. *unguiculata*; *Lespedeza* spp.; millet, *Setaria* spp.; orchardgrass, *Dactylis glomerata* L.; peanuts, *Arachis hypogaea* L.; *Sorghum* spp.; etc. in small forest openings or within sparse stands can increase the health and numbers of turkeys and other wildlife (Halls and Stransky 1968, Shaffer and Gwynn 1967). These plantings should be justified both biologically and economically before extensive use.

A valuable technique to ameliorate the effect of clearcutting is to leave strips of mature vegetation along stream courses (figure 9-3). These streamside zones are especially important to gray and fox squirrels, amphibians, reptiles, and birds. Streamside zones should be identified early, maintained in a variety of hardwood and pine trees and shrubs (including fruit-bearing trees and shrubs), and given permanent protection from fire. Strips of natural vegetation 50 to 100 m in width [the width of a streamside management zone is the sum of the widths on both sides of the stream] consistently support more squirrels, amphibians, and reptiles, and more numbers and varieties of birds than do those 40 m or less in width (Thill and others 1991, Dickson 1989). Squirrels are rare in zones less than 40 m wide (Dickson and Huntley 1986, McElfresh and others 1980). Strips more than 30 m wide support many more amphibians and reptiles than do narrower zones (Rudolph and Dickson 1990). However, many small mammals (especially the fulvous harvest mouse and white-footed

Effects of site preparation and plantation management on wildlife. Mechanical site preparation treatments that cause little soil disturbance can increase plant diversity, wildlife diversity, wildlife food production, and pine production (Locascio and others 1989). Plant abundance and diversity after chemical site preparation frequently exceed plant abundance and diversity after mechanical site preparation (Carter and others 1975). Hot summer fires are excellent for promoting an abundance of food plants for game (Cushwa and Redd 1966; Cushwa and others 1966, 1969, 1970). Cool burns for hazard reduction have little effect on the quantity and quality of deer forage (Wood 1988). Because snags are important for wildlife shelter, they should be protected from fire. Before burning, combustibles should be raked at least 3 m away from snags.

Intensive site preparation treatments such as disking, chopping, and bedding often destroy the aboveground portions of wildlife food plants. Most bird populations are low for the first year after site preparation, but the sites are suitable for use by the eastern meadowlark, *Sturnella magna* (L.), and wild turkey. Once sprouts and seedlings begin to grow, prepared sites quickly develop into superior habitats for small mammals, birds, and white-tailed deer. One- to two-year-old plantations of loblolly pines often have dense stands of forbs and perennial grasses, which make superior habitats for small herbivores such as the cotton rat and small seed-eating mammals such as the white-footed mouse as well as for quail, turkey, and numerous songbirds including the blue grosbeak, *Guiraca caerulea* (L.); indigo bunting, *Passerina cyanea* (L.); and prairie warbler. By the third and fourth years, annual and perennial grasses decrease while fruit-producing shrubs (for example, *Rubus* spp. and *Vaccinium* spp.) increase. This habitat change results in a decrease in the numbers of small seed-eating mammals and early successional birds but an increase in the number of small herbivores and birds such as the Carolina wren, *Thryothorus ludovicianus* (Latham); field sparrow, *Spizella pusilla* (Wilson); northern cardinal; white-eyed vireo; and yellow-breasted chat. The overall result is an increased complexity of wildlife, especially birds, as succession proceeds from a newly established plantation to crown closure. After crown closure, the complexity of wildlife decreases with the decrease in layering and complexity of vegetation (Dickson and others 1984, Schultz and Wilhite 1974, Stransky and Richardson 1977, Stransky and Roese 1984).

Quail, turkeys, and deer make extensive use of young loblolly pine plantations, both for food and for raising their young (figure 9-4). Newly regenerated plantations provide the most and the best food for these animals. Quail and turkeys living in 3- and 4-year-old plantations may have diets that are more restricted than those of birds living in younger stands, primarily because of the demise of seed-producing plants in the older planta-

Figure 9-4—A white-tailed deer doe with her fawn in loblolly pine regeneration in central Louisiana.

tions (Atkeson and Johnson 1979, Brunswig and Johnson 1973, Felix and others 1986, Kennamer and others 1980, Larkin 1989, Perkins and others 1989, Scanlon and Sharik 1986, Sweeney and others 1981).

Numbers and species of birds and mammals continue to decrease as stands age and tree size increases because habitat diversity and complexity decrease. Understory vegetation on intensively cultured sites usually remains lush until trees reach about 5 to 8 years of age, at which time tree crowns begin to shade out the understory. Grass and total herbage decrease in a curvilinear relationship with increasing tree cover or tree basal area. Reduction is most rapid when tree cover increases from 0 to 20% or basal area increases from 0 to 2 m²/ha. Once crowns close, the typical unburned and unthinned plantation provides very poor habitat for most wildlife species (Atkeson and Johnson 1979, Johnson and others 1974). Young, fast-growing trees may also harbor few bark arthropods, an important food of bark-gleaning birds. Fifteen-year-old, fully stocked loblolly pine stands are probably the poorest of all loblolly pine habitats for most birds and mammals (Atkeson and Johnson 1979, Dickson 1982, Dickson and others 1984, Dickson and Segelquist 1979, Halls and Schuster 1965, Meyers and Johnson 1978, Moore and others 1974, Whiting and Fleet 1987).

General patterns of plant succession and wildlife use in loblolly pine plantations are similar over large geographical areas. This similarity is partly an effect of single-species planting. Subtle differences in lesser vegetation, caused by differences in soil, drainage characteristics, and silvicultural treatments, can alter the type and quantity of wildlife present. Converting a hardwood stand to loblolly pine generally has a greater negative impact on small bird species than has replacing one pine stand with another largely because biological diversity is greater in hardwood stands than in pine stands.

Windrows or brush piles and patches of grass in or along the edges of clearcuts add heterogeneity to plantations. These microsites provide excellent hiding and nesting areas for small mammals such as wood rats and cotton rats (Fleet and Dickson 1984) and for birds. Bedded areas also provide dry nesting sites for birds in regions that are generally wet during the breeding season (Schultz and Wilhite 1974). Newly established and burned windrows may also have high concentrations of fleshy fungi, which is not available on typical plantation sites (Hurst and Johnson 1980).

Natural stand management and wildlife populations. Regeneration by seed tree, shelterwood, or selection methods generally has less drastic effects on wildlife populations than clearcutting. Even so, these techniques can alter the diversity and concentration of wildlife substantially. In one seed-tree harvested stand, 36 birds of 7 species nested in each 40-ha tract the second season after logging. By the third season, 116 birds nested in each 40-ha tract, which demonstrates how rapidly birds make use of changing habitats as vegetative complexity increases (Noble and others 1980). Squirrels are also more likely to thrive in seed-tree or shelterwood stands than in clearcuts because there are no periods when vegetation is totally absent, successional stages are longer, and vertical plant diversity and within-stand heterogeneity are enhanced. Small mammals use naturally regenerated stands as often as they use artificially regenerated stands. Site preparation by chopping and burning have the same effect on small mammal use of naturally and artificially regenerated stands (Mengak and others 1989).

Interspersion of forest types. Interspersion of forest types provides the best all-round wildlife habitat. An abundance of deer and turkeys and a diversity of nongame species can be sustained where hardwood stands, mixed pine–hardwood stands, and loblolly pine stands of various ages are interspersed. Regeneration areas, burned areas, and thinned areas normally supply enough forage for deer (Speake and others 1975). Ideal turkey habitat usually requires long pine rotations with controlled burns every 2 to 4 years. This regime keeps some areas open and promotes fruit production by various shrubs in years of fire exclusion. Unfortunately, this management regime also reduces the structural diversity that most other wildlife species require. Stand size, especially for hardwoods, should be relatively large (at least 40 ha) because turkeys readily move from one stand to another to meet seasonal needs.

Intermediate stand management. Silvicultural treatments can have modest to profound effects on wildlife habitats. Growing timber at the minimum density that yields an acceptable economic return admits more light to the understory and improves the environment for growth of wildlife food and cover vegetation. Treatments that increase layering of vegetation are most apt to increase breeding bird density and diversity (Dickson and Segelquist 1979). Practices that can promote layering include prescribed burning, thinning, and occasionally, the use of herbicides or fertilizers.

Prescribed burning. Controlled fires cause little wildlife mortality. However, they have a substantial indirect influence on the abundance and species composition of wildlife through regulation of lesser vegetation. The numbers of animals may decrease for varying lengths of time, depending on the amount of food and shelter destroyed (Landers 1987, Lyon and others 1978). Under pure loblolly pine or mixed pine–hardwood stands, prescribed burning at 3- to 6-year intervals increases the quantity, quality, palatability, and accessibility of grasses, forbs, and shrubs that provide seeds, fruits, and browse for a wide variety of game (including doves, quail, and turkeys) and nongame animals. For best deer management, loblolly stands should be burned on a 3- to 4-year rotation to keep leafy browse at an easily accessible level.

Fires should be cool enough so that dogwood and other valuable hardwoods survive in the midstory.

Annual burning is generally not recommended; it can weaken browse plants and so restrict their growth that they seldom produce much fruit. Persistent annual burning can also destroy oaks and other producers of hard mast unless special provisions are made to protect specific mast-producing areas or individual trees. It may be necessary to exclude fire for several years during a rotation to permit some large shrubs and midstory hardwoods to reach fruit-bearing size (Blair 1968, Byrd and Holbrook 1974, Chen and others 1975, Cushwa and others 1971, Grand and Mirarchi 1988, Halls 1973, Lay 1967).

For the purpose of wildlife management, winter is the best time to burn under loblolly pine or mixed pine–hardwood stands. Plants are dormant in winter, and winter burning destroys little palatable forage. Summer burns give better hardwood control, but they are generally less effective than winter burns in promoting the development of wildlife foods. Summer burns may kill desirable browse plants and may temporarily eliminate forage needed by game animals during the fall and winter. Summer burning is also more likely to result in increased soil erosion (Blair 1968, Halls 1973).

Thinning. Thinning at 5- to 10-year intervals (even beginning with precommercial thinning) allows light to reach the forest floor and increases the number, growth rate, and quality of wildlife food plants such as blackberries, blueberries, woody vines, and hardwood trees. Thinning usually stimulates renewed use of older stands. Yields of browse in a 30-year-old loblolly pine plantation thinned at ages 20 and 25 were directly proportional to the amount of pines removed and ranged from 172 ovendry kg/ha under light thinning to 223 kg/ha with heavy thinning. However, at stand age 35 (five growing seasons after a third thinning), browse yields were inversely related to thinning intensity because browse plants released in earlier thinnings had grown beyond the reach of deer and formed a multilayered midstory that inhibited understory plant growth. When this midstory was removed at stand age 40, herbage dry matter quickly increased to 866 kg/ha and browse to 1,051 kg/ha (Blair 1967, Blair and Enghardt 1976, Blair and Feduccia 1977, Hurst and others 1982, Wood and others 1974).

The combination of thinning and prescribed burning usually increases browse weight and the variety and abundance of understory species (including mushrooms) more than either treatment does separately (Hurst and Warren 1983).

Herbicide treatments. The effects of herbicides on wildlife habitat are usually of short duration, and acute toxicity to most wildlife species is unlikely if materials are applied properly (McComb and Hurst 1987). Herbicides can improve habitat by making new openings, maintaining old openings, and changing understory species composition. Selective injection or basal spraying of undesirable overstory and midstory trees can favor production of high-quality wildlife foods such as vines, forbs, and hardwood sprouts. If herbicide treatments reduce the number of hardwood stems and increase the number of herbaceous plants, the effect is similar to that of successful prescribed burnings. In one case, aerial application of granular hexazinone herbicide to 4-year-old loblolly pine plantations for hardwood brush control increased deer forage (primarily forbs) more than 50%

Figure 9-5—Red-cockaded wood peckers on heart-rot-infected loblolly pine trees in central Louisiana (***right***) and east Texas (***above***).

during the following 2 years (Hurst and Warren 1986). However, herbaceous weed control with liquid hexazi-none can reduce plant biomass and deer forage for 1 year after treatment. Applying the liquid herbicide in bands along tree rows minimizes this adverse effect because the strips of vegetation between rows provide deer forage (Blake and others 1987). Broadcast spraying of herbicides may have long-term harmful effects on wildlife habitat when it damages or kills mast-bearing trees and shrubs that are important wildlife food sources (Blair 1971, Blair and Fedducia 1977).

Forest fertilization. Fertile forest soils grow nutritious forage that enhances wildlife growth, development, and reproduction (Blair and Halls 1968, Crawford 1950, Halls 1970, Short 1969). The opposite is true on infertile soils. A low level of phosphorus (P) in forage tissues throughout the year hampers deer development in young loblolly pine plantations (Blair and others 1977).

In addition to promoting tree growth, fertilization increases the volume of understory plants, alters the nutritional content of important wildlife foods for 1 or 2 years, and accelerates succession. However, it may decrease plant species diversity by as much as 43%. Although fertilization decreases plant species diversity on both Coastal Plain and Piedmont sites, the problem seems to be more frequent on Coastal Plain sites (Haines and Sanderford 1976, Hurst and others 1982, Wood 1986).

Protection and Promotion of Endangered Animal Species

Several endangered or threatened wildlife species live in the loblolly pine ecosystem. The habitats of these species should be protected and, if possible, expanded to increase the populations of the species. Forest management practices should be flexible enough so that they can be modified immediately when endangered or threatened plant and animal species are identified.

The endangered red-cockaded woodpecker (RCW) occurs in much of the loblolly pine range (figure 9-5). Old-growth loblolly pine stands are preferred habitats of the RCW. The birds live in family units consisting of a single breeding pair and birds from previous broods. The birds from previous broods assist their parents in raising

new broods. Red-cockaded woodpeckers forage almost exclusively in living pines. A single family unit may require 50 ha or more of relatively open, pine-dominated stands for nesting and foraging (Chipley 1979, Locke and others 1983, Porter and Labisky 1986). However, one family may thrive in as little as 28 ha of high-quality habitat (Conner R. 1989. Personal communication). Stands adequate for RCW habitat contain at least 1.7 m^2 of pine basal area/ha. The presence of many hardwoods in the overstory may reduce the quality of RCW habitat by attracting other woodpecker species and increasing competition for pine food resources. Unwanted hardwoods can be removed gradually by using chemical injections. Even manual removal of hardwoods does not seem to be harmful to RCW colonies, as long as it is not done during the breeding season (Conner and Rudolph 1991).

Numerous tree characteristics (age, diameter, bole length, presence of red heart fungus, heartwood diameter, resin characteristics, and growth history) and stand characteristics (basal area, midstory development, and canopy height) influence cavity tree selection by the RCW (Conner and Locke 1982, Conner and O'Halloran 1987, Conner and Rudolph 1991, Jackson and others 1979, Locke and others 1983, Rudolph and Conner 1991). The birds form nesting and roosting cavities by excavating holes in trees infected with red heart fungi. *Phellinus pini* (Thore:Fr.) Ames (= *Fomes pini*) is the most common red heart fungus, but *Lentinus lepideus* Fr., *Lenzites saepiaria* (Wulf. ex. Fr.) Fr., *Phaeolus schweinitzii* (Fr.:Fr.) Pat., and *Phlebia radiata* Fr. also occur in cavity trees. These fungi decay portions of the heartwood of trees while leaving sound living exteriors (Conner and Locke 1982). The average loblolly pine cavity tree is more than 75 years old and greater than 23 cm in dbh and has a small crown ratio due to suppression or growth under substantial early competition. In stands with limited numbers of midstory trees, woodpeckers often use trees older than 150 years and 50 to 75 cm in dbh In east Texas, birds consistently select trees that are 16 to 25 years older than the stand average (Rudolph and Conner 1991). Each colony occupies about 4 cavity trees that are at least 58 m from one another (Teitelbaum and Smith 1985, Wood 1983). Old cavity trees have considerable bole pitch, which makes them very susceptible to intense understory fires. For this reason, colony sites should be protected from fire by raking fuel at least 3 m away from the bases of cavity trees and by burning the areas separately and regularly with cool backfires (Conner and Locke 1979).

There are several potential ways to promote the strict ecological conditions required by the RCW. Trees as young as 26 years of age have been artificially inoculated with red heart fungus, suggesting that the age requirement for quality cavity trees could be reduced (Conner and Locke 1983). Shelterwood cutting seems capable of providing a sustained supply of potential cavity trees— trees that are first suppressed and then released, as are most natural cavity trees (Conner and O'Halloran 1987, Conner and Rudolph 1989). Human activity does not disturb the RCW, so it is possible that highway rights-of-way and similar highly visible public lands can be used to support many family units if sufficiently mature trees are present (Chipley 1979). On wildlife manage-

ment areas, the loblolly pine component of low-quality hardwood stands could be increased to develop trees suitable for use by future woodpecker clans (Thomas and Buckner 1981).

The gopher tortoise, *Gopherus polyphemus* Daudin, is another endangered inhabitant of specific parts of the loblolly pine ecosystem. Because the tortoise feeds principally on herbaceous vegetation and requires sunlight for egg incubation, open conditions are essential to its well-being. Clearcutting followed by fire or intensive mechanical site preparation creates sunny sites for productive nesting areas and for production of important grass foods. When tree crowns shade out the understory, the tortoise population decreases. It is essential to keep cutting areas small and arranged so that these animals can migrate to nearby newly prepared sites (Lohoefener and Lohmeier 1981). Long, soil-filled windrows can hamper tortoise movement. Burrows made by the gopher tortoise are used by several snake and frog species (Seehorn 1982).

Several other sensitive animal species live in association with loblolly pines, but little is known about them. They include the Houston toad, *Bufo houstonensis* Sanders, which occurs on well-drained sandy soil in southeastern Texas, and the pine barrens treefrog, *Hyla andersonii* Baird, found in the pocosins of North Carolina (Seehorn 1982).

Range Resources in the Loblolly Pine Ecosystem

Forest range includes forest lands that produce native forage for grazing or browsing animals and those that are revegetated to provide forage that is managed along with trees. Forest range in the loblolly–shortleaf–hardwood ecosystem is estimated at 21.9 million ha and extends from east Texas to northeast Virginia (figure 9-6). Raising livestock together with loblolly pines can result in relatively high production of timber and beef. Overstory tree density, or percentage of canopy cover, is the most important influence on forage yield. Yields decrease as overstory density increases. Without tree competition, forage yields even on marginal sites can average more than 2,800 kg of herbage dry matter/ha/yr and may occasionally exceed 8,900 kg/ha/yr (Fribourg and others 1989). Native forage production drops rapidly as crowns begin to close; however, it can increase again during the latter part of a pine rotation if stand density decreases. Forage produced in low-density pine stands and in natural openings within the forest provide feed for substantial numbers of range

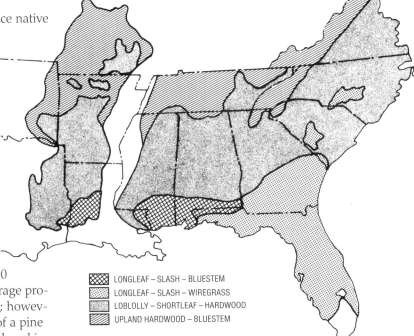

LONGLEAF – SLASH – BLUESTEM
LONGLEAF – SLASH – WIREGRASS
LOBLOLLY – SHORTLEAF – HARDWOOD
UPLAND HARDWOOD – BLUESTEM

Figure 9-6—Major range types in the southern United States (adapted from Byrd and Lewis 1976).

Figure 9-7—Cattle grazing in loblolly pine regeneration in central Louisiana: new regeneration—fire was used to move cattle from the area and the same adequately stocked stand 9 years later.

Coastal Plain of Georgia (Harwell and Dangerfield 1991). When cattle and slash pine were grown together for 20 years in central Louisiana, livestock returns were highest during the first 10 years of the pine rotation, averaging $6.62/ha/yr. Grazing yields and beef production diminished as pine stocking increased. Thinning helped restore beef productivity (Pearson 1982). Fencing is a necessary part of any timber and cattle operation and must be included in any cost analysis. Byrd and Lewis (1976) estimated the following annual forage production levels (air-dry basis) for managed southern pine forests:

Size class	kg/ha
Open seedling and sapling stage	2,910–3,360
Trees up to 15 cm in dbh	1,570–2,900
Poles and small sawtimber	730–1,570
Sawtimber	730–1,680

However, yields may exceed 5,600 kg/ha/yr in seedling and sapling plantations on highly productive sites (Byrd and others 1984, Smeins and Hinton 1987).

Forage production is affected not only by overstory tree density but also by other interrelated factors. Shrubs and hardwood trees compete with and shade forage species, lowering forage yields (Wolters and others 1982). Mature stands with abundant midstory and overstory hardwoods yield as little as 85 to 340 kg/ha/yr of herbage (Smeins and Hinton 1987, Wolters and others 1977).

Water stress commonly limits annual forage production under closed stands. When annual rainfall on a central Louisiana site was 188 cm, understory biomass was 360 kg/ha during the spring and 353 kg/ha during the summer. Understory biomass dropped to 265 kg/ha in the spring and 300 kg/ha in the summer the following year, when rainfall was only 142 cm (Reed and Noble 1987). Other factors such as soil, physiography, environmental conditions, grass species, and frequency of prescribed burning also affect herbage production significantly.

In the loblolly–shortleaf–hardwood ecosystem, the most important grass in openings and under open pine stands is usually either little bluestem, *Schizachyrium scoparium* (Michx.) Nash (= *Andropogon scoparius* Michx.), or pinehill bluestem, *S. scoparium* var. *divergens* (Hack.) Gould (= *A. divergens* (Hack) Andress. ex Hitchc.). Longleaf uniola, *Chasmanthium sessiliflorum* (Poir.) Yates (= *Uniola sessiliflora* Poir.), and spike uniola, *C. laxum* (L.)

cattle. Twelve hectares of sawtimber or 40 ha of dense pine poletimber can usually support 1 animal year-round (Wolters and Wilhite 1974). Stands of loblolly, like most other forest stands, provide shade for livestock in the summer and shelter in the winter.

Growing timber and livestock together may generate more income per hectare than growing timber alone and can help stabilize income by providing a wider array of market opportunities (figure 9-7). During the early part of a pine rotation, livestock returns exceed timber returns; this gradually reverses during later years. A computer model predicted that net present value would increase from $1,369 to $2,343/ha when production of beef cattle was combined with production of loblolly pines on marginal cropland in the upper

Table 9-7—Frequency of occurrence of range vegetation under 638,000 ha of the loblolly–shortleaf pine forest type and 331,000 ha of the oak–pine forest type in southwest Louisiana

Understory vegetation	Percent of total vegetation*		Understory vegetation	Percent of total vegetation*	
	Loblolly–shortleaf pine	Oak–pine		Loblolly–shortleaf pine	Oak–pine
BROWSE			HERBAGE		
Blackberries *Rubus* spp.	21.5	15.2	Bluestems (broomsedge) *Andropogon* spp.	31.5	17.2
Elliott's blueberry *Vaccinium elliottii* Chapm.	9.1	9.6	Broomsedge bluestem *Andropogon virginicus* L.	8.5	10.1
Flowering dogwood *Cornus florida* L.	3.9	7.1	Common carpetgrass *Axonopus affinis* Chase	9.4	11.5
American beautyberry *Callicarpa americana* L.	10.5	12.9	Cutover muhly *Muhlenbergia expansa* (DC.) Trin.	3.8	2.3
Grapevines *Vitis* spp.	51.3	45.0	North American erect grasses *Uniola* spp.	18.9	25.9
Greenbriers *Smilax* spp.	21.0	24.8	Panic grasses *Panicum* spp.	43.8	41.1
Hawthorns *Crataegus* spp.	8.7	8.7	Slender bluestem *Schizachyrium tenerum* Nees	10.8	8.3
Oaks *Quercus* spp.	30.8	29.6	Threeawns *Aristida* spp.	8.3	5.0
Southern waxmyrtle *Myrica cerifera* L.	15.2	10.8	Other grasses	40.1	39.0
Sumacs *Rhus.* spp.	4.1	5.0	Grasslike species	33.5	40.8
Yaupon *Ilex vomitoria* Ait.	2.6	1.1	Legumes	37.4	23.6
Other trees & shrubs	53.2	64.5	Other forbs	72.4	71.3
Other vines	51.3	45.0			
All browse	86.6	88.3	All herbage	89.4	88.7

Source: adapted from Pearson (1976).

* Expressed as a percentage of occurrence on all sample plots.

Yates (= *U. laxa* (L.) B.S.P.), are mixed with the bluestems where the overstory is moderately dense. On heavily shaded sites, uniola grasses form sparse but almost pure stands. Various forbs and legumes contribute to forage production on all sites (Lewis 1974; table 9-7). Browse and herbs each make up about one-third of the ground cover in both the loblolly-shortleaf and the oak-pine ecosystems.

The nutritive value and digestibility of forest forage are relatively low throughout the year. However, both canopy cover and season of the year affect nutrient levels. Nutrition is at its highest level in spring, when plants are growing rapidly, and at its lowest level in winter, when growth is slowest (Lewis 1974, Lewis and others 1982). Forage that grows in the shade contains higher concentrations of protein and P than forage that grows in the open (Wolters 1973). Browse species, including shrubs and small hardwood trees, provide cattle with nutrients that are unavailable, or of limited availability, in grasses and forbs. With implanted electrodes and biotelemetry, it is possible to record the activity level and feeding characteristics of cattle—including the separation of dry roughage and green herbaceous material swallowed under forest cover (Stuth and others 1981).

Cultural Treatments and Loblolly Pine Regeneration

Clearcutting combined with site preparation can be very beneficial to livestock by providing the opportunity for new forage species to seed into and grow rapidly on forest sites. In an east Texas pine–hardwood forest, total forage yield increased from 359 kg/ha before clearcutting to 2,917 kg/ha 1 year after clearcutting and then declined gradually as tree and shrub competition increased. Clearcutting followed by burning increased peak forage levels to 3,540 kg/ha at 1 year after clearcutting. Clearcutting followed by chopping or shearing resulted in slightly higher peak forage yields (3,619 and 3,774 kg/ha, respectively), but it took 3 years for forage to reach these levels. Five years after site preparation, total available forage was still about 5 times greater than under the uncut forest, and yields were directly proportional to intensity of site preparation (Stransky and Halls 1978, 1981).

Tree density greatly affects the amount of forage available on a site. Wide spacing of trees (spacing greater than 3.0 m by 3.7 m) yields much more forage than close spacing. Direct seeding or natural seeding usually reduces forage production sooner than does planting because seeding normally results in denser stands. For example, annual production of forage in direct-seeded slash pine stands was approximately equal to annual production of forage in planted slash pine stands in central Louisiana until trees finished their 6th growing season. From the 7th through the 12th years, the direct-seeded stands consistently yielded about 340 kg less forage/ha than did plantations (Pearson 1974).

Prescribed fire is essential to successful grazing under loblolly pine stands. Long-term fire protection results in increased pine overstory density and increased hardwood competition, and these result in greatly reduced forage production. Annual or periodic burning increases the quantity and improves the quality (nutritive content, palatability, and digestibility) of forage by removing litter, reducing the number and thrift of shrubs and hardwoods, and increasing the number and density of herbaceous species (Duvall and Whitaker 1964, Grelen and Epps 1967, Lewis and others 1982).

Burning in February or March, before the onset of spring growth, is best for cattle management because it seldom kills dormant browse species. It also favors sprouting of plants that are near the ground, which provide food for cattle that is higher in protein and P than 1- or 2-year-old plants. Cattle concentrate on newly burned areas within a few weeks. The length of the interval between burning and use by cattle depends on date of burning and growth of new vegetation. Grazing on fresh burns is usually uniformly heavy through the summer, with little selectivity among grass species. By late summer, grazing declines on burned areas and increases on surrounding unburned areas. The combination of burning and grazing reduces the crown cover of blackberry and other species that compete with loblolly pine for light, moisture, and nutrients (Halls and Homesley 1966, Lewis and Harshbarger 1976).

It is possible to burn loblolly pine stands as young as 3 years old, growing in grazed coastal bermudagrass, by backfiring strips up to 3 m in width. Such burning promotes forage production and reduces development of lower limbs on trees. Reduction of lower limb development can increase the area that can be grazed by 10%. However, it can also reduce tree growth, depending on the amount of needle damage from crown scorch (see chapter 8).

Both commercial and precommercial thinnings reduce overstory stocking and increase forage. At age 12, direct-seeded slash pines (precommercially thinned at age 3 to densities ranging from 1,235 to 13,100 trees/ha) had herbage yields ranging from 627 kg/ha where basal area was 11.6 m²/ha to 2,498 kg/ha where basal area was 5.0 m²/ha. Forage yields were the same with strip thinnings and selection thinnings (Grelen and others 1972). Precommercial thinning will affect forage production under loblolly pines in the same manner. Stands of pole-sized and mature trees provide almost half as much forage as a

treeless range does if they are thinned and burned regularly, even though debris left from log-length thinning and harvesting restricts forage growth and cattle movement until materials deteriorate. Prescribed burning accelarates decomposition of tree tops (Derr and Enghardt 1969, Grelen and Enghardt 1973).

Fertilization at time of plantation establishment can increase annual yields of native forage by 340 to 5,600 kg/ha for up to 5 years. After plantation age 5, forage response to fertilization declines as pines begin to dominate sites. In a central Louisiana trial, fertilizing newly planted loblolly pines in May with 672 kg of 16-30-13/ha tripled herbaceous production 3 months later. The effect gradually decreased during the next 3 years (figure 9-8). Similarly, fertilizing loblolly pine–bluestem sites in Louisiana at planting time with 73 kg of P as triple superphosphate/ha increased total herbage by 480, 394, and 258 kg/ha during the first, second, and third years, respectively (Shoulders and Tiarks 1984).

Responses of trees and herbaceous vegetation vary with cultural treatment combinations. Disking and fertilizing of loblolly pine stands along the Mississippi gulf coast doubled tree growth at age 12. However, herbage yields with disking and fertilization were less than one-third as great as herbage yields without disking and fertilization. Common carpetgrass, *Axonopus affinis* Chase, was the only herb to increase in yield with intensive culture. Fertilizers applied at the time of thinning may increase forage yields by 670 to 2,130 kg/ha for the first 1 or 2 years after application (Wolters and Schmidtling 1975).

Effects of Cattle on Loblolly Pines

Loblolly pines are rarely damaged seriously if cattle have adequate forage and are managed properly. Cattle may browse or trample young trees and may rub or chew bark from older trees. Removal of needles or shoots of trees up to 30 months old does not kill most trees. Recovery is usually rapid once cattle are removed from the area. However, trees die if cattle girdle them completely by eating their bark or knocking it off with their hooves (Lewis 1980a, 1980b).

The key to success in grazing new plantations is to maintain a balance between good forage and the number of animals. Uncontrolled livestock grazing and congregation may result in trampling of pine regeneration. The problem is usually most severe before new grass emerges in the spring. Damage to 1-year-old loblolly pines increased from 10% at 20% forage use to more than 40% at 60% forage use (King and others 1978). To minimize tree damage, it is best to defer grazing until trees are 2.4 to 3.0 m tall or to allow only seasonal grazing until that time (Pearson 1981, 1983). Where moisture is limited during the growing season, pine growth is promoted if forage is grazed before moisture becomes depleted. There may be a period of only 8 to 12 weeks in the early summer when grazing very young plantations is most appropriate

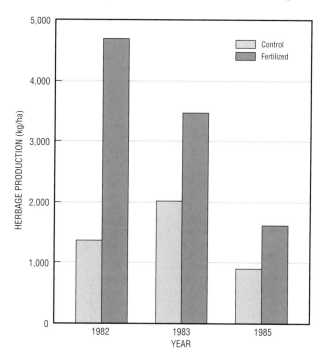

Figure 9-8—Herbaceous standing crop on control and fertilized plots during August of the treatment year (1982) and during August of 1983 and 1985. The study area consisted of 20 ha of loblolly pine seedlings, planted in February 1982. In May 1982, 16-30-13 granular fertilizer formulation was applied by helicopter at a rate of 672 kg/ha (adapted from Thill and Bellemore 1986).

(Pearson 1981). Neither light nor moderate grazing by cattle (33 and 47% utilization) affected establishment or survival of planted or seeded slash pines to age 5 years in central Louisiana. Where utilization was 56%, grazing reduced pine survival by 18 to 24% at age 5. However, stocking was still good and was distributed well, and grazing did not reduce height growth. Average dbh at age 18 was greater in heavily grazed areas than in lightly grazed areas, but volume yield was 10 to 13% lower in heavily grazed areas than in lightly grazed areas (Grelen and others 1985, Pearson 1982, Pearson and others 1971). Grazing should affect loblolly pines much as it affects slash pines.

The type of site preparation influences the amount of damage done to trees by cattle. On intensively prepared sites, horseweed and other unpalatable annuals may constitute most of the forage. Under such conditions, cattle may have to travel extensively in search of palatable plants. Increased travel increases the likelihood that cattle will browse or trample young pines. It may be necessary to exclude cattle from recently planted bedded areas or to keep only small numbers of cattle on such sites. Cattle tend to walk along the tops of beds, especially if the areas between beds are wet, which can result in trampling of newly planted seedlings.

Effects of Cattle on Native Forage and Soils

Grazing intensity does not significantly affect total herbage yields from the native southern pine forest range, but it can change the herbaceous species composition. For example, moderate to heavy grazing can reduce the frequency of pinehill bluestem and increase the relative frequency of carpetgrass. Responses of herbs to seasonal and yearlong grazing are similar on treeless range and forested range (Clary 1979, Pearson and Whitaker 1974).

Intensive grazing is potentially harmful to soil supporting loblolly pines. Heavy or even moderate grazing over long periods compacts the soil and restricts infiltration and percolation of water, especially during intense storms. Reduced infiltration and percolation during storms can result in erosion on fragile sites (Linnartz and others 1966). Moderate grazing for 10 years increased bulk density of medium-textured soils in the longleaf–bluestem range by 5% in the surface 13 cm, by 2% at depths of 15 to 25 cm, and by 1% at 30 to 40 cm (Duvall and Linnartz 1967). Compaction is especially severe around water sources and supplemental feeding stations. Stations can be moved regularly and the sites ameliorated. However, it may be less expensive and less environmentally damaging to designate specific areas for use only as feeding stations.

Integrating Pines, Pastures, and Cattle

Pines, pastures, and cattle can be effectively integrated in several ways:

- Trees can be established and grown in pastures. First-year survival of loblolly pines planted at a 1.8- by 3.0-m spacing in a pasture of grazed subterranean clover, *Trifolium subterraneum* L., was 78%. Pine mortality attributable to cattle damage was less than 7% even though 7 to 8 cows/ha grazed the pasture from March through May. Pine survival in grazed plots did not differ significantly from pine survival in ungrazed plots (Pearson 1987). In another instance, the 20-year survival rate for slash pines in fertilized pastures in south Georgia was lower than the 20-year survival rate for slash pines growing in competition with native vegetation in plantations. However, the fertilized pasture stands produced about 136 m³ of wood/ha, whereas the plantation stands produced only about 105 m³ of wood/ha. Over 15 years, beef production on the forested pastures was about 59% as great as beef production on treeless pastures (Lewis and others 1983).

- Openings can be created in stands and seeded with subterranean clover to supplement native forage in winter (Ribbeck and others 1987).

- Improved grasses can be cultivated under maturing plantations. Where this is done, plantations can produce both quality sawlogs and cattle (Clason and Oliver 1984).

- Tree spacing can be altered to create treeless strips. For instance, planting double rows of loblolly pines at 1.2- by 2.4-m spacing with 12-m open strips between sets of double rows yields as much wood volume but more forage, through age 13, than planting an area uniformly at 2.4- by 3.7-m spacing (Lewis and others 1985).

- Firebreaks (at least 9 m wide) surrounding and dissecting plantations can provide high- quality food for cattle and wildlife throughout a timber rotation. They should be disked at 2- to 3-year intervals or disked and seeded annually with a grain. Fertilizing these areas can increase food quantity and improve food quality (Stransky and Halls 1968).

- Logging roads and skid trails can be seeded to preferred grass species to increase the quantity and improve the quality of cattle and wildlife foods.

- Forest range can be supplemented with adjacent improved pasture.

- Crossbreeding cattle to adapt them for piney woods range can improve resource use. Brahman cows crossbred with British breeds and dairy breeds are very efficient producers on southern forest range (Duvall and Halls 1963, Whitaker and others 1970).

Exotic Forage

Native forages are normally warm-season plants that die or become dormant during the winter. When grown under stands of loblolly pines, cool-season exotic grasses such as tall fescue, *Festuca arundinacea* Schreber, provide high-quality green forage during the winter when native forage is least available. These exotic grasses may also be higher in crude protein, ether extract, ash, P, vitamin A, and digestibility than native bluestems (Pearson and Lewis 1989).

Some varieties of subterranean clovers are shade tolerant as well as nutritious: 'Nangeela' produced 92% of its potential yield under 50% shade and performed well even under 75% shade; 'Woogenellup' can be established under mature loblolly pine stands with densities as great as 20 m² of basal area/ha. Unlike other clovers, subterranean clover reseeds even if heavily grazed during the flowering stage (Johnson and others 1986, Lewis and Pearson 1987, Watson and others 1984).

Exotic grasses and legumes have been successfully added to native forest range only with site preparation, fertilization, and regular shrub control (Burton 1973). Liming to raise soil pH to 6.0 is important where subterranean clover is to be grown on acid soils. Subterranean clover should be fertilized annually during the first few years to maintain good production. It normally does not do well where soils are wet for prolonged periods (Davis and others 1984, Johnson and others 1986).

Integrating Range, Wildlife, and Timber Resources

Profits from managing wildlife, livestock, and loblolly pine timber on the same land can be greater than profits from producing one commodity only (Lundgren and others 1984, Ribbeck and others 1987). The potential for simultaneously producing large quantities of high-quality timber, wildlife, and livestock is greater in the loblolly–shortleaf pine ecosystem than in any other large forest ecosystem in the United States because of the unique combinations of soils, climate, and understory vegetation. In fact, good forest range management can benefit many wildlife species if the total vegetative resource is not overutilized. Grazing can improve wildlife habitat by stimulating the growth of browse food and reducing dense brush. Openings in the pine forest kept in subterranean clover to provide supplemental cattle feed in the winter also provide excellent turkey and quail habitat (Ribbeck and others 1987).

However, there may be substantial overlap in cattle and deer diets on forested sites during winter and early spring. Diets are largely complementary during the remainder of the year. On clearcuts, diets do not overlap at any time of the year; deer primarily eat leafy browse and forbs, and cattle concentrate on grasses and grasslike plants (Thill 1983, 1984). Where livestock and wildlife, especially big game, overutilize food supplies, forest resources can be damaged.

Water Resources and Loblolly Pine Management

Loblolly pine stands promote soil development and site stability that rarely permit surface runoff and accompanying sheet or rill erosion. Planting of loblolly has limited surface erosion and returned many thousands of hectares of degraded north Mississippi farmlands to productivity (Ursic and Thames 1960, USDA FS 1988). Undisturbed forests usually produce the highest quality water, although each watershed has unique hydrological and chemical characteristics. Suspended sediments, pH, and cation nutrients in runoff generally increase in proportion to site disturbance, even in lower Coastal Plain flatwoods (Riekerk and Korhnak 1985). Erosion control measures include construction of dips and bars along road rights-of-way; seeding, fertilizing, and mulching newly disturbed slopes; and retaining tree cover along stream courses. Such measures can reduce road construction and maintenance costs, increase timber yields and fish production, and improve water quality (Dissmeyer and Foster 1987).

Water Yield

Most rainfall not lost through evapotranspiration either recharges forest soil and ground water or leaves the watershed as streamflow. Annual water yields from Coastal Plain and Piedmont forests average about 40 cm and range from 25 to 50 cm (Van Lear and Douglass 1983). As stand density increases, intercepted rainfall and transpiration increase, decreasing the amount of water reaching the soil surface and the amount of streamflow. In steep and rolling terrain, increased streamflow (or stormflow) and sedimentation are the predominant responses to harvesting and site preparation on forested watersheds (Douglass and others 1983).

In flat terrain, the predominant response is a rise in the water table. Hydrologic responses to harvesting and site preparation vary greatly depending on soil conditions (for example, remaining cover, depth of soil, and water storage capacity) and channel characteristics. Burrows dug by small animals can reduce stormflow volumes and increase water storage under pines, especially in older stands (Ursic and Esher 1988).

Thinning or clearcutting can substantially increase the amount of water lost from a forest area. In areas where rainfall exceeds 122 cm/yr, average stream depth has increased by 28 to 46 cm in the first year following clearcutting. Cutting 50% of the basal area commonly increases average first-year streamflow by 13 cm (Anderson and others 1976, McMinn and Hewlett 1975). Cutting 80% of the basal area from a dense stand increased throughfall from 77 to 94% and increased the amount of precipitation reaching the ground by 20 cm/yr (Rogerson 1968). If intensive site preparation accompanies clearcutting, 40 to more than 70% of the soil surface is exposed. This exposure can result in a five-fold to tenfold increase in stormflow and up to a hundredfold increase in sediment compared to an undisturbed forest (Beasley and Granillo 1983; Blackburn and others 1986a, 1986b).

Generally, the water table rises following clearcutting on flat terrain in the lower Coastal Plain or other areas. The water table usually rises most following clearcutting on fine-textured soil, especially where the water table is relatively deep before logging. However, even light cutting can raise the water table. In addition to raising the water table, canopy removal in the pine flatwoods also increases first-year runoff (Riekerk and Korhnak 1985, Trousdell and Hoover 1955, Williams and Lipscomb 1981).

Water Quality

The widely held belief that Americans should protect or improve water quality resulted in the enactment of both national and state environmental and forest practice laws in the 1970's. Undisturbed stands of loblolly pines are very effective in protecting and improving water quality. Sediment concentrations are usually at or below 60 mg/liter of runoff water from undisturbed stands. Sediment concentration in runoff increases as the amount of overstory decreases. The variation in sediment concentrations among undisturbed catchments results primarily from differences in channel characteristics and percentages of ground cover. Sediment yields average 16 to 90 kg/ha/yr and rarely exceed 180 kg/ha/yr in well-stocked loblolly stands in the Piedmont because there is almost no runoff from these stands. One or more intense storms may cause as much as 70% of this annual loss, much of which results from streambed scouring (Beasley 1979, Hewlett 1979, Rogerson 1971, Yoho 1980). Nutrient losses increase proportionally with

sediment losses. Even under undisturbed stands, significant portions of total nitrogen (N) and P losses in stormflow result from sediment losses. In one case, sediment transported at least 40% of the N and at least 70% of the P in stormflow. The potential for large losses of critical macroelements demonstrates the need to maintain low sediment yields when managing loblolly pine (Duffy 1985, Duffy and others 1986). Sloping areas and particularly fragile soils (for example, loess soils) are most prone to damage when left unprotected. However, even flatwoods sites are subjected to greater overland flow and runoff sediment loss as disturbance increases (Douglass and Goodwin 1980, McClurkin and others 1987, Riekerk 1987).

Any removal, disturbance, or alteration in the composition of natural vegetation reduces normal water infiltration and accelerates soil and nutrient loss through sheet or rill erosion. For example, prescribed fire and clearcutting significantly increased cation export, compared to no harvesting, the first year after treatment on a South Carolina Piedmont site (Van Lear and others 1985). Managers can minimize stormflow and sedimentation by keeping the forest floor and streamsides intact during harvesting and site preparation. Roller chopping up and down slopes of 25% or less should have little effect on sediment or nutrient loss and should not degrade site productivity, because the depressions created by the cutting blades are perpendicular to the slopes and trap rainfall (Blackburn and others 1986a, 1986b). Ground cover percentages recommended for minimizing erosion after disturbance are given in table 9-8.

Loblolly pines control erosion primarily by shedding needles that quickly form a loose, interwoven cover that resists water movement. A dense protective litter layer is formed in less than 5 years after seedling establishment. Within 15 years after loblolly pines are planted on actively eroding, abandoned fields, sediment production can be reduced to levels little higher than those in undisturbed natural forests. Much of the sediment leaving reforested areas comes from minor channels developed during former land use and not from the reforested slopes (Ursic 1986, Ursic and Dendy 1965). By the time loblolly plantations reach 8 to 10 years of age, the forest floor is more than 2.5 cm deep, and litter can average 16.4 tonnes/ha (t/ha) (Thames 1962, Williston 1965). This accumulation is twice that produced by slash pines, the next best species for erosion control in the South. Even when trees are the same height, loblolly pines produce two to three times as much litter as shortleaf pines produce on bare, compacted parent material.

Loblolly pines also control soil loss more effectively than do low-grade hardwoods. In one instance, the forest floor under 23- and 32-year-old loblolly pine plantations weighed 13.4 and 31.8 t/ha, respectively, whereas the forest floor under depleted hardwood stands of the same ages weighed only 9.0 and 11.4 t/ha. Soil loss under the hardwoods was seven times as great as soil loss under

Table 9-8—Recommended ground cover percentages (litter plus living vegetation) for minimizing erosion after soil disturbance

Percent slope	Ground cover needed	
	Fragile soils	Stable soils
0	25	0
5	50	25
10	65	50
15	75	60
20	90	75
25	95	85

Source: adapted from Dissmeyer (1978).

Table 9-9—Average annual runoff and sediment from three cover types over a period of 3 years in North Mississippi

Cover type	Runoff (cm)		Ovendry soil loss (kg/ha)
	Loess soils	Loess and Coastal Plain soils*	
Abandoned fields	28.4	7.9	405
Depleted hardwoods	13.7	7.4	284
Loblolly pine plantations	5.1	0.5	40

Source: adapted from Ursic (1963).

* Average of two watersheds for each cover type.

loblolly. Similarly, runoff under hardwoods was 2.7 to 14.0 times as great as runoff under loblolly (table 9-9).

Because herbicides do not compact soil or disturb the protective litter layer, they are valuable as a non-sediment-producing method of site preparation and vegetation control. Most herbicides used in loblolly pine management are low-toxicity chemicals applied only one or two times over a rotation of 20 to 35 years. When properly applied to forest sites, they will top-kill large hardwoods and increase the development of more desirable vegetation (such as loblolly pines and wildlife forage species) without harming surrounding ecosystems, surface water, or groundwater supplies (Segal and others 1987). Seven months of monitoring two Tennessee watersheds following the aerial application of 17 kg/ha of hexazinone pellets (for hardwood control) detected no residues (Neary 1983). The hexazinone concentration in the runoff water of an Arkansas watershed, during a 3-month period after stem application, ranged from less than 1 ppb to 15 ppb, with the higher concentrations occurring during periods of high runoff (Bouchard and Lavy 1983). Residues of hexazinone, following hand–broadcast application over Georgia Piedmont

watersheds, could not be detected in aquatic invertebrates and macrophytes, and no major changes could be found in aquatic insects (Mayack and others 1982). The greatest hazard of herbicides to surface and ground water relates to point-source pollution, such as mishandling of concentrates during transportation, storage, and mixing; cleaning of equipment; and disposal of used containers, rather than nonpoint source forest application (Neary 1985). However, intensive (often annual) use of pesticides in orchards and nurseries can result in high concentrations over time.

Moderate fertilization of loblolly pine stands does not lower water quality because the forest floor is a good natural filter. Fertilizing young seedlings on eroded sites can reduce the time needed, by 1 or more years, to produce an expanded root system and adequate foliage to form a protective litter cover on severely eroded sites. For example, applying NPK at a rate of 168-37-69 kg/ha around newly planted seedlings increased the weight of foliage 1.6 times during the first 2 years without reducing survival (Duffy 1977). Fertilizing 34-year-old planted loblolly and natural pine–hardwoods in the North Carolina Piedmont with 110, 24, and 47 kg of N, P, and potassium (K) per ha, respectively, had no detrimental effect on water quality (Sanderford 1975). Nitrate leaching into the soil water following fertilization is greater in uneven-aged stands than in even-aged stands (Wheeler and others 1989). During aerial fertilization, care must be taken to ensure that materials are not sprayed directly onto, or permitted to drift onto, water surfaces. Applying an herbicide at the same time as, or shortly after, fertilization can increase leaching of nitrate and probably other nutrients due to reduced plant uptake (Wheeler and others 1989).

Using Loblolly Pines to Rehabilitate Severely Degraded Sites

There are localized areas of severe degradation caused by past land abuses (surface mines and mine spoils, borrow pits, and eroded loess and clay slopes) throughout the South. They reduce the quality of water in nearby streams, are of no value for wildlife habitat, and grow no forest products. Even when ameliorated by cultural treatments and soil amendments, badly disturbed areas constitute harsh microenvironments where vegetation grows with difficulty. These abused sites range from less than one-half hectare to thousands of hectares in size. Their soils are extremely variable in acidity and other

physical and chemical characteristics and rarely contain much organic matter.

Loblolly pines can be established to stabilize degraded sites and return them to a productive state. Under suitable conditions, planted and seeded loblolly survive well, grow fast, and quickly produce a layer of protective litter that minimizes the impact of raindrops and halts overland flow. Planting seedlings with the root collar well below the soil surface or planting short seedlings with good root systems can often increase survival on adverse sites (Tuttle and others 1987). Failures of planted nursery stock and direct seeding are mainly the result of unfavorable environmental conditions (such as extreme temperatures or severe drought) at seeding or planting time. Use of container seedlings may increase survival by extending the planting season and increasing the speed of planting (Dickerson 1973, Moditz and Buckner 1983, Ruehle 1980). The undisturbed root systems and extensive mycorrhizae of container seedlings aid early survival, especially under dry conditions. Container seedlings can be specifically conditioned in a greenhouse, by withholding water, reducing day length, and lowering temperatures to prepare for severe outplanting conditions (Barnett 1983). It may be possible to develop hybrid lines of loblolly that excel under specific adverse conditions. For example, pitch pine × loblolly pine hybrids performed as well as or better than either species on Alabama and Tennessee coal spoils (Berry 1982b).

Erosion Control

Loblolly pines have been used to control erosion throughout the South (Williston and Ursic 1979). The Piedmont region of the Southeast contains many thousands of hectares of overworked, abandoned farms that have little or no topsoil, low fertility, poor physical characteristics, and continuous erosion. Loblolly can stabilize these soils and restore their productivity, especially when tree establishment is complemented by site amelioration treatments. Subsoiling promotes tree growth on compacted sites. The addition of dried sewage sludge can also increase pine growth on some eroded sites (Berry 1979, Berry and Marx 1976).

Plantation spacing on eroded sites depends on microsite conditions. About 2,220 trees/ha (1.8- by 2.5-m spacing) is satisfactory for most eroded ungullied sites, including eroded logging roads. As many as 2,965 trees/ha (1.8- by 1.9-m spacing) may be required on barren, sheet-eroded, and gullied segments of abandoned fields and along gully rims. Until they grow large enough to produce effective litter layers, trees on gully outwashes may have to be spaced as closely as 1.2 by 1.2 m (Ursic 1963). The best planting technique is for hand planters to take advantage of favorable spots behind natural barriers, in grassy areas, along the edges of gullies or intermittent watercourses, and in loose soil whenever possible. Where conditions are especially severe, as on bare gully slopes, it may be necessary to build brush dams, add mulch, and even dig holes and add topsoil when planting (Ursic 1966). Efforts to improve planting conditions by leveling gullies can accelerate erosion and are rarely effective.

Seedlings should be planted about 5 cm below the normal groundline on eroded sites. Deeper planting does not increase survival (Ursic 1963). Sowing grasses at the time of pine planting can greatly increase the level of early ground cover. However, the grass species used must be selected very carefully because severe competition by some grasses can greatly reduce pine survival

(Duffy and McClurkin 1974). Loblolly pine mortality is greatest the first year, but the average losses (12 to 25%) are no greater than expected first-year losses on standard planting sites. Second- and third-year losses generally are less than 6% (Ursic 1962). Fertilization of eroded sites may not increase tree growth (McClurkin 1961).

Nitrogen-fixing legumes have been used to raise soil nutrient levels on eroded sites. Some legumes, such as the perennial legume *Lespedeza cuneata* (Dum.–Cours.) G. Don, may strongly compete with trees for a few years. However, by the sixth year, trees begin to respond rapidly to the N produced by this legume (Mays and Bengtson 1985, Nix 1985). Even without fertilization, planting loblolly pines may be very profitable on eroded slopes. For example, 2 ha of eroded submarginal hillside in the North Carolina Piedmont were planted or direct seeded to loblolly and shortleaf pines in 1927. Thirty-seven years later, total yield per hectare (standing plus removals) was 390 m³, or 10.6 m³/ha/yr. In addition, erosion was halted and the soil improved (Maki 1964).

Thinning can start when trees average 15 cm in dbh, and it should be primarily from below—that is, poorer trees should be removed so future diameter growth can be concentrated on selected crop trees. Thinnings must be light enough to maintain a cover that does not permit erosion to resume (Ursic 1963).

Eroded Loess Soils
(The Yazoo–Little Tallahatchie Story)

In the 1800's, exploitative agriculture on rolling erosive soils, especially in the hills of western Tennessee and western Mississippi (the Yazoo and Little Tallahatchie River Basins), changed an area of pine–hardwood forests to the most severely eroded portion of the eastern United States. The productivity of millions of hectares of uplands was reduced greatly. Debris from eroded hillsides buried rich bottomlands, and extremely heavy runoff caused frequent and serious flooding. In the 1940's researchers began working to develop ways to stop the soil loss and to rejuvenate the land. Planting proved to be the best method for establishing trees on eroded sites; seeds are too easily washed from slopes by rain. Among all the conifers planted on eroded loess ridges, only loblolly pine survived well and grew rapidly (table 9-10). More than 918 million loblolly pine seedlings were planted on more than 338,000 ha between 1948 and 1982. The success of these plantings proved that severely degraded sites can be returned to a productive state by proper handling and careful planting of high-quality loblolly pine seedlings (Williston 1988).

The best seed sources for regenerating these north Mississippi loess hills are from northwest Georgia, north Alabama, and northeast Mississippi, although trees from the lost pines area of Texas also survive and grow well (Thames 1962, Ursic 1963). Only dormant seedlings of grades 1 and 2 should be used for these plantings. The general guide is that seedlings should have root collar diameters no smaller than 0.3 cm.

Roadbank Stabilization

Loblolly pine is also an excellent species for stabilizing new roadcuts, which are unsightly and which can erode severely. Treatments are much the same as for eroded forest sites. The more trees planted, the quicker the site is protected. Depending on aspect and site conditions, 2,220 to 4,450 trees/ha should be planted to ensure that at least 1,730 trees/ha survive at the end of the third growing season (Williston 1967, table 9-11). Wider spacings are often successful on north aspects or where seedlings are planted in prepared holes because survival is improved. Periodic thinning is usually required to maintain good individual tree vigor. If survival has been very good, precommercial thinning at age 6 may be needed to reduce stocking to about 2,500 trees/ha. Later thinnings can be made as needed to keep trees healthy and producing adequate quantities of needles (Williston 1971).

Borrow Pits

The South is pockmarked with borrow pits (usually 0.1 to 3.0 ha in size) from which the A and B soil horizons have been removed for use in the construction of highways, dams, or buildings. Regeneration of borrow pits is often very difficult because the remaining soil may be compacted as well as nutrient deficient. Twenty-two years after a South Carolina borrow pit was planted with loblolly pines, trees averaged only 2.5 to 5.0 m in height, and many could readily be pulled from the soil by hand (Berry and Marx 1980). As on eroded Piedmont sites, subsoiling, fertilizing with various inorganic formulations or organic amendments such as sewage sludge, pine bark, or ash, and planting bareroot or container seedlings inoculated with mycorrhizae can stabilize the soil and greatly accelerate tree growth on borrow pits (Berry 1985, Berry and Marx 1980, Van Lear and others 1973).

Mine Reclamation

Loblolly pine grows faster and stabilizes soil faster than most other conifers and hardwoods on many types of mine spoils (Barnett and Tiarks 1987). The one exception among the conifers is Virginia pine, which may perform better than loblolly in colder climates (Lyle 1976,

Table 9-10—Survival and growth of conifers 5 and 10 years after planting on dry ridge sites for 4 successive years in north Mississippi

Species	Survival (%)		Total height (m)	
	5 years	10 years	5 years	10 years
Loblolly pine	56	56	2.4	7.2
Longleaf pine	10	8	0.3	3.8
Shortleaf pine	54	54	1.5	4.4
Slash pine	18	17	1.9	6.6
Virginia pine	53	53	1.9	3.9
Eastern redcedar	66	65	0.8	2.2

Source: adapted from Ursic (1963).

Table 9-11—Tree spacings that provide early site protection

Slope	Site quality	Aspect	Spacing (m)
2:1	Average	North and east	1.8 × 1.8
	Average	South and west	1.5 × 1.8
	Low, droughty	All	1.2 × 1.8
3:1	Average	North and east	1.8 × 2.4
or less	Average	South and west	1.8 × 1.8
	Low, droughty	All	1.5 × 1.8
Flat	All	—	2.4 × 2.4

Source: adapted from Williston (1971).

Plass 1979, Torbert and others 1985). Trees on mine spoils grow most vigorously when surface soil pH is 4.0 or greater. The presence of loblolly increases soil pH over time (Geyer and Rogers 1972). In Louisiana, planted loblolly pines grow vigorously on lignite mine pits refilled with a mixture of overburden material, so there is no need to keep topsoil separate during the stockpiling process when mining lignite (Burton and Tiarks 1986).

Pitch pine (loblolly pine hybrids also do well on mixed overburden in the mountains of southwest Virginia if the sites are fertilized (Moss and others 1989). Chemical weed control or fertilization or both can increase early growth of containerized seedlings on mine spoils (Schoenholtz and Burger 1984). Natural mycorrhizal colonization occurs in mine spoils, and colonization is not affected adversely by slow-release fertilizers or chemical weed control (Schoenholtz and others 1987). Mycorrhizae increase the survival and growth of loblolly on reclaimed surfaces reducing the need for fertilization (Hendrix and others 1985; Walker and others 1981, 1985, 1989). After 2 years on a Virginia coal spoil, seedlings with *Pisolithus tinctorius* (Pt) were more than twice as large as those with *Thelephora terrestris* indicating that the type of mycorrhizae can affect seedling development (Marx 1977).

Although the addition of nutrients, and especially additions of N and P, can substantially increase the vigor and growth of trees on mine spoils (Mays and Bengston 1985), care must be taken in determining the method and time of fertilizer application. Broadcast application of 15-15-15 granular fertilizer to achieve a rate of 336 kg/ha of NPK (as N, P_2O_5, and K_2O equivalents) on an east Tennessee coal mine spoil at seedling planting time resulted in profuse weed growth that reduced loblolly pine survival from 62% to only 27% at the end of 2 years. The growth of surviving trees was not increased by fertilization (Walker and others 1989). Controlling heavy competition during early stand development on mine sites can increase pine survival and early growth significantly (Torbert and others 1985). However, light to moderate grass or legume ground cover has little effect on survival of young planted loblolly. Although competition with legumes probably reduces tree growth somewhat during the first few years, legumes ultimately increase tree growth greatly (Mays and Bengston 1985, Vogel 1973). Mulching around newly established seedlings increases survival, probably by conserving soil moisture (Carpenter and others 1978).

Direct seeding can be used to regenerate loblolly pine on some spoils. However, direct seeding is unlikely to succeed on areas that have been compacted heavily during contouring and leveling operations or where grass competition is heavy. Aerial seeding can be successful on areas that are too rocky to plant. Freshly turned mine spoil harbors few animals that eat seeds and few plants that compete with tree seedlings (Biesterfeldt and Mann 1969, Mergen and others 1981, Thor and Kring 1964). Coarse-textured sandstones and hard shales may provide a better seedbed than do fine spoil materials (Plass 1974).

Timber yields on spoils can be good, considering the original site conditions. In Alabama, experimental plantings of loblolly and shortleaf pines yielded 126 and 107 m³/ha, respectively, at age 20 (Plass and Burton 1967). Twenty-two years after coal spoil plantings in Kansas, loblolly pine basal area was 4.7 m²/ha, and loblolly standing volume was 57 m³/ha. Standing volume of loblolly was almost twice as great as that of any of the other 13 species planted, including shortleaf and Virginia pines (Geyer and Rogers 1972). Loblolly should not be grown close to black locust, *Robinia pseudoacacia* L., in the expectation that the N-fixing legume will promote pine growth. When these species were planted in alternate rows on the banks of Tennessee coal strip-mines, the black locust was three times as tall as the loblolly (8.1 m versus 2.7 m) at age 6 and provided severe competition (Kring 1967).

Metals such as cadmium (Cd), copper (Cu), iron (Fe), and zinc (Zn) accumulate primarily in the root systems of loblolly pines growing on spoils. This storage helps remove metals from the food chain. However, the potential effects of large accumulations in loblolly, over long periods of time, are unknown (Svoboda and others 1979).

Land Denuded by Air Pollution

In the 19th century, sulfur dioxide pollution produced in primitive copper-smelting operations destroyed the vegetation on 9,300 ha of land in east Tennessee. Subsequent erosion severely depleted the soils of organic matter and nutrients. Planting of loblolly pines reversed this

Table 9-12—Effect of fertility treatments and ectomycorrhizae on growth of loblolly pine seedlings after 4 years in the Tennessee Copper Basin

Treatment		Survival (%)	Height (cm)	Diameter (m)	Volume (cm³)
Fertility*	Mycorrhizae				
Sludge	NI†	80.4 a	201.2 a	50.7 a	6,155 a
	Pt†	83.8 a	180.2 a	48.4 a	5,008 a
Fertilizer	NI	75.0 a	118.5 a	31.9 b	1,682 b
	Pt	83.8 a	124.0 b	33.9 b	1,876 b

Source: adapted from Berry (1982a).

Volume is determined from diameter squared times height. All values within a column followed by the same letter are not significantly different at the 95% probability level.

* Sewage sludge applied at a broadcast rate of 1.25 cm deep or approximately 34,000 kg/ha. Fertilizer (10-10-10) applied at 896 kg/ha, and burnt lime applied at a rate of 1,417 kg/ha.

† NI = seedlings naturally inoculated; Pt = seedlings inoculated with *Pisolithus tinctorius*.

trend. Tree survival and growth have been satisfactory even on areas without any other vegetation when NPK tablets or dried sewage sludge was applied in the planting holes. After 3 growing seasons, seedlings planted with 21-g tablets of 20-10-5 had a mean volume of 298 cm³. Those planted with 90 mg of sludge had a mean volume of 125 cm³, and unfertilized seedlings had a mean volume of only 14 cm³ (Berry 1979). Treatment with large quantities of sludge may increase tree growth more than does fertilization through tree age 5 years (McNab and Berry 1985; table 9-12). However, sludge can contain toxic levels of chemicals, and sludge from different sources has very different effects on trees (Berry 1982a). Inoculation of seedlings with *Pisolithus tinctorius* has some potential for increasing growth on these sites (Berry and Marx 1978), but it may not be effective when combined with inorganic fertilizer or sewage sludge treatments.

Other Areas

Loblolly pines can be used to stabilize kaolin clay spoils. The application of sewage sludge at rates of 34 to 138 t/ha can increase early tree growth on these spoils by 50% or more and can stimulate mycorrhizal development. Although inorganic fertilizer and lime help to establish vegetation on these sites, the lack of organic matter still limits tree growth (Berry and Marx 1976).

Growing Loblolly Pines With Agricultural Crops

Agricultural crops and loblolly pines can be produced simultaneously on the same site for several years in new plantations. Becaue trees use very little space during the first 2 to 3 years, crops such as soybeans, *Glycine max* (L.) Merr.; tomatoes, *Lycopersicon lycopersicum* (L.) Karsten; watermelons, *Citrullus lanatus* (Thunb.) Matsum. & Nakai var. Lauatus; and corn can be grown between the rows of pines. This type of operation provides immediate

economic returns that help defray plantation establishment costs. To make such a system work, it is necessary to make extensive changes in plantation spacing and management operations. For example, more rows of annual crops can be grown when tree rows are 5 to 8 m apart than when tree rows are the usual 3 m apart. Some loss in wood productivity can be expected, but financial analyses indicate that intercropping can be more profitable, under some conditions, than growing pines only (McNeel and Stuart 1984).

Planting one or two rows of closely spaced (1.0 to 1.2 m apart) trees on one or more sides of a field can provide substantial protection to agricultural crops where winds are a continuous problem (Maki and Allen 1978). Some loblolly pine genotypes may be more wind resistant than others. Breeding for wind resistance could produce trees that are especially suited for windbreaks (Telewski 1986).

Using Loblolly Pines to Manage the Landscape for Esthetics

Landscape management, or emphasis on visual effects, has only recently become an important part of forest management. Visual effects are increasingly important in the management of loblolly pines even in the Coastal Plain, where opportunities to emphasize species diversity in the overstory are limited and where there are few spectacular changes in the landscape. Only 3% of the timberland in Louisiana and 1% of that in east Texas is located on slopes greater than 15% (Rudis 1988a, 1988b). The Piedmont has a much more broken and diverse landscape in which the effects of recent cutting can be seen for great distances.

The public reacts to forest management primarily by sight. Forest management activities are normally most noticeable and controversial along the sides of heavily traveled roads. Generally, diversifying vegetation types, decreasing stand density, and increasing stand age increase scenic beauty. Less productive sites are usually considered more appealing. Atmospheric conditions and season of the year also affect appearance (Hughes 1974, Palazzo 1974).

Negative visual impact of management is greatest during harvesting and stand regeneration—a cut-over area covered with debris next to a stand of tall trees can be displeasing. As distance from a cutting unit increases, visual differences and concomitant displeasure decrease. The scars left by harvesting and intensive site preparation are usually hidden by rapidly growing vegetation within 2 years. To preserve visual appeal, clearcuts should be designed so that they merge smoothly with other stand types and ages, conform to land contours, and include uncut streamside or pondside management zones that lessen the visual impact of vegetational changes. Site preparation treatments that minimize initial disruption of soil and understory vegetation and speed site recovery and tree growth are best from esthetic and recreational viewpoints. Some large, old trees and standing snags may be kept in cut-over areas for their visual effects. Similarly, it is esthetically pleasing to view dogwoods or other attractive hardwood trees and shrubs in the understories or midstories of pine stands along roadways or in special-use areas.

The visual contrast between clearcuts and adjacent stands is less harsh if the edges of adjoining stands are thinned and if small trees and shrubs in transition zones are retained. Areas along skylines and at higher elevations should not be clearcut. Shelterwood or selection cutting in front of openings, especially along well-traveled roads, can preserve a forest landscape. Alternatively, uncut buffer strips can minimize the visual effect of clearcutting along highways. Once a new stand is established, treatments such as thinning and prescribed burning do not normally pose significant visual problems. The visual impact of properly timed and implemented prescribed burning is of very short duration. Thinnings normally make little change in the color, form, or texture of the overall landscape. Small openings in uneven-aged stands provide contrast. Long rotations generally increase esthetic appeal because people consider large, old trees especially attractive.

Hull and Buhyoff (1986) compared the visual appeal of four types of loblolly pine stands. They found that natural stands are most scenic, unthinned planted stands are less scenic, heavily thinned planted stands are still less scenic, and lightly thinned stands are least scenic. They concluded that scenic beauty should not be assessed on the basis of a single year or stage in the life of a stand, but rather assessed over an entire rotation. This would improve the visual assessment of newly harvested stands, which are unduly criticized for 2 to 3 years of very low visual quality. Similarly, lengthening a rotation increases the scenic beauty available over the life of a stand.

Using Loblolly Pine Forests for Recreation

About half of forest recreational use in the South is in mixed pine–hardwood stands. Recreational use is concentrated in stands near water. The most common forms of recreation are fishing, picnicking, sightseeing, and hunting. Both hunting and fishing can provide income to landowners through annual leases or other land-use permits. Other popular forms of forest recreation include hiking, camping, birdwatching, berrypicking, and photography (Rudis 1985, 1987). Much recreation takes place in areas undergoing regeneration or in areas that have been thinned one or more times. Berrypicking is best in recently disturbed areas or along roadsides, and birdwatchers find the greatest variety of species in areas undergoing rapid succession. If logging roads and skid trails are constructed properly and repaired following harvesting, they can be used as hiking trails or access roads and paths to camping spots, springs, waterfalls, lakes, and scenic vistas. Mature mixed pine–hardwood stands make superior camping areas and are excellent places for observing nature because they support a multitude of wildlife and plant species. Very large, old loblolly pines are majestic, and groups of such trees can produce a cathedral effect. Thus, some loblolly in recreation areas should be retained far beyond maturity if they do not create safety hazards. Removing large trees from recreation areas is normally difficult and costly because surrounding trees and structures must be protected. Pine is excellent campfire wood, so trees that could cause great damage if removed as logs can be cut in short lengths and left for campers.

Using Loblolly Pines in Urban Settings

Loblolly pines make excellent ornamental trees (figure 9-9) that give many years of beauty and service if properly located and cared for. They offer a pleasing contrast when intermingled with various deciduous trees or with monocots such as palms or palmettos. Because they retain needles throughout the year, they ameliorate the microclimate and beautify homesites or public areas even in the winter when deciduous trees have lost their leaves.

Landscapers should take certain precautions when using loblolly pines in yards. If a house has gutters, trees should be planted at least 10 m away to minimize clogging of gutters with cones and needles. If many trees are used, litterfall may make it very difficult to maintain a lawn. Even though most needles and cones drop during the fall of the year, some drop throughout the year. In any case, if a green lawn is desired, trees should be spaced at least 10 m apart so that they develop well-formed crowns that allow adequate light to reach the grass surface, and fallen needles should be removed regularly. Trees should be planted at least 2 m from sidewalks, patios, or other concrete surfaces to minimize the potential for heaving and cracking as roots grow under these structures. Trees should not be grown in or near septic drain fields because roots can clog drain pipes which ultimately results in high repair costs. Similarly, trees should not be planted under power lines, where they will require costly top-pruning that spoils their form. Where trees are desired and little space is available, property should be protected with physical or chemical rooting barriers, crushable pads beneath sidewalks, gutter screens, and regular roof cleaning (Wagar and Barker 1986).

Figure 9-9—Twenty- to twenty-five-year-old loblolly pines providing shade and beauty in a south Louisiana suburb. The few needles deposited on the roof will be swept away with the next wind. The house has no gutters, so that clogging with needles is not a problem.

The stresses to which trees are subjected in urban settings are more severe than those to which trees are subjected in forests. Thus, tree vigor and tree lifespans are shorter in urban environments. Common stresses include drought, flooding, air pollution, chemical imbalance, and physical damage to small boles from lawn care equip-ment. Genetic selections for tolerance to low moisture, high salt levels, and air pollutants such as sulfur dioxide and ozone, as well as for planting in tension zones and on adverse sites may provide genotypes better adapted to urban situations in the future.

Summary

Loblolly pine forests and individual trees have many valuable nontimber uses. These include diverse wildlife habitat, cattle forage, erosion control, water quality improvement, land reclamation and rehabilitation, agroforestry, esthetics, and a wide array of recreational opportunities. Loblolly pine and associated grass, herb, shrub, and tree species are important to the well-being of many of the South's 400 species of amphibians, reptiles, birds, and mammals. An estimated 21.8 million ha of forest range are available for cattle grazing in the loblolly–shortleaf pine–hardwood ecosystem, which stretches from east Texas to northern Virginia. Many of the South's municipalities rely on loblolly pine ecosystems to provide all of their clean drinking water. Preservation of the esthetic value of forests is becoming increasingly important to the public. The esthetic value and energy conservation value of individual trees are also important in many urban and suburban settings.

Interspersion of forest types provides the best all-round wildlife habitat. Loblolly pine stands or mixed loblolly pine–hardwood stands or both should be intermixed with hardwood stands, and narrow strips of forest cover should be maintained along all permanent streams. Intermixed stands should be of modest size and of various ages. Mixed pine–hardwood stands provide good habitat for more wildlife species than do stands of any other type. Overstory and understory hardwoods are especially valuable to a diversity of wildlife species. Extensive unbroken tracts of pure loblolly are not good habitat for most wildlife. In pure loblolly pine and mixed loblolly pine–hardwood stands, the number of wildlife species and the number of individuals increase as vertical layering of vegetation increases. To obtain high levels of plant and animal diversity, adjacent even-aged stands of loblolly should be kept small and irregular. Adjacent even-aged stands should differ in age by at least 7 years. Uncut or sparsely cut management zones 50 to 100 m wide should be maintained along streams to improve wildlife and fish habitats, increase water quality, and improve the esthetic quality of clearcuts.

Early successional vegetation that develops after harvest cutting is especially rich and diverse and makes good to excellent habitats for a multitude of game and nongame wildlife species. The effect is most pronounced for the first 3 to 5 years after clearcutting and site prepa-ration. Cultural treatments such as burning, thinning, pruning, and fertilizing all increase abundance of wildlife food and cover in young stands. The diversity and quantity of good wildlife habitats decrease as stands age and overstory crowns close. Cultural treatments, such as thinning, fertilizing, and burning can stimulate renewed use of maturing or mature stands by wildlife. Increases in use following burning or fertilizing may last only for about 1 year, but increases following combinations of burning, thinning, and fertilizing may last for as long as 3 years. Open, regularly burned stands are critical habitat for the bobwhite quail; the eastern indigo snake, *Drymarchon corais couperi* (Holbrook); the gopher tortoise; the red-cockaded woodpecker; and other species. In the fall, older loblolly stands provide high-energy seeds that are especially important to birds and rodents.

Carefully planned and managed integration of wildlife, livestock, and loblolly pine production can provide increased economic returns, especially during the first 10 years after planting, when forage levels are high. Cattle damage to pine seedlings can be minimized by decreasing grazing or excluding cattle during winter and spring until sufficient forage is produced. If cattle are to graze an area throughout a pine rotation, fewer trees should be planted per hectare, and stands should be thinned at 5-year intervals after mean dbh reaches 15 cm to maintain open conditions. Judicious burning can be used to move livestock continuously, or supplemental feeding can be used to concentrate cattle in areas not devoted to timber production. Wood yield is reduced in forage-timber operations because lightly stocked stands do not produce maximum timber volume. However, production of large, high-quality sawlogs is compatible with continuous beef production.

Loblolly pine stands are very effective in protecting water quality, but will reduce the quantity available because of high levels of evapotranspiration. Erosion is generally less than 180 kg of soil/ha/yr in undisturbed watersheds, and most of this is from stream channels rather than from the general forest area. Harvesting and site preparation cause temporary but sometimes very large increases in stormflow and peak discharge rates. Overland flow and erosion are most likely to occur on intensively prepared sites (such as sheared and wind-rowed sites). Soil losses from intensively prepared sites can range from 9 to 31 t/ha/yr until vegetation stabilizes the soil surface. Controlling erosion at the source can mean significant economic benefit to a landowner through reduced road maintenance costs, increased timber production, increased fish production, and improved water quality.

Use of best management practices (especially revegetating severely degraded sites; constructing dips and water-bars along forest roads; seeding, fertilizing, and mulching unprotected areas; and leaving residual timber in streamside management zones) may reduce gross timber sale revenue by 3 to 5% (Lickwar and others 1990) but should prove economical when the value of improved water quality, esthetics, and wildlife protection is taken into account.

Research Needs

▪ Detailed understanding is needed of how loblolly pine management affects populations of nongame wildlife species. For example, more data are needed on the long-term effects of forest fertilization on individual wildlife species.

▪ Better understanding is needed of the effect of sizes and shapes of clearcuts and associated streamside management zones on many wildlife species.

▪ Detailed evaluation is needed of threatened, endangered, or sensitive plant species associated with loblolly pine forest types, their importance in forest ecosystems, and techniques to maintain their viability.

▪ Quantification is needed of long-term productivity improvements (for timber, wildlife, and water) of severely degraded sites, such as surface mine spoils, severely eroded clay slopes, and borrow pits that are revegetated with loblolly pines.

▪ Detailed understanding is needed of the effects of small mammal activity on the hydrology of loblolly pine forests, especially in the rejuvenation of damaged ecosystems

Literature Cited

Anderson HW, Hoover MD, Reinhart KG. 1976. Forests and water: effects of forest management on floods, sedimentation, and water supply. Gen. Tech. Rep. PSW-18. Berkeley, CA: USDA Forest Service, Pacific Southwest Forest and Range Experiment Station. 115 p.

Atkeson TD, Johnson AS. 1979. Succession of small mammals on pine plantations in the Georgia Piedmont. American Midland Naturalist 101(2):385–392.

Barnett JP. 1983. Containerized pine seedlings for revegetating difficult sites. Journal of Soil and Water Conservation 38(6):462–464.

Barnett JP, Tiarks AE. 1987. Reforesting disturbed sites in the South with pine species. In: Proceedings, 4th Biennial Symposium on Surface Mining and Reclamation on the Great Plains and 4th Annual Meeting of the American Society for Surface Mining and Reclamation; 1987 March 17–19; Billings, MT. Billings, MT: American Society for Surface Mining and Reclamation: H-5-1–H-5-7.

Beasley RS. 1979. Intensive site preparation and sediment losses on steep watersheds in the Gulf Coastal Plain. Soil Science Society of America Journal 43(2):412–417.

Beasley RS, Granillo AB. 1983. Sediment losses from forest practices in the Gulf Coastal Plain of Arkansas. In: Proceedings, 2nd Biennial Southern Silvicultural Research Conference; 1982 November 4–5; Atlanta, GA. Gen. Tech. Rep. SE-24. Asheville, NC: USDA Forest Service, Southeastern Forest Experiment Station: 461–467.

Berry CR. 1979. Slit application of fertilizer tablets and sewage sludge improve initial growth of loblolly pine seedlings in the Tennessee Copper basin. Reclamation Review 2:33–38.

Berry CR. 1982a. Dried sewage sludge improves growth of pines in the Tennessee Copper Basin. Reclamation and Revegetation Research 1:195–202.

Berry CR. 1982b. Survival and growth of pine hybrid seedlings with *Pisolithus* ectomycorrhizae on coal spoils in Alabama and Tennessee. Journal of Environmental Quality 11(4):709–715.

Berry CR. 1985. Subsoiling and sewage sludge aid loblolly pine establishment on adverse sites. Reclamation and Revegetation Research 3:301–311.

Berry CR, Marx DH. 1976. Sewage sludge and *Pisolithus tinctorius* ectomycorrhizae: their effect on growth of pine seedlings. Forest Science 22(3):351–358.

Berry CR, Marx DH. 1978. Effects of *Pisolithus tinctorius* ectomycorrhizae on growth of loblolly and Virginia pines in the Tennessee Copper Basin. Res. Note SE-264. Asheville, NC: USDA Forest Service, Southeastern Forest Experiment Station. 6 p.

Berry CR, Marx DH. 1980. Significance of various soil amendments to borrow pit reclamation with loblolly pine and fescue. Reclamation Review 3:87–94.

Biesterfeldt RC, Mann WF Jr. 1969. New hope for strip-mine reclamation. Forest Farmer 28(12):6–8, 16, 18.

Blackburn WH, Wood JC, DeHaven MG. 1986a. Stormflow and sediment losses from site-prepared forestland in East Texas. Water Resources Research 22(5):776–784.

Blackburn WH, Wood JC, Weichert AT, Fazio PM, Nevill MB. 1986b. The impact of harvesting and site preparation on stormflow and water quality in East Texas. Final Project Report. College Station, TX: Texas A&M University, Texas Agricultural Experiment Station. 174 p.

Blair RM. 1967. Deer forage in a loblolly pine plantation. Journal of Wildlife Management 31(3):432–437.

Blair RM. 1968. Keep forage low to improve deer habitat. Forest Farmer 27(11):8–9, 22–23.

Blair RM. 1971. Forage production after hardwood control in a southern pine-hardwood stand. Forest Science 17(3):279–284.

Blair RM, Brunett LE. 1976. Phytosociological changes after timber harvest in a southern pine ecosystem. Ecology 57(1):18–32.

Blair RM, Brunett LE. 1977. Deer habitat potential of pine–hardwood forests in Louisiana. Res. Pap. SO-136. New Orleans: USDA Forest Service, Southern Forest Experiment Station. 11 p.

Blair RM, Brunett LE. 1980. Seasonal browse selection by deer in a southern pine–hardwood habitat. Journal of Wildlife Management 44(1):79–88.

Blair RM, Enghardt HG. 1976. Deer forage and overstory dynamics in a loblolly pine plantation. Journal of Range Management 29(2):104–108.

Blair RM, Feduccia DP. 1977. Midstory hardwoods inhibit deer forage in loblolly pine plantations. Journal of Wildlife Management 41(4):677–684.

Blair RM, Halls LK. 1968. Growth and forage quality of four southern browse species. In: Proceedings, 21st Annual Conference of the Southeastern Association of Game and Fish Commissioners; 1967 September 24–27; New Orleans, LA. Columbia, SC: Southeastern Association of Game and Fish Commissioners: 57–62.

Blair RM, Short HL, Epps EA. 1977. Seasonal nutrient yield and digestibility of deer forage from a young pine plantation. Journal of Wildlife Management 41(4):667–676.

Blake PM, Hurst GA, Terry TA. 1987. Responses of vegetation and deer forage following application of hexazinone. Southern Journal of Applied Forestry 11(4):176–180.

Bouchard DC, Lavy TL. 1983. Persistence and movement of hexazinone in a forest watershed [abstract]. Proceedings of the Weed Science Society of America: 91.

Brunswig NL, Johnson AS. 1973. Bobwhite quail foods and populations in the Georgia Piedmont during the first seven years following site preparation. In: Proceedings, 26th Annual Conference of the Southeastern Association of Game and Fish Commissioners; 1972 October 22–25; Knoxville, TN. Columbia, SC: Southeastern Association of Game and Fish Commissioners: 96–107.

Buckner JL, Perkins CJ. 1975. A plan of forest wildlife habitat evaluation and its use by international paper company. In: Proceedings, 28th Annual Conference of the Southeastern Association of Game and Fish Commissioners; 1974 November 17–20; White Sulphur Springs, WV. Columbia, SC: Southeastern Association of Game and Fish Commissioners: 675–682.

Burton GW. 1973. Integrated forest trees with improved pastures. In: Proceedings, Range Resources of the Southeastern United States Symposium; 1972; Miami Beach, FL. ASA Spec. Publ. 21. Madison, WI: American Society of Agronomy: 41–49.

Burton JD, Tiarks AE. 1986. Available nutrients and early growth of woody plants vary with overburden material in lignite minesoils of Louisiana. In: Proceedings, National Meeting of the American Society of Surface Mining and Reclamation; 1986 March 17–20; Jackson, MS. Princeton, WV: American Society for Surface Mining and Reclamation: 79–85.

Byrd NA, Holbrook HL. 1974. How to improve forest game habitat. Forest Management Bulletin (May). Atlanta: USDA Forest Service, Southeastern Area, State and Private Forestry. 10 p.

Byrd NA, Lewis CE. 1976. Managing southern pine forests to produce forage for beef cattle. Forest Management Bulletin (September). Atlanta: USDA Forest Service, Southeastern Area, State and Private Forestry. 7 p.

Byrd NA, Lewis CE, Pearson HA. 1984. Management of southern pine forests for cattle production. Gen. Rep. R8-GR-4:22. Atlanta: USDA Forest Service, Southern Region: 1–22.

Carpenter SB, Graves DH, Kruspe RR. 1978. Individual tree mulching as an aid to the establishment of trees on surface mine spoil. Reclamation Review 1:139–142.

Carter MC, Martin JW, Kennamer JE, Causey MK. 1975. Impact of chemical and mechanical site preparation on wildlife habitat. In: Bernier B, Winget CH, ed. Proceedings, Forest Soils and Forest Land Management: 4th North American Forest Soils Conference; 1973 August. Quebec: Les Presses de l'Université Laval: 323–332.

Chen MY, Hodgkins EJ, Watson WJ. 1975. Prescribed burning for improving pine production and wildlife habitat in the hilly Coastal Plain of Alabama. Bulletin 473. Auburn, AL: Alabama Agricultural Experiment Station. 19 p.

Childers EL, Sharik TL, Adkisson CS. 1986. Effects of loblolly pine plantations on songbird dynamics in the Virginia Piedmont. Journal of Wildlife Management 50(3):406–413.

Chipley R. 1979. The red-cockaded woodpecker. Natural Conservancy News 29(5):24–25.

Clary WF. 1979. Grazing and overstory effects on rotationally burned slash pine plantation ranges. Journal of Range Management 32(4):264–266.

Clason T, Oliver WM. 1984. Timber-pastures in loblolly pine stands. In: Proceedings, 33rd Annual Forestry Symposium: Agroforestry in the Southern United States; 1984; Baton Rouge, LA. Baton Rouge, LA: Louisiana Agricultural Experiment Station: 12–-137.

Conner RC, Rudolph DC. 1989. Red-cockaded woodpecker colony status and trends on the Angelina, Davy Crockett and Sabine National Forest. Res. Pap. SO-250. New Orleans, LA. USDA Forest Service. Southern Forest Experiment Station: 1–15.

Conner RN. 1978. Snag management for cavity nesting birds. In: Gen. Tech. Rep. SE-14. Proceedings, Symposium on the Management of Southern Forests for Nongame Birds. Asheville, NC: USDA Forest Service: 120–128.

Conner RN, Locke BA. 1979. Effects of a prescribed burn on cavity trees of red-cockaded woodpeckers. Wildlife Society Bulletin 7(4):291–293.

Conner RN, Locke BA. 1982. Fungi and red–cockaded woodpecker cavity trees. Wilson Bulletin 94(1):64–70.

Conner RN, Locke BA. 1983. Artificial inoculation of red heart fungus into loblolly pines. In: Proceedings, Red-cockaded Woodpecker Symposium II; 1983 January 27–29; Panama City, FL. Tallahassee, FL: Florida Game and Fresh Water Fish Commission: 81–82.

Conner RN, O'Halloran KA. 1987. Cavity-tree selection by red-cockaded woodpeckers as related to growth dynamics of southern pines. Wilson Bulletin 99(3):398–412.

Conner RN, Rudolph DC. 1991. Effects of midstory reduction and thinning in red-cockaded woodpecker cavity tree clusters. Wildlife Society Bulletin 19(1):63–66.

Conner RN, Dickson JG, Locke BA, Segelquist CA. 1983. Vegetation characteristics important to common songbirds in east Texas. Wilson Bulletin 95(3):349–361.

Conner RN, Dickson JG, Williamson JH. 1981. Raptor use of an East Texas clearcut. Texas Ornithological Society Bulletin 14(1/2):22–23.

Crawford BT. 1950. Some specific relationships between soils and wildlife. Journal of Wildlife Management 14(2):115–123.

Cushwa CT, Redd JB. 1966. One prescribed burn and its effects on habitat of the Powhatan game management area. Res. Note SE-61. Asheville, NC: USDA Forest Service, Southeastern Forest Experiment Station. 2 p.

Cushwa CT, Brender EV, Cooper RW. 1966. The response of herbaceous vegetation to prescribed burning. Res. Note SE-53. Asheville, NC: USDA Forest Service, Southeastern Forest Experiment Station. 2 p.

Cushwa CT, Czuhai E, Cooper RW, Julian WH. 1969. Burning clearcut openings in loblolly pine to improve wildlife habitat. Res.

Pap. 61. Macon, GA: Georgia Forest Research Council. 5 p.

Cushwa CT, Hopkins M, McGinnes BS. 1970. Response of legumes to prescribed burns in loblolly pine stands of the South Carolina Piedmont. Res. Note SE-140. Asheville, NC: USDA Forest Service, Southeastern Forest Experiment Station. 6 p.

Cushwa CT, Martin RE, Hopkins ML. 1971. Management of bobwhite quail habitat in pine forests of the Atlantic Piedmont. Res. Pap. 65. Macon, GA: Georgia Forest Research Council. 5 p.

Davis LG, Johnson MK, Pearson HA. 1984. Subclover in pine forests. In: Linnartz NE, Johnson MK, eds. Proceedings, 33rd Annual Forestry Symposium: Agroforestry in the Southern United States; 1984; Baton Rouge, LA. Baton Rouge, LA: Louisiana Agricultural Experiment Station: 89–104.

Derr HJ, Enghardt HG. 1969. Growth in a young managed longleaf pine plantation. Journal of Forestry 67(7):501–504.

Dickerson BP. 1973. Containerized loblolly pines promising for erosion control planting. Tree Planters' Notes 24(1):35–37.

Dickson JG. 1982. Impact of forestry practices on wildlife in southern pine forests. In: Increasing Forest Productivity: Proceedings, 1981 Society of American Foresters National Convention; 1981; Orlando, FL. SAF Publ. 82-01. Washington, DC: Society of American Foresters: 224–230.

Dickson JG. 1989. Streamside zones and wildlife in southern U.S. forests. In: Gresswell RE, Barton BA, Kersher JL, eds. Practical Approaches to Riparian Resource Management: An Educational Workshop; 1989 May 8–11; Billings, MT. Billings, MT: U.S. Department of the Interior, Bureau of Land Management: 131–133.

Dickson JG, ed. 1992. The wild turkey: biology and management. Harrisburg, PA: Stackpole Books. 463 p.

Dickson JG, Conner RN. 1982. Winter birds and snags in a east Texas clearcut. In: Proceedings, 36th Annual Conference of the Southeastern Association of Fish and Wildlife Agencies; 1982 October 31–November 3; Jacksonville, FL. Knoxville, TN: Southeastern Association of Fish and Wildlife Agencies: 638–642.

Dickson JG, Huntley JC. 1986. Riparian zones and wildlife in southern forests: the problem and squirrel relationships. In: Forests, the World, & the Profession: Proceedings, National Convention of the Society of American Foresters; 1986 October 5–8; Birmingham, AL. Washington, DC: Society of American Foresters: 169–171.

Dickson JG, Segelquist CA. 1979. Breeding bird populations in pine and pine-hardwood forests in Texas. Journal Wildlife Management 43(2):549–555.

Dickson JG, Williamson JH. 1988. Small mammals in streamside management zones in pine plantations. In: Proceedings, Symposium on Management of Amphibians, Reptiles, and Small Mammals in North America; 1988 July 19–21; Flagstaff, AZ. Gen. Tech. Rep. RM–166. Fort Collins, CO: USDA Forest Service, Rocky Mountain Station: 375–378.

Dickson JG, Conner RN, Williamson JH. 1980. Relative abundance of breeding birds in forest stands in the Southeast. Southern Journal of Applied Forestry 4(4):174–179.

Dickson JG, Conner RN, Williamson JH. 1983. Snag retention increases bird use of a clear–cut. Journal Wildlife Management 47(3):799–804.

Dickson JG, Conner RN, Williamson JH. 1984. Bird community changes in a young pine plantation in east Texas. Southern Journal of Applied Forestry 8(1):47–51.

Dissmeyer GE. 1978. Forest management principles revealed by recent water quality studies. In: Proceedings, Soil Moisture ... Site Productivity Symposium; 1977 November 1–3; Myrtle Beach, SC. Atlanta: USDA Forest Service, Southeastern Area, State and Private Forestry: 97–110.

Dissmeyer GE, Foster B. 1987. Some economic benefits of protecting water quality. In: Dickson JG, Mughan OE, eds. Gen. Tech. Rep. SO- 65. Proceedings, Symposium on Managing Southern Forest for Wildlife and Fish. New Orleans: USDA Forest Service, Southern Forest Experiment Station: 6–11.

Douglass JE, Goodwin OC. 1980. Runoff and soil erosion from forest site preparation practices. In: What Course in the 80's?— An Analysis of Environmental and Economic Issues; Proceedings, Symposium on U.S. Forestry and Water Quality; 1980 June 19–20; Richmond, VA. Washington, DC: Water Pollution Control Federation: 51–74.

Douglass JE, Van Lear DH, Valverde C. 1983. Stormflow changes after prescribed burning and clearcutting pine stands in the South Carolina Piedmont. In: Proceedings, 2nd Biennial Southern Silvicultural Research Conference; 1982 November 4–5; Atlanta, GA. Gen. Tech. Rep. SE-24. Asheville, NC: USDA Forest Service, southeastern forest Experiment Station: 454–460.

Duffy PD. 1977. Fertilization to accelerate loblolly pine foliage growth for erosion control. Res. Note SO-230. New Orleans: USDA Forest Service, Southern Forest Experiment Station. 4 p.

Duffy PD. 1985. Nutrient gains and losses for loblolly pine plantations. In: Blackmon BG, ed. Proceedings, Forestry and Water Quality—A Mid-South Symposium; 1985 May 8–9; Little Rock, AR. New Orleans: USDA Forest Service, Southern Forest Experiment Station: 42–54.

Duffy PD, McClurkin DC. 1974. Difficult eroded planting sites in north Mississippi evaluated by discriminant analysis. Soil Science Society of America Proceedings 38(4):676–678.

Duffy PD, Schreiber JD, Ursic SJ. 1986. Nutrient transport by sediment from pine forests. In: Proceedings, 4th Federal Interagency Sedimentation Conference; 1986 March 24–27; Las Vegas, NV. [Place of publication and publisher unknown]: 57–65.

Duvall VL, Halls LK. 1963. Outlook for beef cattle on southern forest ranges. Proceedings, Society of American Foresters National Convention; 1962 October 21–24; Atlanta, GA. Bethesda, MD: Society of American Foresters: 76–79.

Duvall VL, Whitaker LB. 1964. Rotation burning: a forage management system for longleaf pine–bluestem ranges. Journal of Range Management 17(6):322–326.

Duvall VL, Linnartz NE. 1967. Influences of grazing and fire on vegetation of soil of longleaf pine–bluestem range. Journal of Range Management 20(4):241–247.

Felix AC III, Sharik TL, McGinnes BS. 1986. Effects of pine conversion on food plants of northern bobwhite quail, eastern wild turkey, and white tailed deer in the Virginia Piedmont. Southern Journal of Applied Forestry 10(1):47–52.

Fleet RR, Dickson JG. 1984. Small mammals in two adjacent forest stands in east Texas. In: Proceedings, Workshop on Management of Nongame Species and Ecological Communities; 1984 June 11–12; Lexington, KY. Lexington, KY: University of Kentucky, Department of Forestry: 264–269.

Fribourg HA, Wells GR, Calonne H, and others. 1989. Forage and tree production on marginal soils in Tennessee, USA. Journal of Production Agriculture 2(3):262–268.

Furrh PL, Ezell AW. 1983. Pine utilization by deer in young loblolly pine plantations in east Texas. In: Proceedings, 2nd Biennial Southern Silvicultural Research Conference; 1982 November 4–5; Atlanta, GA. Gen. Tech. Rep. SE-24. Asheville, NC: USDA Forest Service, Southeastern Forest Experiment Station: 496–503.

Geyer WA, Rogers NF. 1972. Spoils change and tree growth on coal-mined spoils in Kansas. Journal of Soil and Water Conservation 27(3):114–116.

Grand JB, Mirarchi RE. 1988. Habitat use by recently fledged mourning doves in eastcentral Alabama. Journal of Wildlife Management 52(1):153–157.

Grelen HE, Enghardt HG. 1973. Burning and thinning maintain forage in a longleaf pine plantation. Journal of Forestry 71(7):419–425.

Grelen HE, Epps EA Jr. 1967. Herbage responses to fire and litter removal on southern bluestem range. Journal of Range Management 20(6):403–404.

Grelen HE, Pearson HA, Thill RE. 1985. Response to slash pines to grazing from regeneration to the first pulpwood thinning. In: Proceedings, 3rd Biennial Southern Silvicultural Research

Conference; 1984 November 7–8; Atlanta, GA. Gen. Tech. Rep. SO-54: New Orleans: USDA Forest Service, Southern Forest Experiment Station: 523–526.

Grelen HE, Whitaker LB, Lohrey RE. 1972. Herbage response to precommercial thinning in direct-seeded slash pine. Journal of Range Management 25(6):435–437.

Haines LW, Sanderford SG. 1976. Biomass response to fertilization in the Piedmont. In: America's Renewable Resource Potential: 1975—The Turning Point; Proceedings, Society of American Foresters National Convention; 1975 September 28–October 2; Washington, DC. Washington, DC: Society of American Foresters: 425–440.

Halls LK. 1970. Nutrient requirements of livestock and game. In: Proceedings, Range and Wildlife Habitat Evaluation: A Research Symposium; 1968 May; Flagstaff and Tempe, AZ. Misc. Publ. 1147. Washington, DC: USDA Forest Service: 10–18.

Halls LK. 1973. Managing deer habitat in loblolly–shortleaf pine forest. Journal of Forestry 71(12):752–757.

Halls LK. 1975. Economic feasibility of including game habitats in timber management systems. In: Proceedings, 40th North American Wildlife and Natural Resources Conference; 1975 March 16–19; [Location unknown]. Washington, DC: Wildlife Management Institute: 168–176.

Halls LK, ed. 1977. Southern fruit-producing woody plants used by wildlife. Gen. Tech. Rep. S0-16. New Orleans: USDA Forest Service, Southern Forest Experiment Station. 235 p.

Halls LK, Boyd CE. 1982. Influence of managed pine stands and mixed pine/hardwood stands on well being of deer. Res. Pap. SO-183. New Orleans: USDA Forest Service, Southern Forest Experiment Station. 18 p.

Halls LK, Epps EA Jr. 1969. Browse quality influenced by tree overstory in the South. Journal of Wildlife Management 33(4):1028–1031.

Halls LK, Homesley WB. 1966. Stand composition in a mature pine-hardwood forest of southeastern Texas. Journal of Forestry 64(3):170–174.

Halls LK, Schuster JL. 1965. Tree–herbage relations in pine–hardwood forests of Texas. Journal of Forestry 63(4):282–283.

Halls LK, Stransky JJ. 1968. Game food plantings in southern forests. In: Proceedings, 33rd North American Wildlife and Natural Resources Conference; 1968 March 11–13; [Location unknown]. Washington, DC: Wildlife Management Institute: 217–222.

Hamilton RB, Lester GD. 1987. Bird habitat use and its measurement on the Catahoula District of Kisatchie National Forest. In: In: Ecological, Physical, and Socioeconomic relationships Within Southern National Forests; Proceedings, Southern Evaluation Project Workshop; 1987 May 26–27; Long Beach, MS. Gen. Tech. Rep. SO-68. New Orleans: USDA Forest Service, Southern Forest Experiment Station: 92–102.

Hamilton RB, Ellsworth SW, Smith JC. 1987. Mammalian use of habitat in the loblolly–shortleaf pine type of Louisiana. In: Ecological, Physical, and Socioeconomic Relationships Within Southern National Forests; Proceedings, Southern Evaluation Project Workshop; 1987 May 26–27; Long Beach, MS. Gen. Tech. Rep. SO-68. New Orleans: USDA Forest Service, Southern Forest Experiment Station: 81–91.

Harris LD, Smith WH. 1978. Relations of forest practices to non-timber resources and adjacent ecosystems. In: Proceedings, Symposium on Principles of Maintaining Productivity on Prepared Sites; 1978 March 21–22; Mississippi State, MS. New Orleans: USDA Forest Service, Southern Forest Experiment Station: 28–52.

Harwell RL, Dangerfield CW. 1991. Multiple use on marginal land: a case for cattle and loblolly pine. Forestry Chronicle 67(3):249–253.

Hendrix JW, Hunt CS, Maronek DM. 1985. Relationship between the ectomycorrhizal fungus Pisolithus tinctorius associated with loblolly pine and acid-generating Thiobacillus spp. on an acidic strip mine site. Canadian Journal of Microbiology 31(9):878–879.

Hewlett JD. 1979. Forest water quality: an experiment in harvesting and regenerating Piedmont forests. Georgia Forest Res. Pap. Athens, GA: University of Georgia, School of Forest Resources. 22 p.

Holbrook HT, Vaughan MR, Bromley PT. 1987. Wild turkey habitat preferences and recruitment in intensively managed Piedmont forests. Journal of Wildlife Management 51(1):182–187.

Hughes WM. 1974. Landscape management and young pines. In: Proceedings, Symposium on Management of Young Pines; 1974 October 22–24; Alexandria, LA/December 3-5; Charleston, SC. Asheville, NC: USDA Forest Service, Southeastern Forest Experiment Station: 9–18.

Hull BR IV, Buhyoff GJ. 1986. The scenic beauty temporal distribution method: an attempt to make scenic beauty assessments compatible with forest planning efforts. Forest Science 32(2):271–286.

Hurst GA, Johnson JC. 1980. Mushroom biomass on burned windrows and mixed pine–hardwood forests. In: Proceedings, 3rd Southeast Deer Study Group Meeting; 1980 [dates unknown]; Nacogdoches, TX. [Place of publication and publisher unknown]: 1 p.

Hurst GA, Warren RC. 1983. Impacts of silvicultural practices in loblolly pine plantations on white-tailed deer habitat. In: Proceedings, 2nd Biennial Southern Silvicultural Research Conference; 1982 November 4–5; Atlanta, GA. Gen. Tech. Rep. SE-24. Asheville, NC: USDA Forest Service, Southeastern Forest Experiment Station: 484–487.

Hurst GA, Warren RC. 1986. Deer forage on pine plantations after a herbicide application for pine release [abstract]. Proceedings of the Southern Weed Science Society 39:238.

Hurst GA, Campo JJ, Brooks MB. 1982. Effects of precommercial thinning and fertilization on deer forage in a loblolly pine plantation. Southern Journal of Applied Forestry 6(3):140–144.

Jackson JA, Lennartz MR, Hooper RG. 1979. Tree age and cavity initiation by red-cockaded woodpeckers. Journal of Forestry 77(2):102–103.

Johnson MK, Davis LG, Ribbeck KF, and others. 1986. Management of subterranean clover in pine forested range. Journal of Range Management 39(5):454–457.

Johnson SA. 1987. Pine plantation as wildlife habitat: a perspective. In: Dickson JG, Maughan OE, eds. Proceedings, Symposium on Managing Southern Forests for Wildlife and Fish. Gen. Tech. Rep. SO-65. New Orleans: USDA Forest Service, Southern Forest Experiment Station: 12–17.

Johnson SA, Landers JL, Atkeson TD. 1974. Wildlife in young pine plantations. In: Proceedings, Symposium on Management of Young Pines; 1974 October 22–24; Alexandria, LA/December 3–5; Charleston, SC. Asheville, NC: USDA Forest Service, Southeastern Forest Experiment Station: 147–159.

Kennamer JE, Gwaltney JR, Sims KR. 1980. Food habitats of the eastern wild turkey on an area intensively managed for pine in Alabama. In: Proceedings, 4th National Wild Turkey Symposium; 1980 March 2–5; Little Rock, AR. Edgefield, SC: National Wild Turkey Federation: 245–250.

King DR, Bailey RL, Walston PW. 1978. Predicting cattle damage in first-year loblolly pine plantations. Journal of Range Management 31(3):234–235.

Kring JS. 1967. Spoil bank planting. Tennessee Farm and Home Science Oct/Dec: 6–8.

Krochmal A, Kologiski R. 1974. Understory plants in a mature loblolly pine plantation in North Carolina. Res. Note SE-208. Asheville, NC: USDA Forest Service, Southeastern Forest Experiment Station. 8 p.

Lalo J. 1987. The problem of road kill. American Forests 93(9/10):50–52.

Landers JL. 1987. Prescribed burning for managing wildlife in Southeastern pine forests. In: Dickson JG, Maughan OE, eds. Proceedings, Managing Southern Forests for Wildlife and Fish.

Gen. Tech. Rep. SO-65. New Orleans: USDA Forest Service, Southern Forest Experiment Station: 19–27.

Larkin RE. 1989. Utilization of intensively-managed pine forests by eastern wild turkeys in the Coastal Plain of South Carolina. Clemson, SC: Clemson University. 51 p. M.S. thesis.

Lay DW. 1967. Browse palatability and the effects of prescribed burning in southern pine forests. Journal of Forestry 65(11):826–828.

Lewis CE. 1974. Grazing considerations in managing young pines. In: Proceedings, Symposium on Management of Young Pines; 1974 October 22–24; Alexandria, LA/December 3–5; Charleston, SC. Asheville, NC: USDA Forest Service, Southeastern Forest Experiment Station: 160–170.

Lewis CE. 1980a. Simulated cattle injury to planted slash pine: combinations of defoliation, browsing, and trampling. Journal of Range Management 33(5):340–345.

Lewis CE. 1980b. Simulated cattle injury to planted slash pine: girdling. Journal of Range Management 33(5):337–339.

Lewis CE, Harshbarger TJ. 1976. Shrub and herbaceous vegetation after 20 years of prescribed burning in the South Carolina Coastal Plain. Journal of Range Management 29(1):13–18.

Lewis CE, Pearson HA. 1987. Agroforestry using tame pastures under planted pines in the southeastern United States. In: Gholz HL, ed. Proceedings, Agroforestry: Realities, Possibilities, and Potentials; [Dates and location unknown]. Dordrecht, The Netherlands: Martinus Nijhoff Publishers: 195–212.

Lewis CE, Burton GW, Monson WG, McCormick WC. 1983. Integration of pines, pastures, and cattle in south Georgia, USA. Agroforestry Systems 1(4):277–297.

Lewis CE, Grelen HE, Probasco GE. 1982. Prescribed burning in southern forest and rangeland improves forage and its use. Southern Journal of Applied Forestry 6(1):19–25.

Lewis CE, Tanner GW, Terry WS. 1985. Double vs. single-row plantations for wood and forage production. Southern Journal of Applied Forestry 9(1):55–61.

Lickwar PM, Cubbage FW, Hickman CA. 1990. Current southern state programs for control of forestry nonpoint source pollution. Southern Journal of Applied Forestry 14(2):64–69.

Linnartz NE, Hse CY, Duvall VL. 1966. Grazing impairs physical properties of a forest soil in central Louisiana. Journal of Forestry 64(4):239–243.

Locascio CG, Lockaby BG, Caulfield JP, and others. 1989. Effects of mechanical site preparation intensities on white-tailed deer forage in the Georgia Piedmont. In: Miller JH, comp. Proceedings, 5th Biennial Southern Silvicultural Research Conference; 1988 November 1–3; Memphis, TN. Gen. Tech. Rep. SO-74. New Orleans: USDA Forest Service, Southern Forest Experiment Station: 599–602.

Locke BA, Conner RN, Kroll JC. 1983. Factors influencing colony site selection by red-cockaded woodpeckers. In: Proceedings, Red-cockaded Woodpecker Symposium 2; 1983 January 27–29; Panama City, FL. Tallahassee, FL: Florida Game and Fresh Water Fish Commission: 46–50.

Lohoefener R, Lohmeier L. 1981. Comparison of gopher tortoise (Gopherus polyphemus) habitats in young slash pine and old longleaf pine areas of southern Mississippi. Journal of Herpetology 15(2):239–242.

Lundgren GK, Conner JR, Pearson HA. 1984. An economic analysis of five forest-grazing management systems in the southeastern United States. MP-1551. College Station, TX: Texas A&M University, Texas Agricultural Experiment Station. 7 p.

Lyle ES Jr. 1976. Grass, legume and tree establishment on Alabama coal surface mines. In: Proceedings, Conference on Forestation of Disturbed Surface Areas; 1976 April 14–15; Birmingham, AL. Atlanta: USDA Forest Service: 12–19.

Lyon LJ, Crawford HS, Czuhai E, and others. 1978. Effects of fire on fauna. Gen. Tech. Rep. WO-6. Washington, DC: USDA Forest Service. 41 p.

Maki TE. 1964. From poverty grass to pine timber. Research and Farming 23(1):4–5.

Maki T, Allen LH Jr. 1978. Turbulence characteristics of a single line pine tree windbreak. Proceedings of the Soil and Crop Science Society of Florida 37:81–92.

Marx DH. 1977. Manipulation of selected mycorrhizal fungi to increase forest biomass. In: 1977 TAPPI Forest Biology Wood Chemistry Conference; 1977 June 20–22; Madison, WI. Atlanta: TAPPI Press: 139–149.

Mayack DT, Bush PB, Neary DG, Douglass JE. 1982. Impact of hexazinone on invertebrates after application of forested watersheds. Archives of Environmental Contamination and Toxicology 11:209–217.

Mays DA, Bengtson GW. 1985. 'Interstate' Sericea lespedeza: a long-term nitrogen source for loblolly pine growing on coal mine spoil. Tree Planters' Notes 36(3):9–12.

McClurkin DC. 1961. Fertilizer no help to loblolly seedlings. Southern For. Notes 131. New Orleans: USDA Forest Service, Southern Forest Experiment Station. 4 p.

McClurkin DC, Duffy PD, Nelson NS. 1987. Changes in forest floor and water quality following thinning and clearcutting of 20-year-old pine. Journal of Environmental Quality 16(3):237–241.

McComb WC, Hurst GA. 1987. Herbicides and wildlife in southern forests. In: Dickson JG, Maughan OE, eds. Proceedings, Managing Southern Forests for Wildlife and Fish. Gen. Tech. Rep. SO-65. New Orleans: USDA Forest Service, Southern Forest Experiment Station: 28–36.

McElfresh RW, Inglis JM, Brown BA. 1980. Gray squirrel usage of hardwood ravines within pine plantations. In: Proceedings, 29th Annual Forestry Symposium: Integrating Timber and Wildlife Management in Southern Forests; 1980; [location unknown]. Baton Rouge, LA: Louisiana State University, School of Forestry and Wildlife Management, Division of Continuing Education: 79–89.

McMinn JW, Hewlett JD. 1975. First-year water yield increase after forest cutting: an alternative model. Journal of Forestry 73(10):654–655.

McNab WH, Berry CR. 1985. Distribution of aboveground biomass in three pine species planted on a devastated site amended with sewage sludge or inorganic fertilizer. Forest Science 31(2):373–382.

McNeel JF, Stuart WB. 1984. Feasibility of agri-silviculture for pine plantations in the South. Paper 84-1609. St. Joseph, MI: American Society of Agricultural Engineers. 14 p.

Mengak MT, Guynn DC, Van Lear DH. 1989. Ecological implications of loblolly pine regeneration for small mammal communities. Forest Science 35(2):503–514.

Mergen F, Abbot HG, Mann WF Jr, and others. 1981. Sowing forests from the air. Washington, DC: National Academy Press: 61 p.

Meyers JM, Johnson AS. 1978. Bird communities associated with succession and management of loblolly-shortleaf pine forests. In: Proceedings, Management of Southern Forests for Nongame Birds Workshop; 1978 January 24–26; Atlanta, GA. Gen. Tech. Rep. SE-14. Asheville, SC: USDA Forest Service, Southeastern Forest Experiment Station: 50–65.

Moditz P, Buckner E. 1983. Container-grown pine seedlings enable extended planting season on surface mines in east Tennessee. In: Proceedings, 2nd Biennial Southern Silvicultural Research Conference; 1982 November 4–5; Atlanta, GA. Gen. Tech. Rep. SE-24. Asheville, NC: USDA Forest Service, Southeastern Forest Experiment Station: 141–143.

Moore C, Finley J, Debetaz L. 1974. Mixed pine hardwood forest. American Birds 28(6):10–16.

Moss SA, Burger JA, Daniels WL. 1989. Pitch × loblolly pine growth in organically amended mine soils. Journal of Environmental Quality 18(1):110–115.

Neary DG. 1983. Monitoring herbicide residues in springflow after an operational application of hexazinone. Southern Journal of Applied Forestry 7(4):217–223.

Neary DG. 1985. Fate of pesticides in Florida's forests: an overview of potential impacts on water quality. Soil and Crop Science Society of Florida Proceedings 44:18–24.

Nix LE. 1985. Legume interplanting reduces growth of young loblolly pine on eroded Piedmont sites. In: Proceedings, 3rd Biennial Southern Silvicultural Research Conference; 1984 November 7–8; Atlanta, GA. Gen. Tech. Rep. SO-54. New Orleans: USDA Forest Service, Southern Forest Experiment Station: 375–378.

Noble RE, Hamilton RB. 1976. Bird populations in even-aged loblolly pine forests of southeastern Louisiana. In: Proceedings, 29th Annual Conference of the Southeastern Association of Game and Fish Commissioners; 1975 October 12–15; St. Louis, MO. Columbia, SC: Southeastern Association of Game and Fish Commissioners: 441–450.

Noble RE, Hamilton RB, McComb WC. 1980. Some effects of forestry on nongame birds. In: Proceedings, 29th Annual Forestry Symposium: Integrating Timber and Wildlife Management in Southern Forests; 1980; [location unknown]. Baton Rouge, LA: Louisiana State University, School of Forestry and Wildlife Management, Division of Continuing Education: 65–78.

Palazzo RP. 1974. Landscape management. In: Proceedings, Symposium on Management of Young Pines; 1974 October 22–24; Alexandria, LA/December 3–5; Charleston, SC. Asheville, NC: USDA Forest Service, Southeastern Forest Experiment Station: 143–146.

Pearson HA. 1974. Range and wildlife opportunities. In: Proceedings, Symposium on Management of Young Pines; 1974 October 22–24; Alexandria, LA/December 3–5; Charleston, SC. Asheville, NC: USDA Forest Service, Southeastern Forest Experiment Station: 19–27.

Pearson HA. 1976. Multiple-use inventories in Louisiana forests. In: Proceedings, 29th Annual Conference of the Southeastern Association of Game and Fish Commissioners; 1975 October 12–15; St. Louis, MO. Columbia, SC: Southeastern Association of Game and Fish Commissioners: 682–686.

Pearson HA. 1981. Forest and range interactions. In: Proceedings, 1st Biennial Southern Silvicultural Research Conference; 1980 November 6–7; Atlanta, GA. Gen. Tech. Rep. SO-34. New Orleans: USDA Forest Service, Southern Forest Experiment Station: 339–342.

Pearson HA. 1982. Economic analysis of forest grazing. The Stockman 39(10):26–32.

Pearson HA. 1983. Forest grazing in the southern United States. In: Hannaway DB, ed. Proceedings, Foothills for Food and Forests. Oregon State University College of Agricultural Sciences Symposium Series 2; 1983; Corvallis, OR. Beaverton, OR: Timber Press: 247–259.

Pearson HA. 1987. Southern pine plantations and cattle grazing. Journal of Forestry 85(10):36–37.

Pearson HA, Lewis CE. 1989. Agroforestry in the southeastern United States. In: Proceedings, 16th International Grassland Congress; 1989 October 4–11; Nice, France. Nice, France: International Grassland Congress: 1637–1638.

Pearson HA, Sternitzke HS. 1976. Deer browse inventories in the Louisiana Coastal Plain. Journal of Wildlife Management 40(2):326–329.

Pearson HA, Whitaker LB. 1974. Yearlong grazing of slash pine ranges; effects on herbage and browse. Journal of Range Management 27(3):195–197.

Pearson HA, Whitaker LB, Duvall VL. 1971. Slash pine regeneration under regulated grazing. Journal of Forestry 69(10):744–746.

Perkins CJ, Hurst GA, Roach ER. 1989. Relative abundance of small mammals in young loblolly pine plantations. In: Proceeding, 5th Biennial Southern Silvicultural Research Conference; 1988 November 1–3; Memphis, TN. Gen. Tech. Rep. SO-74. New Orleans: USDA Forest Service, Southern Forest Experiment Station: 58–591.

Plass WT. 1974. Direct-seeded pine on surface-mine spoils. Res. Pap. NE-290. Upper Darby, PA: USDA Forest Service, Northeastern Forest Experiment Station. 5 p.

Plass WT. 1979. The use of southern pines for surface mine reclamation. In: Proceedings, Management of Pines of the Interior South; 1978 November 7–8; Knoxville, TN. Technical Publication SA-TP 2. Atlanta: USDA Forest Service: 176–182.

Plass WT, Burton JD. 1967. Pulpwood production potential on strip-mined land in the South. Journal of Soil and Water Conservation 22(6):235–238.

Porter ML, Labisky RF. 1986. Home range and foraging habitat of red-cockaded woodpeckers in Northern Florida. Journal of Wildlife Management 50(2):239–247.

Reed DP, Noble RE. 1987. Vegetative analysis in the loblolly pine-shortleaf pine-upland hardwood forest type, Louisiana. In: Proceedings, Ecological, Physical, and Socioeconomic Relationships Within Southern National Forests: Southern Evaluation Project Workshop; 1987 May 26–27; Long Beach, MS. Gen. Tech. Rep. SO-68. New Orleans: USDA Forest Service, Southern Forest Experiment Station: 73–76.

Ribbeck KF, Johnson MK, Dancak K. 1987. Subterranean clover on southern pine range: potential benefits to game. Journal of Range Management 40(2):116–118.

Riekerk H. 1987. Hydrologic effects of flatwoods silviculture. In: Proceedings, 4th Biennial Southern Silvicultural Research Conference; 1986 November 4–6; Atlanta, GA. Gen. Tech. Rep. SE-42. Asheville, NC: USDA Forest Service, Southeastern Forest Experiment Station: 321–330.

Riekerk H, Korhnak LV. 1985. Environmental effects of silviculture in pine flatwoods. In: Proceedings, 3rd Biennial Southern Silvicultural Research Conference; 1984 November 7–8; Atlanta, GA. Gen. Tech. Rep. SO-54. New Orleans: USDA Forest Service, Southern Forest Experiment Station: 528–534.

Rogerson TL. 1968. Thinning increases throughfall in loblolly pine plantations. Journal of Soil and Water Conservation 23(4):141–142.

Rogerson TL. 1971. Hydrologic characteristics of small headwater catchments in the Ouachita mountains. Res. Note SO-117. New Orleans: USDA Forest Service, Southern Forest Experiment Station. 5 p.

Rowse LA, Marion WR. 1981. Effect of silvicultural practices on birds in a north Florida flatwoods. In: Proceedings, 1st Biennial Southern Silvicultural Research Conference; 1980 November 6–7; Atlanta, GA. Gen. Tech. Rep. SO-34. New Orleans: USDA Forest Service, Southern Forest Experiment Station: 349–357.

Rudis VA. 1985. Timber surveys: potential for dispersed recreation resource assessments. In: Proceedings, 1984 Southeastern Recreation Research Conference; 1984 February 16–17; Asheville, NC. Athens, GA: University of Georgia, Institute for Behavioral Research: 51–58.

Rudis VA. 1987. Recreational use of forested areas by Alabama residents. Res. Pap. SO-237. New Orleans: USDA Forest Service, Southern Forest Experiment Station. 37 p.

Rudis VA. 1988a. Nontimber values of east Texas timberland. Resource. Bull. SO-139. New Orleans: USDA Forest Service, Southern Forest Experiment Station. 34 p.

Rudis VA. 1988b. Nontimber values of Louisiana's timberland. Resource. Bull. SO-132. New Orleans: USDA Forest Service, Southern Forest Experiment Station. 27 p.

Rudolph DC, Conner RN. 1991. Cavity tree selection by red-cockaded woodpeckers in relation to tree age. Wilson Bulletin 10(3):458–467.

Rudolph DC, Dickson JG. 1990. Streamside zone width and amphibian and reptile abundance. Southwestern Naturalist 35(4):472–476.

Ruehle JL. 1980. Growth of containerized loblolly pine with specific ectomycorrhizae after 2 years on an amended borrow pit. Reclamation Review 3:95–101.

Sanderford SG. 1975. Forest fertilization and water quality in the

North Carolina Piedmont. Tech. Rep. 53. Raleigh, NC: North Carolina State University, School of Forest Resources. 42 p.

Scanlon JJ, Sharik TL. 1986. Forage energy for white-tailed deer in loblolly pine plantations. Journal of Wildlife Management 50(2):301–306.

Schoenholtz SH, Burger JA. 1984. Influence of cultural treatments on survival and growth of pines on strip-mined sites. Reclamation and Revegetation Research 3(3):223–237.

Schoenholtz SH, Burger JA, Torbert JL. 1987. Natural mycorrhizal colonization of pines on reclaimed surface mines in Virginia USA. Journal of Environmental Quality 16(2):143–146.

Schultz RP, Wilhite LP. 1974. Changes in a flatwoods site following intensive preparation. Forest Science 20(3):230–237.

Seehorn ME. 1982. Reptiles and amphibians of southeastern national forests. Atlanta: USDA Forest Service: 1–85.

Segal DS, Neary DG, Best GR, Michael JL. 1987. Effect of ditching, fertilization, and herbicide application on groundwater levels and groundwater quality in a flatwood spodosol. Proceedings of the Soil and Crop Science Society of Florida: 107–112.

Shaffer CH, Gwynn JV. 1967. Management of the eastern turkey in oak-pine and pine forests of Virginia and the southeast. In: Hewitt OH, ed. The wild turkey and its management. Washington, DC: The Wildlife Society: 303–342.

Short HL. 1969. Physiology and nutrition of deer in southern upland forests. In: Proceedings, Symposium on the White-tailed Deer in the Southern Forest Habitat; 1969 March 25-26; Nacogdoches, TX. New Orleans: USDA Forest Service, Southern Forest Experiment Station: 14–18.

Short HL. 1971. Forage digestibility and diet of deer on southern upland range. Journal of Wildlife Management 35(4):698–706.

Shoulders E, Tiarks AE. 1984. Response of pines and native forage to fertilizer. In: Proceedings, 33rd Annual Forestry Symposium: Agroforestry in the Southern United States; 1984; Baton Rouge, LA. Baton Rouge, LA: Louisiana Agricultural Experiment Station: 105–126.

Smeins FE, Hinton JZ. 1987. Vegetation of the loblolly-shortleaf pine-hardwood type, Angelina National Forest, Texas. In: Proceedings, Ecological, Physical, and Socioeconomic Relationships Within Southern National Forests: Southern Evaluation Project Workshop; 1987 May 26–27; Long Beach, MS. Gen. Tech. Rep. SO-68. New Orleans: USDA Forest Service, Southern Forest Experiment Station: 31–37.

Speake DW, Hill EP, Carter VE. 1975. Aspects of land management with regard to production of wood and wildlife in the southeastern United States. In: Proceedings, 4th North American Forest Soils Conference; 1973 August; Université Laval, Québec. Québec: L'Presse de Université Laval: 333–349.

Stransky JJ, Halls LK. 1968. Timber and game food relations in pine-hardwood forests of the southern United States. In: Proceedings, IUFRO Congress; 1967 September 4–9; Munich, Germany. Freiburg, Germany: [Publisher unknown]: 208–217.

Stransky JJ, Halls LK. 1978. Forage yield increased by clearcutting and site preparation. In: Proceedings, 32nd Annual Conference Southeastern Association ofFfish and Wildlife Agencies; 1978 November 5–8; Hot Springs, AR. Knoxville, TN: Southeastern Association of Fish and Wildlife Agencies: 38–41.

Stransky JJ, Halls LK. 1981. Forage and pine growth with clearcutting and site preparation. In: Proceeding, 1st Biennial Southern Silvicultural Research Conference; 1980 November 6–7; Atlanta, GA. Gen. Tech. Rep. SO-34. New Orleans: USDA Forest Service, Southern Forest Experiment Station: 343–348.

Stransky JJ, Richardson D. 1977. Fruiting of browse plants affected by pine site preparation in east Texas. In: Proceedings, 31st Annual Conference of the Southeastern Association of Fish and Wildlife Agencies; 1977 October 9–12; San Antonio, TX. Knoxville, TN: Southeastern Association Fish and Wildlife Agencies: 5–7.

Stransky JJ, Roese JJ. 1984. Promoting soft mast for wildlife in intensively managed forests. Wildlife Society Bulletin 12:234–240.

Stransky JJ, Halls LK, Nixon ES. 1976. Plants following timber harvest: importance to songbirds. Texas For. Pap. 28. Nacogdoches, TX: Stephen F. Austin State University, School of Forestry. 13 p.

Strelke WK, Dickson JG. 1980. Effect of forest clear-cut edge on breeding birds in east Texas. Journal of Wildlife Management 44(3):559–567.

Stuth JW, Hunter JF, Kanouse KJ, Pearson HA. 1981. Multiple electrode impedance plethysmography system for monitoring grazing dynamics. Biomedical Sciences Instrumentation 17:121–124.

Svoboda D, Smouth G, Weaver GT, Roth PL. 1979. Accumulation of heavy metals in selected woody plant species on sludge-treated strip mine spoils at the Palzo site, Shawnee National Forest. In: Sopper WE, Kerr SN, eds. Proceedings, Utilization of Municipal Sewage Effluent and Sludge on Forest and Disturbed Land; 1977 March 21–23; Philadelphia, PA. University Park, PA: The Pennsylvania State University Press: 395–405.

Sweeney JM, Wenger CR, Yoho NS. 1981. Bobwhite quail food in young Arkansas loblolly pine plantations. Bull. 852. Fayetteville, AR: University of Arkansas, Agricultural Experiment Station, Division of Agriculture. 18 p.

Teitelbaum RD, Smith WP. 1985. Cavity-site characteristics of the red-cockaded woodpecker in Fontainebleau State Park, Louisiana. Proceedings of the Louisiana Academy of Sciences 48:116–122.

Telewski FW. 1986. Physiological responses of trees to mechanical perturbation: implication for genetic evaluation for wind tolerance. In: Proceedings, International Symposium on Windbreak Technology; 1986 June 23–27; Lincoln, NE. Great Plains Agricultural Council Publication 117. Bozeman, MT: Montana State University, Cooperative Extension Service: 251–252.

Thames JL. 1962. Litter production as influenced by species of southern pine. Journal of Forestry 60(8):565.

Thill RE. 1983. Deer and cattle forage selection on Louisiana pine–hardwood sites. Res. Pap. SO-196. New Orleans: USDA Forest Service, Southern Forest Experiment Station. 35 p.

Thill RE. 1984. Deer and cattle diets on Louisiana pine-hardwood sites. Journal of Wildlife Management 48(3):788–798.

Thill RE, Bellemore JC. 1986. Understory responses to fertilization of eroded Kisatchie soil in Louisiana. Res. Note SO-330. New Orleans: USDA Forest Service, Southern Forest Experiment Station. 6 p.

Thill RE, Wigley TB, Melchiors MA. 1991. Wildlife values of streamside management zones in the Ouachita Mountains, Arkansas. Unpublished Progress Report Summary. FS-SO-4251-1.3, problem 1. 1 p. [On file with USDA Forest Service, Southeastern Forest Experiment Station, Asheville, NC.]

Thomas JD, Buckner E. 1981. Re-establishing yellow pine habitat for the red cockaded woodpecker on the Cumberland plateau. In: Proceedings, 1st Biennial Southern Silvicultural Research Conference; 1980 November 6–7; Atlanta, GA. Gen. Tech. Rep. SO-34. New Orleans: USDA Forest Service, Southern Forest Experiment Station: 358–361.

Thor E, Kring JS. 1964. Planting and seeding of loblolly pine on steep spoil banks. Journal of Forestry 62(8):575–576.

Torbert JL Jr, Burger JA, Lien JN, Schoenholtz SH. 1985. Results of a tree species trial on a recontoured surface mine in southwestern Virginia. Southern Journal of Applied Forestry 9(3):150–153.

Trousdell KB, Hoover MD. 1955. A change in ground-water level after clearcutting of loblolly pine in the Coastal Plain. Journal of Forestry 53(6):493–498.

Tuttle CL, Golden MS, South DB, Meldahl RS. 1987. Survival of loblolly pine seedlings on adverse sites is influenced by initial height. Highlights of Agricultural Research [Alabama Agricultural Experiment Station] 34(4):15.

USDA FS [U.S. Department of Agriculture, Forest Service]. 1988. The Yazoo–Little Tallahatchie flood prevention project: a history of the Forest Service's role. For. Rep. R8-FR8. Atlanta: Forest Service, Southern Region. 63 p.

Ursic SJ. 1962. Early survival of loblolly plantings on eroded lands. Tree Planters' Notes 53:27–28.

Ursic SJ. 1963. Planting loblolly pine for erosion control in north Mississippi. Res. Pap. SO-3. New Orleans: USDA Forest Service, Southern Forest Experiment Station. 20 p.

Ursic SJ. 1966. Mulch improves loblolly pine survival on Coastal Plain parent materials. Journal of Forestry 64(11):728–730.

Ursic SJ. 1986. Sediment and forestry practices in the South. In: Proceeding, 4th Federal Interagency Sedimentation Conference; 1986 March 24–27; Las Vegas, NV. Washington, DC: USDA. Volume 2: 28–37.

Ursic SJ, Dendy FE. 1965. Sediment yields from small watersheds under various land uses and forest covers. In: Proceedings, Federal Inter-agency Sedimentation Conference; 1963 January 28–February 1; Jackson, MS. Misc. Publ. 970. Washington, DC: U.S. Department of Agriculture, Agricultural Research Service: 47–52.

Ursic SJ, Esher RJ. 1988. Influence of small mammals on stormflow responses of pine-covered catchments. Water Resources Bulletin 24(1):133–139.

Ursic SJ, Thames JL. 1960. Effect of cover types and soils on runoff in northern Mississippi. Journal of Geophysical Research 65(2):663–667.

Van Lear DH, Douglass JE. 1983. Water in the loblolly pine ecosystem—eastern region. In: Proceedings, Symposium on the Loblolly Pine Eecosystem—East Region; 1982 December 8–10; Raleigh, NC. Raleigh, NC: North Carolina State University, School of Forest Resources: 285–296.

Van Lear DH, Douglass JE, Cox SK, Augspurger MK. 1985. Sediment and nutrient export in runoff from burned and harvested pine watersheds in the South Carolina Piedmont. Journal of Environmental Quality 14(2):169–174.

Van Lear DH, Saucier JR, Goebel NB. 1973. Growth and wood properties of loblolly pine on a Piedmont subsoil as influenced by early fertilization. Soil Science Society of America Proceedings 37(5):778–781.

Vogel WG. 1973. The effect of herbaceous vegetation on survival and growth of trees planted on coal-mine spoils. In: Proceedings, Bituminous Coal Symposium; 1978 March 7–8; [location unknown]. [Place of publication and publisher unknown]: 197–207.

Wagar JA, Barker PA. 1986. Controlling the roots of urban trees. In: Proceedings, Forests, the World, & the Profession: 1986 Society of American Foresters National Convention; 1986 October 5–8; Birmingham, AL. Bethesda, MD: Society of American Foresters: 329–334.

Walker RF, West DC, McLaughlin SB. 1981. *Pisolithus tinctorius* ectomycorrhizae enhance the survival and growth of *Pinus taeda* on a southern Appalachian coal spoil. In: Proceedings, 1st Biennial Southern Silvicultural Research Conference; 1980 November 6–7; Atlanta, GA. Gen. Tech. Rep. SO-34. New Orleans: USDA Forest Service, Southern Forest Experiment Station: 29–33.

Walker RF, West DC, McLaughlin SB, Amundsen CC. 1985. The performance of loblolly, Virginia, and shortleaf pine on a reclaimed surface mine as affected by *Pisolithus tinctorius* ectomycorrhizae and fertilization. In: Proceedings, 3rd Biennial Southern Silvicultural Research Conference; 1984 November 7–8; Atlanta, GA. Gen. Tech. Rep. SO-54. New Orleans: USDA Forest Service, Southern Forest Experiment Station: 410–416.

Walker RF, West DC, McLaughlin SB, Amundsen CC. 1989. Growth, xylem pressure potential, and nutrient absorption of loblolly pine on a reclaimed surface mine as affected by an induced *Pisolithus tinctorius* infection. Forest Science 35(2):569–581.

Watson VH, Hagedorn C, Knight WE, Pearson HA. 1984. Shade tolerance of grass and legume germ plasm for use in the southern forest range. Journal of Range Management 37(3):229–232.

Wheeler L, Ku TT, Colvin RJ. 1989. The effects of silvicultural practices on soil water chemistry of southern pine forests. Gen. Tech. Rep. SO-74. New Orleans: USDA Forest Service, Southern Forest Experiment Station: 473–476.

Whitaker LB, Pearson HA, Monroe WM. 1970. Crossbred cattle: custom-built for piney woods range. Louisiana Cattleman 70(9):8–9.

Whiting RM Jr, Fleet RR. 1987. Bird and small mammal communities of loblolly–shortleaf pine stands in east Texas. In: Proceedings, Ecological, physical, and Socioeconomic Relationships Within Southern National Forests: Southern Evaluation Project Workshop; 1987 May 26–27; Long Beach, MS. Gen. Tech. Rep. SO-68. New Orleans: USDA Forest Service, Southern Forest Experiment Station: 49–66.

Whiting RM Jr, Fleet RR, Rakowitz VA. 1987. Herpetofauna in loblolly-shortleaf pine stands of east Texas. In: Proceedings, Ecological, Physical, and Socioeconomic Relationships Within Southern National Forests: Southern Evaluation Project Workshop; 1987 May 26–27; Long Beach, MS. Gen. Tech. Rep. SO-68. New Orleans: USDA Forest Service, Southern Forest Experiment Station: 39–48.

Williams KL, Mullin K. 1987. Amphibians and reptiles of loblolly-shortleaf pine stand in central Louisiana. In: Proceedings, Ecological, Physical, and Socioeconomic Relationships Within Southern National Forests: Southern Evaluation Project Workshop; 1987 May 26–27; Long Beach, MS. Gen. Tech. Rep. SO-68. New Orleans: USDA Forest Service, Southern Forest Experiment Station: 77–80.

Williams TM, Lipscomb DJ. 1981. Water table rise after cutting on Coastal Plain soils. Southern Journal of Applied Forestry 5(1):46–48.

Williston HL, Ursic SJ. 1979. Planting loblolly pine for erosion control: a review. Tree Planters' Notes 30(2):15–18.

Williston HL. 1965. Forest floor in loblolly pine plantations as related to stand characteristics. Res. Note SO-26. New Orleans: USDA Forest Service, Southern Forest Experiment Station. 3 p.

Williston HL. 1967. Improving loblolly pine survival in roadbank stabilization. Tree Planters' Notes 18(3):18–20.

Williston HL. 1971. Guidelines for planting and maintaining loblolly pine and other cover for roadbank stabilization. Tree Planters' Notes 22(2):14–17.

Williston HL. 1988. The Yazoo–Little Tallahatchie flood prevention project: a history of the Forest Service's role. Forestry Report R8-FR 8. Atlanta: USDA Forest Service, Southern Region. 63 p.

Wolters GL. 1973. Southern pine overstories influence herbage quality. Journal of Range Management 26(6):423–426.

Wolters GL, Martin A Jr, Clary WP. 1977. Timber, browse, and herbage on selected loblolly–shortleaf pine–hardwood forest stands. Res. Note SO-223. New Orleans: USDA Forest Service, Southern Forest Experiment Station. 9 p.

Wolters GL, Martin A, Pearson HA. 1982. Forage response to overstory reduction on loblolly-shortleaf pine-hardwood forest range. Journal of Range Management 35(4):443–446.

Wolters GL, Schmidtling RC. 1975. Browse and herbage in intensively managed pine plantations. Journal of Wildlife Management 39(3):557–562.

Wolters GL, Wilhite AT Jr. 1974. Loblolly–shortleaf pine–hardwood range of the South. Bull. NS 9. Tifton, GA: University of Georgia, Coastal Plain Experiment Station: 20–23.

Wood DA. 1983. Foraging and colony habitat characteristics of the red-cockaded woodpecker in Oklahoma. In: Proceedings, Red-cockaded Woodpecker Symposium No. 2; 1983 Jan 27–29; Panama City, FL. Tallahassee, FL: Florida Game and Fresh Water Fish Commission: 51–58.

Wood GW. 1986. Influences of forest fertilization on South Carolina deer forage quality. Southern Journal of Applied Forestry 10(4):203–206.

Wood GW. 1988. Effects of prescribed fire on deer forage and nutrients. Wildlife Society Bulletin 16(2):180–186.

Wood GW, Beland JM, Lynn TE. 1974. Potential responses of wildlife habitat and populations to precommercial thinning in a young pine stand. In: Proceedings, Symposium on Management of Young Pines; 1974 October 22–24; Alexandria, LA/December 3–5; Charleston, SC. Asheville, NC: USDAForest Service, Southeastern Forest Experiment Station: 312–316.

Yoho NS. 1980. Forest management and sediment production in the South: a review. Southern Journal of Applied Forestry 4:27–35.

Chapter 10

Protection

Contents

Continued on next page...

Contents (cont'd)

Protection

Introduction

Before the 1930's, loblolly pine grew mainly in relatively balanced natural ecosystems that included trees of various species and ages. Since the 1930's, the creation of large, even-aged stands of rapidly growing loblolly pine has reduced or eliminated some of the natural controls on the proliferation of forest pests. As a result, damage caused by pests and environmental conditions has become increasingly severe and widespread in the loblolly pine forests of the South. In some states, more than one-fifth of the trees are damaged by insects, diseases, or environmental conditions (table 10-1). Intensive forest management is often the primary cause of severe attacks by fusiform rust, *Cronartium quercuum* (Berk.) Miyabe ex Shirai f. sp. *fusiforme* (Hedgc. & Hunt) Burdsall and Snow; annosum root rot, *Heterobasidion annosum* (Fr.:Fr.), Bref. = *Fomes annosus* (Fr.:Fr.) Cooke; and by insects such as southern pine beetle, *Dendroctonus frontalis* Zimmermann; Nantucket pine tip moth, *Rhyacionia frustrana* (Comstock); and pales weevil, *Hylobius pales* (Herbst). Trees weakened or stressed by one pest or adverse environmental condition (for example, drought, flooding, or competition) may be more susceptible to, and even provide attractants for, a wide range of other pests.

Because plant, animal, and disease pests are integral parts of the loblolly pine ecosystem, their management must be integrated with overall pine management. Loblolly pine pest management requires an understanding of interrelationships among pests and host plants and an understanding of the influence of site factors and environmental changes on the protection needs of trees. With this knowledge, systematic manipulations of soil, vegetation, and animals can be planned and accomplished in ways that are economical and ecologically and socially acceptable. Integrated pest management should emphasize pest prevention, containment, and exclusion to reduce pest populations to levels that do not cause serious harm rather than the eradication of unwanted species.

The following sections highlight specific pests of loblolly pines and how tree losses can be minimized by appropriate and judicious application of pest management strategies combined with sound silviculture.

Table 10-1—Loblolly pine trees in Southern States damaged by insects, diseases, animals, and environmental factors

State	Year	Damage (%)			Source
		Saplings	Poletimber	Sawtimber	
Alabama	1983	23.9	25.8	26.4	Mistretta and Bylin (1986)
Florida	1980	20.0 +	19.0 +	28.0 +	Anderson and others (1983)
Georgia	1982	28.0 +	33.0 +	31.0 +	Huber and others (1984)
Louisiana	1985	15.5	16.1	13.5	Mistretta and Bylin (1987)
North Carolina	1984	12.0	12.0 +	11.0 +	Huber and others (1985)
South Carolina	1977–78	16.7	18.5	14.8	Anderson and others (1981)
Tennessee	1982	2.0	8.4	17.8	Mistretta and others (1986)
Virginia	1986	3.0 +	3.0 +	7.0 +	Huber and others (1987)

Diseases of Loblolly Pines

Loblolly pine is subject to infection and damage by a number of diseases during various parts of its life cycle (table 10-2). These diseases, especially fusiform rust and annosum root rot, cause extensive growth losses and tree mortality in loblolly pine forests each year.

Fusiform Rust

Fusiform rust is a native disease. It occurred only sporadically during the 1930's but is now perhaps the most widespread and destructive pest of intensively managed

Table 10-2—Diseases of loblolly pine and tree growth stages affected

Common and scientific name	Primary growth stage(s) affected				Common and scientific name	Primary growth stage(s) affected			
	Seedling	Sapling	Pole	Sawtimber		Seedling	Sapling	Pole	Sawtimber
Annosum root rot *Heterobasidion annosum* (Fr.:Fr.) Bref. [= *Fomes annosus* (Fr.:Fr.) Cooke]			■	■	Heart rot fungus *Phellinus pini* (Thore ex. Fr.)				■
Blue-stain fungus *Ceratocystis minor* (Hedgcock) Hunt				■	Littleleaf disease Caused by *Phytophthora cinnamoni* Rands and *Pythium* spp.			■	■
Brown-spot needle blight *Mycosphaerella dearnessii* Barr. [=*Scirrhia acicola* (Dearn.) Siggers]	■				Needle cast fungi *Lophodermella cerina* (Darker) Darker, *Ploioderma (Hypoderma)* *lethale* (Dearn.) Darker, and *P. Hedgcockii* (Dearn.) Darker			■	■
Comandra blister rust *Cronartium comandrae* Peck	■	■			Pine needle rust *Coleosporium* spp.		■		
Fusiform rust *Cronartium quercuum* (Berk.) Miyabe ex Shirai f. Sp. *fusiforme* (Hedge & Hunt) Burdsall and Snow	■	■		■	Pitch canker *Fusarium moniliforme* Sheld. Var. *subglutinans* Wollenw. & Reink.	■	■	■	■
					Sweetfern blister rust *Cronartium comptoniae* Arth.	■	■		

loblolly pine (Miller and Schmidt 1987). Although loblolly co-evolved with the rust fungus (Burdsall and Snow 1977, Czabator 1971, Snow 1985), intensive plantation management altered the natural balance between the two species. Control of wildfires permitted the oak alternate host to proliferate. Many of the first loblolly seeds collected for nursery production came from susceptible trees that produced abundant cones. These infected nursery seedlings were planted widely. Intensive site preparation and postplanting cultural measures stimulated tree growth, which made more succulent needle and shoot tissue available for infection by the pathogen. The combination of these factors created conditions favoring buildup of the pathogen, and the severity of the disease rapidly increased over much of the loblolly pine range.

Annual losses of loblolly and slash pines caused by fusiform rust are estimated at more than $100 million (Anderson and Mistretta 1982). These include more than

$35 million in the five-state area from Virginia to Florida where 3.6 million of the 9.7 million ha of loblolly and slash pine stands contain at least 10% infected trees (Anderson and others 1986b). About 11% of all planted loblolly in Texas are infected, and 7% of the planted loblolly in Texas have stem infections (Hunt and Lenhart 1986). Damage occurs in all age classes (table 10-3), but its greatest impact is in young plantations, where infection can exceed 90%. Loss is primarily the result of pre-

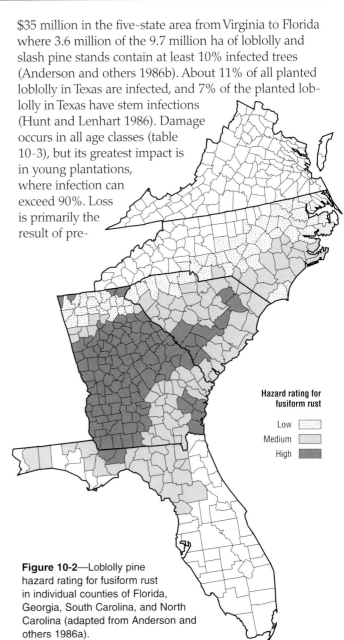

Figure 10-2—Loblolly pine hazard rating for fusiform rust in individual counties of Florida, Georgia, South Carolina, and North Carolina (adapted from Anderson and others 1986a).

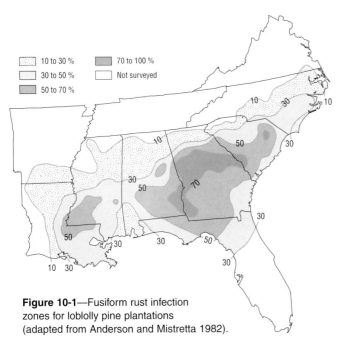

Figure 10-1—Fusiform rust infection zones for loblolly pine plantations (adapted from Anderson and Mistretta 1982).

Table 10-3—Loblolly pine damage incidence and associated cull caused by fusiform rust in various southern States

State	Year	Incidence of damage (%)			Accumulated volume loss (m³)		Source
		Saplings	Pole-timber	Saw-timber	Pole-timber	Saw-timber	
Alabama	1983	11	15	16	NM	NM	Mistretta and Bylin (1986)
Florida	1980	17	17	22	0	5,544	Anderson and others (1983)
Georgia	1982	23	29	27	4,872	29,932	Huber and other (1984)
Louisiana	1983–85	11	10	7	NM	NM	Mistretta and Bylin (1987)
North Carolina	1984	9	10	7	2,212	21,560	Huber and others (1985)
South Carolina	1977–78	16	17	12	5,040	3,557	Anderson and others (1981)
Tennessee	1982	0	<1	<1	NM	NM	Mistretta and others (1986)
Virginia	1986	1	1	1	1,288	6,300	Huber and others (1987)

NM = not measured.

mature mortality and an increase in stem defect. In addition, infected trees are often smaller in diameter and height than those without infections (Mann and Derr 1970, Zutter and others 1987).

Certain areas of the South have higher incidence of fusiform rust than others, even though there are periods of high infection for many locations. Incidence of fusiform rust is highest in a band extending from northeast to southwest across the central portion of the range of loblolly pine, with decreased incidence to the north and south (Squillace 1976; figures 10-1 and 10-2). In areas where fusiform rust may be a problem, stands should be evaluated for infection between ages 3 and 5. If 50% or more of the trees in a stand have galls on the stem or on living branches within 30 cm of the main stem, the site should be rated as high hazard. Stem infection rates of 25 to 50% indicate moderate hazard, and rates less than 2% indicate low hazard. Stem infection at age 5 is a reliable indicator of rust-associated mortality at age 10 (Wells and Dinus 1978). Approximately half of all infections are lethal (Anderson and others 1986a). In Georgia progeny tests, 7% of the loblolly pines that had visible galls at age 3 were dead by age 15, whereas only 7% of those that were rust free at age 3 were dead by age 15 (Sluder 1977). Where

fusiform rust incidence is high, more trees should be planted to offset mortality due to rust and to maintain adequately stocked stands of rust-free trees.

Life cycle. The causal fungus of fusiform rust disease does not spread from pine to pine, but requires an alternate host to complete its life cycle, which typically takes 2 or more years (figure 10-3). Part of the cycle is spent in pine tissues and the remainder in the leaves of red oaks, especially willow oak, *Quercus phellos* L., and water oak. From late February to early April, galls on infected pines produce enormous numbers of orange aeciospores (asexual spores produced by the fruiting body of the rust fungus). Windborne aeciospores infect the leaves of nearby oaks. Brown, hairlike structures are subsequently produced on the undersides of oak leaves, and these structures in turn produce teliospores. When the temperature is between 16 and 27 °C and relative humidity is between 97 and 100% for 4 or more hours, the teliospores germinate. Teliospores can remain viable until early June. Each teliospore produces four basidiospores (sporidia). Basidiospores are

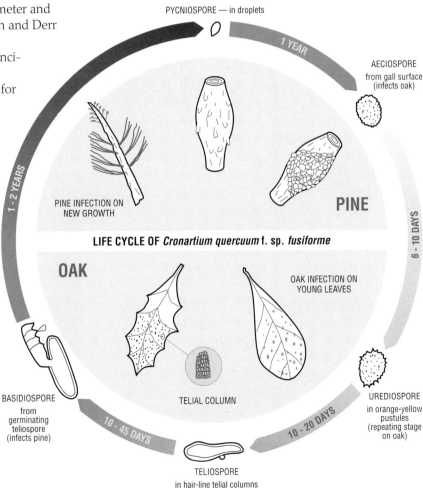

Figure 10-3—Schematic diagram of the life cycle of fusiform rust (adapted from Phelps and Czabator 1978).

carried by wind and infect pines—primarily succulent new shoot tissue and wounds. In total, the fungus remains active for less than 2 months in oak leaves, and oaks become free of the disease in the winter following leaf-fall. Once the loblolly pine host is infected, the developing fungus grows through the host tissue and colonizes the branch or stem cambium. Branch infections within 30 cm of the main stem may spread into the bole.

Gall development. Basidiospores germinate after landing on new pine tissue, and hyphae usually penetrate directly through the cuticle and cell walls of the epidermal cells of hypocotyls, cotyledons, stems, branches, and primary and secondary needles. Occasionally, hyphae grow through the guard cells or subsidiary cells of stomata (Jacobi and others 1982, Miller and others 1980). Rust usually infests young nursery seedlings through cotyledons or primary needles. Within 9 to 12 months, the hyphae have grown into the stems, creating a visible swelling (Jewell and others 1962). A slight swelling and discoloration of the epidermis (gall or canker) generally appears 4 to 6 months after direct infection of a succulent stem or branch.

Hyphae advance radially along the phloem rays through the cambium and along the wood rays to a depth of two to three rings. Infection increases the size and number of cells in the wood rays, reduces wall thickness and length of tracheids, produces abnormally shaped tracheids, and increases the proportion of ray parenchyma (Jackson and Parker 1958, Kuhlman 1988, Rowan 1970b). Various patterns of red pigmentation usually predominate in galls (figure 10-4). In early spring, galls appear yellow to orange as the fungus produces powdery aeciospores for reinfection of oaks. In some cases, galls may not be obvious for a year or more. The most easily recognized symptom of infection is a fusoid (or spindle-shaped) stem or branch gall that is largest in the middle and tapers to each end. However, galls can be globose, intermediate between fusoid and globose, or can even change in form from globose to fusoid or from fusoid to globose over a period of several years (Kais 1966, Powers 1971; figure 10-5). Galls can grow to a length of 60 cm or more. The age of a gall in years is about equal to two-thirds of the length of the gall in inches. This relationship may be useful in setting up pruning or thinning guides (Jackson 1968).

The number of rust infections on individual trees usually increases gradually for the first few years after planting or natural regeneration, then rapidly increases to a maximum by tree age 10, and then declines. However, when conditions are unfavorable for spore development or movement, few infections may occur regardless of

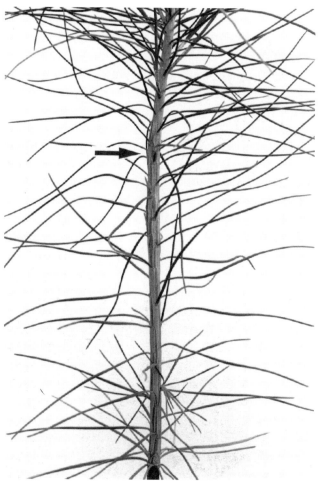

Figure 10-4—Slight swelling and epidermal discoloration (gall) from fusiform rust on a young, tender shoot of loblolly pine. Various patterns of red pigmentation predominate. The **arrow** points to the pigmented spot on the slight swelling.

Figure 10-5—Typical fusiform rust branch gall (USDA Forest Service Collection, National Agricultural Library).

tree size or susceptibility. Infection rates increase again with the return of environmental conditions that favor spore development (Wells and Dinus 1978). A tree may have from one to several dozen galls. Larger trees may have more galls than smaller trees of the same age; the larger trees have more succulent tissue (Barber and Van-Haverbeke 1961). However, rapid height growth of trees does not result in faster expression of rust symptoms (Kuhlman 1978), and tall trees, with their greater vigor, are more likely to survive an infection than their shorter neighbors. Although any tree can be infected, resistant trees survive by resisting the spread of the infection. Trees that are infected at an older age have a better chance of surviving to economic maturity than trees that are infected at a young age (Shoulders and Nance 1987). As host tissue is killed, older galls may become flat or somewhat depressed. Galls often girdle and seriously weaken trees, so wind breakage at the gall may occur. Stem infections seriously degrade tree value. The primary causes of gall death include natural pruning of shaded and galled branches as canopies close in young stands (Kuhlman 1981) and the breaking of main boles at infection sites.

Gall tissue has a higher lignin content and higher yields of turpentine and extractives, but lower burst and breaking strength than rust-free wood (Veal and others 1974). It generally has higher specific gravity than normal wood because it contains 3 to 4 times as much extractives as normal wood contains. Specific gravity is highest where the diameter of the gall is largest. Tannin accumulates in actively growing galls, apparently as a response to development of the pathogen (Walkinshaw 1978). Cytokinin activity is greater in galls than in healthy tissue of loblolly pine seedlings, suggesting that these compounds are important in gall formation (Rowan 1970a, 1970b). It has been estimated that stands lightly infected with fusiform rust yield 1% less pulp/ha than uninfected stands and that heavily infected stands yield 3% less pulp/ha than uninfected stands. It takes slightly more chemical to pulp infected wood by the kraft process than to pulp uninfected wood (Blair and Cowling 1974, Franklin 1975).

Associated insects and fungi.   Insects attack about half the gall tissue by the time trees are age 6 and almost 100% of the gall tissue by the time trees are age 15. Common gall invaders are a chalcid wasp, *Eurytoma sciromatis* Bugbee; the deodar weevil, *Pissodes nemorensis* Germar; and southern pine coneworm, *Dioryctria amatella* (Hulst). Insect galleries serve as infection courts for various opportunistic basidiomycetes; bluestain fungi, *Ceratocystis* spp.; and imperfect fungi (Myren 1964).

Fusiform rust resistance.   The factors that contribute to rust resistance are (1) regional and family differences in loblolly pine, (2) variability of the rust

pathogen, and (3) growth rate or area of potential infection (faster growth of pines means more new tissue for infection). Loblolly pines from different regions show great variability in rust resistance when outplanted on sites of high rust hazard. For example, trees from Livingston Parish, Louisiana, have only one-half to one-tenth as much rust infection when planted in many high-hazard areas of the Southeast as do trees native to these high-hazard areas. Loblolly pines from west of the Mississippi River are also more resistant than those from east of the river (Grigsby 1973; Pait and others 1985; Powers 1986; Wells 1966, 1985; Wells and Wakeley 1966). To date, rust-resistant Livingston Parish loblolly pines have been planted successfully on more than 120,000 ha of high-hazard sites. It is probable that widespread planting of resistant loblolly in areas where rust incidence is high can protect against early infection and significantly suppress rust (Schmidt and others 1986, Wells and Dinus 1978).

Although regional differences in susceptibility to rust seem to be most obvious, there can be significant genetic variation in rust resistance among families within a region or even within a stand. Even the most resistant families from Livingston Parish or other areas may be highly susceptible to rust inoculum from one or more sources (Powers and others 1977). This suggests that phenotypic selection in heavily infected stands can be used to find trees with resistant genes (Kinloch and Zoerb 1971). For example, offspring of gall-free parents selected at random from a natural stand in south Georgia had infection rates ranging from 18 to 100% (Kinloch and Stonecypher 1969).

Genetically distinct families growing at equal rates may differ markedly in susceptibility to rust. Thus, the size of the potential infection court is not the only factor determining susceptibility or resistance (Rowan 1977a). Loblolly pine saplings that have low concentrations of beta-phellandrene in the branch cortex seem to be more resistant to rust infection than trees with high concentrations of beta-phellandrene (Rockwood 1973). Conversely, slash pines with high concentrations of beta-phellandrene are more resistant to rust (Rockwood 1974). In some cases, infected trees resist the disease by confining the fungus to a small area of cortical cells, leaving only a small gall walled off by healthy xylem (Miller and Powers 1973, Snow and others 1963).

Round galls may indicate resistance to the rust pathogen (Snow 1987). Galls longer than 25 mm seem to be more common than shorter galls in 9-month-old seedlings of resistant families. Round galls form on some resistant families, whereas short galls occur on other resistant families (Kuhlman and Powers 1988). The most desirable resistant tree is obviously one that has no galls. However, the development of trees that form a few round galls may be the most realistic goal for tree breeders. Shortleaf pines typically form a few round galls, and the species is thought to have evolved to a balance with the pathogen (Snow 1985). A similar balance may be developing in resistant populations of loblolly pine, in which there is a high frequency of trees without galls and in which many of the galls that do form tend to be round.

There is significant variability within the fusiform rust fungus. Inocula derived from resistant loblolly pine families may be more virulent than those derived from woods-run trees (Powers and others 1977, 1978). Although there was no significant difference in rust virulence for collections made 25 years apart on the same trees, virulence was more variable in younger sources than in older sources (Powers and Dwinell 1978). Because the level of fusiform rust virulence varies, care must be taken to minimize selection for more virulent strains of the fungus when selecting resistant strains of loblolly pine (van Buijtenen 1982).

Resistance screening.   Greenhouse screening of 4- to 8-week-old seedlings is the most widespread technique for determining rust resistance. It is a reliable and cost-effective method for identifying resistant loblolly pines. However, inoculating such young trees may result in heavy infection that largely obscures genetic differences (Carson and Young 1987, Skoller and others 1983, Wells and Dinus 1974). Artificial inoculation with a concentrated basidiospore spray makes possible rapid evaluation of many families in the greenhouse with close correlation to field tests (Matthews and Rowan 1972, Matthews and others 1978). Resistance screening must be done carefully because even resistant sources become more susceptible as the amount of inoculum increases (Schmidt and others 1986).

Laboratory screening assays for disease resistance may eventually be practical. There is an indication that isozyme differences in pollen can be used to determine rust resistance or susceptibility (Powers and others 1986). Responses of loblolly pine embryos to infection have been noted as early as 36 hours after inoculation, suggesting that *in vitro* assay is possible (Gray and Amerson 1983, Spaine and others 1985). Progeny testing can also be used to screen for resistance, but it takes longer and is more costly (Redmond and Anderson 1986).

Breeding for rust resistance.   From as few as 2% to more than 95% of the progenies of loblolly pine can be free of fusiform rust, depending on seed source and planting site. Open-pollinated progenies from Crossett, Arkansas, were totally free of rust after 10 years on a Georgia site (Sluder 1973). Powers (1985) found that families originating in South Carolina tended to be more severely infected by rust found in that state than by rust from anywhere else.

Breeding can increase resistance substantially without adversely affecting growth (Foster and Anderson 1989, Kuhlman and Powers 1988, Miller and Matthews 1988, Powers and Duncan 1976). In both clonal and seedling seed orchards, fewer than 10% of seedlings in families selected for rust resistance had rust infection after exposure to 3 years of natural infection, and height growth of seedlings in resistant families was not reduced (Powers

1981). A study in central Georgia indicated that family selection for rust resistance should be based on the number of galls per tree rather than on percentage of infected trees (Sluder 1989). Variability among progenies of rust-free parents is sufficient to permit additional gain from culling after progeny testing (Dinus 1971). Individual tree histories for second-generation and later selections must be maintained carefully to minimize the influence of trees that became rust-free through natural pruning or other means that do not constitute resistance. Although a considerable effort has gone into breeding loblolly pine for rust resistance, fewer than 30 highly rust-resistant tree selections had been identified by 1989 (Snow G. 1989. Personal communication).

Relative resistance of loblolly and slash pines. Geographical patterns in rust incidence in loblolly and slash pines are generally similar within their overlapping natural ranges, although the high-incidence zone is farther south for slash (Phelps 1977, Squillace 1976). Southwide, the incidence of rust infection is lower for loblolly than for slash pine (Phelps 1974, 1977). In both species, rust incidence is greatest on sites with well- or moderately well-drained soils with loamy sand or sandy loam surface texture and is least on sites with poorly or somewhat poorly drained soils with a sandy surface texture (Schmidt and others 1988). The average number of infections per tree decreases as stand age increases in both species (Goggans 1957).

Rust incidence varies for the two species depending on location and genotype. Rust incidence is highest for both planted loblolly and planted slash pines in Alabama, Georgia, Mississippi, and South Carolina (table 10-4). When loblolly and slash are planted on the same sites within their overlapping natural ranges, the infection rate can be higher for loblolly pine (Schmidtling 1985) or higher for slash pine (Brightwell 1971), or the infection rate can be the same for both species (Hatchell and others 1972). Slash pine generally has a much higher infection rate than loblolly pine at the northern extremity of the natural range of slash pine (in central Georgia) and outside its natural range (Mann and Derr 1970, Schmidt and others 1986, Squillace 1976). Variability in resistance to infection and tolerance to rust once infection occurs seems to be greater for planted loblolly than for planted slash (Shoulders and Nance 1987). Progenies of resistant loblolly are less resistant to rust than are progeny of resistant slash pine (Sluder and Powers 1986).

Resistance in hybrids.   Because both loblolly and slash pines are very susceptible to rust, hybrids between the two species are prone to heavy infection (Dorman 1976). Shortleaf and pitch pines are quite resistant to rust, and loblolly–shortleaf hybrids and loblolly–pitch hybrids are more rust resistant than loblolly pines (Garrett and Trew 1986, Kraus 1986, LaFarge and Kraus 1980, Powers 1985). Even resistant hybrids may show a slight swelling of tissue shortly after infection, but this swelling disap-

Table 10-4—Fusiform rust incidence in 8- to 12-year-old loblolly and slash pine plantations in the South

State	Loblolly pine (%)				Slash pine (%)			
	Healthy	Stem cankers	Branch cankers	Non-merchantable and dead	Healthy	Stem canker	Branch scankers	Non-merchantable and dead
Alabama	60	19	27	4	46	29	33	7
Arkansas	90	3	8	0	NM	NM	NM	NM
Florida	58	17	25	3	83	10	12	2
Georgia	45	31	45	3	39	41	45	5
Louisiana	72	12	20	2	48	25	40	5
Mississippi	67	13	23	3	53	21	32	7
North Carolina	79	9	17	2	65	16	30	2
South Carolina	64	22	37	3	38	38	41	9
Texas	91	9	7	2	70	30	15	5
Virginia	96	2	1	1	—	—	—	—

Source: adapted from Phelps (1977).

NM = not measured. More than 310,000 loblolly pines in more than 1,300 plantations and more than 310,000 slash pines in more than 1,200 plantations were sampled. Percentages of trees do no add to 100% because of category combinations.

pears as stem diameter increases (Garrett and Trew 1986).

Crossing shortleaf with loblolly pine does not increase resistance of the progeny to the form of gall rust, *Cronartium quercuum* (Berk.) Miyabe ex Shirai f. sp. *echinatae* Burdsall & Snow, that infects shortleaf pine (Kraus and others 1982). The greater resistance of loblolly from sources west of the Mississippi River to infection by fusiform rust may be due to introgression of loblolly pine with shortleaf pine (Florence 1973, Hare and Switzer 1969, Henry and Jewell 1963, Powers 1975, Wells and Switzer 1971, Wells and Wakeley 1966). Alternatively, the increased resistance could be the result of selection pressure of the fungus on the host (Snow 1986a).

Relationship of rust infection to surrounding oak vegetation. Variables most closely related to the incidence of fusiform rust on loblolly pines include the kind and abundance of infected oaks and the distance between pines and infected oaks. Water and willow oaks are the most common hosts for the rust fungus. The natural range of water oak is almost identical to that of loblolly pine. Black oak, *Quercus velutina* Lam., and post oak, *Q. stellata* Wangenh., have very low susceptibility to the disease (table 10-5). The incidence of rust infection in loblolly is generally higher when loblolly are planted near willow oak, water oak, or both than when loblolly are planted near most other oak species. In a 10-year-old Mississippi plantation, the incidence of rust decreased from a high of 9 galls/tree on trees located within 25 m of numerous water oaks to a little more than 2 galls/tree on trees located 150 to 200 m from oaks (Snow and others 1986).

Rust management strategies. Rust infection and its subsequent impact on stand development, growth, and yield should be considered when making forest management decisions. Because rust incidence varies both in time and in space, rust control and salvage mea-

sures must be flexible. Computer models can project losses and effects of alternative management schemes based on site index, stocking, geographic location, plantation age, cultural treatment, and other variables. However, in many cases, an initial estimate of rust infection or rust-associated mortality is necessary to project changes in management methods satisfactorily (Borders and Bailey 1986, Lloyd 1983, Moore 1984, Schmidt and others 1979).

Several management techniques can be used to ameliorate the effect of fusiform rust on loblolly pine based on anticipated disease levels. Rust-resistant trees should be used on high-hazard areas (Powers and Kraus 1988, Schmidt and others 1986, Sluder 1988). Seeds can be treated for rust control, and seedlings with obvious galls should be culled. The following other techniques can be used to minimize the effects of rust:

1. Increasing planting density to offset expected mortality.

2. Thinning to salvage potential mortality.

3. Removing nearby oaks to minimize frequency of the alternate host.

4. Substituting more resistant species (such as shortleaf or longleaf pine) for loblolly on areas of high risk.

5. Using natural stand management.

Newly regenerated trees are less susceptible to fusiform rust when growing under a pine overstory than when growing in the open because overtopped seedlings grow slowly, exposing less new tissue to infection and altered environmental conditions. Infection rates are lower when overstory basal area is greater (Rowan and others 1975).

Cultural practices in plantations of juvenile loblolly pine have variable effects on fusiform rust incidence. There are no data indicating that fire changes the incidence of fusiform rust (Lotan and others 1981). Herbaceous weed control may increase infection levels (Kane 1982, Zutter and others 1987), possibly because more succulent growing

Table 10-5—Relative susceptibility of seven oak species to fusiform rust and weights assigned for computing weighted total oak volumes

Species	Ave. no. of telia/cm^2 leaf surface area	Weight, relative to water oak
Water oak (*Quercus nigra* L.)	44.8	1.000
Willow oak (*Q. phellos* L.)	40.0	0.893
Southern red oak (*Q. falcata* Michx.)	14.5	0.324
Northern red oak (*Q. rubra* L.)	12.0	0.268
Laurel oak (*Q. laurifolia* Michx.)	7.2	0.161
Black oak (*Q. velutina* Lam.)	1.5	0.033
Post oak (*Q. stellata* Wangenh.)	0.4	0.009

Source: adapted from Dwinnell (1974) and Squillace and others (1978).

pine tissue is exposed to rust inoculum. Nitrogen (N), phosphorus (P), and potassium (K) fertilizers may increase rust incidence and, on some occasions, increase the number of rust galls per infected tree (Cordell and Filer 1985, Matziris and Zobel 1976, Powers and Rowan 1983). However, fertilizing rust-resistant trees can increase early growth without increasing rust infection (Stone and Powers 1989). Both fertilization and mechanical site preparation seem to increase rust infection in slash pine more than in loblolly pine (Burns and others 1981, May and others 1973, Miller 1972, Pritchett and Smith 1972). When resistant and susceptible populations of loblolly pine are fertilized or cultivated, the resistant populations consistently show less infection than do the susceptible ones (Dinus and Schmidtling 1971, Powers and Rowan 1983). However, even susceptible populations may be unaffected by fertilization (Kane 1981).

Although it should be feasible to prune infected branches to reduce the number of rust infections, such preventive prunings have not been very effective (Enghardt and others 1969). Pruning has been ineffective chiefly because branch infections often reach the stem before pruning and because pruning wounds can be new infection sites (Miller and Matthews 1984). Pruning should not be done during the spring or early summer when basidiospores are likely to be present.

High-value trees—such as those in seed orchards or in urban settings—that are less than 18 cm in dbh and have stem infections that do not completely encircle the stem can often be saved by surgery. The bark and cambium covering and slightly beyond the swollen portion of a stem should be completely removed. The incision should be longer than it is wide and form a V-shape at the bottom and the top to promote healing. Chemical treatments have proven either ineffective or too toxic to be practical (Davis and Luttrell 1967, Matthews and others 1976).

Fusiform rust is particularly damaging to loblolly pines grown on pulpwood rotations during which there are no thinnings or salvage cuts. When rotations are short, the main problem is reduced stocking. Adequately stocked sapling stands have at least 740 disease-free trees/ha. Where rust incidence is expected to exceed 60%, sawtimber rotations may be preferable to short pulpwood rotations. In such cases, 1,235 to 1,480 surviving trees/ha are needed after the first growing season, and regular thinnings are needed to remove diseased trees and concentrate growth on high-quality individuals. By the time a stand reaches minimum merchantability, there should be at least 14 m^2 of basal area/ha of healthy trees to economically manage it through a sawtimber rotation (Anderson and Mistretta 1982, Froelich 1987).

Fusiform rust does not appear to reduce the growth rate of diseased trees that survive to rotation. However, trees that develop stem galls by age 5 have a much higher probability of death in later years than those that are free of cankers (Nance and others 1985). Eighty-five percent of the galls occur on the lower 2.4 m of trees, so there is a large loss of solid wood products. Heavy stem infection in older stands can reduce sawtimber volume by 50% (Geron and Hafley 1988, Webb and Patterson 1984).

Rust-associated mortality is essentially independent of tree size. Given equal exposure to the disease, more large trees than small trees develop stem galls. However, large trees survive stem infections more frequently than do small trees, so cumulative rust-associated mortality is about the same for all size classes.

Rust-associated mortality does not alter the expected diameter distribution in loblolly pine plantations up to 20 years of age. The impact of rust on development of unthinned plantations can be incorporated into existing growth and yield models by including cumulative rust-associated mortality as an independent variable in the survival function (Nance and others 1985).

Sanitation and salvage cutting reduces the number of diseased trees, reduces the loss of merchantable trees, and improves the quality of pole-sized timber. However, preliminary analyses of sanitation and salvage cutting in slash pine plantations indicated that such cutting is of questionable economic value if stands are managed on short pulpwood rotations (Miller and others 1985). The following factors must be evaluated when sanitation and salvage cutting is being considered:

- **The amount of rust**—If fewer than 30% of the loblolly pines in a fully stocked stand are infected, sanitation cutting may not be economical. Fully stocked stands in which more than 60% of the trees are infected should be considered for harvest and regeneration.

- **The condition of the trees**—High-risk trees have one or more galls that more than half encircle the main stem. Such trees are likely to die before rotation age. Moderate-risk trees have one or more galls that encircle less than half the stem, but the location of the gall combined with the size of the gall indicates that tree survival is questionable. Low-risk trees have small galls that do not appear to affect normal tree growth and development (Belanger and others 1985).

- **The probability of associated pest problems**—If sanitation and salvage thinning is likely to increase bark beetles, root diseases, or other pest problems through soil compaction or crop tree injury associated with felling and removal, *no cutting* may be the wisest choice.

Pitch Canker Disease

Pitch canker, *Fusarium moniliforme* Sheld. var. *subglutinans* Wollenw. & Reink. (commonly called *Fusarium subglutinans*), is a fungus that affects loblolly pines from Virginia to east Texas. It causes branch and bole lesions, resinous bleeding, and shoot dieback of the terminal and upper lateral branches of trees from seedling to sawtimber size. Damage is usually confined to the current year's growth. Effects of the disease include stem deformity, reduced growth rate, and occasional mortality. Pitch canker can also result in flower, cone, and seed loss when cone-bearing branches are killed (Blakeslee and others 1980, Dwinell and Barrows-Broaddus 1985). However, cone and seed losses do not always occur, even during epidemic periods (Kuhlman and others 1982). Infected seeds may serve as an inoculum source for damping-off and other diseases in nursery beds. Even when the terminals are only lightly damaged by pitch canker, both height and diameter growth of young planted loblolly trees can be reduced significantly (Kuhlman and Cade 1985).

The fungus attacks parenchyma cells, causing gaps in the cortex, rays, and pith (Barrows-Broaddus and Dwinell 1983). Pitch flows freely from diseased tissue, even on small shoots. The wood beneath cankers becomes discolored and resin soaked (Blakeslee and others 1980). Initially, only a few needle fascicles distal to a lesion die. As the disease develops, more needles turn reddish brown. Once a stem is girdled, all needles distal to the girdle dehydrate and die. Shoot dieback is easily noted in the fall, when fully developed needles turn yellow to reddish brown. Shoot dieback may resume the following spring if one or more of the buds have not been killed by an infection. Expanding buds, unable to obtain water through the girdled stem, quickly wilt and rapidly change from green to brown (Dwinell and others 1977). Cankers are annual on small-diameter shoots and perennial on larger shoots.

Because pitch canker spores are abundant in the air, on dead branches, and on wounded tissue, no vector is necessary for this disease to spread. Branches are susceptible throughout the year, but susceptibility is lower in the spring and summer than in the fall and winter (Kuhlman and others 1982). Susceptibility to infection is not limited to new tissue. In older tissues, wounds caused by insects, diseases, or weather-related injuries seem to be necessary for infection. The fungus can develop in wounds up to 3 weeks old, but the older the wound, the lower the chance of dieback. On 1- to 2-year-old seedlings, dieback ranged from 88% for infections in fresh wounds to 50, 32, and 20% for wounds 1, 2, and 3 weeks old, respectively (Kuhlman 1987). The pitch canker fungus can rapidly colonize fusiform rust-infected tissue. There is no correlation between fusiform rust resistance and pitch canker susceptibility (Dwinell and Barrows-Broaddus 1985). Tip moth larvae and pupae harbor the pitch canker fungus internally and externally, and tip moth infestations probably promote the spread of pitch canker (Runion and Bruck 1985). The addition of NPK fertilizers appears to favor canker development (Fraedrich and Witcher 1982, Solel and Bruck 1989, Wilkinson and others 1977). Soil-applied systemic insecticides (such as phorate or thiabendazole) may control the disease (Runion and Bruck 1988, Wilkinson and others 1977).

Fusarium equiseti (Corda) Sacc. is also pathogenic to loblolly pine if it enters a wound. Low infectivity of mature branches makes this species an unlikely threat to loblolly stands (Solel and others 1988).

The level of *Fusarium* infection in loblolly pine seeds can be rapidly determined by crushing representative seeds on blue filter paper in a plastic tray, spraying the seeds and paper with a liquid medium semiselective for *Fusarium* spp., incubating the specimens for about 14 days at 20 °C, and microscopically examining for the diagnostic polyphialides (Anderson 1986).

Annosum Root Rot

Annosum root rot is a major fungal disease of loblolly and other southern pines. Eastern redcedar, which grows intermixed with and underneath loblolly in many areas, is also highly susceptible to the pathogen (Howell and Stambaugh 1972). The fungus decays roots, often killing them. Trees that survive grow more slowly and are susceptible to windthrow and bark beetle attacks. Once the disease becomes established in the roots of one tree, all nearby trees, whether dominant or suppressed, are subject to attack and death. Trees are usually killed in small groups as the disease spreads out from an infection center (figure 10-6). The disease is most

Figure 10-6—A group of loblolly pines killed by annosum root rot.

damaging to stands growing on sandy soils with low organic matter. These high-hazard sites occur in all states from Virginia to Florida to Texas (figure 10-7). There are no known loblolly seed sources resistant to annosum root rot (Kuhlman 1972).

Some infected loblolly pines die quickly with no apparent visual symptoms of annosum root rot. Most, however, show signs of decline (shortened needles and internodes, yellowish needles, and often a heavy crop of cones) for one or more years before dying. As the fungus grows in the wood, incipient decay may show up as pink to violet stains. Infected roots then become resin soaked and brownish red. More advanced decay includes narrow, elongated, white pockets and scattered black flecks. Yellow stringy rot occurs during the latest stages of decay (USDA FS 1985). Trees killed by annosum root rot often look water soaked as a result of excretion of resin (Froelich and others 1977).

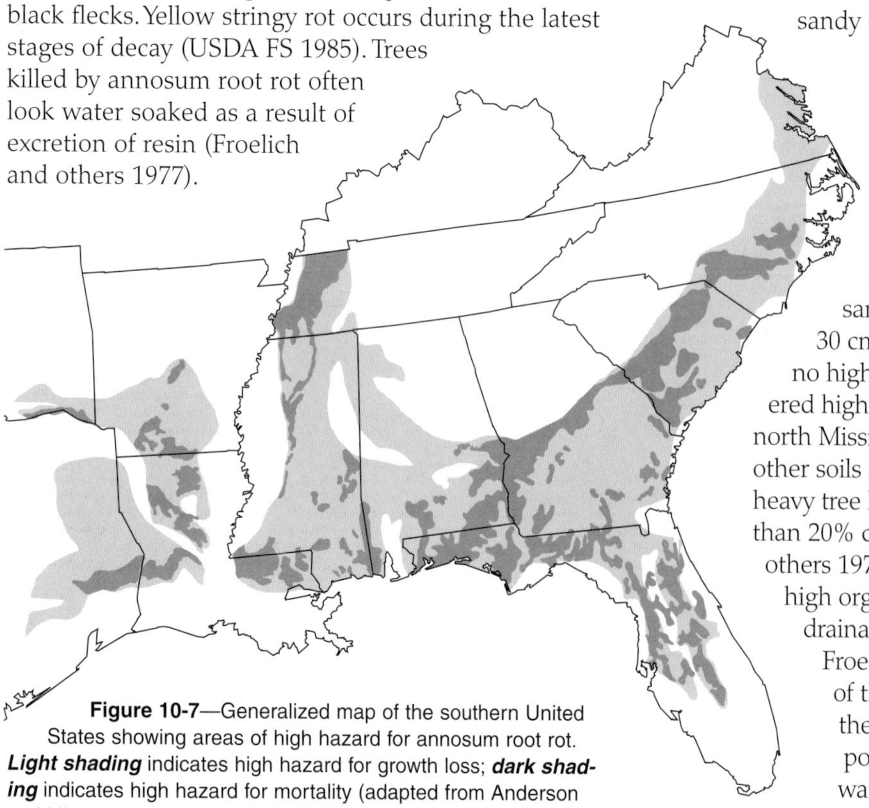

Figure 10-7—Generalized map of the southern United States showing areas of high hazard for annosum root rot. **Light shading** indicates high hazard for growth loss; **dark shading** indicates high hazard for mortality (adapted from Anderson and Mistretta 1982).

Life cycle. The annosum fungus produces fruiting bodies, which are called conks. Conks are normally attached to the bark of trees at the root collar and may not be visible unless the surface litter is brushed away. Conks have light gray to dark grayish brown upper surfaces and creamy-white undersurfaces that darken with age. They are irregular in shape and can range from single sporophores 0.3 cm in diameter to groups of brackets each 5 or more centimeters in diameter. Conks are perennial, but they can dry up and deteriorate during the hot summer months, giving them the appearance of being annual (Robbins 1984).

Basidiospores, which are produced in small pores on the undersurface of conks, are distributed by wind. Wind is the primary mechanism by which the disease is spread

over long distances. Spores germinate readily on the surface of fresh stumps, producing mycelia that colonize the stumps. A stump surface is highly susceptible to infection by *Heterobasidion annosum* for at least 12 days after a tree is cut in winter (Ross 1968). In newly thinned areas, the fungus grows through stump roots and into roots of adjacent living trees at points of root grafting or root contact, or even when roots are up to 0.3 cm apart (Towers 1964).

Insects like the black turpentine beetle, *Dendroctonus terebrans* (Olivier), can act as a vector for *Heterobasidion annosum* (Himes and Skelly 1972). Spores can also be washed through the soil by rain and then infect damaged roots. Conidiospores can be washed to depths of 9.5 cm in undisturbed loamy sand and 0.5 cm in sandy clay loam (Alexander and others 1975).

Hazard rating. Trees on some sites are killed more frequently than those on other sites even when rates of stump infection are equally high. The best way to determine the hazard rating of a site for *H. annosum* is by examining the soil carefully. Sites with sandy, silty, or sandy–loam soil (65% or more sand) at least 30 cm deep with good internal drainage and no high seasonal water table should be considered high-hazard sites. The thick loess soils of north Mississippi are also high-hazard sites. Most other soils are low hazard; however, moderate to heavy tree losses can occur on some soils with more than 20% clay in the surface 15 cm (Kuhlman and others 1976). Soils of low-hazard sites typically have high organic matter, low pH, and poor internal drainage (Anderson and Mistretta 1982; Froelich and others 1966, 1977). The flatwoods of the Atlantic and Gulf Coastal Plains are the lowest hazard sites because they have poor internal drainage and high seasonal water tables. Because there is great variability in soils and microsites, there can be high-hazard sites within low-hazard areas and vice versa. The number of diseased trees in stands thinned in the fall, winter, or spring is a good indicator of the relative hazard of a site and of the need for preventive measures.

Annosum root rot is easily overlooked in its early stages, and damage is sometimes attributed to bark beetles or other causes. Searching for conks or evaluating increment cores from the root collar zone greatly underestimate root rot incidence in stands. Examination of isolations from suspected roots is the best way to estimate infection levels. Alexander and Skelly (1974) found that isolations from roots revealed that 31.6% of the trees in thinned loblolly pine plantations were infected with *H. annosum*, whereas conks and surface increment cores indicated 2.5 and 10.1% infection levels, respectively. Severity of infection can be estimated within 10% of actual infection when all pine root segments in 20 soil samples distributed throughout an infected stand are examined. Each soil sample should be 0.028 m³ in volume and reach from the soil surface to a depth of 30 cm (Alexander and others 1985).

Heterobasidion annosum occurs more often in loblolly pine plantations than in natural stands. Plantation volume losses to annosum root rot usually average less than 3.0% across the range of loblolly, for both thinned (Applegate 1971; Bradford and others 1978a, 1978b) and unthinned stands (Powers and Verrall 1962). Unthinned plantations located on high-hazard sites in Virginia had an 8.3% infection rate, as compared to a 3.3% infection rate for plantations on low-hazard sites (Webb and others 1981). In high-hazard areas, more than 30% of all plantation trees can be killed by the disease, and stand growth losses can exceed 3 m³/ha/yr (which equals 50% or more of total growth) for at least 7 years after thinning (Hodges 1974, Morris 1970, Powers and Verrall 1962).

Annosum root rot has seldom been a problem in thinned or unthinned natural stands of loblolly pine (Powers and Verrall 1962) probably due to a combination of the following factors. Natural stands are less likely than plantations to occur on high-hazard deep sands. Undisturbed natural sites may have more organic matter in the surface soil and correspondingly more individual organisms and types of organisms competing with *H. annosum*. Spacing is less uniform in natural stands than in plantations, and natural stands are often older than plantations when thinned.

Management options for minimizing annosum root rot. Generally, a stand should be harvested and regenerated if more than 20% of the trees are dead or infected within 5 years after thinning. However, the cut can be delayed a few years if trees are expected to grow into the sawlog class, where value will increase greatly. Clearcutting and regenerating an area with a high level of *H. annosum* does not pose a threat to future regeneration because diseased root systems decay rapidly. Losses of new seedlings planted immediately after final harvesting usually range from 1 to 5% (Froelich and others 1977, Kuhlman 1986).

Summer thinning. Frequent thinnings should be avoided on high-hazard sites. Wide plantation spacing minimizes the need for thinning, especially during short rotations. If thinning is required, heavier than normal removals should be considered so that only one intermediate harvest is necessary. Summer thinning minimizes the incidence of stump top infection at latitudes below 34% N, because few *H. annosum* spores are formed during the hot months of May through August and high temperatures often kill any spores produced during that period (Gooding and others 1966). No disease control is necessary if thinning is done during this period, even on high-hazard sites, except during long periods of heavy rainfall and low temperatures. However, summer thinning is not recommended in areas of high southern

pine beetle (SPB) activity because such thinning aggravates SPB problems (Froelich and others 1977). Above latitude 34% N, summer thinning is less effective in controlling *H. annosum*.

Chemical control. *Heterobasidion annosum* can be controlled in newly thinned stands by sprinkling dry, granular borax liberally over the entire surface of each stump immediately after each tree is cut. An applicator can also be attached to a feller-buncher so that an operator can treat each stump with a borax solution immediately after felling (Lowman 1995). The borax is a chemical barrier to wood-destroying organisms. Ideally, borax should also be applied to logging scars on crop trees. If applied after *H. annosum* has colonized a stump, borax may prevent natural competitors of *H. annosum* from entering the stump and thus may aggravate the disease problem. If used properly, however, borax limits stump surface colonization and is safe to handle, easy to apply in any weather, inexpensive, and not detrimental to the environment. The treatment is generally cost-effective unless losses are expected to be very light without treatment (Hodges 1974, Hokans and others 1985). If borax is not applied during the first thinning, applications of borax during subsequent thinnings are usually ineffective.

Prescribed burning. Two prescribed burns before thinning, one within 6 months before thinning, and one post-thinning burn may reduce *H. annosum* infection. Post-thinning burns alone are not recommended. The burns reduce spore levels by destroying litter under which most conks develop. The beneficial effects of fire are greatest where the disease is most serious. Growing legumes following burning does not alter the level of root rot infection. Prescribed burning is less effective than summer thinning or use of borax in reducing the incidence of annosum root rot (Froelich and others 1977, 1978).

Biological control. The fungus *Phlebia gigantea* (Fr.) Donk = *Peniophora gigantea* (Fr.) Massee is an important natural competitor of *H. annosum* in stump roots, even when initial stump infection by *H. annosum* is heavy (Hodges 1964). When sprayed on stumps, *P. gigantea* colonizes rapidly and prevents colonization by *H. annosum*. Application can be by hand or by an applicator attachment to a feller-buncher (Lowman 1995). Use of *P. gigantea* is especially beneficial when *H. annosum* infection is already established (for example, at the time of second thinnings). *Phlebia gigantea* applied under these conditions prevents spreading of the disease (Froelich and others 1977). *Phlebia gigantea* can be applied in water suspension to stump surfaces. When freezing temperatures preclude the use of water suspensions the fungus can be mixed in chain lubricating oil and applied to the stump surface as the chain is cutting the tree (Artman 1972). Natural inoculum levels of *P. gigantea* in a stand can be increased to afford additional protection against stump invasion by *H. annosum* by cutting scattered understory pines several months before a regular thinning (Boyce 1966).

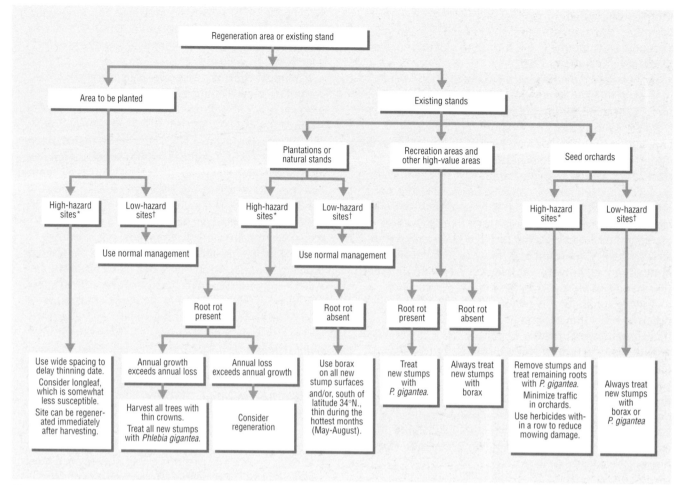

Figure 10-8—Decision key for managing stands with annosum root rot (adapted from Robbins 1984).

* Includes soils with sandy loam textures to a depth of 30 cm or more, without internal drainage or high seasonal water tables.

† Includes all soils with poor internal drainage or high seasonal water tables. Also includes well-drained sites where heavy clay is within 30 cm of the surface.

Although all major southern pines are attacked by *H. annosum*, longleaf pine is the least susceptible and may be a preferable alternative on sandy sites that are high hazards for loblolly pine. Options for managing stands with annosum root rot are summarized in figure 10-8 (Robbins 1984).

Littleleaf Disease

Littleleaf disease results in the gradual killing of feeder roots, followed by crown decline and volume growth loss. It is caused by a complex interaction between parasitic soil fungi (*Phytophthora cinnamomi* Rands and *Pythium* spp.), low soil fertility, poor drainage, and sometimes nematodes. Symptoms begin at about tree age 35 to 40, and affected trees die in 3 to 10 years. Littleleaf disease is a serious problem for shortleaf pine on about 0.6 million ha of Piedmont soils from Virginia to Alabama (Belanger and others 1986, Oak and Tainter 1988). Loblolly pine has replaced shortleaf pine on many sites where the disease is common because loblolly

grows faster and is usually less susceptible to the disease. Unfortunately, loblolly is also adversely affected on high-hazard sites where a rotation of 50 or more years is required for large wood products. A recent survey indicated that maturing loblolly infected with littleleaf disease had only half the wood volume of healthy trees on the same site (Oak 1985).

Littleleaf disease that results in severe tree damage typically occurs on sites having shallow, eroded, clay soils with poor internal drainage. These soils provide the intermittently waterlogged and anaerobic conditions that minimize root regeneration and nutrient and water absorption and provide ideal habitat for fungus spore dispersal and root infection (Fraedrich and Tainter 1989). However, even under the most adverse conditions, loblolly pine roots remain healthier than shortleaf pine roots. At low spore concentrations, about 40 to 80% more spores are needed to infect 50% of a loblolly pine's root tips than are needed for a similar infection of a shortleaf pine. At high spore concentrations, 100% infection occurs for both species (Fraedrich 1985, Fraedrich and others 1989).

Littleleaf disease hazard ratings should be developed for loblolly pine stands growing on long rotations. These ratings should be based on soil series, internal drainage, and presence and age class of susceptible pines. Areas of high hazard should either be ameliorated to increase pine growth or converted to hardwoods. Where site conditions most favor the occurrence of littleleaf disease, loblolly should be managed on a reduced rotation, and frequent cuttings should be made to salvage affected trees. Also, stands should be monitored during SPB outbreaks because disease-weakened trees are preferred hosts for bark beetles (Oak 1985, Oak and Tainter 1988).

Blue-Stain Fungi

Bluestain fungi are pathogenic to loblolly pines. *Ceratocystis minor* (Hedgcock) Hunt is the principal fungus causing blue stain in sapwood. Other fungi causing blue stain include *C. ips* (Rumb.) C. Mor., *C. montia* (Rumb.) Hunt, and *C. pilifera* (Fr.) C. Mor. (Basham 1970). Bark beetles (especially SPB and *Ips* spp.) are important vectors of the fungi; they introduce spores throughout their galleries in the inner phloem of trees. Fungi then colonize the cambium and outer sapwood. Blue-stain fungal growth disrupts normal water movement in the xylem, and disruption of water movement rapidly leads to severe water stress and wilting. Secondary effects include reduced turgor pressure, reduced oleoresin exudation pressure, and drying of the outer bole tissue. Infections by blue-stain fungi predispose host trees to continuous beetle attacks and greatly increase the likelihood of tree death. (This interaction is discussed in the section on the SPB.) Damage from blue-stain fungi is primarily to pole- and sawtimber-sized trees, but seedlings and saplings (especially suppressed individuals) can also be killed (Basham 1970, DeAngelis and others 1986a).

Comandra Blister Rust

Comandra blister rust, caused by the fungus *Cronartium comandrae* Peck, infects loblolly and other southern pines. Its alternate host is an herbaceous plant, false toadflax, *Comandra umbellata* (L.) Nutt. ssp. *umbellata* Piehl. The disease is a problem only in northern Arkansas, eastern Tennessee, and northern Alabama, where the alternate host and loblolly pine grow together naturally, and in plantings north of loblolly's native range. Blister rust was first found on loblolly pine in 1951 in eastern Tennessee and probably was introduced to the area on infected ponderosa pine, *Pinus ponderosa* Laws., planting stock from the West (Cordell and Knighten 1969, Cordell and Wolfe 1969, Matuszewski 1973, Powers and others 1967).

The fungus infects pines through young needles and then grows into the branch and the main stem where it forms a gall. Galls are generally spindle shaped and covered with rough ridges. Spores produced on the surface of a gall in the spring are windblown to comandra plants (false toadflax), where leaves or stems are infected. Within a few weeks, urediospores produced on the

underside of the comandra leaf are disseminated by wind and infect other comandra plants. Telia developed from infections on comandra plants produce spores that are windblown to the loblolly pine host to complete the life cycle of the fungus (USDA FS 1985).

Shortleaf is the pine species most susceptible to this disease, but loblolly pine is very susceptible also. Pitch pine (loblolly hybrids are relatively resistant, as are pitch pine and Virginia pine (Powers 1972). In a loblolly pine plantation, comandra blister rust may be confined to just a few individuals or may infect more than 90% of the trees (Matuszewski 1973). After a tree is infected, the rust gall takes at least 2 years to develop. The tree dies within 1 year after the gall develops (Kauffman and others 1980).

Sweetfern Blister Rust

Sweetfern blister rust, caused by *Cronartium comptoniae* Arth., results in stem galls on young loblolly pines in the northeastern part of the loblolly range. Like fusiform and comandra rusts, sweetfern blister rust requires an alternate host—either sweetfern, *Comptonia peregrina* (L.) Coulter, or sweetgale, *Myrica gale* L.—to complete its life cycle, which takes 2 years under ideal conditions. Infections on young trees are difficult to see, but careful examination can detect either the yellow-orange pustules during spring sporulation or aecial scars during much of the summer. Infected woody tissue usually dies, but not immediately after infection. Infections may appear as depressed streaks on one side of a stem or branch (Artman and Reeder 1977). In one southern New Jersey area, 38% infection was found on 13- to 14-year-old loblolly pines that were planted or grown from seeds (Little 1979).

Most sweetfern blister rust infections occur within 0.6 m of the ground and when sweetfern is within 15 m of a tree. Careful removal of sweetfern from around nursery sites or fungicidal protection of nursery seedlings keeps this disease a minor problem.

Pine Needle Rust

Pine needle rust, caused by *Coleosporium* spp., generally does not damage loblolly pine seriously, but occasionally entire stands are infected. It is most prevalent on young trees and is of greatest concern in nurseries and young plantations. Symptoms include small white-orange blisters on needles (usually lower needles) in the spring. The rust needs an alternate host, such as goldenrod, *Solidago* spp., or aster, *Aster* spp., to propagate itself. Wilson (1961) suggested that ironweed, *Vernonia* spp., was the probable alternate host for *Coleosporium vernoniae* Berk. & Curt. in one severely infected 3-year-old loblolly plantation on a bottomland site in southern Arkansas. Mowing or herbicides can be used to reduce the numbers of the alternate host around high-value areas such as nurseries. No control is needed in forest stands (USDA FS 1985).

Brown-Spot Needle Blight

Brown-spot needle blight, caused by *Mycosphaerella dearnessii* Barr [= *Scirrhia acicola* (Dearn.) Siggers], typically infects longleaf pine seedlings but can also infect needles of loblolly pines of all ages and sizes. Older needles are the most susceptible. When a loblolly pine is infected, there is a severe but limited collapse of mesophyll cells (even with a very limited presence of hyphae). This reaction suggests that a toxin may be produced as the host and pathogen interact. Initially, the needles develop yellow or yellow-brown spots, but they eventually die and turn brown. Dead needles have considerable deterioration of all tissues. The primary adverse effect of this disease is a reduction in shoot growth (Boyce 1952; Jewell 1986; Parris 1967, 1969; Parris and Killebrew 1969).

Needle Cast Fungi

The needles of loblolly pines can be infected and killed by numerous fungi, especially *Lophodermella cerina* (Darker) Darker, *Ploioderma* (= *Hypoderma*) *lethale* (Dearn.) Darker, and *P. hedgcockii* (Dearn.) Darker. These pathogens can infect both new and old needles, causing premature needle shedding and thin, tufted crowns. Fungi generally colonize new needles in the spring or summer, turning them yellow and later, brown. Fruiting bodies formed in the brown needles produce spores that reinfect needles on other trees during wet weather. Needles turn brown from the center to the tip and eventually die. Infection occurs primarily on poletimber and sawtimber trees, but can be found on saplings and even seedlings during severe outbreaks (Snow G. 1989. Personal communication). The loss in photosynthetic area reduces tree growth, but the overall impact is not normally great because these needle pathogens seem to have erratic and localized distributions. However, in the winter of 1970–71, needle cast fungi damaged 22 million ha of southern pine forests along the Atlantic and Gulf Coasts from Georgia and Florida to Texas. Infection was heavy (more than 50% of the crowns were infected) on 0.8 million ha in Mississippi and Alabama (Wolfe and others 1971). Since 1970–71, the blight has recurred each November or December, but damage has been much less severe (Czabator and others 1971, Snow 1986b, USDA FS 1985).

Heart Rot Fungus

Heart rot (commonly called redheart) in loblolly pine is usually caused by *Phellinus pini* (Thore: Fr.) Ames. This disease normally gains entrance to the bole of a tree through branch stubs and on rare occasions through fire-damaged tissue. Slow growth and old age are primary contributors to heart rot (Gruschow and Trousdell 1958). When loblolly pine is grown on rotations of 50 years or less, heart rot is rarely if ever a problem. Trees that grow for more than 70 years can be expected to have gradually increasing amounts of heart rot. Trees with heart rot are used for nesting by the endangered red-cockaded woodpecker and are necessary for that species' survival (see chapter 9).

Other Disease Problems

Loblolly pine is also susceptible to the western gall rust, *Endocronartium harknessii* (J.P. Moore) Y. Hiratsuka, which is distributed throughout the northern part of North America. Plantations of Scotch pine, *Pinus sylvestris* L., as far south as Maryland may already have provided an infection bridge to loblolly (Merrill 1972). The fungus *Fusarium equiseti* (Corda) Sacc. is pathogenic to loblolly seedlings, but not to older trees (Solel and others 1988).

Insect Pests of Loblolly Pine

Loblolly pine is subject to damage by a number of insects during its life cycle (table 10-6). The primary insect problems are pine bark beetles, which account for more than 95% of the total economic loss caused by forest insects. Pales weevil causes the greatest damage to seedlings, and pine tip moths cause the most damage to saplings. Insect problems in nurseries are discussed in a later section.

Southern Pine Beetle

The southern pine beetle (SPB), the black turpentine beetle, and engraver beetles, *Ips* spp., are included in the category of pine bark beetles. Southern pine beetles are the single-most destructive insect pest of loblolly pines, causing the death of several thousand hectares of mature forests annually. Beetles can occur in any stand older than age 5 (Cameron and Billings 1988). There are endemic populations in most stands of pole-sized and larger loblolly pine throughout the species range. Beetles tend to disperse during the spring, enlarge existing infestations in the summer, and disperse again in the fall. By winter, the populations are often scattered throughout the forest in single-tree or small spot infestations (Payne 1980). Epidemic SPB populations usually occur somewhere in loblolly pine's range almost every year. Across the South, approximately 17 million m³ of pine timber (mostly loblolly pine) valued at $225 million were destroyed by SPB's between 1960 and 1978.

In 1985, SPB's destroyed more than $49 million worth of timber in Texas (Flamm and others 1988).

Host selection and tree susceptibility. Host selection is made by females that fly from the bole of one pine to another. They can fly up to 2.6 km to new hosts but normally travel much shorter distances (Kinn 1986). Initial attack on a tree by pioneer beetles is not understood but must involve discrimination between host and nonhost species and possibly between resistant and susceptible trees. Colonization is regulated by a combination of host-produced volatiles and insect-produced pheromones. Male beetles produce compounds such as endo-brevicomin and verbenone that subsequently mask the attractive odors of females to prevent overcrowding of adults on a tree (Payne 1980).

High stand density or tree overmaturity is commonly associated with initial attacks by SPB's. Lorio (1978) found that 85% of all infestations occurred in stands that were 35 years old and older on good to excellent sites but with declining tree growth. Excessive crowding of trees results in small crowns and slow growth, as well as limited synthesis and flow of oleoresin, which provide conditions favorable for successful bark beetle attack (Lorio 1986). Older, slower growing trees tend to be more susceptible to SPB attack at least partially because radial resin duct formation is slower in older trees. The resin-producing system is a primary defense against SPB's (DeAngelis and others 1986b). Trees also become more susceptible to beetle colonization when moisture stressed, and mortality can be expected to increase in stressed trees (Paine and others 1988a). Beetles are especially attracted to trees that are damaged by lightning,

wind, or ice, or that are weakened by other insects or diseases (Lorio 1978). As much as 50% of the beetle infestations are associated with trees damaged by summer lightning storms (Thatcher and Conner 1985). Drought or excess moisture over an extended period can also promote major outbreaks of the SPB. During periods of severe moisture stress, oleoresin flow is reduced, permitting egg laying and rapid larval development (Lorio and Hodges 1977). Under both endemic and epidemic conditions, attacks by a large number of beetles can overcome even a healthy tree. Once trees are killed, nutrients (especially N, P, and K) leach rapidly from both needles and bark (Williams and others 1989).

Close tree spacing favors successful SPB colonization of trees on the periphery of existing SPB infestations. New trees are usually colonized by SPB's along active fronts at points of highest tree density (Schowalter and others 1981) because pheromones from new tree colonization provide a continuous focal point for attracting beetles emerging from recently attacked neighboring trees. Distance is less critical in large SPB infestations than in small infestations because many new trees are attacked each day and multiple pheromone sources are available (Johnson and Coster 1978). As beetles bore through the bark to the cambium, they release pheromones that attract other beetles from the same or nearby infestations. Attacks typically occur about mid-stem, with 320 to 375 beetles/m^2 of bark. Subsequent attacks occur above and below this area until there is no more room, and late-arriving beetles are forced to attack nearby pines. Paine and Stephen (1987c) report that tree response to attacks is the same throughout the bole, indicating that the tendency of beetles to attack first at

Table 10-6—Insect pests of loblolly pine in forest situations and tree growth stages affected

Common and scientific name	Primary growth stage(s) affected				Common and scientific name	Primary growth stage(s) affected			
	Seedling	Sapling	Pole	Sawtimber		Seedling	Sapling	Pole	Sawtimber
Black turpentine beetle *Dendroctonus terebrans* (Olivier)			■	■	Pine sawflies *Neodiprion* spp.	■	■	■	■
Cinaran aphids *Cinara* spp.	■	■	■	■	Pine webworm *Tetralopha robustella* Zeller	■			
Deodar weevil *Pissodes nemorensis* Germar		■	■	■	Pitch blister moth *Retinia taedana* (Miller)		■	■	■
Geometrids *Nepytia semiclusaria* (Walker) and *Lambdina pellucidaria* (Grote and Robinson)		■	■	■	Pitch-eating weevil *Pachylobius picivorus* (Germar)	■			
Gypsy moth *Lymantria dispar* (L.)		■	■	■	Pitch pine tip moth *Rhyacionia rigidana* (Fernald)	■	■		
Ips engraver beetles *Ips.* spp.			■	■	Southern pine beetle *Dendroctonus frontalis* Zimmermann			■	■
Nantucket pine tip moth *Rhyacionia frustrana* (Comstock)	■	■			Speckled pine needle aphid *Essigella pini* Wilson	■	■	■	■
Pales weevil *Hylobius pales* (Herbst)	■				Subtropical pine tip moth *Rhyacionia subtropica* Miller	■	■		
Pine colaspis *Colaspis pini* Barber			■	■	Texas leafcutting ant *Atta texana* (Buckley)	■	■		
Pine needle sheath midge *Contarinia acuta* Gagni		■	■	■	White grubs *Phyllophaga* spp.	■			

Source: adapted from USDA FS (1985).

Figure 10-9—Southern pine beetle gallery development in the phloem of loblolly pine.

midstem is related to factors other than induced host defense. One factor controlling the attack site may be the number of phoretic mites carried on the body of a beetle. Large numbers of mites can hamper the flight of a beetle and influence the distance it can fly and the height at which it arrives at a host tree (Kinn and Witcosky 1978).

Life cycle. The SPB undergoes a complete metamorphosis consisting of egg, larval, pupal, and adult stages. Adults are cylindrical and somewhat stout to elongated, reddish brown, and about the size of a grain of rice. Eggs are opaque, pearly white, and shiny; slightly oblong to oval with rounded ends; and measure about 1.5 mm long by 1.0 mm wide. Larvae are subcylindrical, wrinkled, legless, and have 3 thoracic and 10 abdominal segments. They are yellowish white and about 2.0 mm long at emergence. Mature larvae are 5.0 to 7.0 mm long and have essentially straight bodies and reddish heads. Pupae are yellowish white, 3.0 to 4.0 mm long, and shaped like adults, but have wing pads and legs folded beneath the body.

Duration of a complete generation (from egg to adult) ranges from about 30 to 54 days, depending on the season of the year. Cycles are slowest during winter. Larvae generally emerge within 2 to 11 days after eggs are laid if the temperature is from 15 to 30 °C. Eggs may take 30 or

more days to hatch at temperatures as low as 10 °C. Larvae feed on the inner bark for a short distance (figure 10-9) before boring into the corky outer bark where they pupate (Payne 1980). The pupal stage lasts 5 to 17 days if the temperature is between 15 and 30 °C (Payne 1980; Thatcher 1960, 1967). Young adults chew individual exit holes through the bark, then fly to nearby trees or disperse into the surrounding forest to initiate new infestations. There may be as few as 3 generations/year in the northern part of the range of loblolly pine and more than seven at the southern extreme. Thus, a sparse population can increase to epidemic proportions in a single favorable year. The SPB can have different genetic population structures even within a localized area (Roberds and others 1987).

After mating, female beetles construct S-shaped egg galleries in the inner bark and deposit eggs in individual niches on either side of the galleries. The winding galleries frequently cross each other and girdle a tree. After depositing eggs, the adults frequently reemerge and attack other trees. Typically, a tree must die before the various brood stages develop (Coulson 1980). However, fall- and winter-infested trees can produce broods before a tree dies, and new attacks can occur even after broods are in the late larval, pupal, or callow-adult stage.

Risk rating. Identification of stands at high risk for SPB's is critical to good forest management. High-risk stands in Louisiana and Texas may have 25 to 32 infestations/1,000 ha, which is 4 to 5 times as many infestations as in low-risk stands (Lorio and others 1982).

The probability of beetle infestation increases as site index, stand age, tree size, amount of understory vegetation, and stand damage (from lightning, wind, logging, etc.) increase and as hardwood basal area, pine bark thickness, and soil pH decrease (Hedden and Belanger 1985, Hedden and Lorio 1985, Ku and others 1980, Kushmaul and others 1979). Routine forest inventory data (species composition, stand condition class, size class, and site index) and soil mapping, which indicates landform, soil texture, and water regime class, can be used to predict stand susceptibility to SPB attack (Lorio and Sommers 1985; table 10-7). Historical records and data easily obtained from aerial photos may be all that is needed to

Table 10-7—Characteristics of natural pine stands susceptible to southern pine beetles in the southern Coastal Plain and Piedmont

Southern Coastal Plain	Piedmont
Dense stocking	Well-stocked stands
Large proportion of sawtimber	Small sawtimber
Declining radial growth	Slow radial growth during last 10 years
Poorly-drained solids and low-lying areas	More than 27% clay in surface and subsurface soils
High percentage of shortleaf and/or loblolly pine in the stand	Slopes exceed 10%
	More than 50% shortleaf pine in the stand

Source: adapted from Belanger and Malac (1980) and Belanger and others (1986).

determine hazard rating (DeMars and others 1982, Mason and Bryant 1984). It may also be possible to predict beetle infestation trends with pheromone traps (Billings 1988).

Numerous hazard- or risk-rating systems have been developed, and most are based on combinations of variables. The variables usually include pine basal area or other estimates of stand density or vigor (for example, recent tree growth, live crown ratio, tree height, and number of trees per hectare), site disturbance, soil type and landform, and hardwood basal area if appropriate (Hedden and Lorio 1985, Hicks and others 1980, Ku and others 1980, Kushmaul and others 1979, Lorio 1978, Mason and others 1981, Sader and Miller 1976, Zarnoch and others 1984). Prediction models can simulate the effects of environmental conditions, parasites, and predators on SPB spot growth expansion (Feldman and others 1980, Stephen and Lih 1985). Beetle-caused damage on a stand basis can also be modeled (Hedden 1985).

Tree defense mechanisms. The tree's first defense against beetle attack is its bark—the thicker the bark, the more energy a beetle must expend to penetrate to the cambium. If a beetle penetrates the bark, it severs canals in the phloem, releasing preformed oleoresin. Loblolly pines have both quantitative and qualitative defense mechanisms in their oleoresin systems that help ward off beetle attacks by cleansing wounds and containing infestations. Resistance to attack is strongly related to physical properties of the oleoresin and can be predicted by measuring these properties (Hodges and others 1977, 1979). High oleoresin flow (in both amount and duration) increases resistance to SPB's. Trees with oleoresin flow in excess of 0.20 ml/hr are able to resist beetle attacks better than trees with very low flow rates. Oleoresin combats beetles by flowing into tunnels that are being excavated, where it can entomb boring beetles, force them out, or inhibit beetle brood development. Other physical characteristics of oleoresin, such as viscosity and rate of crystallization, can also be important in this process. Viscosity, total flow, and probably rate of crystallization of oleoresin are under strong genetic control in loblolly pine. The wide tree-to-tree variation in these properties suggests that genetic selection for beetle resistance is feasible (Cook and Hain 1986, Hain and others 1985, Hodges and others 1979).

Qualitative changes in oleoresin composition brought on by conditions, such as moisture stress or insect and fungal damage, may subsequently influence tree susceptibility to attacks by bark beetles and associated fungi (Bridges 1987; Cook and Hain 1985, 1986; Hodges and Lorio 1975). However, the effects of changes in oleoresin composition are not well understood. For example, trees can produce significant amounts of 4-allylanisole in lesion tissue contaminated with mycangial fungi. This chemical, which is not found in preformed oleoresin, inhibits the growth of symbiotic fungi of SPB's and may be an important loblolly pine defense mechanism

against beetle attack (Bridges 1987). High levels of limonene and myrcene may also contribute to host tree resistance because these chemicals are quite toxic to SPB's. Other monoterpenes, such as alpha-pinene, beta-phellandrene, and camphene, may also be toxic to SPB's under some conditions (Cook and Hain 1988, Coyne and Lott 1976, Gollob 1980).

Hain and others (1983) suggest that, if trees are to resist or tolerate an SPB attack, the entire defense response process must be completed with minimum interference from invading organisms because xylem tissue can be rendered nonconductive by the buildup of terpenes and other compounds around lesions. Cook and Hain (1985) found that the size of lesions produced by the loblolly pine's induced defense system increases when either of the fungi *Ceratocystis minor* (Hedgc.) Hunt or *C. minor* var. *barrassii* J. Taylor infect a mechanical wound. Paine and Stephen (1988) postulate that lesions can both limit the growth of fungi during the attack phase of beetle colonization and limit the survival of bark beetle progeny after trees have succumbed.

The time of the year affects the value of the tree's oleoresin defense system. Even very vigorous trees are particularly vulnerable to successful SPB attacks during the spring, when heavy consumption of photosynthates in growth processes limits oleoresin synthesis and yield (Lorio 1986). Also, earlywood does not produce vertical oleoresin ducts, so most of the stored oleoresin is in the previous year's latewood, which is relatively far from where it is needed. Thus, the oleoresin system may not be able to counteract rapid beetle gallery construction during warm spring weather, even though overwintering spots are small and scattered. Strong oleoresin flow in the summer increases tree resistance. Adult beetles are also smallest and have the lowest fat content in summer, so their dispersal capacity is minimized at that time (Hedden and Billings 1977, Lorio 1986, Stephen and Paine 1985). In the fall, decline in oleoresin synthesis and yield favors SPB attack. In the winter, trees have little resistance to beetle attacks, and wounded trees, which form only small lesions, are especially vulnerable. However, environmental conditions are also usually unfavorable for beetle activity in winter (Cook and others 1986, Paine and others 1985b, Stephen and Paine 1985). Trees wounded during the winter can remain focal points for beetle colonization for as long as 150 days (Coulson and others 1986). Trees infested in winter generally remain green two to three times longer than trees infested from March to September. Broods tend to emerge from winter-infested trees after foliage has begun to fall and to emerge from summer-infested trees when the foliage is a fading yellow color (Billings and Kibbe 1978).

Management options for promoting loblolly pine stand resistance. Southern pine beetle infestations typically occur in slow-growing, overstocked loblolly pine stands in which tree vigor and resistance to

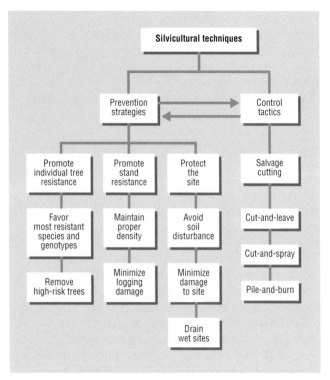

Figure 10-10—Silvicultural guidelines to reduce losses from the southern pine beetle (adapted from Belanger 1981).

attack are low. Appropriate stand management can minimize losses to SPB's (figure 10-10). However, forest management activities must not be aimed just at eliminating losses from this one insect. Managers must consider the effects of treatment for SPB's on other pests.

Favoring most-resistant species. Consideration should be given to regenerating high-hazard Coastal Plain sites to longleaf or slash pine instead of loblolly pine because longleaf and slash are more resistant to SPB's. In the Piedmont, loblolly is more resistant than shortleaf and should be favored on high-hazard sites. Mixed pine–hardwood stands may be more appropriate on some sites because they are more resistant to attack than are monocultures of loblolly.

Removal of high-risk trees. Prescribed burning can eliminate some small, high-risk trees in overstocked stands of young loblolly pine (McNab 1977). Trees with low vigor (primarily trees in overtopped or in intermediate crown classes and with small, thin crowns) should be removed in early harvest cuts. Trees damaged by wind, ice, lightning, or other causes should be removed in salvage or sanitation cuts.

Maintenance of optimum stand density. Trees in dense stands usually grow slowly and produce relatively little oleoresin. Moreover, trees in dense stands—and especially older trees in dense stands—are less likely to survive stressful conditions than are trees in well-spaced stands. Thinning makes more space, water, light, and nutrients available to individual trees, resulting in increases in starch concentrations in phloem, oleoresin exudation pressure, crown development, phloem thick-

ness, and growth of leave trees. All of these changes combine to reduce the risk of beetle attack (Brown and others 1987, Matson and others 1987). Changes in soil moisture availability on an upland site in southeastern Tennessee accounted for 34% of the short-term summer fluctuation in mean oleoresin exudation flow in a 12-year-old plantation of loblolly pine (Mason 1971).

Although few loblolly pine stands would be thinned just to prevent or reduce SPB losses, the knowledge of how stand density affects potential risk is important in establishing intermediate and final harvest schedules. Stand basal area should generally be kept below 23 m²/ha. However, the actual amount of basal area that can be grown safely depends on site quality (Belanger 1980, Hicks and others 1979, Nebeker and others 1985). For greatest effectiveness, thinning should take place in winter, when beetles are least active. Heavy thinning should be avoided in areas where stands are subject to severe wind, snow, or ice damage. Special precautions must be taken when thinning is conducted in stands where annosum root rot hazard is high.

Root pruning is more likely to increase tree susceptibility to beetle attack than is stem pruning; root pruning decreases oleoresin flow, whereas bole scarring stimulates oleoresin flow for a few months (Blanche and others 1985b).

Regulation of age–class structure. Southern pine beetles are most destructive in large stands of trees that are uniform in size. Stands of overmature, slow-growing trees are especially susceptible and should be harvested and the areas regenerated. Overmature stands kept for ecological study, wildlife, or esthetic purposes must be watched carefully, and host trees must be removed before epidemic populations destroy them and spread to surrounding areas. Surrounding older stands with young ones of various age classes can help isolate beetle attacks because seedlings and saplings are attacked much less often than older trees (Lorio 1978).

Modification of sites or competition. Loblolly pines growing in low areas that are flooded frequently can be attractive to beetles (Lorio and others 1972). In such areas, new trees should be planted on spots with higher microrelief, or sites should be bedded or drained so that trees grow vigorously and can withstand beetle attacks. Some soil conditions (for example, spodic layers that limit rooting, low fertility, or low pH) can also make trees more susceptible to SPB attack by reducing vigor. Site preparation, fertilization, or alternative species management may be required on these areas. Soil compaction should be avoided at all costs. Fertilized loblolly pine stands have not exhibited increased resistance to SPB's (Haines and others 1976, Moore and Layman 1978). However, it seems reasonable that if fertilization improves tree health and vigor, then fertilization should reduce the effects of SPB's. Because fertilization can increase pitch canker problems (see earlier discussion), treatments must be applied prudently.

Physical control of outbreaks. Damage to leave trees and to the site can be minimized by selecting appropriate harvesting systems and by planning skid trails carefully. Haphazard felling, tree-length logging, and careless operation of logging equipment tend to injure both aboveground and belowground portions of leave trees, making the leave trees more susceptible to attack by SPB's. Rapid salvage and utilization of infested trees and piling and burning of infested wood can control beetle outbreaks. Cutting and leaving infested trees on the ground may reduce brood emergence, as compared with leaving infested trees standing. However, results of this practice seem to vary greatly and may vary with the season of felling and with the condition of felled trees (Hertel and Wallace 1983, Hodges and Thatcher 1976, Palmer and Coster 1978). Southern pine beetles may attack, colonize, and reproduce in green felled trees or decked logs. When this occurs, most galleries are on the sides and bottom of the trees or logs (Moser and others 1987). Such beetle behavior can significantly reduce the usefulness of cut-and-leave buffer strips.

Salvage cutting is especially effective and economical when large infestations are treated. Usually, uninfected trees around the active head of an infestation are marked as a buffer strip. The buffer can range from 3 to 30 m in width depending on the stage of brood development, stand density, and number of newly attacked and brood-producing trees (Billings and Pase 1979). Harvesting should be done immediately, with the removal sequence depending on the season of the year. In May to October, buffer zone trees should be removed first, then freshly attacked trees, and finally trees with living SPB broods. This sequence reduces the spreading of a spot. During the remainder of the year, the sequence should be reversed to reduce spot proliferation (Belanger and others 1983).

Most small infestations of SPB's do not continue to expand, and spots of 10 or fewer trees should be given low priority for control and salvage during outbreaks (Lorio 1984). However, trees killed in sawtimber stands are usually the largest and most valuable individuals. If many such trees are present, it may be appropriate to give high priority to control and salvage operations in endemic years to capture this valuable resource (Lorio 1984).

Chemical control of outbreaks. The success of chemical pest control treatments varies. Chemical treatments are generally ecologically unsatisfactory because the conditions responsible for the problem or problems are left largely unchanged. However, some preventive or remedial insecticide sprays can be used to protect high-value trees. Pine oil-based chemicals have shown some repellency to SPB's but are ineffective in preventing attacks by *Ips grandicollis* and black turpentine beetles (Berisford and others 1986). Application of materials containing endo-brevicomin and verbenone (which are excreted naturally by male beetles) to the boles of trees may control beetle population growth on newly infected trees. Beetles from a specific geographic region seem to be most responsive to pheromones produced by other beetles from the same region. Aerial application of behav-

ioral chemicals may ultimately become a feasible means of preventing the spread of SPB's (Berisford and Payne 1988, Billings 1987). Because registration requirements change frequently, local regulatory agencies should be consulted before chemical control strategies are planned.

Biological control of outbreaks. Moore (1972) found that biological agents such as insects, birds, mites, diseases, and nematodes killed an average of 24% of each SPB brood in loblolly pine trees growing in the Piedmont of North Carolina. The most effective parasites were the hymenopterous insects *Roptrocerus xylophagorum* Ratzeburg and *Coleoides pissodes* Ashmead. The most effective predators included woodpeckers; the clerid, *Thanasimus dubius* (F.); and the anthocorid, *Scoloposcelis mississippensis* Drake & Harris. Downy woodpeckers, *Picoides pubescens* (Gmelin); hairy woodpeckers, *P. villosus* (L.); and pileated woodpeckers, *Dryocopus pileatus* (L.) all exploit beetles, especially the later and larger instars and emerging adults, as a food source. Woodpeckers do not fly long distances in search of beetles, so stand conditions favoring nesting and foraging must be maintained near susceptible pine stands. The woodpeckers have their greatest value as a control during periods of low beetle populations. Woodpeckers are an important part of an integrated pest management program. However, once beetle populations reach an epidemic level, the buffering effect of predation by woodpeckers is reduced greatly (Kroll and Fleet 1979, Kroll and others 1980).

Interaction of southern pine beetles with other pathogens. Female SPB's have specialized body structures (mycangia) in which two species of symbiotic fungi are carried. One of the mycangial fungi commonly carried is *Ceratocystis minor* var. *barrasii*, which is thought to aid the beetles in killing trees (Barras and Taylor 1973). Another fungal associate, the principal blue-stain fungus, *C. minor*, is not found in the mycangium but is carried externally by attacking adult beetles and associated phoretic mites (Barras and Taylor 1973, Bridges 1985, Bridges and Moser 1983). The beetle and blue-stain fungus combination is more lethal than beetle invasion alone. Loblolly pines usually produce relatively large bole lesions that are soaked with oleoresin in response to SPB invasion and *C. minor* infection (Paine and others 1985b, 1988b). If it becomes extensive, this plugging of xylem tissue causes a reduction in tree moisture content that can inhibit beetle brood development. Previous exposure to *C. minor* does not seem to reduce a tree's defenses and predispose it to colonization by beetles, nor does it seem to stimulate a tree's defenses to produce a greater response to subsequent infection (Paine and Stephen 1987a, Stephen and Paine 1985).

Unlike infections by *C. minor* and other blue-stain fungi, infections by mycangial fungi stimulate little defense response by trees and cause only small lesions. Mycangial fungi compete with blue-stain fungi and create conditions for optimal beetle development (Bridges and Perry 1985; Paine and others 1985a, 1988b; Paine and Stephen 1987b). Trees that are suppressed and growing slowly react less to infection by mycangial fungi associated with the SPB than do rapidly growing trees in the same stand (Paine and Stephen 1987c).

Loblolly pines that are weakened by annosum root rot are preferred host trees for SPB's (Alexander and others 1981). Similarly, *Ips* spp. beetle attacks on felled loblolly pines are more frequent for trees infested with SPB's than for uninfested ones (Berisford 1974).

Ips Engraver Beetles

Next to southern pine beetles, the southern pine engraver beetles—*Ips avulsus* (Eichhoff), *I. calligraphus* (Germar), and *I. grandicollis* (Eichhoff)—are the insects most destructive to loblolly pines. Engraver beetles are usually most active and the principal tree killers during hot and dry periods in the summer. Logging slash and damaged or weakened trees (especially those struck by lightning) are their normal hosts. However, any factor that places stress on a tree (including careless felling and skidding) creates a risk of attack by one or more of these insects. During droughts, they can successfully attack normally healthy trees. If residual trees are not damaged and cut trees are not left lying in the woods, summer thinning generally does not increase engraver beetle damage in healthy stands (Mason 1969).

Concentration of attacks by engraver beetles varies among trees. Attacks are often confined to the bole within the crown of a tree. This may be partially because engraver beetles usually attack trees after SPB's have become established in the mid- and lower boles, thus limiting the choice of attack sites. Egg densities of both engraver beetles and SPB's are reduced where the two species compete (Flamm and others 1987). Infestations by engraver beetles tend to be localized and of short duration, but their continuous presence results in significant cumulative losses throughout the range of loblolly pine. Losses probably total substantially more than $3 million/year.

Engraver beetles can travel up to 6.4 km in a single flight (Kinn 1986). Male beetles usually initiate attacks on wounded trees in response to olfactory stimuli from the loblolly pine host. However, females frequently initiate attacks also. As with SPB's, a chemical attractant released by pioneer beetles leads to mass attack (All and Anderson 1972, Thatcher and Connor 1985, Werner 1972). Attack success increases as the oleoresin exudation rate of trees decreases. Attacks generally do not succeed where the oleoresin exudation rate from wounds exceeds 0.1 ml/hr (Anderson and Anderson 1968).

Depending on the tree species and environmental conditions, engraver beetle populations can complete their development from egg deposition to adult emer-gence in as little as 18 days, but it usually takes 21 to 40 days during the summer and several months during the winter. From 7 to 12 overlapping generations of beetles can occur in a single year, and populations can increase with great rapidity under favorable conditions (Thatcher and Connor 1985; USDA FS 1972). The sex ratio (male–female) of brood beetles is usually 1:1 but the ratio of attacking adults may range from 1:1 to 1:3. More males are lost when searching for a suitable host than are females when responding to pheromones from an attacked tree (Cook and others 1983, Wagner and others 1988). The actions of engraver beetles and associated fungi within a tree are similar to those of SPB's, but gallery construction and larval anatomy are distinctive. Adults can be distinguished from other bark beetles by their scooped-out posterior with 4 to 6 spines on each side (USDA FS 1985).

Control of engraver beetle infestations is usually impractical because the beetles usually emerge before attacks are detected. Salvage of attacked trees before they deteriorate is usually the only alternative available to a forest manager. Beetle populations can be reduced by rapidly moving logs from the woods and by destroying slash from harvesting or salvage operations (Drake 1974). High-value trees can be protected from attack for 1 year by a single surface spray of lindane (Berisford and Brady 1976).

Black Turpentine Beetle

The black turpentine beetle (BTB) is the largest of the southern pine bark beetles, with adults reaching a length of about 0.85 cm. The life cycle takes from 10 to 16 weeks depending on temperature. Black turpentine beetle attacks are most severe in the Gulf States, where up to four generations of the insect can occur each year (Thatcher and Connor 1985; USDA, FS 1985). The life cycle includes eggs, larvae, pupae, callow adults, and adults. Adult females construct egg galleries in the inner bark of pines. They deposit clusters of eggs in one or several widened areas on either or both sides of the gallery. After eggs hatch, the larvae of one brood, feeding side by side away from the gallery, can kill as much as 0.09 m² of inner bark. When feeding is complete, pupal cells are constructed in and around the area consumed by younger larvae. Brood adults feed beneath the bark and, when mature, bore through the bark to attack other places on the same tree or, more often, to initiate new attacks in surrounding areas.

Adult BTB's usually attack freshly cut stumps or the lower 45 to 120 cm of living trees damaged by logging, fire, lightning, drought, stress, or other beetle attacks. Infestations following thinning can be reduced substantially by minimizing logging injuries to residual trees and by preventing excessive root damage by not harvesting on waterlogged soils. Beetle flights and attacks on new trees occur principally from March through October, peaking in midsummer. In most cases, attacks cease within 5 weeks after the initial attack (Godbee and Franklin 1976). However, attacks on the same tree may continue for up to 1 year, eventually extending from the base of larger roots to 3 m up the bole. On rare occasions, attacks are initiated 4.5 to 6.0 m above the ground, and infestations have been found as high as 16.8 m (Clark 1970, Thatcher and Connor 1985).

Large numbers of loblolly pines can be killed during BTB outbreaks. However, most attacks are sublethal, probably because BTB's do not carry blue-stain fungi into wounded tissue as do SPB's and engraver beetles. Unlike trees infested by SPB's or engraver beetles, standing trees with BTB's may be saved if attacks are detected early. Infected portions of trees must be sprayed with lindane in diesel oil (Feduccia and Mann 1975). Drake (1974) suggested that one can determine whether it is possible to save or salvage a tree by searching for ambrosia beetle (*Platypus* spp.) dust at the tree base (Coulson and Witter 1984). If the tree has not been attacked by ambrosia beetles, there is a good chance of saving it. If ambrosia beetle boring dust is present around two-thirds of the base of a tree, the tree should be cut and removed.

Trunk attacks by southern pine coneworms normally cause only minor damage. However, they can be confused with attacks by BTB's because both induce a copious flow of oleoresin. The pitch tubes formed by BTB's are no larger in diameter than a half-dollar, and gum flow lasts for only a few weeks (Goolsby and others 1972). In contrast, the pitch tubes formed by southern pine coneworms are irregular in shape and size, and gum flows for many months.

Interrelationships of Bark Beetles

Even though any one of the bark beetles can kill loblolly pines, two or more species are typically present in a dying tree. Zones of occupancy may overlap, making it difficult to determine whether SPB's, BTB's, or engraver beetles attacked first or the role of each in killing a tree. Engraver beetle and BTB populations often build up during the later stages of SPB outbreaks and can cause additional mortality in surrounding forest stands. Such attacks on surrounding uninfested trees can disrupt SPB spot growth, forcing these beetles to disperse to other areas (Thatcher and Connor 1985).

Other Beetles

Numerous other beetles, including the southern pine sawyer, *Monochamus titillator* (F.), invade loblolly pines weakened or killed by bark beetles or injured or weakened by other agents. The scolytid twig borer *Pityophthorus pulicarius* Zimmerman infests the terminals of trees damaged by cold weather (Clark 1972). None of these insects adversely affect healthy loblolly pines.

Pine Tip Moths

Three species of tip moths attack loblolly pine. The most common is the Nantucket pine tip moth, *Rhyacionia frustrana* (Comstock), which is prevalent throughout the natural range of loblolly pine (Berisford 1988). Two other species—the pitch pine tip moth, *Rhyacionia rigidana* (Fernald), and the subtropical pine tip moth, *R. subtropica* Miller—occur in the eastern range of loblolly but are less common than the Nantucket pine tip moth. The pitch pine tip moth is often found in small numbers in many of the same stands and trees in which the Nantucket pine tip moth occurs. In 20 northeastern Georgia loblolly stands, the pitch pine tip moth accounted for 0 to 7.3% (usually 3.0% or less) of the total tip moth population (Baer and Berisford 1975). The subtropical pine tip moth is restricted to Florida and the southern parts of Georgia, Mississippi, and South Carolina (Yates and others 1981). The three tip moth species are similar in many respects. Although the species are hard to distinguish in some stages of development, specimens in most stages can be identified to species using guides developed by Miller and Wilson (1964) and Yates (1967a, 1967b). The sexes of pupae can also be separated for the three species (Yates 1969).

Tip moths of all three species attack succulent new tissues of terminal and lateral shoots of trees from 0.3 to about 6 m in height. Larvae feed inside both buds and growing shoots and may kill up to 13 cm of a new shoot tip by severing conductive tissue. Loblolly pines can be damaged seriously because larvae can promote the crystallization of oleoresin at lesions, thereby minimizing the ability of trees to inhibit growth and development of the insects (Yates 1965). Tip moth damage is evidenced by browning, curling, and dieback of infested shoots. Shoot dieback prevents full development of potential photosynthetic tissue, temporarily reduces growth, and causes stem deformation. Continual attacks reduce the length of growing tips and increase the number of new shoots.

Life cycle. The following discussion concentrates on how the Nantucket pine tip moth affects loblolly pines, but it generally applies to the actions of the other two tip moth species as well. The Nantucket pine tip moth usually completes from 1 to 5 generations/year, depending on location and weather. There are usually 3 generations in the northern part of the loblolly pine range, 4 in the midrange, and 5 in Florida and and other areas close to the Gulf of Mexico. Pupae overwinter in the tips of infested shoots. As soon as warm weather begins, adults emerge, mate, and lay eggs. Activity may begin as early as December in the southernmost areas. The adult female oviposits individual eggs on the inner surface of a needle or at the needle base, where the eggs receive some protection from parasites, predators, and adverse weather. (Unlike the Nantucket pine tip moth, the pitch pine tip moth and the subtropical pine tip moth deposit eggs in clusters.) Eggs may take as long as 30 days to hatch in cool spring weather but only 5 to 10 days in warm summer weather. The species goes through five larval instars and then pupates. The first- and second-instar larvae mine needles and fascicle sheaths. The third, fourth, and fifth instars bore into buds and shoots and into conelets on older trees. Development of each instar generally takes 7 days or less. Pupae complete development in 13 to 30 days. Insect mortality is high during the egg and pupal stages (Gargiullo and Berisford 1982, 1983; Haugen and Stephen 1984; Hood and others 1985; Yates 1971; Yates and others 1981).

Factors affecting tree susceptibility. Tip moths cause little or no damage when natural regeneration systems are employed because the overstory cover protects new seedlings. Uneven-aged management is especially effective in inhibiting this insect, even in high-hazard areas or during widespread outbreaks. Tip moths are most damaging in large, open reforestation areas (Yates and others 1981). Trees planted in clearcuts usually have higher infestation rates than those that are direct seeded or naturally regenerated because they are easier to find. Sprouted seedlings are generally more susceptible to tip moth damage than normal seedlings (Thames 1962).

Tip moth damage is positively related to the intensity of site preparation. Loblolly pines growing on mechanically prepared areas are more susceptible to tip moth infestation than are loblolly on burned or herbicide-treated sites because seedlings on mechanically prepared sites are more exposed and easier for the moths to find (Hood and others 1988, Lantagne and Burger 1988, Thomas and others 1982). Young trees may be hidden from adult moths if site preparation is kept to a minimum, especially in high-hazard areas (White and others 1984). For example, a 1-year-old, northwest Louisiana plantation in an old field that was fallow for 1 year had 8% tip moth infestation. Disk harrowing before planting increased seedling infestation to 99%, with 79% of all growing tips infested (Warren 1963). Similarly, trees planted on a bare mine spoil in northern Alabama had 10 times more tip moth damage than did trees that were protected by other vegetation (Cross and others 1981). However, understory vegetation does not always protect seedlings from tip moth damage (Miller and Stephen 1983), and seedling growth is reduced as competition from other vegetation increases (see chapter 11).

Infestations are usually heaviest on trees 1 to 3 m tall and on the top half of trees where exposure to sunlight is greatest (Andersen and others 1984). Typically, infestation of planted seedlings is relatively light in the first year, builds to a high level in the second year, and either stabilizes or declines in the third and subsequent years (Cross and others 1981, Thomas and others 1982). On rare occasions, severe and prolonged infestation by larvae kills 1-m-tall trees (Yates and others 1981). Gargiullo and Berisford (1983) describe a method for estimating tip moth populations accurately.

Infestation rates are generally higher and infestations generally last longer on poor sites in the upper Piedmont Plateau. Low soil calcium (Ca) and a shallow horizon are also associated with tip moth infestation. Soil texture seems to influence severity of attack, probably through its effect on site quality. In the upper Piedmont, the highest tip moth hazard was associated with high clay content (small particle size) throughout the A horizon on land where site index was low (Hood and others 1988). In the east Texas Coastal Plain, sites characterized by high silt content in the surface soil (Kulhavy and others 1989) or high sand content in subsurface layers (White and others 1984) had a much higher tip moth hazard than had sites with clay. Trees planted on droughty sites (those best suited for longleaf pines) can be so seriously damaged by tip moths, over a period of several years, that they may look like bushes.

Loblolly pine is more susceptible than slash pine to tip moth attacks. When loblolly and slash pines are growing near each other, female moths seem to be able to select a susceptible loblolly pine host in preference to a resistant slash pine (Hertel and Benjamin 1975, Hood and others 1985). Hybrids between loblolly and slash pines are more resistant to tip moths than are loblolly pines. Crossing south Florida slash pine, *Pinus elliottii* var. *densa* Little and Dorman, with loblolly pine may provide greater tip moth resistance than crossing typical slash pine with loblolly pine (Grigsby 1959). Although loblolly is very susceptible to Nantucket pine tip moth attacks, there is some evidence that resistance may vary by seed source (Hertel and Benjamin 1975).

Effects on tree growth and development. Tip moth control can increase tree growth (Stephen and others 1982) and improve wood quality. Hedden and Clason (1979) concluded that early tip moth control can reduce compression wood content in 20-year-old trees by as much as 50%. Although tip moth damage appears to reduce early height growth considerably, the reduction is often temporary, especially on better sites (Beal 1967; Box 1961; Hedden and Haugen 1987; Hedden and others 1981; Lashomb and others 1978; Merrifield and others 1967; Warren and others 1975a, 1975b; Williston and Barras 1977). Thus, most tip moth control treatments are not cost effective. However, on some medium-to-good sites, protection may be economically beneficial when tip moth damage is severe (Cade and Hedden 1987, Grano and Grigsby 1968, Thomas and Oprean 1984). Tip moth injuries can act as infection points for fusiform rust. Controlling the two pests by treating the insect may be cost effective in stands managed for sawtimber (Hedden and others 1991, Powers and Stone 1988).

Control methods. Granular chemicals provide systemic tip moth control. For example, as little as 1 g of the systemic insecticide carbofuran applied to the soil around each young tree protected the trees from tip moths in one test (Merkel and Hertel 1976). The efficacy of granular systemics is strongly dependent on soil moisture. An abundance of rainfall or irrigation washes these chemicals out of sandy soils, but if there is too little moisture, the chemicals are not dissolved and cannot be absorbed by roots. Sprays of several different chemicals can be as effective as systemics if they are applied at exactly the right times during the moths' life cycle. Optimum control occurs when most, but not all, eggs have hatched, and the best time for spraying can be determined by correlating time-temperature and pheromone trap data (Berisford and others 1984; Chatelain and others 1977; Gargiullo and others 1984, 1985; Pickering and others 1989). In a Southwide experiment, chemically controlling tip moths on planted loblolly pines during the first 6 years of growth increased overall yields by 24.6 m³/ha at tree age 16. However, the increase was not deemed sufficient to justify the cost of control (Williston and Barras 1977). In addition to reducing tip moth damage, carbofuran also decreases fusiform rust infection (Powers and Stone 1988).

It may be possible to control tip moths biologically because they have numerous predators. These predators include many species of spiders that trap adult moths in their webs and also hunt them directly among needles and along branches (Bosworth and others 1970, Eikenbary and Fox 1968, Peck and others 1971). Various parasites combine to provide a high level of natural control when tip moth density is low (Eikenbary and Fox 1968; Lashomb and Steinhauer 1975, 1982; Lashomb and others 1980). Parasites are especially common on tip moth eggs and larvae (Gargiullo and Berisford 1983). Backpack spraying with a granulosis virus of the codling moth, *Cydia pomonella* (L.), can significantly reduce the concentration of tip moths in young plantations. Effects of the virus may even carry over to the next generation of moths (McLeod and others 1983).

Reproduction Weevils

The pales weevil and the pitch-eating weevil, *Pachlobius picivorus* (Germar), eat the tender bark of young loblolly pines. The life cycles, population trends, and feeding habits of the two species are very similar. They are the most serious insect pests of loblolly reproduction in the South and are principally a problem in plantation management. Large numbers of adults are attracted into newly harvested areas by the odor of fresh pine oleoresin (Thomas and Hertel 1969). The adults then breed in pine stumps and roots, and in buried slash. Weevils are also attracted to pines infested with SPB's, BTB's, and engraver beetles (Beal and McClintick 1943, Hill and Fox 1972).

The life cycle of reproduction weevils lasts between 3 and 12 months depending on the time of year that a stand is cut (Nord and others 1984). If the temperature is between 20 and 30 °C, eggs hatch in 5 to 10 days, and larvae feed on the inner bark of roots for about 1 month. At maturity, larvae usually excavate pupal chambers in the wood and pupate for 4 to 6 weeks (Salom and others 1987). Emerging adults feed at night on the tender stems of nearby newly planted seedlings or on twigs of older trees. They remove small irregular patches of bark down to the wood, eventually girdling seedlings and causing their death. Adults also feed below the root collar, especially where planted seedlings have loosely packed roots. Some adult weevils are active throughout most of the year, whenever the temperature exceeds about 15 °C (Nord and others 1984).

Pales weevils can be a problem throughout the range of loblolly pine. Susceptibility of new plantations to damage can vary widely, but where weevils are active, mortality commonly reaches 20 to 25%. Seedling losses to pales weevils may exceed 90% when conditions are good for weevil development. Damage caused by the pitch-eating weevil is greatest in the Gulf States, where mortality of young seedlings can exceed 30%.

Protection from weevils. Decisions about controlling these insects are best made before planting, so an assessment of hazard should be a part of the regeneration plan. Weevils are not a problem on areas formerly in annual crops or hardwoods because such areas lack the pine roots in which the weevils complete their life cycle. Weevils usually leave direct-seeded areas before new regeneration is large enough to feed upon. In pine stands, the risk of weevil buildup is minimized if clearcuts are kept small and scattered. To prevent large weevil populations from mass-migrating short distances and becoming epidemic, clearcuts should not be made next to clearcuts of the previous year. Burning cut-over areas consumes residual debris and may help reduce weevil buildup (Fox and Hill 1973). The overwintering population of weevils and potential for severe damage the following spring are larger the later in the year that an area is harvested and adult weevils are attracted. Areas logged in the winter and spring can generally be planted safely the following winter because weevil populations diminish to low levels by planting time (Speers 1974, Speers and Rauschenberger 1971). Areas logged after July 1 should not be planted with bareroot seedlings the following winter. Lynch and Hedden (1984) found that early-season seedling mortality was directly related to late-season seedling mortality in southeast Oklahoma. The level of damage or mortality at the end of summer can be predicted by measuring damage and mortality 20 weeks after planting. Lightly damaged seedlings usually survive, but those girdled more than 50% often do not survive dry periods.

Control methods. Container seedlings suffer less weevil damage than bareroot stock and have been planted successfully from June to August on high-hazard sites in North Carolina (Doggett and others 1978). If bareroot planting cannot be delayed for about 9 months after harvesting, loblolly pine seedlings may be treated with registered insecticides to prevent damage. Treatments include dips before planting, soil systemics during planting, and sprays after planting (Cade and others 1981; Nord and others 1975, 1978; Werner 1974). Users should consult a state forest entomologist or county agricultural extension agent for information on registered insecticides used specifically for pine weevils.

Few biological control agents of pine weevils are known, and little information is available on their effect in forest ecosystems. White and green muscardine fungi, *Beauveria bassiana* (Balsamo) Vuillemin and *Metarhizium anisopliae* (Metsch.) Sorok., infect weevils at all stages of development. Larvae and adult weevils are frequently infected with a gregarine protozoan. Several species of mites have also been associated with pales weevils, but the relationship between mites and weevils is not known (Nord and others 1984).

Extracts of pine phloem have been used to lure weevils, suggesting that baited traps could capture significant numbers of insects before seedlings are attacked (Thomas and Hertel 1979).

Other Insects

Loblolly pine stands are affected by several additional insect species. Although none of these insects is now a widespread problem, each has the potential to cause significant damage in the future.

Deodar weevil (eastern pine weevil). The deodar, or eastern pine, weevil is found throughout the South. Although primarily associated with cedar hosts, it attacks loblolly and other southern pines. It is not normally a serious problem but can be important in localized areas. There is one generation per year. Adults emerge from April to May and feed briefly on the inner bark of leaders and lateral branches of nearby trees. These attacks cause needle necrosis and, if severe, needle drop and terminal leader mortality on saplings and larger trees. Heavy feeding can kill small trees (Ollieu 1971). Adults are dormant during the summer but resume activity and lay eggs in the fall. They deposit from 1 to 4 eggs in feeding punctures. Newly hatched larvae bore into the inner bark, where they construct winding galleries that can girdle the stem. Evidence of such infestations is often not displayed until January, when branches begin to turn brown. Winter is spent in the larval stage. The larvae pupate in March or April, completing their life cycle. Keeping trees vigorous minimizes damage by this insect (USDA FS 1985).

White grubs. White grubs, *Phyllophaga* spp., the larvae of May or June beetles, can damage loblolly pine seedlings on abandoned fields or on sod. Young grubs normally feed on the roots of grasses and forbs but will eat pine root tips and rootlets. Older larvae can girdle or devour larger roots and may sever taproots. Affected seedlings succumb to drought, turn brown, and can be pulled from the soil easily because they have few roots.

Grubs can easily be detected by spading the soil and breaking clods. Sampling for the insect should be done in the months of July or August before planting the following winter. Significant mortality can be expected when 2 or more grubs are found/0.03 m³ of soil. Infestations can be reduced by furrowing or disking deep enough to destroy the sod cover. Treatment is most effective when done during the summer, when many exposed larvae are killed by heat of direct sunlight and drying of overturned clods.

Aphids. Cinaran aphids, *Cinara* spp., feed on new terminal growth of loblolly pines of all ages. They prefer rapidly growing vigorous trees and, depending on the number of individual aphids and the duration of their feeding, can measurably reduce both diameter and height growth of young trees (Fox and Griffith 1977). Although they undoubtedly reduce the vigor of older loblolly, their effect on the growth of older trees has not been demonstrated (Hood and Fox 1980). The speckled pine needle aphid, *Essigella pini* Wilson, feeds on the needles of loblolly. In high numbers, they can adversely affect the development of seed orchard trees. Soil applications of granular insecticides have reduced the numbers of these aphids (Hood and Fox 1980). Because fungi of the genus *Entomophthora* infest the aphids and numerous species of spiders prey on the aphids, it may be possible to develop biological control treatments if aphids become a serious problem (Carner and others 1977, Fox and Griffith 1976).

Leafcutting ants. The Texas leafcutting ant (also called "town ant"), *Atta texana* (Buckley), can be a major problem. These ants destroy individual seedlings or saplings by stripping off needles, bark, and terminal buds, which they use as a substrate for the fungi that each ant colony cultures. Leafcutting ants also cut radicle and cotyledonary tissues from germinating seeds. During the winter, when other green vegetation is scarce, a leafcutting ant colony can destroy a loblolly pine plantation within its foraging range in only a few days. A single ant nest caused an estimated loss of $653 in stumpage over the 30-year life of a plantation (Moser 1986).

There is no known natural control for the leafcutting ant. Chemical treatment of nests with the fumigant methyl bromide is presently the only readily available and registered control measure. To be most effective, methyl bromide gas must be applied directly to the central nest during moist conditions when there is little wind. Winter may be the best time to apply the chemical because ants are usually concentrated deep in the central part of the nest during cold weather. The top of a nest can be identified from above ground by a number of closely spaced vent, exit, and dirt removal holes. A large nest may have up to 500 holes. A tube is run deep into a nest through one of the holes. After as many of the other holes as possible are filled with soil or blocked with a plastic covering, the gas is released into the nest (Cameron S. 1989. Personal communication). Baiting may ultimately be the safest and most cost-effective means of controlling this pest. Although a number of chemical baits have been tested, none are registered for use.

Geometrids (loopers). The larvae of two geometrids—the pine conelet looper, *Nepytia semiclusaria* (Walker), and *Lambdina pellucidaria* (Grote and Robinson)—feed on loblolly pine foliage and probably on female flowers. Little is known about these insects, but they can cause considerable defoliation in localized areas. They are more likely to be a problem in a seed orchard than in a general forest area (USDA FS 1971, Yates and Ebel 1972).

Pine webworm. The pine webworm, *Tetralopha robustella* Zeller, usually attacks 1- and 2-year-old seedlings but occasionally infests saplings and larger trees. Although attacks are rarely fatal, heavy infestations may reduce seedling growth. Attacks usually peak during the second growing season. Eggs are laid on needles, and newly hatched instar larvae mine needles. By the second or third instar, larvae burrow into the main stem and from there construct masses of frass and webbing. Depending on tree size, from 1 to 20 larvae may occupy each frass nest. Last-instar larvae migrate to the ground, spin cocoons, and pupate (Hertel and Benjamin 1975). There are usually two generations per year. Both handpicking and systemic chemicals control webworms effectively, but control is rarely necessary (Merkel and Hertel 1976, USDA FS 1985).

Pine sawflies. At least 8 species of sawflies, *Neodiprion* spp., defoliate loblolly pines from the seedling stage to maturity (Drake 1974). The loblolly pine sawfly, *N. taedae linearis* Ross, occurs throughout the range of loblolly and is the major defoliator of medium-to-large trees in forest stands. It has a single generation each year and overwinters in the egg stage in needles. Eggs hatch in late winter and early spring. Caterpillarlike larvae feed in groups on host needles, generally devouring older needles first, but they eat all needles when a large population is present. Affected trees may suffer reduced growth but usually recover in 1 to 2 years. Severe infestations may stunt or malform individual trees, and successive defoliations sometimes kill young trees (Coyne 1970, USDA, FS 1972). The blackheaded pine sawfly, *N.*

excitans Rohwer, can also be a serious defoliator of medium-to-large loblolly pines in the Southeast and in Texas. The insect is most active in the summer and fall, and heavily infested trees may remain without needles through the winter. Under conditions most favorable for the insect, 4 to 5 generations of blackheaded pine sawflies may occur each year. Most of the insects overwinter in cocoons, but a few persist as eggs or older larvae (Thatcher 1971).

Sawflies are a minor problem in most forest situations. Sawfly infestations often appear suddenly, continue for 1 to 2 years, and quickly disappear. Short-lived outbreaks seldom warrant artificial control measures (Long and others 1974). A polyhedrosis virus that infects larvae is an important natural control agent. It has been tried as a management control agent with varying levels of success (Yearian and others 1973; Young and Yearian 1986, 1987). Other natural control agents include feral hogs, *Sus scrofa*; armadillos, *Dasypus novemcinctus*; mice, *Peromyscus* spp. and *Reithrodontomys fulvescens*; and shrews, especially *Blarina brevicauda*. These animals help minimize outbreaks by destroying cocoons (Thatcher 1971).

Pine colaspis. The pine colaspis beetle, *Colaspis pini* Barber, usually is not a serious pest and generally prefers slash pine to loblolly pine. Adults chew the edges of needles, producing irregular, sawlike patterns that turn brown. Entire needles may die, causing browning of entire crowns. Occasionally, only tips of needles are injured. Attacks usually occur in early summer. By late summer, trees appear green and healthy again. Trees do not die, and little growth loss occurs (USDA FS 1985).

Pine needle sheath midge. The pine needle sheath midge, *Contarinia acuta* Gagni, feeds within the needle sheath on elongating needles. Needle droop and partial defoliation occur in heavily infested trees. Adult emergence from overwintering sites in the soil, oviposition, and egg hatch of the first generation coincide with the first growth flush of trees in the spring. Three instars occur in each generation, and four generations can take place during the summer. Damage to loblolly pine is generally minor, except when the insect infects seed orchards (Overgaard and others 1976, Weatherby and others 1989).

Pitch blister moth. The pitch blister moth, *Retinia taedana* (Miller), attacks the leaders and uppermost branches of loblolly pines throughout the South. Adults are active in May and June, when they attack 1-year-old shoots between the nodes. Pitch blister moths overwinter as caterpillars in tunnels. The insects feed on bark, cambium, and pith, but damage to trees is minor. The occasional shoot that is killed is quickly replaced. (Miller 1978, Thompson 1987).

Gypsy moth. First-instar larvae of the European strain of the gypsy moth, *Lymantria dispar* (L.), are unable to consume loblolly pine foliage. However, later instars can consume, survive on, and grow on loblolly pine foliage (Barbosa and others 1983). It also appears that the Asian gypsy moth could be a threat to loblolly pine if it became permanently established in the United States. (Wallner W. 1994. USDA Forest Service, Hamden, CT. Personal communication).

Root Parasites

At least 18 plant species native to the South (table 10-8) can parasitize the roots of loblolly pine. Senna seymeria, *Seymeria cassioides* (J.F. Gmel.) Blake, a member of the figwort family (Scrophulariaceae), is the most damaging of these. No other root parasite has been found in large numbers in commercial plantings of loblolly (Musselman and others 1978).

Senna seymeria is an annual herb that can reduce tree growth and even kill seedlings, saplings, and occasionally pole-sized trees when it parasitizes roots. It grows from southern Louisiana to the southeastern part of Virginia and is most common on moist sandy soils of the lower Gulf and Atlantic Coastal Plains. Senna seymeria produces normal-sized plants only after it parasitizes pines. Because pine roots interlace extensively, it may be difficult to isolate individual host trees. If pines are not available, seymeria plants grow to the cotyledonary stage, linger a few weeks, and then die (Fitzgerald and others 1975; Grelen and Mann 1973; Mann and others 1969, 1971).

Intensive site preparation promotes the development of senna seymeria. Loblolly pine seedlings and saplings are usually subject to infestation from the beginning of the second growing season until dense herbaceous vegetation or litter excludes seymeria. However, trees are subject to attack at any stage of development if cultural treatments expose the soil surface enough to allow senna seymeria seeds to germinate.

Senna seymeria infestation following prescribed burning in stands of pole-sized loblolly pine commonly causes the premature loss of lower, older needles. Needles become chlorotic and appear tufted at the twig terminals. Such infestations usually result in growth loss but rarely in mortality. Growth loss begins during the year of infestation and continues into the second season. The growth loss results from shrinkage of and mechanical damage to the host root system. Reduced storage of carbohydrates resulting from foliage loss and reduced photosynthesis probably contribute to growth loss (Fitzgerald and Terrell 1972, Fitzgerald and others 1977).

Haustoria (food-absorbing outgrowths) of senna seymeria penetrate pine roots, and their sheathed vessels ramify throughout the pine root cortex. Modified protrusions of vascular tissue enter pine tracheids through bordered pits and absorb water and nutrients for transport back to the parasite. Senna seymeria is capable of producing at least part of its own food and probably is not dependent on the pine host for sugars or other foodstuffs (Fitzgerald and others 1975).

Another figwort, *Agalinis purpurea* (L.) Penn. (purple gerardia), was an extensive parasite in one young loblolly pine planting but did not seem to affect tree growth during the first year of infestation. Purple gerardia grows on a wide variety of soils and sites throughout the South and, like senna seymeria, is most common on cleared and disturbed sites. It is not host-specific but is never abundant in areas without woody plants. Increased shading as trees mature gradually reduces the density of this parasite (Musselman and Mann 1978, Musselman and others 1978).

Table 10-8—Plant species native to the southern United States that parasitize loblolly pine roots

Family	Scientific name	Common name
Olacaceae (Olax family)	*Ximenia americana* L.	Hog plum, tallowwood
Santalaceae (Sandalwood family)	*Buckleya distichophylla* (Nutt.) Torr.	Buckleya, piratebush
Scrophulariacea (Figwort family)	*Agalinis aphylla* (Nutt.) Raf.	Leafless gerardia
	A. fasciculata (Ell.) Raf.	Fascicled gerardia, beach gerardia
	A. linifolia (Nutt.) Britt.	Perennial gerardia
	A. purpurea (L.) Penn.	Purple gerardia
	A. tenuifolia (Vahl) Raf.	Slender gerardia
	Aureolaria flava (L.) Farw.	Large false foxglove
	A. grandiflora (Benth.) Penn.	Showy false foxglove, big-leaf oakleech
	A. laevigata (Raf.) Raf.	Smooth false foxglove
	A. pedicularia (L.) Raf.	Fernleaf false foxglove
	A. virginica (L.) Penn.	Downy false foxglove
	Buchnera americana L.	Bluehearts
	Dasistoma macrophylla (Nutt.) Raf.	Mullein foxglove
	Macranthera flammea (Bartr.) Penn.	Macranthera, orange blackherb
	Schwalbea americana L.	Chaffseed
	Seymeria cassioides Blake	Senna seymeria
	S. pectinata Pursh	Combleaf seymeria

Source: adapted from Musselman and Mann (1978).

Allelopathy

In allelopathy, one plant species adversely affects another by releasing chemicals into the environment. Leachates from leaves are the usual source of allelopathic chemicals. Root systems contribute little or no inhibitory chemicals, and accumulation of toxic chemicals in soil is unlikely. Allelopathy should disappear when the undesirable plant is removed (Gilmore 1985). Loblolly pine is not known to be allelopathic to other plants, but its needles do contain substances that inhibit the growth of bacteria (Maksymiuk 1970). Conditions under which allelopathy affects loblolly pines in nature are not well defined, but the presence of any of the following species in large numbers should be viewed as an adverse condition for natural loblolly regeneration and early seedling growth:

SPECIES	REFERENCE
Tall fescue (*Festuca arundinaceae* Schreber)	Wheeler and Young (1979)
Dogfennel (*Eupatorium capillifolium* (Lam.) Small)	Hollis and others (1982)
Fetterbush (*Lyonia lucida* (Lam.) K. Koch)	Hollis and others (1982)
Broomsedge (*Andropogon virginicus* L.)	Priester and Pennington (1978)
Giant foxtail grass (*Setaria faberi* Herrm.)	Gilmore (1980, 1985)
Shining sumac (*Rhus copallina* L.)	Smith (1987)
Chinese tallowtree (*Sapium sebiferum* (L.) Roxb.)	Gresham (1987)

Animal Damage

Miller (1987) estimated that annual wildlife damage to southern forest resources exceeded $11 million/year and that another $1.6 million is spent in efforts to control damage on 28.8 million ha of land. Animal damage can occur throughout the life cycle of loblolly pine. Trampling, browsing, grazing, and girdling reduce growth and may cause some stem deformity, but trees usually live unless they are totally girdled. Even then, some seedlings sprout below a girdle.

Small rodents and birds can severely deplete seed production. The most abundant rodents in the loblolly–shortleaf pine type are several species of mice (family Cricetidae). Population densities of mice range from near 0 to 10 animals/ha, depending on the density of understory vegetation (Hatchell 1964, Stephenson and others 1963). Small animals usually abandon a newly burned area for several months after a fire but return as new annual grasses, forbs, and planted pines provide suitable habitat (Layne 1974). Small amounts of endrin can be mixed with thiram to protect loblolly seeds from rodents and birds and to permit high levels of germination in nurseries and in forest settings following direct seeding (Campbell 1981). Prairie crayfish, *Cambarus* spp., seldom feed on pine seeds on wet upland sites. However, the crayfish can excavate 7,400 to 12,000 burrow holes/ha, and significant numbers of seeds applied by a direct seeding can be washed into these holes during wet periods. Such loss of seeds can greatly reduce potential germination (Campbell 1971).

Eastern cottontail rabbits often cause extensive damage and some mortality in first-year loblolly pine plantings by cutting off the stems of seedlings. However, damage cannot be assessed immediately because seedlings clipped even within 2.5 to 5.0 cm of the ground often sprout and grow about as well as unbrowsed trees. When seedlings are clipped, one new bud usually dominates, and the injury may be almost totally masked within 2 years. Better quality seedlings and those clipped higher above the ground are most likely to sprout, and their sprouts are generally more vigorous. Long-term effects of rabbit damage may be moderate to negligible if first-year damage does not exceed approximately 10% (Hunt 1968; table 10-9). Longleaf pines are rarely damaged by rabbits, so they can be used to replace loblolly where rabbit damage is severe. Slash and shortleaf pines are just as susceptible to rabbit damage as loblolly. Where rabbit concentrations are high, a chemical repellent such as endrin or protective polyethylene sleeves can be employed (Mason and Davidson 1964).

Numerous other animals can damage or destroy loblolly pine trees, but the problems are generally very limited. White-tailed deer eat the buds of newly established seedlings, especially in plantations where the animals can walk down recognizable rows. Normally, pines are not a preferred food for deer. Deer repellents are available and effective, but local conditions affect the level of protection (Robinette and Causey 1978). Wild (or feral) hogs can be found throughout

Table 10-9—Survival and mean dimensions of undamaged and rabbit-damaged loblolly pines and contribution of damaged trees to volume at age 30 in plantations established at spacings of 1.8 by 1.8 m to 2.4 by 2.4 m on several soils in southeast Louisiana

Condition of trees	% survival*	Height (m)	dbh (cm)	Volume (%)† Pulp-wood	Volume (%)† Saw-timber
Undamaged	57	17.7	19.3	89	88
Rabbit-damaged‡	56	18.0	19.0	11	12

Source: adapted from Wakeley (1970).

* Based on trees alive at age 1.

† Of total volume in undamaged plus rabbit-damaged trees.

‡ Eleven % of all trees had rabbit damage at age 1.

most of loblolly pine's range. They occasionally eat the tops of loblolly pine seedlings, but mostly damage loblolly pine roots while digging for roots of grasses and shrubs in the spring and summer. Except where hog populations are high, damage to pines is limited, and loblolly seems to be the least preferred pine species (Wahlenberg 1960, Wood and Lynn 1977, Wood and Roark 1980). If not properly managed, cattle sometimes do considerable damage to pine trees. If beaver (*Castor canadensis*) ponds flood low-lying loblolly stands, trees are killed quickly. However, this problem is normally confined to sites where hardwoods

predominate. Beavers eat loblolly pine bark occasionally, so trees growing near beaver ponds are subject to girdling. Bird roosting damage is rare, but roosting damage to developing loblolly stands can be severe locally. Overwintering of large flocks of birds (grackles, *Quiscalus* sp.; blackbirds, *Agelaius* sp.; cowbirds, *Molothrus* sp.; and starlings, *Sturnus* sp.) can kill almost all trees in individual stands. Tree mortality results from physical damage done by the birds and from high concentrations of nutrients from bird excrement in the soil and on tree needles, limbs, and stems (Gilmore and others 1984, Hardy 1978).

Damage Caused by Climatic Conditions

Extremes in weather may have little influence on healthy, well-stocked stands of loblolly pine, but they can have very adverse effects on certain genetic families or following certain types of thinning or insect or disease attacks.

Ice and Snow Damage

New shoots of loblolly pine are relatively brittle. When snow or freezing rain accumulates on them, severe bending and breakage can occur. The prevalence of wet snowfalls, ice, and glaze (freezing rain) storms increases in frequency from one storm every 10 years in the central portion of loblolly's range to one storm every 3 years across the northern portion of the range. The frequent and severe stem and branch breakage caused by snow and ice storms along the northern edge of loblolly's natural range

can greatly reduce stand productivity and length of rotation. The injury usually caused by snow or ice is crown loss. The dense foliage and branches of loblolly readily intercept and accumulate wet snow or glaze. Ice from 0.6 to 1.3 cm in radial thickness can be expected to form on needles and branches somewhere in the central or northern part of loblolly's natural range once every 6 years. Deposits can accumulate to thicknesses greater than 2.5 cm and can increase sapling weight three to five times (Bennett 1959, Brender and Romancier 1965). As the snow and ice burden increases during a storm, the rapidly growing juvenile wood offers little resistance to bending and occasionally breaks (figure 10-11). Often, entire branches are ripped from the boles of older trees, or the trees break off at the base of the crown. Leader and stem breakage is more severe for trees from southern or coastal areas than for trees from inland sources, but the superior

Figure 10-11—Snow and ice damage to loblolly pines: seedlings will often fully recover even if bent to the ground by snow or ice (**a** and **b**); saplings usually will not recover from severe bending caused by snow or ice (**c**); pole and sawtimber trees often break with heavy ice accumulations (**d**).

growth rate of southern or coastal stock more than offsets the greater damage sustained (Jones and Wells 1969).

Recovery from ice or snow damage is directly related to tree size and the amount of damage. Younger and smaller trees are more capable of rapid and complete recovery than older and larger trees (figure 10-11). Young trees bent to less than an angle of 40% from the vertical can be expected to recover and ultimately show little stem deformity. Those bent at an angle of 40% to 50% can recover but will have varying amounts of crook and sweep. Trees bent more than 60% do not recover sufficiently to be retained as crop trees, but they often remain alive for many years (Brewer and Linnartz 1973, Reamer and Bruner 1973).

Trees in the poorest form class, or those that developed under open conditions, are most resistant to ice and snow damage (Cool and others 1971). Ice damage is most severe in the densest stands, where trees have the smallest crowns. However, because the trees in dense stands support one another, dense stands also have the greatest basal area and number of stems per hectare of undamaged or lightly damaged trees following a severe storm. Fusiform rust–damaged trees are highly likely to break at the canker during storms. Well-stocked stands can be managed to a fruitful rotation following most storms. However, if storms occur in 2 successive years, a stand may be completely destroyed (Shepard 1978, Wahlenberg 1960).

Heavy selection thinning or row thinning, followed by heavy ice or snow buildup on branches, increases tree bending and both branch and stem breakage. Pruning also results in more tree loss (table 10-10). For minimal ice and snow damage, stands should be lightly thinned early and often so that crop trees will develop large, sturdy crowns and root systems (Fountain and Burnett 1979). Trees with symmetrical crowns should be favored because uniform distribution of snow and ice reduces the possibility of bending. Although loblolly pines are usually less susceptible than slash pines to glaze or snow damage, they are sometimes as vulnerable as slash pines and may recover more slowly than slash pines from stem damage that occurs between ages 5 and 20 (Cool and others 1971, Kuprionis 1970, Shepard 1981).

Freezing water can damage exposed loblolly seeds significantly. Fully imbibed and frozen seeds have 10 to 20% lower germination than frozen dry seeds (Barnett and Hall 1977). The probable cause of seed damage is swelling of the megagametophyte and embryo within unyielding seedcoats.

Wind Damage

Trees grow fastest and largest from just above to just below the groundline, where maximum physical support is provided. In seedlings, wind stress can reduce both the rate of stem elongation and needle length (Telewski and Jaffe 1981). Continuous wind stress increases the relative size of the lower trunk and upper roots as trees age. Trees growing with little or no competition are highly wind resistant because they have large bases and rapid taper. Trees growing in dense stands rely largely on their neighbors for wind protection.

High winds (generated mostly by hurricanes) can cause extensive bending and breakage in loblolly pine stands, particularly after trees exceed 6 m in height. Roots can also be broken or displaced, and trees blown down. In 1989, the very destructive Hurricane Hugo significantly reduced the area and volume of loblolly pine in South Carolina. Trees in recently thinned stands are most vulnerable to high winds because they have not had time to develop additional crown and roots to replace the support lost when neighboring trees were removed. Also, when soils with impervious layers that restrict normal root development get wet, they are usually less able to support trees, and excessive blowdown can result. Especially valuable trees (such as those kept for seed production or seed orchard stock) should not be grown on soils that restrict rooting (Trousdell and others 1965).

Lightning and Fire Damage

Lightning is common in the South and an important ecological factor in succession. Loblolly pines have the same probability of being struck by lightning as any other dominant tree species in an area. Some trees live a considerable time after being struck, but most eventually die. Browning of all needles usually takes place over a period of 2 weeks to several months following a lightning strike. There is a close relationship between lightning and insect or disease damage, especially in older trees. Lightning-struck trees have extremely low oleoresin flow for several days and altered monoterpene composition, both of which contribute to susceptibility to insects and diseases (Blanche and others 1985a). Moreover, most lightning strikes occur during the growing season, when insects are particularly abundant and active. Soon after a tree is struck, it is usually invaded by one or more species of *Ips* or *Dendroctonus* (see earlier discussion on bark beetles). This beetle invasion is probably the most common cause of loblolly death after trees have been weakened by lightning (Baker 1974).

Wildfires can destroy young trees and varying amounts

Table 10-10—Basal area of undamaged and lightly damaged loblolly pines when a glaze storm followed thinning and pruning

| Pruning level | Basal area (m²/ha) | | | | |
	Very heavy thinning	Heavy thinning	Light thinning	Very light thinning	Pruning means
High	5.3	7.3	8.5	8.5	7.3 a
Medium	7.3	9.6	13.8	14.5	11.3 b
Low	7.1	11.7	14.7	18.6	13.1 c
Thinning means	6.7 a	9.6 b	12.4 c	13.8 c	10.6

Source: adapted from Burton (1981).

Means followed by the same letter within a row or column are not significantly different at the 95% level of probability.

of the protective organic matter on the soil surface, volatilize N and sulfur (S), transform some elements to soluble forms, and cause some changes in the physical and biological properties of soils. None of these changes are substantial enough to reduce site productivity on flat or gently rolling Coastal Plain or Piedmont soils (Metz and others 1961, Moehring and others 1966, Ralston and Hatchell 1971, Wells 1971). However, fire followed by heavy rainfall on unprotected slopes can cause severe local erosion. At the northern extremes of loblolly's range, fires that remove the protective litter layer cause deeper freezing of the surface soil, which may affect root development and tree growth adversely.

Saltwater Damage

Salt water periodically damages low-lying coastal stands of loblolly pine. Hurricane-force winds can spray water with salt concentrations high enough to temporarily damage trees up to 1,200 m inland. Dominant trees are most affected. Trees within 100 m of the dune line can be killed. High tides can force brackish water into coastal pine forests. Where subsequent drainage is slow, high uptake of chloride and sodium ions may damage trees. Some evidence suggests that there is genetic variation in salt tolerance in loblolly (Gresham 1981, Land 1974, Little and others 1958).

Damage From Airborne Pollutants

Airborne particles and vapors can increase levels of nutrients, such as N, Ca, and K, and pollution loads in forest stands (Garner and others 1989, Hanson and others 1989, Lindberg and others 1986, Lorenz and Murphy 1985). Fire transfers 2.5 to 82.0 kg of particulate matter per tonne of fuel burned from place to place (Sandberg and others 1979). Computer models can be used to estimate inputs of fire-caused air pollutants to forest stands (Murphy and others 1977).

Airborne chemicals known to adversely affect loblolly pines include S, nitrogen oxides, and chlorine gas. In the early 1900's, large emissions of sulfur dioxide from smelters in the North Carolina–Virginia–Tennessee region caused the destruction of many thousands of hectares of pine and hardwood forests. Sulfur concentration on needles is a reliable indicator of S pollution patterns in an area; however, S pollution can cause diameter growth loss without producing obvious visual symptoms (Bieberdorf and others 1958, Lindberg and Garten 1988, Phillips and others 1977). The first symptom of chlorine gas damage is necrosis of the newest needles. Higher concentrations of chlorine gas also affect older needles, but there is no tendency to defoliate. Bromine also accumulates in needles, but its effects on loblolly are unknown. Accumulations in 1-year-old needles of trees near chemical plants in Arkansas exceeded 900 ppm, but accumulations were less than

100 ppm at distances greater than 1.6 km from a bromine source. The bromine content of 2-year-old needles was twice that of 1-year-old needles at any given distance from a source (Tainter 1978).

The addition of acidic precipitation to forest soils may lower soil pH enough to mobilize aluminum (Al) and cause Al toxicity. Aluminum concentrations as low as 5.0 mg/l significantly reduce the number of roots per seedling when seedlings are grown in sand culture. At about 20.0 mg of Al/l, both the number and length of roots decline greatly (Paganelli and others 1987, Tepper and others 1989). Photosynthesis and respiration are among the first physiological processes to be affected by pollution. New needles that accumulate even low levels of sodium fluoride can have substantially reduced photosynthesis and respiration. Old needles are less sensitive but are still affected (McLaughlin and Barnes 1975). Loblolly pines are more sensitive to the effects of pollution when growing under stress.

Although substantial progress has been made in reducing airborne levels of many prominent pollutants in the last decade, rising ozone (O_3) and carbon dioxide (CO_2) levels continue to pose severe environmental problems, especially around industrial and urban centers (Ludwig and Shelar 1980, Schneider 1989, Seinfeld 1989). High O_3 levels seem to have no effect on stomatal control in loblolly pine (Sasek and Richardson 1989), but increased O_3 levels cause injury to epicuticular wax, cytolysis of subsidiary and mesophyll cells of needles, and depression of photosynthesis by as much as 80%. The result is that the growth rate of young trees is reduced by as much as 40% (Barnes 1972, Krause and others 1987, Kress and others 1989, Shafer and Heagle 1989, Ward and Kress 1980), but the reduction may not occur until the year following exposure (Sigal and others 1988). Response differs by genotype, which indicates that loblolly can be bred to withstand high levels of O_3 (Adams and others 1988, Hanson and others 1988, Krause and others 1987, Kress and others 1982). Mycorrhizae help roots absorb oxygen (O_2) where the O_3 or sulfur dioxide (SO_2) levels are high, thereby ameliorating the adverse effects of O_3 or SO_2 pollution (Carney and others 1978, Garrett and others 1982, Mahoney and others 1985).

Growing seedlings in containers poses unique problems, especially if they are grown within an enclosed environment like a greenhouse. Although nurseries are not normally near areas subject to severe industrial or urban air pollution, toxic levels of SO_2 and ethylene can build up in enclosed growing areas, especially in the winter, when gasoline or diesel generators are used and good air exchange does not occur. Sulfur dioxide and ethylene can be harmful to young plants at concentrations below 1 ppm (Mastalerz 1977).

Accumulations of heavy metals in southern pine ecosystems through both crown absorption and soil deposition of atmospheric fallout have increased (Adriano and Pinder 1977, Altshuller 1984, Gschwandtner and others

1985). Lead (Pb) concentrations in soil generally range from 20 to 200 ppm, but high concentrations of Pb in soil do not necessarily reduce tree growth. In one case, seedling growth was not affected adversely by soil Pb levels of 600 ppm, and photosynthesis was not inhibited at 1,200 ppm (Seiler and Paganelli 1987). However, additions of as little as 207 ppm of Pb to soil and soil Pb levels as low as 320 ppm can reduce growth significantly if the Pb is translocated to the foliage (Davis and Barnes 1973, Rolfe and Bazzaz 1975). The addition of as little as 100 ppm of cadmium (Cd) to a forest soil inhibits loblolly seedling growth (Kelly and others 1979).

High levels of ionizing radiation reduce loblolly pine seed germination and tree growth. Greater dosages yield greater adverse effects. Acute exposure to as little as 1,250 roentgens (R) of gamma radiation alters the pattern of CO_2 exchange in seedlings and depresses the rate of net photosynthesis and CO_2 evolution by stems (Hadley and Woodwell 1965). Most young trees die when exposure exceeds 1,800 R (Davis 1962). Water stress makes loblolly more susceptible to damage by chronic ionizing radiation (Miller 1965, 1966).

Nursery Protection

Numerous insects and diseases attack loblolly pines in seedling nurseries. Many problems are caused by soilborne organisms. Most fungi and bacteria are either soil organic matter saprophytes or nitrification agents, and most are beneficial rather than harmful. However, many can affect nursery seedlings adversely (table 10-11). Ectomycorrhizal fungi (especially *Pisolithus tinctorius*) protect roots from most diseases. Both the Hartig net and the fungal mantle appear to be involved in this process. The mechanism is nonsystemic, however, because nonmycorrhizal roots on

the same tree can become infected (Marx 1973).

Normally, seedlings can be protected against pathogens by soil fumigation, chemical seed treatments, soil pesticides, foliar sprays, systemic pesticides, or combinations of these treatments (Cordell and Filer 1985). It is also important to rogue diseased or insect-infested seedlings and to eliminate pest host plants in and around a nursery site to help reduce the spread of nursery pests. Culling diseased trees during the lifting and packing process minimizes the spread of infections to field locations.

Table 10-11—Loblolly pine nursery pests

Causal organism	Common name	Portion of tree affected	Causal organism	Common name	Portion of tree affected
Coleosporium spp,	Needles casts and rusts	Foliage	*Sclerotium rolfsii* Sacc.	Damping-off and root rot fungi	Root/basal stem
Diprion spp.	Sawflies	Foliage	*Rhizoctonia solani*	Damping-off and root rot fungi	Root/basal stem
Neodiprion spp.	Sawflies	Foliage	*Trichothecium* spp.	Damping-off and root rot fungi	Root
Paratetranychus spp.	Spider mites	Foliage	*Scapteriscus acletus* Rehn & Hebard	Southern mole cricket	Root
Tetranychus spp.	Spider mites	Foliage	*Prionus* spp.	Root borers	Root
Aphididae family	Aphids	Stem/foliage	*Brachyrhinus* spp.	Root weevils	Root
Toumeyella spp.	Pine tortoise scales	Stem/foliage	*Hylobius pales*	Pales weevil	Root/stem
Phenacaspis spp.	Pine needle scales	Stem/foliage	*Pachylobius picivorus*	Pitch-eating weevil	Root/stem
Sparganothis spp.	Bell moths	Stem/foliage	Noctuidae family	Cutworms	Root/stem
Atta texana	Leafcutting ant	Stem/foliage	*Elasmopalpus lignosellus* (Zeller)	Lesser corn stalk borer	Root/stem
Solenopsis geminata	Fire ant	Stem/foliage	*Phyllophaga* spp.	White grubs	Root
Pogonomyrmex badius (Latreille)	Florida harvester ant	Stem/foliage	*Meloidogyne* spp.	Root-knot nematodes	Root
Cronartium quercuum f. sp. *fusiforme*	Gall rust fungus	Stem	*Xiphinema* spp.	Dagger nematodes	Root
C. comandrae	Gall rust fungus	Stem	*Meloidodera* spp.	Pine cyctoid nematodes	Root
C. comptoniae	Gall rust fungus	Stem	*Hoplolaimus galeatus*	Lance nematode	Root
Fusarium moniliforme var. *subglutinans*	Pitch canker fungus	Root/stem	*Prarylenchus* spp.	Root-lesion nematodes	Root
Pythium spp.	Damping-off and root rot fungi	Root/basal stem	*Tylenchorhynchus* spp.	Stunt nematodes	Root
Phytophthora spp.	Damping-off and root rot fungi	Root/basal stem	*Trichodorus christiei*	Stubby-root nematodes	Root
Fusarium spp.	Damping-off and root rot fungi	Root/basal stem	*Bursaphelenchus* spp.	Pinewood nematodes	Root
Cylindrocladium spp.	Damping-off and root rot fungi	Root/basal stem	*Rhyacionia frustrana*	Nantucket pine tip moth	Stem/foliage
Macrophomina phaseolina	Damping-off and root rot fungi	Root/basal stem	*Eucosma* spp. (Cone and shoot borers)	Tip and shoot moths	Stem/foliage

Source: adapted from Cordell and Filer (1985), May (1985), Ruehle (1964 & 1969), and Ruehle and Marx (1971).

Seed Pests

Seeds of loblolly pine, like those of most tree species, can be infested with parasitic and saprophytic microorganisms. Pathogens may be present within seeds or on seedcoats. Some of the fungi present on the outside of seeds can cause new germinants to damp-off (rot). Damping-off can kill more than 15% of young seedlings in nurseries. *Fusarium moniliforme* can cause 60 to 100% top infection damping-off, whereas *Trichothecium* spp. disrupt and disorganize radicle development of young seedlings (Mason and Van Arsdel 1978). Several species of *Pythium* fungi can cause postemergence damping-off (Hendrix and Campbell 1968). Excessive application of N to soils low in Ca and P during early spring may increase damage by damping-off fungi (Cordell and Filer 1985). Once stems begin to develop woody tissue, about 4 to 6 weeks after germination, susceptibility to damping-off diseases declines rapidly (Filer and Peterson 1975).

Many fungicides can protect seeds against diseases without inhibiting seed germination or ectomycorrhizal development (Pawuk and Barnett 1979). sterilization can also control microorganisms infesting seedcoats. Soaking seeds in 30% hydrogen peroxide for 15 minutes usually eliminates fungal infection without reducing germination (Barnett 1976, Pawuk and Barnett 1979). Most loblolly pine seeds are coated with a fungicide–latex sticker mixture before sowing. The mixture reduces damping-off and repels birds (Cordell and Filer 1985).

Fusiform Rust

Fusiform rust can be a severe problem in nurseries. The long-term incidence of rust in Georgia and Florida nurseries has averaged 24%, with more than 90% infection in some years. Nursery cultivation, fertilization, and irrigation practices increase seedling growth rate and the number of lateral branches, which often promotes rust infection (Rowan 1976, 1977b; Rowan and Steinbeck 1977). Seedlings with obvious galls are usually culled either during packing or during the planting operation. Unfortunately, significant numbers of infected seedlings do not exhibit symptoms before they are lifted from the nursery (Rowan and Muse 1981).

The fungicide triadimefon (Bayleton®), applied as a seed treatment or as a seedling foliar spray, is very effective for controlling fusiform rust on nursery stock. Foliar spraying usually is not initiated until after more than 50% of seedlings have emerged, so a seed treatment reduces loss by protecting early-emerging seedlings. Seeds can be treated either by soaking or application of a wettable powder. Seeds should be soaked in a solution of 30 g a.i./20 liters of water for 24 hours at room temperature. Seed dressing should be at a rate of 25 g a.i./kg of seeds. A seed treatment provides complete protection for about 4 weeks after germination. When triadimefon is not used as a seed treatment, the first foliar spray should be applied within 14

days of germination. Foliar sprays prevent infection for up to 14 days after spraying and eradicate infections established up to 14 days before spraying. Rates as low as 0.28 kg a.i./ha in a water and surfactant mix are effective. Time of application during the day is unimportant. Three or four foliar spray applications to a nursery bed during the year are sufficient to control the disease because the chemical is systemic and acts both as a protectant and an eradicant. Chemical control of rust in the nursery does not increase susceptibility of seedlings after outplanting (Kelley 1980, 1984; Kelley and Rowan 1985; Mexal and Snow 1978; Rowan 1984a; Rowan and Kelley 1986; Skoller and others 1983; Snow and others 1979).

Triadimefon is also effective when incorporated into nursery soil before sowing. However, it suppresses ectomycorrhizal development on nursery seedlings and subsequent seedling growth, especially when applied at high rates (Kelley 1985, 1988; Marx and others 1986; Mexal and Snow 1978). Unless outplanting stock is adequately inoculated with ectomycorrhizae, pine seedlings will perform poorly, especially on stressed sites and during drought years (see chapter 6).

Newly outplanted seedlings are susceptible to rust infection even if they have had seed and foliar treatments. When outplanted on high-hazard sites, up to 40% of sprayed stock may still become infected if fungal control is not continued (Rowan 1976). Top- or root-dipping bareroot nursery stock in a solution of 1,500 mg of granular triadimefon/l of water will prevent natural rust infections during the first infection season after outplanting (Rowan 1984b). However, applying the fungicide to seedling roots or to the rooting zone during the outplanting process does not reduce infection (Snow and others 1986).

Triadimefon is compatible with the animal repellent and fungicide thiram (Kelley and Williams 1985), so seeds can be treated with both chemicals before direct seeding.

Nematodes

Nematodes (unsegmented roundworms) can be either endoparasitic (living in internal tissues of the host) or ectoparasitic (living on the exterior of the host) to loblolly pines. They occur in all forest soils and are the most serious microorganism pests of forest nurseries. The life cycle of plant parasitic nematodes consists of egg, larval, and adult stages. The time spent in each stage can vary greatly. Because nematodes are rarely more than 1 mm in length, they are hard to see. They feed on roots of seedlings and create points of entry for other pathogenic organisms such as root rots. When there are 800 or more individuals/100 cm^3 of soil, stunting of growth, needle discoloration, and some seedling mortality can be expected. Some common parasitic nematodes found in forest nurseries are listed in table 10-11. Loblolly seedlings can be stunted severely when grown in soil infested with the stubby-root nematode, *Trichodorus christiei* Allen (Ruehle 1969). The lance nematode, *Hoplolaimus galeatus* Cobb, is also pathogenic to loblolly (Ruehle and Marx 1971). Loblolly is moderately susceptible to the pinewood nematode, *Bursaphelenchus xylophilus* (Steiner & Buhrer) Nickle (= *B. lignicolus* Mamiya & Kiyohara) (Dwinell 1985).

Root Rots

Black root rot, caused by *Fusarium oxysporum* Schlechtend.:Fr., destroys loblolly pine roots. It can be a severe problem in nurseries. The effect of this root rot on outplanting survival of seedlings is directly related to the percentage of roots affected. The disease can be controlled by methyl bromide–chloropicrin soil fumigation or fungicide drenches of benomyl or thiabendazole. Unfortunately, the soil drenches reduce ectomycorrhizal development (Rowan 1981, 1983).

Tip Dieback

There can be numerous causes of terminal mortality in nursery seedlings, including excess use of fertilizers or pesticides and insect damage. However, managers should be aware that dieback of terminal shoots can also be caused by the pathogens *Diplodia gossypina* Cke. and *Fusarium moniliforme* var. *subglutinans*. The number of trees affected is usually small, and the problem does not reduce survival and growth of the trees following outplanting (Affeltranger 1983, Rowan 1982).

Insect Damage

White grubs, *Phyllophaga* spp., can damage or kill large numbers of nursery seedlings. They feed on young roots, causing rapid seedling mortality, especially in the early spring. Infestations cause patches of seedlings to wither and turn yellow, then brown. Affected seedlings are easy to pull up because their taproots are cut off 2.5 to 7.5 cm below the groundline. White grubs can be controlled with diazinon, chloropicrin, ethylene dichloride, or methyl bromide. The larvae of click beetles, as well as root borers, *Prionus* spp.; root weevils, *Brachyrhinus* spp.; and southern mole crickets, *Scapteriscus acletus* Rehn & Hebard, also feed on pine roots and may cause local problems in nurseries. Nantucket pine tip moth larvae attack terminal buds of nursery seedlings but can be controlled with dimethoate. The lesser cornstalk borer, *Elasmopalpus lignosellus* (Zeller), and the pales weevil feed on stembark near the ground, stunting or killing seedlings; their damage is often confused. The lesser cornstalk borer may cause enough damage in a nursery to justify treatments with malathion (May 1985). Other minor insect pests are listed in table 10-11.

Animal Control

Control of bird predation is critical in loblolly pine nurseries. Spring sowing of seeds comes at a time when native foods for birds are scarce. Bird damage rises to a peak during germination and may continue until seedcoats have dropped. Birds can kill or severely injure newly germinated seedlings by clipping off cotyledons while seedcoats are still attached (Wakeley 1954). Mourning doves damage or destroy more nursery-sown seeds than do other birds, but eastern meadowlarks; bobolinks, *Dolichonyx oryzivorus*; blackbirds; crows, *Corvus* spp.; northern cardinals; bobwhite quail; pigeons, especially *Columba oivia*; and numerous species of sparrows (Fringillidae family) can be a problem in certain areas. Maintaining a few hectares of annual cover (for example, soybeans and sorghum) in a nursery area can keep birds away from newly sown nursery beds (Dorward 1965). Early bird predation can be minimized by ensuring that all newly sown seeds are covered with soil, that seeds are pretreated with repellents, and that beds are irrigated to promote rapid germination and early seedling growth (see chapter 6).

Mammals can also affect nursery seedling production. Deer can be a great nuisance. They trample seeds and seedlings and occasionally browse seedlings. Fences high enough to exclude deer are expensive and must be maintained continuously. Meadow or field mice, *Microtus* spp., occasionally damage many seedlings in small areas when mouse populations are high. Mice are easily controlled by eliminating breeding areas and habitats favorable for their development near seedbeds. Rabbits occasionally chew the tops off a few nursery seedlings, but they are rarely a significant problem.

Cold Injury

Prolonged exposure to freezing temperatures kills the cambium of loblolly pine nursery stock, especially in succulent new germinants. A "hard freeze" following a warm day may cause needles to turn brown and succulent shoots of 9- to 12-month-old seedlings to wilt. Even extended above-freezing cold periods can injure unprotected nursery seedlings. Damage is greatest to seedlings from the southernmost sources. During an extended cold period, roots of seedlings in an Arkansas nursery were killed by soil temperatures that reached −8 °C at a depth of 6.0 mm. This reduced early outplanting survival, delayed bud break, and reduced early height growth (Carlson 1984). Nurseries located in central and southern Alabama, northern Florida, and central and southern Georgia are most likely to be affected by severe cold. Damage is most severe where one or more of the following nursery conditions occur (Lantz 1984):

- Nursery beds are oriented in an east-west direction or have a northern aspect.

- Soils are fine textured.

- Soil moisture is high just prior to a freeze.

Strong winds associated with hurricanes, tornadoes, or severe thunderstorms can blow mulch and surface soil from seedbeds. This can damage seedlings and expose root systems. The effects of strong spring winds can generally be ameliorated by a combination of the following actions:

- Using strategically placed windbreaks to shield nursery beds.

- Early sowing with pretreated seeds to ensure early establishment of a full stand of seedlings.

- Keeping a continuous layer of mulch on seedbeds even after germination and throughout the winter when sowing in the fall.

- Using heavy or coarse mulch material.

- Increasing soil organic matter to minimize the number of single grain particles on the soil surface because these can damage trees when moved by wind.

- Extra watering during dry, windy periods.

Cultural practices, such as root pruning or withholding fertilizer or water, can help to harden-off seedlings (see chapter 6). Frost hardiness of a seedling or a family can be determined by exposing tissue to freezing temperatures (Johnson and Landis 1984). Freeze damage can be assessed in the laboratory by the electrolyte leakage method or by measurement of ethane production by seedlings (Johnson and Gagnon 1988). Evidence of freeze damage includes discoloration of cambium near the root collar, bark slippage, browning of the interior of roots, and sponginess and looseness of bark. Freeze damage becomes more evident as time passes.

Frost heaving, which results from repeated freezing and thawing of nursery soil, primarily in the spring, can severely damage fall-sown seedlings that have not had time to develop long taproots that would firmly anchor them in the soil. Frost heaving is most frequent on fine-textured and poorly drained soils and in northern nurseries.

Controlling Pests of Container Seedlings

Because *Fusarium* spp. can cause root rot and damping-off even in container-grown loblolly pines, soil used in the production of containerized seedlings should be selected with care and fumigated if necessary (Pawuk and Barnett 1974). However, chemical treatments may not eliminate *Fusarium* spp. entirely, because the fungus has been found in megagametophytes and embryos of seeds (Miller and Bramlett 1978). Algal growth in styroblock containers can be controlled by using fungicides such as maneb (Pawuk 1983). Airborne diseases are of minor importance (Pawuk 1982).

Foliage diseases are not a problem in container culture, probably because the time required to produce plantable seedlings is short. If there is a possibility that seedlings will be infected with fusiform rust, they can be sprayed with a systemic fungicide containing triadimefon. Aphids, whiteflies (Aleyrodidae family), scales (*Toumeyella* spp. and *Phenacaspis* spp.), and thrips (especially slash pine flower thrips, *Gnophothrips fuscus* (Morgan)) are generally the most serious insect pests of container stock; mites, Tetranychidae family, are also serious pests. Controlling these insects usually requires regular application of approved insecticides. Other common insect pests, such as ants and caterpillars, are rarely a problem in container culture. They can usually be controlled by good sanitation, baiting, or physical barriers.

Seed Orchard Protection

Cones and seeds are highly subject to damage by insects, diseases, and weather during the 20-month maturation period. More than half of the female strobili are lost between the flower and mature cone stages of development (Fatzinger and others 1980). Although 50% or more of the potential seeds per cone can be obtained in orchards when pollination is controlled, the average is approximately 25%. Sometimes seed production is as low as 14% of potential production (Snyder and Squillace 1966, Yates and Ebel 1978). The major destructive agents are insects and spontaneous strobilus abortion, which seems to be unrelated to insect feeding (Chatelain and Goyer 1980, Ebel 1974, Fatzinger and others 1980, Goyer and Nachod 1976, Kucera 1973, McLemore 1977, Yates and Ebel 1978).

Insect Pests

The grafts, shoots, buds, and needles of orchard trees are all susceptible to insect damage. Spider mites, *Tetranychus* spp., can weaken newly transplanted grafts. Stem borers, reproduction weevils, tip moths, sawflies, and other insects may also damage young grafted stock. The striped pine scale, *Toumeyella pini* (King), occasionally feeds on shoot tips and needles of seed orchard trees from May to early November. Outbreaks of this scale can occasionally cause mortality but attacks usually result in growth loss and reduced tree vigor (Clarke and others 1988, 1989a). Tree parts are not injured seriously unless heavily infested. Scale insects that affect large branches and the main stem of loblolly pines include the pine tortoise scale, *Matsuccous gallicola* (Morrison), and *Toumeyella parvicornus* (Cockerell).

Periodic careful checks of orchard trees will usually reveal these problems early. In the case of scale insects, spraying the immature or crawler stage with chemicals is most effective in decreasing populations (Flavell 1974). Scale problems in seed orchards often occur when chemicals applied to control other pests kill natural enemies of the scale insects. Continued chemical control may lead to future severe outbreaks because of reduced natural predators (Clarke and others 1988, 1989a). Other insects that damage orchard trees include geometrids, the speckled pine needle aphid, and the pine needle sheath midge.

Many insect species feed on loblolly pine flowers and cones (table 10-12). They can destroy from 10 to 75% of a cone crop and probably cause a high percentage of conelet abortion, which can range from near zero to more than 70% for a particular year. The leaffooted pine seed bug, *Leptoglossus corculus* (Say), is probably the single greatest

cause of conelet abortion (DeBarr and Ebel 1973, DeBarr and Kormanik 1975). The loblolly pine coneworm, *Dioryctria taedivorella* Neunzig & Leidy, is the most destructive insect pest in seed orchards, damaging up to 75% of the cones in an orchard in any one year (Ebel 1974; Hanula and others 1985; Kucera 1973; Neunzig and Leidy 1989; Sartor and Neel 1971a, 1971b). Feeding by the shieldbacked pine seed bug, *Tetyra bipunctata* (Herrich-Schäffer), and by the leaffooted pine seed bug can result in up to 10% seed mortality (DeBarr 1974, Goyer and Williams 1981, Williams and Goyer 1980). Although common, seedworms, *Laspeyresia* spp., seldom infest more than 20% of loblolly cones and generally destroy fewer than 4% of the seeds produced in any specific orchard in 1 year (Ebel and others 1980, Fatzinger and others 1980, Goyer and Nachod 1976, USDA FS 1972).

May beetles, *Phyllophaga micans* (Knoch); midges of the family Cecidomyiidae; the Virginia pine sawfly, *Neodiprion*

Table 10-12—The primary feeding periods and general ranges of flower-, conelet-, cone-, and seed-damaging insects in loblolly pine seed orchards

Common name	Scientific name	Range*	Jan.	Feb.	Mar.	Apr.	May	Jun.	Jul.	Aug.	Sep.	Oct.	Nov.	Dec.
Flower- and conelet-damaging insects														
Nantucket pine tip moth	*Rhyacionia frustrana* (Comstock)	a				▓	▓	▓						
Pine conelet looper	*Nepytia semiclusaria* (Walker)	d		▓	▓	▓	▓							
Virginia pine sawfly	*Neodiprion pratti pratti* (Dyar)	e				▓	▓	▓						
May beetles	*Phyllophaga* spp.	a			▓	▓								
Pine catkin sawflies	*Xyela* spp.	a	▓	▓	▓									
Leaffooted pine seed bug	*Leptoglossus corculus* (Say)	a						▓	▓	▓	▓	▓	▓	
Cone feeding midges	*Cecidomyiidae* (Diptera)	a	▓	▓	▓	▓	▓	▓	▓	▓	▓	▓	▓	
South coastal coneworm	*Dioryctria ebeli* Mutuura & Monroe	c			▓	▓	▓	▓						
Loblolly pine coneworm	*D. merkeli* Mutuura & Monroe†	a	▓	▓	▓	▓								
Southern pine coneworm	*D. amatella* (Hulst)	b	▓	▓	▓	▓								
Blister coneworm	*D. clarioralis* (Walker)	a	▓	▓	▓	▓	▓	▓	▓	▓	▓	▓	▓	
Cone-damaging insects														
Southern pine coneworm	*Dioryctria amatella* (Hulst)	b						▓	▓	▓	▓	▓	▓	
Blister coneworm	*D. clarioralis* (Walker)	a	▓	▓	▓	▓	▓	▓	▓	▓	▓	▓	▓	▓
Webbing coneworm	*D. disclusa* Heinrich	a				▓	▓	▓	▓	▓	▓			
South coastal coneworm	*D. ebeli* Mutuura & Munroe	c						▓	▓	▓				
Loblolly pine coneworm	*D. merkeli* Mutuura & Munroe†	a					▓	▓	▓					
Shortleaf pine cone borer	*Eucosma cocana* Kearfott	g					▓	▓	▓	▓				
Cone feeding midges	*Cecidomyiidae* (Diptera)	a				▓	▓	▓	▓	▓	▓	▓		
Seed-damaging insects														
Slash pine seedworm	*Laspeyresia anaranjada* Miller	c					▓	▓	▓	▓	▓			
Longleaf pine seedworm	*L. ingens* Heinrich	a					▓	▓	▓	▓	▓	▓		
Eastern pine seedworm	*L. toreuta* (Grote)	a						▓	▓	▓	▓	▓		
Leaffooted pine seed bug	*Leptoglossus corculus* (Say)	a				▓	▓	▓	▓	▓	▓	▓	▓	
Shieldbacked pine seed bug	*Tetyra bipunctata* (Herrich-Schaeffer)	a					▓	▓	▓	▓	▓	▓	▓	

Source: adapted from Ebel and others (1980).

* Location where the insect can be found within the loblolly pine range: a = natural and introduced range of loblolly; b = natural range of loblolly; c = Coastal Plain of Georgia, Florida, Alabama, Mississippi, and southeast Louisiana; d = natural range of loblolly except northeast Texas and south Arkansas; e = North Carolina, north Tennessee, and northward; f = highlands from north Georgia to Maryland; g = Atlantic Coastal States plus east Tennessee.

† Neunzig and Leidy (1989) reported that *Dioryctria merkeli* feeds mainly on slash pine, whereas a similar species, *D. taedivorella* Neunzig & Leidy is a more widespread coneworm associated with loblolly pine.

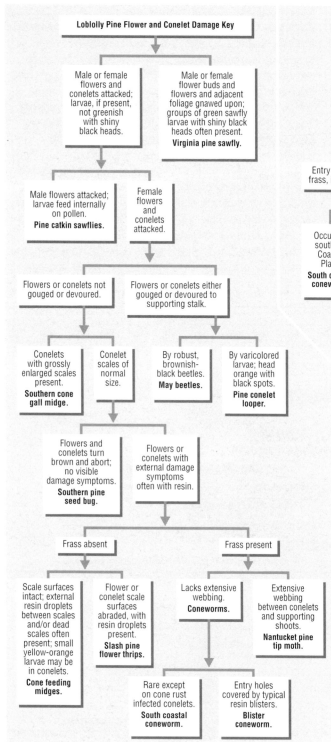

Figure 10-12—Key to loblolly pine flower and conelet damage (adapted from Ebel and others 1980).

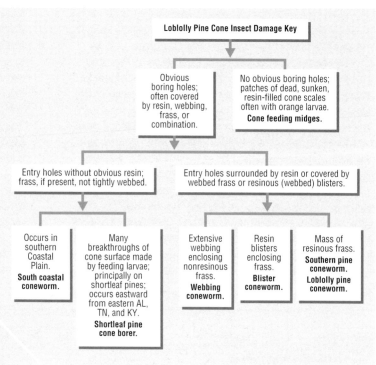

▲ **Figure 10-13**—Key to loblolly pine cone insect damage (adapted from Ebel and others 1980).

ers 1980, McLemore 1973, Neel and Sartor 1969, Yates and Ebel 1972, Yearian and Warren 1964). Tip moths destroy both female flowers and conelets, but they are a relatively minor problem for loblolly. Controlling seed and cone insects with chemicals can precipitate attacks by the woolly pine scale, *Pseudophilippia quaintancii* (Cockerell), and the loblolly pine mealy bug, *Oracella acuta* (Lobdell). Their buildup is probably the result of insecticidal killing of their natural enemies (Nord and others 1985). The characteristic symptom of the woolly pine scale is cottony wax secretions on shoots and needles of infested trees. Woolly pine scale is most prevalent in the upper part of tree crowns. Some tree clones are more susceptible to the scale than others (Clarke and others 1989b).

Most losses of strobili occur during the first 3 to 5 months of strobilus development. Most second-year cones are lost in the spring (Fatzinger and others 1980, Kucera 1973). Damage is unique and can be used to identify individual insect species (figures 10-12 and 10-13). Control-pollinated conelets can be protected from the seed bugs *Leptoglossus corculus* and *Tetyra bipunctata* if they are covered with screen wire cages as soon as pollination bags are removed. The cages must remain in place until cone maturity. The screens do not exclude coneworms of the genus *Dioryctria*, which probably enter the cages as small larvae (Bramlett and others 1977).

Grasshoppers—the twostriped, *Melanoplus bivittatus* (Say), the redlegged, *M. femurrubrum* (De Geer), and especially the American, *Schistocerca americana* (Drury)— can cause severe damage to individual orchard seedlings and saplings by feeding on the buds and needles at

pratti pratti (Dyar) and other sawflies, *Xyela* spp.; small larvae of the pine conelet looper, *Nepytia semiclusaria* (Walker); *Oscinella conicola* (Greene); and *Asynapta keeni* (Foote) are other important pests of loblolly pine cones. These insects usually damage only small portions (1 to 6%) of orchard seed crops but can occasionally cause major damage (Ebel and DeBarr 1973, Fatzinger and oth-

night during dry hot weather when grasses and forbs are scarce. Both nymphs and adults have been observed feeding, primarily on branch tips, especially in and around the center of a new orchard. Observers found as many as 52 individuals feeding on a single seedling branch but found fewer than 5 grasshoppers on most trees (Feaver 1985). Grasshoppers also feed on loblolly pine seedlings growing in the woods when other food is scarce, but the damage is usually minor.

Secondary insects reported to infest strobili of dead loblolly pines or strobili dying from other causes include the moths *Battaristis vittella* (Busch), *Moodna ostrinella* (Clemens), and *Holcocera* spp. and the beetles *Ernobius* spp. and *Pityophthorus* spp. (Goyer and Nachod 1976, Neel and Sartor 1969, Yearian and Warren 1964).

Chemical treatments are presently the most practical and successful means of controlling insect pests in seed orchards. However, Federal registrations are constantly in jeopardy, and few new chemicals are being tested for use in seed orchards or for other minor applications. In addition, broad-spectrum insecticides frequently kill beneficial insects, as well as target pests. Azinphos-methyl (Guthion®), carbofuran (Furadan®), fenvalerate (Pydrin®), and permethrin (Ambush®) are registered for control of coneworms and seed bugs in loblolly pine seed orchards. Their use does not reduce seed set, seed yield, or seed germination if recommended concentrations are applied (Cameron and others 1987, DeBarr and Matthews 1985, Fatzinger and others 1985). *Bacillus thuringiensis*, a microbial insecticide considered harmless to mammals, also reduces coneworm and seedworm damage in loblolly (Gage 1975, McLeod and others 1984). Loblolly shows genetic variability in resistance to insects and diseases (see chapter 7), and this suggests that selection can produce resistant trees and reduce the need for pesticides (Dwinell and Barrows-Broaddus 1985).

Depending on tree size and orchard size, chemicals can be applied by hand, ground machine, or aircraft. Low- or high-volume sprayers mounted on a truck or trailer can disperse pesticides from the ground to the tops of trees. Aerial application is advantageous in many cases because spray deposits concentrate in the upper tree crowns where most new cones develop and because the chemical can be applied in a short time. The density of foliage and viscosity of spray material determine how much material filters to lower levels (Barry and others 1984, Johansen and Shimmel 1967). Disadvantages of aerial spraying include unwanted drift to populated areas, shortness of periods when weather is satisfactory for spraying, and waste of chemical in young stands in which the crown surface occupies only a small part of the area sprayed.

Insect trapping can increase the efficiency of a control program by providing continuous information about species presence, population size, and periods of high activity. Insecticide applications can be timed based on trap catches, and areawide trends in insect populations can be estimated to increase the effectiveness of general pest management programs. The use of pheromones to disrupt communications between male and female pests may prove a safe and effective method of reducing insect reproduction success and population size.

Diseases

Pitch canker can be particularly severe in loblolly pine seed orchards, where branch dieback in the upper crown causes the loss of strobili, cones, and seeds. Symptoms of the disease (predominately shoot dieback in the upper crown, but also bleeding resinous cankers on the trunk and larger branches, reduction in the quality and quantity of viable seeds, and mortality and deterioration of internal seed tissues) occur throughout the year (Barrows-Broaddus and Dwinell 1985, Dwinell and others 1977, Miller and Bramlett 1978). Branch scars created when cones are removed are common infection courts (Blakeslee and others 1980). There is considerable clonal variation in susceptibility to pitch canker (Dwinell and others 1977, Kelley and Williams 1982). This suggests that breeding could reduce susceptibility. There seems to be no correlation between pitch canker susceptibility and fusiform rust resistance in loblolly families (Dwinell and Barrows-Broaddus 1985).

Fusiform rust can infect new field grafts although some genotypes are resistant to the disease. Pruning rootstock stimulates formation of succulent epicormic sprouts on the rootstock that provide excellent infection points for the pathogen, especially in the spring and early summer when spores are most prevalent. Branches of large orchard trees should not be pruned when the danger of infection is high. Wound paint or spray can reduce the incidence of infection of newly cut surfaces (Long and others 1974).

Rust cankers on orchard trees provide overwintering sites for coneworm larvae, and especially for larvae of the southern pine coneworm, *Dioryctria amatella* (Hulst). These cankers also support high resident beetle populations.

Special care must be taken to protect seed orchard trees from infection by annosum root rot. In low-hazard areas, stumps of rogued trees must always be treated with borax or *Phlebia gigantea*. On high-hazard sites, stumps should be removed and remaining roots treated with *P. gigantea*. Also, vehicle traffic should be kept to a minimum, and herbicides should be used for weed control to eliminate bole or root damage that can be caused by mowing or disking (Robbins 1984).

Fungi of the genera *Aspergillis*, *Curvularia*, *Fusarium*, *Pestalotia*, and *Phomopsis* commonly infest more than half of the seeds of loblolly pine, whether seeds are collected directly from cones or after falling into nets on the ground (Ammon 1987).

Rodents

During the winter, gopher (family Geomyidae) feeding and burrowing can destroy the root systems of young loblolly pines in orchards. Gopher activity is usually spotty and associated with fresh piles of soil. Unfortunately, by the time damage to specific trees can be detected, it is usually too late to save those individuals. However, additional tree mortality can usually be prevented. Fall and winter application of poisoned bait with a gopher machine may be necessary to control these animals before colonies build. The machine, which is similar to a subsoiler, creates false tunnels and deposits poisoned bait in the tunnels (Long and others 1974).

Squirrels can destroy many mature cones by chewing off bracts and eating seeds. Scattered remnants of cones and individual bracts on the ground provide evidence of squirrel activity and the extent of damage. Good acorn or cone crops in surrounding forest land usually limit squirrel movement into orchards. Hunting pressure in surrounding forest land normally keeps squirrel populations to levels that will do little damage. If the situation is severe, hunting in the orchard or fixing a wide band of sheet metal around the lower bole of each tree protects cones.

Summary

Damage caused by pests and environmental stresses has become increasingly severe in southern pine forests over the past 50 years principally because many ecosystems of mixed species have been converted to rapidly growing, even-aged stands of loblolly or other single species. Conversion to pine monoculture has reduced or eliminated many natural influences that previously kept pathogenic organisms in check.

Major diseases affecting loblolly pine include fusiform rust and annosum root rot. Both predominate in plantations. Annosum root rot damage is greatest following thinning in stands of pole-sized timber. It usually infects newly cut stumps and destroys roots in pockets sur-

rounding infection courts. The principal control methods include thinning only in summer below latitude 34% N, application of granular borax, a borax solution, or *Phlebia gigantea* in liquid suspension to the cut surfaces of stumps, or application of two prescribed burns before thinning. Fusiform rust commonly causes galls to form on the stems of nursery seedlings and on both stems and branches of planted seedlings and saplings. The disease requires an oak alternate host during its approximately 2-year life cycle. Growing galls often badly deform and weaken loblolly stems, causing stem breakage. Newly regenerated trees under a pine overstory are less susceptible to fusiform rust than are newly regenerated trees in

Table 10-13—Major insect and disease pests of loblolly pine associated with regeneration, intermediate stand management, and harvesting

Loblolly pine stand development stages and management activities*	Repro-duction weevils	Leaf-cutting ants	SPB	Ips/BTB	Annosum root rot	Fusiform rust
Stage 1— Regeneration to age 10 (seedling/sapling stands)						
Site preparation						
1. Burn						■
2. Herbicides						■
3. Chop/disk/shear/pile	■					■
4. Bed	■					■
Regeneration						
1. Natural regeneration						
a. See tree		■				■
b. Clearcut in strips		■				
c. Shelterwood		■				■
d. Seed-in-place		■				
e. Seedling-in-place	■	■				
2. Artificial regeneration						
a. Direct seed		■				
b. Plant	■	■		■		■
• Seed source/species				■		■
• Spacing			■	■		
• Matching species to site			■	■		■

Loblolly pine stand development stages and management activities*	Repro-duction weevils	Leaf-cutting ants	SPB	Ips/BTB	Annosum root rot	Fusiform rust
Early stand treatment						
1. Herbicides						■
2. Fertilization						■
3. Release spray						■
Stage 2—Age 10 to harvest (pulpwood/sawtimber stands)						
Intermediate culture						
1. Precommercial thin			■	■	■	■
2. Thin (pine)			■	■	■	■
3. Pine release cut (hardwoods)			■			■
4. Improvement cut			■		■	■
5. Fertilization						■
6. Burn					■	■
Stage 3—Harvest						
1. Seed tree			■	■	■	■
2. Shelterwood			■	■	■	■
3. Selection			■	■	■	■

Source: adapted from Hertel and others (1985).

SPB = southern pine beetle, BTB = black turpentine beetle.

* An ■ indicates a stand/age treatment impact on the pest. Refer to table 10-14 or text to determine specific stand/pest interactions.

Table 10-14—Recommendations for management of some insects and diseases affecting loblolly pines

Pest	Stand class	Prevention	Suppression
Reproduction weevils	Seedling	Delay planting 1 year in high-hazard areas if pine lands are harvested (or site-prepared with significant number of residual pines being felled) in July or later. Treat seedlings with registered insecticides prior to or at planting time if area has many fresh stumps.	Spray seedling with registered insecticides if significant weevil damage occurs.
Texas leaf-cutting ant	Seedling	Survey sites with deep sandy soils and treat ant colonies with registered insecticides prior to planting. If insecticides are not used, do not plant seedlings in vicinity of active colonies.	Treat new colonies with registered insecticides.
Southern pine beetle (SPB)	Seedling/ sapling	Favor mixed pine or pine–hardwood stands. Improve drainage in low-lying areas subject to flooding.	NA
	Pole/ sawtimber	Perform frequent surveillance in high-hazard stands or areas. Avoid damage to site and/or trees. Salvage cut and thin to remove high-risk trees and to maintain vigorously growing stands. Promote multispecies stands. Use uneven-aged management. Avoid damage to site and roots and trunks of residual trees when making partial cuts. Treat stumps to control annosum root rot (see below).	Preform frequent surveillance. Consider control techniques such as: • salvage* • cut-and-leave* • cut-and-spray • pile-and-burn.
Ips/black turpentine beetle (BTB)	Pole/ sawtimber	Promote healthy, rapidly growing trees. Avoid damage to site, as well as roots and trunks of residual trees.	Early detection and immediate spraying of infected boles with lindane in diesel oil can protect trees from BTB. N/A for Ips.
Annosum root rot	Seedling	Increase initial spacing of seedlings to delay thinnings and reduce root contacts on high-hazard sites. Consider establishing more resistant species on high-hazard sites (e.g., longleaf on sandy sites).	NA
	Pole/ sawtimber	Consider prescribed burning before and after thinning. Reduce oak population. Treat stumps with borax when thinning on deep sandy soils in winter above latitude 34° N. Thin and use *Phlebia gigantea* if root rot is present. Make partial cuts in the summer below latitude 34° N. or treat fresh stumps with borax. If annosum is already present, treat fresh stumps with *P. gigantea*. Liquidate and regenerate stand if disease-free residual stand stocking is inadequate to maintain to harvest.	Remove diseased trees and a buffer of healthy neighbors, and treat fresh stumps with *P. gigantea*. If disease-free residual stand stocking is inadequate, regenerate.
Fusiform rust	Seedling/ sapling	Cull rust-infected stock. Regenerate high-hazard sites with resistant seed source. Minimize site preparation. Increase planting density to offset future losses (note conflict with annosum and SPB). Delay fertilization until age 8 to 10. Delay prescribed burning until trees are at least 8 years old. Reduce oaks in or adjacent to regeneration area.	Treat nursery seedlings with registered fungicides. Use a rust impact prediction model to determine stand treatment needs.
	Pole/ sawtimber	Remove severely infected trees to prevent inoculation of younger age classes in adjacent stands to recover potential lost volume. Remove oaks during harvest. Select uninfected parents when using seed-tree or shelterwood system.	Liquidate stand and regenerate if disease-free residual stand stocking is inadequate.

Source: adapted from Hertel and others (1985).

* If cutting green buffer on deep sandy soil, treat stumps with borax to control annosus root rot.

open, planted areas, so shelterwood or all-age management may be preferable on some high-risk sites. Control of fusiform rust in loblolly pine stands has improved significantly over the past decade. The systemic fungicide triademefon (Bayleton®) provides excellent protection to nursery seedlings when applied 3 to 5 times/infection season. Use of disease-resistant seedlings, especially those from east Texas and south Louisiana, have reduced infection in plantations by more than 50%.

The southern pine beetle (SPB), pine engraver beetles, and the black turpentine beetle are the most destructive insect pests of loblolly. In most years, SPBs account for more than 80% of the insect-caused economic loss of loblolly pine. The other bark beetles are responsible for another 10% of the loss. Populations of each of these species can increase rapidly and can cause substantial tree mortality in stands of pole-sized or larger pine if conditions favor their development. They all feed and construct egg galleries in the phloem and hasten tree death by plugging water-conducting tissues. Their success in killing trees can be attributed partly to their symbiotic relationships with fungi. Beetle-induced fungal infections are thought to be important in overcoming host resistance and are also important to larval nutrition.

Beetles readily attack loblolly in pure stands or in mixtures with hardwoods. Heavily stocked older stands are generally most susceptible to attack by beetles. However, as many as 50% of the bark beetle infestations in loblolly are associated with lightning-damaged trees.

Insects other than bark beetles account for less than 5% of the annual insect-caused losses of loblolly pine. New loblolly pine regeneration is most seriously affected by the pales weevil, whereas most damage in sapling stands is caused by tip moths.

Incorporation of existing pest management techniques into silvicultural systems costs little and can have substantial and long-lasting benefits. This requires careful planning and a knowledgeable assessment of the risk of attack for each stand or area. Table 10-13 summarizes known effects of management practices on insect pests and diseases, and table 10-14 provides management recommendations for minimizing problems during regeneration, intermediate, and harvesting stages.

The presence of multiple hazards (for example, SPB's and littleleaf disease, SPB's and annosum root rot) can pose special problems for management. These can best be managed by silvicultural manipulation—that is, by regenerating loblolly pine on appropriate sites, preparing sites properly, and controlling stocking at planting, and by thinning, salvage cutting, and adjusting rotation length. Similarly, controlling environmental conditions in nurseries through integrated programs of fumigation, seed and seedling treatments, crop rotation, and proper selection of cover crops has greatly reduced multiple insect and disease control problems and seedling losses.

Research Needs

■ An effective littleleaf disease hazard rating system for loblolly pine stands grown for long rotations on high hazard sites needs to be developed.

■ A better understanding is needed of the effects of different naturally occurring chemicals in oleoresin of loblolly pine resistant to southern pine beetles (SPB's) in order to permit the selection of tree strains with improved resistance to SPB's.

■ More research is needed on breeding trees that physically resist SPB's through high oleoresin flow rates and/or high total oleoresin flow. Research should also incorporate site variability to take full advantage of variability in host resistance.

■ Loblolly pine genotypes with high tolerance to destructive stresses (for example, air pollution, unfavorable soil or site conditions, and water stress) in both rural and urban settings need to be identified and selected.

■ Genotypes with superior resistance to a wide range of insect and disease problems need to be identified and selected.

■ New or improved ways to control insect populations with naturally occurring pheromones need to be developed.

Literature Cited

Adams MB, Kelly JM, Edwards NT. 1988. Growth of *Pinus taeda* L. seedlings varies with family and ozone exposure level. Water, Air, and Soil Pollution 38(1/2):137–150.

Adriano DC, Pinder JE III. 1977. Aerial deposition of plutonium in mixed forest stands from nuclear fuel reprocessing. Journal of Environmental Quality 6(3):303–307.

Affeltranger CE. 1983. The effect of tip blight on survival and growth of outplanted loblolly pine after two years. In: Proceeding, 1982 Southern Nursery Conferences; 1982 August 9–12; Oklahoma City, OK/July 12–15; Savannah, GA. Tech. Publ. R8-TP4. Atlanta: USDA Forest Service, Southern Region: 192–194.

Alexander SA, Hokans RH, Fanelli ES, Kurdyla TM. 1985. Methods for estimating annosus root rot in loblolly pine stands. In: Proceedings, Integrated Pest Management Symposium; 1985 April 15–18; Asheville, NC. Gen. Tech. Rep. SO-56. New Orleans: USDA Forest Service, Southern Forest Experiment Station: 56–57.

Alexander SA, Skelly JM. 1974. A comparison of isolation methods for determining the incidence of *Fomes annosus* in living loblolly pine. European Journal of Forest Pathology 4(1):33–38.

Alexander SA, Skelly JM, Morris CL. 1975. Edaphic factors associated with the incidence and severity of diseases caused by *Fomes annosus* in loblolly pine plantations in Virginia. Phytopathology 65(5):585–591.

Alexander SA, Skelly JM, Webb RS. 1981. Effects of *Heterobasidion annosum* on radial growth in southern pine beetle-infested loblolly pine. Phytopathology 71(5):479–481.

All JN, Anderson RF. 1972. Initial attack and brood production by females of *Ips grandicollis* (Coleoptera: Scolytidae). Annals of the Entomological Society of America 65(6):1293–1296.

Altshuller AP. 1984. Atmospheric concentrations and distribution of chemical substances. In: The acid deposition phenomenon and its effects. EPA-600/8-83-016AF. Washington, DC: U.S. Environmental Protection Agency: 323–423.

Ammon V. 1987. Incidence of fungi on seed collected from cones and from plastic netting in a loblolly pine seed orchard in Mississippi [abstract]. Phytopathology 77(17):1758.

Andersen BC, Kulhavy DL, Johnson PC. 1984. Estimating infestation rates of the Nantucket pine tip moth (Lepidoptera: Tortricidae) through sequential sampling. Environmental Entomology 13(6):1593–1597.

Anderson NH, Anderson DB. 1968. Ips bark beetle attacks and brood development on a lightning-struck pine in relation to its physiological decline. Florida Entomologist 51(1):23–30.

Anderson RL. 1986. New method for assessing contamination of slash and loblolly pine seeds by *Fusarium moniliforme* var. *subglutinans*. Plant Disease 70(5):452–453.

Anderson RL, Mistretta PA. 1982. Integrated pest management handbook: management strategies for reducing losses caused by fusiform rust, annosus root rot and littleleaf disease. Agric. Handbk. 597. Washington, DC: USDA Forest Service. 30 p.

Anderson RL, Cost ND, McClure JP, Ryan G. 1986a. Predicting severity of fusiform rust in young loblolly and slash pine stands in Florida, Georgia, and the Carolinas. Southern Journal of Applied Forestry 10(1):38–41.

Anderson RL, McClure JP, Cost ND, Hoffard WH. 1983. Incidence and impact of damage to Florida's timber, 1980. Resource Bull. SE-64. Asheville, NC: USDA Forest Service, Southeastern Forest Experiment Station. 20 p.

Anderson RL, McClure JP, Cost N, Uhler RJ. 1986b. Estimating fusiform rust losses in five southeast states. Southern Journal of Applied Forestry 10(4):237–240.

Anderson RL, McClure JP, Hoffard WH, Cost ND. 1981. Incidence and impact of damage to South Carolina's timber, 1979. Resour. Bull. SE-56. Asheville, NC: USDA Forest Service, Southeastern Forest Experiment Station. 34 p.

Applegate HW. 1971. Annosus root rot mortality in once-thinned loblolly pine plantations in Tennessee. Plant Disease Reporter 55(7):625.

Artman JD. 1972. Further tests in Virginia using chain-saw applied *Peniophora gigantea* in loblolly pine stump inoculation. Plant Disease Reporter 56(11):958–960.

Artman JD, Reeder TN Jr. 1977. Sweetfern blister rust found in young loblolly pine plantations in Maryland and Delaware. Journal of Forestry 75(3):136–138.

Baer RG, Berisford CW. 1975. Species composition of pine tip moth, *Rhyacionia* spp., infestations in northeast Georgia. Journal of the Georgia Entomological Society 10(1):64–67.

Baker WW. 1974. Longevity of lightning-struck trees and notes on wildlife use. In: Proceedings, Tall Timbers Fire Ecology Conference; 1973 March 22–23; Tallahassee, FL. Tallahassee, FL: Tall Timbers Research Station: 497–504.

Barber JC, VanHaverbeke DF. 1961. Growth of outstanding nursery seedlings of *Pinus elliottii* Engelm. and *Pinus taeda* L. Sta. Pap. 126. Asheville, NC: USDA Forest Service, Southeastern Forest Experiment Station. 12 p.

Barbosa P, Waldvogel M, Martinat P, Douglass LW. 1983. Development and reproductive performance of the gypsy moth *Lymantria dispar* (L.) (Lepidoptera: Lymantriidae), on selected hosts common to mid-Atlantic and southern forests. Environmental Entomology 12(6):1858–1862.

Barnes RL. 1972. Effects of chronic exposure to ozone on photosynthesis and respiration of pines. Environmental Pollution 3(2):133–138.

Barnett JP. 1976. Sterilizing southern pine seeds with hydrogen peroxide. Tree Planters' Notes 27(3):17–19, 24.

Barnett JP, Hall O. 1977. Subfreezing conditions after seeding can reduce southern pine seed germination. Tree Planters' Notes 28(1):3–4, 37.

Barras SJ, Taylor JJ. 1973. Varietal *Ceratocystis minor* identified from mycangium of *Dendroctonus frontalis*. Mycopathologia et Mycologia Applicata 50(4):293–305.

Barrows-Broaddus J, Dwinell LD. 1983. Histopathology of *Fusarium moniliforme* var. *subglutinaus* in four species of southern pines. Phytopathology 73(6):882–889.

Barrows-Broaddus J, Dwinell LD. 1985. Branch dieback and cone and seed infection caused by *Fusarium moniliformme* var. *subglutinans* in a loblolly pine seed orchard in South Carolina. Phytopathology 75(10):1104–1108.

Barry JW, Barber LR, Kenney PA, Overgaard N. 1984. Feasibility of aerial spraying of southern pine seed orchards. Southern Journal of Applied Forestry 8(3):127–131.

Basham HG. 1970. Wilt of loblolly pine inoculated with blue-stain fungi of the genus *Ceratocystis*. Phytopathology 60(5):750–754.

Beal JA, McClintick KB. 1943. The pales weevil in southern pines. Journal of Economic Entomology 36(5):792–794.

Beal RH. 1967. Heavy tip moth attacks reduce early growth of loblolly and shortleaf pine. Res. Note SO-54. New Orleans: USDA Forest Service, Southern Forest Experiment Station. 3 p.

Belanger RP. 1980. Silvicultural guidelines for reducing losses to the southern pine beetle. Tech. Bull. 1631. Washington, DC: USDA Forest Service and Science and Education Administration: 165–177.

Belanger RP. 1981. Silvicultural considerations in developing integrated southern pine beetle management procedures. In: Proceedings, 1st Biennial Southern Silvicultural Research Conference; 1980 November 6–7; Atlanta, GA. Gen. Tech. Rep. SO-34. New Orleans: USDA Forest Service, Southern Forest Experiment Station: 276–286.

Belanger RP, Malac BF. 1980. Silviculture can reduce losses from the southern pine beetle. Agric. Handbk. 576. Washington, DC: USDA Forest Service. 17 p.

Belanger RP, Godbee JF, Miller T, Webb RS. 1983. Salvage cutting in southern pine forests. In: Proceedings, 2nd Biennial Southern

Silvicultural Research Conference; 1982 November 4–5; Atlanta, GA. Gen. Tech. Rep. SE-24. Asheville, NC: USDA Forest Service, Southeastern Forest Experiment Station: 382–386.

Belanger RP, Hedden RL, Tainter FH. 1986. Integrated pest management handbook: managing Piedmont forests to reduce losses from the littleleaf disease–southern pine beetle complex. Agric. Handb. 649. Washington, DC: USDA Forest Service and USDA Cooperative State Research Service. 18 p.

Belanger RP, Miller T, Godbee JF. 1985. Fusiform rust: guidelines for selective cutting of rust-infected trees in merchantable slash pine plantations. In: Proceedings, Integrated Pest Management Research Symposium; 1985 April 15–18; Asheville, NC. Gen. Tech. Rep. SO-56. New Orleans: USDA Forest Service, Southern Forest Experiment Station: 254–257.

Bennett I. 1959. Glaze: its meteorology and climatology, geographical distribution, and economic effects. Tech. Rep. EP-105. Natick, MA: US Army Headquarters, Quatermaster Research & Engineering Command Center. 173 p.

Berisford CW. 1974. Parasite abundance in *Ips* spp. infestations as influenced by the southern pine beetle. Environmental Entomology 3(4):695–696.

Berisford CW. 1988. The Nantucket pine tip moth. In: Berryman AA, ed. Dynamics of forest insect populations: patterns, causes, implications. New York: Plenum Publishing: 141–161.

Berisford CW, Brady UE. 1976. Duration of protection of loblolly pines from *Ips* bark beetles by lindane. Journal of Economic Entomology 69(3):357–358.

Berisford CW, Payne TL. 1988. Regional variation: a potential factor in the integration of behavioral chemicals into southern pine beetle management. In: Payne TL, Saarenmaa H, eds. Integrated control of Scolytid bark beetles: Proceedings, IUFRO Working Party and 17th International Congress of Entomology Symposium; 1988 July 4; Vancouver, BC. Blacksburg, VA: Virginia Polytechnic Institute and State University: 275–282.

Berisford CW, Brady UE, Fatzinger CW, Ebel BH. 1986. Evaluation of a repellent for prevention of attacks by three species of southern pine bark beetles (Coleoptera: Scolytidae). Journal of Entomological Science 21(4):316–318.

Berisford CW, Gargiullo PM, Canalos CG. 1984. Optimum timing for insecticidal control of the Nantucket pine tip moth (Lepidoptera: Tortricidae). Journal of Economic Entomology 77(1):174–177.

Bieberdorf FW, Shrewsbury CL, McKee HC, Krough LH. 1958. Vegetation as a measure indicator of air pollution: 1. The pine (*Pinus taeda*). Bulletin of the Torrey Botanical Club 85(3):197–200.

Billings RF. 1987. Southern pine beetle inhibitor. Texas Forestry News 66(2):7–9.

Billings RF. 1988. Forcasting southern pine beetle infestation trends with pheromone traps. In: Payne TL, Saarenmaa H, eds. Integrated control of Scolytid bark beetles: Proceedings, IUFRO Working Party and 17th International Congress of Entomology Symposium; 1988 July 4; Vancouver, BC. Blacksburg, VA: Virginia Polytechnic Institute and State University: 295–306.

Billings RF, Kibbe CA. 1978. Seasonal relationships between southern pine beetle brood development and loblolly pine foliage color in east Texas. Southwestern Entomologist 3(2):89–98.

Billings RF, Pase HA III. 1979. A field guide for ground checking southern pine beetle spots. Agric. Handbk. 558. Washington, DC: USDA Forest Service. 19 p.

Blair RL, Cowling EB. 1974. Effects of fertilization, site, and vertical position on the susceptibility of loblolly pine seedlings to fusiform rust. Phytopathology 64:761–762.

Blakeslee GM, Dwinell DL, Anderson RL. 1980. Pitch canker of southern pines: identification and management considerations. Fors. Rep. SA-FR 11. Atlanta: USDA Forest Service, Southeastern Area. 15 p.

Blanche CA, Hodges JD, Nebeker TE. 1985a. Changes in bark beetle susceptibility indicators in a lightning-struck loblolly pine. Canadian Journal of Forest Research 15(2):397–399.

Blanche CA, Nebeker TE, Hodges JD, Karr BL, Schmitt JJ. 1985b. Effect of thinning damage on bark beetle susceptibility indicators in loblolly pine. In: Proceedings, 3rd Biennial Southern Silvicultural Research Conference; 1984 November 7–8; Atlanta, GA. Gen. Tech. Rep. SO-54. New Orleans: USDA Forest Service, Southern Forest Experiment Station: 471–478.

Borders BE, Bailey RL. 1986. Fusiform rust prediction models for site-prepared slash and loblolly pine plantations in the Southeast. Southern Journal of Applied Forestry 10(3):145–151.

Bosworth AB, Raney HG, Eikenbary RD, Flora NW. 1970. Nocturnal observations of spiders in loblolly pines at Haworth, OK. Journal of Economic Entomology 63(1):297–298.

Box BH. 1961. Comparison of loblolly and slash pine growth in a twelve-year-old plantation in southeastern Louisiana. LSU Forestry Note 49. Baton Rouge, LA: Louisiana State University and A&M College, Louisiana Agricultural Experiment Station. 4 p.

Boyce JS Jr. 1952. A needle blight of loblolly pine caused by the brown-spot fungus. Journal of Forestry 50(9):686–687.

Boyce JS Jr. 1966. Sporulation by Peniophora gigantea with reference to control of annosus root rot. Forest Science 12(1):2–7.

Bradford B, Alexander SA, Skelly JM. 1978a. Determination of growth loss of Pinus taeda L. caused by Heterobasidion annosus (Fr.) Bref. European Journal of Forest Pathology 8(3):129–134.

Bradford B, Skelly JM, Alexander SA. 1978b. Incidence and severity of annosus root rot in loblolly pine plantations in Virginia. European Journal of Forest Pathology 8(3):135–145.

Bramlett DL, Lewis WG, DeBarr GL. 1977. Screen cages to protect control-pollinated pine cones from seedbugs. Tree Planters' Notes 28(2):25–28.

Brender EV, Romancier RM. 1965. Glaze damage to loblolly and slash pine. In: Wahlenberg WG, ed. A guide to loblolly and slash pine plantation management in southeastern USA. Rep. 14. Macon, GA: Georgia Forest Research Council: 156–159.

Brewer CW, Linnartz NE. 1973. The recovery of hurricane-bent loblolly pine. For. Notes 104. Baton Rouge, LA: Louisiana State University and A&M College, School of Forest and Wildlife Management. 2 p.

Bridges JR. 1985. Relationship of symbiotic fungi to southern pine beetle population trends. In: Integrated Pest Management Research Symposium; 1985 April 15–18; Asheville, NC. Gen. Tech. Rep. SO-56. New Orleans: USDA Forest Service, Southern Forest Experiment Station: 186–194.

Bridges JR. 1987. Effects of terpenoid compounds on growth of symbiotic fungi associated with the southern pine beetle. Phytopathology 77(1):83–85.

Bridges JR, Moser JC. 1983. Role of two phoretic mites in transmission of bluestain fungus, Ceratocystis minor. Ecological Entomology 8:9–12.

Bridges JR, Perry TJ. 1985. Effects of mycangial fungi on gallery construction and distribution of bluestain in southern pine beetle–infested pine bolts. Journal of Entomological Science 20(2):271–275.

Brightwell CS. 1971. Comparative performance of slash and loblolly pine. Woodlands Research Notes 25. Savannah, GA: Union Camp Corporation, Woodlands Research Department. 3 p.

Brown MW, Nebeker TE, Honea CR. 1987. Thinning increases loblolly pine vigor and resistance to bark beetles. Southern Journal of Applied Forestry 11(1):28–31.

Burdsall HH Jr, Snow GA. 1977. Taxonomy of Cronartium quercuum and C. fusiforme. Mycologia 69(3):503–508.

Burns PY, Hu SC, Awang JB. 1981. Relationship of fusiform rust infection to intensive culture of slash pine. In: Proceedings, 1st Biennial Southern Silvicultural Research Conference; 1980 November 6–7; Atlanta, GA. Gen. Tech. Rep. SO-34. New Orleans: USDA Forest Service, Southern Forest Experiment Station: 366–369.

Burton JD. 1981. Thinning and pruning influence glaze damage in a loblolly pine plantation. Res. Note SO-264. New Orleans: USDA Forest Service, Southern Forest Experiment Station. 4 p.

Cade SC, Lynch AM, Hedden RL, Walstad JD. 1981. Seedling debarking weevils: a site hazard-rating system case history. In: Proceedings, Hazard-rating Systems in Forest Insect Pest Management Symposium; 1980 July 31–August 1; Athens, GA. Gen. Tech. Rep. WO-27. Washington, DC: USDA Forest Service: 27–30.

Cade SC, Hedden RL. 1987. Growth impact of pine tip moth on loblolly pine plantations in the Ouachita Mountains of Arkansas. Southern Journal of Applied Forestry 11(3):128–133.

Cameron RS, DeBarr GL, Godbee JF, Taylor JW. 1987. Potential alternative insecticides for insect control in southern pine seed orchards. In: Proceedings, 19th Southern Forest Tree Improvement Conference; 1987 June 16–18; College Station, TX: Southern Forest Tree Improvement Committee: 182–189.

Cameron RS, Billings RF. 1988. Southern pine beetle: factors associated with spot occurrence and spread in young plantations. Southern Journal of Applied Forestry 12(3):208–214.

Campbell TE. 1971. Prairie crayfish: a hazard in direct seeding. Tree Planters' Notes 22(4):20–24.

Campbell TE. 1981. Effects of endrin in repellent seed coatings on caged rodents. Research Pap. SO-174. New Orleans: USDA Forest Service, Southern Forest Experiment Station. 5 p.

Carlson WC. 1984. Cold damage to loblolly pine seedlings. In: Proceedings, Southern Nursery Conferences; 1984 June 11–14; Alexandria, LA/July 24–27; Asheville, NC. Atlanta: USDA Forest Service, Southern Region: 1–12.

Carner GR, Griffith KH, Fox RC. 1977. Entomophthora spp. infecting cinaran aphids in South Carolina. Journal of the Georgia Entomological Society 12(2):121–124.

Carney JL, Garrett HE, Hedrick HG. 1978. Influence of air pollutant gases on oxygen uptake of pine roots with selected ectomycorrhizae. Phytopathology 68(8):1160–1163.

Carson SD, Young CH. 1987. Effect of inoculum density and fertilization on greenhouse screening of loblolly pine seedlings for resistance to fusiform rust. Phytopathology 77(8):1186–1191.

Chatelain MP, Finger CK, Goyer RA. 1977. Imidan® for control of the Nantucket pine tip moth on loblolly and slash pines in Louisiana. For. Notes 119. Baton Rouge, LA: Louisiana State University and A&M College, School of Forestry and Wildlife Management. 3 p.

Chatelain MP, Goyer RA. 1980. Seasonal attack periods of cone-feeding insects of loblolly pine cones. Annals of the Entomological Society of America 73(1):49–53.

Clark EW. 1970. Attack height of the black turpentine beetle. Journal of the Georgia Entomological Society 5(3):151–152.

Clark EW. 1972. The role of Pityophthorus pullcarius Zimmerman in tip dieback of young loblolly pine. Journal of the Georgia Entomological Society 7(2):151–152.

Clarke SR, DeBarr GL, Berisford CW. 1988. Differential susceptibility of Toumeyella pini (King) (Homoptera: Coccidae) to pyrethroid and organophosphate insecticides: a factor in outbreaks in southern pine seed orchards. Journal of Economic Entomology 81(5):1443–1445.

Clarke SR, DeBarr GL, Berisford CW. 1989a. The life history of Toumeyella pini (King) (Homoptera: Coccidae) in loblolly pine seed orchards in Georgia. Canadian Entomologist 121(10):853–860.

Clarke SR, DeBarr GL, Berisford CW. 1989b. Life history of the woolly pine scale Pseudophilippia quaintancii Cockerell (Homoptera: Coccidae) in loblolly pine seed orchards in Georgia. Journal of Entomological Science 24(3):365–372.

Cook SP, Hain FP. 1985. Qualitative examination of the hypersensitive response of loblolly pine, Pinus taeda L., inoculated with two fungal associates of the southern pine beetle, Dendroctonus frontalis Zimmerman (Coleoptera: Scolytidae). Environmental Entomology 14(4):396–400.

Cook SP, Hain FP. 1986. Defensive mechanisms of loblolly and shortleaf pine against attack by southern pine beetles, *Dendroctonus frontailis* Zimmermann, and its fungal associates, *Ceratocystis minor* (Hedgecock) Hunt. Journal of Chemical Ecology 12(6):1397–1406.

Cook SP, Hain FP. 1988. Toxicity of host monoterpenes to *Dendroctonus frontalis* and *Ips calligraphus* (Coleoptera: Scolytidae). Journal of Entomological Science 23(3):287–292.

Cook SP, Hain FP, Nappen PB. 1986. Seasonality of the hypersensitive response by loblolly pine and shortleaf pine to inoculation with a fungal associate of the southern pine beetle (Coleoptera: Scolytidae). Journal of Entomological Science 21(3):283–285.

Cook SP, Wagner TL, Flamm RO, Dickens JC, Colson RN. 1983. Examination of sex ratios and mating habits of *Ips avulsus* and *I. calligraphus* (Coleoptera: Scolytidae). Annals of the Entomological Society of America 76(1):56–60.

Cool BM, Goebel NB, Wooten TE, Loadholt CB. 1971. Glaze damage to pine trees in the Sandhills area of South Carolina. For. Res. Ser. 21. Clemson, SC: South Carolina Agricultural Experiment Station. 13 p.

Cordell CE, Filer TE Jr. 1985. Integrated nursery pest management. In: Lantz CW, ed. Southern pine nursery handbook. Atlanta: USDA Forest Service, Southern Region, Cooperative Forestry: chapter 13.

Cordell CE, Knighten JL. 1969. Comandra blister rust on young loblolly pine in eastern Tennessee. Journal of Forestry 67(5):332–333.

Cordell CE, Wolfe RD. 1969. Comandra blister rust, a threat to southern hard pines. Phytopathology 59(8):1022.

Coulson RM. 1980. Population dynamics. In: Thatcher RC, Searcy JL, Coster JE, Hertel GD, eds. The southern pine beetle. Tech. Bull. 1631. Washington, DC: USDA Forest Service and Science and Education Administration: 71–106.

Coulson RM, Flamm RO, Pulley PE, and others. 1986. Response of the southern pine bark beetle guild (Coleoptera: Scolytidae) to host disturbance. Environmental Entomology 15(4):850–858.

Coulson RM, Witter JA. 1984. Forest entomology: ecology and management. New York: John Wiley & Sons: 565–567.

Coyne JF. 1970. *Neodiprion taedae* Linearis: a sawfly pest of loblolly and shortleaf pines. Revised. Forest Pest Leaflet 34. New Orleans: USDA Forest Service, Southern Forest Experiment Station. 4 p.

Coyne JF, Lott LH. 1976. Toxicity of substances in pine oleoresin to southern pine beetles. Journal of the Georgia Entomological Society 11(4):301–305.

Cronan CS, Goldstein RA. 1989. ALBIOS: a comparison of aluminium biogeochemistry in forested watersheds exposed to acidic deposition. In: Adriano DC, Havas M, eds. Advances in environmental science: acidic precipitation, vol. 1: case studies. New York: Springer-Verlag: 113–135.

Cross EA, Gabrielson FC, Bradshaw DK. 1981. Some effects of vegetative competition and fertilizer on growth, survival, and tip moth damage in loblolly pine planted on alkaline shale surface mine spoil. In: Proceedings, Symposium on Surface Mining Hydrology, Sedimentology, and Reclamation; 1981 December 7–11; Lexington, KY. Lexington, KY: University of Kentucky, OES Publications: 59–63.

Czabator FJ. 1971. Fusiform rust of southern pines—a critical review. Research Pap. SO-65. New Orleans: USDA Forest Service, Southern Forest Experiment Station. 39 p.

Czabator FJ, Staley JM, Snow GA. 1971. Extensive southern pine needle blight during 1970-1971, and associated fungi. Plant Disease Reporter 55(9):764–766.

Davis JB, Barnes RL. 1973. Effects of soil-applied fluoride and lead on growth of loblolly pine and red maple. Environmental Pollution 5(1):35–44.

Davis TS. 1962. Effect of cobalt-60 gamma radiation on pine seed and one-year-old seedlings. Forest Science 8(4):411–412.

Davis TS, Luttrell ES. 1967. Frequency of sporulation of fusiform rust galls on loblolly pine and effectiveness of surgical and antibiotic treatments. Plant Disease Reporter 51(6):505–507.

DeAngelis JD, Hodges JD, Nebeker TE. 1986a. Phenolic metabolites of *Ceratocystis minor* from laboratory cultures and their effects on transpiration in loblolly pine seedlings. Canadian Journal of Botany 64(1):151–155.

DeAngelis JD, Nebeker TE, Hodges JD. 1986b. Influence of tree age and growth rate on the radial resin duct system in loblolly pine (*Pinus taeda*). Canadian Journal of Botany 64(5):1046–1049.

DeBarr GL. 1974. Quantifying the impact of seedbugs. In: Seed yield from southern pine seed orchards: Proceedings of a colloquium; 1974 April 2–3; Macon, GA. Macon, GA: Georgia Forest Research Council: 34–41.

DeBarr GL, Ebel BH. 1973. How seedbugs reduce the quantity and quality of pine seed yields. In: Proceedings, 12th Southern Forest Tree Improvement Conference; 1973 June 12–13; Baton Rouge, LA. Baton Rouge, LA: Louisiana State University Division of Continuing Education: 97–103.

DeBarr GL, Kormanik PP. 1975. Anatomical basis for conelet abortion on *Pinus echinata* following feeding by *Leptoglossus corculus* (Hemiptera: Coreidae). Canadian Entomologist 107:81–86.

DeBarr GL, Matthews FR. 1985. Insecticide applications during the pollination period do not adversely affect seed yields of loblolly pine. Southern Journal of Applied Forestry 9(4):240–243.

DeMars CJ, Slaughter GW, Greene LE, Ghent JH. 1982. Mapping pine mortality by aerial photography, Umstead State Park, NC. Research Pap. PSW-158. Berkeley, CA: USDA Forest Service, Southwest Forest and Range Experiment Station. 14 p.

Dinus RJ. 1971. Phenotypic selection for fusiform rust resistance. In: Proceedings, 11th Southern Forest Tree Improvement Conference; 1971 June 15–16; Atlanta, GA. Macon, GA: USDA Forest Service, Eastern Tree Seed Laboratory: 68–75.

Dinus RJ, Schmidtling RC. 1971. Fusiform rust in loblolly and slash pines after cultivation and fertilization. Research Pap. SO-68. New Orleans: USDA Forest Service, Southern Forest Experiment Station. 10 p.

Doggett C, Lawrence L, Killingsworth D. 1978. Containerized seedlings: a new tool in seedling debarking weevil control. Tree Planters' Notes 29(4):18–19.

Dorman KW. 1976. The genetics and breeding of southern pines. Agric. Handbk. 471. Washington, DC: USDA Forest Service. 407 p.

Dorward RE. 1965. Nursery bird control through cover crops. Tree Planters' Notes 70:12.

Drake LE. 1974. Control of insects affecting pine plantations. In: Proceedings, Symposium on Management of Young Pines; 1974 October 22–24; Alexandria, LA/December 3–5; Charleston, SC. Asheville, NC: USDA Forest Service, Southeastern Forest Experiment Station: 28–32.

Dwinell LD. 1974. Susceptibility of southern oaks to *Cronartium fusiforme* and *Cronartium queuccum*. Phytopathology 64:400–403.

Dwinell LD. 1985. Relative susceptibilities of five pine species to three populations of the pinewood nematode. Plant Disease 69(5):440–442.

Dwinell LD, Barrows-Broaddus J. 1985. Infection of fusiform rust galls on slash and loblolly pines by the pitch canker fungus, *Fusarium moniliforme* var. *subglutinans*. In: Proceedings, Rusts of Hard Pines Working Party; 1984 October 1–6; Athens, GA. IUFRO, S2.06-10. Athens, GA: Georgia Center for Continuing Education, University of Georgia: 239–248.

Dwinell LD, Ryan PL, Kuhlman EG. 1977. Pitch canker of loblolly pine in seed orchards. In: Proceedings, 14th Southern Forest Tree Improvement Conference; 1977 June 14–16; Gainesville, FL. Macon, GA: USDA Forest Service, Eastern Tree Seed Laboratory: 130–137.

Ebel BH. 1971. Distribution and incidence of *Laspeyresia* spp. seedworm infestation in Virginia, loblolly and shortleaf pine cones in the southern States. In: Proceedings, 11th Southern Forest Tree Improvement Conference; 1971 June 15–16; Atlanta, GA. Macon, GA: USDA Forest Service, Eastern Tree Seed Laboratory: 95–97.

Ebel BH. 1974. Cone and seed insects of shortleaf and loblolly pines in the Georgia Piedmont. In: Seed yield from southern pine seed orchards: Colloquium proceedings; 1974 April 2–3; Macon, GA. Macon, GA: Georgia Forest Research Council: 26–33.

Ebel BH, DeBarr GL. 1973. Injury to female strobili of shortleaf and loblolly pines by *Nepytia semiclusaria* (Lipidoptera: Geometridae). Florida Entomologist 56(1):53–55.

Ebel BH, Flavell TH, Drake LE, and others. 1980. Seed and cone insects of southern pine. Revised. Gen. Tech. Rep. SE-8. Asheville, NC: USDA Forest Service, Southeastern Forest Experiment Station. 41 p.

Eikenbary RD, Fox RC. 1968. Arthropod predators of the Nantucket pine tip moth, *Rhyacionia fustrana*. Annals of the Entomological Society of America 61(5):1218–1221.

Enghardt HG, Smith LF, Wells OO. 1969. Pruning to reduce fusiform rust damage not justified on young slash pines. Res. Note SO-87. New Orleans: USDA Forest Service, Southern Forest Experiment Station. 3 p.

Fatzinger CW, Hertel GD, Merkel EP, and others. 1980. Identification and sequential occurrence of mortality factors affecting seed yields of southern pine seed orchards. Res. Pap. SE-216. Asheville, NC: USDA Forest Service, Southeastern Forest Experiment Station. 43 p.

Fatzinger CW, Yates HO III, Hammond WJ, Hutto R. 1985. Insect-caused cone and seed losses in treated and untreated loblolly pine seed orchards. Res. Note SE-333. Asheville, NC: USDA Forest Service, Southeastern Forest Experiment Station. 4 p.

Feaver M. 1985. Niedzlek grasshopper (*Orthroptera: Acrididae*) damage to pine seedlings at night in a seed orchard. Florida Entomologist 68(4):694–696.

Feduccia DP, Mann WF Jr. 1975. Black turpentine beetle infestations after thinning in a loblolly pine plantation. Res. Note SO-206. New Orleans: USDA Forest Service, Southern Forest Experiment Station. 3 p.

Feldman RM, Curry GL, Coulson RN. 1980. The use and structure of the TAMBEETLE spot dynamics model. In: Stephen FM, Searcy JL, Hertel GD, eds. Proceedings, Modeling Southern Pine Beetle Populations Symposium; 1980 Feb 20–22; Asheville, NC. Tech. Bull. 1630. Atlanta: USDA Forest Service, Southeastern Area, State and Private Forestry: 20–29.

Filer TH, Peterson GW. 1975. Damping-off. In: Forest nursery diseases in the United States. Agric. Handbk. 470. Washington, DC: USDA Forest Service: 6–8.

Fitzgerald CH, Reines M, Terrell S, Kormanik PP. 1975. Early root development and anatomical parasite-host relationships of black senna with slash pine. Forest Science 21(3):239–242.

Fitzgerald CH, Schultz RC, Fortson JC, Terrell S. 1977. Effects of *Seymeria cassioides* infestation on pine seedling and sapling growth. Southern Journal of Applied Forestry 1(4):26–30.

Fitzgerald CH, Terrell S. 1972. *Seymeria cassioides*, a parasitic weed on pine. Sch. For. Resour. Bull. Athens, GA: University of Georgia, School of Forest Resources. 2 p.

Flamm RO, Coulson RN, Payne TL. 1988. The southern pine beetle. In: Berryman AA, ed. Dynamics of forest insect populations: patterns, causes, implications. New York: Plenum Press. 531–553.

Flamm RO, Wagner TL, Cook SP, and others. 1987. Host colonization by cohabiting *Dendroctonus frontalis*, *Ips avulsus*, and *I. calligraphus* (Coleoptera: Scolytidae). Environmental Entomology 16(2):390–399.

Flavell TH. 1974. Insect pests of young pines. In: Proceedings, Symposium on Management of Young Pines; 1974 October 22–24; Alexandria, LA/December 3–5; Charleston, SC.

Asheville, NC: USDA Forest Service, Southeastern Forest Experiment Station: 243–248.

Florence LZ. 1973. Prospects for using natural loblolly (shortleaf hybrids for resistance to fusiform rust. In: Proceedings, 12th Southern Forest Tree Improvement Conference; 1973 June 12–13; Baton Rouge, LA. Baton Rouge, LA: Louisiana State University, Division of Continuing Education: 302–309.

Foster GS, Anderson RL. 1989. Indirect selection and clonal propagation of loblolly pine seedlings enhance resistance to fusiform rust. Canadian Journal of Forest Research 19(4): 534–537.

Fountain MS, Burnett FE. 1979. Ice damage to plantation-grown loblolly pine in South Arkansas. Arkansas Farm Research 28(3):3.

Fox RC, Griffith KH. 1976. Predation of pine cinaran aphids by spiders. Journal of Georgia Entomological Society 11(3):241–243.

Fox RC, Griffith KH. 1977. Pine seedling growth loss caused by cinaran aphids in South Carolina. Journal of Georgia Entomological Society 12(1):29–34.

Fox RC, Hill TM. 1973. The relative attraction of burned and cutover pine areas to the pine seedling weevils *Hylobius pales* and *Pachylobius picivorus*. Annals of the Entomological Society of America 66:52–54.

Fraedrich BR, Witcher W. 1982. Influence of fertilization on pitch canker development on three southern pine species. Plant Disease 66(10):938–940.

Fraedrich SW. 1985. Susceptibility of shortleaf and loblolly pine seedlings to *Phytophthora cinnamomi* [abstract]. Phytopathology 75(11):1337–1338.

Fraedrich SW, Tainter FH. 1989. Effect of dissolved oxygen concentration on the relative susceptibility of shortleaf and loblolly pine root tips to *Phytophthora cinnamomi*. Phytopathology 79(10):1114–1118.

Fraedrich SW, Tainter FH, Miller AE. 1989. Zoospore inoculum density of *Phytophthora cinnamomi* and the infection of lateral root tips of shortleaf and loblolly pine. Phytopathology 79(10):1109–1113.

Franklin EC. 1975. Phenotypic and genetic variation of sulfate naval stores yields in loblolly pine. In: Proceedings, 1974 Forest Biology Conference; 1974 September 18–20; Seattle, WA. Atlanta: TAPPI: 99–102.

Froelich RC. 1987. Sawtimber as an alternative forest management strategy for sites with a high fusiform rust hazard. Southern Journal of Applied Forestry 11(4):228–231.

Froelich RC, Dell TR, Walkinshaw CH. 1966. Soil factors associated with *Fomes annosus* in the Gulf States. Forest Science 12(3):356–361.

Froelich RC, Hodges CS Jr, Sackett SS. 1978. Prescribed burning reduces severity of annosus root rot in the South. Forest Science 24(1):93–100.

Froelich RC, Kuhlman EG, Hodges CS, and others. 1977. *Fomes annosus* root rot in the South: guidelines for prevention. Atlanta: USDA Forest Service, State and Private Forestry, Southeast Area. 17 p.

Gage EV. 1975. Evaluation and timing of selected insecticides for control of *Dioryctria* coneworms in a loblolly pine seed orchard. Fayetteville, AR: The University of Arkansas. 28 p. M.S. thesis.

Gargiullo PM, Berisford CW. 1982. Number of instars of the pitch pine tip moth, *Rhyacionia rigidana* (Lepidoptera: Tortricidae, olethreutinae). Canadian Entomologist 114(6):531–534.

Gargiullo PM, Berisford CW. 1983. Life tables for the Nantucket pine tip moth, *Rhyacionia frustrana* (Comstock), and the pitch pine top moth, *Rhyacionia rigidana* (Fernald) (Lepidoptera: Torticidae). Environmental Entomology 12(5):1391–1402.

Gargiullo PM, Berisford CW, Canalos CG, and others. 1984. Mathematical descriptions of *Rhyacioni fustrana* (Lepidoptera: Tortricidae) cumulative catches in pheromone traps, cumulative eggs hatching, and their use in timing of chemical control. Environmental Entomology 13(6):1681–1685.

Gargiullo PM, Berisford CW, Godbee JF Jr. 1985. Prediction of optimal timing for chemical control of the Nantucket pine tip moth, *Rhyacionia frustrana* (Comstock) (Lepidoptera: Tortricidae), in the Southeastern Coastal Plain. Journal of Economic Entomology 78(1):148–154.

Garner JHB, Pagano T, Cowling EB. 1989. An evaluation of the role of ozone, acid deposition, and other airborne pollutants in the forests of eastern North America. Gen. Tech. Rep. SE-59. Asheville, NC: USDA Forest Service, Southeastern Forest Experiment Station. 172 p.

Garrett HE, Carney JL, Hedrick HG. 1982. The effects of ozone and sulfur dioxide on respiration of ectomycorrhizal fungi. Canadian Journal of Forest Research 12(2):141–145.

Garrett PW, Trew IF. 1986. Resistance of pitch (loblolly pine hybrids to fusiform rust (*Cronartium quercuum* F. sp. *fusiforme*). Plant Disease 70(6):564–565.

Geron CD, Hafley WL. 1988. Impact of fusiform rust on product yields of loblolly pine plantations. Southern Journal of Applied Forestry 12(4):226–231.

Gilmore AR. 1980. Phytotoxic effects of giant foxtail on loblolly pine seedlings. Comparative and Physiological Ecology 5(3):183–192.

Gilmore AR. 1985. Allelopathic effects of giant foxtail on germination and radicle elongation of loblolly pine seed. Journal of Chemical Ecology 11(5):583–592.

Gilmore AR, Gertner GZ, Rolfe GL. 1984. Soil chemical changes associated with roosting birds. Soil Science 138(2):158–163.

Godbee JF Jr, Franklin RT. 1976. Attraction, attack patterns, and seasonal activity of the black turpentine beetle. Annals of the Entomological Society of America 69(4):653–655.

Goggans JF. 1957. Southern fusiform rust: some factors affecting its incidence in Alabama's Coastal Plain region. Bull. 304. Auburn, AL: The Alabama Polytechnic Institute, Agricultural Experiment Station. 19 p.

Gollob L. 1980. Monoterpene composition in bark beetle-resistant loblolly pine. Naturwissenschaften 67(8):409–410.

Gooding GV Jr, Hodges CS Jr, Ross EW. 1966. Effect of temperature on growth and survival of *Fomes annosus*. Forest Science 12(3):325–333.

Goolsby RP, Ruehle JL, Yates HO. 1972. Insects and diseases of seed orchards in the South. Rep. 28. Macon, GA: Georgia Research Council. 25 p.

Goyer RA, Nachod LH. 1976. Loblolly pine conelet, cone, and seed losses to insects and other factors in a Louisiana seed orchard. Forest Science 22(4):386–391.

Goyer RA, Williams VG. 1981. The effects of feeding by *Leptoglossus corculus* (Say) and *Tetyra bipunctata* (Herrich and Schaffer) on loblolly pine (*Pinus taeda* L.) conelets. Journal of the Georgia Entomological Society 16(1):16–21.

Grano CX, Grigsby HC. 1968. Spraying southern pines not practical for tip-moth control. Res. Note SO-77. New Orleans: USDA Forest Service, Southern Forest Experiment Station. 2 p.

Gray DJ, Amerson HV. 1983. In vitro resistance of embryos of *Pinus taeda* to *Cronartium quercuum* F. sp. *fusiforme*: ultrastructure and histology. Phytopathology 73(11):1492–1499.

GrelenHE, Mann WF Jr. 1973. Distribution of senna seymeria (*Seymeria cassioides*), a root parasite of southern pines. Economic Botany 27(3):393–342.

Gresham CA. 1987. Potential allelopathic interactions of *Sapium sebiferum* on loblolly pine seed germination and seedling growth. In: Proceedings, 4th Biennial Southern Silvicultural Research Conference; 1986 November 4–6; Atlanta, GA. Gen. Tech. Rep. SE-42. Asheville, NC: USDA Forest Service, Southeastern Forest Experiment Station: 331–334.

Gresham CA. 1981. A survey of salt spray damage of beach vegetation along the northern beaches of South Carolina. For. Bull. 27. Clemson, SC: Clemson University, Department of Forestry. 3 p.

Grigsby HC. 1959. Two promising pine hybrids for the mid-South. Southern Lumberman 198(2466):32–33.

Grigsby HC. 1973. South Carolina best of 36 loblolly pine seed sources for southern Arkansas. Res. Pap. SO-89. New Orleans: USDA Forest Service, Southern Forest Experiment Station. 10 p.

Gruschow GF, Trousdell KB. 1958. Incidence of heart rot in mature loblolly pines in coastal North Carolina. Journal of Forestry 56(3):220–221.

Gschwandtner G, Gschwandtner KC, Eldridge K. 1985. Historic emissions of sulfur and nitrogen oxides in the United States from 1900 to 1980. EPA Proj. Sum. 600/S7-85/009. Research Triangle Park, NC: US Environmental Protection Agency, Air and Energy Engineering Research Laboratory. 8 p.

Hadley EB, Woodwell GM. 1965. Effect of ionizing radiation on rates of CO_2 exchange of pine seedlings. Radiation Research 24(4):650–656.

Hain FP, Cook SP, Matson PA, Wilson KG. 1985. Factors contributing to southern pine beetle host resistance. In: Proceedings, Symposium on Integrated Pest Management; 1985 April 15–18; Asheville, NC: Gen. Tech. Rep. SO-56. New Orleans: USDA Forest Service, Southern Forest Experiment Station: 154–160.

Hain FP, Mawby WD, Cook SP, Arthur FH. 1983. Host conifer reaction to stem invasion. Zeitschrift für Angewandte Entomologie 96(3):247–256.

Haines LW, Haines SG, Liles FT Jr. 1976. Effects of fertilization on susceptibility of loblolly pine to the southern pine beetle. Tech. Rep. 58. Raleigh, NC: North Carolina State University, School of Forest Resources. 55 p.

Hanson PJ, McLaughlin SB, Edwards NT. 1988. Net CO_2 exchange of *Pinus taeda* shoots exposed to variable ozone levels and rain chemistries in field and laboratory settings. Physiologia Plantarum 74(4):635–642.

Hanson PJ, Rott K, Taylor GE, and others. 1989. NO_2 deposition to elements representative of a forest landscape. Atmospheric Environment 23(8):1783–1794.

Hanula JL, DeBarr GL, Berisford CW. 1985. Adult activity of *Dioryctria amatella* (Lepidoptera: Pyralidae) in relation to development of immature stages in loblolly pine cones. Environmental Entomology 14(6):842–845.

Hardy JW. 1978. Damage to loblolly pine by winter roosting blackbirds and starlings. In: Proceedings, 30th Annual Conference of the Southeastern Association of Fish and Wildlife Agencies; 1976 October 24–27; Jackson, MS. Montgomery, AL: Southeastern Association of Fish and Wildlife Agencies: 466–471.

Hare RC, Switzer GL. 1969. Introgression with shortleaf pine may explain rust resistance in western loblolly pine. Res. Note. SO-88. New Orleans: USDA Forest Service, Southern Forest Experiment Station. 2 p.

Hatchell GE. 1964. Small-mammal species and populations in the loblolly–shortleaf pine forest type of Louisiana. Res. Pap. SO-10. New Orleans: USDA Forest Service, Southern Forest Experiment Station. 12 p.

Hatchell GE, Dorman KW, Langdon OG. 1972. Performance of loblolly and slash pine nursery selections. Forest Science 18(4):308–313.

Haugen DA, Stephen FM. 1984. Development rates of Nantucket pine tip moth, *Rhyacionia fustrana* (Lepidoptera: Tortricidae), life stages in relation to temperature. Environmental Entomology 13(1):56–60.

Hedden RL. 1985. Simulation of southern pine beetle-associated timber loss using CLEMBEETLE. In: Proceedings, Integrated Pest Management Research Symposium; 1985 April 15–18; Asheville, NC. Gen. Tech. Rep. SO-56. New Orleans: USDA Forest Service, Southern Forest Experiment Station: 288–291.

Hedden RL, Belanger RP. 1985. Predicting susceptibility to southern pine beetle attack in the Coastal Plain, Piedmont, and Southern Appalachians. In: Proceedings, Integrated Pest Management Research Symposium; 1985 April 15–18;

Asheville, NC. Gen. Tech. Rep. SO-56. New Orleans: USDA Forest Service, Southern Forest Experiment Station: 233–238.

Hedden RL, Billings RF. 1977. Seasonal variations in fat content and size of the southern pine beetle in east Texas. Annals of the Entomological Society of America 70(6):876–880.

Hedden RL, Clason T. 1979. Nantucket pine tip moth impact on loblolly pine wood and product quality. Fors. Res. Rep. 1979. Homer, LA: Louisiana State University and Agricultural and Mechanical College, North Louisiana Hill Farm Experiment Station, Center for Agricultural Sciences and Rural Development: 57–71.

Hedden RL, Haugen DA. 1987. Impact of pine tip moth attack on loblolly pine seedlings. In: Proceedings, 4th Biennial Southern Silvicultural Research Conference; 1986 November 4–6; Atlanta, GA. Gen. Tech. Rep. SE-42. Asheville, NC: USDA Forest Service, Southeastern Forest Experiment Station: 535–537.

Hedden RL, Lorio PL Jr. 1985. Rating stand susceptibility to southern pine beetle attack on national forests in the Gulf Coastal Plain. Res. Pap. SO-221. New Orleans: USDA Forest Service, Southern Forest Experiment Station. 5 p.

Hedden RL, Belanger RP, Powers HR, Miller T. 1991. Relation of Nantucket pine tip moth attack and fusiform rust infection in loblolly pine families. Southern Journal of Applied Forestry 15(4):204–208.

Hedden RL, Richmond JA, Thomas HA, Lashomb JH. 1981. Impact of Nantucket pine tip moth attack on young loblolly pine biomass. In: Proceedings, 1st Biennial Southern Silvicultural Research Conference; 1980 November 6–7; Atlanta, GA. Gen. Tech. Rep. SO-34. New Orleans: USDA Forest Service, Southern Forest Experiment Station: 238–241.

Hendrix FF Jr, Campbell WA. 1968. Pythiaceous fungi isolated from southern forest nursery soils and their pathogenicity to pine seedlings. Forest Science 14(3):292–297.

Henry BW, Jewell FF. 1963. Resistance of pines to southern fusiform rust. In: Proceedings, World Consultation on Forest Genetics and Tree Improvement; 1963 August 23–30; Stockholm. Rome: FAO: 1–4.

Hertel GD, Benjamin DM. 1975. Tip moth and webworm attacks in Southwide pine seed source plantations. Res. Note SE-221. Asheville, NC: USDA Forest Service, Southeastern Forest Experiment Station. 6 p.

Hertel GD, Mason GN, Cade SC, Kucera RC. 1985. Strategies for reducing insect and disease losses. In: Proceedings, Symposium on Loblolly Pine Ecosystem—West; 1984 March 20–22; Jackson, MS. Mississippi State, MS: Mississippi Cooperative Extension Service, Extension Forestry Department: 217–231.

Hertel GD, Wallace HN. 1983. Effect of cut-and-leave and cut-and-top control treatments on within-tree southern pine beetle populations. Res. Note SO-299. New Orleans: USDAForest Service, Southern Forest Experiment Station. 4 p.

Hicks RR Jr, Coster JE, Watterston KG. 1979. Reducing southern pine beetle risks through proper management planning. Forest Farmer 38(7):6–7, 18.

Hicks RR Jr, Howard JE, Watterston KG, Coster JE. 1980. Rating forest stand susceptibility to southern pine beetle in east Texas. Forest Ecology and Management 2(4):269–283.

Hill TM, Fox RC. 1972. Two pine seedling weevils attracted to pines infected by the black turpentine beetle. Annals of the Entomological Society of America 65(1):269.

Himes WE, Skelly JM. 1972. An association of the black turpentine beetle Dendroctonus terebrans and Fomes annosus in loblolly pine [abstract]. Phytopathology 62(6):670.

Hodges CS. 1964. The effect of competition by Peniophora gigantea on the growth of Fomes annosus in stumps and roots [abstract]. Phytopathology 54(6):623.

Hodges CS Jr. 1974. Cost of treating stumps to prevent infection by Fomes annosus. Journal of Forestry 72(7):402–404.

Hodges JD, Thatcher RC. 1976. Southern pine beetle survival in trees felled by the cut and top-cut and leave method. Res. Note

SO-219. New Orleans: USDA Forest Service, Southern Forest Experiment Station. 5 p.

Hodges JD, Elam WE, Watson WF. 1977. Physical properties of the oleoresin system of the four major southern pines. Canadian Journal of Forest Research 7:520–525.

Hodges JD, Elam WW, Watson WF, Nebeker TE. 1979. Oleoresin characteristics and susceptibility of four southern pines to southern pine beetle (Coleoptera: Scolytidae) attacks. Canadian Entomologist 111:889–896.

Hodges JD, Lorio PL Jr. 1975. Moisture stress and composition of xylem oleoresin in loblolly pine. Forest Science 21(3):283–290.

Hokans RH, Fanelli ES, Alexander SA. 1985. Growth following thinning model for loblolly pine plantations infected by annosus root rot. In: Proceeding, Integrated Pest Management Research Symposium; 1985 April 15–18; Asheville, NC. Gen. Tech. Rep. SO-56. New Orleans: USDA Forest Service, Southern Forest Experiment Station: 59–61.

Hollis CA, Smith JE, Fisher RF. 1982. Allelopathic effects of common understory species on germination and growth of southern pines. Forest Science 28(3):509–515.

Hood WM, Berisford CW, Hedden RL. 1985. Oviposition preference of the Nantucket pine tip moth Rhyacionia frustrana (Lepidoptera: Tortricidae) on loblolly and slash pine. Journal of Entomological Science 20(2):204–206.

Hood WM, Fox RC. 1980. Control of aphids on loblolly pine in northwestern South Carolina. Journal of the Georgia Entomological Society 15(1):105–108.

Hood WM, Hedden RL, Berisford CW. 1988. Hazard rating forest sites for pine tip moth, Rhyacionia spp., in the Upper Piedmont Plateau. Forest Science 34(4):1083–1093.

Howell FC, Stambaugh WJ. 1972. Rates of pathogenic and saprophytic development of Fomes annosus in roots of dominant and suppressed eastern redcedar. Plant Disease Reporter 56(11):987–990.

Huber CM, McClure JP, Cost ND. 1984. Incidence and impact of damage to Georgia's timber, 1982. Resour. Bull. SE-75. Asheville, NC: USDA Forest Service, Southeastern Forest Experiment Station. 27 p.

Huber CM, McClure JP, Cost ND. 1985. Incidence and impact of damage to North Carolina's timber, 1984. Resour. Bull. SE-82. Asheville, NC: USDA Forest Service, Southeastern Forest Experiment Station. 27 p.

Huber CM, McClure JP, Cost ND. 1987. Incidence and impact of damage to Virginia's timber, 1986. Resour. Bull. SE-90. Asheville, NC: USDA Forest Service, Southeastern Forest Experiment Station: 23.

Hunt EV Jr. 1968. How serious is rabbit damage on loblolly pine seedlings? Journal of Forestry 66(11):853.

Hunt EV Jr, Lenhart JD. 1986. Fusiform rust trends in east Texas. Southern Journal of Applied Forest 10(4):215–216.

Jackson LWR. 1968. Growth of fusiform branch cankers on loblolly and slash pine. Naval Stores Review 78(4):6–7.

Jackson LWR, Parker JN. 1958. Anatomy of fusiform rust galls on loblolly pine. Phytopathology 48(11):637–640.

Jacobi WR, Amerson HV, Mott RL. 1982. Microscopy of cultured loblolly pine seedlings and callus inoculated with Cronartium fusiforme. Phytopathology 72(1):138–143.

Jewell FF. 1986. Histological studies of Scirrhia acicola (Dearn.) Siggers and other needle-inhabiting fungi on longleaf and loblolly pines. In: Proceedings, Recent Research on Conifer Needle Diseases; 1984 October 14–18; Gulfport, MS. Gen. Tech. Rep. WO-50. Washington, DC: USDA Forest Service: 1–4.

Jewell FF Sr, True RP, Mallett SL. 1962. Histology of Cronartium fusiforme in slash pine. Phytopathology 52(9):850–858.

Johansen RW, Shimmel JW. 1967. Thickening retardents improves adhesion to tree crowns. Res. Note SE-84. Asheville, NC: USDA Forest Service, Southeastern Forest Experiment Station. 3 p.

Johnson CJS, Landis TD. 1984. Frost hardiness testing for nursery stock. In: Proceedings, 1984 Southern Nursery Conference; 1984 June 11–14; Alexandria, LA. Atlanta: USDA Forest Service, Southern Region: 13–19.

Johnson,JD, Gagnon KG. 1988. Assessing freeze damage in loblolly pine seedlings: a comparison of ethane production to electrolyte leakage. New Forests 2(1):65–72.

Johnson PC, Coster JE. 1978. Probability of attack by southern pine beetles in relation to distance from an attractive host tree. Forest Science 24(4):574–580.

Jones EP Jr, Wells OO. 1969. Ice damage in a Georgia planting of loblolly pine from different seed sources. Res. Note SE-126. Asheville, NC: USDA Forest Service, Southeastern Forest Experiment Station. 4 p.

Kais AG. 1966. Sequential field observations of pycnial and aecial sporulation and growth of fusiform rust galls. Final report summary. 1 p. On file with USDA Forest Service, Southern Forest Experiment Station, Gulfport MS.

Kane MB. 1981. Fertilization of juvenile loblolly pine plantations impacts on fusiform rust incidence. In: Proceedings, 1st Biennial Southern Silvicultural Research Conference; 1980 November 6–7; Atlanta, GA. Gen. Tech. Rep. SO-34. New Orleans: USDA Forest Service, Southern Forest Experiment Station: 199–204.

Kane MB. 1982. Effect of hexazinone application on disease and insect incidence in young loblolly pine plantations. Proceedings of the Southern Weed Science Society 35:185–194.

Kauffman BW, Applegate HW, Cordell CE, Thor E. 1980. Susceptibility of eight pine species to comandra blister rust in Tennessee. Plant Disease 64(4):375–377.

Kelley WD. 1980. Evaluation of systemic fungicides for control of Cronartium quercumm F. sp. fusiforme on loblolly pine seedlings. Plant Disease 64(8):773–775.

Kelley WD. 1984. Efficacy of morning vs. afternoon applications of triadimefron for controlling fusiform rust. Southern Journal of Applied Forestry 8(4):231–232.

Kelley WD. 1985. Seed treatment with Bayleton reduces fusiform rust in forest nurseries. Highlights of Agricultural Research [Auburn, AL: Auburn University, Alabama Agricultural Experiment Station] 32(1):8.

Kelley WD. 1988. Effect of short-term storage of triadimefron-treated loblolly pine seed on incidence of fusiform rust. Southern Journal of Applied Forestry 12(1):18–20.

Kelley WD, Rowan SJ. 1985. Fusiform rust and its control in southern forest tree nurseries. In: Proceedings, International Symposium on Nursery Management Practices for the Southern Pines; 1985 August 4–9; Montgomery, AL. Auburn, AL: Auburn University, Alabama Agriculture Experiment Station: 454–459.

Kelley WD, Williams JC. 1982. Incidence of pitch canker among clones of loblolly pine in seed orchards. Plant Disease 66(12):1171–1173.

Kelley WD, Williams JC. 1985. Effects of triadimefon and triadimenol as seed dressings on incidence of fusiform rust on loblolly pine seedlings. Plant Disease 69(2):147–148.

Kelly JM, Parker GR, McFee WW. 1979. Heavy metal accumulation and growth of seedlings of five forest species as influenced by soil cadmium level. Journal of Environmental Quality 8(3):361–364.

Kinloch BB Jr, Zoerb MH. 1971. Genetic variation in resistance to fusiform rust among selected parent clones of loblolly pine and their offspring. In: Proceedings, 11th Southern Forest Tree Improvement Conference; 1971 June 15–16; Atlanta, GA. Macon, GA: USDA Forest Service, Eastern Tree Seed Laboratory: 76–79.

Kinloch BB Jr, Stonecypher RW. 1969. Genetic variation in susceptibility to fusiform rust in seedlings from a wild population of loblolly pine. Phytopathology 59(9):1246–1255.

Kinn DN. 1986. Studies on the flight capabilities of Dendroctonus frontalis and Ips calligraphus: preliminary findings using tethered beetles. Res. Note SO-324. New Orleans: USDA Forest Service, Southern Forest Experiment Station. 3 p.

Kinn DN, Witcosky JJ. 1978. Variation in southern pine beetle attack height associated with phoretic uropodid mites. Canadian Entomologist 110:249–251.

Kraus JF. 1986. Breeding shortleaf × loblolly pine hybrids for the development of fusiform rust-resistant loblolly pine. Southern Journal of Applied Forestry 10(4):195–197.

Kraus JF, Powers HR Jr, Snow G. 1982. Infection of shortleaf × loblolly pine hybrids inoculated with Cronartium quercuum F. sp. echinatae and C. quercuum F. sp. fusiforme. Phytopathology 72(4):431–433.

Krause CR, Shafer SR, Heagle AS. 1987. Ultrastructural effects of ozone to field-grown loblolly pine seedlings [abstract]. Phytopathology 77(12):1758.

Kress LW, Skelly JM, Hinkelmann KH. 1982. Relative sensitivity of 18 full-sib families of Pinus taeda to O$_3$. Canadian Journal of Forest Research 12(2):203–209.

Kress LW, Allen HL, Mudano JE, Heck WW. 1989. Ozone effects on the growth of loblolly pine. In: Bucher JB, Bucher-Wallin I, eds. Air pollution and forest decline: Proceedings, 14th International Meeting for Specialists in Air Pollution Effects on Forest Ecosystems; 1988 October 2–8; Interlaken, Switzerland. Birmensdorf, Switzerland: IUFRO P2.05: 153–158.

Kroll JC, Conner RN, Fleet RR. 1980. Southern pine beetle handbook: woodpeckers and the southern pine beetle. Agric. Handbk. 564. Washington, DC: USDA Forest Service. 23 p.

Kroll JC, Fleet RR. 1979. Impact of woodpecker predation on over-wintering within-tree populations of the southern pine beetle (Dendroctonus frontalis). In: The role of insectivorous birds in forest ecosystems. London: Academic Press: 269–280.

Ku TT, Sweeney JM, Shelburne VB. 1980. Site and stand conditions associated with southern pine beetle outbreaks in Arkansas—a hazard-rating system. Southern Journal of Applied Forestry 4(2):103–106.

Kucera DR. 1973. Cone and seed losses in loblolly pine. Dissertation Abstracts International 33(11):5327.

Kuhlman EG. 1972. Susceptibility of loblolly and slash pine progeny to Fomes annosus. Res. Note SE-176. Asheville, NC: USDA Forest Service, Southeastern Forest Experiment Station. 7 p.

Kuhlman EG. 1978. Postinoculation temperatures and photoperiods: their effect on development of fusiform rust on loblolly pine. Plant Disease Reporter 62(1):8–11.

Kuhlman EG. 1981. Sporulation by Cronartium quercuum F. sp. fusiforme on loblolly and slash pine. Phytopathology 71(3):345–347.

Kuhlman EG. 1986. Impact of annosus root rot minimal 22 years after planting pines on root rot infested sites. Southern Journal of Applied Forestry 10(2):96–98.

Kuhlman EG. 1987. Effects of inoculation treatment with Fusarium moniliforme var. subglutinans on dieback of loblolly and slash pine seedlings. Plant Disease 71(2):161–162.

Kuhlman EG. 1988. Histology and progression of fusiform rust symptoms on inoculated loblolly pine seedlings. Plant Disease 72(8):719–721.

Kuhlman EG, Cade S. 1985. Pitch canker disease of loblolly and pond pines in North Carolina plantations. Plant Disease 69(2):175–176.

Kuhlman EG, Dianis SD, Smith TK. 1982. Epidemiology of pitch canker disease in a loblolly pine seed orchard in North Carolina. Phytopathology 72(9):1212–1216.

Kuhlman EG, Hodges CS Jr, Froelich RC. 1976. Minimizing losses to Fomes annosus in the southern United States. Res. Pap. SE-151. Asheville, NC: USDAForest Service, Southeastern Forest Experiment Station. 16 p.

Kuhlman EG, Powers HR Jr. 1988. Resistance responses in half-sib loblolly pine progenies after inoculation with Cronartium quercuum F. sp. fusiforme. Phytopathology 78(4):484–487.

Kulhavy DL, Ross WG, Meeker JR, Tracey WD. 1989. Site/stand factors influencing Nantucket pine tip moth in loblolly pine plantations. In: Proceedings, 1st Biennial Southern Silvicultural Research Conference; 1980 November 6–7; Atlanta, GA. Gen. Tech. Rep. SO-34. New Orleans: USDAForest Service, Southern Forest Experiment Station: 563–566.

Kuprionis J. 1970. Recovery of loblolly, slash, and shortleaf pines bent by snowfall and/or ice. Bull. 4. Ruston, LA: Louisiana Polytechnic Institute, School of Agriculture and Forestry, Division of Research. 35 p.

Kushmaul RJ, Cain MD, Rowell CE, Porterfield RL. 1979. Stand and site conditions related to southern pine beetle susceptibility. Forest Science 25(4):656–664.

LaFarge T, Kraus JF. 1980. A progeny test of (shortleaf × loblolly) × loblolly hybrids to produce rapid-growing hybrids resistant to fusiform rust. Silvae Genetica 29(5/6):197–200.

Land SB Jr. 1974. Depth effects and genetic influences on injury caused by artificial sea water floods to loblolly and slash pine seedlings. Canadian Journal of Forest Research 4(2):179–185.

Lantagne DO, Burger JA. 1988. Effect of site preparation intensity on the early growth of loblolly pine (*Pinus taeda* L.) and the incidence of pine tip moth (*Rhyacionia* spp.). New Forests 2(4):219–229.

Lantz CW. 1984. Freeze damage to southern pine seedlings in the nursery. In: Proceedings, of the Southern Nursery Conference; 1984 June 11–14; Alexandria, LA. Atlanta: USDA Forest Service, Southern Region: 20–29.

Lashomb JH, Steinhauer AL. 1975. Observations of *Zethus spinipes* Say (Hymenoptera: Eumenidae). Proceedings of the Entomology Society of Washington 77(1):–164.

Lashomb JH, Steinhauer AL. 1982. Within-tree response of Nantucket pine tip moth, *Rhyacionia frustrana* (Lep.: Tortricidae) parasitoids to varying host densities. Entomophaga 27(3):277–282.

Lashomb JH, Steinhauer AL, Dively G. 1980. Comparison of parasitism and infestation of Nantucket pine tip moth in different age stands of loblolly pine. Environmental Entomology 9(4):397–402.

Lashomb JH, Steinhauer AL, Douglass L. 1978. Impact studies of Nantucket tip moth populations on loblolly pine. Environmental Entomology 7(6):910–912.

Layne JN. 1974. Ecology of small mammals in a flatwoods habitat in north-central Florida, with emphasis on the cotton rat (*Sigmodon hispidus*). American Museum Novitates 2544:1–48.

Lindberg SE, Garten CT Jr. 1988. Sources of sulfur in forest canopy throghfall. Nature 336(10):148–151.

Lindberg SE, Lovett GM, Richter DD, Johnson DW. 1986. Atmospheric disposition and canopy interactions of major ions in a forest. Science 231:141–145.

Little S, Mohr JJ, Spicer LL. 1958. Salt-water storm damage to loblolly pine forests. Journal of Forestry 56(1):27–28.

Little S. 1979. Sweetfern blister rust cankers on loblolly pines in a southern New Jersey plantation. Bulletin of the New Jersey Academy of Science 24(2):70–72.

Lloyd FT. 1983. Computer simulated fusiform rust losses from early infections in loblolly plantations. In: Proceedings, Symposium on the Loblolly Pine Ecosystem—East Region; 1982 December 8–10; Raleigh, NC. Raleigh, NC: North Carolina State University, School of Forest Resources: 198–204.

Long EM, van Buijtenen JP, Robinson JF. 1974. Cultural practices in southern pine seed orchards. In: Colloquium Proceedings, Seed Yield From Southern Pine Seed Orchards; 1974 April 2–3; Macon, GA. Macon, GA: Georgia Forest Research Council: 73–85.

Lorenz R, Murphy CE Jr. 1985. The dry deposition of sulfur dioxide on a loblolly pine plantation. Atmospheric Environment 19(5):797–802.

Lorio PL. 1978. Developing stand risk classes for the southern pine beetle. Res. Pap. SO-144. New Orleans: USDA Forest Service, Southern Forest Experiment Station. 9 p.

Lorio PL Jr. 1984. Should small infestations of southern pine beetle receive control priority. Southern Journal of Applied Forestry 8(4):201–204.

Lorio PL Jr. 1986. Growth-differentiation balance: a basis for understanding southern pine beetle–tree interactions. Forest Ecology and Management 14:259–273.

Lorio PL Jr., Hodges JD. 1977. Tree water status affects induced southern pine beetle attack and brood production. Res. Pap. SO-135. New Orleans: USDA Forest Service, Southern Forest Experiment Station. 7 p.

Lorio PL Jr, Howe VK, Martin CN. 1972. Loblolly pine rooting varies with microrelief on wet sites. Ecology 53(6):1134–1140.

Lorio PL Jr, Mason GN, Autry GL. 1982. Stand risk rating for the southern pine beetle: integrating pest management with forest management. Journal of Forestry 80(4):212–214.

Lorio PL Jr, Sommers RA. 1985. Potential use of soil maps to estimate southern pine beetle risk. In: Proceedings, Symposium on Integrated Pest Management; 1985 April 15–18; Asheville, NC. Gen. Tech. Rep. SO-56. New Orleans: USDA Forest Service, Southern Forest Experiment Station: 239–245.

Lotan JE, Alexander ME, Arno SF, and others. 1981. The forest soil environment. In: Effects of fire on flora: a state-of-knowledge review. Proceedings, National Fire Effects Workshop; 1978 April 10–14; Denver, CO. Gen. Tech. Rep. WO-16. Washington, DC: USDA Forest Service: 52–56.

Lowman B. 1995. Missoula Technology and Development Center's 1995 nursery and reforestation programs. Tree Planters' Notes 46(2):36–45.

Ludwig FL, Shelar E Jr. 1980. Empirical relationships between observed ozone concentrations and geographical areas with concentrations likely to be above 120 ppb. Journal of Air Pollution Control Association 30(8):894–897.

Lynch AM, Hedden RL. 1984. Relation between early-and late-season loblolly pine seedling mortality from pales and pitch-eating weevil attack in southeast Oklahoma. Southern Journal of Applied Forestry 8(3):172–176.

Mahoney MJ, Chevone BI, Skelly JM, Moore LD. 1985. Influence of mycorrhizae on the growth of loblolly pine seedlings exposed to ozone and sulfur dioxide. Phytopathology 75(6):679–682.

Maksymiuk B. 1970. Occurrence and nature of antibacterial substances in plants affecting *Bacillus thuringiensis* and other entomogenous bacteria. Journal of Invertebrate Pathology 15(3):356–371.

Mann WF Jr, Derr HJ. 1970. Response of planted loblolly and slash pine to disking on a poorly drained site. Res. Note 110. New Orleans: USDA Forest Service, Southern Forest Experiment Station. 3 p.

Mann WF Jr, Grelen HE, Williamson BC. 1969. *Seymeria cassioides*, a parasitic weed on slash pine. Forest Science 15(3):318–319.

Mann WF Jr, Williamson BC, McGilvray JM. 1971. Parasitic weed—a new pine problem. Forest Farmer 30(6):6–8.

Marx DH. 1973. Mycorrhizae and feeder root diseases. In: Marks GC, Kozlowski TT, eds. Ectomycorrhizae: their ecology and physiology. New York: Academic Press: 351–382.

Marx DH, Cordell CE, France RC. 1986. Effects of triadimefon on growth and ectomycorrhizal development of loblolly and slash pines in nurseries. Phytopathology 76(8):824–831.

Mason GN, Hicks RR Jr, Bryant CM, and others. 1981. Rating southern pine beetle hazard by aerial photography. In: Symposium Proceedings, Hazard-Rating Systems in Forest Insect Pest Management; 1980 July 31–August 1; Athens, GA. Gen. Tech. Rep. WO-27. Washington, DC: USDA Forest Service: 109–114.

Mason GN, Bryant CMV. 1984. Establishing southern pine beetle hazard from aerial stand data and historical records. Forest Science 30(2):375–382.

Mason GN, Van Arsdel EP. 1978. Fungi associated with *Pinus taeda* seed development. Plant Disease Reporter 62(10):864–867.

Mason RR, Davidson FR. 1964. Protecting pine seedlings from rabbits with polyethylene sleeves. Journal of Forestry 62(10):751–752.

Mason RR. 1969. Behavior of Ips populations after summer thinning in a loblolly pine plantation. Forest Science 15(4):390–398.

Mason RR. 1971. Soil moisture and stand density affect oleoresin exudation flow in a loblolly pine plantation. Forest Science 17(2):170–177.

Mastalerz JW. 1977. The greenhouse environment: the effects of environmental factors on the growth and development of flower crops. New York: John Wiley & Sons. 629 p.

Matson PA, Hain FP, Mawby W. 1987. Indices of tree susceptibility to bark beetles vary with silvicultural treatment in a loblolly pine plantation. Forest Ecology and Management 22(1/2):101–118.

Matthews FR, Miller T, Dwinell LD. 1978. Inoculum density: its effect on infection by Cronartium fusiforme on seedlings of slash and loblolly pine. Plant Disease Reporter 62(2):105–108.

Matthews FR, Powers HR, Arnold BG. 1976. Eradication of fusiform rust on loblolly pine rootstock: comparison of sodium arsenite and bark excision. Tree Planters' Notes 27(1):9–10.

Matthews FR, Rowan SJ. 1972. An improved method for large-scale inoculations of pine and oak with Cronartium fusiforme. Plant Disease Reporter 56(11):931–934.

Matuszewski M. 1973. Comandra blister rust in Kentucky. Plant Disease Reporter 57(1):17–18.

Matziris DL, Zobel BJ. 1976. Effect of fertilization on growth and quality characteristics of loblolly pine. Forest Ecology and Management 1(1):21–30.

May JT. 1985. Insects and other animal pests: lifecycles and control. In: Lantz CW, ed. Southern pine nursery handbook. Atlanta: USDA Forest Service, Southern Region, Cooperative Forestry: chapter 14.

May JT, Rahman S, Worst RH. 1973. Effects of site preparation and spacing on planted slash pine. Journal of Forestry 71(6):333–335.

McLaughlin SB Jr, Barnes RL. 1975. Effects of fluoride on photosynthesis and respiration of some southeast American forest trees. Environmental Pollution 8(2):91–96.

McLemore BF. 1973. Loblolly pine flowers damaged by Phyllophaga beetles. Journal of Economic Entomology 66(2):541–542.

McLemore BF. 1977. Strobili and conelet losses in four species of southern pines. Res. Note SO-226. New Orleans: USDA Forest Service, Southern Forest Experiment Station. 5 p.

McLeod PJ, Wallis GW, Yearian WC., Stephen FM, Young SY. 1983. Evaluation of codling moth granulosis virus for Nantucket pine tip moth suppression. Journal of the Georgia Entomological Society 18(3):424–427.

McLeod PJ, Yearian WC, Young SY. 1984. Evaluation of Bacillus thuringiensis for coneworm, Dioryctria spp., control in southern pine seed orchards. Journal of the Georgia Entomological Society 19(3):408–413.

McNab WH. 1977. An overcrowded loblolly pine stand thinned with fire. Southern Journal of Applied Forestry 1(1):24–26.

Merkel EP, Hertel GD. 1976. Pine tip moth and pine webworm control with carbofuran in north Florida. Res. Note SE-236. Asheville, NC: USDA Forest Service, Southeastern Forest Experiment Station. 6 p.

Merrifield RG, Foil RR, Hansbrough T. 1967. Height growth of loblolly pine improved only slightly after ten years of tip moth control. Tree Planters' Notes 18(3):17–18.

Merrill W. 1972. Occurrence of Endocronartium harknessii in Pennsylvania. Plant Disease Reporter 56(12):1058.

Metz LJ, Lotti T, Klawitter RA. 1961. Some effects of prescribed burning on Coastal Plain forest soil. Sta. Pap. 133. USDA Forest Service, Southeastern Forest Experiment Station. 10 p.

Mexal JG, Snow GA. 1978. Seed treatment with systemic fungicides for the control of fusiform rust in loblolly pine. Res. Note SO-238. New Orleans: USDA Forest Service, Southern Forest Experiment Station. 4 p.

Miller FD Jr, Stephen FM. 1983. Effects of competing vegetation on Nantucket pine tip moth (Lepidoptera: torticidae) populations in loblolly pine plantations in Arkansas. Environmental Entomology 12(1):101–105.

Miller JE. 1987. Assessment of wildlife damage on southern forests. In: Forests, the world, and the profession: Proceedings, 1986 Society of American Foresters National Convention; 1986 October 5–8; Birmingham, AL. Bethesda, MD: Society of American Foresters: 180–185.

Miller LN. 1965. Changes in radiosensitivity of pine seedlings subjected to water stress during chronic gamma irradiation. Health Physics 11:1653–1662.

Miller LN. 1966. Radiosensitivity of pines as affected by water stress and growth stage [abstract]. Bulletin of Ecology Society of America 47(3):127.

Miller T, Powers HR Jr. 1973. Differential host responses of slash pine and loblolly pine seedlings to infection by Cronartium fusiforme [abstract]. Phytopathology 63(4):446.

Miller T. 1972. Fusiform rust in planted slash pines: influence of site preparation and spacing. Forest Science 18(1):70–75.

Miller T, Belanger RP, Webb RS, Godbee JF. 1985. Pest assessments after sanitation-salvage cutting in fusiform rust-infected slash pine plantations. In: Proceedings, Integrated Pest Management Research Symposium; 1985 April 15–18; Asheville, NC. Gen. Tech. Rep. SO-56. New Orleans: USDA Forest Service, Southern Forest Experiment Station: 258–262.

Miller T, Bramlett DL. 1978. Fungi associated with damage to strobili cones and seed of slash and loblolly pines [abstract]. Phytopathology News 12(9):207.

Miller T, Matthews FR. 1984. Wounds on loblolly pines are sites of infection for fusiform rust fungus. Southern Journal of Applied Forestry 8(4):205–207.

Miller T, Matthews FR. 1988. Field performance of symptomatic survivors of loblolly pine families inoculated with Cronartium quercuum f. sp. fusiforme [abstract]. Phytopathology 78(12):1607.

Miller T, Patton RF, Powers HR Jr. 1980. Mode of infection and early colonization of slash pine seedlings by Cronartium quercuum f. sp. fusiforme. Phytopathology 70:1206–1208.

Miller T, Schmidt RA. 1987. A new approach to forest pest management. Plant Disease 71(3):204–207.

Miller WE. 1978. Petrova pitch-blister moths of North America and Europe: two new species and synopsis (Olethreutidae). Annals of the Entomological Society of America 71(3):329–340.

Miller WE, Wilson LF. 1964. Composition and diagnosis of pine tip moth infestations in the Southeast. Journal of Economic Entomology 57(5):722–725.

Mistretta PA, Bylin CV. 1986. Incidence and impact of damage to Alabama's timber, 1983. Resour. Bull. SO-112. New Orleans: USDA Forest Service, Southern Forest Experiment Station. 20 p.

Mistretta PA, Bylin CV. 1987. Incidence and impact of damage to Louisiana's timber, 1985. Resour. Bull. SO-117. New Orleans: USDA Forest Service, Southern Forest Experiment Station. 19 p.

Mistretta PA, Bylin CV, Baker R. 1986. Incidence and impact of damage to Tennessee's timber, 1982. Resour. Bull. SO-110. New Orleans: USDA Forest Service, Southern Forest Experiment Station. 18 p.

Moehring DM, Grano CX, Bassett JR. 1966. Properties of forested loess soils after repeated prescribed burns. Res. Note SO-40. USDA Forest Service, Southern Forest Experiment Station. 4 p.

Moore GE. 1972. Southern pine beetle mortality in North Carolina caused by parasites and predators. Environmental Entomology 1(1):58–65.

Moore GE, Layman HF. 1978. Attempts to increase resistance of loblolly pines to bark beetles by fertilization. Res. Note SE-260. Asheville, NC: USDA Forest Service, Southeastern Forest Experiment Station. 4 p.

Moore KE. 1984. Impact of fusiform rust on loblolly pine plantations. In: Proceedings, Research in Forest Productivity, Use, and

Pest Control: Contributions by Women Scientists Symposium; 1983 September 16; Burlington, VT. Gen. Tech. Rep. NE-90. Broomall, PA: USDA Forest Service, Northeastern Forest Experiment Station: 65–68.

Morris CL. 1970. Volume losses from *Fomes annosus* in loblolly pine in Virginia. Journal of Forestry 68(5):283–284.

Moser JC. 1986. Estimating timber losses from a town ant colony with aerial photographs. Southern Journal of Applied Forestry 10(1):45–47.

Moser JC, Sommers RA, Lorio PL Jr, and others. 1987. Southern pine beetles attack felled green timber. Res. Note SO-342. US.DA Forest Service, Southern Forest Experiment Station. 7 p.

Murphy CE Jr, Sinclair TR, Knoerr KR. 1977. A model for estimating air-pollutant uptake by forests; calculation of absorption of sulfur dioxide from dispersed sources. In: Proceedings, Conference on Metropolitan Physical Environment; 1975 August 25–29; Syracuse, NY. Gen. Tech. Rep. NE-25. Broomall, PA: USDA Forest Service, Northeastern Forest Experiment Station: 340–350.

Musselman LJ, Mann WF Jr. 1978. Root parasites of southern forests. Gen. Tech. Rep. SO-20. New Orleans: USDA Forest Service, Southern Forest Experiment Station. 76 p.

Musselman LJ, Harris CS, Mann WF Jr. 1978. *Agalinis purpurea*: a parasitic weed on sycamore, sweetgum, and loblolly pine. Tree Planters' Notes 29(4):24–25.

Myren DT. 1964. Insects and fungi associated with *Cronartium fusiforme* infected tissue and comparisons of the strength of infected and healthy wood [abstract]. Phytopathology 54(8):902.

Nance WL, Shoulders E, Dell TR. 1985. Predicting survival and yield of unthinned slash and loblolly pine plantations with different levels of fusiform rust. In: Proceedings, Integrated Pest Management Research Symposium; 1985 April 15–18; Asheville, NC. Gen. Tech. Rep. SO-56. New Orleans: U.S. Department of Agriculture, Forest Service, Southern Forest Experiment Station: 62–72.

Nance WL, Shoulders E. 1987. Effect of fusiform rust on survival of loblolly pine in unthinned plantations. In: Proceeding, 4th Biennial Southern Silvicultural Research Conference; 1986 November 4–6; Atlanta, GA. Gen. Tech. Rep. SE-42. Asheville, NC: USDA Forest Service, Southeastern Forest Experiment Station: 550–554.

Nebeker TE, Hodges JD, Karr BK, Moehring DM. 1985. Thinning practices in southern pines—with pest management recommendations. Tech. Bull. 1703. Washington, DC: USDA Forest Service. 36 p.

Neel WW, Sartor CF. 1969. Notes on insects infesting pine cones in Mississippi. Entomological News 80(6):159–165.

Neunzig HH, Leidy NA. 1989. A new species of *Dioryctria* (Lepidoptera: Pyralidae: Phycitinae) from the southeastern United States. Proceedings of the Entomological Society of Washington 91(3):321–324.

Nord JC, DeBarr G, Barber LR, and others. 1985. Low-volume applications of Azinphosmethyl, Fenvalerate, and Permethrin for control of coneworms (Lepidoptera: Pyralidae) and seed bugs (Hemiptera: Coreidae and Pentatomidae) in southern pine seed orchards. Journal of Economic Entomology 78(2):44–450.

Nord JC, Flavell TH, Pepper WD, Layman HF. 1975. Field test of chlorpyrifos and carbofuran to control weevils that debark pine seedlings. Res. Note SE-226. Asheville, NC: USDA Forest Service, Southeastern Forest Experiment Station. 7 p.

Nord JC, Flavell TH, Pepper WD, Layman HF. 1978. Field test of four insecticides for control of pales and pitch-eating weevils in first-year pine plantations. Res. Note SE-255. Asheville, NC: USDA Forest Service, Southeastern Forest Experiment Station. 9 p.

Nord JC, Ragenovich I, Doggett CA. 1984. Pales weevil. FIDL 104, rev. Washington, DC: USDA Forest Service. 11 p.

Oak SW. 1985. Adaptation of littleleaf disease hazard rating for use in forest management in South Carolina national forest. In: Proceedings, Integrated Pest Management Symposium; 1985

April 15–18; Asheville, NC. Gen. Tech. Rep. SO-56. New Orleans: USDA Forest Service, Southern Forest Experiment Station: 246–251.

Oak SW, Tainter FH. 1988. Risk prediction of loblolly pine decline on littleleaf disease sites in South Carolina. Plant Disease 72(4):289–293.

Ollieu MM. 1971. Damage to southern pines in Texas by *Pissodes nemorensis*. Journal of Economic Entomology 64(6):1456–1459.

Overgaard NA, Wallace HN, Stein C, Hertel GD. 1976. Needle midge (Diptera: Cecidomyiidae) damage to loblolly pines in the Erambert Federal Seed Orchard, Mississippi. Rep. 76-2-13. Pineville, LA: USDA Forest Service, Southeastern Area, State and Private Forestry, Resource Protection Unit, Forest Insect and Disease Management Group.

Paganelli DJ, Seiler JR, Feret PP. 1987. Root regeneration as an indicator of aluminium toxicity in loblolly pine. Plant and Soil 102(1):115–118.

Paine TD, Stephen FM. 1987a. Fungi associated with the southern pine beetle: avoidance of induced defense response in loblolly pine. Oecologia 74(3):377–379.

Paine TD, Stephen FM. 1987b. Influence of tree stress and site quality on the induced defense system of loblolly pine. Canadian Journal of Forest Research 17(6):569–571.

Paine TD, Stephen FM. 1987c. The relationship of tree height and crown class to the induced plant defenses of loblolly pine. Canadian Journal of Botany 65(10):2090–2092.

Paine TD, Stephen FM. 1988. Induced defenses of loblolly pine, *Pinus taeda*: potential impact on *Dendroctonus frontalis* within-tree mortality. Entomologia Experimentalis et Applicata 46(1):34–46.

Paine TD, Stephen FM, Cates RG. 1985a. Induced defenses against *Dendroctonus frontalis* and associated fungi: variation in loblolly pine resistance. Gen. Tech. Rep. SO-56. New Orleans: USDA Forest Service, Southern Forest Experiment Station: 169–176.

Paine TD, Stephen FM, Cates RG. 1988a. Moisture stress, tree suitability, and southern pine beetle population dynamics. In: Payne TL, Saarenmaa H, eds. Integrated control of Scolytid bark beetles: Proceedings, IUFRO Working Party and 17th International Congress of Entomology Symposium; 1988 July 4; Vancouver, BC. Blacksburg, VA: Virginia Polytechnic Institute and State University: 85–103.

Paine TD, Stephen FM, Cates RG. 1988b. Phenology of an induced response in loblolly pine following inoculation of fungi associated with the southern pine beetle. Canadian Journal of Forest Research 18(12):1556–1562.

Paine TD, Stephen FM, Wallis GW, Young JF. 1985b. Seasonal variation in host tree defense to the southern pine beetle. Arkansas Farm Research 34(1):5.

Pait JA III, Draper L Jr, Schmidt RA. 1985. Third-year comparisons of loblolly and slash pine seed sources for fusiform rust resistance and growth potential in north central Florida. In: Proceedings, 18th Southern Forest Tree Improvement Conference; 1985 May 21–23; Long Beach, MS. Springfield, VA: National Technical Information Service: 320.

Palmer HC Jr, Coster JE. 1978. Survival of southern pine beetles in felled and standing loblolly pines. Journal of the Georgia Entomological Society 13(1):1–7.

Parris GK. 1967. Field infection of loblolly pine seedlings in Mississippi with naturally produced inoculum of *Scirrhia acicola*. Plant Disease Reporter 51(7):552–556.

Parris GK. 1969. Control of the brown spot disease on loblolly pine in Mississippi by spraying [abstract]. Phytopathology 59(2):116–117.

Parris GK, Killebrew JF. 1969. Germination and entrance of the brown spot disease fungus into the loblolly pine needle, and the possible relationship of associated extraneous fungi to infection [abstract]. Phytopathology 59(2):117.

Pawuk WH. 1982. Diseases of container-grown southern pine seedlings and their control. In: Proceedings, Southern Containerized Forest Tree Seedling Conference; 1981 August 25–27; Savannah, GA. Gen. Tech. Rep. SO-37. New Orleans: USDA Forest Service, Southern Forest Experiment Station: 47–50.

Pawuk WH. 1983. Fungicide control of algae in containers. Tree Planters' Note 34(4):5–7.

Pawuk WH, Barnett JP. 1974. Root rot and damping-off of container-grown southern pine seedlings. In: Proceedings, North American Containerized Forest Tree Seedling Symposium; 1974 August 26–29; Denver, CO. Great Plains Agric. Coun. Publ. 68. Lincoln, NE: Great Plains Agricultural Council: 47–50.

Pawuk WH, Barnett JP. 1979. Seed handling practices for southern pines grown in containers. Southern Journal of Applied Forestry 3(1):19–22.

Payne TL. 1980. Life history and habits. In: Thatcher RC, Searcy JL, Coster JE, Hertel GD, eds. The southern pine beetle. Tech. Bull. 1631. Washington, DC: USDA Forest Service and Science and Education Administration: 7–28.

Peck WB, Warren LO, Brown IL. 1971. Spider fauna of shortleaf and loblolly pines in Arkansas. Journal Georgia Entomological Society 6(2):87–94.

Phelps WR, Czabator FL. 1978. Fusiform rust of southern pines. FIDL 26. Washington, DC: USDA Forest Service. 7 p.

Phelps WR. 1974. Evaluation of fusiform rust incidence on loblolly and slash pine in the South. Plant Disease Reporter 58(12):1137–1141.

Phelps WR. 1977. Incidence and distribution of fusiform rust. In: Dinus RJ, Schmidt RA, eds. Proceedings, Management of Fusiform Rust in Southern Pines; 1976 December 7–8; Gainesville, FL. Gainesville, FL: University of Florida: 25–31.

Phillips SO, Skelly JM, Burkhart HE. 1977. Growth fluctuation of loblolly pine due to periodic air pollution levels: interaction of rainfall and age. Phytopathology 67(6):716–720.

Pickering J, Ross DW, Berisford CW. 1989. An automated system for timing insecticidal sprays for Nantucket pine tip moth control. Southern Journal of Applied Forestry 13(4):184–187.

Powers HR Jr. 1971. Variation in shape of rust galls on loblolly pine. Plant Disease Reporter 55(7):623–625.

Powers HR Jr. 1972. Comandra rust on southern pines. Journal of Forestry 70(1):18–20.

Powers HR Jr. 1975. Relative susceptibility of five southern pines to Cronartium fusiforme. Plant Disease Reporter 59(4):312–314.

Powers HR Jr. 1981. Developing fusiform rust-resistant seed orchards using survivors of artificial inoculation tests. In: Proceedings, 1st Biennial Southern Silvicultural Research Conference; 1980 November 6–7; Atlanta, GA. Gen. Tech. Rep. SO-34. New Orleans: USDAForest Service, Southern Forest Experiment Station: 34–37.

Powers HR Jr. 1985. Response of sixteen loblolly pine families to four isolates of Cronartium quercuum F. sp. fusiforme. In: Proceedings, Rusts of Hard Pines Conference: IUFRO Working Party S2.06-10; 1984 [dates unknown]; [Location unknown]. Athens, GA: University of Georgia, Center for Continuing Education: 89–96.

Powers HR Jr. 1986. Performance of Livingston Parish loblolly pine in the Georgia Piedmont. Southern Journal of Applied Forestry 10(2):84–87.

Powers HR Jr, Duncan HJ. 1976. Increasing fusiform rust resistance by intraspecific hybridization. Forest Science 22(3):267–268.

Powers HR Jr, Dwinell LD. 1978. Virulence of Cronartium fusiforme stable after 25 years. Plant Disease Reporter 62(10):877–879.

Powers HR Jr, Kraus JF. 1988. Rust resistant loblolly pines: a comparison of seed sources. Georgia Forest Res. Pap. 74. Macon, GA: Georgia Forestry Commission, Research Division. 7 p.

Powers HR Jr, Rowan SJ. 1983. Influence of fertilization and eco-mycorrhizae on loblolly pine growth and susceptibility to fusiform rust. Southern Journal of Applied Forestry 7(2): 101–103.

Powers HR Jr, Stone DM. 1988. Control of tip moth by carbofuran reduces fusiform rust infection on loblolly pine. Res. Pap. SE-270. Asheville, NC: USDA Forest Service, Southeastern Forest Experiment Station. 4 p.

Powers HR Jr, Verral AF. 1962. A closer look at Fomes annosus. Forest Farmer 21(13):8–9, 16–17.

Powers HR Jr, Hepting GH, Stegall WA Jr. 1967. Comandra rust on loblolly pine in eastern Tennessee. Plant Disease Reporter 51(1):4–8.

Powers HR Jr, Lin D, Hubbes M. 1986. Detection of rust resistance in loblolly pine by isozyme analysis [abstract]. Phytopathology 76(10):1112.

Powers HR Jr, Matthews FR, Dwinell LD. 1977. Evaluation of pathogenic variability of Cronartium fusiforme on loblolly pine in the southern USA. Phytopathology 66(11):1403–1407.

Powers HR Jr, Matthews FR, Dwinell LD. 1978. The potential for increased virulence of Cronartium fusiforme on resistant loblolly pine. Phytopathology 68(5):808–810.

Priester DS, Pennington MT. 1978. Inhibitory effects of broomsedge extracts on the growth of young loblolly pine seedlings. Res. Pap. SE-182. Asheville, NC: USDA Forest Service, Southeastern Forest Experiment Station. 7 p.

Pritchett WL, Smith WH. 1972. Fertilizer response in young pine plantations. Soil Science of America Proceedings 36(1):660–663.

Ralston CW, Hatchell GE. 1971. Effects of prescribed burning on physical properties of soil. In: Proceedings, Prescribed Burning Symposium; 1971; Charleston, SC. Asheville, NC: USDA Forest Service, Southeastern Forest Experiment Station: 68–85.

Reamer LD, Bruner MH. 1973. The recovery of loblolly pine after snow damage. For. Bull. 10. Clemson, SC: Clemson University, Department of Forestry. 5 p.

Redmond CH, Anderson RL. 1986. Economic benefits of using the resistance screening center to assess relative resistance to fusiform rust. Southern Journal of Applied Forestry 10(1):34–37.

Robbins K. 1984. Annosus root rot in eastern conifers. FIDL 76. Washington, DC: USDA Forest Service. 9 p.

Roberds HH, Hain FP, Nunally LB. 1987. Genetic structure of southern pine beetle populations. Forest Science 33(1):52–69.

Robinette DL, Causey MK. 1978. Tests of repellents to protect loblolly seedlings from browsing by white-tailed deer. In: Proceedings, 30th Annual Conference of the Southeast Association of Fish and Wildlife Agencies; 1976 October 24–27; [Location unknown]. Knoxville, TN: Southeast Association of Fish and Wildlife Agencies: 481–486.

Rockwood DL. 1973. Monoterpene-fusiform rust relationships in loblolly pine. Phytopathology 63(5):551–553.

Rockwood DL. 1974. Cortical monoterpene and fusiform rust resistance relationships in slash pine. Phytopathology 64(7):976–979.

Rolfe GL, Bazzaz FA. 1975. Effect of lead contamination on transpiration and phytosynthesis of loblolly pine and autumn olive. Forest Science 21(1):33–35.

Ross EW. 1968. Duration of stump susceptibility of loblolly pine to infection by Fomes annosus. Forest Science 14(2):206–211.

Rowan SJ. 1970a. Fusiform rust gall formation and cellulose, lignin, and other wood constituents of loblolly pine. Phytopathology 60(8):1216–1220.

Rowan SJ. 1970b. Fusiform rust gall formation and cytokinin of loblolly pine. Phytopathology 60(8):1225–1226.

Rowan SJ. 1976. Factors affecting the incidence of fusiform rust in nurseries [abstract]. Proceedings of the American Phytopathological Society 2:48.

Rowan SJ. 1977a. Fertilizer-induced changes in susceptibility to fusiform rust vary among families of slash and loblolly pine. Phytopathology 67(10):1280–1284.

Rowan SJ. 1977b. Incidence of fusiform rust in Georgia forest tree nurseries, 1959-1973. Tree Planters' Notes 28(2):17–18, 29.

Rowan SJ. 1981. Soil fumigants and fungicide drenches for control of root rot of loblolly pine seedlings. Plant Disease 65(1):53–55.

Rowan SJ. 1982. Tip dieback in southern pine nurseries. Plant Disease 66(3):258–259.

Rowan SJ. 1983. Loss of feeder roots lowers seedling survival more than severe black root rot. Tree Planters' Notes 34(1):18–20.

Rowan SJ. 1984a. Bayleton applied to bareroot nursery stock reduces fusiform rust in first year after outplanting. Tree Planters' Notes 35(2):11–13.

Rowan SJ. 1984b. Bayleton seed treatment combined with foliar spray improves fusiform rust control in nurseries. Southern Journal of Applied Forestry 8(1):51–54.

Rowan SJ, Kelley WD. 1986. Survival and growth of outplanted pine seedlings after mycorrhizae were inhibited by use of triadimefon in the nursery. Southern Journal of Applied Forestry 10(1):21–23.

Rowan SJ, Muse D. 1981. Latent fusiform rust infections in slash and loblolly pine nursery stock. In: Proceedings, 1st Biennial Southern Silvicultural Research Conference; 1980 November 6–7; Atlanta, GA. Gen. Tech. Rep. SO-34. New Orleans: USDA Forest Service, Southern Forest Experiment Station: 38–39.

Rowan SJ, Steinbeck K. 1977. Seedling age and fertilization affect susceptibility of loblolly pine to fusiform rust. Phytopathology 67(2):242–246.

Rowan SJ, McNab WH, Brender EV. 1975. Pine overstory reduces fusiform rust in underplanted loblolly pine. Res. Note SE-212. Asheville, NC: USDA Forest Service, Southeastern Forest Experiment Station. 6 p.

Ruehle JL. 1964. Plant-parasitic nematodes and their significance in forest nursery production. In: Proceedings, Region 8 Forest Nurserymen's Conference; 1964 August 19–20; Morganton, NC/September 16–17; Oklahoma City, OK. Atlanta: USDA Forest Service, Southern Region: 92–98.

Ruehle JL. 1969. Influence of stubby root nematode on growth of southern pine seedlings. Forest Science 15(2):130–134.

Ruehle JL, Marx DH. 1971. Parasitism of ectomycorrhizae of pine by lance nematode. Forest Science 17(1):31–34.

Runion GB, Bruck RI. 1985. Associations of the pine tip moth with pitch canker of loblolly pine. Phytopathology 75(11):1339.

Runion GB, Bruck RI. 1988. The effects of thiabendazole on Fusarium subglutinans, the causal agent of pitch canker of loblolly pine. Plant Disease 72(4):297–300.

Sader SA, Miller WF. 1976. Development of a risk rating system for southern pine beetle infestation in Copiah County, MS. In: Proceedings, Remote Sensing of Earth Resources Conference; 1976; [Location unknown]. Tullahoma, TN: NASA 5: 277–294.

Salom SM, Stephen FM, Thompson LC. 1987. Development rates and a temperature-dependent model of pales weevil, Hylobius pales (Herbst), development. Environmental Entomology 16(4):956–962.

Sandberg DV, Pierovich JM, Fox DG, Ross EW. 1979. Effects of fire on air: a state of knowledge review. Gen. Tech. Rep. WO-9. Washington, DC: USDA Forest Service. 40 p.

Sartor CF, Neel WW. 1971a. Impact of Dioryctria amatella on seed yields on maturing slash and loblolly pine cones in Mississippi seed orchards. Journal of Economic Entomology 64(1):28–30.

Sartor CF, Neel WW. 1971b. Variable susceptibility to Dioryctria amatella (Hulst) (Lepidoptera: Phycitidae) among pines in clonal seed orchards. In: Proceedings, 11th Southern Forest Tree Improvement Conference; 1971 June 15–16; Atlanta, GA. Macon, GA: USDA Forest Service, Eastern Tree Seed Laboratory: 91–94.

Sasek TW, Richardson CJ. 1989. Effects of chronic doses of ozone on loblolly pine: photosynthetic characteristics in the third growing season. Forest Science 35(3):745–755.

Schmidt RA, Squillace AE, Swindel BF. 1979. Predicting the incidence of fusiform rust in five-to ten-year-old slash and loblolly pine plantations. Southern Journal of Applied Forestry 3(4):138–140.

Schmidt RA, Holley RC, Klapproth MC, Miller T. 1986. Temporal and spatial patterns of fusiform rust epidemics in young plantations of susceptible and resistant slash and loblolly pines. Plant Disease 70(7):661–666.

Schmidt RA, Miller T, Holley RC, and others. 1988. Relation of site factors to rust incidence in young slash and loblolly plantations in the Coastal Plain of Florida and Georgia. Plant Disease 72(8):710–714.

Schmidtling RC. 1985. Co-evolution of host/pathogen/alternative host systems in fusiform rust of loblolly and slash pines. In: Proceedings, Rusts of Hard Pines Working Party Conference; 1984 October 1–6; Athens, GA. IUFRO S2.06-10. Athens, GA: University of Georgia, Georgia Center for Continuing Education: 13–19.

Schneider SH. 1989. The greenhouse effect: science and policy. Science 243(4892):771–781.

Schowalter TD, Pope DN, Coulson RN, Fargo WS. 1981. Patterns of southern pine beetle (Dendroctonus frontalis Zimm.) infestation enlargement. Forest Science 27(4):837–849.

Seiler JR, Paganelli DJ. 1987. Photosynthesis and growth response of red spruce and loblolly pine to soil-applied lead and simulated acid rain. Forest Science 33(3):668–675.

Seinfeld JH. 1989. Urban air pollution: state of the science. Science 243(4892):745–752.

Shafer SR, Heagle AS. 1989. Growth responses of field-grown loblolly pine to chronic doses of ozone during multiple growing seasons. Canadian Journal of Forest Research 19(7):821–831.

Shepard RK Jr. 1978. Ice storm damage to thinned loblolly pine plantations in northern Louisiana. Southern Journal of Applied Forestry 2(3):83–85.

Shepard RK Jr. 1981. Ice damage to slash and loblolly pine in northern Louisiana. Tree Planters' Notes 32(1):6–8.

Shoulders E, Nance WL. 1987. Effects of fusiform rust on survival and structure of Mississippi and Louisiana loblolly pine plantations. Res. Pap. SO-232. New Orleans: USDA Forest Station, Southern Forest Experiment Station. 11 p.

Sigal LL, Eversman S, Berglund DL. 1988. Isolation of protoplasts from loblolly pine needles and their flow-cytometric analysis for air pollution effects. Environmental and Experimental Botany 28(2):151–161.

Skoller DL, Bridgwater FE, Lambeth CC. 1983. Fusiform rust resistance of select loblolly pine seedlots in the laboratory, nursery and field. Southern Journal of Applied Forestry 7(4):198–203.

Sluder ER. 1973. Open-pollinated progenies from six selected loblolly pines: 10-year performance in central Georgia. Res. Note SE-194. Asheville, NC: USDA Forest Service, Southeastern Forest Experiment Station. 3 p.

Sluder ER. 1977. Fusiform rust in loblolly and slash pine plantations on high hazard sites in Georgia. Res. Pap. SE-160. Asheville, NC: USDA Forest Service, Southeastern Forest Experiment Station. 9 p.

Sluder ER. 1988. Inheritance and gain in a half-diallel cross among loblolly pines selected for resistance to fusiform rust. Silvae Genetica 37(1):22–26.

Sluder ER. 1989. Fusiform rust in crosses among resistant and susceptible loblolly and slash pines. Southern Journal of Applied Forestry 13(4):174–177.

Sluder ER, Powers HR. 1986. Further comparisons between infection of loblolly and slash pines by fusiform rust after artificial inoculation or planting. Res. Note SE-342. Asheville, NC: USDA Forest Service, Southeastern Forest Experiment Station. 4 p.

Smith ML. 1987. Effects of water soluble extracts of shining sumac leaves on germination and growth of loblolly pine. Finel Rep. Summary FS-SO-4104-225. 1 p. On file with USDA Forest Service, Southern Forest Experiment Station, Pineville, LA.

Snow GA. 1985. A view of resistance to fusiform rust in loblolly pine. In: Proceedings, Insects and Diseases of Southern Forests: 34th Annual Forestry Symposium; 1985 March 26–27; Baton Rouge, LA. Baton Rouge, LA: Louisiana State University,

Louisiana Agricultural Experiment Station: 47–51.

Snow GA. 1986a. Geographic patterns of rust resistance in loblolly pine may be the result of coevolution of *Cronartium quercuum* with its pine hosts. In: Tauer CG, Hennessey TC, eds. Physiologic and genetic basis of forest decline: Proceedings, 9th North American Forest Biology Workshop; 1986 June 15–18; Stillwater, OK. Stillwater, OK: Oklahoma State University: 197–202.

Snow GA. 1986b. A needle blight of slash and loblolly pines in south Mississippi. In: Proceedings, Recent Research on Conifer Needle Diseases Conference; 1984 October 14–18; Gulfport, MS. Gen. Tech. Rep. WO-50. Washington, DC: USDA Forest Service: 20–21.

Snow GA. 1987. The tendency for round gall development in loblolly pines that are resistant to *Cronartium quercuum* F. sp. *fusiforme* [abstract]. In: Proceedings, 19th Southern Forest Tree Improvement Conference; 1987 June 16–18; College Station, TX. Springfield, VA: National Technical Information Service: 124.

Snow GA, Froelich RC. 1968. Daily and seasonal dispersal of basidiospores of *Cronartium fusiforme*. Phytopathology 58(11):1532–1536.

Snow GA, Affeltranger CC, Cordell CE. 1986. A cooperative study of granular Bayleton for control of fusiform rust in field plantings of loblolly and slash pine. Final Rep. Summary FS-SO-4503-20.50, Problem 3. On file with USDA Forest Service, Southern Forest Experiment Station, Gulfport, MS.

Snow GA, Jewell FF, Eleuterius LN. 1963. Apparent recovery of slash and loblolly pine seedlings from fusiform rust infection. Plant Disease Reporter 47(4):318–319.

Snow GA, Powers HR Jr, Kais AG. 1969. Pathogenic variability in *Cronartium fusiforme*. In: Proceedings, 10th Southern Forest Tree Improvement Conference; 1969 June 17–19; Houston, TX. College Station, TX: Texas Forest Service, Texas A&M University: 136–139.

Snow GA, Rowan SJ, Jones JP, and others. 1979. Using Bayleton (triadimefon) to control fusiform rust in pine tree nurseries. Res. Note SO-253. New Orleans: USDA Forest Service, Southern Forest Experiment Station. 5 p.

Snow GA, Wells OO, Switzer GL. 1986. Fusiform rust gradient in a loblolly pine plantation. Forest Science 32(2):372–376.

Snyder EB, Squillace AE. 1966. Cone and seed yields from controlled breeding of southern pines. Res. Paper SO-22. New Orleans: USDA Forest Service, Southern Forest Experiment Station. 7 p.

Solel Z, Bruck RI. 1989. Effect of nitrogen fertilization and growth suppression on pitch canker development on loblolly pine seedlings. Journal of Phytopathology 125(4):327–335.

Solel Z, Runion GB, Bruck RI. 1988. *Fusarium equiseti* pathogenic to pine. Transactions of the British Mycological Society 91(3):536–537.

Spaine P, Amerson H, Moyer J. 1985. Detection of *Cronartium quercuum* F. sp.*fusiforme* in *Pinus taeda* embryos using the enzyme linked immunosorbent assay [abstract]. Phytopathology 75(5):628.

Speers CF. 1974. Pales and pitch-eating weevils: development in relation to time pines are cut in the Southeast. Res. Note SE-207. Asheville, NC: USDA Forest Service, Southeastern Forest Experiment Station. 7 p.

Speers CF, Rauschenberger JL. 1971. Pales weevil. Forest Pest Leaflet 104. Washington, DC: USDA Forest Service. 6 p.

Squillace AE. 1976. Geographic patterns of fusiform rust infection in loblolly and slash pine plantations. Res. Note SE-232. Asheville, NC: USDA Forest Service, Southeastern Forest Experiment Station. 4 p.

Squillace AE, Dinus RJ, Hollis CA, Schmidt RA. 1978. Relation of oak abundance, seed source and temperature to geographic patterns of fusiform rust incidence. Res. Paper SE-186. Asheville, NC: USDA Forest Service, Southeastern Forest Experiment Station. 20 p.

Stephen FM, Lih MP. 1985. A *Dendroctonus frontalis* infestation growth model: organization, refinement, and utilization. In: Proceedings, Integrated Pest Management Research Symposium; 1985 April 15–18; Asheville, NC. Gen. Tech. Rep. SO-56. Asheville, NC: USDA Forest Service. Southern Forest Experiment Station: 186–194.

Stephen FM, Paine TD. 1985. Seasonal patterns of host tree resistance to fungal associates of the southern pine beetle. Zeitschrift für Angewandte Entomologie 99(2):113–122.

Stephen FM, Wallis GW, Colvin RJ, and others. 1982. Pine tree growth and yield: influence of species, plant spacing, vegetation, and pine tip moth control. Arkansas Farm Research 31(2):10.

Stephenson GK, Goodrum PD, Packard RL. 1963. Small rodents as consumers of pine seed in east Texas uplands. Journal of Forestry 61(7):523–526.

Stone DM, Powers HR. 1989. Sewage sludge increases early growth and decreases fusiform rust infection of nursery-run and rust-resistant loblolly pine. Southern Journal of Applied Forestry 13(2):68–71.

Tainter FH. 1978. Effect of bromine on pine forests. Arkansas Farm Research 27(2):9.

Telewski FW, Jaffe MJ. 1981. Thigmomorphogenesis: changes in the morphology and chemical composition induced by mechanical perturbation in 6-month-old *Pinus taeda* seedlings. Canadian Journal of Forest Research 11(2):380–387.

Tepper HB, Yang CS, Schaedle M. 1989. Effect of aluminum on growth of root tips of honey locust and loblolly pine. Environmental and Experimental Botany 29(2):165–173.

Thames JL. 1962. Seedling size and soil moisture affect survival of loblolly pine sprouts. Tree Planters' Notes 55:27–29.

Thatcher RC. 1960. Bark beetles affecting southern pines: a review of current knowledge. Occas. Pap. 180. New Orleans: USDA Forest Service, Southern Forest Experiment Station. 25 p.

Thatcher RC. 1967. Winter brood development of the southern pine beetle in southeast Texas. Journal of Economic Entomology 60:599–600.

Thatcher RC, Connor MD. 1985. Identification and biology of southern pine bark beetles. Agric. Handbk. 634. Washington, DC: USDA Forest Service, Cooperative State Research Service. 14 p.

Thatcher RC. 1971. Pine sawfly: *Neodiprion excitans* Roh. Forest Pest Leaflet 105. Revised. Washington, DC: USDA Forest Service. 4 p.

Thomas HA, Hertel GD. 1969. Responses of pales weevil to natural and synthetic host attractants. Journal of Economic Entomology 62(2):383–386.

Thomas HA, Hertel GD. 1979. Response of pales weevils to natural and synthetic traps under field conditions. Journal of Economic Entomology 72(3):342–345.

Thomas HA, Miller T, MacNab WH. 1982. Pine tip moth damage in relation to site preparation and regeneration method for loblolly pine. Res. Note SE-311. Asheville, NC: USDA Forest Service, Southeastern Forest Experiment Station. 3 p.

Thomas HA, Oprean CP. 1984. Growth impact of tip moth control in 23-year-old pines. Res. Note SE-324. Asheville, NC: USDA Forest Service, Southeastern Forest Experiment Station. 6 p.

Thompson LC. 1987. Pitch-blister moth on loblolly pine. Arkansas Farm Research 36(5):10.

Towers B. 1964. Root-contact infection by *Fomes annosus* in a thinned loblolly pine plantation. Plant Disease Reporter 48(10):767–769.

Trousdell KB, Williams WC, Nelson TC. 1965. Damage to recently thinned loblolly pine stands by hurricane Donna. Journal of Forestry 63(2):96–100.

USDA FS [U.S. Department of Agriculture, Forest Service]. 1971. A pine looper, *Lambdina athasaria pellucidaria*. For. Pest Rep. 1. Atlanta: USDA Forest Service, Southeastern Area, State and Private Forestry. 9 p.

USDA FS [U.S. Department of Agriculture, Forest Service]. 1972. Insects and diseases of trees in the South. Atlanta: USDA Forest Service, State and Private Forestry, Southeastern Area. 81 p.

USDA FS [U.S. Department of Agriculture, Forest Service]. 1985. Insects and diseases of trees in the South. Gen. Rep. R8-GR 5. Atlanta: USDA Forest Service, Southern Region. 98 p.

van Buijtenen JP. 1982. A population genetic model of the alternate host system of *Cronartium quercuum* F. sp. *fusiforme*. Forest Science 28(4):745–752.

Veal MA, Blair RL, Jett JB, McKean WT. 1974. Impact of fusiform rust on pulping properties of young loblolly and slash pine. In: Proceedings, 1974 Forest Biology Conference; 1974 September 18–20; Seattle, WA. Atlanta: TAPPI: 47–58.

Wagner TL, Hennier PB, Flamm RO, Coulson RN. 1988. Development and mortality of *Ips avulsus* (Coleoptera: Scolytidae) at constant temperatures. Environmental Entomology 17(2):181–191.

Wahlenberg WG. 1960. Loblolly pine: its use, ecology, regeneration, protection, growth, and management. Durham, NC: Duke University, School of Forestry/Washington, DC: USDA Forest Service. 603 p.

Wakeley PC. 1954. Planting the southern pines. Agric. Monogr. 18. Washington, DC: USDA Forest Service. 233 p.

Wakeley PC. 1970. Long-term effects of damage by rabbits to newly planted southern pines. Tree Planters' Notes 21(2):6–9.

Walkinshaw CH. 1978. Cell necrosis and fungus content in fusiform rust-infected loblolly, longleaf, and slash pine seedlings. Phytopathology 68(12):1705–1710.

Ward M, Kress LW. 1980. Variation in response among 33 wind-pollinated families of *Pinus taeda* L. [abstract]. Phytopathology 70(7):693.

Warren LO. 1963. Nantucket pine–tip moth infestations: severity of attack as influenced by vegetative competition in pine stand. Arkansas Farm Research 12(6):4.

Warren LO, Stephen FM, Young JF. 1975a. Control of pine tip moth as influenced by space, competitive vegetation, insect control, and pine species. Spec. Rep. 23:10. Fayetteville, AR: University of Arkansas, Arkansas Agricultural Experiment Station: 23–25.

Warren LO, Stephen FM, Young JF. 1975b. Long-term effects of pine tipmoth control. Spec. Rep. 23/10. Fayetteville, AR: University of Arkansas, Arkansas Agricultural Experiment Station: 26 p.

Weatherby JC, Moser JC, Gagne RJ, Wallace HN. 1989. Biology of a pine needle sheath midge, *Contarinia acuta* Gagne (Diptera: Cecidomyiidae), on loblolly pine. Proceedings of the Entomological Society of Washington 9(3):346–349.

Webb RS, Alexander SA, Skelly JM. 1981. Incidence, severity, and growth effects of *Heterobasidion annosum* in unthinned loblolly pine plantations. Phytopathology 71(6):661–662.

Webb RS, Patterson HD. 1984. Effect of stem location of fusiform rust symptoms on volume yields of loblolly and slash pine sawtimber. Phytopathology 74(8):980–983.

Wells CG. 1971. Effects of prescribed burning on soil chemical properties and nutrient availability. In: Proceedings, Prescribed Burning Symposium; 1971; Charleston, SC. Asheville, NC: USDA Forest Service, Southeastern Forest Experiment Station: 86–97.

Wells OO. 1985. Use of Livingston Parish, Louisiana, loblolly pine by forest products industries in the Southeast. Southern Journal of Applied Forestry 9(3):180–185.

Wells OO, Dinus RJ. 1974. Correlation between artificial and natural inoculation of loblolly pine with southern fusiform rust. Phytopathology 64(5):760–761.

Wells OO, Dinus RJ. 1978. Early infection as a predictor of mortality associated with fusiform rust of southern pines. Journal of Forestry 76(1):8–12.

Wells OO, Switzer GL. 1971. Variation in rust resistance in Mississippi loblolly pine. In: Proceedings, 11th Southern Forest Tree improvement Conference; 1971 June 15–16; Atlanta, GA. Macon, GA: USDA Forest Service, Eastern Tree Seed Laboratory: 25–30.

Wells OO. 1966. Variation in rust resistance among pine seed sources and species in a Mississippi planting. Forest Science 12(4):461–463.

Wells OO, Wakeley PC. 1966. Geographic variation in survival, growth, and fusiform-rust infection of planted loblolly pine. For. Sci. Monogr. 11. Washington, DC: Society of American Foresters. 40 p.

Werner RA. 1972. Aggregation behaviour of the beetle *Ips grandicollis* in response to host-produced attractants. Journal of Insect Physiology 18(3):423–437.

Werner RA. 1974. Penetration and persistence of systemic insecticides in seeds and seedlings of southern pines. Journal of Economic Entomology 67(1):81–84.

Wheeler GL, Young JF. 1979. The allelopathic effect of fescue on loblolly pine seedling growth. Arkansas Farm Research 28:6.

White MN, Kulhavy DL, Conner RN. 1984. Nantucket pine tip moth (Lepidoptera: Tortricidae) infestation rates related to site and stand characteristics in Nacogdoches county, TX. Environmental Entomology 13(6):1598–1601.

Wilkinson RC, Underhill EM, McGraw JR, and others. 1977. Pitch canker incidence and fertilizer-insecticide treatment. Prog. Rep. 77-1. Gainesville, FL: University of Florida, Institute of Food and Agriculture Science, Teaching Research Extension. 4 p.

Williams TM, Gresham CA, Hedden RL, Blood ER. 1989. Impact of southern pine beetle infestation on nutrient retention mechanisms in loblolly pine. In: Proceedings, 5th Biennial Southern Silvicultural Research Conference; 1988 November 1–3; Memphis, TN. Gen. Tech. Rep. SO-74. New Orleans: USDA Forest Service, Southern Forest Experiment Station: 465–472.

Williams VG, Goyer RA. 1980. Comparison of damage by each life stage of *Leptoglossus corculus* and *Tetyra bipunctata* to loblolly pine seeds. Journal of Economic Entomology 73(4):497–501.

Williston HJ, Barras SJ. 1977. Impact of tip moth injury on growth and yield of 16-year-old loblolly and shortleaf pine. Res. Note SO-221. New Orleans: USDA Forest Service, Southern Forest Experiment Station. 5 p.

Wilson CL. 1961. Epidemics of pine needle rust in Arkansas. Plant Disease Reporter 45(12):957.

Wolfe RD, Drake LL, Peacher PH, wilmore DH. 1971. A survey of pine needle blight damage in the South. Rep. 72-2-3. On file with USDA Forest Service, Southern Forest Experiment Station, Asheville, NC.

Wood GW, Roark DN. 1980. Food habits of feral hogs in coastal South Carolina. Journal of Wildlife Management 44(2):506–511.

Wood GW, Lynn TE Jr. 1977. Wild hogs in southern forests. Southern Journal of Applied Forestry 1(2):12–17.

Yates HO III. 1965. The influence of oleoresin on southern pine injury by *Rhyacionia* (Lepidoptera, Olethreutidae). Dissertation Abstracts 26(1):567.

Yates HO III. 1967a. Pupae of *Rhyacionia frustrana*, *R. rigidana*, and *R. subtropica* (Lepidoptera: Olethreutidae). Annals of the Entomological Society of America 60(5):1096–1099.

Yates HO III. 1967b. Radiographic detection of *Rhyacionia* larvae, pupae, parasites, and predators within pine shoots (Lepidoptera: Olethreutidae). Journal of the Georgia Entomological Society 2(3):81–85.

Yates HO III. 1969. Characters for determining the sex of *Rhyacionia* pupae (Lepidoptera: Olethreutidae). Journal of the Georgia Entomological Society 4(2):75–76.

Yates HO III. 1971. Nantucket pine tip moth caused flower and conelet mortality. In: Proceedings, 11th Southern Forest Tree Improvement Conference; 1971 June 15–16; Atlanta, GA. Macon, GA: USDA Forest Service, Eastern Tree Seed Laboratory: 224–229.

Yates HO III, Ebel BH. 1972. Light-trap collections and review of biologies of two species of pine-feeding Geometridae. Journal of the Georgia Entomological Society 7(4):265–271.

Yates HO III, Ebel BH. 1978. Impact of insect damage on loblolly pine seed production. Journal of Economic Entomology 71(2):345–349.

Yates HO III, Overgaard NA, Koerber TW. 1981. Nantucket pine tip moth. FIDL 70. Washington, DC: USDA Forest Service. 7 p.

Yearian WC, Warren WO. 1964.   Insects of pine cones in Arkansas.
    Journal of the Kansas Entomological Society 37(3):259–264.

Yearian WC, Young SY, Livingston JM. 1973.   Field evaluation of a
    nuclear polyhedrosis virus of *Neodiprion taedae linearis*. Journal
    of Invertebrate Pathology 22(1):34–37.

Young SY, Yearian WC. 1986.   Application of a nuclear polyhedro-
    sis virus of *Neodiprion taedae linearis* Ross on pine: persistence
    and effect of timing on larval mortality. Journal of Entomological
    Science 21(3):193–200.

Young SY, Yearian WC. 1987.   Intra-and inter-colony transmission
    of a nuclear polyhedrosis virus of the loblolly pine sawfly, *Neodi-
    prion taedae linearis* Ross, on pine. Journal of Entomological
    Science 22(1):29–34.

Zarnoch SJ, Lorio PL J, Sommers RA. 1984.   A logistic model for
    southern pine beetle stand risk rating in central Louisiana.
    Journal of the Georgia Entomological Society 19(2):168–175.

Zutter BR, Gjerstad DH, Glover GR. 1987.   Fusiform rust inci-
    dence and severity in loblolly pine plantations following herba-
    ceous weed control. Forest Science 33(3):790–800.

Chapter 11

Growth and Yield

Contents

Continued on next page...

Contents (cont'd)

Growth and Yield

Introduction

Growing naturally regenerated loblolly pines is financially competitive with clearcut-and-plant silviculture (Dangerfield and Edwards 1991). There is no single optimum growing-stock level or rotation age for loblolly pines. Each stand has a distinctive density, spacing arrangement, and growth capability (figure 11-1). Many natural stands that contain loblolly pines have distinctive mixed-species composition. Managers need precise tree growth and stand yield information so they can project the effects of stand density control, prescribed cultural treatments, cutting cycles, and rotation lengths on saw timber, pulpwood, or fiber production. During the early 1970's, many growth and yield projection systems were developed for unthinned planted stands on abandoned farmland (old fields) across loblolly's natural range (Burkhart and others 1972a, Goebel and Warner 1969, Lenhart 1972a, Lenhart and Clutter 1971, Smalley and Bailey 1974). By the late 1970's, there were enough data on growth of thinned and unthinned plantations on forested sites to develop specialized yield estimates (Daniels and others 1979, Feduccia and others 1979, Smith 1978, Strub and others 1981).

Monitoring of permanent growth and yield plots in loblolly pine plantations during the past 2 to 3 decades has provided accurate long-term growth data and some baseline data for quantifying soil-site productivity relationships; developing basal area, height growth, and stand structure functions; developing tree survival equations; determining effects of cultural treatments on structure and growth; and quantifying the effects of competing vegetation and pests.

Figure 11-1—This virgin loblolly–shortleaf pine stand averages 215 m³ of sawtimber/ha with trees that are up to 135 cm in dbh and 250 years old.

Tree Measurements and Estimators of Tree Growth

The heights of young loblolly pines can be measured directly for the first several years. Once trees grow taller than about 6 m, direct measurement becomes cumbersome, and estimates made using hand-held instruments are more practical (Rennie 1979). Past tree heights can be estimated from stem analysis data by several methods (Carmean 1972, Lenhart 1972a, Newberry 1978). Carmean's method is the most accurate. In this method, it is assumed that height growth is constant for all years within a bolt and that each crosscut occurs in the middle of a year's growth (Dyer and Bailey 1987). Total height of trees and height at a specific diameter outside bark (dob) can be predicted using equations (Cao and Pepper 1986). Several models are available for projecting height–age curves of planted loblolly pine stands with reasonable accuracy (Brewer and others 1985, Popham and others 1979).

Loblolly pines exhibit more variability in merchantable height than in total height. Taper and branching, and crooks resulting from breakage or damage caused by pathogens, can affect merchantable height of trees having the same total height and diameter at breast height (dbh). The basic relationship between tree height and diameter is the same for loblolly from different seed sources (Buford 1986). In natural stands on the lower Piedmont of Georgia, total and merchantable heights can be predicted from site index and tree diameter class. Total height increases at a fairly uniform rate for trees 15 to 50 cm in dbh. However, merchantable height begins to level off by the time trees reach 35 to 40 cm in dbh, often because the central stem is separated into several large limbs (figure 11-2). Only the lower 30% of the length of the main stem of a loblolly with a dbh of 25 cm yields sawn lumber, whereas the lower 70% of the main stem of a loblolly with a dbh of 50 cm yields sawn lumber (Brender 1986).

Most diameter measurements are taken with a diameter tape or with tree calipers. Circumferential banding, often used to measure change in larger trees precisely, is not practical for small trees or small tree parts because growth directly underneath the band is constricted. A transducer can be used to measure diameter changes in small stems, branches, or roots over periods as short as 3 hours (Kinerson 1973). Equations are available for predicting inside bark diameter from outside bark diameter and both inside and outside bark diameters at breast height (Cao and Pepper 1986).

Measurements of Stand Density

Basal area can be determined precisely and is an excellent measurement of density of loblolly pine stands (Allen and Duzan 1981). Change in basal area over time is a useful predictor of stand growth and can be useful in scheduling intermediate cuttings. The combination of number of stems and basal area may be the best simple measurement of density.

Basal area growth is the product of basal area increment per stem and number of stems per unit area. It is influenced by site index and rises or falls with increasing stand age. Basal area growth increases rapidly at young ages and decreases to almost nothing by age 80 where site indices are 15 to 18 m (base age 50). Basal area growth culminates well before volume growth culminates. Nelson (1963) found that basal area growth of 20-year-old loblolly pines was greatest when basal area was about 80 to 95 ft^2 of basal area/acre (18 to 23 m^2/ha), regardless of site index. However, growth was almost maximum over a wide range of basal areas. For example, where site index was 70 ft (21 m), growth was 90% of maximum at basal areas ranging from 65 to 115 ft^2/acre (15 to 26 m^2/ha). At tree age 50, growth was greatest at about 80 to 90 ft^2 of basal area/acre

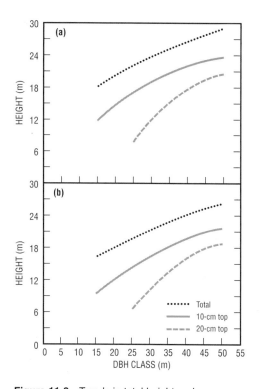

Figure 11-2—Trends in total height and merchantable heights for loblolly pines growing in the Piedmont of Georgia: site index 26 m (**a**) and site index 20 m (**b**) (adapted from Brender 1986).

Table 11-1—Annual basal area growth per acre of natural loblolly pines at ages 20, 50, and 80 in Georgia, South Carolina, and Virginia as related to site index and initial (30–160 ft^2/acre) basal area

| Site Index (ft) | Basal area growth (ft^2/acre) | | | | | | | | | | | | | |
	IBA 30	IBA 40	IBA 50	IBA 60	IBA 70	IBA 80	IBA 90	IBA 100	IBA 110	IBA 120	IBA 130	IBA 140	IBA 150	IBA 160
Age 20														
50	2.58	3.43	4.11	4.62	4.95	5.10	5.09	4.89	4.53	3.98	3.27	2.38	1.31	0.07
60	2.60	3.48	4.18	4.72	5.09	5.29	5.32	5.18	4.87	4.40	3.75	2.94	1.96	0.81
70	2.63	3.52	4.26	4.82	5.23	5.47	5.55	5.47	5.22	4.81	4.24	3.51	2.61	1.54
80	2.65	3.57	4.33	4.93	5.37	5.66	5.79	5.76	5.57	5.23	4.73	4.07	3.25	2.28
90	2.68	3.62	4.40	5.03	5.51	5.84	6.02	6.05	5.92	5.64	5.21	4.63	3.90	3.02
100	2.71	3.66	4.47	5.13	5.65	6.03	6.25	6.33	6.27	6.06	5.70	5.20	4.55	3.76
Age 50														
50	0.40	0.74	1.00	1.20	1.32	1.37	1.35	1.26	1.09	0.86	0.55	0.18	NT	NT
60	0.43	0.78	1.08	1.30	1.46	1.55	1.58	1.55	1.44	1.27	1.04	0.74	0.38	NT
70	0.45	0.83	1.15	1.40	1.60	1.74	1.82	1.83	1.79	1.69	1.53	1.30	1.02	0.68
80	0.48	0.88	1.22	1.51	1.74	1.92	2.05	2.12	2.14	2.10	2.01	1.87	1.67	1.42
90	0.50	0.92	1.29	1.61	1.88	2.11	2.28	2.41	2.49	2.52	2.50	2.43	2.32	2.15
100	0.53	0.97	1.36	1.72	2.02	2.29	2.52	2.70	2.84	2.93	2.99	3.00	2.97	2.89
Age 80														
50	NT	0.06	0.23	0.34	0.41	0.44	0.42	0.35	0.24	0.08	NT	NT	NT	NT
60	NT	0.11	0.30	0.44	0.55	0.62	0.65	0.64	0.58	0.49	0.36	0.19	NT	NT
70	NT	0.16	0.37	0.55	0.69	0.80	0.88	0.92	0.93	0.91	0.85	0.75	0.63	0.47
80	NT	0.20	0.44	0.65	0.84	0.99	1.12	1.21	1.28	1.32	1.34	1.32	1.28	1.20
90	NT	0.25	0.51	0.76	0.98	1.17	1.35	1.50	1.63	1.74	1.82	1.88	1.92	1.94
100	NT	0.30	0.59	0.86	1.12	1.36	1.58	1.79	1.98	2.15	2.31	2.45	2.57	2.68

Source: adapted from Nelson (1963).

IBA = initial basal area (in ft^2/acre); NT = no trees in this class; 1 ft^2/acre = 0.2296 m^2/ha; 1 ft = 0.305 m.

(18 to 21 m²/ha) on poor sites, greatest at 100 to 120 ft² of basal area/acre (23 to 28 m²/ha) on medium sites, and greatest at 130 to 150 ft² of basal area/acre (30 to 34 m²/ha) on high sites (table 11-1).

Stem Form

Stem taper or stem profile (change in stem diameter with tree height) strongly affects merchantable volume and total biomass in both plantations and natural stands (Lloyd 1985, Van Lear and others 1986). For example, Clark and Taras (1976) determined that the midstem form quotient (diameter inside bark [dib] at one-half total tree height – dbh) for sawtimber loblolly pines in natural stands is about 0.63. Stem form is affected by stand density, total tree height, crown ratio, and height to the live crown. Bole taper can be determined by comparing dbh and upper stem diameter measurements, which usually involves felling the tree and making precise measurements at various points along its stem. Stem taper functions for predicting either upper stem diameter inside bark or upper stem dob from dbh and height measurements have been developed for loblolly pine plantations on cut-over sites in east Texas (Lenhart and others 1987) and Louisiana (Baldwin and Feduccia 1991).

When no allowance is made for stem taper, estimated volumes of individual trees can differ from actual volumes by – 26 to +15%. Including stem taper can reduce errors to – 1.8 to +1.0% (Lloyd 1985). However, trees growing in unthinned oldfield plantations, plantations on cut-over areas, and natural stands all have significantly different taper and form. Amateis and Burkhart (1987a) concluded that separate taper and volume equations are needed for each of these growth situations. Volume prediction models employing compatible stem taper functions are available for both planted (Baldwin and Feduccia 1987, Feduccia and others 1979, Lenhart and others 1987) and natural loblolly pines (Farrar and Murphy 1988).

Stand density affects stem form by altering crown ratios. Trees with larger crowns have more taper and less volume in the upper part of the stem than do trees with smaller crowns. Inclusion of crown ratio as an independent variable increases the accuracy of tree volume and stand yield

predictions (Byrne and Reed 1986, Feduccia and others 1979, Liu and Keister 1978, Liu and others 1989, Valenti and Cao 1986; table 11-2). Crown ratio can usually be determined at little cost by measuring the height to the base of the live crown when measuring total tree height. If height to base of live crown is not measured, crown ratios of individual trees can be predicted from combinations of stand age, stand basal area, tree diameter, and tree height (Dell 1979, Dyer and Burkhart 1987, Feduccia and others 1979, Holdaway 1986, Newberry and Burkhart 1985).

Because thinning or fertilization can also change the stem form of crop trees, separate taper, total volume, and merchantable volume prediction equations may be required for treated and untreated stands. Following thinning, diameter growth of the stem is greatest near the base of the tree and in the lower portion of the crown. Thus, trees in thinned stands become more cylindrical, developing less taper in the lower stem and relatively more taper in the upper stem than trees in unthinned stands develop (Baldwin and Feduccia 1991). Fertilization of stands of pole-sized loblolly pines can also result in greater growth on the upper stem than on the lower stem for up to 5 years after treatment. For this reason, response to fertilization is underestimated unless upper stem measurements are incorporated into equations. By 5 years after treatment, a single volume equation should accurately predict volume in both fertilized and unfertilized stands (Jack and others 1988).

Table 11-2— Inside bark volume of loblolly pines between a 15-cm stump and the tip of the main stem by diameter at breast height (dbh) height, and crown length ratio class

Dbh (cm)	Height (m)	Inside bark volume (m³)		
		CLR < 36%	CLR 36-50%	CLR >50%
10	6	0.022	0.020	0.017
15	9	0.067	0.064	0.062
20	12	0.157	0.157	0.143
25	15	0.316	0.316	0.283
30	18	0.571	0.540	0.501
35	21	0.958	0.862	0.823
40	24	1.512	1.288	1.282

Source: adapted from Dell (1979) and Feduccia and others (1979).

CLR = crown length ratio (%) = ratio of crown length to tree height.

Tree Biomass

Tree parts other than the bole cannot be described adequately in terms of volume. Thus, dry weight measurements, green weight measurements, or both must replace or at least supplement traditional volume measurements to accurately describe the total growth of loblolly pine forests and the accumulation of biomass. Also, both the total and relative amounts of biomass in various tree components vary with site quality and stand

age, so weight measurements must be developed for specific forest conditions. Tree age is clearly related to tree weight—older trees weigh more than younger trees of the same dimensions (Baldwin 1987, Burkhart and Clutter 1971). Thinning alters tree weight, so separate equations are needed to determine the green and dry weights of aboveground tree components for thinned and unthinned stands (Baldwin 1987).

Biomass Prediction

Many equations have been developed to estimate total dry- or green-weight biomass of individual loblolly pine trees and stands for diverse sites, environmental conditions, and stand ages throughout the species' range (Baldwin 1987, 1989; Burkhart and Clutter 1971; Burkhart and others 1972a, 1972b; Flowers 1978; Hicks and others 1972; Lenhart and others 1987; Pienaar and Grider 1984; Shelton and others 1984; Williams 1989). Baldwin (1986) summarizes the equations available for predicting biomass of planted loblolly.

One yield model calculates optimum planting density for plantations grown for biomass (Lloyd and Harms 1988). The predictor variables are usually dbh alone or dbh and total height. Other variables, such as bole diameter at the base of the live crown or at the groundline, are also good biomass predictors for young trees. For example, the bole weight of trees up to 4 m in height can be estimated by using the following equation (Shear and Perry 1986):

$$B = 6.67RCD^{2.83}$$

where: B = bole weight (in grams)
RCD = root collar diameter (in centimeters)

Similarly, the dry weight of all aboveground material can be estimated accurately for individual loblolly pine saplings from total tree height and bole diameter at the groundline (Edwards and McNab 1979) or total tree height and dbh (Edwards and McNab 1981). It is possible that similar allometric relationships can be made for larger trees.

High-resolution remote-sensing data can be used to accurately estimate the area of land in the loblolly pine forest type and the amount and spatial distribution of loblolly pine biomass, especially if ground check data are incorporated into the analysis (Jensen and Hodgson 1985, Jensen and others 1986, Shimabukuro and others 1980). Even large-scale 35-mm or infrared aerial photographs can be used to estimate the amount of loblolly pine in the upper crowns of mixed stands (Baldwin 1982, Needham and Smith 1987).

Dry-Weight Biomass of Boles, Branches, and Needles

Newly lifted nursery seedlings may weigh only 30 to 60 g, whereas old monarch loblolly pines can tip the scales at up to 14 tonnes (t). The relative weight of tree components varies by tree size. During the first year of tree life, needles may constitute more than 50% of the tree's total dry weight. As a tree grows, the bole quickly supplants the needles as the dominant component of biomass. In saplings, foliage and stemwood each account for about one-third of the aboveground weight (Smith and others 1971, Switzer and others 1966, Wells and others 1975). For trees aged 15 years and older, foliage makes up only 3 to 5% of the total tree dry weight, whereas the bole makes up about 65 to 70% of the total tree dry weight,

Table 11-3—Size of tree, weight of aboveground tree parts, and percentage of total weight in tree parts for 10 loblolly pine trees of different ages

Age (yr)	Diameter of base (cm)	Height (m)	Ovendry weight (g)				
			Needles	Stemwood	Stembark	Branches	Total
7	7.1	2.4	711.3 (38.0)	532.4 (28.4)	338.1 (18.1)	289.3 (15.5)	1,871.1
7	7.1	3.0	1,253.3 (43.3)	706.8 (24.4)	395.1 (13.6)	541.1 (18.7)	2,896.3
7	10.4	3.2	1,724.9 (29.8)	2,132.3 (36.9)	818.2 (14.2)	1,101.3 (19.1)	5,776.7
7	10.9	4.0	2,722.0 (29.5)	3,174.0 (34.4)	1,100.4 (11.9)	2,240.9 (24.2)	9,237.3
7	12.7	5.2	3,456.8 (26.5)	5,390.0 (41.4)	1,840.7 (14.1)	2,346.0 (18.0)	13,033.5
8	14.2	6.3	3,376.2 (24.2)	6,097.9 (43.6)	1,923.6 (13.8)	2,569.4 (18.4)	13,967.1
8	17.5	7.1	3,563.2 (14.5)	13,093.1 (53.1)	3,403.6 (13.8)	4,585.9 (18.6)	24,645.8
13	21.1	10.9	4,211.9 (9.7)	25,136.2 (57.7)	5,603.2 (12.9)	8,583.2 (19.7)	43,534.5
21	19.0	14.0	2,776.0 (5.0)	39,103.5 (70.9)	6,879.1 (12.5)	6,426.6 (11.6)	55,185.2
21	24.4	14.2	4,171.4 (4.7)	61,686.1 (70.0)	8,848.6 (10.0)	13,475.4 (15.3)	88,181.5

Source: adapted from Metz and Wells (1965).

Values in parentheses beneath each number show the percentage of the total tree weight in that particular part of the tree.

Table 11-4—Average percentage of total dry weight for various components of seven 15-year-old planted loblolly pine trees with diameters at breast height ranging from 11 to 21 cm and heights ranging from 10 to 15 m

Stem		Branches			Roots	
Bark	Wood	Old	New	Needles	Taproot	Lateral
9.4	60.4	8.6	0.8	4.7	7.8	8.3

Source: adapted from Ralston (1973).

and branches 10% (Wells and others 1975; tables 11-3 and 11-4). Roots constitute the remaining 15 to 20% (see Root Biomass and Shoot-to-Root Ratio section).

The dry-weight percentage of wood (xylem) increases as a tree grows, whereas that of bark (phloem) decreases with increasing tree size (figure 11-3). Bark accounts for about 15% of the dry weight of a tree 15 cm in dbh. At tree maturity, about 86% of the dry weight is wood, 10% is bark, and 4% is needles. On the average, 80 to 90% of the aboveground wood in a mature loblolly pine is in the main stem. Branches, however, contain 30% of the bark (Clark 1978, Clark and Taras 1976, Ralston 1978, Taras and Clark 1974).

The weight of individual loblolly pines is directly related to tree size. For example, the bark-free, ovendry wood weight is highly correlated (R =.99) to squared outside-bark dbh and total height or merchantable height in the interior West Gulf Coastal Plain (figure 11-4; appendix B, tables 1 through 4). The center of mass for tree-length stems 12 to 36 cm in dbh and 4 to 19 m in length is about 32 to 44% of the way up the stem from the butt, depending on the amount of tree taper. The whole-tree center of mass is about 2 m farther from the butt than is the tree-length center of mass (Fridley and Tufts 1989).

Crown Biomass

For purposes of this discussion, the crown consists of all branches and all foliage on a tree. On a stand basis, branch weight is affected primarily by site index and stand age. Branch biomass continues to increase in dry weight until at least tree age 25 on all sites (figure 11-5). Needle biomass also varies with site quality in young stands, but it remains fairly constant for a particular site after trees are about 12 to 15 years old. After tree age 15, total crown biomass can range from as little as 10 t/ha (figure 11-5) on poor sites to more than 30 t/ha on good sites. A 41-year-old, twice-thinned plantation on a poor

Piedmont site had 14 t of branch material/ha but only 2.7 t of foliage/ha. Branches and foliage made up 15% of the total aboveground biomass (Van Lear and others 1984). In contrast, 16- to 18-year-old, unthinned plantations growing on better sites in the North Carolina Piedmont and Arkansas Coastal Plain had from 26 to 31 t of crown biomass (including 5 to 8 t of foliage)/ha, and crown biomass constituted 17 to 25% of the aboveground biomass (table 11-5).

In a typical tree, branches with the greatest wood weight are in the lower part of the crown, whereas the branches with the greatest needle weight occur near the middle of the crown (figure 11-6). Needle weight makes up about 60% of crown weight in trees 5 cm in dbh but less than 20% of crown weight in trees with dbh's greater than 30 cm (figure 11-7).

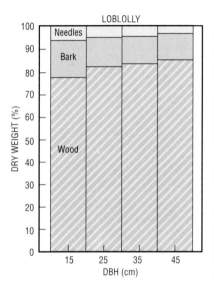

Figure 11-3—Proportion of loblolly pine tree dry weight in wood, bark, and needles (adapted from Clark and Taras 1976).

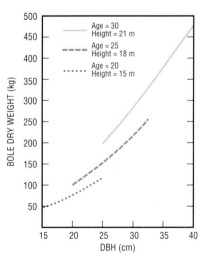

Figure 11-4—Correlation between tree diameter at breast height and bole dry weight of planted loblolly pines in central Louisiana (adapted from Baldwin 1987).

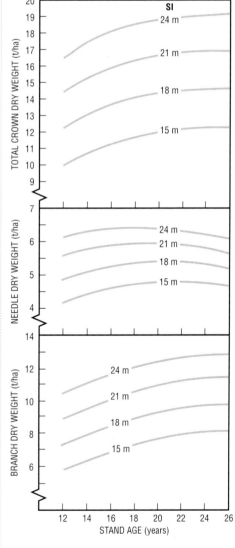

Figure 11-5—Aboveground biomass of loblolly pine branches and needles in the Coastal Plain of North Carolina and South Carolina as affected by site and stand age (adapted from Hepp and Brister 1982).

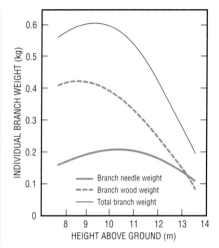

Figure 11-6—Trend in individual branch component weights with increasing height above ground for an average tree 15 m tall and 15 years old in the North and South Carolina Coastal Plain (adapted from Hepp and Brister 1982).

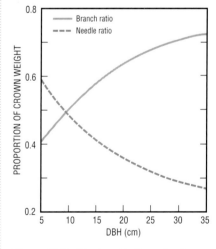

Figure 11-7—The trend in the ratio of branch weight to needle weight with increasing tree diameter at breast height (adapted from Hepp and Brister 1982).

Table 11-5—Dry weight biomass of loblolly pine plantations at varous stand locations and tree ages by stand component

| Location and reference | Average age (yr) | Average height (m) | Dry weight biomass (t/ha) | | | | | | |
| | | | Foliage | Branches | | Stem | | Above-ground total | Roots |
				Live	Dead	Bark	Wood		
Alabama Upper Coastal Plain (Larsen and others 1976)	13	11.6	9.5	12.1	7.9	8.1	50.9	88.5	—
North Carolina Piedmont (Wells and others 1975)	16	15.0	8.0	14.6	8.6	15.2	109.6	156.0	36.3
Arkansas Coastal Plain (Ku and Burton 1973)	18*	18.6	5.9	15.5	8.0	15.4	128.9	173.3[†]	—
	18[‡]	16.2	6.8	15.0	7.8	14.4	114.6	159.1[†]	—
Arkansas loessial soil (Ku and Burton 1973)	18*	16.8	5.0	14.7	6.6	13.3	103.5	143.8[†]	—
	18[‡]	14.9	6.2	16.6	8.7	9.3	84.7	127.2[†]	—
East Texas Gulf Coastal Plain (Pehl and others 1984)	25	20.0	4.6	12.0	5.2	14.5	133.0	169.3	35.4

* Poorly drained soil.

[†] Total tree weights will not equal arithmetic sum of weights of parts because each entry was derived from a separate regression equation.

[‡] Well-drained soil.

Table 11-6—Ovendry weight of dominant and codominant loblolly pine crowns (foliage, branches, and the main stem above 10 cm in diameter) in the South Carolina Coastal Plain and Georgia Piedmont, by tree diameter class, in stands with a basal area of 21 m²/ha and growing on land with a 27-m site index (base age 50)

Tree dbh (cm)	Crown ovendry weight (kg)	Tree dbh (cm)	Crown ovendry weight (kg)	Tree dbh (cm)	Crown ovendry weight (kg)
15	11.3	25	41.8	38	117.1
18	16.8	28	53.6	41	138.0
20	23.6	30	66.7	43	161.2
23	32.2	33	81.7	46	186.1
		36	98.5		

Source: adapted from Wade (1969).

Crown biomass can be predicted from various secondary measurements. Tree dbh can be used to predict the ovendry weight of dominant and codominant loblolly pine crowns with a high level of confidence (Baldwin 1989; table 11-6). Because crown weight increases with crown ratio, stand density is an important component of the equation. For example, a tree 18 cm in dbh with a 20% crown ratio may have a crown weight of only about 5.9 kg, whereas a tree 18 cm in dbh with a crown ratio of 65% may have a crown weight of 23 kg (Hepp and Brister 1982). Crown biomass can also be predicted from the sapwood cross-sectional area at breast height and at the base of the live crown (Baldwin 1989); however, the process is relatively slow. Because the weight of loblolly pine foliage is closely related to tree size, nondestructive sampling can be used to approximate the amount of foliage on a tree. Either tree dbh or tree basal area accounted for 78% of the variation in foliage weight in a 25-year-old northern Mississippi plantation (Rogerson 1964). Shear and Perry (1986) developed equations that nondestructively estimate needle dry weight of 4-year-old loblolly from the number of branches and the size of 4-year-old loblolly by crown position.

The equation for estimating needle dry weight is

$$N = 24.5 + 22.2(L3) + 39.2(L4) + 35.6(M3) + 83.7(M4) + 47.6(U3) - 1.2(U4) \text{ with } R^2 = 0.90$$

where:

N is needle dry weight;

$L3$, $M3$, and $U3$ = the number of live and dead branches in the lower, middle, and upper thirds (respectively) of the crown having branch diameters of 1.0 to 1.5 cm at the bole; and $L4$, $M4$, and $U4$ = the number of live and dead branches in the lower, middle, and upper thirds (respectively) of the crown having branch diameters greater than 1.5 cm at the bole.

The allometric equation for predicting 4-year-old loblolly pine needle weight (Shear and Perry 1986) is

$$N = 0.54 RCD^{3.49} \text{ with } R^2 = 0.80$$

where:

N is needle weight (in grams), and RCD is root collar diameter (in centimeters).

It is possible that similar correlations can be made for larger trees.

Because crown size is closely correlated with basal area and tree diameter, crown ratio can also be used to predict volume and basal area growth (Burton and Shoulders 1983, Sprinz and Burkhart 1987).

Root Biomass and Shoot-to-Root Ratio

In mature loblolly pines, the dry weight shoot-to-root ratio is about 80 to 20. From tree age 6 until tree maturity, the root biomass of loblolly ranges from about 14 to 26% of total biomass depending on stand conditions (tables 11-4 and 11-7). The root biomass of a 25-year-old east Texas plantation having 1,175 trees/ha was 36 t/ha. Taproot biomass made up 63% of the total (Tuttle 1978). Stump-plus-root biomass of a 47-year-old plantation in the Piedmont of South Carolina (with basal area of 19 m²/ha and density of 437 stems/ha) had a dry weight of 29.5 t/ha and accounted for 20% of total stand biomass (Kapeluck and Van Lear 1994). These data are similar to those for other conifers from 3 to 100 years of age (table 11-8).

Biomass Energy

Loblolly pine biomass makes up a large portion of total biomass in most southern states. For example, it accounts for 23% of all woody biomass in Alabama, where shortleaf, longleaf, and slash pines account for only 6, 4, and 3% of woody biomass, respectively (Rosson and Thomas 1986). A considerable quantity of loblolly pine woody biomass remains on a forested site after harvesting—especially after clearcut harvesting.

Table 11-7—Shoot-to-root biomass for loblolly pine plantations across the South by plantation age and site index

Plantation age (yr)	25-yr site index (m)	Biomass (t/ha)			Source
		Above-ground	Below-ground	Total	
6	NA	43 (74)	15 (26)	58	Box (1968)
12	21*	81 (84)	17 (16)	108	Nemeth (1973)
15	NA	93 (81)	22 (19)	115	Ralston (1973)
16	21	156 (81)	36 (19)	192	Wells and others (1975)
22	24	196 (86)	33 (14)	229	Shelton and others (1975
22	24	196 (83)	39 (17)	235	Shelton (1984)
25	18	161 (82)	36 (18)	197	Tuttle (1978), Houser (1980)
25	20	169 (83)	35 (17)	204	Pehl and others (1984)

Numbers in parentheses are percentages of total biomass.   NA = data not available.

* Estimated from site index at age 50 years.

Table 11-8—Root biomass as a percentage of total tree biomass of several *Pinus* species at various locations and ages (adapted from Nemeth 1973)

Species and location	Age (yr)	Percentage of total biomass	Source
Pinus contorta, USA	100	16–18	Johnstone (1972)
P. densiflora, Japan	15	17	Satoo (1966)
P. elliottii, USA	5	13–15	White and others (1971)
P. radiata, Australia	8	16	Ovington and others (1967)
P. resinosa, USA	25	15–22	Hutnik (1964)
P. rigida, USA	41	21	Whittaker and Woodwell (1968)
P. strobus, USA	NA	15–25	Young and others (1964)
P. sylvestris, UK	3–55	22–23	Ovington (1957)
P. sylvestris, UK	33	18	Ovington and Madgwick (1959)

Source: adapted from Nemeth (1973).

NA = data not available.

Some 850,000 ha of land were clearcut in Mississippi between 1977 and 1987, and an average of 34.5 dry tonnes of material/ha was left on the ground. Loblolly pine made up the largest portion of this tonnage (26%). Loblolly with dbh's greater than 2.5 cm also made up 14% of all standing, live, woody biomass on Mississippi's cut-over areas that were not site prepared (Rosson 1988).

The intensively cultured, short-rotation plantation is a biologically feasible means of producing large quantities of fiber and energy. Wherever it can be established, loblolly pine outproduces most hardwoods (Kellison and others 1979). However, culture on very short rotations is not the best way to produce loblolly pine biomass. Growth of loblolly to about age 4 is relatively slow compared to growth during the "grand" years from tree age 5 to tree age 15, when biomass yields of almost 20 t/ha/yr can be attained. Moreover, loblolly pine does not coppice and must be replanted at substantial cost after each harvest. Evaluations of energy storage and flow in a loblolly plantation and in a natural oak–pine system in southeast Oklahoma indicated that the pine plantations were twice as efficient as oak–pine at using the total amount of available energy. However, the costs of devel-

oping and maintaining the artificial system is such that the net energy gains from the two systems are about equal (Klopatek and Risser 1981).

The energy content of biomass material can be increased and transportation cost reduced by transpirational drying—that is, by permitting transpiration to reduce the moisture in felled trees before the trees are limbed and removed from the felling site (Stokes and others 1987). Delaying the harvest of logging residues by 3 months in the winter decreased the heartwood moisture content by 50% and the sapwood moisture content by 60% in an east Texas study. This delay increased the net fuel values of sapwood and heartwood by 72 and 33% (Rogers 1981).

Natural Stand Biomass

A dense stand of natural loblolly pine regeneration can soon shade out all but the most tolerant competitors and can increase loblolly pine from about 2% of the total biomass on a site 2 years after regeneration to as much as 86% of total biomass after 5 years (Cox and Van Lear 1985). The higher the stocking, the greater the total dry weight is for at least the first 15 years. However, the dry weight increase over stands with less (but still good) stocking may be very small. When more than 9,500 stems/ha survived through age 14 on a high-quality site on the lower Coastal Plain of South Carolina, the total dry weight of biomass (87 t/ha) was only 1% greater than when age-14 stocking was 6,000 stems/ha and only 10% greater than when age-14 stocking was 3,700 stems/ha (table 11-9). A 77-year-old, naturally regenerated, uneven-aged, loblolly–shortleaf pine stand growing on a medium-quality site on the upper Coastal Plain of southern Arkansas produced 111 t of dry biomass/ha. There were 80 t of stemwood, 8 t of stem bark, 16 t of live branches, 2 t of dead branches, and 5 t of needles per ha (Ku and others 1981b).

On many sites, understory biomass makes up a significant portion of the total biomass in natural stands. If loblolly pine regeneration is patchy or light, hardwoods (primarily sweetgum, red maple, blackgum, oaks, and hickories) may invade and account for much of the biomass during a rotation. Low levels of management usually mean more hardwood understory. Stand conditions

Table 11-9—Dry weight of tree components for five stand densities of 14-year-old natural loblolly pines

Density (trees/ha)		Dry weight yield* (t/ha)					% of maximum dry weight
age 3	age 14	Foliage	Branches	Stemwood	Stembark	Total	
2,500	2,045	4.7	5.6	44.9	8.1	63.3	73
5,000	3,744	5.3	6.4	54.6	11.0	77.3	89
10,000	6,022	5.5	6.8	60.0	13.1	85.4	98
20,000	8,183	5.2	6.5	59.6	14.1	85.4	98
40,000	9,571	5.0	6.5	60.4	14.9	86.8	100

Source: adapted from Harms and Langdon (1976).

* 50-year site index of 32 m.

Table 11-10—Trends in aboveground biomass development for planted loblolly pine*

Biomass total (t/ha)	Biomass during 1 year (t/ha/yr)	Age (yr)	Stocking (trees/ha)	Physiographic region	Source
6	4.0	4	9,260†	Mississippi Coastal Plain	Nelson and others (1968)
16	9.0	5	9,260†	Mississippi Coastal Plain	Nelson and others (1968)
43	NA	6	NA	Louisiana Coastal Plain	Box (1968)
54	26.0	10	900	North Carolina Coastal Plain	Nemeth (1973)
81	14.0	11	1,220	North Carolina Coastal Plain	Nemeth (1973)
88	NA	11	2,990	Arkansas uplands	Pope and Graney (1979)
91	12.8	13	1,400	North Carolina Coastal Plain	Nemeth (1973)
88	NA	13	1,439	Alabama Coastal Plain	Larsen and others (1976)
102	17.8	14	1,497	North Carolina Piedmont	Ralston (1973)
114	12.3	15	1,497	North Carolina Piedmont	Ralston (1973)
156	7.5	16	2,243	North Carolina Piedmont	Wells and others (1975)
173	NA	18	NA	Arkansas Coastal Plain	Ku and Burton (1973)
159	NA	18	NA	Arkansas Coastal Plain	Ku and Burton (1973)
144	NA	18	NA	Arkansas loess	Ku and Burton (1973)
127	NA	18	NA	Arkansas loess	Ku and Burton (1973)
196	NA	22	NA	Mississippi	Shelton (1984)
169	NA	25	1,175	Texas Coastal Plain	Pehl and others (1984)

NA = data not available

* Studies vary widely in site and stand structure so specific comparisons may not be meaningful.

† Initial spacing.

and species composition vary so much in mixed pine–hardwood stands that understory biomass cannot be estimated with reasonable precision from overstory conditions alone. The biomass in understory trees must be measured or estimated directly (Phillips and Saucier 1982).

Depending on site quality, understory hardwood biomass in north Louisiana and south Arkansas ranged from 9 to 53 t/ha and averaged 24 t/ha. Understory biomass averaged 28 t/ha on poor sites and 21 t/ha on good sites. About 4, 19, and 77% of the understory biomass was in foliage, branches, and stems, respectively. There was no difference in understory biomass between summer and winter harvests, but material harvested in the winter had lower nutrient content (Ku and others 1981a, Ku and Baker 1987, Lockaby and Adams 1986). Understory biomass and

20 or more tonnes/ha of pine residues from harvesting could provide substantial amounts of energy, but total removal would substantially reduce the nutrient reservoir on many sites. Lockaby and Adams (1986) found that the nitrogen (N), phosphorus (P), potassium (K), calcium (Ca), and magnesium (Mg) in 53 t of understory hardwoods/ha amounted to 117, 10, 68, 177, and 30 kg/ha, respectively.

Plantation Stand Biomass

Numerous studies document the effects of site quality and stand age on dry-weight biomass of planted stands (table 11-10). During the first few years of stand growth, most biomass is tied up in annual plants and hardwood sprouts. By stand age 4, aboveground dry weight of pine trees is about 5 t/ha. Growth accelerates rapidly at about this time, and pine biomass may more than double in a single year (Nelson and others 1968). Total biomass exceeds 50 t/ha by stand age 10 and can exceed 170 t/ha by age 18. Dry-weight yields of boles, branches, and foliage can be predicted for any stage of plantation development from age 10 through age 45 on cut-over sites in east Texas, southern Mississippi, and Louisiana (Baldwin and Feduccia 1987).

Genetic and Environmental Effects on Total Biomass and the Distribution of Biomass

Individual trees can differ greatly in total biomass and distribution of biomass. For example, four half-sib families growing in north-central Arkansas had 66.5, 77.5, 96.5, and 113.5 t of aboveground biomass/ha at age 11. The family that grew fastest produced 71% more wood volume than the slowest growers (Pope and Graney 1979).

Biomass distribution can vary greatly among trees of the same age. In one study, needle biomass of 7-year-old

Table 11-11—Distribution of forest biomass (total aboveground green weight) for individual southern pine species, other softwoods, and total hardwoods by diameter class (5 to 40+ cm)

Species	All Classes	Total above ground green weight							
		5 cm	10 cm	15 cm	20 cm	25 cm	30 cm	35 cm	40+ cm
Percent of total soft woods									
Loblolly pine	38	26	24	30	32	35	41	47	54
Longleaf pine	7	3	3	4	5	9	11	11	6
Shortleaf pine	10	9	8	9	12	12	11	8	4
Slash pine	19	22	32	29	24	18	15	13	9
Other yellow pines	14	22	22	19	18	16	12	9	6
Other softwoods	12	18	11	9	9	10	10	12	21
Total softwoods	100	100	100	100	100	100	100	100	100
Actual weight (million t)*									
Total softwoods	2,235	50	171	308	378	378	329	246	376
Total hardwoods	3,521	246	346	369	392	421	416	369	962
All species	5,756	296	517	676	769	799	745	615	1,338

Source: adapted from Phillips and Sheffield (1984).

* Numbers in columns may not add to total due to rounding.

Table 11-12—Predicted total tree green weight including foliage of sapling-sized loblolly, slash, and longleaf pines in the Coastal Plain of Georgia by diameter at breast height (dbh) and total tree height (15 to 60 ft)

Dbh (in)	Predicted total tree green weight (lb)									
	15 ft	20 ft	25 ft	30 ft	35 ft	40 ft	45 ft	50 ft	55 ft	60 ft
Open grown*										
1	4	5	6	7	9	10	NT	NT	NT	NT
2	14	1	23	28	32	36	40	NT	NT	NT
3	31	40	49	58	67	76	84	93	101	NT
4	52	68	83	99	114	128	143	157	172	186
5	79	102	126	148	171	193	215	237	258	279
6	110	143	175	207	238	269	300	330	360	390
Understory†										
1	3	5	6	7	8	90	NT	NT	NT	NT
2	14	17	21	25	28	32	36	39	NT	NT
3	27	36	44	51	59	67	74	81	89	NT
4	46	60	73	86	994	112	124	136	149	161
5	69	902	109	129	148	167	185	203	222	240
6	96	124	152	179	205	231	257	282	307	332
Combined‡										
1	4	5	6	7	8	9	NT	NT	NT	NT
2	14	18	22	26	30	34	38	42	NT	NT
3	29	38	46	55	63	71	79	87	95	NT
4	49	64	78	92	106	119	133	146	159	172
5	49	96	117	138	158	178	198	218	238	257
6	102	133	167	191	220	240	248	275	303	357

Source: adapted from Phillips and McNab (1982).

Shaded area indicates range of data. NT = no trees in this class. Results are based on samples of 20% loblolly, 40% longleaf, and 40% slash pine.

* Based on the equation $Y = 0.35824(D^2Th)^{0.91084}$, where Y = total tree green weight, D = dbh, and Th = total tree height.

† Based on the equation $Y = 0.35147(D^2Th)^{0.89240}$.

‡ Based on the equation $Y = 0.36137(D^2Th)^{0.89825}$.

Table 11-13—Predicted total tree green weight including foliage of sapling-sized loblolly, shortleaf, and Virginia pines in the Piedmont of Georgia by diameter at breast height (dbh) and total tree height (15 to 60 ft)

Dbh (in)	Predicted total tree green weight (lb)									
	15 ft	20 ft	25 ft	30 ft	35 ft	40 ft	45 ft	50 ft	55 ft	60 ft
Open grown*										
1	6	8	9	11	12	NT	NT	NT	NT	NT
2	20	25	30	35	40	45	NT	NT	NT	NT
3	39	50	60	70	80	89	98	108	NT	NT
4	63	81	97	113	129	144	159	174	189	203
5	92	117	142	165	188	210	232	253	274	295
6	125	159	192	224	255	285	310	343	372	400
Understory†										
1	3	4	5	6	7	8	NT	NT	NT	NT
2	12	16	19	23	27	31	34	38	NT	NT
3	26	34	43	51	59	67	75	88	90	NT
4	45	60	74	88	102	115	129	143	145	170
5	69	91	113	134	155	176	197	218	239	259
5	98	129	160	190	220	249	279	308	337	366
Combined‡										
1	4	6	7	9	10	11	NT	NT	NT	NT
2	16	21	25	30	45	38	42	47	NT	NT
3	33	42	52	61	69	78	86	95	103	NT
4	55	70	85	100	115	129	143	156	170	183
5	81	104	126	148	169	190	210	231	251	270
6	111	143	173	203	232	261	289	317	344	371

Source: adapted from Phillips and McNab (1982).

Shaded area indicates range of data. NT = no trees in this class. Results are based on samples of 40% loblolly, 40% longleaf, and 20% Virginia pine.

* Based on the equation $Y = 0.83469(D^2Th)^{0.83469}$, where Y = total tree green weight, D = dbh, and Th = total tree height.

† Based on the equation $Y = 0.25533(D^2Th)^{0.94684}$.

‡ Based on the equation $Y = 0.47411(D^2Th)^{0.86800}$.

trees made up 26 to 43% of the total aboveground weight and stemwood made up 24 to 41% (table 11-3). On a good Georgia site, weight per tree and per hectare at tree age 8 were more than 20 and 50% greater, respectively, for trees with abundant *Pisolithus tinctorius* (Pt) ectomycorrhizae than for trees without Pt. An abundance of ectomycorrhizae at planting increases tree survival and growth during dry periods before root systems and crowns expand fully (Marx and others 1988).

Green-Weight Biomass

Loblolly pine accounts for 15% of all aboveground green-weight biomass and 38% of all softwood biomass on commercial forest lands in the Atlantic Coastal States from Virginia to Florida (table 11-11). On Coastal Plain sites, the total green-weight of individual, open-grown, naturally regenerated saplings (including foliage) ranges from 1.8 kg (4 lb) for trees 2.5 cm (1 inch) in dbh and 4.6 m (15 ft) in height to 67.2 kg (148 lb) for trees 12.7 cm (5 inches) in dbh and 9.2 m (30 ft) in height. Understory loblolly of these diameters and heights

Table 11-14—Average green weight of total tree and stem components of natural loblolly pines growing throughout the state of Georgia by diameter at breast height (dbh)

Dbh (cm)	No. of trees sampled	Average green weight (kg)				
		Top diameter outside bark			Total weight	
		23 cm	18 cm	10 cm	Stem	Tree
15	65	NT	NT	99	127	150
20	64	NT	130	248	268	315
25	65	182	344	451	468	553
30	66	467	621	688	703	844
35	65	822	928	981	994	1,191
40	66	1,220	1,296	1,340	1,353	1,637
45	57	1,590	1,649	1,691	1,705	2,096

Source: adatped from Saucier and others (1981).

NT = no trees in this class.

weighed 1.4 kg (3 lb) and 58.6 kg (129 lb) (table 11-12). On Piedmont sites, open-grown saplings weighed from 2.7 to 74.9 kg (6 to 165 lb), whereas understory trees of the same diameters and heights weighed from 1.4 to 60.8 kg (3 to 134 lb) (table 11-13).

Green weight of the bole (wood and bark to a 7.5-cm top) of plantation-grown loblolly pines in the Piedmont of Georgia ranges from about 23 kg for a tree 12.7 cm in dbh and 6.1 m in height to 715 kg for a tree 30 cm in dbh and 24.4 m in height (Burkhart and Clutter 1971). The total green weight of a loblolly pine 45 cm in dbh, including wood, bark, and foliage, can be 2.1 t, with 19% of this weight in branches and foliage (table 11-14). Green weight of the crown of a tree is strongly influenced by tree height. In Georgia, naturally grown loblolly, 45 cm in dbh and 18.3 m in height, had a crown weight of 287 kg while a tree of the same diameter but 30.5 m tall had a crown weight of 469 kg (table 11-15).

As with dry weight, mutual competition greatly affects the relative green weight in crown and bole. When there are only 250 mature trees/ha, about 30% of the aboveground green weight is in the crowns. The proportion of aboveground green weight in the crowns decreases to about 20% when there are 500 trees/ha and to about 12% when there are 1,500 trees/ha (Sprinz and others 1979). Prediction equations for green-weight yields of boles, branches, and foliage have been formulated for plantations aged 10 to 45 years on cut-over sites in east Texas, southern Mississippi, and Louisiana (Baldwin and Feduccia 1987).

Table 11-15—Green weight of wood, bark, and foliage in the crown (all branches plus main stem above 4-inch diameter outside bark) of natural loblolly pines growing in Georgia by diametter at breast height (dbh) and total tree height (40-110 ft)

Dbh (in)	Green weight (lb)							
	40 ft	50 ft	60 ft	70 ft	80 ft	90 ft	100 ft	110 ft
6	77	89	100	111	122	—		
7	93	109	124	139	154	—		
8	112	132	152	171	191	—		
9	133	158	183	208	233	258		
10	156	187	218	249	280	311		
11	182	220	257	295	332	369		
12	211	255	300	344	389	433	478	
13	242	294	346	398	451	503	555	
14	275	336	396	457	517	578	638	
15	311	380	450	519	589	658	728	797
16		428	507	586	666	745	824	903
17		479	569	658	747	836	926	1,015
18			633	734	834	934	1,034	1,134
19			702	814	925	1,037	1,148	1,260
20			774	898	1,021	1,145	1,269	1,329
21			850	986	1,123	1,259	1,395	1,531
22			930	1,079	1,229	1,378	1,528	1,678
23				1,177	1,340	1,504	1,667	1,830
24				1,278	1,456	1,634	1,812	1,990

Source: adapted from Saucier and others (1981).

Shaded area indicates range of data. $Y = 32.91827 + 0.03089 (D^2Th)$ where: Y = weigh of crown, D = dbh, and Th = total height.

Table 11-16—Relative size of components of southern pine species of three ages and on three sites in northern Louisiana

Pine species	Dbh (cm)		Total height (m)		Taproot length (m)		Stand age (yr)
	Average (n = 12)	Range	Average (n = 12)	Range	Average (n = 12)	Range	
Loblolly	13.7	5.8 – 20.6	14.0	7.0 – 18.0	2.1	1.5 – 3.0	26
Longleaf	15.5	8.1 – 22.4	15.6	9.5 – 20.1	2.2	1.5 – 3.4	26
Shortleaf	12.4	4.8 – 21.6	13.4	7.0 – 18.9	2.0	1.2 – 3.2	26
Slash	15.2	7.9 – 21.8	15.2	8.5 – 19.8	1.9	1.6 – 2.6	26
Intermediate site							
Loblolly	17.0	11.7 – 22.4	17.7	14.9 – 19.5	1.5	1.1 – 1.8	27
Longleaf	16.0	7.6 – 26.7	18.0	11.3 – 21.7	1.3	0.8 – 1.8	27
Shortleaf	16.8	12.4 – 24.9	18.3	16.8 – 20.1	1.4	1.1 – 1.8	27
Slash	20.1	7.6 – 26.7	18.0	11.3 – 21.7	1.3	0.8 – 1.8	27
Wet site							
Loblolly	16.3	11.9 – 21.1	16.5	12.8 – 19.5	1.3	0.9 – 1.6	25
Longleaf	12.7	6.1 – 18.8	13.4	7.3 – 19.2	1.0	0.6 – 1.4	25
Shortleaf	10.2	5.8 – 17.0	9.1	5.2 – 12.2	0.9	0.6 – 1.4	25
Slash	16.5	9.7 – 24.1	17.7	13.1 – 21.3	1.2	0.7 – 1.5	25

Source: adapted from Gibson and others (1975).

Biomass Differences Between the Major Southern Pines

When growing in natural, closed, uneven-aged sawtimber stands, loblolly pine, longleaf pine, and shortleaf pine trees of similar size have about the same proportions of tree weight in wood (83%), bark (13%), and needles (4%); slash pine has 1 to 4% more of its total weight in bark. The distribution of wood in stem and crown material does not differ greatly from species to species. Typically, 89 to 91% of all aboveground wood is in the main stem and 9 to 11% is in the crown, for all major southern pines (Clark and Taras 1976).

Southern pines of identical heights and dbh's differ significantly in total-tree green and dry weight. Longleaf pine trees are about 19% heavier on a dry-weight basis than loblolly pines of similar sizes and are about 6% heavier than slash pines of similar sizes largely because of species-to-species differences in stem form and water content of wood and bark. Forty-five percent of the green weight of slash and longleaf pines is water weight, and 50 to 52% of the green weight of loblolly and shortleaf pines is water weight (Clark and Taras 1976). The biomass of dead loblolly pine branches is greater than that of slash pine branches during the early years of development because the lower branches of loblolly pines tend to live longer than those of slash pines and to persist on the tree longer after they die (Nemeth 1972). In one study, loblolly and slash pines had similar green weights per unit volume at age 18, but at age 30, loblolly was significantly heavier than slash pine (Lohrey 1991). Growth differences between loblolly and other southern pines vary with site moisture (table 11-16). Longleaf tends to grow better on dry sites than on wet sites, whereas slash and loblolly grow better on wet sites than on dry sites.

Stand Growth and Yield

Because loblolly pine grows on widely diverse sites over many millions of hectares, general growth and yield models may not be applicable in specific situations. At least 24 models have been developed to predict plantation or natural stand growth and yield for specific site conditions or physiographic regions. Even so, factors affecting both growth and yield (site quality, stand density, stand age, genetic makeup, and management regime) must be incorporated into models before accurate yield projections can be made. In some cases,

site index for loblolly pine can be predicted from site index for shortleaf pine and vice versa (Harrington 1987), suggesting some interspecific continuity in yield projections.

Volume growth in a stand during any interval of time ($V_1 - V_2$) can be partitioned into four basic components: survivor growth (S), ingrowth (I), mortality (M), and cut (C) (Beers 1962):

$$V_1 - V_2 = S + I - M - C$$

Growth and Yield Estimation

There are many growth and yield prediction models for loblolly pine. They are practical aids for stand management and valuable conceptual tools for organizing and projecting knowledge about factors affecting forest development. They allow the simulation of tree growth as affected by various silvicultural treatments over a range of stand densities, harvest intervals, sites, and species combinations. The economic value of thinning, fertilization, tree improvement, and hardwood control treatments can be predicted, providing a sound basis for management decisions. Models capable of forecasting tree size distribution within stands are extremely useful to those who must assess the economic value of treatments.

Variables commonly used in growth and yield estimation include dominant height over time (height–age relationships), diameter distribution by height over time (height–diameter relationships), and tree mortality over time. When comparing yields of planted and direct seeded or naturally seeded stands, it is important to consistently express tree age as age from seed so that results are interpreted accurately (Smalley and Bailey 1974, Smalley and Bower 1971). Environmental conditions, such as intensity and timing of wet and dry weather during the growing season, may be important enough to consider as variables in future growth and yield models (Murphy and Farrar 1987, Zahner and Grier 1990).

Modeling Methods

Growth and yield models include whole-stand models, size-class distribution models, and individual-tree models.

- **Whole-stand models** are used to predict aggregate stand volume. They can also be used to predict net growth, which is the difference between predicted yields at two points in time. Whole-stand models do not provide the size-class information necessary for evaluation of utilization options and products,

and they generally cannot be used to analyze a wide range of stand treatments (Burkhart 1982, Clutter and others 1983, Munro 1974).

- **Size-class distribution models** estimate the number of trees per unit area in each diameter class and predict tree heights for given diameters under particular stand conditions (Burkhart and Strub 1974, Feduccia and others 1979, Lenhart 1972a, Lenhart and Clutter 1971, Smalley and Bailey 1974). Size-class models can be used to evaluate alternative utilization options.

- **Individual-tree models** simulate the growth of each tree, then aggregate the results to provide estimates of stand growth and yield. They can be distance dependent or distance independent. Distance-dependent, individual-tree models require data on individual tree locations as input; distance independent models do not (Munro 1974).

The three types of growth and yield models perform similarly for simple yield estimates, providing cubic-volume estimates that are sufficiently accurate for many uses. Selection of a model depends on the amount of stand detail desired and the management practices or biological responses to be evaluated. Although individual-tree models provide the greatest detail and flexibility, they also require more detailed data and are more time consuming and costly to execute (Borders and others 1987, Burkhart and others 1987a, Daniels and others 1979, Strub and others 1986). Explicit yield prediction models such as whole-stand (or stand-level) models estimate the total cubic volume of timber on an area directly from average total height of the tallest trees and the surviving number of trees. These models predict total stand yields more accurately than do implicit yield prediction models such as diameter-distribution models, which estimate the total amount of timber indirectly by summing across diameter classes (Lenhart 1988a).

Predicting Mortality

As crowns close in dense stands, individual trees in the upper crown classes continue to grow rapidly, whereas those in lower crown classes rapidly decline in vigor and often die quickly (Nance and others 1985). Mortality increases as the ratio of individual-tree basal area to total basal area within a competitive sphere decreases (Glover and Hool 1979).

The rate of tree mortality decreases as stand age increases, but site quality has an effect on this relationship. For a given site quality, higher initial stand densities result in more mortality and earlier mortality than do lower initial densities. By about stand age 35 to 40 years, however, the numbers of surviving trees in stands growing on similar sites tend to equalize (Schultz 1975). If stand density is held constant, survival rate is negatively correlated with site quality. That is, survival over time decreases more as site index increases. Early survival is generally greatest where site index is high, but competition among fast-growing trees increases mortality on high-quality sites from about stand age 15 to 20 years onward. The final difference between survival on high-quality and low-quality sites may be as little as 10% or as much as 30% (figures 11-8 and 11-9). Clearly, initial stand density should be dictated by site quality.

Predicting Diameter Distribution, Basal Area, Volume, and Yield

Models are available for predicting individual tree volumes and stand yields by tree size class for oldfield plantations (Amateis and others 1986, Newberry and Burk 1985) and cut-over forest site plantations (Amateis and others 1984; Lenhart 1987, 1988b; Matney and others

1986). Even the basal areas of individual trees and aggregate distributions of basal area can be predicted (Green and others 1984). Analysis of published data indicates that a single prediction system could be used to estimate total and merchantable volume for oldfield, plantation-grown loblolly pines throughout much of the Coastal Plain and Piedmont (Van Deusen and others 1981). Similarly, Burkhart and others (1985) suggest that a single equation adequately predicts total cubic-volume yield for loblolly plantations on cut-over, site-prepared land throughout the Coastal Plain and Piedmont. However, McClure and others (1987) subsequently found that yield regressions for Piedmont and Coastal Plain populations of loblolly pine can differ significantly.

It may be necessary to derive separate equations to accurately predict total and merchantable volumes of trees growing in unthinned, oldfield plantations, planted trees growing on cut-over sites, and trees in natural stands because trees growing under these different conditions have different height–dbh relationships and different tree form characteristics (Amateis and Burkhart 1987b).

For greatest versatility, total cubic volume of each tree (inside or outside bark) should be the basic computation in any yield model. Computer programs can easily convert total volumes into merchantable volumes. They can also be used to estimate other measurements, such as number of stems per unit area by diameter class, average height, and cubic volume inside and outside bark to any height. Computer programs can also be used to identify the products that can be obtained from trees in each diameter class (Guldin 1984b). For example, there are equations that predict the number of 2.7-m veneer bolts in plantation-grown trees in the interior western Gulf Coastal Plain. The only predictors needed are dbh and total tree height (Lenhart and Hyink 1976). In

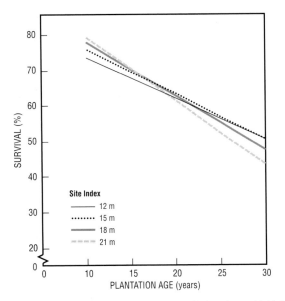

Figure 11-8—Survival percentage by site index class of loblolly pine plantations on cutover sites in the West Gulf region (adapted from Feduccia and others 1979).

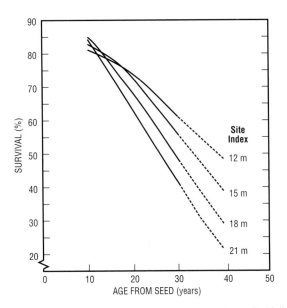

Figure 11-9—Survival percentage by site index class of loblolly pine plantations on old fields of the Tennessee, Alabama, and Georgia highlands (adapted from Smalley and Bailey 1974).

northwest Louisiana, sawlog volume, chip-and-saw volume, chip volume, and total volume have been predicted accurately from local volume tables, which are derived only from dbh (Clason and Cao 1986).

Options for thinning, fertilization, length of rotation, and type of harvest (such as seed tree, shelterwood, or clearcut) have been incorporated into volume prediction equations and yield tables (Ballard and others 1981, Cao and others 1982, Frazier 1981, Matney and Sullivan 1982, Myers 1977, Smith and Hafley 1986, Strub and others 1981). Growth and yield models and yield tables have been prepared specifically for thinned plantations on cut-over sites in east Texas, southern Mississippi, and Louisiana (Baldwin and Feduccia 1987) and on loess soils of northern Mississippi, Arkansas, and Tennessee (Sullivan and Williston 1977). Growth projection equations are also available for thinned, natural, even-aged as well as thinned, natural, uneven-aged loblolly–shortleaf pine stands. When used with local data, these equations should be applicable throughout the South (Bailey and Ware 1983; Murphy and Farrar 1983, 1988a, 1988b).

Projections of mortality and product degrade resulting from fusiform rust are available, as are projections of lumber degrade resulting from sweep (Smith and others 1987). Options are also available that allow the user to project the amount of stem sweep and to identify the percentage of cull in total sawtimber volume for particular diameter classes and the maximum sawtimber diameter class where this cull percentage applies. Branch size can be predicted accurately from stocking, site index, tree dbh, and rotation age (Busby and others 1990, Schroeder and Clark 1970, Smith 1988, Strub and others 1986). Total sawtimber, volume of chip-and-saw logs, yield of veneer-grade wood, weight of fuel chips, and weight of all products can be calculated. Available models can even predict the merchantability of an individual tree. Taken together, the many available growth and yield models give forest and mill managers superb planning data and data on present resources.

Land managers must be aware, however, that most growth and yield models need considerable refinement before they can be useful on a site-specific or condition-specific basis. In many cases, underlying assumptions on which the models are based have not been tested adequately, primarily because of insufficient data. Also, a model may be very sensitive to small changes in site index, making it invalid beyond the boundaries of the data (Matney and others 1986). Thus, field checks should always be incorporated when applying estimates to specific management situations.

Volume and Yield Tables

Individual-Tree Volume Tables for Plantations

Tables that provide cubic-volume estimates of individual trees over a range of sizes are available for planted loblolly pine on a variety of sites, across the entire range of the species (table 11-17).

Stand Yield Tables for Plantations

Equations and tables are available to project board foot and cubic foot yields per unit area in oldfield loblolly pine plantations over a wide range of site and stocking conditions (table 11-18). Input data include stand age, number

Table 11-17—Published tables and equations for estimating total and merchantable cubic-foot volumes of individual planted loblolly pine trees (all original measurements in English units)

Source	Physiographic region	No. of trees in samples	Type of volume tables and equations	Source	Physiographic region	No. of trees in samples	Type of volume tables and equations
Plantations				**Cut-over forest sites**			
Bailey and Clutter (1970)	Georgia Piedmont	608	Total volume inside bark and outside bark; merch. volume to 3-inch top inside bark and outside bark for trees 5 to 12 inches in dbh	Amateis and Burnhart (1987a)	Southwide	445	Total and merchantable volume inside bark or outside bark to any height or top diameter limit
Hasness and Lenhart (1972)	Interior western Gulf of Arkansas, Louisiana, Oklahoma, Texas	632	Total volume of trees 5 to 14 inches; merch. volume inside bark and outside bark to 2-inch, 3-inch, and 4-inch top	Baldwin and Feduccia (1991)	Central Louisiana	NA	Total and merchantable volumes, inside bark or outside bark to any height or top diameter limit of thinned and unthinned stands
Romancier (1961)	Georgia Piedmont	116	Merchantable volume to 2.0 and 3.6-inch top inside bark for trees 5 to 12 inches in dbh	Clutter and others (1984)	Lower Coastal Plain North Florida, South Carolina, Georgia, North Carolina	762	Total and merchantable stem volume inside bark and outside bark for trees 2 to 14 inches dbh
Schmidt and Bower (1970)	Mississippi flatwoods	600	Total cubic volume inside bark of planted 7-year-old trees 1 to 8 inches in dbh				
Smalley and Bower (1968)	Cumberland Plateau and Highland Rim	340	Total and merch. cubic-foot volumes, inside bark and outside bark for 2-inch top, 3-inch top, 4-inch top or entire stem of trees 5 to 13 inches dbh	Lenhart and others (1987)	East Texas Coastal Plain	65	Total wood or wood and bark volume of trees 2 to 11 inches dbh

Table 11-18—Yield tables of loblolly pines for oldfield plantations (all original measurements are in English units)

Source	Physiographic region	No. of plots*	Stand age (yr)	Site index† ft	Site index† m	Surviving trees per acre	Surviving trees per ha
Burkhart and others (1972b)	Piedmont and Coastal Plain of Virginia and Coastal Plain of Maryland, Delaware and North Carolina	189	9–35	47–84	14–26	300–2,900	740–7,170
Coile and Schumacher (1964)	Coastal Plain from Texas to North Carolina plus the Piedmont of the Carolinas and Georgia	373 plus 28 plots on cutover sites‡	5–35+	NA	NA	NA	NA
Daniels and Burkhart (1975)	Coastal Plain and Piedmont of Virginia	189 plus 51 plots on cutover sites‡	8–35	47–84	14–26	300–2,900	740–7,170
Goebel and Warner (1969)	South Carolina	220	9–25	40–75	12–23	500–1,400	1,235–3,460
Goggans and Schultz (1958)	Alabama Coastal Plain	46	5–16	NA	NA	~400–1,000	990–2,470
Lenhart (1972a)	Interior western Gulf of Louisiana, Oklahoma, Arkansas, Texas	219	9–30	40–70	12–21	500–1,200	1,235–2,965
Lenhart and Clutter (1971)	Georgia Piedmont	226	9–33	40–80	12–24	500–1,650	1,235–4,075
Smalley and Bailey (1974)	Tennessee, Alabama, and Georgia Highlands	302	10–31	40–70	12–21	202–2,240	499–5,335

* In most of the studies the number of trees measured is not identified. Plots often contain 64 original planting locations, so the number of trees measured for each plot depends on survival.

† Base age 25 years.

‡ Cutover plots were lumped with oldfield plantations; NA = not available.

of surviving trees per unit area, and average height of dominant and codominant trees. The number of surviving trees can be estimated from the number of trees planted, and average tree height can be calculated from site index.

Yields (inside or outside bark) are also available for loblolly pine plantations growing on many prepared Piedmont and Coastal Plain sites from Texas to Virginia (figure 11-10 and table 11-19). Site factors that affect growth in important ways include rainfall, slope, soil texture, surface soil thickness, and soil organic matter content (Shoulders and Walker 1979).

Effect of Site on Yields

Site quality, or the productive capacity of land, is probably the most important influence on tree growth. Site quality has commonly been expressed in terms of site index, which is the total height of dominant trees at a specific age. For natural loblolly pine stands, the base age is generally 50 years from seed. For plantations, the base age is usually 25 years from planting. Physiographic factors exert a general influence on site quality, but local variation in soil, slope, aspect, and moisture are the most important determinants of the growth capability of individual stands. Soil differences and related moisture and nutrient differences have caused mature tree heights to range from 15 to 34 m within a short distance (Brender 1973). In a single 3.6-ha tract on the hilly upper Coastal Plain of Alabama, 29-year-old loblolly averaged 25 cm in dbh and 20 m in height on eroded hills, 28 cm in dbh and 23 m in height on slopes, 35 cm in dbh and 25 m in height on flats, and 37 cm in dbh and 23 m in height along water channels. The maximum difference in elevation from the eroded hills to the permanently wet branch bottoms was only 9 m (Livingston 1972). Loblolly pines planted at 1.8- by 1.8-m spacing in the Georgia Piedmont produce from 88 to 277 m³ of merchantable wood/ha by age 19, depending on site quality (Belanger and Brender 1968).

Site index curves are usually derived by stem analysis of dominant and codominant trees. They have been prepared for natural stands and plantations on a variety of sites across the South (appendix C, figures 1 through 12). For greatest accuracy in assessing the site index of a

Figure 11-10—Twenty-five-year-old loblolly pines planted at a 3- by 3-m spacing (**left**) or a 1.2- by 1.2-m spacing (**right**) in north Louisiana. Table 11-20 presents detailed data for this study.

Table 11-19—Studies that have produced models, equations, and yield tables for estimating cubic and board measure yields of loblolly planted on cutover sites with a base age of 25 years (all original measurements in English units)

Source	Physiographic regions	No. of Plots	Stand age (yr)	Site index* ft	Site index* m	Trees planted per acre	Trees planted per ha
Amateis and others (1984)	Entire Coastal Plain and Piedmont	186	8+	33–97	10–30	275–950[†]	680–2,345[†]
Bailey and others (1985)	Piedmont and upper Coastal Plain of Alabama, Georgia, South Carolina	291	10–21+	40–70	12–21	300–1,500	740–3,710
Baldwin and Feduccia (1987)	Gulf Coastal Plain of Texas, Louisiana, and Mississippi	527	3–45	42–78	13–24	100–2,700	245–6,670
Clutter and others (1984)	Lower coast of north Florida, South Carolina, North Carolina	226	10+	40–70	12–21	300–900	740–2,220
Ledbetter and others (1986)	Gulf Coastal Plain of Alabama, Arkansas, Louisiana, Mississippi	230	4–28	42–80	13–24	435–1,137	1,075–2,810
Matney and others (1988)	Alabama, Louisiana, Mississippi	230	1–26+	50–70+	15–21+	400–800+	990–1,975+
Shoulders and Walker (1979)	Coastal Plain of Louisiana and Mississippi	113	2–15	NM	NM	1,210	2,990

NM = Not measured.
* Base age 25.
[†] Number of surviving trees at measurement age.

particular site, one should use curves or tables that were developed from stands of the same geographic area, similar physiographic or soil conditions, and similar origins (for example, oldfield plantations, site-prepared plantations, or natural stands) (Lloyd 1981).

Rangewide site index curves for natural stands were first produced for the entire loblolly pine range in a comprehensive publication (USDA 1929). Since then, more specific curves have been assembled for the Atlantic and eastern Gulf Coastal Plain (Schumacher and Coile 1960); the Coastal Plain of Virginia, North Carolina, and South Carolina (Trousdell and others 1974); northern Louisiana and southern Arkansas (Zahner 1962); and the states from North Carolina to Maryland and Delaware (Devan and Burkhart 1982).

Oldfield plantation site index curves are available for the Coastal Plain of North Carolina to Delaware and the Piedmont of Virginia (Devan and Burkhart 1982); coastal North Carolina to southwestern Arkansas (Golden and others 1981); the interior western Gulf Coastal Plain (Lenhart 1971, Lenhart and Fields 1970); the Piedmont of Georgia (Clutter and Lenhart 1968); the South Carolina Piedmont (Goebel and Warner 1969, Shipman 1960); the Tennessee, Alabama, and Georgia Highlands (Smalley and Bower 1971); and southern Illinois (Gilmore 1979). Plantation site index curves are available for cut-over, site-prepared forest sites throughout the Coastal Plain and Piedmont (Amateis and Burkhart 1985); the Carolina flatwoods (Pienaar and Shiver 1980); the western Gulf Coastal Plain (Popham and others 1979), and east Texas (Lenhart and others 1986, Shipman 1960).

Because early tree growth varies widely, site index estimation and curve development have normally been confined to stands older than 10 years of age. However, site productivity can be predicted successfully in stands less than 5 years old in some instances (Lenhart and others 1986). Daniels and others (1986) concluded that a measurement of the area potentially available to each tree (the inverse of stand density) should be an effective predictor of the growth of individual loblolly pine trees in stands over 7

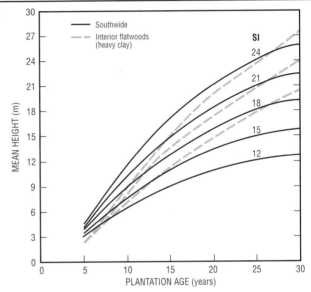

Figure 11-11— Site index curves for oldfield plantations ranging from coastal North Carolina to southwestern Arkansas (excluding the interior flatwoods of central Mississippi) compared to those of the interior flatwoods of central Mississippi (adapted from Golden and others 1981).

years old when combined with tree size and stand density.

Managers must be cautious when using site index to estimate productivity, because height growth of loblolly pines varies with stand density within the normal range of densities for plantation establishment (about 750 to 3,000 stems/ha) (Anderson 1981, Lloyd and Jones 1983, Shepard 1971). For example, 20-year-old loblolly growing on sites with a site index of 23 m (base age 25 years) in the Piedmont of South Carolina averaged 16.7, 17.2, 17.8, and 18.5 m tall in stands with 2,113, 1,458, 993, and 694 surviving trees/ha, respectively (Harms and Lloyd 1981). In addition, the shapes of height-over-age curves can vary for sites with the same site index (figure 11-11).

Effect of Stocking on Plantation Yield

Mortality trends over large areas are predictable for loblolly pine. If all trees are left to grow to maturity, the number of trees per unit area tends to equalize regardless of initial stocking. For example, a north Louisiana plantation established with 6,729 trees/ha had only 1,485 more trees/ha at age 25 and only 501 more trees/ha at age 33 than a comparable plantation established with 1,075 trees/ha (table 11-20). However, the equalization process may be much slower on some sites (figure 11-12 and table 11-21). Many loblolly pine survival curves are available (Bailey 1986, Feduccia 1982, Hansbrough and others

1964, Owens 1974). Mortality accelerates and yields decrease with increasing hardwood competition (Burkhart and Spring 1984a; figure 11-13). Hardwood competition is usually more prevalent on cut-over forest lands than in oldfield plantations. When seed sources are near, naturally regenerated loblolly seedlings become established in plantations—roughly in inverse proportion to the density of planted seedlings (Little and Somes 1958).

Very large pine growth responses to herbaceous weed control can be obtained if herbicides are used properly (Creighton and others 1987, Dougherty and Lowery 1991, table 11-22).

Both diameter growth and height growth of loblolly pine are inversely related to the amount of competition, so competition between individual pines must be kept at an acceptable level and the amount of hardwood competition must be limited; 21-year-old trees spaced at 3 by 3 m averaged 19.2 m in height. Those spaced at 1.8 by 2.4 m averaged 16.5 m in height, and those spaced at 1.2 by 1.2 m averaged 14.3 m in height (table 11-23). Heights at these three spacings were 26.6 m, 24.5 m, and 21.6 m at age 33 (Ayers and others 1987). Similar results have been obtained for loblolly plantations up to 33 years of age in other locations around the South (Arnold 1981, Balmer and others 1975, Campbell and Mann 1974, Hansbrough 1968, Harms and Lloyd 1981, Lloyd and Jones 1983, McClurkin 1976). When survival is reasonably uniform, average tree diameter is closely related to initial spacing throughout a normal loblolly pine rotation (figure 11-14). This trend holds for tree heights also.

Maximum merchantable cubic-volume yields are normally obtained in even-aged plantations, up to about age 20, when the number of stems per hectare is relatively high. The merchantable volume of 10- to 12-year-old, even-aged plantations is usually maximized at stocking levels of 3,000 to 4,000 stems/ha. However, the volume in

Table 11-20—Surviving loblolly pine trees in a north Louisiana plantation as affected by spacing (1.2 by 1.2 to 3.0 by 3.0 m) and age

Age (yr)	Trees/ha				
	1.2 by 1.2 m	1.8 by 1.8 m	1.8 by 2.4 m	2.4 by 2.4 m	3.0 by 3.0 m
0	6,729	2,990	2,244	1,683	1,075
6	5,560	2,273	2,019	1,364	1,023
13	4,275	2,115	1,661	1,450	946
18	4,097	2,110	1,661	1,436	946
21	3,375	1,915	1,532	1,337	917
22	3,044	1,858	1,458	1,315	887
25	2,343	1,547	1,240	1,275	857
28	1,787	1,359	1,090	1,201	798
29	1,670	1,300	1,082	1,161	739
33	1,166	852	904	739	665

Source: adapted from Ayers and others (1987) and Shepard (1971).

Table 11-21—Expected survival of loblolly pines to age 25 based on stand densities at ages 10, 15, and 20 in the interior western Gulf Coastal Plain

Age (yr)	No. of trees/ha							
10	1,235	1,483	1,730	1,977	2,224	2,471	2,718	2,965
15	1,149	1,371	1,579	1,791	2,004	2,204	2,412	2,609
20	1,077	1,275	1,458	1,643	1,831	1,997	2,177	2,340
25	1,016	1,196	1,359	1,525	1,685	1,833	1,989	2,132
15	1,235	1,483	1,730	1,977	2,224	2,471		
20	1,156	1,369	1,594	1,806	2,019	2,226		
25	1,087	1,280	1,478	1,663	1,574	2,029		
20	1,235	1,483	1,730	1,977	2,224			
25	1,164	1,379	1,599	1,814	2,024			

Source: adapted from Lenhart (1972b).

Table 11-22 — Size of loblolly pine trees 4 years after applications of hexazinone (Velpar®), oxyfluorfen (Goal®), glyphosate (Roundup®), and triclopyr (Garlon®) to a newly established plantation growing in competition with grasses (*Andropogon* spp. and *Panicum* spp.), ragweed (*Ambrosia* spp.), goldenrod (*Solidago* spp.), and blackberries (*Rubus* spp.), and a few small hardwoods of various species

Weed control treatment	Total height (m)	Groundline diameter (cm)	Volume index (cm³)
Broadcast—2 years[*]	3.57 a	9.55 a	9,195 a
Band—2 years[†]	2.90 b	7.80 b	5,212 b
Broadcast—1 year[*]	2.58 c	6.45 c	3,360 c
Band—1 year[†]	2.58 c	6.98 c	3,393 c
Control	1.81 d	4.44 d	1,311 d

Source: adapted from Knowe and others (1985).

Means followed by the same letter in each column are not significantly different at the 95% probability level using Duncan's new multiple range test.

[*] Weed control was maintained as needed by broadcast applications of selective herbicides and direct application of nonselective herbicides made with CO_2 pressurized and hand-pumped backpack sprayers.
[†] Weed control was accomplished by applying selective herbicides in a 1.2-m-wide strip over each row of planted trees. Spot treatments with directed sprays were used to maintain weed control in bands.

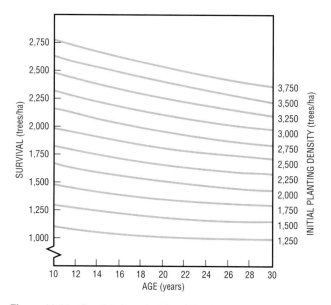

Figure 11-12—Predicted survival for oldfield loblolly pine plantations in the Georgia Piedmont (adapted from Lenhart and Clutter 1971).

Table 11-23—Growth of loblolly pines planted at various spacings in north Louisiana over a 21-year period

Spacing (m)	No. of seedlings planted	No. of trees at age 21	Avg. dbh (m)	Avg. height (m)	Merch. volume (m³)	Mean annual increment (m³)
1.2 by 1.2	6,729	3,375	12.7	14.3	197.8	9.4
1.8 by 1.8	2,995	1,915	17.1	16.2	250.0	12.0
1.8 by 2.4	2,244	1,532	18.3	16.5	236.2	11.3
2.4 by 2.4	1,683	1,337	20.3	17.1	248.1	12.0
3.0 by 3.0	1,075	917	23.6	19.2	280.9	13.2

Source: adadpted from Shepard (1971).

such stands is in very small trees. In 15- to 20-year-old, even-aged plantations, greatest merchantable yields are usually obtained at stocking rates between 900 and 2,200 trees/ha (table 11-23). The only variation from this general trend is on the very poorest sites, where maximum productivity can occur at stocking levels as low as 500 stems/ha. In unthinned stands older than 25 years, merchantable volume is maximized at stocking of 750 to 1,000 stems/ha (Arnold 1981). The relationship between stocking and yield in natural stands is much like the relationship between stocking and yield in plantations.

Close spacings have the following other advantages over wide spacings:

- Decreased chance of total stand failure.
- Wider selection of potential crop trees.
- Trees with smaller branches and less stem taper.
- Reduced period of acute fire hazard (because weed vegetation is suppressed quickly).
- Reduced competition from nonpine vegetation and reduced site-preparation cost for the next rotation.
- Decreased risk of wind or ice damage or rise in the water table.
- Increased soil stability on slopes.

Wide spacings have the following advantages:

- Lower establishment costs.
- Larger tree diameters at young tree ages.
- Shorter rotations.
- More diverse wildlife food production.

Effect of Tree Improvement on Plantation Yield

Genetically improved trees now make up the great majority of all artificially regenerated loblolly pines. First-generation genetic gain in volume of superior loblolly may be as low as 2% (Lowerts 1987). However, when first-generation improved loblolly pines are planted on recommended sites in the primary range, volume yield can be as much as 10 to 20% greater than that of unimproved plantations. Value improvement over an entire rotation might be as high as 18 to 32% on uniform areas within the natural range of loblolly (Gladstone and others 1987; Grigsby 1975; Kellison and Weir 1980; Kitchens 1985; Kraus and LaFarge 1982; Nichols 1974; Porterfield 1974; Talbert 1982; Talbert and others 1983, 1985). Loblolly shows a differential ability to absorb and utilize nutrients, so some interregional crosses may grow well on sites low in available nutrients (Woessner and others 1975). Most projections of gain are based on trials that are less than 10 years old, but it is clear that tree improvement can increase yields greatly.

Even if genetic selection increases average tree diameter and average tree height, standard growth and yield equations can be used to predict yields of improved stands (Buford and Burkhart 1987, Janssen and Sprinz 1987). However, caution must be used when projecting rotation yields based on rapid early growth of superior trees because superiority does not always show up in

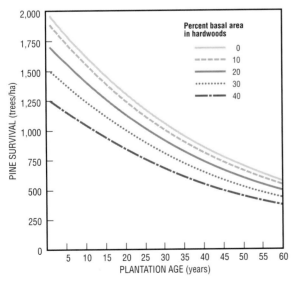

Figure 11-13—Surviving loblolly pine trees per hectare as related to percentage of basal area in hardwoods, based on planting 1,975 trees/ha (adapted from Burkhart and others 1987b).

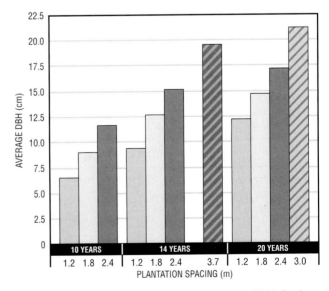

Figure 11-14—Effect of initial spacing on diameter of loblolly pine trees planted on comparable sites in three locations measured at ages shown (adapted from Brender 1965).

juvenile growth. For example, apparent height gain at age 11 was unrelated to total yield at age 31 in an Arkansas comparison of 7 seed sources (Sprinz 1987). In a provenance trial in southwest Arkansas, both dbh and height growth of dominant trees were 3 to 8% greater for East Coast sources than for the local source through tree age 29. The differences were statistically significant. However, height-over-age patterns did not begin to show up until about tree age 12 (Talbert and Strub 1987).

Second- and third-generation trees are being bred for superior growth combined with other traits, including improved stem form. Once the form of superior trees has been improved substantially, standard yield equations will have to be altered to account for this important change. Similarly, as tree breeding increases specific gravity, weight tables will require adjustment.

Growth and Yield of Direct-Seeded Stands

Direct-seeded stands can compare favorably with planted stands in terms of basal area and yield. A 324-ha area in southeast Louisiana, which was direct seeded in spots 1.8 m apart, produced 548 m³ of wood/ha over a 55-year period despite early predation by birds and insects (including the Nantucket pine tip moth), fire, and a 1947 hurricane (Campbell 1976). However, stocking, tree diameters, and spacing are generally less uniform in direct-seeded stands than in plantations, and direct-seeded stands usually have more unmerchantable stems than do plantations (tables 11-24 and 11-25). There are no yield tables specifically for direct-seeded loblolly pine. However, Daniels and others (1979) describe methods for constructing a model of tree growth and stand development for direct-seeded stands. Yield tables for natural stands can probably be used to estimate yields in stands established by broadcast seeding, whereas yield tables developed for plantations should be appropriate for spot- or row-seeded stands.

Table 11-24—Growth and yield of direct-seeded and planted loblolly pines in central Louisiana at age 22

Stand characteristics	Seeded-rough*	Seeded-disked†	Planted‡
Total volume (m³)	312.4	334.4	350.8
Merchantable volume (m³)	273.3	292.9	315.5
Basal area (m²)	17.9	18.3	19.3
Tree height (m)	14.6	14.9	16.8
Average tree diameter (cm)	16.8	16.0	18.3
No. of trees/ha	2,088	2,394	1,801
Unmerchantable trees/ha (%)	18	23	2

Source: adapted from Campbell (1975).

* A cutover longleaf pine site that had been burned 1 year prior to seeding a light grassy rough.
† Same as seeded-rough except that the seeds were sown only in 1.8-m-wide disked strips that were 1.8 m apart.
‡ Planted trees are 1 year older than trees grown from seed.

Table 11-25—Twenty-year growth of direct seeded and planted loblolly pines on a typical lower Coastal Plain site in the western Gulf Region

Treatments	Volume (m³/ha)		No. of trees/ha	
	Total stand	Merchantable trees	Total stand	Merchantable trees
Planted in grass rough*	335 a	313 a	1,604 d	1,596 d
Broadcast-sown grass rough†	270 b	226 d	2,679 ab	2,160 ab
Broadcast-sown flat strips‡	301 ab	247 cd	2,774 a	2,380 a
Broadcast-sown bedded strips§	322 a	278 abc	2,824 a	2,298 a
Swath-sown flat strips‖	316 ab	282 abc	2,355 bc	2,034 abc
Swath-sown bedded strips#	323 a	294 ab	2,016 c	1,778 bcd
Furrow-sown¶	295 ab	264 bcd	2,051 c	1,787 cd

Source: adapted from Campbell (1985).

Treatment means followed by the same letter are not significantly different at the 90% probability level using Duncan's multiple range test.

* Trees were hand planted as 1+0 seedlings at 1.8- by 2.4-m spacing. They are 1 year older than trees grown from seed.
† 42,000 seeds/ha hand-broadcast on 1-year rough.
‡ Same as broadcast-sown grass rough but over alternating flat-disked and undisked strips each 2.1 m wide.
§ Same as broadcast-sown grass rough but over alternating bedded and undisked strips each 2.1 m wide.
‖ 21,000 seeds/ha in swath-sown flat strips but on flat-disked strips only.
Same as swath-sown flat strips but on bedded strips only.
¶ 247,000 seeds/ha sown with an H-C furrow seeder.

Growth and Yield of Natural Stands

Equations for volume and basal area growth are available for natural loblolly stands in the West Gulf Coastal Plain (Murphy and Farrar 1983, Murphy and Sternitzke 1979), the Atlantic and East Gulf Coastal Plain (Burk and Burkhart 1984, Nelson and others 1961, Rockwood and others 1980, Schumacher and Coile 1960), and the Piedmont (Burk and Burkhart 1984, Nelson and others 1961). Most models provide little information on size class—trees are characterized only as sawtimber or pulpwood—and incorporate little information on intensive management. One exception is a diameter–distribution yield model for the Piedmont and Coastal Plain of Virginia and the Coastal Plain of North Carolina (Burk and Burkhart 1984). It includes stand and stock tables for 30-year projections from age 20 for various combinations of site index and initial basal area.

Stem profile (taper) functions have been developed for natural loblolly pine trees in stands west of the

Mississippi River. When incorporated into growth and yield equations, these functions can improve the accuracy of volume predictions for natural stands (Farrar and Murphy 1988).

In natural stands, volume growth increases rapidly as basal area increases to about 18 m²/ha, but then quickly levels off (figure 11-15). On good sites, cubic yields can exceed 6 m³/ha/yr through age 30. On medium sites, cubic yields reach about 4 m³/ha/yr through age 30 and on poor sites only about 2.5 m³/ha/yr (table 11-26). However, trees in natural stands are generally in random clumps (Mengak and others 1987), and spacings and densities are seldom consistently uniform even after thinning. Moreover, natural stands can be even- or uneven-aged, and trees in uneven-aged stands vary greatly in diameter. These departures from uniformity make it more difficult to predict volume and yield for natural stands than for plantations.

Even-Aged Stands

Growth and yield data on natural, even-aged loblolly pine stands are very limited. The most current information (table 11-27) consists of stand-level volume and volume growth predictors for thinned and unthinned stands. Variable density volume tables developed by Murphy (1983b) are applicable under a wide range of management regimes and are useful even when species other than loblolly constitute up to 50% of stand basal area. They provide information on merchantable pulpwood and both cubic and board-measure volumes of sawtimber. Sullivan and Clutter (1972) give simultaneous stand volume and volume growth predictors. Brender and Clutter (1970) provide lump-sum estimates of merchantable cubic volumes. None of these models can estimate volume distribution by tree size. There is no system available that estimates yields by diameter classes or yields of individual trees in thinned, even-aged, natural stands.

Table 11-26—Average stocking and volume per hectare of natural loblolly pine stands* in North Carolina and east Virginia as affected by stand age and site

Stand age (yr)	Trees 12.7 cm in dbh and larger					Net volume of sawtimber†	
	No. of sample plots	No. of plots	Average dbh (cm)	Basal area (m²/ha)	Net volume (m³/ha)	fbm International 1/4-inch/acre	m³/ha
Good sites							
20	7	254	20.1	21.1	120	3,375	47.2
25	23	240	21.3	23.4	150	6,250	87.5
30	37	237	22.4	25.0	175	8,575	120.0
35	27	221	23.6	26.2	195	10,450	146.2
40	40	201	24.6	27.1	212	11,950	167.2
45	31	191	25.7	27.6	223	12,950	181.2
50	29	200	26.4	28.0	232	13,825	193.5
55	19	198	27.4	28.2	239	14,525	203.3
60	7	191	28.2	28.5	245	15,025	210.3
65	12	153	28.7	28.7	247	15,350	214.8
70	10	148	29.2	28.7	248	15,500	216.9
Medium sites							
20	66	232	18.3	16.3	83	1,625	22.7
25	42	246	19.3	18.6	105	3,075	43.0
30	64	233	20.1	20.2	122	4,325	60.5
35	64	234	21.1	21.2	138	5,475	76.6
40	65	213	21.8	21.8	150	6,525	91.3
45	54	204	22.6	22.3	160	7,425	103.9
50	38	172	23.1	22.7	169	8,150	114.1
55	36	184	23.6	23.0	175	8,775	122.8
60	22	166	24.1	23.2	179	9,275	129.8
65	9	173	24.4	23.2	181	9,650	135.0
70	11	171	24.6	23.2	181	9,925	138.9
Poor sites							
20	7	211	17.3	12.6	45	875	12.2
25	4	198	18.0	15.2	62	1,550	21.7
30	2	239	18.5	16.8	76	2,150	30.1
35	3	241	19.0	17.9	89	2,725	38.1
40	3	247	19.8	19.1	99	3,200	44.8
45	1	243	20.3	19.7	108	3,625	50.7
50	1	281	20.8	20.2	115	3,950	55.3
55	2	193	21.3	20.7	121	4,175	58.4
60	0	212	21.6	20.9	125	4,350	60.9
65	1	231	21.8	20.9	127	4,450	62.3
70	0	179	22.1	20.9	127	4,475	62.6

Source: adapted from Knight (1978).
* Based on a survey of more than 3,400 sample plots in well-stocked stands.
† Conversion of m³ = 176.57 fbm International 1/4-inch rule.

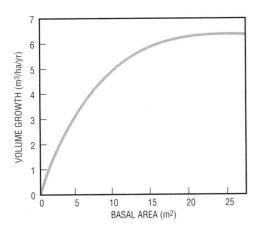

Figure 11-15—Relationship of stand volume growth to stand basal area for natural uneven-aged loblolly–shortleaf pine stands in south Arkansas (adapted from Murphy 1981).

Table 11-27—Models and yield tables for natural, even-aged stands of loblolly pine

Source	Physiographic region	Range in data			
		Stand No. of plots	Site age (yr)	index* (m)	Basal area (m²/ha)
Brender and Clutter (1970)	Lower Piedmont of Georgia	179	15–70	15.2–30.5	2.3–27.6
Burkhart and others (1972b)	Coastal Plain of North Carolina and Virginia Piedmont	121	13–77	16.2–28.1	8.0–49.8
Murphy (1983a, 1983b)	West Gulf (east Texas, south Arkansas, Louisiana)	145	20–51+	21.3–30.8	4.6–23.2
Schumacher and Coile (1960)	Coastal Plain from Maryland to Alabama	420	20–80†	18.3–36.6†	22.0–45.5†
Sullivan and Clutter (1972)	Georgia, Virginia, South Carolina	102	21–69	16.2–33.5	6.9–35.4

Source: adapted from Burkhart and others (1981).
* Base age 50 years.
† Range of data extrapolated from yield tables (actual range not given).

Uneven-Aged Stands

There are no published data on the growth and yield of natural, uneven-aged loblolly pine in pure stands. However, growth and yield data are available for mixed loblolly–shortleaf pine stands managed under the selection system (Farrar and others 1984b, Murphy and Farrar 1983). Murphy and Farrar (1988c) found that height growth of the tree of maximum diameter can be predicted adequately by models for even-aged stands. They also determined that heights of trees in lower diameter classes can be derived as a function of their diameter, the maximum diameter, and the height of the tree of maximum diameter. Optimum stocking of pines per unit area by diameter class approximates a reverse J-shaped curve (figure 11-16). Merchantable cubic volumes or sawtimber volumes can be predicted under current or future basal area conditions using tables 11-28 and 11-29. Managed, uneven-aged, loblolly–shortleaf pine stands, on sites of 26 to 29 m at a base age of

50 years, that are adequately stocked should grow at an annual rate of about 0.7 m² of merchantable basal area/ha, 6 m³ of pulpwood, and 7.0 to 7.7 m³ of sawtimber (1,235 to 1,360 fbm International /-inch rule) per ha (Murphy 1983c). In southwest Arkansas, 33 years of selection management resulted in an average of 1,023 fbm (Doyle)/ha in annual sawtimber growth and an average annual cut of 890 fbm of lumber/ha (Farrar and others 1984a). In contrast, 25 years of selection management in east-central Mississippi on a similar site produced only 570 to 740 fbm (Doyle)/ha/year, even with annual or 5-year cutting cycles designed to increase standing volumes (Farrar and others 1989).

Comparing Yields of Even-Aged and Uneven-Aged Stands

Yields of uneven-aged stands of loblolly pine did not differ greatly from yields of even-aged stands over 36-year and 50-year management periods (tables 11-30 and 11-31). Even-aged stands have higher cubic-volume yields than do uneven-aged stands because they are more fully stocked with trees of merchantable size. However, managed uneven-aged stands have higher lumber yields in large, valuable stems because the proportion of basal

Table 11-28—Merchantable stand volume for various merchantable basal areas in uneven-aged loblolly–shortleaf pine stands on average sites in the western Gulf Region

Merchantable basal area (m²/ha)	Merchantable volume (m³/ha)	Merchantable basal area (m²/ha)	Merchantable volume (m³/ha)
7	57.7	19	160.2
8	66.2	20	168.8
9	74.6	21	177.4
10	83.2	22	186.1
11	91.6	23	194.5
12	100.2	24	203.1
13	108.7	25	211.8
14	117.3	26	220.5
15	125.7	27	229.2
16	134.2	28	237.9
17	142.9	29	246.6
18	151.5	30	255.3

Source: adapted from Farrar and others (1984b).

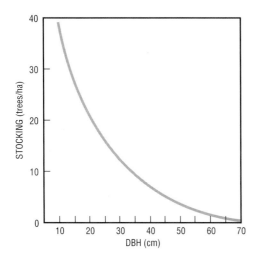

Figure 11-16—Optimum stocking of uneven-aged loblolly pine trees per acre by diameter class (adapted from Reynolds 1969).

Table 11-29—Cubic and board-foot volumes for various sawtimber basal areas in uneven-aged loblolly–shortleaf pine stands on average sites in the western Gulf Region

Sawtimber basal area (ft²/acre)	Sawlog volume (ft³/acre)	Board-foot volume		
		Doyle (fbm/acre)	Scribner (fbm/acre)	International 1/4-inch (fbm/acre)
10	198	922	1,161	1,417
15	311	1,457	1,832	2,204
20	429	2,014	2,532	3,015
25	551	2,590	3,254	3,845
30	675	3,181	3,995	4,691
35	803	3,785	4,751	5,549
40	932	4,400	5,520	6,418
45	1,063	5,024	6,302	7,297
50	1,196	5,658	7,095	8,184
55	1,331	6,300	7,897	9,080
60	1,467	6,949	8,709	9,983
65	1,605	7,605	9,529	10,893
70	1,743	8,267	10,357	11,810
75	1,883	8,936	11,193	12,732
80	2,024	9,610	12,035	13,660
85	2,166	10,290	12,884	14,593
90	2,309	10,974	13,739	15,531
95	2,453	11,664	14,601	16,473
100	2,598	12,358	15,467	17,420
105	2,744	13,057	16,340	18,371
110	2,891	13,760	17,217	19,327
115	3,038	14,467	18,099	20,268
120	3,186	15,177	18,987	21,249
125	3,335	15,892	19,878	22,216

Source: Farrar and others (1984b).

Conversion factors: ft²/acre x 0.2296 = m²/ha; ft³/acre x 0.07 = m³/ha; fbm/acre x 2.471 = fbm/ha.

Table 11-30—Total and mean annual production of loblolly pines and cost/benefit ratio for even and uneven-aged management systems over a 50-year rotation

Management system	Production/ha				
	Total		Mean Annual		
	Total merchantable (m³)	Board feet Doyle	Total merchantable (m³)	Board feet Doyle	Benefit to cost ratio*
Uneven-aged (HS)	412.8	52,487	8.3	1,050	3.71
Uneven-aged (LS)	287.4	43,534	5.7	870	3.11
Even-aged (natural)	546.5	40,559	10.9	810	5.40
Even-aged (plantation)	594.2	51,782	11.9	1,035	3.13

Source: adapted from Baker (1987).

HS = high stocking, LS = low stocking.

* Seven-percent discount rate.

Table 11-31—Volume production of loblolly pine in southeast Arkansas associated with alternative natural reproduction methods during a 36-year management period

Treatment	Total production*/ha			Average annual production/ha		
		Board ft†			Board ft†	
	m³‡	Doyle	International-1/4-inch	m³‡	Doyle	International-1/4-inch
Clearcut	234.4 b	23,129 b	35,404 b	6.5 b	642 b	983 b
Heavy seed tree	294.8 a	32,202 a	44,923 a	8.2 a	895 a	1,243 a
Diameter limit	269.6 a	29,355 a	47,858 a	7.5 a	815 a	1,329 a
Selection	211.7 b	33,536 a	43,677 a	5.9 b	93.2 a	1,213 a

Source: adapted from Baker and Murphy (1982).

Treatment means, followed by the same letter in the same column, are not significantly different at the 95% probability level.

* Total production = present standing volume plus intermediate harvests minus volume after initial treatment.

† Trees >29.2 cm in dbh.

‡ Trees >8.9 cm in dbh.

area in sawtimber is greater in uneven-aged stands and because such stands always include sawtimber-size trees. Thirty-year yield projections for medium-quality sites in the Piedmont indicate an 11.9% internal rate of return for even-aged natural stands (133.5 m³/ha) and an 11.0% return for plantations (177 m³/ha). Establishment costs for plantations were nearly double those for natural stands, and the increased costs more than offset the 44 m³ increase in yield (Mengak and others 1987). However, the risk of natural regeneration failure can be high if regeneration is not properly planned (see chapter 5).

Species-to-Species Differences in Growth and Yield

Loblolly pine is more adaptable than any other southern pine, is especially competitive on intermediate pine sites, and responds well to management. However, seed source, stand condition, and age largely determine whether loblolly does or does not outperform other southern pines. If stands are left to grow 50 years or more, growth differences between loblolly, longleaf, shortleaf, and slash pines often become insignificant (Strub and Sprinz 1988).

Lobolly Pine Versus Slash Pine

On wet Coastal Plain sites (especially on Spodosol soils of the lower Coastal Plain), slash pine does as well as or better than loblolly pine and should be the favored species for regeneration (Caulfield and others 1989, Outcalt 1982, Wilhite 1976; table 11-32). These include wet sites of the western Gulf Coastal Plain where slash pine has been introduced (Shoulders 1973). However, intensive culture may accelerate the growth of loblolly more than the growth of slash on wet sites. For example, a combination of cultivation and fertilization at establishment increased the basal area of loblolly more than it increased the basal area of slash after 25 years in southern Mississippi. However, 16% more of the loblolly basal area was in juvenile wood (Clark and Schmidtling 1989).

On dry or moist but well-drained sites within the overlapping natural ranges of loblolly and slash pines, and even somewhat north of the natural range of slash pine, it is often difficult to anticipate which species will perform better. Performance may depend on seed source, rust resistance, or minor topographic changes. In several studies loblolly grew more rapidly than slash at young ages (Brightwell 1971, Cole 1975, Malac and Brightwell 1973). In other instances, growth of the two

Table 11-32—Difference between species in total volume at age 20 in Mississippi and Louisiana plantings by site condition

	Percent of sites showing difference			
	Wet site (%)	Intermediate site (%)	Dry site (%)	All (%)
Loblolly vs. slash				
Loblolly significantly greater	0	8	0	5
Slash significantly greater	53	11	0	21
No significant difference	47	81	100	74
Loblolly vs. longleaf				
Loblolly significantly greater	67	75	25	67
Longleaf significantly greater	0	0	0	0
No significant difference	33	25	75	33
Loblolly vs. shortleaf				
Loblolly significantly greater	50	9	0	11
Shortleaf significantly greater	0	0	0	0
No significant difference	50	91	100	89

Source: adapted from Shoulders (1983).

Statistical significance was at the 95% probability level using Duncan's new multiple range test.

Table 11-33—Mean annual total stem volume increment per hectare of planted pines larger than 11.4 cm dbh in the transition zone of the upper Coastal Plain and the Piedmont Plateau of east-central Alabama by type of topography (maximum difference in elevation, 9.1 m)

Pine species	Age	Mean annual total stem volume (m³/ha)			
		Hill	Slope	Flat	Average
Slash	31	12.3 a	17.4 b	16.2 ab	15.4 b
Loblolly	29	10.4 a	17.2 b	15.7 b	14.4 b
Shortleaf	31	4.4 a	5.2 a	1.7 a	3.8 a
Longleaf	30	6.5 a	2.9 a	2.0 a	3.8 a
Average	30	8.4 a	10.7 a	8.9 a	9.3

Source: adapted from Livingston (1972).

Values in rows or columns not followed by the same letter are significantly different at the 95% probability level.

Table 11-34—Average height, diameter at breast height, and survival of 6 species of southern pines in the South Carolina Piedmont after 13 growing seasons

Pine species	Average		
	Height (m)	Dbh (cm)	% Survival
Loblolly	12.68 a	15.75 a	97 a
Slash	12.40 a	16.38 a	94 a
Shortleaf	9.34 b	13.56 b	92 a
Longleaf	8.34 b	11.00 c	75 b
Virginia	6.84 b	12.24 bc	64 bc
Eastern white	5.90 b	8.99 d	50 c

Source: adapted from Branan and Porterfield (1971).

In each column, all averages not identified by a common letter are significantly different at the 95% probability level.

(figure 11-17). Available data strongly indicate that loblolly should be preferred over slash on all but wet sites west of the Mississippi River.

Loblolly Pine Versus Longleaf Pine

Early growth of loblolly pine is more rapid than that of longleaf, making loblolly more suited to short-rotation management on most sites (Caulfield and others 1989; tables 11-32 and 11-33). Even on wet flatwoods, loblolly can be expected to produce considerably more pulpwood than longleaf, or than Sonderegger pine (a naturally occurring hybrid between a loblolly male parent and a longleaf female parent), over short rotations. In central Louisiana and north Florida, merchantable volume of loblolly exceeded that of longleaf at ages 20 to 26 by 44 to 88 m³/ha (Lohrey 1974, Outcalt 1982, Wilhite 1976). The growth rate of longleaf may approach that of loblolly as early as age 20 if the site or intensity of management is low but not until later than age 35 if site or intensity of management is high (Livingston 1972, Lohrey 1974, Schmidtling 1987). Generally, if rotations exceed 50 years, longleaf outperforms loblolly on most sites. However, longleaf grows better than loblolly even on short rotations in the dry sandhills of the Carolinas (Kellison and Jett 1978, Shain and Jenkins 1974). Longleaf is much more resistant to both fire and fusiform rust than is loblolly. This advantage may more than offset longleaf's generally slower growth rate.

species was about equal through rotations of up to 30 years (Caulfield and others 1989, Jones 1969, Schmidtling 1987, Shoulders 1983; tables 11-32 and 11-33). A Southwide study showed that plantations of 15- to 20-year-old loblolly in sites diverted from farm crop production produced an average of 24% more volume per hectare than plantations of 15- to 20-year old slash pine produced on comparable sites (Alig and others 1980).

Even outside its native range, slash pine grows as fast as loblolly pine on some intermediate sites (Shoulders 1983; table 11-34). However, 10-year volume growth of loblolly exceeded that of slash by 22% in progeny test plantings in the upper Coastal Plain of east Texas (Long 1979). Slash pine can grow as fast as loblolly over a 30-year rotation on some sites as far north as northwestern Louisiana (Clason and Cao 1983). Efforts to mix slash and loblolly in the same plantation in north Louisiana showed that slash pine cannot compete with loblolly

Loblolly Pine Versus Shortleaf Pine

Loblolly pine grows faster than shortleaf pine on all but the very driest pine sites where the species' ranges overlap and even north of the natural range of loblolly (Branen and Porterfield 1971, Livingston 1972; tables 11-32, 11-35, and 11-36). Loblolly out-competes shortleaf even where hardwood brush is present. In the mid-South, loblolly is preferred well into the range of shortleaf because it produces 1.6 to 6.3 m³/ha/yr more cellulose than shortleaf (Williston 1958, 1967a, 1972). At age 26, an unthinned loblolly plantation on a north Mississippi creek bottom had 6% more volume than a neighboring shortleaf plantation of the same age (Williston 1985). In a south Arkansas test, the average 17-year-old loblolly tree had

Figure 11-17—Twenty-four-year-old loblolly and slash pines planted in alternate rows in north Louisiana. Small slash pines are in the middle row.

two to three times more wood volume than the average shortleaf of the same age (Stephen and others 1982). In another south Arkansas comparison, a plantation of 19-year-old loblolly had 3.2 m² more basal area/ha than had a 19-year-old plantation of shortleaf, even though 168 m³/ha of loblolly and only 97 m³/ha of shortleaf had been removed. In southern Illinois, 31-year-old loblolly reached a maximum volume of 352 m³/ha as compared with 312 m³/ha for shortleaf of the same age (Arnold 1981). Even on low-quality mountain sites in central Tennessee, 10-year-old loblolly pines were 2.1 m taller and 2.5 cm larger in diameter than shortleaf (Loftus 1974).

When natural mixed stands of loblolly and shortleaf pines are placed under management, loblolly increases in dominance because it responds more rapidly to cultural treatments. In the first 10 years after an uneven-aged mixed stand was released from understory hardwood competition, loblolly pine trees less than 25 cm in dbh grew 10.3 cm in dbh (table 11-35) and decreased their taper sufficiently to increase volume by 6 to 8%. The diameter response of shortleaf was 7.4 cm, and taper changes were insignificant. However, shortleaf pine stands can generally be grown with more stems and more basal area than can loblolly stands, especially on dry sites. Once shortleaf stands reach about age 20, they generally grow rapidly enough so that it is not prudent to clearcut them and replace them with loblolly before maturity (Williston and Dell 1974). When stand rotations longer than 50 years are planned for dry or infertile sites, shortleaf should be considered as an alternative to loblolly.

Table 11-35—Average diameter growth response of natural, uneven-aged loblolly–shortleaf pine stands chemically released from understory hardwood competition in 1955

Period	Diameter increment (cm)		Period	Diameter increment (cm)	
	Loblolly	Shortleaf		Loblolly	Shortleaf
1950-54	3.94	3.48	1965-69	3.96	2.69
1955-59	5.82	4.19	1970-74	3.81	2.59
1960-64	4.52	3.17	1975-79	3.20	2.26

Source: adapted from Guldin (1984a).

Table 11-36—Average survival, height, diameter and basal area of 16-year old pine trees planted at a 1.8 by 1.8 m initial spacing on an abandoned field in the Virginia Piedmont

Pine species	% Survival	Height (m)	Diameter (cm)	Basal area (m²/ha)
Loblolly	76	13.1	14.5	11.7
Virginia	74	11.3	12.2	8.3
Shortleaf	80	10.7	11.7	8.7

Source: adapted from Kormanik and Hoekstra (1963).

Loblolly Pine Versus Virginia Pine

Where their natural ranges overlap, loblolly pine is almost always preferred over Virginia pine because loblolly grows faster and has better form. Loblolly pine grows faster than native Virginia pine on the Virginia Piedmont (table 11-36) and on some highland areas, and has been planted widely in those areas. Loblolly also outgrows Virginia pine on many mountain sites in Tennessee and Alabama. Ten years after planting on ridges, bottoms, and cleared, north-facing slopes in the Cumberland Plateau of northern Alabama, loblolly averaged 10 m in height and 13.7 cm in dbh, Virginia pine averaged 8.4 m in height and 11.4 cm in dbh. Loblolly grew better than Virginia pine on all sites (Smalley and Pierce 1972). On plateau and ridge sites, loblolly averaged 1.2 m taller and 1.3 cm more in diameter than Virginia pine at age 10 (Loftus 1974). Even on the Highland Rim of Tennessee, loblolly is a preferred species for rotations of up to 25 years (Miller 1982). However, loblolly pine plantings risk severe ice and snow damage every year on all natural Virginia pine sites (see chapter 10).

Loblolly Pine Versus Sand Pine

Sand pine grows better than loblolly or other southern pines on dry sandhill sites (and especially on the Florida sandhills) even though loblolly may grow faster during the first few years after stand establishment (Kellison and Jett 1978). In Georgia and South Carolina sandhills, yield from 15-year-old sand pine plantations averaged 63 to 106 m³/ha and yield from loblolly pine plantations of the same age averaged 31 to 60 m³/ha. Yields of slash and longleaf were similar to yields of loblolly (Hebb 1982).

Increasing Growth and Yield Through Site Manipulation and Management of Young Stands

Stand yields at rotation age are greatest when competing vegetation is minimized without removing debris or soil from the planting site (Burkhart and others 1985). Also, the greatest financial returns usually occur when the intensity of site preparation or vegetation control in young stands is moderate (Burger and Kluender 1983). Where the level of herbaceous competition, hardwood competition, or both is moderate to high, control usually results in substantial growth and value increases in

young loblolly pine stands. In southern Arkansas, both early vegetation control and early tip moth control promoted the growth of loblolly. Early tip moth control increased growth by about 0.07 m³ of wood/tree at age 17 (Stephen and others 1982). Controlling herbaceous vegetation in pole-sized and larger stands probably has little or no effect on tree growth, but controlling hardwoods increases tree growth.

Site Preparation

Burning, mechanical treatments that incorporate surface organic matter into the soil and minimize soil loss (for example, disking; chopping on well-drained sites; and bedding on moderately well-drained to poorly drained sites), and chemical weed control (alone or in various combinations) increase survival and growth of loblolly pines on a wide variety of sites. Mechanical or chemical treatments are usually more effective than fire alone (Arbour and Ezell 1981; Buckner and others 1987; Haines and others 1975; Haywood 1983, 1987; Haywood and Burton 1989; Haywood and others 1981; Outcalt 1984; Stransky and others 1985; table 11-37). Chemical site preparation is probably the most cost-effective type of treatment when residual hardwood stocking is moderate to heavy. If there is little or no hardwood competition, mechanical site preparation is more economical (Hickman and others 1987).

Bedding can increase survival on poorly drained or somewhat poorly drained, clayey, Coastal Plain soils by 10 to 20%. Similarly, bedding can increase the 25-year site index for sites with these soils by as much as 3.7 m (Gent and others 1986, Hammond 1987, McKee and Wilhite 1986). Bedding consistently increases tree growth only on sites where the water table is at or near the soil surface for several consecutive weeks (Cain 1978, Derr and Mann 1977). Subsoiling can also increase survival and early growth on soils with compacted layers while scalping

Table 11-37—Key to managing Atlantic Coastal Plain sites

Site group	Representative soil classes	Typical series	Drainage class
Organic soils (Pocosins)	Humaquepts Umbraquults	Portsmouth Pantego Bayboro Pamlico	Very poorly to poorly drained
Wet soils with sand or sandy loam subsoil (pond pine flats)	Aquults Aquods	Lynn Haven Rutlege Leon	Very poorly to poorly drained
Wet soils with loam to clay subsoil (wet flats)	Albaquults Paleaquults Albaqualfs	Bladen Bethera Coxville Megget Yonges	Poorly drained
Moderately wet soils with sand or sandy loam subsoils (sand ridges)	Paleaquults Paleudults Psamments	Lynchburg Seewee Chipley Goldsboro Eulonia	Somewhat poorly to moderately well drained
Moderately wet soils with loam to clay subsoils (middle Coastal Plain)	Ochraquults Ochraquafs Hapludults	Okeetee Wahee Nemours Duplin Dunbar Craven	Somewhat poorly to moderately well drained
Dry soils (upper Coastal Plain)	Paleudults Psamments Entisols	Orangeburg Lucy Eustis Norfolk Lakeland Caroline	Well to excessively drained

Source: adapted from McKee (1989).

promotes early tree development where herbaceous ground cover is heavy (Beers and Bailey 1985, Lantagne and Burger 1983, Posey and Walker 1969, Stransky 1964).

Removing surface vegetation by windrowing often increases survival, improves tree distribution, and increases early growth by reducing vegetative competition and increasing soil moisture (Cathey and others 1989, DeWit and Terry 1983, Edwards 1986a, Pehl 1983, Stafford and others 1985, Tuttle and others 1987). However, if a significant amount of topsoil is removed from the planting zone during the windrowing operation, the loss of nutrients can cause reduced tree growth by age 10 to 15 (Burkhart and others 1985). The fact that 4-year-old trees growing in windrows may be as much as 10 times as large as those growing in stripped areas (Miller 1990) is abundant proof that loss of topsoil is serious. An extreme loss of topsoil can reduce site index by 3.4 to 5.5 m and yields by more than 20% over a 25- to 30-year rotation on upper Coastal Plain or Piedmont sites (Fox and others 1989, Golden and Isaacson 1987). Recovery is very slow; even after 50 years, the mean height of dominant and codominant trees was reduced by 4.3 m (Fox and others 1989, Glass 1976). There are many other published examples of yield losses caused by improper site preparation (Buford and McKee 1987, Goebel 1968, Haywood 1980, Pehl and Bailey 1983). Large losses of topsoil and resulting reductions in yield are environmentally and economically unacceptable.

Most evidence indicates that grade 1 seedlings (including those that are exceptionally tall) grow faster than grade 2 or 3 seedlings for many years, especially on good sites (Barber and VanHaverbeke 1961, Hatchell and others 1972, Hunt and Gilmore 1967, South and others 1985, Zarger 1965). For 13 years after planting in southwestern Georgia, the annual growth of grade 3 trees was only 75% as great as that of grade 1 or 2 trees. By age 30, grade 1 stock yielded 86 to 154% more volume per unit area than did grade 3 stock, proving that planting only the best seedlings is an effective way of increasing growth (Wakeley 1969).

Weed Control in Established Stands

Site preparation before planting increases stand growth more than does releasing established pines (Edwards 1986b). However, early control of herbaceous plants should increase survival where there is little rainfall during the growing season, where soil moisture holding capacity is low, and where there is severe competition (Creighton and others 1987, Haywood and Tiarks 1990). Under less demanding conditions, weed control may have no effect on survival (Zutter and others 1987). Loblolly pines grow best if released early—at the beginning of the second growing season after planting. Release after the first growing season is also very effective. Generally, diameter growth is more responsive than height growth to vegetation control. Combined

Table 11-38—Loblolly pine growth increases associated with drainage

Source	Soil type	Age (yr)	Mean distance to canal (m)	Annual growth (m³/ha) Drained	Annual growth (m³/ha) Undrained	% Increase of drained over undrained
Miller and Maki (1957)	Portsmouth fine sandy loam	0–17	61 m	17.9	1.23	1,298
Terry and Hughes (1975)	Bayboro-Bladen	0–13	10 m	4.3	0.54	696
White and Pritchett (1970)	Leon fine sand	0–5	WT = 46*	7.6	1.3	585
	Leon fine sand		WT = 92†	4.9	1.3	277

* Water table constantly maintained at 46 cm below groundline.

† Water table constantly maintained at 92 cm below groundline.

Table 11-39—Effects of different precommercial thinning treatments at age 7 on subsequent loblolly pine growth

Thinning treatment*	Age 7 Basal Area (m²/ha)	Age 7 No. of Trees/ha	Age 19 No. of Trees/ha	Age 19 Basal area (m²/ha)	Age 19 Dbh (cm)	Age 21 Height† (m)
Control	11.7	75,410	6,714	27.6	7.1	13.4
Machine	2.6	13,340	4,169	25.2	8.9	14.6
Machine + hand	1.2	4,570	1,352	23.6	15.0	15.9

Source: adapted from Grano (1969).

* Control = not treating a 7-year-old naturally regenerated stand established after an intense wildfire; machine thinning = cutting parallel swaths 2.4 m wide and leaving strips of pines 0.9 m wide (hardwoods over 10 cm in dbh were removed by hand); machine plus hand thinning = machine removal (as above) plus hand removal of all hardwoods and thinning residual pines to about a 0.9 m spacing at age 7 and a second hand thinning at age 16 to increase spacing to about 2.4 m within strips.

† Average height of 250 tallest trees/ha.

treatments that control both woody and herbaceous vegetation increase growth most during the first 5 years of tree development in both plantations and natural stands. Herbaceous control alone is the next best treatment. Woody vegetation control alone has the least effect on early growth (Bacon and Zedaker 1987, Cain 1991, Miller and others 1991, Zutter and others 1987).

One or more applications of herbaceous weed control treatments shortly after stand establishment also increase survival and individual tree and stand volume growth where there is substantial competition to young pines. Merchantable volume increases associated with early herbaceous weed control averaged 30% at stand age 10 in Southwide studies (Creighton and others 1986, 1987). Loblolly pines grow rapidly when herbaceous weeds are controlled chemically, if chemicals are used properly (Creighton and others 1986, 1987; Dougherty and Lowery 1991). When applied to 2- to 5-year-old loblolly pine stands at rates determined on the basis of soil type and tree age, pellet and liquid (foliar spray) hexazinone increased volumes, 5 to 6 years later, by 7% (pellets) and 9% (liquid) over a wide range of sites (Glover and others 1991). In planted stands, controlling woody weeds generally results in much greater wood yields over a rotation than does herba-

ceous weed control (Dangerfield and Merck 1990); however, thinning may be required to maintain early growth increases (Martin 1981). In north Louisiana, suppressing hardwoods at age 7 increased loblolly pine stand volume by 25% at age 22, and merchantable volume should be increased by 59 m³/ha at the end of a 35-year rotation (Clason 1991).

Drainage

Young loblolly pine trees tend to grow slower on poorly drained soils than on similar but better drained soils. Artificial drainage measures, such as ditching, may be essential before stands can even be established on very poorly drained pocosin sites. Such water-control measures can permit young stands to grow rapidly (table 11-38). Once a stand reaches crown closure, transpiration alone is often sufficient to keep the water table at levels that permit continued rapid growth. Thus, drainage may be needed only during the first few years of the life of new stands, especially on seasonally wet sites. To get acceptable yields on very wet sites, managers may have to employ artificial drainage throughout the rotation.

Precommercial Thinning

Precommercial thinning can substantially increase the growth rate of dense, even-aged, natural or direct-seeded stands of loblolly pine, especially when thinning takes place between stand ages 2 and 7 (Dierauf 1985, Lohrey 1977; table 11-39). Even stands as old as age 15 respond to precommercial thinning (Bower 1965). If competing hardwoods are present, hardwoods should be controlled at the time of precommercial thinning (table 11-40). The main benefits of precommercial thinning are increased diameter growth, shortened time to first commercial harvest, and increased merchantable yield at final harvest. A dense natural loblolly–shortleaf stand that was precommercially thinned at age 6 produced 20 times as much sawlog volume (8.9 m³/ha) at age 22 as a similar but unthinned stand produced (Cain 1990). However, total cubic-volume yields are decreased by precommercial thin-

Table 11-40—Merchantable cubic meter growth and yield at different ages of naturally regenerated loblolly pines as affected by hardwood control and precommercial thinning at age 6

Stand treatment	Age 10 Yield (m³/ha)	Age 10 % TBA in hdwd	Age 15 Yield (m³/ha)	Age 15 % TBA in hdwd	Age 20 Yield (m³/ha)	Age 20 %TBA in hdwd	Mean annual growth (cm³/yr)
1. Hardwoods not controlled	0.7	51	20.3	46	59.4	47	2.9
2. Large hardwoods (> 12.5 cm) chemically controlled after harvest cut	4.9	21	54.7	22	124.3	22	6.2
3. Treatment 2 plus precommercial thinning of pines and cutting of all small hardwoods at age 6	8.4	14	83.9	14	178.8	17	8.9

Source: adapted from Langdon and Trousdell (1974).

TBA = total basal area; hdwd = hardwoods.

ning until about stand age 15, when high mortality begins to occur in stagnated stands. Growth of individual trees is fastest when precommercial thinning leaves no more than 1,850 well-spaced trees/ha. Individual-tree selection results in the greatest merchantable yield and product quality, but strip thinning by machine is the least expensive way to thin precommercially and usually is the most cost effective, especially on large areas. Strip and selection precommercial thinning can be combined to increase merchantable yields by 40 to 70% at ages 23 to 25 (Balmer and Williston 1973, Mann and Lohrey 1974; tables 11-41 and 11-42). Precommercial thinning stimulates diameter growth of crop trees in planted stands also, but reduced stocking results in reduced yields of pulpwood (Foil and others 1964).

The economic feasibility of precommercial thinning can be estimated by means of break-even analysis (Fox 1988). For example, if precommercial thinning at stand age 5 costs \$124/ha (\$50/acre), if pulpwood stumpage is expected to bring \$15/2.55 m^3 (that is, \$15/cord) at har-

vest time, and if an 8% return on investment at age 30 is required, then the equation for determining the total volume increase (V_r) needed to break even is

$$V_r = [\$124/ha + 1.08^{25}] - \$15/2.55 \, m^3 =$$
$$143.6 \, m^3/ha \, (22.8 \, cords/acre).$$

Therefore, precommercial thinning would have to increase growth of the stand by 5.7 m^3/ha/yr (0.9 cords/acre/yr) over the 25-year growth period to return 8% on the investment at the end of the rotation. Such a calculation does not take into account added value associated with moving some of the product into sawtimber, poles, or other more valuable products.

Effects of Commercial Thinning on Growth and Yield

Thinning affects natural and planted stands similarly if pretreatment conditions (for example, crown ratio and stocking) are similar. Growth following thinning is greatly affected by stand age, stand density, and site quality. Both volume growth and basal area growth increase as site index and residual basal area increase. On average or better sites, between 23 and 32 m^2 of basal area/ha are needed to maintain near maximum cubic-volume growth for loblolly pine stands 10 to 30 years of age. Sawtimber-volume growth is fastest when basal area is kept at 21 to 23 m^2/ha (Nix and others 1987). In most stands, thinning initially reduces cubic-volume growth because it reduces growing stock below the optimum level (Burton 1981, 1982). However, growth loss is usually not excessive, provided that comparisons are not made with drastically thinned or extremely dense stands (table 11-43). Heavy thinning at young ages can greatly reduce sawtimber-volume growth and pulpwood-volume growth for the next 10 years (table 11-44). Compatible cubic volume and basal area projection equations are available for thinned, oldfield, loblolly pine plantations (Burkhart and Sprinz 1984b).

Although total volume may be 25% greater in closely spaced than in widely spaced stands, the cellulose is in many small trees that are hard to handle and low in value (Goebel and others 1974, Somberg and Haas 1971, Williston 1967b). For example, a stand planted at a spacing of 1.2 by 1.2 m and only lightly thinned still had 12% of its trees in the 10- to 15-cm diameter classes at age 45. In contrast, only 2% of trees planted at 2.4- by 2.4-m spacings were as small as 18 cm in diameter at stand age 45 (Feduccia and Mosier 1977).

Table 11-41—Increase in tree size and stand volume at age 16 after precommercial thinning of densely stocked, direct-seeded loblolly pines in Louisiana at age 3

Thinning treatment	No of trees/ha at age 3	No. of tree/ha at age 16	Height of dominant & codominant trees (m)	All trees	Dbh (m) Trees ≥9.1 cm	Trees ≥14.2 cm	All trees*	Volume (m³/ha) Trees ≥9.1 cm†	Trees ≥14.2 cm‡
Unthinned check	12,437	5,782	11.9	9.1	11.7	15.5	253.8	132.2	44.0
Selection thin	10,749	6,153	10.8	8.6	11.9	15.5	204.7	100.0	30.6
Selection thin	7,165	4,653	11.7	9.9	12.4	16.0	214.7	123.6	52.0
2.0-m strip§	6,986	4,678	11.7	9.9	12.4	16.3	226.4	135.7	60.1
2.3-m strip§	3,887	3,328	10.5	10.2	12.7	16.0	152.5	95.5	55.8
Selection thin	3,583	3,047	12.3	12.4	13.7	16.5	209.0	170.7	106.5
Checkerboard‖	3,788	2,982	12.1	11.9	14.0	17.5	207.8	155.7	108.0
Strip plus selection#	6,926	3,032	12.3	12.4	14.0	16.8	229.6	171.5	115.4
Selection thin	1,853	1,705	12.4	15.0	15.7	17.8	184.0	155.0	128.1

Source: adapted from Lohrey (1977).

* Volume outside bark in trees > 1.5 cm in dbh to a 0.0-cm top diameter outside bark (dob).

† Volume outside bark in trees > 9.1 cm in dbh to a 10-cm top dob.

‡ Volume outside bark in trees > 14.2 cm in dbh to a 10-cm top dob.

§ Alternating strips of the same width left and removed.

‖ Two 2-m strip thinnings made at right angles to each other leaving clumps of trees.

Thinned to 3,583 trees/ha at age 5.

Table 11-42—Precommercially thinning a 4-year-old, direct-seeded loblolly pine stand substantially increased yield and average tree size at age 23 in the Virginia Piedmont

Treatment	Spacing (m)	Mean dbh of 100 largest trees (cm)	Pulpwood vol. (m³/ha)
Check	*	18.3	113
Mechanical thinning with bulldozer†	2.1	20.8	142
Mechanical plus hand thinning‡	1.8	22.1	157
Hand thinning only	2.1-2.4	21.3	174

Source: adapted from Dierauf (1985).

* Initial stocking ranged from 3,625 to 11,532 seedlings/ha.

† Bulldozed strips approximately 2.1 m wide separated by leave strips approximately 1.2 m wide.

‡ Bulldozed as in mechanical thinning with bulldozer, with pines in the leave strips hand-thinned to an approximate spacing of 1.8 m between trees.

Table 11-43—Basal areas and relative reduction of yields of young planted loblolly pines

| Location | Age (yr) | | Basal area at measurement age (m²/ha) | | % Periodic annual increment* |
	Thinning	Measurement	Thinning	No thinning	
Georgia	10	12	17.0	28.9	87
Oklahoma†	10	12	18.6	36.7	96
Georgia	11	13	23.0	35.8	80
Georgia‡	11	21	23.0	35.5	101
Alabama	13	16	20.2	32.4	89
Illinois	13	17	18.6	30.3	101
Tennessee	14	17	17.9	39.0	76
Tennessee	19	24	26.4	33.1	105

Source: adapted from Schultz (1975).

* Most effective thinning treatment as a percentage of merchantable yield of unthinned stands from thinning to measurement age.

† Cregg and others (1988).

‡ Xydias and others (1983).

The volume and size of trees to be cut in a commercial thinning, and timing of the thinning, depend on site quality, the level of tree competition, and the economic objectives of the landowner. Increment cores or periodic diameter measurements best indicate when growth rate begins to decline and when thinning should take place. For optimum tree growth, thinnings should begin before tree age 20. A 5-year thinning cycle with three to five thinnings beginning at about age 10 to 15 produces high-quality sawlogs at rotation age. However, if thinning takes place before crown closure occurs or is so heavy that the stand must grow for several years before it again fully occupies the site, total yield is reduced (Wheeler and others 1982). Response to thinning is concentrated in diameter growth; there is little if any increase in height growth (Nix and others 1987). The very largest trees are relatively unaffected by thinning over a rotation of 25 to 60 years because they are already outcompeting neighboring trees (Andrulot and Williston 1974, Goebel and others 1974).

Frequent light thinnings provide the best opportunity to increase production of high-quality trees and to salvage potential mortality. Thinning in young stands

increases cubic-volume yields consistently only when it salvages material that would otherwise be lost through natural mortality (Feduccia and Mann 1976). In Georgia, one unthinned plantation with an average of 1,586 trees/ha at age 11 and with a basal area of 40 m²/ha lost 8.4% of its total volume during the next 10 years as a result of 33% tree mortality (table 11-44). Natural mortality may be even greater in older stands. Between tree ages 35 and 50, natural mortality can reduce net cubic volume in well-stocked stands by at least 20% in the absence of thinning (Andrulot and others 1972).

If trees in plantations or natural stands need to be released, careful thinning from above, once or twice between tree ages 15 and 20, can be silviculturally sound and can produce more early revenue than can low thinning. For example, cubic-volume yields differed little when even-aged, natural, loblolly-shortleaf pine stands in Arkansas and Louisiana were thinned from above or from below. However, sawtimber yields and total financial returns were reduced by crown thinning (Arthaud and Klemperer 1986, Bassett 1966, Burton 1980; table 11-45). Generally, thinning from below reduces the time required to produce sawtimber and veneer logs, whereas merchantable pulpwood can be obtained earlier with judicious thinning from above. Thinning from above should never be done on a continuous basis, however (see chapter 8).

Although thinning normally results in increased thickness of growth rings, most literature indicates that thinning does not affect specific gravity or latewood percentage in annual rings, even when thinning is combined with pruning of green limbs and vegetation control (Andrulot and others 1972, Burton and Shoulders 1974, Choong and Chang 1974, Cregg and others 1988, Taylor and Burton 1982). However, heavy thinning may increase wood specific gravity for a short time (Smith 1968). Some other physical properties may be affected by thinning. For instance, trees that are thinned have earlywood tracheids that are narrower and latewood tracheids that are wider than those of trees in unthinned stands (Smith 1968). Trees having fewer than 1.6 rings/cm have structurally weaker wood than trees with more rings per cen-

Table 11-44—Cellulose production of a 21-year-old loblolly pine plantation on an old field in Georgia, having a site index above 24 m at base age 25, by thinning treatment

| Trees/ha remaining after thinning at age 11 | Stand volume after thinning at age 11 | Volume (m³/ha) | | | Volume at age 21 (m³/ha) | | |
| | | Removals* | | Total growth from age 11 to 21 | Total | Total less mortality | Total sawtimber† ≥20 cm in dbh |
		Thinning	Mortality				
247	65	156	2.8	128	351	348	44.8
494	118	118	3.1	165	405	402	56.0
741	154	75	12.8	178	420	407	58.8
1,586 (control)	217	0	37.0	186	440	403	71.4

Source: adapted from Xydias and others (1983).

* At age 11.

† Based on a conversion rate of 1 m³ of sawtimber = 176.57 fbm.

Table 11-45—Merchantable volume and number of trees in loblolly pine stands at age 35 following thinning from above and thinning from below

| Treatment | Merchantable volume (m³/ha) at age 35 | | No. of trees/ha |
	Pulpwood	Sawtimber*	
Site index 74†			
Thinned from above	163	36.0	813
Thinned from below	171	47.6	689
Site index 92†			
Thinned from above	211	131.2	497
Thinned from below	214	203.0	413

Source: adapted from Burton (1968).

* Based on a conversion rate of 1 m³ of sawtimber = 176.57 fbm.

† Base age 50.

timeter (for example, less stiffness, lower modulus of elasticity, and lower bending strength) that can greatly reduce the yield of high-grade veneer (MacPeak and others 1987).

Thinning plantations. At most stand densities, thinning reduces total cubic yield but results in larger and presumably more valuable crop trees. Clason (1989) determined that plantation growth and development are optimized when age and stocking density are related as follows:

Age (years)	Trees/ha
8 to 14	750 to 1,500
14 to 20	250 to 1,000
20 to 25	125 to 500
25 to 30	125 to 250

The effects of various kinds of thinnings on pulpwood yield are listed in table 11-46. A typical plantation thinning consists of selection removal of about 36% of the merchantable volume and 41% of the basal area from a previously unthinned stand having an average tree dbh of 20 cm. When stands are thinned to equal basal areas, selection thinning from below results in greater stand yields than does row thinning, and growth is on larger trees (Baldwin and others 1989). However, a combination of row and selection thinning can result in yields nearly as great as those resulting from selection thinning only (Grano 1971). Multiproduct yield tables for loblolly pine plantations thinned once by a combination of row and selection removal are available for initial planting densities of 1,327, 1,683, and 2,194 trees/ha on site indices of 17, 20, and 23 m at base age 25 years (Smith and Hafley 1984).

Thinning from below tends to remove trees of lower form class and to leave trees of higher form class. Removal of trees of lower form class can account for at least 8% of the increase in sawtimber volume associated with thinning from below (Shearin and others 1985). Nix and others (1987) found that trees 15, 30, and 45 cm in dbh had average form classes of 72, 81, and 78, respectively. Such differences are not a factor when thinning removes trees from all crown classes, as in row thinning. In one instance, the average form class of trees in row-thinned plots increased from 66 to 75 over a 10-year period that included three thinnings, whereas the average form class of trees in unthinned plots increased from

67 to 74 during the same period (Williston 1967b).

When stand density exceeds 1,975 trees/ha, row thinnings should remove every third row to keep many of the best trees and still increase growth significantly. Lighter cuttings do not stimulate growth on enough trees, whereas cutting every other row may leave an insufficient number of desirable crop trees in some spots. Cutting every fourth or fifth row in a dense, 17-year-old, loblolly pine plantation in Maryland produced no growth response through age 22. In contrast, cutting every third row increased average diameter growth of trees in each crown class by 0.5 to 0.8 cm, increased average crown ratio, and increased stand volume by 12% over no thinning (Little and Mohr 1963). Removing every fourth or fifth row normally provides sufficient growing space for most leave trees in 15- to 20-year-old stands stocked

Table 11-46—Effect of varying kinds and levels of thinning on long-term, cubic-meter yields of loblolly pine plantations

Source	Summary of treatments	Age (yr)		Final yields (m³/ha)	
		First thin	Final yield	Best	Worst
Selection thinning					
Louisiana middle Coastal Plain (Feduccia and Mosier 1977)	Multiple thinnings of single blocks 1.2- by 1.2-m, 1.8-m by 1.8-m, 2.4- by 2.4-m, 3.0- by 3.0-m spacings to varying basal areas (BA's) on an average site	20	45	409 when 2.4- by 2.4-m spacing maintained at BA 23 m²/ha	341 for 1.8- by 1.8-m spacing maintained at BA 20.5 m²/ha
South Carolina Piedmont (Goebel and others 1974)	Multiple thinnings of single permanent plots at 1.8- by 1.8-m, 1.8- by 2.1-m, and 1.8- by 2.4-m spacings, thinned to BA of 17 to 31 m²/ha	13	30–34	395 when 1.8- by 2.1-m spacing thinned to BA 23 m²/ha	294 when 1.8- by 2.4-m spacing thinned to BA 17 m²/ha
Loess hills of north Mississippi (Williston 1979)	Three thinnings of 1.8- by 1.8-m, spacings to BA 16 or 23 m²/ha on sites 24 or 27 m (base age 50)	17	37	435 when site 27 m thinned to BA 23 m²/ha	307 when site 24 m thinned to BA 16 m²/ha
Row thinning					
Eastern Maryland (Little and others 1968)	Four levels of row thinning (every other row to every fifth row with spacing probably 1.8- by 1.8-m)	17	27	234 when no thinning occurred	149 when every other row was removed
Combination thinning					
Upper Coastal Plain of southeastern Arkansas (Grano 1971)	1.8- by 1.8-m plantation with multiple-row thinnings followed by multiple selection thinnings to 22 m²/ha and single-row thinnings to 20.5 m²/ha are compared with multiple-pure selection thinnings to 22 and 20.5 m²/ha	14	29	454 when site selectively thinned to BA 22 m²/ha	408 when site selectively thinned to BA 20.5 m²/ha
Upper Coastal Plain of west Tennessee (Williston 1967b)	Row thinnings followed by multiple selection thinnings compared with selection thinning only on sites averaging 24 m (base age 50)	19	29	232 when site thinned to approx. BA 24 m²/ha	183 when site thinned to approx. BA 16 to 17 m²/ha
Accelerated sawlog production					
Southeastern Arkansas (Burton 1982)	Thinnings to crop tree only stands at ages 9 or 12 and multiple low thinnings to 20.5 m²/ha beginning at age 12	9–12	33	375 when thinned to BA 20.5 m²/ha	238 removing all but sawtimber at age 9
Upper Coastal Plain of northern Louisiana (Sprinz and others 1979)	Variously spaced plantations precommercially thinned at age 5 to 1,000 trees/ha, then selectively thinned to 250, 500, or 750 trees/ha at age 11	11	27	297 when thinned to 750 trees/ha*	204 when thinned to 250 trees/ha

* Unthinned stands 1.8- by 1.8-m, 1.8- by 2.4-m, 2.4- by 2.4-m, or 3.0- by 3.0-m all produced greater merchantable volumes than this amount.

with fewer than 1,480 trees/ha. Although row thinning does not improve the quality of the trees in a stand, it does not reduce tree quality if the site and remaining trees are not damaged.

Survival curves for thinned, oldfield, loblolly pine plantations in the Coastal Plain and Piedmont of Virginia are shown in figure 11-18. In the normal range of densities for managed stands, the survival curves are approximately linear.

Thinning even-aged natural stands. Long-term studies in natural stands of central Louisiana and southern Arkansas provide an overview of the effects of regular thinnings on stand yields through age 50. When several crown thinnings were applied between the ages of 17 and 43, sawtimber production at Urania, Louisiana, was 63,611 fbm/ha (International ¼-inch rule) at age 50. When thinning was delayed until at least age 35, saw-

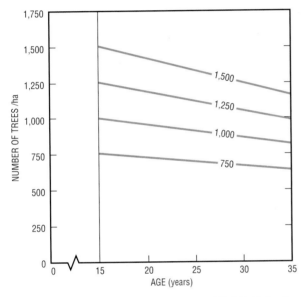

Figure 11-18—Survival curves for thinned oldfield loblolly pine plantations in the Coastal Plain and Piedmont of Virginia after thinning at age 15 to 750, 1,000, 1,250, and 1,500 trees/ha (adapted from Lemin and Burkhart 1983).

Table 11-47—Effect of intensity of thinning from below to various basal areas at 5-year intervals beginning at age 20 on pulpwood and sawtimber yields in natural loblolly–shortleaf pine stands in southern Arkansas

Stand age (yr)	Pulpwood (m³/ha)			Sawtimber (m³/ha)[†]		
	16 m²/ha	23 m²/ha	Increasing*	16 m²/ha	19.5 m²/ha	Increasing*
25	188	186	190	NM	NM	NM
30	244	251	255	69	88	84
35	323	343	344	198	203	209
40	396	420	426	288	292	305
45	449	467	486	367	342	395

Source: adapted from Burton (1980).

NM = Not measured.

* Thinning to basal area of 16 m²/ha at age 20, increasing to 17 m²/ha at age 25, to 18 m²/ha at age 30, to 19.5 m²/ha at age 35, to 21 m²/ha at age 40, and to 22 m²/ha at age 45.

† Based on a conversion rate of 1 m³ of sawtimber = 176.57 fbm.

timber yield was 55,845 fbm/ha at age 50, and stands that were not thinned yielded 42,476 fbm/ha. Unthinned plots also had net cubic-volume yields 20% less than plots that received crown thinning due to high mortality after age 35 (Andrulot and others 1972). Thinning natural loblolly–shortleaf stands every 5 years to different stocking levels produced different yields at Crossett, Arkansas (table 11-47). The greatest yields occurred when basal area was permitted to increase with age.

Individual-tree competition and self-thinning in dense natural stands are predictable processes and have been modeled so that long-term growth can be evaluated (Harms 1981, Lloyd and Harms 1986). Early release of potential crop trees in such stands is very important to healthy long-term growth and development. If crowded stands are left unthinned for a long time, crown lengths can eventually be reduced so much that overall stand response to thinning may be very limited. Also, release of young trees from hardwood competition promotes rapid growth. For example, releasing pine seedlings from all hardwoods 5 cm in dbh and larger, followed by selection harvesting of pines and hardwoods for 25 years, significantly increased pine pulpwood and sawlog volume at stand age 47. The benefit-to-cost ratio of the single release treatment was 1.5 to 1 (Cain 1988). To maximize production of high-quality sawlogs, the first thinning should be implemented no later than stand age 15 (Ruark and others 1991).

Pruning

Managed natural stands normally produce high-quality sawtimber, but it may be necessary to prune plantation loblolly pines artificially to obtain logs of equal quality (Guldin and Fitzpatrick 1991). Green-limb pruning to a height of 5.2 m yields 1 clear 4.9-m log from the most valuable part of the main stem. However, green-limb pruning can reduce tree diameter growth, and to a lesser extent height growth, for several years if a significant portion of the live crown is removed. Diameter growth is reduced as soon as live branches are removed. Reduced diameter growth may last for as long as 3 years (table 11-48). The smaller the tree is when pruned, the more severe is the detrimental effect of pruning on sub-

Table 11-48—Effect of pruning, at age 6, on average annual diameter and height growth of loblolly pine crop trees on a north Louisiana oldfield site

Treatment	7 yr	8 yr	9 yr	10 yr	11 yr
Average dbh growth (cm)					
Check	2.0	2.5	2.3	0.5	0.5
Pruned*	1.5	2.3	1.8	1.5	0.8
Average height growth (m)					
Check	1.2	1.4	1.5	1.1	1.1
Pruned*	1.0	1.3	1.5	1.3	0.8

Source: adapted from Foil and others (1964).

* Trees were pruned to half their total height or to a maximum of 2.4 m.

sequent growth. When open-grown loblolly pines 10- to 18-cm in diameter were pruned to 5.2 m in one operation, there was a 2.3-cm diameter growth loss during the next 14 years even though one-third of each tree was kept in green crown. Height growth was not affected (Brender 1961). If pruning is very severe, unpruned surrounding trees may grow faster than the pruned trees (Banks and Prevost 1976).

Two-step pruning is required for maximum formation of clear wood in butt sawlogs. Two-step pruning (to 2.4 m at age 6, then to 5.2 m at age 11) yielded about 4% more cubic-foot volume and 9% more sawn-wood volume, and trees had less taper than those pruned once at age 11 (Valenti and Cao 1986). Two-step pruning (ages 6 and 11) plus thinning to 250 or 500 trees/ha at age 11 produced 24 to 29% clear wood at age 29, whereas one-step pruning at age 11 and the same thinning regime produced 15 to 18% clear wood at age 29 (Clason and Stiff 1981). If thinning is heavy, pruning significantly improves stem form. When combined with light or very light thinning, pruning does not seem to improve stem form (Burton 1981).

Fertilization

Fertilizers often promote tree growth and alter stand structure (for example, diameter distribution and stem form) and mortality patterns (Allen and Duzan 1983, Gent and others 1986). The overall effectiveness of fertilization may be substantial and long-lasting, may last for only a short time, or may be of no value at all on some sites (even on infertile sites). Consequently, treatment must be selective and site specific (Fisher 1981, Moschler and others 1970, Shepard 1973, Torbert and Burger 1984) (see chapters 4 and 8). Trees with less than 25% of their height in live crowns tend to be unresponsive to fertilization even after thinning (Comerford and Mollitor 1982).

Fertilization in young stands.
Volume gains attributable to P fertilization of young stands can average 1.0 to 3.5 m³/ha/yr throughout a rotation (Allen and Ballard 1983, Comerford and Mollitor 1982, Fisher 1981, Fisher and Garbett 1980, Pritchett and Comerford 1982, Tiarks 1983; figure 11-19). Response may even continue into a second rotation. Phosphorus fertilization is critical for stand establishment on some wet Coastal Plain sites (figure 11-20). However, if soluble phosphates are used, a subsequent application may be needed at about tree age 10 to 15 on fine-

textured wet soils (Pritchett 1976, Pritchett and Gooding 1975, Wells and Allen 1985, Wells and Crutchfield 1969). Combining bedding with P fertilization on wet Coastal Plain sites results in greater cubic-volume increases and a higher net present value than either fertilization or bedding alone (Gent and others 1986, McKee and Wilhite 1986). On poorly drained clay soils in the lower Coastal Plain, application of N and P at planting time consistently increases growth more than does application of P alone. Growth responses to P fertilization on upper Coastal Plain and Piedmont sites are much smaller than the responses on lower Coastal Plain sites.

Nitrogen fertilization can also substantially increase the growth of young loblolly pines on a wide variety of sites (Baker and others 1974). Unlike the effects of P,

Figure 11-19—Seven-year-old loblolly pines growing on a bedded South Carolina coastal site. Trees were fertilized with 56 kg of phosphorus/ha at planting.

Figure 11-20—Eight-year-old loblolly pines that received 90 kg of phosphorus/ha in bands around each seedling at planting (background) and unfertilized trees (foreground).

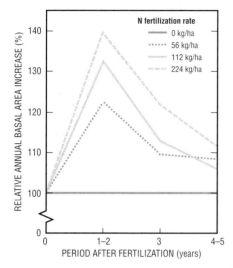

Figure 11-21—Average relative annual basal area increase of seven loblolly pine trials receiving application rates of 0, 56, 112, and 224 kg of nitrogen/ha (adapted from Ballard 1981).

Table 11-49—Effect of fertilization on growth of established southern pine stands by location and age

Location	At fertilization	At measurement	Unit of measurement*	Best fertilization treatment (kg/ha)	Best treatment	Control	% Increase over control
VA Piedmont	5	7	TCY	24–N + 3-P	NA	NA	28
SC Coastal Plain	7	9	TCY	112–N	29.0	27.7	5
VA Piedmont	1 & 4	10	TCY	296–P	6.9	6.0	15
SC Piedmont	7 & 9	12	ATV	269–K + 224–N	NA	NA	33
VA Piedmont	11	14	TCY	168–N	20.4	16.6	23
SC Piedmont	18	20	TCY	101–N	11.0	8.7	26
SC Coastal Plain	20	22	TCY	112–N	33.9	17.9	89
AR Coastal Plain	14–18	16–20	MCY	336–N + 84–P	15.0	10.9	38
AR Ouachita Mtns.	28–48	29–49	BA	168–N	NA	NA	6

The "Age (yr)" heading spans "At fertilization" and "At measurement". The "Annual increment after fertilization (m³/ha/yr)" heading spans "Best treatment" and "Control".

Source: adapted from Schultz (1975).

All stands are plantations, except the 20-year-old South Carolina Coastal Plain stand, which is naturally regenerated.

* TCY = total cubic yield; NA = data not available; ATV = average tree volume; MCY = merchantable cubic yield to a 10-cm top; BA = basal area.

annual gains from N fertilization peak during the first two growing seasons following fertilization and then gradually decline toward insignificance by the fifth growing season (Haines and Maxwell 1976, Moehring 1966, Zahner 1959; figure 11-21). Low levels of N fertilization sometimes increase tree growth almost as much as do high levels of fertilization. Trees do not respond to N fertilization on P-deficient sites unless P is also applied (Buford and McKee 1987).

Young loblolly pine stands are consistently more responsive to combinations of N and P than to any other fertilizer or combinations of fertilizers. It costs very little more to treat with N and P than to treat with P alone, and the combined treatment at planting time or within a few years of planting can increase growth substantially on severely P-deficient sites on the lower Coastal Plain (Sarigumba 1978). Bolstad and Allen (1987) found significant height and diameter responses to combined N and P fertilization 5 years after treating stands as young as 3 to 4 years old across the Piedmont and Coastal Plain. Overall, the best combination was 112 kg of N plus 56 kg of P per ha.

The addition of K occasionally increases growth (Haines and Maxwell 1976). Liming may increase or reduce tree growth depending on specific conditions (see chapter 8).

Fertilization response in established plantations. A second opportunity to fertilize loblolly pines occurs once trees have dominated a site—usually after about age 7. Established stands are usually most responsive to N or combinations of N and P. At least 75% of stands on most soils in the southeastern Coastal Plain show significant volume growth increases following applications of 112 to 168 kg of N and 56 kg of P per ha (Bolstad and Allen 1987, Comerford and Mollitor 1982). Phosphorus, applied alone, usually produces a small

Table 11-50—Average annual volume increase above no-fertilization levels for 5 years after fertilization of 15- to 25-year-old loblolly pine stands in the lower Coastal Plain, upper Coastal Plain, and Piedmont

Fertilization treatment (kg/ha)	Lower Coastal Plain (24 studies)	Upper Coastal Plain (28 studies)	Piedmont (49 studies)
112 N	2.1	2.7	3.5
56 P	1.8	0.5	0.9
112:56 N/P	3.9	3.2	3.3
112:56:56 N/P/K	3.5	3.7	4.1

The three data columns are spanned by the heading "Annual volume increase (m³/ha)".

Source: adapted from Wells and Allen (1985).

response or no growth response (Anonymous 1987, Gerig and others 1978). As with young stands, the greatest response to fertilization, especially N fertilization, occurs during the first few years after treatment (Allen and Ballard 1983, Buckley and Farmer 1974); however, some response may continue for an extended period. For example, fertilizing stands of pole-sized loblolly with N can result in gross volume increases of 14 to 56 m³ of wood/ha during the ensuing 4 to 5 years on very responsive sites (Ballard 1981, Wells and Allen 1985). Fertilization is more likely to increase the growth of large trees rather than of overtopped or intermediate ones, probably because the larger trees have larger root systems and absorbing surfaces (Ballard and others 1981).

Mid- to late-rotation (ages 15 to 25) fertilization is normally very cost effective because expenses can be recouped by harvesting within a few years after treatment. Volume response can vary greatly depending on site quality, initial stand density, and mortality following treatment, but gains greater than 2.8 m³/ha/yr are common (tables 11-49 and 11-50). Generally, N fertilization increases growth enough so that fertilization is economically advantageous if (1) site index is greater than 15 m (base age 25), (2) stocking is between 6.5 and 11.2 m² of basal area/ha,

(3) soil moisture does not limit growth, and (4) foliar N concentration is less than 1.2%. A growth model suggests that response increases with increasing basal area but decreases with increasing site index (Duzan and Allen 1981). If foliar P concentration is less than 0.12%, P should be applied with N (Allen and Ballard 1983, Duzan and others 1982). Prediction equations are available to estimate 5- to 8-year responses to N and P fertilization on Ultisols of the Coastal Plain and Piedmont from Maryland to Alabama (McNeil and others 1984).

Applications of sewage sludge can increase the growth of loblolly pines. However, sludge should not be applied until several years after planting because the treatment causes weeds to grow rapidly. Spreading liquid sewage sludge under 8-year-old planted loblolly on sandy Coastal Plain soils in South Carolina increased the dry weight of stemwood by 21% but did not alter the proportion of biomass in wood, bark, or foliage over a 4-year test period (Clark and Saucier 1988).

Fertilization has no long-term effect on form class (Jack and others 19880 and seems to have only a minor effect on wood quality. It does not change the percentage of latewood or change fiber length (Schmidtling 1973). Increased growth following fertilization may keep wood specific gravity from increasing for several years after treatment, but it usually does not decrease it (Clark and Schmidtling 1989). Heavy fertilization is likely to alter wood specific gravity more than moderate fertilization (Beckwith and Reines 1978, Zobel and others 1961). When the soil moisture level favored rapid growth and modest quantities of N (56 kg/ha) were applied in 6 consecutive years, the bending strength and stiffness of pole-sized loblolly pines in southern Illinois were increased (Hsu and Walters 1975). After N was applied at the rate of 179 kg/ha in an unthinned plantation in the North Carolina Piedmont, Girard form class increased significantly, and stocking decreased from 5,040 to 2,915 stems/ha between age 11 and age 23 (Pegg 1966).

Water Management

Tree growth and stand yields are greatly affected by the amount of available moisture and the timing of precipitation, especially growing season rainfall (Murphy and Farrar 1987). On many wet sites, surface drainage alone can alter conditions enough to permit adequate growth of loblolly pines (DeBell and others 1982). However, both primary and secondary drainage systems may be needed to increase tree growth substantially on excessively wet areas (table 11-51).

Table 11-51—Growth response of planted loblolly pines to wetland drainage

Study	Soils	Age* (yr)	Distance to canal	Basal area† (m²/ha) Drained	Basal area† (m²/ha) Undrained	% Increase over undrained
Miller and Maki (1957)	Bladen, very fine sandy loam	0–17	51.8 m	4.6	0.3	1,433
White and Pritchett (1970)	Leon fine sand	0–5	46.0 cm‡	7.6§	1.3§	485
			92.0 cm‡	4.9§	1.3§	277
Terry and Hughes (1975)	Bayboro-Bladen sandy loam	0–13	10.0 m	4.3	0.5	760

Mean annual growth spans the Basal area and % Increase over undrained columns.

Source: adapted from Terry and Hughes (1975).

* Ages from beginning of drainage to time of final measurement.
† Inside bark at a height of 1.3 m above ground.
‡ Water table constantly maintained at this depth below the ground surface.
§ Basal area measurements were probably taken outside bark.

Relationship of Fertilization and Water Control

The effects of fertilization and water control on growth are usually additive on wet, nutrient-deficient forest sites; however, application of one treatment may partially offset the need for the other treatment. Phosphorus fertilization can lessen the need for drainage under some conditions (Hook and others 1983, McKee and others 1984) but may be useless without water control on the Carolina pocosins. A combination of higher stocking levels and fertilization may increase growth and yield on wet areas (Langdon and Hatchell 1977, McKee and Wilhite 1986). Five-year height growth and diameter growth were 18 and 9% greater with combined fertilization and water control than with water control alone,

and were 69 and 78% greater than with fertilization alone (White and Pritchett 1970).

On an upland site in southeast Arkansas, supplemental fertilization and irrigation beginning at age 2 increased volume growth of the average tree, at age 8 by 23% and volume growth of dominant trees at age 8 by 154% (Moehring 1964). Hsu and Walters (1975) found that the growth of poles with superior bending strength and stiffness or pulpwood with higher fiber yield could be accelerated by maintaining soil moisture in the range of 30 to 60% and providing a moderate amount of nitrate fertilizer (56 kg /ha N) to young loblolly pines in southern Illinois.

Combining Cultural Treatments

Tree growth response can be excellent if beneficial cultural treatments are combined in appropriate ways (table 11-52 and figure 11-22). At age 5, trees in a south Louisiana loblolly pine plantation that received fertilization, irrigation, and insect and vegetation control treatments averaged 7.7 m in height and 11.7 cm in dbh. Trees that received no culture averaged only 4.6 m in height and 5.3 cm in dbh (Brewer and Linnartz 1971). On an intensively prepared site, a complete fertilizer treatment and total control of vegetation increased loblolly volume at age 5 from 11.8 m³/ha to 25.9 m³/ha. Herbaceous plant control was the most effective single treatment, increasing volume from 11.8 to 19.2 m³/ha (Tiarks and Haywood 1986).

Thinning and fertilization can interact to increase growth greatly under many conditions (table 11-53 and figure 11-23). Thinning from below removes the weaker, slower growing trees. Fertilization then stimulates growth, especially diameter growth, of the remaining trees (Allen and Ballard 1983, Jones and Broerman 1977). The adverse effect of thinning on total growing stock is partially offset by N fertilization because stands thinned from below respond more to fertilization than do unthinned stands (Ballard and others 1981).

Response to intensive culture can continue for an entire rotation. Intensive site preparation, plus early fertilization and cultivation, greatly increased survival, diameter growth, and height growth of loblolly pines for 25 years on a relatively unproductive Coastal Plain site in south Mississippi. Loblolly was more responsive to culture than either slash or longleaf pine. At age 25, loblolly trees that were cultivated and heavily fertilized averaged 8 m taller and 9.8 cm greater in diameter than uncultivated unfertilized controls (Smith and Schmidtling 1970; table 11-54 and figure 11-24).

Table 11-52—Combinations of cultural treatments improve growth of loblolly pines

Source	Locations	Age at treatment (yr)	Best treatment	Total cubic volume increase over control percent	Total cubic volume increase over control m³/ha	Period of growth (yr)
Tiarks and Haywood (1986)	Louisiana	0	Fertilization and vegetation control	119	14.1	5
Unpublished industry data	Georgia	0	Cultivation, fertilization, and insect control	180	NA	8
Haywood and Tiarks (1990)	Louisiana	0	Fertilization and vegetation control	35	55.2	11
White and Pritchett (1970)	Florida	0	Fertilization and water regulation	680	31.7	5
Moehring (1964)	Arkansas	2	Fertilization and irrigation	150	67.2	8
Schmidtling (1973)	Mississippi	0	Cultivation for 3 years and fertilization	636	99.0	9
Bittle and Holt (1972)	Arkansas	0	Chemical vegetation and insect control	214	NA	10
Unpublished industry data	Florida	0	Chopping and chemical insect control	860	NA	10

Source: adapted from Schultz (1975).

NA = data not available

Table 11-53—Four-year volume and diameter growth response of 12 loblolly pine stands following fertilization with 168 kg of N/ha with or without thinning

	Fertilizer response T	Fertilizer response NT	Difference T–NT	Range of difference
Net volume (m³/ha)	12.9	8.7	+4.2	−21.7 to +27.6
Sawlog volume (m³/ha)	9.2	5.6	+3.6	−10.2 to +16.8
Average diameter (cm)	0.48	0.25	+0.23	−0.23 to +0.53

Source: adapted from Allen and Ballard (1983).

T = thinned, NT = nonthinned; 1 m³ = 176.57 fbm.

Figure 11-22—Fourteen-year-old loblolly pines fertilized with 4,480 kg/ha of 10-5-5 fertilizer at planting, disked between rows at ages 1, 2, and 3, and then mowed at ages 4 and 5 (*left*) versus no cultural treatments after planting (*right*).

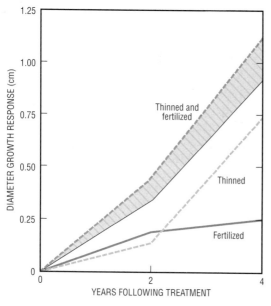

Figure 11-23—Average diameter growth response for 12 loblolly pine stands after fertilization with 168 kg nitrogen/ha and/or varying intensities of thinning. The shaded area represents the gain in measured response for fertilization and thinning in combination as compared to the sum of the single effects of the two treatments (adapted from Allen and Ballard 1983).

Table 11-54—Average tree height and diameter at breast height at 25 years for longleaf, loblolly, and slash pines under five different cultural treatments

Pine species	C	F-0	F-1	F-2	F-4
Height (m)					
Longleaf	15.8	14.2	17.7 a	18.3 a	18.1
Loblolly	12.5	13.0	17.9 a	18.6 a	20.5
Slash	17.6	15.7	18.0 a	18.9 a	18.3
Dbh (cm)					
Longleaf	17.8	15.4 a	20.4 a	22.0 a	21.8
Loblolly	15.4	15.9 a	22.4 a	23.6 a	25.2
Slash	16.3	17.6 a	21.2 a	22.4 a	22.9

Source: adapted from Schmidtling (1987).

Height or dbh values within a column followed by the same letter are not significantly different at the 95% probability level.

C = control, no cultivation or fertilizer;

F-0 = cultivation, but no fertilizer;

F-1 = cultivation and a single application of 112 kg N, 24 kg P, and 47 kg K per ha;

F-2 = cultivation and a single application of 224 kg N, 47 kg P, and 94 kg K per ha; and

F-4 = cultivation and a single application of 448 kg N, 95 kg P, and 187 kg K per ha.

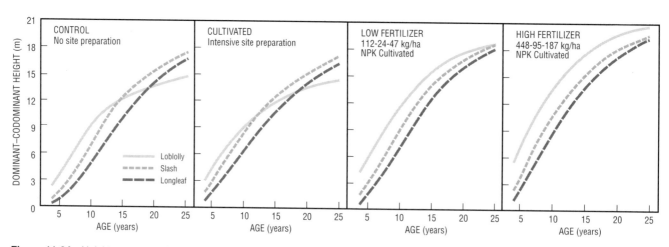

Figure 11-24—Height over age relationships, for a 25-year period, between loblolly, slash, and longleaf pines growing in southern Mississippi (adapted from Schmidtling 1987).

Yields of Oleoresin and Other Extractives

Naval stores are produced from loblolly and other southern pines as byproducts in the sulfate pulping process. If treated with chemicals such as paraquat, diquat, or ethephon while growing, loblolly pines can be stimulated to produce increased amounts of turpentine and resin acids, which are stored in xylem tissue. The resin-soaked wood, which is called lightwood, yields increased valuable quantities of extractives when pulped. Paraquat stimulation can increase the turpentine content and the resin acid content in the wood of loblolly pine trees 13 cm in dbh and larger by an average of 160 and 100%, respectively, within 9 months of treatment (Drew and Roberts 1978; table 11-55). Because oleoresin production is stimulated for at least 12 to 15 months following treatment (Conley and oth-

ers 1977, Drew and Roberts 1977, Holton 1978), at least 15 months' development time should be allowed to maximize profits (Krumbein 1978). A second treatment does not increase resin yield.

Simple tools such as basal injectors, axes, drills, or bark hacks can be used to wound the lower boles of trees to stimulate resin production. Stubbs and others (1984) concluded that the most cost-effective treatment is to apply 2% paraquat with a tree injector at 13-cm intervals around the bole of a tree either in the spring or fall. A good alternative is to remove a strip of bark from around one-third the circumference of a tree and apply 5% paraquat to the stripped surface. This can be done at any time of the year. A 10% ethephon solution can be added to the paraquat to further increase yields if treatment takes place during the fall and winter. Some treatment-associated mortality can be expected. South of middle Georgia, an insecticide spray must be applied during or shortly after stem treatment to prevent bark beetle buildup.

Although most resin soaking occurs near the wound, some increase has been found as far as 8.2 m up the stem (Roberts and Peters 1977). Resin soaking occurs higher in the stems of trees treated with 8% paraquat than it occurs in the stems of trees treated with lower concentrations. However, paraquat is a highly toxic substance, and high concentrations are more likely to slow tree growth, increase cambial necrosis, and reduce resin soaking near the application point. Paraquat treatments have reduced volume growth of pole-sized loblolly pines by 20 to 30% over the first year, but height and branch extension do not seem to be affected (Clason 1978, Nix 1979). Nevertheless, paraquat concentrations as high as 24% should cause only slight tree mortality (Drew and Roberts 1977). If paraquat could be introduced into trees in a quickly mobile form, it would probably be much more effective in distributing resin soaking (Nix 1976). Adding the fungicide benomyl along with paraquat has been shown to reduce diameter growth loss caused by

Table 11-55—Oleoresin content of paraquat-treated, pulpwood-sized loblolly pines growing in the South Carolina Piedmont at 0 to 2.4 m above wound

% Paraquat	Method of wounding	Oleoresin content above wound (%)		
		0 m	1.2 m	2.4 m
0	Control*	3.1 e	3.0 c	2.7 c
2	Axe—frill	16.3 ab	8.3 a	4.5 a
2	Bark—face	17.4 a	7.6 a	5.0 a
2	Axe—twice	19.4 a	7.8 a	3.5 b
2	Bark—twice	15.0 b	6.3 a	3.3 b
8	Axe—frill	12.3 c	7.3 a	4.1 ab
8	Bark—face	10.4 c	6.4 a	3.9 b
8	Axe—twice	6.6 d	4.9 b	2.4 c
8	Bark—twice	9.0 c	7.5 a	3.6 b

Source: adapted from Nix (1977).

Values within a column followed by the same letter are not significantly different at the 95% probability level.
* Control means are pooled for all methods of wounding.

paraquat, significantly increase the quantity of extractives produced, and reduce the adverse effects of blue stain infection (Clason 1987).

Summary

Stand density, site quality, competing vegetation, and tree improvement can have significant effects on loblolly pine tree growth and stand yield. Stocking levels that maximize profits are much lower than levels that maximize physical production. Where integrated products are grown on average sites (site index 25 m, base age 50), maximum merchantable yield can be obtained by establishing 1,700 to 2,200 trees/ha and then keeping basal area between 20 and 23 m^2/ha. Removal of both herbaceous and woody vegetation at or shortly before planting and then keeping trees free of competition normally results in the most rapid growth of young trees.

Precommercial thinnings have proven valuable in the management of dense natural stands but should not be necessary in plantations where initial spacing is 1.8 by 1.8 m or greater. Commercial thinning before age 25 may reduce total yield somewhat but increases average tree diameter and product value. To maximize the amount of high-quality sawtimber in crop trees, make the first thinning at about stand age 15—the age when trees no longer produce juvenile wood. After about age 20, well-managed stands can produce 5.6 to 7.0 m^3 of high-quality sawtimber/ha/yr for many years. By age 30 years, total yields can range from 290 to 380 m^3/ha/yr and merchantable yields from about 250 to 330 m^3/ha/yr—much of which will be sawtimber. Yield tables for both planted and natural stands are available for many sites and stand densities. Natural regeneration of stands is financially competitive with clearcutting and planting.

Phosphorus fertilization can greatly increase seedling growth on wet Coastal Plain sites. Nitrogen fertilization alone or together with P fertilization can increase the growth of loblolly pines from seedling stage to maturity on many soils throughout the South. Application of as little as 56 kg/ha P, or 56 kg/ha P and 40 kg/ha N, may result in optimum growth of newly established trees. Increases in tree volume of 5 to 89% for at least 3 to 5 years can occur when 56 to 168 kg/ha N are applied to pole-sized loblolly stands on clay soils.

First-generation tree improvement can increase volumes by 2 to 7% and can increase stand value at rotation age by 18% or more depending on site quality. Increases from future generations may be even higher.

Maintaining moist but not wet conditions promotes increased tree growth. Bedding, or drainage, or both are necessary for fastest growth on wet sites.

Sophisticated computer simulation systems that make use of current research information can accurately project the effects of some genetic, environmental, and cultural treatments on product yields.

Research Needs

There is an expanding need for both plantation and natural stand growth and yield information that:

■ Improves the accuracy of predicting potential gains from tree improvement opportunities.

■ Matches genotypes with sites to maximize genetic gains.

■ Accurately incorporates environmental conditions (for example, droughts, extremely wet conditions, and site nutrient status) during the growing season into growth models and yield tables.

■ Accurately projects the effects of cultural treatments such as site preparation, repeated thinning, fertilization, competition control, and combinations of intensive culture on genetically improved plantings.

■ Accurately predicts the effects of intensive pine plantation silviculture on long-term forest site productivity.

■ Accurately predicts the effects of cultural treatments on wood quality.

■ Quantifies the effects of insect and disease pests on plantation and natural stand yields.

Although some whole-stand equations are available for natural stands of pure loblolly pine and for stands where loblolly is mixed with shortleaf pine or with hardwoods, there is relatively little information on size-class distributions or responses to alternative cultural treatments. The most critical needs for natural stands include:

■ Flexible models that predict size-class distributions over a range of sites.

■ Models that predict species responses to alternative thinning regimes over an array of sites and stand densities.

■ Quantification of response to cultural practices, such as control of competing vegetation or fertilization.

Other areas where basic research could make substantial improvements in future forest management technology include:

■ Accurate quantification of short-term, or even daily, growth rates using sophisticated estimates of growth processes (for example, photosynthesis and respiration) obtained from high-resolution satellite imagery (Tucker and others 1986).

■ Quantification of tree improvement opportunities in natural stand management (for example, seed tree pollination, direct seeding, and thinning based on outstanding physical and chemical characteristics of trees).

Literature Cited

Alig RJ, Mills TJ, Shackelford RL. 1980. Most soil bank plantings in the South have been retained, some need follow-up treatments. Southern Journal of Applied Forestry 4(1):60–64.

Allen HL, Ballard R. 1983. Forest fertilization of loblolly pine. In: Proceedings, Symposium on the Loblolly Pine Ecosystem—East Region; 1982 December 8–10; Raleigh, NC. Raleigh, NC: North Carolina State University, School of Forest Resources: 163–181.

Allen HL, Duzan HW Jr. 1981. What measure of stand density is best for growth predictions in loblolly pine plantations. In: Proceedings, 1st Biennial Southern Silvicultural Research Conference; 1980 November 6–7; Atlanta, GA. Gen. Tech. Rep. SO-34. New Orleans: USDA Forest Service, Southern Forest Experiment Station: 175–178.

Allen HL, Duzan HW Jr. 1983. Nutritional management of loblolly pine stands: a status report of the North Carolina State forest fertilization cooperative. Gen. Tech. Rep. 163. Portland, OR: USDA Forest Service, Pacific Northwest Forest and Range Experiment Station: 379–384.

Amateis RL, Burkhart HE. 1985. Site index curves for loblolly pine plantations on cutover site-prepared lands. Southern Journal of Applied Forestry 9(3):166–169.

Amateis RL, Burkhart HE. 1987a. Cubic-foot volume equations for loblolly pine trees in cutover, site-prepared plantations. Southern Journal of Applied Forestry 11(4):190–192.

Amateis RL, Burkhart HE. 1987b. Tree volume and taper of loblolly pine varies by stand origin. Southern Journal of Applied Forestry 11(4):185–189.

Amateis RL, Burkhart HE, Burk TE. 1986. A ratio approach to predicting merchantable yields of unthinned loblolly pine plantations. Forest Science 32(2):287–296.

Amateis RL, Burkhart HE, Knoebel BR, Sprinz PT. 1984. Yields and size class distributions for unthinned loblolly pine plantations on cutover site-prepared lands. Publ. FWS-2-84. Blacksburg, VA: Virginia Polytechnic Institute and State University, School of Forestry and Wildlife Resources. 69 p.

Anderson JD. 1981. Changes in site quality on seriously eroded old-field sites with loblolly pine plantations in the Piedmont of South Carolina. Clemson, SC: Clemson University. 48 p. Ph.D. dissertation.

Andrulot EA, Williston HL. 1974. Growth and yield of second-growth loblolly in central Louisiana. In: Proceedings, Symposium on Management of Young pines; 1974 October 22–24; Alexandria, LA/December 3–5; Charleston, SC. Asheville, NC: USDA Forest Service, Southeastern Forest Experiment Station: 116–120.

Andrulot ER, Blackwell LP, Burns PY. 1972. Effects of thinning on yield of loblolly pine in central Louisiana. Bull. 6. Ruston, LA: Louisiana Tech University, College of Life Sciences. 145 p.

Anonymous 1987. Developing the technology to better manage the nutritional resources of loblolly pine stands. 16th Ann. Rep. Raleigh, NC: North Carolina State University, School of Forest Resources, North Carolina State Forest Nutrition Cooperative. 35 p.

Arbour SJ, Ezell AW. 1981. Effect of mechanical site preparation treatments on height growth of loblolly pine in east Texas sandy soils. In: Proceedings, 1st Biennial Southern Silvicultural Research Conference; 1980 November 6–7; Atlanta, GA. Gen. Tech. Rep. SO-34. New Orleans: USDA Forest Service, Southern Forest Experiment Station: 96–99.

Arnold LE. 1981. Gross yields of rough wood products from 31-year-old loblolly and shortleaf pine spacing study. For. Res. Rep. 81-1. Champaign–Urbana, IL: University of Illinois, Agricultural Experiment Station, 4 p.

Arthaud GJ, Klemperer WD. 1986. An economic approach to thinning in loblolly pine plantations. In: Forest economics gumbo New Orleans style: Proceedings, 1986 Southern Forest Economics Workshop; 1986 April 16–18; New Orleans, LA. Raleigh, NC: North Carolina State University: 93–100.

Ayers GD, Clason TR, Smith WD. 1987. Impact of intensive competition management. In: Proceedings, 4th Biennial Southern Silvicultural Research Conference; 1986 November 4–6; Atlanta, GA. Gen. Tech. Rep. SE-42. Asheville, NC: USDA Forest Service, Southeastern Forest Experiment Station: 576–580.

Bacon CG, Zedaker SM. 1987. Third-year growth response of loblolly pine to eight levels of competition control. Southern Journal of Applied Forestry 11(2):91–95.

Bailey RL. 1986. Rotation age and establishment density for planted slash pine (Pinus elliottii) and loblolly pine (Pinus taeda). Southern Journal of Applied Forestry 10(3):162–168.

Bailey RL, Clutter JL. 1970. Volume tables for old-field loblolly pine plantations in the Georgia Piedmont. Rep. 22. Macon, GA: Georgia Forest Research Council. 4 p.

Bailey RL, Ware KD. 1983. Compatible basal-area growth and yield model for thinned and unthinned stands. Journal of Forest Research 13(4):563–571.

Bailey RL, Grider GE, Rheney JW, Pienaar LV. 1985. Stand structure and yields for site-prepared loblolly pine plantations in the Piedmont and upper Coastal Plain of Alabama, Georgia, and South Carolina. Res. Bull. 328. Athens, GA: University of Georgia, College of Agriculture. 118 p.

Baker JB. 1987. Production and financial comparisons of uneven-aged and even-aged management of loblolly pine. In: Proceedings, 4th Biennial Southern Silvicultural Research Conference; 1986 November 4–6; Atlanta, GA. Gen. Tech. Rep. SE-42. Asheville, NC: USDA Forest Service, Southeastern Forest Experiment Station: 267–274.

Baker JB, Murphy PA. 1982. Growth and yield following four reproduction cutting methods in loblolly–shortleaf pine stands: a case study. Southern Journal of Applied Forestry 6(2):66–67.

Baker JB, Switzer GL, Nelson LE. 1974. Biomass production and nitrogen recovery after fertilization of young loblolly pines. Soil Science Society of America Proceedings 38(6):958–961.

Baldwin VC Jr. 1982. A procedure to obtain even-aged forest stand structure and volume predictions using aerial photographic information. In: Proceedings, In-place Resource Inventories: Principles and Practices National Workshop; 1981 August 9–14; Orono, ME. Orono, ME: University of Maine: 308–314.

Baldwin VC Jr. 1986. A summary of equations for predicting biomass of planted southern pines. In: Estimating tree biomass regressions and their error: Proceedings, Workshop on Tree Biomass Regression Functions and Their Contribution to the Error of Forest Inventory Estimates; 1986 May 26–30; Syracuse, NY. Gen. Tech. Rep. NE-117. New Orleans: USDA Forest Service, Southern Forest Experiment Station: 157–171.

Baldwin VC Jr. 1987. Green and dry-weight equations for above-ground components of planted loblolly pine trees in the West Gulf Region. Southern Journal of Applied Forestry 11(4):212–218.

Baldwin VC Jr. 1989. Is sapwood area a better predictor of loblolly pine crown biomass than bole diameter? Biomass 20:177–185.

Baldwin VC Jr, Feduccia DP. 1987. Loblolly pine growth and yield prediction for managed West Gulf plantations. Res. Pap. SO-236. New Orleans: USDA Forest Service, Southern Forest Experiment Station. 27 p.

Baldwin VC Jr, Feduccia DP. 1991. Compatible tree-volume and upper stem diameter equations for loblolly pines in the West Gulf region. Southern Journal of Applied Forestry 15(2):92–97.

Baldwin VC Jr., Feduccia DP, Haywood JD. 1989. Postthinning growth and yield of row-thinned and selectively thinned loblolly and slash pine plantations. Canadian Journal of Forest Resources 19(2):247–256.

Ballard R. 1981. Nitrogen fertilization of established loblolly pine stands: a flexible silvicultural technique. In: Proceedings, 1st Biennial Southern Silvicultural Research Conference; 1980 November 6–7; Atlanta, GA. Gen. Tech. Rep. SO-34. New Orleans: USDA Forest Service, Southern Forest Experiment Station: 223–229.

Ballard R, Duzan HW, Kane MB. 1981. Thinning and fertilization of loblolly pine plantations. In: Proceedings, 1st Biennial Southern Silvicultural Research Conference; 1980 November 6–7; Atlanta, GA. Gen. Tech. Rep. SO-34. New Orleans: USDA Forest Service, Southern Forest Experiment Station: 100–104.

Balmer WE, Owens EG, Jorgenson JR. 1975. Effects of various species on loblolly pine growth 15 years after planting. Res. Note SE-211. Asheville, NC: USDA Forest Service, Southeastern Forest Experiment Station. 7 p.

Balmer WE, Williston HL. 1973. The need for precommercial thinning. For. Mgmt. Bull. (July). Atlanta: USDA Forest Service, State and Private Forestry. 6 p.

Banks PF, Prevost MJ. 1976. Sawlog pruning regimes for Pinus patula, P. elliottii and P. taeda in Rhodesia. Southern African Forestry Journal 99:44–48

Barber JC, VanHaverbeke DF. 1961. Growth of outstanding nursery of seedlings of Pinus elliottii Engelm. and Pinus taeda L. Station Pap. 126. Asheville, NC: USDA Forest Service, Southeastern Forest Experiment Station. 12 p.

Bassett JR. 1966. Thinning loblolly pine from above and below. Res. Note SO-44. New Orleans: USDA Forest Service, Southern Forest Experiment Station. 3 p.

Beckwith JR III, Reines M. 1978. Fertilization increases volume and weight of planted loblolly pine. Southern Journal of Applied Forestry 2(4):118–120.

Beers BL, Bailey RL. 1985. Yields, stand structure and economic conclusions. Georgia For. Res. Pap. 55. Macon, GA: Georgia Forestry Commission. 7 p.

Beers TW. 1962. Components of forest growth. Journal of Forestry 60(4):245–248.

Belanger RP, Brender EV. 1968. Influence of site index and thinning on the growth of planted loblolly pine. Georgia Forest Res. Pap. 57. Macon, GA: Georgia Forest Research Council. 7 p.

Bolstad PV, Allen HL. 1987. Height and diameter growth response in loblolly pine stands following fertilization. Forest Science 33(3):644–653.

Borders BE, Souter BA, Ware KD. 1987. Percentile-based distributions characterize forest stand tables. Society of American Foresters 33(2):570–576.

Bower DR. 1965. Precommercial thinnings accelerate diameter growth of loblolly pine. Journal of Forestry 63(3):210.

Box BH. 1968. A study of root extension and biomass in a six-year-old loblolly pine plantation in southeast Louisiana. Dissertation Abstracts 28(9):3545–3546.

Branan JR, Porterfield EJ. 1971. A comparison of six species of southern pines planted in the Piedmont of South Carolina. Res. Note SE-171. Asheville, NC: USDA Forest Service, Southeastern Forest Experiment Station. 3 p.

Brender EV. 1961. Pruning open-grown loblolly pine. Southern Lumberman 203(2357):134–136.

Brender EV. 1965. A guide to loblolly and slash pine plantation management in southeastern USA. Rep. 14. Macon, GA: Georgia Forest Research Council: 39–46.

Brender EV. 1973. Silviculture of loblolly pine in the Georgia Piedmont. Rep. 33. Macon, GA: Georgia Forest Research Council. 74 p.

Brender EV. 1986. Relationship of total height and merchantable height to d.b.h. and site index in natural even-aged stands of loblolly pine in the lower Piedmont. Southern Journal of Applied Forestry 10(1):4–6.

Brender EV, Clutter JL. 1970. Yield of even-aged, natural stands of loblolly pine. Rep. 23. Macon, GA: Georgia Forest Research Council. 7 p.

Brewer CW, Linnartz NE. 1971. Results of eight years of intensive cultural management of loblolly pine in southeast Louisiana. Note 95. Baton Rouge, LA: Louisiana State University and A&M College, School of Forestry and Wildlife Management, Agricultural Experiment Station. 4 p.

Brewer JA, Burns PY, Cao QV. 1985. Short-term projection accuracy of five asymptotic height-age curves for loblolly pine. Forest Science 31(2):414–418.

Brightwell CS. 1971. Comparative performance of slash and loblolly pine. Woodlands Res. Note 25. Savannah, GA: Union Camp Corporation, Woodlands Research Department. 3 p.

Buckley WB, Farmer RE Jr. 1974. Fertilization of Tennessee Valley pines and hardwoods: response during the second 5 years after application. Tree Planters' Notes 25(4):14–15.

Buckner E, Evans R, Mullins J, Thor E. 1987. Converting "the Barrens" from low-quality hardwoods to high-yielding loblolly pine plantations. In: Proceedings, 4th Biennial Southern Silvicultural Research Conference; 1986 November 4–6; Atlanta, GA. Gen. Tech. Rep. SE-42. Asheville, NC: USDA Forest Service, Southeastern Forest Experiment Station: 50–52.

Buford MA. 1986. Height-diameter relationships at age 15 in loblolly pine seed sources. Forest Science 32(3):812–818.

Buford MA, Burkhart HE. 1987. Genetic improvement effects on growth and yield of loblolly pine plantations. Forest Science 33(3):707–724.

Buford MA, McKee WH Jr. 1987. Effects of site preparation, fertilization and genotype on loblolly pine growth and stand structure: results at age 15. In: Proceedings, 4th Biennial Southern Silvicultural Research Conference; 1986 November 4–6; Atlanta, GA. Gen. Tech. Rep. SE-42. Asheville, NC: USDA Forest Service, Southeastern Forest Experiment Station: 378–383.

Burger JA, Kluender RA. 1983. Site preparation—Piedmont. In: Proceedings, Symposium on the Loblolly Pine Ecosystem—East Region; 1982 December 8–10; Raleigh, NC. Raleigh, NC: North Carolina State University, School of Forest Reseources: 58–74.

Burk TE, Burkhart HE. 1984. Diameter distributions and yields of natural stands of loblolly pine. Publ. FWS-1-84. Blacksburg, VA: Virginia Polytechnic Institute and State University, School of Forestry and Wildlife Resources. 46 p.

Burkhart HE. 1983. Growth and yield of loblolly pine. In: Proceedings, Symposium on the Loblolly Pine Ecosystem—East Region; 1982 December 8–10; Raleigh, NC. Raleigh, NC: North Carolina State University, School of Forest Resources: 205–221.

Burkhart HE, Clutter JL. 1971. Green and dry weight yields for old-field loblolly pine plantations in the Georgia Piedmont. Rep. 2, Ser. 4. Macon, GA: Georgia Forest Research Council. 11 p.

Burkhart HE, Sprinz PT. 1984a. A model for assessing hardwood competition effects on yields of loblolly pine plantations. Publ. FWS-3-84. Blacksburg, VA: Virginia Polytechnic Institute and

State University, School of Forestry and Wildlife Resources. 55 p.

Burkhart HE, Sprinz PT. 1984b. Compatible cubic volume and basal area projection equations for thinned old-field loblolly pine plantations. Forest Science 30(1):86–93.

Burkhart HE, Strub MR. 1974. A model for simulation of planted loblolly pine stands. In: Fries J, ed. Growth models for tree and stand simulation: Proceedings, 1973 IUFRO Meetings, Working Party S4.01-4. Stockholm: Royal College of Forestry: 128–135.

Burkhart HE, Cao QV, Ware KD. 1981. A comparison of growth and yield prediction models for loblolly pine. Publ. FWS-2-81. Blacksburg, VA: Virginia Polytechnic Institute and State University, School of Forestry and Wildlife Resources. 59 p.

Burkhart HE, Cloeren DC, Amateis RL. 1985. Yield relationship in unthinned loblolly pine plantations on cutover, site-prepared lands. Southern Journal of Applied Forestry 9(2):84–91.

Burkhart HE, Farrar KD, Amateis RL, Daniels RF. 1987. Simulation of individual tree growth and stand development in loblolly pine plantation on cutover, site-prepared areas, 1987. Publ. FWS-1-87. Blacksburg, VA: Virginia Polytechnic Institute and State University, School of Forestry and Wildlife Resources. 47 p.

Burkhart HE, Glover GR, Sprinz PT. 1987. Loblolly pine growth and yield response to vegetation management. In: Walstad JD, Kuch PJ, eds. Forest vegetation management for conifer production. New York: Wiley: 243–271.

Burkhart HE, Parker RC, Oderwald RG. 1972a. Yields for natural stands of loblolly pine. Publ. FWS-2-72. Blacksburg, VA: Virginia Polytechnic Institute and State University, School of Forestry and Wildlife Resources. 63 p.

Burkhart HE, Parker RC, Strub MR, Oderwald RG. 1972b. Yields of old-field loblolly pine plantations. Publ. FWS-3-72. Blacksburg, VA: Virginia Polytechnic Institute and State University, School of Forestry and Wildlife Resources. 51 p.

Burton JD. 1968. Thinning from above and below in loblolly pine. Southern Lumberman 217(2704):185–186.

Burton JD. 1980. Growth and yield in managed natural stands of loblolly and shortleaf pine in the West Gulf Coastal Plain. Res. Pap. SO-159. New Orleans: USDA Forest Service, Southern Forest Experiment Station. 23 p.

Burton JD. 1981. Some short-term effects of thinning and pruning in young loblolly pine plantations. In: Proceedings, 1st Biennial Southern Silvicultural Research Conference; 1980 November 6–7; Atlanta, GA. Gen. Tech. Rep. SO-34. New Orleans: USDA Forest Service, Southern Forest Experiment Station: 111–114.

Burton JD. 1982. Sawtimber by prescription—the sudden sawlog story through age 33. Res. Paper SO-179. New Orleans: USDA Forest Service, Southern Forest Experiment Station. 9 p.

Burton JD, Shoulders E. 1974. Fast-grown, dense loblolly pine sawlogs: a reality. Journal of Forestry 72(10):637–641.

Burton JD, Shoulders E. 1983. Crown size and stand density determine periodic growth in loblolly pine plantations. In: Proceedings, 2d Biennial Southern Silvicultural Research Conference; 1982 November 4–5; Atlanta, GA. Gen. Tech. Rep. SE-24. Asheville, NC: USDA Forest Service, Southeastern Forest Experiment Station: 283–287.

Busby RL, Ward KB, Baldwin VC Jr. 1990. COMPUTE–MECHLOB: a growth and yield prediction system with a merchandising optimizer for planted loblolly pine in the west gulf region. Res. Pap. SO-255. New Orleans: USDA Forest Service, Southern Forest Experiment Station. 22 p.

Byrne JC, Reed DD. 1986. Complex compatible taper and volume estimation systems for red and loblolly pine. Forest Science 32(2):423–443.

Cain MD. 1978. Planted loblolly and slash pine response to bedding and flat disking on a poorly drained site -and update. Res. Pap. SO-237. New Orelans: USDA Forest Service, Southern Forest Experiment Station. 6 p.

Cain MD. 1988. A low-cost technique for increasing pine volume production in mixed pine–hardwood stands. Res. Pap. SO-246.

New Orelans: USDA Forest Service, Southern Forest Experiment Station. 9 p.

Cain MD. 1990. Precommercial thinning and management of natural loblolly pine stands for rapid sawlog production. Unpublished progress reprot summary. FS-SO-4106-5, Problem 2. [On file with USDA Forest Service, Southern Forest Experiment Station, Monticello, AR.]

Cain MD. 1991. The influence of woody and herbaceous competition on early growth of naturally regenerated loblolly and shortleaf pines. Southern Journal of Applied Forestry 15(4):179–185.

Campbell TE. 1975. Yields of direct-seeded loblolly pine at age 22 years. Res. Note SO-199. New Orleans: USDA Forest Service, Southern Forest Experiment Station. 3 p.

Campbell TE. 1976. The nation's oldest industrial direct seeding. Forest and People 3rd Quarter: 22–24.

Campbell TE. 1985. Development of direct-seeded and planted loblolly and slash pines through age 20. Southern Journal of Applied Forestry 9(4):205–211.

Campbell TE, Mann WF Jr. 1974. Growth in a loblolly pine spacing study in southwest Louisiana. In: Proceeding, Symposium on Management of Young Pines; 1974 October 22–24; Alexandria, LA/December 3–5; Charleston, SC. Asheville, NC: USDA Forest Service, Southeastern Forest Experiment Station: 108–115.

Cao QV, Burkhart HE, Max TA. 1980. Evaluation of two methods for cubic-volume prediction of loblolly pine to any merchantable limit. Forest Science 26(1):71–80.

Cao QV, Pepper WD. 1986. Predicting inside bark diameter for shortleaf, loblolly, and longleaf pines. Southern Journal of Applied Forestry 10:220–223.

Cao QV, Burkhart HE, Lemin RC Jr. 1982. Diameter distributions and yields of thinned loblolly pine plantations. Publ. FWS-1-82. Blacksburg, VA: Virginia Polytechnic Institute and University, School of Forestry and Wildlife Resources. 62 p.

Carmean WH. 1972. Site index curves for upland oaks in the central states. Forest Science 18(2):109–120.

Carmean WH, Hahn JT, Jacobs RD. 1989. Site index curves for forest species in the eastern United States. Gen. Tech. Rep. NC-128. St. Paul, MN: USDA Forest Service, North Central Forest Experiment Station. 142 p.

Cathey TN, Torbert JL, Burger JA, O'Conner G. 1989. Sixth year results from a stand regeneration project. In: Proceedings, 5th Biennial Southern Silvicultural Research Conference; 1988 November 1–3; Memphis, TN. Gen. Tech. Rep. SO-74. New Orleans: USDA Forest Service, Southern Forest Experiment Station: 141–146.

Caulfield JP, Shoulders E, Lockaby BG. 1989. Methods for including risk in species-site selection decisions. In: Proceedings, 5th Biennial Southern Silvicultural Research Conference; 1988 November 1–3; Memphis, TN. Gen. Tech. Rep. SO-74. New Orleans: USDA Forest Service, Southern Forest Experiment Station: 181–186.

Choong ET, Chang BY. 1974. Effect of cultural treatments on density and growth in a loblolly pine plantation. Louisiana State University Wood Utilization Notes 25. Baton Rouge, LA. School of Forestry & Wildlife Management. 4 p.

Clark A III. 1978. Total tree and its utilization in the southern U.S. Forest Products Journal 28(10):47–52.

Clark A III, Saucier JR. 1988. Biomass response of loblolly pine to applied sewage sludge four years after treatment. In: Proceedings, 9th Annual Southern Forest Biomass Workshop; 1987 June 8–11; Mississippi State, MS. Mississippi State, MS: MSU Department of Forestry; Mississippi Agricultural and Forestry Experiment Station; Mississippi Forest Products Laboratory; and Mississippi Cooperative Extension Service: 126–138.

Clark A III, Schmidtling RC. 1989. Effect of intensive culture on juvenile wood formation and wood properties of loblolly, slash, and longleaf pine. In: Proceedings, 5th Biennial Southern Silvicultural Research Conference; 1988 November 1–3;

Memphis, TN. Gen. Tech. Rep. SO-74. New Orleans: USDA Forest Service, Southern Forest Experiment Station: 211–217.

Clark A III, Taras MA. 1976. Comparison of above ground biomasses of the four major southern pines. Forest Products Journal 26(10):25–29.

Clason TR. 1978. Utilization of paraquat in a silvicultural thinning regime: first-year results. In: Proceedings, Lightwood Research Coordinating Council; 1978 January 10–11; Atlantic Beach, FL. [Place of publication and publisher unknown]: 14–18.

Clason TR. 1987. The influence of benomyl on blue stain infestation, oleoresin synthesis, and growth in paraquat-treated loblolly pine. Forest Science 33(2):552–557.

Clason TR. 1989. Stocking control measures affect individual pine growth and development. In: Proceedings, 5th Biennial Southern Silvicultural Research Conference; 1988 November 1–3; Memphis, TN. Gen. Tech. Rep. SO-74. New Orleans: USDA Forest Service, Southern Forest Experiment Station: 205–210.

Clason TR. 1991. Thinned loblolly pine stand growth improved by early hardwood suppression. Southern Journal of Applied Forestry 15(1):22–27.

Clason TR, Cao QV. 1983. Comparing growth and yield between 31-year-old slash and loblolly pine plantations. In: Jones EP Jr, ed. Proceedings, 2nd Biennial Southern Silvicultural Research Conference; 1982 November 4–5; Atlanta, GA. Gen. Tech. Rep. SE-24. Asheville, NC: USDA Forest Service, Southeastern Forest Experiment Station: 291–298.

Clason TR, Cao QV. 1986. A product volume table for loblolly pine planted in northwest Louisiana. Bull. 775. Baton Rouge, LA: Louisiana Agricultural Experiment Station. 20 p.

Clason TR, Stiff CT. 1981. Influence of pruning on wood growth and product volume in a loblolly pine plantation. In: Proceedings, 1st Biennial Southern Silvicultural Research Conference; 1980 November 6–7; Atlanta, GA. Gen. Tech. Rep. SO-34. New Orleans: USDA Forest Service, Southern Forest Experiment Station: 105–110.

Clutter JL, Lenhart JD. 1968. Site index curves for old-field loblolly pine plantations in the Georgia Piedmont. Rep. 22, Ser. 1. Macon, GA: Georgia Forest Research Council. 4 p.

Clutter JL, Forston JC, Pienaar LV, and others. 1983. Predicting growth and yield. In: Timber management: a quantitative approach. New York: John Wiley and Sons: 88–139.

Clutter JL, Harms WR, Brister GH, Rheney JW. 1984. Stand structure and yields of site-prepared loblolly pine plantations in the lower Coastal Plain of the Carolinas, Georgia, and north Florida. Gen. Tech. Rep. SE-27. Asheville, NC: USDA Forest Service, Southeastern Forest Experiment Station. 173 p.

Coile TS, Schumacher FX. 1964. Soil-site relations, stand structure, and yields of slash and loblolly pine plantations in the Southern United States. Durham, NC: T.S. Coile, Inc.: 12–13.

Cole DE. 1973. Comparisons within and between populations of planted slash and loblolly pine: a seed source study. In: Proceedings, 12th Southern Forest Tree Improvement Conference; 1973 June 12–13; Baton Rouge, LA. Baton Rouge, LA: Louisiana State University, Division of Continuing Education: 277–292.

Cole DE. 1975. Comparisons within and between populations of planted slash and loblolly pine. Georgia For. Res. Pap. 81. Macon, GA: Georgia Forest Research Council. 12 p.

Comerford NB, Mollitor AV, eds. 1982. Guide to classification and management of southeastern Coastal Plain forest soils. Gainesville, FL: University of Florida, School of Forest Resources and Conservation. 85 p.

Conley JM, Crowell EP, McMahon DH, Barker RG. 1977. Increases in turpentine, rosin, and fatty acid content of slash and loblolly pines by paraquat treatment. TAPPI Journal 60(12):114–116.

Cox SK, Van Lear DH. 1985. Biomass and nutrient accretion on Piedmont sites following clearcutting and natural regeneration of loblolly pine [abstract]. In: Proceedings, 3rd Biennial Southern Silvicultural Research Conference; 1984 November 7–8; Atlanta,

GA. Gen. Tech. Rep. SO-54: New Orleans: USDA Forest Service, Southern Forest Experiment Station: 501–506.

Cregg BM, Dougherty PM, Hennessey TC. 1988. Growth and wood quality of young loblolly pine trees in relation to stand density and climatic factors. Canadian Journal of Forest Research 18(7): 851–858.

Creighton JL, Glover GR, Zutter BR. 1986. Loblolly pine growth response to herbaceous weed control: a summary of fifteen studies [abstract]. Proceedings of the Southern Weed Science Society 39:193.

Creighton JL, Zutter BR, Glover GR, Gjerstad DH. 1987. Planted pine growth and survival responses to herbaceous vegetation control, treatment duration, and herbicide application technique. Southern Journal of Applied Forestry 11(4):223–227.

Dangerfield CW Jr, Edwards MB. 1991. Economic comparison of natural and planted regeneration of loblolly pine. Southern Journal of Applied Forestry 15(3):125–127.

Dangerfield CW Jr, Merck HL. 1990. Helping pines earn more with weed control. Tech. Pub. R8-TP 14. Atlanta: USDA Forest Service, Southern Region. 23 p.

Daniels RF, Burkhart HE. 1975. Simulation of individual tree growth and stand development in managed loblolly pine plantations. Blacksburg, VA: Virginia Polytechnic Institute and State University, Division of Forestry and Wildlife Resources. 69 p.

Daniels RF, Burkhart HE, Clason TR. 1986. A comparison of competition measures for predicting growth of loblolly pine trees. Canadian Journal of Forest Research 16(6):1230–1237.

Daniels RF, Burkhart HE, Strub MR. 1979. Yield estimates for loblolly pine plantations. Journal of Forestry 77(9):581–583.

DeBell GR, Askew GR, Hook DD, and others. 1982. Species suitability on a lowland site altered by drainage. Southern Journal of Applied Forestry 6(1):2–9.

Dell TR. 1979. Potential of using crown ratio in predicting product yield. In: Frayer WE, ed. Proceedings, Forest Resource Inventories Symposium, Vol. 2; 1979 July; Fort Collins, CO. Fort Collins, CO: Colorado State University, Department of Forest and Wood Science: 843–851.

Derr HJ, Mann WF Jr. 1977. Bedding poorly drained sites for planting loblolly and slash pines in southwest Louisiana. Res. Pap. SO-134. New Orleans: USDA Forest Service, Southern Forest Experiment Station. 5 p.

Devan JS, Burkhart HE. 1982. Polymorphic site index equations for loblolly pine based on a segmented polynomial differential model. Forest Science 28(3):544–555.

DeWit JN, Terry TA. 1983. Site preparation effects on early loblolly pine growth, hardwood competition, and soil physical properties [abstract]. In: Proceedings, 2nd Biennial Southern Silvicultural Research Conference; 1982 November 4–5; Atlanta, GA. Gen. Tech. Rep. SE-24. Asheville, NC: USDA Forest Service, Southeastern Forest Experiment Station: 39–46.

Dierauf TA. 1985. Results at age 23 of a loblolly pine pre-commercial thinning study. Occas. Rep. 65. Richmond, VA: Virginia Division of Forestry, Department of Conservation and Economic Development. 11 p.

Dougherty PM, Lowery RF. 1991. Spot-size of herbaceous control impacts loblolly pine seedling survival and growth. Southern Journal of Applied Forestry 15(4):193–199.

Drew J, Roberts DR. 1977. Developments in paraquat treatment of trees to induce lightwood formation. Forest Products Journal 27(7):43–47.

Drew J, Roberts DR. 1978. Extractive enhancement in pines by paraquat treatment. Forest Products Journal 28(9):21–26.

Duzan HW Jr, Allen HL. 1981. Estimating fertilizer response in site-prepared pine plantations using basal area and site index. In: Proceedings, 1st Biennial Southern Silvicultural Research Conference; 1980 November 6–7; Atlanta, GA. Gen. Tech. Rep. SO-34. New Orleans: USDA Forest Service, Southern Forest Experiment Station: 219–222.

Duzan HW Jr, Allen HL, Ballard R. 1982. Established loblolly pine plantations with basal area and site index. Southern Journal of Applied Forestry 6(1):15–19.

Dyer ME., Bailey RL. 1987. A test of six methods for estimating true heights from stem analysis data. Forest Science 33(1):3–13.

Dyer ME, Burkhart HE. 1987. Compatible crown ration and crown height models. Canadian Journal of Forest Research 17(6):572–574.

Edwards MB. 1986a. Loblolly pine growth after four treatments for site preparation and pine release in the Georgia Piedmont [abstract]. Proceedings of the Southern Weed Science Society 39:228.

Edwards MB Jr. 1986b. Three year performance of planted loblolly pine seedlings on a lower Piedmont site after six site-preparation treatments. Res. Note SE-337. Asheville, NC: USDA Forest Service, Southeastern Forest Experiment Station. 3 p.

Edwards MB, McNab WH. 1979. Biomass prediction for young southern pines. Journal of Forestry 77(5):291–292.

Edwards MB, McNab WH. 1981. Biomass prediction for young southern pines: an addendum. Journal of Forestry 79(5):291.

Farrar RM Jr, Murphy PA. 1988. A versatile volume-defining function for natural loblolly pine trees. Res. Pap. SO-243. New Orleans: USDA Forest Service, Southern Forest Experiment Station. 9 p.

Farrar RM Jr, Murphy PA, Colvin R. 1984a. Hope Farm woodland: 33-year production in an uneven-aged loblolly-shortleaf pine stand. Journal of Forestry 82(8):476–479.

Farrar RM Jr, Murphy PA, Willett RL. 1984b. Tables of estimating growth and yield of uneven-aged stands of loblolly–shortleaf pine on average sites in the West Gulf area. Bull. 874. Fayetteville, AR: University of Arkansas, Division of Agriculture, Agricultural Experiment Station. 21 p.

Farrar RM Jr, Straka TJ, Burkhardt CE. 1989. A quarter-century of selection management on the Mississippi State Farm forestry forties. Tech. Bull. 164. Mississippi State, MS: Mississippi State Agricultural and Forestry Experiment Station. 24 p.

Feduccia DP. 1982. Initial planting density in southern pine plantations. In: Proceedings, Regeneration of Southern Pines; 1982 October 19–21; Woodworth, LA. Long Beach, MS: Forestry and Harvesting Training Center: 150–166.

Feduccia DP, Mann WF Jr. 1976. Growth following initial thinning of loblolly pine planted on a cutover site at five spacings. Res. Pap. SO-120. New Orleans: USDA Forest Service, Southern Forest Experiment Station. 9 p.

Feduccia D, Mosier J. 1977. The Woodworth spacing and thinning study: an obituary. Forests & People 27(1):18–21.

Feduccia DP, Dell TR, Mann WF Jr, and others. 1979. Yields of unthinned loblolly plantations on cutover sites in the West Gulf Region. Res. Pap. SO-148. New Orleans: USDA Forest Service, Southern Forest Experiment Station. 88 p.

Fisher RF. 1981. Soils interpretations for silviculture in the southeastern Coastal Plain. In: Proceedings, 1st Biennial Southern Silvicultural Research Conference; 1980 November 6–7; Atlanta, GA. Gen. Tech. Rep. SO-34. New Orleans: USDA Forest Service, Southern Forest Experiment Station: 323–330.

Fisher RF, Garbett WS. 1980. Response of semimature slash and loblolly pine plantations to fertilization with nitrogen and phosphorus. Soil Science Society of America Journal 44(4):850–854.

Flowers WR Jr. 1978. Individual tree width and volume equations for site prepared loblolly pine plantations in the Coastal Plain of the Carolinas, Georgia, and north Florida. Athens, Georgia: University of Georgia. 53 p. M.S. thesis.

Foil RR, Hansbrough T, Merrifield RG. 1964. Development of loblolly pine as affected by early cultural treatments. Hill Farm Facts 5. Homer, LA: North Louisiana Hill Farm Experiment Station. 5 p.

Fox B. 1988. Estimating returns on forest investments using

break-even yield analysis. Southern Journal of Applied Forestry 12(4):264–266.

Fox TR, Morris LA, Maimone RA. 1989. The impact of windrowing on the productivity of a rotation age loblolly pine plantation. In: Proceedings, 5th Biennial Southern Silvicultural Research Conference; 1988 November 1–3; Memphis, TN. Gen. Tech. Rep. SO-74. New Orleans: USDA Forest Service, Southern Forest Experiment Station: 133–140.

Frazier JR. 1981. Compatible whole-stand and diameter distribution models for loblolly pine plantations. Blacksburg, VA: Virginia Polytechnic Institute and State University, School of Forestry and Wildlife Resources. Thesis summary. 3 p.

Fridley JL, Tufts RA. 1989. Analytical estimates of loblolly pine tree center of mass and mass moment of inertia. Forest Science 35(1):126–136.

Gent JA, Allen HL, and others. 1986. Magnitude duration and economic analysis of loblolly pine (Pinus-taeda) growth response following bedding and phosphorus fertilization. Southern Journal of Applied Forestry 10(3):124–128.

Gerig TM, Schreuder HT, Crutchfield DM, Wells CG. 1978. The two-way median fit: a sensitive statistical procedure to detect response of trees to fertilization. Forest Science 24(3):358–362.

Gibson MD, McMillin CW, Shoulders E. 1985. Preliminary results for weight and volume of even-aged, unthinned, planted southern pines on three sites in Louisiana. In: Proceedings, 6th Annual Meeting of the Southern Forest Biomass Working Group; 1984 June 5–7; Athens, GA. Asheville, NC: USDA Forest Service, Southeastern Forest Experiment Station: 69–74.

Gilmore AR. 1979. Revised site-index curves for plantation-grown loblolly pine in southern Illinois. Fores. Res. Rep. 79-2. Champaign–Urbana, IL: University of Illinois, Department of Forestry, Agricultural Experiment Station. 1 p.

Gladstone WT, Bean PM, Hughes JH, Talbert CB. 1987. A challenge for tree improvement. In: Proceedings, 19th Southern Forest Tree Improvement Conference; 1987 June 16–17; College Station, TX. Sponsored Pub. 41. College Station, TX: Southern Forest Tree Improvement Committee: 1–7.

Glass GG Jr. 1976. The effects from rootraking on an upland Piedmont loblolly pine (Pinus taeda L.) site. Tech. Rep. 56. Raleigh, NC: North Carolina State University, School of Forest Resources, NC State Forestry Cooperative. 44 p.

Glover GR, Hool JN. 1979. A basal area ratio predictor of loblolly pine plantation mortality. Forest Science 25(2):275–282.

Glover GR, Zutter BR, Minogue PJ, Gjerstad DH. 1991. Effect of hexazinone rate and formulation on loblolly pine in broadcast release applications. Southern Journal of Applied Forestry 15(1):54–61.

Goebel NB. 1968. Subsoiling and its effects on growth of certain forest tree species in the Piedmont. For. Bull. 3. Clemson, SC: Clemson University, Department of Forestry. 3 p.

Goebel NB, Warner JR. 1969. Volume yields of loblolly pine plantations for a variety of sites in the South Carolina Piedmont. For. Res. Ser. 13. Clemson, SC: Clemson University, Department of Forestry, South Carolina Agricultural Experiment Station. 15 p.

Goebel NB, Warner JR, Van Lear DH. 1974. Periodic thinnings in loblolly pine stands: growth, yield, and economic analyses. For. Res. Ser. 28. Clemson, SC: Clemson University. 11 p.

Goggans JF, Schultz EF Jr. 1958. Growth of pine plantations in Alabama's Coastal Plain. Bull. 313. Auburn, AL: Alabama Polytechnic Institute, Alabama Agricultural Experiment Station. 19 p.

Golden MS, Isaacson CV. 1987. Effect of site preparation soil movement on loblolly pine height growth in 12-and 14-year-old plantations in the Hilly Coastal Plain of Alabama. In: Proceedings, 4th Biennial Southern Silvicultural Research Conference; 1986 November 4–6; Atlanta, GA. Gen. Tech. Rep. SE-42. Asheville, NC: USDA Forest Service, Southeastern Forest Experiment Station: 368–372.

Golden MS, Meldahl R, Knowe SA, Boyer WD. 1981. Predicting

site index for old-field loblolly pine plantations. Southern Journal of Applied Forestry 5(3):109–114.

Grano CX. 1969. Precommercial thinning of loblolly pine. Journal of Forestry 67(11):825–827.

Grano CX. 1971. Growth of planted loblolly pine after row and selective thinning. Res. Note SO-123. New Orleans: USDA Forest Service, Southern Forest Experiment Station. 3 p.

Green EJ, Burkhart HE, Clason TR. 1984. A model for basal area distribution in loblolly pine. Forest Science 30(3):617–628.

Grigsby HC. 1975. Performance of large loblolly and shortleaf pine seedlings after 9 to 12 years. Res. Note SO-196. New Orleans: USDA Forest Service, Southern Forest Experiment Station. 4 p.

Guldin JM, Fitzpatrick MW. 1991. Comparison of log quality from even-aged and uneven-aged loblolly pine stands in south Arkansas. Southern Journal of Applied Forestry 15(1):10–17.

Guldin RW. 1984a. Economic returns from spraying to release loblolly pine. Proceedings of the Southern Weed Science Society 37:248–254.

Guldin RW. 1984b. MERCHANDIZER: adapting USLYCOWG to the marketplace. Gen. Tech. Rep. SO-52. New Orleans: USDA Forest Service, Southern Forest Experiment Station. 36 p.

Haines LW, Maxwell KF. 1976. Response of 7-year-old loblolly pine to nitrogen and phosphorus fertilization. In: Proceedings, 6th Southern Forest Soils Workshop; 1976 October 19–21; Charleston, SC. Atlanta: USDA Forest Service, Southeastern Area, State and Private Forestry: 133–135.

Haines LW, Maki TE, Sanderford SG. 1975. The effect of mechanical site preparation treatments on soil productivity and tree (Pinus taeda L. and P. elliottii Engelm. var. elliottii) growth. In: Proceedings, 4th North American Forest Soils Conference, 1973. Quebec, Canada; Les Presses de l'Université Laval. 379–395 p.

Hammond WJ. 1987. Bedding fertilization and herbicide effects on planted loblolly pines. Proceedings of the Southern Weed Science Society 40:189–193.

Hansbrough T. 1968. Stand characteristics of 18-year-old loblolly pine growing at different initial spacings. Hill Farm Facts/Forestry 8:1–4.

Hansbrough T, Foil RR, Merrifield RG. 1964. The development of loblolly pine planted at various initial spacings. Hill Farm Facts [North Louisiana Hill Farm Experiment Station, Homer, LA] 4:1–4.

Harms WR. 1981. A competition function for tree and stand growth models. In: Proceedings, 1st Biennial Southern Silvicultural Research Conference; 1980 November 6–7; Atlanta, GA. Gen. Tech. Rep. SO-34. New Orleans: USDA Forest Service, Southern Forest Experiment Station: 179–183.

Harms WR, Langdon OG. 1976. Development of loblolly pine in dense stands. Forest Science 22(3):331–337.

Harms WR, Lloyd FT. 1981. Stand structure and yield relationships in a 20-year-old loblolly pine spacing study: USDA Forest Service, Charleston, SC, USA. Southern Journal of Applied Forestry 5(3):162–166.

Harrington CA. 1987. Site-index comparisons for naturally seeded loblolly pine and shortleaf pine. Southern Journal of Applied Forestry 11(2):86–91.

Hasness JR, Lenhart JD. 1972. Cubic-foot volume for loblolly pine trees in old-field plantations in the interior West Gulf Coastal Plain. Texas For. Pap. 12. Nacogdoches, TX: Stephen F. Austin State University, School of Forestry. 7 p.

Hatchell GE, Dorman KW, Langdon OG. 1972. Performance of loblolly and slash pine nursery selections. Forest Science 18(4):308–313.

Haywood JD. 1980. Planted pines do not respond to bedding on an Acadia-Beauregard-Kolin silt loam site. Res. Note SO-259. New Orleans: USDA Forest Service, Southern Forest Experiment Station. 4 p.

Haywood JD. 1983. Response of planted pines to site

preparation on a Beauregard-Caddo soil. In: Proceedings, 2nd Biennial Southern Silvicultural Research Conference; 1982 November 4–5; Atlanta, GA. Gen. Tech. Rep. SE-24. Asheville, NC: USDA Forest Service, Southeastern Forest Experiment Station: 14–17.

Haywood JD. 1987. Effects of site amelioration on growth and yield of slash and loblolly pines planted on a Caddo silt loam in southwestern Louisiana. In: Proceedings, 4th Biennial Southern Silvicultural Research Conference; 1986 November 4–6; Atlanta, GA. Gen. Tech. Rep. SE-42. Asheville, NC: USDA Forest Service, Southeastern Forest Experiment Station: 389–394.

Haywood JD, Burton JD. 1989. Loblolly pine plantation development is influenced by site preparation and soils in the West Gulf Coastal Plain. Southern Journal of Applied Forestry 13(1):17–21.

Haywood JD, Tiarks AE. 1990. Eleventh-year results of fertilization, herbaceous, and woody plant control in a loblolly pine plantation. Southern Journal of Applied Forestry 14(4):173–177.

Haywood JD, Thill RE, Burton JD. 1981. Intensive site preparation affects loblolly pine growth on upland sites. Proceedings of the American Society of Agricultural Engineers 10-81:224–231.

Hebb EA. 1982. Sand pine performs well in the Georgia–Carolina sandhills. Southern Journal of Applied Forestry 6(3):144–147.

Hepp TE, Brister GH. 1982. Estimating crown biomass in loblolly pine plantations in the Carolina flatwoods. Forest Science 28(1):115–127.

Hickman CA, Anderson WC, Guldin RW. 1987. Economic assessment of chemical versus mechanical site preparation. In: Proceedings, 4th Biennial Southern Silvicultural Research Conference; 1986 November 4–6; Atlanta, GA. Gen. Tech. Rep. SE-42. Asheville, NC: USDA Forest Service, Southeastern Forest Experiment Station: 274–282.

Hicks DR, Lenhart JD, Somberg SI. 1972. Merchantable green weights for loblolly pine trees in old-field plantations in the interior West Gulf Coastal Plain [USA]. Texas For. Pap. 16. Nacogdoches, TX:, Stephen F. Austin State University, School of Forestry. 4 p.

Holdaway MR. 1986. Modeling tree crown ratio. Forestry Chronicle 62(5):451–455.

Holton RW. 1978. Tall oil and turpentine analyses of Virginia and loblolly pines treated with paraquat in east Tennessee. In: Proceedings, Lightwood Research Coordinating Council; 1978 January 10–11; Atlantic Beach, FL. [Place of publication and publisher unknown]: 77–80.

Hook DD, DeBell DS, McKee WH Jr, Askew JL. 1983. Responses of loblolly pine (mesophyte) and swamp tupelo (hydrophyte) seedlings to soil flooding and phosphorus. In: Atkinson D, and others, eds. Tree root systems and their mycorrhizas. The Hague: Martinus Nijhoff/Dr. W. Junk Publishers: 387–394.

Houser JN. 1980. Estimation of aboveground biomass and inorganic nutrient content of a 25-year-old loblolly pine (Pinus taeda L.) plantation. College Station, TX: Texas A&M University. 56 p. M.S. thesis.

Hsu JK, Walters CS. 1975. Effect of irrigation and fertilization on selected physical and mechanical properties of loblolly pine (Pinus taeda). Wood and Fiber 7(3):192–206.

Hunt EV Jr, Gilmore G. 1967. Taller loblolly pine seedlings grow faster in a Texas plantation. Tree Planters' Notes 18(2):25–28.

Hutnik RJ. 1964. Accumulation and production of dry matter in red pine (Pinus resinosa Ait.) plantations at various spacings. Durham, NC: Duke University, School of Forestry. Dissertation Abstracts.

Hyink DM, Lenhart JD, Somberg SI. 1972. Ovendry weights for loblolly pine trees in old-field plantations in the interior West Gulf Coastal Plain. Texas For. Pap. 17. Nacogdoches, TX: Stephen F. Austin State University, School of Forestry. 3 p.

Jack SB, Stone EL, Swindel BF. 1988. Stem form changes in unthinned slash and loblolly pine stands following midrotation fertilization. Southern Journal of Applied Forestry. 12(2):90–97.

Janssen JE, Sprinz PT. 1987. Modeling distributions of stem characteristics of genetically improved loblolly pine. Proceedings,

19th Southern Forest Tree Improvement Conference; 1987 June 16–18; College Station, TX. College Station, TX: Southern Forest Tree Improvement Committee, Texas Forest Service, and the Texas Agricultural Experiment Station: 367–375.

Jensen JR, Hodgson ME. 1985. Romote sensing forest biomass: an evaluation using high resolution remote sensor data and loblolly pine plots. Professional Geographer 37(1):46–56.

Jensen JR, Hodgson ME, Mackey HE Jr. 1986. Remote sensing forest biomass for loblolly pine using high resolution airborne remote sensor data. In: Cole DW, Henry CL, eds. The forest alternative for treatment and utilization of municipal and industrial wastes. Seattle: University of Washington Press: 324–334.

Johnstone WD. 1972. Total standing crop and tree component distributions in three stands of 100-year-old lodgepole pine. In: Forest Biomass Studies; Proceedings, Working Group on Forest Biomass Studies, Section 25, Growth and Yield, IUFRO Congress; 1971 March 15–20; Gainesville, FL. Orono, ME: University of Maine, College of Life Sciences and Agriculture : 81–89.

Jones EP Jr. 1969. Growth comparison slash and loblolly pine in Georgia. Forest Farmer 28(5):11–12.

Jones SB, Broerman FS. 1977. Thinning and fertilization of sixteen-year-old loblolly pine. Woodlands Res. Note 34. Savannah, GA: Union Camp Corporation, Woodlands Research Department. 2 p.

Kapeluck PR, Van Lear DH. 1994. [Unpublished data.]

Kellison RC, Jett JB Jr. 1978. Species selection for plantation establishment in the Atlantic Coastal Plain and Sandhills Provinces. In: Proceedings, Soil Moisture ... Site Productivity Symposium; 1977 November 1–3; Myrtle Beach, SC. Atlanta: USDA Forest Service, Southeastern Area, State and Private Forestry: 196–202.

Kellison RC, Slichter TK, Frederick DJ. 1979. Matching species to site for increased wood production. TAPPI Journal 62(8):77–79.

Kellison RC, Weir RJ. 1980. How forest genetics is helping grow better trees for tomorrow. TAPPI Journal 63(2):57–62.

Kinerson RS Jr. 1973. A transducer for investigations of diameter growth. Forest Science. 19(3):230–232.

Kitchens RN. 1985. One-quarter century of tree improvement in the southern region. In: Proceedings, National Silviculture Workshop; 1985 May 13–16; Rapid City, SD. Washington, DC: USDA Forest Service, Timber Management: 284–288.

Klopatek JM. Risser PG. 1981. Energy analyses of forestry practices in oak-pine forests and loblolly pine plantations. Forest Science 27(2):365–376.

Knight HA. 1978. Average timber characteristics of the better stocked, natural stands in North Carolina and eastern Virginia. Res. Note SE-257. Asheville, NC: USDA Forest Service, Southeastern Forest Experiment Station. 10 p.

Knowe SA, Nelson LR, Gjerstad DH, and others. 1985. Four-year growth and development of planted loblolly pine on sites with competition control. Southern Journal of Applied Forestry 9(1):11–15.

Kormanik PP, Hoekstra PE. 1963. A comparison of loblolly, white, Virginia, and shortleaf pine in the Virginia Piedmont. Res. Note SE-11. Asheville, NC: USDA Forest Service, Southeastern Forest Experiment Station. 3 p.

Kraus JF, LaFarge T. 1982. Georgia's seed orchard trees: a report on the first-generation selections. For. Res. Pap. 37. Macon, GA: Georgia Forest Research Council. 10 p.

Krumbein JP. 1978. An economic evaluation of the paraquat application for oleoresin production in conifers. In: Esser MN, comp. Proceedings, Lightwood Research Coordinating Council; 1978 January 10–11; Atlantic Beach, FL. [Place of publication and publisher unknown]: 168–178.

Ku TT, Baker JB. 1987. Impact of harvesting southern pine understory biomass on site productivity. In: Proceedings, Seminar on Forest Productivity and Site Evaluation; 1987 November 10–11; Taipei, Taiwan. Taipei, Taiwan: Council of Agriculture: 95–103.

Ku TT, Burton JD. 1973. Dry matter and minerals in loblolly pine plantations on four Arkansas soils. Arkansas Academy of Science Proceedings 27:21–25.

Ku TT, Baker JB, Blinn CR, Williams RA. 1981a. Understory biomass for energy fuel. In: Proceedings, 1st Biennial Southern Silvicultural Research Conference; 1980 November 6–7; Atlanta, GA. Gen. Tech. Rep. SO-34. New Orleans: USDA Forest Service, Southern Forest Experiment Station: 230–233.

Ku TT, Wheeler L, Young JF, and others. 1981b. Biomass and nutrient accumulations of an uneven-aged southern pine stand in Arkansas. In: Proceedings, 1st Biennial Southern Silvicultural Research Conference; 1980 November 6–7; Atlanta, GA. Gen. Tech. Rep. SO-34. New Orleans: USDA Forest Service, Southern Forest Experiment Station: 248.

Langdon OG, Hatchell GE. 1977. Performance of loblolly, slash, and pond pines on a poorly drained site with fertilization at ages 11 and 14. In: Proceedings, 6th Southern Forest Soils Workshop; 1976 October 19–21; Charleston, SC. [Place of publication unknown]: Southern Forest Soils Council: 121–126.

Langdon OG, Trousdell KB. 1974. Increasing growth and yield of natural loblolly pine by young stand management. In: Proceedings, Symposium on Management of Young Pines; 1974 October 22–24; Alexandria, LA/December 3–5; Charleston, SC. Asheville, NC: USDA Forest Service, Southeastern Forest Experiment Station: 288–295.

Lantagne DO, Burger JA. 1983. First-year survival of loblolly pine (Pinus taeda L.) as affected by site preparation on the South Carolina and Georgia Piedmont. In: Proceedings, 2nd Biennial Southern Silvicultural Research Conference; 1982 November 4–5; Atlanta, GA. Gen. Tech. Rep. SE-24. Asheville, NC: USDA Forest Service, Southeastern Forest Experiment Station: 5–10.

Larsen HS, Carter MC, Gooding JW, Hyink DM. 1976. Biomass and nitrogen distribution in four 13-year-old loblolly pine plantations in the Hilly Coastal Plain of Alabama. Canadian Journal of Forest Research 6(2):187–194.

Ledbetter JR, Sullivan AD, Matney TG. 1986. Yield tables for cutover site-prepared loblolly pine plantations in the Gulf Coastal Plain. Tech. Bull. 135. Mississippi State, MS: Mississippi State University, Mississippi Agricultural and Forestry Experiment Station. 31 p.

Lemin RC Jr, Burkhart HE. 1983. Predicting mortality after thinning in old-field loblolly pine plantations. Southern Journal of Applied Forestry 7(1):20–23.

Lenhart JD. 1971. Site index curves for old-field loblolly pine plantations in the interior West Gulf Coastal Plain. Texas For. Pap. 8. Nacogdoches, TX: Stephen F. Austin State University, School of Forestry. 4 p.

Lenhart JD. 1972a. Predicting survival of unthinned, old-field loblolly pine plantations. Journal of Forestry 70(12):754–755.

Lenhart JD. 1972b. Cubic-foot yields for unthinned old-field loblolly pine plantations in the interior West Gulf Coastal Plain. Texas For. Pap. 14. Nacogdoches, TX: Stephen F. Austin State University, School of Forestry. 46 p.

Lenhart JD. 1987. Estimating the amount of wood per acre in loblolly and slash pine plantations in east Texas. In: Proceedings, 4th Biennial Southern Silvicultural Research Conference; 1986 November 4–6; Atlanta, GA. Gen. Tech. Rep. SE-42. Asheville, NC: USDA Forest Service, Southeastern Forest Experiment Station: 485–488.

Lenhart JD. 1988a. Diameter-distribution yield-prediction system for unthinned loblolly and slash pine plantations on non-old-fields in east Texas. Southern Journal of Applied Forestry 12(4):239–242.

Lenhart JD. 1988b. Evaluation of explicit and implicit yield prediction in loblolly and slash pine plantations in east Texas. Proceedings, IUFRO Conference on Forest Growth Modelling and Prediction; 1987 August 24–28; Minneapolis, MN. Gen. Tech. Rep. NC-120. St. Paul, MN: USDA Forest Service, North Central Forest Experiment Station: 747–753.

Lenhart JD, Clutter JL. 1971. Cubic-foot yield tables for old-field loblolly pine plantations in the Georgia Piedmont. Rep. 22/Ser. 3. Macon, GA: Georgia Forest Research Council. 13 p.

Lenhart JD, Fields HL. 1970. Site index curves for old-field loblolly pine plantations in northeast Texas. Texas For. Pap. 3. Nacogdoches, TX: Stephen F. Austin State University, School of Forestry. 4 p.

Lenhart JD, Hyink DM. 1976. Number of 8.7-foot veneer bolts in loblolly pine trees of old-field plantations in the interior West Gulf Coastal Plain. Texas For. Pap. 27. Nacogdoches, TX: Stephen F. Austin State University, School of Forestry. 5 p.

Lenhart JD, Hackett TL, Laman CJ, and others. 1987. Tree content and taper functions for loblolly and slash pine trees planted on non-old-fields in east Texas. Southern Journal of Applied Forestry 11(3):147–151.

Lenhart JD, Hunt EV, Blackard JA. 1986. Site index equations for loblolly and slash pine plantations on non-old-fields in east Texas. Southern Journal of Applied Forestry 10(2):109–112.

Little S, Mohr JJ. 1963. Five-year effects from row thinnings in loblolly pine plantations of eastern Maryland. Res. Pap. NE-12. Upper Darby, PA: USDA Forest Service, Northeastern Forest Experiment Station. 15 p.

Little S, Somes HA. 1958. Results 18 years after planting loblolly pines at different spacings. Res. Note 80. Radnor, PA: USDA Forest Service, Northeast Forest Experiment Station. 3 p.

Little S, Mohr JJ, and others. 1968. Ten-year effects from row thinnings in loblolly pine plantations of eastern Maryland. Res. Note NE-77. Upper Darby, PA: USDA Forest Service, Northeastern Forest Experiment Station. 8 p.

Liu CJ, Keister TD. 1978. Southern pine stem form defined through principal component analysis. Canadian Journal of Forest Research 8(2):188–197.

Liu CM, Leuschner WA, Burkhart HE. 1989. A production function analysis of loblolly pine yield equations. Forest Science 35(3):775–788.

Livingston KW. 1972. Minor topographic changes affect growth and yield of planted southern pines. Bull. 439. Auburn, AL: Auburn University, Alabama Agricultural Experiment Station. 15 p.

Lloyd TF. 1981. How many tree heights should you measure for natural, Atlantic Coastal Plain loblolly site index? Southern Journal of Applied Forestry 5(4):180–183.

Lloyd TF. 1985. Tree form effects on volume prediction precision from taper models. In: Proceedings, 3rd Biennial Southern Silvicultural Research Conference; 1984 November 7–8; Atlanta, GA. Gen. Tech. Rep. SO-54: New Orleans: USDA Forest Service, Southern Forest Experiment Station: 466.

Lloyd TF, Harms WR. 1986. An individual stand growth model for mean plant size based on the rule of self-thinning. Annals of Botany 57:681–688.

Lloyd TF, Harms WR. 1988. A biomass yield model constrained by growing space availability. In: Proceedings, 9th Annual Meeting of the Southern Forest Biomass Working Group; 1987 June 8–11; Biloxi, MS. Mississippi State, MS: Mississippi State University, Department of Forestry: 110–114.

Lloyd TF, Jones EP. 1983. Density effects on height growth and its implications for site index prediction and growth projection. In: Proceedings, 2nd Biennial Southern Silvicultural Research Conference; 1982 November 4–5; Atlanta, GA. Gen. Tech. Rep. SE-24. Asheville, NC: USDA Forest Service, Southeastern Forest Experiment Station: 329–333.

Lockaby BG, Adams JC. 1986. Dry weight and nutrient content of fuelwood biomass from loblolly pine stands in northern Louisiana. Forest Science 32(1):3–9.

Loftus NS Jr. 1974. Performance of pine and yellow-poplar planted on low-quality sites in central Tennessee. Res. Note SO-176. New Orleans: USDA Forest Service, Southern Forest Experiment Station. 5 p.

Lohrey RE. 1974. Growth and yield in a longleaf pine plantation.

In: Proceeding, Symposium on Management of Young Pines; 1974 October 22–24; Alexandria, LA/December 3–5; Charleston, SC. Asheville, NC: USDA Forest Service, Southeastern Forest Experiment Station: 88–96.

Lohrey RE. 1977. Growth responses of loblolly pine to precommercial thinning. Southern Journal of Applied Forestry 1(3):19–22.

Lohrey RE. 1991. Green weight per standard rough cord by pine species and tree diameter in central Louisiana. Unpublished final report summary. FS-SO-4101-243, Problem 3. [On file with USDA Forest Service, Pineville, LA.]

Long EM. 1979. Comparison of growth and volume production of slash and loblolly pine test plantations on two planting sites. In: Proceedings, 15th Southern Forest Tree Improvement Conference; 1979 June 19–21; Mississippi State, MS. Macon, GA: USDA Forest Service, Eastern Tree Seed Laboratory: 166–169.

Lowerts GA. 1987. Tests of realized genetic gain from a coastal Virginia loblolly pine first generation seed orchard. In: Proceedings, 19th Southern Forest Tree Improvement Conference; 1987 June 16–18; College Station, TX. Springfield, VA: National Technical Information Service: 423–431.

MacPeak MD, Burkhart LF, Weldon D. 1987. A mill study of the quality, yield, and mechanical properties of plywood produced from fast-grown loblolly pine. Forest Products Journal 37(2):51–56.

Malac BF, Brightwell CS. 1973. Effect of site preparation on growth of planted southern pines. Woodlands Res. Note 29. Savannah, GA: Union Camp Corp., Woodlands Research Department. 9 p.

Mann WF Jr, Lohrey RE. 1974. Precommercial thinning of southern pines. Journal of Forestry 72(9):557–560.

Martin JP. 1981. Mechanical weed control in southern forests. In: Holt HA, Fischer BC, eds. Weed control in forest management: Proceedings, 1981 John S. Wright Forestry Conference; 1981 February 3–5; [Location unknown]. [Place of publication and publisher unknown]: 103–107.

Marx DH, Cordell CE, Clark A III. 1988. Eight-year performance of loblolly pine with Pisolithus ectomycorrhizae on a good-quality forest site. Southern Journal of Applied Forestry 12(4):275–280.

Matney TG, Sullivan AD. 1982. Compatible stand and stock tables for thinned and unthinned loblolly pine stands. Forest Science 28(1):161–171.

Matney TG, Sullivan AD, Ledbetter JR. 1986. Diameter distributions and merchantable volumes for planted loblolly pine on cutover site-prepared land in the West Gulf Coastal Plain. Tech. Bull. 132. Mississippi State, MS: Mississippi State University, Mississippi Agricultural and Forestry Experiment Station. 12 p.

Matney TG, Sullivan AD, Ledbetter JR. 1988. Stand-level cubic-foot volume ratio equations for planted loblolly pine on site-prepared land in the Mid-South Gulf Coastal Plain. Southern Journal of Applied Forestry 12(1):7–10.

McClure JP, Anderson J, Schreuder HT. 1987. A comparison of regional an site-specific volume estimation equations. Res. Paper SE-264. Asheville, NC: USDA Southeastern Forest Experiment Station. 9 p.

McClurkin DC. 1976. Influence of spacing on growth of loblolly pines planted on eroded sites. Res. Note SO-209. New Orleans: USDA Forest Service, Southern Forest Experiment Station. 4 p.

McKee WH Jr. 1989. Preparing Atlantic Coastal Plain sites for loblolly pine plantations. Gen. Tech. Rep. SE-57. Asheville, NC: USDA Forest Service, Southeastern Forest Experiment Station. 17 p.

McKee WH Jr, Wilhite LP. 1986. Loblolly pine response to bedding and fertilization varies by drainage class on lower Atlantic Coastal Plain sites. Southern Journal of Applied Forestry 10(1):16–21.

McKee WH Jr, Hook DD, DeBell DS, Askew JR. 1984. Growth and nutrient status of loblolly pine seedlings in relation to flooding and phosphorus. Soil Science Society of America Journal 48:1438–1442.

McNeil RC, Ballard R, Duzan HW Jr. 1984. Prediction of mid-term from short-term fertilizer responses for southern pine plantations. Forest Science 30(1):264–269.

Mengak MT, Van Lear DH, Nodine SK, Guynn DC Jr. 1987. Growth and economic comparisons of selected naturally and artificially regenerated stands. In: Proceedings, 4th Biennial Southern Silvicultural Research Conference; 1986 November 4–6; Atlanta, GA. Gen. Tech. Rep. SE-42. Asheville, NC: USDA Forest Service, Southeastern Forest Experiment Station: 283–288.

Metz LJ, Wells CG. 1965. Weight and nutrient content of the aboveground parts of some loblolly pines. Res. Pap. SE-17. Asheville, NC: USDA Forest Service, Southeastern Forest Experiment Station. 20 p.

Miller DC. 1982. Species, spacing and their interactions in four southern pines. Knoxville, TN: University of Tennessee. 52 p. Ph.D. dissertation.

Miller JH. 1990. Herbaceous weed control trials with a planting machine sprayer and a crawler-tractor sprayer—fourth year pine response. Proceedings of the Southern Weed Science Society 43:233–244.

Miller JH, Zutter BR, Zedaker SM, and others. 1991. A regional study on the influence of woody and herbaceous competition on early loblolly pine growth. Southern Journal of Applied Forestry 15(4):169–179.

Miller WD, Maki TE. 1957. Planting pines in pocosins. Journal of Forestry 55:659–663.

Moehring DM. 1964. Speeding up growth of the loblolly. Forest Farmer 23(6):9–14.

Moehring DM. 1966. Diameter growth and foliar nitrogen in fertilized loblolly pines. Res. Note SO-43. New Orleans: USDA Forest Service, Southern Forest Experiment Station. 3 p.

Moschler WW, Jones GD, Adams RE. 1970. Effects of loblolly pine fertilization on a Piedmont soil growth, foliar composition, and soil nutrients 10 years after establishment. Soil Science Society of America Proceedings 34(4):683–685.

Munro DD. 1974. Forest growth models: a prognosis. In: Growth Models for Tree and Stand Simulation; Proceedings, Joint Meetings of S4.01 and S6.02, IUFRO; 1973 August 20–24; Vancouver, BC. Res. Notes 30. Stockholm: Institutionen for Skogsproduktion: 7–21.

Murphy PA. 1981. Growth and yield of uneven-aged loblolly-shortleaf pine stands—a progress report. In: Proceedings, 1st Biennial Southern Silvicultural Research Conference; 1980 November 6–7; Atlanta, GA. Gen. Tech. Rep. SO-34. New Orleans USDA Forest Service, Southern Forest Experiment Station: 305–310.

Murphy PA. 1983a. A nonlinear timber yield equation system for loblolly pine. Forest Science 29(3):582–591.

Murphy PA. 1983b. Merchantable and sawtimber volumes for natural even-aged stands of loblolly pine in the West Gulf Region. Res. Pap. SO-194. New Orleans: USDA Forest Service, Southern Forest Experiment Station. 38 p.

Murphy PA. 1983c. Predicting growth and yield in uneven-aged pine stands. In: Hotvedt JE, Jackson BD, ed. Predicting growth and yield in the mid-South; 31st Annual Forestry Symposium; [dates unknown]; [location unknown]. Baton Rouge, LA: Louisiana State University, Division of Continuing Education: 61–73.

Murphy PA, Farrar RM Jr. 1983. Sawtimber volume predictions for uneven-aged loblolly-shortleaf pine stands on average sites. Southern Journal of Applied Forestry 7(1):45–50.

Murphy PA, Farrar RM Jr. 1987. Incorporating precipitation into a basal area growth model. In: Proceedings, 4th Biennial Southern Silvicultural Research Conference; 1986 November 4–6; Atlanta, GA. Gen. Tech. Rep. SE-42. Asheville, NC: USDA Forest Service, Southeastern Forest Experiment Station: 527–531.

Murphy PA, Farrar RM Jr. 1988a. A framework for stand structure projection of uneven-aged loblolly-shortleaf pine stands. Forest Science 34(2):321–332.

Murphy PA, Farrar RM Jr. 1988b.   Basal-area projection equations for thinned natural even-aged forest stands. Canadian Journal of Forest Research 18(7):827–832.

Murphy PA, Farrar RM Jr. 1988c.   Tree height characterization in uneven-aged forest stands. In: Forest growth modelling and prediction, Vol. 1. Gen. Tech. Rep. NC-120. St. Paul, MN: USDA Forest Service, North Central Forest Experiment Station: 118–125.

Murphy PA, Sternitzke HS. 1979.   Growth and yield estimation for loblolly pine in the West Gulf. Res. Pap. SO-154. New Orleans: USDA Forest Service, Southern Forest Experiment Station. 8 p.

Myers CA. 1977.   A computer program for variable density yield tables for loblolly pine plantations. Gen. Tech. Rep. SO-11. New Orleans: USDA Forest Service, Southern Forest Experiment Station. 31 p.

Nance WL, Shoulders E, Dell TR. 1985.   Predicting survival and yield of unthinned slash and loblolly pine plantations with differ-ent levels of fusiform rust. In: Proceeding, Integrated Pest Management Research Symposium; 1985 April 15–18; Asheville, NC. Gen. Tech. Rep. SO-56. New Orleans: USDA Forest Service, Southern Forest Experiment Station: 68–72.

Needham TD, Smith JL. 1987.   Stem count accuracy and species determination in loblolly pine plantations using 35-mm aerial photography. Photogrammetric Engineering and Remote Sensing 53(12):1675–1678

Nelson TC. 1963.   Basal area growth of natural loblolly pine stands. Res. Note SE-10. Asheville, NC: USDA Forest Service, Southeastern Forest Experiment Station. 4 p.

Nelson TC, Lotti T, Brender EV. 1961.   Merchantable cubic-foot volume growth in natural loblolly pine stands. Sta. Pap. 127. Asheville, NC: USDA Forest Service, Southeastern Forest Experiment Station. 12 p.

Nelson LE, Switzer GL, Smith WH. 1968.   Dry matter and nutrient accumulation in young loblolly pine (*Pinus taeda* L.). In: Youngberg CT, Davey CB, eds. Tree growth and forest soils. Proceedings, 3rd North American Forest Soils Conference; 1968 August; Raleigh, NC. Corvallis, OR: Oregon State University Press: 261–273.

Nemeth JC. 1972.   Dry matter production and site factors in young loblolly and slash pine plantations. Raleigh, NC: North Carolina State University. 95 p. Ph.D. dissertation.

Nemeth JC. 1973.   Dry matter production in young loblolly pine (*Pinus taeda*) and slash pine (*Pinus elliottii* Engelm.) plantations. Ecological Monographs 43(1):21–41.

Newberry JD. 1978.   Dominant height growth models and site index curves for site-prepared slash pine plantation in the Lower Coastal Plain of Georgia and north Florida. [Location and school name unknown]. 47 p. M.S. thesis.

Newberry JD, Burk TE. 1985. S_B distribution-based models for individual tree merchantable volume-total volume ratios. Forest Science 31(2):389–398.

Newberry JD, Burkhart HE. 1985.   Variable-form stem profile mod-els for loblolly pine. Canadian Journal of Forest Research 16(1):109–114.

Nichols CR. 1974.   Interrelation of tree improvement and manage-ment objectives—small ownerships. In: Proceedings, Symposium on Management of Young Pines; 1974 October 22–24; Alexandria, LA/December 3–5; Charleston, SC. Asheville, NC: USDA Forest Service, Southeastern Forest Experiment Station: 175–179.

Nix LE. 1976.   Paraquat induction of resin soaking in pines in the South Carolina Piedmont. In: Proceedings, Lightwood Research Coordinating Council; 1976 January 20–21; Jacksonville, FL. [Place of publication and publisher unknown]: 102–108.

Nix LE. 1977.   Seasonal aspects of the response of slash, loblolly, and shortleaf pines to paraquat. In: Proceedings, Annual Light-wood Research Conference; 1977 January 1819; Atlantic Beach, FL. [Place of publication and publisher unknown]: 84–89.

Nix LE. 1979.   The effects of paraquat treatment on height growth, branch extension, and cambial activity of loblolly pine. In: Proceedings, 6th Annual Lightwood Research Conference; 1979 January 17–18; Atlanta, GA: [Place of publication and publisher unknown]: 21–27.

Nix LE, Shearin AT, Cox SK. 1987.   Update of long term loblolly pine plantation growth and yield study on the Clemson Experimental Forest. In: Proceedings, 4th Biennial Southern Silvicultural Research Conference; 1986 November 4–6; Atlanta, GA. Gen. Tech. Rep. SE-42. Asheville, NC: USDA Forest Service, Southeastern Forest Experiment Station: 489–495.

Outcalt KW. 1982.   Selecting pine species for flatwoods sites. Tree Planters' Notes 33(1):18–19.

Outcalt KW. 1984.   Influence of bed height on the growth of slash and loblolly pine on a Leon fine sand in northeast Florida. Southern Journal of Applied Forestry 8(1):29–31.

Ovington JD. 1957.   Dry-matter production by *Pinus sylvestris* L. Annals of Botany 21:287–314.

Ovington JD, Madgwick HAI. 1959.   Distribution of organic matter and plant nutrients in a plantation of Scots pine. Forest Science 5(4):344–355.

Ovington JD, Forrest WD, Armstrong JS. 1967.   Tree biomass esti-mation. In: Proceedings, Symposium on Primary Production and Mineral Cycling in Natural Ecosystem; [dates unknown]; [Location unknown]. Orono, ME: University of Maine Press: 4–31.

Owens EG. 1974.   The effects of initial tree spacing and regenera-tion method on stand development in loblolly pine after 10 years. In: Proceeding, Symposium on Management of Young Pines; 1974 October 22–24; Alexandria, LA/December 3–5; Charleston, SC. Asheville, NC: USDA Forest Service, Southeastern Forest Experiment Station: 340–349.

Pegg RE. 1966.   Stem form of fertilized loblolly pine. Journal of Forestry 64(1):19–20.

Pehl CE. 1983.   Site preparation influences on young loblolly pine plantations in east Texas. Southern Journal of Applied Forestry 7(3):140–145.

Pehl CE, Bailey RL. 1983.   Performance to age ten of a loblolly pine plantation on an intensively prepared site in the Georgia Piedmont. Forest Science 29(1):96–102.

Pehl CE, Tuttle CL, Houser JN, Moehring DM. 1984.   Total bio-mass and nutrients of 25-year-old loblolly pines (*Pinus taeda* L.). Forest Ecology Management 9(3):155–160.

Phillips DR, McNab WH. 1982.   Total-tree green weights of sapling-size pines in Georgia. Georgia For. Res. Pap. 39. Macon, GA: Georgia Forest Research Council. 18 p.

Phillips DR, Saucier JR. 1982.   Estimating understory biomass. Southern Journal of Applied Forestry 6(1):25–27.

Phillips DR, Sheffield RM. 1984.   The small timber resource in the Southeast. In Proceedings, Conference on "Harvesting the South's Small Trees"; 1983 April 18–20; Biloxi MS. [Place of pub-lication unknown]: Forest Products Research Society: 7–17.

Pienaar LV, Grider GE. 1984.   Standard volume and weight equa-tions for site-prepared loblolly pine plantations in the Piedmont of South Carolina, Georgia, and Alabama. Tech. Rep. 1984-3. Athens, GA: University of Georgia, School of Forest Resources, Plantation Management Research Cooperative. 13 p.

Pienaar LV, Shiver BD. 1980.   Dominant height growth and site index curves for loblolly pine plantations in the Carolina flat-woods. Southern Journal of Applied Forestry 4(1):54–59.

Pope PE, Graney DL. 1979.   Family differences influence the aboveground biomass of loblolly pine plantations. Res. Pap. SO-155. New Orleans: USDA Forest Service, Southern Forest Experiment Station. 6 p.

Popham TW, Feduccia DP, Dell TR, and others. 1979.   Site index for loblolly plantations on cutover sites in the West Gulf Coastal

Plain. Res. Note SO-250. New Orleans: USDA Forest Service, Southern Forest Experiment Station. 6 p.

Porterfield RL. 1974. Predicted and potential gains from tree improvement programs: a goal programming analysis of program efficiency. Tech. Rep. 52. Raleigh, NC: North Carolina State University. 112 p.

Posey CE, Walker R. 1969. Scalping improves growth and survival of loblolly pine seedlings during drought. Tree Planters' Notes 19(4):25–28.

Pritchett WL. 1976. Phosphorus fertilization of pine in the Atlantic Coastal Plain. In: Proceedings, 6th Southern Forest Soils Workshop. 1976 October 19–21; Charleston, SC. [Place of publication unknown]: Southern Forest Soils Council: 52–56.

Pritchett WL, Comerford NB. 1982. Long-term response to phosphorus fertilization on selected southeastern Coastal Plain soils. Soil Science Society of America Journal 46(3):640–644.

Pritchett WL, Gooding JW. 1975. Fertilizer recommendations for pines in the southeastern Coastal Plain of the United States. Bull. 774. Gainesville, FL: University of Florida, Institute of Food and Agricultural Sciences, Agricultural Experiment Stations. 23 p.

Ralston CW. 1973. Annual primary productivity in a loblolly pine plantation. In: Proceedings, IUFRO Working Party on the Mensuration of the Forest Biomass Meeting (S4.01); IUFRO biomass studies; 1973 June 25–29; Nancy, France/1973 August 20–24; Vancouver, BC. Orono, ME: University of Maine Press: 105–117.

Ralston CW. 1978. Mineral cycling in temperature forest ecosystems. In: Proceedings, 5th North American Forest Soils Conference; 1978 August; Fort Collins, CO. Fort Collins, CO: Colorado State University, Department of Forestry and Wood Sciences: 320–340.

Rennie JC. 1979. Comparison of height-measurement techniques in a dense loblolly pine plantation. Southern Journal of Applied Forestry 3(4):146–148.

Reynolds RR. 1969. Management of southern pine for size and quality. Forests and People 19(1):22–23, 44–45.

Rockwood DL, Arvanitis LG, Hodgkins PE. 1980. Southern pine volume equations and associated conversion factors for southern Georgia. Bull. 813. Gainesville, FL: University of Florida, Florida Agricultural Experiment Station. 49 p.

Rogers KE. 1981. Preharvest drying of logging residues. Journal of Forestry 31(12):32–36.

Rogerson TL. 1964. Estimating foliage on loblolly pine. Res. Note SO-16. New Orleans: USDA Forest Service, Southern Forest Experiment Station. 3 p.

Romancier RM. 1961. Weight and volume of plantation-grown loblolly pine. Res. Note SE-161. Asheville, NC: USDA Forest Service, Southeastern Forest Experiment Station. 2 p.

Rosson JF. 1988. Residual woody biomass on harvested timberland in Mississippi. In: Proceeding, 9th Southern Forest Biomass Workshop; 1987 June 8–11; Biloxi, MS. Mississippi State, MS: Mississippi State University: 152–162.

Rosson JF, Thomas CE. 1986. The woody biomass resource of Alabama. Res. Pap. SO-228. New Orleans: USDA Forest Service, Southern Forest Experiment Station. 31 p.

Ruark GA, Saucier JR, Campbell RG. 1991. Managing dense, seed-origin loblolly stands to utilize the favorable juvenile wood core for sawlog production: a case study. Southern Journal of Applied Forestry 15(1):5–9.

Sarigumba TI. 1978. Fertilization of young pines on Georgia Coastal Plain soils. Southern Journal of Applied Forestry 2(2):38–41.

Satoo T. 1966. Production and distribution of dry matter in forest ecosystems. Miscellaneous Information of Tokyo University Forests 16:1–16.

Saucier JR, Phillips DR, Williams JG Jr. 1981. Green weight, volume, board-foot, and cord tables for the major southern pine species. Georgia For. Res. Pap. 19. Macon, GA: Georgia Forestry Commission. 63 p.

Schmidtling RC. 1973. Intensive culture increases growth without

affecting wood quality of young southern pines. Canadian Journal of Forest Resources 3:565–573.

Schmidtling RC. 1987. Relative performance of longleaf compared to loblolly and slash pines under different levels of intensive culture. In: Phillips DR, comp. Proceeding, 4th Biennial Southern Silvicultural Research Conference; 1986 November 4–6; Atlanta, GA. Gen. Tech. Rep. SE-42. Asheville, NC: USDA Forest Service, Southeastern Forest Experiment Station: 395–400.

Schmitt D, Bower D. 1970. Volume tables for young loblolly, slash, and longleaf pines in plantations in south Mississippi. Res. Note SO-102. New Orleans: USDA Forest Service, Southern Forest Experiment Station. 4 p.

Schroeder J, Clark A III. 1970. Predicting veneer grade-yields for loblolly pine. Forest Products Journal 20(2):37–39.

Schultz RP. 1975. Intensive culture of southern pines: maximum yields on short rotations. Iowa State Journal of Research 49(3):325–337.

Schumacher FX, Coile TS. 1960. Growth and yields of natural stands of the southern pines. Durham, NC: T.S. Coile, Inc. 115 p.

Shain WA, Jenkins WB. 1974. Growth and yield of loblolly, longleaf, and slash pines (Pinus taeda, Pinus palustris, Pinus elliottii) in the South Carolina Sandhills. For. Bull. 15. Clemson, SC: Clemson University, Department of Forestry: 1–3.

Shear TH, Perry TO. 1986. Nondestructive estimation of the needle weight and stem weight of small loblolly pine trees (Pinus taeda). Canadian Journal of Forest Research 16(2):403–405.

Shearin AT, Nix LE, Collins RT. 1985. Thinning from below affects the Girard form class and final volume of loblolly pine plantations. In: Proceedings, 3rd Biennial Southern Silvicultural Research Conference; 1984 November 7–8; Atlanta, GA. Gen. Tech. Rep. SO-54: New Orleans: USDA Forest Service, Southern Forest Experiment Station: 227–230

Shelton MG, Nelson LE, Switzer GL. 1984. The weight, volume and nutrient status of plantation-grown loblolly pine trees in the interior flatwoods of Mississippi. Tech. Bull. 121. Starkville, MS: Mississippi State University, Mississippi Agricultural and Forestry Experiment Station. 27 p.

Shelton MG. 1984. Effects of the initial spacing of loblolly pine plantations on production and nutrition during the first 25 years. Starkville, MS: Mississippi State University, Department of Agronomy. 161 p. Ph.D. thesis.

Shepard RK. 1971. The development of loblolly pine planted at various initial spacings (Pinus taeda). Louisiana Agriculture 15(2):8–9, 11.

Shepard RK. 1973. The influence of fertilizers on height growth of loblolly pine (Pinus taeda). For. Res. Rep. Homer, LA: North Louisiana Hill Farm Experiment Station: 11–14.

Shimabukuro YE, Filho PH, Koffler NF, Chen SC. 1980. Automatic classification of reforested pine and eucalyptus using Landsat data. Photogrammetric Engineering and Remote Sensing 46(2):209–216.

Shipman RD. 1960. Site quality of loblolly pine plantations in the South Carolina Piedmont. For. Res. Ser. 1. Clemson, SC: South Carolina Agricultural Experiment Station. 2 p.

Shoulders E. 1973. Rainfall influences female flowering of slash pine. Res. Note SO-150. New Orleans: USDA Forest Service, Southern Forest Experiment Station. 7 p.

Shoulders E. 1983. Comparison of growth and yield of four southern pines on uniform sites in the gulf Coastal Plain. In: Predicting growth and yield in the Mid-South; Proceedings, 31st Annual Forestry Symposium; 1982; Baton Rouge, LA. Baton Rouge, LA: Louisiana State University, Division of Continuing Education: 75–100.

Shoulders E, Walker FV. 1979. Soil, slope, and rainfall affect height and yield in 15-year-old southern pine plantation. Res. Pap. SO-153. New Orleans: USDA Forest Service, Southern Forest Experiment Station. 52 p.

Smalley GW, Bailey R. 1974. Yield tables and stand structure for loblolly pine plantations in Tennessee, Alabama, and Georgia highlands. Res. Pap. SO-96. New Orleans: USDA Forest Service, Southern Forest Experiment Station. 81 p.

Smalley GW, Bower DR. 1968. Volume tables and point sampling factors for loblolly pines in plantations on abandoned fields in Tennessee, Alabama, and Georgia highlands. Res. Pap. SO-32. New Orleans: USDA Forest Service, Southern Forest Experiment Station. 13 p.

Smalley GW, Bower DR. 1971. Site index curves for loblolly and shortleaf pine plantations on abandoned fields in Tennessee, Alabama, and Georgia highlands. Res. Note SO-126. New Orleans: USDA Forest Service, Southern Forest Experiment Station. 6 p.

Smalley GW, Pierce K. 1972. Yellow-poplar, loblolly pine, and Virginia pine compared in Cumberland Plateau Plantations. Res. Note SO-141. New Orleans: USDA Forest Service, Southern Forest Experiment Station. 6 p.

Smith DM. 1968. Wood quality of loblolly pine after thinning. Res. Pap. FPL-89. Madison, WI: USDA Forest Service, Forest Products Laboratory. 10 p.

Smith JL. 1978. Volume yields of site prepared loblolly pine plantations in the lower Coastal Plain of the Carolinas, Georgia and north Florida. Athens, GA: University of Georgia. 58 p. M.S. thesis.

Smith LF, Schmidtling RC. 1970. Cultivation and fertilization speed early growth of planted southern pines. Tree Planters' Notes 21(1):1–3.

Smith WD. 1988. Modeling tree quality in loblolly pine plantations. In: Proceedings, Conference on Forest Growth Modeling and prediction; 1987 August 23–27; General Tech. Rep. NC-120. Minneapolis, MN: USDA Forest Service, North Central Forest Experiment Station: 1053–1057.

Smith WD, Geron CC, Hafley WL. 1987. Modeling the impact of tree quality on product yields. In: Forests, the world, and the profession; Proceedings, 1986 Society of American Foresters National Convention; 1986 October 5–8; Birmingham, AL. Bethesda, MD: Society of American Foresters: 93–97.

Smith WD, Hafley WL. 1984. Multiproduct yield tables for single-thinned loblolly pine plantations. Tech. Rep. 2. Raleigh, NC: North Carolina State University, School of Forest Resources, Southern Forest Research Center. 75 p.

Smith WD, Hafley WL. 1986. Evaluation of a loblolly pine plantation thinning model. Southern Journal of Applied Forestry 10(1):52–63.

Smith WH, Nelson LE, Switzer GL. 1971. Development of the shoot system of young loblolly pine: II. Dry matter and nitrogen accumulation. Forest Science 17(1):55–62.

Somberg SI, Haas RE. 1971. Heavy thinnings can increase income form east Texas loblolly pine stands. Texas For. Pap. 10. Nacogdoches, TX: Stephen F. Austin State University, School of Forestry. 4 p.

South DB, Boyer JN, Bosch L. 1985. Survival and growth of loblolly pine as influenced by seedling grade: 13-year results. Southern Journal of Applied Forestry 9(2):76–81.

Sprinz PT. 1987. Effects of genetically improved stands on growth and yield principles. Proceedings of the Southern Conference on Forest Tree Improvement 41:338–348.

Sprinz PT, Burkhart HE. 1987. Relationships between tree crown, stem, and stand characteristics in unthinned loblolly pine plantations. Canadian Journal of Forest Research 17(6):534–538.

Sprinz PT, Clason T, Bower D. 1979. Spacing and thinning effects on the growth and development of a loblolly pine plantation. For. Res. Rep. Homer, LA: North Louisiana Hill Farm Experiment Station. 42 p.

Stafford CW, Torbert JL, Burger JA. 1985. An evaluation of site preparation methods for loblolly pine regeneration on the Piedmont. In: Proceedings, 3rd Biennial Southern Silvicultural Research Conference; 1984 November 7–8; Atlanta, GA. Gen.

Tech. Rep. SO-54: New Orleans: USDA Forest Service, Southern Forest Experiment Station: 57–60.

Stephen FM, Wallis GW, Colvin RJ, and others. 1982. Pine tree growth and yield: influence of species, plant spacing, vegetation, and pine tip moth control. Arkansas Farm Research 31(2):10.

Stokes BJ, Watson WF, Miller DE. 1987. Transpirational drying of energywood. ASAE Pap. 87-1530. St. Joseph, MI: American Society of Agricultural Engineers. 14 p.

Stransky JJ. 1964. Site-preparation effects on early growth of loblolly pine. Tree Planters' Notes 64:4–6.

Stransky JJ, Roese JH, Watterson KG. 1985. Soil properties and pine growth affected by site preparation after clearcutting. Southern Journal of Applied Forestry 9(1):40–43.

Strub MR, Sprinz PT. 1988. Comparisons of southern pine height growth. In: Proceedings, Conference on Forest Growth Modelling and Prediction; 1988 August 23–27; Minneapolis, MN. Gen. Tech. Rep. NC-120. St. Paul, MN: USDA Forest Service, North Central Forest Experiment Station: 428–434.

Strub MR, Feduccia DP, Baldwin VC Jr. 1981. A diameter distribution method useful in compatible growth and yield modeling of thinned stands. In: Proceedings, 1st Biennial Southern Silvicultural Research Conference; 1980 November 6–7; Atlanta, GA. Gen. Tech. Rep. SO-34. New Orleans: USDA Forest Service, Southern Forest Experiment Station: 127–130.

Strub MR, Green EJ, Burkhart HE, Pirie W. 1986. Merchantability of loblolly pine: an application of nonlinear regression with discrete dependent variable. Forest Science 32(1):254–261.

Stubbs J, Roberts DR, Outcalt KW. 1984. Chemical stimulation of lightwood in southern pines. Gen. Tech. Rep. SE-25. Asheville, NC: USDA Forest Service, Southeastern Forest Experiment Station. 51 p.

Sullivan AD, Clutter JL. 1972. A simultaneous growth and yield model for loblolly pine. Forest Science 18(1):76–86.

Sullivan AD, Williston HL. 1977. Growth and yield of thinned loblolly pine plantations in loessial soil areas. Tech. Bull. 86. Mississippi State, MS: Mississippi State University, Mississippi Agricultural and Forestry Experiment Station. 16 p.

Switzer GL, Nelson LE, Smith WH. 1966. The characterization of dry matter and nitrogen accumulation by loblolly pine (Pinus taeda L.). Soil Science Society of America Proceedings 30:114–119.

Talbert JT. 1982. One generation of loblolly pine tree improvement: results and challenges. In: Proceedings, 18th Meeting of the Canadian Tree Improvement Association; 1981 August 18–21; Duncan, BC. Chalk River, ON: Canadian Forestry Service, Petawawa National Forestry Institute: 106–120.

Talbert CB, Strub MR. 1987. Dynamics of stand growth and yield over 29 years in a loblolly pine source trail in Arkansas. Proceedings of the Southern Conference on Forest Tree Improvement (41):30–38.

Talbert JT, Weir RJ, Arnold RD. 1983. Loblolly pine tree improvement: an attractive forestry investment. In: Proceedings, Southern Forest Economics Workshop; 1983 April 7–8; Mobile, AL. [Place of publication and publisher unknown]: 16 pp.

Talbert JT, Weir RJ, Arnold RD. 1985. Costs and benefits of a mature first generation loblolly pine tree improvement program. Journal of Forestry. 83(3):162–166.

Taras MA, Clark A III. 1974. Aboveground biomass of loblolly pine in a natural, uneven-aged sawtimber stand in central Alabama. In: Proceedings, 1974 Biology Conference; 1974 September 18–20; Seattle, WA. Atlanta, GA: TAPPI Research and Development Division: 107–116.

Taylor FW, Burton JD. 1982. Growth ring characteristics, specific gravity, and fiber length of rapidly grown loblolly pine. Wood and Fiber 14(3):204–210.

Terry TA, Hughes JH. 1975. The effects of intensive management on planted loblolly pine (Pinus taeda L.) growth on poorly drained soils of the Atlantic Coastal Plain. Forest soils and forest land management. Quebec: Les Presses de l'Université Laval: 351–77.

Tiarks AE. 1983. Effect of site preparation and fertilization on slash pine growing on a good site. In: Proceedings, 2nd Biennial Southern Silvicultural Research Conference; 1982 November 4–5; Atlanta, GA. Gen. Tech. Rep. SE-24. Asheville, NC: USDA Forest Service, Southeastern Forest Experiment Station: 34–39.

Tiarks AE, Haywood JD. 1986. *Pinus taeda* L. response to fertilization, herbaceous plant control, and woody plant control. Forest Ecology and Management 14(2):103–112.

Torbert JL Jr, Burger JA. 1984. Long-term availability of applied phosphorus to loblolly pine on a Piedmont soil. Soil Science Society of America Journal 48:1174–1178.

Trousdell KB, Beck DE, Lloyd TF. 1974. Site index for loblolly pine in the Atlantic Coastal Plain of the Carolinas and Virginia. Res. Pap. SE-115. Asheville, NC: USDA Forest Service, Southeastern Forest Experiment Station. 11 p.

Tucker CJ, Fung IY, Keeling CD, Gammon RH. 1986. Relationship between atmospheric CO_2 variations and a satellite-derived vegetation index. Nature 319:195–203.

Tuttle CL. 1978. Root biomass and nutrient content of a 25-year-old loblolly pine (*Pinus taeda* L.) plantation in east Texas. College Station, TX: Texas A&M University. 60 p. M.S. thesis.

Tuttle CL, Golden MS, Meldahl RS. 1987. Effect of soil removal and herbicide treatment on sol properties and early loblolly pine growth. Bull. 588. Auburn, AL: Alabama Polytechnic Institute, Alabama Agricultural Experiment Station: 3–22.

USDA [U.S. Department of Agriculture]. 1929. Volume, yield, and stand tables for second-growth southern pines. Misc. Pub. 50. Washington, DC: USDA Forest Service. 202 p.

Valenti MA, Cao QV. 1986. Use of crown ratio to improve loblolly pine taper equations. Canadian Journal of Forest Research 16(5):1141–1145.

Van Deusen PC, Sullivan AD, Matney TG. 1981. A prediction system for cubic foot volume of loblolly pine applicable through much of its range. Southern Journal of Applied Forestry 5(4):186–189.

Van Lear DH, Taras MA, Waide JB, Augspurger MK. 1986. Comparison of biomass equations for planted vs. natural loblolly pine stands of sawtimber size. Forest Ecology and Management 14(3):205–210.

Van Lear DH, Waide JB, Teuke MJ. 1984. Biomass and nutrient content of a 41-year-old loblolly pine (*Pinus taeda* L.) plantation on a poor site in South Carolina. Forest Science 30(2):395–404.

Wade DD. 1969. Estimating slash quantity from standing loblolly pine. Res. Note SE-125. Asheville, NC: USDA Forest Service, Southeastern Forest Experiment Station. 4 p.

Wakeley PC. 1969. Results of southern pine planting experiments established in the middle twenties. Journal of Forestry 67(4):237–241.

Wells CG, Allen L. 1985. When and where to apply fertilizer. Gen. Tech. Rep. SE-36. Asheville, NC: USDA Forest Service, Southeastern Forest Experiment Station. 23 p.

Wells CG, Crutchfield DM. 1969. Foliar analysis for predicting loblolly pine response to phosphorus fertilization on wet sites. Res. Note SE-128. Asheville, NC: USDA Forest Service, Southeastern Forest Experiment Station. 4 p.

Wells CG, Jorgensen JR, Burnett CE. 1975. Biomass and mineral elements in a thinned loblolly plantation at age 16. Res. Pap. SE-126. Asheville, NC: USDA Forest Service, Southeastern Forest Experiment Station. 10 p.

Wheeler GL, Meade FM, Russell MW. 1982. Growth of loblolly pine in Arkansas Ozarks. Southern Journal of Applied Forestry 6(4):215–217.

White EH, Pritchett WL. 1970. Water table control and fertilization for pine production in the flatwoods. Tech. Bull. 743. Gainesville, FL: University of Florida, Florida Agricultural Experiment Station. 41 p.

White EH, Pritchett WL, Robertson WK. 1971. Slash pine root bio-

mass and nutrient concentrations. In: Young HE, ed. Forest biomass studies; Proceedings, 15th IUFRO Congress, section 25, growth and yield; [dates unknown]; [location unknown]. Gainesville, FL: University of Florida: 165–176.

Whittaker RH, Woodwell GM. 1968. Dimension and production relations of trees and shrubs in the Brookhaven Forest, New York. Journal of Ecology 56:1–25.

Wilhite LP. 1976. Slash, loblolly, longleaf, and Sonderegger pines 20 years after planting on Leon sand in northeastern Florida. Res. Pap. SE-153. Asheville, NC: USDAForest Service, Southeastern Forest Experiment Station. 8 p.

Williams RA. 1989. Use of randomized branch and importance sampling to estimate loblolly pine biomass. Southern Journal of Applied Forestry 13(4):181–184.

Williston HL. 1958. Shortleaf versus loblolly pine in north Mississippi. Journal of Forestry 56(10):761.

Williston HL. 1967a. Growth of pine planted for erosion control in north Mississippi. Res. Note SO-67. New Orleans: USDA Forest Service, Southern Forest Experiment Station. 4 p.

Williston HL. 1967b. Thinning desirable in loblolly pine plantations in west Tennessee. Res. Note SO-61. New Orleans: USDA Forest Service, Southern Forest Experiment Station. 7 p.

Williston HL. 1972. Shortleaf and loblolly pine growth in the Mid-South. Journal of Forestry 70(5):209–291.

Williston HL. 1979. Growth and yield to age 37 in north Mississippi loblolly plantations. Southern Journal of Applied Forestry 3(3):127–130.

Williston HL. 1985. Growth and yield of planted loblolly and shortleaf pines in a north Mississippi creek bottom. Southern Journal of Applied Forestry 9(4):247–249.

Williston HL, Dell TR. 1974. Growth of pine plantations in north Mississippi. Res. Pap. SO-94. New Orleans: USDA Forest Service, Southern Forest Experiment Station. 15 p.

Woessner RA, Davey CB, Crabtree BE, Gregory JD. 1975. Nutrient content of the aboveground tissues of 12-week-old loblolly pine intraprovenance and interprovenance crosses. Canadian Journal of Forest Research 5:592–598.

Xydias GK, Gregory AH, Sprinz PT. 1983. Ten-year results from thinning an eleven-year-old stand of loblolly pine on an excellent site. In: Proceedings, 2nd Biennial Southern Silvicultural Research Conference; 1982 November 4–5; Atlanta, GA. Gen. Tech. Rep. SE-24. Asheville, NC: USDA Forest Service, Southeastern Forest Experiment Station: 193–199.

Young HE, Strand L, Altenberger R. 1964. Preliminary fresh and dry weight tables for seven tree species in Maine. Tech. Bull. 12. Orono, ME: Maine Agricultural Experiment Station. 76 p.

Zahner R. 1959. Fertilizer trials with loblolly pine in southern Arkansas. Journal of Forestry 57(11):812–816.

Zahner R. 1962. Loblolly pine site curves by soil groups. Forest Science 8(2):104–110.

Zahner R, Grier CE. 1990. Concept for a model to assess the impact of climate on the growth of the southern pines. In: Dixon RK, Meldahl RS, Ruark GA, Warren WG, eds. Process modeling of forest growth responses to environmental stress. Portland, OR: Timber Press: 383–392.

Zarger TG. 1965. Performance of loblolly, shortleaf, and eastern white pine superseedlings. Silvae Genetica 14:182–186.

Zobel BJ, Goggans JF, Maki TE, Henson F. 1961. Some effects of fertilizers on wood properties of loblolly pine. Tappi Journal 44(3):186–192.

Zutter BR, Glover GR, Gjerstad DH. 1987. Vegetation response to intensity of herbaceous weed control in a newly planted loblolly pine plantation. New Forests 4:257–271.

Chapter 12

International Importance of Loblolly Pine

Contents

LOBLOLLY PINE (*PINUS TAEDA* L.)

International Importance of Loblolly Pine

Introduction

Although loblolly pine is native only to the southern United States, its adaptability and potential for culture in other parts of the world has long been recognized. The species was first introduced into South Africa about 1898, and plantations were established there as early as 1908. It was first planted on the island of Mauritius in the Indian Ocean in 1911 and in Australia in 1917 (Lindsay 1932). It was first introduced into South America in 1948 (Golfari 1970). During the last two decades, loblolly pine was planted on a trial basis in dozens of countries under a wide range of environmental conditions. The most extensive programs are in China and Brazil, which together produce and plant more than 320 million seedlings annually. The most successful exotic plantings are usually between latitudes 24° and 30° N or S and at elevations of 500 to 900 m. Loblolly often grows rapidly and is often harvested at early ages in exotic locations. When this is the case, the percentage of juvenile wood is high. Loblolly pine wood that consists largely of juvenile wood is normally undesirable for products that require strength but is excellent for paper products (Zobel 1985).

Seed sources from the southern part of loblolly pine's native range perform especially well in subtropical climates. Most physical characteristics of individual loblolly trees and stands planted in exotic locations are the same as those of trees in the native range. However, growth can be exceedingly rapid under some conditions, and self-pruning is poor in almost all foreign locations.

Loblolly Pine in South America

In South America, loblolly pine is grown on 15- to 25-year rotations for both fiber and solid wood products. A number of forest product companies and multiple-product farms have committed themselves to intensive, long-term programs of loblolly pine plantation management, including tree improvement and nursery production. Under some multiple-use management regimes, slash pine is substituted for loblolly on lower slopes and along wet fringes of streams or in depressions. Slash may grow somewhat more slowly than loblolly, but it can be tapped for oleoresin to provide a more diverse income. Many farmers and private landowners have planted small plots and hedgerows with loblolly. Most management plans project continuous planting of superior trees for succeeding generations; however, natural regeneration is becoming more prevalent along hedgerows and in open areas as the area and range of planted loblolly increases.

History

Fast-growing loblolly pine plantations have become important economically as a part of Brazil's and Argentina's rapidly expanding pulp and paper, particleboard, packaging, lumber, and veneer industries. Brazil, where more than 120 million trees were planted annually in the late 1970's and early 1980's, has the largest loblolly pine program in South America. Plantings, which exceeded 460,000 ha between 1966 and 1981, were confined mostly to the southern states of Parana and Santa Catarina (Machado 1984). In some locations, loblolly stands are in their second rotation. Growth rates of 25 to 39 m^3/ha/yr (CIEF 1987) are up to three times faster than stands growing on excellent sites in the United States.

More than 170,000 ha of underused land in the Misiones and Corrientes Provinces of northern Argentina (approximate latitudes 27° to 29° S) have been planted with loblolly and slash pines since 1962, and these plantings have made these provinces the mainstay of Argentina's kraft pulp industry (Crotto 1987). Because loblolly grows so well in specific areas of northern Argentina (especially on Latosols, Lithosols, and hydromorphic soils) (CIEF 1987, Golfari 1979), rates of planting by some companies have grown exponentially in recent years.

Small numbers of loblolly pines are grown in Colombia, Uruguay, and Venezuela on a regular basis. For example, 641,000 loblolly seedlings were planted in Uruguay in 1984 (McDonald and Krugman 1985).

Habitat

In South America, loblolly pine grows best between latitudes 24° S and 32° S and at elevations between 500 and 1,500 m (EMBRAPA 1986; Krall 1969; Machado 1978, 1984). Krall (1969) determined that trees from origins where growing seasons are longer make a greater percentage of their growth in the later part of the growing season and that trees from areas where droughts are frequent grow more slowly.

If planted closer to the Equator than 24° S latitude, loblolly pine grows satisfactorily only at higher elevations where climatic conditions are similar to those of its native range. For example, at latitude 22° S in Brazil, loblolly grew slower than any of the other seven species tested, reaching only one-third the size of *Pinus caribaea* Morelet and about one-half the size of slash pine (Garrido and Negreiros 1976). However, it grows at latitude 9° N at an elevation of 2,200 m in the Venezuelan Andes (Quijada and Zapata 1978) and seems to grow very well at an elevation of about 2,500 m in the Colombian Andes (latitude 2° to 10° N). The best seeds for the Andean region of Colombia come from central Florida and from the coasts of Georgia, Alabama, South Carolina, and Louisiana (Ladrach 1983, 1985). Seeds from southernmost coastal areas of the United States also grow at an acceptable rate of 27 m³/ha/yr on volcanic soils at 1,750 m in the Popayan altiplano of Colombia, which is only about 2° north of the Equator (Ladrach 1983).

Loblolly pine grows from hilltops to the fringes of stream bottoms on all but very sandy soils of southern Brazil and northeast Argentina. Tree growth is especially rapid on rolling red clay hills of moderate to poor fertility. Plantings of loblolly have helped to stabilize these and other eroded areas by producing a thick litter and duff layer that increases the soil's organic matter content and water-holding capacity (Souza and others 1982). Even on severely eroded sites, height growth of 1 to 2 m is common between tree ages 5 and 15 years. The capability of loblolly to rejuvenate soil is demonstrated by its producing 37 tonnes (t) of organic matter/ha and 292 kg of nitrogen (N)/ha in a 19-year-old plantation growing on eroded soil (Lopes and others 1983). Loblolly increases the acidity of soil more than does native vegetation (Haag and others 1978, Lopes and others 1983). The decrease in pH is about 0.2 to 0.4 units in the surface 60 cm over a 20- to 25-year period.

It is extremely important to match native climatic requirements, such as amount and distribution of rainfall, range in annual mean temperatures, and absolute minimum temperature, when growing loblolly pine in South America. It adapts best where rainfall is uniformly distributed (no dry season), where the temperature does not fall below – 23 °C, and where mean annual precipitation is between 920 and 1,550 mm. In Brazil, loblolly grows best where the mean annual temperature is between 13 and 19 °C (EMBRAPA 1986). However, it shows considerable resistance to freezing temperatures throughout South America (Golfari 1962).

Tree Improvement

The production of genetically improved seeds in quantities that meet internal demand is a goal in all countries growing loblolly pine on a large scale. Most loblolly seeds for early plantings in both Argentina and Brazil came from bulk seeds collected in a few locations in the southern United States (especially Marion County, Florida; Beaufort County, North Carolina; and Livingston Parish, Louisiana). Most of the plantings grew well; however, specific seed sources or original stands were not identified, so original seed collections were almost impossible to duplicate. In the early 1970's, a broad range of specific seed sources was tested in several climatic zones of northern Argentina and southern Brazil. In a test at 534 m above sea level in the Misiones Province of Argentina (latitude 26°56′ S, longitude 54°24′ W), 15-year-old loblolly from Livingston Parish produced 664 m³ of fiber/ha, 72% more than the local commercial standard for the species and 12 to 28% more than *P. caribaea*, *P. oocarpa* (Schiede), and *P. patula* (Schiede and Deppe) produced (Fahler and others 1986).

In Brazil, Coastal Plain sources of loblolly pine from north Florida, Georgia, and South Carolina generally had the greatest height, diameter, and cubic volume growth through ages 6 to 9. Specific sources from other parts of the natural range of loblolly also proved superior for use in certain locations (Baldanzi 1978, Baldanzi and Malinovski 1976, Monteiro and others 1983, Shimizu and Higa 1981, Speltz and Bonisch 1972). In a test of 17 seed sources at latitude 24°20′ S, volume per hectare at age 9 ranged from a low of 249 m³ for a south Mississippi source to 500 m³ (55.6 m³/yr) for a northeast Florida source (Barrichelo and others 1977). Tests of United States seed sources in the State of Rio Grande do Sul, at latitude 31°45′ S and an altitude of 10 m, resulted in the following average growth (outside bark wood volumes) through age 9.5 years (Fishwick 1978):

Seed source	Volume/ha (m³)	Volume/ha/yr (m³)
Berkeley County, South Carolina	242	25.5
Jackson County, Florida	231	23.2
Noxubee County, Mississippi	214	22.3
Bastrop County, Texas	209	22.0
Northeast Georgia	206	21.7
Southeast Virginia	194	20.4
Coastal Virginia	193	20.3

Of more than 50 different loblolly seed sources tested in Uruguay, an east Texas source was found to be superior with a growth rate of 24.5 m³/ha/yr through age 10. Growth was about 15.5 m³/ha/yr for trees from Louisiana, Arkansas, and Georgia (Krall 1987).

Based on seed source trials, genetically superior seed orchards have been established in many locations in South America, especially in southern Brazil and northern Argentina, and some organizations expect to produce sufficient quantities of superior seeds for their own use in the early 1990's (Kikuti and others 1984). Outstanding trees are now being selected and bred for second-generation and even third-generation plantings in Argentina. Seed production areas, consisting of 100 to 300 excellent phenotypes/ha, are expected to provide an adequate amount of reasonably good, locally grown, southern pine seeds to supplement available improved seeds (Velazquez 1987). In addition, Marion and Columbia Counties in Florida and Livingston and Washington Parishes in Louisiana continue to provide excellent bulk seeds that produce fast-growing trees. Many organizations import these seeds regularly.

Artificial Regeneration

Almost all loblolly pine forestation in South America has been accomplished by planting seedlings. Direct seeding and the use of rooted cuttings have been limited to small experiments.

Seedling production. Capacities of South American pine nurseries range from 200,000 to 10 million bareroot seedlings/year. Management of large nurseries is highly mechanized and patterned after management of southern pine nurseries in the United States. In small nurseries, there is a considerable amount of hand labor. Loblolly pine seeds generally receive some pretreatment (prechilling) before sowing; however, Campinhos (1965) recommended that seeds obtained from the United States be left untreated. The commonest pretreatment is a 24-hour soak followed by 30 to 60 days of refrigeration at 0 to 5 °C. Other highly successful pretreatments include a 1-hour soak in aerated water followed by 1 week of chilling, a 4-hour soak in 1% hydrogen peroxide followed by 15 days of cold storage, and a 1-hour soak in 40% (by volume) hydrogen peroxide followed by 12 days of damp storage. Water soaking for as little as 48 hours without chilling yields 75% germination within 30 days. Chilling increases germination by about 10 to 15% (Bianchi and others 1984). After cold soaking, a fungicide can be applied to minimize damping-off (Pasztor 1963).

Seeds are sown in September or October in six to eight rows along 1-m-wide beds that are raised about 15 cm (figure 12-1). Pine needles, rice straw, and leaf mold mulches provide equally good germination, but Oliveira and Bridi (1976) showed that seedling height

Figure 12-1—The Papel Misiones bareroot loblolly pine nursery in which 20- to 30-cm-tall seedlings (at 400 plants/m²) are grown for 6 to 8 months with 3 to 4 undercuttings at depths of 10 to 15 cm.

growth was superior with a pine straw mulch. When seeds are sown at an optimum density of about 220 to 270 seeds/m², seedlings average 15.5 cm tall with root-collar diameters of 3.7 mm at 8 months. Up to 625 seedlings/m² can be grown successfully during an 8-month nursery cycle. Seedlings grown at this density average about 3.0 cm taller than those grown at optimum density, and they have root-collar diameters about 0.3 mm smaller than those of seedlings grown at optimum density. Seedlings grown at this high density have slightly reduced field survival rates but otherwise seem to be acceptable planting stock (Carneiro 1985).

Irrigation, fertilization, and herbicide treatments are applied as necessary. To increase development of secondary root systems, two to four undercuttings are made with a fixed blade at depths of 10 to 15 cm. The shallow undercutting results in a relatively small total root system and a high shoot-to-root ratio, but survival is generally good because trees are planted only during or shortly after rains. Hand lifting, culling, and packing followed by immediate transport and outplanting is the normal practice.

In 1987, the following system was used in an unmechanized private nursery in Uruguay that grew about 200,000 bareroot loblolly and slash pine seedlings annually (Schultz 1987):

1. Nutrient-rich riverbed soil was used to make seedbeds that were 15 cm high by 1 m wide.

2. In September or October, seeds were hand-sown 2 to 3 cm apart in shallow trenches spaced at 15-cm intervals across the seedbed (220 to 330 seedlings/m²) and covered lightly with soil.

3. Following seed germination, chemical treatments were applied weekly, or as needed, to control damping-off and to spot control chlorosis caused by nutrient deficiency.

4. Beds were weeded by hand.

5. In early March, a sharp spade was used to cut lateral roots on one side of each 1-m row. The spade entered the ground at an angle of 45% and severed taproots 10 to 15 cm below the soil surface. Two weeks later, the same treatment was performed on the other side of each row.

6. In June, the 15- to 25-cm-tall seedlings were lifted by hand, culled, bundled into 500- seedling groups, and sold for about 5 U.S. cents/seedling.

7. About every 2 to 3 years, old river sand was manually replaced with new river sand, so that fertility was maintained without costly inorganic fertilizers.

Container loblolly pine seedlings are also used to varying degrees in South American countries, depending on specific needs of landowners. Container type and sowing season greatly influence root system development and behavior (Carneiro 1987). Campinhos and others (1984) concluded that the best medium for growing container loblolly seedlings is a mixture of two parts peat humus to one part vermiculite.

There is a positive correlation between the amount of mycorrhizal inoculum and the growth and needle color of loblolly pine seedlings in nurseries (Inoue 1972). When loblolly was first introduced in South America, it did poorly because mycorrhizal fungi were absent. Fungi, such as *Scleroderma vulgare* Horn., were then introduced from the United States for use in inoculating trees (Takacs 1964a, 1964b). The mycorrhizae quickly became self-perpetuating. Mature trees near nurseries now provide adequate nursery inoculation.

Planting and stocking. Most plantings are made with bareroot seedlings. Success is greatest when bareroot seedlings are about 11 months old and dormant and they have root-collar diameters of at least 3.7 mm and some secondary needles (Carneiro 1977). Nine- to ten-month-old seedlings also do well in most areas. Even 6- to 8-month-old seedlings that have been undercut 3 or 4 times have satisfactory survival. Seedling height is not a good indicator of quality class. Top pruning, as well as root pruning, may increase early survival. Trees can be kept in cold storage (2 to 4 °C and 90% relative humidity) for up to 80 days with 70 to 90% outplanting survival. Storage for 4 to 5 months often reduces survival to 30 to 40%, whereas 6 months of storage reduces survival to only about 3 to 25% (Kikuti and others 1984).

Most planting is done by hand during the winter (May to July) on areas that have been spot or broadcast site-prepared. It is best to plant early in the season on upland soils so seedlings can become established before dry weather sets in. One- or two-row machine planters are used on well-prepared level sites. Planting usually takes place within 48 hours after seedlings are lifted from the nursery. Bareroot seedlings are normally planted to, or just above, the root collar. However, deeper planting is usually not detrimental to survival or growth. In trials on an upland loam and a lowland organic soil in Argentina, planting at normal depth, to midstem, or to the base of the terminal bud did not influence tree height after 4 years. Seedlings should be planted to normal depth on wet soils, but the planting period can be extended if necessary (Alonzo and Sancho 1967).

Traditionally, planting density has been 2,000 to 2,500 seedlings/ha and spacings have been 2.0 by 2.0 m, 2.5 by 1.6 m, 2.5 by 2.0 m, 3.0 by 1.5 m, and 3.0 by 2.0 m. More recent recommendations call for planting at lower densities (1,100 to 1,600 seedlings/ha) to promote rapid growth on fewer stems and to minimize planting costs and mortality before harvest. Some managers use container stock to replace dead trees during the first few months after bareroot outplanting. After that, seedlings are too big, and containerized replacements cannot compete successfully. Bareroot seedling survival of 95% or more can be achieved with good stock and outplanting care (Ladrach 1974).

Machado (1979a) followed the survival of loblolly pines in closely spaced plantations in central Parana, Brazil (figures 12-2 and 12-3). At tree age 6, survival exceeded 95% on all sites. By age 15, it varied from 65% on high-quality sites to near 90% on lower quality sites. The following prediction model accounted for 94% of the total variation:

$$\log (T_p/T_s) = A\,(0.001907\,H - 0.006322\,\sqrt{H})$$

where:

T_p = planted trees,

T_s = surviving trees,

A = plantation age, and

H = average height of dominant and codominant trees.

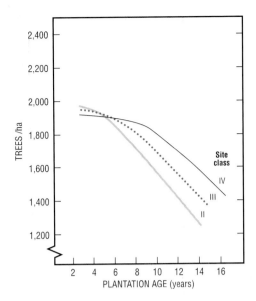

Figure 12-2—Natural survival of loblolly pines planted at 2.0- by 2.5-m spacing (2,000 trees/ha) as related to site class and plantation age (adapted from Machado 1979a). Median tree height at age 14 for site class II is 21.0 m; class III, 18.1 m; and class IV, 15.4 m.

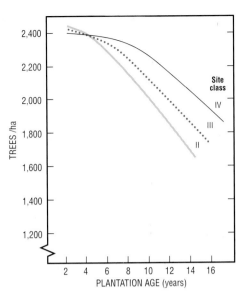

Figure 12-3—Natural survival of loblolly pines planted at 2- by 2-m spacing (2,500 trees/ha) as related to site class and plantation age (adapted from Machado 1979a). Median tree heights at age 14 are the same as those in figure 12-2.

Loblolly pine survival remains higher than that of 9 other exotic pines even when initial spacings are low. This is clearly demonstrated in the Misiones Province of Argentina, where survival rates of widely spaced pines of several species and varieties were compared over a 15-year period (Fahler and others 1986). Most species had less than 15% mortality through age 5, but by age 15, from 20 to more than 50% of the original trees were dead. In contrast, only one of three loblolly sources had any mortality at age 5 (6% for Livingston Parish, Louisiana), and mortality was only 4 to 7% through age 15.

Natural Regeneration

Natural regeneration of loblolly pine will occur under and around maturing stands (Seitz 1987; figure 12-4). Natural reproduction in the understory of thinned stands may surpass 60,000 stems/ha and is quite often sufficient to produce fully stocked stands following clearcutting. There are no data on how best to plan natural regeneration of loblolly. A study with slash pine at approximate latitude 23° N suggests that thinning loblolly plantations at about 20 years to densities of 167 to 500 stems/ha would result in the production of enough seeds for successful natural regeneration between stand ages 20 and 30 (Garrido and others 1984).

Maximum seed dissemination under a 19-year-old loblolly pine stand near Curitiba, Brazil, was 690 seeds/m²/year. As many as 151 seeds/m² were deposited 40 m outside the stand. Seedfall can begin as early as the last week of April and may continue until February. Seedfall peaks in mid-July, and about 77% of all seeds fall during the winter months of June and July. Another 15% fall in August and September, and the remaining 8% fall throughout the rest of the year. About 70% of the seeds germinate (Jankovski 1985, Seitz 1987).

Figure 12-4—Natural regeneration of 2- to 4-year-old loblolly pine trees in Parana, Brazil.

Stand Management

Pruning. Loblolly pine does not self-prune well in South America at any level of stocking (figure 12-5). Even though lower limbs may die within a few years, many dead limbs remain attached for 3 to 10 years—resulting in numerous dry knots that greatly reduce tree value. Low stand density promotes retention of both green and dry limbs. The fact that loblolly self-prunes well at high densities in its native habitat but not in South America suggests that one or more natural pathogenic organisms that decompose dead limbs attached to trees have not been transferred to South America.

Green-limb pruning must be done early in the life of a stand if high-quality trees are to be produced. Stohr and others (1987) found that 25 to 40% of the live crown of a young tree can be removed by green pruning without significantly affecting growth, primarily because the crown is quickly recovered as a result of rapid height growth. Removing up to 60% of the live crown of loblolly pine saplings slows height and diameter growth for a year or two, but does not significantly reduce total

Figure 12-6—A cross section, 25 cm in diameter at 6 m in height, of a 15-year-old loblolly pine thinned from a plantation in Misiones Province, Argentina.

growth during the first 4 years after pruning because crown development is so rapid. The first pruning normally takes place at tree age 4 or 5 and removes all limbs to 2.5 m above the ground. Crop trees should be pruned again immediately after the first thinning (at about age 8). At this time, trees can be pruned to 6.5 m in one operation if they are about 12 to 13 cm in dbh and if no more than 40% of the live crown is removed.

Pruning is normally done by hand, and a variety of pruning knives or saws are used. Saws prune better, but knives do the job faster. Low pruning (to 2.5 m) by saw is most economical with a "Manasa" saw, a lightweight, slightly curved blade adapted for extension handles. High pruning by saw, especially from 4.5 to 6.0 m, is fastest with a "Dauner" saw, which resembles a hacksaw attached to an extension handle (Nogueira 1978).

Thinning. Depending on management philosophy and objectives, loblolly pine stands may receive zero to four thinnings over rotations of 15 to 25 years (Burger and others 1980, McTague and Bailey 1987a). Trees planted exclusively for cellulose and reconstituted products can be planted at densities of 1,100 to 2,500 stems/ha and managed either without thinnings or with two thinnings—the first at approximately age 7 or 8 and the second between ages 10 and 12. When both sawn materials and cellulose are required, three to four thinnings are made at 3- to 4-year intervals beginning approximately at age 8 (figure 12-6). On rare occasions, loblolly is managed for sawlog production on a 30-year rotation. When this is the case, five thinnings may be made, beginning at age 8 and then at 4-year intervals. Five to ten percent of first thinnings can be sawn, and as much as 50 to 70% of the total production of loblolly plantations can be sawn over 20- to 30-year rotations (Burger and others 1980).

Thinnings can make up a high percentage of total stand yield on good sites in South America. The first thinning should remove at least 25% of the basal area of

Figure 12-5—A 10-year-old loblolly pine plantation. The tree in the foreground shows typical poor self pruning. The tree behind and to the left was pruned at age 5 (University of Parana Experimental Forest, Parana, Brazil).

Table 12-1—Yield of loblolly pine plantations in Santa Catarina, Brazil, and South Carolina, United States, at two thinning ages

Type of measurement	Santa Catarina, Brazil 9 yr	Santa Catarina, Brazil 14 yr	South Carolina, United States 9 yr	South Carolina, United States 15 yr
Max. Height (m)	14.9	—	8.2	—
Max. dbh (cm)	21.6	—	13.5	—
Thinning yield (m³/ha)	69.3	132.3	—	69.3
Total thinned (m³/ha)	—	201.5	—	69.3

Source: Luke D, 1978. Westvaco; corporate citizen/Brazil. Presented at the international conference, USDA Forest Service; 1978 May 22; [city unknown], Brazil

the stand. A rapidly growing plantation in Santa Catarina, Brazil, yielded 69.3 m³/ha in a thinning at age 9 and an additional 132.3 m³/ha when thinned at age 14. A comparable planting in South Carolina yielded only 69.3 m³/ha in a first thinning at age 15 (table 12-1).

Thinning alters loblolly pine wood quality. Wood produced two seasons after growth acceleration in Brazil had higher lignin content, larger ring width, and lower density than wood from unthinned stands. Thinning also results in increases in lumen diameter and amounts of extractives and holocellulose. Pulp produced from wood that has undergone accelerated growth has increased tensile strength, specific weight, and porosity, but it has reduced tear strength (Muner and Barrichelo 1983).

Tree nutrition and fertilization.   Generally, there is an adequate supply of most nutrients in the soils where loblolly pine does well, but nutrient deficiencies—especially phosphorus (P) deficiency—do occur on some sites (Flor 1977).

Table 12-2—Soil analysis under different overstory conditions on a red-yellow podzolic soil at Piracicaba, Brazil

Soil parameter	0–10 cm soil depth No cover	0–10 cm soil depth Pinus taeda	0–10 cm soil depth Eucalyptus citriodora	10–20 cm soil depth No cover	10–20 cm soil depth Pinus taeda	10–20 cm soil depth Eucalyptus citriodora
pH	5.50	5.30	5.12	5.50	5.10	5.15
% C	0.54	0.78	0.84	0.54	0.32	0.48
ion conc. (mg/100 g)						
PO_4^{-3}	0.03	0.05	0.04	0.03	0.04	0.04
K^+	0.17	0.10	0.33	0.10	0.06	0.21
Ca^{+2}	1.90	1.57	1.03	1.10	0.99	0.84
Mg^{+2}	0.56	0.30	0.51	0.40	0.22	0.27
Al^{+3}	0.50	0.80	1.21	1.20	1.26	1.23
H^+	3.04	3.98	4.34	3.04	3.96	4.25

Source: adapted from Haag and others (1978).

The content of potassium (K), calcium (Ca), magnesium (Mg), and zinc (Zn) in current needles is positively correlated with tree growth, and the concentrations of K, Ca, and Mg in the upper mineral soil are closely correlated with their presence in needles (Reissmann and Zottl 1984, Rocha Filho and others 1978). A red-yellow podzolic soil (Ultisol) at Piracicaba, Brazil (latitude 22°43′S, longitude 47°38′W, elevation 590 m), supported a 24-year-old stand of planted loblolly pine and a 20-year-old stand of planted *Eucalyptus citriodora* Hook. Nutrient levels in soil samples from the plantations were compared (table 12-2). Although both species changed the soil nutrient content, *E. citriodora* supplied greater amounts of litter to the soil, and this litter was higher in nutrients than were the needles of loblolly pine. Nevertheless, replacing native vegetation with loblolly pine can substantially increase the amount of nutrients recycled from deep horizons to surface soil and surface organic matter (Haag and others 1978).

More than 70% of the loblolly pine needles fall during April, May, June, and July, with 25% falling in May. Loblolly has a higher litterfall in northern Argentina and southern Brazil than in its natural range, probably because it grows faster there than in the United States (figure 12-7). On the Rio Negro Forest in Parana, Brazil, the ovendry moisture content of loblolly needles averages 172% at the beginning of the growing season (October) and gradually decreases to about 116% as buds elongate. Oleoresin

Figure 12-7—Thick litter layer under a 19-year-old loblolly pine stand on a good clay site at Las Marias Farm, Corrientes, Argentina.

content of needles ranges from a maximum of 15% during the summer (January and February) to a minimum of 2% during the winter. Periods of high crown combustibility occur in the spring and in the middle of the winter when the moisture content of foliage is low and the percentage of oleoresin is high (Fernandes 1981, Fernandes and Soares 1981).

An organic layer rapidly builds up under loblolly pine stands. Even in plantings on denuded sites, 3 years of fallen needles and other detritus produce a litter and duff layer up to 5 cm thick. This material contributes organic matter to the surface soil and protects soil fauna and minerals during controlled burns (Goldammer 1983). By stand age 5, needlefall equals about 2.5 t/ha/yr. It quickly increases to 6.5 t/ha/yr by stand age 7, and then gradually increases to 8.3 t/ha/yr by age 15. It then declines at different rates depending on intensity of thinning or other management activities (figure 12-8). Needles begin decomposing rapidly soon after falling. Although newly fallen needles contain few microorganisms (mycelial length of 4.4 m/g of dry mass), fungal biomass increases to a maximum mycelial length of 23.4 m/g of dry mass within a year. The most important needle decomposers are fungi and *Thecamoebas* spp. (Godeas 1987).

Loblolly pines are rarely fertilized in South America, so there is little published information about response to fertilizers. Where loblolly pines were planted in the grassland area of Parana, Brazil, adding P to the planting holes increased diameter growth by 7% and height growth by 9% by tree age 7. Adding N or K did not increase growth (Muniz and others 1975). Loblolly pines can successfully revegetate strip mine spoils in Brazil, but growth is very poor without liming and NPK fertilization (Chiaranda and others 1983, Simoes and others 1978).

Growth and Yield

Loblolly pine trees grow rapidly, attain large sizes, and have the potential for long life in many South American locations. During the first 9 years, annual height growth often averages 1.5 m, and annual diameter growth often averages 2.8 cm (Baldanzi 1978). In dense stands, the rate of growth is often very high during the first 10 to 13 years and then declines rapidly. Stands of moderate density grow rapidly through age 20. Even when density is as low as 1,100 stems/ha, the canopy closes by about stand age 10 to 15 (Machado 1980). Rotations as short as 15 years yield up to 10% sawtimber. On the best sites, dominant trees easily attain a diameter of 55 cm by age 20 (Schultz RP. 1987. Personal observations). Growth curves developed for plantations in Parana, Brazil, indicate heights of 27 to 32 m by age 20 on the best sites and 19 to 23 m on average sites (figure 12-9). McTague and Bailey (1987a) suggest that the histories of loblolly stands in southern Brazil can be inferred from the diameter distribution percentiles.

Individual-tree volume tables, for volume with and without bark, are available for various parts of Brazil (Machado 1979b, Rosot 1980, Ubialli 1981; appendix D tables 1 and 2), Argentina (Kolln and Viola 1987), and Uruguay (Sorrentino 1987). Total and merchantable volume equations incorporating stem form are available for plantations in southern Brazil (Ahrens and Holbert 1981, McTague and Bailey 1987b). Stand yields of 15 to 25 m³/ha/yr are common (Blackman 1980, Castillo and others 1987, Golfari 1978), and yields of 35 m³/ha/yr occur on better sites. Nine-year-old plantations growing

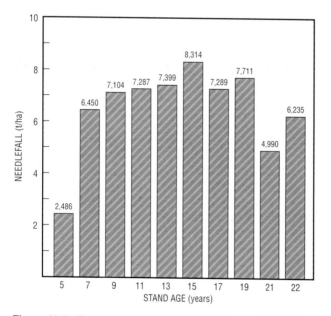

Figure 12-8—Total yearly needlefall in 5- to 22-year-old loblolly pine stands in Monte Alegre, Parana, Brazil, during 1981–82 (adapted from Goldammer 1983).

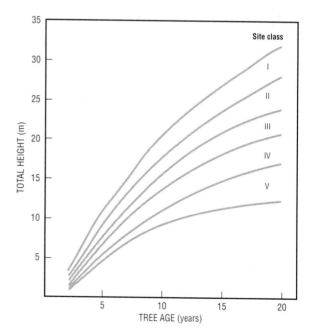

Figure 12-9—Polymorphic site index curves (total height over age) constructed from 64 stems aged 6 to 17 years on excellent to poor sites in the central region of the State of Parana, Brazil (adapted from Machado 1980).

at an elevation of 850 m at latitude 24°20′ S in Brazil yielded 56 m³/ha/yr (Barrichelo and others 1977).

Where initial stocking is less than 1,000 stems/ha, sites are not used fully during 20- to 25-year rotations. In the central part of Parana, unthinned plantations with initial stockings of 1,100 to 4,440 stems/ha should reach common asymptotic basal areas of from 40 to 65 m²/ha, depending on site quality, as early as age 20. Before that time, stands with higher stocking have higher basal areas on average to good sites (Machado 1981).

Harvesting

Plantation harvesting is generally mechanized in South America. Chain saws are used regularly, and a few companies use hydraulic fellers and feller-bunchers. Chain saws are normally used for all thinning operations (felling, limbing, and bucking). As in the United States, plantation thinning is often a combination of row and selection thinning. Either shortwood or whole-tree removal is used depending on particular conditions (Grammel 1985). In whole-tree removal, trees are felled and then moved to yarding areas where they are limbed, bucked, and loaded onto logging trucks. At times, gate delimbing is used. Lightweight agricultural tractors with rubber tires and hydraulically operated bar and fixed choker chains are commonly and efficiently used to extract thinned material (Stohr and Baggio 1981). Horses and oxen are used effectively in small operations, especially for early thinnings on steep and broken terrain.

Agroforestry

Many private landowners and family-controlled companies in South America raise cattle, annual crops, and perennial crops such as yerba mate, *Ilex paraguariensis* St. Hil., together with pines. Common tree spacings of 1,100 to 1,500 stems/ha result in substantial competition by understory vegetation and provide opportunities for grazing cattle. Grazing can start in 2- or 3-year-old stands depending on the concentration and timing of animal use. Some cattle are grazed under older, open loblolly pine stands, but little is known about maximizing the efficiency of combined timber and cattle production.

Intercropping of annual crops with loblolly pines is successful for about 2 years if tree stand density is not excessive. However, dense young loblolly pine plantations quickly shade out other vegetation, making dual cropping unprofitable. In southern Parana, Brazil, survival of loblolly spaced at 3 by 2 m was not reduced during the first 29 months when as many as 83,000 corn plants/ha were grown in 4 rows between each 2 rows of trees. Tree height was reduced significantly when there were 83,000 corn plants/ha, but 50,000 corn plants/ha were not detrimental to tree growth. After 2 years, loblolly crowns shade out too much of the corn to make joint production profitable (Schreiner and Baggio 1984).

Pest Management

Loblolly pine trees in South America are attacked by very few insects or diseases. The most serious problem is leafcutting ants (*Atta* spp. and *Acromyrmex* spp.), which can defoliate a tree in 1 or 2 days. Where ant colonies are present, control must begin before planting and may have to continue throughout the rotation. Methyl bromide or vaporized chlorinated hydrocarbons, such as heptaclor, are fumigants commonly used for ant control. However, dechlorane (Mirex®) baits seem to be more effective and less costly for ant control (Hodges and McFadden 1987). The wood-boring wasp, *Sirex noctilio* F., was first observed attacking loblolly in southern Brazil in 1988. This insect, which was introduced from Australia, has gradually spread from Argentina through Uruguay and is gradually moving northward in Brazil. The fungus *Cylindrocladium clavatum* (Hodges & May) sp. n. has been found in several areas of southern Brazil. Because it can quickly kill young loblolly pines, it is considered a potential threat (Hodges and May 1972). The nematode *Xiphinema brevicolle* has been found in association with loblolly in Itirapino, Sao Paulo, Brazil; however, there is no indication that it is harmful to the tree (Zem 1977). Rodents (*Clyomys* spp., *Agouti* spp., and *Coendou* spp.) occasionally chew off patches of bark or even completely girdle both the lower bole and upper bole of saplings and larger trees. *Agouti paca* L. chews the lower boles of pines as beavers do (Carvalho and Bueno 1975).

Loblolly Pine in Africa

History

Loblolly pine was first planted in southern Africa in about 1900, but plantings failed because mycorrhizal fungi were not present. Trial and commercial plantings were established in the Republic of South Africa; Southern Rhodesia, now Zimbabwe; and Nyasaland, now Malawi, from the 1930's to the 1950's. These were followed by large-scale plantings in the late 1960's, when improved seeds became widely available (Schutz and Wingfield 1979, Southern Rhodesia Forestry Commission 1957). The Republic of South Africa is Africa's major producer of loblolly pines. Of the 604,070 ha of softwood plantations in the country in 1984, 54,893 ha (9%) were in loblolly plantations (Wessels 1987). Loblolly is also locally important in Zimbabwe. Its development and management in South Africa and in Zimbabwe are well documented (Marsh 1978, Mullin and others 1978, Norskov-Lauritsen 1963). Small numbers of loblolly are planted annually in Malawi (Ingram 1984), Swaziland, and Tanzania (McDonald and Krugman 1985).

Habitat

In the Republic of South Africa, loblolly pine grows best where droughts are of short duration and in cool areas where there is only a winter dry period. It is particularly suited to low-lying areas of the lowveld, bordering the escarpment, where soils are deep but quite sensitive to drought (Grey and Taylor 1983). It is managed for sawtimber, veneer, and pulpwood in northern Transvaal, eastern Transvaal, southern Transvaal, Natal, eastern Cape, southern Cape, and Tsitsikamma forestry regions, and to a lesser extent in the western Cape region (Esterhuyse 1985). This geographic range extends from latitude 24° S to latitude 34° S. In Natal (27.5° S to 31° S), it does well wherever mean annual precipitation exceeds 950 mm, mean July temperature is not lower than 8 °C, mean January temperature is not above 26 °C, and elevation is less than 1,800 m (Schonau and Schulze 1984).

Tree Improvement

Government forestry organizations in South Africa, Zimbabwe, and Malawi began local breeding programs with loblolly pines during the late 1950's and early 1960's when superior trees were selected from the local populations. Selections were based on comparisons with 10 dominant, neighboring trees (Barnes 1977). Loblolly has responded well to the efforts of tree breeders. Volume increases with acceptable timber qualities are considered the most important objectives in a breeding program. Although first-generation selections in South African seed orchards have upgraded loblolly stem form, this characteristic is not given high priority as long as it is above average (Hagedorn 1976). Loblolly seed production is generally superior to that of other pines in young orchards. For example, a 7- to 8-year-old loblolly pine orchard in Transvaal, South Africa, produced from 20 to 26 kg of seeds/ha, whereas a slash pine orchard produced 8 to 9 kg/ha and a *P. patula* orchard produced only 0.3 kg of seeds/ha (Pederick 1974). Some second-generation seed orchards have been established in South Africa (South African Forestry Research Institute 1985).

Provenance trials of loblolly pine from across its natural range were installed in widely scattered areas of South Africa in 1937. The species grew well over a wide range of environmental conditions. These trials have shown clearly that improved seeds from the southern-most United States populations (southern Texas, southern Louisiana, and Florida) are most desirable. Growth of seedlings from the best and the poorest provenances differed by as much as 119%. At one location, the best provenances grew at rates of 32 to 44 m³/ha/yr through age 35. The best loblolly provenances could usually be determined at age 2 to 3 and could always be determined by age 9 (Falkenhagen 1978).

Genotype × environment interactions are not common in the Republic of South Africa, indicating that loblolly pine grows satisfactorily on many environmentally different areas (van Wyk and Falkenhagen 1984). Loblolly seems to be more susceptible to snow damage in South Africa than in the United States, perhaps because the South African winters are not uniformly cold and permit the development of new growth that is unable to support snow burdens (Marsh 1978). Drought-resistant genotypes from east Texas seem to perform best in areas of Zimbabwe where fairly long drought periods occur (Banks 1966).

Comparison of Species and Hybrids

Loblolly and slash pines have been compared in many locations in southern Africa because both species grow well in the region and because their environmental requirements are similar. Loblolly generally yields more timber than slash pine, but relative growth is site specific and dependent on seed source. Growth rates of the two species are about the same on many intermediate sites, and slash may grow up to 10 to 20% faster than loblolly on very wet or very dry sites. However, under the right conditions, loblolly can be at least 30% more productive than slash pine (Falkenhagen 1978, Mullin and Falkenhagen 1979, Mushi and Madoffe 1984). Loblolly captures sites more rapidly, is more tolerant of cold conditions, is much more resistant to windthrow and wind breakage at higher altitudes, and is more resistant to the pine woolly aphid, *Pineus pini* (L.), and the honey fungus, *Armillaria mellea* (Vahl:Fr.) Kumm. Conversely, slash pine is more drought resistant; more tolerant of poor drainage; less severely affected by the rhizina root rot fungus, *Rhizina undulata* Fr.:Fr. = *R. inflata* (Schaeff.) Karst.; less susceptible to fire; has better stem and branch characteristics; and can be used for oleoresin production (Barnes and Mullin 1978). In the Natal Midlands and the eastern Transvaal, the well-drained valley bottoms should be planted with loblolly pine because it is the most demanding pine. The foot slopes and lower middle slopes should be reserved for *P. patula*, whereas slash pine should be established on the crests, upper middle slopes, and in poorly drained valley bottoms (Schonau and Fitzpatrick 1981). On some nutrient-deficient sites, *P. patula* grows twice as fast as loblolly or slash pine (table 12-3). *Pinus patula* generally grows faster than loblolly or slash pine even on areas where all

Table 12-3—The effect of phosphorus (P) fertilization (applied as 2:3:2 fertilizer) on the growth of three *Pinus* species 8.75 years after application on a planted and weeded site in South Africa

Species	Growth (m³/ha/yr)			
	0 kg/ha P	10 kg/ha P	20 kg/ha P	30 kg/ha P
Pinus elliottii	8,652	10,307	11,388	10,978
P. Patula	17,594	18,248	20,003	19,272
P. Taeda	9,759	13,060	14,179	14,843

Source: adapted from Donald and others (1987).

three species grow well. However, log recovery differs little from species to species. In the southern and eastern Cape, loblolly pine does not compete economically with *P. radiata* D. Don. The two species grow best on similar soils but *P. radiata* produces timber of higher quality. However, loblolly is a worthwhile alternative to *P. radiata* on Cape soils with low P content and in areas subject to periodic hail damage. Also, loblolly is less subject to attack by *Sphaeropsis sapinea* (Fr.:Fr.) Dyko & Sutton (= *Diplodia pinea* (Desmaz.) Kickx) (Marsh 1978, Schonau and Grey 1987, Swart and others 1988).

The flowering times of loblolly and slash pines overlap in Zimbabwe, so adjacent stands may produce hybrids. Many more seeds are produced when loblolly is the male parent. The F_1 hybrids can exhibit heterosis in height growth, and general combining ability variance is high, suggesting that the potential value of hybridization may be particularly good where species are grown as exotics in plantations because hybrid habitats could develop (Barnes and Mullin 1978).

Artificial Regeneration

South Africa produces much of its own loblolly pine seeds from 39 ha of open-pollinated, clonal seed orchards established in 1968 and 1969 (Gavidia 1978). The standard pretreatment for loblolly pine seeds (see chapter 8) is also used in the Republic of South Africa (Daniels and van der Sijde 1975). Mechanical sowing of seeds in nurseries is becoming increasingly common (Hodgson 1980).

Bareroot systems, single-plant container systems (polypot or sleeve systems), and the box system are all used to grow loblolly pine seedlings. The cost of producing bareroot stock is about one-half that of producing seedlings by the container system or box system because most bareroot seedlings are produced in large, centralized nurseries. Seeds germinate best in nurseries when covered by a layer of sawdust 0.5 to 1.0 cm thick (Daniels 1975a). Fertilization with NPK as a 2:3:2 compound mixture is recommended. The fertilizer should be applied as a top dressing at the rate of 0.5 g of 2:3:2 per plant 1 month after germination or pricking out (Daniels 1975b). Undercutting or root wrenching is done when seedlings are 15 to 20 cm tall. In 1960, 25,000 loblolly seedlings were raised in nurseries (Donald 1965). By

1983, nursery production of loblolly had increased to 6.4 million seedlings (McDonald and Krugman 1985). In Zululand, one 6.5-ha nursery that grows loblolly and slash pines on a production basis has a capacity of 4 million seedlings (Young 1983).

Loblolly pine has been planted on about 83,600 ha, or about 7.5% of the land suitable for exotic pine management in South Africa (Barnes 1977, Donald 1986). Site preparation methods used include preparing the spot where each tree is planted, plowing 0.5-m-wide strips in one or two directions before planting, and agricultural plowing and harrowing of entire sites (Wessels 1987). Intensive site preparation can include the creation of planting pits 45 by 45 cm wide and 20 cm deep, which are made several months prior to planting to permit soil settling. On grasslands, shrubs are removed, and the ground is often subsoiled in one direction at the desired spacing for planting.

Seedlings are outplanted when about 8 to 12 months old (Darrow 1979). Trees should not be taller than 30 cm at outplanting (Wessels 1987). Container seedlings are often used at planting sites that are distant from the nursery or where soil or other environmental conditions are unfavorable. Survival may be slightly higher when half of the stem is buried than when seedlings are planted at root-collar depth (Donald 1970). For sawtimber rotations, trees are generally planted at spacings of 2.7 by 2.7 m (1,372 trees/ha) to 3.5 by 3.5 m (816 trees/ha). The closer spacings are used when stands are to be thinned before final harvesting. For pulpwood rotations, trees may be planted at 2.1- or 2.4-m intervals. Growth of new plantations is generally good, especially on well-prepared areas; trees reach heights of 1.8 to 2.4 m during the first 2 years (Cawse 1979, 1983; Darrow 1979; Wessels 1987).

Stand Management

Various management techniques, including pruning, thinning, fertilizing, and prescribed burning, are used to increase loblolly pine growth and quality in southern Africa.

Pruning. At normal plantation densities, most branches remain alive until trees reach the 13-cm diameter class. For this reason, live branch pruning must be considered when loblolly pine is managed for high-quality products. As a rule, removing as much as 25% of the length of the living crowns of young trees does not affect growth if all stems in the stand are pruned. Pruning 50% of the live crown on all stems normally causes a significant but temporary reduction in diameter growth, but the loss in volume is negligible after a few years. If more than 50% of the live crown is removed, significant and long-lasting growth reductions occur. Loss of growth is likely to be greater on good sites than on poor ones because the length of the live crown is less on the latter.

Table 12-4—Pruning regime for loblolly pine stands in Zimbabwe planted at a spacing of 2.4 by 2.4 m (1,736 stems/ha); measurements are for 250 dominant stems/ha

dbhob (cm)	Mean height (m)	Age (years)	Average height of pruning (m)	Pruning height as percentage of living crown (%)	Maximum unpruned stem diameter ob at time of pruning (cm)	Pruning core size (cm)	Pruning instructions
10.2	5.9	4.7	2.6	25	11.4	16.5	Prune all stems to 7.6 cm dob or 2.6 m, whichever is higher, before first thinning.
14.0	7.9	5.7	4.6	38	11.4	15.2	Prune all stems to 7.6 cm dob or 4.6 m, whichever is higher, before first thinning.
18.8	10.7	7.5	6.7	41	12.7	17.8	Prune all stems to 6.7 m after first thinning.
25.4	15.4	10.5	11.0	48	17.3	22.4	Prune 250 stems/ha to 11.0 m, final crop stems only.

Source: adapted from Banks and Prevost (1976).

dbhob = diameter at breast height outside bark; ob = outside bark.

Table 12-5—Typical planting and thinning schedule when growing loblolly pines on public lands in South Africa (all sites combined)

Age (yr)	Trees to be left per hectare (no.)	Proportion of trees removed in thinning (%)
0	1,334	NA
8	633	46*
13	388	31
18	242	38

Source: adapted from Darrow (1979).

NA = not applicable.

* Assumes the normal 2.7- by 2.7-m spacing with 90% survival at 8 years.

For a given intensity of live-crown pruning, loblolly pine tree growth is reduced somewhat more than growth of slash pine but less than growth of *P. patula* (Banks and Prevost 1976).

First-quality stands may be pruned to 11 m in four operations (table 12-4). Wessels (1987) presents the following schedule for pruning high-quality sawtimber stands to 7 m in three operations:

Prune to 3 m when dominants are 6 m tall

Prune to 5 m when dominants are 9 m tall

Prune to 7 m when dominants are 12 m tall

If veneer logs are desired, the trees may be pruned again—to 10.5 m—when the dominants are 16.0 m tall. An equation that predicts the ages at which stands will attain these specific top heights is available (Bredenkamp 1985). Pruning to 7 m can usually be completed before the first thinning is undertaken. Pruning on poor sites, or pruning above 7 m on good sites, can rarely be justified. In pulpwood stands, trees are often pruned once—to about 3 m—when average tree height is about 6 m. This improves stand access and wood quality (Marsh 1978).

Thinning. Thinning schedules for plantings vary by management philosophy. Stands can be clearfelled for pulpwood as early as age 12; however, thinning at age 10, followed by clearfelling at age 15, provides some small sawtimber and improves the overall fiber characteristics of the pulped material (Darrow 1979). Higher stand densities can be maintained on high-quality sites than on low-quality sites. Higher densities tend to shorten the time required to reach carrying capacity, but they reduce average stem size (Strub and Bredenkamp 1985).

Where the objective is to produce pulpwood, Cawse (1983) suggests that loblolly pines be planted at 2.4 by 2.4 m on all sites, that every third row be removed by

thinning at age 11 or 12, that stands be thinned to 694 stems/ha at age 18, and that stands be clearfelled at 25 years. Where stands are not to be thinned, trees should be planted at 3.3 by 3.3 m and clearcut at 30 years. If stands of widely spaced trees are thinned, one-third of the trees should be removed selectively at age 12 to 15 years.

On public lands in the Republic of South Africa, stands on low-quality sites are first thinned at age 6 or 7. On better sites, initial thinning is delayed until about age 8 to 10. Each thinning removes about 30 to 50% of the trees (table 12-5). The practice is to thin at stand ages 8, 13, and 18. The final thinning reduces the stand to about 250 final crop trees per hectare at age 18, and these trees may be pruned to 7 m for production of high-quality sawlogs. Clearfelling and whole-tree removal are then accomplished approximately at stand age 30 to 40 with a variety of modern ground or high-lead skidding systems. Stands grown at high densities show decline by age 40 to 50 years without any obvious pathogenic problems. Rapid tree growth may result in earlier overmaturity in South Africa than in the United States of America, especially if stands are overstocked. Regular thinnings should minimize this potential problem (Schutz and Wingfield 1979).

Both row and selection thinning are effective and give similar results (Bredenkamp and others 1983). Row thinning is especially effective for the first thinning, whether sawtimber or pulpwood is the product, because it is inexpensive and the remaining low-quality trees can be removed during subsequent selection thinnings (Scott 1977).

Other management techniques. Loblolly pine plantations seldom require fertilization, but applications of 10 to 30 kg of P/ha as superphosphate, or 10 to 30 kg of P in 2:3:2 mixtures of NPK, can increase growth significantly in some areas (Donald and others 1987, Mackenzie and Donald 1983). Soils exhibiting P deficiency are characteristically wet or derived from gabbro, a basic igneous rock. Once P requirements have been met, responses to N and K may also occur. However, applying N or K or both without P can depress early tree growth. A combination of fertilizing with NPK and weeding can also stimulate early tree growth. Where weed competition is severe, tree growth can be promoted by hoeing or by applying herbicides around individual trees 1 or 2 times during the first year after planting. Combining thinning with fertilizing can increase loblolly yields under some conditions. For example, a second broadcast application of 50 to 90 kg of P/ha at the time of the first thinning ensures maximum growth on P-deficient sites if crop trees are provided adequate space to grow. Fertilization with P or N + P following a second thinning stimulates the growth of sawtimber trees enough to make the treatment economical if stand basal area is below 30 m²/ha (Donald 1983, 1987; Donald and others 1987).

Burning can control competing vegetation and consume some of the litter under older stands (Donald and others 1987, Haigh 1980, Wattle Research Institute 1983). However, wildfires can damage young stands severely. Trees in the 1- to 10-year age range are most susceptible, and loblolly pine saplings are much more susceptible than slash pine saplings. In areas of high risk, loblolly pine stands should be control burned at 2- to 3-year intervals (De Ronde and others 1986, Germishuizen and Smale 1982, van Loon 1967).

Growth and Yield

The mean annual increment of loblolly pine plantations in State forests in South Africa is about 18 m³/ha/yr. On favorable sites where rainfall occurs throughout the year, annual volume increments can exceed 28 m³/ha (Marsh 1978). Depending on site quality and stocking, recommended rotation lengths range from 18 to 35 years (Cawse 1983). Trees reach a height of about 30 m and a dbh of 45 cm at age 35 (Marsh 1978).

Loblolly pine stands in eastern Transvaal have attained a mean dominant height of 30 m at age 20 and a maximum height of 42.7 m at ages 35 to 45 years (Darrow 1979). On good sites, loblolly can yield more than 600 m³/ha at age 35 (table 12-6). This is generally more than slash pine yields but substantially less than *P. patula* yields. Loblolly pine volume tables are available

Table 12-6—Loblolly pine sawtimber yields in South Africa to a minimum top diameter of 18 cm for normal rotations assuming 1,334 planted trees/ha, 80% survival at 10 years, and thinnings at 8, 13, and 18 years

Site class	Recommended clearfelling age (yr)	Volume (m³/ha)			MAI*
		Thinning	Clearfelling	Total	
I	35	236.3	400.8	639.7	18.3
II	35	121.6	245.3	366.9	10.4
III	40	28.7	113.3	142.0	3.5

Source: adapted from Darrow (1979).

MAI = Mean annual increment.

for the eastern part of Zimbabwe. They include volumes and inside-bark to outside-bark relationships for trees 7.6 to 38.1 m in height and 12.7 to 63.5 cm in dbh outside bark (Prevost 1971).

The aggregate density of fast-grown loblolly pines is as high as that of slow-grown trees. For example, the ovendry density of experimental trees spaced at 1.8 by 1.8 m reached 0.61 g/cm³ at tree age 16, and that of trees spaced at 4.6 by 4.6 m reached 0.56 g/cm³ at tree age 16 (Banks and Schwegmann 1957). Some trees growing on a variety of sites in the summer rainfall areas of South Africa produce wood that has no annual rings and that has abnormal tracheids, fewer pits, and greater numbers of rays and proto-rays than either normal wood or compression wood. This abnormal wood generally forms to a height of about 3 m and is exhibited externally by a severe taper. The cause is not known, but climate, site quality, and silvicultural practices do not appear to be causative (Herman 1985, van der Sijde and others 1985). Plant growth regulators can induce the same severe taper in seedlings (Herman 1988).

Volume of a planted loblolly tree to a 75-mm top diameter can be obtained from the following equation (Bredenkamp and Loveday 1984):

$$\log V = b_0 + b_1 \log (D+d) + b_2 \log H$$

where:

log	=	common logarithm to the base 10
V	=	stem volume (in cubic meters)
D	=	diameter at breast height (in millimeters)
d	=	20 mm
H	=	tree height (in meters)
b_0	=	− 6.91292
b_1	=	2.03735
b_2	=	1.18149

Pest Management

Spiders from at least 23 different families live in loblolly pine plantations in Africa. They are found in plantation soil, litter, stem bark, and foliage. Their great diversity and large numbers may be an important part of the complex that keeps pests in loblolly plantations at endemic levels (van den Berg and Dippenaar-Schoeman 1988).

No single pest has emerged as a serious threat to loblolly pine plantation forestry in southern Africa. The black pine aphid, *Cinara cronartii* Tissot & Pepper, feeds on the crown in winter and can infest trees heavily. Rogueing the most susceptible families has essentially eliminated this problem (South African Forestry Research Institute 1985). The parasite *Pauesia* spp. (Hymenoptera: Aphidiidae) may provide a biological control mechanism for the black pine aphid (Kfir and others 1985).

The pine woolly aphid, *Pineus pini* (L.), was introduced into Zimbabwe in 1962 through loblolly scions from Australia. Trees can be damaged moderately, but many individuals are immune. Most damage occurs when trees are under physiological stress because they have been planted on unsuitable sites or where the climate is generally unsuitable (Barnes and others 1976). *Pineus* spp. have not been recorded in Malawi or Zambia (Katerere 1983a, 1983b).

The pine needle aphid, *Eulachnus rileyi* (Williams), occurs in Malawi, Zambia, and Zimbabwe, and causes extensive defoliation when present in large numbers (Katerere 1983b, Odendaal 1980). Other insects that feed on loblolly pines in Africa include *Thericles* spp. and *Chrysolagria* spp. Both adults and larvae of *Chrysolagria* spp. are leaf feeders (Katerere 1983a).

Lundquist (1986, 1987) identified 12 fungi associated with loblolly pines in the Republic of South Africa. The fungus *Sphaeropsis sapinea* (Fr.:Fr.) Dyko & Sutton (= *Diplodia pinea*) can cause severe stress in loblolly pines. Symptoms include chlorosis, needlefall, and sometimes dieback (Wingfield and Knox-Davies 1980). However, loblolly seems to be more resistant to this fungus than are most other exotic pines planted in southern Africa (Swart and others 1988). Rhizina root rot infects both newly planted and older plantations throughout southern Africa. Management controls for this disease include winter planting in the summer rainfall region and clearcutting without subsequent slash burning to minimize the development of rhizina fruiting bodies

(Lundquist 1984). Root rots caused by *Armillaria* spp. can substantially reduce the growth of young loblolly pines. Eight-year-old trees showing early symptoms of the disease had growth reductions of 13 to 39%. Growth loss reached 57 to 70% the year before trees died (Lundquist 1988).

New plantings can be damaged severely by various species of deer that eat young shoots, especially during the winter. Effective repellents are not available (Schutz and others 1978). Monkeys strip the bark of trees, and this damage results in stained and decayed boards after milling. Most damage occurs when the animals are en route to other food sources (Droomer 1985, von dem Bussche and van der Zee 1985). In one instance, Samango monkeys, *Cercopithecus* (*mitis*) *albogularis*, damaged hundreds of hectares of loblolly pine plantations in northern Transvaal. Most damage occurs before trees reach 20 years of age (Droomer 1985). At higher elevations in Malawi, plantings have been damaged heavily and in some cases destroyed by blue monkeys (*Cercopithecus mitis*) and yellow baboons (*Papio cynocephalus*) (Ingram 1984).

Chlorosis and necrotic needle mottling associated with air pollution are beginning to show up in loblolly pine plantations in South Africa's eastern Transvaal (Botha and others 1988).

Loblolly Pine in Asia

Although loblolly pine has been tested in many Asian countries, including China, India, Japan, South Korea, Taiwan, and Vietnam, it has been accepted for use as a forest tree species only in China.

China

Loblolly and slash pines are the most widely planted exotic species in China, where they are grown in 14 provinces (Krugman and others 1983). The first plantings were made in the 1930's. The combined planting rate for the 2 species was estimated to be between 350 and 500 million seedlings/year in the early 1980's (McDonald and Krugman 1985). About equal numbers of loblolly and slash pines are planted. The planting rate is expected to grow as the quantity of available seeds increases. Plantings are concentrated between latitudes 19° N and 36° N and longitudes 105° E and 122° E, in three climatic zones (tropical and southern subtropical region, eastern subtropical region, and warm temperate region). Tree growth increases as latitude decreases. Loblolly is used for both timber and fuelwood in China (FAO 1982).

Loblolly pine outperforms the native Masson pine, *Pinus massoniana* Lamb., especially on soils of the Red and Yellow Earth group (south from the Yangtze River to the Tropic of Cancer) and throughout most of the lower Yangtze River drainage when planted at lower elevations (Carter and others 1981, Kellison 1985). Best growth occurs where the soil is at least 50 cm deep and the soil bulk density does not exceed 1.40 g/cm^3 (Zhang 1984). Forty-year-old loblolly at latitude 26° N and longitude 119° E attained more than twice the volume of the native Masson pine and 43% more volume than slash pine (table 12-7). The loblolly pine seed sources that

Table 12-7—Comparison of loblolly, slash, and Masson pine growth in Minhou, China, at latitude 26° N and longitude 119° E

Age (yr)	Height (m)			Dbh (cm)			Volume (m³/tree)		
	Slash pine	Loblolly pine	Masson pine	Slash pine	Loblolly pine	Masson pine	Slash pine	Loblolly pine	Masson pine
10	7.6	8.3	5.5	7.2	8.3	5.6	0.02	0.02	0.10
20	15.6	16.7	11.2	15.6	18.8	14.0	0.14	0.24	0.08
30	22.3	23.6	18.1	21.5	26.1	19.3	0.40	0.64	0.23
40	27.3	28.2	22.1	26.6	31.0	23.9	0.78	1.11	0.44

Source: adaped from Pan CK. 1981. Unpublished data on southern pines in China.

perform best in southern and central subtropical regions of China are from coastal regions of Florida and South Carolina, and from Livingston Parish, Louisiana. In the northern subtropical region, loblolly from Piedmont and inland sources are better than coastal sources because they have greater cold tolerance (Zhigang 1989).

Both bareroot and container stock are grown and outplanted. Container stock may make up as much as 25% of total planting stock. Seedling mortality caused by *Fusarium* spp. is a common nursery problem. Fusiform rust and tip moths damage pines native to China and may eventually affect loblolly pine in China (Kellison 1985). In Jiangxi Province, loblolly completes 5% of its combined annual height and diameter growth during June through August, about 1 month earlier than native Masson pine and exotic slash pine complete similar percentages of their growth. Fourteen percent of loblolly growth occurs after October, compared to 9% for Masson pine (Liang 1984). Unlike in the United States, young loblolly pines are highly resistant to the pinewood nematode, which adversely affects many pines native to China (Yang and others 1987).

Taiwan

Loblolly pine has been tested in many parts of Taiwan but is not recommended for commercial planting. Its growth is comparable to that of slash pine at middle elevations (750 m) and better than slash pine at higher elevations (1,250 m) in the southern part of the island (latitude 22° N, longitude 121° E) (Lin 1965). Ten-year-old loblolly pine trees average 6 to 7 m in height and 6 to 10 cm in dbh (Liang 1965). At one southern location, volume of 24-year-old loblolly was 346 m³/ha as opposed to 315 m³/ha for slash pine. In the central and northern parts of the island (latitude 24° N to 25° N), growth of loblolly is only about half as great as that of slash pine. For example, two 20-year-old stands of loblolly pine had volumes of 125 m³ and 145 m³, whereas two slash pine stands of the same age had volumes of 279 m³ and 278 m³. Pine shoot borers, *Dioryctria* spp., can be severe pests of young loblolly pines (Chang and Sun 1984).

Japan

Loblolly pine was introduced into Japan in 1911, and 1,640 ha of plantations had been established by 1972 (Mikami and Iwakawa 1973). Trees from Maryland and North Carolina seed sources are able to withstand the normally cold conditions in the hilly regions (about 600 m in elevation) of central Japan approximately at latitude 36° N. (Mikami and Iwakawa 1973). Because young trees are susceptible to damage by high winds, plantings should be confined to sheltered areas (Yoshida and others 1981). Control of competing vegetation is often necessary for the first 2 years after planting, and NPK fertil-

izer treatments can increase tree growth substantially (Tsuge 1971). Biomass of a dense, heavily fertilized, loblolly pine plantation in the Wakayama Prefecture reached 113.9 t/ha at age 7 (Akai and others 1968).

Volume tables have been calculated using the following regression equations (Wada and others 1971):

$$V = 0.09878 \, D^{1.91773} \, H^{0.68771}$$
(for trees with dbh greater than 6.0 cm)

$$V = 0.05773 \, D_{0.3}{}^{1.79330} \, H^{0.89350}$$
(for trees with dbh less than 6.0 cm)

where:

V = stem volume (in cubic decimeters)
D = dbh (in centimeters)
$D_{0.3}$ = diameter (in centimeters) at 30 cm aboveground
H = tree height (in meters)

Loblolly pine's growth is superior to that of the indigenous pines, *P. densiflora* (Sieb. and Zucc.) and *P. thunbergii* (Parl.), under some conditions. One 7-year-old loblolly pine plantation on the Shirahama Experimental Station of Kyoto University in Wakayama Prefecture had basal areas ranging from 18.5 m²/ha at a stocking of 2,151 trees/ha to 34.6 m²/ha at a stocking of 6,543 trees/ha. Needle dry weight ranged from 8 to 13 t/ha. Living branch dry weight ranged from 9 to 13 t/ha. By stand age 9, minimum and maximum stocking had decreased to 2,101 and 5,934 trees/ha, respectively, but the corresponding basal areas had increased to 24.5 and 44.8 m²/ha. Needle dry weight for minimum and maximum stocking rose to 12 and 21 t/ha, respectively. Annual litterfall at ages 8 and 9 ranged from 5 to 8 t/ha depending on stand density (Akai and Furuno 1971). Tadaki and Kagawa (1968) found that annual litterfall in an 8-year-old loblolly stand equalled 100% of the leaf biomass as opposed to 40 to 50% in 14-year-old *Castanopsis cuspidata* and about 30% in 40-year-old *Chamaecyparis obtusa* (Sieb. & Zucc.) Endl. A 34-year-old loblolly pine plantation at an elevation of 200 m in the Nishikihara National Forest in the Kumamoto Prefecture had the following characteristics (Akai and others 1972):

- 320 m³ of stem volume/ha
- 197 t of total dry weight/ha (160 t of stem, 21 t of live branches, 7 t of dead branches, 9 t of foliage, and 0.4 t of cones)
- 14 m³ of current annual increment

Loblolly pine trees growing in Japan are attacked by both insects and diseases. The adult striated chafer, *Anomala testaceipes* Motschulsky, and the pine caterpillar, *Dendrolimus spectabilis*, can cause a small amount of needle loss (54 to 204 kg of dry weight/ha/yr), but this has little effect on tree growth (Furuno 1972a, 1972b; Furuno and Uenaka 1976). Adult trees can also be damaged by the sawyer *Monochamus alternatus* Hope. However, loblolly is resistant to the pinewood nematode,

Bursaphelenchus xylophilus (Steiner and Buhrer 1934, Nickle 1970), which causes wilting and death of native Japanese pines (Bentley and others 1985, Furuno and others 1977, Furuno and Futai 1986, Yang and others 1987). A disease caused by the fungus *Ascocalyx pinicola* Kobayashi et Kondo develops at the base of dead branches and gradually works into the stem cambium. Most lesions begin to form when trees are 5 to 9 years old (Kondo and Kobayashi 1984). Dothistroma needle blight, caused by *Dothistroma pini* Hulbary var. *pini*, also damages trees but seems to be only a minor problem (Ito and others 1975).

South Korea

Loblolly pines generally grow well in the southern part of the country (south of latitude 36° N). However, there were substantial survival and volume growth differences between 13 seed sources planted at Naju (latitude 35°01′ N), Wolsong (latitude 35°40′ N, and Wanju (latitude 35°48′ N). The trees that survived and grew best came from Jasper, Texas; Berkeley, South Carolina; and Kershaw, South Carolina (Han and others 1985). Volume growth of 24-year-old loblolly averaged 200% greater than volume growth of pitch pine when grown at five locations (Han and others 1987b).

Pitch pine × loblolly pine hybrid seedlings have been mass-produced in South Korea since the early 1950's (Hyun 1972, Hyun and Ahn 1959), and growth patterns are known for stands up to 30 years of age (Han and others 1987a, 1987b). The cross grows much faster than the mother species (pitch pine) and is more cold hardy than the loblolly pollen parent. The northernmost loblolly seed sources provide the highest level of cold hardiness and are preferred for planting stock (Hyun 1974). Superiority of the cross is not the result of heterosis, because F_2 hybrids do not lose hardiness and loblolly grows faster than the cross where it is not too cold for loblolly to perform well (Han and others 1985). The relative performance of parental species, F_1 hybrids, backcrosses, and F_2 populations is closely tied to characteristics of the planting site. Vigor of the F_2 populations has been maintained only in southern South Korea, where mild weather presumably allowed development of segregants more similar to cold-sensitive loblolly (Hyun 1972). Thus, the environment in which loblolly hybrids are to be used may dictate selection of the crossing strategy.

Individual needle fascicles of 2-year-old pitch pine × loblolly pine hybrids can be propagated into as many as 24 new plants when the appropriate cultural media and hormones are used (Park and others 1984). Loblolly cuttings root best when scions are taken from plants younger than 5 years old (Ooyama and Toyoshima 1965). Nursery inoculation with the mycorrhizal fungus *Pisolithus tinctorius* increases the height growth of hybrid seedlings substantially (Lee and Koo 1983) and will probably increase the height growth of cuttings.

Insects can damage the pitch pine × loblolly pine hybrid. For example, the cone insects *Dioryctria abietella* Denis and Schiffermuller, *D. sylvertrella* Ratzeburg, and *Petrova cristata* severely damaged 70 to 100% of the cones and destroyed 50% of the seeds in experimental pitch pine × loblolly pine F_1 seed orchards in Suwon and Cjungwon, South Korea. A 3% carbofuran (Furadan) systemic insecticide generally controlled the problem (Chung and others 1984).

Loblolly pine has also been crossed successfully with *Pinus thunbergii*. Controlled crosses (loblolly female flowers and pollen of *P. thunbergii*) have produced high yields of cones and sound seeds, but growth of young trees was only 8% greater than that of pitch pine (Ahn 1977). Crosses with loblolly as the pollen parent are not successful (Nakai and others 1976).

India

Foresters in India have tried loblolly pine in small experimental plantings. The species has shown some promise for reforestation at an elevation of approximately 1,500 m in the United Khasi and Jaintia Hills (Rajkhowa 1966). One provenance survived and grew about as well as *P. oocarpa* and *P. caribaea* over 3 years at an altitude of 1,067 m in the Nilgiri Hills of Tamil Nadu (Chowdhary and others 1987). Loblolly has performed successfully at elevations up to 2,050 m in the Himalayan region, although *P. patula* grows much faster than loblolly in that environment (Guhathakurta 1972, Seth 1972). Loblolly has also been established on hot, bare, rocky slopes at an elevation of 2,135 m in the Punjab. The species is not recommended for planting on these sites because it suffers greatly from snow and severe summer droughts. However, some individual trees have grown to a height of 13.7 m and a dbh of 36 cm by age 24 (Das and Chand 1958). Rajkhowa (1966) found that P fertilization can increase seedling growth at Shillong (1,500 m in elevation) in the United Khasi and Jaintia Hills.

The pine woolly aphid and two species of curculionid beetles, *Dereodus pollinosus* and *Xanthochelus faunus*, attack loblolly pines in India. The beetles defoliate trees by cutting new needles (Gupta 1980).

Loblolly Pine in
Australia and New Zealand

Australia

Loblolly pine is not grown extensively in Australia. However, it yields more cellulose than any other pine on the better soils of the coastal escarpment of New South Wales and southern Queensland (about latitude 25° to 33° S) at elevations of 300 to 950 m (Forestry Commission of New South Wales 1978, Smith 1978a). Nurseries in Queensland produced 13,000 loblolly seedlings in 1981 compared to 1.5 million slash pine seedlings and 4.8 million Caribbean pine (*P. caribaea*) seedlings (McDonald and Krugman 1985). Loblolly was inoculated with strains of mycorrhizal fungi to improve growth as early as 1939 (Bevege 1978).

A breeding program that made use of families from across the natural range of loblolly pine was begun in 1966. The program was designed to improve stem form and accelerate tree growth (Burgess 1968, 1978). The main breeding strategy was to take advantage of population–and genotype–edaphic environment interactions to maximize output with minimum use of fertilizers, equipment, and labor.

In loblolly pines, height extension and earlywood production occur concurrently during a 2.2- to 2.5-month period beginning in early spring. This is followed by terminal dormancy and a transition to latewood production in early summer. Latewood production persists for approximately 6.2 months. Cambial dormancy begins in early winter and lasts for 3.2 to 3.5 months. Continued height extension and earlywood production are associated with mean daily temperatures greater than 12 °C, a high rate of evaporation (more than 110 mm/month), and a fairly high rate of daily sunshine (more than 6 hours). A decrease in daily sunshine to less than 6 hours seems to be the main factor triggering the onset of terminal dormancy and a transition to latewood production (Smith 1978b). Volume equations for loblolly pine in Queensland have been compiled by Vanclay (1982) and Vanclay and Shepherd (1983).

Loblolly pines respond rapidly to cultivation and fertilization when planted on Lateritic Podzolic soils of the coastal lowlands of subtropical Queensland (Richards and Bevege 1967). A stand planted at a density of 2,224 stems/ha can sustain a pulpwood thinning at age 7, if established with the aid of cultivation and N fertilization. On P-deficient sites, measurable growth response can occur within 4 months after P fertilization and cultivation. Foliar P should be at least 0.09% for good loblolly pine growth. The optimum foliar level is about 0.1%. Even without fertilization, planted loblolly pines improve the soil N status sufficiently in a period of 5 to 6 years to permit successful growth of hoop pine, *Araucaria cunninghamii* Ait. This level of N improvement (22 to 50 kg/ha/yr) is similar to that obtained when a legume cover crop is grown for 1 or 2 years. Nitrogen fixation by mycorrhizal fungi associated with loblolly pine roots is considered to be the basis of the site improvement (Bevege and Richards 1972, Richards 1962, Richards and Bevege 1967). Five-year-old loblolly pines that were planted at a spacing of 1.5 by 1.5 m immobilized 269 kg of N/ha in biomass (Queensland Department of Forestry 1966).

Loblolly pine has few pest problems in Australia. Possums damage planted trees by debarking and sometimes girdling them. The mountain possum, *Trichosurus caninus* (Ogilby), and the brush-tailed possum, *T. vulpecula* (Kerr), strip smooth bark between 50 and 300 cm from growing tips, primarily on saplings (beginning about tree age 5) and poles. This damage often causes death of the terminal and forking and sometimes even kills the tree. Most damage occurs primarily where plantations border native wet sclerophyll forests and rain forests. From only a few trees to more than 60% of a stand may be damaged (Barnett and others 1977, How 1976). The pine bark weevil, *Aesiotes notabilis* Pasc., is a pest of hoop pine in eastern Queensland. Pine bark weevils have also been recorded on loblolly, indicating that the species is not immune to this insect (Wylie and Yule 1978).

New Zealand

Loblolly pine was planted on a small scale in the northern part of New Zealand (north of latitude 38° S) during the late 1960's and early 1970's. There, it forms productive stands on moderately leached clay soils. Unfortunately, very little latewood is formed in trees during the early stages of growth, so the wood tends to be of low density and is mechanically weak (Harris and Birt 1972). In 1976, there were 3,861 ha of southern pine (loblolly, longleaf, and slash) plantations in the country. All plantings of southern pines were phased out during the late 1970's and early 1980's in favor of *P. radiata* (McDonald and Krugman 1985).

Loblolly Pine in Europe

Loblolly pine has a limited use as a forest tree in the moist lowlands between the Black Sea and the Caspian Sea (about latitude 42° N) in the Republic of Georgia (Matinjan 1961, Mzavija 1965). In Ajaria, southwest Georgia, the mean annual increment of loblolly reached 33 m³/ha/yr at age 30 (Manvelidze 1972).

Loblolly pine is considered a promising species for diversification of large blocks of planted *P. pinaster* Ait. in southwest France. In that region, loblolly should be planted only on the best soils and should be managed intensively (Chaperon and Arbez 1981). Trial plantings indicate that loblolly will grow on clay soils covered by a shallow sandy layer in the western part of the Sologne (latitude 47°15′ N, 100 m in elevation) (Godron and Destremau 1983) and in the Landes district (latitude 44° N) of France (Guinaudeau 1971).

Trials also indicate that loblolly pine will grow at elevations of 800 to 950 m near Tripolis in the central Peloponnese (about latitude 37°30′ N) of Greece (Georgevits 1976). One advantage of loblolly is that it seems to be resistant to the fungus *Cronartium flaccidum* (Alb. et Schw.) Wint., which causes a severe blister rust on native Mediterranean pines (Raddi and Fagnani 1978).

On a poor site in Emsland, northwestern Germany (latitude 52°45′ N), two F₁ progenies of Korean crosses between pitch and loblolly pines grew as well as *P. sylvestris* and *P. nigra* Arnold for 19 years. On the same site, only one-third of the trees with a pollen parent from a Virginia (USA) source died, whereas two-thirds of the trees with a loblolly pollen parent from a Georgia (USA) source died. The difference between mortality rates resulted from differences in frost resistance (Stephan 1984).

Loblolly Pine in Hawaii, the Caribbean Islands, and Mauritius

Hawaii

Loblolly pine has been planted and grown successfully for more than 27 years on a variety of sites at elevations around 1,130 m on the islands of Maui and Molokai (about latitude 21° N) where rainfall averages about 137 cm/yr. Total volume of 25-year-old test plantings exceeds 600 m³/ha, which is twice that expected for most stands in the southeastern United States. Survival at 9 years is about 98% and can be as high as 87% at stand age 25 (DeBell and others 1989, Schubert and Korte 1969, Whitesell 1974). Specific gravity of wood of 19- to 25-year-old trees averaged 0.419 and ranged from 0.333 to 0.524 (Skolmen 1963). This is substantially lower than the specific gravity of wood of loblolly of similar age in the species' native range (see chapter 2). On dry, marginal sites, slash pine produces greater volumes of wood than does loblolly. As sites improve, growth differences between the two species lessen. Nine-year-old loblolly planted at an elevation of 1,130 m on the island of Maui grew up to 16 cm in dbh and 10 m in height at a spacing of 2.4 by 2.4 m (Schubert and Korte 1969). For maximum loblolly pine growth, spacing should be less than 3 by 3 m (Buck and Imoto 1982).

Pathogens found on loblolly pines in Hawaii include an aphid, *Cinara carolina* Tissot., and various fungi. *Cinara carolina* has been observed on seedlings on the island of Maui (Hawaii Department of Agriculture 1962). Needle cast fungi, *Lophodermium* spp., and the fungus *Sphaeropsis sapinea* (= *Diplodia pinea*), which causes tip dieback, caused only minor damage to loblolly in Hawaii (Bega and others 1978). *Botryosphaeria dothidea* (Moug.:Fr.) Ces. & de Not. has also been recorded infecting roots

and sometimes killing overstocked, drought-ridden trees (Hodges 1983).

The Caribbean Islands

Loblolly pine is not recommended for planting anywhere in the Caribbean. Small test plantings were made in various locations in Puerto Rico (about 17° N) beginning in 1955. The lack of native mycorrhizae severely hampered early growth (Briscoe 1959). Even with the addition of mycorrhizal fungi, growth is only about one-third that of *P. caribaea*, which is native to the neighboring islands. In one plot, 8-year-old loblolly averaged 5.5 m in height and 9 cm in dbh, whereas a single 8-year-old, *P. caribaea* tree planted on the same plot was 18.3 m in height and 28 cm in dbh (Unpublished information on file at USDA Forest Service, International Institute of Tropical Forestry, Rio Piedras, PR).

Mauritius

Mauritius is located in the Indian Ocean approximately at latitude 20° S and longitude 56° E. Pines (mostly slash, but some loblolly) have been planted there since the 1950's. Southern pine plantings now occupy about 7,600 ha, and most were established between 1966 and 1980. Preferred sites are at altitudes above 540 m where soils are fairly deep and not waterlogged. Presently, seeds are collected from established stands and raised in local nurseries. During 1984, about 70,000 loblolly pine seedlings and about 1.1 million slash pine seedlings were raised for use in new plantations (Mauritius Forestry Service 1987).

Summary

Loblolly pine is now a valuable forest resource in Africa, Asia, and South America. Some 400 million seedlings are presently being planted annually on these continents. Two hundred to 300 million seedlings are planted annually in China and more than 100 million annually in Brazil. Smaller but locally important numbers of loblolly are planted annually in Argentina, South Africa, Uruguay, and Zimbabwe. Most of these countries have made long-term commitments to continuous loblolly pine regeneration and management. Trial plantings have been made in more than a dozen other countries.

Tree improvement and proper site selection are the keys to growing loblolly pines successfully in exotic locations. Planted trees have displayed outstanding growth and vigor on degraded sites, old fields, and pastures in many locations. Careful control of planting sites has resulted in superior growth for a variety of products. Fertilization is not necessary for rapid growth on most sites, and pest control measures must be taken only where leafcutting ants are a problem.

Although loblolly pine is very adaptable, it has not been used to its full potential in many exotic locations. Many plantings have failed because the wrong seed sources were used or because plantings were made in environments for which the species or the seed sources were not adapted. Seed sources from the southernmost United States perform especially well in subtropical climates. In some cases, hybrids may outgrow pure loblolly in harsh environments. As genetically improved trees become more available and the species' geographic diversity is more fully recognized and used, interest in loblolly as a superior exotic pine should continue to increase.

Research Needs

- Poor self-pruning is a problem in loblolly pines grown in South America. A method of promoting decomposition of dry limbs is needed so that dry limbs will drop from trees shortly after dying rather than remaining on trees for a decade or more. Alternatively, genetic variability may permit the selection of fast-growing genotypes that have rapid self-pruning.

- Breeding programs, using families from appropriate segments of the natural range, are needed to improve growth in many exotic locations. Emphasis on genotype–environment interactions should maximize volume growth with limited stand culture and labor.

Literature Cited

Ahn KY. 1977. Studies on the characteristics of loblolly × pitch and loblolly × Korean black pine hybrids. Bulletin of the Seoul National University College of Agriculture 2(1):471–482.

Ahrens S, Holbert D. 1981. A taper and volume model for loblolly pine. Boletim de Pesquisa Florestal 3:37–68.

Akai T, Furuno T. 1971. Amounts of litter-fall and grazing in young loblolly pine forest. Bulletin of the Kyoto University Forests 42:83–95.

Akai T, Ueda S, Furuno T. 1972. Mechanisms related to (dry) matter production in a thrifty loblolly pine (Pinus taeda) forest. Bulletin of the Kyoto University Forests 43:85–105.

Akai T, Furuno T, Ueda S, Sano S. 1968. Mechanisms of matter production in a young loblolly pine forest. Japan Forestry Bulletin 43:26–49.

Alonzo AE, Sancho R. 1967. Depth and season of bare root planting of Pinus elliottii and P. taeda in Buenos Aires providence. IDIA (Suplemento Forestal) 4:12–20.

Baldanzi G. 1978. Research on Pinus taeda at the Rio Negro Forest Research Station, Parana. Revista Floresta 9(1):5–7.

Baldanzi G, Malinovski JR. 1976. Comparative trial of different provenances of Pinus taeda and P. elliottii. Revista Floresta 7(2):5–8.

Banks CH, Schwegmann LM. 1957. The physical properties of fast-and slow-grown Pinus patula and P. taeda from South African sources. South African Journal of Forestry 30:44–59.

Banks PF. 1966. Early height growth in Rhodesia of progenies of Pinus taeda from Texas. Rhodesia, Zambia, and Malawi Journal of Agricultural Research 4:3–7.

Banks PF, Prevost MJ. 1976. Sawlog pruning regimes for Pinus patula, P. elliottii and P. taeda in Rhodesia. Southern African Forestry Journal 99:44–48

Barnes RD. 1977. Population improvement through selection and hybridization in Pinus patula, P. elliottii, and P. taeda in southern Africa. In: Third World Consultation on Forest Tree Breeding; 1977 March 21–26; Canberra, Australia. FO-FTB-77-3/3. Rome: FAO/IUFRO: 489–505.

Barnes RD, Jarvis RF, Schweppenhauser MA, Mullin LJ. 1976. Introduction, spread and control of pine wooly aphid, Pineus pini (L.) in Rhodesia. South African Forestry Journal (96):1–11.

Barnes RD, Mullin LJ. 1978. Three-year height performance of Pinus elliottii Engelm. var. elliottii × P. taeda L. hybrid families on three sites in Rhodesia. Silvae Genetica 27(6):217–223.

Barnett JL, How RA, Humphreys WF. 1977. Possum damage to pine plantations in north-eastern New South Wales. Australian

Forest Research 7:185–195.

Barrichelo LEG, Kageyama PY, Speltz RM, and others. 1977. Trials of provenances of *Pinus taeda* from the point of view of their industrial use. Instituto de Pesquisas e Estudos Florestais, Piracicaba 15:1–14.

Bega RV, Smith RS Jr, Martines AP, Davis CJ. 1978. Severe damage to *Pinus radiata* and *P. pinaster* by *Diplodia pinea* and *Lophodermium* spp. on Molokai and Lanai in Hawaii. Plant Disease Reporter 62(4):329–331.

Bentley MD, Mamiya Y, Yatagai M, Shimzu K. 1985. Factors in *Pinus* species affecting the mobility of the pine wood nematode, *Bursaphelenchus xylophitus*. Annals of the Phytopathological Society of Japan 51(5):556–561.

Bevege DI. 1978. Nutritional and other edaphic considerations concerning growth, and their interactions with populations of southern and tropical pines in Queensland. In: Proceedings, Joint IUFRO Workshop; 1977 April 4–7; Oxford, UK: Commonwealth Forestry Institute: 237–251, vol. 1.

Bevege DI, Richards BN. 1972. Principles and practice of foliar analysis as a basis for crop-logging in pine plantations: 2. determination of critical phosphorus levels. Plant and Soil 37:159–169.

Bianchi M, Nieto A, Sorrentino A. 1984. Pretreatments' seeds of *Pinus elliottii* Engelm var. *elliottii* and *Pinus taeda* L.: their effects on germinative power. In: Proceedings, Methods of Production and Quality Control of Forest Seeds and Seedlings; 1984 March 19–23; Curitiba, Brazil. Curitiba, Brazil: Federal University of Parana: 96–108.

Blackman T. 1980. Pulpwood forestry in Brazil: Olinkraft amasses experience. World Wood 21(4):28–29.

Botha AT, Wessels DCJ, Moore LD. 1988. Are injury symptoms on pine trees in the Eastern Transvaal (South Africa) air pollution related? Phytopathology 78(12 part 1):1581.

Bredenkamp BV. 1985. A planning strategy for the pruning of pines. South African Forestry Journal 134:33–34.

Bredenkamp BV, Loveday NC. 1984. Volume equations for diameter measurements in millimeters. South African Forestry Journal 130:40.

Bredenkamp BV, Venter JSJ, Haigh H. 1983. Early respacement and fewer thinnings can increase profitability of coniferous sawtimber production. South African Forestry Journal 124:36–42.

Briscoe CB. 1959. Early results of mycorrhizal inoculation of pine in Puerto Rico. Caribbean Forester 20:73–77.

Buck MG, Imoto RH. 1982. Growth of 11 introduced tree species on select forest sites in Hawaii. Res. Paper PSW-169. Honolulu: USDA Forest Service, Pacific Southwest Forest and Range Experiment Station. 12 p.

Burger D, Machado SA, Hosokawa RT. 1980. Thinnings in Brazilian plantations of fast growing species. In: Proceedings, 1980 IUFRO Project Group 4.02, Economics and Harvesting of Thinnings; 1980 September 29–October 4; Göttingen, Germany. [Place of publication and publisher unknown]: 12 p.

Burgess IP. 1968. Thoughts on the *P. taeda* tree improvement programme. In: Proceedings, 5th Silvicultural Research Officers' Conference; 1967 April 10–13; Tumut, Australia. Tech. Pap. 14. [Sydney], Australia: Forestry Commission of New South Wales: 53–57.

Burgess IP. 1978. Performance of selected *Pinus taeda* L. families in northern New South Wales. In: Proceedings, Joint IUFRO Workshop; 1977 April 4–7; Brisbane. Oxford, UK: Commonwealth Forestry Institute: 819–823, vol. 2.

Campinhos E Jr. 1965. Comparative trials in breaking dormancy of *Pinus elliottii* and *P. taeda* seed produced in Brazil and in the USA. Anais Brasileiros de Economia Florestas Instituto Nacional do Pinho 17:105–122.

Campinhos E Jr, Ikemori YK, Martins FCG. 1984. Determination of the most adequate growth medium to the production of seedlings of *Eucalyptus* (from cuttings and seeds) and *Pinus* (from seeds) in rigid plastic containers. In: Proceedings, Methods of Production and Quality Control of Forest Seeds and Seedlings;

1984 March 19–23; Curitiba, Brazil. Curitiba, Brazil: Federal University of Parana: 350–378.

Carneiro JG de A. 1977. Determination of the standard of quality of *Pinus taeda* seedlings for planting out. Revista Floresta 8(1):63–68.

Carneiro JG de A. 1985. Efeito da densidade sobre o desenvolvimento de alguns parametros morfofisiologicos de mudas de *Pinus taeda* L. em viveiro e apos o plantio. Curitiba, Brazil: Federal University of Parana. 125 p.

Carneiro JG de A. 1987. Types of containers and sowing season influences on root system behavior and morphological parameters of *Pinus taeda* and *Pinus elliottii* seedlings. Project in cooperation with the Federal University of Parana and Albert Ludwig University, Freiburg, Germany. Curitiba, Brazil: Setor de Ciencias Agrarias Departmento de Silvicultura e Manejo. 81 p.

Carter WG, Boucher M, Turnbull JW. 1981. Forestry planning and development in the People's Republic of China with special reference to production forestry in the South. Report of a visit under the China/Australia Agricultural Exchange Scheme; 1980 April 16–May 10; Canberra, Australia: Department of Primary Industry. 41 p.

Carvalho CT de, Bueno RA. 1975. Animals causing damage to plantation (Mammalia, Rodentia). Silvicultura em Sao Paulo 9:39–46.

Castillo EM del, Gil MN, Ortin EA, and others. 1987. Determinacion del crecimiento de *Pinus taeda* y *Pinus patula*. In: Proceedings, 1987 Simposio Sobre Silvicultura y MejorAmiento Genetico de Especies Forestales; 1987 April 6–10; Buenos Aires. Buenos Aires: Forest Research and Experimental Center [CIEF]: 40–52.

Cawse JCL. 1979. Dry season plantings and related establishment techniques. South African Forestry Journal 111:34–38.

Cawse JCL. 1983. Industrial wood regimes for plantations of *P. patula*, *P. taeda* and *P. elliottii*. South African Forestry Journal 125:35–57.

Chang YC, Sun JC. 1984. Survey on insect-pests of economic tree (or bamboo) species in Taiwan: 5. The important insect-pests of *Pinus* species. Quarterly Journal of Chinese Forestry 17(4):37–45.

Chaperon H, Arbez M. 1981. Introduction of *Pinus taeda* into southwest France. Annals of Silvicultural Research. 1980. Paris: Association Foret-Cellulose: 92–121.

Chiaranda R, Poggiani F, Simoes JW. 1983. Tree growth and litterfall in forest stands planted on soils affected by oil shale mining. Instituto de Pesquisas e Estudos Florestais, Piracicaba (25):25–28.

Chowdhary RL, Bari PA, Prasad KG. 1987. Performance of tropical pines and their provenances in Tamil Nadu. Indian Forester 113(2):101–111.

Chung DY, Kwon HM, Tak WS, and others. 1984. Control of cone insects of four pine species by soil application of furadan carbofuran at two locations. Research Report of the Institute of Forest Genetics (Immok Yukcong Yonku-So Yongu Pogo) 20:70–73.

CIEF [Forest Research and Experimental Center]. 1987. Untitled report. Buenos Aires.

Crotto JE. 1987. Ensayo de origenes en *Pinus elliottii* Engelm y *Pinus taeda* L. impatacion y 2 anos de crecimientos. In: Proceedings, 1987 Simposio Sobre Silvicultura y Mejoramiento Genetico de Especies Forestales; 1987 April 6–10; Buenos Aires. Buenos Aires: Forest Research and Experimental Center [CIEF]: 11–19.

Daniels FW. 1975a. Effect of seed-cover upon germination of pine seed [*Pinus elliottii*, *Pinus taeda*, *Pinus patula*]. Forestry in South Africa (16):69–71.

Daniels FW. 1975b. Nursery fertilizer experiments in *Eucalyptus grandis* and *Pinus taeda*. Forestry in South Africa (17):57–61.

Daniels FW, van der Sijde HA. 1975. Cold stratification of *Pinus elliottii*, *Pinus taeda* and *Pinus patula* seed. Forestry in South Africa (16):63–68.

Darrow WK. 1979. Silviculture of the southern pines in South Africa. Journal of Forestry 77(10):682–685.

Das ES, Chand B. 1958. Experimental afforestation of bare, dry and rocky slopes in high hills. Indian Forester 84(7):402–406.

DeBell DS, Harms WR, Whitesell CD. 1989. Stockability: a major factor in productivity differences between Pinus taeda plantations in Hawaii and the southeastern United States. Forest Science 35(3):708–719.

De Ronde C, Bohmer LH, Droomer EAP. 1986. Evaluation of wildlife damage in pine stands. South African Forestry Journal 138:45–50.

Donald DGM. 1965. A study of the history, practice and economics of forest nurseries in South America. Annale, Universiteit van Stellenbosch: 40A(1):107.

Donald DGM. 1970. The effect of planting depth on the survival of Pinus radiata, Pinus pinaster and Pinus taeda. South African Forestry Journal (74):17–19.

Donald DGM. 1983. The application of fertilizer to pole stage pine crops. In: Schonau APG, Stubbings JA, comp. Proceedings, Symposium of the Southern African Institute of Forestry; 1983 June 23; Pietermaritzburg, South Africa. [Place of publication and publisher unknown]: 59–71.

Donald DGM. 1986. South African nursery practice—the state of the art. South African Forestry Journal 139:36–47.

Donald DGM. 1987. The application of fertiliser to pines following second thinning. South African Forestry Journal 142:13–16.

Donald DGM, Lange PW, Schultz CJ, Morris AR. 1987. The application of fertilizers to pines in southern Africa. South African Forestry Journal (141):53–62.

Droomer EAP. 1985. Volume and value loss owing to samango monkey damage in pine stands in the Northern Transvaal. South African Forestry Journal 134:47–51.

EMBRAPA [Empresa Brasileira de Pesquisa Agropecuaria]. 1986. Zoneamento ecologico para plantios florestais no estado do parana. Curitiba, Brazil: Ministry of Agriculture. 89 p.

Esterhuyse CJ. 1985. Site requirements of the most important commercial trees planted in South Africa. South African Forestry Journal 133:61–66.

Fahler JC, Orozco EG, Di Lucca CM, Gimenez S. 1986. Evaluation de especies del genero Pinus en el departamento Guarani—Missiones, Argentina. Informe Tecnico no. 44. Buenos Aires: Instituto Nacional De Tecnologia Agropecuaria: 1–19.

Falkenhagen ER. 1978. Thirty five-year results from seven Pinus elliottii (Engelman.) and Pinus taeda (L.) provenance trials in South Africa. South African Forestry Journal 107:22–36.

Fernandes RR. 1981. Variacoes Estacionas dos teores de umidade e oleoresina em folhagem de Pinus elliottii Engelm, Pinus taeda L. E. Araucaria angustifolia (Bert) O. Ktze. E. sua influencia no potencial de inflamabilidade das copas. Curitiba, Brazil: Federal University of Parana: 121–122. M.S. thesis.

Fernandes RR, Soares RV. 1981. Seasonal variation of moisture content of foliage of Pinus elliottii, Pinus taeda and Araucaria angustifolia in Parana, Brazil. Revista Floresta 12(2):5–12.

Fishwick RW. 1978. A preliminary assessment of a nine-year-old southern pine (Pinus elliottii and P. taeda) trial with some observations on these species in South Brazil. In: Third World Consultation on Forest Tree Breeding; 1977 March 21–26; Canberra, Australia. FO-FTB-77-3/3. Canberra: CSIRO: 336–339.

Flor H de M. 1977. Studies of production and stem form of Pinus taeda L. in a fertilizer trial area of the Canguiri Farm (Brazil). Revista Floresta 8(1):69–70.

FAO [Food and Agricultural Organization of the United Nations]. 1982. Forestry in China. Pap. 35. Rome: FAO: 3, 7, 151, 181, 257.

Forestry Commission of New South Wales. 1978. Pine plantings in New South Wales. G-26914-1 Sydney: Forestry Commission, NSW: 8–19.

Furuno T. 1972a. Effects of artificial defoliation upon growth of loblolly pine (Pinus taeda Linn.). Bulletin of the Kyoto University Forests 43:73–84.

Furuno T. 1972b. Primary consumption by leaf-eating insects in loblolly pine canopies. Bulletin of the Kyoto University Forests 44:20–37.

Furuno T, Uenaka K. 1976. Studies on the insect damage upon the pine-species imported in Japan: 3. On the feeding of adult of striated chafer (Anomala testaceipes Motschulsky). Bulletin of the Kyoto University Forests 48:9–21.

Furuno T, Watanabe H, Uenaka K. 1977. Studies on the insect damage upon the pine-species imported (introduced) in Japan: 4. On the Japanese pine sawyer, Monochamus alternatus Hope, infesting loblolly pine, Pinus taeda Linn., and lace-bark pine, Pinus bungeana Zucc. Bulletin of the Kyoto University Forests 49:8–19.

Furuno T, Futai K. 1986. Effects of pine wood nematode upon the growth of pine-species. Bulletin of the Kyoto University Forests 57:112–127.

Garrido MA de O, Negreiros OC de. 1976. Competition between different species of the genus Pinus in Assis and Teodoro Samaio districts. Techical Bulletin of the San Paulo, Brazil, Forestry Institute 22:1–15.

Garrido MA de O, Garrido LM do AG, Ribas C, Assini JL. 1984. Density influence in seed production by Pinus elliottii. In: Proceedings, Methods of Production and Quality Control of Forest Seeds and Seedlings; 1984 March 19–23; Curitiba, Brazil. Curitiba, Brazil: Federal University of Parana: 134–139.

Gavidia AT. 1978. Produçao mundial de sementes em Pinus tropicais e sub-tropicais. Revista Floresta 9(2):9–17.

Georgevits RP. 1976. Observations on two pine shoot moths, Rhyacionia buoliana var. thurificana Led. and Rhyacionia buoliana Den. & Schiff. (Lep., Tortricidae) in Greece. Zeitschrift für Angewandte Entomologie 80(3):289–299.

Germishuizen PJ, Smale PJ. 1982. The use of controlled burning in an established pine stand as a means of fire protection at Usutu Pulp Company Limited (Swaziland). Swaziland: Usutu Pulp Company Fire Seminar; 7 May 1982; [Location unknown]. [Place of publication and publisher unknown]: 10–12.

Godeas AM. 1987. Decomposition studies on Pinus taeda forest: 2. Decomposition of leaf litter. Pedobiologia 30(5):323–331.

Godron M, Destremau DX. 1983. Advice on reforestation in the Sologne Region, France. Informations Foret 1:1–20.

Goldammer JG. 1983. Controlled burning as a method of fire management in pine plantations in southern Brazil. Freiburg, Germany: Freiburger Waldschutz-Abhandlungen 4: 211–239.

Golfari L. 1970. Report to the government of Brazil: conifers suitable for the reafforestation of the States of Parana, Santa Catarina and Rio Grande do Sul. Rome: FAO. 86 p.

Golfari L. 1978. Effect of ecological factors on the choice of species for reforestation. In: Proceedings, 7th World Forestry Congress; 1972 October 4–18; General San Martin, Argentina. Buenos Aires: World Forestry Congress: 1626–1629.

Golfari L. 1979. Conifers suitable for the afforestation of the States of Parana Santa Catarina and Rio Grande Do Sul. FAO TA-2858. Rome: FAO: 2–86.

Golfari L. 1962. Resistencia a las heladas de pinos exoticas en Misiones. Buenos Aires: Administracion Nacional de Bosques, Direccion de Investigaciones Forestales. 6 p.

Grammel RH. 1985. Harvesting fast-growing timber plantations in South America. Holz-Zentralblatt 113:1596–1597.

Grey DC, Taylor GI. 1983. Site requirements for commercial afforestation in the Cape. South African Forestry Journal 127:35–38.

Guhathakurta P. 1972. Introduction trials of pines in North Bengal. In: Burley J, Nikles DG, comp. Selection and breeding to improve some tropical conifers: Proceedings, 15th IUFRO Congress; 1971; Gainesville, FL. Oxford, UK: Commonwealth Forestry Institute: 318–324.

Guinaudeau J. 1971. Tests in mineral fertilization on a Pinus taeda plantation in Landes district. French Forestry Review 23(4):443–447.

Gupta BK. 1980. New pests of tropical pines in India. Indian Forester 106(4):312–313.

Haag HP, Rocha Filho JV de C, Oliveira GD de. 1978. Nutrient cycling in *E. citriodora* and *P. taeda*: 2. nutrient distribution in litter fall. Solo 70(2):28–31.

Hagedorn SF. 1976. A phenotypic assessment of *Pinus taeda* progenies in the Eastern Transvaal. South African Forestry Journal 97:58–62.

Haigh H. 1980. A preliminary report on controlled burning trails in pine plantations in Natal. South African Forestry Journal 113:53–58.

Han YC, Hong SH, Sohn SI, and others. 1987a. Studies on late growth performance of *Pinus rigida* × *Pinus taeda*. Research Report of the Institute of Forest Genetics (Immok Yukcong Yonku-So Yongu Pogo) 23:11–15.

Han YC, Lee KY, Choi SK, and others. 1987b. Growth performance of 24-year-old loblolly pine (*Pinus taeda* L.) in five locations. Research Report of the Institute of Forest Genetics (Immok Yukcong Yonku-So Yongu Pogo) 23:96–100.

Han YC, Ryu KO, Lee KY, and others. 1985. A ten-year-old loblolly pine provenance test in Korea. Research Report of the Institute of Forest Genetics (Immok Yukcong Yonku-So Yongu Pogo) 21:78–88.

Harris JM, Birt DV. 1972. Use of beta rays for early assessment of wood density development in provenance trials. Silvae Genetica 21:21–25.

Hawaii Department of Agriculture, Division of Plant Industry. 1962. Annual Report 1961–1962. Honolulu: Hawaii Agricultural Experiment Station 83:11–12.

Herman B. 1985. The anatomy of some abnormal wood formation in *P. taeda*. In: Proceedings, Symposium on Forest Products Research International—Achievements and the Future; 1985 April 22–26; Pretoria, South Africa. Pretoria, South Africa. International Association of Wood anatomy Bulletin 6(2):84–85.

Herman B. 1988. Effects of 1-napthaleneacetic acid (NAA) and gibberellin A_3 (GA_3) on abnormal wood formation in *Pinus taeda*. South African Forestry Journal 144:30–32.

Hodges CS, McFadden MW. 1987. The current status of forest insects and diseases in Latin America. In: Proceedings, 1987 Simposio Sobre Silvicultura y Mejoramiento Genetico de Especies Forestales; 1987 April 6–10; Buenos Aires. Buenos Aires: Forest Research and Experimental Center [CIEF]: 225–234.

Hodges CS. 1983. Pine mortality in Hawaii associated with *Botryosphaeria dothidea*. Plant Disease 67(5):555–556.

Hodges CS, May LC. 1972. A root disease of pine, araucaria and eucalyptus in Brazil caused by a new species of *Cylindrocladium*. Phytopathology 62(8):898–901.

Hodgson TJ. 1980. Pine seed grading: the implication for orchard seed. South African Forestry Journal 112:10–14.

How RA. 1976. Reproduction, growth and survival of young in the mountain possum, *Trichosurus caninus* (Marsupialia) in a *Pinus taeda*/*P. elliottii* plantation in New South Wales. Australian Journal of Zoology 24(2):189–199.

Hyun SK. 1972. The possibility of F_2-utilization in pine hybridization. In: Proceedings, IUFRO Genetics–SABRAO Joint Symposia; 1972; Tokyo. Tokyo: Government Forest Experiment Station: 1–10.

Hyun SK. 1974. Pine hybridization and performance of hybrids in Korea. Indian Journal of Genetics 34A:375–386.

Hyun SK, Ahn KY. 1959. Principal characteristics of × *Pinus rigitaeda*. Research Report of the Institute of Forest Genetics (Immok Yukcong Yonku-So Yongu Pogo) 1:35–50.

Ingram CL. 1984. Provenance research on *Pinus elliottii* Engleman and *P. taeda* Linnaeus in Malawi. In: Proceedings, Provenance and Genetic Improvement Strategies in Tropical Forest Trees Joint Work Conference; 1984 April 9–14; Mutare, Zimbabwe. Harare, Zimbabwe: Zimbabwe Forest Commission and Oxford: Commonwealth Forestry Institute: 265–277.

Inoue MT. 1972. A comparative trial for assessing the effects of inoculating seedlings of *Pinus taeda* with mycorrhizal fungi, in relation to the amount of inoculum present in the soil. Revista Floresta 4(1):63–68.

Ito K, Zinno Y, Suto Y. 1975. Dothistroma-pini-var-pini needle blight of pines in Japan. Bull. 272. Tokyo: Forest Protection Research, Government Forest Experiment Station: 123–140.

Jankovski T. 1985. Avaliacao da producae e disseminacao de sementes em um provoamento de *Pinus taeda* L. Curitiba, Brazil: Federal University of Parana. 74 p. M.S. thesis.

Katerere Y. 1983a. The fungus *Entomophthora planchoniana* Cornu (non thaxter): the pine needle aphid *Eulachnus rileyi* (Williams). Commonwealth Forestry Review. 62(4):271–273.

Katerere Y. 1983b. Insect pests of pine plantations in the eastern districts of Zimbabwe. Zimbabwe Journal of Agricultural Research 21:101–105.

Kellison RC. 1985. Seed procurement and nursery management of the southern pines in the People's Republic of China. In: Proceedings, International Symposium on Nursery Management Practices for the Southern Pines; 1985 August 4–9; Montgomery, AL. Auburn, AL: Auburn University, Alabama Agricultural Experiment Station: 20–24.

Kfir R, Kirsten F, Van Rensburg NJ. 1985. *Pauesia* sp. (Hymenoptera: Aphidiidae): a parasite introduced into South Africa for biological control of the black pine aphid, *Cinara cronartii* (Homoptera: Aphididae). Environmental Entomology 14(5):597–601.

Kikuti P, Monteiro RFR, Cordeiro JA. 1984. Production of genetically improved seed of *Pinus taeda* L. In: Proceedings, Methods of Production and Quality Control of Forest Seeds and Seedlings; 1984 March 19–23; Curitiba, Brazil. Curitiba, Brazil: Federal University of Parana: 244–252.

Kolln RF, Viola J. 1987. Tablas de volumen con corteza para *Pinus elliottii* y *P. taeda* en El Norte de Missiones. In: Proceedings, 1987 Simposio Sobre Silvicultura y Mejoramiento Genetico de Especies Forestales; 1987 April 6–10; Buenos Aires . Buenos Aires: Forest Research and Experimental Center [CIEF]: 134–152.

Kondo H, Kobayashi T. 1984. A new canker disease of loblolly pine, *Pinus taeda* L., caused by *Ascocalyx pinicola* sp. nov. Journal of the Japanese Forestry Society 66(2):60–66.

Krall J. 1969. Growth of loblolly pine in Uruguay. Journal of Forestry 67(7):481.

Krall J. 1987. Introducion de especies y origenes de pinos y eucalyptus en el Uruguay. In: Proceedings, 1987 Simposio Sobre Silvicultura y Mejoramiento Genetico de Especies Forestales; 1987 April 6–10; Buenos Aires. Buenos Aires: Forest Research and Experimental Center [CIEF]: 97–104.

Krugman SL, Ching KK, Dinus RJ, and others. 1983. Forest genetics and tree improvement in the People's Republic of China. Washington, DC: USDA Office of International Cooperation and Development and Society of American Foresters. 84 p.

Ladrach WE. 1974. Recommendations on initial spacing and management of density of conifer plantations. Investigacion Forestal (2):1–5.

Ladrach WE. 1983. Ten year growth of the Chupilluata Arboretum (Columbia). Investigacion Forestal 82:1–8.

Ladrach WE. 1985. Comparisons between provenances and sources of fourteen conifers in the Columbian Andes after five years. Investigacion Forestal 102:1–3.

Lee KJ, Koo CD. 1983. Inoculation of pines in a nursery with *Pisolithus tinctorius* and *Thelephora terrestris* in Korea [abstract]. In: Atkinson D, and others, eds. Tree root systems and their mycorrhizas. The Hague: Nijhoff/Junk Publishers: 325–329.

Liang JH. 1965. Investigation and study on the yield of turpentine and other some things about plantation of exotic pines which are planted in Taiwan. Bulletin of the Taiwan Forestry Research Institute 107:1–20.

Liang YZ. 1984. Growth differences of slash, loblolly and Masson's pines at seedling stage. Forest Science and Technology 2:11–13.

Lin WC. 1965. Study on the growth of various species of pine in relation to elevations and climatic factors. Bulletin of the Taiwan Forest Research Institute 119:1–38.

Lindsay AD. 1932. Loblolly pine (*Pinus taeda*). Leaflet 36. Canberra: Commonwealth Forestry Bureau. 5 p.

Lopes MIMS, Mello f de AF de, Garrido MA de O. 1983. Effect of *Pinus* culture on litter and chemical properties of a dark-red latosol original under cerrado vegetation: 1. Effect on quantity and composition of litter. Instituto Anaisda Escola Superior de Agricultura "Luis de Queiroz" 40:423–426.

Lundquist JE. 1984. The occurrence and distribution of rhizina root rot in South Africa and Swaziland. South African Forestry Journal 131:22–24.

Lundquist JE. 1986. Fungi associated with *Pinus* in South Africa: 1. The Transvaal. South African Forestry Journal 138:1–14.

Lundquist JE. 1987. Fungi associated with *Pinus* in South Africa: 3. Natal, the Orange Free State and the Republic of Transkei. South African Forestry Journal 143:11–19.

Lundquist JE. 1988. Methods for describing the effect of Armillaria root rot on growth of young *Pinus taeda*. Phytopathology 78(12/1):1555.

Machado S do A. 1978. Studies in growth and yield estimation for *Pinus taeda* L. plantations in the state of Parana—Brazil. Seattle: University of Washington. 170 p. Ph.D. dissertation.

Machado S do A. 1979a. Estimativa de sobrevivencia de *Pinus taeda* em plantios homogeneos. Revista Floresta 10(1):73–76.

Machado S do A. 1979b. Tabela de volume para *Pinus taeda* na regiao de telemaco borba-pr. Revista Floresta 10(1):29–35.

Machado S do A. 1980. Curvas de indice de sito para plantacoes de *Pinus taeda* L. na Regiao central do estado do Parana. Revista Floresta 11(2):4–18.

Machado S do A. 1981. The use of a flexible biological model for basal area growth and yield studies of *Pinus taeda*. In: Proceedings, IUFRO Forest Resources Inventory, Growth Models, Management, Planning, and Remote Sensing; [dates unknown]; Nigata, Japan. [Place of publication and publisher unknown]: 75–91.

Machado S do A, coord. 1984. Inventario florestal nacional florestas plantadas nos Estados do Parana e Santa Catarina. Brasilia: Instituto Brasileiro de Desenvolvimento Florestal. 284 p.

Mackenzie AA, Donald DGM. 1983. Weed control and fertilizer use in South African forest establishment. In: Proceedings, Jubilee Symposia of the Faculty of Forestry; 1982 September 23–24; Stellenbosch, South Africa. Mededeling, Fakulteit Bosbou, Universiteit Stellenbosch 1(98): 295–304.

Manvelidze KM. 1972. Growth rhythm cambium action characteristics and wood formation of North American wood species. Bulletin of the Academy of Sciences of the Georgian SSR 64(3):659–662.

Marsh EK. 1978. The cultivation and management of commercial pine plantations in South Africa. Bull. 56. Pretoria, South Africa: Department of Forestry. 140 p.

Matinjan AB. 1961. North American plants at Batumi [on the Black Sea] Coast. Byulleten Glavnogo Botanicheskogo Sada 43:8–12.

Mauritius Forestry Service. 1987. Annual report of the Forestry Service of the Ministry of Agriculture, Fisheries, and Natural Resources for the year 1984. Port Louis, Mauritius: L.C. Achille, Government Printer. 28 p.

McDonald S, Krugman SL. 1985. Worldwide planting of southern pines. In: Proceedings, 1985 International Symposium on Nursery Management Practices for the Southern Pines; 1985 August 4–9; Montgomery, AL. Auburn, AL: Auburn University, Alabama Agricultural Experiment Station: 1–29.

McTague JP, Bailey RL. 1987a. Compatible basal area and diameter distribution models for thinned loblolly pine plantations in

Santa Catarina, Brazil. Forest Science 33(1):43–51.

McTague JP, Bailey RL. 1987b. Simultaneous total and merchantable volume equations and a compatible taper function for loblolly pine. Canadian Journal of Forest Research 17(1):87–92.

Mikami S, Iwakawa MA. 1973. Provenance trial of loblolly pine: eleven year results at Oneyama test plantation. Meguro, Japan: Bulletin of the Government Forest Experiment Station 255:47–60.

Monteiro RFR, Spelts RM, Cordeiro JA. 1983. Fast growing trees. Silvicultura 30:211–213.

Mullin LJ, Barnes RD, Prevost MJ. 1978. A review of the southern pines in Rhodesia. Bull. For. Res. 7. Salisbury, Zimbabwe: Rhodesia Forestry Commission. 328 p.

Mullin LJ, Falkenhagen ER. 1979. *Pinus elliottii* and *P. taeda* provenance trials in South Africa. South African Forestry Journal 109:51.

Muner TS, Barrichelo LEG. 1983. Effect of thinning on the quality of wood from *Pinus taeda* L. used for producing kraft pulp. In: Proceeding, Association of the Brazilian Pulp and Paper Industry (ABCP) 16th Annual Meeting and 3rd Latin-American Cellulose and Paper Congress; 1983 November 21–26; Sao Paulo. Sao Paulo: ABCP: 93–112.

Muniz PJ da C, Baldanzi G, Pellico Netto S. 1975. Experiment in applying fertilizers to *Pinus elliottii* and *Pinus taeda* in southern Brazil. Revista Floresta 6(1):5–13.

Mushi JA, Madoffe S. 1984. Performance of two *Pinus taeda* L. provenance trials at Lushoto and Sao Hill, Tanzania. In: Proceedings, IUFRO Working Parties S2.02-08 (Tropical Species Provenances), S2.03-01 (Breeding Tropical Species), and S2.03-13 (Breeding Southern Pines); 1984 April 9–14; Mutare, Zimbabwe. Harare, Zimbabwe: Zimbabwe Forestry Commission: 404–415.

Mzavija AI. 1965. Raising the productivity of the forests of the Colchis lowland [Caucasia]. Lesn Hoz 18(2):4–12.

Nakai I, Fujimoto H, Inamori Y. 1976. Studies on the cross-breeding of genus *Pinus*: on the process of fertilization in the interspecific pollination of *Pinus thunbergii* Parl. with *P. densiflora* Sieb. et Zucc. and other pine species. Bulletin of the Kyoto University Forests 48:31–45.

Nogueira AC. 1978. Estudo de rendimento de poda em povoamentos de *Pinus taeda* L. Curitiba, Brazil: Federal University of Parana. 113 p. M.S. thesis.

Norskov-Lauritsen G. 1963. Notes on the growth habits of the main pine species of the Eastern Transvaal region. Forestry in South Africa 3:67–83.

Odendaal M. 1980. *Eulachnus rileyi*: a new pest on pines in Zimbabwe. South African Forestry Journal 115:69–71.

Oliveira JJP de, Bridi GL. 1976. Effect of needles, rice straw and leaf mould on the germination and development of *Pinus taeda* seedlings. Revista do Centro de Ciencias Rurais 6(2):197–201.

Ooyama N, Toyoshima A. 1965. Rooting ability of pine cuttings and its promotion. Bulletin of the Meguro (Japan) Government Forest Experiment Station 179:99–125.

Park JI, Kim JH, Lee BC. 1984. Regeneration of plantlets by culturing needle fascicles of 2-year-old *Pinus-rigida*-(-*Pinus taeda* seedlings in-vitro. Research Report of the Institute of Forest Genetics (Immok Yukchong Yonku-So Yongu Pogo) 20:102–107.

Pasztor YP de Castro. 1963. Effect of two fungicides on the germination of *Pinus taeda*. Silvicultura em Sao Paulo 1(2):67–70.

Pederick LA. 1974. Seed orchards and their importance in the genetic improvement of forest tree species. Indian Journal of Genetics 34A:347–358.

Prevost JJ. 1971. Volume tables for *Pinus patula*, *Pinus elliottii*, and *Pinus taeda* in the eastern districts of Rhodesia. Rhodesia Bulletin of Forest Research 3:6–69.

Queensland Department of Forestry. 1966. Annual report of the Department of Forestry for the year 1965–66. Brisbane, Australia: S.G. Reid, Government Printer. 27 p.

Quijada M, Zapata A. 1978. Survival and growth at 4 years of provenances of *Pinus elliottii* and *P. taeda* planted at La Mucuy, Merido State, Venezuela. Revista Forestal Venezolana 26:45–59.

Raddi P, Fagnani A. 1978. Relative susceptibility to blister rust caused by *Cronartium flaccidum* of several species of pine. European Journal of Forest Pathology 8(1):58–61.

Rajkhowa S. 1966. The effect of inorganic fertilizers on the height growth of *Pinus taeda* and *Pinus caribaea* seedlings. Indian Forester 92(4):260–263.

Reissmann CB, Zottl HW. 1984. Mineral nutrition and growth of pine plantations in southern Brazil. In: Proceedings, IUFRO Symposium on Site and Productivity of Fast Growing Plantations; 1984 April 30–May 11; Pretoria and Pietermaritzburg, South Africa. Pretoria, South Africa: South African Forest Research Institute: 647–658.

Richards BN. 1962. Increased supply of nitrogen brought about by *Pinus*. Ecology 43(3):538–541.

Richards BN, Bevege DI. 1967. The productivity and nitrogen economy of artificial ecosystems comprising various combinations of perennial legumes and coniferous tree species. Australian Journal of Botany 15(3):467–480.

Rocha Fihlo JV de C, Haag HP, Oliveira GD, de Pitelli RA. 1978. Nutrient cycling in *Eucalyptus citriodora* and *Pinus taeda*: 1. Nutrient distribution in soil and litter. Anais de Escola Superior de Agricultura "Luis de Queiroz" 35:113–123.

Rosot NC. 1980. Estimative do peso de madeira seca de *Pinus taeda* L. por ocasiao do primeiro desbaste. Curitiba, Brazil: Federal University of Parana. M.S. thesis: 59, 64–64.

Schonau APG, Fitzpatrick RW. 1981. A tentative evaluation of soil types for commercial afforestation in the Transvaal and Natal. South African Forestry Journal 116:28–39.

Schonau APG, Grey DC. 1987. Site requirements of exotic tree species. In: von Gadow K, and others, eds. South African forestry handbook. Pretoria, South Africa: South African Institute of Forestry: 82–94.

Schonau APG, Schulze RE. 1984. Climatic and altitudinal criteria for commercial afforestation with special reference to Natal. South African Forestry Journal 130:10–18.

Schreiner HG, Baggio AJ. 1984. Intercropping of corn (*Zea mays* L.) with *Pinus taeda* L. planted stands located in Southern Parana, Brazil. Boletim de Pesquisa Florestal 8/9:26–49.

Schubert TH, Korte KH. 1969. Early growth and development of 4 pine species in Hawaii, USA. Res. Note PSW-189. Berkeley, CA: USDA Forest Service, Pacific Southwest Forest and Range Experiment Station. 4 p.

Schultz RP. 1987. Unpublished field notes.

Schutz CJ, Kunneke C, Chedzey J. 1978. Towards an effective buck repellant. South African Forestry Journal 104:46–48.

Schutz CJ, Wingfield MJ. 1979. A health problem in mature stands of *Pinus taeda* in the Eastern Transvaal. South African Forestry Journal 109:47–49.

Scott RWS. 1977. Application of line thinnings in practice. South African Forest Journal 102:67–72.

Seitz RA. 1987. Aspectos da silvicultura no Sul do Brasil. In: Proceedings, 1987 Simposio Sobre Silvicultura y Mejoramiento Genetico de Especies Forestales; 1987 April 6–10; Buenos Aires. Buenos Aires: Forest Research and Experimental Center [CIEF]: 16–35.

Seth SK. 1972. Selection and breeding to improve some tropical conifers. In: Burley J, Nikles DG, comp. Selection and Breeding to Improve Some Tropical Conifers: Proceedings, 15th IUFRO Congress; 1971; Gainesville, FL. Oxford, UK: Commonwealth Forestry Institute: 1–3.

Shimizu JY, Higa AR. 1981. Racial variation of *Pinus taeda* L. in Southern Brazil up to 6 years of age. Boletim de Pesquisa Florestal 2:1–25.

Simoes JW, Poggiani F, Balloni EA, and others. 1978. Adaptability of fast-growing tree species on shale strip mined spoil. Instituto de Pesquisas e Estudos Florestais [IPEF], Piracicaba 16:1–12.

Skolmen RG. 1963. Wood density and growth of some conifers introduced to Hawaii. Res. Pap. PSW-12. Berkeley, CA: USDA Pacific Southwest Forest and Range Experiment Station. 20 p.

Smith WJ. 1978a. The phenology of growth and wood information in three Queensland-grown exotic conifers. In: Nikles DG, Burley J, Barnes RD, comp. Progress and problems of genetic improvement of tropical forest trees: vol. 1. Wood quality of tropical species in relation to provenance and tree breeding; Proceedings, IUFRO Workshop S2.02-08 & S2.03-01; 1977 April 4–7; Brisbane, Australia. Oxford, UK: Commonwealth Forestry Institute: 100–124.

Smith WJ. 1978b. Variation in wood quality and productivity of some Queensland plantation-grown softwoods. In: Nikles DG, Burley J, Barnes RD, comp. Progress and problems of genetic improvement of tropical forest trees: vol. 1. Wood quality of tropical species in relation to provenance and tree breeding; Proceedings, IUFRO Workshop S2.02-08 & S2.03-01; 1977 April 4–7; Brisbane, Australia. Oxford, UK: Commonwealth Forestry Institute: 74–89.

Sorrentino A. 1987. Tablas locales de volumen commercial par pino maritimo (*Pinus pinaster* Ait.), elliottii (*P. elliottii* Engelm.) y taeda (*P. taeda* L.). Bull. 135. Montevideo, Uruguay: Universidad de la Republica. 34 p.

South African Forestry Research Institute. 1985. Research review 1985. Pretoria, South Africa: South African Forestry Research Institute. 2 p.

Southern Rhodesia Forestry Commission. 1957. State afforestation in southern Rhodesia. In: Proceedings, 7th British Commonwealth Forestry Conference; May 1957; [cities unknown] Australia and New Zealand. Salisbury, Rhodesia: Art Printing Works. 12 p.

Souza ML de P; Souza DM de P, Lucchesi LAC. 1982. Water holding capacity of soil under 12 year old slash stand (to 50 cm.). Revista do Setor de Ciencias Agrarias 4(1/2):17–22.

Speltz RM, Bonisch HJ. 1972. Ensaio de competicâo entre origens de *Pinus taeda* L. Proceedings, Congresso Florestal Mundial; 1978 October 4–18; Buenos Aires. Monte Alegre, Parana, Brasil: [Indústrias Klabin do Paranà de Celulose S/A, Departmento Florestal]: 1–15.

Stephan BR. 1984. Results of a 19-year-old trial with *Pinus rigida* × *taeda* in northwestern Germany. Mitteilungen der Deutschen Dendrologischen Gesellschaft 75:127–133.

Stohr GW, Baggio AJ. 1981. Comparison of two skidding systems in thinning of *Pinus* plantations. Boletim de Pesquisa Florestal 2:89–131.

Stohr GW, Emerenciano DB, Faber J. 1987. Green pruning of *Pinus taeda* and its influence on growth in Parana-Brazil. In: Proceedings, 1987 Simposio Sobre Silvicultura y Mejoramiento Genetico de Especies Forestales; 1987 April 6–10; Buenos Aires: Buenos Aires: Forest Research and Experimental Center [CIEF]: 197–204.

Strub MR, Bredenkamp BV. 1985. Carrying capacity and thinning response of *Pinus taeda* in the CCT experiments. South African Forestry Journal 133:6–11.

Swart WJ, Wingfield MJ, Knox-Davies PS. 1988. Relative susceptibilities to *Sphaeropsis sapinea* of six *Pinus* spp. cultivated in South America. European Journal of Forest Pathology 183/4:184–189.

Tadaki Y, Kagawa T. 1968. Studies on the production structure of forest: seasonal change of litter-fall in some evergreen stands. Journal of the Japanese Forestry Society 50(1):7–13.

Takacs EA. 1964a. The inoculation of subtropical pines with mycorrhiza in *Pinus taeda* with *Scleroderma vulgare*. IDIA (Suplemento Forestal) 12:41–44.

Takacs EA. 1964b. The use of hydrogen peroxide for stimulating the germination of *Pinus tadea*. IDIA (Suplemento Forestal) 12:45–46.

Tsuge T. 1971. Studies on the nutrition and fertilizing of trees: the fertilizing effects for growth and nutrient uptakes of afforestation tree seedlings transplanted in wood land, and the movement in wood soils of fertilizer nutrients applied at transplanting. [*Cryptomeria japonica*, *Pinus taeda*]. Memoirs of the Faculty of Agriculture Kinki University (Kinki Daigaku Nogakubu Kiyo) 4: 65–79.

Ubialli JA. 1981. Tabelas de volume para *Pinus taeda* L. nos principais eixos de reflorestamento do estado do Parana. Curitiba, Brazil: Federal University of Parana: M.S. thesis: 69–70, 105–109.

USDA FS [USDA Forest Service]. 1990. Unpublished information [On file with the USDA Forest Service, International Institute of Tropical Forestry, Rio Piedras, PR].

van den Berg AM, Dippenaar-Schoeman AS. 1988. Spider communities in a pine plantation at Sabie, Eastern Transvaal: a preliminary survey. Phytophylactica 20(3):293–296.

van der Sijde HA, Shaw MJP, van Wyk G. 1985. Reaction wood in *Pinus taeda*: a preliminary report. South African Forestry Journal 133:27–32.

van Loon AP. 1967. Some effects of a wild fire on a southern pine plantation. Res. Note 21. Taree, New South Wales, Australia: Forestry Commission of New South Wales. 38 p.

van Wyk G, Falkenhagen ER. 1984. Genotype × environment interaction in South African breeding material. In: Proceedings, Symposium on Site and Productivity of Fast Growing Plantations; 1984 April 30–May 11; Pretoria and Pietermaritzburg, South Africa. Pretoria, South Africa: South African Forest Research Institute: 215–231.

Vanclay JK. 1982. Volume to any utilization standard for plantation conifers in Queensland. Res. Note 36. Brisbane, Queensland, Australia: Department of Forestry. 8 p.

Vanclay JK, Shepherd PJ. 1983. Compendium of volume equations for plantation species used by the Queensland Department of Forestry. Tech. Pap. 36. Brisbane, Queensland, Australia: Department of Forestry. 21 p.

Velazquez JD. 1987. Creacion de un rodal semillero de *Pinus elliotti* var. *elliotti*, origen Saint Johns. In: Proceedings, 1987 Simposio Sobre Silvicultura y Mejoramiento Genetico de Especies Forestales; 1987 April 6–10; Buenos Aires. Buenos Aires: Forest Research and Experimental Center [CIEF]: 23–36.

von dem Bussche GH, van der Zee D. 1985. Damage by samango monkeys, *Cercopithecus* (*mitis*) *albogularis*, to pine trees in northern Transvaal. South African Journal of Forestry 133:43–48.

Wada S, Yamamoto T, Sano S. 1971. Construction of volume tables for young trees of loblolly, slash and Japanese black pine [*Pinus taeda, Pinus elliotti, Pinus thunbergii*]. Bulletin of the Kyoto University Forests 42:174–189.

Wattle Research Institute. 1983. Report for 1982–1983. South Africa: Wattle Research Institute: 63–79.

Wessels NO. 1987. Silviculture of pines. In: von Gadow K, and others, eds. South African forestry handbook. Pretoria, South Africa: South African Institute of Forestry: 95–105.

Whitesell CD. 1974. Effects of spacing on loblolly pine in Hawaii after 11 years. Res. Note PSW-295. Berkeley, CA: USDA Forest Service, Pacific Southwest Forest and Range Experiment Station. 4 p.

Wingfield MJ, Knox-Davies PS. 1980. Association of *Diplodia pinea* with a root disease of pines in South Africa. Plant Disease 64(2):221–223.

Wylie FR, Yule RA. 1978. Pine bark weevil. Advisory Leaflet 1. Brisbane, Queensland, Australia: Department of Forestry. 3 p.

Yang B, and others. 1987. The resistance of pine species to pine wood nematode, *Bursaphelenchus xylophilus*. Acta Phytopathologica Sinica 17(4):211–214.

Yoshida M, Tsuzuki K, Satake K. 1981. On the growing process of loblolly pine and slash pine planted in the Shikoku region: 1. Height growth and preparation of the volume tables for standing trees. Bull. 313. Japan: Forestry and Forest Products Research Institute: 1–35.

Young C. 1983. The open-rooted nursery and establishment system for pines. In: Proceedings, Jubilee Symposia of the Faculty of Forestry; 1982 September 23–24; Stellenbosch, South Africa. Mededeling, Fakulteit Bosbou, Universiteit Stellenbosch 1(98): 233-245.

Zem AC. 1977. Nematodes associated with wild and cultivated plants of cerrado in Itirapina, Sao Paulo. Revista de Agricultura 52(2/3):112.

Zhang NQ. 1984. A preliminary discussion on the effects of physical properties of soils on growth of *Pinus taeda*. Forest Science and Technology 11:10–12.

Zhigang P. 1989. Eight year results of slash and loblolly pine provenance tests in China. In: Proceedings, 20th Southern Forest Tree Improvement Conference; 1989 June 26–30; Charleston, SC. Charleston, SC: Southern Forest Tree Improvement Committee: 211.

Zobel BJ. 1985. Juvenile wood in tropical forest plantations: its characteristics and effect on the final product. CAMCORE Bull. Trop. For. 2. Raleigh, NC: North Carolina State University, School of Forest Resources. 17 p.

Appendix

Technical Appendices

Contents

Appendix A

Appendix A-1—Plants associated with loblolly pine by site type

Scientific name	Common name	Well	Mod.	Poor
TREES				
Acer rubrum L.	red maple		■	■
* Albizia julibrissin Durazzini	mimosa silktree		■	
Carpinus caroliniana Walt.	American hornbeam		■	■
Carya cordiformis (Wangenh.) K. Koch	bitternut swamp hickory	■	■	■
C. glabra (Mill.) Sweet	pignut hickory	■	■	■
C. ovalis (Wangenh.) Sarg.	red hickory	■		
C. pallida (Ashe) Engl. & Graebn.	sand hickory	■		
C. texana Buckl.	black hickory	■		
C. tomentosa (Poir.) Nutt.	mockernut hickory	■	■	■
* Cercis canadensis L.	eastern redbud		■	■
Chamaecyparis thyoides (L.) B.S.P.	Atlantic white-cedar			■
Cornus florida L.	flowering dogwood	■	■	
Diospyros virginiana L.	common persimmon	■		
Fagus grandifolia Ehrh.	American beech			■
Fraxinus americana L.	white ash			■
F. caroliniana Mill.	Carolina ash			■
F. pennsylvanica Marsh.	green ash			■
F. profunda (Bush) Bush	pumpkin ash			■
* Gleditsia triacanthos L.	honeylocust	■	■	
Ilex opaca Ait.	American holly	■	■	■
Juniperus viginiana L.	eastern redcedar	■	■	
Liquidambar styraciflua L.	sweetgum	■	■	■
Liriodendron tuhpifera L.	yellow-poplar	■	■	
Maclura pomifera (Raf.) Schneid.	Osage-orange		■	■
Magnolia grandiflora L.	southern magnolia		■	■
M. virginiana L.	sweetbay			■
Morus rubra L.	red mulberry			■
Nyssa aquatica L.	water tupelo			■
N. sylvatica Marsh. var. sylvatica	black tupelo, blackgum		■	■
Ostrya virginiana (Mill.) K. Koch	eastern hophornbeam		■	■
Oxydendrum arboreum (L.) DC.	sourwood	■	■	
Persea borbonia (L.) Spreng.	redbay			■
Pinus echinata Mill.	shortleaf pine	■		
P. elliottii Engelm.	slash pine		■	■
P. glabra Walt.	spruce pine		■	■
P. palustris Mill.	longleaf pine	■	■	
P. rigida Mill.	pitch pine	■		
P. serotina Michx.	pond pine		■	■
P. virginiana Mill.	Virginia pine	■	■	
Populus deltoides Bartr ex Marsh.	eastern cottonwood			■
P. heterophylla L.	swamp cottonwood			■
Prunus serotina Ehrh.	black cherry		■	
Quercus alba L.	white oak	■	■	■
Q. coccinea Muenchh.	scarlet oak	■		
Q. falcata Michx.	southern red oak	■		
Q. falcata var. pagodifolia Ell.	cherrybark oak		■	■
Q. laevis Walt.	turkey oak	■		
Q. laurifolia Walt.	laurel oak		■	■
Q. marilandica Muenchh.	blackjack oak	■		
Q. michauxii Nutt.	swamp chestnut oak			■
Q. nigra L.	water oak		■	■
Q palustris Muenchh.	pin oak			■
Q. phellos L.	willow oak		■	■
Q. rubra L.	northern red oak	■	■	
Q shumardii Buckl.	Shumard oak			■
Q. stellata Wangenh.	post oak	■	■	
Q. stellata var. margaretta (Ashe) Sarg.	sand post oak	■		
Q. velutina Lam.	black oak	■		
Q virginiana Mill.	live oak		■	
* Robinia pseudoacacia L.	black locust	■	■	■
Sassafras albidum (Nutt.) Nees	sassafras	■		
Taxodium distichum (L.) Rich.	baldcypress			■

Scientific name	Common name	Well	Mod.	Poor
SHRUBS				
Aesculus pavia L.	red buckeye	■	■	■
Arundinaria gigantea (Walt.) Chapm.	cane			
Asimina parviflora (Michx.) Dunal	dwarf paw paw			
Baccharis halimifolia L.	eastern baccharis,. silverling	■		
Callicarpa americana L.	American beautyberry	■	■	■
Castanea pumila (L.) Mill.	Allegheny chinkapin	■	■	
Ceanothus americanus L.	New Jersey tea	■		
Clethra spp.	white alder	■	■	■
C. acuminata Michx.	clethra		■	■
C. alnifolia L.	sweet pepperbush		■	■
Corylus cornuta Marsh.	beaked hazelnut		■	■
Crataegus spp.	hawthorn		■	■
Cyrilla racemiflora L.	swamp cyrilla, titi			■
Decumaria barbara L.	climbing hydrangea		■	■
Euonymus americana L	strawberry-bush		■	■
Euphorbia corollata L	flowering spurge	■	■	
Gordonia lasianthus (L.) Ellis	gordonia, loblolly-bay			■
Hamamelis virginiana L.	witch-hazel		■	■
Hypericum hypericoides L.	St. Andrew's cross	■	■	
Ilex cassine L.	dahoon			■
I. decidua Wait.	possumhaw. deciduous holly	■		
I. glabra (L.) Gray	bitter gallberry		■	■
I. vomitoria Ait.	yaupon	■	■	■
Kalmia latifolia L.	mountain-laurel		■	■
Ligustrum spp.	privet		■	■
L. vulgare L.	common privet		■	■
Lyonia lucida (Lam.) K. Koch	fetterbush		■	■
L. mariana (L.) D. Don	lyonia	■		
Myrica cerifera L.	waxmyrtle, southern bayberry			■
Penstemon laevigatus Ait.	smooth beardtongue		■	
Rhododendron spp.	rhododendron	■	■	■
Sebastiania ligustrina (Michaux) Muell-Arg.	Sebastian bush		■	■
Sorbus arbutifolia (L.) Heynhold	red chokeberry			■
Symplocos tincloria (L.) L' Her.	sweetleaf	■	■	■
Vaccinium. arboreum Marsh.	tree sparkleberry	■		
V. elliottii Chapm.	Elliot's blueberry		■	■
V. stamineum L.	gooseberry	■	■	
V vacillans Torr	dryland blueberry	■	■	■
Viburnum spp.	vibumum	■	■	■
V. dentatum L.	arrow-wood		■	■
V. rufidulum Raf	rusty blackhaw	■		

Scientific name	Common name	Well	Mod.	Poor
WOODY VINES				
Ampelopsis arborea (L.) Koehne	peppervine	■	■	■
Berchemia scandens (Hill) K. Koch	Alabama supplejack			■
Campsis radicans (L.) Seem. Ex Bureau	trumpet-creeper	■	■	
Gelsemium sempervirens (L.) Ait. f.	yellow jessamine	■	■	■
Ipomoea spp.	morning-glory	■	■	
Lonicera japonica Thunb.	Japanese honeysuckle	■		
Parthenocissus quinquefolia (L.) Planch.	Virginia creeper	■	■	■
Pueraria lobata (Willd.) Ohwi	kudzu	■	■	
Rhus copallina L.	shining sumac	■	■	
Rubus spp.	blackberries	■	■	■
R. arbutus Link	blackberry	■	■	
R. trivialis Michx.	southern dewberry	■	■	
Smilax spp.	greenbrier	■	■	■
S. bona-nox L.	sawbrier	■	■	■
S. glauca Walt.	cat greenbrier	■	■	■
S. laurifolia L.	laurel greenbrier		■	■
S. rotundifolia L.	common greenbrier. horse/bullbrier	■	■	■
Toxicodendron radicans (L.) Kuntze	poison ivy	■	■	■
Vitus spp	grape	■	■	■
V. aestivalis Michx.	summer grape		■	■
V. rotundifolia Michx.	muscadine grape	■	■	■

Scientific name	Common name	Well	Mod.	Poor
GRASSES AND FORBS				
Amaranthus spp.	pigweed	■		
Ambrosia artemisiifolia L.	common ragweed	■	■	■
A. trifida L.	giant ragweed	■		
Andropogon spp.	bluestems, broomsedges	■	■	■
Arisaema triphyllum (L.) Torrey	Jack-in-the-pulpit		■	■
Aristida stricta Michx.	threeawn grass	■		
A. purpurescens Poir.	arrowfeather threeawn			■
Arundinaria spp.	switch cane		■	■
Aster spp.	aster		■	■
A. dumosus L.	bushy aster			■
A. lateriflorus (L.) Britt.	starved aster			■
A. linariifolius L.	stiff-leaved aster	■	■	
A. paternus Cronquist	white-topped aster	■		
Athyrium asplenioides (Michx.) A.A. Eaton	southern lady fern		■	■
Axonpus affinis Chase	common carpetgrass		■	■
Bromus spp.	bromegrass	■	■	
Carex spp./*Cyperus* spp.	sedges	■	■	■
* *Cassia fasciculata* Michx. (= *Chamaecrista fasciculata* (Michx.) E. Green)	partridge pea	■	■	

Scientific name	Common name	Well	Mod.	Poor
* C. obtusifolia L. (= Senna (obtusifolia (L.) Irwin & Barneby	sicklepod	■		
* C. nictitans L.	wild sensitive plant		■	■
Centella asiatica (l.) Urban	centella			■
Centrosemia virginianum (L.) Benth.	butterfly pea	■	■	
Chenopodium spp.	lamb's-quarters, pigweed	■		
Chimaphila maculata (L.) Pursh	spotted wintergreen	■	■	
Chrysogonum virginianum L.	goldenstar	■	■	
Coreopsis major Walt.	tickseed	■	■	
Croton capitatus var. lindheimeri (Engelm. & Gray) Muell. Arg.	woolly croton	■	■	
Cynodon dactylon (L.) Pers.	bermudagrass	■	■	
Cyperus spp.	nutsedge			■
Dactyloctenium aegyptium (L.) Willd.	crowfoot grass	■	■	
* Desmodium spp.	tick-trefoil, beggar lice	■	■	
* D. ciliare (Muhl. ex Willd.) DC.	hairy beggar's ticks		■	
* D. laevigatum (Nutt.) DC.	smooth tick-trefoil		■	
* D. rotundifolium DC.	dollarleaf	■	■	
* D. viridiflorum (L.) DC.	beggar's ticks	■	■	
Digitaria spp.	crabgrass	■	■	
Diodia teres Walt.	poor-joe	■	■	
Echinochloa crusgalli (L.) Beauv. var. crus-galli	barnyard grass		■	■
Elephantopus tomentosus L.	elephant's-foot, hairy elephantfoot			
Eleusine indica (L.) Gaertn.	goosegrass	■	■	
Epilobium anguslifolium L.	fireweed	■		
Eragrostis spp.	lovegrass	■	■	■
Erianthus giganteus (Walt.) Muhl.	sugarcane, plumegrass			■
Erigeron canadensis L. (= Coryza canadensis L. Cronq.)	horseweed	■	■	
E. strigosus Muhi ex. Willd.	daisy fleabane		■	
Eupatorium spp.	thoroughwort	■	■	■
E. capillifolium (Lam.) Small	dogfennel	■	■	
E. hyssopifolium L.	hyssopleaf eupatorium	■	■	
Euphorbia corollata L.	flowering spurge	■	■	
Festuca spp.	fescue		■	■
Fragaria virginiana Duchesne	wild strawberry		■	■
Galactia spp.	milkpea			■
Galium spp.	bedstraw		■	■
Gerardia spp.	gerardia			
Gnaphalium spp.	endweed	■	■	
G. obtusifolium L.	rabbit tobacco, fragrant cudweed		■	
G. pupureum L.	purple cudweed		■	
Goodyera pubescens (Willd.) R. Br.	downy rattlesnake-plantain	■	■	■
Gymnopogon spp.	skeletongrass			■
Helianthus spp.	sunflowers	■	■	
Heteropogon melanocarpus (Ell.) Benth.	sweet tanglehead			■
Heterotheca graminifolia (Michx.) Shinners	grassleaf goldaster	■	■	
H. mariana (L.) Shinners	mad plantain, Maryland goldenstar	■	■	
Juncus spp.	rushes	■	■	
Lactuca floridana (L.) Gaertn.	wild lettuce		■	■
* Lathyrus hirsutus L.	rough pea	■		
Lechea spp.	pinweed	■		
* Lespedeza spp.	lespedeza	■	■	■
L. capitata Michx.	roundhead lespedeza			■
* L. cuneata (Dum.-Cours) G. Don	sericea lespedeza	■		
* L. intermedia (S. Wats.) Britt	sericea lespedeza	■		
* L. repens (L.) Bart	creeping bush-clover		■	
* L. virginica (L.) Britt	Virginia bush-clover	■		
Liatris graminifolia (Walt.) Willd.	grass-leaved blazing star	■		
Mecardonia acuminata (Walt.) Small	mecardonia	■	■	
Medeola virginiana L.	Indian cucumber-root			■
Melilotus alba Medikus	white sweet clover		■	
Mollugo verticillata L.	carpet-weed		■	
Muhlenbergia expansa (DC) Tnn.	cutover muhley			■
Osmunda cinnamomea L.	cinnamon fern		■	■
O regalis L.	royal fern			■
Oxalis spp.	woodsorrel	■	■	■
O. stricta L.	Yellow woodsorrel	■		
Panicum spp.	panicum grasses	■	■	■
P. anceps Michx.	beaked panicum	■	■	
P. hemitomon Schultes	maidencane, paille fine			■
Paspalum spp.	paspalum grasses	■	■	■
Phytolacca americana L	common pokeweed	■	■	
Polypremun procumbens L.	juniperleaf	■		
Polystichum acrostichoides (Michx.) Schott	Christmas fern	■	■	■
Portulaca oleracea L.	purslane	■	■	
Potentilla canadensis L.	common cinquefoil. five-fingers	■		
Pteridium aquilinum (L.) Kuhn	bracken fern			■
Pycnathemun spp.	mountain mints	■		
Rhexia mariana L.	Maryland meadowbeauty	■	■	
Rhus aromatica Ait.	fragrant sumac	■		
Rhrynchospora globularis (Chapm.) Small var. recognita Gale	pinehill beakrush	■		
R. copallina L. shining sumac	shining sumac			
Richardia scabra L.	Florida pusley, Mexican clover	■	■	
Rudbeckia spp.	black-eyed Susans	■	■	
Scutellaria integrifolia L.	rough skullcap	■	■	
Senecio smallii Britt.	Small's ragwort	■		
Sisyrinchium angustifolium Mill.	blue-eyed-grass		■	■

Scientific name	Common name	Site drainage type		
		Well	Mod.	Poor
Solidago erecta Pursh	slender goldenrod		■	
S odora Ait.	simple goldenrod, fragrant goldenrod	■	■	
S petiolaris Ait.	goldenrod	■	■	
Sorgrastum spp.	Indiangrass			■
Stylosanthes biflora (L.) BSP	pencil flower	■	■	
Tephrosia spp.	tephrosia			■
T. virginiana (L.) Pers.	goatsrue	■	■	
Thelypteris novaboracensis (L.) Nieuwland	New York fern		■	■
Toxicodendron pubescens Miller	poison oak	■	■	
* *Trifolium arvense* L.	rabbit foot clover	■	■	

Scientific name	Common name	Site drainage type		
		Well	Mod.	Poor
* *T. campestre* Schreber	low hop clover	■	■	
* *T. pratense* L.	red clover	■	■	
* *T. repens* L	white clover	■	■	
Trilisia paniculata (Walt. Ex Gmel.) Cass.	hairy Trilisia			■
Uniola sessiliflora Poir.	longleaf uniola		■	
U. laxa (L.) BSP	spike uniola		■	
Vicia spp.	vetch	■	■	■
Woodwardia areolata (L.) Moore	netted chain-fern			■
Xanthium spp.	cocklebur	■	■	■
Yucca filamentosa L.	Adam's needle, spoonleaf yucca	■	■	

Sources: adapted from Beckett and Golden (1982), Gjerstad and Barber (1987), Gresham and Lipscomb (1985), Haywood (1980), Haywood and Melder (1982), Krochmal and Kologiski (1974), Lewis and Harshbarger (1976), Palmer (1986), Schuster (1967). Snyder (19800. Wahlenberg (1960), Wolters and Schmidtling (1975).

* Nitrogen-fixing legume.

Appendix A-2—Bryophytes associated with loblolly pine on well-drained sites in Durham Co. , North Carolina

Scientific name
Dicranum montanum Hedw.
Dicranum scopaium Hedw.
Isopterygium tenerum (Sw) Min.
Leucobryum albidum (Bnd.) Lindb.
Lophocolea heterophylla (Schrad.) Dumort.
Platygyrium repens (Brid.) BSG
Sematophyllum adnatum (Michx.) Bnn.
Thuidium delicatulum (Hedw.) BSG

Source: adapted from Palmer (1986).

Literature Cited

Beckett S, Golden MS. 1982. Forest vegetation and vascular flora of Reed Brake Research Natural Area, Alabama. Castanea 47(4):368-392.

Gjerstad DH, Barber BL. 1987. Forest vegetation problems in the South. In: Walstad JD, Kuch PJ, eds. Forest vegetation management. New York: John Wiley and Sons: 55-75.

Gresham CA, Lipscomb DJ. 1985. Selected ecological characteristics of *Gordonia lasianthus* in coastal South Carolina, USA. Bulletin of the Torrey Boptanical Club 112(1):53-58.

Haywood JP. 1980. Control of dogfennel (*Eupatorium capillifolium* (Lam.) Small) does not increase loblolly pine yields. Res. Note S0-258. New Orleans: USDA Forest Service, Southern Forest Experiment Station. 5 p.

Haywood JD, Melder TW. 1982. How site treatment affects pine and competing plant cover. Proceedings of the Southern Weed Science Society 35:224-230.

Krochmal A, Kologiski R. 1974. Understory plants in mature loblolly pine plantations in North Carolina. Res. Note SE-208. Asheville, NC: USDA Forest Service, Southeastern Forest Experiment Station. 8 p.

Lewis CE, Harshbarger TJ. 1976. Shrub and herbaceous vegetation after 20 years of prescribed burning in the South Carolina Coastal Plain. Journal of Range Management 29(1):13-18.

Palmer MW. 1986. Pattern in corticolus bryophyte communities of the North Carolina Piedmont: do mosses see the forest or the trees? Bryologist 89(1):59-65.

Schuster JL. 1967. The relation of understory vegetation to cutting treatments and habitat factors in an east Texas pine-hardwood type. Southwestern Naturalist 12(4):339-364.

Snyder JR. 1980. Contributions to the knowledge of flora and vegetation in the Carolinas. [In: Lieth H, Landolt E, eds. Proceedings, 16th International Phytogeographical Excursion (1978) Through the Southeast United States.] Veröffentlichungen des Geobotanische Institute der Eidgenössische Technische Hochschule Stiftung Rübel in Zürich 2(69):60-63.

Wahlenberg WG. 1960. Loblolly pine: its use, ecology, regeneration, protection, growth, and management. Durham, NC: Duke University, School of Forestry. 603 p.

Wolters GL, Schmidtling RC: Browse and herbage in intensively managed pien plantations. Journal of Wildlife Management 39(3):557- 562.

Appendix B

These tables are adapted from Hyink and others (1972).

Appendix B-1—Ovendry bark-free weight, in pounds, of the total stem, for loblolly pine trees

Dbh (in)	Total height (ft)											
	20	25	30	35	40	45	50	55	60	65	70	75
5	23.6	30.5	37.4	44.3	51.1	58.0	64.9	71.8	78.7			
6		45.6	55.5	65.5	75.4	85.3	95.2	105.1	115.0	124.9	134.8	
7			77.0	90.5	104.0	117.5	131.0	144.5	157.9	171.4	184.9	
8			101.8	119.4	137.0	154.6	172.3	189.9	207.5	225.1	242.7	
9			129.9	152.2	174.5	196.8	219.0	241.3	263.6	285.9	308.2	
10				188.8	216.3	243.8	271.3	298.9	326.4	353.9	381.4	409.0
11						295.8	329.1	362.5	395.8	429.1	462.4	495.7
12						352.8	392.5	432.1	471.7	511.4	551.0	590.6
13						414.7	461.3	507.8	554.3	600.8	647.3	693.9
14							535.6	589.5	643.5	697.4	751.4	805.3

Appendix B-2—Ovendry bark-free weight, in pounds, to a 2.0-inch top diameter outside bark (dob), for loblolly pine trees

Dbh (in)	Total height (ft)											
	20	25	30	35	40	45	50	55	60	65	70	75
5	22.6	29.5	36.4	43.3	50.2	57.0	63.9	70.8	77.7			
6		44.7	54.6	64.5	74.4	84.3	94.2	104.1	114.0	123.9	133.9	
7			76.0	89.5	103.0	116.5	130.0	143.5	157.0	170.5	184.0	
8			100.8	118.4	136.1	153.7	171.3	188.9	206.5	224.2	241.8	
9			128.9	151.2	173.5	195.8	218.1	240.4	262.7	285.0	307.3	
10				187.8	215.3	242.9	270.4	297.9	325.5	353.0	380.5	408.1
11						294.9	328.2	361.5	394.8	428.2	461.5	494.8
12						351.9	391.5	431.2	470.8	510.5	550.1	589.8
13						413.8	460.4	506.9	553.4	599.9	646.5	693.0
14							534.7	588.7	642.6	696.6	750.5	804.5

Appendix B-3—Ovendry bark-free weight, in pounds, to a 3. 0-inch top dob, for loblolly pine trees

Dbh (in)	Total height (ft)											
	20	25	30	35	40	45	50	55	60	65	70	75
5	18.2	25.2	32.1	39.0	45.9	52.8	59.8	66.7	73.6			
6		40.4	50.3	60.3	70.3	80.2	90.2	100.2	110.1	120.1	130.1	
7			71.9	85.5	99.1	112.6	126.2	139.8	153.3	166.9	180.4	
8			96.9	114.6	132.3	150.0	167.7	185.4	203.1	220.9	238.6	
9			125.1	147.5	169.9	192.3	214.8	237.2	259.6	282.0	304.5	
10				184.3	212.0	239.7	267.4	295.0	322.7	350.4	378.1	405.8
11						292.0	325.5	359.0	392.5	426.0	459.5	493.0
12						349.3	389.2	429.0	468.9	508.7	548.6	588.4
13						411.6	458.4	505.1	551.9	598.7	645.5	692.2
14							533.1	587.3	641.6	695.8	750.1	804.4

Appendix B-4—Ovendry bark-free weight, in pounds, to a 4.0-inch top dob, for loblolly pine trees

Dbh (in)	Total height (ft)											
	20	25	30	35	40	45	50	55	60	65	70	75
5	06.6	13.6	20.6	27.6	34.6	41.7	48.7	55.7	62.7			
6		29.0	39.1	49.2	59.4	69.5	79.6	89.7	99.8	109.9	120.0	
7			61.0	74.8	88.6	102.3	116.1	129.9	143.6	157.4	171.1	
8			86.3	104.3	122.3	104.2	158.2	176.2	194.2	212.1	230.1	
9			11 5.0	137.7	160.5	183.2	206.0	228.7	251.5	274.2	297.0	
10				175.1	203.2	231.2	259.3	287.4	315.5	343.6	371.7	399.8
11						284.3	318.3	352.3	386.3	420.3	454.2	488.2
12						342.5	382.9	423.3	463.8	504.2	544.7	585.1
13						405.6	453.1	550.6	548.0	595.5	643.0	690.4
14							528.9	584.0	639.0	694.1	749.1	804.2

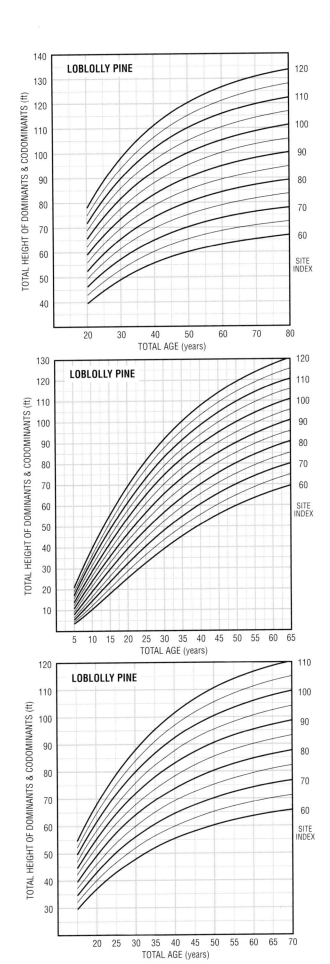

Appendix C

These figures are adapted from Carmean and others (1989). Site Index curves for forest tree species in the eastern United States. Gen. Tech. Rep. NC–128. St. Paul, MN: USDA Forest Service, North Central Forest Experiment Station. 142 p.

Figure C-1—Loblolly pine

Coastal Plain from Chesapeake Bay, Maryland to Mobile Bay, Alabama

- 420 plots having 8 dominant and codominant trees on each plot
- Total height and total age, anamorphic, logarithm equation

Convert dbh age to total age by adding years
according to site index (BH = 0.0):

SI:	60-75	76+
Years:	4	3

	b_1	b_2	b_3	b_4	b_5	R^2	SE	Maximum difference
H	1.1421	1.0042	−0.0374	0.7632	0.0358	0.99	0.73	2.2
SI	0.8485	1.0038	−0.0389	−1.0031	−0.0145	0.99	0.82	3.0

Figure C-2—Loblolly pine

Coastal Plain of Virginia, North Carolina, and South Carolina

- 22 plots having 2 dominant and codominant trees on each plot
- Stem analysis, polymorphic, nonlinear regression

Convert dbh age to total age by adding years
according to site index (BH = 0.0):

SI:	60-75	76+
Years:	4	3

	b_1	b_2	b_3	b_4	b_5	R^2	SE	Maximum difference
H	3.0849	0.8076	−0.0341	26.2342	−0.6702	0.99	1.45	5.2
SI	0.5694	1.0415	−0.0204	−1.4874	−0.1242	0.98	2.70	6.5

Figure C-3—Loblolly pine

North Louisiana and southern Arkansas

- 211 plots on poorly aerated soils, number of dominant and codominant trees not given, additional site index curves given for loess soils and well-aerated soils
- Total height and total age, anamorphic, age coefficient from soil-site regression

Convert dbh age to total age by adding years
according to site index (BH = 0.0):

SI:	60-75	76+
Years:	4	3

	b_1	b_2	b_3	b_4	b_5	R^2	SE	Maximum difference
H	1.1643	0.9999	−0.0413	1.1057	−0.0002	0.99	1.12	3.5
SI	0.7973	1.0165	−0.0408	−1.6634	−0.0974	0.99	1.22	4.6

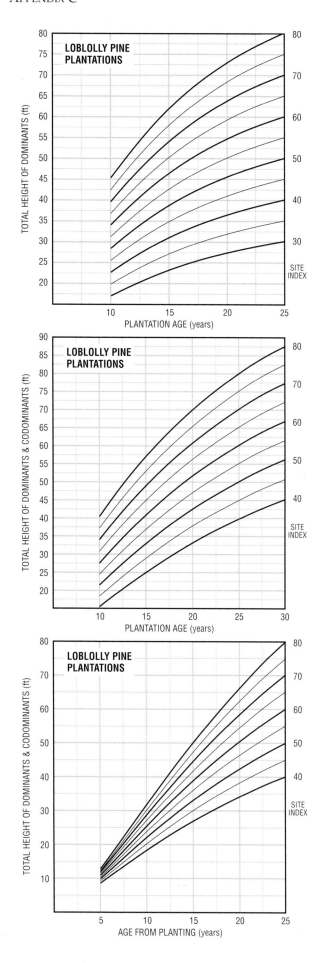

Figure C-4—Loblolly pine plantations

South Carolina Piedmont

- 220 plantations, number of dominant trees not given
- Total height and plantation age, anamorphic, logarithm equation
- Site index is total height at 25 years plantation age

Convert dbh age to plantation age by adding years
according to site index (BH = 0.0):

SI:	<50	>50
Years:	3	2

	b_1	b_2	b_3	b_4	b_5	R^2	SE	Maximum difference
H	1.1579	1.0000	−0.0930	1.4274	0.0001	0.99	0.15	0.3
SI	0.9150	0.9936	−0.1123	−1.5988	0.0347	0.99	0.74	2.2

Figure C-5—Loblolly pine plantations

Georgia Piedmont

- 141 dominant and codominant trees, number of plots not given
- Stem analysis, polymorphic, nonlinear regression
- Site index is total height at 25 years plantation age

Convert dbh age to plantation age by adding years
according to site index (BH = 0.0):

SI:	<50	>50
Years:	3	2

	b_1	b_2	b_3	b_4	b_5	R^2	SE	Maximum difference
H	2.9579	0.8274	−0.0581	9.3221	−0.4616	0.99	0.37	1.3
SI	0.1483	1.2560	−0.0155	−2.5747	−0.2990	0.99	0.66	2.6

Figure C-6—Loblolly pine plantations—Piedmont

Piedmont throughout most of natural range

- 68 plots, cutover and site prepared land, 1 dominant and 1 codominant tree on each plot
- Stem analysis, differential equation, polymorphic
- Site index is total height at 25 years since planting

Convert dbh age to age since planting by adding years
according to site index (BH = 0.0):

SI:	<50	>50
Years:	3	2

	b_1	b_2	b_3	b_4	b_5	R^2	SE	Maximum difference
H	1.0060	1.1098	−0.0535	0.5548	0.2433	0.99	0.01	0.4
SI	0.8459	1.0028	−0.1241	−1.4067	0.2398	0.99	0.01	3.4

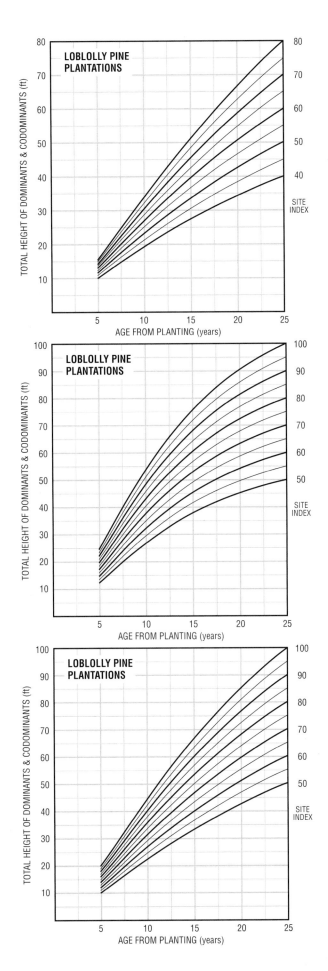

Figure C-7—Loblolly pine plantations—Coastal Plain

Coastal Plain throughout most of natural range

- 105 plots, cutover and site prepared land, 1 dominant and 1 codominant tree on each plot
- Stem analysis, differential equation, polymorphic
- Site index is total height at 25 years since planting

Convert dbh age to age since planting by adding years according to safe index (BH = 0.0):

SI:	<50	>50
Years:	3	2

	b_1	b_2	b_3	b_4	b_5	R^2	SE	Maximum difference
H	1.0107	1.1384	−0.0393	0.4584	0.2413	0.96	0.78	0.5
SI	0.9172	0.9646	−0.0982	−1.0330	0.2288	0.99	1.96	3.5

Figure C-8—Loblolly pine plantations—well drained

Coastal plains of North and South Carolina
—all except very poorly drained soils

- 154 plots, site prepared lands, 2 dominant and codominant trees on each plot
- Stem analysis, nonlinear regression, anamorphic
- Site index is total height at 25 years since planting

Convert dbh age to age since planting by adding years according to site index (BH = 0.0):

SI:	<50	>50
Years:	4	3

	b_1	b_2	b_3	b_4	b_5	R^2	SE	Maximum difference
H	1.1519	1.0000	−0.1003	1.6640	0.0001	0.99	0.08	0.01
SI	0.8680	1.0000	−0.1003	−1.6650	−0.00004	0.99	0.10	0.02

Figure C-9—Loblolly pine plantations—poorly drained

Coastal Plains of North and South Carolina
—very poorly drained soils in pocosins

- 25 plots, site prepared lands, 2 dominant and codominant trees on each plot
- Stem analysis, nonlinear regression, anamorphic
- Site index is total height at 25 years since planting

Convert dbh age to age since planting by adding years according to site index (BH = 0.0):

SI:	<50	>50
Years:	4	3

	b_1	b_2	b_3	b_4	b_5	R^2	SE	Maximum difference
H	1.5177	1.0000	−0.0551	1.4360	−0.0001	0.99	0.08	0.01
SI	0.6596	0.9998	−0.0551	−1.4347	0.0002	0.99	0.11	0.02

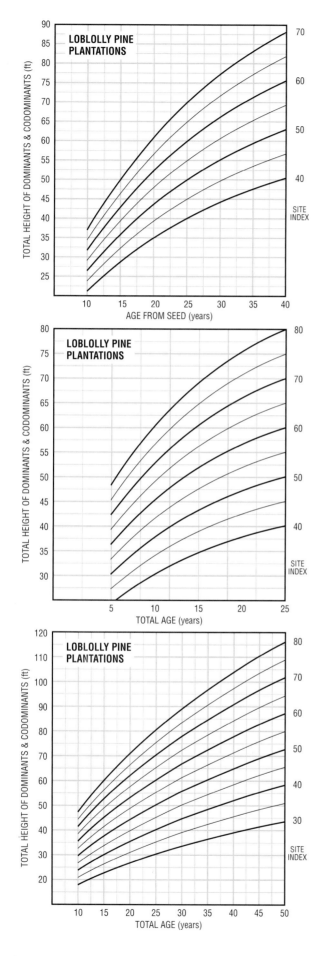

Figure C-10—Loblolly pine plantations

Central Tennessee, Northern Alabama, and Northwest Georgia

- 270 plantations, number of dominant and codominant trees not given
- Total height and age from seed, anamorphic, logarithm equation
- Site index is total height at 25 years age from seed

Convert dbh age to age from seed by adding years
according to site index (BH = 0.0):

	SI:	<50	>50				
	Years:	4	3				

	b_1	b_2	b_3	b_4	b_5	R^2	SE	Maximum difference
H	1.5861	0.9999	−0.0390	0.9753	−0.0017	0.99	0.28	0.7
SI	0.5990	1.0131	−0.0394	−1.0892	−0.0272	0.99	0.32	1.1

Figure C-11—Loblolly pine plantations

Interior western Gulf Coastal Plain of Texas, Louisiana, and Arkansas

- 699 plots, number of dominant and codominant trees not given
- Total height and total age, anamorphic, logarithm equation
- Site index is total height at 25 years total age

Convert dbh age to total age by adding years
according to site index (BH = 0.0):

	SI:	<50	>50				
	Years:	4	3				

	b_1	b_2	b_3	b_4	b_5	R^2	SE	Maximum difference
H	1.1547	0.9973	−0.0915	1.2294	0.0029	0.96	0.59	0.8
SI	0.8550	1.0066	−0.0931	−1.3579	−0.0163	0.97	0.65	1.2

Figure C-12—Loblolly pine plantations

Lower western Gulf Coastal Plain of eastern Texas, Louisiana, Arkansas, and Alabama

- 293 permanent growth plots on cutover sites, number of dominant and codominant trees not given
- Remeasurements of total height and total age, anamorphic, regression equations
- Site index is total height at 25 years total age

Convert dbh age to total age by adding years
according to site index (BH = 0.0):

	SI:	<50	>50				
	Years:	4	3				

	b_1	b_2	b_3	b_4	b_5	R^2	SE	Maximum difference
H	2.7644	0.9991	−0.0090	0.6293	0 0003	0 99	1.20	4.9
SI	0.2937	1.0738	−0.0112	−0.9033	−0.0801	0.99	1.42	6.9

Appendix D

Appendix D-1—Volume table for the Telemaco Borba region of Parana, Brazil; total volume (cubic meters per tree) with bark for trees 5 to 78 years old adapted from Machado 1979)

dbh (cm)	Height (m)																	
	7.0	8.0	9.0	10.0	11.0	12.0	13.0	14.0	15.0	16.0	17.0	18.0	19.0	20.0	21.0	22.0	23.0	24.0
5.0	0.008	0.009	0.010	0.011	0.011	0.012												
6.0	0.011	0.012	0.013	0.015	0.016	0.017												
7.0	0.014	0.016	0.018	0.020	0.022	0.023	0.025	0.027										
8.0	0.018	0.020	0.023	0.025	0.028	0.030	0.032	0.035										
9.0	0.022	0.025	0.028	0.031	0.034	0.038	0.041	0.044	0.047	0.050	0.053							
10.0	0.027	0.031	0.034	0.038	0.042	0.046	0.050	0.053	0.057	0.061	0.065							
11.0	0.032	0.036	0.041	0.046	0.050	0.055	0.059	0.064	0.069	0.073	0.078							
12.0	0.037	0.043	0.048	0.054	0.059	0.065	0.070	0.075	0.081	0.087	0.092	0.098						
13.0	0.043	0.049	0.056	0.062	0.069	0.075	0.081	0.088	0.094	0.101	0.107	0.114						
14.0	0.049	0.057	0.064	0.071	0.079	0.086	0.094	0.101	0.109	0.116	0.124	0.131						
15.0	0.056	0.064	0.073	0.081	0.090	0.098	0.107	0.115	0.124	0.133	0.141	0.150						
16.0		0.072	0.082	0.092	0.101	0.111	0.121	0.130	0.140	0.150	0.160	0.170	0.180					
17.0		0.081	0.092	0.102	0.113	0.124	0.135	0.146	0.158	0.169	0.180	0.191	0.203					
18.0			0.090	0.102	0.114	0.126	0.138	0.151	0.163	0.176	0.188	0.201	0.214	0.226				
19.0			0.099	0.112	0.126	0.140	0.153	0.167	0.181	0.195	0.209	0.223	0.237	0.251	0.266	0.280	0.294	
20.0				0.124	0.139	0.154	0.169	0.184	0.199	0.215	0.231	0.246	0.262	0.278	0.294	0.309	0.325	
21.0				0.135	0.152	0.168	0.185	0.202	0.219	0.236	0.253	0.270	0.288	0.305	0.323	0.340	0.358	
22.0				0.147	0.165	0.184	0.202	0.220	0.239	0.258	0.277	0.296	0.315	0.334	0.353	0.373	0.392	0.412
23.0				0.160	0.180	0.200	0.220	0.240	0.260	0.281	0.301	0.322	0.343	0.364	0.385	0.407	0.428	0.449
24.0				0.194	0.216	0.238	0.260	0.282	0.305	0.327	0.350	0.373	0.396	0.419	0.442	0.465	0.489	0.512
25.0				0.210	0.233	0.257	0.281	0.305	0.329	0.354	0.378	0.403	0.428	0.453	0.478	0.504	0.529	0.555
26.0				0.226	0.251	0.277	0.302	0.329	0.355	0.381	0.408	0.435	0.462	0.489	0.517	0.544	0.572	0.600
27.0					0.269	0.297	0.325	0.353	0.381	0.410	0.439	0.468	0.497	0.527	0.556	0.586	0.616	0.646
28.0					0.288	0.318	0.348	0.378	0.409	0.440	0.471	0.502	0.533	0.565	0.597	0.629	0.661	0.694
29.0					0.308	0.340	0.372	0.404	0.437	0.470	0.504	0.537	0.571	0.605	0.639	0.674	0.709	0.743
30.0					0.349	0.362	0.397	0.431	0.466	0.502	0.538	0.574	0.610	0.646	0.683	0.720	0.757	0.795
31.0					0.370	0.385	0.422	0.459	0.497	0.534	0.573	0.611	0.650	0.689	0.728	0.768	0.808	0.848
32.0						0.409	0.448	0.488	0.528	0.568	0.609	0.650	0.691	0.733	0.775	0.817	0.860	0.903
33.0						0.433	0.475	0.517	0.560	0.603	0.646	0.690	0.734	0.778	0.823	0.868	0.913	0.959
34.0						0.458	0.503	0.547	0.592	0.638	0.684	0.731	0.778	0.825	0.872	0.920	0.969	1.017
35 0						0.484	0.531	0.578	0.626	0.675	0.723	0.773	0.822	0.873	0.923	0.974	1.025	1.077
36.0							0.560	0.610	0.661	0.712	0.764	0.816	0.869	0.922	0.975	1.029	1.084	1.138
37.0							0.590	0.643	0.696	0.751	0.805	0.860	0.916	0.972	1.029	1.086	1.144	1.201
38.0							0.620	0.676	0.733	0.790	0.848	0.906	0.965	1.024	1.084	1.144	1.205	1.266
39.0							0.652	0.710	0.770	0.830	0.891	0.953	1.015	1.077	1.140	1.204	1.268	1.333
40.0							0.684	0.746	0.808	0.872	0.936	1.000	1.066	1.132	1.198	1.265	1.333	1.401
41.0							0.716	0.781	0.847	0.914	0.981	1.049	1.118	1.187	1.257	1.328	1.399	1.471
42.0									0.887	0.957	1.028	1.099	1.172	1.244	1.318	1.392	1.467	1.542
43.0									0.928	1.001	1.076	1.151	1.226	1.303	1.380	1.458	1.536	1.615
44.0									0.970	1.047	1.124	1.203	1.282	1.362	1.443	1.525	1.607	1.690
45.0									1.012	1.093	1.174	1.256	1.339	1.423	1.508	1.594	1.680	1.767
46.0									1.056	1.140	1.225	1.311	1.398	1.486	1.574	1.664	1.754	1.845
47.0									1.100	1.188	1.277	1.367	1.457	1.549	1.642	1.735	1.830	1.925
48.0												1.423	1.518	1.614	1.711	1.808	1.907	2.006
49.0												1.481	1.580	1.680	1.781	1.883	1.986	2.089
50.0												1.540	1.643	1.747	1.853	1.959	2.066	2.174

Appendix D-2—Volume table for the Telemaco Borba region of Parana, Brazil; total volume (cubic meters per tree) without bark for trees 5 to 18 years old (adapted from Machado 1979)

dbh (cm)	Height (m)																	
	7.0	8.0	9.0	10.0	11.0	12.0	13.0	14.0	15.0	16.0	17.0	18.0	19.0	20.0	21.0	22.0	23.0	24.0
5.0	0.006	0.007	0.008	0.008	0.009	0.010												
6.0	0.008	0.009	0.011	0.012	0.013	0.014												
7.0	0.011	0.013	0.014	0.016	0.017	0.019	0.020	0.022										
8.0	0.014	0.016	0.018	0.020	0.022	0.024	0.026	0.028										
9.0	0.017	0.020	0.022	0.025	0.028	0.030	0.033	0.035	0.038	0.041	0.043							
10.0	0.021	0.024	0.027	0.030	0.034	0.037	0.040	0.043	0.047	0.050	0.053							
11.0	0.025	0.028	0.032	0.036	0.040	0.044	0.048	0.052	0.056	0.060	0.064							
12.0	0.029	0.033	0.038	0.042	0.047	0.052	0.057	0.062	0.067	0.071	0.076	0.081						
13.0	0.033	0.038	0.044	0.049	0.055	0.060	0.066	0.072	0.078	0.083	0.089	0.095						
14.0	0.038	0.044	0.050	0.057	0.063	0.070	0.076	0.083	0.090	0.096	0.103	0.110						
15.0	0.043	0.050	0.057	0.064	0.072	0.079	0.087	0.095	0.102	0.110	0.118	0.126						
16.0		0.056	0.064	0.072	0.081	0.090	0.098	0.107	0.116	0.125	0.134	0.144	0.153					
17.0		0.062	0.072	0.081	0.091	0.100	0.110	0.120	0.131	0.141	0.151	0.162	0.173					
18.0		0.069	0.080	0.090	0.101	0.112	0.123	0.134	0.146	0.158	0.169	0.181	0.193					
19.0		0.076	0.088	0.100	0.112	0.124	0.136	0.149	0.162	0.175	0.188	0.202	0.215	0.229	0.243	0.257		
20.0			0.096	0.110	0.123	0.137	0.151	0.165	0.179	0.194	0.208	0.223	0.238	0.254	0.269	0.285		
21.0			0.105	0.120	0.135	0.150	0.165	0.181	0.197	0.213	0.229	0.246	0.263	0.279	0.297	0.314		
22.0			0.115	0.131	0.147	0.164	0.181	0.198	0.215	0.233	0.251	0.269	0.288	0.307	0.326	0.345	0.364	
23.0			0.125	0.142	0.160	0.178	0.197	0.215	0.235	0.254	0.274	0.294	0.315	0.335	0.356	0.377	0.399	
24.0				0.154	0.173	0.193	0.213	0.234	0.255	0.276	0.298	0.320	0.342	0.365	0.388	0.411	0.434	0.458
25.0				0.166	0.187	0.208	0.230	0.253	0.276	0.299	0.323	0.347	0.371	0.396	0.421	0.446	0.472	0.498
26.0				0.178	0.201	0.224	0.248	0.273	0.298	0.323	0.349	0.375	0.401	0.428	0.455	0.483	0.511	0.539
27.0				0.191	0.216	0.241	0.267	0.293	0.320	0.348	0.376	0.404	0.433	0.462	0.491	0.521	0.552	0.582
28.0					0.231	0.258	0.286	0.315	0.344	0.373	0.403	0.434	0.465	0.497	0.529	0.561	0.594	0.627
29.0					0.247	0.276	0.306	0.337	0.368	0.400	0.432	0.465	0.499	0.533	0.567	0.602	0.638	0.673
30.0					0.263	0.294	0.326	0.359	0.393	0.427	0.462	0.497	0.533	0.570	0.607	0.645	0.683	0.722
31.0					0.297	0.313	0.347	0.383	0.419	0.455	0.493	0.531	0.569	0.609	0.648	0.689	0.730	0.771
32.0						0.333	0.369	0.407	0.445	0.484	0.524	0.565	0.606	0.648	0.691	0.734	0.778	0.823
33.0						0.352	0.392	0.432	0.472	0.514	0.557	0.600	0.645	0.689	0.735	0.781	0.828	0.876
34.0						0.373	0.414	0.457	0.501	0.545	0.591	0.637	0.684	0.732	0.781	0.830	0.880	0.931
35.0						0.394	0.438	0.483	0.530	0.577	0.625	0.674	0.725	0.776	0.827	0.880	0.933	0.988
36.0						0.416	0.462	0.510	0.559	0.609	0.661	0.713	0.766	0.820	0.875	0.931	0.988	1.046
37.0							0.487	0.538	0.590	0.643	0.697	0.753	0.809	0.867	0.925	0.984	1.045	1.106
38.0							0.513	0.566	0.621	0.677	0.735	0.793	0.853	0.914	0.976	1.039	1.103	1.168
39.0							0.539	0.595	0.653	0.713	0.773	0.835	0.898	0.963	1.028	1.095	1.162	1.231
40.0							0.565	0.625	0.686	0.749	0.813	0.878	0.945	1.013	1.082	1.152	1.223	1.296
41.0							0.592	0.655	0.720	0.786	0.853	0.922	0.992	1.064	1.137	1.211	1.286	1.363
42.0									0.754	0.823	0.894	0.967	1.041	1.116	1.193	1.271	1.351	1.431
43.0									0.789	0.862	0.937	1.013	1.091	1.170	1.251	1.333	1.417	1.502
44.0									0.825	0.902	0.980	1.060	1.142	1.225	1.310	1.396	1.484	1.574
45.0									0.862	0.942	1.024	1.108	1.194	1.281	1.370	1.461	1.553	1.647
46.0									0.899	0.983	1.069	1.157	1.247	1.339	1.432	1.527	1.624	1.723
47.0									0.938	1.026	1.116	1.208	1.302	1.398	1.495	1.595	1.696	1.800
48.0												1.259	1.357	1.458	1.560	1.664	1.770	1.878
49.0												1.311	1.414	1.519	1.626	1.735	1.846	1.959
50.0												1.365	1.472	1.581	1.693	1.807	1.923	2.041

Index

Subject and Species Index

D

E

F

Correction Sheet

Please make the following underlined changes to your copy.

pg.

xii	metric units for light are lumen/$\underline{m^2}$
2-13	Table 2-11, the aboveground total value for copper (cu) is 0.499$\underline{2}$
3-8	Table 3-3, under Deep loess, ranges are $\underline{24\text{-}26}$ for Loess hills and bluffs and $\underline{24\text{-}27}$ for Loess plains
3-12	Figure 3-9, the y axis label is NEEDLE LENGTH (cm) $\underline{AND}$ OVEN DRY WEIGHT (mg)
5-9	Table 5-2, the straddle heading is No. of sound seeds/$\underline{ha}$
6-29	Figure 6-18, the y axis label is $\underline{ROOT}$ LENGTH (cm)
6-32	Figure 6-22, the legend for part b is ...two fiberglass greenhouses with a common sidewa$\underline{ll}$
7-5	Table 7-3, the values for Ratio of perimeter to cross section are $\underline{1 \text{ to } .104, 1 \text{ to } .095, 1 \text{ to } .099, 1 \text{ to } .084}$
10-41	Table 10-14, in asterisked footnote, ... to control annosu$\underline{m}$ root rot.
10-56	Reference is Wolfe, Drake, Peacher, $\underline{Wilmore}$
11-9	Table 11-7, Aboveground biomass for 12 years of plantation age is 9$\underline{1}$
11-10	Table 11-11, title is Distribution of biomass ($\underline{\text{total green weight}}$) ...; Actual weight for total hardwoods with 20-cm diameter is 39$\underline{1}$
11-12	Table 11-16, the first four headings in the left column should be subheads of $\underline{Dry site}$
11-15	Table 11-17, add footnote $\underline{NA = sample size not given.}$
11-16	Table 11-18, the per-hectare value for surviving trees from Goggans and Schultz (1958) is $\underline{\sim9900\text{–}2{,}470}$
11-27	Table 11-40, units of Mean annual growth are $\underline{(m^3/ha)}$
11-28	Table 11-41, units of Dbh are $\underline{(cm)}$
11-29	Table 11-44, units of Stand volume after thinning at age 11 are $\underline{(m^3/ha)}$
11-46	Martin 1981, publication information is $\underline{\text{East Lansing, MI: Michigan State University Press}}$
11-50	Zobel and others 1961, $\underline{TAPPI}$ Journal
12-13	Table 12-3, P. $\underline{patula}$ and P. $\underline{taeda}$
12-26	Takacs 1964b, Pinus $\underline{taeda}$
A-7	The complete citation for Hyink and others (1972) can be found on page 11-44

ISBN 0-16-049279-3